FOR KATE
*with love*

# The English

A Social History
1066–1945

By the same author

# The English

## A Social History
## 1066–1945

CHRISTOPHER HIBBERT

W·W·NORTON & COMPANY
New York          London

First American edition, 1987
All rights reserved.

Copyright © Christopher Hibbert 1987

*Library of Congress Cataloging in Publication Data*

Hibbert, Christopher, 1924–
   The English: a social history, 1066–1945.
   Includes index.
   1. England—Social life and customs.   2. National
characteristics, English.   I. Title.
   DA110.H48   1986   941   86–8752

ISBN 0-393-02371-0

W.W. Norton & Company, Inc., 500 Fifth Avenue,
New York, NY 10110.
W.W. Norton & Company, Ltd.,
37 Great Russell Street, London WC1B 3NU.

Printed in Great Britain

1 2 3 4 5 6 7 8 9 0

# Contents

PART FOUR · From the Victorians to
Modern Times

# Author's Note

I had originally intended to call this book *Scenes of English Life*. This title would have indicated the limits of its scope. It cannot pretend to be a work of original scholarship or even of synthesis. It is intended for the general reader. References to sources are given in the text but these are provided to give the reader the opportunity of turning to those works of scholars and experts on which I have relied – as well as to the literature which I have quoted – and as a means of acknowledging the debt which writers such as myself owe to the professional historian. I can at least claim that the book is the result of a lifetime's reading and of thirty years of writing on historical subjects. Not all the reading for this book has been done by myself. And I am most grateful to the many friends who have read books for me and have taken extracts from them. I would like especially to thank Liz McLeod, Dawn Marriott, J. T. Cooper, Godfrey Whitelock, Guy Hibbert and Thérèse Pollen. I am also most grateful to Janet Law, Alison Riley, Tessa Street, Nonie Rae and Margaret Lewendon; to my wife for having compiled the comprehensive index; to the staffs of the British Library, the Bodleian Library, the London Library and the Institute of Historical Research, to Richard Johnson, Deputy Editorial Director of Grafton Books, and Anne Charvet, Senior Editor; to my agent, Bruce Hunter; to Thomas C. Wallace of W. W. Norton & Co; and to Marianne Taylor and Katherine Everett who have helped me choose the illustrations.

Professor A. Goodwin and Donald Pennington, sometime Fellow of Balliol College, Oxford, have been kind enough to read the manuscript and have given me much useful advice for the book's improvement.

C.H.

# A Note on Money

Sums have been given throughout in pre-decimal currency in which there were twelve pence (12d) to a shilling (1s) and twenty shillings to a pound (£1). When conversion took place shillings were abolished and there were henceforth to be one hundred pence (100p) to a pound. Because of the fluctuating rate of inflation and other reasons it is not really practicable to give modern real-worth equivalents of old monetary units. As a very rough guide it may be taken that in 1600–1610 prices were four to five times as high as they had been in 1500 and throughout the later Middle Ages. In 1700–1710 they were 5½ to 6½ times as high as in 1500. Wages rose much more slowly. Multiplying eighteenth-century sums by at least sixty will also give some rough guide. An income then of £300 ($420) a year might be said to have been worth at least £18,000 ($25,600) in 1986.

# Chronology of Reigns

**Norman Kings**
William I    1066
William II    1087
Henry I    1100
Stephen    1135

**House of Plantagenet**
Henry II    1154
Richard I    1189
John    1199
Henry III    1216
Edward I    1272
Edward II    1307
Edward III    1327
Richard II    1377

**House of Lancaster**
Henry IV    1399
Henry V    1413
Henry VI    1422

**House of York**
Edward IV    1461
Edward V    1483
Richard III    1483

**House of Tudor**
Henry VII    1485
Henry VIII    1509
Edward VI    1547
Mary I    1553
Elizabeth I    1558

**House of Stuart**
James I    1603
Charles I    1625

**The Commonwealth**    1649–60

**House of Stuart** (restored)
Charles II    1660
James II    1685
William III and Mary II    1689
Anne    1702

**House of Hanover**
George I    1714
George II    1727
George III    1760
George IV    1820
William IV    1830
Victoria    1837

**House of Saxe-Coburg**
Edward VII    1901

**House of Windsor**
George V    1910
Edward VIII    1936
George VI    1936
Elizabeth II    1952

# Prologue

In his riverside palace outside London's western gate the King of England lay dying. A pious man, known to history as Edward the Confessor, the great-great-great-great-grandson of Alfred the Great, he had no children to whom his crown might be bequeathed. And as soon as he had died four powerful men laid claim to it, two of them brothers of the queen, another the King of Norway. The fourth was Edward's cousin, William, Duke of Normandy, whose claim was genealogically the strongest. But, ignoring Duke William's rights, King Edward nominated his brother-in-law, Harold Godwinson, Earl of Essex, his successor; and on 6 January 1066, the very day that the Confessor was buried there, Harold had himself crowned in Westminster Abbey.

Soon afterwards the queen's other brother and the King of Norway invaded England. They were both defeated in battle in the north, and both killed. But, having led his tired soldiers south to face the Duke of Normandy whose knights had now also landed on the English coast, Harold was himself defeated and killed near Hastings. Thus William, Duke of Normandy, became King of England.

Having conquered the country, however, his more difficult task was to hold it and to govern it. He did so with great skill. Within scarcely more than a generation of his victory more than 500 Norman castles had been built; royal officials, mostly churchmen, were administering the country efficiently; Saxon prelates had been gradually replaced by Normans; Norman French had become the language of the law; all land had passed by conquest into the hands of the crown and had been granted, in return for specified services, to tenants-in-chief, bishops, abbots and barons, who in turn had passed much of it on to tenants owing allegiance to them. By the time of William the Conqueror's death in 1087 about half the cultivated land in the country was in the hands of tenants-in-chief, nearly all Norman or

French; a quarter was in the hands of churchmen, only two of them Englishmen; most of the rest was held directly by the Crown. Subordinate to these great lords were the mass of the people, some two and a half million of them, speaking their different versions of English, a race apart.

# PART ONE

---

# The Middle
# Ages

# 1 · *Castles, Lords and Chatelaines*

The castles to which the horsemen ride in the fourteenth-century poem, *Sir Gawain and the Green Knight*, are like fairy palaces, with painted pinnacles and crenellations, cusped turrets and chalk-white chimneys, with 'carven finials curiously chisel'd' and 'many a lovely casement that closed full clean'. The reality was very different. Most of the castles by which the Normans helped to establish their rule in England were built at first of wood. On some commanding site a deep ditch or moat was dug, the earth removed being thrown up to create a mound or to increase the height of an existing hill upon which a timber tower was constructed. Around the tower above the ditch a palisade was made with felled trees whose ends were sharpened to points; and, enclosed by this palisade, at the foot of the mound, a large yard or bailey was formed with huts for the garrison, stables for horses, workshops, granaries and cattle-sheds. The bailey was usually entered by way of a drawbridge across the moat. This led to a gatehouse from the upper floors of which a portcullis could be lowered to keep out enemies and intruders.

Gradually the palisades were replaced by curtain walls and the wooden structures by buildings of stone or of flint or rubble faced with stone. The walls of the tower or keep were immensely thick and pierced at intervals by windows which, very narrow at the bottom, might grow wider on the upper floors where they were more easily defended during times of siege or assault. The lower floor, where the castle's well was dug, was usually used for the storage of food and military equipment and for dungeons; the guard room, chapel and the great hall were on the floor above; and, as castles became homes as well as fortresses, sleeping chambers were formed on the upper storeys and approached by circular staircases within the corner towers. These towers led on to the battlemented roof from which the castle guard could keep watch over the surrounding countryside. In some castles, as at

Kenilworth, the staircase was on an outside wall and led to a well-protected door opening directly into the hall.

By the beginning of the fourteenth century castles were no longer being built primarily for intimidation and defence, although a castellated appearance, complete with battlements, gatehouse and portcullis, was still imposed upon manor houses erected for great families, as it was to be upon sixteenth-century Oxford and Cambridge colleges and Victorian prisons. At the same time licences to crenellate were sought from the king by owners of existing manor houses who wished to strengthen and ornament them by building a tower and curtain wall and digging a moat as the owner of Stokesay in Shropshire had done at the end of the thirteenth century. Over 180 licences to crenellate were issued in the reign of Edward III from 1327 to 1377; but only sixty were granted in the next reign; and no more than seventeen in the first eighty years of the fifteenth century, towards the end of which brick walls began to replace stone as a favourite building material, it being recognized that thick stone walls were no protection against determined battering by heavy artillery and that to withstand a siege was far less conclusive than victory in a pitched battle beyond the castle walls. Nevertheless, both with new castles and those stark Norman keeps which were being developed into huge and rambling structures, their builders, bishops as well as lay lords, wished to present a formidable aspect to the world so as to reflect and emphasize their power and riches.[1]

The larger of these castles covered extensive tracts of land – in Henry II's time Windsor Castle extended over thirteen acres – and they comprised upper and lower baileys, inner and outer courtyards and numerous out-houses. The main stone buildings were often roofed with lead, and, looking down from the battlements, the guard would have seen an extraordinary variety of structures inside the long curtain wall. As well as stables and workshops, pigsties and byres, there were farrieries and dovecotes, kitchens and hen-coops, and perhaps a chapel in addition to the small one in the keep. Covered passages and corridors led to chambers set aside for guests who could not be accommodated elsewhere and to those series of rooms known collectively as the wardrobe in which clothes were kept and tailored and valuable household stores, including expensive spices, were kept in locked chests with jewels and plate.[2]

Most Norman halls, like most early Norman castles, were of wood; but some, like that at Oakham in Leicestershire, were of stone and have survived. Oakham's hall was built in about 1190 by the rich Walkelin de Ferrers. Although exceptional in its finely carved stonework, its design was common to most halls of the period. Since builders could not at that time roof a wide span, it was constructed like a church with a nave and two side aisles. Light came from small windows in the walls of the aisles; warmth from a fire burning in a central hearth such as the one which can still be seen at Penshurst Place in Kent, wall chimneys being virtually unknown until the fourteenth century. In one of the gable walls three doors led respectively to the buttery, where the yeoman of the buttery served out bread, the pantry, where the yeoman of the pantry issued candles and beef, and the kitchen which, like that preserved at Stanton Harcourt in Oxfordshire, was a building detached from the hall because of the dangers of fire.

The smoke from the hall fire escaped through a hole in the roof which was fitted by the thirteenth century with a pottery louvre; and, so as to prevent the smoke from blowing about the hall when the doors were opened, screens, at first movable and later fixed, were placed in front of them. Over the passage formed by the fixed screen a gallery might be built so that minstrels could play their pipes and tabors while the lord had his dinner at a table on a raised platform at the other end of the hall, the walls of which were covered with paintings and hung with tapestries. Below him sat the members of his household. They sat at trestle tables in the main body of the hall, the floor of which was more often of rammed earth than of stone and was so littered with scraps of food as well as with straw and rushes that it was commonly referred to as 'the marsh'. As late as the 1520s Erasmus described such floors as being 'usually of clay, strewed with rushes under which lie unmolested an ancient collection of beer, grease, fragments, bones, spittle, excrements of dogs and cats, and everything that is nasty'.[3]

Whatever the state of the marsh, dinner in a great man's hall was a formal occasion, announced by 'blowynges and pipynges' and conducted with due ceremony. It was generally eaten before noon, supper being served at about four o'clock in the afternoon. Two meals a day were then considered 'suffycyent for a rest man', though a 'laborer may eate three tymes a day': 'he that eate often lyveth a beestly lyfe'.

First, cloths were drawn over the tables, then spoons and cups or tankards laid out. Utensils were usually of earthenware or wood, pewter being rare until the fifteenth century; but on side tables or cupboards there would be displays of gold and silver, of bowls and dishes and ornamental pieces to demonstrate the lord's riches.

From the kitchen beyond the hall, where cooks had sweated by the heat of the roaring fires, and scullions, in dirty rags if not entirely naked, had turned the handles of the spits and washed up urgently-needed pots and pans, the food was carried across the courtyard or along the covered passage to the door which led into the hall by the screens' passage. Then the door, the centre one of the three opposite the lord's dais and larger than the doors on either side, would open and, as in the hall into which 'the largest man alive' rides unannounced in *Sir Gawain and the Green Knight*:

> Then comes the first course with loud trumpets' blare,
> (Those golden reeds which painted banners bear)
> The noble pipes, the little kettles sound,
> Wild warbles wakening startle the clear air
> Till the heart leaps for joy, and all around,
> Grave seneschals direct bright platters overground
>
> So plenteously 'twere hard to set arights
> One silver dish the more, clean upon cloth,
> Fresh food was there, abundance of delights,
> To each twain dishes twelve and, nothing loth,
> Goblets of beer and of the bright wine both.[4]

The procession of servants bearing food was led by the marshal of the hall, carrying a white staff, or, on the occasions of the grandest banquets, by a household officer on horseback. The procession approached the lord's table which usually stood beneath a canopy. And, after the lord and his family had been served, dishes were carried to the table where the gentlemen of the household sat with the steward, then to those tables where the lesser servants sat, presided over by the marshal of the hall and the clerk of the kitchen. The food was served on trenchers, thick slices of bread or scooped-out crusts which might afterwards be distributed to the poor or the family's dogs. Grace was said by the almoner and then all fell to, grabbing the spoons on the table – forks were then unknown – or using the knives which each man carried to the table with him in a case in his belt.

Table manners were far from meticulous and the noise was tremendous as dogs barked under the boards; falcons sitting on perches behind the benches uttered their sharp cries; and the ushers of the hall marched up and down between the tables calling out, 'Speak softly my masters, speak softly'. Even noble pages in the fifteenth century had to be advised in books of etiquette such as *The Babees Book* that wine must not be drunk when the mouth was full; that the upper part of the body must not lean forward over the table with the head hanging into the dish; that neither nose nor nails must be picked at meal times; that salt should not be flicked out of the cellar with a knife; that dirty spoons should not be put down on the cloth; that the knife should not be used to carry food to the mouth; that meat should not be cut in the manner of 'field men who have such an appetite that they reck not in what wise, where or when or how ungoodly they hack at their meat', and that when the meal was finished, the guest must 'ryse uppe withoute lauhtere, japynge, or boystrous words'.[5] In his *Booke of Nurture*, John Russell, marshal of Humphrey, Duke of Gloucester, thought it necessary to add that young gentlemen must not spit or 'retch too loud', or put their fingers into cups 'to seek bits of dust', or lick dishes with their tongues. Another well-known book of etiquette, the *Booke of Courtesy*, cautioned against spitting on the table, cleaning the teeth with the tablecloth, wiping the hands on skirt or tippet after the nose had been blown into them, and against playing with the animals that scratched about under the table eating scraps:

> Whereso thou sitt at mete in borde,
> Avoide the cat at on bare worde,
> For yf thou stroke cat other dogge,
> Thou are lyke an ape teyghed with a clogge.[6]

The food served was various and plentiful, for it was considered that the provision of good fare was essential to a great lord's standing in the world. Provisions would be transported from other manors or bought in a wide variety of markets. At Blakemere, Lord Talbot's home in Shropshire, one of several Talbot households, supplies were purchased not only from the local market at Whitchurch, but also from Nantwich, Shrewsbury, Chester, Worcester and Gloucester as well as from London. Even when Lord Talbot was away in 1417–18 fighting with the king in France, his steward recorded that, at an average cost of 2½d each, over 15,700 meals were served at Blakemere, well over 2000 of them to 'strangers who turned up at various times'.[7]

By the beginning of the sixteenth century three meals a day had become more common than two. In the *Northumberland Household Book*, which contains the regulations drawn up for the household of the fifth Earl of Northumberland, this Lenten 'Braikfaste for my Lords and my Lady' is prescribed: 'Furst a Loaf of Bread in Trenchers; two Manchetts [fine white loaves], a Quart of Beer; a Quart of Wine; two Pieces of Saltfish; six pieces of baconed Herring; three pieces of white herring or a dish of Sprats.'[8]

The Earl's two eldest sons were served much the same, though they had no wine and a dish of butter instead of the baconed herring; while the children in the nursery had bread and butter, salt fish, herring or sprats, and beer.

After Lent was over the Earl allowed himself half a chine of boiled beef or mutton for breakfast instead of the fish; the two boys had chicken; and the smaller children in the nursery boiled mutton bones.[9]

At other meals in the Northumberland household and in other grand houses, the food served was divided into portions, known as messes, by the server and distributed to each person according to his rank, a distinguished guest having a whole mess all for himself. Less distinguished guests had a mess for two, while others helped themselves to a mess for four.[10]

Bread, baked by the household's own baker, was eaten at every meal, usually the fine white bread known as wastel, though coarse loaves, dark and gritty and made from scraps which even hungry scullions found unpalatable, were sometimes given to visitors. Meat was served in large quantities, beef and mutton regularly, pork and veal almost as often, venison more rarely. Poultry, too, was a common dish, geese and capons as well as ordinary fowl, though partridge appears to have been too expensive for regular consumption and peacocks were rarely seen except on the tables of the very rich. Gallons of milk and pounds of butter were regularly supplied to the cooks in the kitchen; so were large quantities of cheese which was mostly made on the farm but also bought elsewhere, and enormous quantities of eggs, not eaten on their own but used extravagantly in cooking. The accounts of Eleanor de Montfort, Countess of Leicester, which have recently been studied by Margaret Wade Labarge, show that no less than 3700 eggs were consumed by the countess's admittedly large household and guests in a single week of 1265.[11]

Fish, a staple diet during Lent and on fast days, came from the manor's fishponds or, more commonly, in the form of salted herrings, smoked mackerel or dried cod. On manors near the sea the range of fish was naturally wider; and while a household of an inland manor might have to content themselves with bream or pike or eels, usually salted and dried or boiled in paste, households by the coast enjoyed fresh sole and mullet, crabs and oysters, sturgeon, porpoise and even whale, a dish then highly prized. 'Wolde to Gode I wer one of the dwellers by the see syde', wrote a fifteenth-century schoolboy, expressing a common sentiment, 'for ther see fysh be plenteous and I love them better than I do this fresh water fysh.'[12]

The variety of vegetables, though it became much wider from the fourteenth century onwards, was far narrower than it is today. Dried peas and beans were served often enough, so were onions, leeks, turnips and garlic; but the early medieval gardener was much more likely to concentrate on herbs, and the medieval cook on spices, than they were on the kinds of fresh green vegetables which were enjoyed in France. Sage and parsley, fennel and borage, were all widely grown in England; while the amounts of spices handed over to the cook from the wardrobe were immense. Both mustard and pepper were used lavishly in cooking; so was ginger which was valued for its medicinal properties as well as its culinary effects. Cummin and cloves, saffron, mace and nutmeg, cinnamon, coriander and galingale, an aromatic root from East Asia, were to be found in the wardrobes of all households which could afford them. So were such exotic spices as zedoary, a ginger-like substance made from the rootstock of an East Indian plant, and cubebs, the pungent and peppery berries of a Javanese shrub, though these had to be used more sparingly, being so costly. One fourteenth-century recipe for a preserve containing nuts, carrots, turnips, pumpkins, peaches and pears required a pound of mustard seed for every 500 nuts, half a pound each of anise and horseradish, as well as liberal measures of fennel, coriander, cloves, cinnamon, pepper, ginger, saffron, nutmeg, red cedar, grain of Paradise, caraways (pounded and soaked in vinegar), two pounds of mashed raisins, wine, and twelve pounds of honey.

Honey was frequently employed for sweetening and for the making of gingerbread; but sugar, expensive though it was at up to 2s a pound, was as familiar to cooks as honey in all large households, and was even used, together with almonds, cloves, onions and ginger, to flavour oysters. The Countess of Leicester's household was getting through about eight pounds of sugar a month in 1265. Her accounts also reveal purchases of rice, another delicacy; and large amounts of almonds which were often eaten with rice and, when dried, were served with other dried fruits such as dates, raisins and figs, mostly imported from Spain.[13]

By the end of the fourteenth century it had become a common practice to commit recipes and suggested bills of fare to writing. One bill of fare of the reign of Richard II, which has survived with its attendant recipes, lists three courses beginning with larded boar's head and a pottage made from slowly boiled pork liver and kidneys, the whites of leeks, minced onions, and bread steeped in broth and drawn up with blood and vinegar, pepper and cloves. The first course also included beef, mutton, pork, swan, roasted rabbit and 'tart'.

The second course comprised duck, pheasant and chicken stuffed with a mixture of yolks of egg, dried currants, cinnamon, mace, cubebs and cloves, and two other pottages. One of these pottages was made of ground almonds seethed with good meat broth, minced onions, small parboiled birds – sparrows, thrushes, starlings and linnets were all consumed as well as magpies, rooks and jackdaws – and, again, cinnamon and cloves. The other pottage contained powdered rice boiled in almond milk, the brawn of capons and hens – beaten in that essential item of a medieval kitchen, a large mortar – mace and the inevitable cloves and cinnamon, the whole being coloured with finely ground sandalwood.

The third and last course included rabbits, hares, teals, woodcocks, snipe, a dish known as 'flampoyntes' whose ingredients comprised ground pork, grated cheese, sugar and pepper baked in a pie, and 'raffyolys' which were patties made of chopped pork, grated cheese, powdered ginger and cinnamon.

This was a relatively modest dinner. For a more ambitious meal the recommended bill of fare, again arranged in three courses, included duck; teals; herons; roasted veal, pork and capon; small birds in an almond milk sauce; a mixed meat tart; and a 'leche lumbarde' made from pounded pork, eggs, raisins, currants, minced dates, red wine and almond milk, flavoured with sugar, cinnamon, ginger, cloves, salt and pepper, and coloured with

saffron. Finally there came a 'sarsed browet' into which, in a most complicated recipe which involved pounding with pestle and mortar, chopping,
parboiling, seething, stirring and frying, was stirred a wild mixture of
almonds, beef broth, cloves, mace, figs, currants, ginger (both powdered
and minced), rabbits, squirrels, sugar, partridges ('fried whole for a lord but
otherwise chopped into gobbets'), sandalwood, saffron, vinegar, cinnamon
and wine.

That was the first course. With the second course came more ducks and
rabbits; pheasant; venison; hedgehog; jelly; another 'leche'; 'browet of
Almayne' which, in addition to more familiar ingredients, including pork
and rabbit, ginger and cloves, vinegar and mace, contained pine-cones and
wild bugloss; and 'viande royale', a concoction of Greek or Rhenish wine,
clarified honey, ground rice, pepper, cinnamon, cloves, saffron, sugar,
sandalwood and mulberries. The third course provided yet another 'leche'
and a different kind of pottage; more partridges and boar; roasted cranes,
kids and curlews; a peacock served in the skin which was sewn back on to the
roast flesh complete with feathers, head and tail; a dish known as 'pome de
oringe' which was, improbably, made of spiced pork liver, garnished with
parsley, rendered shiny with yolk of egg and coloured with indigo.[14]
Colouring food was considered almost as important as flavouring it. As well
as indigo to dye it blue and saffron to make it yellow, burnt toast crusts were
used to turn it black and blood to make it red.[15]

Cookery books of the fifteenth century emphasize the need for the main
courses to be accompanied by 'subtilties', ornamental concoctions in pastry
or sugar, such as 'a black bore enarmede with golde' or 'a castelle of sylver
with [flags] of golde'. These 'subtilties' were frequently constructed with
great elaboration as a compliment to some notable guest and might display
his coat of arms or depict some event in which he had played a distinguished
part. They were brought into the hall to the sound of trumpets, and no great
feast was complete without one.

The amount of food consumed during these feasts, which might continue
over a number of days, was enormous. When, in September 1465, the
enthronement of George Neville as Archbishop of York was celebrated at
Cawood Castle to demonstrate the riches and power of his family, twenty-
eight peers, fifty-nine knights, ten abbots, seven bishops, numerous lawyers,
clergy, esquires and ladies, together with their attendants and servants
arrived at the castle. Counting the archbishop's own family and servants
there were about 2500 to be fed at each meal. They consumed 4000 pigeons
and 4000 crays, 2000 chickens, 204 cranes, 104 peacocks, 100 dozen quails,
400 swans and 400 herons, 113 oxen, six wild bulls, 608 pikes and bream,
twelve porpoises and seals, 1000 sheep, 304 calves, 2000 pigs, 1000 capons,
400 plovers, 200 dozen of the birds called 'rees', 4000 mallards and teals, 204

kids and 204 bitterns, 200 pheasants, 500 partridges, 400 woodcocks, 100 curlews, 1000 egrets, over 500 stags, bucks and roes, 4000 cold and 1500 hot venison pies, 4000 dishes of jelly, 4000 baked tarts, 2000 hot custards with a proportionate quantity of bread, sugared delicacies and cakes. Three hundred tuns of ale were drunk, and 100 tuns of wine, a tun containing 208 gallons according to the thirteenth-century treatise known as *Fleta*, or 252 gallons according to the more usual reckoning. In any event there must have been well over sixty pints of wine for each person.[16]

Although there were various vineyards in England, such as that at Ledbury which yielded Bishop Swinfield seven tuns of white wine in 1290, most wine was imported from the Continent, much of it from Bordeaux, and regular shipments also came from the Rhine and Spain. It had a short life and within a few months was often undrinkable, so disgusting indeed, that Peter of Blois, one of Henry II's clerks, complained that even at the king's peregrinating court the wine frequently 'turned sour and mouldy, thick, greasy, stale, flat and smacking of pitch'. 'I have sometimes seen great lords,' Peter of Blois continued, 'served with wine so muddy that a man must needs close his eyes and clench his teeth, wry-mouthed and shuddering, and filtering the stuff rather than drinking it.'[17]

At feasts, of course, even the roughest bastard wine provided for the servants was never as dreadful as this, while the Gascon wine seems always to have been of a high quality. Drunk in cups or in mazers, shallow bowls of maple-wood often fitted with a silver rim and sometimes with a silver cover, it was passed in these vessels from hand to hand, books of etiquette requiring one hand only to be used when handing a cup to a neighbour but both hands to be used when drinking, so that there should be less danger of spilling.

It was very rare for anyone to refuse wine. Teetotalism was extremely rare, the word itself unknown until 1834. Drinkwater and Boileau were distinctive and uncommon surnames. Indeed, Englishmen had a reputation for heavy drinking.

> The English delight in drink and make it their business to drain full goblets [the Italian friar, Salimbene, wrote in about 1285]. For an Englishman will take a cup of wine and drink it, saying, 'Ge bi: a vu', which is to say, 'It behoveth you to drink as much as I shall drink', and therein he thinketh to say and do great courtesy, and he taketh it exceeding ill if any do otherwise than he himself hath taught in word and shown by example.[18]

Much as they might have preferred to eat elsewhere, the lord and his lady customarily continued to have their meals in the hall with their household until the middle of the fourteenth century. Writing in the previous century for the benefit of the Countess of Lincoln for whom he drew up household regulations, Bishop Grosseteste emphasized the need for her to sit 'in the middle of the high board', so that her 'visage and cheer be showed to all men'.

'So much as you may without peril of sickness and weariness eat you in the hall afore your many,' he added in another passage, 'for that shall be to your profit and worship.' The countess ought also, the bishop considered, make the senior officers of her household sit in the hall as often as she could. Yet while the servants in manorial households were still generally having their meals in the hall when William Langland was writing his *Vision of Piers Plowman* in about 1362, the lord and his family were not so frequently to be seen there, and might, indeed, appear only upon special occasions:

> Wretched is the hall . . . each day in the week
> There the lord and lady liketh not to sit.
> Now have the rich a rule to eat by themselves
> In a privy parlour . . . for poor men's sake,
> Or in a chamber with a chimney, and leave the chief hall
> That was made for meals, for men to eat in.[19]

By Langland's time this 'chamber with a chimney' had become the usual dining-room of the rich. In the past, when the meal was a festive one, the ladies of the household had nearly always dined in an upper chamber; but now their husbands and sons were habitually climbing the stairs to eat there, too, at first in the apartment where they also slept, but later in great chambers, finely panelled and decorated with carved stonework and brightly painted wooden ceilings, the cupboards glittering with polished plate and shining ornaments, the chests covered with rich damasks, light streaming perhaps through a large oriel window filled with expensive, greenish glass which was usually fixed in removable frames and transported with the rest of the household equipment to other houses. By the middle of the fifteenth century it was presumed in the *Booke of Courtesy* that the lord would eat in such a chamber, while his steward would preside over his former table in the hall.

Yet if less formality was now observed at the hall's high table, the ceremonies attendant upon serving dinner in the upstairs chamber were as extravagant as ever, if not more so. A contemporary set of regulations, listing the formalities ideally to be followed in the household of an earl and requiring the services of at least twenty servants, has been described by Mark Girouard. There had to be grooms of the chamber to set out the trestle tables; and a yeoman of the ewer and a yeoman of the chamber, assisted by a third yeoman, to lay the earl's own table, bowing to the board and kissing their hands before spreading the cloth. In laying the cloth they formed 'a state', a fold into which their master's knife and spoon were later tucked. There had to be a yeoman of the cellar to place the requisite cups on the cupboard, to fill the shelves with their ostentatious display of plate, and to bring up the wine from the cellar. There had also to be a yeoman of the buttery to fetch the beer, and a yeoman of the pantry to bring up the bread, knives and spoons and the huge and elaborate dish, often in the shape of a ship, in which the salt was kept. This was reverently placed to the left of the earl's place with three ceremonial bows.

These preparations duly completed by the yeomen servants, the presence of the gentlemen sewer and carver was now required. These officials were both ritually washed by the yeoman of the ewer who presented them with towels which the one placed over his shoulder and the other hung round his neck like a scarf, folding it crosswise over his chest and tucking the ends into his belt. The carver was also equipped with napkins on which he wiped his knife before cutting slices of bread from all the loaves on the earl's table. He did this so that he could take 'sayes' of them, a precautionary measure of tasting observed since the days when poison was likely to be suspected.

Ceremonial 'sayes' were also taken by the sewer in the servery before the various dishes were allowed to be taken in procession by the gentlemen and yeomen through the hall and up into the chamber. At the door the marshal of the hall received the leader of the procession, calling out, 'By your leave, my masters', as an order for all the servants to stand up, bareheaded and in silence. The food, growing ever colder, was then arranged on the tables while the carver took 'sayes' to confirm the findings of the sewer downstairs, being careful when he was cutting the meat to follow the rules of the *Boke of Kerving* which instructed him never to set on 'fyshe, flesche, beefe, ne fowle more than two fyngers and a thombe'.

At last informed that his meat was 'on the board', the earl and those who were to dine at his table now appeared. The earl was deferentially approached by two gentlemen. One, carrying a bowl of water, sank to his knees as the earl washed his hands; the other, 'with suitable bowing and kissing', dried them with a towel. The gentleman usher having, with two assistants, shown the earl to his chair, then disposed the guests at his table, having taken great care to ensure that the exact order of precedence was followed and no one given grounds for feeling offended. The most worthy and important guests were placed on the right hand of the earl, above the salt, at the end of the table known as the 'reward'. Usually one side of the table only was used, and there was a significantly wide space between the earl and his guests below the salt, and even between him and his neighbour above the salt if it were felt that the difference in rank merited the separation. Conversation was consequently very difficult.

Lesser guests were placed at a separate table in the chamber. The yeomen ushers sat with the 'ladies' gentlewomen' at a board laid outside the chamber door; while those guests considered unworthy of dining upstairs at all were found places at the steward's table in the hall.

After grace had been said by the almoner or the clerk of the closet, eating could at last begin. The gentleman cupbearer attended only to the earl, holding the cup for him on bended knee and carrying in his other hand a second cup into which he caught any drops that might fall from his master's lips. The sewer and carver, helped by gentlemen waiters, looked after the earl and his guests above the salt, while another sewer, without a napkin and assisted by yeomen, waited upon those at the less favoured end of the board.

The second course was welcomed into the chamber with even more elaborate ceremony than the first, being met at the door by two yeomen ushers carrying their rods of office and escorted to the board by the sewer who made three obeisances on the way before kneeling down to take the prescribed 'sayes' from dishes held up to him by kneeling gentlemen.

When the meal had been finished, the tables cleared and the guests' hands washed, all stood up to bow or curtsey to the earl and then retired to the end of the chamber where they stood in rows in order of seniority. The earl himself now stood up; his hands were also washed; grace was said; the gentlemen attendants and yeomen servants who had served the meal left the room, their places being taken by other gentlemen and servants who had dined in the hall. Musicians were called in and dancing began.[20]

The most popular form of dancing was the *carole* in which the ladies and gentlemen held each other by alternate hands and moved round in a circle, singing to the tune. There was often, as in *Sir Gawain and the Green Knight*, 'much noise and merriment' and 'all the mannerly mirth that men tell of', although dances were usually then less energetic than the lively, almost acrobatic skips and jumps later to be enjoyed at the court of Queen Elizabeth I.

As well as dancing there were often entertainments by tumblers, buffoons, jugglers, knife-dancers and acrobats, story-tellers, minstrels and musicians. The musicians played a variety of instruments, viols and timbrels, tabors and citoles, citherns, bagpipes and drums, representations of which are to be seen, carved as label-stops, on the blind arcading in the north aisle of the nave in Beverley Minster.

Harps were a source of particular pleasure; and in several richer families a harpist, as well as a wayte to pipe the watch, was a permanent member of the household. In the later Middle Ages the instruments became both more refined and more numerous; and a cultivated man able to afford them might have virginals, clavichords and portable organs as well as flutes, gitterns (early guitars) and shawms (types of oboe).

While listening to the music, women might take up their embroidery if the light was strong enough, or fondle a pet, a cat, a monkey or a lap dog whose feeding at table books of etiquette still regularly condemned. And after the music they might play games, on summer evenings in the garden, bowls perhaps, or hand-ball, or whip and top, or a sort of nine-pins known as kayles after the French *quilles* in which the players threw balls or, more commonly, sticks at rows of pins or pegs, endeavouring to knock them all down at once.

On winter evenings guests would play games indoors, games of chance or games of skill like chess. Tables, a kind of backgammon, was popular; so was an early form of noughts and crosses; so were all the many different ways of playi           names of ten of which were listed by John of Salisbury in th                              he                         or checkers which was                                       h square instead of roui

C                                              ngland as it was on the                                            me, was played with pie                                        ed into Europe in the ter                                       es had to be modified. T                                         there were no queens, these Europea..                        r. Also there were, of course, no bishops which were  ... : Saracenic board by an elephant. The European sets were, however, often as elaborately carved, in wood, ivory and semi-precious stone, as their Middle Eastern and Asian counterparts; and the boards upon which the pieces were moved were, as frequently, valuable slabs of precious metals or crystal. The pieces were of large dimensions, a king of the twelfth century, belonging to one of several sets found off the coast of Scotland in 1831, being no less than seven inches in circumference and over four inches high. And, since the game, like so many others, was generally played for money and quarrels often arose, the pieces made handy and, on occasions, dangerous missiles. Bauduin, the illegitimate son of Ogier, is said to have received such a violent blow with a rook from the young Prince Charles that both his eyes flew out of his head. And there is a similar story of King John as a boy losing his temper when playing, and battering his opponent over the head with a heavy board.

The rules for playing chess were less complicated then than now, although there were numerous variations of the game, among them 'The Damsel's Game', 'The Chase of the Knight' and 'The Battle of the Rooks'. The rules were available in Latin verse from the twelfth century; and by the sixteenth there were instructions in English on how to 'Learn the Game Easily and Play it Well'.[21]

Playing cards were also introduced into England from the East by way of France or Spain; though these were not known until the fourteenth century, the date 1379 being ascribed by an Italian writer to their first arrival in Viterbo 'from the country of the Saracens'. But Chaucer and his contemporaries never refer to them; and it was not until after his death that card games began to rival tables as a popular medieval pastime. By 1463 they had become so popular and so many packs were being brought in from the Continent, particularly from Germany, France and the Netherlands, that Parliament forbade their importation at the request of the English manufacturers; and by 1497 apprentices were spending so much time playing cards, and presumably quarrelling over the money won and lost, that a statute was passed forbidding them to play except in their masters' houses at Christmas. A few years later, when Margery Paston wrote to one Lady Morley asking what kinds of game were considered suitable for a house in mourning over the Christmas holidays, she received the reply that in the Morley family 'there were none disguisings, nor harpings, nor luting, nor none loud disports, but playing at the tables, and the chess, and cards'. An inquiry addressed to Lady Stapleton elicited a similar response.[22]

For those too high-spirited to settle down to play cards, there were numerous more lively and frolicsome games, some of them of unknown antiquity. Among the most popular, particularly with ladies, or so it seems from contemporary illuminations, was blindman's buff, then known as hoodman blind, and hot-cockles in which one of the party knelt down blindfolded with her face on the knee of another while the rest of the players sat round her in a circle. One of these would hit her on the hand or on the back; and from the strength of the blow or otherwise she had to guess who the striker was. If she guessed aright, the striker took her place; if not, she had to submit to further punishment. An even livelier and potentially painful game was frog-in-the-middle in which the frog was required to sit on the ground while the other players surrounded and buffeted him, or more usually her, until one of them was caught and held so firmly that escape was impossible. These games were particularly rowdy at Christmas when they came under the control of a lord of misrule who, arrayed in the most elaborate costume and carrying a wand of office, was allowed to make up new rules during his term of office.

There were also less energetic games, among them *roy-qui-ne-ment* (the king who does not lie) in which one of the party asked another questions, often extremely indelicate questions, designed to provoke laughter by their phrasing and the answers they were expected to elicit; and ragman in which the participants drew at random strings attached to rolls of verses – often again very coarse verses – describing the supposedly good or evil character of the person who selected them.

When it was time to go to bed, the guests dispersed to their lodgings where beds would have been prepared for them.

In the bedchamber let a curtain go round the walls decently, or a scenic canopy, for the avoiding of flies and spiders [one early medieval book advised]. A tapestry should hang appropriately. Near the bed let there be placed a chair to which a stool may be added, and a bench nearby the bed. On the bed itself should be placed a feather mattress to which a bolster is attached. A quilted pad of striped cloth should cover this on which a cushion for the head can be placed. Then sheets of muslin, ordinary cotton, or at least pure linen, should be laid. Next a coverlet of green cloth or of coarse wool, of which the fur lining is badger, cat, beaver, or sable, should be put over all . . . A perch should be nearby on which can rest a hawk . . . From another pole let there hang clothing . . . and let there be also a chambermaid whose face may charm and render tranquil the chamber, who, when she finds time to do so may knit or unknit silk thread, or make knots of orphryes [gold lace], or may sew linen garments and woollen clothes, or may mend.[23]

In most great houses these might be either a single room or, in the case of the most distinguished guests, a set of rooms to which he and his personal servants only had access. The sets of rooms might contain a principal chamber for the guest's own use, two other chambers, sometimes known as pallet chambers, for his servants, a closet in which he could be on his own to pray or read, a wardrobe and a privy. If he were accompanied by his wife, she might have her own chamber, with another chamber for her gentlewomen leading out of it. The wardrobe was a room in which the servants could sit by a fire and perhaps mend clothes; the privy, which often led off it and was sometimes consequently known by the Norman-French word garderobe, was a small apartment – also called the withdraught, jakes, latrine, or gong – in which the seat was positioned over a shaft leading to a pit or drain or was suspended over the moat. In royal houses the privy was in the care of a groom of the stool or stole, a servant whose title was later to be borne by one of the most senior officers of the royal household. As well as privies, chamber pots were available in all large households; and, for those who wanted to have a bath, big tubs were available, and in these the guest sat while servants poured warm water over him.

While important guests were conducted to the lodgings assigned to them, others, less favoured, had to make do with a shared room or even with a shared bed; while many of the lord's servants had no beds at all. The steward and one or two senior officials might have rooms of their own; and other gentlemen servants would sleep in what was called the knights' chamber. But the less favoured were required to sleep on pallets, or to share a pallet, outside their master's door. And for many the best places they could find would be on the straw by the hall fire or by the still warm ovens of the high-ceilinged kitchen.[24]

# 2 · Cottagers and Peasants

Dwarfed by the church, the castle and the manorial hall, the cottages of the villagers were squat and dark. They had no chimneys, the smoke from the fire being allowed to escape as best it could through the partially open door or the small window apertures which were closed in cold weather with wooden shutters or pieces of cloth. The interiors were commonly divided into two main rooms, one for sleeping, the other for eating, animals frequently grunting or clucking in both, or rustling about in the straw on the floor of trodden earth. Light when required for some essential task was provided by flickering rush-lights that momentarily dispelled the gloom. Furniture was rarely to be seen, other than a few stools, a trestle table, a bench, a chest for the clothes reserved for Sundays, and frames for the bags of straw on which the occupants slept. In a corner might be glimpsed some cooking pots and dishes, a tub for washing and a home-made broom. Outside in the open, or in a shed, there might be a farm implement or two; and men fortunate enough to possess these were constantly called upon to lend or hire them, and frequently seem to have had difficulty in getting them back.[1]

Very few of the cottages were of stone, even in those areas where good stone was readily found. Most were built on wooden frames, the walls being made of rows of sticks between which long twigs were intertwined, creating a lattice-work; and on these frames, layers of mud, or mud mixed with straw, were plastered and left to dry. In the simplest, triangular structures the side wall timbers were planted in the earth at an angle and fixed overhead to a ridge pole; in others the wall timbers, or crucks, were curved so that it was easier to stand up inside. In those more elaborate still, the side timbers stood straight up from the earth, their tops being fixed to rafters, and the rafters in turn to the ridge pole. The roofs were usually thatched with straw, or with reeds or sedge where these grew nearby, or occasionally covered with wooden shingles.

Between each cottage and the village lane grew a few onions or cabbages, peas or beans, leeks or garlic; and, beside the path, there were perhaps a few rows of parsley and other herbs. Behind, in a small enclosed plot, grew more vegetables, a fruit tree or two, cherries, apples and pears. Some cottages had a pig snuffling about beside a mud-splashed sty and fed on nothing but waste; several had hens, capable of providing, so Walter of Henley said in the middle of the thirteenth century, as many as 180 eggs a year each; several, also, had geese – in some villages there were enough of these to warrant the employment of a gooseherd – and a few, very few, had a cow.[2] By the later Middle Ages, however, a man with a holding of more than eight or ten acres would probably have a cow, as well as other animals. In 1414, so Professor Hilton has recorded, the possessions of a tenant from the Worcestershire village of Ombersley were confiscated while he was apparently on the run as a horse thief. He held nineteen and a half acres, mostly wheat, but also rye, oats, and vetch for his animals' forage. It was valued by his neighbours at 50s for which price one of them bought it. The man also owned, in addition to a wagon, a winnowing fan, a riddle, a plough, three cartloads of firewood, three vats of malt, and a bacon, four hogs, twenty geese, a cock with four hens, and two oxen as well as his cow.[3]

In most cottages, though, a bowl of milk was not as often seen on the peasant's table as an earthenware jug of ale; nor was a piece of beef as frequently to be found in the metal pot that hung over his fire as a mess of vegetables and oatmeal pottage which, with a hunk of dark-coloured bread, had generally to serve for his evening meal. Sometimes there would be cheese and curds or on special occasions a chicken or a rabbit snared on a poaching expedition. Yet, while peasants – not commonly known by that name in England – rarely went hungry, except in winters of exceptional hardship, when, in William Langland's words, they 'suffered much hunger and woe', they seem not to have enjoyed as a general rule even the modest fare of the widow of Chaucer's 'Nun's Priest's Tale' who 'had a yard that was enclosed about by a stockade and a dry ditch without':

> Sooty her hall, her kitchen melancholy,
> And there she ate full many a slender meal;
> There was no *sauce piquante* to spice her veal,
> No dainty morsel ever passed her throat,
> According to her cloth she cut her coat.
> Repletion never left her in disquiet
> And all her physic was a temperate diet,
> Hard work for exercise and heart's content.
> And rich man's gout did nothing to prevent
> Her dancing, apoplexy struck her not;

She drank no wine, nor white, nor red had got.
Her board was mostly served with white and black,
Milk and brown bread, in which she found no lack;
Broiled bacon or an egg or two were common,
She was in fact a sort of dairy-woman.[4]

Work in the village began as soon as it was light. The peasants trudged out to work, their shirts tucked into the waistbands of their breeches; those with coats wore them to the knee; many of them were bare-legged. They made their way either to the parallel strips into which their land was divided or, if their services were required that day, to the fields of the lord of the manor. Their strips, about half an acre or an acre in extent, were divided from each other by rows of stones or ridges of unploughed land; and one man's holding would consist of several strips, usually scattered about the village rather than in a single block. So it was in each man's interest to work in cooperation with his neighbour, as they had to do when yoking their animals together to plough the lord's demesne. A selfish and difficult man, however, might prefer to work independently and this would give him an opportunity to cheat his neighbour, as the dishonest peasant does in *Piers Plowman* by allowing his plough to gnaw into land which is not his, and, when reaping, to swing his sickle over his own boundary and cut corn he had not sowed.

When the ground was ready for sowing, the peasants carried sacks of seeds on to their strips and either filled a basket or box, which was slung around their neck or tied round their waist, or they poured a quantity of seed into an apron which they held up for the purpose with one hand. They then scattered the seed as their wives kept away the 'crowes, doves and other byrdes' with stones cast from slings or arrows shot from bows. Afterwards the ground was harrowed, usually by means of a rough wooden implement drawn across the ground at the tail of some animal, a horse or an ox, a beast which Walter of Henley believed to be the more useful, since, 'when the horse is old and worn out, then there is nothing but the skin; but when the ox is old, with ten pennyworth of grass, he shall be fit for the larder'. Peas and beans were dropped into holes made in the ground with pointed sticks.[5]

The peasant's constant concern was to procure enough manure, for the lord usually maintained that all dung found on his demesne and in the village streets was his; and the peasant was consequently driven to sweeping up the straw of the previous year's harvest, which had been used in cowsheds during the winter, mixing this with earth, and throwing it on to the streets before ploughing it back into the fields. When his crop had grown, he mowed it with a scythe, an implement much like those still occasionally to be seen, managing to cut about an acre a day. He then thrashed his corn with flails made of two pieces of some wood such as blackthorn tied together by strips of leather, then either winnowed it with a fan or cast it into the air by the open door of a barn where the wind would carry off the chaff and allow the separated grain to fall to the ground.

When the sowing and reaping had been done there was always much other work to do. Every year there were hedges to cut and ditches to clear, draining to do, animals to look after, gardens to hoe, wood to cut, and assarts to cultivate. Assarts were pieces of forest waste which had been converted into arable land by cutting down the trees and grubbing up the brushwood, the peasant having either paid an agreed rent to the lord or a fine – in the case of royal forests a fine to the king – for having done so without permission. Once in possession of an assart the peasant would cultivate it in his own way whenever he had time to do so.

Finding time was always a problem for him, since most serfs were bound to work for their lords on many days every year. They were kept to their tasks by overseers carrying white wands of office in their hands, by haywards whose duty it was to supervise the pasture and the work of the harvest, by the beadle who was there to make sure there was no trouble and to deal with it if there were, and by the reeve, the manorial official who was ultimately responsible for the serfs. As a man appointed from their kind, the reeve knew all the serfs and, as a trusted servant of his master, was generally well rewarded for his arduous task. The serfs, too, were rewarded when the hayward's horn sounded and their day's work was done. Already at noon, on those days when they were required to work until dusk, a midday meal of bread and cheese and ale, better no doubt than any they tasted at home, had been brought out to them from the manor. In the evenings they sat down at trestle tables in a courtyard or outhouse and were provided with more bread and ale, and, on occasions to be remembered, with roast meat and as much cheese as they wanted. After the last day of the harvest on some manors a sheep was let loose among the serfs and, provided it remained in the field with them, was deemed to be theirs. On other manors each man was allowed to approach a large haycock and carry off as big a bundle as he could balance on his scythe.

Hard as their lives so often were, many, if not most, peasants had other customary rights which made existence more endurable. They had use of the common meadows, known as Lammas lands, once the crop on them had been gathered; and, when their turn came round or they drew an entitling lot in the shape of a specially marked apple or piece of wood, they could grow a crop on part of the meadows themselves. They also had rights over the waste lands where they could pasture their animals and gather timber for use as fuel, for repairs to their cottages and for the construction of their tools and household utensils. They were usually allowed to gather not only wood that had fallen to the ground, but as much as they could pull down or knock off

trees 'by hook or by crook'. They might also be allowed to cut turf for banking
or roofing, to dig out gravel for building, to gather bracken for their animals'
litter or for their own bedding, to pick nuts, berries and wild fruit, or even to
fell a certain number of trees, though customs varied from village to village
and from manor to manor. These two terms were not necessarily the same,
since a manor might extend over several villages while a village might belong
to two or more different manors. The rights of one villager might well,
therefore, not be the same as his near neighbours'.[6]

The villagers' rights almost never extended, however, to the trapping of
animals in the forest. Poaching nevertheless seems to have been practised
continuously on the most widespread scale. Countless birds were netted and
rabbits snared; and the more daring peasant would emerge from the thickets
having trapped and speared a deer or a wild boar. The rivers, too, were a
plentiful source of supply for the villagers' cooking pots. Eels were trapped at
night; and, from time to time, a salmon would be smuggled beneath a
peasant's smock into the concealing gloom of his cottage.

Sir, for God's sake do not take it ill of me if I tell thee the truth [a peasant
charged with poaching explained in a manorial court]. I went the other
evening along the bank of this pond and looked at the fish which were
playing in the water, so beautiful and so bright, and for the great desire I
had for a tench I laid me down on the bank and just with my hands quite
simply, and without any other device, I caught that tench and carried it
off; and now I will tell thee the cause of my covetousness and my desire.
My dear wife had lain abed a right full month, as my neighbours who are
here know, and she could never eat or drink anything to her liking, and for
the great desire she had to eat a tench I went to the bank of the pond to take
just one tench; and that never other fish from the pond did I take.[7]

Another poacher here describes the pleasures of the illicit chase:

In May, when there are many things to enjoy, and in the summer season
when airs are soft, I went to the wood to take my luck, and in among the
shaws to get a shot at hart or hind, as it should happen. And as I stood in
that place the idea of stalking came to me, so I covered both body and bow
with leaves, turned in behind a tree and waited there awhile. And as I
gazed in the glade near by me I saw a hart with tall antlers: the main stem
was unburnished and in the middle very strong. And he was full grown and
adorned with horns and large, broad and big of body: whoever might catch
him, he was a dish for a king.

I let the leash fall to the ground quietly, and settled down my hound by
the bole of a birch tree, and took careful note of the wind from the

fluttering of the leaves. I stalked on very quietly so as to break no twigs, and crept to a crab-apple tree and hid underneath it.

Then I wound up my bow and prepared to shoot, I had to stand without moving and to stir no foot, although gnats grievously troubled me and bit my eyes, for if I had tried to move, or made any sign, all my sport, that I had so long awaited, would have been lost. The hart paused, went on cautiously, staring here and there, but at last he bent down and began on his feed. Then I hauled to the hook [the trigger of the cross-bow] and smote the hart. It so happened that I hit him behind the left shoulder and the blood streamed out on both sides. He stopped: brayed and then brushed through the thickets, as if everything in the wood had crashed down at the same moment. I went to my hound, and quickly grasped him and untied his leash, and let him cast about. The briars and the bracken were smeared with blood, and the hound picked up the scent and pursued the hart to where he was, for he had crept into a cave, and, crouched to the earth, had fallen down – dead as a door-nail.[8]

The prizes of a poaching expedition were considered by the peasant fair compensation for the manifold services and hardships which his lord imposed upon him. For there was not only work to be done on the lord's demesne, regular 'week-works' and occasional 'boons', there were all manner of payments to be made for what were considered the serf's privileges. He might be asked to pay a tax known as wood-penny for the right to pick up wood; he might be required to take a basket of eggs to the manor house in recognition of his being allowed to keep hens; he might be asked to pay the lord a proportion of the proceeds on the sale of a cow; and when he died he would probably be liable for heriot which entailed giving up his best beast or most valuable chattel, a relic of the days when a man's weapons of war, his horse and harness – his *heregeatwa* was the Old English word – had to be returned to his lord upon his death. The serf might also be liable for tallage, a tax, later usually of a fixed amount calculated on the basis of what a man could afford to pay, but often originally an arbitrary demand at the discretion of the lord. This, so a respected thirteenth-century professor of divinity decided, the serfs were bound to pay, since they and their possessions were the property of their master or, as the lord of a monastic estate once put it more crudely, serfs owned nothing but their own bellies.

Then there were many limitations placed upon the serf's personal freedom: he could not leave the manor without permission, nor give his daughter in marriage without payment nor send his son to school without leave. He was not allowed to bake his own bread, even if he could have done so without bringing his cottage down about his ears in flames, but had to use the oven belonging to the lord. Yet more resented than this, because he could easily have done it at home – more resented even than the doves that clattered out of the lord's dovecote to fatten themselves for the lord's table at the expense of the peasants' crops – was the obligation imposed upon the serf to have his corn ground at a mill belonging to the lord and run by one of his servants, or by his tenant, the miller.

Mills, usually watermills but, after their first appearance in England towards the end of the twelfth century, sometimes windmills, were a hated feature of the countryside; and the miller was often a detested character, blamed alike for cheating those who were bound to use his services, for grumpily dealing out ill-ground meal, for rigorously supervising the collection of multure – that proportion of grain that had to be contributed either to himself or to the lord as an additional profit – and for delays that were not always his fault and might be caused by a breakdown of his machinery, or by drought or a windless day that left his wheels and sails motionless. Chaucer provides a portrait of a miller that any mediaeval peasant would quickly have recognized:

> The Miller was a chap of sixteen stone,
> A great stout fellow big in brawn and bone.
> He did well out of them, for he could go
> And win the ram at any wrestling show.
> Broad, knotty and short-shouldered, he would boast
> He could heave any door off hinge and post,
> Or take a run and break it with his head.
> His beard, like any sow or fox, was red
> And broad as well, as though it were a spade;
> And, at its very tip, his nose displayed
> A wart on which there stood a tuft of hair
> Red as the bristles in an old sow's ear.
> His nostrils were as black as they were wide.
> He had a sword and buckler at his side,
> His mighty mouth was like a furnace door.
> A wrangler and buffoon, he had a store
> Of tavern stories, filthy in the main.
> His was a master-hand at stealing grain.
> He felt it with his thumb and thus he knew
> Its quality and took three times his due.[9]

There were, of course, honest millers, just as there were forbearing and lenient lords. While there are records of lords confiscating private handmills – the Abbot of St Albans used the stones from them to pave his parlour floor – there are records, too, of mere token fines being levied for their use. The severity with which heriot was enforced depended, too, upon local custom and the character of the lord. Some lords did not claim heriot at all when the serf had little to offer; and Giraldus Cambrensis, writing in the late twelfth century, tells a story of St Hugh of Lincoln who 'was so utterly uncovetous of earthly things' that, when his servants had carried off the ox of a certain dead peasant, he ordered it to be restored to the widow when she came to him in tears, begging for mercy.

> Hereupon the steward of the manor said unto him, 'My Lord, if you remit this and other similar perquisites, you will never be able to keep your land.' But Hugh, hearing this, leapt straight down from his horse to the ground, which in that spot was deep in mire; and grasping both hands full of mud, he said, 'Now I hold my land, and none the less do I remit to this poor woman her ox.' Then, casting away the mud and looking upwards, he added, 'For I seek not to cling to earth beneath but to heaven above. This woman had but two workfellows. Death hath robbed her of the better and shall we rob her of the other? God forbid that we should be so grasping.'[10]

Many, if not most lords *were* grasping, however, and quite ready to take advantage of a manorial custom which might allow them to seize far more than the usual best beast or most valuable chattel. Sometimes a full third of a dead man's assets had to be surrendered. On the manor of Hedenham, whose lord was the Bishop of Rochester, custom allowed him to compel the sale of an animal if that was all the widow had to offer and to share the proceeds with her; and on the manor of Barchester a reeve was ordered to take into the hands of the lord the land of a widow who could not afford to keep it once her cow and her ox had been seized. On another manor the customs were so exceptionally severe as to decree that:

> . . . when any [bondman] dieth, the lord shall have all the pigs of the deceased, all his goats, all his mares at grass, and his horse (if he had one for his personal use), all his bees, all his bacon-pigs, all his cloth of wool and flax, and whatever can be found of gold and silver. The lord shall also have all his brass pots . . . because the lord ought to have all things of metal.[11]

Although such harsh customs were very rare, and apparently interpreted without too strict a regard for their very letter, there can be no doubt that a death in the family was usually an expensive and occasionally a ruinous calamity. It may be true that the sorry lot of the early medieval peasant has sometimes been exaggerated, and that starvation and famine were not common, yet at times in some parts of the country peasants could no doubt be seen struggling piteously to survive like the poor couple described by Langland:

> As I went by the way, weeping for sorrow, I saw a poor man hanging on to the plough. His coat was of a coarse stuff which was called cary; his hood was full of holes and his hair stuck out of it. As he trod the soil his toes peered out of his worn shoes with their thick soles; his hose hung about his hocks on all sides, and he was all bedaubed with mud as he followed the plough. He had two mittens, made scantily of rough stuff, with worn-out fingers and thick with muck. This man bemired himself in the mud almost to the ancle, and drove four heifers before him that had become feeble, so that men might count their every rib so sorry looking they were.
>
> His wife walked beside him with a long goad in a shortened cotehardy looped up full high and wrapped in a winnowing-sheet to protect her from the weather. She went barefoot on the ice so that the blood flowed. And at the end of the row lay a little crumb-bowl, and therein a little child covered with rags, and two two-year-olds were on the other side, and they all sang one song that was pitiful to hear: they all cried the same cry – a miserable note. The poor man sighed sorely, and said 'Children be still.'[12]

The wife working beside her husband in the fields, the daughter beside her father, or the single woman harrowing on her own were not uncommon sights. Women were more often to be found cooking and gardening, brewing ale, milking the cows or feeding the pigs, looking after the poultry or winnowing the grain. But their capacity to do such heavy work as driving plough oxen and breaking stones for road-mending was never doubted; and they were apparently in general rewarded at the same rate as their male counterparts. Female servants usually received less than men; but female reapers and binders at Minchinhampton, Gloucestershire, in 1380 received the men's daily rate of 4d, while female thatchers at Avenham nearby were being paid the same as men.[13] Indeed, compared with the ladies of the manor, peasant women enjoyed a certain independence; and, while they did not sit on juries and were not considered eligible as stewards or reeves, they were regarded as fully capable of taking over their husbands' holdings.

Prejudices against women as a sex existed, of course, since they were, after all, the descendants of Eve as well as sisters to the mother of God; and English manorial custom preferred succession of a holding to a male rather than a female heir. Yet daughters and widows did inherit and, although pressure was put upon them to marry or remarry as soon as possible, many of them continued to hold their land even though no marriage took place. An analysis of a number of family holdings in the West Midlands between 1350 and 1450 shows that, apart from those which came into the hands of the lord and were subsequently reissued outside the families, over 60 per cent went to female heiresses, nearly all widows.[14]

Both widows and widowers as well as bachelors were, however, under constant pressure to remarry as the lord was anxious to maintain the amount of labour he needed for the farming of his demesne. On the manor of Hales in 1274, for example, John of Romsey and Nicholas Sewal were 'given till next court to decide as to the widows offered them'. In 1279 on the same manor Thomas of Oldbury was ordered to take one Agatha of Halesowen to wife. He said he would rather be fined; and as he could find no guarantors for the fine he was ordered to be distrained. On the manor of Brightwaltham in 1335 as many as six widows who had come into their husbands' holdings without being able to provide the labour that was due, were each ordered to provide themselves with husbands if they wished to keep their land.[15]

Remarriage did, however, present problems. Few difficulties were encountered when the widow's new husband came from the same manor, as both parties would remain the property of the lord and so would any children they might have. But a marriage outside the manor which entailed the loss of property to one lord or the other was a different matter, and in these cases a fine would have to be paid. These fines were sometimes extremely heavy. On the Worcester Cathedral estate in the fourteenth century they could be as high as 13s 4d, the equivalent of about six weeks' wages. Other estates, however, were more lenient. In the 1350s Gloucester Abbey generally charged between 3s and 5s; and in 1356 a woman from Pattingham in Staffordshire was fined the relatively modest sum of 3s 4d for permission to leave the manor, though she would, no doubt, have been charged more had she not been so old and feeble.[16]

Fines were also imposed for fornication and adultery. These offences were really a matter for the Church; but the lord was concerned in them not only because a fine paid to the Church by the serf was so much loss to himself but also because unchastity might well depreciate the value of a bondswoman and this was his loss, too. So the lord ensured that fines were imposed upon those guilty of sexual offences whether or not the Church was involved in the case; and the culprits, both men and women, were liable to be flogged and put in the stocks as well as excommunicated.

The daily lives and conditions of peasantry varied from year to year and from district to district, just as did the ways in which lords made use of their land. In some cases the lord farmed his own land, advised by stewards and bailiffs and employing men for wages: by the early thirteenth century about half the men working on the land in England were receiving wages either for a full day's work or part-time work. In other cases the lord let his land to tenants who paid him, if not with their services, in kind or in money; in yet others he let it to one single tenant, a farmer, who for an agreed sum would buy his rights and the services due to him. These services were far from uniform. In Northumbria, for example, husbandmen were mostly shepherds and were rarely required to work on the lord's land; and in the east of England there were more men who had acquired their freedom from service than there were in the Midlands.[17]

This freedom was gained in a variety of ways. Some had paid for their manumission; others had been granted it by some such charter as that granted in 1355 to a serf of little use to him by the Bishop of Exeter:

> Whereas thou, being now come to thy fifty years, hast no longer any wife or offspring lawfully begotten of thy body, and art so insufficient in wordly goods that thou must needs live from thine own labour, and knowest no art but that of a boatman, therefore we cannot hold it unprofitable to us or to Our Church of Exeter to restore thee to thy natural liberty. Wherefore, in order that thou mayest be able to labour more freely and seek thy daily food and clothing by boatmanship, we do hereby manumit thee and restore to natural liberty both thyself and all goods and chattels whatsoever, specially reserving for Ourselves and Our successors and Our Church the patronage of thyself, and all thine offspring if perchance thou do beget any such.[18]

In this case the boatman was set completely free, though 'patronage', probably meaning heriot, was reserved both for himself and his children. But often the serf was granted his manumission only on condition that he continued to supply some service. The Prior of Bath, for instance, agreed to free one of his serfs on the understanding that he would continue throughout his life to be on call when required as a plumber and glazier.

Other serfs had gained their freedom by running away, usually to a town where – though the laws were vague, variable and contradictory – it seems that provided his lord had not succeeded in recapturing him within four days, a court order would be required to bring him back into servitude. If he succeeded in escaping to a chartered town and remained there for a year and a day, becoming a burgess or a member of a merchant guild, his lord was powerless to force him to go back to his manor, so long as he remained in the borough. If he did not stay in the borough, however, trouble might well be in store for him, as it was for Simon de Paris who although humbly born, had done so well for himself that he had become an alderman and sheriff of London. In 1306 he returned to his family home at Necton in Norfolk and was promptly arrested by the lord's bailiff who ordered him to take up the appointment of reeve. Simon refused and was put in prison, the lord maintaining that the man had been a villein, that is to say a feudal serf, and was, therefore, always a villein. He had been caught in his 'villein's nest' and was liable for villein's service. The justice agreed with the lord when the case came to court, but the jury did not. The influence of the City of London was powerful and Simon was released.[19]

Yet it was not always possible to escape from servitude even if the former villein remained in a town. Some town charters expressly excluded serfs from the privileges they granted. The charter of Plympton did so, for instance. Here the Earl of Devon decreed that 'our born serfs, who if they happen to remain or sojourn in the aforesaid borough, cannot claim or usurp any liberty by reason of the aforesaid liberty granted to our aforesaid burgesses, without our consent'. Also, it was often extremely difficult and occasionally impossible for the serf to enter a guild. In many towns no one who was a serf could be enrolled as an apprentice or admitted to a guild, a serf being defined as the son of a man who was himself a serf at the time of the child's birth. Yet if a man could survive as a porter, a roadmender or servant or in some other occupation for which guild membership was not necessary, his descendants might one day become burgesses and even rich citizens.

A serf might also become free if his lord decided for some reason to enfranchize a village and convert it into a borough. The Earl of Derby did this in 1251 when he created the borough of Higham Ferrers; and the ninety-two men whose names are listed in the charter, 'their families and tenements and chattels', were suddenly freed from servitude. Moreover, in the case of royal boroughs, their residents might bring freedom to serfs in villages outside their walls when their towns were prosperous and needed to expand. In 1256, for example, the townsmen of Scarborough received from the king permission to absorb the manor of Wallesgrave 'with all its appurtenances and 60 acres' into their town. Thus all the serfs on the manor were made free overnight. In the same way when a new borough was created, land and burgage rights were offered to all those who would come and settle in it. Such rights were offered by Edward I in 1286 when royal deputies were ordered to 'lay out, with sufficient streets and lanes, and adequate sites for a market and church, and plots for merchants and others, a new town with a harbour in a place called Gotowre-super-mare [Dorset]'.[20]

By these various means more and more serfs gained their freedom as the years passed; and whereas in the middle of the fourteenth century over half the population of England were serfs, by the end of the sixteenth all men were free. Because a man was free, however, it did not necessarily follow that he was better off than a serf. Some serfs held far more land than free men, as much as fifty or sixty acres, and could well afford to pay not to fulfil the obligations to their lords which were demanded of them, or even to send servants in their place. A free man, on the other hand, might well be driven to work on the land of a man who was still technically a serf in order to survive. And in the thirteenth and early fourteenth centuries survival for many became increasingly difficult. At least fifteen acres were needed to support a family of five, yet it is probable that less than half the number of families had as much land as that. Many peasants accordingly found it more profitable to work regularly for a master; and as more and more men paid for exemption from labour services, so there were more lords who could afford to, or were obliged to, pay men to work for them full time. The lord's workers not only had the benefit of a steady wage, in good seasons and in bad, something like 4d a day at the end of the thirteenth century, but they were also provided when necessary with living quarters in the manor's outbuildings or in barns on a more distant farm which were no more uncomfortable than the cottages of the other villagers; and they commonly enjoyed better food than the cottagers could supply for themselves. On one Norfolk manor in 1272 the lord's labourers were given beef as well as peas-pottage and bread, good beer and cheese, cod and herrings and even, on special occasions as a recompense for particularly heavy work, a goose.

Nor were lords the only employers of labour. Tenants, widows in particular, would pay other tenants to work for them, ploughing, harrowing, manuring or carting, and they would either pay them money or allow them a share of the crop when harvested. Men in regular and comparatively well rewarded work were, nevertheless, rare. They became proportionately rarer as the population of the country grew; and, while the number of mouths to feed expanded, the soil declined in fertility, agricultural prices and rents rose steeply, as much as 50 per cent in the first half of the century, and wages fell against the high cost of living. Poor harvests became frequent, that of 1315 being calamitous; and, while famine spread, cattle perished from murrain. At the same time the profits to be made from wool were so enticing that it was no longer considered worth while to reclaim land for arable farming. Fines imposed in the manorial courts had to be waived because the offenders were quite unable to pay them. And then in the summer of 1348 help for the agricultural labourer came with the consequences of a fearful pestilence that spread across the land.

# 3 · *Plague and Revolt*

'In the year of our Lord 1348, about the feast of the Translation of St Thomas,' wrote a monk of Malmesbury, 'the cruel pestilence, terrible to all future ages, came from parts over the sea to the south coast of England, into a port called Melcombe in Dorsetshire.'[1]

From Dorset the pestilence spread rapidly throughout the West Country, infecting Somerset and Devon, reaching Bristol on 15 August, then extending its ravages to Gloucester, sweeping east to Oxford then south to London.

> It passed most rapidly from place to place [recorded Robert of Avesbury, Registrar of the Court of Canterbury], swiftly killing ere mid-day many who in the morning had been well, and without respect of persons (some few rich people excepted), not permitting those destined to die to live more than three, or at most four, days. On the same day twenty, forty, sixty and very often more corpses were committed to the same grave.[2]

At Bristol and in other towns, existing graveyards were soon overflowing with the dead and new graves had to be dug elsewhere.

The victim's symptoms were first the eruption of hard, dry swellings in various parts of the body, particularly in the groin, on the legs, neck and under the arms, then of small black pustules, known as tokens. These were followed by delirium and the vomiting of blood. It was so infectious, said John Clynn of the Order of Friars Minor, that those who so much as touched the bodies of victims, were immediately infected themselves and buried with them. In some cases the whole process of infection and death occupied but a single day.[3]

No one knew whence the plague or Great Mortality, much later to be known as the Black Death, originated and even recently it was supposed that it was caused by exhalations from the earth which corrupted the air. Now it is known that bubonic plague is a disease not of man but of that species of black rat known as *Rattus rattus* which then scurried in their thousands through the streets and into houses, nesting in walls and rafters and darting out in search of food. The plague bacterium was transmitted from one rat to the next by fleas which, gorging on the animals' blood, became so saturated with bacteria that they could no longer digest them and jumped to the skin of human beings to feed there instead. The disease – which may not have been bubonic plague but anthrax[4] – seems to have originated in the East whence it was brought to the shores of the Black Sea by a Tartar horde which infected Genoese traders who in turn brought it to Europe.[5]

The spread of the plague was halted by the onset of the cold winter months, but it renewed its course more virulently than ever with the advent of spring, causing further deaths in Oxford and London, reaching Kent and the eastern counties, infecting East Anglia by March and Yorkshire by May. Only the remote areas of the north-west, the mountainous regions of Wales and Scotland and west Cornwall remained immune.

Kent suffered as badly as anywhere. According to William Dene, a contemporary monk of Rochester:

The Bishop of Rochester, out of his small household, lost four priests, five gentlemen, ten serving men, seven young clerks, and six pages so that not a soul remained who might serve him in any office . . . The mortality swept away so vast a multitude of both sexes that none could be found to carry the corpses to the grave. Men and women bore their own offspring on their shoulders to the church and cast them into a common pit. From these there proceeded so great a stench that hardly anyone dared to cross the cemeteries . . . In this pestilence many chaplains and paid clerics refused to serve, except at excessive salaries . . . and priests betook themselves to places where they could get larger stipends than in their own benefices . . . So great also was the deficiency of labourers and workmen of every kind in those days that more than a third of the land over the whole kingdom remained uncultivated.[6]

The worst affected places were the large towns where the often filthy and normally congested conditions in which people lived and rats thrived were more common than in the countryside. Small villages did not escape, however, once the contagion had caught hold. Some were entirely wiped out. It was said that the old and infirm were less susceptible than the young and healthy, but the pestilence struck all classes. The Archbishop of Canterbury died; so did all the Wardens of the Goldsmiths' and Hatters' Companies. Some religious houses lost all their inmates, Luffield and St Mary Magdalen at Sandon among them. But others were scarcely affected at all. At Christchurch, Canterbury, only four of the eighty monks lost their lives. Indeed, the pattern of mortality throughout the country varied considerably, as have modern estimates as to the number of lives lost. Professor Shrewsbury suggested that the death toll cannot have been more than a twentieth of the population; other estimates make it a third or even a half.[7] What the population of the country was in 1348 is unknown. It is likely, however, that there were about 1.25 million people when Domesday Book was compiled in 1086, that there were about 3.5 million in the middle of the thirteenth century, that by 1300 this figure had risen to some 4.25 million, but that by 1380 the population was less than 2.5 million, some areas, particularly in the north, being very thinly inhabited, others, in such good arable areas as East Anglia and Leicestershire, being more densely populated. There were reasons other than the Black Death for the sharp fall, among them occasional famine and the decline in corn growing which required a large labour force and the expansion of sheep farming which did not. Yet there can be no doubt that the mortality in 1348–9 was extremely high, and that, followed by less virulent epidemics, it accelerated a change which was already occurring in English society.[8]

As the thirteenth century progressed, the system of commuting service on the lord's farmland for money had begun to be less common and, on some manors, to be reversed. The growth in population had increased the demand for land and had enabled the lord to ask for both higher rents and more frequent services. But now there was plenty of land for the surviving peasants and an acute labour shortage. Indeed, in the years immediately following the Black Death there were plentiful supplies of corn, cattle and sheep which had not been affected by the pestilence: seven years after the Black Death some 40,000 sacks of wool were being exported annually. And many peasants were able to increase their holdings by taking over the strips of those who had perished. Others, who had no land, were able to demand greater rewards for their services – as much as two and a half times as much as they had earned before the pestilence – and if they did not receive these increases, they fled to another manor or to a town where labour was short and sure to be well rewarded.

Many landlords thus deprived of labour chose to let their land either for a money rent or for payment in kind; and their tenants – some growing crops, others becoming sheep farmers, yet others doing both – developed into quite well-to-do yeoman farmers whose interests were more closely identified with the lesser gentry than with the landless labourers whose discontents they no longer shared. Parliament supported the yeoman farmers in their disagreements with the landless labourer. So did the lords of the manor, both lay and ecclesiastical, who feared that the labourers' demand for higher wages might make their rents from the farmers difficult to collect. And so did the law officers of the Crown whom many peasants saw as the greatest predators of all. This combined resentment towards the labourers resulted in 1351 in a Statute of Labourers which vainly endeavoured to keep wages down, to ensure, for instance, that no one was to be paid for haymaking more than the 1d a day he might have expected to earn before the Black Death, and that charity should not be given to able-bodied beggars. A subsequent statute proposed that any labourer who left his place of work to seek higher wages should be branded with the letter F on his forehead as a sign of falsehood. It became a crime for a labourer to wear clothes suited only to a higher station in life, for a servant to pay more for his cloth than a prescribed amount, for 'common lewd women' to dress like 'good noble dames' and so make it difficult to discover 'what rank they are'.

As the difference between the labourers and those more fortunate widened, so there developed an increasing concern for social status. The term gentleman began to be generally used as well as yeoman and husband-man. Also, in the higher ranks of society, the range of hereditary titles was extended; and those below them in the social hierarchy were expected to show due respect to their betters, to their 'very dear, honourable and rightful lord'. As *The Mirror of Magistrates* put it,

> No subject ought for any kind of course
> To force the lord, but yield him to the laws.[9]

Subjects were, however, no longer content to submit themselves to this subordination and were becoming ever more unruly. They declared themselves 'to be quit and utterly discharged of all manner of serfage, due as well of their body as of their tenures,' according to the preamble to a statute of 1377, 'and they will not suffer any distress or other justice to be made upon them. They do menace the ministers of their lords of life and member, and, which more is, gather themselves in great routs and agree by such confederacy that every one shall aid the other to resist their lords with strong hand.'[10]

These unruly villeins had many allies. There were burghers in the towns who, dissatisfied with their own landlords, sympathised with them. So did many friars and priests; one of these was John Ball, who had on three occasions been committed to the Archbishop of Canterbury's prison for his utterances and, despite a subsequent sentence of excommunication, had moved about the country from churchyard to market-place, demanding the abolition of all bishops and abbots and preaching upon the text:

> When Adam dalf [dug] and Eve span,
> Who was thanne a gentilman?

Ball warmly supported many of the doctrines of John Wyclif, especially Wyclif's claim that men had the right to withhold tithes from unworthy clergymen, his condemnation of monasticism, the secular riches of the church and the celibacy of the clergy. And, although Wyclif had as many if not more supporters in Parliament as among the common people (who were not particularly anxious to have the Bible translated into English), there were several Lollards, as Wyclif's followers were called, on the rebels' side. Also on their side was a motley collection of outlaws and vagabonds, discharged soldiers and bowmen, poachers and other fugitive offenders against the laws of the forest.

Their growing discontent was exacerbated by a series of taxes levied on everyone and known as poll taxes, the third of which, imposed in 1381 and three times as heavy as its predecessor, was not graded by rank as that one had been. There were violent and evidently spontaneous protests against this tax and its often corrupt collectors in widely separated parts of the country, in Essex and Suffolk, Hertfordshire, Norfolk and Kent. In all of these counties and elsewhere armed bands, villagers and townsmen, rose in arms. Manors and religious houses were attacked; lords and priors were murdered; and the cries went up, 'Death to all lawyers. John Ball hath rungeth your bell!'

The men of Kent and Essex marched on London, after plundering Rochester and Canterbury, releasing Ball from Maidstone gaol and destroying all lawyers' houses on the line of march. Their leader was one Walter, perhaps an ex-soldier, a man who worked on the tiling of roofs and was consequently known as Wat Tyler. Under Tyler's command, the rebels encamped at Blackheath where they waited for an interview with the king, Richard II, who was then only fourteen years old. The king agreed to appear personally before the rebels, but pressure of the crowds prevented him from landing at Greenwich; and, as the frustrated rebels entered Southwark and broke down the doors of the Marshalsea prison, he returned to his refuge with his mother in the Tower. The rebels, having plundered Lambeth Palace, burning books, accounts and furniture and smashing open wine casks, crossed London Bridge, joined by the London mob. They made their way to Fleet Street, opened the Fleet prison, destroyed the lawyers' rolls in the Temple; attacked foreign artisans, broke into the houses of the city merchants and, so the chronicler Froissart said, 'fell on the food and drink that was found. In the hope of appeasing them, nothing was refused them . . . They destroyed several fine houses, saying they would burn all the suburbs, take London by force, and burn and destroy everything.' The Savoy Palace, home of the king's uncle, John of Gaunt, Duke of Lancaster, was burned to the ground; the Tower was besieged. On 14 June, the king, who from his room in the Tower had looked down upon the mob, 'howling like men possessed', managed to arrange an interview with the rebels at Mile

End where, among other concessions, he granted their requests for the abolition of feudal services and their right to rent land at 4d an acre. Satisfied, some of the rebels went home. Others remained, however, and meanwhile the violence continued with renewed fury.

Before leaving the Tower the king had advised Simon of Sudbury, Archbishop of Canterbury and Chancellor, as well as his other threatened ministers, to seize the opportunity to escape by one of the watergates and to slip away downstream. But as Sudbury appeared on the river stairs he was recognized by the rebels and the London mob still congregating in thousands outside; and, as he hurriedly retreated within the walls, they stormed across the causeway and the drawbridges, smashed their way through the gates, poured into the outer yard and then into the inner bailey. Pushing their way through the Great Hall and into the Wardrobe, they ransacked the kitchens, bedchambers and armoury, and forcing down the door of the Queen Mother's private apartments, they smashed her furniture, tore down the hangings from the walls and cut her bedclothes into ribbons. The queen herself, smuggled out of the Tower in the confusion by her pages, managed to escape and was rowed away upstream. But in the Chapel of St John the shouting rabble came upon the Archbishop, Sir Robert Hales, the Lord Treasurer, John of Gaunt's physician, and John Legge who had devised the poll tax. They were all at prayer before the altar. Dragged away from the chapel, down the steps and out of the gates onto Tower Hill, where traitors were executed, they were beheaded one after the other. Their heads were stuck on pikes and carried in triumph around the city.

The next day the king met the rebels again, this time at Smithfield, the open land north-west of the tower where horse sales were held in more peaceful times. Further concessions were made to the rebels: all bishoprics and all lordships, except that of the king, would be abolished; the estates of the church would be confiscated; the rebels would be pardoned and emancipated. But the insolent arrogance of Wat Tyler, who rode right up to the king, his 'horse's tail under the very nose of the king's horse', made the mayor of London, Sir William Walworth, a fishmonger, lose his temper. Riding forward and calling Tyler a 'stinking wretch', he knocked him clean off his horse with the flat of his broadsword. As he lay on the ground one of the king's squires dismounted and stabbed him in the stomach, killing him. Seeing this, the rebels cried out in horror, and brandishing their weapons they advanced upon the king's retinue. But with remarkable self-control Richard trotted forward to hold them back, calling out to them, 'Sirs, will you kill your king? I am your captain. Follow me.' And he led them north towards the fields of Clerkenwell.

The Peasants' Revolt as it was later to be called was over. The mayor galloped back to the city to raise a volunteer force and soon had the rebels surrounded. Tyler's head was cut from his corpse and displayed on London Bridge. John Ball who had fled from Smithfield was hanged, drawn and quartered in the presence of the king at St Albans and his quarters were displayed in four other towns as a warning to traitors. Jack Straw, another leading rebel, whose followers had burned down the Priory of St John, Clerkenwell, was also executed and his head displayed on London Bridge. Other rebels, both in London and in Norfolk, Suffolk, Cambridgeshire, Hertfordshire and other counties where simultaneous revolts had also erupted, were severely punished. The promises made to them were withdrawn on the grounds that they had been obtained under duress. The poll tax was abandoned, however, and Parliament thereafter became more than ever determined that the king should not endeavour to supplement the income which he drew from traditional and hereditary rights and land by exceptional taxes except in special circumstances and with their approval. It was to be very many years before the violence and repercussions of the Peasants' Revolt were to be forgotten.[11]

# 4 · *Churches, Monks and Friars*

On Sundays the villagers entered the church, dipped their fingers in the stoup of holy water, crossed themselves, then stood in the aisles whispering to each other, occasionally moving across the rush-covered floor of the nave to murmur a greeting to a friend or to share a muttered joke, the voice of the priest rising above their own, the Latin words of the service familiar in their ears, though rarely intelligible, except for the *Paternoster* and the *Ave* in which some of them would join. On the walls all around them were paintings, some of them frightening pictures of Judgement Day and Souls in Torment; and at the east end where the priest stood were the benches and pews for the clergy, for the lord and his family and for the parish clerk. There were no seats for the rest of the congregation; and, if a priest gave a sermon, the people in the nave would sit down upon the rushes. Sermons, however, were not given nearly as regularly as conscientious bishops would have liked. There are no pulpits in English churches of a date earlier than the middle of the fourteenth century. Nor was music often heard during ordinary services until the fourteenth century when organs began to be installed. But there was often much loud noise from the congregation. The Knight of La Tour-Landry described a service evidently far from unusual, in which there was such 'chattering, laughing, jangling and jesting aloud' that the priest 'smote his hand on the book to make them hold their peace; but there were some that did not'.[1]

Priests were in what were known as Major Orders, but there were also thousands of men in Minor Orders, clerks, accountants, doctors and lawyers. In the Earl of Northumberland's household, for example, there were no less than eleven upper servants in orders, apart from the family chaplain. These included the surveyor, the almoner, the earl's secretary and his children's master of grammar.[2] Such men, having been tonsured as all university students and even some grammar schoolboys had to be, were classed as clerics and, having at least enough Latin to read a verse of the Bible, could claim benefit of clergy, which meant, originally, that if charged with a felony they could be tried only in an ecclesiastical court. The Major Orders were divided into two classes, those, like monks, living in seclusion and subject to the *regula* of a religious order, and known therefore as regular clergy, and those, like priests, living in the world (*in seculo*) and hence known as the secular clergy. In all there were perhaps as many as 40,000 ordained men in England in the thirteenth century, that is to say, one for about twenty-five or thirty of the adult population.[3]

Most priests, if their superiors are to be believed, were neither dutiful nor competent. They were 'dumb dogs', Archbishop Stephen Langton asserted; while Archbishop Peckham complained in 1281, 'The ignorance of the priests casteth the people into the ditch of error. The folly and unlearning of the clergy, who are bidden to instruct men in the Catholic faith, sometimes tendeth rather to mistaken than to sound doctrine.' Roger Bacon agreed with him: 'Clerks and country priests recite the Church services, of which they know little or nothing, like brute beasts.' Although some came from rich and even noble families, a large proportion of priests were of peasant stock and seem to have come to holy orders by way of assisting at services as a boy, by acting as server or 'holy water clerk', and then, perhaps, having picked up some skill at reading and writing and a little Latin from some helpful parson, by attending a grammar school. Most of them were poor, despite the glebe land, which was assigned to them by the manor, and the tithes, which, if too strictly demanded, alienated them from their even poorer parishioners. Many were obliged to work on the land as though they were peasants themselves. Others, like the uncouth and lazy fellow in *Piers Plowman*, went about from village to village 'singing for silver', offering such services as they were licensed to perform to any who could pay for them. Those resident in a parish generally lived in small, dark houses little more comfortable than those of the peasantry around them. The annual value of their livings, even in the middle of the fifteenth century, was only about £9, and although this might seem a lot compared with the £3 or so that a peasant with about twenty acres might be able to spend on his family, the priest usually had to find money out of his stipend for service books, the upkeep of the chancel and occasional alms.[4]

The reports of diocesan visitations revealed a lamentable situation. These reports were compiled after the bishop's representatives had been to every parish to gather evidence from clergy and 'synodsmen' or sidesmen. They were intended to note faults rather than to record virtues; but the evidence of widespread malpractices which they present seems incontrovertible. In many places priests, like several of their bishops, lived openly with wives and children, despite the stern prohibition of the Lateran Council of

1074 and the many subsequent demands from Rome, Canterbury and diocesan synods. John Peckham, the Franciscan who became Archbishop of Canterbury in 1279, felt obliged to rule that priests' children should not inherit their father's benefices. Also, in many parishes, the clergy were notorious tavern-haunters. A visitation in Oxfordshire revealed that in nearly a third of the parishes the parson was an absentee, and that in nearly half the church was in need of extensive repairs. In the city of Norwich in 1373 ten clergy were accused of incontinence, one of them with two different women, Beatrice and Juliana, for which he was fined 5s. In Devonshire in 1301 the parishioners of Clyst Honiton reported that the chancel was so ruinous that Mass could not be said at the high altar, that there was no chalice and that 'all other appurtenances of the church' were insufficient. Thirty years later, in the same parish, the priest was reported to be unchaste with three different women, one of them the wife of a sidesman. At Dawlish a priest 'hath kept his concubine for ten years and more, or longer still; and, though often corrected on that account, he incorrigibly persists'. In another parish the clergy spent 'their time not in offering to God due sacrifice of praise, but rather in gabbling through the service, with frequent interruptions of vain and unprofitable discourse, and unlawful murmurs to each other'. At Marychurch, where the priest was suspected of embezzlement, there was neither pyx nor chalice, and the sidesmen said

> . . . that the vicar puts all sorts of beasts into the churchyard, whereby it is evilly trodden down and foully defiled. Item, he appropriates the trees in the churchyard that are blown down, and uses them for his own buildings. Item, he causes his malt [for his brewing] to be prepared in the church, and stores his corn and other things therein; whereby his servants, in their exits and their entrances, open the door, and at times of tempest the wind comes in and is wont to [loosen the tiles] . . . He often absents himself and stays at Moreton-Hampstead, sometimes for fifteen days, sometimes for eight.[5]

A visitation carried out in the admittedly rather more than usually disreputable diocese of Hereford in 1397 found only forty-four of 281 parishes well administered. In the remainder priests were accused of fornication with their maidservants or with their parishioners' wives, of neglect and absenteeism, of allowing their churches to fall into disuse and even into ruins. One rector was charged with threshing his corn in the churchyard, another with drunkenness, yet others with setting themselves up as tradesmen, with lending money at exorbitant rates, with refusing to conduct funerals or baptisms, with forging wills, with selling the Sacrament, with disclosing confessions made under the Sacrament of Penance, with seducing women in church, and even with practising Black Magic.

Hereford diocese, however, was exceptional; and there were certainly priests enough in the Church who, like Chaucer's parson, the brother of a ploughman, were 'rich in holy thought and work, who truly knew Christ's gospel and could preach it devoutly to parishioners and teach it'.

Yet, as Chaucer well knew, the virtues of such parsons as these were offset by the only too common priest

> Who set his benefice to hire
> And left his sheep encumbered in the mire
> Or ran to London to earn easy bread
> By singing masses for the wealthy dead.

The clergy, wrote John Wyclif,

haunten tavernes out of all mesure and sterin lewid men to dronkenesse, ydelnesse and cursed swerynge and chydynge and fightynge . . . Thei fallen to [gambling] at tables, chess and hasard, and beten the stretis, and sitten at the taverne til thei hav lost their witt . . . and suntyme neither have eighe ne tonge ne hond ne foot to helpe hem self for dronkenesse.[6]

In the next century there are still more records of parsons being arrested for coining, poaching and even highway robbery.

Yet, although he appears often to have had scant respect for the priest and to have attended Mass on Sundays and on some holy days more out of habit than piety, the peasant's whole vision of the world was in turns illuminated and overcast by thoughts of God and the Devil. The friars who came to preach on the village green, filling his mind with dreams of heaven and hell, the images on the walls of the church and the mystery plays which were performed there, stories of the miraculous properties of the nearby shrine (the one place outside the village which he was ever likely to see unless he went to a fair), the holy wells which had once been under the protection of pagan gods, the legends in which Christian and heathen heroes and villains were inextricably intertwined, the superstitious beliefs handed down to him – the magical qualities of consecrated bread which, placed beside his hives, would protect his bees, or if sprinkled over cabbage would keep off cater-pillars – all these helped to make him aware of other worlds in which he would be rewarded or punished according to his deserts, worlds far beyond his village which was itself dominated by the church and by the manor which the Church as an institution taught him to respect.

He had reason enough to find the ministers of the Church oppressive. First of all there were tithes to pay, and these worked out at about 10 per cent of a parishioner's gross revenue; there were 'great tithes' on crops and cattle and 'lesser tithes' on all manner of other produce and possessions. The Vicar of Tadcaster in Yorkshire in 1290 was entitled to receive 'lesser tithes' on 'wool, flax, pot-herbs, leeks, apples, cheese, butter, milk, eggs, calves, chicken, geese, hens, sucking-pigs, bees and honey'. Then there were Mass pennies to be contributed and occasional Peter's pence, light-scot and church-scot and, most resented of all, the mortuary which could entail handing over to the Church the head of the family's second best beast upon his death, the best having already been appropriated by the lord of the manor as heriot.

These impositions led to widespread dislike of the clergy. In the early sixteenth century a Spanish envoy reported home from London, 'Nearly all the people here hate the priests.' And he might well have said the same a hundred years earlier. It was considered bad luck to meet a priest in the road, and passers-by were advised that if they did so they should 'leave him on their left hand'. 'Some men,' it was said, 'had [rather] to mete with a [toad] or a frogge in the way than with . . . any man of Holy Church.'[7]

Much as the clergy as a whole were distrusted, however, and much as their impositions were resented, the church was accepted as the natural centre of village life – even though the peasantry rarely attended service there except on Sundays and on certain holy days – and in many parishes sabbath-breaking was considered a serious offence to be punished with both fines and beating. In 1450 in the diocese of Durham a man working at a mill 'on the day of the Lord's Ascension' was sentenced 'to go before the procession on three Sundays in his shirt and drawers, after the fashion of a penitent', and was warned that a second offence would entail a fine of 10s. The next year two women caught washing linen on St Mary Magdalene's day were sentenced to be beaten 'with a hank of linen yarn'; and a man who mowed his meadow on St Oswald's day was also sentenced to be beaten and to be publicly paraded about the village with a bundle of hay in his hands.

Meetings were held in church and announcements were made there. Business and farming matters were discussed in the nave, and the bells in the tower were rung to bring people's attention to the seasonal demands of the agricultural year, the planting of beans, or the pruning of apple trees. Plays were performed in church, and festivals celebrated with music and dancing. Here manorial courts and sometimes even markets were held. And here, with much drinking of ale in the churchyards afterwards, baptisms, marriages and funerals all took place.

Babies were baptized as soon as possible, often on the very day of birth, the midwife holding the child by the font round which acolytes carried lighted tapers while the priest intoned the words of the service. It was a brief ceremony, as was that of a wedding which was celebrated at the church door. First banns of marriage were published, as they still are now. A book of instruction required the priest to 'thryes ask in holy chyrche . . . eche day on this manner: N. of V. has spoken with N. of P. to have her to his wife, and to ryght lyve in forme of holy chyrche. If any mon knowe any lettying qwy they may not come togedyr say now or never on payne of cursying.'

This same book of instruction for priests sets down the following form for the marriage itself:

N: Hast thou wille to have this wommon
  to thi wedded wif

R: Ye Syr

N: My thou wel fynde at thi best to love
  hur and hold ye to hur and to no other
  to thi lives end

R: Ye Syr

N: Then take her by yor hande and saye
  after me: 'I N, take thee N, in forme of
  holy chyrche, to my wedded wyfe, for-
  saking alle other, holdying me hollych
  to thee, in sekeness and in hele, in
  ryches and in poverte, in well and in
  wo, tyl deth us departe, and there to I
  plyght ye my trowthe.'[8]

The ceremony of a funeral was generally far more elaborate than that of a wedding. At John Paston's funeral at St Peter's Hungate in Norwich there were thirty-eight priests in attendance, twenty-three nuns and sixty-five choristers, both men and boys, as well as a prioress with her maid, an anchoress and four torch-bearers. Later at Bromholm Priory, where Paston's body was taken, fourteen ringers were employed to toll the priory bells and ninety-four servitors, paid at the rate of 3d or 4d a day, to wait upon the guests.[9]

The amount of food and drink consumed by these guests was enormous. So it was at the funeral feast given in memory of Thomas Stonor a few years later. A document in the *Stonor Papers* lists an extraordinary variety of dishes served on this occasion, including, 'for priests etc.', 'first: chicken broth, capons, mutton, geese, custard; the second course, soup, hotch-potch of meat and herbs, capons, lamb, pork, veal, roasted pigeons, baked rabbits, pheasants, venison, jelly'.[10]

Yet the funeral and its subsequent feast were often the least heavy expenses in bereaved well-to-do families. There were Masses for the souls of the departed to be paid for, sometimes in perpetuity, chantry chapels to be endowed, monuments to be raised, effigies carved, tombs inscribed, stained glass windows to be fitted, chapels built, or vestments and sacred vessels purchased. And by such means as these, the churches of the country became increasingly rich, commodious and ornate.[11]

By the end of the thirteenth century there were already more than 8000 churches in England, the responsibility for whose upkeep lay partly with the priests, partly with his parishioners who commonly raised money at church ales. These events, at which villagers were encouraged to drink as much as they could, were usually held in the churchyard or in a building known as the church house nearby. The ale-wife was generally asked to suspend her brewing for as long as they lasted. Some went on for three days. At the Deverills in Wiltshire in the thirteenth century, bachelors who could still stand up were allowed to go on drinking for nothing. Other parishes resorted to blackmail: at St Andrew's Church, Plymouth, only the second-best copes were used for the funerals of parishioners who had not been sufficiently generous to the church in their wills.[12]

As the number of churches steadily grew, so did the number of monasteries. After the formation of the Benedictine monastery at Canterbury by St Augustine towards the end of the sixth century, there had been no foundations other than Benedictine in England until the reformist order of Cluny etablished a priory at Lewes in 1077. Less than thirty years later over half of England's seventeen cathedrals were monastic; and in the twelfth century Cistercian and Carthusian houses were founded in various parts of the country, such as the Cistercian houses of Rievaulx and Fountains Abbey in Yorkshire and the Carthusian Witham in Somerset. In 1131 Gilbert, grandson of a rich Norman knight, founded the Gilbertine Order, the only monastic order to originate in England. He persuaded seven good women of the parish to live in a building adjoining the church and to abide by a rule of life like that of the Cistercians. Lay sisters were encouraged to join the Order and then lay brothers to help farm the land. Finally priests were appointed to serve the joint community. Other foundations rapidly followed; and by the time of St Gilbert's death in 1189 there were nine Gilbertine houses of both men and women in the country and four of canons only. In the double houses nuns were required to keep to the north side of the church, the canons to the south, and an ordinance provided for a partition wall 'high enough so that canons and nuns cannot see each other, but not so high that the nuns cannot hear the celebration of Masses at the canons' altar'.[13]

This was the period in which monasticism flourished most usefully and profitably in England. Many monasteries were seats of learning and centres of art. In them noble chronicles were compiled and beautifully illuminated; charity and hospitality were dispensed; abbots were called upon to lend their wisdom to the rulers of their country; kings and nobles made gifts of land and money to respected houses and hoped in return to save their souls; schools and hospitals were established; lovely buildings were erected; the wool industry expanded as sheep, under the skilful care of the monks, cropped the grass of the dales.

Since then, however, these earlier virtues of monasticism had been gradually eroded, as religious houses grew so wealthy that their income seems to have been at one time almost a fifth of the whole national income. The original strict rules imposed upon the orders began to be widely ignored. No longer did monks confine themselves to the cloister, observe the regulations about obedience and poverty, conscientiously say the Masses enjoined upon them by past benefactors, or pay too strict a regard to the rules framed to limit their diet. Meat, once provided only for the sick, was now enjoyed by all in the infirmary; and when this was forbidden by papal statute, a special room was set aside, a kind of half-way house, usually known as the 'misericorde', 'the chamber of mercy', between the infirmary and the refectory, where meat was freely allowed upon the table. This, too, was prohibited by papal statute; but in 1339 the pope, recognizing that the prohibition was unenforceable, conceded that the monks might continue to relish their meat in the 'misericorde' provided that only half their number did so at a time, the other half maintaining the vegetarian rule elsewhere.[14]

As early as 1177 Giraldus Cambrensis had been astonished by the extravagant fare enjoyed by the monks of Canterbury. In his autobiography, written in the third person, Giraldus recorded:

Sitting then in the hall with the Prior and the greater monks at the high table he noted there, as he was wont to relate, two things, these were the excessive superfluity of gestures [by the monks who were forbidden to speak to each other] and the multitude of the dishes. For the Prior sent so many gifts of meat to the monks who served him, and they on their part to the lower tables, and the recipients gave so many thanks and were so profuse in their gesticulations of fingers and hands and arms and in the whisperings whereby they avoided open speech, (wherein all showed a most unedifying levity and licence) that Gerald felt as if he were sitting at a stage play or among a company of actors and buffoons; for it would be more appropriate to their Order and to their honourable estate to speak modestly in plain human speech than to use such a dumb garrulity of frivolous signs and hissings. Of the dishes themselves and their multitude what can I say but this, that I have oft-times heard him relate how six courses or more were laid in order (or shall I not say in disorder?) upon the table; and these of the most sumptuous kind. At the very last, in the guise of principal courses, masses of herbs were brought to all the tables, but they were scarcely touched, in face of so many kinds of fishes, roast and boiled, stuffed and fried – so many dishes tricked out by the cook's art with eggs and pepper – so many savouries and sauces composed by that same art to stimulate gluttony, and to excite the appetite. Add to this, that there was such abundance of wine and strong drink – of new wine and mead and mulberry wine, and all intoxicating liquors in so much abundance – that even beer, which the English brew excellently (especially in Kent), found no place; but rather beer stood as low in this matter as the pot-herbs among other dishes. I say, ye might see so excessive and sumptuous a superfluity here in meats and dishes as might weary not only the guest who partook thereof, but even the beholder. What then would Paul the Hermit have said to this? or Anthony? or Benedict, father and founder of monastic life? . . . The Church, in proportion as she hath grown in wealth, hath much decreased in the virtues.[15]

In the later Middle Ages most monks seem to have done quite as well for themselves as those Giraldus saw guzzling at Canterbury. At Westminster the abbey's household records show that the fish supplied was required to be the best obtainable in the market, and that each monk was to have a plentiful supply of bream or mullet, flounders or herring or 'salted Cambridge eels'. At the far less well endowed abbey at Spalding, the daily allowance of four eggs or fish for each monk was increased, under the terms of an abbot's will, to six. All may not have been eaten, but the reports of visitations suggest that the surplus was less often given to the poor than to friends of the monks who came to meals with them.[16]

While food and drink were enjoyed in abundance, manual labour, which had been insisted upon by St Benedict, was gradually abandoned as being both beneath a monk's dignity and unnecessary in foundations which had become so affluent. Work in the fields was not only given up but also work in the monastery where the duties of cooking, washing, and even shaving the brethren were performed by servants who also worked in the gardens and cut the cloister grass. In the richer houses there were more servants than monks. At the same time, although monasteries were still the principal distributors of charity to the poor – for whom the State as a whole made no provision – the money given away was, in most cases, a very small proportion of total income. Indeed, the surviving accounts of English monasteries indicate that never so much as a tenth of their income was paid out in charity.[17]

The strict observance of celibacy had long been abandoned with that of poverty. A visitation of Flaxley Abbey in 1397 revealed that nine monks were fornicators and that the abbot himself was 'defamatus' with three different women. Discipline at Flaxley was unusually lax, but there is no doubt that celibacy in monastic houses was no longer strictly observed, and that the monk, far from living in conditions of austerity and abnegation, was more likely to resemble Chaucer's whose passion was hunting and whose clothes were as expensive as any knight's:

> The Rule of good St Benet or St Maur
> As old and strict he tended to ignore;
> He let go by the things of yesterday
> And took the modern world's more spacious way.
> He did not rate that text at a plucked hen
> Which says that hunters are not holy men
> And that a monk uncloistered is a mere
> Fish out of water, flapping on the pier,
> That is to say a monk out of his cloister.
> That was a text he held not worth an oyster . . .
> This Monk was therefore a good man to horse;
> Greyhounds he had, as swift as birds, to course.
> Hunting a hare or riding at a fence
> Was all his fun, he spared for no expense.
> I saw his sleeves were garnished at the hand
> With fine grey fur, the finest in the land,
> And on his hood, to fasten it at his chin
> He had a wrought-gold cunningly fashioned pin . . .
> Supple his boots, his horse in fine condition.
> He was a prelate fit for exhibition,
> He was not pale like a tormented soul.
> He liked a fat swan best, and roasted whole.[18]

While monks came from all classes, until the later Middle Ages nuns were recruited almost exclusively from the richer families, often from those which had failed to find husbands for them. Abbesses of the Benedictine Barking Abbey included three queens and two princesses. Illegitimate daughters were also sent to nunneries; so were the wives of noble rebels, young women of fortune whose guardians or families wanted to get their own hands on their money, daughters of weak health or unsound mind as well as those of recognized vocation. They were usually required to bring a dowry with them and they were expected to be able to read and sing, though not necessarily to write. They were for the most part at least sixteen years old before they were accepted as novices, though much younger girls were taken by some nunneries where they were educated to the required level of literacy.

The number of nuns in the country was never great, perhaps no more than 2000 at the most; and most nunneries were very small institutions. A few had schools attached; others had hospitals to which not only sisters were admitted when ill but also relatives. Yet, as in monasteries, most of the hard work in nunneries was carried out by lay servants, the nuns themselves being occupied in more leisurely pursuits such as needlework. Many nunneries, indeed, were more like pleasant holiday retreats than the religious houses which would have once satisfied St Benedict. Private sleeping chambers seem to have been more usual than dormitories, and small dining-rooms than communal refectories.

There were severe prioresses such as the one at Catesby who dragged her nuns about 'even in choir'; but most appear to have been as easy-going as the Abbess of Shaftesbury who, in the fourteenth century, secured a dispensation to take a year's holiday so that she could 'reside in her manors for the sake of air and recreation'.[19] The records of visitations indicate that, although dancing and entertainments by minstrels were forbidden except at Christmas, there was widespread jollity in many nunneries at all seasons. The Prioress of Stamford had to confess to the Bishop of Lincoln that one of her nuns had run off with a harpist with whom she had gone to live in Newcastle-on-Tyne. In 1387 it was discovered that at Romsey the nuns habitually took their pets, rabbits, birds and dogs, into church with them. At another nunnery they took their squirrels.[20] And at Langley, a guest staying in the convent took with her 'a great abundance of dogs, insomuch that whenever she comes to church there follow her twelve dogs, who make a great uproar'.[21]

In many convents the nuns were permitted to bring their own clothes. And even when wearing the habits required by their order's regulations, they did not always deny themselves the pleasure of jewellery; while wimples, originally intended to conceal as much of the face as possible, were so arranged as to reveal the temples and the chin and were elegantly pleated like that worn by Chaucer's prioress whose 'forehead, certainly was fair of spread':

> Her cloak, I noticed, had a graceful charm.
> She wore a coral trinket on her arm,
> A set of beads, the gaudiest tricked in green,
> Whence hung a golden brooch of brightest sheen
> On which there first was graven a crowned A,
> And, lower, *Amor vincit omnia*.

The friar, who accompanied the prioress on the pilgrimage to Canterbury, was equally well dressed, though far less pleasant. Indeed, he appears in a less favourable light than anyone else on the journey. As with the monk, the portrait in the earlier Middle Ages would have been much different. There were four main orders, the Carmelites, also known as white friars because of the colour of their mantles, the Franciscans or grey friars, the Dominicans, the black friars, and the Austin Friars. Later they were joined by the Crutched Friars, or Friars of the Holy Cross, the Trinitarians, or Red Friars, the Pied Friars, or Friars of the Blessed Mary, and the Friars of the Penance of Jesus Christ, the Friars of the Sack. Unlike monks they did not lead a cloistered life but went about the country and into the poorest districts of the towns as evangelists, preaching the word of God, hearing confessions and ministering to the sick. Most of their founders had laid great stress on the need for poverty not only for individual friars but for the order as a whole. The Franciscans, for example, had been enjoined to live by manual labour or by begging for sustenance but were not allowed to accept money or to own property. They preached wherever a congregation could be assembled, usually in the open, and gathered around them large and silent crowds who listened fascinated to their sermons, to stories of miracles and fearful punishments, tales of the apostles, the disciples and the prophets, the extraordinary and exciting legends of the saints, and the news that they brought of life in the outside world. Often they offended the parish clergy whose own eloquence was no match for theirs, and whose sermons, when given, were so much more prosaic; and frequently they annoyed the bishops whose indolence or avidity they roundly condemned.

But by the end of the thirteenth century those friars who still adhered to the strict rules of conduct laid down by the founders of their orders were few and far between. With munificent bequests from royal and noble patrons, all the main orders had acquired riches and had been enabled to begin the construction of buildings of great splendour, often on the sites of much poorer houses where their former indigence and good intentions had once aroused the admiration of laity and clergy alike. Henry III, Edward I and Edward II were particularly generous to the Dominicans whose property in London, where their first community had been founded in Chancery Lane in 1221, had spread down to the river and by 1278 included those two huge Thameside strongholds, Baynards Castle and Montfichet Tower. Henry III's brother, the Earl of Cornwall, as well as Henry III himself, Edward I and John of Gaunt had helped the Carmelites to develop an equally large area upon which a splendid priory appeared. Margaret, second queen of Edward I, Queen Isabella and Queen Philippa were all benefactors of the Franciscans whose Greyfriars Monastery was to be one of the finest in London with a large library built at the expense of Richard Whittington. There were similar magnificent friaries and friary churches throughout England, notably at Coventry where the Carmelites' church was as impressive as any cathedral, and at King's Langley where the Dominicans prayed for the soul of Edward II's beloved Piers Gaveston. Most of the priories, like those at Reading,

Southampton, Northampton, Bristol, Newcastle and Chelmsford, have disappeared; but enough remains of the Carmelite friary at Aylesford in Kent for posterity to realize how far, by the time its cloister and sleeping chambers had been completed, the white friars had departed from their founder's ideals.[22]

Certainly, by Chaucer's time, the friar was more often a 'very festive fellow', 'glib with gallant phrase and well-turned speech'. The friar in *The Canterbury Tales* is a limiter, one granted an area in which to beg so as to limit his activities. A disreputable, grasping, ingratiating fellow, he is ready to grant absolution after hearing confessions – for which he claims to have a special licence from the Pope – provided he is decently rewarded.

> He kept his tippet stuffed with pins for curls,
> And pocket-knives to give to pretty girls.
> And certainly his voice was gay and sturdy,
> At sing-songs he was champion of the hour.
> His neck was whiter than a lily-flower
> But strong enough to butt a bruiser down.
> He knew the taverns well in every town
> And every innkeeper and barmaid too
> Better than lepers, beggars and that crew,
> For in so eminent a man as he
> It was not fitting with the dignity
> Of his position, dealing with a scum
> Of wretched lepers; nothing good can come
> Of commerce with such slum-and-gutter dwellers,
> But only with the rich and victual-sellers.

# 5 · *Drinking and Playing*

As well as in the church, villagers met in the alehouse, a drinking place far less expensive than the large inns in the towns and on the main highways where the more prosperous wayfarers stayed and rather less so than the taverns which sold wine and which became more socially distinguishable from alehouses as the Middle Ages progressed. In the earlier years of the fourteenth century French wine cost only about 3d a gallon but by the late fifteenth century, after the Hundred Years' War with France and the loss of Gascony, it rose to as much as 8d and by the end of the sixteenth century it could not be bought for much less than 2s 8d.[1] The taverns where wine was sold – usually advertised by branches and leaves hung over the door – were mostly in towns and kept by vintners. In 1309 in London, where the population was between 30,000 and 40,000, there were apparently as many as 354 taverners and the Vintners' Company was gaining virtual monopoly of the retail trade. There seems to have been proportionately as many in every large town; but as one pilgrim grumpily complained, 'Taverns are for the rich and for lovers of good wine.'[2] The poor had to be content with the alehouse.

Ale, however, was not cheap. The Assize of Ale of 1266 fixed the maximum price of ½d a gallon in the towns and about ¼d elsewhere. But a royal ordinance of 1283 raised the maximum to 1½d a gallon for strong ale and 1d for the weaker, so that for four pints even of the weaker brew a labourer, as Peter Clark has estimated, would have to part with about a third of his daily earnings. Nor was the ale supplied by the average village brewster as good as that to be enjoyed in baronial households where an expert ale-wife would be employed. The brew dispensed by most ale-sellers was much thicker, flatter and sourer than the best Kentish ale so highly praised by Gerald of Wales in the twelfth century. Fermentation was frequently incomplete and, although long-peppers were added to the mixture to help preserve it, the liquor soon went off. One fourteenth-century drinker complained that it was 'muddy, foggy, fulsome, puddle, stinking'.[3] Manor servants and day labourers were, therefore, grateful that they received food and drink as part of their wages, since the ale placed on the board in the hall and in the outbuildings where workers were fed after fulfilling their obligations in the masters' fields was much more palatable than that the independent ale-seller could be relied upon to supply.

Most ale-sellers and brewers were women. At Wallingford in the early thirteenth century there were nearly sixty brewers and only four of them were men. And most male brewers had other occupations. At Norwich among those listed as brewers were a smith, a parchment dealer, a carter and a gate-keeper. In the earlier Middle Ages few of those who brewed and sold ale kept open house for drinking on their premises. Their customers came with jugs and buckets to take the brew away. It was also hawked about the streets, and, at fairs and festivals, sold from stalls in the market-place. But by the end of the fourteenth century the number of alehouses in towns and large villages seems to have been growing fast, and those who kept them were increasingly relying for their supplies on local brewers who were operating on quite a large scale. In 1454 a petition from Norfolk protested that a gang of marauders was rampaging about the country 'with bows and arrows shooting and playing in men's closes among men's cattle, going from alehouse to alehouse and menacing such as they hated'.[4]

By then the alehouse had become a much more common sight all over the country; and the quality of the ale had much improved, particularly that brewed at Burton-on-Trent and in London. This was partly owing to the introduction of hops instead of spices and partly to the more extensive equipment available to the professional brewer. As early as 1335 the inventory of a brewhouse in St Martin's, Ludgate, listed, among several other vessels, tubs and utensils, a lead cistern, a tap-trough, a mash-vat, a fining vat and an ale vat. At the same time ale was becoming more easily within the reach of the ordinary working man. Whereas the thirteenth-century labourer had been hard put to it to afford even a pint or two, two centuries later rising wages would have allowed a building craftsman in southern England to buy four gallons of good ale with his daily wage had he wanted to. Certainly the alehouse had by then become a convivial meeting-place where the customers, mostly from the lower orders of society, could drink from earthenware or pewter pots, talk and sing, gamble, sometimes eat and occasionally, as the customers of Julian Fox of Thornbury had been able to do in the 1370s, enjoy the services of a prostitute.[5] Breton, the ale-seller in *Piers Plowman*, keeps a house in which

> Ther was lauhyng and lakeryng and 'let go the coppe!'
> Bargeynes and bevereges: by-gunne to aryse,
> And seten so til evesong rang.

Among the customers were a shoemaker, a warner and his wife, Tim the tinker and two of his apprentices, Hick the hackneyman, Hugh the needle-seller, Daw the ditcher, the clerk of the parish, a rat-catcher, a priest, a ropemaker, a hayward, a hermit, a hangman, porters and cut-purses, bald-headed tooth-drawers, a dozen harlots and 'a whole heap of upholsterers'. One of the bibulous company is Glutton whom Breton has waylaid as he was walking to church:

> But Breton the brewster bad him good morrow,
> And asked him with that whither he was going:
> 'To holy church', said he, 'to hear the service,
> And so I will be shriven and sin no longer.'
> 'I have good ale, gossip: Glutton, will you try it?'
> 'What have you?' he asked – 'any hot spices?'
> 'I have pepper and peonies', she said, 'and a pound of garlic
> And a farthing worth of fennel seed for fasting seasons.'
> Then Gluttony goes in with a great crowd after . . .

He eventually gulps down 'a gallon and a gil' after which

> He could neither step nor stand till a staff held him,
> And then began to go like a gleeman's bitch,
> Sometimes aside and sometimes backwards,
> Like one who lays lures to lime wild-fowl.
> And he drew to the door all dimmed before him,
> He stumbled on the threshold and was thrown forwards.[6]

Heavy drinking was not, of course, confined to alehouses and taverns. At most family celebrations, baptisms, marriages and funerals, large quantities of ale were consumed. In about 1223 Bishop Richard Poore of Salisbury found it necessary to order that marriages must be 'celebrated reverently and with honour, not with laughter or sport or at public potations or feasts'. But the frequency with which similar decrees had to be issued over the years indicates the difficulty, if not the impossibility, of making marriage celebrations more decorous and of eradicating the 'bride ales', the customary parties which were held after the church ceremony and at which the guests drank quarts of ale specially brewed for the occasion, the profits going to the bride.

While Bishop Poore was vainly protesting against irreverent marriages,

other bishops were denouncing the loose manner in which funeral ceremonies were conducted, particularly wakes and their attendant singing,
games and drunken merriment, not to mention the fornication and theft for
which, so a church council of 1342 maintained, they provided opportunities.
Yet frolicsome wakes continued unabated; and a death in the family at the
manor remained the occasion for such festivities as those held after the
funeral of the fourth Lord Berkeley in 1368 when the reeve was instructed to
fatten up 100 geese and 'divers other Reeves the like, in geese, duckes, and
other poultry'.[7]

As well as 'bride ales', there were all manner of other 'ales' which provided
excuses for heavy drinking, in addition to church ales. There were 'scot ales'
and 'play ales', 'lamb ales' and 'Whitsun ales' and the 'scythale' which was
held on the completion of a season of mowing. The cost of some of these 'ales'
was born by the lord of the manor as a reward for satisfactory service, but
others were held for his profit and tenants were expected to attend and to
bring a fixed amount of beer money with them.[8]

On most manors at Christmas time the tenants were invited to a feast and
asked to bring their dishes and mugs as well as logs for the yule fire in the hall.
At this time of year, according to William FitzStephen, Thomas Becket's
*clericus*, friend and biographer, writing in the second half of the twelfth
century, 'every man's house, as also their parish churches, were decked with
holme [holly], Ivie, Bayes, and whatsoever the season afforded to be greene'.
As well as Christmas, May Day and Midsummer Day were particularly
joyful holidays. In London on May Day, as FitzStephen related, 'every man,
except impediment, would walke into the sweete meadows and greene
woods, there to rejoyce their spirites with the beauty and savour of sweete
flowers, and with the harmony of birds'. Elsewhere, in every town and
village, there would be May Day celebrations, dances and ceremonies so old
that none knew when they had first been performed. Young men and girls
would go out into the woodlands to the sound of music to gather the May
blossom with which, bound in wreaths, they would decorate the windows
and doors of their cottages; and they would carry back to their villages 'their
Maie pole, whiche they would bring home with great veneration, as thus':

They have twentie or thirtie yoke of oxen, every oxe having a sweet
nosegaie of flowers tyed on the tippe of his hornes, and these oxen draw
home this Maiepole . . . which is covered all over with flowers and
hearbes, bounde rounde about with strings, from the top to the bottome,
and sometyme painted with variable colours, with two or three hundred
men, women and children following it, with great devotion. And thus
beyng reared up, with handkerchiefs and flagges streamyng on the toppe,

they strawe the grounde aboute, binde greene boughes aboute it, sette up Sommer haules, Bowers, and Arbours hard by it. And then fall they to banquet and feast, to leape and daunce aboute it, as the Heathen people did at the dedication of their Idolles, whereof this is a perfect patterne, or rather the thyng itself.[9]

In other villages the maypole stood in a convenient part of the village 'in the whole circle of the year, as if it were consecrated to the goddess of Flowers'. On occasions, a maypole would be set up in the courtyard or grounds of a manor house, and here also pageants and displays of archery were performed, the actors and contestants often dressed as Robin Hood and his merry men. One such pageant was held at a baronial mansion in the fifteenth century:

A large square was staked out in the grounds and fenced with ropes. Six young men first entered the square, clothed in jerkins of leather, with axes upon their shoulders like woodmen, and their heads bound with large garlands of ivy-leaves, intertwined with sprigs of hawthorn. Then followed six young maidens of the village, dressed in blue kirtles, with garlands of primroses on their heads, leading a fine sleek cow decorated with ribbons of various colours, interspersed with flowers; and the horns of the animal were tipped with gold. These were succeeded by six foresters, equipped in green tunics, with hoods and hosen of the same colour; each of them carried a bugle-horn attached to a baldrick of silk, which he sounded as he passed the barrier. After them came the baron's chief falconer, who personified Robin Hood. He was attired in a bright grass-green tunic, fringed with gold . . . A page as Little John walked at his right hand; and Cecil Cellerman, the butler, as Will Stukely, at his left. These, with ten others of the jolly outlaw's attendants who followed, were habited in green garments, bearing their bows bent in their hands, and their arrows in their girdles. Then came two maidens, in orange-coloured kirtles with white courtpies, strewing flowers, followed immediately by the Maid Marian, elegantly habited. She was supported by two bridemaidens, in sky-coloured rochets girt with crimson girdles, wearing garlands upon their heads of blue and white violets. After them came four other females in green courtpies, and garlands of violets and cowslips. Then Sampson the smith, as Friar Tuck, carrying a huge quarter-staff on his shoulder; and Morris the mole-taker, who represented Much the miller's son, having a long pole with an inflated bladder attached to one end. And after them the Maypole, drawn by eight fine oxen, decorated with scarfs, ribbons, and flowers of divers colours; and the tips of their horns were embellished with gold. The rear was closed by the hobby-horse and the dragon. When the May-pole was drawn into the square, the foresters sounded their horns, and the populace expressed their pleasure by shouting incessantly until it reached the place assigned for its elevation: and during the time the ground was preparing for its reception, the barriers of the bottom of the inclosure were opened for the villagers to approach, and adorn it with ribbons, garlands, and flowers as their inclination prompted them . . . And when it was elevated the woodmen and the milk-maidens danced around it according to the rustic fashion.

The baron's chief minstrel accompanied the dance on his bagpipes, his assistants playing pipe and tabor. Then the jester frisked up and down the square on his hobby-horse, followed by the ranger 'who personated a dragon, hissing, yelling, and shaking his wings with wonderful ingenuity'; while the mole-taker pranced about, throwing meal into the faces of the spectators or rapping them over the head with the bladder at the end of his pole, and Friar Tuck 'walked with much gravity around the square, and occasionally let forth his heavy staff upon the toes of such of the crowd as he thought were approaching more forward than they ought to do . . . Then the archers set up a target and made trial of their skill in regular succession.' The pageant was finished with the archery; and the procession began to move away to make room for the villagers who afterwards assembled in the square and 'amused themselves by dancing round the maypole in promiscuous companies'.[10]

Archery, which was a principal feature of this pageant, was practised everywhere, although it was a constant complaint by those in authority that young men were neither so assiduous nor so skilful as their ancestors had been and that, in the words of John Stow, young men had long since abandoned this healthy and useful exercise to 'creepe into bowling-alleys and ordinarie dicing-houses where they hazard their money at unlawful games'.

During the Hundred Years' War with France numerous proclamations had been issued to encourage the practice of archery. 'Cause public pro-clamation to be made,' ran one Act of 1369, 'that everyone of the said City of London strong in body, at leisure times and on holidays, use in their recreation bows and arrows.' To foster the exercise – deemed essential for the provision of well-trained bowmen for the army – handball and football were forbidden under pain of imprisonment; and further ordinances, prohibiting all other sports on Sundays and Feast Days, decreed that if an archer killed a man while practising, the misadventure should not be considered a crime. Spaces were set aside beyond the city walls where earthen butts were set up. In the country, men were urged to practise in churchyards and on village greens, using arrows about three feet long with sharp tips of steel – capable of penetrating through an oak door four inches thick – smooth wooden shafts, and flights of duck or peacock feathers or, more rarely, of parchment. The bows were about five feet long and the best of them were made of yew, though, to prevent too many yews being cut down for the purpose, bowyers were instructed from time to time to make four bows of witch-hazel, ash or elm to every one they made of yew. The best bowstrings, according to Roger Ascham's *Toxophilus, the Schole of Shooting*, were made of good hemp, flax or silk. The bowstring was drawn back to the ear unlike the string of the shortbow which was drawn back only to the chest, and a skilled long-bowman could shoot accurately at distances up to 300 yards. It was the archers of South Wales who had first shown Edward I the range and power of the long-bow and this had thereafter become the principal weapon of English infantry; and, by becoming so, had revolutionized both the organization and tactics of the English army. Edward I's army on the Continent in 1297 had contained 7810 infantry, three-quarters of them Welsh, and only 895 cavalry. Edward III's army contained a higher proportion of cavalry, but not of knights, for the additional mounted men were horse-archers who could pursue the retreating enemy at great speed after his cavalry attack had been stopped and broken by the line of armoured knights and foot-archers.[11]

Other warlike skills practised by young men were fighting with the broad-sword; cudgelling, in which victory was obtained when blood poured down the opponent's scalp; quarter-staff which was played, or rather fought, with poles over six feet long held firmly in the middle by one hand and loosely by the other between the middle and the end, at, in fact, the quarter-mark. The object of this exercise was merely to knock the opponent over, preferably senseless, unlike single-stick which, as with cudgelling, was ended by the drawing of blood.

Wrestling was a universally popular pastime, both with rich and poor, although, as Touchstone said, it was not considered a suitable spectacle for ladies. The rules, when observed at all, varied in different parts of the country. In some counties certain holds and throws were disallowed; in others there were no holds barred; in Devon wrestlers were permitted to wear heavy soles to their shoes with which they delivered vicious kicks to their opponents. In London wrestling was given official encouragement by the lord mayor who presided over annual matches on St Bartholomew's Day, a practice of 'old time', said Stow. The victors were rewarded by bags of money thrown to them by the lord mayor and aldermen in a large tent erected at Clerkenwell. 'And after this,' another chronicler relates, 'a parcel of wild rabbits are turned loose in the crowd and are hunted by boys with great noise, at which the mayor and aldermen do much besport themselves.'[12]

In FitzStephen's twelfth-century account of Londoners amusing themselves, they are described watching cockfights, playing football, practising 'feates of warre' with 'disarmed launces and shields', casting stones, dancing, leaping, going out into the fields 'on warlike horses'. 'The girls, as the moon rises, dance to the stringed instrument. In the winter before dinner . . . there are boar fights, or tusked pigs or bulls and large bears are baited with dogs.' And in all seasons there were riders to be seen tilting at the quintain, galloping towards a wooden figure on a pivot and attempting to strike it on the spot which would ensure that the figure did not quickly swivel round and hit the horsemen on the back with its sword. A variety of this game was played upon the river.

> A shield is hanged on a pole, in the middle of the stream [John Stow explained in a résumé of FitzStephen's account]. A boat is prepared without oares to bee carried by the violence of the water, and in the fore part thereof standeth a young man readie to give charge upon the shield with his launce; if so be hee breaketh his launce against the shield, and doth not fall, he is thought to have performed a worthy deed. If so be without breaking his launce he runneth strongly against the shield, downe he falleth into the water, for the boat is violently forced with the tide; but on each side stand great numbers to see, and laugh thereat . . . In the holy dayes all the Somer . . . the Maidens trip in their Timbrels, and daunce as long as they can see . . .
>
> When the great fenne or Moore, which watreth the walls of the Citie on the north-side [Moorfields] is frozen, many young men plye upon the yce; some, striding as wide as they may, do slide swiftly . . . Some tie bones to their feete, and under their heeles, and shoving themselves by a little picked staffe, doe slide as swiftly as a bird flieth in the ayre, or an arrow out of a Crossbowe.[13]

Beyond the walls of most manor houses were orchards and fishponds, complete perhaps with fish-house and curing furnace, and, sheltered by the walls from the winds, there grew not only the herbs which were such essential ingredients of medieval cookery, but also flowers. Ideally, so Alexander Neckham wrote in his *De Naturis Rerum* towards the beginning of the thirteenth century:

> The garden should be adorned with roses and lilies, the turnsole or heliotrope, violets, and mandrake, there you should have parsley, cost, fennel, southernwood, coriander, sage, savery, hysop, mint, rue, ditanny, smallage, pellitory, lettuce, garden cress, and peonies. There should also be beds planted with onions, leeks, garlic, pumpkins, and shallots. The cucumber, the poppy, the daffodil, and brank-ursine ought to be in a good garden. There should also be pottage herbs, such as beets, herb mercury, orach, sorrel, and mallows.

There should also, he added, be a good supply of medicinal herbs including borage and purslane, hazelwort, colewort and ragwort, valerian and myrtle, thyme and saffron. Recent archaeological work, corroborating and extending the evidence of the records, has shown that a large variety of plants and fruits were, indeed, grown in gardens. In addition to those already named, goosefoot and sorrel were grown, penny-cress and whortleberry, borage, black mustard and, for use as a laxative, corncockle, as well as strawberries and blackberries, sloes, plums and raspberries. In the nearby orchard grew apples, plums and pears, cherries and quinces.[14]

Contented as they might have been in the contemplation of their gardens and orchards, most members of the upper classes found their greatest pleasure in the chase. They spent day after day between 24 June and 14 September and from 10 November to 2 February hunting deer; they also hunted wild boar and foxes with packs of wolf-hounds, mastiffs, greyhounds, terriers and beagles, riding with swords, with bows and arrows and with spears. They brought down pheasants and partridges with hawks; netted smaller birds such as larks, as well as badgers; snared rabbits; coursed hares. Women as well as men joined in the sport. In the early fourteenth-century manuscript known as the *Taymouth Horae* there are several pictures of ladies hawking and hunting, sticking boars, cutting up stags, blowing the mort on a horn as the slaughtered stag's head is displayed on the point of a spear. Even nuns enjoyed hunting. The Bishop of Winchester had to order the abbesses of the three principal nunneries in his diocese to get rid of their hunting dogs which were consuming food that should have been given to the poor and which, defiling both church and cloister, 'frequently troubled' divine service with 'their inordinate noise'.[15]

The nobles' passion for hunting and hawking was severely criticized by some clerics. In the middle of the twelfth century John of Salisbury said that the sports made them as brutal as the beasts they chased, that peasants were evicted for the sake of the beasts, and that if a great and merciless hunter passed your home you were obliged to find for him and his party all the refreshment possible. Otherwise you might be ruined or even accused of treason.[16]

Yet clerical condemnation had not the slightest effect on the hunter's pleasure. In *The Master of Game*, the oldest book on hunting in English, written at the beginning of the fifteenth century, Edward, second Duke of York, cousin of Henry V, undertook 'to prove how hunters live in this world more joyfully than any other men':

For when the hunter riseth in the morning, and he sees a sweet and fair morn and clear weather and bright, and he heareth the song of the small birds, the which sing so sweetly with great melody and full of love, each in its own language in the best wise . . . and when the sun is arisen, he shall see fresh dew upon the small twigs and grasses, and the sun by his virtue shall make them shine. And that is great joy and liking to the hunter's heart. After when he shall go to his quest or searching, he shall see or meet anon with the hart without great seeking, and shall harbour [trace to the lair] him well and readily within a little compass. It is great joy and liking to the hunter . . . And when he has come home he shall doff his clothes and his shoes and his hose, and he shall wash his thighs and his legs, and peradventure all his body. And in the meanwhile he shall order well his supper, with the neck of the hart and of other good meats, and good wine or ale. And then he shall go and drink and lie in his bed in fair fresh clothes, and shall sleep well and steadfastly all the night without any evil thoughts of any sins, wherefore I say that hunters go into Paradise when they die, and live in this world more joyfully than any other man.[17]

Hunting was not for the poor. Good greyhounds were extremely expensive; a goshawk could cost £5; and a female peregrine, the most prized of all hunting birds, even more. They were fed most extravagantly, King John's being given doves, pork and chicken once a week; and they were taken into the dining-hall as well as being provided with perches in their masters' bedrooms. The Abbot of Westminster, Nicholas Litlington, thought so highly of his falcon that he paid for a waxen image of it to be bought for the abbey altar when it was ill.[18]

A statute of Edward III issued in 1360 decreed that anyone finding a hawk must immediately hand it over to the sheriff of the county who was to proclaim the discovery in all the towns for which he was responsible. 'And if any man take such Hawk,' the statute continued, 'and the same conceal from the Lord whose it was, or from his Falconers . . . shall have Imprisonment of Two Years, and yield to the Lord the price of the Hawk so concealed and carried away, if he have whereof; and, if not, he shall the longer abide in prison.'[19]

Giraldus Cambrensis records a story which well illustrates the excitement of hawking, and the occasional victory of the quarry:

King Henry the Second of England (or his son Richard, I name both, but shun to distinguish clearly since my tale is to his dishonour) in the early days of his reign cast off his best falcon at a heron, for the sake of that cruel pastime. The heron circled higher and higher; but the falcon being swifter, and already wellnigh overtaken him, when the king felt certain of victory and cried aloud, 'By God's eyes or His Gorge . . . that bird shall not now escape, even though God Himself had sworn it!' (for they had learned thus to swear in their youthful insolence; and such habits may scarce be unlearnt; even as Henry II.'s grandfather Henry I., was wont to swear *By God's Death*.) At these words the heron turned forthwith to bay; and, by a most miraculous change from victim to tormentor, stuck his beak into the falcon's head, dashed out his brains, and (himself whole and unhurt) cast the dying bird to the earth at the King's very feet.[20]

# 6 · *Wayfarers and Pilgrims*

A long journey in medieval England was never undertaken lightly, although the roads were not as bad as has sometimes been maintained, and, as the maps of Matthew Paris show, a network of highways did exist. It had been accepted in Norman times that a road should be wide enough for two wagons to pass each other, for sixteen knights to ride abreast, or for two oxherds to touch together the tips of their goads.[1] And on most stretches of the main roads which led out of London this width seems to have been maintained, then and thereafter. But on minor roads constant encroachments caused maddening bottlenecks, while the surfaces were repeatedly falling into ruinous disrepair either through neglect or through wilful destruction. In 1286, for example, the people of Cambridge were prosecuted for ploughing up the road to Hinton.[2] Packhorse routes were notoriously difficult. Although often paved in boggy terrain, and then known as 'causeys', a corruption of the Latin for trodden, they were usually so narrow that two trains of horses could not pass each other and after long arguments one or other of them would have to give way and move down into the mud.[3]

Foul weather, snow and floods were likely to close any road in winter when the very track itself was difficult to discern, even though large stones often marked the verges in desolate country. In the winter of 1324–5 a man from Nottingham, travelling on the king's business in the eastern counties, managed to cover only six miles a day, though he usually covered over twenty-five; and in 1339 Parliament had to be adjourned because those who were due to attend it were prevented by bad weather and impassable roads from doing so.

The condition of roads in the towns in winter was frequently scarcely better than that of those in the country, as the number of prosecutions for blocking or polluting highways indicate. Citizens were repeatedly fined for letting pigs run wild, leaving dung heaps in the road, butchering animals there, blocking the gutters with rubbish. The Norwich Leet Rolls for 1390–91 are replete with records of fines imposed for such offences:

> Isabella Lucas has and maintains a foul gutter running from her messuage into the King's highway . . . Fined 6d . . . Wm Gerard has had a horse lying for a long time in the King's highway, near the church of St Michael de Colegate to the abominable offence and poisoning [of the air] . . . Fined 12d . . . The churchwardens of St Martyn's of the Bale for noyeing the King's highway with muck and compost [are] fined 3d.[4]

At Norwich, as in other towns, citizens were obliged to maintain the stretch of road outside their own doors, while tolls were charged on goods coming into the town from outside to pay for the repair of other stretches. The tollgate would be set up some distance from the town gate to prevent strangers skirting the town if their business did not oblige them to enter it; a token would be given in exchange for the toll paid; and the token handed over to the keeper of the town gate. But the tolls rarely realized enough money for the amount of work that was required. And town authorities frequently had to petition Parliament for powers to compel citizens to fulfil neglected obligations, as the stewards and bailiffs of Gloucester did in 1473 when they had cause to complain that the citizens' dereliction had left their town 'feebly paved and full perilous and jeopardous'.[5] Occasionally the king intervened. Edward III did so in 1352 when he ordered those citizens who lived beside the notoriously ill-kept road from Westminster to Temple Bar to improve it by digging a ditch, raising a pavement seven feet wide and making a paved roadway. Even so, a few years later this road was in as parlous a condition as ever.

The streets of London were quite as bad as those elsewhere. In the middle of the fourteenth century it was claimed that 'the highway between Temple-bar and Westminster [was] rendered so deep and miry by the carts and horses carrying merchandise . . . that it was dangerous to pass upon it'.[6] It was also claimed that

> all the folk who bring victuals and wares by carts and horses to the City do make grievous complaint that they incur great damage and are oftentimes in peril of losing what they bring, and sometimes do lose it, because the roads without the City are so torn up and the pavement so broken as may be seen by all persons.[7]

It was to be many years before the state of England's roads improved. In the middle of the sixteenth century those in London were described in a preamble to an Act as being 'very foul and full of pits and sloughs, very perilous and noyous as well for all the King's subjects on horseback as well as on foot and with carriages';[8] while in Yorkshire the conveyance of lead from the roof of Jervaulx Abbey had to be postponed until the summer months because, 'the ways in that countrie are so foule and deep that no carriage can pass in winter'.[9] As late as the time of Henry VIII the roads of the country were still 'full of great Paynes, Perils and Jeopardie'.[10]

The trouble was that, although the maintenance of roads and bridges was deemed a service for which the whole nation was responsible, and although the Statute of Winchester of 1285 placed an obligation upon all landowners to maintain the highways passing through their manors – upon which they could charge strangers tolls for using them – roadmending was an irksome duty and tolls, when authorized and collected, were used by the less conscientious landowners for other purposes. Even the queen of Edward III, who had been granted the revenues of London Bridge by the king, appropriated them all to herself, neglecting to repair the structure which became so ruinous that collectors had to be sent all over the country to raise donations for its reconstruction. At the same time the clergy had to be enjoined to address their congregations with 'pious exhortations' on the bridge's behalf.[11]

The repair of roads and bridges for the benefit of travellers was, indeed, considered a pious duty. 'It is meritorious to mend dangerous roads and perilous bridges,' the local people were reminded when a bridge over the Trent was in urgent need of attention. After all, the Latin word for priest, *pontifex*, meant bridge-builder. Bishops granted indulgences to those who contributed to rebuilding funds, as witness the Bishop of Durham in 1394:

Whereas the bridge at Chollerford, as we hear, is decayed by the inundation of the waters . . . and now wants repair, whereby the inhabitants in the neighbourhood are in great want. We, therefore, confiding in the mercy of almighty God, and the sufferings of His Holy Mother, and all the Saints, do release unto all our parishioners . . . thirteen days of their enjoined penance, upon condition they lend a helping hand to the repairing of the said bridge, or contribute their pious charity thereto.[12]

Devout testators left money in their wills for the mending of bridges and specified stretches of highway, an example followed by Henry VII who bequeathed £2000 for 'the repair of the highways and bridges from Windsor to Richmond Manor and thence to St George's church beside Southwark and thence to Greenwich manor and thence to Canterbury'.[13] Hermits, whose huts were often to be seen by fords and whose blessings were valued by devout wayfarers, sometimes took over the care of roads and bridges as a religious duty, and were occasionally authorized to collect charges for doing so. William Philippe, a hermit who lived to the north of London, was officially permitted by Edward III to collect tolls 'from our people passing between Heghgate and Smethfelde' to pay for the repair of the Hollow Way.[14] The abbots of monasteries, too, considered it a holy duty to care for the roads that passed by their houses. 'Such abbeys as were near the danger of seabanks,' wrote Roger Aske in the sixteenth century, 'were great maintainers of sea-walls and dykes, maintainers and builders of bridges and highways and such other things for the commonwealth.'[15]

Many bridges, built at first of oak and later of stone, had chapels attached to them. Among these were London Bridge, whose large chapel built over the middle pier was dedicated to St Thomas of Canterbury, and 'the faire bridge of stone of nine arches' at Wakefield, under which, in the words of the antiquary John Leland, 'runneth the river of Calder; and on the east side of this bridge is a right goodly chapel of Our Lady and two cantuarie preestes founded in it'.

In many cases both chapel and bridge were beneficiaries under wills and in receipt of regular income from rents in the towns which they served. Yet these bequests served to keep few of them in good condition. Many, indeed, were in the ruinous state of the bridge over the Trent at Heybethebridge near Nottingham 'to the making and repair of which', as Parliament was informed in 1376, 'Nobody is bound and alms only are collected . . . so that oftentimes several persons have been drowned, as well horsemen as carts, man, and harness.'[16] The sad history of the bridge over the Tweed, one of the longest bridges in the country, was not exceptional. This bridge is first known to have collapsed during the floods of 1199. It was subsequently rebuilt on several occasions, sometimes in wood, at others in stone; but no structure stood for long; and in 1294, after a devastating inundation, a ferry guarded by cross-bowmen had to be established. Half a century later, after a toll of sixpence had been collected from every ship entering the harbour, a new bridge was constructed, 'but not in such a way as not to fall again, which has since happened to it many times'.[17]

In particularly hard winters few bridges anywhere were safe. In the winter of 1281–2, when 'there was such a frost and snow, as no man living could remember the like', 'five arches of London Bridge, and all Rochester Bridge were borne downe, and carried away with the streame, and the like happened to many bridges in England'.[18] Always most at risk were those country bridges with no endowments and with insufficient alms to maintain them properly. As the piers of these were gradually worn away and the stones of the parapets were knocked into the river by clumsily driven and heavily laden carts, their passage became an extremely risky undertaking; and frequently on stormy nights a driver and load would crash with the splintering wood or crumbling masonry into the waters beneath.

ABOVE: Cooks and scullions at work in the kitchen. The scullion on the right is turning a spit on which carcasses are roasting. Because of the great heat from the fire the scullion often worked naked. His duties at the spit handle were sometimes performed by dogs obliged by painful persuasion to walk in circles, while the scullion scoured pots and pans.

RIGHT: Two illustrations from the Luttrell Psalter depict servants preparing a meal and taking it in to serve their master, Sir Geoffrey Luttrell, and his guests. Highly spiced food was commonly served on trenchers, thick slices of bread or scooped-out crusts which might afterwards be distributed to the poor or to dogs. Knives were carried to the table in cases attached to belts or girdles; spoons were laid on the board or cloth, but forks were then unknown.

dedit filiis hominum

ipius : ipius : a factendum ta

ABOVE: Ladies travelling in a coach in the 14th century. Carriages such as this were often elaborately decorated, not only being brightly painted but also being embellished with carved figures of animals standing on the shafts. The interiors were hung with tapestries and furnished with couches and pillows. Edward III paid the then immense sum of £1,000 for one such coach.

RIGHT: A 14th-century manuscript depicting a physician administering medicine to his patient. All manner of concoctions were prescribed – from ivory shavings in wine to 'borage root and saffron soaked in ale', boiled hedgehog fat and the wings of insects, and from mandrake as a narcotic to comfrey, liquorice and calamine for cases of bronchitis.

BELOW: A pilgrim inspects a (miraculous) mirror shown to him in a display of other toilet articles.

**TOP LEFT**: A monk and his mistress punished in the stocks for their impurity. By the end of the 14th century morals in many religious houses had become lax. A visitation of Flaxley Abbey in 1397 revealed that nine monks were fornicators and that the Abbot himself was 'defamatus' with three different women. For centuries, stocks, in which the feet were secured by the ankle, were used for the public punishment of all kinds of offences.

**CENTRE LEFT**: Chess was introduced into Europe from the Moslem world in the tenth century. Sets were often elaborately carved in wood, ivory and semi-precious stones, and the pieces usually of large dimensions. The game was generally played for money.

**BELOW**: Bear-baiting attracted large crowds throughout the Middle Ages and was not much condemned as a 'full ugly sight' until the second half of the 16th century. Bears were generally muzzled, as shown here, and expected to do most damage with their claws. Their keepers carried sticks to beat off over-ferocious dogs.

ABOVE: Country people at their various pursuits, including scything, stooking, transporting the harvest with great difficulty up a steep hill, threshing, and carrying the corn to the miller. This miller has a windmill. Although windmills had been introduced into England towards the end of the 12th century, they were not as common at this time (*circa* 1340) as watermills.

RIGHT: Craftsmen at work on the construction of a building, using augers, adzes and other tools. An illustration from a life of St Alban who was martyred at the beginning of the fourth century on the site of the abbey named after him. This was started in 1077, the builders using Roman bricks from nearby Verulamium. During the Middle Ages, however, bricks were a most unusual building material in England, except for fireplaces, the word 'brick' from the French *brique* not entering the language until the beginning of the 15th century.

Occasionally a rickety bridge might be repaired by royal command. Edward III, for instance, once required the 'Sheriff of Oxfordshire to declare that all bridges should be repaired and all fords marked out with stakes for the crossing of the King with his falcons during the approaching winter season'.[19] But it was not until 1531 that a statute enabled Justices of the Peace to levy a county rate to pay for the regular maintenance of bridges.[20]

While it was difficult enough to get old bridges repaired, it was far more so to get new ones built, even when a royal grant was available – as it was in 1248 to the 'good men of Doncastre' who were permitted to take a '1d on every cart with merchandise' which crossed the bridge they were required to build there – and even when, as an added inducement, the priest of the bridge's chapel was asked to pray for the souls of contributors. For whoever built a bridge was, legally, responsible for its upkeep. Bridge construction was, accordingly, not an undertaking that those who could afford it would willingly enter into. So burdensome was it, indeed, that one of the clauses of Magna Carta expressly stipulated that no 'village or individual shall be compelled to make bridges at river banks except those who from of old were legally bound to do so'. On the Continent an order of bridge friars undertook the task of bridge building; and the Pont St Esprit as well as the bridge at Avignon were the result of their endeavours. But no such order existed in England.[21]

Hard as journeys often were, particularly in winter, the medieval wayfarer managed nevertheless to cover long distances and to travel fast when necessary. Everyone who could afford to do so rode a horse. But horses were expensive, a knight's warhorse in the thirteenth century costing as much as £80, more than a poor man could expect to earn in a lifetime. Even a rouncy, an ordinary riding-horse incapable of carrying the great weights which warhorses were bred to do, might cost over £3 at a time when a cow could be bought for 9s 5d, an ox for 13s, a sheep for 1s 5d and a fowl for 1d. Palfreys, the saddle-horses most commonly used, could not be bought for much less than £15 each although at the end of the thirteenth century a brother of the Earl of Gloucester managed to purchase a palfrey and a cart-horse for just over £5 each. Prices clearly varied considerably, depending to a large extent upon the quality of the animal. The cost of horses hired at staging-posts, however, was generally fixed; and in the 1280s on the London to Dover road, where there were regular staging-posts, the charge for hiring a horse, conspicuously branded so that it would be difficult to sell if stolen, was 1s from Southwark to Rochester, 1s also from Rochester to Canterbury, and 6d from Canterbury to Dover.[22]

On a good horse and a dry road a rider could usually manage about forty miles a day: the Mayor of Exeter, riding in 1447 from his house to London, a distance of 170 miles, allowed himself four to five days for the journey; and a merchant with packhorses travelling from York to London, 200 miles, would expect to take five days. Riders on their own could travel even faster if they wished. When visiting the Praemontarians in his diocese in 1494 Bishop Redman regularly covered fifty miles a day; and a messenger, riding by night as well as by day, could manage sixty. Even a cumbersome household could cover thirty miles a day in the summer, as the Countess of Leicester's did when she was in a hurry to reach the safety of Dover Castle in 1265, though in winter an average of fifteen miles a day was rarely exceeded by large parties such as hers.[23]

Foot messengers could sometimes manage more than thirty miles a day and, if in royal service in the time of Edward II, were allowed 4s 8d a year to buy shoes and paid 3d a day on the road, a meagre sum but often hugely increased for bearers of good news: the queen's messenger was rewarded with forty marks pension for life when he brought news to King Edward III of the birth of the future Black Prince.[24]

All women rode astride until the invention of a woman's saddle in the fourteenth century allowed them to ride side-saddle instead. Many women preferred to keep to the old style, however. The Ellesmere manuscript of *The Canterbury Tales* shows the Prioress riding side-saddle, but the Wife of Bath astride, wearing large spurs and carrying an intimidating whip.

For those too ill or old to ride, and for delicate ladies, there were litters, tunnel-like structures slung between two horses head to tail and decorated with tapestries and upholstered with cushions. William of Malmesbury relates that the body of William II was brought back in a litter from the New Forest after he had been killed while hunting; and later on in the twelfth century Abbot Hugh of Bury St Edmunds was carried back to Bury by litter, having injured his knee on a pilgrimage to Canterbury. There were also carriages, although these cumbersome machines were scarcely more comfortable than the rough carts which peasants used and in which judges sometimes ordered juries to be rattled about until they had reached a unanimous verdict. Nor did carriages become less uncomfortable as the centuries passed: Queen Elizabeth I once complained to the French ambassador that after a journey in a carriage in London she could not sit down for several days. They were usually drawn by four horses one behind the other, the driver mounted on one of them, wielding a thonged whip. The long body of the carriage was rounded, its wooden sides frequently brightly painted and gilded. The windows were hung with curtains and when these were pulled back a horseman riding by might catch a glimpse of an interior hung with tapestries or a lady reclining on piles of embroidered cushions. An illustration in the Louterell Psalter depicts an elaborately decorated carriage of the fourteenth century with ladies looking out at front and back and the faces of others framed by the windows. Such carriages as these, with carved figures of animals standing on the shafts, were most valued possessions. Edward III paid £1000 for a carriage for Lady Eleanor, as much as he would have had to pay for a herd of 1600 oxen.[25]

If carriages like these were rare, carts could be seen rattling along drawn by oxen or horses on every highway, large carts drawn by up to eight horses, and with their wooden wheels rimmed with iron bands and studded with iron nails or spikes to give them a firmer grip, and lighter carts or wains with two wheels only. All manner of goods were transported in these rough conveyances. Manorial court rolls and other records refer to the cartage of lead and stone and sand for building; of limestone and coal, alum and dyes; of 'stones and cinders from the Park to the Castle for repairing and mending the way from the Hall to the Gate'; of hogsheads of salted venison. Tolls on fish, meat, iron, timber, hay, rushes, faggots and brushwood were all charged 'by the cartload'. In the twelfth century 265 cartloads of lead were sent from Derbyshire to Boston in Lincolnshire for transshipment to Waltham Abbey by way of London; and in 1333 Edward III ordered various abbots and priors to provide enough carts for carrying his tents and other military supplies for the campaign against the Scots. In 1367, when parts of an alabaster table for St George's Chapel at Windsor were brought down from Nottingham in ten carts each drawn by eight horses, the journey, a distance of some 120 miles, took seventeen days. And this was considered by no means an excessively slow rate, particularly in winter when the going was so slow that the cost of transporting certain loads, such as casks of wine, doubled. Twenty carts carrying the records of the Exchequer and the Court of Common Pleas took eleven days to reach Westminster from York in 1327, twice the time that a train of packhorses would have taken. Four years before, Edward II had ordered that sumpter-horses should in future be brought on military campaigns in addition to carts which were far too slow.[26]

Packhorses were, indeed, always used in preference to carts if speedy delivery were essential and cost was a secondary consideration. A train of packhorses could get to London from York in five days, as quickly as a rider could; and the loads that horses could carry were surprisingly heavy. The thirteenth-century knight, Bogo de Clare, carried his entire wardrobe, his buttery as well as his bedding on three sumpter-horses; the servants of some Lichfield merchants travelling to Stafford market in 1342 required no more than two horses to carry their extremely expensive and weighty supplies of 'spicery and mercery'; Richard of Gloucester needed only one horse to transport the whole of his supply of spices and dates from Odiham to Kenilworth.[27]

For heavy and bulky loads like building materials, manure and military supplies, however, carts were indispensable. And because they were so essential and so troublesome to manage, lords of manors still maintained their rights to demand 'cartage' of their tenants after most other feudal obligations had disappeared. Lords normally exercised this right in order to get their tenants to cart manure to their fields or brushwood to the manor house; but much longer journeys were also occasionally demanded: the tenants of Ramsey Abbey had to undertake journeys to St Albans and London and as far as Bury St Edmunds, Cambridge and Ipswich. And when royal officers requisitioned corn for the king's use, they had the right to demand cartage as well.[28]

For those who had neither subjects nor tenants to call upon, there were both hirers of carts and carriers. The movement of large households usually involved the hiring of carts which in the fourteenth century could be had for 4d a day. Carrying wine, a load that needed special care, was more expensive, but, even so, the Countess of Leicester in 1265 was charged only 18s 6d for the transport of two tuns of wine from London to Kenilworth. From the end of the fourteenth century there were professional carriers on all the main roads, carrying passengers as well as goods, parcels and letters. One of the most successful was named Pickford. The Pastons regularly availed themselves of the services of the Norwich to London carrier; and in 1484 a witness who appeared before the Star Chamber said that he had been a carrier on the Exeter to London route for thirty-five years. For short distances in large towns porters were available. In 1322 twenty-four London porters were paid £1 to carry fifty-two barrels, each containing £500, from the Treasury to Queen's Bridge and then, having been rowed down the Thames, from the waterfront to a chapel in the Tower.[29]

Travel by river was in general easier and cheaper, though a good deal slower, than travel by road. This was clearly demonstrated at Christmas 1319 when the scholars of King's Hall, Cambridge, were invited to spend the holiday with Edward II at York. The older scholars went by road and arrived in three days. The younger ones, presumably more impoverished, chose to go by boat from Cambridge to Spalding. This took them two days. They then went by horse from Spalding to Boston, their luggage following in carts. From Boston they took another boat which carried them up the Witham to Lincoln, a journey which lasted a further two days. At Lincoln they hired two further boats and went on their way up the Foss Dyke to Torksey where they transferred to a larger boat which took them at last to York. Their whole journey occupied nine days; and they were three days late for Christmas.[30]

On their way they would have seen all kinds of boats ferrying both goods and passengers – flat-bottomed towboats, ferry-boats and shells, row-boats, barges with oars and barges with sails, sailing-boats and wherries; and they would have passed all manner of cargoes. Most of the goods required by Ely Cathedral, lead for the roof, tallow, wax and cloth, arrived by river from

Boston. And from Boston, as early as 1184, lead from Derbyshire was being shipped out to Rouen.[31]

Every major medieval town was on a river; and all had wharfs catering for water-borne traffic. The Trent, the Humber and the Ouse were as busy as any road; and boats were constantly docking by the banks of the Thames in London with goods from all over the country. Oxfordshire wool came to London from Henley, marble from Wareham, reeds from Newcastle, stone from Devon.[32] And while these cargoes were being unloaded, passenger boats passed up and down river and from bank to bank, usually charging 2d a head between Westminster and the Tower. The Thames boatmen, a notoriously unruly set, were subject to numerous regulations: in 1391, for example, they were forbidden to carry customers to the brothels of Southwark between sunrise and sunset; and a few years later they were prohibited from crossing the river at all after nightfall.[33]

Travellers by water naturally faced as many hazards as those who journeyed by land. Rivers frequently silted up, as the Ouse did in 1399 – boats had to unload at Selby and continue their journey by road – and as the Yare did at Norwich in 1422 when all the town's citizens were required to turn out between five and seven o'clock in the morning on certain days of the week to help to dredge the river or pay 4d for a deputy to do the work for them. In 1492 the shallows in the Orwell at Ipswich were rendered even more perilous by bargees who carried ballast to throw overboard in an attempt to raise their craft in the water; and it had to be decreed that 'every ship that shall throw their ballast into the river shall pay 12d for each ton thrown out, and the informer shall have 12d'.[34] Rivers also became unnavigable when obstructions were built by those who lived by their banks: grain boats from the east were once prevented from sailing up the Don when the villagers of Barnby Dun in Yorkshire blocked the river with stepping-stones so that they and their sheep could cross from bank to bank.[35]

There was also the danger of sharing the fate of the forty men, women and their goods who lost their lives in the Yare when an overloaded boat sank in 1343; and there was danger, too, from pirates, even on rivers deep inland. In 1429 the people of Tewkesbury were driven to petition the House of Commons about attacks on navigators on the Severn by 'rovers of the Forest of Dean'; and the next year an Act had to be passed for the protection of boatmen on their way to 'Gloucester, Worcester and other places' who were attacked by 'many Welshmen and ill-disposed persons [who] were used to assemble in manner of war', stopping 'boats and floats or drags with merchandise . . . and hewing these craft in pieces and beating the sailors'. In the open sea the pirate was an even more deadly peril, 'one plague the devill hath added to make the sea more terrible than a storme'.

The pirate's heart is so hardened in that rugged element that hee cannot repent, though he view his grave before him continually open. He hath so little of his owne that even the house he sleeps in is stoln . . . His rule is the horriblest tyranny in the world for he gives license to all rape, murder and cruelty. He is a cruell hawke that flies at all but his own kind: and as a whale never comes ashore but when shee is wounded, so he very seldom but for his necessities . . . He is a perpetual plague to noble traffique, the hurrican of the sea.[36]

To pilgrims who sailed regularly from south-coast ports bound for Rome or Santiago de Compostella, the pirate was certainly a perpetual menace. There was also, as one pilgrim who made the journey to Spain recorded in rhyme, the added unpleasantness of fearful seasickness in a small boat crowded with a hundred passengers; of sickening smells; of the rough manners of the sailors who pushed the landlubbers about the deck under the pretext of working the ship and who bawled out to anyone who appeared particularly ill, 'Cheer up, be merry! We shall soon be in a storm!' The captain, as coarse as his men, shouted above the roar of the wind and the splash of the rain:

> 'Hale the bowelyne! Now, vere the shete!
> Cooke, make redy anoon our mete,
> Our pylgryms have no lust to ete,
> I pray God geve hem rest!'

> 'Go to the helm! What, howe! No nere?
> Steward, falow! A pot of bere!
> Ye shalle have sir, with good chere,
> Anon alle of the best' . . .

> Thys mene whyle the pylgryms ly
> And have theyr bowlys fast theym by,
> And cry after hot malves.[37]

They had all made their wills before they set out and commended themselves to their personal patron saints and to those other saints, St Botolph and St Christopher among them, who were known to keep a kindly eye upon travellers. Nor was it only pilgrims embarking upon adventurous voyages overseas who took these precautions: anyone setting out upon a long journey would be sure to do so, for the dangers of the way were legion and nobody was safe. In 1216 King John himself 'journeying towards the north, in the river which is called Wellestren, by an unexpected accident,' in the words of Roger of Wendover, 'lost all his wagons, carts, and sumpter horses with the treasures, precious vessels and all the other things which he loved with so much care. For the ground was opened in the midst of the waves, and bottomless whirlpools swallowed them all up, with the men and the horses, so that not one foot escaped.'[38]

This was an exceptional disaster; but at all times roads were likely to be threatened by floods so that 'no one could have passed there, nor take any carriage there without danger of losing their lives, goods, chattels and Merchandises'.[39] In 1250 several carts, horses and a man of Simon de Montfort's household were washed away at Dorking; and in 1376 a clerk, carrying a hundred marks for the king, was drowned in the Severn when a bridge collapsed. His body not being found was said to have been dragged ashore and eaten by wolves.

Natural disasters were, however, not so common as attacks by highwaymen and gangs of robbers, particularly in times of civil war and general social unrest. 'There is no country in the world where there are so many thieves and robbers as in England,' an Italian envoy recorded; 'insomuch that few venture to go alone into the country excepting in the middle of the day, and fewer still in the towns at night, and least of all in London.'[40] In 1348 the House of Commons deplored the dangers of roads 'throughout all the shires of England' on which 'robbers, thieves and other malefactors, both on foot and horseback, ride in divers places, committing larcenies and robberies'.[41]

A few years earlier the servants of some Staffordshire merchants had been attacked by robbers in Cannock Wood in an incident which was not considered at all out of the ordinary. The gang of marauders was led by Sir Robert de Rideware who took the servants and their masters' goods to the grounds of Lappeley Priory where he divided the booty among his men and some accomplices, 'each one a portion, according to his degree'. The gang then rode on to a nunnery at Blythebury where, being refused shelter, they broke down the door, fed their horses and spent the night. By now, however, one of the robbed servants had managed to escape and had run for help. A pitched battle ensued. Four of the highwaymen were taken prisoner and beheaded on the spot; but Sir Robert escaped and, with some of his men, lived to terrorize the servants once they had returned home to Lichfield 'so that they dared not go anywhere out of the said town'.[42]

The Coroners' Rolls of the period are full of accounts like this, of stories of robberies, of murders, of ambushes, of such fates as that which befell a certain Walter Ingham who, being waylaid, was 'grievously beat and wounded, as well upon his head as upon his legs, and other full grievous strokes and many upon his back, so that he is maimed upon his right leg, and fain to go on crutches, and so must do all the days of his life to his utter undoing'.[43] Other reports describe travellers being attacked with knives, shot with arrows, struck on the head with pole-axes, dragged into churchyards where their toes were cut off, or fighting back successfully like Nicholas Cheddleton who 'while going along the King's highway with linen and cloth and other goods', according to the report of a coroner's inquest at Marston, Staffordshire, was 'met by certain thieves who tried to kill and rob him. And the said Nicholas, in self-defence, struck one of the robbers right over the head with a staff worth a penny, of which blow he died forthwith.'[44]

The *Paston Letters* well indicate how apprehensive people were about their own safety and that of their families and friends when a journey had to be undertaken. 'Beware how you ride or go, for naughty and ill-disposed fellowships,' Margaret Paston warns her husband. 'I should send you money,' another letter runs, 'but I dare not put it in jeopardy, there be so many thieves stirring . . . John Loveday's man was robbed unto his shirt as he came homeward.' Margaret Paston's anxiety was only too well justified. Her uncle, Philip Berney, was shot by robbers who ambushed him 'in the highway under Thorpe wood' and then 'over-rode him and took him and beat him and spoiled him'. He never recovered from his wounds and, after fifteen months' illness, 'passed to God with the greatest pain'.[45]

Repeatedly measures were taken to make travelling less dangerous. An Act of 1285, intended to protect wayfarers from ambush, ordered that on highways between market towns 'there be neither dyke, tree or bush whereby a man may lurk to do hurt within two hundred feet on either side of the way'.[46] When fairs were held mounted guards were often placed on the major roads approaching them to encourage traders to attend them; and, on their own account, merchants with valuable loads would always hire a guard to accompany them upon their journeys. Oxford undergraduates, forbidden to bear arms during term time, were permitted to do so on their journeys to and from the university, a journey which they often made in a carrier's cart, as cheap and safe if not as comfortable a method of transportation as any other.[47]

In most towns curfews were imposed. At Norwich 'all men dwelling in the city, of whatever condition they may be, shall warn their servants that they shall not be absent outside the houses of their masters after the eighth hour, under the penalty of imprisonment'.[48] And at Beverley, imprisonment might also be imposed upon any inhabitant wandering 'in the street beyond the franchises by night after nine o'clock', and upon any stranger after eight o'clock 'without a light and reasonable cause'.[49]

There was safety, of course, in numbers; and, whenever they could, medieval wayfarers contrived to travel in large parties, ideally in the wake of the well-guarded royal household which was constantly on the move from one part of the kingdom to another. It might be travelling from one of the numerous castles in royal hands to the next, there being about sixty of these to choose from in the twelfth century, or to a monastery, or to the castle of some magnate whose dues included *firma unius noctis* – one night's entertainment for the immense and peripatetic household of the king.

The household had to be peripatetic not only because so large a retinue of men and animals could neither be satisfactorily fed nor hygienically accommodated in one place for too long, but also because the king's court was the government of the country and it was necessary for it to rule, and to show itself to be ruling, elsewhere than in London. Edward I, in the twenty-eighth year of his reign, moved his household no less than seventy-five times.[50] The household had also to be large, for all its many officers had attendant clerks and servants; and they, as well as the king, had to be provided with food and drink, with chaplains and guards, with limners and ushers and clerks, with hornblowers, archers, watchmen and cooks. There was the Lord High Chancellor to consider, the Lord High Steward and the Lord High Treasurer, the Lord President of the Council, the Lord Great Chamberlain, the Lord High Constable, the Keepers of the Seals and the King's Marshals. In the separate departments of the Keepers of the Cups and of the Dishes, of the Master Steward of the Larder and the Usher of the Spithouse, of the Chamberlain of the Candles, of the Keeper of the Gazehounds and the Keeper of the Brachs, of the Cat Hunters and Wolf Catchers and of the Keeper of the Tents, there were bakers and butchers and confectioners, poulterers and fruiterers, servitors and butlers, scullions and kennelmen, grooms and storekeepers. There were heralds and actors, singers, buffoons and barbers, express messengers whose duty it was to give warning of the court's approach and to order tenants and owners of estates on the route to collect provisions or provide accommodation. There was a 'Clerke of Markette' who according to the regulations drawn up for the household of Edward IV, 'ridith in the contries before the Kinges commyng to warn the people to bake, to brewe, and to make redy other vytale and stuffe in to their logginges'.[51]

There was a washerwoman to wash the king's clothes and a water-carrier to give him his bath. And, straggling for miles along the roads, splashing through the mud in winter, in clouds of dust in summer, were the sprawling lines of horses and pack animals, the carriages and carts piled high with leather pouches and bundled bags, with boxes and chests, with barrels of coins and caskets of jewels, cases of documents, kitchen utensils, hunting spears, altar cloths and chalices, tables and feather-beds, quills and parchment, chamber pots and scent bottles.

As the cavalcade approached the place where a halt was to be made for the night, twenty-four archers leading the way, the king's marshals marked with chalk those houses considered most suitable for requisition as lodgings. They also made sure that all suspected malefactors within twelve leagues of the castle were arrested and that the castle itself was cleared of harlots. The Inner Marshal, who was responsible for the security of the castle, fined each whore who remained 4d for the first time he arrested her. If she were to return she was brought before the steward and given a solemn warning never to approach a royal castle again. Were she to do so, she would be thrown into prison and her hair cut off. A fourth offence would result in the loss of her upper lip. Severe punishments were also inflicted upon disorderly hangers-on, those 'laundresses and gamesters', as Peter of Blois described them in the reign of Henry II, 'perfumiers and hucksters, vassals, mimes and barbers', as well as tiresome suitors, petitioners and parties with lawsuits who hoped to have their cases attended to when the king's law officers sat to dispense justice.

The ordinances of the household of Edward IV paid particular attention to these troublesome hangers-on, decreeing that masterless men who followed the court should be put in irons for forty days on bread and water, that female camp-followers should be branded on the forehead, and that all those whose duties compelled them to accompany the royal household should leave their wives at home. These ordinances also dealt minutely with the duties of all the king's officers, with those of the Treasurer of the Household, who had to keep the accounts, of the Marshal of the Hall, who had to ensure that no intruders, dogs or lepers found their way into any of the apartments under his control, and of the Chamberlain who had, amongst other duties, 'to arrange decently for the King's bed, and to see that the rooms be arranged with carpets and benches'.[52]

It was customary for the marshal to consult the mayor and sheriffs and other town officers when quarters were required for the court; and if this were not done there could be trouble. In the reign of Edward II, when the king was himself established in the Tower of London, the people of his household were quartered, without previous arrangements, in various near-by houses, the mansion of a distinguished sheriff being marked with chalk and occupied by the king's secretary. When the sheriff came home and found this royal official in his chamber, strange servants in his kitchen and numerous horses in his stables, he had them all thrown out and with his own hands rubbed the chalk marks off his walls. He was cited to appear before the king's steward and required to pay an indemnity of at least £1000. But he refused to submit and appealed to the mayor and citizens who produced charters of the city's privileges in his defence. These charters were quite clear on the subject and could not be denied. The matter was quietly dropped.[53]

Towns less powerful than London, however, had to put up with much inconvenience not only from the king but also from the households of great lords, whose retinues were sometimes almost as large, and even from bishops on the move in their dioceses. A rich baronial household was likely to move almost as often as the king's; and it would contain a similar hierarchy, with a marshal to arrange about supplies; a clerk of the marshalcy to deal with the horses, the purchase of oats and straw and horseshoes and the payment of the smith and the grooms; another official to keep an eye on the sumpter-horses and the carts; and messengers to deliver urgent letters and give warning of the retinue's approach.

The size of these rich households made it impossible for them to be accommodated at such inns as then existed; but hospitality was usually offered at castles and large houses where men of rank received each other with a readiness which would seem highly eccentric today. When special rooms for guests were available these would be offered to the lord and his lady, or the lord might be invited to spend the night in his host's own chamber, while the visiting servants would be provided with places to sleep in the hall on the rushes covering the floor or on mattresses thrown over them. Accommodation was also available in monasteries, rooms in the monastery itself being allotted to those of high rank, the rest normally being shown to a guest-house, many of which had bedrooms radiating from a central hall.

For smaller parties with enough money to spare there were inns where travellers would be shown to rooms containing several beds which they were likely to be asked to share with another or even two other guests. Yet these places were usually more expensive than most travellers could afford, and complaints of outrageous charges were extremely common. From time to time statutes were promulgated in an effort to force 'hostelers et herbergers' to sell food at reasonable prices; one in the reign of Edward III endeavoured to put an end to the 'great and outrageous cost of victuals kept up in the realm by inn-keepers and other retailers of victuals, to the great detriment of the people travelling all over the country'.[54]

It was, however, possible to travel without incurring expense as the experiences of the Warden and two Fellows of Merton College showed when they made a winter journey on horseback in 1331 with four servants from Oxford to Durham and Newcastle. Their expenses for one day, a Sunday, at an inn at Alfreton, were fairly typical. The total cost was 2s 3¼d, 10d of this being spent on fodder for the horses, and only 2d for beds. Bread came to 4d, beer to 2d, wine to 1½d, meat to 5½d and potage to ¼d. They spent 2d on fuel and ¼d on candles. Once they got lost and had to employ a guide, but his charge was no more than 1d. Their most expensive day was that upon which they had to cross the Humber, a wide river and in winter a difficult one to navigate; and for this crossing they had to pay 8d.[55]

A few years earlier a party of twenty-six Cambridge scholars had travelled from their university to York. They found the cost of beds even cheaper than the Oxford men, never paying more than 8d for the whole group.[56]

\*

By the end of the Middle Ages it was generally agreed that English inns had much improved and there was little need for those fourteenth-century phrasebooks taken on foreign travels that gave the French for such snatches of conversation as the following:

'I hope there are no fleas, landlord, nor bugs nor other vermin.'

'No, sir, please God, for I make bold that you shall be well and comfortably lodged here – save that there is a great peck of rats and mice . . .'

'William [addressed to a servant], undress and wash your legs, and then dry them with a cloth, and rub them well for the love of fleas, that they may not leap on your legs, for there is a peck of them lying in the dust under the rushes. Hi! The fleas bite me so! And do me great harm for I have scratched my shoulders till the blood flows.'

Most English inns were, indeed, comparatively clean and wholesome. William Harrison praised them in the warmest terms:

Those townes that we call throwfares have great and sumptuous innes builded in them for the receiving of such travellers and strangers as pass to and fro. The manner of harbouring wherein is not like that of some countries, in which the host or goodman of the house doth challenge a lordlie authoritie over his ghests, but clean otherwise, with everie man may use his inne as his owne house in England, and have for his money how great or how little varietie of vittels or what other service himself shall think expedient to call for. Our innes are also very well furnished with naperie, bedding and tapisterie especiallie with naperie . . . Each comer is sure to lie in clean sheets, wherein no man hath beene lodged since they came from the laundresse . . . It is a word to see how each owner contendeth with other for goodnesse of enterteinement of their ghests, as about finesse and change of linnen, furniture of bedding, beautie of roomes, service at the table, costliness of plate, strengthe of drink, varietie of wines or well using of horses.[57]

Inns were still not for the poor, however, and while merchants, the better-paid messengers and more prosperous itinerant packmen could afford to stay in them regularly, most tinkers, pedlars and chapmen, who went about selling everything from pins and gloves to rabbit skins, could not. Nor could many pilgrims and nor could drovers who, covering about twelve miles a day, moved flocks and herds of animals, cows, ewes, lambs, or swine, from manor to manor and one part of the country to another. These men, when they could afford a roof over their heads at all, had to be content with what comfort and warmth could be found in an alehouse, an establishment readily recognized by the pole with a bush at the end of it sticking out of the wall, often so far across the highway that riders struck their heads against them until an Act of 1375 restricted their length to seven feet. But few alehouses, it seems, offered accommodation; and a traveller was lucky to find one with a spare bed. They were principally drinking places and so favoured a haunt of pilgrims that William Thorpe, the Lollard, complained of their wasting their time there, 'spending their goods upon vitious hostelars, which are oft women uncleane of their bodies'.[58]

Pilgrims generally travelled in groups for safety as Chaucer's did; and they were commonly as colourful and lively a band as that which the miller in *The Canterbury Tales* led out of Southwark, blowing his bagpipes while the monk's bridle jingled 'as loud as doth the chapel-belle'. Among them would be men like the friar, 'a wanton one and merry'; or the monk 'who was not pale like a tormented soul'; or the summoner who loved 'drinking strong red wine till all was hazy' and 'would shout and jabber as if crazy'; or the franklin who 'lived for pleasure and had always done, for he was Epicurus' very son'.

In the opinion of William Thorpe, there were far too many pilgrims like these.

> They will ordain beforehand to have with them both men and women that can well sing wanton songs [he complained]. And some other pilgrims will have with them bagpipes; so that every town they come through, what with the noise of their singing and with the sound of their piping, and with the jangling of their Canterbury bells, and with the barking out of dogs after them, they make more noise than if the King came there, with all his clarions and many other minstrels.[59]

Some were on foot, carrying the characteristic pilgrim's staff with its pointed iron base like that of an alpenstock and its knob at the other end, perhaps inscribed with an encouraging motto such as, 'May this safely guide thee on thy way'. Others were on horseback or in carts. Several were on their way abroad, their expenses partially paid by a trade guild like the fourteenth-century Taylors' Guild at Lincoln whose statutes provided that 'if anyone desire to make a pilgrimage to the Holy Land, each brother and sister shall give him a penny; and if to St James of Galicia or Rome, a halfpenny; and they shall go out with him outside the gates of Lincoln; and on his return they shall meet him again and go with him to his mother-church.'[60]

Most pilgrims, however, were on their way to or from one or other of the pilgrimage shrines of England of which there were about sixty or seventy. Two of the principal ones were at Canterbury and Walsingham. Thousands of pilgrims flocked to Canterbury to make offerings at the shrine of St Thomas Becket who had been murdered in the cathedral by four knights on the evening of 29 December 1190. Thousands more made their way to Walsingham where the miraculous statue of the Virgin was bedecked with jewels and where so many precious gifts had been bestowed upon the place that Roger Ascham – after visiting the celebrated shrine of the wise men of the East at Cologne – came to the conclusion that 'the three kings be not so rich as the Lady of Walsingham'. Pilgrimages were also regularly made to the shrines of St Edward the Confessor at Westminster, of the holy Confessor Cuthbert at Durham, of St Swithin at Winchester, to Waltham where a miraculous cross of black marble had been found in the days of King Cnut, to Beverley, Lincoln, York and Peterborough, and to Glastonbury where St Joseph of Arimathea had, so it was said, deposited the chalice of the Last Supper and where the Glastonbury Thorn had sprung up from his staff.

Pilgrims returning from these places generally wore badges or emblems associated with them, little metal flasks of well-water with holes so that they could be sewn on clothes, medallions depicting the supposed features of a saint, and sometimes such a variety of other favours, vernicles and brooches that they looked like the man in Erasmus's dialogue who is asked by his sceptical friend in astonishment: 'I pray you, what arrays is this that you be in? Me thynke that you be clothyd with cockle schelles, and be laden on every side with bunches of lead and tynne. And you be pretely garnyshed with wrethes of straws, and your arms is full of snakes eggs.'

The curators of shrines vied with each other in the attractions they had to offer and were constantly endeavouring to increase their supply of holy relics for the greater profit of their church or monastery or order. The College of St George at Windsor possessed parts of the skulls and skeletons of at least sixteen saints, including a section of the jawbone of St Mark with fourteen teeth; a piece of the brain of St Eustace; the fingers of St George; a candle end and a girdle which had belonged to the Blessed Virgin Mary together with a fragment from her tomb and some of her milk; a thorn of Christ's crown; part of his supper table; a slither of wood from the Holy Cross; and, next to a large iron money-box with numerous slots for the offerings of pilgrims, the bones of John Schorne, a priest who had possessed an astonishing power of curing the ague and who had once forced the Devil into a boot.[61]

Abbeys which had no such enticing relics to offer would occasionally employ an artist to manufacture an image which looked as though it were capable of working miracles. Thus, one Yorkshire abbot ordered a crucifix to be made for the choir of his chapel. 'And the artist never worked at any fine and important part, except on Fridays, fasting on bread and water,' wrote one of the abbot's successors towards the end of the fourteenth century. 'And he had all the time a naked man under his eyes, and he laboured to give to his crucifix the beauty of the model. By the means of this crucifix, the Almighty worked open miracles continually. It was then thought that if access to this crucifix were allowed to women, the common devotion would be increased and great advantage would result from it for our monastery.' Unfortunately in this case the scheme did not prove profitable. Numerous women came to see this to them extraordinary example of sculpture made from a nude living model; but they came from curiosity and the abbot found that the expenses incurred by his having to receive them were far greater than the offerings they made to his monastery.[62]

# 7 · *Tournaments, Pageants and Miracles*

For Sir Walter Scott chivalry was the shining glory of the Middle Ages, an institution and a code of ethics to be considered worthy of comparison with Christianity itself. Certainly the ideals enshrined in the Arthurian legends, the bravery and loyalty of the knights, their magnanimity in victory, their sense of *noblesse oblige*, their courtly manners, their honour of womanhood, their gentleness, not only in the sense of *gens*, men of race and of good breeding, but also of mercy and consideration, were all qualities to be admired. The heroic knights of the Round Table to whom, like their king, wrong was 'exceedingly loathsome and right ever dear', rode through a magical and dreamlike world as paragons of courage in their battles with dragons and evil giants and as models of constancy in their service of ladies whom they rescued from oppression, disgrace and death. Bound 'never to do outrageously, nor murder and always to flee treason, also by no means to be cruel, but to give mercy unto him that asketh mercy . . . and always to do ladies, damsels, and gentlewomen succour upon pain of death', they are seen living up to their vows; and if the knightly code was, in fact, frequently violated, it nevertheless, as Maurice Keen has shown, remained the object of universal veneration.[1]

To these impulsive and generous heroes, sentiment was not weakness. They could weep, as Launcelot weeps, copiously like 'a child that had been beaten', and as soldiers were then never ashamed to do, as the followers of John Chandos did when he lay dying at the bridge of Lussac, crying 'piteously', so Froissart tells us, wringing their hands, tearing their hair and making pitiful complaint, 'and specially such as were of his own house'.[2]

The lower orders play no part in Malory's narration of the Arthurian stories. Who the author was is a mystery. He was certainly a prisoner when he wrote *Le Morte d'Arthur* – that 'noble and joyous book', as it was described by Caxton who published it in July 1485 from the sign of the Red Pale in

Westminster – though it is full of a strange sense of doom that foreshadows the 'dolorous death and departing of this world' of its great hero and his valiant knights. Yet, apart from his imprisonment and his longing for the day of his deliverance, little else is known about him. He may have been a Thomas Malory of Studley and Sutton in Yorkshire who was a prisoner of war in France, or he may have been Sir Thomas Malory, a Warwickshire gentleman who, after serving as Member of Parliament for his county, evidently turned to a life of crime involving accusations of cattle thieving, extortion, rape and attempted murder and culminating in his incarceration in the noisome prison of Newgate. Whoever he was, he allowed a peasant to appear only once in his narrative and then briefly and to receive a knock on the head for refusing to lend a knight his cart.[3]

As Sir Edmund Chambers pointed out, 'the distinction between noble and churl is fundamental' to *Le Morte d'Arthur*. 'If there are sparks of nobility in a cowherd's son, like Tor, or a kitchen knave, like Gareth, you may be sure he will turn out to be a king's son in disguise.'[4] Such class distinctions were not confined to the literature which chivalry promoted. Ruskin, who regarded the Middle Ages with almost as benign an eye as Scott, noted chivalry's contempt for the manual worker. Ideally the knight should protect the poor.

> What is the function of orderly knighthood? [asked John of Salisbury in the fourteenth century] To protect the Church, to fight against treachery, to reverence the priesthood, to fight off injustice from the poor, to make peace in your own provinces, to shed your blood for your own brethren, and, if needs must, to lay down your own life.[5]

Yet a contemporary of John of Salisbury, Peter of Blois, Archdeacon of Bath, writes to a friend in a condemnation of chivalry which, while exaggerated in tone, was not unjustified:

> I cannot bear the vaunting and vainglory of the Knights your nephews . . . The Order of Knighthood, in these days of ours, is mere disorder. For he whose mouth is defiled with the foulest words, whose oaths are most detestable, who least fears God, who vilifies God's ministers, who feareth not the Church – that man nowadays is reputed bravest and most renowned of the knightly band . . . Aspirants receive their swords from the altar in order that they may profess themselves sons of the Church, acknowledging themselves to have received their weapons for the honour of the priesthood, the defence of the poor, the avenging of wrongs and the freedom of their country. Yet in practice they do the contrary. If these knights of ours are sometimes constrained to take the field, then their sumpter-beasts are laden not with steel but with wine, not with spears but

with cheeses, not with swords but with wineskins, not with javelins but with spits. You would think they were on their way to feast, and not to fight.[6]

Knights did not always receive their swords from the altar as Peter of Blois suggests. There was an essentially religious ceremony which was performed by a bishop. There was also a ceremony in which the candidate kept vigil throughout the preceding night before an altar on which the sword was laid; the next morning he took a ritual bath, as the still existing Order of the Bath indicates, and then heard Mass before his spurs were put on and he was dubbed with the sword. But it was much more usual for the dubbing ceremony to be performed with the most perfunctory religious rites, or without any rites at all, and for the king or a noble to carry it out in a baronial hall or on the field of battle.[7]

The devices emblazoned on the knight's shield and surcoat as distinguishing marks in the muddle and fury of battle had developed into the intricate science of heraldry. The complicated symbols, allusive, allegorical, punning, artistically and skilfully arranged in coloured designs and handed down from generation to generation, were displayed on gatehouses and chantry chapels, on tents and standards, on plate and carriages and were never more proudly worn than when, announced by trumpets and heralds, the knight entered the lists to take part in a tournament.

Brought to England from France in the twelfth century, the tournament was originally a rough and tumble training-ground for a young knight, an opportunity for him to display his strength and prowess. It usually took the form of a ferocious mock-battle fought in an open field with numerous knights on each side lashing out at each other in their efforts to unhorse their opponents. Injuries were common; knights were sometimes so badly injured that they died of their wounds; while squires, overcome with excitement, joined in the *mêlée* and added to the violence and confusion. But since then, having been repeatedly and vainly banned by Henry III who feared that they would be used as excuses for baronial conspiracies, tournaments had become subject to stricter rules. The sorts of weapon which could be used were more severely limited; combats between two horsemen became more common than mock-battles between many; and, rather than brute force, skill and practised horsemanship were likely to bring victory. The contests were still dangerous, as the antagonists rode full tilt at each other in boarded enclosures in which barriers to prevent the horses colliding were not in common use until the fifteenth century; but the numbers of knights who were killed in a bone-shattering crash to the ground were nothing like as many as in the days of mass battering. The Church had at first frowned upon tournaments because of the bloodshed involved, had refused Christian burial to those who were killed in them, and had succeeded in getting them banned in England. It abandoned its opposition in 1316, however, when Pope John XXII was persuaded that they were an essential military exercise for potential crusaders.

As well as an exercise in arms, the tournament had also become a form of love-play. Almost every knight had a lady whom he wanted to impress, to whom he prayed for victory, while also praying to Our Lady that, after victory, his prowess in the lists might be rewarded by an opportunity to demonstrate his prowess as a lover. After the jousts he would approach the stand where the ladies sat, remove his helm, bow to them and then return to his lodgings to await their verdict upon the prizes which it was in their gift to bestow. Having come to their decision, they would address the successful knight with formal courtesy:

> Sir, theis ladyes and gentilwomen thank you for your disporte and grete labour yt ye have this day in their presences. And the seide ladyes and gentilwomen seyen that ye, Sir —— have done the best joust this day. Therefore the seide ladyes and gentilwomen gevyn you this diamonde and send you much worship and joy of yor lady.[8]

Prizes of rubies and sapphires were presented to

> . . . the othir two next the best Justers. This doon then shall the heraulde of armes stonde up all on high. And shall say wt all an high voice: John hath wele justid, Ric[har]d have justid bettir and Thomas hath justid best of all, then shall hee that the diamount is geve unto take a lady by the hande and begynne the daunce.[9]

On occasions the ladies did not merely award the prizes, but constituted the prizes themselves; for according to the ethos of chivalry an act of infidelity was no disgrace. Adultery had, indeed, become an accepted social diversion of the upper classes, with a recognized code of behaviour compatible with chivalrous ideas; and it was expected that a knight would have already made love to another knight's wife before making a *mariage de convenance* himself. Provided he observed the manners of polite society and was prepared to fight and to die for the lady he professed to love, he might otherwise behave as he liked. As Dr Coulton put it, 'woman-hunting was, it may be said, a normal sport'. Chastity girdles were not worn by ladies at court, since the virtue of a lady, if it were to be protected at all, must be preserved by the sword and not by the key in the manner of an Italian merchant.[10]

By the middle of the thirteenth century a new kind of tournament, referred to in 1252 by Matthew Paris as the Round Table, had developed. This was a social occasion, often lasting for several days, during which all kinds of sports were practised: wrestling, casting the stone and the lance, high jumping and long jumping, as well as the usual jousts. The knights who took part sat down to eat with their shields at their backs at a table, like that of King Arthur, so shaped as to set aside all distinctions of rank and quality. Such an event was held at Windsor Castle by Edward III in 1344 when, from all over England and from 'parts beyond the seas', 'an indescribable host of people' came to the castle 'to delight in so great solemnity'. The feasts that followed the games and joustings were most lavish, 'abounding in the most alluring' of drinks; and, as the guests ate and drank, minstrels, wearing new tunics specially provided for the occasion, played in the gallery. Afterwards one guest recalled, 'dances were not lacking, embraces and kissings, alternately commingling'.[11] It was during a later tournament at Windsor in 1348 that Edward III founded the Order of the Garter, the oldest order of chivalry in Europe, the original members of which were mostly young knights who apparently wore a garter as their badge during the joustings.

One of the most popular of all forms of tournament was that known as the *pas d'armes* in which a knight had to fight his way through a defended obstacle, or a series of obstacles, to his goal. At first these displays usually took place in open country where a bridge or a narrow file would be defended by the knight's adversary; but by the fifteenth century it was more common for artificial obstacles to be erected in the shape of castle keeps, gateways or drawbridges. The knight would then appear in armour at the beginning of the course, driving up in a chariot or striding forth dramatically from a pavilion. An allegorical fantasy, involving a lady, would be devised to explain his presence there to the spectators; and he would then ride off to battle with the enemy.

No one who was not a gentleman could take part in tournaments, but all conditions of men and women could watch, provided they could gain access to the ground. Most townspeople, however, were well content with the spectacles which could be seen from the windows of their own houses and workshops. Some of these were modest enough – a few students, perhaps, celebrating by marching through the streets with pipes, drums and flowers, or a group of apprentices with flags and the symbols of their trades. But there were grand spectacles, particularly those staged in London, such as water pageants; parades through streets beneath damask awnings, velvet-covered poles, escutcheons, shields and standards, tapestries, arches of halberds and triumphal bridges; or the processions, more splendid year by year, in which the mayor, or lord mayor as he has been commonly known since 1545, went to Westminster to receive the approval of the king to his election, going at first by road, then more often by river, and after 1452 in a magnificent barge rowed by silver oars.

Almost every year pageants were staged in the streets to celebrate both national and civic occasions, royal weddings and coronations, visits by distinguished foreigners and military victories as well as such events as the anniversary of the granting of a charter. By the middle of the thirteenth century in London it had already become an established tradition for the entry of the king into the city from his palace at Westminster to be marked by formal pageantry. The city fathers would meet the king and the officers of his household outside the city boundaries. They would then ride back into the city along a route beside which the citizens were paraded in the liveries of their respective trade guilds. By the end of the century the western limits of the city were marked by a chain which was stretched between posts across the road to Westminster; and by 1351 this boundary, known as Temple Bar, was more imposingly distinguished by a gate with a prison above it. Here in later times a ceremony was always performed – and still is performed – on state occasions when the sovereign wishes to enter the city: permission was asked of the mayor who offered his sword of state as a demonstration of loyalty; the sword was immediately returned and carried before the royal procession to indicate that the sovereign was in the city under the mayor's protection.

It was usual in the thirteenth and fourteenth centuries for the royal party to proceed to St Paul's, the fine Norman cathedral which had been built on the site of a Saxon building destroyed by fire in 1087; and, having heard Mass, to be escorted back to the Palace of Westminster, the various trade guilds competing with each other to make the grandest spectacle, the Fishmongers' Company often apparently being considered the most ingenious and extravagant of all. In 1298 when the city celebrated the defeat of the Scots by Edward I at Falkirk, this Company, which had received its first charter twenty-six years before, outdid the other Companies as the 'solemne Procession passed through the Citie [by] having amongest other Pageants and shews, foure Sturgeons guilt, carried on four horses; then foure Salmons of Silver on foure horses, and after them six and fortie armed knights riding on horses, and then one representing Saint Magnes'. In 1313 the Fishmongers excelled themselves when, in celebration of the birth of Edward III, they constructed a large ship in full sail emblazoned with the heraldic devices of the English and French royal houses.[12]

The inventive concoctions of the Fishmongers were again 'notably excellent' when the city staged a pageant to celebrate the coronation of Richard II in 1377. But on this occasion other companies, too, were singled out for praise:

> Nor did these great guilds lack a large company of flutes and trumpets: for every guild is led by its own trumpeters. Trumpeters had been stationed by the Londoners above the Conduit, as above the tower in the same

street, which had been built in the King's honour, to sound a fanfare on his approach . . . A kind of castle had been constructed, having four towers, in the upper part of the shopping street called Cheapside: and from two of its sides wine flowed abundantly. In its towers, moreover, four very beautiful maidens had been placed, of about the King's own age and stature and dressed in white garments . . . On the King's approach being sighted, they scattered golden leaves in his path and, on his coming nearer, they showered imitation gold florins on to both him and his horse. When he had arrived in front of the castle, they took gold cups and, filling them with wine at the spouts of the said castle, offered them to him and his retinue. In the top of the castle, and raised above and between its four towers, a golden angel was stationed, holding in its hands a golden crown. This angel had been devised with such cunning that, on the King's arrival, it bent down and offered him the crown.[13]

Enormous sums of money were expended on occasions like these and wine flowed abundantly. Gates and market crosses were elaborately decorated; tableaux were staged upon the covered tops of water cisterns; flags and banners fluttered from windows and chimneys; the richest costumes were made for those who were to take part in the drama – an inventory of the properties required for the festivities attendant upon the coronation of Edward IV's queen, Elizabeth Woodville, includes an item specifying 900 peacocks' feathers – and handsome sums were paid to poets and schoolmasters for devising pageants: at the beginning of the seventeenth century Thomas Middleton received no less than £282 for composing a pageant for the Grocers' Company.[14]

One of the most memorable of all London pageants was that held to celebrate Henry V's victory at Agincourt in 1415 when a triumphant cavalcade of scarlet-clad aldermen, citizens and craftsmen attended the king from London Bridge to St Paul's. Each of the twin towers of the gatehouse on the bridge was surmounted by a statue 'of amazing magnitude', one representing a giant holding a battle-axe in his right hand and the keys of the city in his left, the other a woman clothed in a red cloak, sparkling with jewels and other ornaments. Beyond the bridge were other jewel-bedecked figures of animals and warriors standing on both sides of the roadway between columns painted to resemble white marble and green jasper, or in tapestry-lined pavilions. And beneath triumphal arches and inside velvet tents were 'innumerable boys, representing the angelic host, arrayed in white with their faces painted gold and with glittering wings and virgin locks set with precious sprigs of laurel', singing anthems to the sound of organs.

As the procession of great men wound its way through the narrow streets to St Paul's, the king bareheaded and in a purple robe like a Roman emperor marching in triumph down the *Sacra Via*, his knights following him in armour, his attendants wearing the insignia of their various offices, his forlorn and noble prisoners of war walking in their wake, they passed old men of 'venerable hoariness' dressed in golden mantles and representing prophets, martyrs and ancient kings. These men sang psalms of thanksgiving, offered the king silver leaves, a cup filled with wine from the conduit pipes, and then let fly 'great quantities of sparrows and little birds that alighted on the King's breast and shoulders and fluttered about him'. Beyond were pavilions in which 'the most beautiful girls, standing motionless like statues', blew from cups, 'with gentle breath scarcely perceptible', leaves of gold upon the king's head as he passed beneath them. Then there were choirs of girls 'singing with timbrel and dance'; and white-clad cherubs feathered like angels throwing down gilded laurel leaves from the towers of model castles; and, on the steps of St Paul's, eighteen bishops in their pontificals waiting to conduct him to the high altar.[15]

The enjoyment of spectacles like this was limited to those who lived in London and in the few other towns such as York and Coventry which could afford to stage them. But all over the country, on a lesser scale, theatrical performances were regularly produced. These had developed from the liturgical drama of the early Church. The Mass itself with its ceremonial and symbolism was a dramatic spectacle, while the antiphonal singing in church services lent itself readily to dialogue. As early as 970 St Ethelwold of Winchester was speaking of 'the strengthening of faith in the unlearned vulgar'; and since then the primitive dramas enacted in churches at Easter, in which the Angel appeared before the Marys by the tomb of the Resurrection, had become increasingly elaborate and more sophisticated. Other characters had been introduced, among them Doubting Thomas and the Seller of Spices; the Marys sang lyric laments. Nativity plays were introduced with yet further characters, the Magi, the Shepherds, and, later to become a stock character of broad comedy, the rowdy, hectoring Herod, who was a popular character, too, in those entertainments staged by the minor clergy in cathedrals and collegiate churches known as the Feast of Fools. During these revels, held at New Year at Lincoln, Beverley, St Paul's, Salisbury and probably elsewhere, the clergy, giving free rein to their high spirits, appointed 'a King' who presided over the festivities and took a leading part in the noisy merriment and farcical pantomime.[16]

At first, in churches, the parts were taken – the dialogue being chanted not sung – by priests, nuns and choirboys. But later laymen, though not lay women, were allowed to appear; and eventually, it seems, a few professional performers, mostly musicians. The action took place both in the nave and in those parts of the aisle which were intended to represent the Garden of

Gethsemane, Herod's Palace, the Mount of Olives or whatever scenes the play demanded. Those playing the parts of prophets delivered their lines from the pulpit.

As time passed, as the congregations, or audiences, grew in numbers, and as increasingly comical and even bawdy characters were added to the cast, many clergy expressed themselves in agreement with Abbess Herrad of Landsberg who, though she, like St Ethelwold, acknowledged that the plays had been instituted 'in order to strengthen the belief of the faithful and to attract the unbeliever', regretted they had now been spoiled by 'buffoonery, unbecoming jokes . . . and all sorts of disorder'. They still had their advocates. In 1300 Robert Manning of Bourn warmly commended them, provided that the clergy did not wear unseemly masks. Their good purpose was:

> To make men be in belief of God,
> That He rose in flesh and blood . . .
> To make men to believe steadfastly
> That God was born of Virgin Marie.

Yet in several dioceses the performance of plays in church had already been forbidden, as it had been by Bishop Grosseteste of Lincoln who in 1244 had written, 'The clergy [of our diocese], as I hear, make plays which they call Miracles', and had ordered his archdeacons to 'exterminate these altogether', in so far as it was in their power. Other bishops, including Walter de Chanteloup, Bishop of Worcester, also pronounced against plays in church; and about 1250 the university of Oxford banned all masked students from taking part in performances in all churches within the city. So religious drama gradually moved out of churches and was performed instead in churchyards, in market places or on carts which were paraded about the town, the actors performing their particular scene before a group of spectators who waited in their places at the various 'stations' – in York there were up to sixteen of these, in Beverley six – for the next cart and the next scene to appear. Or a play might be performed on a site leased for the occasion by the corporation to an individual citizen who might want to entertain guests outside his own house or make money by selling seats on platforms he created around the performing area. The actors now were no longer clergymen and choirboys but members of trade guilds and, possibly, a few actors employed by the guilds to give credit to their performances. Amateur craft members were encouraged to take part by the offer of free food and drink both during and after the performance and at rehearsals which were usually held in the morning before the day's work began. The smiths of Chester, for example, were given 'flesh at the breakfast and bacon'. Payments of money are also recorded: in 1494 at Hull a player received 10d for taking the part of God; and in 1490 at Coventry payments were made of 2s to Christ and to Pilate's wife, 3s 4d to Herod, and 4s to Pilate himself. At Perth, Adam and Eve both got 6d, the Devil and St Erasmus 8d each, while the torturers of the saint whose intestines were wound out of his body on a windlass, were given 1s each. One Fawston of Coventry was less well rewarded with 4d for 'hanging Judas' though he did get another 4d for 'coc croying'.[17]

Each guild might be responsible for a particular scene in a play; Noah's ark, for example, would be the responsibility of the shipwrights, Jonah and the Whale that of the fishmongers, Joseph's workshop would be assigned to the carpenters, the Last Supper to the Bakers, the retinue of the Magi to the Goldsmiths. Or a guild might be responsible for one entire miracle or mystery play, the town authorities often deciding which were most suited to a particular guild. This sometimes led to resentment, as it did in York in 1431 when the masons' guild 'murmured among themselves concerning their own pageant on Corpus Christi Day, when Fergus was scourged, seeing that the matter of the pageant is not contained in Holy Scripture, and that it caused rather laughter and clamour than devotion, and sometimes quarrels, contentions and fights proceeded therefore among the people'. The city council acceded to the guild's request and granted them permission to perform the Herod play instead. The apocryphal play was not suppressed altogether, however; and, ribald and contentious though it was, it was later performed in York by the guild of linen-weavers.[18]

The town authorities were not only responsible for allocating the plays; they also took it upon themselves to arrange for auditions to discover the best performers.

> Yearly in the time of Lent [the York city council ordained] there shall be called before the Mayor four of the most conyng, discrete and able players within this city, to search for, hear and examine all the players throughout all the artificers belonging to the Corpus Christi play. And all such as they shall find sufficient in person and conyng to the honour of the city and the worship of its crafts they shall admit, and all other insufficient persons either in conyng, voice or person they shall discharge, ammove and avoide.[19]

The York city council also decreed, as did Wakefield council, that plays should be staged at authorized places only and nowhere else on pain of a fine, that every player should 'be ready in his pagiaunt' at a specified time (half past four in the morning at York, five o'clock at Wakefield), and that if a guild failed to produce a play 'by good players well arrayed and openly spekyng' 100s should be 'paide to the chambre without any pardon'.[20]

At Coventry it was also an offence for a member of one guild to appear in another's production without permission from the mayor. And at Beverley fines were imposed for incompetent productions, and one unfortunate player was fined for forgetting his lines. In certain towns close supervision by the authorities was clearly necessary since quarrels and even fights between rival guilds were far from uncommon. At Chester in 1399 there was a pitched battle between the Weavers and the Fullers during the procession; at York in 1419 the Carpenters and Cordwainers attacked the Skinners with clubs and axes; and at Newcastle-upon-Tyne measures had to be taken to abate 'the dissension and discord that hath been amongst the Crafts of the said Towne as of man slaughter and murder and other mischiefs in time comeing which hath been lately attempted amongst the fellowship of the said crafts'.[21]

Although the York Masons complained that their play provoked laughter, most guilds welcomed plays that had funny interludes and went out of their way to emphasize the comic element in their performances. The workmen at the Tower of Babel were normally given comic dialogue, as, sometimes, were the shepherds in the nativity plays. Noah's wife was invariably a raging harridan; Noah himself a laughable drunkard; Herod an absurdly bombastic figure; Satan and his devils caused as much mirth as horror as they diligently prodded the souls of the damned into the mouth of hell.

Audiences demanded horror as well as humour. There had to be bladders of blood, severed heads, lambs for sacrifices, fearsome masks, instruments of torture and full-throated cries of anguish. When Christ suffered on the cross, the actor must be seen to be suffering, too.[22]

The theatrical effects were cunningly devised and extremely realistic. There were earthquakes and floods and fire; the Devil appeared from concealed traps in clouds of sulphurous smoke; God and his angels descended to the stage by means of wires and cranes hidden in clouds; one contraption representing hell's mouth required sixteen men to work the mechanism.[23]

The cost of these performances was naturally heavy. The guilds levied 'pageant-pence' or 'pageant-silver' upon their members. The fifteenth-century Glovers of York had to pay 2d a year towards the expenses of the guild's play if they were born within the community, 4d if 'strangers'.[24] In the next century in Chester the Smith's Company collected as much as 2s 4d a year from their guildsmen and about 1d each from their journeymen; and a dyer went to prison rather than make a contribution towards his guild's pageant. At Chelmsford 'the summer dramatic festival' of plays in the town and its neighbourhood was supported by loans from nine leading citizens who contributed over £20 between them.[25] Money was also raised by church-ales at which collections were made; by sales of unwanted costumes from previous performances; by payments from citizens who could afford to 'have pageantry played before their own doores'; by the allocation of proportions of rents and tithes; by gifts from private and municipal benefactors; and by such bequests as that of the Coventry man who left a scarlet gown to the tanners for their plays, together with 3s 4d to every craft charged with the maintenance of a pageant.[26] And, although it seems that spectators were not charged for watching the plays, a hat was taken round after each performance for contributions towards the cost.[27]

In the countryside the opportunities for seeing a well-presented play with striking effects and expensive costumes were limited; but all over England village amateurs had for long been putting on mumming plays whose distant origins in dumb show seem to have been the rites performed at the various seasons of the agricultural year and whose later developments, spoken in rhyming couplets, featured some such heroic figure as St George who would introduce himself with the words,

> I am St George, a noble knight
> Come from foreign parts to fight
> To slay that fiery dragon who is bold
> And cut him down with his blood cold.

There would then be fights with Turkish swordsmen after which a doctor would appear to demonstrate his prowess of healing wounds and bringing back the dead to life; and, as in the mystery plays and bible stories of the guilds, various stock characters, broadly lampooned, would find their way into the action, without too much concern for their relevance, the Fool with cap and bells, the Devil and Father Christmas. In the similar Plough Monday plays, which were performed on the Monday after Twelfth Night and were also, no doubt, relics of primitive folk festivals, the characters were farm workers and ordinary country people, the deaths that occurred among them being the results of accidents rather than combat.[28]

The authorities kept a wary eye on these mumming plays, which were inclined to degenerate into riots and to keep men from more gainful occupations. Indeed, they kept a watchful eye upon all dramatic performances which were, from time to time, suppressed, as they were in London in 1318 when the mayor and aldermen were 'chargen on the Kynges behalf that no manere persone, of what astate, degre or condicioun that evere be, duryng this holy tyme of Cristemes be so hardy in eny wyse to walk by nyght in any mere mommyng, pleyes, enterludes, or other disgisynges with eny feynd berdis, peynted visers, diffourmyd or colourid visages in eny wyse.'[29]

Morris-dancing, too, was often frowned upon, for in its origins this was far less innocent than might be gathered from the performances of its present practitioners. Derived from the sword-dance or from the Morisco or Moorish dance, morris-dancing was normally performed by six persons with bells on their legs and coloured scarves or sticks in their hands. They were generally accompanied by a fool who carried a cow's tail and a bladder often blown up to represent a phallus; by a crowned man on a hobby horse; and at Maytime by a Jack-in-the-Green. In the later Middle Ages characters representing Robin Hood, Maid Marian and Friar Tuck were also of the troupe who danced to the accompaniment of pipe and tabor. The faces of the dancers were blackened, possibly a relic of the old pagan rite of smearing the face with ashes from a sacrificial fire.[30]

Minstrels were also censured by the Church, for, while the most celebrated of their calling, men like Rahere, the Augustinian founder of St Bartholomew's Hospital, and Blondel de Nesle, the favourite minstrel of Richard I, were respected figures at court, there were others who were condemned as harshly as any of those *histriones* anathematized by Thomas de Chatham, Sub-Dean of Salisbury, at the beginning of the thirteenth century:

> Some transform and transfigure their bodies with indecent dance and gesture, now indecently unclothing themselves, now putting on horrible masks . . . There are, besides, others who have no definite profession, but act as vagabonds, not having any certain domicile. These frequent the courts of the great and say scandalous and shameful things concerning those who are not present so as to delight the rest . . . There is yet a third class of *histriones* who play musical instruments for the delectation of men, and of these there are two types. Some frequent public meeting-places and lascivious gatherings, and there sing stanzas to move men to lasciviousness. Beside there are others, who are called *jongleurs* who sing the gestes of princes and the lives of saints.[31]

The most successful and highly regarded minstrels were well-paid members of rich households; and at feasts given by the most wealthy families many of them were employed to entertain the guests. The records of the Whitsuntide feast of 1306 given by Edward I in London include a long list of minstrels together with the sums paid to each. The most handsomely rewarded were the minstrels who were given the title of *le roy*; then came those known as *maistres*; the less important had names which indicate the kind of entertainment they provided or the instruments they played – Janin le Lutour, Baudee le Taboureur, Gillotin le Santreour, Reginaldus le Menteur, Guillaume sanz Maniere and the female comedian, Matill' Makejoye.[32]

The licence allowed to the comedians was considerable, though Henry I is alleged to have put out the eyes of a Norman minstrel who composed and sang songs against him. Many minstrels took advantage of all the opportunities they had of ingratiating themselves with their employers, to whom they had free access, and making as much money out of their privileged positions as they could. Henry I's wife, Matilda, is believed to have squandered most of her revenues upon rapacious minstrels in her household; one of Edward II's favourite minstrels, William de Morlei, known as Roy de North, was awarded a grant of land; Edward III's minstrels were paid the satisfactory sum of 7½d a day in peace time and 12d a day when they were required to go to war as a military band. These included five trumpeters, one citoler, five pipers, one tabouretter, two players of clarions, one nakerer and one fiddler. There were also three additional performers listed as waits.[33]

By Edward III's time, as Professor Holt has observed, 'there was the first of many signs that the profession was getting out of hand'. An ordinance of 1315 indicates that indolent persons, pretending minstrelsy, were going about in search of hospitality and money. It was accordingly decreed that no one except a professed minstrel should seek food or drink in the houses of prelates, earls or barons. Two years later, in 1317, a woman dressed as a minstrel managed to gain access to Westminster Hall at the time of the royal Whitsun banquet and insulted the king by leaving a manifesto attacking his government. In 1496 Edward IV incorporated the royal minstrels as a guild and in an ineffective decree granted them authority to seek out those 'rough peasants and craftsmen of various mysteries of our realm of England pretending to be minstrels [and carrying] our letters not issued by us and . . . under colour of the art or occupation of minstrels fraudulently collect and receive great sums of money from our lieges'.[34]

As well as the king all great lords had minstrels in their households. The Earl of Derby took minstrels with him on his foreign expeditions in 1390 and 1392; while the *Household Book* of the Earl of Northumberland indicates that he was able to call upon 'a Taberett, a Luyte and a Rebecc' as well as six 'trompettes'. Municipal corporations also employed minstrels to play at all local celebrations and festivities, allowing them a salary and the right to wear the town livery with a silver badge. And although the Church frequently condemned them, they were often to be heard performing at the festivities of religious guilds and even in the halls of monasteries.[35]

These were the fortunate ones. The rest had to make their living on the open road, playing their instruments, telling their stories and jokes by the wayside, in the market-place, wherever a crowd could be gathered. For these life could be hard. In the worst times even the most skilful of them, like the poet Rutebeuf, were close to starvation. Unless they were protected by licences such as those issued in Chester to *bona fide* performers, or by the livery of a lord for whom they played on special occasions, they were liable to be treated as vagabonds. And minstrels were known to adopt liveries to which they were not entitled so as to avoid arrest as vagrants. In an attempt to stop this, Edward IV – whose own minstrels' livery had been usurped by 'certain rude husbandmen and artificers' fancying themselves as entertainers – created the guild of minstrels whose officers had authority over their profession throughout the country, except in Chester. It seems that admission to the guild was limited to 'minstrels of honour', in the same way that membership of the later guild of minstrels in Beverley was confined to those who could claim to be 'mynstrell to some man of honour or worship or waite of some towne corporate or other ancient town, or else of such honestye and conyng as shal be thought laudable and pleasant to the hearers'.[36]

Hard though the life of some unfortunate minstrels was, however, most of them managed to do well for themselves.

They wandered at their will from castle to castle, and in time from borough to borough [in the words of Sir Edmund Chambers, their historian], sure of a ready welcome alike in the village tavern, the guildhall, and the baron's keep. They sang and jested in the market-places, stopping cunningly at a critical moment in the performance to gather their harvest of small coin from the bystanders. In the great castles, while lords and ladies supped or sat around the fire, it was theirs to while away many a long bookless evening with courtly *geste* or witty sally. At wedding or betrothal, baptism or knight-dubbing, treaty or tournament, their presence was indispensable. The greater festivities saw them literally in their hundreds, and rich was their reward in money and in jewels, in costly garments, and in broad acres. They were licensed vagabonds with free right of entry into the presence-chambers of the land. You might know them from afar by their coats of many colours, gaudier than any knight might respectably wear, by the instruments upon their backs and those of their servants, and by the shaven faces, close-clipped hair and flat shoes proper to their profession.[37]

Often to be seen in their wake were the itinerant entertainers whose appeal was largely to the unlettered, the rope-walkers and acrobats, the conjurors, the jugglers and the puppet-masters, and all those other entertainers whose audiences were not so depleted as were those of the more sophisticated minstrels by the advent of printing.

# 8 · *Town Life*

Although country people were constantly being drawn into towns, these strange and noisy places with their crowded streets and huddled buildings never seemed welcoming to outsiders and, on occasions, could be positively hostile. The rebel priest, John Ball, is believed to have warned some of his associates at the time of the rising of 1381, 'Bee war [beware] of guile in borough'. Certainly this warning reflects the countryman's suspicions of the town-dweller which were already centuries old.[1]

Even such fairly large towns as, say, Nottingham and Warwick had what would be considered today a decidedly rural atmosphere; and the rights of the inhabitants to common pastures were still jealously guarded. In some smaller towns, indeed, there were burgesses who were full-time farmers, while most of the local craftsmen, as at Oakham in Rutland and Congleton in Cheshire, were also husbandmen in what time they could spare from their other avocations. And in larger towns, Coventry, Leicester, Worcester and Gloucester among them, husbandry still occupied a considerable part of the inhabitants' day.[2] Yet not only in such towns as these but also in those smaller places with less than 500 inhabitants, those *villes marchandes* as official documents describe them, the people's occupations and concerns were essentially different from those of the peasant: they were engaged in commerce and manufacture, and in providing services; and the weekly market was 'the focus of their lives'.[3] These towns were not necessarily larger than the biggest of the surrounding villages; but the villages were almost exclusively agricultural. In Sherborne, a village with as many inhabitants as a small town, all the taxpayers in 1380–81 were listed as cultivators, though some had surnames indicating that they also practised a craft; whereas in the small town of Stow-on-the-Wold – whose population at this time was probably about 300, and certainly less than that of Sherborne – there were, as Professor Hilton has recorded, no more than four households whose heads were listed in the poll-tax list as being cultivators of the soil. A few of the more well-to-do inhabitants, naturally, held land outside the town; but they did not farm these holdings personally. Their occupations are listed as smith, merchant, *velbrugger*, that is to say, dealer in sheepskins, and brewstress. In all, twenty-eight separate crafts and trades were practised in this one small town.[4]

Most towns were small. A Venetian nobleman who was in England in about 1500 thought the country 'very thinly inhabited' with 'hardly any towns of importance'. And, even a century later, another Italian considered that there were only about twenty-four large towns in the entire country, though 'populous villages and small towns' were very frequently encountered. Certainly, throughout this period as much as 95 per cent of the population was still rural; and there were very few towns indeed with over 1000 inhabitants. The provincial capital of York had a population of no more than 8000 in the late Middle Ages. London was exceptional with some 50,000.[5]

Yet, although they were small, towns were usually rich in comparison with the surrounding countryside, however poor they might have been when first founded. Colchester, for instance, a largish town of some 2200 inhabitants at the time of the Conquest, had not increased in size for two and a half centuries. A toll levied on their goods in about 1300 revealed that one of the richest men in the town was a butcher whose valuation came to no more than £7 15s 2d. The stock-in-hand of his fellow butchers was mostly limited to brawn, lard and a few salting tubs, though one had two carcasses of oxen valued at 2s each, and another had meat worth 30s. In addition to the butchers, there were thirteen well-to-do tanners and fourteen mercers, but otherwise there were no men of even moderate wealth in the town. During the fourteenth century, however, clothiers came to settle and to make money in the town; so did weavers, fullers, dyers and wool-mongers. In 1373 the undercroft beneath the old Moot Hall was converted into a spacious Wool Hall with a fine porch and adjoining shops. Further shops had by then been built in other parts of the town with living accommodation over them; the poor hovels had been replaced with larger timber-framed dwellings; and the population of the now prosperous town had doubled.[6]

It was the same in other towns all over the country. In the fourteenth and fifteenth centuries, in town after town, old churches were restored and new ones constructed; hospitals, schools and almshouses were founded; market crosses were set up; bridges, aqueducts and wharfs were built, as well as guild halls and common halls in which the town's charters and other precious documents were kept in chests with many locks. Inns were provided for travelling merchants and traders, and for the 'mayors and clerks of distant boroughs come to negotiate a commercial treaty'.[7]

As they became rich, towns also became powerful, often able to extract from the king privileges for themselves which villages, even if larger in area and population, could never have done. In their turn, successive kings found the towns useful allies against an insubordinate aristocracy, and were ready to grant royal recognition to those trading associations in the boroughs, the guilds.

These guilds, established to control the trade within the borough, had originated from organizations with a purely benevolent or religious basis and from associations formed to ensure that the men practising any particular craft never grew too numerous, that standards of quality and skill were maintained, that tools might be shared, raw materials readily supplied, and that charitable assistance might be made available to those who could no longer work, such as an old loriner no longer able to grasp his hammer with sufficient strength or a goldsmith blinded by the fire and smoke of quicksilver. The ordinances of the developing guilds established an increasingly strict control over their particular crafts. The 1307 ordinances of the craft of Girdlers of York, for instance, forbade their members to work by night or to farm out surplus work, restricted master craftsmen in the number of apprentices they could take on, and decreed that all apprentices must serve a minimum of four, later raised to seven, years. Yet, concerning themselves with the spiritual and moral as well as the social welfare of their members, laying down rules for the celebration of Masses for the dead, for regular church attendance, and for the ostracism of those guilty of adultery, the guilds not only endeavoured to ensure that their members led a respectable life and received a fair price for their goods but also that their customers were not overcharged, that the community as a whole benefited from their supervision and regulations. Their members, women as well as men, were subject to strict rules, forbidden, for example, to withhold supplies until demand increased the price, to discuss the guild's business in public, or to conduct themselves indecorously at their meetings. Punishment for breaches of the rules were often severe and carried out in public, the offender being beaten, fined or placed in the pillory, a placard indicating his offence placed about his neck for the benefit of those who could read and some other indication of his misdemeanour, such as a rotting fish tied under his chin, for those who could not.

As the guilds grew in authority and the burgesses in wealth, so the hold of the aristocracy on the towns, strong if not paramount when Domesday Book was compiled, was gradually weakened. Towards the end of the Middle Ages it became common for the richer burgesses to leave the towns and set themselves up as country gentlemen, and to aspire to socially superior marriages for their daughters. But for a century and a half, from about 1200 to the middle of the fourteenth century, there were families of burgesses in most towns whose members, generation after generation, were evidently quite content to remain in them. This family continuity, as Dr Colin Platt has suggested, reflected a profound satisfaction with urban living that can have only come from a unique combination of independence and economic success.[8]

The interests of these wealthy burgess families were promoted by frequent intermarriage. In London, of the ninety-five aldermen elected before 1293 over two-thirds belonged to a single complex of interrelated families, ten of them from the family of Henry Fitzailwyn, first Mayor of London, eight from the Blunds and six from the Buckerels, all of these families being connected to each other by marriage and all being extremely rich. Men like these were considerably better off than country gentlemen and some were more wealthy than all but the richest nobility. Fitzailwyn owned property in Kent, Surrey and Middlesex as well as in London; while the fortune of his successor as Mayor, the mercer, Richard Whittington, was so immense that he was not only able to rebuild London's main prison and found its principal almshouses but also to bestow money upon numerous charitable enterprises all over the capital. In several county towns there were men with comparable fortunes. William Canynges, a fifteenth-century Bristol merchant, employed 800 men to work his ships and had a further 100 in his pay in the town. And Thomas Horton, clothier of Bradford-on-Avon, was so rich that he personally paid 70 per cent of the entire subsidy of the town. The families to which such men belonged managed over the years to accumulate most of their communities' wealth. Well over half the wealth of Norwich was in the hands of only 6 per cent of the population; while almost half of Coventry's was held by 2 per cent.[9]

These rich burgesses had a virtual monopoly of power. There was, traditionally, a system in medieval boroughs by which all their inhabitants held themselves liable for conscription in times of trouble; and at the muster-at-arms, held twice a year, both rich and poor were expected to appear in military array with such weapons as they could afford, the poor bringing knives, daggers or hatchets, the prosperous burghers presenting themselves 'after their degree' with mail or padded coats, bucklers, swords, bows and arrows and, in later times, a gun. But in few towns after the fourteenth century did the rich actually appear, choosing to pay deputies to represent them. Also, each householder was bound to take his turn in keeping nightly watch and ward in the streets; but this duty, too, was performed for the rich by substitutes. It was also upon the poor that the task fell of ensuring that the common rights of a town were not diminished and that its common land and properties remained in good heart and good repair. In Romney, for example, the poor had to keep the marshes drained and free of encroachments, and in Sandwich they were responsible for the maintenance of the dykes and for the protection of the harbour.[10]

Those prosperous burgesses who paid others to fulfil their duties for them occupied the town's offices as though of right. At meetings in the common hall a select group of them, summoned by the mayor, was commonly taken to represent the general body of inhabitants and to give their assent to measures on behalf of the burghers at large. All important offices were confined to men of a certain station in society, 'the rank of a mayor' or 'the rank of a sheriff' being well-known medieval phrases intended to express a comfortable social position maintained by an adequate income.[11] At Ipswich twelve portmen regularly divided among themselves all the posts of bailiffs, coroners and councillors; and elsewhere from generation to generation, the chief munici- pal offices were handed down in the few leading families of the place.[12] From time to time there were revolts against this assumption that only the members of these families should be considered worthy of high municipal office and enabled to parade about the town in their richly coloured, fur-trimmed robes. In Exeter in 1339 there were 'impetuous clamours' against the constant re-election of one or two men as mayor; but this attempt by the common people to assert themselves was not successful, and matters con- tinued much as they had done in the past. So they did at Lincoln where, in 1325, the inhabitants complained that they were without defence against 'the great lords of the said city', that these 'grauntz Seigneurs' paid nothing while the 'mean people' were arbitrarily taxed without their consent, that the money raised by the murage tax for building the city wall was used for their own purposes by the rich burgesses in office who rendered no accounts to the people, that the common people alone were forced to keep the nightly watch. At Oxford the people complained vainly more than once that the mayor and other officers were exacting taxes without the town's consent, pocketing the money raised, collecting money for their expenses on juries and assizes while leaving the poor to pay their own costs. At York in 1342 Nicholas Langton was elected mayor for the seventeenth time; and at Liverpool for eighteen years between 1374 and 1406 two men shared office between them. Similar stories could be told of almost every town in England.[13]

This rich élite lived in town mansions in the grandest style. The earliest town houses, like those in the country, were of timber-frame construction with walls of wattle and daub; but the ravages of fire and the requirements of a burgess's reputation had soon led to the widespread use of stone. At Canterbury there were at least thirty stone houses by the early thirteenth century; and at Southampton for many years, among several others of the same material, 'the "great stone houses" of Richard of Leicester, an early thirteenth-century notable of Southampton, remained a landmark of the port'.[14]

Town houses differed little in plan from many houses in the country. There was the same hall built over store-rooms and approached, perhaps, by an outside staircase; there were the same chambers and the same separate kitchen. But there were, except for the most fortunate town-dweller, problems presented by congestion. In rows of houses whose gable ends faced on to a narrow street, there was little space on the site for anything other than a small yard into which rubbish might be tipped; and the street itself was usually littered with rubbish already. Even in London, which had more scavengers and rakers to call upon than other towns, a foreign visitor said that the streets were 'so badly paved that they got wet at the slightest quantity of water'. They were also clogged with rubbish and excrement which lay rotting and stinking in the gullies running down the middle of the cobbled streets whence it was occasionally washed away by heavy rainfalls into ditches, streams and eventually the river.

From time to time the rakers carted the filth in the streets away to tip it into the great pits or lay-stalls that were dug outside the city gates or down to the river where boats were moored, waiting to ferry it away. But no sooner had a street been cleaned and its rubbish carted off than it was filled up again with kitchen refuse and excrement thrown out of doors and windows, with rushes discarded from hall floors and straw cleared out of stables, with rotting animals' heads and entrails from butchers' shops, with rubble from builders' yards, stale fish from fishmongers' yards, and feathers from poulterers. Year after year attempts were made to prevent citizens from throwing their rubbish into the streets, from building pigsties outside their front doors, from blocking the gutters with offal, oyster shells and fish-heads and from throwing dead animals into the river and into the city ditch. But the very frequency of the orders and proclamations, issued by the king and the city corporation, indicates how little regard was paid to them.[15]

London was far from exceptional in this respect. In Nottingham, a wealthy and thriving borough, streets were blocked with piles of cinders thrown out smoking hot from the bell-foundry and iron workshops, or with heaps of corn which the householders winnowed – or as they called the process 'windowed' – by throwing it in handfuls from the upper floors so that the wind might carry away the chaff. In the even wealthier city of Norwich, the market-place, which was still not paved in 1507, was pitted with holes excavated by builders as sand-pits. And in Hythe, so an early fifteenth-century jury declared, streets were alternately choked with refuse and flooded with water. Timber dealers threw trunks across the highway; dyers poured their waste water over it; butchers, swine-keepers and even respectable merchants such as the Honywodes cast their waste on to it or established 'hoggestocks' which were 'abominable to all men coming to the market as well as to all dwelling in the town'. The 'Cherche Weys' were occupied by the pits of a skinner. There was 'no carrying through Brokhellislane'. The Holy Well and the well in West Hythe were both choked with rubbish, while 'the water in the cart of Geoffrey Waterleader by which the whole community is refreshed' was made foul by the refuse from the butchers' shambles. Everywhere gates and bridges were falling into ruins, walls decaying, hedges overgrown and ditches undrained.[16]

Yet progress was slowly made. The dangers consequent upon pollution of the soil had long been recognized; and the lining and regular cleaning of cesspits had been advocated by town authorities since the twelfth century. By the fourteenth century building contracts were specifying the provision of both adequate cesspits and privies; and in some new buildings the privies were so arranged that they could be cleared from the street by those who were paid to cart away night-soil. In London there were public latrines at the gates and on platforms overhanging the Walbrook; and by the late Middle Ages there were public latrines also at Leicester, Winchester, Southampton, Hull and Exeter and, no doubt, elsewhere. Nor was London alone in enjoying a supply of fresh water: pipes or open conduits served Exeter, Bristol and Southampton in the fourteenth century, and Gloucester and Hull in the fifteenth.[17] At the same time more and more towns were paying serious attention to the paving of streets. In 1482 a paviour was appointed in Southampton and paid a salary to inspect the town's paving, to order repairs where necessary and to collect the cost from the householders who, here as elsewhere, were responsible for that part of the street outside their own dwelling. A few years later Nottingham also had a municipal paviour who was paid 33s 4d a year and provided with an official gown.[18]

The houses of the poor were also being improved. In earlier times they had been little better than the cottages of the villagers, though several had been on two floors, the upper storey projecting over the lower. They were still mostly timber-framed, but they were now more conveniently designed and often more spacious. The house in which a moderately successful shopkeeper or master craftsman lived might expect to have a shop or work-room on the ground floor, a hall, larder and kitchen on the floor above, and bedchambers and a privy on a third floor reached by a staircase from the hall. There might also, perhaps, have been a cockloft in the gable of the roof. As with the earlier houses, each storey commonly projected over the one below so that in very narrow streets people standing at the upper floor windows of houses facing each other could almost touch hands. The poorest workers had to be content with far smaller and less salubrious houses in the suburbs of the town or in dwellings converted from some abandoned defensive work on the town wall. But in several towns speculators had built rows of cottages for working people closer to their work; and, although these were excessively small, they seem to have been a distinct improvement upon the majority of those cottages which, with the help of a local carpenter, the countryman built for himself.

There is, however, little evidence of much concerted effort to develop towns to a preconceived plan. Some, on the sites of Roman settlements, tended to follow the original grids for the sake of convenience; but most grew haphazardly, the streets winding in accordance with the whims of individual builders, the houses in groups at odd angles, spare plots providing dumping grounds for rubbish in which pigs and hens grunted and strutted in constant search of sustenance. Castles or abbeys often provided a nucleus for a town; while rivers and natural harbours frequently influenced the shape of a town's development. So, sometimes, did a busy fair or market, held perhaps at some important crossroads.

At the time of Domesday Book there were only about fifty markets in England and Wales; but thereafter numerous other places had acquired market rights, particularly in the years 1227 to 1350 when 1200 new markets were recognized.[19] The regulations of these markets usually kept traders localized in a specific area. Some traders were required to separate themselves from the rest because of the unpleasant smells or sights with which they were associated, butchers, fishmongers and tanners among them. Others, like smiths and potters, were made to keep their distance because of the dangers of fire. Some, like dyers and fullers, had to locate themselves near running water. Yet others chose to carry on business close to men in the same trade as a matter of convenience. Several towns had separate corn, hay and livestock markets; in many others a central market locality would be divided into separate areas where specialized traders were concentrated. In London the names of the streets still leading off Cheapside – Wood Street, Milk Street, Ironmonger Lane, Poultry, Bread Street – all indicate where the stalls of the various trades were kept in the market before its open ground was covered with buildings; while the names of other London streets indicate the former centre of a trade or craft or the place where its goods were sold in the market. So Fish Street Hill is where the fishmongers had their stalls, Sea Coal Lane where the coal merchants were established by the Fleet river from the time of Henry III, Goldsmith Street where goldsmiths congregated even before the Goldsmiths' Company received its first charter in 1327, Lombard Street where the Italian bankers settled after the expulsion of the Jews from London in 1290, and Jewry Street and Old Jewry where the Jewish money-lenders lived in their ghettoes before that time. Likewise in Salisbury, Butcher Row, Cordwainer Row, Pot Row, Ironmonger Row, Wheeler Row and Fish Row all owe their names to market traders.

\*

While markets, usually held weekly, were designed to satisfy the needs of ordinary shoppers, fairs, held annually, were established for trading on a larger scale. Many of them originated with the congregation of pilgrims at holy shrines in abbeys and cathedrals on saints' days when, taking advantage of such an influx of visitors, traders and merchants would set up stalls to tempt them to part with what money they had not reserved as an offering at the shrine and for their journey home. Fairs are known to have existed in Anglo-Saxon times, though their charters were not granted until after the Conquest, a large proportion of them being issued in the thirteenth century. In the county of Somerset alone no less than ninety-four fairs were established by charter before 1500, several of them in 1304 and the years immediately following as rewards for service in the Scottish wars granted to lords of the fair who had the right to demand rent from the stallholders.[20]

Some fairs specialized in a particular commodity. Bartholomew Fair at Smithfield – where Rahere, founder of St Bartholomew's Hospital and Lord of the Fair, was not above performing juggling tricks for the entertainment of those who attended it – was a cloth fair. Barnet had a horse fair; Abingdon a cattle fair; several ports had fishing fairs; other places, like the celebrated Stourbridge Fair which belonged to the Corporation of Cambridge, had a conglomeration of stalls selling all manner of goods from gingerbread to tuning forks.

Bailiffs were appointed to ensure that ordinary shops were kept closed and the lords of the fair received their proper profit, that the regulations governing the conduct of traders were observed, that weights and measures were tested, and that the food and wine offered was of a satisfactory standard. Defaulters, and those responsible for the affrays that so frequently erupted, were brought before Courts of Pie Powder whose name was probably derived from the French *pieds poudreux* signifying the dusty feet of the travellers dealt with in them.

The craftsman whose wares were sold at fairs and markets had usually served out his apprenticeship in the house of a master who undertook to teach him his trade, and who might additionally be required to give him a general education, as well as bed, board and clothing, in return for complete subservience and a hard day's work as soon as he was qualified to provide it. His apprenticeship complete, he became a journeyman and could thereafter work for a wage, either for his original master or for another. If skilful and ambitious he might then submit an example of his craft to his guild which would decide upon its merits whether or not he could become a master himself.

Travelling craftsmen, such as the masons and wood-carvers whose skill took them from city to city to work upon cathedrals and churches, were accommodated in lodges in which up to about twenty lived at a time. But most craftsmen slept above the workshops where they spent their day, working long hours and as closely tied to their town as the peasant was to his village.

# 9 · *Daughters and Wives*

Although a woman was seen as subordinate to her father or her husband, and her goods were theoretically not under her own control, she was not left defenceless at the man's mercy. The Church recognized separation in cases of gross cruelty, fornication and apostasy; while the law accepted a woman's right to hold land, to make a will or a contract, to sue and to appear as her own or her husband's attorney, and, if widowed, to be the guardian of her children. She could also appeal against her husband to her family when in urgent need of their help. In the case of poorer women, manorial custom would usually make allowances for her if she were having a baby: her obligations to the lord of the manor might well be waived for the time being, or she might even be sent a present, though less perhaps because the lord felt moved by compassion than because he recognized the importance of her function in providing the estate with fresh labourers.[1]

Whatever her customary privileges or legal rights, however, the married woman was not considered to stand on the same level as her husband; and it cannot be doubted that many wives were beaten almost as often as their children. A man fined at Sporle Manor Court for thrashing his servant expressed a common sentiment when he indignantly expostulated that he did not know what the world was coming to, that the day would soon come when a man might not beat his own wife.[2]

A marriage in families of property was a matter of business like any other: a poor man might choose a wife because he loved her; but parents with money or land would expect their children to marry with an eye to the family fortune. Love might come later but was not considered prerequisite. The marriage of Elizabeth Paston is a case in point. When she was about fifteen her parents decided that she would marry a rich widower, Stephen Scrope, a man of fifty who, so he himself recorded, 'had suffered a sickness that kept me a thirteen or fourteen years ensuing, whereby I am disfigured in my

person and shall be whilst I live'. Elizabeth naturally had no inclination to
marry him and at first declined to do so. Her mother therefore kept her at
home so that she should see no other more attractive man and saw to it that for
three months she was 'beaten once in the week or twice, sometimes twice in
one day, and her head broken in two or three places'. This treatment
eventually induced the girl to give way; but for some reason the marriage did
not take place, and for the next ten years various other possible husbands
were considered and their circumstances investigated, the greatest importance always being attached to the Paston family's 'worship and profit and to
the lands of the man under consideration standing clear'. Two country
squires were rejected, presumably because they were not rich enough; and
then Elizabeth's brother, John, received a letter from Lord Grey of Hastings: 'If your sister be not yet married, I trust to God I know where she may
be married to a gentleman of 400 marks of livelode, the which is a great
gentleman born and of good blood.'

This sounded promising; but it transpired that the gentleman in question
was a ward of Lord Grey whose interest in the marriage was prompted by the
hope that he could get his hands on the Paston dowry himself. So these
negotiations were abandoned, and yet others entered into with a man to
whom Elizabeth was at last married, whether or not happily is unknown.

Other members of her family, however, did find happiness; and one at
least did marry for love. This was Margery, the youngest sister of Sir John
Paston, for whom a profitable match was confidently expected. Several offers
were made to her family, but none had been considered worthy of her, and
her mother had taken her to St Saviour's Abbey, Bermondsey, to pray 'that
she may have a good husband'. Suddenly after several years in which various
matches were considered, the Pastons were horrified to be told that Margery
Paston had pledged herself to Richard Calle, Sir John's chief bailiff. The
reactions of the family, from whom she had long kept the pledge secret out of
fear, were as violent as she had feared. Her brother wrote scornfully of his
sister selling 'candle and mustard in Framlingham'; her mother was furious;
the family chaplain was as cross as anyone and advised that the matter should
be submitted to the consideration of the Bishop of Norwich. It was a very
serious affair because plights of troth were then binding and the Church,
while disapproving of them, did recognize them if properly made. The
bishop closely examined Margery Paston as to the exact words she had used.
She repeated them and added spiritedly that 'if those words made it not sure
she would make it sure ere she went thence, for she thought in her conscience
she was bound whatever the words were'. The bishop emphasized all the
disadvantages of the marriage, the shame to her family and the disapproval of
her friends. But she remained unshaken, as did Calle during his examination.
The bishop then said he would reserve judgement until after Michaelmas to

give time for any possible impediments to the marriage to be disclosed. Margery begged him to give a ruling earlier than that, but he declined to do so; and so she set out to go home. On the way, however, she was met by the family chaplain who told her she was no longer welcome there: her mother would not receive her nor would any of her mother's friends. She had to go back to Norwich where the bishop found her lodgings from which she eventually moved to Blackborough nunnery near Lynn. Her mother remained unreconciled to the marriage and wrote to her son,

> I pray you and require you that ye take it not pensively, for I know it goeth right near your heart, and so it doth to mine and to others. But remember you, and so do I, that we have lost of her but a worthless person, and set it the less to heart . . . If he [Calle] were dead at this hour, she should never be at my heart as she was.

Since there were no legal grounds upon which the marriage could be prevented, it did in the end take place. Margery was apparently never forgiven and seems not to have been received into the family again, though her eldest son did receive £20 under the terms of his grandmother's will.[3]

Harsh as her behaviour to her daughter appears to us, Margaret Paston was nevertheless a woman capable of deep affection. Her own marriage had been arranged and yet, as was so often the case, it proved a happy union. She subordinated her interests to those of her husband, as wives were expected to do; but evidently she did not resent her subordination, and proved a competent housewife. Like other wives in her position, she kept a careful eye on her larder so that supplies of essential foods were always available but not ordered in extravagant quantities and therefore wasted. She presided over the baking in the household, the smoking and salting of meat, the making of preserves and wine. She watched, too, over the clothing of the family, supervising the spinning and weaving that was carried out in the house, and ordering what could not be made at home from Norwich or London, specifying how much should be paid for silk laces, hose-cloth, 'a girdle of plunket ribbon' (6d), 'a bonnet of deep murrey' (21s 4d) or pattens. 'I was wont to pay but 2½d for a pair,' she wrote, 'but I pray you let them not be left behind though I pay more. They must be low pattens; let them be long enough and broad upon the heele.'

> I pray that you will . . . buy some frieze to make your child's gowns [she wrote in another letter to her husband who was in London]. And that you will buy a yard of broad-cloth of black for an hood for me at 3s 8d or 4s a yard, for there is neither good cloth nor good frieze in this town [Nor-

wich]. As for the child's gowns if I have [the material], I will get them
made [here] . . .

As for cloth for my gown [she told her husband in November 1453], I
cannot get anything better than the sample I am sending you, which is, I
think, too poor both in cloth and colour, so please buy me 3¼ yards of
whatever you think is suitable for me, of what colour you like, for I have
really searched all the drapers' shops in this town, and there is a very poor
choice. Please buy a loaf of good sugar as well, and half a pound of whole
cinnamon, for there is no cinnamon in this town.

Just as John Paston was frequently commissioned to shop for his wife, so
she was instructed to do all kinds of errands for him in his long absences away
from home, and was asked frequently for confirmation that they had been
done or would be done: 'Thomas Howes [a friend's agent] has got four great
beams for the private room, the malthouse and the brewery,' runs one
characteristic letter when alterations to the Pastons' house were being carried
out, a letter such as many husbands of rank all over the country might have
expected to receive.

As to the laying of these beams, they will be laid this coming week . . . . As
to the rest of the work I think it must wait until you come home because I
cannot get either joists or boards yet. I have measured the private room
where you want your chests and accounting-board to be kept for the time
being and there is no room beside the bed even if it was moved to the door,
to put both your board and chests there and to have space to move and sit
down as well. So I have arranged that you shall have the same private room
as you had before.

Margaret Paston's letters to her husband begin and end with customary
formality, being addressed to her 'right reverend and worshipful husband'
and typically subscribed, 'The Holy Trinity have you in their keeping and
send you health. Written in haste at Norwich on the Wednesday after St
Peter's Day.' But there can be no doubt of the affection she held for him. On
28 September 1443, after hearing that he had been ill, she wrote:

Right worshipful husband, I commend myself to you, desiring with all my
heart to hear how you are and thanking God for your recovery from your
great illness. And I thank you for the letter that you sent me, for by my
truth, my mother and I were nought in heart's ease from the time that we
knew of your sickness till we knew truly of your recovery. My mother-in-
law promised another image of wax weighing as much as you for Our Lady
of Walsingham, and she sent four nobles [26s 8d] to the four Orders of

Friars at Norwich to pray for you, and I have promised to go on Pilgrimage
to Walsingham and to St Leonard's [Priory] for you. By my troth, I had
never so heavy a season as I had from the time that I knew of your sickness
till I knew of your complete recovery, and yet my heart is still in no great
ease, nor shall be, till I know that ye be really well . . . If I might have had
my will, I should have seen you ere this time. I would you were at home
. . . I pray you if your sore be whole so that you may endure to ride . . .
come home . . . For I hope you should be kept as tenderly here as ye be at
London. I have not time to write half a quarter as much as I should say to
you if I might speak with you. I shall send you another letter as hastily as I
may. Almighty God have you in his keeping, and send you health. Written
in Oxmead in very great haste on St Michael's Eve . . . Your son is well,
blessed be to God.[4]

Devoted as she was to her husband, Margaret Paston, like most women of
her class, appears to have been far less affectionate towards her children.

# 10 · *Pupils and Masters*

The want of affection in the English is strongly manifested towards their children [an Italian visitor to England noted]. For after having kept them at home till they arrive at the age of seven or nine years at the utmost, they put them out, both males and females, to hard service in the houses of other people . . . And few are born who are exempted from this fate, for every one however rich he may be, sends away his children into the houses of others, whilst he, in return, receives those of strangers into his own. And on enquiring the reason for the severity, they answered that they did it in order that their children might learn better manners. But I for my part, believe that they do it because they like to enjoy all their comfort themselves.[1]

It was also hoped that the children would have a better opportunity of advancing in the world under the protection of some great lord, that they would learn to be obedient as well as mannerly, that they would gain some sort of education and some knowledge of how matters were conducted in a great house, and, perhaps, that they would be set on the way to making a profitable marriage. Their happiness was rarely a consideration. When Agnes Paston's daughter bitterly complained of her unhappiness living in another house, her mother curtly replied that she must accustom herself 'to work readily as other gentlewomen do'.

From their earliest years children were expected to hold their parents and, in particular, their fathers in the deepest respect; and even when they came of age would not sit down in their presence without permission. When young, most were regularly beaten, girls as well as boys, in accordance with the advice given in books written for the guidance of parents in the upbringing of their offspring. The experiences of Lady Jane Grey were shared by many a medieval girl who, when the time came, thought it her duty to treat her own children in the same way:

> One of the greatest benefites that God ever gave me, is, that he sent me so sharpe and severe Parentes . . . For when I am in presence of father or mother, whether I speke, kepe silence, sit, stand, or go, eate, drinke, be merie or sad, be sawying, plaiying, dauncing, or doing anie thing els, I must do it, as it were, in soch weight, mesure and number, even so perfitelie as God made the world, else I am so sharpelie taunted, so cruellie threatened, yea presentlie some tymes with pinches, nippes and bobbes, and other waies which I will not name for the honor I beare them . . . that I thinke myself in hell.[2]

Even if they were not beaten at home they could certainly expect to be whipped at school. Agnes Paston, when inquiring about the progress of her son's lessons, told his master that if he had not done well, 'nor would not amend', no pains need be spared to 'belash him truly till he will amend. So did his last master.' Indeed, there were very few masters who did not. Medieval woodcuts invariably depict them with a birch; and a master of grammar at Cambridge was presented with two insignia of office when he had qualified; one was a psalter, the other a birch. And he was required to use the birch on a local boy to show that he had no aversion to corporal punishment, the boy being paid 4d for his 'labour'.[3]

The thirteenth-century rules of Westminster almonry school indicate how much the birch was then relied upon to maintain discipline, and how much disorder there nevertheless seems to have been. In the morning the boys were required to say their prayers

> without shouting and confusion; if anyone neglects these good things, let them be punished . . . Whether they are standing or sitting in the choir let them not have their eyes turned aside to the people, but rather toward the altar; not grinning or chattering or laughing aloud; not making fun of another if he does not read or sing psalms well; not hitting one another secretly or openly or answering rudely if they happen to be asked a question by their elders. Those who break the rules will feel the rod without delay . . . Likewise if anyone who knows Latin does speak English or French with his companion, or with any clerk, for every word he shall have a blow with the rod. Likewise for rudeness in word or deed anywhere, or for any kind of oath, let not the rod be spared . . . Again whoever at bed time has torn to pieces the bed of his companions or hidden the bedclothes, or thrown shoes or pillow from corner to corner, or roused anger, or

thrown the school into disorder, shall be severely punished in the morning.[4]

In all other schools birching seems to have been as common a punishment as at this one. A few voices were raised against it, among them those of Roger Ascham, Greek reader at St John's College, Cambridge, and Sir Thomas Elyot who in *The Governour* suggested that children should not be 'inforced by violence to lerne but . . . swetely allured with praises and such praty gyftes as [they] delite in'.[5] Also, parents occasionally sought redress in the courts for the excessive beating of their children. But most boys had to grow accustomed to regular thrashings, and would well have sympathized with the pupil in the late fifteenth-century poem *The Birched Schoolboy*, whose life was made a misery by his master's sharp 'birchen twiggis'.

> On Monday in the morning when I shall rise
> At vi. of the clock, it is the gise
> To go to school without a-vise
> I had rather go twenty mile twice!
>   What availeth it me though I say nay?
>
> My master looketh as he were mad:
> 'Where hast thou been, though sorry lad?'
> 'Milking ducks, my mother bade:'
> It was no marvel that I were sad.
>   What availeth it me though I say nay?
>
> My master peppered my arse with well good speed:
> It was worse than fennel seed;
> He would not leave till it did bleed.
> Much sorrow has been for his deed!
>   What availeth it me though I say nay?
>
> I would my master were a wat [hare]
> And my book a wild cat,
> And a brace of greyhounds in his top.
> I would be glad for to see that!
>   What availeth it me though I say nay?
>
> I would my master were an hare,
> And all his bookis houndis were,
> And I myself a jolly hunter:
> To blow my horn I would not spare!
> For if he were dead I would not care.
>   What availeth it me though I say nay?[6]

Scenes in a late 15th-century farmyard showing simple forms of harrow and plough, woodmen with axes and billhooks, cowherds, a man sowing with a bag of seeds around his neck and, in front of their enclosed hives, two beekeepers beating iron drums in simulation of thunder to bring down the swarming bees.

ABOVE: A physician supervising the collection of herbs in his walled herb garden. Astrology, magical potions and charms played a large part in medieval medicine, but herbs were also widely used. As late as the 17th century the successful physician, John Radcliffe, admitted that his only pieces of medical equipment were a few phials, a skeleton and a herbal.

LEFT: Attended by her ladies, a mother gives birth in her bedchamber. Tapestries hang on the wall and a fire blazes in an elaborate fireplace, but even in wealthy households such as this there was little furniture in the bedchambers apart from the richly curtained bed. Beds, indeed, were valued possessions, frequently mentioned in wills and, carefully packed, transported from house to house when the family moved from one of its manors to another.

ABOVE: The marriage of John of Portugal to Philippa of Lancaster, a picture painted for Edward IV in the late 15th century, showing the elaborate costumes of the time.

ABOVE: A 15th-century tournament under royal patronage. By this time the earlier rough-and-tumble *mêlée* in which numerous knights endeavoured to unhorse each other in mock battles had given way to more skilful and orderly jousts subject to recognized rules. The knights are wearing armour of steel plate which had by now taken the place of the heavier mail except for gussets and as an extra protection round the neck between the back and breastplates and the helmet.

RIGHT: A knight as he would have appeared in armour in the early years of the Hundred Years War between England and France (1337–1453). This is Sir Geoffrey Luttrell with his wife and daughter.

In the Peasants' Revolt of 1381, artisans as well as peasants rose in rebellion, protesting against a variety of social and economic grievances. Armed rebels from Kent and Essex and elsewhere marched upon London. Here their leader, Wat Tyler, is shown being killed by the Mayor, William Walworth, at Smithfield.

William of Wykeham, Bishop of Winchester, founded New College, Oxford, in 1379, and in 1382 a school at Winchester where pupils could be properly grounded in Latin grammar before passing on to Oxford. Six colleges had by then already been founded at Oxford, most of them principally for graduates studying theology. Winchester college is shown here, *circa* 1463.

Birching, of course, however severe and regular, could not be relied upon to bring all pupils to submit to their masters; and in some schools the statutes provided for the incorrigible to be expelled. At Wotton-under-Edge in 1384 scholars were required to be 'of good behaviour attending school and obedient to their master' and 'compelled continually to devote their time to learning and study'. If they were undisciplined and 'after due warning and chastisement refused to amend', they were to be expelled.[7]

At this time elementary education was gained in a variety of schools of different origins – widely scattered throughout the country and ever growing in numbers – giving clever boys of humble origins an opportunity to rise in the world. By the second half of the thirteenth century there were already schools in sixty places in England, including all the cathedral towns, and many more had been founded since then. In Lincolnshire, Nottinghamshire and Yorkshire there were almost three times as many schools in the fourteenth century as there had been a hundred years before.[8] There were small, informal schools kept by parish clerks or clergy in minor orders who taught their pupils at the parish church, perhaps in the vestry, as at North Cadbury, Somerset, where vestiges of the alphabet can still be seen on the whitewashed walls. There were chantry schools whose founders had provided money for teaching children to serve as altar boys or choristers for the chantry priests. There were song schools attached to most cathedrals and almonry schools attached to monasteries. There were small schools run by the various orders of friars for their young novices, although the elementary monastery schools which had flourished in the late eleventh and twelfth centuries had gradually disappeared after 1215 when canon law discouraged the practice of committing children to a monastic life before the age of fourteen. There were guild schools, preparatory schools for grammar schools and grammar schools themselves. And there were those private foundations like 'Seinte Marie College of Wynchestre' established in 1382 by William of Wykeham, Bishop of Winchester, and Eton College founded by Henry VI.

At the humblest of these schools the curriculum was simple. It began with the alphabet and song and 'other petite lernunge as . . . redyng of the mateyns and of the psalter . . . and redyng of Englissh'; and progressed, as at Childrey chantry school, to 'learning prayers and psalms, collects and graces to be said before and after meals, the articles of faith in English, the ten commandments, the seven deadly sins and seven sacraments'.[9] At some schools the emphasis was more secular. At a school in Rotherham, founded in 1483 by Thomas Rotherham, Archbishop of York, accountancy was taught as well as grammar, because 'that county [Yorkshire] produces many youths endowed with the light and sharpness of ability who do not all wish to attain the dignity and elevation of the priesthood . . . and these may be better fitted for the mechanical arts and other concerns of this world'.[10]

Normally, the teaching of grammar was left to the grammar schools whose pupils were expected to have a grounding in basic education before they came. Parents wishing to enter their sons at St Paul's School were told, 'If your chylde can rede and wryte Latin and Englysshe sufficiently, so that he be able to rede and wryte his owne lessons, then he shall be admytted into the schole for a scholer.'[11]

Once admitted to a school like St Paul's a child's principal subject would be Latin grammar, probably based on Donatus's *Ars Minor* which was written in fourth-century Rome in question and answer form. All the other main textbooks were common to the whole of western Europe and, as teaching methods were oral rather than visual, they were generally written in verse.

The lower forms began with attempts to translate sentences from English into Latin, simple sentences, often intended to amuse and known as *vulgaria*: 'The blind eateth many a fly' or 'His nose is like a shoeing-horn'. Then the pupils progressed to disputations, stylized debates conducted in Latin, and, ideally, to the composition of Latin verse: fourteenth-century pupils at Bredgar in Kent were not considered fit to take part in the chapel liturgy until they could 'read, sing, construe and compose twenty-four verses in a single day'.[12]

To familiarize them with Latin, pupils were usually forbidden to speak English. A *vulgarium* of the late fifteenth-century ran, 'If I had not used my English tongue so greatly for which the master hath rebuked me oft times, I should have been more cunning in grammar. Wise men say that nothing may be more profitable than to speak Latin.' Boys at schools in Wells were specifically ordered at meal times 'to ask for anything they want in Latin not in English'.[13] In many grammar schools, however, French was also permitted, though the use of this language was gradually dying out by the fourteenth century, much to the chagrin of conservative commentators, one of whom, writing in 1385, complained that nowadays children 'know no more French than their left heel knows, and that is harm for them if they cross the sea and travel in foreign lands, and in many other circumstances. Also gentlemen have now largely ceased teaching their children French.'[14] Greek was also rarely taught in grammar schools, though it seems to have formed part of the curriculum at both Eton and Winchester in the fifteenth century.[15]

The school day was arduous and long, beginning as early as six o'clock and in summer at five. There were lessons before breakfast, from eight o'clock to nine, more morning lessons after breakfast until twelve, and still more lessons in the afternoon from two to six.[16] The timetable remained unvaried throughout the year, there being breaks for feast days only, and holidays of less than a fortnight at Christmas, Easter and Whitsun, although at some places there were short traditional holidays at other times, as during the annual carnival at St Andrew's where the scholars were customarily given three days' holiday for cock-fighting.[17] Boarders, however, usually spent their holidays at school, and even on Sundays were given work to do to keep them out of mischief.

They were not well fed; nor were their living conditions in the least comfortable. At St Paul's School the pupils' urine was collected in tubs and sold to dyers and tanners, the profits going towards the school funds. 'For other causes, if need be, they shall go to the water-side.'[18]

Classes were generally large. In 1412 the hundred or so pupils at Winchester were all taught in one room; and Eton's rather larger numbers in the fifteenth century were also all crammed into a single classroom. At St Paul's, at the beginning of the next century, the pupils were instructed in one large rectangular chamber divided into four by curtains. This provided space for three classes and a chapel. The boys sat on long benches or forms, sixteen to a form, each of which was supervised by a head boy.[19]

Yet, despite the discomfort and severely limited facilities, education was not cheap. Certain schools had been founded on a charitable basis: William of Wykeham had established his school at Winchester for 'seventy poor and needy scholars'; Eton provided for the teaching of poor local boys for nothing; so did a school founded in 1515 at Liverpool by one John Crosse who left lands for a priest 'to keep a grammar school and take his advantage from all the children except those whose names be Crosse, and poor children that have no succour'. At Wotton-under-Edge grammar school the master was enjoined to 'keep the school faithfully . . . and kindly receive all scholars whatsoever, howsoever and whencesoever coming for instruction in the said art of grammar, without exacting, claiming or taking from them any advantage or gain for their labour'. And at Sevenoaks grammar school, founded by William Sevenoke, a local man who had done well as a grocer in London, the master was required in about 1432 to 'teach and instruct all poor boys whatsoever coming there for the sake of learning, taking nothing of them or their parents or friends for the teaching and instructing of them'. Similarly the statutes of Queen's College, Oxford, provided for the teaching of seventy poor grammar pupils when finances permitted, though the finances were rarely deemed to allow it and it was not often that more than one or two pupils were provided for by the college.[20]

Also, almonry schools gave free education, usually for the sons of those connected with the religious house to which they were attached or for relatives of the monks. At Durham almonry school 'there were certain poor children called the children of the almonry, who only were maintained with learning and relieved with the alms and benefactions of the whole house, having their meat and drink in a loft on the north side of the Abbey gates.'[21] At several other schools the pupils received alms from outside patrons. The scholars at Pontefract School in 1267 were being sent forty loaves a week from Pontefract Hospital; and in 1310 those in St Albans were receiving twenty-eight loaves a week from the abbot. Sometimes an appeal for help to a rich patron might bring variety to the scholars' diet. In 1222 Thomas of Holland begged an acquaintance, the Chancellor of England, for a little venison on behalf of the scholars of Lincoln. 'You being established in power and enjoying your lord's favour,' he wrote, 'could easily satisfy a friend in such a thing. And it would be glorious to me if, through your bounty, I could get something so rare on the table for my companions.'[22]

By the early years of the sixteenth century free places were additionally to be had at the endowed grammar schools which by then most counties possessed. These were usually founded, like the grammar school at Seven-oaks, by some local man who had made good; and they tended to be in the smaller towns. There were six in Gloucestershire, not in such relatively large towns as Gloucester itself but in places like Chipping Campden where education was otherwise hard to obtain. There were three in Norfolk, two in Somerset and as many as twelve in Lancashire.

Yet most pupils at grammar schools in England were charged for attending them. In 1395 at Nottingham parents had to find 8d a quarter for each child and at Maldon in 1420 12d a quarter, while grammar pupils at Merton College, Oxford, were charged 4d a term in 1277, a fee which had doubled by the 1380s. At Ipswich in 1477 the grammar schoolmaster was entrusted with 'the jurisdiction of all scholars in the liberty and precinct of this town, except the petties called ABCs and song', and he was authorized to take from them, 'according to a scale fixed by the Lord Bishop of Norwich, viz for a grammarian 10d, psalterian 8d, and primerian 6d'.[23] These were fees for day boys. Boarders had to pay considerably more, 7d a week at Beccles in 1403, 10d a week at Stevenage in 1312 and as much as 1s a week at Croydon in 1394. School fees were, therefore, beyond the pockets of most parents; and the twelfth-century Abbot Sampson of Bury St Edmunds was, no doubt, far from being alone in confessing that he would never have become a monk if he could have afforded to continue at school. When he could afford to do so, he arranged for others to enjoy the advantages which had been denied him, and bought 'some stone houses in the town of St Edmund and assigned them to the master of the schools' so that every poor scholar might be relieved of the burden of paying 'a penny or a halfpenny twice a year . . . whether he could or could not'.[24]

Nor were boarding and masters' fees the only expenses. There were clothes to pay for, in some schools uniforms, in most, pens, penknives and ink-horns, writing tablets and, in winter, candles. In 1500 one contented schoolboy wrote, 'the last feir my unkle on my fathers syde gave me a pennare [a sheath in which pens were carried] and an ynkehorne and my unkle on my mothers syde gave me a penn knyff. Now [if I had] a payre of tabullys [writing tablets] I [would lack] nothynge.'[25] There were also books to buy, but these were so expensive that few pupils could afford them, even those tattered copies that went through the hands of one generation of boys after the next. Schools which had libraries bequeathed to them were rare; and most pupils had to do without books altogether, relying upon the lessons of the master.

Much, therefore, depended upon the qualities of the master, usually a clergyman. As in all professions, there were those who were conscientious and worthy and those who were not. The names of unruly or disreputable schoolmasters are certainly not absent from the records of the courts. In 1225 a Huntingdonshire schoolmaster and his under-master were arrested for poaching; in 1381 a master was among those found guilty of riotous behaviour in Suffolk; in 1450 an Oxford teacher packed the church of St Michael with his own pupils so that they could seize the priest if he attempted to read a threatened sentence of excommunication upon him; and this same man was in trouble again three years later for helping two chaplains beat up an Oxford citizen.[26] Certainly, many schoolmasters were ill-qualified. In the fifteenth century it was easy enough to obtain a teaching licence which was often claimed as a degree. The applicant seems merely to have had to assure the authorities that he had taught or studied grammar for a particular period and to take a fairly simple test such as writing a poem in praise of the university.[27] In the opinion of Sir Thomas Elyot 'the name of schole maister [was] moche had in contempte', while the tutors employed in private houses were chosen with 'lasse diligence' than was employed 'in takynge servantes': parents 'chiefely enquire with howe small a salary he will be contented, and never to inserche howe moche good Lernynge he hath, and how amonge well lerned men he is esteemed'.[28]

The salary with which private tutors had to be content was never high. The grammar master in Edward IV's household received 4d a day together with his food, fuel, light and clothing; and in 1511 a tutor in a Northumberland household was in receipt of £5 a year with food, beer and fuel.

In schools a master's salary would not be much more than this. At Winchester in 1400 the headmaster, known as the warden, received £10 a year, plus 17s worth of cloth and a room which he shared with the usher. In lesser schools, with seventy to eighty pupils, the master might receive about £10 a year but out of this he had to keep himself and sometimes to pay the rent of the schoolroom and the wages of an assistant. At the school founded by the

Archbishop of York at Rotherham in 1483 the grammar master had £10 a year, but the song master only £6 13s 4d and the writing master £5 6s 8d.[29]

To make ends meet it was often necessary for the master's wife to take in boarders. The masters at cathedral schools were usually unmarried clerics; but in endowed grammar schools by the fifteenth century they were often not, and the statutes of these schools frequently made a point of specifying that they need not be. At Sevenoaks in 1342 the master had to be '. . . an honest man, sufficiently advanced and expert in the science of grammar, Bachelor of Arts [but] by no means in holy orders'.[30]

Many honest and expert men did become schoolmasters, occupying a position in the social hierarchy similar in status to the middle ranks of the clergy, above a chantry priest but below a rector;[31] and it is clear that, despite Sir Thomas Elyot's strictures, they may even have been in the majority. Certainly Edmund de Stonor appears to have been perfectly content with the schoolmaster to whom his son, also named Edmund, was sent in 1380. The Stonors' chaplain, who was told to see the boy when he was ill, reported:

> I have observed your son Edmund and observed his condition for two nights and a day. His illness grows less from day to day and he is not in bed . . . He is beginning to learn Donatus slowly and does well . . . Truly, I have never seen such care given a boy as he had during his illness. The master and his wife prefer that some of his clothes be left at home for he has too many and fewer would suffice and it is possible, though they would not wish it, that some clothes might easily be torn and spoilt.[32]

For those who were to have any schooling at all, formal education in reading and song schools began at about the age of seven and lasted normally for two or three years. Boys sometimes went to grammar schools when they were eight, but a more usual age was ten or eleven. At Wotton-under-Edge ten was the minimum age; and this was also the age at which most boys entered Eton and Winchester, though both these schools did accept boys as young as eight. A pupil was expected to stay at grammar school for five or six years; but some boys were still at school at eighteen, which was the upper limit at Eton; and when Robert Buck of Skipton ran away from school, because he was savagely beaten, he was twenty.[33]

Very few children, even of those who went to school, achieved a high standard of literacy; and many had no more knowledge of Latin than Langland's cleric who, although he was supposed to be able to read the language accurately and had been 'priest and parson passing thirty winters', could 'neither solfa, nor sing nor read saints' lives'. Among the upper classes there was a common feeling that learning was for clerks and not for noblemen, that, as it was expressed in the *Jestes of Sloggin*, 'a Mayster of Arte is not worth a Farte'. This was an opinion violently expressed at a dinner party at which

> there happened to be present one of those whom we call gentlemen, who always carry some horn hanging at their backs, as though they would hunt during dinner. He, hearing letters praised, roused with sudden anger, burst out furiously with these words, 'A curse on these stupid letters! All learned men are beggars! . . . I swear by God's body I'd rather my sons should hang than study letters. For it becomes the sons of gentlemen to blow the horn nicely, to hunt skilfully and elegantly carry and train a hawk. But the study of letters should be left to the sons of rustics.'[34]

In fact, it was not easy for the sons of rustics to study letters, since the lords of manors were aware that education might lead to the taking of holy orders and the escape from servile status of a potential labourer. Until the fifteenth century villeins had to obtain a licence from the lord of the manor to send one of their children to school; and these licences were not cheap: in the fourteenth century the Abbot of St Albans charged no more than a week's wages, but the payments demanded on a Warwickshire manor, where they could be as high as 13s 4d, seem to have been more usual.[35]

The court was not much affected by upper-class prejudices against well-educated men and women. It was true that few Norman or Plantagenet kings had a very firm grasp of Latin; that, with the possible exception of Henry I, Edward III was probably the first English king to have more than a few words of the English language; and that until his reign there is no evidence of a king writing. But from Edward III's time onwards, the court took due notice of the twelfth-century proverb, '*Rex illiteratus, asinus coronatus*'; and the education of the heir to the throne in subjects other than military skills and courtly accomplishments became a matter of serious concern. From the age of seven he was placed in charge of a respected knight together with various companions of his own age, usually the king's wards. They were instructed in polite behaviour, and given lessons by a well-trained master. At an early age Henry VI learned to read and write Latin as well as French and English; and Edward V began his education at the age of three, his daily timetable including lessons in both morning and afternoon as well as sports and exercise, Matins, Mass and Evensong and readings during dinner from 'such noble stories as it behoveth a prince to understand'.[36]

In most early medieval noble households less emphasis was placed upon book learning than upon manners, etiquette and social graces, the daughters in particular receiving little other education unless they were sent to nunneries where the standard of education was not impressive. Letters to nuns seem invariably to have been written in English or French, rather than Latin which they could not be expected to understand; and even their French was likely to resemble that of Chaucer's Prioress who spoke

> After the scole of Stratford atte Bowe
> For French of Paris were to her unknowe.

When not sent to nunneries aristocratic ladies of an intellectual bent might absorb some learning from the family chaplain, provided that they did not live in one of those households, described by the Knight of La Tour-Landry, in which it was considered that women should 'knowe no things' about reading, even of the scriptures. But if they received no encouragement at home, there was little likelihood of their being taught outside it: in London in the fifteenth century there were only three licensed schoolmistresses as opposed to twenty-one in Paris in 1380. It was not in the least unusual for ladies to be unable to write more than their own name, and some could not even do that. Nor, for that matter, could some gentlemen do much better. It has been emphasized that the accounts of medieval bailiffs and the bills of artisans show that such people had learned to write quite adequately; and both the *Paston Letters* and the *Stonor Letters* indicate that many of the friends, business acquaintances, stewards and upper servants of both these families were capable of putting pen to paper.

> Sir William Stonor, his father and brothers wrote their own letters, and spelt passably well [wrote C. L. Kingsford, editor of the *Stonor Letters*]. Jane Stonor wrote tolerably well but spelt atrociously. Her daughter-in-law Elizabeth generally employed an amanuensis but could write well enough if she pleased. Generally the country squires of Oxfordshire and their women-folk, and the better class merchants could write with ease. The worst writers and spellers are the inferior . . . clergy . . . or humble mercantile people.[37]

Nevertheless, there were still in the fifteenth century many women and some men of good families who were either barely literate or wrote with extreme difficulty. Those who could do so usually relied on scribes; and as rich and influential a landowner as Sir John Fastolf could apparently do little more than sign his name, and towards the end of his life he left his secretary to do this for him. He evidently found his inability as little hindrance to him in his business affairs, as had St Godric the highly successful merchant, international trader and shipowner who taught himself to write only in his old age.[38]

As the Middle Ages drew to a close, however, and the upper classes were expected to play a fuller part in assisting the king in formulating policies and in bearing office as justices of the peace, sheriffs and members of Parliament, literacy became increasingly important. Even so there are not many instances of the sons of the nobility attending university unless they were intended for the Church.[39]

# 11 · *Scholars and Students*

Oxford had become a celebrated place of scholarship, with about 1500 students, by the end of the twelfth century and was unrivalled by Cambridge until the fifteenth century.[1] But at first it was not clear that either would become acknowledged as one of the two leading seats of learning in England. In the 1170s Lincoln cathedral school had a reputation for teaching law which was equal to that of Paris or Bologna; while Hereford, Exeter and Northampton all had claims to be considered on a par with Oxford. Why Oxford should have risen to preeminence was not clear. A Saxon settlement by the river ford had been overshadowed by a Norman castle around which a moderately prosperous market town had developed. But its central position in the country no doubt helped its growth as a university town as did the proximity of two monastic establishments and the royal manor of Woodstock as well as 'an influx of English scholars from Paris'.[2]

The university's days, however, were so beset by violent disruptions that it seemed at first unlikely to survive. Some of these outbreaks throw such an illuminating light upon the riotousness of the times, upon the rivalries between the townspeople and the scholars, and upon the dissensions between the different 'nations' of students, the southern and northern English (the dividing line being taken to be the river Nene), the Welsh, the Irish and the Scots, that they are worth describing in some detail.

The first serious outbreak, which took place in 1209, is thus reported by Roger of Wendover:

About this time a certain clerk who was studying in Arts at Oxford slew by chance a certain woman and finding that she was dead sought safety in flight. But the mayor and many others, coming to the place and finding the dead woman, began to seek the slayer in his lodging where he had lived with three other fellow-clerks. And not finding the guilty man they took his three fellow-clerks, who knew nothing whatsoever of the killing and cast them into prison. After a few days . . . these clerks were led out from the city and hanged. Whereupon some 3000 clerks, both masters and scholars departed Oxford, so that not one of the whole University was left. Some pursued their studies . . . at Cambridge, and others at Reading, leaving Oxford utterly empty.[3]

A few years later there was further uproar after the mayor and bailiffs, 'at the Instance and Complaint of the Chancellor and Masters', ordered that all 'Lewd Women then in Gaol' should be released on condition they undertook to leave the town and no more resort to the scholars' chambers.

On the Publication of the Writ many loose women were expelled from hence [despite] the Tumults then made by some of the *French* students whose infamous Lust had engag'd them in their Quarrels, and by haunting Stews and Brothels, had contracted the foul Disease almost in an Epidemical Manner. [This] deprav'd Course of Life . . . brought over the Pope's Legate into *England*, sent hither to reform the Corruptions of the Place, and residing at Osney [Abbey].

One day a party of students went to see the legate; but being rudely repelled by the porter 'in his loud *Italian* voice', they forced open the door and burst into the building. A fight ensued with the legate's retinue; and a cook, who threw a cauldron of boiling water over an Irish scholar, was shot dead, 'which caused an uproar throughout the House'. The legate took shelter in the belfry from which he fled in the middle of the night to seek the king's protection at Wallingford. On this occasion the university was suspended altogether and the students once again departed, this time to Northampton and Salisbury.[4]

Twenty years after this there was an outright battle between the various national factions, the 'Northern English and the Welsh' – 'with banners and flags among them to distinguish each division' – winning the victory over the 'Southern English' after 'divers on both sides [had been] slain and pitifully wounded'.[5]

Then, towards the end of the century, there was more serious rioting when, on Friday before the feast of St Mathias 1298, the bailiff 'was at Carfax carrying his mace, as is due'. 'There came some clerks at the University to fight and disturb the peace, and laid hands on the Bailiff and trampled on him and took away his mace; whereupon hue and cry was made.' One of the students was arrested; immediately 'a multitude of clerks with their followers with force of arms' appeared upon the scene, released him and attacked the bailiff's house. 'Further on Saturday morning following, came the clerks to

St Mary's Church and took all the lay-folk they could find, beat them and wickedly trampled on them, and they killed one . . . and dragged [another] into the church, and beat him before the high altar, wounded and evil treated him, and threatened all the burgesses with robbery and murder.'[6]

One of the most serious of all riots occurred in 1354 when a party of scholars were drinking at Swyndlestock Tavern and, having been served some indifferent wine by the landlord, John of Croydon, 'several snappish words passed between them'. 'At length the Vintner giving them stubborn and saucy language', they threw the wine and vessel at his head. His friends then rang the bell of St Martin's, and a crowd of townsfolk attacked the students, 'some with bows and arrows, others with divers weapons'.

> The Chancellor [of the University] perceiving what great danger they were in, caused the University Bell at St Mary's to be rung out, whereupon the Scholars got bows and maintained the fight with the Townsmen till dark night, at which time the fray ceased . . . On the next day . . . the Townsmen subtilly and secretly sent about fourscore men armed with bows and arrows and other manner of weapons into the parish of St Giles in the north suburb; who . . . having discovered certain Scholars walking after dinner in Beaumont (being the same place we now call St Giles's Field), issued out of St Giles's Church, shooting at the said Scholars . . . One Scholar they killed without the Walls, some they wounded mortally, others grievously and used the rest basely. All which being done without any mercy, caused an horrible outcry in the Town; whereupon the Town bell being rung out first and after that the University bell, divers Scholars issued out armed with bows and arrows in their own defence and of their companions, and having first shut and blocked up some of the Gates of the Town (lest the country people who were then gathered together in innumerable multitudes might suddenly break in upon their rear in an hostile manner and assist the Townsmen who were now ready prepared in battle array and armed with their targets also) they fought with them and defended themselves till after Vesper tide; a little after which time, entered into the Town by the west gate about two thousand countrymen with a black dismal flag, erect and displayed. Of which the Scholars having notice, and being unable to resist so great and fierce a company, they withdrew themselves to their lodgings.
>
> The countrymen advanced crying Slea, Slea . . . Havock, Havock . . . Smyt fast, give gode knocks . . . Finding no Scholars in the streets to make any opposition, [they] pursued them, and that day they broke open five Inns, or Hostles of Scholars with fire and sword . . . Such Scholars as they found in the said Halls or Inns they killed or maimed, or grevously wounded. Their books and all their goods which they could find, they

spoiled, plundered and carried away. All their victuals, wine, and other drink they poured out; their bread, fish &c. they trod under foot. After this the night came on and the conflict ceased for that day.

The next day, however, there was more violence. Although the surviving and subdued scholars remained indoors, 'the Townsmen, desiring to heap mischief upon mischief . . . with hideous noises and clamours came and invaded the Scholars' houses which they forced open with iron bars and other engines; and those that resisted . . . they killed or else in a grievous sort maimed.'

Some innocent wretches, after they had killed, they scornfully cast into houses of easment, others they buried in dunghills, and some they let lie above ground. The crowns of some Chaplains, viz. all the skin so far as the tonsure went, these diabolical imps flayed off in scorn of their Clergy. Divers others whom they had mortally wounded, they haled to prison, carrying their entrails in their hands in a most lamentable manner . . .

The wickedness and outrage continuing . . . all the Scholars being fled divers ways, our Mother the University of Oxon which had but two days before many sons is now almost forsaken and left forlorn.[7]

Eighteen months later the king was still issuing pleas to the masters to re-establish lectures in the town.

After this 'great slaughter of 1354' there were no comparable battles in Oxford between the scholars and the townsmen. But there were still occasional fights between the two, while the skirmishing between the 'nations' continued unabated. In 1389 a gang of English scholars

. . . fought after all the Welshmen abiding and studying in Oxford, shooting arrows before them in diverse streets and lanes as they went, crying out, 'War, war, sle, sle, sle, the Welsh doggys and her whelps and ho so looketh out of his howese, he shall in good sorte be dead.'

And certain persons they slew and others they grievously wounded, and some of the Welshmen who bowed their knees to abjure the town, they the Northern Scholars led to the gates, causing them first to piss on them, and then to kiss the place on which they had pissed. But being not content with that, they, while the said Welshmen stooped to kiss it, would knock their heads against the gates in such an inhuman manner, that they would force blood out of the noses of some, and tears from the eyes of others.[8]

There were occasional assaults, too, upon Jews, upon the so-called '*ludi*' who spied on scholars whom they caught not speaking Latin, and upon proctors who, armed with poleaxes and accompanied by assistants, patrolled the streets of the town in an effort to keep the peace. Oxford was also frequently disturbed, so it was reported in 1410, 'by persons who in the guise of scholars abide in divers places within the university . . . who sleep all day and at night lurk about taverns and brothels, bent on robbing and homicide'. Towards the middle of the century there was such a sharp decline in the number of scholars that it was feared that the university might disintegrate. In 1435 the Duke of Gloucester received a letter in which he was warned that it was 'reduced to the greatest misery'. Lectures had ceased and 'a complete ruin of education' was imminent. In 1456–7 only twenty-seven scholars took the Master of Arts degree.[9]

Cambridge was no less riotous than Oxford. There was a savage fight between the scholars and townspeople in 1261; in 1381 the townsmen destroyed the University's charter and records; and in 1418 the mayor, bailiffs and commonalty of Cambridge were driven to complain to the king:

> That on the vigil of St James the Apostle, many scholars, with the assent and at the excitation and abetting of the before mentioned persons, armed in a warlike manner, caused great terror to the mayor, by laying in wait to kill him and his officers, if they on that night had issued out of their houses; and that when they perceived they could not effect their malicious purpose, they affixed on the mayor's gate a certain schedule, to his great scandal, and so that the mayor and burgesses dared not to preserve the peace.[10]

In an attempt to maintain discipline students at both Oxford and Cambridge were heavily fined for a variety of offences. In 1432 at Oxford, where the 'unrestrained continuance of execrable dissensions' had 'almost blackened its charming manners, its famous learning and its sweet reputation', the masters of the university unanimously ordered that whoever was convicted of disturbing the peace should be fined 'according to the quantity and quality of his crime, over and above the usual penalties, viz':

> For threats of personal violence, twelvepence; for carrying of weapons against the statute, two shillings; for drawing weapons of violence, or pushing with the shoulder or striking with the fist, four shillings; for striking with a stone or club, six shillings and eight-pence; for striking with a knife, dagger, sword, axe, or other weapon of war, ten shillings; for carrying a bow and arrow with intent to harm, twenty shillings; for gathering armed men or other persons and conspiring to hinder the execution of justice or to inflict bodily harm on anyone, thirty shillings; for

resisting the execution of justice, or going about by night, forty shillings as well as satisfaction to the injured party.[11]

Fines proving ineffective, however, the birch was commonly used from the end of the fifteenth century for numerous offences other than riotousness. The Statutes of Brasenose College, for instance, ordered birching for unprepared lessons, playing or talking during lectures, and for speaking in English rather than Latin. There were disagreements as to how old an undergraduate should be before flogging was considered an inappropriate punishment: Dr John Caius of Cambridge fixed the age limit at eighteen; Thomas Wolsey of Oxford decided that it should be twenty.

Unruly as the scholars so often were, the crown displayed great interest in preserving Oxford and Cambridge and in supporting the university authorities in their disputes with those of the town. The university at Northampton was suppressed in 1265 as it offered a threat to Oxford; and in about 1334 a royal writ forbade seventeen masters from lecturing at Stamford and instituting what promised to be a successful university there.[12] The burgesses of both Oxford and Cambridge were in regular receipt of rebukes from the court for not treating the scholars with due respect. In 1300 King Edward I ordered the townspeople of Oxford to clean up their town, to stop dumping rubbish in the streets and boiling fat on the pavement. 'The air is so corrupted and infected,' his letter continued, 'that an abominable loathing [is] diffused among the aforesaid masters and scholars.'[13]

King Henry III delivered an equally severe reprimand to the burgesses of Cambridge on another matter:

> You are aware that a multitude of scholars from divers parts, as well from this side the sea as from overseas, meets at our town of Cambridge for study, which we hold a very gratifying and desirable thing . . .
>
> We have heard, however, that in letting your houses you make such heavy charges to the scholars lying among you, that unless you conduct yourselves with more restraint and moderation towards them in this matter, they will be driven by your exactions to leave your town and, abandoning their studies, leave our country which we by no means desire.[14]

Fairer rents were, therefore, to be agreed between two Masters of the University and 'two good and lawful men' of the town.

At Oxford as at Cambridge, scholars lived in private houses as lodgers or in hospices which were established by the townspeople for profit. After about

1200, however, halls were established and students were encouraged to live in these rather than in ordinary lodging-houses so that the university authorities would have more control over them. In 1313 the principals or wardens of halls at Oxford were required to take an oath that 'should they know of anyone from their society who is organising meetings or showing agreement with those organising them, or going to gatherings . . . or disturbing the peace of the University . . . or holding a brothel in the house or carrying arms or causing in whatever way discord between southerners and northerners, they should within three days of learning about it report it to the Chancellor who shall punish all the disturbers of the peace with imprisonment'.[15]

Since university halls were usually so uncomfortable and so strictly supervised, most students preferred to take lodgings which, while often spare enough, might be made quite comfortable like those of Chaucer's Oxford student, the lodger in the house of a carpenter, who had made

> Some studies in the arts, but all his fancy
> Turned to astrology and geomancy . . .
> This lad was known as Nicholas the Gallant,
> And making love in secret was his talent,
> For he was very close and sly, and took
> Advantage of his meek and girlish look.
> He rented a small chamber in the kip
> All by himself without companionship.
> He decked it charmingly with herbs and fruit
> And he himself was sweeter than the root
> Of liquorice, or any fragrant herb.
> His astronomic text-books were superb,
> He had an astrolabe to match his art
> And calculating counters laid apart
> On handy shelves that stood above his bed.
> His press was curtained coarsely and in red;
> Above there lay a gallant harp in sight
> On which he played melodiously at night
> With such a touch that all the chamber rang;
> It was *The Virgin's Angelus* he sang,
> And after that he sang *King William's Note*,
> And people often blessed his merry throat.
> And that was how this charming scholar spent
> His time and money, which his friends had sent.[16]

Had he lived a few years later this student would not have been able to live in lodgings, for in about 1410 residence in halls became compulsory for all undergraduates. By then several colleges had also been founded, originally as self-governing religious bodies, principally for graduates but later becoming undergraduate societies.[17] University College, Balliol and Merton were all established in the thirteenth century, as was Peterhouse at Cambridge. Merton was founded in 1264 by Walter de Merton, 'formerly Chancellor of the illustrious Lord the King of England'. Its statutes were promulgated in 1270 and, among other rules, decreed:

> There is to be one person in every chamber where scholars are resident, of maturer age than the others, who is to have a superintendence of the others and who is to make report of their morals and advancement . . . While in their chambers the scholars must abstain from noise and interruption to the fellows and apply themselves with all diligence to study and when they speak they must use the Latin tongue . . . Care and diligent solicitude must be taken that no persons be admitted but those that are chaste, of good conduct, peaceful, humble, indigent, of ability for study and desirous of improvement . . . The scholars who are appointed to the duty of studying in the house are to have a common table, and a dress as nearly alike as possible . . . The scholars are to have a reader at meals, and in eating together they are to observe silence and to listen to what is read . . . There shall be a constant succession of scholars devoted to the study of letters, who shall be bound to employ themselves in the study of Arts or Philosophy, the Canons or Theology. Let there be also one member of the collegiate body who shall be a grammarian, and must entirely devote himself to the study of grammar.[18]

Other colleges later specifically proscribed walking on the grass and destroying plants; keeping ferrets, hawks or hunting dogs; preventing their fellow-scholars from studying by 'noisiness, shouting, playing a musical instrument or any sort of clamour or noisiness'; 'struggling, chorus-singing, leaping, singing, shouting, tumult and inordinate noise'; playing dice in public and 'tumultuous games' in hall. At New College even chess was included in a list of forbidden 'noxious, inordinate and unhonest Games'. Yet the regulations at most colleges seem to have been widely disregarded. Some fifty years after its foundation in 1458 Magdalen College, Oxford, was revealed by an inspection ordered by the Visitor, the Bishop of Winchester, to contain an inordinate number of miscreant fellows:

> Stokes was unchaste with the wife of a tailor.
> Stokysley baptized a cat and practised witchcraft.

Gregory climbed the great gate by the tower, and brought a Stranger into College.

Kendall wears a gown not sewn together in front.

Pots and cups are very seldom washed, but are kept in such a dirty state that one sometimes shudders to drink out of them.

Gunne has had cooked eggs at the Taberd in the middle of the night.

Kyftyll played cards with the butler at Christmas time for money.

Smyth keeps a ferret in College, Lenard a sparrow-hawk, Parkyns a weasel, while Morcott, Heycock and Smyth stole and killed a calf in the garden of one master Court.[19]

The University as a whole at that time forbade swearing, games of chance, being out after eight o'clock at night in winter and nine o'clock in summer, sharing a bed with a friend without permission, walking abroad with a companion, not attending lectures, recitations and disputations which were all compulsory, and making 'odious comparisons of country to country, nobility to ignobility, Faculty to Faculty'. Every offence carried an appropriate fine, from ¼d for speaking in a language other than Latin to 6s 8d for an assault which led to the spilling of blood. Many of these regulations applied not only to undergraduates but also to the citizens of Oxford, over whom the Chancellor had wide-ranging authority. Citizens were, for example, punished for keeping late hours and for playing cards all night as well as for such offences as brewing bad ale. In 1440 the Chancellor expelled from the city one Lucy Colbrand, a prostitute, who had caused 'litigation, fornication, fights and homicides in the University'.[20]

Living conditions for the scholars were far from comfortable. The bedrooms were unlikely to have either fires or glass in the windows: as late as 1598 the junior fellows of King's College, Cambridge, still had to be content with wooden shutters rather than glass panes. Rooms were usually shared with at least one other scholar, and those under fifteen were commonly allotted a companion with whom they must share a bed. Furniture was sparse and seems usually to have been limited to forms, stools, chests, chairs and truckle beds with straw palliasses. Occasionally pitchers and bowls for washing are mentioned in inventories or a 'cistern and trough of lead'. Rarely could a scholar afford the luxury of hangings or the bed-coverings described in the will of a chaplain in 1447 as comprising, among other items, 'one coverlyt of reed and blew with ostryche fetherys . . . one coverlyt of grene and yellow poudred with roses'.[21]

The food provided at most colleges at both Oxford and Cambridge was equally spare. There were two meals a day, one at about ten, the other at about five, although at New College, Oxford, only one meal was provided on

Fridays and Saturdays and in Lent. No butter was served in Lent; and on Lenten Fridays there were raisins, almonds, honey and rice instead of fish. Salt cellars were available as well as cups and dishes, but the scholars had to provide their own trenchers in addition to their knives. Oxford fare was considered so meagre that when he fell foul of the king and lost his office, Sir Thomas More said to a member of his household, 'My counsel is that we fall not to the lowest fare first; we will not therefore descend to Oxford fare, nor to the fare of New Inn, but we will begin with Lincoln's Inn diet.'[22]

Yet a university education was usually very expensive. The scholar had to pay for his teaching as well as his books and his board and lodging. He also, of course, had to pay for his clothes, 8d for a shirt, so the principal of St Mildred's Hall, Oxford, John Arundell, estimated in 1424, 1d for a belt and 4d for clogs. There was also the cost of a gown – in the case of a scholar at Queen's College, a 'blood red' gown – which was worn over a green, blue or red cassock; and at Oxford, so it was decreed in 1358, the gown should be longer and more flowing than the usual garment since it was 'decent that those to whom God had given preference with internal mental gifts' should also 'be different outwardly in dress'.[23] Then there were candles to be paid for, not to mention the journey – perhaps, a very long journey – to and from home. John Arundell estimated that the scholars under his care in the 1420s could not manage on less than 16s 4½d for the first term of their third year, which, after paying 6s 10d for commons and battels, 1s for a gaudy, 1s 8d for lectures, and small sums for other items, allowed only 6d for books.

> Since I cannot get through without heavy costs [runs one characteristic letter from a needy scholar who could not make both ends meet] I have scarcely enough money for my expenses till the bearer of this letter returns. For in commons I cannot manage with less than 8d a week, but in other necessaries also I have spent the money allowed to me, and I have to go on spending. To wit, in my journey to Oxford, for myself and my horse, 3s 4d. In the purchase of two books at Oxford, namely the Codex and the Digestum of Vetus, after I got here, 6s 8d, to the teacher from whom I hear my 'ordinary' lectures, 2s. And when you reckon in the wages of our manciple and cook, the hire of my study and many other necessities with which I need not trouble you because of their number, it will be obvious that my expenses are not unreasonable.[24]

I am studying at Oxford with the greatest diligence [another scholar wrote to his father], but the matter of money stands greatly in the way of my promotion, as it is now two months since I spent the last of what you sent me. The city is expensive and makes many demands. I have to rent lodgings, buy necessaries, and provide for many other things which I cannot now specify. There I respectfully beg your paternity that by the promptings of divine pity you may assist me so that I may be able to complete what I have well begun. For you must know that, without Ceres and Bacchus, Apollo grows cold. Farewell.[25]

Although many scholars were the sons of knights, burgesses or merchants who could afford to meet these demands, there were others whose fathers were not in a position to do so. These paid their way by actings as 'battelers', that was to say waiting on richer scholars during meals and acting generally as their servants, or they went begging by reciting poems at rich men's doors, or were maintained by patrons or friends or by bequests such as that made in the will of Lady Margaret Chocke who in 1483 left one John Langley, 'six marks yerely during 4 years for to goo to Oxford to scole'.[26] Also they might benefit from a fine imposed upon miscreants: in 1208, when the burgesses of Oxford were punished for hanging two clerks, they were required 'to give annually fifty 2s for the use of poor scholars . . . and also feed a hundred poor scholars with bread, cereals, drink and a fish or meat course each year on St Nicholas's Day . . . They shall also swear to sell to the scholars all necessary provisions at a just and reasonable price'.[27] Later Henry VIII ordered that any clergyman with an income of £100 or more must support at least one scholar at grammar school or university. Also, for the poorest scholars, university chests or strongboxes were established and financed by benefactors, and from these money could be borrowed in return for a pledge of a book, say, or pieces of clothing which were auctioned if not redeemed at the end of the year. Yet, despite these charitable arrangements, many scholars were very poor, and looked very poor like those dressed in tattered clothes who gathered around the university chests on a loan day in St Mary's Church, or like the Oxford cleric who accompanied Chaucer's pilgrims to Canterbury:

> An Oxford Cleric, still a student though,
> One who had taken logic long ago,
> Was there; his horse was thinner than a rake,
> And he was not too fat, I undertake,
> But had a hollow look, a sober stare;
> The thread upon his overcoat was bare.
> He had found no preferment in the church
> And he was too unworldly to make search
> For secular employment. By his bed
> He preferred having twenty books in red
> And black, of Aristotle's philosophy,
> Than costly clothes, fiddle or psaltery.
> Though a philosopher, as I have told,

> He had not found the stone for making gold.
> Whatever money from his friends he took
> He spent on learning or another book
> And prayed for them most earnestly, returning
> Thanks to them thus for paying for his learning.
> His only care was study, and indeed
> He never spoke a word more than was need,
> Formal at that, respectful in the extreme,
> Short, to the point, and lofty in his theme.
> A tone of moral virtue filled his speech
> And gladly would he learn, and gladly teach.

At least Chaucer's student could afford books. When he was at Oxford, St Richard, who became Bishop of Chichester in 1244, was so poor that he and two companions with whom he shared a room could only afford one gown between them. 'When one, therefore, went out with the gown to hear a lecture, the others sat in their room, and so they went forth alternately; and bread with a little wine and pottage sufficed for their food.'[28]

While some fellows of colleges were fairly well off, most were almost as poor as the students they taught. Between 1382 and 1444 the Fellows of King's Hall, Cambridge, received a commons allowance of 1s 2d a week; but, since the average charge for commons was 1s 8½d a week, they were usually out of pocket and were obliged to find other sources of income. It was not until 1479 that the first lectureship was established and a fellow was paid a regular salary for delivering a course of lectures.

Lectures were given in Latin and, as books were so expensive, they were the principal, and for some students the only form of education, though copies of extracts from essential textbooks, which were both bought and hired by students, had been available since the thirteenth century. Not all colleges had libraries; and few libraries were well stocked: in the 1470s there were still only 135 books in the library of Lincoln College, Oxford. All libraries had to take note of what books the Chancellor proscribed. In about 1340 he forbade the study of Ovid and 'any other book' that might 'provoke scholars to what is not allowed'.[29]

The average age of students on entry into the universities was between fifteen and seventeen. Some were much younger: one of the Paston boys seems to have been no more than thirteen when he went to Cambridge. But some halls and colleges fixed minimum ages. In 1380 the minimum age for King's Hall was fourteen, and for New College sixteen. Many students left after a year or two; yet others remained for far longer than that. It took seven years of study of Latin, Greek and Hebrew, of moral, metaphysical and natural philosophy, and of grammar, logic, rhetoric, music, arithmetic, geometry and astronomy to qualify for the degree of Master of Arts. By the sixteenth century it took sixteen years to become a Doctor of Theology.

In the earliest days of the universities theology had been of the utmost importance. There were then few students who were not intent upon becoming clerks or priests; and Oxford had been dominated by the mendicant friars, Dominican, Franciscan, Carmelite and Augustinian, all of whom had houses there. Three of the greatest theologians and philosophers of the thirteenth century were closely associated with Oxford. Robert Grosseteste, Chancellor of the University, became first rector of the Franciscans at Oxford in 1224; Duns Scotus, also believed to be a Franciscan, is supposed to have composed his principal theological treatise, *Opus Oxoniense*, there; and Roger Bacon, another Franciscan, studied and lectured there for several years. These 'regular' clergy, the monks and friars, had remained a powerful influence in Oxford during the following century. But by then the 'secular' clergy, the priests and deacons and clerks in lower orders, had come to consider themselves the proper authority in the university; and in the furious controversy which centred around the religious reformer, John Wyclif, who was Master of Balliol in 1360, they had taken Wyclif's side. Since those days religion and religious teaching has played a less intense part in university life; and by the fifteenth century Oxford had become as much a centre of business studies as a training-ground for men intent upon a career in the church or the cloister. Indeed, in a sense it always had been so. 'If you are a real scholar you are thrust out into the cold,' John of Garland had written as early as 1241. 'Unless you are a money-maker, I say, you will be considered a fool, a pauper. The lucrative arts, such as law and medicine are now in vogue, and only those things are pursued that are of cash value.' Two hundred years later no one could doubt that, even though they might have taken or intended to take minor orders, many if not most undergraduates were at the university to obtain an administrative or secretarial appointment at court or in some large household by the study of letter-writing, accountancy or the law. Robert Wodelarke, who founded St Catherine's College, Cambridge, in 1473, specifically to improve the quality of England's teachers, considered the ills of the country had their roots in the universities having become schools of law for careerists rather than places of spiritual uplift.[30]

The study of law, however, particularly the English Common Law which was not taught at the universities, was by then better undertaken in London at the Inns of Court. These establishments took their name from the inns or town houses, particularly those used as hostels for students and practitioners of law, which had developed in the fourteenth century within easy reach of the courts at Westminster. After the establishment in about 1422 of Lincoln's

Inn – which probably took its name from the third Earl of Lincoln, one of Edward I's most influential advisers, whose family had acquired land in the area – the inns grew and prospered and by the 1470s there were about 1000 students attached to them. Since it cost a minimum of £13 6s 8d a year to study at the Inns, only the sons of the rich could afford to go to them; and some contemporaries cited this as one good reason why there was so little delinquency at the Inns of Court compared to the state of affairs in Oxford.

Writing between 1464 and 1470, Sir John Fortescue, who was a Governor of Lincoln's Inn in 1425 and was appointed Chief Justice in 1442, suggested that a student could 'not well be maintained for under eight and twenty pounds a year'.

If he have servants to wait on him, as for the most part they have [Fortescue continued], the expense is proportionately more: for this reason, the students are sons to persons of quality; those of an inferior rank not being able to bear the expenses of maintaining and educating their children in this way. As to the merchants, they seldom care to lessen their stock in trade by being at such large yearly expenses. So that there is scarce to be found, throughout the kingdom, an eminent lawyer, who is not a gentleman by birth and fortune; consequently they have a greater regard for their character and honour than those who are bred in another way. There is both in the Inns of Court, and the Inns of Chancery, a sort of academy, or gymnasium, fit for persons of their station; where they learn singing, and all kinds of music, dancing and such other accomplishments and diversions, which are called revels, as are suitable to their quality, and such as are usually practised at court. At other times, out of term, the greater part apply themselves to the study of the law . . . All vice is discouraged and banished. So that knights, barons, and the greatest nobility of their kingdom, often place their children in those Inns of Court; not so much to make the laws their study, much less to live by the profession, having large patrimonies of their own, but to form their manners and to preserve them from the contagion of vice. The discipline is so excellent, that there is scarce ever known to be any piques or differences, any bickerings or disturbances amongst them. The only way they have of punishing delinquents is by expelling them the society: which punishment they dread more than criminals do imprisonment and irons: for he who is expelled out of one society is never taken in by any of the other.[31]

# 12 · *Crime and Punishment*

During the anarchic reign of King Stephen in the twelfth century, so the *Peterborough Chronicle* reported, the dungeons of the barons' castles were full of 'both men and women put in prison for their gold and silver, and tortured with pains unspeakable'. Crimes such as these seem to have been common throughout England at all times of unrest. When the misgovernment of Henry III provoked Simon de Montfort into leading his followers into civil war, marauding gangs of robbers, for centuries one of the hazards of English life, overran the entire country. Commissioners appointed in 1305 found that these gangs had not only forcibly seized and held estates, bought others for paltry sums by threats, 'impeded and corrupted constables, bailiffs and the King's officers', but had invaded manor houses and plundered them from cellar to loft, attacked and maimed jurors and witnesses to prevent them telling the truth at assizes, and hired assassins for battery, assault and mayhem. Later on in the century Bristol was for some years in the hands of a brigand who had taken possession of the port, seized its cargoes and issued proclamations in the royal style. In Norfolk, 300 men marched about the country under their own banner like an army of invasion, defying all authority. In Suffolk, a gang of versatile criminals exported stolen wool, imported counterfeit money, forged documents and seals and abducted people from their homes and from church and held them to ransom. When a 'great multitude of men', including one of his former chaplains, marched in military array upon one of his manors, demolished his fences and gates, broke into his buildings, and carried off 300 head of cattle and 1000 sheep, the Bishop of Exeter believed at first that a 'foreign enemy had landed' and was collecting supplies for an army. The Archbishop of Canterbury, in a similar raid, lost not only his animals and trees but even his corn. The Countess of Lincoln also lost all her timber and most of her game when her estate at Kingston Lacy was attacked by a band of fifty men, including the

Abbots of Sherbourne and Middleton. In a raid upon an estate in Wiltshire, in which the Prior of Bristol took part, all the inmates of the manor house were murdered, the lady of the house was raped, and her chaplain died of fright. Some years later a gang of 400 armed men rode to Walsingham while the sessions were being held there and secured the acquittal of all their friends. All over the country rival claimants to land were demanding payment of rent from tenants who were either forced to pay twice over or to suffer the consequences of failing to do so.[1]

The manor courts were often powerless to redress wrongs. In peaceable times these courts – presided over by a senior official of the lord or by the lord himself attended by clerk and beadle – conducted their business well enough. They normally dealt with such matters as disputes over labour service and trespass, with allegations of immorality and slander; they fined men for brawling or poaching or using false weights, and punished girls for reducing their value by losing their virginity. But in years of unrest there were more serious crimes to consider; and the manor courts were unable to deal with them. On some manors the lord, declining to wait for the royal coroner, usurped the king's authority by setting up gallows and hanging offenders, even those found guilty of crimes committed elsewhere.

During the Wars of the Roses, official records and private correspondence alike provided sad and vivid testimony of appalling lawlessness, of what a petition set out in the Rolls of Parliament for 1459 described as 'robberies, ravishments, extortions, oppressions, riots and unlawful assemblies . . . universally [committed] throughout every part of [the] realm [by] misdoers favoured and assisted by persons of great might'. Twelve years later the state of the realm was said to be more disordered than ever. A petition of 1472 complained of further 'great abominable murders, robberies . . . affrays and assaults . . . committed by such persons as either be of great might or else favoured under persons of great power in such wise as their outrageous demerits as yet remain unpunished'.[2]

Gangs of brigands, often in the pay of powerful magnates, remained for years in complete control of towns and of large areas of the countryside. One gang, representative of many, 'would issue out at their pleasure', in the words of the information laid against them, 'sometimes six in number, sometimes twelve, sometimes thirty or more, armed, jacked and salleted, with bows arrows, spears and bills, and over-ride the country and oppress the people and do many horrible and abominable deeds'.[3] They invaded churches and attacked men at Mass; battered down the doors of houses, stole the contents, murdered the inmates; and rode about the country rounding up sheep and cattle. In the west of England the ferocious feud between the Earl of Devon and Lord Bonville provoked 'great and grievous riots by which some men have been murdered, some robbed, and children and women taken'. At the same time in East Anglia, as the *Paston Letters* show, veritable armies were on the move in the attempted settlement of private claims, and had long been so. In one letter Margaret Paston advises her husband in London to 'get some crossbows, and windlasses to wind them with, and crossbow bolts, for your houses here are so low that no one can shoot out of them with a longbow . . . And I would also like you to get two or three short pole-axes to keep indoors, and as many leather jackets if you can.' In a subsequent letter she adds: 'It would be a good idea it seems to me, for you to order now a neat defensive jacket for yourself, for there [in London] they make the best and the cheapest ones.' She feared that Lord Moleyns, who laid claim to a property at Gresham which the Paston family had bought, would attempt to seize it by force; and her fears were justified, as a petition to the king from her husband soon afterwards makes clear:

[Lord Moleyns] sent to the said mansion [Gresham] riotous people to the number of a thousand . . . arrayed in manner of war with cuirasses, body armour, leather jackets, headpieces, knives, bows, arrows, shields, guns, pans with fire and burning tinder in them, long crowbars for pulling down houses, ladders, pickaxes with which they mined the walls, and long trees with which they broke up gates and doors, and thus came into the said mansion. The wife of your petitioner was in the house, and twelve people with her, whom they drove out of the said mansion, and they mined through the walls of the room where the wife of your petitioner was and carried her out of the gates; and they cut through the posts supporting the house and let them fall. They broke up all the rooms and chests in the said mansion, and rifled them; and as in a robbery they carried off the goods, clothes and money that your petitioner and his servants had there, to the value of £200, and sold part of it, gave part of it away and divided the rest amongst themselves, to the great and outrageous hurt of your petitioner, saying openly that if they had found your petitioner there and one John Damme who is his adviser and various other servants of his, they would have been killed.[4]

John Paston placed little faith in this petition which, in fact, merely resulted in the sheriff receiving a letter from the king ordering him to ensure that such a panel was formed as would acquit Moleyns. Paston resignedly remarked that such letters could easily be bought for 6s 8d, for justice was utterly corrupt. Paston's father had advised a man to drop a suit as soon as he learned that the opponent was a friend of the Duke of Norfolk. And, as a correspondent of Paston himself observed, 'Nowadays, ye know well that the law goeth as it is favoured.' Bribes were a continuous necessity in any law suit unless a great man's influence rendered them superfluous; and perjury was common.

For the poor, trials were always uncertain. The laws of earlier times had invested those who had been wronged with the power to inflict punishments summarily and personally once proof of guilt had been obtained; and in the absence of incontrovertible proof the guilt of the accused was decided by the ordeal. Before the Norman Conquest this ancient ceremony of 'God's judgement' had taken place inside a church; soon after the Conquest it was transferred to specially prepared pits outside it. A fire was lit and while water was being brought to the boil, a priest walked up and down between the two rows of spectators sprinkling them with holy water and giving it to them to sip, and the Gospels and cross for them to kiss. They were required to be 'fasting and to have abstained from their wives during the night'. The accused had also been made to eat nothing for three days but bread, salt and herbs. When the water had boiled he was instructed to thrust his hand, or his arm up to the elbow, into it and pick out a stone. The skin was then bandaged and if, after three days when the cloth was removed, there was evidence of scalding this was taken to be proof of guilt.

As an alternative to the ordeal by water the accused was sometimes required to walk over red-hot ploughshares without being seared, place his hand in a glove of red-hot iron, or to pick up a red-hot iron bar and hold it in his bare hand while he walked three paces. As with the ordeal with water, the hands or feet were then bandaged for three days; and if at the end of the third day a blister the size of half a walnut had appeared, this was accepted as proof of guilt. The priests themselves, if accused of crimes, were not made to undergo these ordeals; but instead had to stand before the altar and eat a piece of cheese on consecrated bread. God was called upon to send down the angel Gabriel to stop the throat of a guilty priest and prevent him from swallowing.

Guilt could also be decided by compurgation in which a number of compurgators were asked to swear to the innocence of the accused. Such oaths were taken as proof of innocence, just as the absence of compurgators, or an insufficient number of them at the time of the trial, was taken as proof of guilt. Forms of trial of this sort were common to many primitive societies and in them may be seen some inchoate germs of the jury system which was developed and greatly extended in scope and significance by William I and Henry II who encouraged the growth of a common law in England long before France and Germany had outgrown their local customs.[5]

Trial by ordeal was formally abolished in England in 1219. But the equally ancient trials by combat survived into the fourteenth century. These were more often used to settle civil disputes, but a man accused of felony might establish his innocence by challenging his accuser to a duel. Knights fought with swords or lances; commoners with staves made lethal by iron heads; women and priests, the old and infirm could appoint champions to fight for them. The funeral brass of Wyville, Bishop of Salisbury, who died in 1375 bears the figure of the bishop's champion standing in a fortified gateway, and presumably represents his victory over his opponent in a battle fought to determine the ownership of Sherborne Castle.[6]

Trials by battle were rare, however, even in the thirteenth century; and by the time they were abandoned the various courts which had been established were administering the law with some regard to the rules of evidence. They were also administering it with increasing, if fluctuating, severity; for the conception of sin which had by now been absorbed into the criminal law had altered its character. Those guilty of serious crimes such as murder, robbery and rape could no longer make amends by compensation; they were required to do penance as sinners. They were also regarded, under the influence of the traditions of the rediscovered Roman law, as offenders against society at large whom the king, as leader of that society, was entitled to punish.

In earlier centuries jurisdiction had been seen by the king – or by the prelates and lords of the manor to whom, under the feudal system, jurisdiction had been granted in return for specified services – largely as a source of revenue. It was now more often regarded as a method of repression, deterrence and retribution; and it was felt that only by the threat of savage punishments could the people's growing predisposition to crime be checked. When crime was not checked, it was generally supposed that the punishments had not proved savage enough. Thus it was, for example, that although the laws of Ethelstan had provided that a coiner should have his hand cut off, by the time of Henry I, when this punishment had not deterred others from committing what the more general use of money had made a common offence, coiners could be castrated as well. A century later, coining was still widespread and, after an inquiry in Edward I's time, 280 Jews were hanged in London for this offence alone.[7]

The idea that criminal jurisdiction should be a source of revenue was not, of course, forgotten. Fines and forfeiture of goods were still commonly imposed in the king's courts. So were sentences of outlawry by which the goods of the outlaw fell to the Crown. In 1279 all but three of the men who had been found guilty after trials for murder were outlawed. The ecclesiastical courts, while imposing severe punishments, such as the whipping and branding of heretics, also took care to ensure that their rights of jurisdiction were profitable ones.

For the guilty who could not pay the fines imposed upon them, or whose goods were worthless, there was scant mercy. She had deserved death, a court decided in the case of a woman found guilty of perjury (a capital offence) in a murder trial, 'but by way of dispensation let her eyes be torn out'. Even less mercy was shown to traitors whose public punishments were intended to add horror to the sentence of death.

> The award of the court, [the Earl of Carlisle was told in the reign of Edward II] is that for your treason you be drawn, and hanged, and beheaded; that your heart, and bowels and entrails, whence came your traitorous thoughts, be torn out and burnt to ashes and that the ashes be scattered to the winds; that your body be cut into four quarters, and that one of them be hanged upon the tower of Carlisle, another upon the tower of Newcastle, a third upon the Bridge of York and the fourth at Shrewsbury; and that your head be set upon London Bridge, for an example to others that they may never presume to be guilty of such treasons as yours against their liege Lord.[8]

For the punishment of lesser crimes than treason there were the stocks, the pillory, and the ducking- or drowning-stool. The stocks, which held the miscreant by his ankles, were to be seen by the fifteenth century in every town and village in England where they were used to hold criminals until they could be taken to the place of their trial, and to expose vagabonds and local offenders to the ignominy of public vilification. The pillory held the culprit by the neck and wrists and was also used to shame offenders. A Londoner, accused of slander against some important city officials, was sentenced to a year's imprisonment in Newgate and, during the year, was to be put in the pillory four times:

> The said John shall come out of Newgate without hood or girdle, barefoot and unshod, with a whetstone hung by a chain from his neck, and lying on his breast, it being marked with the words, – 'A false liar'; and there shall be a pair of trumpets, trumpeting before him on his way to the pillory; and there the cause of his punishment shall be solemnly proclaimed. And the said John shall remain on the pillory for three hours of the day, and from thence shall be taken back to Newgate in the same manner.[9]

The pillory was a more painful punishment than the stocks. Occasionally the culprit's ears were nailed to the wooden board so that he could not hang his head when the spectators of his misery threw stones or rubbish at him; and sometimes his feet did not reach the platform and he was throttled. Death in the pillory was not uncommon; and women are known to have drowned when tied on the ducking-stool, a common punishment for 'immoral', 'nagging' and 'scolding' women, and later for witches, who were plunged by it into the waters of a pond.

\*

A sentence to imprisonment could also prove a sentence to death, particularly for those who could not pay the fees customarily demanded by gaolers for habitable accommodation and what was known as 'easement of irons'. In Newgate alone there were numerous deaths every year; and in one year almost half the cases recorded in the *Coroners' Rolls for the City of London* are inquests on men who died in that prison. When the debtors' prison at Ludgate was closed and the prisoners were transferred to Newgate, an order was made for reopening Ludgate on these grounds:

> Whereas through the abolition and doing away with the Prison of Ludgate, which was formerly ordained for the good and comfort of citizens and other reputable persons, and also, by reason of the fetid and corrupt atmosphere that is in the hateful gaol of Newgate, many persons who were lately in the said Prison of Ludgate . . . and who for divers great offences which they had there compassed, were committed to the said gaol [of Newgate], are now dead, who might have been living, it is said, if they had remained in Ludgate, abiding in peace there.[10]

All over the country there were prisons as appalling, though not as large, as Newgate; and prisoners, in good health when they entered them, died in them in hundreds. In 1358 fifty approvers died in York Castle alone.[11] All over the country, too, there were corrupt sheriffs and other officials who took innocent men, unlawfully indicted them, and imprisoned them in order to extract money from them.[12] Prisoners were tortured in gaol to force them to give evidence against their supposed accomplices and were afterwards left in prison to die. From time to time efforts at reform were made: the commissions which Edward I was compelled to appoint to inquire into the misdeeds of his legal officers were not the first nor the last of many commissions appointed for this purpose. Yet justice remained difficult and sometimes impossible to obtain; bribery and corruption continued to infect the whole system; and it was still lamented that jurors could not be induced to bring in true verdicts against criminals.

If not bribed or intimidated, juries often took the side of the accused as a matter of course, believing that he was frequently no more reprehensible than the judge who presided over his trial. And so long as not only inferior lawyers but a Chief Justice of England could be shown to be in receipt of bribes, as William Thorpe was in 1350; and so long as the Chancellor himself could make illegal profits from his high office, as William of Wykeham was believed to have done in 1371, the honesty of ordinary men who served on juries was not likely to be assured. Nor were their prejudices against the courts likely to be overcome when so many men enjoyed special privileges. Benefit of clergy, which meant originally that an ordained clerk charged with felony could be tried only in ecclesiastical courts, had changed its nature. It had come to be accepted as a plea against capital punishment in any court, and the benefit could be claimed by anyone who could show that he was an educated man. The ability to read a line or two of a prescribed text, which could, in any case, be learned by heart, was often taken as being sufficient evidence of education. As late as 1613 two men convicted of burglary at the house of the Earl of Sussex received different sentences: 'The said Paul reads, to be branded; the said William does not read, to be hanged.'[13]

For those who could not otherwise evade the law, there was the protection of sanctuary. As it had been considered sacrilege to remove the criminal fugitive from the temples of ancient Egypt and Rome, so it was recognized in Christian Europe that those who sought the protection of sacred ground were inviolate. Not only churches and monasteries offered protection but also any place which the Church, and the laws inspired by the Church, recognized as a sanctuary, as well as any area granted the privilege of sanctuary by royal charter. In London the numbers of these areas was constantly growing, and, although the right of sanctuary was legally suppressed in the reign of James I, several survived until the eighteenth century, including the Minories, the Mint, Whitefriars, Ram Alley, Mitre Court, Salisbury Court, Montague Close and Deadman's Place. A malefactor who reached sanctuary, however, was not necessarily safe, even though to drag men out of sanctuary was a sacrilege punishable by whipping, fine, excommunication or even death. One Nicholas le Porter, who had helped snatch some refugees from the church of the Carmelites at Newcastle, was ordered to be whipped:

We order [wrote Bishop Richard to the parson of St Nicholas at Durham] that on Monday, Tuesday, and Wednesday of the Whitsun week just coming, he shall receive the whip from your hands publicly, before the chief door of your church, in his shirt, bareheaded, and barefoot. He shall there proclaim in English the reason for his penance, and shall admit his fault; and when he has thus been whipped the said Nicholas will go to the cathedral church of Durham, bareheaded, barefoot and dressed as above, he will walk in front, you will follow him; and you will whip him in the same manner before the door of the cathedral these three days, and he will repeat there the confession of his sin.[14]

Other offenders against the laws of sanctuary were excommunicated. Yet when William Longbeard took refuge in the London church of St Mary le Bow, in 1196, the Archbishop of Canterbury set fire to the building in order to smoke him out; in 1182 the Constable of the Tower dragged some escaped prisoners out of St Paul's and beheaded them in the churchyard; and during the Peasants' Revolt the abbey at Westminster, the chapel royal in the Tower, St John's Clerkenwell and St Martin's Vintry were all invaded by the pursuers of wanted men.[15]

A fugitive who gained sanctuary had to confess his crime, give up his arms and, if he had entered a religious house, swear to obey its rules. Theoretically he was then safe for forty days; and during that time he could either come out to surrender or swear 'to abjure the realm'. If he chose to leave the country he had to go 'ungert, unshod, bare-headed in his bare-shirt, as if he were to be hanged on the gallows', having received a cross in his hands. He was instructed to go to a specified port, usually Dover, given a fixed time in which to complete the journey, usually a day for every twenty-five miles, and forbidden to turn off the high road, on which alone he had the protection of the law against his enemies. If there were no ships at the port ready to sail, he had to walk into the sea to demonstrate his readiness to leave, and this he had to do every day until he sailed.[16] Offenders often did abjure the realm, as many as 1000 a year. In Wiltshire in the reign of Henry III sixty-six malefactors, six of them women, chose to go into exile rather than surrender to the law; and some years later in Cornwall, seventy-eight malefactors did so, most of them robbers.[17]

While malefactors frequently escaped by seeking sanctuary or by bribing court officials and jurors when they did come to trial, they could also evade justice by taking advantage of the pardons offered to them in return for a year's campaigning in the army. Many did so; and the far from universal adoption of surnames ensured that these pardons often passed from hand to hand without the possibility of a court being able to determine whether or not those who held them were entitled to do so.

Yet although thousands of malefactors escaped justice by one means or another, there did exist systems of law enforcement which were intermittently successful in making arrests. Since the time of the Saxon kings, the underlying principle of law enforcement had been one of mutual responsibility. Men had been associated in tithings, originally groups of ten men responsible for each other's good behaviour, and in territorial divisions known as hundreds which William the Conqueror had found a useful instrument. Whenever a member of his Norman garrison was found dead within its boundaries, for instance, the murderer was presumed, without proof to the contrary, to have been a Saxon; and the hundred had accordingly to assume the responsibility for paying the fine for murder. By the end of the thirteenth century much of the significance of the hundred had been lost; but, theoretically at least, it still held a responsibility for crimes committed within its boundaries and had to answer the summons of the king's officers in times of danger.

In 1283 the Statute of Winchester reiterated this mutual responsibility and emphasized the ancient English tradition that every man was a policeman. In order to keep the peace more effectively, and to 'abate the power of felons', it specified the type of weapon which every man had for generations been expected to possess both to fight the king's enemies and to keep the peace. The statute also confirmed the responsibility of all able-bodied men to follow the 'hue and cry' which required them to down tools when the call was made and to dash off in pursuit of malefactors caught in the act. Nor did their responsibilities end here, for they were also liable to be called to serve as constables when their turn came, only 'Religious Persons, Knights, Clerkes and Women' being excepted.

In towns able-bodied men were also expected to perform regular duty as watchmen; each of London's twenty-four wards, for example, was required by an Act of 1283 to provide six men chosen from all the householders, to parade as watchmen under the orders of an alderman. As the years passed, however, busy merchants and artisans found it increasingly irksome to abandon their counting-houses and work-benches when the 'hue and cry' was raised or when their turn came to act as constables or watchmen. So, gradually, the 'hue and cry' fell into disuse to be replaced by the practice of paying a proxy to perform the duty of constable and to act as assistant to the justice of the peace, an officer whose origins can be traced back to the twelfth century but whose importance did not emerge until a statue of 1360 defined his considerable powers.[18]

Yet if improved methods of law enforcement did lead to more arrests, punishment for crime remained so uncertain and arbitrary, and acquittal could so often be bought by bribes or influence that men continued to settle their own grievances by private methods. In the Northumberland Roll of 1279, seventy-two murders are listed and only forty-three accidental deaths. In the murder cases eighty-one culprits are identified. Of these no more than three were hanged. Six escaped to sanctuary, one was imprisoned, one fined, one pleaded benefit of clergy and sixty-nine escaped altogether.[19] In 1348 there were eighty-eight known cases of murder in Yorkshire, whose population at that time was probably about the same as that of Sheffield today. If murders were committed on this scale now, there would not be less than 10,000 a year in England and Wales instead of the average of between 500 and 600. Most murderers today commit suicide or, if sentenced, are imprisoned. But nearly all murderers then were allowed to become outlaws, since this was more profitable financially; and many of these outlaws returned to commit depredations in a different part of the country.

Almost as common a method of private vengeance as murder was mutilation which the law allowed as a punishment, though it was not often inflicted except upon the very poor. Guy Mortimer, rector of Kingston-upon-Hull, attacked one of his parishioners against whom he bore a grudge and, with the help of a fellow clergyman and some other friends, he cut off his upper lip. The court before which Mortimer was brought declared he was guilty of mere trespass and imposed a fine. Not until the fifteenth century was cutting out the tongue of an enemy or putting out his eyes considered a felony.[20]

# 13 · Doctors and Patients

A doctor too emerged as we proceeded;
No one alive could talk as well as he did . . .
The cause of every malady you'd got
He knew, and whether dry, cold, moist or hot;
He knew their seat, their humour and condition
He was a perfect practising physician.

Like all other conventional practitioners of his craft, the doctor in Chaucer's portrait knew that the properties of the four elements – earth, air, fire and water – were all present in a person's body in varying proportions. These proportions were responsible for a person's character, his or her 'humour', the cause of his being either sanguine, choleric, phlegmatic or melancholy. The earth was deemed to be cold and dry, the air to be hot and moist, fire hot and dry, and water cold and moist. The melancholy man was predominantly cold and dry, the choleric hot and dry, the phlegmatic cold and moist, and the sanguine man, like air, was hot and moist, and this gave him his high colour and his cheerful good nature. It was the doctor's object to recognize the natural temperament of his patient, and to know how to treat him when the elements making up his character became unbalanced and he consequently fell ill.

To help him in his task the doctor could turn to astrology. This enabled him to fix the best time for medicines to be given, for purges to be administered, for cuppings and bleedings, for the application of leeches, for the use of the pig's bladder equipped with a tube which served him as an enema. Astrology was also of use in helping the apothecaries – from whom the doctor bought his more complex remedies – to mix them in their proper proportions, for there were some prescriptions such as theriac, an antidote to poison, which contained some fifty ingredients each of which had to be incorporated at the appropriate time.

Chaucer's doctor, who makes a great show of his knowledge and talks a good deal of Hippocrates, Galen and Discorides and other ancient masters of his science, seems to have relied heavily upon 'Natural Magic' and horoscopes for his treatment, and placed effigies of his patients round their necks so that healing powers could descend into them and thence into the patients when the planets were favourably placed. He also follows the example of most of his fellow-doctors by never setting too light a value upon his skills:

> All his apothecaries in a tribe
> Were ready with the drugs he would prescribe
> And each made money from the other's guile;
> They had been friendly for a goodish while . . .
> In blood red garments, slashed with bluish-grey
> And lined with taffeta, he rode his way;
> Yet he was rather close as to expenses
> And kept the gold he won in pestilences.
> Gold stimulates the heart, or so we're told.
> He therefore had a special love of gold.

In his demands for high fees for his services, he was obeying the precepts of John of Aderne, the successful fourteenth-century surgeon who had had much practice in his craft during the Hundred Years' War, and strongly advised doctors, or leeches as he calls them, to beware 'of scanty askings', since they 'set at nought both the market and the thing'.

> Therefore for the cure of fistula [John of Aderne continued] when it is curable, ask competently of a worthy man and a great forty pound, take he not less than an hundred shilling. For never in all my life took I less than an hundred shilling for cure of that sickness . . . And if the patients or their friends or servants ask how much time he hopeth to heal it, evermore let the leech promise the double that he supposeth to speed by half; that is, if the leech hope to heal the patient in twenty weeks – that is the common course of curing – add he so many over . . . Have the leech also clean hands and well shapen nails, and cleansed from all blackness and filth. And be he courteous at lords' tables, and displease he not in words or deeds to the guests sitting by; hear he many things but speak he but few . . . And when he shall speak, be the words short, and, as much as he may, fair and reasonable and without swearing. Learn also a young leech good proverbs pertaining to his craft in comforting of patients . . . Also it speedeth that a

leech can talk of good tales and of honest that may make the patients to laugh, as well of the Bible as of other tragedies.[1]

According to Johannes Mirfield who worked at St Bartholomew's, Smithfield, in the fourteenth century, very few doctors lived up to John of Aderne's ideals. They were, in fact, mostly 'ignorant amateurs' or what Johannes considered 'worse and more horrible', 'worthless and presumptuous women'. In any case, whichever their sex, they made

> the greatest possible mistakes (thanks to their stupidity) and very often kill their patients; for they work without wisdom . . . in a casual fashion [unacquainted with] the causes or even the names of the maladies which they claim to be able to cure . . . Modern physicians appear to possess three special qualifications, namely, to be able to lie in a subtle manner, to show an outward honesty, and to kill with audacity.[2]

The cures they advocated were frequently taken from such books of traditional recipes as the fourteenth-century Welsh *Meddygon Myddfai* (Physician of Myddfai). This, as a cure for toothache for instance, proposes that the patient should 'take a candle of mutton fat, mingled with seed of sea holly. Burn this candle as close as possible to the tooth, holding a basin of cold water beneath it. The worms [which are gnawing the tooth] will fall into the water to escape the heat of the candle.' Another book, agreeing that toothache was caused by worms 'itchynge and tyckelinge and contynuall dyggynge and thrylynge [boring] at the roots', recommended killing the offending creatures with a mixture of myrrh and opium. Yet another cure was 'to goe thryse about a church yarde'.[3]

For the treatment of stone the remedy discovered by John of Gaddesden, physician at the royal court, was said to have been efficacious. John, having long pondered the problem, 'at last bethought of collecting a good number of those beetles which in summer were found in the dung of oxen, also of the crickets which sing in the fields'.

> I cut off the heads and wings of the crickets [he wrote], and put them with the beetles and common oil into a pot. I covered it and left it afterwards for a day and night in a bread oven. I drew out the pot and heated it at a moderate fire. I pounded the whole and rubbed the sick parts. In three days the pain had disappeared.[4]

For skin diseases the patient was recommended to take gold filings 'in meate or in drinke or in medicine'; while 'thyn plates of gold, firy hot, quenced in wine maketh the wine profittable ayenst the evill of the splene, and ayenst many other evills and passions malincolik'.[5] Doctors treating jaundice in the fourteenth century were recommended to wash the patient with water in which wormwood had been steeped, and for medicine to give him either ivory shavings in wine, borage root and saffron soaked in ale, or saffron and ivory shavings in holy water. And for those suffering from quinsy this was the cure: 'Take a fat cat, skin it, draw out the guts and take the grease of a hedgehog and the fat of bear, and fennugreek, and sage, and gum of honeysuckle and virgin wax. All this crumble small and stuff the cat, roast it whole and gather the grease and anoint [the patient] therewith.'[6]

Magical potions and charms, such as inscribed parchments hung round the neck, were also widely used; and even John Aderne recommended 'the following charm against spasm' as having been found 'most sovran':

A charm written on parchment and placed in a purse and put on the neck of the patient . . . In nomine patris ✠ et filii ✠ et Spiritus sancti ✠ Amen. ⊕ Thebal ⊕ Enthe ⊕ Enthanay ⊕ In nomine Patris ⊕ et Filii ⊕ et Spiritus sancti ⊕ Amen. ⊕ Ihesu Nazarenus ⊕ Maria ⊕ Iohannes ⊕ Michael ⊕ Gabriel ⊕ Raphael ⊕ Verbum caro factum est ⊕.

Let it be closed afterwards in the manner of a letter so that it cannot be opened easily, and for this reason I used to write it in Greek letters that it might not be understanded of the people. And if one carries that written charm fairly in the name of God Almighty, and believes, without doubt, he will not be troubled with cramp.[7]

While, as Keith Thomas has said, it would be 'a gross travesty to suggest that the medieval Church deliberately held out to the laity an organized system of magic designed to bring supernatural remedies to bear upon earthly problems', the leaders of the Church did abandon the struggle against superstition whenever it seemed in their interest to do so.[8] And it was, indeed, impossible, even had it been desirable, to prevent medieval patients from believing in the magical properties of holy relics and devotional incantations. It was widely held that the wearing of verses from the gospels and of an *agnus dei* was a protection against calamity, disease and death; that the key of a church door was an efficacious remedy against rabies; that a Bible placed on the forehead was a cure for sleeplessness; that soil from a churchyard could ward off sickness; that the sign of the cross could keep evil spirits at bay; that splinters of martyrs' bones, chips from the holy cross or drops of Christ's blood were remedies for all manner of ills.

More than one authority maintained that it was possible to obtain a prognostication by 'taking the herb cinquefoil and, while collecting it, saying a Paternoster on behalf of the patient, and boiling it in a new jar with some of the water which the patient is destined to drink, and if the water be red in colour after this boiling, then the patient will die'. His death could also be foretold by counting up all the letters in the patient's name, the name of the servant sent to summon the doctor and the name of the day upon which the summons first arrived. 'If an even number result, the patient will not escape. If the number be odd then he will recover.'[9]

For the relief of pain during surgery there was little the doctor could do either by magic or by any other means, although it was claimed that by applying to the skin an ointment made from a variety of ingredients including henbane, mandragora, hemlock and black and white poppies 'he shall mow [be able to] suffre kuttyng in any place of the body without felying or akyng . . . Also the sede alon [of henbane] giffen in wyne to drynk maketh the drinker alsone for [immediately go] to sleep, that he schal noght fele whatso-ever is done to hym.' Certainly henbane could render a man unconscious, but if carelessly administered it could also kill him.

Some more enlightened doctors emphasized the importance of diet and exercise. Johannes Mirfield of St Bartholomew's suggested that invalids should be encouraged to drink wine and barley water and to eat honey, river-crab and dried figs.

Milk is of the greatest possible value [he also suggested for consumptives] especially if it be that of women; asses milk is next to be preferred, and then that of goats. The milk ought to be imbibed direct from the udder; but should this be impossible, then take a salver, which has been washed in hot water, and allow it to stand over another full of hot water; then let the animal be milked into the salver and the milk immediately proferred . . .

Moreover, wine should not be drunk during the whole period in which the milk remains in the stomach, for the wine causes the milk to coagulate, and this changes it into the nature of poison . . . The patient can also eat the flesh of all the usual kinds of fowl which fly, except of those which live on the water; likewise the flesh of kids, lambs, and unweaned calves, or of the young rabbit; also the extremities of animals (such as the feet and legs of little pigs), hens and their chickens, and the flesh of a year-old lamb: and of all these only a little should be taken, and but rarely, except in the case of flying fowl, and even this should be taken only in such a small quantity as to be digestible.

As for exercise, Johannes Mirfield considered that:

The first and most important [kind] of [exercise is] to walk abroad, choosing the uplands where the air is pure; this is the best of all. Riding is another form of exercise but this is only for the wealthy. It behoves prelates, however, to have some other method of taking exercise. Let such a man therefore, have a stout rope, knotted at the end, hanging up in his chamber; and then grasping the rope with both hands, let him raise himself up, and remain in that position for a long time without touching the ground . . . Another method of taking exercise is to hold the breath and impel it towards the head, or towards the belly, and this is extremely useful . . . Or if this pastime does not please him, let him hold in his hands a stone, weighing thirty pounds, in which a ring has been fixed, and carry it about frequently from one part of his dwelling to another; or let him hold this same stone up in the air for a long time before setting it down, or lift it to his neck, or between his hands.[10]

In the sixteenth century Andrew Boorde, the physician, whose *Dyetary of Health* and *Brevyary of Health* were both highly influential, emphasized the importance of a balanced diet and of ensuring that patients were given food suited to their temperaments. The phlegmatic man, for instance, should avoid white meat and fruit, the choleric hot spices; while fried meat was bad for the melancholic man, and garlic for the sanguine.

A good cook is half physician [Boorde wrote]. For the chief physic (the counsil of a physician excepted) doth come from the kitchen; wherefor the physician and the cook must consult together for the preparation of meat . . . For if the physician, without the cook, prepare any meat except he be very expert, he will make a worse dish of meat, that which the sick cannot take.[11]

The regulation of sleep was also important. Men and women of the sanguine and choleric temperaments needed only seven hours' sleep, but the phlegmatic ought to have nine and the melancholic even longer.

In Boorde's day new and efficacious drugs were coming into use. Ipecacuana, later to be used in the treatment of dysentery and as a constituent of expectorant mixtures in the treatment of bronchitis, had already been brought over from the New World. So had quinine although the uses of this as an antiseptic and anti-pyretic and in the treatment of malaria were not discovered until later. Tobacco had also been found in America and was used as a fumigant and, less dangerous than mandrake, as a narcotic during operations. Many supposed cures still relied upon magic: a garnet worn around the neck was supposed to alleviate melancholia, while spring water drunk from the skull of a murdered man was believed to cure the falling sickness. But there were far more remedies which were scientifically based, and the indisputably curative properties of various herbs and plants were now more widely known and made use of everywhere. Comfrey, as well as liquorice and calamint, was, for example, used effectively in the treatment of bronchitis. Drinking and bathing in the waters of spas benefited those who could afford to visit them.

At the same time the medical profession was becoming more respected. At the beginning of the sixteenth century there were still only a very few physicians who held a university degree, and of these most had taken a degree without actually examining a patient. There were even fewer surgeons who had obtained a licence from a university after having satisfied the authorities as to their competence. Most of those practising the craft were barber-surgeons, belonging to different guilds and allowed only to operate locally. Apothecaries were also grocers and pepperers. By the end of the century all this had changed.

The first step was taken in 1511 with a Medical Act whose preamble stated the problem with which it intended to deal:

> Physic and Surgery is daily within this Realm exercised by a great multitude of ignorant persons as common artificers, smiths, weavers and women who boldly and customably take upon them great cures and things of great difficulty in the which they partly use sorcery and witchcraft to the grievous hurt, damage, and destruction of many of the King's liege people.[12]

The Act required all physicians and surgeons to be graduates of a university or to be licensed by a bishop after examination by experts. Those who continued to practise in defiance of the Act were liable to be fined £5 a month. Shortly after this, Thomas Linacre, the king's physician and translator of Galen, who held a medical degree from Padua, obtained a royal charter authorizing him to establish a Company of Physicians. This company, whose meetings were held in Linacre's house near St Paul's, later became the Royal College of Physicians, the oldest medical institution in England. It was authorized to examine and grant licences to physicians throughout the country.

Soon after its establishment, the king's surgeon, Thomas Vicary, was granted permission to amalgamate all the various guilds of barbers and surgeons into one United Company of Barber-Surgeons. In the eighteenth century the surgeons were to leave the barbers and to form the Company of Surgeons which in 1800 became the Royal College of Surgeons of England. But, although united in name in 1540, the two practitioners had different crafts assigned to them: the surgeons operated on the body, the barbers on the teeth. Later, the apothecaries followed the example of the surgeons and the physicians by separating themselves from the ancient Grocers' Company and by setting up the Society of Apothecaries.

By then the hospitals of the country had also been reformed.

Numerous hospitals had been built in England since 1123 when Rahere had founded St Bartholomew's Hospital in London in fulfilment of a vow he is supposed to have made when recovering from malarial fever in a hospice on the Tiber island of S. Bartolomeo in Rome. By 1300 there were some 750 hospitals of various kinds in England. Many were established by the Church, others by trade and professional guilds, some, like Bartholomew's, by private benefactors. In addition to these, infirmaries were maintained by abbeys and monasteries. But these, as the medical historian Frederick F. Cartwright has observed, were mainly for the religious houses' own sick and aged brethren and only occasionally for travellers and strangers, the part played by the monastery in caring for the laity having been overestimated in the past, and the function of the parish church and priest being virtually overlooked. Churches, in fact, were often used as hospitals, the patients being crowded into the aisles in time of pestilence; and the more conscientious clergy considered it part of their duty not only to visit the sick but to use what medical knowledge they had in order to treat them. When hospitals were built, they, like manorial halls, frequently followed the design of churches, with beds in the aisles, perhaps divided into cubicles, a day-room in the centre where the nave of the church would have been, and a chapel at the east end.[13]

The treatment in these hospitals was necessarily primitive. Patients were commonly nursed by those less ill, though in some hospitals and infirmaries there were paid attendants. The doctors, intent upon the care rather than the cure of their charges and generally clinging to the orthodox Christian view that illness being divinely inflicted must be supernaturally alleviated, rarely administered any medicaments, relying upon the soothing qualities of various herbs and spices to bring relief. The remedies, potions, elixirs, nostrums and panaceas of itinerant quacks, such as decoctions of hog-lice as a cure for consumption, were, therefore, much sought after by the sick while the services of outside surgeons and barbers were necessary when any operations, including the usual blood-letting, were to be performed. These surgeons were laymen since churchmen, by decree of the Council of Tours of 1163, were forbidden to practise any treatment involving the shedding of blood; and while not actually forbidden – though it has been widely held to have been so because of a misreading of a papal bull prohibiting the boiling of the corpses of crusaders so that their bones could be more easily returned home for burial – dissection was disapproved of by the Church which believed in physical resurrection. The Church, indeed, disapproved of the study of medicine generally by clergy since the body was not a matter for their concern and 'men vowed to religion should not touch those things which cannot honourably be mentioned in speech'. The early twelfth-century Abbot Faricius of Abingdon was considered unsuitable for a bishopric because he had practised as a physician before he became a monk.

At universities, which were under the jurisdiction of the Church, medical teaching was almost exclusively oral, consisting of the reading of and commenting on inaccurate Latin versions of Greek and Arabian writers; and for anatomical instruction the student had to rely upon surgical works in manuscript or upon private tutors. This contributed to extraordinary errors of belief, it being generally held that the stomach was a kind of cauldron in which food was cooked by the heat of the liver and that in the words of Bernard de Gourdon, professor at Montpelier, the stomach 'possesses the power of attracting food to itself'.

Yet if anything approaching expert surgery could not be expected in early medieval hospitals, most of those received into them were not in need of surgery anyway. The varieties of patient admitted into such a hospital as St Bartholomew's or St Thomas's, also originally a twelfth-century foundation, were described by Robert Copland's gate-porter:

> They that be at such mischief
> That for their living can do no labour
> And have no friends to do them succour:
> As old people sick and impotent,
> Poor women in childbed here have easement,
> Weak men sore wounded by great violence
> And sore men eaten with pox and pestilence,
> And honest folk fallen in great poverty
> By mischance or other infirmity;
> Wayfaring men and maimed soldiers
> Have their relief in this poor-house of ours;
> And all others which we deem good and plain
> Have their lodgings here for a night or twain;
> Bedrid folks and such as cannot crave
> In these places most relief they have,
> And if they hap within our place to die
> Then are they buried well and honestly.
> But not every unsick stubborn knave
> For then we should over many have.[14]

Most hospitals in England, however, were as ready to open their doors to all those in need of their protection as St Mary's, Chichester, which was founded in 1172 and which undertook gladly to receive and assign a bed to 'anyone in infirm health and destitute of friends . . . until he shall recover. In regard to the poor people who are received late at night and go forth early in the morning, let the warden take care that their feet are washed and, as far as possible, their necessities attended to.' Most hospitals also undertook to take care of sick and weary travellers and pilgrims; and many were accordingly established on the roads to such places as Canterbury and Walsingham.

All over the country there were hospitals for lepers, perhaps as many as 100 in all, leprosy being so dreaded a disease from the tenth until the fifteenth century that, although probably no more than five in 1000 of the population suffered from it at any one time, it was treated as a crime and sufferers from it as outcasts under the statute *De Leproso Amovendo*. Archbishop Lanfranc built a leper hospital for over 100 lepers at Harbledown near Canterbury, but most lazar houses — as they were called after the beggar who, in the parable recorded by St Luke, lay at the rich man's gate 'full of sores' — were small establishments caring for less than forty sufferers; many had less than five inhabitants; twelve was considered ideal, this being a number coinciding with that of Christ and his eleven apostles. They were often endowed with land so that the inmates could be largely self-sufficient. The hospital dedicated to St James the Less, Bishop of Jerusalem, a lazar house for young women which was transformed by King Henry VIII into St James's Palace, had extensive grounds in what is now St James's Park where the lepers kept their hogs. Other leper hospitals possessed farmland, some-times tilled by labourers who did not suffer from the disease, the only outsiders whom the inmates ever saw, apart perhaps from the occasional glimpse of a procurator who went about collecting money for their main-tenance. The master or warden was generally a leper himself, so were the prioresses who governed the lazar houses for women and the segregated parts of those hospitals where both sexes were accommodated, usually in groups of primitive cottages around a chapel situated near a mineral spring whose waters might alleviate, though never cure, the disease. Conditions in all lazar houses were unpleasantly severe. In 1313 the inmates of a lazar house at Kingston rioted against the strictness of their regime and destroyed their own hospital. It was not only that their movements were so closely watched, but also that the futile attempts at curing their disease were so unpleasant. Being washed in the curative waters of a holy well, such as that beside which the leprosaria was built in the Leicestershire village of Burton Lazars, was no doubt perfectly unexceptionable. After all Naaman, the leprous captain of the host of the King of Syria, had been cured, as recorded in the Second Book of Kings, by dipping himself seven times in the waters of Jordan. But painful plastering, restricted diets, blood-letting and purging were also regularly prescribed, as was a remedy concocted from leeks boiled with adders.[15]

Once diagnosed as a leper by a jury or a panel of clergy, the leper was outcast from society; and a special Church office, not, however, usually followed in all its particulars, was prescribed for his banishment. He was taken from his house to church as though he were already dead; and in church he was told to kneel down before the altar between two trestles upon which black cloths had been hung. After he had heard Mass a priest cast earth on his feet with a spade and pronounced, 'Be thou dead to the World, but alive unto God.' The priest then made him swear never

> . . . to enter churches, or go into a market, or a mill, or a bakehouse, or unto any assemblies of people. Also I forbid you ever to wash your hands or even your belongings in spring or stream of water of any kind; and if you are thirsty you must drink water from your cup or from some other vessel. Also I forbid you ever henceforth to go out without your leper's dress, that you may be recognised by others; and you must not go outside your house unshod. Also I forbid you, wherever you may be, to touch anything which you wish to buy.[16]

The leper was also made to swear never to eat or drink with clean persons, nor even talk to them unless standing to the windward side; never to touch a child; always to stand clear of strangers when begging for the scraps of food which would be thrown at him from a distance. He must give warning of his approach by a bell of wooden clappers and wear a distinctive cloak and hood. Female lepers had to wear thick veils. Unless a place was found for him in a lazar house, the leper was provided with a primitive hut in which to shelter, with a bowl in which he could keep such alms as he might collect, and the bell or rattle prescribed by the Church office.[17]

As the incidence of leprosy increased in the thirteenth century, so the regulations governing the control of lepers became ever more stringent. In 1276 the Assize of London decreed that no leper should, under any circumstances, be allowed into the city; and in 1310 barbers were placed at the gates to assist the porters in detecting any leprous person who might illegally endeavour to gain admittance. At Berwick-on-Tweed it was ordained that no leper should come within the gates of the borough; and, if one got in by chance, the sergeant was enjoined 'to put him out at once'. 'If one wilfully forces his way in,' the regulations continued, 'his clothes shall be taken off him and burned, and he shall be turned out naked. For we have already taken care that a proper place for lepers shall be kept outside the town, and that alms shall be given there to them.'[18]

It being supposed, with some justification, that one of the causes of leprosy was the consumption of rotten fish, town authorities frequently issued regulations, such as that made at Berwick: 'If there be no leper-folk, the rotten pork or salmon shall be utterly destroyed.' At Oxford, when the city granted the Chancellor of the university jurisdiction over the market, he was required to forfeit 'all flesh or fish that shall be found to be putrid, unclean, vicious or otherwise unfit . . . on this condition that the things forfeited be given to the Hospital of St John'.[19]

Leprosy began to decline in England at the beginning of the fourteenth century when, in those lean and hungry years, lepers were the first to die. In the subsequent years of plague more lepers were carried off, particularly in the more densely populated areas of the south and east; and by the end of the Black Death there was no further need for the establishment of new lazar houses while some of those already in existence were being converted to other purposes. The only foundation after 1347 is that of William Pole in 1411 on land granted by Henry IV who, it has been suggested, may have had leprosy himself, though it is evidently more likely that he was suffering from an unusually painful form of eczema. By the end of the fifteenth century, leprosy had been wiped out except in the extreme north and west.[20]

As the number of lazar houses declined, other hospitals began to offer more specialized treatment than those of the early Middle Ages. In some the old were cared for, in others sick travellers and pilgrims, in a few the insane, in several orphans and unmarried mothers. Holy Trinity Hospital, Salisbury, established in 1379, cared for 'lying-in women until delivered, recovered and churched' as well as for the 'mad until their senses return'. Both St Mary Without Bishopsgate and St Bartholomew's in London undertook to provide for the babies of women who died in childbirth until the children were seven years old. St Thomas's Hospital had eight beds, endowed in 1423 by Richard Whittington who stipulated that women should be treated in confidence so that their chances of marriage should not be impaired. The Priory Hospital of St Mary's Within Cripplegate, known as Elsing Spital after its founder, a rich mercer, William de Elsing, was established in about 1329 for blind men and women. Bethlehem Hospital, which was founded as the Priory of St Mary Bethlehem outside Bishopsgate in 1247 and had a hospital attached in 1329, cared for 'distracted' patients from 1377, that was to say it kept them chained to the wall by leg or ankle and, when violent, had them ducked in water or whipped.[21]

Many hospitals were closed by the Dissolution of the Monasteries, and for long the king, preoccupied with other problems, had resisted their re-establishment. In 1538 the citizens of London petitioned the king and sought leave to refound the hospitals themselves once their old possessions had been returned to them:

For the aid and comfort of the poor sick, blind, aged and impotent persons, being not able to help themselves, nor having any place certain wherein they may be lodged, cherished and refreshed till they be cured and holpen of their diseases and sickness. For the help of the said poor people, we inform your Grace that there be near or within the City of London three hospitals or spitels, commonly called Saint Mary Spitel, Saint Bartholomew Spitel, and Saint Thomas Spitel, founded of good devotion by ancient fathers and endowed with great possessions and rents . . . [If permission to refound these hospitals were to be granted] a great number of poor, needy, sick and indigent persons shall be refreshed, maintained, comforted, found, healed and cured of their infirmities, frankly and freely by physicians, surgeons and apothecaries . . . so that all impotent persons not able to labour shall be relieved and all sturdy beggars not willing to labour shall be punished, so that with God's grace few or no persons shall be seen abroad to beg or ask alms.[22]

The petition went unheeded. St Mary Spital, which had been founded in 1197 and which, when it was closed in 1538, had 180 beds with two patients in each, lay deserted. So did St Bartholomew's, which was described in 1540 as 'vacant and altogether destitute of a master and all fellows and brethren'. So, also, did St Thomas's which, established in about 1106 and later dedicated to St Thomas the Martyr, had been closed after a visitation by Thomas Cromwell who described it as Southwark's 'bawdy hospital' and recommended that Becket should be 'decanonised'.[23]

Of these three hospitals, St Mary Spital was never reopened; but in the reign of Edward VI permission was granted to re-establish St Thomas's as a hospital for the sick and aged, at first with twenty beds. At about the same time Christ's Hospital was founded for orphans who were to be provided with the distinctive long blue coats and yellow stockings which are still worn by the boys of the school, now rehoused at Horsham in Sussex, the colour of the stockings being chosen, so it is said, to keep away the rats from the orphans' ankles. Three hundred and eighty orphans were collected for the hospital but 'many of them, taken from the dunghill, when they came to swete and cleane keping and to pure dyett, dyed down righte'.[24] Also at this time, the royal palace of Bridewell, which had been built for Henry VIII on the banks of the Fleet river, was made over to the City of London for the reception of vagrants and homeless children and for the punishment of petty offenders and disorderly women.[25] And the hospital of St Mary Bethlehem, more commonly known as Bedlam, was re-established as a lunatic asylum. By then St Bartholomew's had also reopened; in 1549 three surgeons were appointed, and in 1568 Dr Rodrigo Lopez, soon afterwards to be hanged at Tyburn accused of trying to poison Queen Elizabeth I, became the hospital's first physician.[26]

Elsewhere in the country other hospitals were restored and refounded and, while conditions in many of them were little better than they had been in the medieval past, they were slowly improving.

Plague, however, had become endemic and was now as widely feared as leprosy. At the beginning of the century there had been several outbreaks of what became known as sweating sickness, the last of which, in 1551, started in Shrewsbury and carried off almost a thousand people within a few days. Apart from profuse sweating and 'grete stynking', the disease was characterized by a sense of deep foreboding, high fever, a violent headache, dizziness, abdominal pains and, in some sufferers, a vesicular rash, 'grete pricking in their bodies' and black spots. Death came with frightening suddenness. A French doctor, who was in England at the time of the first epidemic, recorded:

> We saw two priests standing together and speaking and both of them die suddenly. The wife of a tailor was also taken and died as suddenly. Another young man walking by the street fell down suddenly. Also another gentleman riding out of the city . . . Also many others the which were too long to rehearse we have known that have died suddenly.[27]

In this epidemic 'a wonderful number' died in London including the lord mayor and the man elected to succeed him, as well as five aldermen; and there were numerous deaths in other towns as well. In a third epidemic 400 students were reported to have died in Oxford; others perished in Cambridge; several deaths occurred in Cardinal Wolsey's household and after the king's Latin secretary died, Sir Thomas More told Erasmus that there was 'less danger in the ranks of war' than in London. During a subsequent outbreak the French ambassador was on a visit to the Archbishop of Canterbury in whose household 'there died eighteen persons in four hours and hardly anyone escaped'. People left the towns to seek safety in the countryside, but the sweating sickness might strike anywhere.[28] In 1551 in the small Devonshire parish of Uffculme, where there were thirty-eight burials in the whole year, twenty-seven of them took place in the first fortnight of August and all those interred were listed in the register as having died of 'the hock-sickness or stop-gallant'. It was known by this name, a contemporary clergyman explained, because it 'posted through England and spared none. There were some dancing in the court at nine o'clock that were dead at eleven.'[29]

Virulent as was the sweating sickness, however, the plague which broke out in England in 1563 was much more so. In that year, so John Stow recorded, there died in London alone 'of all diseases 70,372, and of the plague, being part of the number aforesaid, 17,404'. There had been previous outbreaks almost as malignant. In 1499–1500 there were 20,000 deaths; in September 1513 the Venetian envoy said that it was perilous to remain in London where there were 200 deaths a day; all the Venetian merchants had taken houses in the country and there was no business doing. In February 1514 Erasmus declared himself disgusted with London where it was unsafe to walk the streets because of plague: in going to St Paul's the king preferred to be on horseback 'to avoid contact with the crowd by reason of the plague'. Three years later when contagion returned the court kept away from London altogether until public criticism led to its return in March, where-upon three pages died and it withdrew again to Berkshire. In 1531 it with-drew from London once more, first to Greenwich, then, feeling unsafe there, to Southampton. Four years after this, plague once more drove the court from London to Thornbury in Gloucestershire. On each occasion the richer citizens left with them. 'I met with wagones, cartes and horses full laden,' a beggar says in Bulein's *Dialogue* of 1564. 'For years of the blacke Pestilence [they left the city, taking] with them boxes of medicens and sweete perfumes. O God! How fast did they run, and were afraid of eche other for feare of smitying.' But most could not afford to leave and had nowhere to go; and of these hundreds died.[30]

From time to time plague regulations were issued in an attempt to check the spread of the pestilence which was believed to be largely due to 'stinking carrion . . . and the corruption of privies cast into the water nigh to cities or towns . . . the casting of foul things in the streets [which makes] the air corrupt . . . the keeping of stinking matters in houses or latrines long time', and the wandering through the streets of infected dogs. In London orders were given to 'cause all the welles and pumps to be drawen iii times everye weke . . . and to cast down into the canelles [gutters] at everye such drawying xii bucketts full of water at the least, to cleanse the streets wythall . . . All persons having dogs in their houses other than hounds, spaniels or mastiffs necessary for the custody or safe keeping of their houses' were to 'convey them forthwith out of the city, or cause them to be killed and carried out of the city and buried at the common laystall'. Bonfires containing frankincense and herbs were to be lit in the streets to fumigate the air.[31]

A 'precept issued to the aldermen' in 1543 contains further regulations:

That no person who should be afflicted with the plague, should go abroad or into any company for one month after his sickness, and that all others who could not live without their daily labour should as much as in them lay refrain from going abroad . . .

That every person whose house had been infected should, after a visitation, carry all the straw and clothes of the infected in the fields to be cured.

That no housekeeper should put any person diseased out of his house into the street or other place unless they provided housing for them in some other house . . .

That the churchwardens of every parish should employ somebody to keep out all common beggars out of churches on holy days, and to cause them to remain without doors.

That all the streets, lanes, etc. within the wards should be cleansed.

That the aldermen should cause this precept to be read in the churches.[32]

Infected houses were at first distinguished by bundles of hay or straw hanging from the windows, then by a blue – later a red – cross of St Anthony painted on canvas or on board and nailed to the post of the street door with the legend, 'Lord have mercy on us'. Their occupants were required when walking abroad to carry in their hands a white rod two feet – after 1581 a yard – long. With each fresh outbreak the regulations were repeated and grew more severe. More and more dogs were slaughtered, and by 1563 cats, too, were being killed. The regulations of 1568 made quarantine more severe by ordering that 'all infected persons be shutt up and noe person to come forth in twenty dayes after the infection'; and in 1581 the two 'honest and discrete matrons', who were appointed in each parish to examine the bodies of all the dead and report to the parish clerk the names of the victims of plague, were threatened with 'imprisonment in such sorte as may serve the terror of others' should they 'through favour or corruption give a wrong certificate'. For the protection of the queen at Windsor Castle a gallows was set up in the market-place of the town 'to hang all such as should come there from London'; and it was decreed that 'no wares to be brought to, or through, or by Windsor; nor anyone on the river by Windsor to carry wood or other stuff to or from London upon pain of hanging without any judgement'. 'Such people as received any wares out of London into Windsor were turned out of their houses and their houses were shut up.'[33]

Yet no measures taken to prevent the spread of plague proved fully effective; and epidemics, if not as frequently as in the past, continued to break out with equal violence until the Great Plague of 1664–5 brought them to a fearful climax. There were at least 10,000 deaths from plague in 1593; and in 1603 almost 3000 people died in the city of London alone. All who had the means fled, but they were not well received in the country: 'The sight of a Londoner's flat cap was dreadful, a treble ruff threw a village into a sweat.' After one outbreak John Taylor, the 'Water Poet', wrote:

> Milk maids and farmers' wives are grown so nice
> They think a citizen a cockatrice.

In London, so Taylor said,

> All trades are dead, or almost out of breath,
> But such as live by sickness and by death.

Many, if not most, physicians fled with the other refugees, and the care of the sick was left in the hands of quacks and herbalists who made large profits, as did the parish sextons. But none of the cures recommended proved effective, though many were tried, including the strapping of cakes of arsenic under the armpits. Water was still polluted by the shambles, most of which were left undisturbed within the city; and orders for the erection of pest houses 'and other places of abode for infected persons' were not issued until 1635 when about 10,400 people died in London. When the last epidemic was over it is believed that 156,463 victims in all had been claimed.[34]

Meanwhile, people were also dying in large numbers of syphilis, a highly infectious disease which seems to have been reintroduced to Europe from Africa or the West Indies in about 1490 and which became widespread after the return from America of Columbus's sailors. The disease was at first not always sexually transmitted. King Henry VIII was alleged to have been infected by the 'perilous and infective breath' of Wolsey, according to the Articles of Arraignment which charged the cardinal with all manner of offences. It was known as the Neapolitan disease, since the soldiers of Charles V contracted it in Naples, as the *lues venera*, as the Spanish pox, but more often as the French pox.[35]

> If one were to seek among the diseases of the body for that which ought to be awarded the first place, [Erasmus wrote in 1525] it seems to my judgement that it is due to that evil, of uncertain origin, which has now been raging with impunity in all the countries of the world . . . What clings more tenaciously? What repels more vigorously the art and care of physicians? What passes more easily by contagion to another? What brings more cruel tortures . . . This *lues* is a foul, cruel contagious disease, dangerous to life, apt to remain in the system and to break out anew not otherwise than the gout.[36]

There was no satisfactory cure. Some doctors prescribed cauterization with red-hot irons, others various medicines. John Barrister, author of a book on ulcers published in 1575, recommended 'a thinne diet with the decoction of guaiacum or universal unctions ex Hydrargyro'. Many sufferers consulted quacks such as the Flemish mountebank who set up his stall in Gloucester and hung forth 'his pictures, his flags, his instruments and his letters of mart with long lybells, great tossells, broad scales in boxes and the like counterfeit shows and knacks of knavery, cozening the people of their money, without either learning or knowledge'.[37]

William Clowes, surgeon to St Bartholomew's Hospital and author of *A Short and Profitable Treatise touching the Cure of the Disease called (Morbus Gallicus) by Unctions*, was as bewildered by the disease, its origins and constitutional effects as anyone else. He believed it was not spread only by sexual licence and wrote of 'good poor people that be infected by unwary eating or drinking or keeping company with those lewd beasts, and which either for shame will not bewray it, or for lack of good chirurgions know not how to remedy it'. But he believed its main cause was the 'licentious and beastly disorder of a great number of rogues and vagabonds, the filthye lyfe of many lewd and idell persons, both men and women, and the great number of lewd alehouses which are very nests and harbourers of such filthy creatures . . . By means of which disordered persons some other of better disposition are many times infected.'

In St Bartholomew's alone Clowes claimed to have treated over 1000 patients suffering from the disease; and he spoke 'nothing of St Thomas Hospital and other howses about the city wherein an infinite multitude [were] dayly in cure'.[38]

Occasional measures were taken to combat the spread of the disease. In 1506 an order was given to shut down the stews of Bankside in Southwark where eighteen wooden brothels, their steps running down to the river, were distinguished by painted signs like taverns. Yet twelve of them soon opened their doors again and customers were entertained as usual. By the beginning of the next century, however, syphilis was becoming less virulent and starting to take on its present characteristics as a chronic venereal disease.

Smallpox, though, was now beginning to be dreaded as much as the plague had once been. The symptoms of this disease were described by Thomas Phaer in his *Book of Children* as

> . . . itch and fretting of the skin as if it had been rubbed with nettles, pain in the head and back, sometimes as it were a dry scab or lepry spreading over all the members, other whiles in pushes, pimples and whaylys with much corruption and matter, and with great pains of the face and throat, dryness of the tongue, hoarseness of voice, and in some, quiverings of the heart.

If the patient were to recover the skin was likely to be badly pitted.

In treating Edward of Caernarvon, first Prince of Wales, however, John of Gaddesden, his mother's physician, had prevented the appearance of the characteristic and unsightly marks by adopting an old Arabic custom and wrapping the patient in red cloth and hanging red material over the windows.

Yet, although Queen Elizabeth I herself contracted smallpox, the disease never became as widespread as either the plague or syphilis in Tudor England. The full effects of its ravages were to be suffered later.

# PART TWO

## The Ages of Shakespeare and Milton

# 14 · *Villagers, Vagrants and Vagabonds*

In the late 1530s the King's Antiquary, John Leland, 'a most vainglorious man' in the opinion of a friend, embarked upon a tour of England which lasted for six years. When his journey was over he told the king:

> I have travelled in your dominions both by the sea coasts and in the middle parts, sparing neither labour nor costs . . . There is almost neither cape nor bay, haven, creek or pier, river or confluence of rivers, beaches, washes, lakes, meres, fenny waters, mountains, valleys, moors, heaths, forests, woods, cities, boroughs, castles, principal manor places, monasteries and colleges, but I have seen them; and noted in so doing a whole world of things very memorable.[1]

He planned to publish his findings in fifty volumes, describing both the present aspect of all the counties of England and Wales and their remains. But before he had finished his exhausting work he was pronounced incurably insane, and it was left to others to bring out his *Itinerary* from his mountainous assortment of topographical notes.

Much of the country which Leland saw had altered little from the land that Chaucer knew. It was still open land, without hedges or fences, the huge fields, divided by ridges and grass-covered paths into strips and patches, spreading endlessly across the countryside. There were the same meadows where grass for the hay harvest grew, the same crops of wheat and barley, the same fallow fields and downland pasture, the same waste patches in which pigs snuffled in their endless search for bits of food. For mile after mile in the Midlands, in Northamptonshire and Hampshire, in Berkshire, Wiltshire and Dorset, in Norfolk and elsewhere the landscape rolled away like this, largely unaffected by the passing years. In the still undrained fens of Cambridge, Lincoln and Huntingdon men could be seen moving about over the water-logged land in skerries or on stilts, going to milk the thin and scrawny cows on the islands surrounding their village or bringing home baskets full of wild duck and geese and the thousands of eels with which they paid their rents. To the north were the moors and dales of Yorkshire, and beyond them the wild border country of the Percy and Neville families, Earls of Northumberland and Westmorland, where men, regardless of the laws of the south, rode out on cattle and kidnapping raids through the high grass and heather and the wildernesses of moss. And to the west was Wales, no longer an alien place kept in check by the lords of the marches in their castles along the border, but now an integral part of the country, whose people were proud to retain their language, their music and their poetry but proud also to have supplied in the Tudors a Welsh dynasty for the English throne and content to have their counties represented in the Parliament at Westminster. There were those, of course, who regretted the passing of the old Welsh feudalism and tribalism; and there were those Englishmen who found, as William Camden was to do, that the wild and mountainous parts of the principality were 'rough all over and unpleasant to see, with craggy stones, hanging rocks and rugged ways', that Radnor, in particular was 'hideous after a sort to behold, by reason of the turning and crooked by-ways and craggy mountains'.[2] Yet elsewhere in Wales the countryside was charming, the small farms well tended in the traditional way, the fields, like those in Flintshire, 'in some places barley, in others wheat, but generally throughout rye . . . and afterwards four or five crops together of oats'.[3]

While the appearance of much of the landscape had remained unchanged for centuries, however, there were large areas that were being transformed by new methods of agriculture which were bringing the common-field system to an end. Large village farms were being split up into various smaller farms; land was being enclosed and fenced to turn arable into pasture; common land was being encroached upon and brought within more profitable holdings. This was happening in several parts of the country, from Essex in the east to Devon in the west; and experts were generally agreed that it made for far more remunerative farming. John Norden, the mapmaker, who toured England some years after Leland had done, estimated that one acre farmed in the new way was half as profitable again as it had been when farmed in the old;[4] while Thomas Tusser, the Old Etonian East Anglian farmer, thought that enclosures made land three times as remunerative:

> More plenty of mutton and beef,
> Corn, butter and cheese of the best,
> More wealth anywhere (to be brief)
> More People, more handsome and prest
> Where find ye – go search any coast,
> Than there where enclosure is most.[5]

The numbers of sheep to be seen were, indeed, enormous. At one place in Norfolk, so John Norden wrote, there were fed 'above 30,000 sheep and the place is so fruitful that if overnight a wand or rod be laid upon it, by the morning it shall be covered with grass of that night's growth and not to be discerned'. The Spencers in Northamptonshire also had 30,000 sheep; and it was upon their flocks that the fortunes of the family were built.[6] Between 1540 and 1546 the price of wool rose from 6s 8d a tod (28 lb) to 20s 8d, having already risen between 1510 and 1520; and increasing numbers of landlords converted their land to sheep pasture so as to enjoy the higher profits. It was a process which was widely condemned and held responsible for the inflation of prices which began in about 1530. The author of the *Decaye of England* expressed a common belief when he wrote:

> The more shepe, the dearer is the woll,
> The more shepe, the dearer is the mutton,
> The more shepe, the dearer is the beefe,
> The more shepe, the dearer is the corne,
> The more shepe, the skanter is the white meat,
> The more shepe, the fewer eggs for a penny.[7]

Later in the century the price of wool fell, while that of wheat rose and a return to arable farming consequently took place. But by then many agricultural labourers had been thrown out of work by the change to sheep farming, which required fewer men than arable, and those who could not find work again swelled the growing ranks of the unemployed.

In most parts of the country the same crops had been grown and the same sorts of implements used for centuries; but new ones were being introduced. Wooden ploughs were still in general use, though these were often now to be seen shod with iron; and horses, if still less common than oxen, were not so rarely used as draught animals. Since the 1520s hops had been grown in Suffolk as well as in Kent and the slightly bitter beer flavoured with them was preferred by most men to the traditional ale now normally reserved for the old and ill, women and children.[8] Flax was grown in Lincolnshire; hemp in Sussex, Dorset and Somerset; saffron widely in Essex where Saffron Walden had been so called for some time past. Kent and Devon were celebrated for their orchards, Suffolk for its horses, Cheshire, Worcestershire and Suffolk for their cheeses. The increasing demands of the towns, particularly of London, strongly influenced the produce supplied by the surrounding countryside, while the needs of growing industries, of shipbuilding and housing, hop-growing and glass-making all entailed the continuous supply of large loads of fuel.

Forests were certainly shrinking in size; and contemporaries constantly lamented the loss of trees and protested that the whole aspect of the countryside was being ruined. 'As the woods here decay,' wrote a man from Worcestershire, 'so the glass houses remove and follow the woods with small change.' William Camden observed the thinning of the woods in Wiltshire and Dorset; while, writing of the Forest of Arden in Warwickshire, the poet, Michael Drayton, quoted by Dr Rowse, complained:

> For, when the world found out the fitness of my soil
> The gripple wretch began immediately to spoil
> My tall and goodly woods and did my grounds enclose:
> By which in little time my bounds I came to lose.[9]

To be sure there were still vast tracts of the countryside covered with timber – much of Staffordshire was still a huge oak forest – and recent research has shown that the price which it fetched rose more slowly than those of any other agricultural product;[10] yet the concern felt at the time was widespread, and industry was undoubtedly beginning to be voracious in its demands for wood and charcoal.

Textiles remained the most profitable industry. The work was still largely done at home, looms being set up in cottages and hired out by clothiers. But already there were fulling-mills; and one clothier, John Winchcomb, known to posterity as Jack of Newbury, was credited, later in the sixteenth century, by a popular ballad with having a large and improbably jolly factory:

> Within one room, being large and long
> There stood two hundred looms full strong.
> Two hundred men, the truth is so,
> Wrought in these rooms all in a row.
> By every one a pretty boy
> Sate making quilts with mickle joy.
> And in another place hard by
> A hundred women merrily
> Were carding with joyful cheer
> Who singing sat with voices clear.[11]

This is a fanciful picture, both as to numbers and to merriment; but although the overwhelming majority of the working population of the country still laboured on the land, the beginnings of England's industrial future could already be discerned. An ingenious clergyman, William Lee, saddened, so it is said, by the sight of his wife spending evening after evening knitting stockings by hand, put his mind to the invention of a knitting frame which was soon in use in the hosiery industry in Leicestershire and Nottinghamshire.

There had long been tin-mines in Cornwall and Devon. Now there was widespread mining for lead and copper, iron and coal, in several places supervised by foreign immigrants. In 1561 overtures were made to an experienced German firm to help with the opening up of mines in the north. The Germans were at first reluctant to share their secrets with Englishmen. But four years later fifty German miners landed at Newcastle, a copper-mine was opened up at Newlands, and soon, so the queen was informed, 'fine and perfect copper' was being made. The immigrants settled down well in England: several married English wives; another, according to an entry in the Crosthwaite register, had an illegitimate child. They went to church in Crosthwaite; they bought an island on the lake, planted fruit trees and built a brewery and a pig-house; they acted in plays, practised archery, baited bears; they sent home money and asked for fishing tackle and books.[12]

While these Germans were working happily in the Lake District, other foreigners were helping in the development of mines in the West Country where ore of zinc, mixed with copper for the making of brass, had been found near Bath. Soon a profitable wire works had been established at Tintern. There were lead-mines in the Mendips and silver-mines in Devon. Saltpetre was being dug and there were several mills in Surrey where George Evelyn, grandfather of the diarist, had obtained a monopoly for the manufacture of gunpowder, a right which added immensely to the family's fortunes. Elsewhere there were ironworks and salt pans, paper-mills and gun foundries. In the Weald of Kent there were blast furnaces beside the forges, and by 1565 steel was also being produced there. Coal, known as sea-coal because it was shipped down the coasts by boat, was being mined in ever-increasing quantities, and was being used not only in numerous manufacturing processes but also in private houses whose hearths and chimneys had to be reconstructed on account of the thick smoke which it gave off. By 1564 as many as 33,000 tons of coal a year were being shipped from Newcastle to London; and by 1598 these shipments had risen to 163,000 tons.[13]

The colliers that plied between the northern ports and London, were, as G. M. Trevelyan observed, one of the two chief nurseries of English seamen. The other was the fishing fleets that sailed out of the harbours of Devon and Cornwall – bringing cod back from as far away as the shores of Newfoundland – and from Lynn and Yarmouth and other east coast ports in search of herring. The fishermen, many of them fighting sailors in time of war, were helped by the government which insisted upon the observance of 'fish days' for economical as much as religious reasons, insisting upon the punishment of such offenders as the woman pilloried for serving meat in her tavern during Lent, and stressing the importance of maintaining the skills and numbers of seafaring men in an age when England's interests were becoming more and more maritime. By encouraging the fishing industry the government also helped to revive wasted towns, to keep down the consumption of beef and mutton, to reduce the amount of arable land converted into pasture and thus the numbers of workless men, the constant worry of every Tudor administration.[14]

The maintenance of order, both in the repression of the rebellious poor and the subjugation of the over-ambitious rich, was seen as the prime responsibility of government. Every part of society, wrote Richard Hooker in his influential *Laws of Ecclesiastical Polity*, expressing a commonly held opinion, must have 'one head or governor'. This held true of the family, just as it held true of the State as a whole. Men were learning to accept the authority of the Crown as their ordained ruler; and local authorities and local customs were giving way to central government. At the same time the power of the craft guilds was declining; and wages and prices, conditions of trade, industry and of apprenticeship were all coming under the control of the State. A Statute of Artificers, for example, which was enacted in 1563 decreed that all craftsmen, whether in town or country, had to learn their crafts for seven years under a responsible master, since 'until a man grows into 23 years, he for the most part, though not always, is wild, without judgement and not of sufficient experience to govern himself'. Not until that age could he either become a master on his own or offer himself as a journeyman for hire. The statute also directed magistrates in each county to fix rates of wages for all grades of labour according 'to the plenty or scarcity of the time'.[15]

Neither increasing respect for local government, nor the activities of the most conscientious justices of the peace in dealing with miscreants and social and political malcontents could, however, prevent the frequent eruption of riots and local disturbances and the occasional widespread rebellion. On Evil May Day in London in 1517, an immense mob of apprentices, ruffians and disillusioned clerics, incited by a preacher at St Paul's Cross and led by a xenophobic broker, attacked the houses and workshops of foreign merchants and craftsmen and was brought under control only after troops had been called in, guns fired from the Tower and 400 prisoners taken. In 1536 a protest in Lincolnshire against the dissolution of smaller monasteries sparked off the Pilgrimage of Grace in which feudal magnates, opposed to the extension of royal control over the northern counties, and peasants, protesting against the enclosure of arable lands for pasture, joined forces in improbable alliance against the Crown. A few years later two other rebel armies were up in arms, while there were further serious anti-enclosure riots;

and in 1554 some 3000 men from Kent, led by Sir Thomas Wyatt, marched upon London in protest against the proposed marriage of Queen Mary to Philip II of Spain. The rebels got as far as London Bridge but so many cannon were brought against them they had to retire to Kingston. Wyatt was arrested and brought to the Tower, and he and about 100 of his followers were executed. Within the next few years there were yet more riots by apprentices in London, this time against the city government, and by poor people in the country, once more against enclosures.

There was no doubt that the grievances of the country people were justified. There was widespread unemployment, appalling destitution and a burning resentment that the Dissolution of the Monasteries had accelerated an inclination by landowners to consider their estates as commercial assets to be fully exploited for quick profits, rather than as valued possessions enabling whole communities to supply their own needs. Most of the land appropriated by the Crown did not pass from the religious houses to the so-called 'new man' of Tudor society, but into the hands of existing local landowners, two-thirds of all peers being granted or purchasing monastic estates. Yet both those 'new men' who did manage to acquire them, and those more numerous older families that did so – as well as those speculators who turned refectories into forges and monastic guest-houses into factories – were anxious to make money out of their possessions, to increase rents, evict tenants, change the terms of leases, and enclose common land at the expense of the poor villager.[16]

In a celebrated sermon, Hugh Latimer, the son of a yeoman who rented a farm for £3 or £4 a year, contrasted his father's state with that of his successor. His father, so Latimer said, was able to keep 100 sheep and thirty cows and had enough tillage to support half a dozen men; he had paid for the education of his son; had provided his daughters with generous portions on their marriage; had offered hospitality to his neighbours and alms to the poor. His successor, on the other hand, paid over four times as much in rent, and was unable 'to do anything for his Prince, for himself, nor his children, nor give a cup of drink to the poor'.[17] Many another man, so the Rev. William Harrison contended, considered himself lucky to have a roof over his head, an acre of ground, and a few 'cabbages, radishes, parsnips, carrots, melons and pumpkins by which he and his poor household liveth as their principal food, sith they can do no better'.[18]

The hired labourers, whose numbers had much increased with the decline in those of smallholders, were no better off. Some, such as hedgers and ditchers, harvesters and thatchers, were paid at a daily rate; others, like shepherds and milkmaids, who offered their services at fairs, were usually paid by the year; but few were well rewarded. On the Darell family estates at Littlecote and Axford in Wiltshire, field-workers were paid 2d or 3d a day, the more skilled hedgers 7d, ploughmen 1s a week with board, and shepherds 6d a week also with board. Threshers received from 3d to 7d a day according to the grain, the shepherd's boy 2½d, thatchers 2s for five days' work.[19] These rates seem to have been fairly typical, though in Cheshire in 1594 some thatchers were getting no more than 1d a day and reapers only 2d, both without meat or drink; and in Yorkshire in 1593 threshers were also being paid 1d a day in winter, 2d in summer, but these did have their food as well. According to an East Riding assessment of that year a woman servant in charge of 'brewing, baking, kitching, milk house, or malting that is hired with a gentleman or rich yeoman' was not permitted to receive more than 17s a year in addition to her board and lodging.[20] At least, this woman had enough to eat but there were thousands who did not; and in times of dearth, of murrain in cattle, of foot-rot in sheep, and of steeply rising prices, there were outbreaks of famine. In December 1596 there were seven deaths from starvation in the streets of Newcastle, and twenty-five in two successive months the next autumn.[21]

There was disagreement as to who or what was responsible for this sorry state of affairs. There were those who laid it at the door of a wicked people justly punished by an avenging God; there were others who blamed the inherent idleness of working men; some said the debasement of the coinage was at the root of the evil, or inflation, or the gold pouring into Europe from America; or the tendency of merchants to concentrate on the importation of foreign luxuries rather than on the expansion of markets for home-based industries. A few placed the responsibility upon the decline of charity; in fact, a recent study of wills and benefactions has shown that there was no such decline, that charitable institutions and causes benefited from handsome endowments far more regularly towards the end of the sixteenth century than they had done at the beginning.[22] It was at least agreed by many that the selfishness of grasping landlords had, indeed, thrown thousands of country people out of work, and that the crowds of vagrants, rogues and vagabonds had been enlarged by the Statute of Liveries of 1504 which, by denying a lord's traditional right to be served by a retinue of liveried retainers, forced yet more troublesome and masterless men out of employment, and onto the roads.

As the ballad 'Now-a-Dayes' put it:

> Temporall lordes be almost gone,
> Householdes kepe thei few or none,
> Which causeth many a goodly man
>     ffor to beg his bredd:
> Iff he steele ffor necessite,

ther is none other remedye
But the law will shortlye
Hange him all save the hedd.[23]

It was also generally agreed that the numbers of vagrants had been swollen by the Dissolution of Monasteries. The new vagrants were not monks who were given pensions and mostly went into other occupations, but servants and dependants – whose services were not required by the new owners of the monasteries' lands – and the poor who had begged at the gates and had often been indulged, whether deserving charity or not.

The actual numbers of these beggars and vagabonds was a subject of constant speculation. In 1577, William Harrison wrote, 'It is not yet full three-score yeares since this trade began, but how it hath prospered since that time it is easie to judge, for they are now supposed of one sex and another, to amount unto about 10,000 persons, as I have heard reported.'[24]

Other estimates put the number much higher. In 1594 the Lord Mayor of London suggested there were as many as 12,000 beggars in the city alone; and in 1569 a search by constables throughout the country initiated by the Privy Council seems to have resulted in the apprehension of 13,000 rogues and masterless men.

They were of two main types, the filthy, ragged vagabonds, as described in Thomas Harman's *Caveat for Common Cursetors* (1568), who roamed about the country, alternately begging and stealing and sometimes wreaking havoc in the villages through which they passed, and the smartly dressed and cunning tricksters, the 'conny-catchers', whose ploys were revealed in various pamphlets by Robert Greene and whose activities were mostly limited to London and a few other of the larger towns.

According to Harman the roaming vagabonds, who often travelled about in large companies, tended to specialize in a particular form of preying upon the respectable public and to be distinguished from each other by cant names. There were the masterful 'Upright Men' who were regarded as leaders of their gangs; bullying 'Rufflers' who begged from the strong and were strong enough themselves to rob the weak; 'Hookers' or 'Anglers' who stole clothing from open windows by means of hooked poles; 'Priggers of Prancers' who were horse thieves; 'Palliards' who obtained money by exhibiting scars revoltingly exacerbated with arsenic and ratsbane; 'Fraters' who pretended to be collecting money for hospitals; 'Whip-Jacks' who made out that they were shipwrecked sailors; 'Counterfeit Cranks' who feigned the symptoms of the falling sickness; 'Dommerers' who presented themselves as deaf mutes; and 'Abraham Men' who faked insanity like the 'Bedlam Beggars' described by Edgar in *King Lear*. These men, 'with roaring voice',

Strike in their numb'd and mortified bare arms
Pins, wooden pricks, nails, sprigs of rosemary;
And with this horrible object, from low farms,
Poor pelting villages, sheep-cotes, and mills,
Sometime with lunatic bans, sometime with prayers
Enforce their charity.[25]

Another authority, John Awdeley in his *Fraternitye of Vacabondes* (1561), added to their number 'Jarckmen' who forged licences to beg; 'Patricios' or hedge-priests who performed marriages which were to hold until death did part, that was to say until the couple agreed to separate by shaking hands over the carcass of a dead animal they happened to pass on the road; and 'Curtsey Men' who pretended to be well-to-do people fallen on hard times. 'These kind of ydle vacabondes will go commonly well apparelled without any weapon, and in places where they meete together at their hosteryes they wyll bear the part of right good gentlemen . . . but commonly they will pay them with stealing a pair of sheetes or coverlet.'[26] All were followed by 'Doxies', women who had been 'broken and spoiled of their maidenhead'; by 'Dells', 'young wenches not yet broken'; by 'Walking Morts', unmarried whores; by 'Kynchin Coes' and 'Kynchin Morts', male and female children; and by 'Bawdy Baskets', female pedlars who 'go with baskets and cap-cases on their arms, wherein they have laces, pins, needles and silk girdles of all colours. And for their trifles they will procure of maiden-servants when their mistress or dame is out of the way, either some good piece of beef, bacon or cheese, that shall be worth twelve pence, for two pence of their toys.'[27]

Also on the road, though not necessarily of their company, were bands of strolling players and performers who had no patron to grant them his protection, jugglers, quacks and acrobats, tinkers, pedlars, and gipsies who were described by Thomas Dekker in his *Lanthorne and Candle-light*: 'Their apparell is old and phantasticke, tho it be never so full of rents: the men weare scarfes of Callico, or any other base stuffs having their bodies like Morris dancers with bells and uther toyes to intice the countrey people to flocke about them, and to wounder at their fooleries or rather rancke knaveryes'.[28]

When Dekker wrote this gipsies had been the subject of several punitive Acts. In 1554 it had been declared a felony for a gipsy to remain in England after twenty days from the proclamation of the Act; and in 1563 it was made a capital offence for anyone to consort with gipsies. This statute, for breach of which five men were hanged at Durham in 1596, was not repealed until 1783 as a law of 'excessive severity' and one which had never been effective.[29]

Many vagabonds had been born on the road and their fathers before them. 'I once rebuking a wyld rogue because he went idelly about,' wrote Harman, 'he shewed me that he was a beggar by enheritance – his grandfather was a beggar, his father was one, and he must nedes be one by good reason.' It was difficult for wanderers like this to grow accustomed to any other life. The *Records of the Borough of Leicester* refer to a destitute ten-year-old boy covered with lice and sores, who was taken in by a kindly family who cleaned him, fed him and cared for him. But after four or five months the call of the road proved irresistible and he fell to wandering again, and no doubt eventually became like one of those rovering pilferers described by the satirist, Samuel Rowlands:

> As perfect lousy as they both could crawl
> Each had a hat and nightcap for the cold,
> And cloaks with patches . . .
> Great satchel scrips that shut with leather flaps
> And each a dog to eat his master's scraps.
> Their shoes were hob-nail proof, soundly bepegged,
> Wrapt well with clouts to keep them warmer legged.[30]

Those not born to the vagabond's life and who wished to become members of the fraternity were initiated by 'Upright Men' who took them off to 'the bowsing Ken, which is to some typpling house next adjoyninge':

Then doth this upright man call for a gage of bowse, whiche is a quarte pot of drinke [Harman recorded] and he powres the same upon peld pate, adding these words: 'I G.P. do stalle thee W.T. to the Roge, and that from hence forth it shall be lawefull for thee to Cant' – that is to aske or begge – 'for thy living in al places.' Here you se that the upright man is of great auctorite. For all sortes of beggers are obedient to his hests, and surmounteth all others in pylfring and stealings.[31]

Harman and several other writers of contemporary pamphlets provide entertaining and macabre examples of the vagabonds' skills and tricks, a 'Hooker's' expertise in plucking the sheets and coverlet from a bed in a farmer's house – 'in which laye three parsones (a man and two bygge boyes)' and leaving them 'lying a slepe naked' – a juggler killing himself having drunkenly forgotten to place in position the metal plate between his stomach and the bladder full of calf's blood into which it was his practice to thrust a dagger in a horribly realistic representation of disembowelment.

Whether or not we can believe all the stories which give so vivid a picture of life on the English road in the sixteenth century, there can be no doubt of the government's deep concern both about masterless men and vagabonds and about 'Movers of Sedition and Spreaders of Falce Rumores' who went around the country alienating 'the people's mind' and who were punished in the pillory and by mutilation in a series of increasingly cruel measures.

At the beginning of the century it was enacted that impotent beggars should hold licences from the justices of the peace permitting them to beg within certain limits. All vagabonds and beggars without licences and all able-bodied men found begging were to be stripped from the waist upward and whipped until bloody, or set in the stocks for three days and nights on bread and water. They were then to be sent to their usual place of residence, when this could be discovered. It often happened, however, that the place of residence, once discovered, would not accept responsibility for the beggar. This was the case with one poor widow and her six children who, for two years, were sent back from one village to another, both places denying that they had any responsibility for them. When accepted, the vagrants were to be cared for if they could not work and to be put to labour if they could. A second offence of vagrancy might entail the loss of an ear, a third of two ears. Anyone harbouring a sturdy vagabond was liable to a fine and imprisonment at the discretion of the court.

These measures proving ineffective and the numbers of vagabonds increasing, the early laws were repealed in 1547 and a severer statute was passed. This decreed that all those who were capable of work but remained idle should be deemed to be vagabonds, branded with a V on the breast and made slaves for two years. As slaves they could be chained, driven to work with whips, and given food little better than that provided for animals. Those for whom private masters could not be found were to become slaves of local communities and put to road-mending or other public works. Should they run away they were to be branded on the chest with the letter S and made slaves for life. If they ran away again they were to be executed. This statute, however, was so severe that it was soon repealed and the previous law revived.

Yet, determined as were the efforts made to stamp them out, and active as several towns were in levying compulsory rates to help the deserving poor before Parliament decided to do so on a national scale, the bands of vagabonds continued to grow. And by 1572 further legislation was essential, since all parts of the kingdom were 'presently with rogues, vagabonds and sturdy beggars exceedingly pestered, by means whereof daily happeneth horrible murders, thefts and other great outrages'. In that year a statute considerably widened the definition of vagabond to include all idle persons using 'subtyll craftye and unlawfull games or playes'; all able-bodied persons not working and with no excuse for being idle; all players and minstrels 'not belonging to any baron of this realm or some honourable personage of greater degree'; all pedlars, tinkers and petty chapmen without licences from two

Justices of the Peace; university scholars begging without licence from their Vice-Chancellors; and released prisoners caught begging without permission and without means to support themselves on their way home.

Exceptions were specifically made for harvest workers returning to their villages; servants who had been dismissed or whose masters had died; persons who had been robbed on the highway; and discharged soldiers and sailors. But all others who could not give a satisfactory account of themselves and were over fourteen years old were to be whipped and burned through the gristle of the right ear with a hot iron unless a master undertook to give them employment for a year. For second offences they were to be hanged as felons, unless given employment for two years. For leaving their employment or for a third offence they were to be hanged without benefit of clergy. Three years later it was ordered that stocks of wool, hemp, iron and other materials should be provided by each parish and that houses of correction should be established in each county, so that there was always work for rogues to do and places in which to do it. Overseers of the Poor were to be appointed and empowered to assess each parish so that funds could be collected for the relief of the aged, impotent and sick. A subsequent statute of 1597 modified the previous legislation, moderated the punishments to be inflicted on the able-bodied and elaborated the methods by which a compulsory poor rate to aid the deserving poor was to be collected and distributed.[32]

Punishments seem to have been severely inflicted where they were considered necessary. At the Middlesex Sessions alone between 1570 and 1575 forty-four vagabonds were branded and eight were hanged. It was some years, however, before the numbers of vagabonds over the country as a whole were reduced; and then the improvement was doubtless due more to the overseers of the poor than to the officers of law enforcement, and to the tardy recognition that savage punishments were no defence against men who could find no work or who would, as one Somerset Justice of the Peace put it, 'rather hazard their lives than work'. This same justice of the peace complained to the Privy Council in 1596 that, although forty felons had been executed in his county that year, far more than this had been allowed to escape justice, while no more than a fifth of those who committed felonies were apprehended. Even when they were arrested they often obtained their freedom by restoring the stolen goods, or through the corruption or carelessness of incompetent officers of the law:

And these that thus escape ynfect great numbers, ymboldenynge them by ther escapes. And they will change both name and habytt and commonly go ynto other sheeres so as no man shall knowe them . . . I do not see howe yt ys possible for the poore cuntryman to beare the burthens dewly layde uppon hym and the rapynes of the Infynytt numbers of the wicked wandrynge Idell people of the land . . . And I may Justlye saye that the Infynyte numbers of the Idle Wandrynge people and robbers of the land . . . spend dobly as myche as the laborer dothe, for they lye Idely in the Ale houses daye and nyght eating and drinkynge excessively. And within these iii monethes I tooke a thief that was executed these last assizes that confessed unto me that he and two more laye in an Alehouse three weeks in which tyme they eate xx<sup>ti</sup> fatt sheepe whereof they stole every night . . . And such numbers beynge growen to this Idle and thevyshe lif ther ar scant sufficyent to do the ordynary tillage of the land, for I know that some having had their husbandmen sent for Soldiers they have cost a great parte of ther tyllage and others are not to be gotten by reason so manye are abroad and practysinge all kind of villanye.[33]

Soon after this letter was written conditions in the countryside did begin to improve, though in the towns, mainly in London, cheats and rogues remained as great a menace as ever, haunting bowling alleys, taverns and dicing houses and the cheaper of those eating houses known as ordinaries where, according to George Whetstone, author of *Touchstone for the Time* (1584), 'the dayly guests are maisterless men, needy shifters, theves, cut-purses, unthriftie servants, both serving men and prentises'.

There was your gallant extraordinary thief that keeps his college of good fellows, and will not fear to rob a lord in his coach for all his ten trencher-bearers on horseback [wrote Thomas Middleton of the company of one such ordinary]; your deep-conceited cutpurse, who by the dexterity of his knife will draw out the money, and make a flame-coloured purse show like the bottomless pit; your cheating bowler . . . your cheverill-gutted catchpoll, who like a horse-leech sucks gentlemen; and, in all your twelve tribes of villany.[34]

The pickpockets and cut-purses to be found in these places were highly skilful, carefully trained criminals, proud of their skills and jealous of their territories. There were 'Nips' who cut purses with a knife and a horn thumb, and 'Foists' who used their fingers only and so disdained the use of knives that they did not carry them even to cut their meat for fear lest they be thought to need them in their profession. Active at fairs and executions and upon all occasions when crowds gathered, they hired accomplices to climb steeples to get people to look up into the air, exhibited freaks and worked with the singers of bawdy ballads. William Fletewood, Recorder of London, reported to Lord Burghley of a training-school which was established by 'one Wotton, a gentleman borne, and sometyme a marchaunt man of good credyt, who falling by tyme into decay, kepte an alehouse at Smart's Key, neere Byl-lingsgate':

> There were hung up two devyses, the one was a pocket, the other was a purse. The pocket had in it certain cownters, and was hung about with hawkes' bells and over the top did hang a little sacring bell; and he that could take out a cownter without any noyse was allowed to be a publique foyster, and he that could take a piece of sylver out of the purse, without the noyse of any of the bells, he was adjudged a judiciall nypper. Nota, that a foyster is a pick-pocket, and a nypper is termed a pickpurse, or a cutpurse.[35]

Fletewood and others described the numerous tricks practised upon the unwary and gullible by the denizens of the London underworld, the card tricks, the frauds with loaded dice, the cozenage at bowls, the shop-lifting, the trap known as 'cross-biting' by which a whore enticed a countryman into her room whereupon her bully appeared, in the guise of an outraged husband, sword in hand, to relieve his victim of all he had. Many of these criminals lived in gaols, keeping themselves loaded with suits for debt, escaping the searches made for them by the watch, and paying the keeper to let them out and to receive them back again after the commission of their crimes.[36]

The authorities could do little to cope with the cony-catchers who generally got off lightly when they were brought to justice, which was not often. In 1537, for instance, a man who had acquired a horse 'per fraudem deceptionem et astutiam vocat Cosenyage' was fined 40s and put in Cheapside pillory. Had he stolen the horse and not got it by deceit he would probably have been hanged.

There were statutes enough to limit the opportunities of cony-catchers: bowling, quoits, tables, dice and cards were all, at one time or another, proscribed; and, in order to encourage archery, the practice of which was declining fast, bow-makers were forbidden to charge more than 6s 8d for a long-bow of the best quality. Yet archery continued to decline, while men persisted in playing cards and dice. Indeed, the government issued licences for what proved impossible of restraint. When Thomas Cornwallis, Queen Elizabeth's groom-porter, sought a patent to license gaming-houses in London, the failure of the government to enforce the law was freely admitted. 'Seying that the inclination of menne to be geven and bent to the aforesayd pastymes and plays, and that no penaltye of the lawes or statutes aforesayd hath heretofore restrained them', Cornwallis's request for a patent was granted.[37]

# 15 · *Priests, Parishioners and Recusants*

Between 1536 and 1540, with varying degrees of justification, some eight thousand monastic houses were suppressed and their property transferred to the Crown as a means of increasing royal income. A few years before this Dissolution of the Monasteries a pamphlet addressed to King Henry VIII condemned the 'idle beggars and vagabonds' of the Church who had 'gotten into their hands more than a third part of all your Realm'.

> The goodliest lordships, manors, lands and territories are theirs [the pamphleteer continued]. Besides this they have the tenth part of all corn, meadow, pasture, grass, wool, colts, calves, lambs, pigs, geese and chickens. Yea, and they look so narrowly upon their profits, that the poor wives must be countable to them of every tenth egg, or else she getteth not her rights at Easter, and shall be taken as heretic . . . Who is she that will set her hands to work to get 3d a day and may have at least 20d a day to sleep an hour with a friar, a monk or a priest?[1]

Such outbursts of anti-clericalism were not in the least uncommon, even if, as Professor Scarisbrick has said, 'On the whole, English men and women did not want the Reformation and most of them were slow to accept it when it came.'[2] Erasmus, while deploring what he took to be the excesses of Martin Luther, unfavourably compared 'contemptible friars' with 'itinerant mountebanks' and roundly condemned the greedy monks, 'gorging the carcase to the point of bursting', while scrupulously observing 'a lot of silly ceremonies and paltry traditional rules'.[3] It was widely suggested that the immense wealth of these monks and friars and such princes of the Church as Cardinal Wolsey should be transferred to more deserving hands; and, except in the north, the people of the country as a whole were in general agreement that this transference at least was overdue. So were many of the clergy themselves. Most reforming clergy, however, believed that the monastic wealth, if appropriated, should go towards the endowment of charitable, religious and educational enterprises; while the King saw the Dissolution as an opportunity to place his finances on a sounder footing, Parliament as a means of avoiding unpopularity by taxation, the landed gentry as a means of enlarging their estates, and the urban middle class as a chance of becoming landed gentry themselves. Some endowments were made: Trinity College, Cambridge was founded by the King in 1546 not long after Christ Church, originally Cardinal College, had been founded by Wolsey at Oxford; and other benefits were bestowed upon the nation by the fortification of harbours and the improvement of arsenals which were paid for out of the money received from the spoliation of monastic lands. But those who profited most from the Dissolution were initially the King and ultimately, and to a far greater extent, the families into whose hands the lands and tithes and coal-fields of the monasteries passed.[4]

The pensioned monks, about five thousand of them, in addition to two thousand nuns and 1,600 friars, were for the most part not ill treated. Many of them became clergymen, and in the years to come seem to have been as ready as those whose ranks they had joined to accept the changes required by the Protestant regime of Edward VI, by the Catholic revival of Mary, and by the ecclesiastical compromise which was eventually contrived in the reign of Elizabeth.

Under Elizabeth there were, of course, extreme Protestants who could not accept the settlement, who could not believe with John Jewel, Bishop of Salisbury, that 'every soul, of what calling soever he be' was subject to the monarch and magistrates, and that the State must decide what the one religion of the country must be. There were also unreconciled Catholics who could not accept Cranmer's English Prayer Book as a replacement of the Latin Mass. Several revolts, notably in the western counties and in Oxfordshire, erupted against the new liturgy. Among fifteen demands which some insurgents made were these: 'We will have the Sacrament hung over the high altar and thus to be worshipped as it was wont to be, and they which will not thereunto consent, we will have them die like heretics against the holy Catholic faith . . . We will have holy bread and holy water every Sunday, palms and ashes at the time accustomed, images to be set up again in every church, and all other ancient ceremonies held heretofore by our Mother Holy Church.'[5] At Sampford Courtenay in Devon, so David Mathew tells us, the parishioners forced their priest to defy the law by saying Mass publicly in Latin, 'the common people all the country round clapping their hands for joy'.[6] But Roman Catholics were not at first harried, except those who were notorious papists or whose loyalty was suspect. They were required to attend Anglican services and were fined a shilling for not doing so; but they were otherwise left largely to their own devices. John Trevelyan, a Catholic Cornish squire, attended church to avoid the fine; yet he always left before the sermon, calling out cheerily to the parson: 'When thou hast said what thou hast to say, come and dine with me.'[7] There were Catholics in all counties – more in Lancashire and Yorkshire, Cheshire and Shropshire than elsewhere – who were allowed to practise their own religion, provided they did so discreetly. Several of them still had their private chaplains; and noblemen were not even required to take the oath required of others. There were Catholics, too, at court; one of them, William Byrd, was organist at the Chapel Royal.[8] Queen Elizabeth herself had candles on the altar and a crucifix in her private chapel, and did not at all care for sermons, particularly from Puritan-minded preachers. 'Do not talk about that!' she called out when one of these spoke against images and implied criticism of the crucifix. '*Leave that!*' she cried in an even louder voice when, not having heard her, the preacher continued his sermon. '*Leave that!* It has nothing to do with your subject and the matter is now threadbare.'[9] On another occasion she opened the window of her closet to thank a bishop for a sermon to which she had obviously not been listening.

Many of her subjects were shocked by the trappings of popery which were permitted to remain in churches. 'Our churches stand full of such great puppets, wondrously decked and adorned,' wrote Bishop Jewel in a homily against the 'Perils of Idolatry'. 'Garlands and coronets be set on their heads, precious stones hanging about their necks; their fingers shine with rings set with precious stones; their dead and stiff bodies are clothed with garments stiff with gold.'[10] Rosaries were still used in some churches; the shrines of saints were still revered and the passing bell was rung at Hallow-tide. Several former holy days were no longer celebrated; but others, like vigils and patronal festivals, remained as before. The parish clerk still led the responses, while the ecclesiastical courts still functioned, punishing parishioners for working on Sundays and keeping a stern eye upon their morals, as upon those of one John Gill of Adderbury who got Mary Spenser with child and who was required

> . . . to come into the church on Sunday sennight next and there tarry the whole evening prayer and after evening prayer in some convenient place of the church before Mr Rawlins the vicar . . . and confess his fault and deliver 6s 8d to Mr Rawlins for the use of the poor and undertake 6s 8d more to the same use at the feast of St Michael next.[11]

In certain parts of the country, indeed, the old religion continued almost as before. 'In Lancashire and the parts thereabouts,' according to Strype, 'papists [showed] themselves to be numerous, Mass was commonly said, priests harboured, the Book of Common prayer and the church established by law laid aside. Many churches were shut up and cures unsupplied, unless with such popish priests as had been ejected.' In Yorkshire recusancy was common. In York itself numerous citizens were examined as to their failure to go to church:

> William Bowman, locksmith, sayeth he refuseth to come to the church because he thinketh it is not the Catholic Church, for there is neither priest, altar, nor Sacraments . . . Isabel Bowman sayeth she cometh not to the church, for her conscience will not serve her, because there is not the Sacrament hung up and other things as hath been aforetime . . . Janet Strickett, widow, sayeth she cometh not to the church because her conscience will not serve her, for the bread and wine is not consecrate, as it hath been in the past . . . John Wood, tailor, cometh not to the church . . .[12]

In Ribblesdale in north Yorkshire, so it was complained, people continued to use the 'Popish rites of Burial':

> They set forth the corpse in their houses all garnished with crosses, and sit round about with tapers and candles burning night and day, till it be carried to the Church. All which time the neighbours . . . visit the corpse and there everyone do say a Pater Noster or De Profundis for the soul: the bells all the while being rung many a solemn peal. After which they are made partakers of the dead man's dole or banquet of charity. Thus all things being accomplished in right Popish order at home, at length they carry the corpse towards the Church all garnished with crosses (wrapped in a shroud & uncoffined) which they set down by the way at every Cross, and there all of them devoutly on their knees make prayer for the dead. And when in this superstitious sort they have brought the corpse to the Church, some with haste prevent the Minister and bury the corpse themselves, because they will not be partakers of the service said at the burial . . . And when the corpse is ready to be put into the grave, some by kissing the dead corpse, others by wailing the dead with more than heathenish outcries, others with open invocations for the dead and another sort with jangling bells, so disturb the whole action that the Minister is often compelled to let pass that part of the service appointed for the burial of the dead & to withdraw himself from their tumultuous assembly. After which burial, at their banquet in the ale house, they oftentimes have a Pater Noster for the dead.[13]

All over the country there were Catholics who condemned what Nicholas Fitzherbert called the 'pernicious opinion' that 'it was permitted them to attend the heretical churches and meetings without committing any great crime or separating themselves from the Catholic church'. One of the recusants was Cardinal Allen, former Fellow of Oriel College, Oxford, and Principal of St Mary's Hall, who left England in 1561 for Flanders whence a mass of Catholic literature and propaganda was imported into England, despite government legislation against it. Some years later Allen established at Douay a seminary for English students abroad and from this and other colleges and religious communities on the Continent a regular flow of missionary priests entered England.

> They took shipping and, wind and weather being both prosperous, they sailed along the coast of England and meant to have landed on Essex side [runs a contemporary account of one secret landing of missionary priests]. But for their sakes the master of the bark lingered that evening until it was two hours within the night, and being come near unto Scarborough, there came out a little boat with divers rovers or pirates in it, to have surprised them, who shot at them divers times with muskets, but had no harm; for the wind being then somewhat contrary, the master turned his ship and sailed back into the main sea, where in foul weather they remained three days; and so at last being driven eastward, they landed near unto Whitby in Yorkshire on the side of a high cliff, with great danger to their lives. At last they came to Whitby, where going into an inn they found there one Ratcliffe, a pursuivant, who after an exact view of them all questioned with them about their arrival in that place, whence they came and whither they would? They answered that coming from Newcastle, they were by tempest driven thither. And so after refreshing of themselves, they all went to a Catholic gentleman his house (whose name for divers respects I suppress) within two or three miles of Whitby, by whom they were directed some to one place, some to another, according to their own desires.[14]

The searches of houses which were made for such missionaries led to the construction of hiding places in the houses of Catholic families. They were often behind chimneys, or concealed in fireplaces or hidden behind sliding panels in attics and lofts; and are still to be seen in such houses as Stonor Park where Edmund Campion and his companions had their secret printing press in 1581. Some of these so-called priests'-holes were actually built into the house at the time of its construction as was done at the house of the Caryll family at West Grinstead. Nicholas Owen, a Welsh carpenter and Jesuit lay brother, 'developed a very resourceful invention' over the course of twenty-five years. He was twice captured, on the second occasion being starved out of his refuge at Hindlip after a search lasting four days.[15]

The presence of Mary Queen of Scots on English soil and the fulminations of Pope Pius V against Queen Elizabeth led to firmer measures being taken against the recusants. A list of leading Catholics was drawn up. Heavy fines were imposed upon the rich – the annual fine to be imposed upon the Stonor family was set in 1577 at a figure which today would represent well over £50,000 – and those who declined to recant were arrested and put on trial.

'The priests they succeed in capturing are treated with a variety of terrible tortures', wrote William Allen. '[One] is to drive spikes between the nails and the quick . . . When they would not confess under this torture, the nails of their fingers and toes were turned back.' Edmund Campion and other Jesuits were executed at Tyburn after repeated torturing upon the rack. And at York, Margaret Clitherow, the daughter of a wax chandler and wife of a butcher, was subjected to the punishment known as *peine forte et dure* for refusing to plead to the charge of having harboured priests and heard Mass.

> She was stripped naked [in the words of her biographer and friend, John Mush], after this they laid weight upon her, which when she felt it she said, 'Jesu! Jesu! Have mercy upon me!' which were the last words she was heard to speak. She was in dying one quarter of an hour. A sharp stone, as much as a man's fist, was put under her back; upon her was laid to the quantity of seven or eight hundredweight at the least, which breaking her ribs, caused them to burst forth of the skin.[16]

Between 1581 and 1588, the year of the defeat of the Spanish Armada, at least sixty-four priests, eighteen laymen and two women were executed for their religion, as opposed to nearly 300 Protestants who had perished in the fires of Smithfield and elsewhere during the reign of Queen Mary. But the flow of missionary priests into England continued unabated, as a Proclamation against Jesuits of 21 November 1591 indicates:

> And furthermore, because it is known . . . that they do come into the same realm by secret creeks, and landing places, disguised both in names and persons; some in apparel as soldiers, mariners, or merchants, pretending that they have heretofore been taken prisoners, and put into galleys, and delivered. Some come in as gentlemen, with contrary names, in comely apparel, as though they had travelled into foreign countries for knowledge . . . and many as gallants; yea in all colours, and with feathers and such like, disguising themselves; and many of them in their behaviours as ruffians, far off to be thought or suspected to be friars, priests, jesuits, or popish scholars.[17]

By the time that this proclamation was issued, however, measures against Catholics were being relaxed, while changes could be observed in churches everywhere except in the most remote parishes. Images were being destroyed; medieval wall paintings replaced by religious texts or by the Ten Commandments; and railed altars at the east end of the church were removed to make way for communion tables in the nave. There was now no chanting during the services; psalms were sung in rhymed versions, sometimes to the accompaniment of viols and wind instruments, and prayers were said. Queen Elizabeth and Archbishop Whitgift had 'weathered the storm, and the Anglican vessel slipped safely on between the dashing rocks of Romanism and Puritanism'. Most of the Puritan clergy, gentry and clergy had been loyal to the queen and 'the younger generation brought up on Bible and Prayer Book, and sharing the struggle for national existence against Spain, Pope and Jesuits, became for the most part fervent Protestants. Bible reading and family prayer were becoming customs of the English'.[18]

Listening to sermons, however, was not customary yet, though those clergy who did preach often did so for two hours or more. In the earlier years of the sixteenth century there had been many clergymen who could not preach the shortest of sermons, who could scarcely even read the prayer book. And as late as 1561–2 in the archdeaconry of Leicester, then in the diocese of Lincoln, only fifteen out of 129 clergymen were able to preach a sermon. Nor was the general behaviour of the clergy much better than it had been in the previous century. In the diocese of Norwich a rector was said to spend more time farming than in tending his human flock; in that of Lincoln one rector was fined for allowing a puppeteer to make use of the church for his performance, another was found guilty of adultery, and more were known to have been guilty of the same offence. In Kent a vicar was described as 'a common cow-keep and one that useth commonly to drive beasts through the town of Faversham . . . and other open places, in a jerkin with a bill on his neck, not like a prelate but rather like a common rogue, who hath oft-times been warned thereof, and he will not be reformed'.[19] Elsewhere, parsons were accused of forgetting that the church was a house of prayer; of allowing it to become a house of 'talking, of walking, of brawling, of minstrelry, of hawks and dogs'; and of not ensuring that men and women sat apart from each other as they were meant to do. They guzzled flesh on Fridays and let belief 'revolve with the wind'.[20]

By the end of the century, however, both the behaviour of the clergy and their educational standards had been much improved by the bishops; while their social standing had also been enhanced. Formerly they had as often as not been extremely poor. Harrison had said that 'the incumbent thinketh himself well acquitted if [on an income of £20 a year], all ordinary payments being discharged, he may reserve £13 6s 8d towards his own sustenation or maintenance of his family'. A poorer living than this was not able to maintain 'a mean scholar much less a learned man'. 'The greater part of the more excellent wits,' Harrison continued, 'choose rather to employ their studies unto physic and the laws, utterly giving over the study of the Scriptures for fear lest they should in time not get their bread by the same.'[21] Priests had been allowed to marry since 1547, and their children had put further strain upon their resources. But now the stipends of clergy had increased; and the parsonage was becoming a more comfortable house than its neighbours with better furniture and with books in the study. The parson was just beginning to be accepted on equal terms by the squire.

# 16 · *Country Houses and Country People*

During his prolonged tour of England in the 1530s and 1540s, John Leland was struck by the number of ruined castles he found upon the way. Many of these like Belvoir Castle, the property of the Earl of Rutland, were being converted into great houses. So were many former religious houses, such as Lacock Abbey in Wiltshire, which had been bought by Sir William Sharington, and the priory in the same county which was now the property of Sir John Thynne, begetter of Longleat.

These two men were representative of many of those who were building grand new houses in every county in the middle of the sixteenth century. Sir John Thynne, a nephew of Sir William Thynne, Clerk Comptroller of the Royal Household, had made his fortune as steward to the Duke of Somerset; Sir William Sharington had made his, much more dubiously, as vice-treasurer of the Bristol Mint. Whether self-made men or the inheritors of great wealth, the builders of this new age wanted their country houses to appear no less splendid, and usually more eccentrically fanciful, than the castles and fortified manor houses of the medieval past. The earlier Gothic styles of architecture, which were later to be known as Early English and Decorated, had gradually given way to the Perpendicular and this was now being overlaid with what has been termed Tudor-Gothic. Cupolas sprang up on top of towers; chimney stacks, protruding from the walls, clustered in a variety of shapes over the roofs; gables were surmounted by painted weather vanes and heraldic beasts; finials sprouted from the summits of the entrance porch; glass was used with increasing liberality, almost entirely replacing oiled linen and horn panels. Indeed, at Hardwick Hall in Derbyshire, which was built in the 1590s by the immensely rich and overpoweringly bossy Countess of Shrewsbury, the windows occupied so much of the façade that it gave rise to the jingle, 'Hardwick Hall, more glass than wall'.

Stone for these houses was plundered from monasteries which the Dissolu-

ABOVE: Sir Thomas More (1478–1535) and various members of his family, drawn by Holbein in 1527. He built himself a house, Beaufort House, in Chelsea in the early 1520s. It was, said Erasmus, 'not mean, nor invidiously grand, but comfortable'. Most houses at this time were sparsely furnished by later standards, but carved oak dressers and lantern clocks like the ones shown were common features in parlours.

RIGHT: Anne Askew, the Protestant martyr, was burned at Smithfield after torture on the rack in 1546. She perished with three other martyrs, all men, watched by the Lord Mayor and various Privy Councillors sitting on a bench beneath St Bartholomew's church. Gunpowder was strapped to the victims' bodies to spare them the sooner of their pain.

The following labels appear within the engraving:

S. PAULES CHURCH

Hamsted Mills
Hamsted
S.Brides
the Water house
Pauls Wharfe
Quene hythe
Three Cranes
The Roll Schipes
The Gally fuste
THAMESIS
The Bear Gardine
The Globe

ABOVE: A view of London as it appeared in 1616, the year of Shakespeare's death. In the right foreground can be seen the Globe theatre on Bankside in Southwark. It had reopened two years before, after its predecessor, built in 1598–9, had been destroyed by fire. The flying flag gives notice that the afternoon's performance is about to begin. To the left of it are ale-houses, brothels, watermen's tenements and the Bear Garden. Dominating the far bank is old St Paul's Cathedral as it was before being destroyed in the Great Fire 50 years later. The jumbled waterfront below it was described by the poet William D'Avenant whose father kept a tavern at Oxford frequented by Shakespeare: 'Here a palace, there a woodyard; here a garden, there a brewhouse; here dwelt a lord, there a dyer.'

BELOW: Four London scenes during the Great Plague in 1665. In the first, multitudes are seen 'flying from London by water in boats and barges', with old St Paul's, shortly to be destroyed in the Great Fire, in the background. In the second, crowds are shown escaping by road; in the third, a burial party proceeds through Covent Garden by the railings in front of the church of St Paul's, designed by Inigo Jones and completed in 1633; and, in the fourth, are 'carts full of dead to bury'. There were probably in all some 100,000 victims, many of them buried in shallow pits like the ones shown, only inches beneath the surface so that 'the air stank with the smell of death'.

Matthew Hopkins, the self-styled 'Witchfinder General', who was himself hanged in 1647. He went about the country offering his services and extracting confessions by sticking pins into suspects and making them walk until their feet blistered. Two of his victims are here depicted with him. The one on the left is Elizabeth Clark, a one-legged beggar-woman, who gave the names of three of her imps as Holt, Jarmara, and Soake and Sugar. The other confessed that her imps were called Ilemanzar, Pyewackett, Pecke in the Crowne, and Griezell Greedigutt, names, said Hopkins, which 'no mortal could invent'.

tion had placed, either by gift or by purchase, in the hands of rich laity. There were also stone quarries in most English counties from Devon to East Anglia and Kent to Yorkshire. Timber was also used, of course, in building and altering such manor houses as Little Moreton Hall, that astonishing black and white creation in Cheshire to which, in the late 1550s, William Moreton added extravagantly decorated extensions and a jettied gatehouse. Brick, however, was now more commonly used than any other material.[1]

In earlier times bricks had been imported from the Continent and, known as Flanders tiles, been used mainly in the construction of fireplaces. The thirteenth-century Little Wenham Hall had been constructed of locally-made pink and yellow bricks, but this was an unusual example which had not been followed elsewhere until the brick buildings of France attracted the attention of English knights fighting there well over 100 years later. The English word 'brick', from the French *brique*, did not enter the language until 1416, and the town wall at Hull, built in the second half of the fourteenth century of locally-made bricks, was probably the first major public work to be constructed in England of the new material.[2] Thereafter brick became an extremely fashionable building material, used not only for palaces which were or became royal, St James's Palace and Hampton Court among them, but even for houses like Compton Wynyates in Warwickshire which were built in districts where the local material was stone.[3]

Many of these houses were built in the shape of an H or an E, it later being supposed that this was to flatter King Henry or Queen Elizabeth. Others were built round a courtyard on to which the main windows looked. Many faced north-east, since it was widely believed that, as the authority on health Andrew Boorde put it, 'the south wind doth corrupt and make for evil vapours', while the east wind was 'temperate, fryske and fragraunt'.[4] Most houses were only one room in thickness, each room intercommunicating with its neighbour. Bur nearly all, of whatever plan, seem to have been closely supervised in their construction by those who were paying for them. At the beginning of the sixteenth century there were no architects as such. The first known use of the word is in a book published in 1563. A master mason would usually draw up a plan based upon his client's requirements, a master carpenter being responsible for the interior details. Some master masons achieved a national reputation; and when Robert Smythson, the mason, died in 1614, the most skilful of them were known as architects. The word was inscribed on Smythson's tombstone.

Smythson himself had worked all over the country. He had advised Sir Matthew Arundel at Wardour Old Castle, Wiltshire; he had helped Sir John Thynne with the design of Longleat, the first great country house to be built in the High Elizabethan style; he was employed by Sir Francis Willoughby whose Woolaton Hall in Nottinghamshire was completed in 1585; soon afterwards he had advised the Countess of Shrewsbury in that dramatic combination of the Gothic and classical, Hardwick Hall; and he had then worked for Sir Henry Griffiths at Burton Agnes in Yorkshire.[5]

By Smythson's time the interiors of great houses had become far more complex than those of the Middle Ages, and far more care was taken to ensure the privacy of their owners' families. The great chamber, the principal room in the house, was now often known as the dining chamber; but it was also used for games, dancing, plays, for the lying-in-state of deceased owners and distinguished members of their families, and, where there was no chapel, for household prayers. Plays were also performed and games sometimes played in the hall which, although still a dining-room for servants, was beginning to be designed more as an imposing entrance to a house than as a room for daily use. In some houses upper servants now ate in a downstairs parlour.

Parlours had originally been rooms in monasteries in which visitors could talk to the monks, and this use was the derivation of their name. They had afterwards fulfilled a similar purpose in private houses, before developing into private sitting- or dining-rooms. Some parlours were also used as bedsitting-rooms or as bedrooms for guests, but by the beginning of the sixteenth century there were few parlours in which beds were to be found. They were more intimate and warmer rooms than the great chamber on the floor above them; but in larger houses they were growing in size and in number. At Longleat there were three parlours, a great parlour, a little parlour and a room known as the shovelboard parlour which was set aside for games.[6]

While a family could enjoy more privacy downstairs, there were more private rooms upstairs, too. It was becoming rare for ladies and gentlemen to sleep in the chamber in which they received their guests. Bedchambers were now becoming common, and withdrawing chambers were created leading off them. In these servants slept within call, still lying on pallets or on those beds known as truckle beds because of the wheels or castors upon which they could be pushed about and concealed in daytime under high-standing beds. Gradually withdrawing chambers began to be used not so much for sleeping in as for sitting in and for receiving visitors and thus eventually developed into the drawing-room. Adjoining the bedroom there might well be a 'stool-house' containing a close-stool, also known as a necessary-stool or night-stool until Victorian delicacy required them to be known as night commodes. At Ingatestone Hall, built in the 1540s, there were at least five of these, each with a close-stool covered with leather, velvet or cloth, and a pewter pan. They also contained one or two chamber pots.[7]

Nearly all large houses now had galleries. At first these were covered walks, often open on one side and used for walking in inclement weather. Some houses had two galleries, one above the other. There were two galleries, for instance, at the Vyne in Hampshire, the upper one of which survives and, dating from about 1520 and extending to seventy-four feet, is the oldest long gallery in England. Originally galleries were sparsely furnished, if furnished at all; but, after a time, when most of them were enclosed, they were provided with chairs and tables and, frequently, with portraits, not only of members of the family but also of great men of the age and of past ages. Sir Henry Wotton, the English connoisseur of Venetian paintings, advised that no room in a house should contain many pictures except the long gallery; and this advice seems to have been generally followed. At Lambeth Palace, in Archbishop Parker's time, all the pictures were in the gallery; at Leicester House there were twenty-eight pictures in the great gallery when the Earl of Leicester died in 1588 and apparently no more than one or two in any other room; at Hardwick Hall in 1601 almost half the pictures in the house were in the long gallery.[8] By the end of the century there were 103 portraits in the long gallery at Woburn Abbey.[9]

As well as for promenading, galleries were, like the hall and the great chamber, the scene of games, dancing, music and fencing matches. They usually had windows along one wall only and were provided with one or more fireplaces, supplemented by braziers in the coldest weather. Their ceilings were often elaborately plastered and their walls wainscoted and brightly painted.

Decorations in most rooms, indeed, were, as an Italian visitor to England wrote, 'marvellously wrought'. Plasterwork on the ceilings was intricately moulded and gaily painted; panelling was carved in the shape of linen folds; arras and coloured cloths hung from the walls; doors were flanked by pilasters or columns or panels of embossed leather; floors were made of highly polished oak or marble slabs strewn with sweet-smelling herbs; chimney pieces were hugely imposing, ablaze with escutcheons and coats of arms, decorated with marble columns and caryatids, sometimes as ostentatious as the tombs by which their families liked to commemorate themselves in parish churches.[10]

The gardens of such houses were often created with as much care and expense as the house itself. One such was the garden of Beaufort House in Chelsea which had belonged to Sir Thomas More. This was described by John Heywood who married Sir Thomas's niece, Elizabeth Raskell, as 'wonderfully charming . . . both from the advantage of its site and also for its own beauty. It was crowned with almost perpetual verdure; it had flowering shrubs and the branches of fruit trees interwoven in so beautiful a manner that it appeared like a tapestry woven by Nature herself.'[11]

In his essay, *Of Gardens*, Francis Bacon advised that gardens were 'best to be square, encompassed on all four sides by a stately arched hedge'. Within this square hedge – which might itself be enclosed by a brick wall and form part of a shady, arcaded gallery – the beds of flowers and shrubs were arranged in intricate patterns, either level with the straight, neat paths or raised above them. As well as flowers and shrubs, the beds contained plants in pots, coloured sands, miniature mazes, or grass in which grew wild flowers, daisies, cowslips and buttercups. In some gardens the beds were divided by painted wooden rails and many were adorned with figures of heraldic beasts, sundials and fountains.[12] At Hampton Court, so a German visitor recorded in the 1590s, there was a 'splendid, high and massy fountain with an ingenious waterwork whereby you can, if you like, make the water play upon the ladies and others who are standing by and give them a thorough wetting'. This visitor also noted that some beds at Hampton Court were 'planted with nothing but rosemary, others laid out with various other plants which are trained, intertwined and trimmed in so wonderful a manner and in such extraordinary shapes that the like could not easily be found'.[13]

The flowers to be seen in the earlier knot gardens had been far less varied than those to be seen by the end of the century. Roses, primroses, violets, gilliflowers, peonies, marigolds and lilies had all long been known. So had pinks which seem to have been introduced by the Normans, although the variety known as carnation – possibly a corruption of coronation since they were frequently used in making chaplets – was not known by that name until 1538. In later years numerous other plants were introduced into England, many of them by émigrés such as the Huguenots who were renowned as gardeners. The tulip came from Asia Minor by way of the Netherlands, sunflowers from Peru, lilacs from Persia, marigolds from Africa, nasturtiums from America. Thomas Linacre, the physician, is credited with having introduced the damask rose; while Edmund Grindal, Bishop of London 1559–70, brought over from Germany the tamarisk which he planted in the gardens of Fulham Palace whence presents of fruit were regularly sent to Queen Elizabeth I. As with flowers, so it was with trees. Oak, elm, pine, beech, alder, lime, birch, sycamore and larch were all known in the early Tudor period, though planes, silver firs, horsechestnuts and lombardy poplars were not introduced until later. In orchards, however, there were to be found nearly all the fruit trees which grow in England today, although there were far more cherry trees in the sixteenth century than there are now, cherries being a favourite fruit with all classes at that time. Six hundred cherry trees, 'at 6d the hundred', were once ordered for the great orchard at Hampton Court.[14]

A notable feature of the garden at Hampton Court was the 'mount' which had been raised for Cardinal Wolsey on a base of 256,000 bricks. Most grand gardens had similar 'mounts' from which all their beauties could be enjoyed;

and on the summit of many of them were built summer or banqueting houses. Some of these were large buildings. The one at Hampton Court was three storeys high. So was that at Holdenby which, finished in 1585, had six rooms to each floor, being less a banqueting house than a lodge. Other banqueting houses were quite small, like that at Rushton in Northamptonshire which was built for Sir Thomas Tresham in 1595. But nearly all were built to fanciful designs. The one at Rushton, known as the Triangular Lodge, had gables topped by extravagantly tall finials, and was covered with mystical symbols in multiples of three, in honour of the Trinity.

The huge sums of money spent upon the creation and maintenance of gardens in great houses severely depleted many fortunes. Lord Burghley, who was advised by John Gerard, author of the classic *Herball*, employed about forty poor people, at a total wage of £10 a week, in the gardens at Theobalds, in addition to his regular gardeners. He complained of the cost but the results were delightful.

> Here are a great variety of trees and Labyrinths made with a great deal of labour [reported the foreign traveller, Paul Hentzner]; and a jet de eau with its basin of white marble, and columns and pyramids of wood and materials up and down the gardens [which are] encompassed by water large enough for one to have the pleasure of going in a boat and rowing between the shrubs.[15]

The Earl of Leicester's garden at Kenilworth was described by Robert Lancham, a court official who accompanied the queen on one of her frequent progresses:

> Close to the wall is a beautiful terrace ten feet high and twelve feet broad, quite level and covered with thick grass which also grows on the slope. There are obelisks on the terrace at even distances, great balls and white heraldic beasts, all made of stone and perched on artistic posts, good to look at. At each end is a bower, smelling of sweet flowers and trees . . . There are also four parterres cut in regular proportions; in the middle of each is a post shaped like a cube, two feet high; on that a pyramid, accurately made, symmetrically carved, fifteen feet high; on the summit a ball ten inches in diameter.[16]

There were similar decorations in the garden at Hatfield, Robert Cecil's house which was built for him by Robert Lyminge. The steps leading from the house into it were decorated with figures of gilded lions; a fountain of exotic design was surmounted by a statue of Neptune towering over the lead fish in the basin. The rose garden was separate from the knot garden; there was a maze and a vineyard, the largest at that time in the country; the plants included several exotic and hitherto unknown varieties brought from the Continent by Cecil's gardener, John Tradescant the elder.[17]

Great houses were more fully furnished than they had been in the Middle Ages, yet, by the standards of the eighteenth and nineteenth centuries, they would still have been considered rather bare. The most prized pieces in many houses remained the beds. These now, instead of having canopies hanging from the ceiling on cords, were more often all of a piece, the tester from which the curtains hung being supported by posts at each corner. Headboards were generally larger and were extravagantly carved, sometimes being provided with recesses for candles at the top of which were holes through which the smoke could escape. Mattresses were stuffed with carded wool or feathers and were laid upon rope or canvas meshes rather than upon the boards of earlier times. Bedrooms would also probably contain carved chests and stools and a cupboard for jugs and basins, brushes and combs, pots of cosmetics, a looking-glass and a chamber pot, perhaps of pewter and known as a 'jordan'. 'Jordans' were sometimes enclosed in close-stools. One of these made for the king in 1547 was covered with black velvet and decorated with ribbons, a fringe and 2000 gilt-headed nails. The water-closet was invented by Sir John Harrington in 1596 and the queen, his godmother, had one installed in Richmond Palace the following year. But it was to be very many years before her example was generally followed; and, in the meantime, as Andrew Boorde complained, there was too much 'pissing in chimnies'.

   This habit was also condemned, together with other bad behaviour on the part of guests, by Thomas Tusser whose *Five Hundreth Goode Pointes of Husbandrie* was published in 1573:

> The sloven and the carles man, the roinish
>    nothing nice,
> To lodge in chamber comely deckt, are seldom
>    suffred twice.
>
> With curteine som make scaberd clene, with
>    coverlet their shoo,
> All dirt and mire some wallow bed, as spanniels
>    use to doo.
>
> Though bootes and spurs be nere so foule, what
>    passeth some thereon?
> What place they foule, what thing they teare,
>    by tumbling thereupon.

Foule male some cast on faire boord, be carpet
    nere so cleene,
What maners careles maister hath, by knave his
    man is seene.

Some make the chimnie chamber pot to smell like
    filthie sink,
Yet who so bold, so soone to say, fough, how
    these houses stink?

They therefore such as make no force what comly
    thing they spil,
Must have a cabben like themselves, although
    against their wil.

But gentlemen will gently doe where gentlenes
    is sheawd,
Observing this, with love abide, or else hence
    all beshreawd.[18]

Chairs were rarely seen in bedrooms and, indeed, were not all that common anywhere. In some houses they were reserved for the owner and favoured guests, hence to take the chair or to become a chairman came to take on its present connotation of precedence. At Hampton Court, where Cardinal Wolsey had no less than 280 beds, there were only five chairs of state, though there were a few other chairs, mostly uncomfortable, for lesser men. Some were box-chairs, others were bobbin chairs. Later in the sixteenth century conversation chairs with arms and low seats, known as *caqueteuses* from the French *caqueter* (to chatter), were introduced from the Continent. By the end of the century, indeed, chairs were more commonly found in large houses, and the seats were usually covered in some material, quilted or cushioned. In an inventory taken of the contents of Sir Henry Unton's house at Wadley in Berkshire in 1596 nearly all the chairs and stools are described as covered. In the great chamber there was a velvet chair and six stools in tuft taffeta; in the parlour there were two chairs in green cloth, one in black wrought velvet laid with silver and gold lace, thirteen stools in green cloth and six leather stools. One of the bedrooms had a chair, two stools and a cushion for the window seat all covered in yellow velvet.[19]

In halls, chambers and parlours there were coffers and cupboards, dressers and stepped sideboards, aumbries and buffets, chests with a single drawer at the bottom which developed into chests of several drawers, and tables, these no longer trestle tables but more often heavy pieces with the tops fixed to bulbous legs. Most were more or less clumsily carved, although many were made of fine woods, rosewood, walnut and oak inlaid with marquetry, and they were often covered with carpets, which, imported from the Continent and from Turkey and Asia Minor, were also hung on the walls, although not until later placed on the floor. Where rushes were used these were now usually changed every month not laid on top of old layers as had been a common practice in the Middle Ages.

Pewter and silver were much in evidence, both as decorative pieces on cupboards and sideboards and as tableware. Ceremonial salts became increasingly elaborate, the Earl of Leicester's being made of mother-of-pearl, and shaped like a galleon. It was 'garnished with silver and divers warlike engines and ornaments; with sixteen pieces of ordnance whereof two [are] on wheels; two anchors in the forepart; and on the stern an image of Dame Fortune standing on a globe with a flag in her hand'.[20] Spice-boxes and pepper-casters were almost as ornate; so were pomanders and candlesticks and clocks. Even chandeliers and warming-pans were sometimes of silver; lidded goblets were made in silver and in gold; and horn tankards were ornamented with silver bands. Silver and pewter trenchers were taking the place of wooden ones and the medieval slices of bread. Spoons were also of silver; knives were now laid on the table rather than brought to it in sheaths; though forks, introduced from Italy, were rarely seen. Thomas Coryate, the English traveller, who set out upon the journey which was to provide material for his *Crudities* in 1608, came across the fork in Italy and, as Fernand Braudel says, 'made fun of it at first, then adopted it – to the great amusement of his friends who christened him *furciferus* (fork-handler, or to be more precise pitchfork-handler)'. 'Was it the fashion for wearing ruffs that led rich diners to use forks?' Braudel continues. 'Probably not, since in England, for example, there is no mention of table forks in any inventory before 1660. Their use only became general in about 1750.'[21]

'Venice glasses' were widely used for drinking. English glass also was now rivalling the Venetian in quality, thanks largely to Continental craftsmen who had been brought over to impart their expertise to English glassworkers. For their beautifully wrought ironwork the English craftsmen had need of no such advice.

The meals consumed were as ample as ever, particularly dinner which was usually served between ten o'clock and noon. But the Rev. William Harrison insisted that, while a gentleman took pride in his kitchen and often employed a French chef, he was not in the habit of overeating. Nor, so a Dutch visitor observed, were most gentlemen at this period heavy drinkers. 'At their tables, although they be very sumptuous and love to have good fare, yet neither use they to overcharge themselves with excess of drink, neither thereto greatly provoke and urge others, but suffer every man to drink in such measure as best pleaseth himself.'[22]

Meat and bread remained the principal foods, the 'gentilitie' eating wheaten bread in Harrison's words, though "their household or poor neighbours in some shires [were] forced to content themselves with rye or barley, [and] in time of dearth many with bread made out of beans, peason or oats and some acorns among.' Vegetables were still not often served with meat, although sometimes used in cooking it – chickens were boiled with leeks – and often used for making pottage. Salads, however, seem to have been popular; and dishes of cucumber, peas, olives and artichokes were more often seen than they had been in the past. The potato, encountered in America by the invading Spaniards – there were at least 220 varieties in Peru – was introduced into England during the second half of the century; but, while grown in private gardens, potatoes were not yet considered by farmers to be a worthwhile commercial crop.[23] Cheese, except for soft or cream cheese which was frequently used in cooking, was now less often eaten by the rich than by the poor who seem to have enjoyed large quantities both of hard cheese, which was made of skimmed milk and became harder the longer it was kept, and of green cheese, a fresh curd cheese commonly flavoured with herbs.

Fynes Moryson, who had travelled extensively on the Continent, thought that English beef and mutton was the best in Europe and that only Westphalia had better bacon.

> The English eat fallow deer plentifully [Moryson recorded], as bucks in summer and does in winter, which they bake in pasties, and this venison pasty is a dainty, rarely found in any other kingdom. England, yea perhaps one county thereof, hath more fallow deer than all Europe that I have seen. No kingdom in the world hath so many dove-houses. Likewise brawn is a proper meat to the English, not known to others. English cooks, in comparison with other nations, are most commended for roasted meats . . . The English inhabitants eat almost no flesh commoner than hens, and for geese they eat them in two seasons, when they are felled upon the stubble after harvest and when they are green about Whitsuntide. And howsoever hares are thought to nourish melancholy, yet they are eaten as venison both roast and boiled. They have plenty of conies [rabbits] the flesh whereof is fat, tender and more delicate than any I have eaten in other parts.[24]

Dinner was generally a leisurely pleasure, 'the nobility, gentlemen and merchant men' often sitting over it until 'two or three o'clock at afternoon,' according to Harrison, 'so that with many it is a hard matter to rise from the table to go to evening prayers'. Wine was commonly kept in a copper tub full of water; and before a glass was refilled it was rinsed.

Supper was usually eaten at about five o'clock, or earlier in the country where dinner might be at eleven; and, although this was meant to be a light meal compared with dinner, one gentleman living in London in 1589 did not consider it unusual to consume a roast shoulder of mutton and three fried rabbits as well as bread, beer and a pint of claret.[25]

Indeed, while the sixteenth-century gentlemen may not have made a habit of overeating, as Harrison maintained, it is clear that most of them and their household did not stint themselves either. The kitchen books of Sir William Petre of Ingatestone Hall, Essex – one of the few surviving records of food and drink consumed in a mid-sixteenth-century country house of moderate size – indicate that both the family and the servants fed very well. There were about twenty servants at the Hall, including the chaplain, the house steward and the acater who received no wages but were permitted instead to lease farms on the estate at low rents. There were four housemaids and one nursemaid, a housekeeper, a clerk of the kitchen, a male cook, a butler, and a part-time brewer. Outside servants included a gardener, two horsekeepers, a stable-boy, two carters and a cart-lad. All the lower servants were hired by the year, and received board and lodging, and an allowance for their grey summer and winter liveries, in addition to their wages which amounted to a total of £40 a year. The cook, butler and housekeeper each received 10s a year, the gardener 10s 6d and the part-time brewer 5s. Occasionally some of the servants were given 'rewards' for extra work: the nursemaid once had 6d for knitting the children 'two pairs of hoses' and the gardener's wife earned a penny or two for occasional weeding. By such means they were able to accumulate a little pocket money to spend at the local fair for which they were given the day off and from which they came back perhaps with a ribbon or a fairing.[26] In some other households servants' wages were liable to be reduced by fines for misbehaviour or negligence. In the household of a Somerset high sheriff, they were fined 1d for swearing, untidy dress, or leaving a bed unmade after eight o'clock in the morning; 2d for not attending family prayers; and 6d for being late in serving dinner. The fines were deducted from their wages every quarter day, together with the cost of breakages, and given to the poor or to 'other godly use'.[27]

If their wages were moderate the Petres' servants had no cause to complain about the amplitude and variety of their meals. One day before the Christmas holiday of 1551, while the family were still in London, they had twelve local people for guests at dinner and between them all they consumed three joints of boiled beef and one of roasted, a neat's tongue, a baked leg of mutton, two rabbits and a partridge. On Christmas day that year six boiled and three roast joints of beef were carried to the dinner table, a neck of mutton, a loin and a breast of pork, a goose, four rabbits, as well as eight baked pear pies.

The following year family, servants and guests at Ingatestone, in forty-six weeks, consumed seventeen oxen, one bull, fourteen steers, four cows, twenty-nine calves, 130 sheep, fifty-four lambs, three boars, thirteen bucks, five does, nine porkers, three goats, seven kids, one stag and five hogs 'killed for bacon'. All kinds of wildfowl were also eaten, mallards, widgeons, wild ducks, teals, cranes, shovelards, woodcocks, curlews, redshanks, plovers and wild pigeons. Pigeons also came regularly from the dovecot, well over 1000 of them between Easter and Michaelmas in 1552. And, as in previous centuries, quantities of small birds came into the cook's hands, larks, blackbirds, starlings and swallows.[28]

The cost of food had risen since the beginning of the century when chickens had cost about 1½d each, eggs were ¾d a dozen, rabbits 1s 4d for nine, and a gallon of gooseberries 2d. By 1558, according to the accounts of a dinner given by the master and wardens of the Stationers' Company, gooseberries had doubled in price, rabbits had more than doubled and chickens had trebled. Seven geese cost 9s 4d, two breasts of veal 2s 4d, two necks of mutton 1s, and thirty-six gallons of beer 4s 8d.[29]

Ingatestone was unusual in having both a drinking water tap in the yard and a piped supply of 'sweet' spring water in the house. Yet, in compliance with Andrew Boorde's advice that water was 'not wholesome by itself for an Englishman', the staff drank beer instead, consuming about eight pints of small beer each, at a cost of 1d the gallon.[30] Wine was considerably more expensive at about 1s a gallon. But Sir William's cellar was always well stocked. Shortly before Christmas 1551 the steward's stocktaking revealed that there was a total of 584 gallons in the wine cellar, comprising:

> A butt of sack and 12 gallons.
> 2 puncheons of French wine and 20 gallons.
> An hogshead of French wine.
> An hogshead of Gascon wine with an half.
> An hogshead of red wine with an half.
> A piece of Rhenisen wine.
> 4 gallons of Malmsey.

The fish served on fast-days was equally varied. Much of it came from the Hall fish ponds, but the acater also bought 'seafish' from Brentwood, Chelmsford and Barking, and presents of fish were regularly received from friends and acquaintances of the family. As well as haberdine and ling, smoked herring, tench, carp, bream, roach and perch, the household also, therefore, enjoyed sole and plaice, whiting and flounders and, less often, mackerel, gurnard and salmon. Oysters were common fare even on those 'four hot months which are void of the letter R' during which, so Harrison said, they were 'generally forborne'. They cost only 8d or 9d a bushel, and as little as 4d a bushel if bought at Battlesbridge at the head of the creek within twenty miles of Ingatestone.

Bread was eaten plentifully, the Hall ovens baking the equivalent of about 20,000 loaves of good to medium quality a year. Cheese, butter and eggs were also in good supply. In 1552 about 2664 pounds of cheese were consumed, possibly as much as 970 pounds of butter and certainly no less than 2657 eggs. As in the past most cooked dishes were highly flavoured. As well as salt and pepper, cloves, mace, saffron, ginger and cinnamon were all bought in large quantities.

Little else, however, had to be purchased, for Ingatestone Hall was largely self-sufficient. All fuels for heating, cooking and brewing came from the estate, as well as most food and most timber for building. What the estate could not supply was generally bought from local joiners, carpenters, turners, wheelwrights and smiths who could put their hands to making furniture and carts, farm implements, garden tools and horseshoes. Bricks were also made locally; so were shoes and pots. Only occasionally did a purchase have to be made further afield, a saddle, for instance, from Chelmsford, a plough and 'two hogsheads' for fish from Billericay, dried fruit, ink, salt and plate and, of course, expensive plate and jewellery and fashionable clothes from London.[31]

# 17 · *Animals and Sportsmen*

The maintenance of Ingatestone Hall and of his London house at Aldersgate – where there were, as in Essex, several servants, including a housekeeper, laundress and cook – cost Sir William Petre about £250 a year. But when the queen came to stay on one of her periodical progresses throughout her realm, by which she showed herself to her people at little expense to herself, he would be expected to spend more in a single day than he would otherwise spend in a month. There was extra silver and plate to buy, new hangings for the rooms to be set aside for the queen as a royal suite, supplies of food and drink to lay in for her entourage, of paper, ink and wax lights. There were new buildings to be erected: on the occasion of her visit to Ingatestone in 1561, Petre's accounts mention, in addition to page after page of unusual expenses, a sum of £3 8s 2d paid to bricklayers, carpenters and labourers, for 'making ranges, sheds and other necessaries against the queen's Majesty's coming'. Even so, Petre's expenses were modest compared with the outlay required of others. A visit of four or five days to Hedingham Castle cost the Earl of Oxford £273; and a visit of similar duration cost Lord Rich of Leighs Priory £389. In 1577 Sir Nicholas Bacon had to spend £577 on entertaining the queen for four days; and in 1602 a three-day visit to Lord Keeper Egerton cost no less than £2000.[1]

Travelling with a huge retinue, which required over 300 carts and more than 2000 horses, the queen obliged some of her subjects not merely to convert their houses but even to enlarge them for her. Presence and audience chambers had to be provided, as well as privy chambers and lodgings for officials, attendants and courtiers, for their servants and their servants' servants. Lord Burghley's household at Theobalds, where the queen was a frequent visitor, was constantly disrupted by these visitations. His own servants had to move out of the house to sleep in a storehouse and they were obliged to have their meals in the joiners' workshop.

My house at Theobalds [Burghley told a friend] was begun by me with a mean measure but increased by occasion of Her Majesty's often coming, whom to please I never would omit to strain myself to more charges than building it. And yet not without some special direction of Her Majesty. Upon fault found with the small measure of her chamber (which was in good measure for me) I was forced to enlarge a room for a larger chamber; which need not be envied of any for riches in it.[2]

As well as Theobalds, Burghley owned Burghley House in Northamptonshire, an enormous mansion where the queen also stayed on several occasions at a cost to its owner of £2000 to £3000 for each visit. Immense as this sum then was, there were several other great men in the country who were anxious to have the honour of entertaining the queen and who waited for a visit in vain. Holdenby House in Northamptonshire – which was built at vast expense by the Lord Chancellor, Sir Christopher Hatton, and all but ruined him – stood ready for ten years, full of servants waiting for the queen to come to stay. During the whole of that time she never did come. Hatton died a bachelor at the age of fifty-one, leaving Holdenby and his debts to a nephew who could not afford to live in it. It was sold a few years later and within fifty years had been demolished.[3]

The better the hunting the more the queen was likely to enjoy herself. Many country houses had two deer parks, one for red, the other for fallow deer. Foxes and badgers were occasionally 'preserved by gentlemen to hunt and have pastime withal', but deer were the principal quarry. They were hunted both in the park and, beyond its pales, in the open countryside where heavy horses thundered over the grass in the wake of the greyhounds and spaniels which all true English gentlemen were said to love. There was, indeed, a familiar proverb: 'He cannot be a gentleman who loveth not a dog.' And greyhounds and spaniels, as well as other breeds, were frequently given as presents in those regular parcels which passed from hand to hand in Tudor England in recognition of past services or in hope of benefits to come. In the *Lisle Letters* references are made not only to presents of food and wine, quails, parrots, oranges, lengths of satin, hawks, singing-birds, monkeys, gold, books, puffins, baked cranes, haunches of venison, marmosets, coral beads, purses and tips of unicorns' horns, but also to frequent gifts of 'pretty dogs', greyhounds, mastiffs, bloodhounds and water spaniels. Many were sporting dogs but others were lap-dogs, one of which, Purkoy, a present from Lord Lisle, gave great pleasure to Anne Boleyn who 'setteth much store by a pretty dog'. 'Her Grace delighted so much in little Purkoy,' so Lady Lisle was told, 'that after he was dead of a fall there durst nobody tell her Grace of it.'[4]

The eastern view of dogs as scavengers, so Keith Thomas has observed, had been transmitted to medieval England by means of the Bible and was still widely held in the sixteenth century.[5] Dogs were still used to turn kitchen spits by running around in 'dog-wheels' and were trained to the task by having hot coals placed beneath their paws to keep them on the move.[6] But attitudes were changing. Distinctions had long been made between the mongrels of tinkers and the watchdogs of merchants on the one hand and the greyhounds and setters of the aristocracy on the other; and in 1567 the mayor of Liverpool had ordered that householders' watchdogs must be kept tied up 'for avoidance of sundry inconveniences as for hurting of greyhounds, hounds and spaniels, *that is gentlemen's* dogs', the kinds of dogs, in fact, to be seen as emblems of fidelity at the feet of their masters' effigies on tombs.[7] Yet by this time dogs were being praised for their faithfulness, their affectionate natures and powers of observation, irrespective of their breeding. In his epigram *In Cineam* of 1594, Sir John Davies wrote:

> Thou sayest thou art as weary as a dog,
> As angry, sick, and hungry as a dog,
> As dull and melancholy as a dog,
> As lazy, sleepy, idle as a dog.
> But why dost thou compare thee to a dog?
> In that for which all men despise a dog,
> I will compare thee better to a dog.
> Thou art as fair and comely as a dog,
> Thou art as true and honest as a dog,
> Thou art as kind and liberal as a dog,
> Thou art as wise and valiant as a dog.[8]

Attitudes to cats, too, were gradually changing. Kept in the Middle Ages as a protection against vermin, 'unclean and impure beasts' that lived by ravening, cats were frequently left unfed to improve their performance as mousers. Keith Thomas cites an early Tudor textbook which contains for translation into Latin the simple sentence and commonly held sentiment, 'I hate cats.'[9] Dick Whittington, four times Mayor of London, who died in 1423, was not provided with his cat until the legends accumulated around his name almost two hundred years later.[10] Yet long before Samuel Johnson became so celebrated as a cat-lover – going out to buy his beloved Hodge oysters in case his servants, being put to that trouble on a cat's behalf, might take against the 'poor creature' – there were numerous examples of men as devoted to cats as he, among them the Earl of Southampton who was comforted by the presence of his pet during his imprisonment in the Tower after Essex's rebellion; John Harrison, the Leeds merchant who had holes cut in his doors so that the cats could enter 'even the best rooms of the house';

and Archbishop Laud who was given one of the earliest tabbies to be imported into England. By the time of Charles II there were said to be few London familes without a pet cat, 'some having several, sometimes five or six in a house'.[11]

Cats, however, were still cruelly used. They were hung up in baskets to be used as targets at country fairs; they were stuffed alive into effigies and placed on bonfires so that their cries could add to the horror of the scene; they were thrown out of garret windows with bladders fastened to them to see how far they could fly. At Ely Cathedral there was 'a great noise and disturbance near the choir' one New Year's Day when a man roasted a live cat on a spit before a large and noisy crowd.[12]

Man's 'charter of dominion over the creatures', as Thomas Fuller called it, was taken to provide an excuse for cruel sports. However bloodthirstily executed, hunting was 'yet without guilt'. In Henry VIII's day it was common practice to have several hundred deer rounded up and then to loose the hounds upon them in a wholesale massacre; and after the slaughter of a deer it was customary for ladies to wash their hands in the blood in the belief that it would make them white.[13] James I was far from unusual in appearing insanely vindictive as he hunted down the quarry, riding after the hounds at a wild gallop and dismounting eagerly to cut the stag's throat as soon as it had been brought down. Then he would rip its belly open, put his hands and sometimes his feet inside and daub his companions with blood. Like so many of his contemporaries – who, according to Fynes Moryson, took more delight in hunting than the people of any other nation – the king not only hunted stags with frenzied enthusiasm, not only killed hares and caught larks, pursued game with hawks and cormorants, he loved to see cocks fighting and bears and bulls being baited to death. To watch bears baited he had a special pit made and once matched a lion with a bear which was to be punished for killing a child, but the lion refused to fight and the bear had to be baited to death by dogs instead.[14]

The king's predecessor, Queen Elizabeth I, also much enjoyed hunting and attended the animal baitings that often followed the sport, as she did during the entertainments provided at Kenilworth Castle by the Earl of Leicester in 1575 when a crew of dogs was let loose upon thirteen bears and there was 'plucking and tugging, scratching and biting and such an expense of blood as a month's licking . . . will not recover'.[15]

Wearing clothes and jewels more suitable for the audience chamber than the hunting field, the queen was not content, even at the age of sixty-seven, to watch the hounds driving the deer along the coursing paddock, and to shoot at the quarry from the stands as her ladies preferred to do. She insisted on going ahead with the men, riding her horse so fast that she tired out her frightened companions, proving that she was quite capable of shooting with a heavy cross-bow and killing the 'great and fat stagge with her owen Hand'.[16]

Hare-coursing was still a popular sport. So was hawking, and most rich gentlemen employed a falconer who trained the hawk to fly from the master's gloved hand and bring the quarry to earth where it was located by the jingling bells tied to its legs. Bows and arrows were still used to bring down wildfowl but by 1559 the 'keeper of my master's park' at Ingatestone was receiving money to buy 'gunpowder to kill fowl with'; and the fowling-piece, or 'birding-piece' as Mistress Ford calls it in *The Merry Wives of Windsor*, was becoming quite common. Birds and beasts were also snared, netted, limed and trapped; and, although fish were usually drawn out of fishponds in nets, angling was becoming more common than it had been in the fifteenth century when Dame Juliana Berners had sung its praises in *A Treatyss of Fysshynge with an Angle* and had compared the pleasure of fishing in the 'swete ayre' and smelling the 'swete savoure of the meede floures' with the laboriousness and frustrations of hunting. 'For the hunter must always renne and folowe his houndes . . . swetynge full sore. He bloweth tyll his lyppes blyster, and when he wenyth it be an hare full oft it is an hegge hogge.' He returns home tired out, his clothes wet and torn, his hounds and hawks lost, and suffering from 'ryght evyll a thurste'.[17]

While hunting remained the favourite pastime of the healthy, the adventurous and energetic, most gentlemen enjoyed quieter sports and games as well. Nearly everyone played bowls, and few country houses were without their bowling-greens or bowling-alleys. The game was still played much as it had been in the time of Edward II, but the introduction of the bias, a heavy metal weight inserted into one side of the bowl, demanded much greater skill in play. Some houses also had courts for the playing of tennis, a game introduced from France where it seems to have originated as a sort of handball played in cathedral cloisters. There the game was known as *jeu de paume*, 'palm game', the ball being struck with the palm of the hand, and its English name was probably derived from the French players' call of 'Tenez!', 'Watch out!', before serving. By the middle of the sixteenth century the game was being played in roofed courts with rackets and with harder balls made of bits of cloth tightly wadded together which were exported to England in large numbers. King Henry VII had had courts constructed at Blackfriars, Greenwich, Westminster and elsewhere; and his son, Henry VIII, a skilful player in his youth, had built tennis courts also at Whitehall, St James's and Hampton Court. By Elizabeth I's day fives, a form of handball played in a walled court with a gloved hand, was also popular; and fencing was becoming as widely practised among the upper classes, both in the Spanish and Italian styles, as archery and wrestling.

A kind of cricket was being played by the end of the century; but it had not yet caught the general fancy, whereas football had been played by the common people for centuries. With no generally accepted rules, it was a violent game in which 'young men propel a huge ball not by throwing it into the air, but by striking and rolling it along the ground with their feet'. It frequently led to quarrels and fights, sometimes to riot and murder. Constant efforts were made to control it. In the fourteenth and fifteenth centuries several proclamations were issued banning it, ordering men to practise archery instead and imposing fines and even imprisonment on those who continued to play it. But it proved impossible to suppress and by the sixteenth century had become established as part of the social life of the country, being played everywhere on public holidays and on Sundays.[18] The way in which it was played varied from place to place but in most there were no regulations as to the number of players on each side, no boundaries and no time limit. At Ashbourne in Derbyshire the goals were three miles apart and the game lasted all day. In Pembrokeshire, as described by George Owen of Henlyss – who carried the scars, 'signes and seales' of it in his 'heade, handes and other partes' – it was played with a wooden ball ('boyled in tallow to make it slipperye') by men stripped to the waist and with hair and beards so short their opponents could not get a grip on them. As many as 2000 players took part; and the confusion and violence was so great that a visitor who chanced upon the scene in 1588 observed, 'If this be but playe, I cold wishe the Spaniardes were here to see our plaies in England. Certes they would be oodielye feare of our warre.'[19]

Football, indeed, according to Philip Stubbes, was 'a bloody and murdering practice'.

Doth not everyone lie in wait for his adversary, seeking to overthrow him and pitch him on the nose, though it be upon hard stones, in ditch or dale, in valley or hill, or what place soever it be? He careth not so he have him downe. And he that can serve the most of this fashion, he is counted the only fellow . . . so that by this means sometimes their necks are broken, sometimes their backs, sometime their legs, sometime their arms; sometime one part thrust out of joint, sometime another; sometime the noses gush out with blood, sometime their eyes start out . . . But whosoever scapeth away the best goeth not scot free, but is either sore wounded, crazed [concussed] and bruised, so that he dieth of it, or else scapeth very hardly; and no marvel, for they have the sleights to meet one betwixt two, to back him against the heart with their elbows, to hit him under the short ribs with their griped fists, and with their knees to catch him upon the hip, and to pitch him on his neck, with a hundred such murdering devices.[20]

There were a few who saw good in the game. Richard Mulcaster, headmaster of St Paul's School, thought that the game 'strengtheneth and brawneth the whole body, and by provoking superfluities downewards, it dischargeth the head and upper parts. It is good for the bowels, driveth downe the stone and gravel from both the bladder and kidneies.' But Mulcaster had to agree that as usually played in England, 'with bursting of shins and breaking of legs, it be neither civil, [nor] worthy'. It it were to become a game for gentlemen, rules would have to be made and referees introduced to enforce them.[21]

As it was, most people agreed with Sir Thomas Elyot who thought that football was 'nothing but beastly fury and extreme violence, whereof proceedeth hurt and consequently rancour and malice do remain with those that he wounded'.[22]

# 18 · *Readers and Music Makers*

Before the age of printing English people rarely read for pleasure. A surprisingly large number of medieval books in manuscript have survived; but most households contained few volumes other than breviaries and psalters, manuals of etiquette, perhaps a technical treatise or two on subjects like medicine and law, guidebooks and collections of moralizing precepts which advised the reader to 'be given more to wakefulness than sleep' or 'to bear poverty with patience since Nature created you a naked infant'. Bibles were not often seen because a licence was required for their possession, and without it the reader might be accused of heresy. Historical chronicles, both in verse and prose, books of travels such as that ascribed to Sir John Mandeville, copies of Chaucer and Langland, and romances, in particular those relating to King Arthur, seem to have been the most widely read books in those households which possessed any books at all. This distressed Roger Ascham who wrote:

> In our forefather's time when papistry, like a standing pool, covered and overflowed England, few books were read in our tongues saving certain books of chivalry, as they said for pastime or pleasure . . . As one, for example *Le Morte d'Arthur*, the whole pleasure of which book standeth in two special points, in open manslaughter and bold bawdry . . . Yet I know when God's Bible was banished the Court, *Le Morte d'Arthur* [was] received into the Prince's chamber.[1]

Most rich men had modest libraries, the books often being prized for their monetary value rather than their literary merit; and many, like Sir John Paston, employed, at great expense, professional scribes and illuminators to copy and embellish texts. At Caister Castle Sir John Fastolf had some twenty books excluding those reserved for use in the chapel. Among them, according to the catalogue, were *The Cronycles of France*, the *Romance da Rose*, *Meditacions Saint Bernard*, *A Book of Julius Caesar*, *Veges de l'arte Chevalerie*, *Vice and Vertues*, a book of etiquette, the *Chronicles of Titus Livius*, *Problemate Aristotelis* and *Liber de Cronykles de Grant Bretayne in Ryme*. These were the kinds of book to be found in most large fifteenth-century households; and some of them would have been found in the public libraries which were beginning to be established. The Guildhall Library in London, a library of mostly theological books chained in their shelves, was established in about 1423 with money left by Richard Whittington, the Lord Mayor; and by 1464 there were also chained libraries at Bristol and Worcester. Both these were open to the public between 10 o'clock in the morning and two in the afternoon. A university graduate acted as librarian, helping visitors and giving a weekly lecture.

Soon after the establishment of these two libraries, William Caxton rented a shop for 10s a year near the entrance to the south transept of Westminster Abbey. Later he took other rooms by the gate leading to the Almonry; and until his death in 1491, from the sign of the Red Pale, he issued seventy-four books printed in English, twenty of them translations into the language made by himself. He was the first English but by no means the first European printer. Johannes Gutenberg had published his celebrated Bible twenty years before Caxton established his press in Westminster; and presses had been set up at Cologne in 1464, at Rome in 1467, at Venice and Paris in 1470 and soon afterwards in Spain, Hungary and Poland. It was at Cologne, where he lived from 1470 to 1472, that Caxton learned the craft of printing.

He had been born in Kent and been apprenticed at the age of sixteen to Robert Large, a rich London mercer. After Large's death he had moved to Bruges, centre of the European wool trade, where he became rich himself. Of a studious turn of mind, and exceedingly industrious by nature, he began to occupy his leisure hours in 1469 by translating Raoul Le Fèvre's *Recueil des Histoires de Troy* during which labours his 'pen became worn, his hand weary, his eye dimmed'. But he was rewarded in 1475 by the pleasure of seeing the book in print, issued by his own press in Bruges. The next year, that of his return to England, saw the appearance both of his translation from the French of *The Game and Playe of Chesse* and of his first item printed in England, an Indulgence dated 13 December 1476.

He had a clear idea of the kinds of people who constituted the great majority of his readers. His friends were wealthy merchants such as he had been; his patrons were Edward IV and his successor, Richard III, as well as noblemen who, from time to time, commissioned books. His English publications covered a wide variety of subjects, history and philosophy, romance, devotion and English literature, from *Dictes and Sayengs of the Phylosophers* by Edward IV's brother-in-law, Anthony Woodville, Lord

Rivers, to Chaucer's *The Canterbury Tales*, John Gower's *Confessio Aman-tis*, much of Lydgate's poetry, and Sir Thomas Malory's *Le Morte d'Arthur* which appeared in 1485. These were the kind of books which English readers preferred and which were provided for them after Caxton's death by Wynkyn de Worde – who probably came to England as his assistant in 1476 and later established himself in Fleet Street – and by those other English printers who catered for the public that Caxton had helped to create.[2]

This public was particularly drawn to books of history and travels, translations of the classics, to theological works, and to herbals, treatises of self-instruction, and manuals on medicine and diet. Sir John Mandeville's wildly fanciful *Travels*, translated from the French in 1496, were especially popular, as were Ranulph Higden's universal history, *Polychronicon*, Robert Fabyan's *The New Chronicles of England and France* and Thomas à Kempis's *On the Imitation of Christ*, first published in English in 1503. *A Treatyse of Fysshynge with an Angle* appeared in 1495, and Roger Ascham's *Toxophilus* in 1545. Fitzherbert's *Boke of Husbandrie* of 1523 was followed by Thomas Tusser's *Hundreth Good Pointes of Husbandrie* in 1557. The mathematician Robert Recorde brought out a whole series of widely read books on his subject, including *Introduction to lerne to recken with the Pen* in 1537, *Grounde of Artes*, which appeared in numerous editions from 1540 onwards, *The Whetstone of Witte, or the second Part of Arithmetike*, *The Pathway of Knowledge, or the first Principles of Geometry*, and *The Treasure of Knowledge*.

Widely read though they were, most books such as Fabyan's *New Chronicles* were printed in what would today be considered extremely small editions, perhaps not more than 200 copies or so, and they were consequently very expensive. It was only those books which were printed in much larger quantities that could be bought for the relatively cheap price of the Book of Common Prayer which was sold at 2s 2d for an unbound copy, 3s 8d bound.[3]

For much of the period the Bible could not be bought at all. In the fourteenth century various translations of New Testament books had appeared; and although these versions 'made in the time of John Wyclif or since' had been suppressed in 1407 at the Council of Oxford, several of them were still in circulation when William Tyndale's translation, printed on the Continent, appeared in England in the 1520s. Miles Coverdale's translation, which contained an unauthorized dedication to Henry VIII, was also printed abroad; and it was not until 1537 that a Bible ascribed to one Thomas Matthew was issued with the official consent of the king. Two years later the 'Great Bible' was issued under the patronage of Thomas Cromwell; and in 1540 'Cranmer's Bible' was published with a notice to the effect that it was 'appointed to the use of churches'. Yet even now not everyone was permitted to read the Bible freely since the king, who had condemned Tyndale's strongly Protestant marginal notes as 'pestilent glosses', considered its unrestricted study 'a dangerous thing'. Noblemen were allowed to read it to their families, and gentlemen and merchants in a satisfactory way of business could read it to themselves, but the common people not at all. The prohibitions, lifted in the reign of Edward VI, were reimposed during that of Mary, in which yet another English version was printed for Protestant exiles and for the first time divided into verses. In the reign of Queen Elizabeth came the Geneva Bible, also known as the Breeches Bible because in it Genesis chapter 3, verse 7 is rendered, 'and they sowed figge-leaves together, and made themselves breeches'. For fifty years this was the most widely read of all translations, until the appearance of the splendid Authorized Version of 1611 which soon displaced its predecessors and has proved unsurpassable.[4]

After the appearance of the Geneva Bible, the reading and listening to the words of the scriptures became an almost universal practice. People no longer had to gather, perhaps in trepidation, around the church lectern to hear the word of God, but could now attend to it at home where for many families the Bible was the only book they possessed, its endpapers becoming, and remaining until Victorian times, a register of births and deaths and a convenient place on which to record cooking recipes and medicines for sick cows. The regular reading of the Geneva Bible, and the Calvinistic marginal annotations with which it was embellished, not only introduced ordinary English people to the kind of religious controversies which flourished on the Continent but also, by the emphasis placed upon the study of the Old Testament, helped to prolong the medieval belief that success in the world depended upon divine favour, and that the world itself was one in which the supernatural was always likely to make a sudden appearance like the *deus ex machina* of the theatre.[5]

Almost as influential as the Bible in maintaining these habits of mind was John Foxe's *Actes and Monuments of These Latter Perilous Times*, later published under its more familiar title of *The Book of Martyrs: A History of the Persecution of the Protestants*. This, with its strong implication that the English people had been chosen by God to fight against Anti-Christ in the person of the pope, was considered so important a work that it was ordained in 1571 that copies should be available in all cathedrals and in the houses of gentry and the upper clergy for the edification of both servants and visitors. It was to be found, indeed, in most libraries in the country. Lady Hoby kept it beside her Bible and her books of sermons; Lady Mary Grey with her works by Whitgift, Luther and Knox, her Psalter, Psalms and Book of Common Prayer, her *Treatise on the Ressurrection of the Dead*, her *Comment on the Four Evangelists*, her *Ship of Assured Safety* and her *Life and Selected Orations of Demosthenes*.[6]

As the reign of Elizabeth progressed, more and more books appeared, so many, in fact, that Thomas Coryat feared that there would soon be more books than readers. In the country they were sold at fairs and by pedlars; in London the stalls of the booksellers sprawled in ever increasing numbers across St Paul's Churchyard. Offered for sale were all kinds of books from digests and encyclopaedias, and works on astronomy, astrology and alchemy, to romances, pamphlets, broadsheets, joke and riddle books, translations of erotic Italian novels and fiction by such English writers as Thomas Lodge, author of *A Margarite from America*; Robert Greene upon whose *Pandosto: The Triumph of Time* Shakespeare (that 'upstart crow') based the plot of *The Winter's Tale*; and Sir Philip Sidney whose *The Arcadia* first appeared in 1590.

No books were more popular, however, than those which told of fabulous animals and extraordinary peoples, of adventures and discoveries in strange lands, works like Edward Topsell's *History of Serpents* which described Ethiopian dragons ninety feet long, even more monstrous than those described by Pliny; Sir Walter Ralegh's *The Discovery of the Large, Rich and Beautiful Empire of Guiana*; and the *Principal Navigations* of the Rev. Richard Hakluyt who proposed that the overseas trade and colonial policies of England would 'increase the Queen's dominions, Enrich her coffers, and reduce many Pagans to the faith of Christ'.[7]

As booksellers flourished, so did music makers. The painters and sculptors of Tudor England might not be considered remotely comparable with those of continental Europe; and only in the painting of miniatures did an English artist, Nicholas Hilliard, achieve a mastery that his European rivals envied. Yet, as musicians, Englishmen were recognized masters, adopting towards their calling a professionalism that was largely lacking in other arts. Admittedly few musicians made their living by composing; most had to live by entertaining at court or in rich men's houses. But, whereas a painter was likely to be either an amateur indulging a hobby or a craftsman who made his money as an engraver or a house decorator, a musician was more likely to be considered, and to consider himself to be, an artist, as well as, perhaps, a scholar.

Before continental universities had begun to do so, Cambridge awarded degrees in music. Oxford followed suit, Robert Fayrfax, the composer, being awarded the degree of Doctor of Music there in 1511. Christopher Tye became a Doctor of Music at Cambridge in 1545 while John Taverner was nearing the end of his life as Master of the Choristers at Christ Church, Oxford. Thomas Tallis – the other great composer of the early Tudor period who was master of the Elizabethan musician, William Byrd – was employed at the Chapel Royal. Both John Dowland and Thomas Morley were awarded the degree of Bachelor of Music at Oxford in 1588.[8]

Queen Elizabeth herself was a talented musician, as her father had been. Her brother, Edward VI, who had employed sixty-five secular musicians at court, played the lute; her sister, Mary, was an expert performer upon the virginals; Elizabeth herself played the virginals 'excellently well' in the opinion of Sir James Melville, the Queen of Scots' ambassador. 'But she left off immediately as soon as she turned her about and saw me,' Melville related. 'She appeared to be surprised to see me, and came forward, seeming to strike me with her hand; alleging she used not to play before men, but when she was solitary, to shun melancholy.'[9]

She takes great pleasure in dancing and music [another diplomat, de Maisse, informed his master Henri IV, in 1598]. She told me she entertained at least sixty musicians; in her youth she danced very well and composed measures and music and had played them herself and danced them. She takes such pleasure in it that when her maids dance she follows the cadence with her hand and foot. She rebukes them if they do not dance to her liking and without a doubt she is mistress of the art having learnt in the Italian manner to dance high.[10]

Many, if not most of her well-to-do subjects, having learned to love music at school, were as musical as she was; and there were few households that did not possess a number of musical instruments. The inventory of Sir Thomas Kitson's goods at Hengrave Hall lists six viols, six violins, seven recorders, four cornets, a bandora, a cittern, two sackbuts, three hautboys, a curtal (a sort of bassoon), a lysarden (a deep-toned bass wind instrument), two flutes, three virginals, four lutes and an organ. There were also over fifty books of part-songs.[11] The Petres at Ingatestone Hall possessed virginals, lutes and viols, a gittern, an organ; and Sir William, though not a performer on all these instruments himself, seems to have played the virginals and organ, and certainly expended large sums of money on hiring musicians and choristers to perform for the entertainment of his family and guests.[12]

In most families, indeed, books of music and musical instruments were left lying about for the pleasure of guests who would also be expected to take part in the singing of madrigals; and if a guest claimed that he had no ear for music, it was as though he had admitted some disgraceful misconduct. 'Yea, some, might whisper to others,' wrote Thomas Morley in *Plaine and Easie Introduction to Practical Musicke*, and would ask how the poor fellow had been brought up.[13] Nor was this love of music confined to the wealthier classes. All over the country, in small private houses and public inns, music was played and madrigals were sung. No civic celebration was complete without musical accompaniment; in barbers' shops lutes were provided for the entertainment of customers as they were waiting for their turn in the chair; even Sir Francis Drake's *Golden Hind* had its own orchestra.[14]

'Manual labourers and mechanical artificers of all sorts,' wrote the author of *Praise of Musicke* in 1588, 'keepe such a chaunting and singing in their shoppes, the tailor on his bulk, the shoemaker at his last, the mason at his wall, the shipboy at his oar, and the tiler on the house top.'[15]

At court, music was an essential accompaniment to the masque, that combination of verse, mime, ballet and spectacle which had its origins in Italy. The first mention of the performance of a masque in England is in Hall's *Chronicle* which describes a night in 1512 when King Henry VIII

> . . . with XI other wer disguised after the maner of Italie, called a mask a thyng not seen afore in England. Thei wer appareled in garments long and brode, wrought all with gold, with visers and cappes of gold, and after the banket doen, these Maskers came in . . . and desired the ladies to daunce . . . And after thei daunced and commoned together, as the fashion of the Maske is, thei tooke their leave and departed . . . It was not a thyng commonly seen.[16]

A hundred years later, however, the masque had become one of the principal and most elaborate entertainments that the court had to offer. It had developed into a kind of stylized pageant, allegorical and spectacular, whose complicated symbolism was expressed in verse, song, dance, theatrically extravagant movement, intricate mechanical devices, and by the declamations of fantastically costumed courtiers. At Whitehall Palace as well as at the riverside palace, Somerset House, which Inigo Jones had restored for James I's consort, Anne of Denmark, huge sums of money were expended on these extraordinary productions in which the queen indulged her passion for display and dressing up.

The first of Queen Anne's masques, the *Masque of Blackness*, was performed in the Elizabethan Banqueting House at Whitehall on Twelfth Night 1605. Its magical theme and setting were characteristic of numerous other masques which were to be staged in various London and country palaces over the next thirty-five years. It told the fantastic story of the twelve daughters of Niger, the Ethiopian river-god, and of their introduction to Albion. Blackamoors and nymphs, tritons and mermaids, monsters and nereids cavorted and sang, appearing from the raging waves in huge conches and disappearing into the fathomless depths of the ocean, all dressed in a marvellous variety of costumes, bejewelled and magnificent.

The *Masque of Blackness* was written by Ben Jonson, whose collaboration with its designer, Inigo Jones, was to bring to the court of James I and of his son, Charles I, as fine a series of entertainments as had ever dazzled the audiences of the Medici court in Florence. Jonson's subsequent *Pleasure Reconciled to Virtue*, which was produced at the Banqueting House in 1618, was witnessed by Orazio Businor, almoner to the Venetian ambassador:

A large hall is fitted up like a theatre, with well secured boxes all round. The stage is at one end and his Majesty's chair in front under an ample canopy. Near him are stools for the foreign ambassadors . . . Whilst waiting for the King we amused ourselves admiring the decoration and beauty of the house . . . Then such a concourse as there was, for although they profess only to admit the favoured ones who are invited, yet every box was filled, notably with most noble and richly arrayed ladies, in number some 600 and more according to the general estimate . . . On entering the house the cornets and trumpets to the number of fifteen or twenty began to play very well a sort of recitative, and then after his Majesty had seated himself under the canopy . . . he caused the ambassadors to sit below him, while the great officers of the crown and courts of law sat upon benches. The Lord Chamberlain then had the way cleared and in the middle of the theatre there appeared a fine and spacious area carpeted all over with green cloth. In an instant a large curtain dropped, painted to represent a tent of gold cloth with a broad fringe. The background was of canvas painted blue, powdered all over with golden stars. This became the front arch of the stage.[17]

Beginning after supper, masques lasted well into the night, and occasionally were not concluded until dawn. Some went on for twelve hours and cost almost as many thousands of pounds, the beauty of the verse being matched by the inventiveness of the costumes and settings and by those marvellous contrivances by which mountains were made to move, angels to fly and devils to sink into hell. To Jonson, indeed, it seemed that Inigo Jones's costumes and settings, mechanical devices and movable scenery were considered more important – certainly by Jones himself – than his own contributions to their joint enterprise. The final break between the two men came in 1631 when Jonson published the text of *Love's Triumph through Gallipolis*, with his name as its author taking precedence on the title page before that of Inigo Jones. For Jones, this was the ultimate insult. Arrogant, self-centred and inordinately vain, he protested indignantly at this suggestion that his own ingenious contrivances, brilliant settings and splendid costumes should be considered of less merit than Jonson's versifications. Thereafter Jonson, quite as arrogant and as much given to self-commendation as his rival, lost court patronage. Jones worked with other poets, among them Sir William

D'Avenant whose *Salmacida Spolia* was the last masque to be performed at Whitehall before the Civil War brought all such delights and extravagances to an end.[18]

# 19 · *Clothes and Class*

Rich men who chose to dress in sombre hues, like Burghley and Walsingham, were rare. Most spent huge amounts on velvet suits trimmed with silver and jewellery, and on silk hats which were commonly worn indoors as well as out. The padded doublet, buttoned down the front, was attached to a man's breeches by tagged laces known as points. The breeches were worn with stockings and, if sewn to them, the garment was known as 'wholehose'. The armhole joins of the doublet were hidden by padded rolls of material or by tabs known as pickadils and, later, by projections like epaulettes. Ruffs, frequently of the most extravagant design and sometimes in layers, were worn both at the neck, and at the wrist; and, towards the end of the century, leg-of-mutton sleeves became more fashionable than close-fitting ones. Over his doublet a gentleman wore a cloak, often faced with gold or silver lace or even embroidered with pearls and with almost equally elaborate linings. He might also wear a heavy gold chain and jewellery, including earrings as well as a neatly trimmed beard.

Ladies' chemises and petticoats, their laced bodices and hooped or padded skirts, their gowns and cloaks and scented gloves, their stomachers, sleeves, farthingales, ruffs and feathers were all as resplendent as the clothes of their husbands.

The Spanish farthingale, held out by cane hoops, remained in fashion until the 1580s when it was replaced by the French farthingale in which a roll of material around the waist pushed out the skirt almost at right angles to fall vertically to the level of the instep. This farthingale was either in the shape of a circle, an oval, or a semi-circle, and held out the skirt at the back only. Silk stockings were also fashionable. So were court shoes and low-cut jewelled slippers which were replaced for outdoor wear by shoes with high cork soles or by overshoes with cloth uppers. Women still usually slept naked or perhaps in night-smocks; and both they and men generally wore either kerchiefs wound around their heads in bed or nightcaps which, medical authorities suggested, ought to have holes in the top.[1]

When the lady was wakened by her maid who pulled back the curtains of the bed, her clothes would be warmed by the fire in her bedroom before she put them on, a linen smock serving for underclothes. She would then have her hair dressed, perhaps with an ivory comb and silver-handled brush, and then attend to her face. In the early sixteenth century cosmetics were not nearly so widely used as they were to be later, and hairstyles were much simpler than they were to become in the days of Queen Elizabeth I whose wigs were clustered with jewels and pearls. Scents, however, were liberally used by both men and women and far more valued than soap. Soap was imported from Spain and Italy, the products of Castile and Venice being particularly prized. It was also made in England at Bristol, and at about 4d a pound it was not too expensive. Baths, however, were rarely taken regularly except for medicinal purposes, and much reliance was, therefore, placed upon pomanders and scent bottles. One popular scent, said to have been invented by Henry VIII, contained rose water, musk, ambergris and civet. Nutmegs, aloes and storax were used in other recipes. Queen Elizabeth was especially fond of the smell of marjoram. All these ingredients were placed in pomanders which were often attached to the sash end of a girdle.[2]

Renaissance ideals of beauty required a white skin and fair hair, a high smooth forehead, thin eyebrows, red lips, and small feet; and those whom nature had not endowed with these qualities did all they could to acquire them. Women bleached their hair sitting in the sun, protecting their faces from its rays by wearing masks which they kept in position by a button held in the teeth. They applied white powder made of ground alabaster to their skin, and a variety of lotions and ointments containing lemon juice, milk of almonds, white wine, white of egg and oil of tartar, honey, beeswax, rose petals, herbs, asses' milk and the ground jawbones of hogs.

As the sixteenth century progressed, efforts to simulate the ideal seem to have grown more ruthless. Hairs were plucked out and dyed as well as bleached; more drastic measures were taken to whiten hands and face, neck and breasts; lips were painted red; cheeks glazed with white of egg; lines representing thin veins were drawn upon the bosom which unmarried women left largely exposed; the waist was pressed in with pieces of metal or wood sewn into the bodice; hips were padded; kohl was used to outline the eyes and belladonna to enlarge the pupils. The face under its artificial glaze frequently resembled polished marble, particularly if attempts had to be made to disguise the effects of smallpox.

Some of the cosmetics used were harmless enough. A lip colouring made of cochineal, white of hard-boiled egg, green figs, alum and gum arabic would have done no damage to the skin. But other preparations were highly dangerous. A white skin was sometimes obtained, for instance, by the application of white lead mixed with vinegar or with borax and sulphur, red lips by madder or red ochre or by red crystalline mercuric sulphide. As a treatment for spots and freckles birch tree sap was innocuous and often effective; but other remedies containing ground brimstone, oil of turpentine and soliman, which was made of sublimate of mercury, eventually led to a skin as ravaged as white lead left it mummified.[3]

Teeth also were ruined by efforts to keep them clean, either by vigorous rubbing with a mixture of powdered pumice-stone, brick and coral, which took off the enamel as well as the stain, or by rinsing with solutions of honey and burned salt, or sugar and honey. Sir Hugh Platt, who considered himself an expert upon such matters, urged his friends not to clean their teeth with aqua fortis, otherwise, 'within a few dressings', they would probably be 'forced to borrow a rank' of false teeth to eat their dinner. The best method of keeping the teeth 'both white and sound', Platt continued, was to 'take a quart of honey, as much vinegar, and half so much white wine, boil them together and wash the teeth therewith now and then'.[4]

Experienced physicians and tooth-drawers recommended wood for tooth-picks, but silver and gold implements were commonly used as being more suited to their owners' standing in the world.

Social standing was a subject much debated, rank being considered much more significant than nationality or even colour – witness Othello. 'We divide our people commonly into four sorts,' wrote William Harrison in 1577. At the summit were the nobles. There were very few of these, no more than fifty-five peers in 1597, the same number as there had been in 1485. Next came 'knights, esquires and simple gentlemen'. There were very few of these, too, certainly less than 3 per cent of the population, though they were rising in influence and numbers, as rich 'new men', particularly those who had done well out of the law or government service, bought land and assumed the trappings of their new estate.

As for gentlemen, they may be made good cheap in England [Sir Thomas Smith, a lawyer and government official, wrote in 1560]. For whosoever studieth the laws of the realm, who studieth in the universities, who professeth liberal sciences and, to be short, who can live idly and without manual labour and will bear the part, charge and countenance of a gentleman, he . . . shall be taken for a gentleman.[5]

After the gentry, in Harrison's classification, came 'citizens and burgesses . . . of some substance to bear office', then 'yeomen of the countryside', men who did not bear coats of arms but might well be better off than gentlemen.

For the most the yeomen are farmers to gentlemen [Harrison explained]; and with grazing, frequenting of markets and keeping of servants . . . so come to great wealth, in so much that many of them are able to buy the lands of unthrifty gentlemen, and often setting their sons to the schools and to the universities and to the Inns of Court, or otherwise leaving them sufficient lands whereupon they may live without labour, do make them by those means to become gentlemen.[6]

Most yeomen, however, content with their lot, did not choose to become gentlemen. 'A man may find sundry yeomen,' wrote William Lambarde, the antiquary, son of a draper, 'although otherwise for wealth comparable with the gentle sort that will not yet for all that change their condition, nor desire to be apparelled with the titles of gentry.'[7] They preferred to spend their money on enlarging their holdings rather than on coats of arms. In Leicester-shire, for example, between 1540 and 1600, as Dr Hoskins has shown, tens of thousands of acres were bought by yeomen, many of whom eventually became owners of the manors upon which their forebears had been tenant farmers a generation or two earlier.[8]

While the wealthy yeomen frequently preferred to remain yeomen despite their affluence, there was nevertheless widespread social mobility, with men of substance moving upwards by virtue of their wealth or occupation irrespective of their birth. It was no disgrace for a gentleman's son to leave home to seek his fortune in trade; and his heirs were proud to read on his elaborate funeral monument some such description of him as 'Citizen and Mercer'. Some 'new men' were undoubtedly brash. Asa Briggs has drawn attention to one *arriviste*, Thomas Dolman, who, in following a fashion for displaying classical mottoes over his mansion's entrance porch, chose the arrogant text, 'The toothless envies the eater's teeth'.[9] Such men delighted to put their money into country estates; and in four counties, widely separated from each other, Derbyshire, Essex, Somerset and Shropshire, more new country houses were built in the fifty years between 1570 and 1620 than in any other half century.[10]

The fourth class of people which Harrison identified were those who were destined 'to be ruled and not to rule others', who had no 'voice or authority in our commonwealth'. These were 'day labourers, poor husbandmen, and all artificers, as tailors, shoemakers, carpenters, and the like'. Yet these men were not 'altogether neglected', Harrison went on to explain, 'for in cities and corporate towns, for default of yeomen, they are fain to make up their inquests of such meaner people. And in villages they are commonly made churchwardens, sidesmen, ale-conners, constables, and many times enjoy the name of headboroughs.' Such official positions were often not welcome.

The unpaid constable, for instance, was a hard-worked man expected to bring malefactors to justice, to raise the hue and cry, follow escaped prisoners, have vagrants whipped, supervise ale-houses, and musters of the militia, superintend the morals of his fellow-parishioners, to ensure that fast days were observed, that church attendance was not shirked, and that proper wages as laid down by the justices were received and paid. Yet, for all the unwelcome duties the office of constable entailed, it did provide a man with a certain position in society; and enabled him, if he were so inclined, to look down upon those whom he considered beneath him, men considered unworthy of office. 'In London the rich disdain the poor,' wrote Thomas Nashe, the dramatist. 'The courtier the citizen. The citizen the countryman. The merchant the retailer. The retailer the craftsman. The better sort of craftsman the baser. The shoemaker the cobbler.'[11] And in the country there were more than a few members of old families who agreed with the Staffordshire reactionary Sampson Erdeswicke that it was a pity there were so many merchants and lawyers buying up property in the shires and taking over land that had formerly been in the hands of persons of more worthy pedigree.[12]

Social distinctions were marked in all kinds of ways, in the clothes people wore and the food they ate, but not in what was in the twentieth century to become the most telling distinction of all, the accent in which they spoke. The children of the gentry frequently attended the same local school as the sons of yeomen and husbandmen, and all would grow up speaking with the same strong regional accents, still using words unknown in other parts of the country, and in Cornwall speaking a different language altogether. When the Marchioness of Exeter signed a letter to her son, 'your lowfyng mothar, Gartrude Exettar', she wrote the words as she would have pronounced them; and Sir Walter Ralegh, who had been born to an ancient family in a Devon manor house and had been at Oriel College, Oxford, 'spake broad Devonshire to his dying day'.[13] So incidentally, did the Tory landowner, Lord Rolle of Stevenstone, who did not die until 1842.

Although there had been times, during years of dearth or plague, when the numbers of deaths exceeded those of births, the population of the country had been steadily rising since the 1470s; and by 1600 there were probably well over 4 million inhabitants of England and Wales. Over half these were under twenty-five years of age and less than 10 per cent were over sixty. The great majority of the population still lived in the country, though towns, while still often rural in atmosphere, were growing fast; and in many of them, suburbs, where once the medieval poor had lived in hovels beneath the walls, were being developed as areas for the richer citizens to live in more peaceful and healthy surroundings than the busy and rowdy town centres could now offer.

# 20 · *Citizens, Masters and Journeymen*

No town could be compared in size with London whose population increased enormously in the sixteenth century. Before the first official census of 1801, which was itself not very reliable, all estimates are essentially the results of guesswork. It seems likely, however, that the population of Roman London in the third century was between 45,000 and 50,000, that it dwindled away during the Dark Ages and that when the Tower of London was built shortly after the Norman Conquest there were some 14,000 to 18,000 people living there. By the end of the twelfth century the numbers had probably risen to about 25,000 and by 1340, largely owing to immigration from abroad and from other parts of England, to about 50,000, the estimated population of the Roman city. This was far more than the population of any other town in England; and it was not large by continental standards: Paris was much bigger, so were Venice, Naples and Milan. After the Black Death there was little increase in the size of London until the end of the fifteenth century; but thereafter there was a sharp rise in the population, again largely due to immigration but not so much of foreigners and of apprentices from elsewhere in England as of unskilled labourers and of the destitute in search of food and work. The government, alarmed by the numbers and by overcrowding, and fearing the spread of disease, fire, social unrest and outbreaks of violence, endeavoured to check the growth.

In the summer of 1580 a proclamation was issued prohibiting, within three miles of any London gate, the building of any new house where no former house was known to have existed within human memory. From that date onwards for over 100 years similar proclamations were repeatedly issued, prohibiting new buildings or the division of existing ones, defining punishments for builders and householders who transgressed the law and providing for the demolition of houses put up without licence. But it proved impossible to prevent overcrowding: the policy of prohibiting new building in the hope of keeping down the population merely served to cram the poor into houses already standing. Nor, despite their constant efforts, were the authorities successful in preventing new buildings from being erected. Knowing that they might, if they were lucky, escape with a fine, builders continued to put up unauthorized houses; yet, knowing, too, that if they were not lucky their buildings might be pulled down, they took care to use the cheapest materials and to expend as little money as possible. Some builders went so far as to erect screens to hide their illicit buildings from the authorities: one man in Cursitor's Alley, Chancery Lane, built high walls round a field where he claimed to be keeping tame rabbits but where he had, in fact, put up a row of squalid tenements. Many other builders selected the narrowest, darkest, most remote alleyways and courts to put together any sort of jerry-built shelter that would command a rent. Also, since additions to existing houses were allowed, it became common practice to patch up a derelict house, add the permitted extension, and dig beneath it a cellar to let as a shop, gaming-room, a 'tippling house' or even as lodgings to some improvident family. So the growth of London continued unchecked; new suburbs sprang up; and Westminster expanded rapidly. By the end of the century the population had risen to about 200,000 and was almost to double within fifty years.[1]

John Stow, the son of a tailor in a poor way of business on Cornhill, whose *Survey of London and Westminster* was published in 1598, much lamented the changes that had occurred in his lifetime. He disapproved of the way the gardens of so many big houses were being turned into bowling-alleys and dicing-houses, of the way in which so many rich men were encroaching upon common lands and open fields to build houses 'like Midsummer pageants with towers, turrets and chimney-tops'. He regretted, too, the encroachments upon the precincts of churches and even upon roadways which were making the streets so narrow that they were constantly blocked by wagons, drays and barrows. Much of the Walbrook, now 'worse cloyed and choken than ever it was before', had disappeared beneath buildings which stretched across the stream from bank to bank. The medieval ditch, although still deep and 200 feet wide in places, was elsewhere a clogged and dirty channel, while between Aldgate and the Tower, where once the water had been deep enough to drown a horse, the moat had been filled up completely and covered with carpenters' yards, kitchen gardens and tenements. In the markets in East-cheap, Knightrider Street and in Faringdon Ward the traders had edged further and further forward, first building roofs over their stalls, then replacing their stalls with bigger sheds, and finally building houses which stretched out over the roadway where their customers had formerly walked.

The Dissolution of the Monasteries had exacerbated the problem. Numerous religious houses had passed into the hands of rich laymen who converted them into large mansions, selling off part of the gardens for building and either turning the chapels into parish churches, pulling them down or converting them to some other use. The chapel of the Crutched Friars was turned into a tennis court; that of St Martin-le-Grand became a wine tavern; the site of the Carmelite priory of the Whitefriars was soon occupied by small tenements, alehouses and poor men's shops. Part of the property of the Austin Friars came into the hands of Thomas Cromwell, the brewer's son who became Henry VIII's Lord Great Chamberlain; and by his acquisition of this land be became a neighbour of John Stow's father. Without giving the old tailor any warning, or offering him compensation, Cromwell had his house dug out of the ground, placed on rollers and pulled over twenty feet away from his own boundary so that he could extend his garden.

John Stow was also saddened by the appearance of the expanding suburbs to the east of the Tower along the roads to the villages of Whitechapel and Stepney, Shadwell and Limehouse and down by the waterfront to Wapping. Here there were continual streets and straggling passages, 'with alleys of small tenements or cottages . . . inhabited by sailors' victuallers' which had destroyed the once beautiful 'fayre hedges and long rows of elms'. All the way now from Radcliffe, past Goodman's Fields – through which as a boy in the 1520s Stow had walked to fetch milk (at ½d for three pints) – to the 'filthy cottages' and laystalls around Aldgate, the 'horrid entrance to the City', there was a long, dirty ribbon development of brick and wood.[2]

To the west of the City the appearance of London was also being transformed. Covering acres of ground on the river front between Charing Cross and Westminster Hall was the new royal Palace of Whitehall, originally York Place which, although it belonged to the see of York and not personally to the Archbishop, the king had taken over, as he had taken over Hampton Court, from the enormously rich Cardinal Wolsey. To the west of it were the red brick walls of St James's Palace, yet another of the thirteen palaces which the king owned within a day's ride of his capital; and between the new Privy Stairs at Whitehall Palace and the mouth of the Fleet river there was an almost continuous line of rich men's palaces for well over a mile. Adjoining Whitehall was Northumberland House, the immense town house of the Dukes of Northumberland. Further downstream were the medieval walls of the Palace of the Savoy and the huge Renaissance mansion built between 1547 and 1550 from monastic ruins by the Lord Protector Somerset. East of Somerset House were the palaces of the Earls of Arundel and Essex; then, before the banks of the Fleet were reached, appeared the rambling halls and courts of the Temple – once the premises of the religious order of the Knights Templar and now the haunt of lawyers – and finally the dark red walls of Bridewell. Behind these riverside palaces, on the other side of the Strand, were the houses of more great men, Craven House, home of the Craven family whose immense fortune had been founded by Sir William Craven, merchant tailor and Lord Mayor of London; Exeter House, the palace of Lord Burghley; and the valuable Covent Garden estate, once the property of the Abbot of Westminster, now in the hands of the Russell family, headed by the Earls of Bedford.

South of the river, Southwark, still frequented by whores and whoremongers, by visitors to bear-gardens, cockpits and bull-baiting rings, was still growing apace; and it was only to the north that large-scale building was inhibited by problems of water supply and by the heavy clay which made it impossible for householders to enjoy any satisfactory and reasonably cheap system of drainage. Yet, even in the north, suburbs were developing. Clerkenwell, Smithfield and Spitalfields were all growing, due in part to the arrival of so many Huguenot refugees; and there were long rows of houses on both sides of the road at Hoxton.[3]

The life of the city had changed little since the days of Richard Whittington. There were the same pageants and processions, the same quarrels and occasional riots, the same sports and pastimes. Young men still tilted at the quintain on Cornhill, still practised archery to the uproarious accompaniment of drums and flutes in Islington, Finsbury and Moorfields, although John Stow noted a growing and worrying interest in artillery which was leading to a sad decline in the trade of the bowyers, fletchers and bowstring-makers in Grub Street and turning the archery ground in Bishopsgate Without into a smoky waste where the gunners from the Tower fired their brass cannon into butts of upturned earth.

Men could still drink sack for less than 4d a pint, and still get drunk at Bartholomew Fair. Pirates were still hanged in chains downstream from the Tower as they had been since Roman times; the heads of traitors were still displayed on London Bridge until blown down on a windy night; the markets, bigger than ever, 'unmeasurably pestred with the unimaginable increase and multiplicity of market-folkes', still continued as before, six days every week.

The largest market was Cheapside which was opened at dawn in winter and six o'clock in the summer by the ringing of a bell. Further east was the sprawling Leadenhall Market, the place to go for the best poultry and milk, leather and cloth, kitchen pans and tools. The butcher's markets were in Eastcheap and Newgate Street; the fish market on Fish Street Hill; and there were other markets in Cornhill, in King Street, Westminster, at Smithfield and Southwark, and on the quays at Queenhythe, Billingsgate and Bear Key.

The noise was tremendous as the market people shouted the price and merit of their wares above the din of rumbling carts, bellowing cattle, haggling, laughing, quarrelling and banter. Carts shod with iron were not allowed in London streets and the fore-horse was supposed to be led, but, as John Stow said, 'these good orders' were not observed. Coaches and wagons were driven along without regard to the convenience of pedestrians who were forced into doorways, splashed with mud or covered with dust; and not a day passed when a street was not blocked by vehicles parked or entangled between the overhanging houses.

> There squeaks a cart wheel, here a tumbrel rumbles,
> Here scolds an old bawd, there a porter grumbles,
> Here two tough carmen combat for the way.[4]

From the markets and the streets, the stalls, and the shops which were piled high with merchandise and outside which apprentices and maid-servants ran to catch the attention of the passers-by, the cries went up: 'What do you lack? Do you buy, sir? See what you lack? Pins, points, garters, Spanish gloves, silk ribbons. Crabs! Pears! Shoes! Small coal! Writing ink!'

Even in St Paul's Churchyard, where the booksellers congregated, carrying on business beneath heavy painted hanging signs depicting ships and mermaids, black boys and bishops' mitres, brazen dragons and saracens' heads, the noise and shouting was just as loud and intense: 'What do you lack, gentlemen. See, a new book come forth, sir, buy a new book, sir . . . Perils of the deep, chronicles and sermons!' And it was just the same at the Royal Exchange which had been built between Cornhill and Threadneedle Street in the 1560s by the rich mercer, Thomas Gresham, as a bourse, like Antwerp's, where merchants from all countries could meet and discuss their business. There were rows of shops on the upper floor, mostly apothecaries, armourers, booksellers, goldsmiths, milliners and drapers selling,

> Such purses, gloves and points
>    Of cost and fashion rare,
> Such cotworks, partlets, suits of lawn,
>    Bongraces and such ware;
> Such gorgets, sleeves and ruffs,
>    Linings for gowns and cauls,
> Coifs, crippins, cornets, billaments,
>    Musk boxes and sweet balls;
> Pincases, pick-tooths, beard-brushes,
>    Combs, needles, glasses, bells,
> And many such like toys as these,
>    That Gain to Fancy sells.[5]

There were also numerous hawkers and street vendors outside the building; and in 1570 several women were prosecuted for selling fruit at the Cornhill Gate and 'amusing themselves in cursing and swearing to the great annoyance and grief of the inhabitants and passers-by'. Yet the row made by such women, by singing chimney-sweeps and itinerant pie-sellers, by bawling apprentices and shouting servant girls, squabbling porters and carters, was often lost in the general hubbub from open windows, workshops and taverns, bear-gardens and builders' yards, for 'hammers are beating in one place, tubs hooping in another, pots clinking in a third, water tankards running at fill in a fourth'.[6] And everywhere carts screeched, dogs barked, the Public Cryer and the Bellman made their rounds and the life of London went on in all its infinite variety.

Although not to be compared with London in importance or size, other towns in England were also growing, so that by the end of the sixteenth century probably as many as a fifth of the population were townspeople. The population of Norwich was about 17,000; York and Bristol were smaller, but were also large towns by medieval standards, Bristol having some 9000 to 10,000 people. Salisbury had about 7000 and Worcester about 4000.

The towns of the more remote western counties and the north, so much less prosperous than those of the eastern counties and of the clothing districts of the Cotswolds in the Middle Ages, were now beginning to rival them. Totnes, Plymouth and Exeter, with a population of almost 9000 by the end of the century, were already important centres. So were Poole because of its fishing industry, and Newcastle because of its coal. The small towns of the Midlands and Yorkshire were also beginning to come into prominence. Birmingham, 'swarming with inhabitants and echoing with the noise of anvils', in William Camden's words, although still only a town of metal-workers, a sixth the size of Coventry, was starting to grow fast, as were Halifax and Leeds, 'a pretty market town standing by its clothing'. Leland described Manchester as 'the fairest, best builded, quickest and most populous town of all Lancashire'. Sheffield, long known for its scythes, was becoming famous for its cutlery.[7]

The pattern throughout the country was far from regular. York, though still the capital of the north, was not as prosperous as it had been; nor was Southampton. The silting-up of rivers led to the decline of other towns. The Dissolution of the Monasteries harmed the economy of places like Canterbury and Bury St Edmunds. Yet other cities profited from the Dissolution and most shared in the general prosperity of the later years of Queen Elizabeth's reign that followed the depression of the earlier years of the century. Many of them were pleasant enough places to live in; their inhabitants had room for gardens or allotments and a large proportion kept animals; the cottages stood usually in individual plots rather than in terraces. Some cottages, as Leland observed, were built of stone, like those in the towns of Northamptonshire, while others, such as those in Loughborough and Leicester, were still almost entirely of wood.

The workers who lived in these cottages were not well paid. In the 1590s in Chester, for example, apprentice linen weavers received no more than 1d a day, joiners and smiths 2d a day, bricklayers 2½d and master carpenters 4d, although they did also receive food which cost their masters about 4d a day for each man. In those days beef cost about 2d a pound, butter 5d, coarse cloth 1s 4d a yard and a pair of children's shoes between 6d and 1s. Such wages and prices were tolerable for the countryman who could find means of augmenting his diet denied to the townsman; but they were less than adequate for many urban workers at a time when wages had not risen nearly as fast as prices had: the cost of wheat was four times as high as it had been in the fifteenth century yet wages had scarcely doubled. At the end of the sixteenth century few workers in London were earning more than 1s a day, while the average weekly wage in the country as a whole seems to have been about 5s.[8]

Not only were the wages of the sixteenth-century worker subject to strict controls, but so also were his hours of work, the conditions of his employment, even the clothes he wore and the length of his hair. Apprentices who could afford to do so, 'did affect to go in costly apparel and wear weapons and frequent schools of dancing, fencing, and music'. Such behaviour was not to be allowed. All apprentices – most of whom were not released from their indentures until they were twenty-four – must forswear silk stockings and padded doublets, gaudy colours and embroidered shirts, ruffs and fancy hats. They must stick to plain materials, leather or thread laces in their shoes, and on Sundays and holy days a respectable woollen cap. They were not permitted to keep clothes elsewhere than under their master's roof; and if they disobeyed these orders and walked abroad in fine array they were subject to severe penalties. A second offence might entail a sound whipping in the hall of their company.

Working hours, as fixed by statute, were long. From March to September labourers and artificers had to work from five in the morning until seven or even eight at night, and from September to March from dawn till dusk. Missing an hour's work was to result in the loss of 1d in wages. Two hours, however, were allowed for their meals, and in the summer they were permitted to sleep for half an hour after their midday meal. A trained worker had to follow his own trade so long as there was work for him in it. If there were not he had to seek work on the land; and if he could find no master in the country, he was to be put to work by the parish as vagrants were.

Yet, despite the regulations to which he was subject and the poor rewards for his labour, the journeyman and the apprentice did enjoy advantages too. Their master's behaviour was also controlled by statute. He could not dismiss his men before their time was up, and he could be heavily fined for doing so. Nor could he underpay them; nor could he employ apprentices in disproportionate numbers to his journeymen: various stipulated masters of crafts were allowed to have three apprentices to each journeyman; were they to take on another apprentice, they must employ another journeyman as well. Also, while there were, of course, harsh taskmasters, they do not appear to have been common. Most journeymen and apprentices seem to have lived with their masters, their master's families and servants as accepted members of the family, taking pride in their joint work and supporting each other in their differences with rivals and outsiders. The relationship between Simon Eyre, Dekker's eccentric master shoemaker, and his servants appears to have been characteristic. They are uncouth and outspoken in their behaviour towards him, but they feel for him a real affection. As he enters the yard in front of his house he calls out, 'Where be these boys, these girls? They wallow in the fat brewiss of my bounty, and lick up the crumbs of my table, yet will not rise to see my walks cleansed. What, Nan, what Madge Mumblecrust? . . . What Firk, I say? What Hodge? Open my shop-windows.'

'O master,' comes Firk's voice in reply. 'Is't thou that speak bandog and Bedlam this morning? I was in a dream and mused what madman had got into the street so early.'[9]

> A huswife good betimes will rise,
> And order things in comelie wise,
>     Her mind is set to thrive:
> Upon her distaffe she will spin
> And with her needle she will winne,
>     If such he hap to wive.

Thomas Tusser's model housewife gets up early and sets all the servants to their tasks, for 'when husband is absent, let huswife be chiefe, and look to the labour that eateth hir biefe'. She must

> Set some to peele hempe or else rushes to twine
> To spin and to card, or to seething of brine . . .
> Set some about cattle, some pasture to vewe,
> Some mault to be grinding against ye do brewe.
> Some corneth, some brineth, some will not be taught,
> Where meat is attainted, there cookrie is naught . . .
> Call servants to breakfast by day starre appeare
> A snatch and to worke, fellowes tarie not here.
> Let huswife be carver, let pottage be heate,
> A messe to eche one, with a morsell of meate.

After breakfast there were brewing and baking to attend to, cooking and washing, work in the dairy and work in the fields. At dinner time the prudent housewife made sure that there was a good meal for the servants but no dainties, since 'seggons [poor labourers] halfe starved worke faintly and dull, and lubbers doo loiter, their bellies too full'.

As soon as the meal was finished there was more work to do, sewing and

mending, making candles, feeding animals, milking cows; and then it was
supper time:

> Provide for thy husband, to make him good cheere,
> Make merrie togither, while time ye be heere.
> At bed and at boord, howsoever befall,
> What ever God sendeth be merrie withall.[1]

Cheerful and conscientious, strict yet just with the servants, beating them
when they deserved it and caring for them when they were ill, the good
housewife was always vigilant. She looked into corners to make sure there
was no dust lurking there; she kept a watchful eye on her maids so that they
did not become lazy in changing their linen; she insisted that food was not
wasted and bread was never baked in such amounts that it went hard and
mouldy. She saved feathers from plucked poultry for her mattresses and
pillows; she kept the cat out of the dairy where there was a mousetrap
instead; at night she brought in all clothes and sheets that had been left in the
garden to dry so that no hooker with his long pole could lift them over the
hedge; and before she went to bed she made her rounds with her keys,
ensuring that all doors were fastened and locks secure.[2]

That was the day of a yeoman's wife. The wife of a farmer who had fewer
servants to help her, perhaps but a single maid, had to work even harder and
more strenuously. *The Boke of Husbandrie* of 1523 told her that 'it is a
wive's occupation to winnow all manner of corn, to make malt, wash and
wring, to make hay, shear corn, and in time of need to help her husband to fill
the muck wain or dung cart, drive the plough, to load hay, corn and such
other . . . to go or ride to the market to sell butter, cheese, milk, eggs,
chickens, capons, hens, pigs, geese, and all manner of corn'. She was also
expected to be in charge of the dairy and of the household accounts, 'to make
a true reckoning and accompt to her husband what she hath received and
what she hath paid'.[3]

Many a lady was kept almost as busy, as is indicated by the diary of Lady
Hoby, wife of Sir Thomas Posthumus Hoby, the thin-legged, hunchbacked
son of a former ambassador to France. Lady Hoby frequently records a
morning spent dyeing wool, winding yarn, busying herself making oil in her
closet, or spinning. 'Went about my stilling; stilled aqua vitas,' she writes in
one entry. 'After private prayer I saw a man's leg dressed, took order for
things in the house, and wrought till dinner time,' she recounts in another.
She dried fruits, made quince jelly and damson jam, dried rose leaves for
pots-pourris, prepared syrups and candied sweetmeats, distilled cordials.
She was a skilled nurse; knew how to apply poultices and tie bandages; well
understood the medicinal qualities of the herbs that grew in her Yorkshire
garden. 'After dinner,' she writes, 'I was busy weighing of wool till almost

night . . . I did see [wax] lights made almost all the afternoon . . . I went to take my bees and saw my honey ordered . . . After I dined I talked and read to some good wives . . . I went to talk to my old women.' She seems to have known as much about the estate as her husband who clearly valued her advice: 'Took horse and rode to Harwoodall to see our farm be bought . . . I walked with Mr Hoby about the town to spy out the best places where cottages might be builded . . . After supper I talked a good deal with Mr Hoby of husbandry and household matters.'

She found time, however, for other pursuits. She played bowls; she sometimes went fishing; she, once at least, went to Scarborough for a boat trip; she went out in a coach to visit friends or rode over her estate; she entertained visitors, not always willingly: 'I was visited by a kinswoman, which was some trouble at the first, but considered all Crosses ought thankfully to be borne.' She was also a most devout Puritan and on Sundays occupied herself with religious pursuits.

> After I was ready, I went to private prayers, then to breakfast [she writes of one Sunday]. Then I walked till church time with Mr Hoby, and after to dinner. After which I walked and had speech of no serious matter till 2 o'clock. Then I writ notes into my bible till 3. And after 4 I came again from the church, walked and meditated a little and again writ some other notes in my Bible of that I had learned till 5, at which time I returned to examination and prayer after I had read some of Bond of the Sabbath, I walked abroad. And so to supper, after to prayers and lastly to bed.[4]

Lady Hoby and her husband had no children, Sir Thomas being thought either impotent or infertile; but her friends had to spend a good deal of time in their nurseries, supervising the nursemaids. A conversational manual describes a mother entering the nursery of a morning and asking the nurse how her baby has slept. The child has been 'somewhat wayward', the nurse says; and this the mother attributes to his cutting a tooth. The baby's 'swaddling bands' are then undone so that he can have a bath. While this is being done, while he is being washed and while being dressed, his mother gives continuous instructions to the nurse in the manner of such manuals:

> Give him his coat of changeable taffeta and his satin sleeves. Where is his bib? Where is his little petticoat? Let him have his gathered apron with strings, and hang a muckinder [bib] to it . . . Where is his biggin [baby's cap] and his little band with an edge . . . You need not yet to give him his coral with the small golden chain, for I believe it is better to let him sleep until the afternoon . . . God sent thee good rest, my little Boykin.[5]

\*

But soon the little 'boykin' will be treated like a miniature adult, although he will probably have his meals separately from the adults, being brought in occasionally to greet his parents' guests, to say grace for them or to read a passage of scripture.[6] And, as likely as not, he will be sent away from home as his forebears had been. And, again like his forebears, he will probably be flogged, although perhaps not as severely as Thomas Tusser was at Eton, where the headmaster, Nicholas Udall, who was imprisoned for buggery, once gave him fifty-three stripes. Certainly, few children escaped flogging altogether, and the textbooks that were used in schools in teaching Latin accepted it as a matter of course. The dialogues of J. L. de Vives, a Spanish friend of Erasmus, which were to be found in several English schools, including Eton, Westminster and Shrewsbury, contain numerous references to the practice.[7] And in a poem written towards the end of the sixteenth century, Edmund Coote, a schoolmaster at Bury St Edmunds, makes it clear that his pupils will be beaten for every kind of offence from bad manners and untidiness to being late for school, laughing in class or spoiling their books.[8]

Most parents agreed that flogging was a necessary corrective for their children. When Sir Peter Carew ran away as a schoolboy from a cruel master at Exeter Grammar School and climbed on to a tower of the city wall, threatening to throw himself off if his tormentor came after him, his father had him brought home tied to a dog and chained him in the dog's kennel.[9]

# 22 · *Actors and Playgoers*

Trumpets blared from the theatres' towers and flags were flown to give notice that the afternoon's performances were about to begin. Outside the audiences had assembled early, for there were few, if any, reserved seats; and there was generally a scramble for the best. In 1599 a penny would secure admittance to the yard where, so Dekker said, the 'stinkards were so glewed together in crowdes with the steames of strong breath that when they came foorth, their faces lookt as if they had been boyled'.[1] A seat in a gallery cost 2d and the better seats with cushions 3d. These were regarded as reasonable prices when a quart of ale in a tavern would cost 4d and an hour or so with a prostitute 6d.[2]

Men and women of all classes went to the theatre, groundlings and gentlemen, apprentices and foreign ambassadors, women of the town who sat in the galleries and ladies of position who, sometimes masked, sat in private rooms. Stern critics of the theatre portrayed the playhouses of the period as being full of 'vagrant persons, maisterles men, thieves, horse stealers, whoremongers, cony-catchers, contrivers of treason and other idele and daungerous persons'.[3] Henry Crosse in *Vertues, Common-Wealth; or, The High-Way to Honour* wrote:

> Nay many poore pincht, needie creatures, that live of almes, and that have scarce neither cloath to their backs, nor foode for the belley, yet wil make hard shift but they will see a Play, let wife and children begge [and] languish in penurie . . . A play is like a sincke in a Towne, whereunto all the filth doth runne: or a byle in the body, that draweth all the ill humours unto it.[4]

Yet other, less prejudiced observers noted that, while the theatre certainly did attract such customers as Crosse described, they were far from being in the majority. A playgoer from the Venetian Embassy, for example, noted that audiences contained large numbers of 'handsome ladies who seat themselves among men without the slightest hesitation'.[5] And the poet and epigrammatist, John Davies, thus described a typical day in the life of an idle gallant:

> *Fuscus* is free, and hath the world at will,
> Yet in the course of life that he doth leade,
> He's like a horse which turning rounde a mill,
> Doth alwaies in the selfe same circle treade:
> First he doth rise at 10, and at eleven
> He goes to *Gyls*, where he doth eate till one,
> Then sees a play til sixe, and sups at seaven,
> And after supper, straight to bed is gone,
> And there till tenne next day he doth remaine,
> And then he dines, then sees a comedy,
> And then he suppes, and goes to bed againe.
> Thus rounde he runs without variety:
> Save that sometimes he comes not to the play
> But falls into a whore-house by the way.[6]

At the end of the sixteenth century, so it has been estimated, there were weekly audiences of about 15,000 at the London theatres. By 1605 and throughout the whole of Shakespeare's theatrical career, as many as two out of every fifteen of the capital's population were going to the theatre every week.[7]

Notified by playbills, which were set up in prominent positions throughout the city and no doubt at the playhouse doors, and by announcements made after the epilogue of previous performances, the audience impatiently waited for the entertainment to begin, drinking ale, smoking tobacco, sampling the books which were hawked up and down between the seats, playing games of cards, eating fruit and sweetmeats, or, like the Citizen's Wife in the *Knight of the Burning Pestle*, unwrapping liquorice, sugar-candy and green ginger, and sending their husbands out for more beer.

Before and after the play, and sometimes between the acts, a variety of other entertainments were also commonly provided. These were sometimes as spectacular as the performances at the Bear Garden in Southwark described by a German visitor in August 1584:

Dogs were made to fight singly with three bears, the second bear being larger than the first, and the third larger than the second. After this a horse was brought in and chased by the dogs, and at last a bull, who defended

himself bravely. The next was, that a number of men and women came
forward from a separate compartment, dancing, conversing and fighting
with each other: also a man who threw some white bread among the crowd,
that scrambled for it. Right over the middle of the place a rose was fixed,
this rose being set on fire by a rocket: suddenly lots of apples and pears fell
out of it down upon the people standing below. Whilst the people were
scrambling for the apples, some rockets were made to fall down upon them
out of the rose, which caused a great fright but amused the spectators.
After this, rockets and other fireworks came flying out of all corners, and
that was the end of the play.[8]

As well as fireworks, songs and dumb-shows, prize-fights, dances and the
antics of clowns and female tumblers were frequently offered as attractions to
accompany the play. Symons, the acrobat, was a leading player in one of
England's most distinguished companies which also employed a Turkish
rope-dancer. After a production of Shakespeare's *Julius Caesar* in 1599, a
Swiss visitor was diverted by a lively dance performed by four members of
the company, two of them dressed as women. There was no interval between
the acts, but during the peformance 'food and drink [were] carried round the
audience'.[9]

There was much contemporary criticism of the rowdy behaviour of theatre
audiences; but, in fact, though noisy enough before the play began they seem
to have fallen into attentive silence once the performance started. And, while
cutpurses, pickpockets and prostitutes were always on the lookout for likely
victims or customers, so they were in all other places where crowds gathered.
As Greene warned his readers, pickpockets were at work in 'all places of
resort and assemblies, therefore their chief walks [are] St Paul's, Westminster, the Exchange, plays, bear-garden, running at tilt, the Lord Mayor's day,
and festival meetings, frays, shootings, or great fairs'. The theatre was
evidently not a place of special risk or criminality. There is record only of a
single stabbing at the Fortune theatre in 1613, but elsewhere in the county of
Middlesex that year there were eleven murders, twelve cases of manslaugh-
ter, twenty-eight cases of assault and battery, and ten other cases of assault.[10]
Yet, in the words of M. C. Bradbrook, 'while the crowd at common theatres
probably did not contain a much higher proportion of ruffians than any other
London crowd [and while] the record of grave disturbances at plays in the
later sixteenth century is negligible, in relation to the number of performances given, it would inevitably be in an excitable mood'.[11] Nor did
audiences hesitate to condemn what they took to be displeasing performances, such as that given by a visiting French cast who were 'hissed, hooted
and pippin-pelted from the stage'.[12]

'In the playhouses at London,' wrote the author of *Playes Confuted in Five*

Circumfula.sedet.digna.parente.cohors
Talis.erat.quondam patriarchae.mensa.Iacobi.
Menſa.fuit.Iobo: sic.cumulata.pio͡s
Fac.Deus.ut.multos.haec.oriʒat.menſa.Iohẽ
Ger͡ minet.ut.Iobi.ſtirps.renouata.fuit;
Fercula.praeclaro.donaſti.laeta.Cobhamo
Haec.habeant.longos.gaudia.tanta.dies:
An.ṁ.1567.

ÆTA 6    ÆTATIS SVÆ 5 GEMELLI

ABOVE: Lord Cobham (1527–96) and his family, painted by Hans Eworth in about 1567. The children are dressed – and were treated – as miniature adults.

RIGHT: The young Elizabeth Vernon, Countess of Southampton, painted in about 1600. She stands by her dressing-table combing her hair with an ivory comb. The embroidered jacket, smock bordered with lace, pink silk corset stiffened with whalebone, the petticoat and diaphanous apron, and the ruff pinned to the curtain are all characteristic of the fashion of the time.

Longleat in Wiltshire, one of the earliest of the great Elizabethan houses – built in the 1560s for Sir John Thynne, as advised by the master mason, Robert Smythson.

RIGHT: Highly athletic dancing at court. Queen Elizabeth's partner is Robert Dudley, Earl of Leicester. In 1602 the Earl of Worcester wrote: 'We are folic here in Court: much dancing in the Privy Chamber of country dances before the Queen's Majesty, who is exceedingly pleased therewith. Irish tunes are at this time most pleasing.'

BELOW: *The Thames at Richmond*, a painting of the Flemish school, *circa* 1600. Morris Dancers had been performing their ritual folk dances in England since earliest times, as, indeed, they still do. The name may be derived from 'morisco', Moorish, in allusion to the dancers blacking their faces as part of their disguise. On the river to the right a party of courtiers are seen being rowed towards Richmond Palace where Queen Elizabeth I often spent the summer in her later years.

A painting by Gerrit Houckgeest of Charles I dining in state in Whitehall Palace. Every day the King's table – where he sat in public, served by attendants on bended knee – was provided with 28 dishes, brought in to a fanfare of trumpets that temporarily stilled the less strident notes of his private orchestra. The Queen's table had 24 dishes. Whitehall Palace was burned down in 1698, only the Banqueting House surviving.

William, second Earl of Salisbury, painted by George Geldorp in 1626 in costume typical of its period. In the background can be seen men hunting and the Earl's family home, Hatfield House, begun by his father, Robert Cecil, first Earl of Salisbury, in 1607.

*Actions* in 1579, 'it is the fashion of youthes to go first into the yarde and to carry theire eye through every gallery, then, like unto ravens where they spye the carion, thither they flye, and presse as nere to ye fairest as they can.'

You shall see suche heaving, and shooing, such ytching and shouldring, too sitte by women [this author continued in another book], such care for their Cappes, that no chippes light in them: Such pillowes to their backes, that they take no hurte: Such masking in their eares, I know not what: Such giving them Pippins to pass the time: Such tickling, such toying, such winking . . . that it is a right Comedie.[13]

In the country the audiences were even livelier:

The people which were in the Roome were exceeding Joviall, and merry before the Play began, Young men and Maids dancing together, and so merry and frolick were many of the Spectators, that the Players would hardly get Liberty that they themselves might Act.[14]

Before the building of the first public theatre in London, plays had generally been performed in the courtyards of inns, and were still occasionally presented in them – notably in those of the Bull, the Bell, the Cross Keys and the Belsavage – long after the theatres had been established. The inns had the advantage of ready supplies of hot food and drink and of other entertainments such as those provided by prostitutes and exhibitions of dwarfs, freaks and monsters in private rooms. But they could not compete with the more convenient seating arrangements and the dramatic special effects which the public theatres could provide.

The first of these theatres, known simply as The Theatre, was opened in 1576 at Shoreditch, just outside the jurisdiction of the City, by James Burbage, a member of the Earl of Leicester's Company of Players, and his rich brother-in-law, John Brayne. The next year another theatre was built in Shoreditch. This was the Curtain and was probably financed by an actors' syndicate. These two theatres were followed by several others, built on the south bank of the river, much to the pleasure and profit of the watermen. Among them were the Swan which, according to a Dutch visitor, had a seating capacity of 3000 and was 'built of a concrete of flint stones . . . supported by wooden columns painted in such exact imitation of marble that it might deceive even the most cunning'; the Rose, where Edward Alleyn, son-in-law of its builder, Philip Henslowe, made his reputation as an actor; the Hope, also built by Philip Henslowe; and the Globe, a round wooden theatre erected by Henslowe's rivals, Richard Burbage and his brother, Cuthbert. Shakespeare was both a player and a shareholder here; and on the stage, where stools were placed for privileged persons, several of his plays were first performed. But shortly before his death, two cannon, fired during a performance of *Henry VIII*, set the thatched roof of the galleries alight and the theatre was destroyed. No one was hurt except a man who had 'his breeches on fire that would perhaps have broyled him if he had not with the benefit of a provident wit put it out with bottle ale'. It was shortly rebuilt, however; and was for long a prominent feature of the waterfront at Bankside.[15]

None of these theatres survived; but from a drawing made by a foreign tourist of the Swan in about 1596 an idea can be formed of their design. The platform-stage, supported on stout columns, jutted out into the unroofed courtyard where the standing spectators surrounded it on three sides. Above the spectators were the circular roofed galleries where the rest of the audience sat. Behind the platform-stage was a wall with doors or curtained doorways giving access backstage and providing exits and entrances for the actors. Above the door was a musicians' gallery; and above that the tower which housed the machinery and from which the flag flew when the theatre was open.[16]

The machinery, and the trapdoors in the stage, were vital parts of the theatre, since Elizabethan audiences relished shocks and surprises as much as they did trumpets, thunder and savage realism in bloody scenes of torture and death which were made all the more horrible by the use of animals' entrails. They loved to see devils springing up suddenly from hell, and wrathful gods descending from the heavens. They were, as Paul Hentzner discovered, 'vastly fond of great noises that fill the ear, such as the firing of cannon, drums, and the ringing of bells'. When a battle scene was being enacted at the Globe the noise of the guns, the shouts and the clash of arms could be heard on the far bank of the river. The din of London Bridge and Billingsgate are singled out by Morose in Ben Jonson's *The Silent Woman* as among the worst of the discordant rackets he would be prepared to undergo for her. 'Nay,' he adds, 'I would sit out a play that were nothing but fights at sea, drum, trumpet and target.'[17]

Such performances were rarely staged in the so-called private theatres which were established in Blackfriars and elsewhere at the turn of the century. The first Blackfriars theatre was opened in 1578 by Richard Farrant, the Master of the Children of the Chapel at Windsor who, in order to evade the prohibition of public theatres in the area by the Court of Common Council, called it a private theatre where his choir could practise 'for the better trayning to do her Majestic service'. James Burbage, Richard's father, a carpenter and part-time actor, bought the building in 1596, and improved it with galleries to hold 600 or 700 people. The next year it was leased to one of

Farrant's successors as Master of the Windsor boys and to Nathaniel Gyles, Master of the Children of the Chapel Royal. The boy actors were extremely popular and rivalled the adult companies, much to the annoyance of Shakespeare who more than once refers to child actors disparagingly in his plays, making Rosencrantz in *Hamlet* refer to 'an aery of children, little eyases, that cry out on the top of question, and are most tyrannically clapp'd for 't: these are now the fashion, and so berattle the common stages, – so they call them, – that many wearing rapiers are afraid of goose-quills, and dare scarce come thither'.[18]

At the beginning of the seventeenth century Richard Burbage took six of his fellow-actors into partnership to run the Blackfriars theatre which thereafter became so popular that the local residents protested against the number of playgoers and their coaches blocking the nearby streets. It was a fashionable audience, for the seats here and at the other private theatres were much more expensive than those at the public theatres, rising as high as 2s 6d. Also, the buildings were smaller and, since they were roofed, plays could be performed in the wettest weather and in the dark by candlelight.[19]

With the advent of the private theatres, the well-to-do did not, however, abandon the public theatres which continued to attract playgoers of all classes and were particularly popular with foreign ambassadors and their suites: the French ambassador was seen at the Globe, the Venetian at the Curtain, and the Spanish ambassador at the Fortune, another large theatre with a seating capacity of over 2000.

The player's life was not an easy one. There were celebrated actors who, largely through having a financial investment in a theatre, made large sums of money. Edward Alleyn retired before he was forty, rich enough to buy the manor of Dulwich for £10,000, to build the College of God's Gift, and to spend £1700 a year upon its maintenance and that of his own household. And Richard Burbage bequeathed his wife and children land worth £300 as well as valuable shares in both the Blackfriars and Globe theatres. But Richard Tarleton, the ugly comic actor who was renowned for his improvisations and was as celebrated in his day as either Alleyn or Burbage, was a poor man, and so were most of his less famous fellow-players. In the days when plays had been performed in inn-yards most of the profits went to the owners or tenants of the building; and so they did when the first theatres were built. The admission fees were divided between the players and the 'housekeeper'; but when all the actors in a company had received their share and paid their expenses, they did not consider themselves well rewarded for their work. As a writer put it in 1609, 'Hee shall be glad to play three houres for two pence to the basest stinkard in London, whose breth is stronger than garlicke, and able to poison all the twelve penny roomes.'[20]

The rare provident actor was, nevertheless, able to do quite well for himself. The 'hired men', that is to say those who played the smallest parts, were paid 10s a week by Philip Henslowe, though they received only 5s a week when they were on tour. They were likely to profit by additional payments, a special reward for playing well at court, perhaps, or fees for private engagements in the evenings when the public theatres were closed. They were also likely to receive compensation when the theatres were shut because of the plague. Moreover, they often had shares in the extensive wardrobe of their respective companies, and in the plays which were written for them. Indeed, their shares in a play were sometimes worth more than the fees the dramatists received for writing them: a play was commonly sold outright for £5 or £6 in Philip Henslowe's time, while no more than £2 or £3 was paid for amending an old play for revival. In 1599 Thomas Dekker earned £35; but he had written at least three successful plays that year and collaborated on several others.[21]

When a play was completed, the stage manager would add the cues for alarms and noises, prepare a 'plot' – an outline of the story with a list of entrances and exits – and an inventory of the properties required. There was never much in the way of scenery, but a list of properties possessed by Alleyn's company includes such items as stairs, steeples, a beacon, a tree, a snake, two mossy banks and two coffins, various 'dead limbs', a tree of golden apples, a cauldron and a dragon. The costumes were always of the most lavish and colourful kind, so resplendent in fact that foreign visitors who could not understand a word of the play derived entertainment in gazing at 'the very costly dresses of the actors', many of them the discarded but by no means threadbare clothes of lords and ladies.

Before the play could be produced it had to be passed by the Lord Chamberlain whose office would return it with offensive lines touching upon political, religious or moral matters crossed out or with notes such as 'mend this' written in the margins. The actor was, therefore, trained to find ways round the censorship with gestures and inflections of voice; he was also required to master a large number of parts in a short time, the women's parts being allocated to boys, who were generally apprenticed to a senior player before their voices broke, though parts such as the Nurse in *Romeo and Juliet* or Mistress Quickly in *The Merry Wives of Windsor* were played by the comedians of the company. One company, the Admiral's Men, put on fifty-five new plays in the three years from June 1594 and no less than sixty-two in 1599–1600.[22]

But while the prompter could always be relied upon to help an actor who had forgotten his lines, there were other hazards of an actor's life from which there was no protection. On his appearance in a play which offended the authorities he was likely to be arrested and imprisoned, the fate of several actors in a 'lewd plaie that was plaied in one of the plaiehowses on the Bancke Side' in 1597.[23] His company would be dissolved upon the death of its patron until his heir took the players over or another patron could be found. And his theatre would usually be closed in Lent, during outbreaks of plague, periods of national mourning and after damage by fire: when the Fortune was burned down 'by negligence of a candle', and plague broke out soon after it was rebuilt, the company that performed there disintegrated. The Phoenix, a playhouse in Drury Lane close to the bawdy houses which were frequently the target of rioting youths, was partially demolished in 1616 on Shrove Tuesday, the apprentices' traditional holiday.

> The Prentizes on Shrove Tewsday last to the number of 3 or 4000 committed extreame insoslencies [wrote Edward Sherburne]. Part of this nomber, taking their course for Wapping, did there pull downe to the ground 4 houses, spoiled all the goods therein, defaced many others; & a Justice of the Peace coming to appease them . . . had his head broken with a brick bat. The' other part, making for Drury Lane, they beset [the Phoenix] round, broke in, wounded divers of the players, broke open their trunckes, & whatt apparell, bookes or other things they found, they burnt & cutt in peeces; & not content herewith, gott on the top of the house, & untiled it, & had not the Justices of Peace & Sherife levied an aide, & hindred their purpose, they would have laid that house likewise even with the ground. In this skyrmishe one prentise was slaine, being shott through the head with a pistoll, & many others of their fellowes were sore hurt, & such of them are taken his Majestie hath commanded shal be executed for example sake.[24]

The players and all their works were also constantly attacked by preachers and moralists; in Puritan tracts and pamphlets; by tradesmen and retailers, 'Vintners, Alewives and Victuallers' who surmised 'if there were no Playes, they should have all the companie that resort to them'; by employers who maintained that the theatre enticed servants out of their masters' houses on afternoons when they ought to be working; and by the City fathers who lamented that more wholesome practices such as archery were being neglected. It was complained that, although it had long been agreed that no plays would be performed during divine service either on Sundays or on Saints' Days, audiences crowded round the theatre doors on those days long before they opened, and that 'the play-houses were already full, while the bells were still ringing' in the empty churches. Actors were condemned as crocodiles, wolves, vipers, drones, wasps, caterpillars, mites and maggots and were likened to thieves and whores. All manner of calamities were ascribed to the public's love of plays both in London and in the country where permanent companies were also established and where, to advertise forthcoming attractions, the players marched through the streets in gaudy clothes, beating drums and playing trumpets. In 1580 an earthquake and three years later the collapse of scaffolding, resulting in the death of eight people, were attributed to 'God's wrath against plays'. Affrays in Whit Week 1584 outside the Theatre and the Curtain provided an excuse for the City corporation to persuade the Privy Council to suppress both houses for a time; and disturbances in Southwark in 1591 led to the banning of all plays there between 23 June and the following Michaelmas.[25]

For Thomas White the 'sumptuous Theatre houses' were 'a continuall monument of London's prodigalitie and folly'; for William Harrison, 'an evident token of a wicked time'; for William Crawshaw, 'a bastard of Babylon, a daughter of error and confusion, a hellish device, the divels owne recreation to mock at holy things'.[26] John Northbrooke, a Bristol divine, in a frequently reprinted tirade, condemned 'these schools of all wickedness and vice' which brought men and women into Satan's snare of 'concupiscence and filthie lustes of wicked whoredome'. He urged the righteous to go to a play at least once

> To see what reward there is given to these Crocodiles . . . If you will learne howe to bee false, and deceive your husbandes, or husbandes their wives, howe to playe the harlottes, to obtayne one's love, howe to ravishe, how to beguyle, how to betraye, to flatter, lye, sweare, foresweare, to allur to whoredone, how to poyson, how to disobey and to rebel against Princes, to consume treasures prodigally, to move to lustes, to ransacke and spoyle cities and townes, to bee ydle and blaspheme, to sing filthe songs of love, to speake filthy, to be prowde, how to mocke, scoffe, and deryde any nation . . . shall not you learne, then, at such enterludes howe to practice them?[27]

Echoing such condemnations as these the lord mayor and aldermen frequently petitioned the Privy Council to suppress the London theatres, those promulgators of 'profane fables, Lascivious matter, cozoning devices, and other unseemly & scurrilous behaviours'.[28]

Two years after this petition was written, in July 1597, the lord mayor and aldermen wrote to the Privy Council again:

> We have signified to your HH many tymes heartofore the great inconvenience which wee fynd to grow by the Common exercise of Stage Playes. Wee presumed to doo, aswell in respect of the dutie wee beare towardes her highnes for the good gouernment of this her Citie, as for conscience sake, being perswaded (under correction of your HH. judgment) that neither in politie nor in religion they are to be suffered . . . Wee have fownd by

th'examination of divers apprentices & other servantes whoe have confessed unto us that the said Staige playes were the very places of theire Randevous appoynted by them to meete with such otheir as wear to joigne with them in theire designes & mutinus attemptes, beeinge allso the ordinarye places for maisterles men to come together & to recreate themselves.[29]

Several specific reasons were offered as to why the theatres should be closed: they were 'a speaciall cause of corruptinge Youth, conteninge nothing but unchast matters . . . & other lewd ungodly practizes'. They were the 'ordinary places for . . . idele and dangerous persons to meet together & to make their matches to the great displeasure of Almightie God & the hurt & annoyance of her Majestie's people'. They maintained 'idleness in such persons as have no vocation & draw apprentices and other servants from their ordinary workes and all sortes of people from the resort unto sermons and other Christian exercises'. And in time of sickness 'many have sores . . . take occasion to walk abroad & to recreate themselves by hearing a play. Whereby others are infected, and themselves also many things miscarry.'[30]

The Privy Council responded to the City's complaints by charging the lord mayor and the justices of Middlesex to arrange for the destruction of all theatres in and about London. This total ban on acting was lifted on 1 November; but on 9 February the next year the Act of Parliament governing both a citizen's right to act professionally and a gentleman's right to maintain a theatrical company was drastically amended. Ten days later the Privy Council informed the magistrates of Middlesex and Surrey that 'licence hath bin graunted unto two companies of stage players retayned unto us, the Lord Admyral and Lord Chamberlain'. All other companies, and in particular a company which 'by waie of intrusion' was playing at the Boar's Head, were to be suppressed.

In June 1600 a further Privy Council order decreed that, since acting was not 'evill in yt self' and might therefore 'with a good order and moderacion be suffered' – and since the queen must be supplied with good entertainment by good actors – there must be 'howses to serve for publique playenge to keepe players in exercise'. There were, therefore, 'to bee about the Cittie two howses . . . to serve for the use of Common Stage plaies'. It was emphasized, however, that no play was to be presented, '(as sometimes they have bin), in the Common Inns', and that there were to be no performances on Sundays, in Lent or in times of plague.

This order, like previous and subsequent orders, was never properly enforced: unlicensed theatres which should have been closed contrived to remain open, while several companies flourished under the protection of royal patronage. Indeed, in the reign of James I, after a statute had deprived the magistrates of their licensing power, the Chamberlain's, the Earl of Worcester's and the Admiral's men were all taken directly into the royal service as the Companies of the King, the Queen and of Prince Henry, the heir apparent. It was not until the change of political power in the reign of Charles I and with the onset of the Civil War that the City authorities were able to overrule the court and deal with the players as they wished. In 1642, a fortnight after the king raised his standard at Nottingham, Parliament finally pronounced that

> Whereas the distressed Estate of Ireland, steeped in her own Blood, and the distracted Estate of England, threatned with a Cloud of Blood, by a Civill Warre, call for all possible meanes to appease and avert the Wrath of God appearing in these Judgements; amongst which, Fasting and Prayer having bin often tryed to be very effectuall, have bin lately, and are still enjoyned; and whereas publike Sports doe not well agree with publike Calamities, nor publike Stage-playes with the Seasons of Humiliation, this being an Exercise of sad and pious solemnity, and the other being Spectacles of pleasure, too commonly expressing lacivious Mirth and Levitie: It is therefore thought fit, and Ordeined by the Lords and Commons in this Parliament Assembled, that while these sad Causes and set times of Humiliation doe continue, publike Stage-Playes shall cease, and bee forborne.[31]

Even after this pronouncement, however, the theatre did not immediately die. An October issue of *Mercurius Melancholicus* announced that 'the Common Inns of sin and Blasphemy, the Playhouses', had begun 'to be custom'd again, and to act filthiness and villainy to the life'[32] That month Beaumont and Fletcher's *A King and no King*, formerly acted at the Blackfriars, was advertised as a forthcoming production at the Salisbury Court Theatre which had been built in 1629.

> The Sheriffes of the City of London with their officers went thither [according to a report in the newsbook, *Perfect Occurrences*] and found a great number of people; some young lords and other eminent persons; and the men and women with the Boxes [in which the admission money was collected] fled. The Sheriffes brought away Tim Reade the Foole, and the people cryed out for their monies, but slunk away like a company of drowned Mice without it.[33]

This raid deterred neither the players nor the playgoers, and in 1648 it was reported that performances were being given not only at the Salisbury Court but at other theatres as well. Provoked by this report, Parliament sent troops of soldiers to the theatres named, arrested all the actors they could find and took away their costumes. The Salisbury Court Theatre was soon afterwards demolished, as the Globe had been in 1644 and the Blackfriars and Hope were to be in 1655 and 1656. The Fortune Theatre was also pulled down after a severe ordinance had been issued by Parliament ordering the authorities in London, Westminster, Middlesex and Surrey,

To pull downe and demolish . . . all stage Galleries, Seates and Boxes, erected or used . . . for the acting, or playing, or seeing acted or plaid . . . Stage-Playes, Interludes, and Playes . . . And to cause to be apprehended all common players and Actors.[34]

# 23 · 'Whole Counties Became Desperate'

When the Royal Standard was raised in the driving rain at Nottingham in 1642 on the outbreak of the Civil War between the supporters of King Charles I and Parliament, there were scarcely more than 1000 men at the king's command. Many of those who had already declared their allegiance shared the reluctance of Sir Edmund Verney, shortly to be killed fighting for him in Warwickshire. 'I do not like the Quarrel,' Sir Edmund wrote, 'and do heartily wish the King would yield.' But his conscience was concerned 'in honour and in gratitude; he had eaten the King's bread and served him near thirty Years', and he would not do 'so base a Thing as to foresake him' now.

Yet this simple loyalty to the Crown, whether displayed by men like Verney or by those who would always support the king, right or wrong, was not sufficiently widespread or deeply felt to gain Charles more than a few supporters. Others who might have supported him hung back: it was harvest time, for one thing, and for another the King was still making overtures to Parliament as though he hoped, even now, to reach a compromise. Men were reluctant to jeopardize their future by openly declaring their support of a cause which might at any moment be abandoned or betrayed.

Charles's behaviour in the months before his arrival in Nottingham had certainly, to say the least, been equivocal. Following the advice of various recent and moderate adherents to his cause, he had appeared to be willing to accept all the reasonable constitutional reforms which had been introduced, and to be concerned to present himself as the upholder of legality and of the Church of England. But at the same time he had shown how ready he still was to be influenced by the firebrands and reactionaries at Court who urged him to crush the rebellion by force, to get help to do this from anyone, foreigners and Catholics included. It was not only his enemies, but also his potential friends who distrusted him. And in the end it was Parliament itself which enabled him to attract sufficient support to offer battle.

For on 6 September its members declared that all men who did not support it were 'delinquents' and that their property was forfeit. This meant that those who would have been happy to stay neutral were virtually obliged to fight in their own defence; it meant, as the Parliamentarian Sir Simonds D'Ewes admitted, that 'not only particular persons of the nobility' but 'whole counties' became 'desperate'. Men whose fortunes might well have been lost had Parliament won, now undertook to raise troops to fight for the king in whose victory their own salvation might be secured; while gentry whose income from land was declining and whose fortunes depended upon the rich perquisites which only the Court could offer, needed no further persuasion to fight.

If self-interest provided the spur for this early surge of support for the Royalist cause, other reasons, no less important, played their part in swelling the numbers of men who eventually decided to throw in their lot with the king. It was not only that the king's majesty was considered by many, including Edmund Verney, to be sacrosanct. 'I beseech you consider,' Verney wrote to his brother who had made up his mind to support Parliament, 'that majesty is sacred; God sayth "Touch not myne anointed."' There was also the strong feeling that the king was the defender of the true Church; and although religion became of much more importance later in the struggle than it was in the beginning, it was even now of grave concern. Moreover, while it was never primarily a class struggle – at least the gentry were fairly equally divided – there was an undeniable fear among many of the king's supporters that the lower classes would use this opportunity to turn upon their masters, that the predominantly Puritan merchants and shopkeepers of the towns were intent upon upsetting the structure of power to their own advantage, that the king's opponents represented rebellion and chaos as opposed to law and order. These fears and beliefs were not, of course, general throughout the country; they were strongest in the north, except for the more industrialized parts of Yorkshire and Lancashire, in the west Midlands and Wales and in the West Country. Parliament, on the other hand, derived its strongest support from south-east England, London and in East Anglia where Oliver Cromwell, himself a gentleman farmer with a small estate near Huntingdon, helped to organize the 'Eastern Association'. But there were no firm lines of division: most trading towns declared for Parliament; many areas endeavoured to remain neutral; a large number of landowners changed from side to side with the fortunes of war; hundreds of families were divided in their loyalties as the Verneys were; thousands of country people found themselves drawn into the conflict on the side that their landlords and masters elected to support; thousands more were not too sure what all the fuss was about or, as Sir Arthur Haslerig said, did not really care what government they lived under 'so long as they may plough and go to market'. Some did not even know there was a conflict at all, and only about three men in every hundred took an active part in it. Long after the war had started, long after the first battles had been fought, a Yorkshire farm labourer, when advised to keep out of the line of fire between the king's men and Parliament's learned for the first time that 'them two had fallen out'.[1]

Yet, even if unaware of all the issues involved, the poor of England had long had cause for grievous discontent. Prices, which had continually risen and so reduced the value of their wages, had not become steadier until the 1620s, and thereafter there were years of bad harvests, of plague, of distress in the woollen industry, of adverse balances of trade. There were seven good years between 1629 and 1635, but these were followed by intermittent years of hardship and unemployment and of outbreaks of discontent. In Yorkshire and Lincolnshire there were riots against the draining of the fens which threatened a way of life traditional there for centuries; in Wiltshire and Cornwall there were riots against enclosures and against interference with the people's rights on common lands. Elsewhere there were widespread protests against the diminishing areas of land around the cottages of farm labourers which, when newly built in the reign of Queen Elizabeth, had been required by law to have four acres at least. There were frequent complaints, too, that the shilling a day upon which most workers were required to live was barely adequate for life's necessities.[2]

Protests found voice in numerous pamphlets. After the lifting of censorship in 1641 their number increased from twenty-two the previous year to 1996 in 1642.[3] They also found expression in the proliferation of Protestant sects, Calvinists and Baptists, Presbyterians and Quakers, Ranters and Seekers and Muggletonians, all offering their own paths to salvation, feeding resentment against the bishops whom the king employed in the administration of his secular affairs.[4]

After the Civil War, in which about 100,000 men were killed, the protests were continued and the demands renewed. The Levellers, those radicals in the Parliamentary army, vigorously pursued their campaign for a greatly widened suffrage and the abolition of tithes. The even more extreme Diggers, demanding 'an end to the ownership of private property and declaring that the poorest man hath as true a title and just right to the land as the richest man', occupied manorial land and cut down manorial trees. Such provocation united conservative-minded men in their determination to resist the extremists; while Oliver Cromwell, a conservative himself at heart, expressed his wish to preserve 'the ranks and order of men whereby England hath been known for hundreds of years: a nobleman, a gentleman, a yeoman'.[5]

It was the noblemen and gentlemen, indeed, who were the eventual beneficiaries of the Civil War and the years that followed it. Land had certainly passed from Royalist into Roundhead hands, but it passed back again after the Restoration. There were certainly Royalist gentry who had contracted such debts that they had to sell their estates either to richer landowners or to successful merchants and yeomen who were rising into the gentry class: the theme of many plays produced in the reign of Charles II was the hatred of small squires and gentry for the rich lords who were buying their land.[6] Yet, while the process of swallowing up small estates in larger as an agricultural advancement had undoubtedly begun, the gentry as a whole emerged from the war with their position in the country enhanced. As Justices of the Peace they exercised greater authority after the Restoration of Charles II than they had in the days of his father, and as landowners they held half the land in the country.[7]

At the same time, so it seems from contemporary estimates, the Civil War had done little to relieve poverty. These estimates were compiled by Gregory King, a genealogist and statistician who was born in Lichfield in 1648. After careful study of the records of the population and wealth of the country towards the close of the seventeenth century, King estimated that out of a total population of 5,500,520 people there were 1,275,000 'labouring people and outservants' with a yearly income of about £15 a year per family, 1,300,000 'cottagers and paupers' struggling to survive on £6 10s per family, and 30,000 'vagrants as gipsies, thieves, beggars etc'.[8]

The Act of Settlement passed in 1662 made no clear distinction between this last group and those poor people who, for reasons beyond their control, found themselves without means of support in a village not their own. All of them were liable to be sent back to the parish where they were last settled when ordered to do so by two Justices of the Peace upon receipt of a complaint from the Overseers of the Poor. Indeed, long before this Act was passed an expensive item in the account books of parish constables was the relief doled out to poor people ordered to return to villages where they had previously lived and where they would almost certainly not be welcome upon their return.

The account books of Upton-by-Southwell in Nottinghamshire record the following doles among many others of the same kind:

Given to a poore man and his wife and five children which lay a day and night in James Bloomer barne . . . 1s 8d.
Given to a cripple woman being sent from constable to constable in a cart being very weake and feeble, she being releifed with meat and money . . . 8d.[9]

Pregnant women and the sick were pushed about with particular haste for fear lest they either gave birth to a child which would then be a charge upon the parish or die in it and require burial. At Wymeswold 'a Bygg belly woman' was given 2d to help speed her 'forth of the towne'; and on 25 June 1631 a Nottinghamshire constable noted in his accounts, 'Given to a woman that was great with child to gett her away . . . 2d. Given to a poor man, his wife and three small children. One child being very sore sicke for fear the child should die in this towne I gave them to be gone . . . 8d.'[10]

Gregory King thought that more than a million people in the country were occasionally in receipt of alms of one sort or another, the poor rate in his day being nearly £800,000 a year, a sum which was often said to be distributed with extravagant largesse as poor relief is commonly alleged to be by those who have never needed it. Richard Dunning maintained in 1698 that the parish dole was frequently three times as much as a common labourer with a wife and three children could afford to spend on himself, that people who had once received outdoor relief refused to work thereafter, seldom drank 'other than the strongest ale-house beer' and never ate any bread save what was 'made of the finest wheat flour'.[11]

The wages of a common labourer which Dunning said were spurned by those who could get relief were certainly low. They were meant to be regulated by schedules setting out maximum figures which were issued for each county by the Justices of the Peace. Although there were statutory penalties for both paying and receiving wages above the official rates, paying higher figures was sometimes agreed to after bouts of private bargaining. Yet most workers had to be content with the low wages given in Gregory King's tables or perhaps with as little as £3 a year if they were provided with food and lodging as well. A worker who had a little land around his cottage and rights on the common might live without fear of hunger. Indeed, Gregory King estimated that half the poor who were in work ate meat every day, the other half at least twice a week, and even the unemployed might do so once a week. But for those who had no land to help feed hungry children life was hard, particularly in years of dearth such as that of 1659 and in those years of rising prices between 1693 and 1699 when the cost of bread doubled. Soon afterwards prices began to fall again; and by 1701 a chicken could be bought for 2d in Yorkshire, but even this was a price beyond the reach of many.

Efforts were made to improve farming methods and so bring food prices down. Numerous books were published offering farmers advice, from Sir Richard Weston's *Discourses of Husbandrie* of 1645 to Leonard Meager's *The Mystery of Husbandry: or Arable, Pasture and Woodland Improved* which appeared in 1697. The Royal Society, founded in 1662, established an agricultural committee to conduct experiments and carry out research; and this committee advocated the growing of potatoes and of crops to feed animals during the winter months, the use of clover and sainfoin to convert arable land temporarily into pasture, and more efficient watering, manuring and fertilizing. Experts visited Holland to see how the Dutch – of whom advice was also sought before the establishment of the Bank of England in 1694 – had converted waterlogged land into profitable farms. At the same time certain practising farmers were turning to new crops and new methods on their own land. Colonel Robert Walpole, father of Sir Robert, the future prime minister, began growing turnips as cattle fodder on his estate in East Anglia in 1673. William Russell, the first Duke of Bedford, continued his father's work on draining the Fen district – despite opposition from the local people who crept out by night to cut the dykes – and he lived to see good crops growing and cattle feeding on the land that had formerly produced little but reeds and wild ducks. In the Thames valley new market gardens appeared. Elsewhere forests were cut down to extend the acreage of farmland. Yet, over the country as a whole, as Maurice Ashley has pointed out, change was slow to come. Most farmers distrusted innovation, preferring to stick to their traditional ways and distrusting the new-fangled methods. As a pamphleteer observed in 1675: 'It is our own negligence and idleness that brings poverty upon us.'[12]

In his estimation of the numbers of persons in the various classes and callings in English society at the end of the seventeenth century, Gregory King listed 750,000 farmers earning on average £42 10s a year, 280,000 'freeholders of the better sort' having £91 a year, and 660,000 'freeholders of the lesser sort' with £55 a year. Other categories listed in his tables were:

| Number of families | Ranks, degrees, titles and qualifications | Heads per family | Number of persons | Yearly income per family £ |
|---|---|---|---|---|
| 160 | Temporal lords | 40 | 6400 | 3200 |
| 26 | Spiritual lords | 20 | 520 | 1300 |
| 800 | Baronets | 16 | 12,800 | 880 |
| 600 | Knights | 13 | 7800 | 650 |
| 3000 | Esquires | 10 | 30,000 | 450 |
| 12,000 | Gentlemen | 8 | 96,000 | 280 |
| 5000 | Persons in greater offices and places | 8 | 40,000 | 240 |
| 5000 | Persons in lesser offices and places | 6 | 30,000 | 120 |
| 2000 | Eminent merchants and traders by sea | 8 | 16,000 | 400 |

| Number of families | Ranks, degrees, titles and qualifications | Heads per family | Number of persons | Yearly income per family £ |
|---|---|---|---|---|
| 8000 | Lesser merchants and traders by sea | 6 | 48,000 | 198 |
| 10,000 | Persons in the law | 7 | 70,000 | 154 |
| 15,000 | Persons in liberal arts and sciences | 5 | 75,000 | 60 |
| 50,000 | Shopkeepers and tradesmen | 4½ | 225,000 | 45 |
| 60,000 | Artisans and handicrafts | 4 | 240,000 | 38 |
| 5000 | Naval officers | 4 | 20,000 | 80 |
| 4000 | Military officers | 4 | 16,000 | 60 |
| 50,000 | Common seamen | 3 | 150,000 | 20 |
| 35,000 | Common soldiers | 2 | 70,000 | 14 |
| 364,000 | Labouring people and out-servants | 3½ | 1,275,000 | 15 |
| 400,000 | Cottagers and paupers | 2 | 1,300,000 | 6.10s[13] |

There were also 12,000 people in the families of 'eminent clergymen' who earned £72 a year per family, and 40,000 in the families of 'lesser clergymen' with an annual income of £50 each. Their Church had emerged from the troubles of the seventeenth century with renewed strength. An Act of Uniformity passed in 1662 had decreed that all clergymen who did not conform to the Prayer Book liturgy by St Bartholomew's Day were to lose their livings, and this had resulted in the expulsion from the Church of some thousand priests. Subsequently, lay Dissenters were, like Roman Catholics, excluded from public office and were otherwise persecuted, though usually for social rather than religious reasons. There was, however, no danger now of the country being overrun by Puritans any more than there was of it being governed by Roman Catholics.

When Charles II's brother, the Roman Catholic James II, threatened to establish a royal despotism backed by a powerful army, the Anglican gentry and the Church of England were essential elements in the forces that overthrew him and brought to the throne in his place his elder daughter Mary and her husband, James's nephew, the Dutch Protestant, William of Orange, who, before becoming William III and Mary II, were required to accept a limitation of royal powers as outlined in a Declaration of Rights. Soon after their accession all Nonconformists, with the exception of Unitarians, a sect which rejected the doctrine of the Trinity, were granted freedom of worship by the Toleration Act of 1689. Nonconformists were also allowed to escape the jurisdiction of most of the penal laws to which Roman Catholics were still subject, though – unless they were prepared to take Holy Communion at least once a year in their parish church – they remained excluded from public life.[14]

Nonconformists were at this time largely confined to towns, and remained so until the Wesleyan movement led to the formation of many dissenting congregations in the country. There were one or two Dissenters among the nobility and a few among the gentry. But most were from the kind of families that produced John Bunyan, whose father made a living by farming nine acres and did tinkering work to make ends meet, and George Fox, founder of the Quakers, who was the son of a weaver. They were proud of their independence and of the seriousness with which they regarded their faith as compared with what they took to be the laxer attitudes of the congregations in the churches where the opinions of the squire were likely to be as dominant as those of the parson, if not more so.

> He has often told me [wrote Addison of Sir Roger de Coverley] that at his coming to his estate he found the Parishioners very irregular; and in order to make them kneel and join in the responses, he gave every one of them a hassock and a Common-Prayer book; and at the same time employed an itinerant singing-master, who goes about the country for that purpose, to instruct them nightly in the tunes of the Psalms. As Sir Roger is landlord to the whole congregation, he keeps them in very good order, and suffers nobody to sleep in it besides himself; for if by chance he has been surprised into a short nap at sermon, upon recovering out of it he stands up and looks about him, and if he sees anybody else nodding, either wakes them himself or sends his servants to them.[15]

Unquestionably the services in many parish churches were already controlled by the squire in this patrician way, and were to be so for generations to come, even in our own century when the patron of a living would, like King Edward VII at Sandringham, place his gold watch prominently on the back of the pew in front of him so that the rector should not be tempted to prolong the sermon for more than the prescribed ten minutes. Yet Anglicans were not so indifferent to their faith, nor so inclined to regard churchgoing as principally a social duty, as many Nonconformists liked to suppose. In most good Anglican homes graces were said before and after meals, and the family and their servants met for daily prayers: in the home of Alice Thornton, daughter of a member of the minor gentry of Yorkshire, the whole family was called to prayers by a little bell at six in the morning, at two in the afternoon and again at night.[16]

*

While the influence of the Puritans had been paramount in England, soldiers had been authorized to enter private houses to ensure that the Sabbath and the fasts ordered by Parliament were being properly observed; maypoles had been cut down, brothels as well as theatres had been demolished; gambling dens had been closed; race-meetings banned; and the number of alehouses diminished. Acts were passed for the punishment of sexual incontinence, making fornication a felony; and acts of public penance during Morning Prayer for sexual offences became more frequent, a girl who had been found engaged in illicit carnal relations being required to parade clothed in white, and carrying a white sheet, bare-headed, bare-legged and barefoot, 'in sight of the congregation'. After the gospel had been read she was required to say 'in a penitent manner and with an audible voyce as folloeth':

> I, A.M., spinster of this parish, not having the fear of God before mine eyes nor regarding my owne soule healthe to the displeasure of Almighty God, the danger of my soule and the evill example of others committed the vile and heinous sinne of fornication.[17]

In 1647 an ordinance decreed that all persons who had acted in any playhouse in London were to be punished as rogues; in 1648 men and women who had acted in public could be whipped and those who had watched them act could be fined; in 1654 cock-fighting was prohibited, not so much because it was cruel as because it was 'commonly accompanied with gaming, drinking and swearing'. Anyone 'profanely or vainly walking' on the Lord's Day was penalized; and stricter rules were made to enforce public worship and to prevent Sunday travelling and trading. A new Act was passed against profane swearing and it became an offence to gamble with cards. It was also an offence for apprentices or servants to remain in a tavern after eight o'clock on a holiday. For six months horse-racing was abolished and it was even considered a crime, in certain circumstances, to play football: one John Bishop, an apothecary, was charged with having at Maidstone, 'wilfully and in a violent and boisterous manner run to and fro' and kicked 'up and down in the common highway and street within the said town and county, called the High Street, a certain ball of leather, commonly called a football'.[18]

Punishments for crimes such as this were unlikely to be severe, but the crime of blasphemy was punished ferociously. James Naylor, who said that he was God, declared that a man might enjoy the pleasure of love with any woman provided she belonged to the same sect. His own sect was mostly composed of women who sat round his chair for hours on end chanting, 'Holy! Holy! To the true God and Great God and Glory to the Almighty!' Naylor was sentenced to be set in the pillory in Palace Yard; to be whipped to the Old Exchange by the hangman; two days later to be pilloried at Old

Exchange and to have a hole bored through his tongue; to be branded with a B; to be taken to Bristol to be publicly whipped and to be sent through the town on a horse's bare back with his face to the tail; then to be placed in solitary confinement at Bridewell.[19]

During the time of the Long Parliament, between 1645 and 1647, witchcraft was also punished with great severity. For generations people had been turning to 'cunning men' and 'wise women', 'sorcerers', conjurers', 'blessers' and 'charmers' for protection against pain and illness and early death, and against fire and dearth, for magical cures and love potions, for help in the recovery of stolen goods or the discovery of buried treasure or missing children. The witches consulted offered all manner of treatment and wizardries, from curing headaches by boiling a lock of the patient's hair in urine, then throwing it into the fire, to treating sick animals by tapping them with magic wands or tying bunches of herbs to their tails. One Northumberland witch placed her lips to the mouths of sick children 'and made such chirping and sucking that the mother of the said child thought that she had sucked the heart out of it and was sore affrighted'. Others made diagnoses by examination and measuring of the ill person's clothes or, as a cure for 'heart-ache', crossed garters over their ears while muttering incantations. Yet it seems that before 1500 it was extremely rare for witches to suffer more than the mildest punishments; and, according to Keith Thomas, examination of medieval judicial records has so far revealed no more than a dozen known cases of supposed witches being executed for the whole period between the Norman Conquest and the Reformation; 'and most of these had been involved in plots against the monarch or his friends'.[20]

Towards the middle of the seventeenth century, however, witch-hunts became much more hysterical than they had been in the past; and, although many judges lamented the vindictiveness with which they were pursued – and some, like the Lord Chief Justice, Sir John Holt, who seemed 'to believe nothing of witchery at all', did their best to bring about acquittals – there were others who showed themselves determined to secure conviction even upon the flimsiest of evidence. Lord Chief Justice North confessed that he had condoned the conviction of three innocent women at Exeter because he feared that acquittal might result in a fresh wave of witch-hunting.[21] As it was, the uproar in court was sometimes so deafening that the evidence could not be heard above the din. At the trial of Mary Spencer in 1634 there was such a row that she could not hear the charges which were brought against her.[22]

Some women, it was supposed, became witches after having fornicated with the devil or having kissed his rectum in which 'lustful women took especial delight', though such charges were much more common on the

Continent than they were in England. Coitus was very painful because the devil had an extremely large and hard penis, sometimes shod with iron, at others covered with brittle fish-scales, and his semen was cold as ice. But this did not necessarily mean that the body of a woman who had been entered by him would show that she had been hurt. It was possible for a woman who was proved in court to be a virgin to have 'committed uncleanness' with the Devil as she could have done so without being deflowered. In the absence of witnesses who were prepared to swear that they had seen the accused fornicating with the Devil or with an incubus, evidence was accepted from distinguished witch-finders such as Matthew Hopkins who could discover whether or not a woman was possessed by the devil by sticking pins into her flesh to discover the places rendered insensitive by the Devil's touch. Witches could also be detected by their habit of throwing back their hair, their inability to cry, their practice of walking backwards and intertwining their fingers, by the devils that took the shape of animals, mostly toads and cats, who were their familiars, and by a third nipple on some part of their body.

Hopkins, the son of a minister of Wenham, Suffolk, was said to have been a lawyer when the Civil War began. He claimed to have had his first experiences of witches in 1644 when he was in practice at Manningtree where he procured the condemnation of twenty-nine women who had made sacrifices to the Devil. Thereafter as the self-styled 'Witch-Finder General' he travelled about the countryside with a male assistant and female searcher, charging a fee for his discovery of witches in the various places where he stayed. Suspected women were urged to confess and were hanged when they did so. Those who declined to confess were stripped and searched for their secret nipple, placed cross-legged and bound on a table in a closed room with a hole in the door through which their 'imps' could enter. They were kept like this for as long as two days without food or sleep, being occasionally untied and made to walk round the room until their feet blistered and they were prepared to admit what was required of them.[23]

These measures taken against supposed witches, usually women who had caused disquiet or offence in their communities, were sanctioned by the authorities. A commission was granted in 1645 for their trial at Bury St Edmunds at which John Godbolt was the judge and before which Samuel Fairclough preached two sermons on the evils of witchcraft. Several victims were tried and hanged, and there were subsequent trials and executions all over Suffolk and Norfolk, Essex and Huntingdonshire and at Cambridge. Not all the victims were women. John Lowes, the ancient vicar of Brandeston, Suffolk where he had been incumbent for fifty years was ducked and otherwise ill-treated until he felt obliged to confess to avoid further suffering. He was hanged at Framlingham, having been permitted to read his own funeral service.

There was little active opposition to these trials; and it was not until John Gaule, a Huntingdonshire clergyman who believed in witches himself raised objections to the methods used to discover them, that Hopkins's career came to an end. 'Every old woman,' wrote Gaule in a book based on several sermons on witchcraft, 'with a wrinkled face, a furr'd brow, a hairy lip, a gobber tooth, a squint eye, a squeaking voyce, or a scolding tongue, having a ragged coate on her back, a skull-cap on her head, a spindle in her hand, and a dog or cat by her side, is not only suspected but pronounced for a witch.'[24] Soon after Gaule's book was published Hopkins was himself accused of witchcraft and made to undergo the same examinations as had his victims. He was hanged in August 1647.

Thereafter trials and executions of witches were not so frequent, but they did not come to an end. The prevalence and danger of witches was emphasized by Sir Matthew Hale, Lord Chief Baron of the Exchequer, who when directing a jury in a trial in 1661 'made no doubt at all of the existence of witches, as proved by the Scriptures, general consent and acts of parliament'. In this case two widows were indicted for causing certain children to be taken with fainting fits, to vomit nails and pins and to see strange ducks, mice and other animals which were invisible to everyone else. A toad had run out of their bed and when thrown on the fire had exploded with a loud crack like a pistol shot. Sir Thomas Browne, author of *Religio Medici*, gave evidence for the prosecution which succeeded in obtaining the conviction and execution of both prisoners.

At a subsequent trial in 1665 Hale sentenced two witches to death on the evidence of a woman who said that her children 'coughed extremely and brought up crooked pins' and once a big 'nail with a very broad head' which she produced together with forty of the pins. A doctor spoke of the 'subtlety of the Devil' while giving his evidence and explained how the working of the humours of the body in relation to this subtlety brought about this 'flux of pins'.[25]

The vomiting of pins was, apparently, a sure sign that the Devil's agency was at work. In 1716 Mary Hicks and her daughter Elizabeth, who was just eleven, were hanged for having, on their own confession, sold their souls to the Devil and obliged their neighbours to perform this painful miracle. But a man who accused a woman of making him vomit pins and of taking away his appetite was eventually arraigned at Surrey Assizes as a cheat and impostor. This was, however, not before he had succeeded in getting the woman convicted by Sir Thomas Lane, a firm believer in her evil powers. The witch's accuser could only get relief, so he told Sir Thomas, by scratching her. He was told to scratch her to prove his point. He did so and, immediately regaining his appetite, ate a big piece of bread and cheese.[26]

In 1736 the statutes against witchcraft were repealed but for many years suspicions continued to centre upon any persons whose eccentricities or secretiveness had aroused the hostility of their neighbours. Ducking and measuring a woman's weight against that of a Bible were still used to discover witches long after the legal punishments had disappeared; while in the middle of the eighteenth century villagers still attacked women whom they considered to be in league with the Devil. In 1751 a notice appeared on market day at Winslow, Leighton Buzzard and Hemel Hempstead to the effect that a man and a woman were 'to be publicly ducked at Tring for their crimes'. The woman was Ruth Osborn who was suspected of casting a spell over a dairyman and his calves. On the day appointed for her ducking she and her husband took sanctuary in the church from which the crowd dragged them to a pond, wrapped in sheets and with their thumbs tied to their toes. The woman died immediately, her husband a few days later. The man, a chimney-sweep, held primarily responsible for their death was executed and his body was hung in chains and remained suspended as a warning to others for a number of years. Charges arising out of the drowning of witches were, nevertheless, not uncommon in country districts up till the beginning of the nineteenth century.[27]

# 24 · *Schoolboys and Schoolgirls*

Throughout the country in the seventeenth century there were still thousands of people like Thomas Tryon who got no education because his father, though 'an honest sober man of good reputation', had so many children that he was 'forced to bring them all to work betimes'.[1] There were, however, increasing numbers of schools for poor children to attend when their labour could be spared. From 1536 parishes had been required to give basic reading lessons and religious instruction to all children; and the duty of providing these lessons usually fell upon the parson, as it did, for instance, at Wigston Magna in Leicestershire where £14 from village funds was paid to the vicar and an assistant to teach poor local boys.[2] Lessons were often given in church. John Evelyn recalled receiving his first lessons in the church porch at Wotton.

Licences were also given to laymen 'to teach boys the abcedarium and English letters', writing and arithmetic. William Swetnam, a fishmonger, was granted a licence by the Archbishop of Canterbury in 1596 to 'teach and instruct children in the principles of reading . . . and also to write and cast accounts'.[3] For children up to the age of seven there were dame schools in which instruction was given in such skills as knitting and spinning, though rarely in reading, and scarcely ever in writing; while for parents who wanted their children taught at home there were textbooks available 'for the private instruction of little children and more ignorant servants'.

Children were instructed with the help of pictorial rhyming alphabets, and of hornbooks, children's primers consisting of a sheet containing the letters of the alphabet mounted on a wooden frame, shaped like a table-tennis bat, and covered by a sheet of transparent horn. The earliest hornbooks had letters, both in large and small type, printed beneath a cross, hence they were known as Christ's Cross Rows. Beneath the letters was the Lord's Prayer and this was followed by a row of Roman or Arabic numerals or both. The hornbook was often attached by its handle to the child's belt. Yet, despite the pupil's familiarity with it, it frequently proved ineffective. 'This course we see hath been very effectual in a short time with some ripe-witted children,' wrote one critic of its general usefulness. 'But others . . . have been thus learning a whole year together and though they have been much chid and beaten for want of heed could scarce tell six of their letters at twelve months' end.'[4]

After leaving their dame school the brighter children might pass on, perhaps through the lower or 'petties' form of a grammar school – in which reading, writing and the rudiments of grammar were taught by undermasters or pupil-ushers – to one of the country's grammar schools. The numbers of these had much grown since the Middle Ages. There were, indeed, more per head of population at this time than there were to be in the Victorian age. By 1547 there was a grammar school in every sizable market town; and a study of ten counties in the 180 years between 1480 and 1660 has revealed the foundation of 410 new schools.[5]

Some of the country's most famous schools were founded in this period. Shrewsbury in 1551, Repton in 1559, Rugby in 1567, Uppingham in 1584, Harrow in 1590. Whitgift, Oakham, Gresham's and Tonbridge were also founded in the sixteenth century; Blundell's in 1604, Charterhouse in 1611. Other new schools were of highly variable quality. Some, particularly those which, like the school at Alford, Lincolnshire, would admit only pupils who could 'read perfectly and write legibly', gained as creditable a national reputation as Shrewsbury and Repton where the sons of the gentry were sent as boarders. Yet there were more than a few which could only attract boys who could not find places elsewhere.

Several of the old endowed schools which offered free places to poor children also provided places for children who paid for their lessons by cleaning the classrooms: at Manchester Grammar School two poor scholars were paid to sweep the premises twice a week and at Lichfield six pupils received £1 6s 8d a year to buy books provided they kept the school clean and well dusted.[6] Moreover, since the establishment of Christ's Hospital, other similar establishments had been founded all over the country, at Bristol, Exeter, Plymouth, Norwich, Nottingham, York, Reading and elsewhere. The children at these schools were usually provided with uniforms, poor boys at the charity school at Skipton in Yorkshire being issued with 'coat, waistcoat, breeches and round cap of purple cloth, two pairs of purple stockings, one pair of shoes, two shirts, two neckcloths and two handkerchiefs'.[7]

After the formation of the Society for the Promotion of Christian Knowledge in 1698 there was a great increase in the number of charity schools in the country. The society itself, the first of whose stated purposes was 'to promote and encourage the erection of charity schools in all parts of England and Wales', established six schools in the first six months of its existence; and by 1704 in its schools in London and Westminster alone there were 1386 boys and 745 girls in attendance.

> This school being only designed for the Benefit of such Poor Children, whose Parents or Friends are not able to give them Learning, [the statutes of one of these charity schools decreed] the Master shall not receive any money of the children's friends . . . [upon] any pretence whatsoever; nor shall the Master teach any children beside the poor of this Parish; but shall content himself with his Salary, upon pain of forfeiting his place.[8]

A typical subscription form declares:

> Whereas Profaneness and Debauchery are greatly owing to a gross Ignorance of the Christian Religion especially among the poorer sort; and whereas nothing is more likely to promote the practice of Christianity and Virtue than an early and pious Education of Youth; and whereas many poor people are desirous of having their Children taught . . . [this school will afford them] a Christian and Useful education.[9]

There were lessons from seven o'clock in the morning to eleven, and from one o'clock to five in the summer; from eight to eleven, and one to four in winter. Before and after lessons there were prayers; reading was concentrated upon the psalter and the Bible; and arithmetic was taught only to those who had mastered reading. Strong emphasis was placed upon good diction and morality; and masters were enjoined to discourage and correct, 'by all proper methods', 'the Beginnings of Vice, and particularly Lying, Swearing, Cursing and taking God's name in vain'.[10] In attaining these ends the masters were to consider corporal punishment as a last resort.[11] They were also required to be:

> A Member of the Church of England, of a sober life and conversation, and not under the age of 25 years.
> One that frequents the Holy Communion.
> One that hath a good Government of himself and his Passions.
> One of a meek temper and humble Behaviour.
> One who can write a good Hand and who understands the grounds of Arithmetic . . .
> One who keeps good order in his Family.[12]

*

In the sixteenth century teaching had been an ill-paid and not highly respected profession. 'Our calling creeps low,' wrote Richard Mulcaster in 1581, 'and hath pain for companion.' Rarely considered a suitable full-time career for a well-educated man, it was practised mostly by those looking for other work, clergy waiting for a benefice, men who had failed in other occupations, or the infirm. One John Bagford, 'a teacher of little children to spell and read English', was 'a very sickly, weak and impotent person, by reason whereof [he was] altogether uncapable to follow any other employment'.[13] A survey of schoolmasters in Worcestershire has shown that only twenty per cent of them were teaching full-time as a career.[14] The experiences of the author of *Mount Tabor* were not exceptional:

> Before Master Downhale came to be our Master in Christ-school [he wrote of his schooldays in the 1560s], an ancient Citizen of no great learning was our schoolmaster; whose manner was to give us out several lessons in the evening, by construing it to every form, and in the next morning to examine us thereupon . . . Now when the two highest forms were despatched some of them whom we called prompters would come to sit in our seats of the lower forms, and so being at our elbows would put into our mouths answers to our master's questions, as he walked up and down by us; and so by our prompters' help, we made shift to escape correction; but understood little to profit by it.[15]

Schoolmasters necessarily had very short holidays and their pay compared unfavourably even with the small stipends of the lower clergy. At Melton Mowbray in about 1600 the grammar schoolmaster was paid £10 a year by the town and the usher £5. At Rotherham the schoolmaster of the free school, 'a bacheler of arte of honest conversacion', also had £10, though he received additional allowances of 12s 'for his gowne; for the fyre to his chamber, 3s 4d and his Barber and launder free'. The master of the song-school at Rotherham was even more poorly paid at £6 3s 4d a year; while some ushers had even less than this. In 1583 the usher at St Bees, Cumbria, received only £3 6s 8d.[16]

Even with all the additional payments he could lay his hands on, for teaching 'modern' subjects as extras, writing letters for the illiterate and accepting bribes from rich parents for giving their children preferential treatment, the sixteenth-century schoolmaster was hard put to it to make a reasonable living.

By the middle of the seventeenth century, however, higher standards were expected of schoolmasters than in the past. At Chigwell in 1629 the Latin schoolmaster was required to be 'a graduate of one of the universities not under seven and twenty years of age, a man skilful in the Greek and Latin tongues, a good poet, of a sound religion, neither papist nor puritan, of a grave behaviour, of a sober and honest conversation, no tippler nor haunter of alehouses, no puffer of tobacco, and above all, that he be apt to teach and severe in his government'.[17] Twenty-five years later ordinances were issued requiring the dismissal of teachers found guilty of 'profane cursing or swearing, perjury . . . adultery, fornication, drunkenness, common haunting of taverns or alehouses, frequent quarrelling or fighting, frequent playing at cards or dice, profaning of the Sabbath day or [encouraging or practising] any Whitsun ales, wakes, morris dances, may poles, stage plays or such like licentious practices'.[18]

And schoolmasters did tend, in general, to be more conscientious and less impatient than they had been formerly. In many schools flogging was still the principal form of discipline. At Eton in the 1660s, when the use of tobacco was considered highly effective in warding off the plague, one boy recalled that he had never been 'so whipped in his life as he was one morning for not smoking'.[19] But nearly all seventeenth-century writers urged that the birch should be used in moderation. 'The great indiscretion and intemperance of masters hath brought a very great contempt and hatred upon the profession,' it was observed in 1661. 'It doth generally more hurt than good, by making those that are dull more dull and dispiriting the ingenious.'[20] This belief was by then quite widely held; and schoolmasters were consequently much more effective instructors.

Adam Martindale, the son of a Lancashire yeoman, who was born in 1623, had sad experiences with a succession of incompetent masters from the age of seven when he was sent to school in St Helen's, two miles from his father's house, 'a great way for a little fat, short-legged lad to travel twice a day'. His first teacher was interested only in money; his second was 'an old humdrum curate', a 'simpleton' and a 'tippler'; his third a woman who had a mere 'smattering of Latin'; his fourth a very poor, young married man who showed open favouritism to boys whose parents could afford to give him presents; his fifth 'beat the children passionately for no good reason'. At the age of twenty-one, in 1644, he himself became a master at Over Whitley Grammar School in Cheshire, a 'newly founded school'. 'The income was not very great but well paid,' Martindale wrote in his autobiography, '. . . and mine accidental gettings (having a full school and pretty store of rich men's sons in it), and opportunities for earning monies by making writings for neighbours were a good adition to my salary . . . My scholars were, for all my youth, submissive and reverent.'[21]

By this time teachers like Martindale were not exceptional, and boys were as likely as not to be as fortunate as William Woolaston of Shenstone in Leicestershire who was born in 1659:

When I was in the tenth year of my age, and had only learned at home to read, there came a straggling fellow (from whence I never knew) to Shenston . . . and opened a Latin school for country lads, such as he was capable of teaching. To this man I went the first hour after I had heard of him . . . and since [then I have] always placed this man's coming amongst the particular providences of my life.[22]

Improvement in the standards of teaching was appropriately matched by an increase in literacy, although the increase was slow and the rate of illiteracy was still high among women and in country districts. It has been calculated that over three-quarters of the population of London was literate in the late Tudor and early Stuart periods; but that over the country as a whole about two-thirds of the people were still illiterate; and since reading was taught before writing, and sometimes to the exclusion of writing altogether, many people who could read could not even write their own name.[23] By the end of the seventeenth century, however, the rate of literacy in England had risen considerably, though whether steadily or by fits and starts is uncertain;[24] and in the 1640s, the percentage of students in the country undergoing higher education was not again to be reached until after the First World War.[25] Visitors to London in 1641 were astonished by the number of bookshops and by the large congregations of people who listened to sermons and took notes. Foreigners also noted the pains which poor people took to obtain schooling for their children.

'Every man strains his fortune to keep his children at school,' wrote the Royalist James Howell in a letter in 1651. 'The cobbler will clout it till midnight, the porter will carry burdens till his bones crack again, the ploughman will pinch both back and belly to give his son learning.'[26] Other contemporary observers agreed with him; and by 1707 there was said to be 'scarce any Husband-man' who would 'take his son from the school to the Plow, till he [had] got some smattering' of Latin.[27] John Bunyan was sent to school. 'Notwithstanding the meanness . . . of my Parents,' he wrote, 'it pleased God to put it into their Hearts to put me to school, to learn both to read and write.'

Charges in schools varied widely. Most, even those that termed themselves 'free', made some charge, though this might be as little as 4d as a registration or admission fee. Others were extremely expensive, charging as much as £18 a year plus £12 a year for clothing. Boarding accommodation was rarely offered, pupils who did not live in the town, being found lodgings near the school at about 2s a week, including laundry. Where boarding accommodation was offered, it was often as uncomfortable as that provided at Bramley grammar school where rats ran through the dormitories and the wind blew snow through the holes in the roof at night.[28] Some schools adjusted their charges in accordance with the status of the parents. At Shrewsbury a lord paid a 10s fee for the admission of his son, a knight 6s 8d, a gentleman 3s 4d for his eldest son, 2s 6d for younger sons. Men of lower degree were charged 2s, a fee reduced to 1s if they were natives of Shropshire and 8d if they lived in Shrewsbury. Burgesses of Shrewsbury paid no more than 4d.[29] At the Merchant Taylors' there were 100 free places for the poor, fifty places for boys whose parents were prepared to pay 2s 6d a quarter, and 100 for those who could afford 5s a quarter.[30]

In all schools the curriculum was still largely devoted to Latin, an emphasis that led 'manie children to bee worse' in English construction after two or three years at school than they were when they started. 'You shall have scholars almost ready to go the University,' one critic of this emphasis on Latin wrote, 'who yet can hardly tell you the number of pages, sections, chapters or other divisions in their books to find out what they should.' In some schools, as at Charterhouse from 1627, pupils were beginning to be taught 'to cypher and cast an account, especially those that are less capable of learning, and fittest to be put to trades'. But it was not until later on in the seventeenth century that 'modern' subjects were recognized as being important enough to take the place of lessons previously devoted exclusively to Latin, and even then parents were often charged extra for these additions to the old curriculum.

Merchant Taylors', where Richard Mulcaster was headmaster, was exceptional in believing that music was 'among the most valuable means in the upbringing of the young' and in having singing and instrumental music taught throughout the school as a 'daily exercise'. In few schools, so it seems, was a modern language taught except as an extra. History and geography were similarly neglected.[31]

The school day was long, and holidays were short, sixteen days at Christmas and twelve at Easter being usual. In one typical school there was a half-holiday on Thursdays but on this day, as on others, homework had to be done. On Sundays and holy days pupils had to 'report in due time to the school house and from thence by two and two, in order to go to divine service'. At Sandwich school 'at every Christmas time, if the master do think it "meet", one comedy or tragedy of chaste matter in Latin was played, the parts [being] divided to as many scholars as may be and to be learnt at vacant times'.[32] Other schools, too, notably St Paul's, performed plays; some organized outings to collections of pictures and curiosities; others took part in public disputations, as various London grammar school pupils did in the churchyard of the priory in Smithfield on the eve of St Bartholomew's Day. Shrewsbury mounted a military parade with a band. But extracurricular activities were rare and leave from the schoolroom seldom permitted.

In the schoolroom pupils still sat on long forms, one form usually accommodating pupils of similar abilities but widely different ages. At a Wolverhampton school in 1609, sixty-nine pupils aged between six and eighteen were grouped into six forms. The top form had only two boys, one seventeen, the other eighteen. A lower form included one boy aged nine and two others of seventeen. Since learning was based on oral instruction and repetition and on reading aloud in unison, schoolrooms were very noisy, particularly so in those many schools in which all the pupils were contained in a single hall or at most two or three large rooms.

The increase in the number of charity schools in the seventeenth century was almost matched by that of 'Dissenting Academies' of which there were about thirty at its close. They were founded by Puritan clergy expelled from the Church, but their pupils were not limited to the sons of Dissenters; and many Anglican parents were drawn to these academies by the greater emphasis then placed upon science and mathematics and upon English and other modern languages rather than upon the classics which were, in some of the more strict, condemned as heathen works all of whose 'filthy places' would be 'wisely passed over'.[33] This rejection of the classics as the dominating subject in a school's curriculum was also apparent in establishments founded by Quakers who had opened fifteen boarding schools by 1671, including two that were co-educational and two for girls.[34]

It was still generally considered, however, that to educate girls to the same standard as boys was unseemly, most people agreeing with Lady Newdigate who expressed a wish in her will that her sons should be brought up in 'good learning' and her daughters in 'virtuous and godly life'.[35] The statutes of some schools, Harrow for example, specifically excluded girls in accordance with the views of a commentator on female education who wrote in 1524, 'Many men put great doubt whether it should be expedient and requisite or not for a woman to have learning in books of Latin or Greek. And some utterly affirm that it is not only neither necessary nor profitable, but also very noisome and jeopardus.'[36] There were, however, by the end of the century several boarding establishments for the daughters of the rich.

> The gentlewoman we spoke of doth continue her course in teaching still [a letter of that time runs]. Her rates are thus, 16 pounds a year apiece, for diet, lodging, washing and teaching them to work, reading, writing and dancing, this cometh to £32 a year. But for music you must pay besides. . . She hath teachers for viol, singing, lute and virginals.[37]

But such establishments were extremely rare as, indeed, were such model pupils as Lady Jane Grey who learned Greek, Latin, Italian, Spanish and French when she was six, and Hebrew, Chaldee and Arabic before she was seventeen. When Roger Ascham visited her and found the rest of her family out hunting, she is said to have commented, 'But I [think] all their sport in the Park is but a shadow to that pleasure that I find in Plato. Alas, good folk, they never felt what true pleasure meant.'[38] Queen Elizabeth I was equally learned. Ascham said of her when he was her tutor, 'She readeth here now at Windsor more Greek every day than some Prebendaries of this Church do in a whole week.' She could read Latin as well, and she could speak it without stopping for a word. She spoke French, Spanish and Italian, too, and even Welsh. She could talk intelligently on any intellectual topic and liked to spend three hours a day reading history. She spent hours, too, with a pen or a needle between her extraordinarily long, white fingers until her handwriting and needlework were both of an exquisite beauty. But the queen and Lady Jane were peculiarly privileged, and it was not until the next century that girls were likely to share the experiences of Lucy Apsley, daughter of the Lieutenant of the Tower of London, who at the age of seven, so she said, had 'at one time eight tutors in different qualities, language, music, dancing and needlework . . . My genius was quite averse from all but my book, and I was so eager of that my mother, thinking it prejudiced my health would moderate me in it; yet this rather animated than held me back, and every moment I could steal from my play I would employ in any book I could find, when my own were locked up for me.'[39]

Such learning in a girl was strongly deprecated by King James I who, refusing to have his daughters taught Latin, expressed the belief that 'to make women learned and foxes tame had the same effect: to make them more cunning'.[40] His great-granddaughter, Queen Mary, was notoriously ill-educated, though she had at least been taught French. Modest, pious, charitable and sweet-natured, she busied herself with gardening, collecting porcelain, embroidery and housework and, when she returned to England from The Hague, where her court had been 'remarkable only for dullness and decorum', she ran about, 'talking a great deal and looking into every closet and conveniency, and turned up the quilts of the bed, just as people do at an inn, with no sort of concern in her appearance'.[41]

Her half-sister, Queen Anne, had as few compelling interests, apart from hunting and racing. She had strong, indeed often obstinate views, but she never seemed fully to understand what was happening in the world or even in her own country. Her knowledge of history and geography, as of art and literature, was lamentable. She is said to have been fond of music and to have played the guitar as a girl, but in later life she did not even listen to her own band. Her conversation was that of a kindly, unambitious and unimaginative woman who liked her food, enjoyed playing cards and gambling, and was excessively concerned with the niceties of etiquette. She spoke chiefly 'upon fashions', the Duchess of Marlborough said, 'and rules of precedence, or observations upon the weather, or some such poor topics'. She had a remarkably retentive memory, 'but chose to retain in it very little besides ceremonies and customs of courts, and such like insignificant trifles'.[42]

Women who had had a good education, or were unusually clever, were expected to hide the fact. There was a well-known proverb, 'Beware of a young wench, a prophetess and a Latin woman'; and although Lucy, Countess of Huntingdon, for instance, had been taught Latin as well as French and Italian and various other accomplishments, she was advised by her mother on her marriage merely to 'make herself fit conversation for her husband'.[43]

Some women were undoubtedly well educated, if not at school, perhaps by their brothers' tutors whose lessons they shared, or under the guidance of an open-minded father who did not resent, as so many of his contemporaries did, what were taken to be masculine accomplishments in a lady. But there were, even in the middle of the seventeenth century, a very high proportion of women in England who were not even barely literate. It has been estimated that in London in 1640 as many as about 80 per cent of all women were illiterate, while in East Anglia the proportion was very nearly 100 per cent.[44]

Even so relatively liberal an educationalist as Richard Mulcaster, who considered it right and proper that girls should be educated, believed that they should be allowed learning only 'with respect to their ends'.[45] And certainly in most girls' schools the curriculum was heavily weighted in favour of needlework and manners, deportment and such accomplishments as might make an appealing wife. Basua Makin, the clever daughter of a Sussex clergyman, lamented that young ladies were taught nothing except how to 'frisk and dance, to paint their faces, to curl their hair and put on a whisk'; while Hannah Woolley, author of *The Gentlewoman's Companion* and other books on domestic practice, commented acidly, 'Most in this depraved later Age think a woman Learned and Wise enough if she can distinguish her Husband's bed from another's.'[46]

Painting was taught in some schools, a form of shorthand in a few. Hannah Woolley thought it as well that a young lady should be taught how to carve a joint of meat, an art not yet adopted by the gentlemen of the household.[47] But there were very few girls' schools indeed that included the subjects offered at Basua Makin's school at Tottenham High Cross, among them Latin, Greek, Hebrew, Italian, French, Spanish and 'Experimental Philosophy'; and even here half the school day was devoted to 'Dancing, Music, Singing, Writing and Keeping Accounts'.[48] As for the education offered to poor girls, this was largely confined to subjects which might prove useful in later life: at one village school in Sussex in 1699, the dame put her children to making clothes. Reading and writing were also occasionally taught but classes in these were given by visiting schoolmasters and were evidently considered of less importance.[49]

At schools run by the Society for the Promotion of Christian Knowledge, as soon as the boys could 'read competently well', so it was observed in 1706, the master taught them 'to write a fair legible hand, with the grounds of arithmetic to fit them for apprentices or service'; while the girls, having been taught how to read, learned how 'to knit their stockings and gloves, to mark, sew, make and mend their clothes'.[50] 'A Shift [was] hung up in the School [at Oswestry in 1713] for the best Spinner, [a Head-dress] for the best Sewer, a Pair of Stockings for the best Knitter.' At the Red Maids' Hospital at Bristol, a charity school run by 'one grave painful and modest woman of good life and conversation', the forty poor girls, all dressed in the red uniforms from which the school took its name, were indentured for seven years to the mistress and taught English and sewing, the profits of the sewing work going to the mistress.[51] At other charity schools in the early eighteenth century it cost £75 a year to provide schooling and clothing for fifty boys, but only £60 for the same number of girls.[52]

For those who could afford the fees there were constantly growing numbers of boarding and day academies for girls in England. In the earlier part of the seventeenth century there were, for example, Mrs Friend's academy at Stepney where £21 a year was charged for teaching writing, needlework and music; Mrs Perwich's school at Putney where 800 girls over seventeen years of age were taught music, dancing, singing and handicrafts by sixteen masters who also helped to organize the school orchestra; at Putney there were several 'schools and colleges for young gentlewomen' to which John Evelyn made a special trip by barge in 1649. By the middle of the century there were, in fact, academies for girls in every large town in England; and, whatever the limitations of their curricula, they did serve a valuable purpose. There were those, of course, like John Aubrey, who looked back to the good old days when 'the boys were educated at the monasteries, the young maids not at Hackney schools, etc, to learn pride and wantonness, but at the nunneries where they had examples of piety, humility, modesty and obedience'.[53] Yet many who had experience of girls' schools had cause to be grateful to them. One of these was Sir Ralph Verney who in the 1640s had a great deal of trouble with his orphan ward, Betty, 'a pestilent wench', in her guardian's opinion, 'of a cross, proud lazy disposition'. Verney decided to send her to a boarding school to learn 'diet, teaching and other things' at a cost of £25 a year. At this Betty violently protested and her guardian commented, 'She is a strange perverse girl and so averse from going hither that she doth not sticke to threaten her own death by her owne hands, though my girls [who have been there] give all the commendation that can be of that school.' Despite her violent objections, Betty was packed off and a few months later 'one ne'er saw soe great a change in countenance, fashion, humour and disposition [and all for the better] in any body, neyther could i imagine it possible it could have beene wrought soe soone'.[54]

# 25 · *Undergraduates and Tutors*

In a book written for the guidance of students in 1622, Henry Peacham wrote, 'For the companions of your recreation consort yourself with gentlemen of your own rank and quality; for that friendship is best contenting and lasting. To be overfree and familiar with inferiors argues a baseness of spirit and begetteth contempt.'[1] This was familiar and often reiterated advice. 'You are maintained with the best of your rank,' Simonds D'Ewes told his younger brother, then at St Catherine's College, Cambridge, 'dishonourate not yourself by your unseemly associating with pensioners and subsizers though of other colleges.'[2]

Oxford and Cambridge were now generally considered as finishing schools for the sons of gentlemen rather than as seminaries for the Church as they had been in the Middle Ages.[3] 'They were erected by their founders at the first only for poor men's sons,' wrote William Harrison:

> But now they have the least benefit of them, by reason the rich do so encroach on them . . . It is in my time an hard matter for a poor man's child to come by a fellowship (though he be never so good a scholar and worthy of that room) . . . and yet, being placed, most of them study little other than histories, tables, dice and trifles . . . Besides this being for the most part either gentlemen or rich men's sons, they oft bring the universities into much slander. For, standing upon their reputation and liberty, they ruffle and roist it out, exceeding in apparel and banting riotous company . . . And for excuse when they are charged with breach of all good order, think it sufficient to say that they be gentlemen.[4]

The poorer, lower-class students, most of them intending to take holy orders, were certainly in a noticeable minority. Many new scholarships had been founded for the poor in recent years, yet, even so, as the numbers of undergraduates grew, the proportion of those from poor families remained very small. In the 1630s the fathers of boys sent to Cambridge from Thetford grammar school were listed as one knight, three esquires, nine gentlemen, two rectors and one tailor; and from Aylsham grammar school as one esquire, thirteen gentlemen, two clergymen and two drapers.[5] It has been estimated that in the seventeenth century half the peerage went to university, though very few undergraduates of noble birth took degrees, leaving this to those plebeians who were headed for the Church and who had to spend up to seven years before attaining the degree of Master of Arts.[6] Some rich and noble undergraduates did conscientiously attend lectures, study Latin and the other subjects which were now an essential part of the curriculum, grammar, rhetoric, logic, arithmetic, music and Greek – Hebrew, Arabic, ancient history and geometry were added in the seventeenth century[7] – but many troubled themselves little with what did not interest them.

Whether or not they took degrees, however, a high proportion of the distinguished men of the day attended either Oxford or Cambridge. The churchmen, Jewel and Hooker; the scholars, Camden and Thomas Harriot; the poet, Donne; the dramatist, Beaumont; the composer, Dowland; the geographer, Hakluyt; the martyrologist, John Foxe; and Sidney and Ralegh were all at Oxford. Burghley, Walsingham, Lord Keeper Bacon, Gresham, Cavendish and Coke, Spenser and Marlowe, and the Earls of Oxford, Essex and Southampton were at Cambridge.[8]

The differences between rich and poor were very marked. Since 1576, while the sons of noblemen and knights had been allowed to wear light-coloured clothes of velvet and silk, others had been restricted to black gowns and black caps. And in hall undergraduates sat at different tables according to their rank, the lowest table – at which sat 'people of low condition' – being served, so Thomas Cogan said, 'with boiled beef and pottage, bread and beer and no more'.[9] At their High Table the rich employed the poor to wait upon them as sizars; the eldest son of Sir William Thorold did so in the 1630s at St John's College, Cambridge, where he paid a former school-fellow at Melton Mowbray school, the son of a draper, to attend to his wants.[10] Indeed, the poor were often compelled to undertake such menial tasks in order to exist. The living costs at Oxford rose from about £20 a year in 1600 to £30 a year in 1660; and even boys with good scholarships found it difficult to raise these sums without making extra money by working.[11] According to his biographer, John Prideaux, later Fellow of Exeter College, Oxford, was one of those who had to put their hands to the most menial tasks at the outset of his university career:

A good gentleman of the Parish [in Devon] took some compassion on him and kept him sometime at school until he had gotten some smattering in the Latin tongue and School learning. Thus meanly furnished, his Genius strongly inclined him to go to Oxford, and accordingly he did so, in a very poor habit and sordid (no better than leather breeches) to seek his Fortune . . . Here [at Exeter College] he is said at the beginning to have lived in very mean Condition and to have gotten his Livelihood by doing servile offices in the kitchen.[12]

All undergraduates, whether rich or poor, now lived in colleges rather than in inns and lodging-houses as their Continental contemporaries did; and they were subject to severe discipline which their youth was deemed to require. The minimum age of entry was fifteen, but this apparently was widely ignored. Sir Philip Sidney was fourteen when he went to Christ Church, Oxford; and in the late sixteenth century almost a fifth of freshmen at Oxford were under fourteen. Some were less than thirteen. Robert Devereux, second Earl of Essex, was sent to Trinity College, Cambridge, at the age of ten, though he did not matriculate until two years later. The average age of entry at Cambridge in Stuart times was sixteen.[13]

From 1536 onwards undergraduates were required to renounce Rome and to take oaths of obedience to the monarchy; and from 1581 at Oxford they had to subscribe to the Thirty-nine Articles. They had to attend the college chapel and from 1616 at Cambridge to attend services at St Mary's as well. Their orthodoxy thus, it was hoped, ensured, their moral behaviour and educational welfare were entrusted to the guidance of tutors – like all fellows of colleges, unmarried clergymen – whose authority they were expected to respect without question. The tutorial system had developed in the sixteenth century. Some tutors gained a reputation for tutoring the rich and thereby became quite rich themselves. Although theoretically Catholics could not attend university, there were Catholic tutors who looked after Catholic boys. At Caius College, Cambridge, in the late sixteenth century one Catholic tutor taught the sons of various wealthy recusants who had rooms near his own. They had their own Catholic sizars and lived almost separately from the rest of the college.[14]

'You must be ordered by your tutor in all things for your good,' Sir Daniel Fleming told his son, James, 'otherwise it will be much worse for you.'[15] Subject to numerous restraints, undergraduates were forbidden, at various times, to bet, to go hunting, to play football (at Oxford, though not at Cambridge), to attend plays and bull baitings. The rules, however, were widely ignored; and Thomas Crosfield, Fellow of Queen's College, Oxford, in the 1620s, frequently went fishing and bull-baiting, and to puppet-shows and plays with his young charges. He gave a cheerful account of his day:

> I' th morning pray'd and heard a Latin sermon . . .
> And to my pupils read Enunciations
> Modificate, and went to disputation.
> That done we din'd, and after did resort
> To bowls i' th' garden and to have some sport.[16]

This seems innocent enough, however, when compared with the be-haviour of Thomas Greenway, President of Corpus Christi, who in the second half of the previous century had been accused by a fellow of the college of all manner of misdemeanours:

> He spoyleth the College wodes, as the common report is, and maketh in every sale a part of money unto himself. He is noted of many men to have had connexion with viii Infamous women . . . He is accompted a Whoremonger, a common drunkard, a mutable papist and an unpreching prelate and one of an Italian faith. He resorteth to bull-beytinge and bearebeyting in London. In Christmas last past he, comming drunke from the Towne, sat in the Hall amonge the Schollers until i of the clock, totering with his legge, tipling with his mouth, and hering bawdy songes with his eares as, My Lady hath a prety thinge, and such like. He kepeth vi horse continually in the stable, whereas the Colledge nedeth and alloweth but five. He ys a faithful friend to all the papistes and a mortall enemy to all the protestants in this house . . . He hath lefte in our fine Box but iis vid, in which, at his cumming, he found ccccli.[17]

In a determined effort to improve the behaviour of both fellows and undergraduates at Oxford and to submit them both to a more rigorous discipline, Archbishop Laud, Chancellor of the University, drew up in 1636 the so-called Laudian Code which was to survive until 1864. This code enacted that scholars should 'keep away during the day, and especially at night, from the shops and houses of the townsmen; but particularly from houses where women of ill or suspected fame or harlots are kept'; that they should also keep away from 'inns, eating-houses, wine-shops and all houses . . . wherein wine or any other drink or the Nicotian herb, or tobacco, is commonly sold; also that if any person does otherwise, and is not eighteen years old, and not a graduate, he shall be flogged in public'. It was further ordained that 'neither rope-dancers nor players (who go on the stage for gain's sake), nor sword-matches, or sword players are to be permitted within the University of Oxford'. No student or other person was to 'carry either offensive arms, such as swords, poignards, daggers (commonly called stilettos), dirks, bows and arrows, guns, or warlike weapons or implements, within the verge of the University, unless when he happens to make a journey to parts remote'. Nor must any 'scholars, particularly the younger sort, and undergraduates idle and wander about the city or its suburbs, nor in the streets, or public market, or Carfax (at Penniless Bench as they commonly call it)'. As for sports and games and personal appearance:

It is enacted that scholars of all conditions shall abstain from every kind of game in which there is a money stake, as for instance, the games of dibs dice and cards, and also ball-play in the private yards and greens of the townsmen. Also, they must refrain from every kind of sport or exercise, whence danger, wrong or inconvenience may arise to others, from hunting wild animals with hounds of any kind, ferrets, nets or toils; and also from all parade and display of guns and cross-bows, and, again, from the use of hawks for fowling. In like manner, no scholars of any condition (and least of all graduates) are to play football within the University or its precinct . . . It is enacted that all the heads, fellows and scholars of colleges, as well as all persons in holy orders, shall dress as becomes clerks. Also that all others (except the sons of barons having the right of voting in the Upper House of Parliament, and also of barons of the Scotch and Irish peerages) shall wear dresses of a black or dark colour, and shall not imitate anything betokening pride or luxury, but hold themselves aloof from them. Moreover they shall be obliged to abstain from that absurd and assuming practice of walking publicly in boots. There must be, also, a mean observed in the dressing of the hair; and they are not to encourage the growth of curls, or immoderately long hair.[18]

Undergraduates continued to grow their hair long, however, much to the annoyance of Dr Ralph Kettell of Trinity College, whose 'fashion was to go up and down the College', so John Aubrey said, 'and peep in at the key-holes to see whether the boys did follow their books or no'. Kettell was

irreconcilable to long hair; called them hairy scalps, and as for periwigs (which were then [in the late 1630s] very rarely worn) he believed them to be the scalps of men cut off after they were hanged, and so tanned and dressed for use. When he observed the scolars' haire longer than ordinary (especially if they were scholars of the house), he would bring a pair of scissors in his muff (which he commonly wore), and woe be to them that eate on the outside of the table.

'I remember,' Aubrey added, 'he cut Mr Radford's hair with the knife that clips the bread on the buttery-hatch, and then he sang (this is in the old play – Henry VIII – of *Gammer Gurton's Needle*), "And was not Grim the collier finely trimm'd?"'[19]

Dr Kettell, in Aubrey's opinion, was 'an excellent governour' who soundly scolded 'the idle young boies of his college'. But there were many heads of colleges who were much laxer than Laud would have wished; and although, towards the end of the century, there were far fewer fellows as dissolute as Matthias Watson of Lincoln College – who, 'after sundry peremptory warnings', was dismissed in 1625 because of his notorious lewd and [debauched] course of life' – or as joyfully and irresponsibly ebullient as Dr Richard Corbet, Dean of Christ Church in the 1620s – who sang ballads 'at the Crosse at Abingdon on market day, who used to drink and be mery at Fryar Bacon's study (where was good liquor sold) and where he once cut a sleeping scholar's good silk stockings full of little holes' – there were still numerous fellows as eccentric as Thomas Goodwin, appointed President of Magdalen College after the Civil War, a 'somewhat whimsycall' scholar who 'in a frolic once pist in old Mr Lothian's pocket'.[20] Yet by Goodwin's day the reputation of both Oxford and Cambridge had, at least temporarily, much improved; and in 1682 when they were still the only two universities in the country–an attempt by Cromwell to found a third university at Durham having proved premature–it could be said with not too pronounced exaggeration that 'in the beautiful fabric of the Kingdom of England the two eyes are the two universities, Oxford and Cambridge, those two nurseries . . . of learning and religion which are not to be paralleled in the whole world'.[21]

# 26 · 'Roasted Chickens – Pease – Lobsters – Strawberries'

The England of Matthew Hopkins's witch-hunts and of Cromwell's major-generals was also that of Dorothy Osborne who, in a letter written in the year that Cromwell became Protector, described how she used to go out in the summer evenings to walk on the common near her house where 'a great many young wenches keep sheep and cows and sit in the shade singing of Ballads'.

> I talk to them [she continued], and find that they want nothing to make them the happiest people in the world, but the knowledge that they are so. Most commonly when we are in the midst of our discourse, one looks about her and spies her cows going into the corn, and then away they all run as if they had wings at their heels.[1]

Dorothy Osborne was born in Bedfordshire, one of the richest counties in England with fertile pasturelands and rolling fields of wheat and barley. Bedfordshire's neighbours, Hertfordshire, Buckinghamshire and Northamptonshire were also rich; but, because of London, no county was richer than Middlesex, though Surrey rivalled it. There were fine pastures in East Anglia and in Devonshire and Somerset, splendid flocks of sheep in Warwickshire, Oxfordshire, Berkshire and Worcestershire. Kent was celebrated for its orchards, its hopfields and market gardens, Wiltshire for its dairy farms, Leicestershire for its cornfields, Dorset for its prodigious quantity of cattle. The lead- and coalmines in the Mendip hills, the forges of Sussex and Durham, the tin-mines of Cornwall, the coalmines of Gloucestershire and the ironworks around Birmingham and in Staffordshire gave employment to thousands of workers, while all along the Thames estuary, and in the coastal ports and fishing villages, thousands more made their living at sea as trawlermen, as merchant seamen, smugglers and as sailors in the Royal Navy, so many of them in Plymouth that one traveller reported that only women and children could be seen in the streets of the town. There were fishermen, too, in Northumberland, Cumberland and Westmorland as well as shepherds; there were textile workers in Lancashire and Yorkshire, knitters and spinners in Norfolk, Suffolk and Lincolnshire, fowlers and reed-cutters in the fen country, working beside the farmers newly settled on the reclaimed lands. There were brewers in Leeds, cutlers in Sheffield, cotton-spinners in Manchester, lace-makers in Exeter.[2]

The south of England was much richer than the north and Wales. It was also more populous, three-quarters of the people living in the southern counties and owning three-quarters of the nation's wealth. York and New-castle, which supplied London with coal, were prosperous cities; but elsewhere in the north the townspeople appeared far less well fed and clothed than they did in the south: Roger North described Kendal in Westmorland 'as being very stony and dirty . . . the common people walked barefoot . . . but it is almost the same all over the north'.[3] Liverpool, soon to become a large and vital port and the centre of the slave trade, was still scarcely more than a fishing village. The custom administration of Hull cost £900 a year, but that was not a twentieth of the cost of London's.

After London, which remained exceptional, Bristol, its cobbled streets worn smooth by horse-drawn sledges, was the busiest port in England, its carriers supplying all the south-west and western Midlands with the goods its merchants shipped up the mouth of the Severn. Norwich, which now had thirty-six churches, was still the second largest town in the country with a population, like Bristol's, of about 30,000 as compared with London's 350,000 to 400,000 in 1650 rising to 575,000 to 600,000 in 1700. But there were few towns remotely comparable with these. Probably as much as four-fifths of the people of England still lived by agriculture and as many as half of the remainder from the sea. The country was still largely self-sufficient, its principal export remaining cloth, although increasingly goods imported from America and the East by enterprising merchants and such trading companies as the East India Company, were being re-exported to Europe at considerable profits.[4]

Throughout the century the contrasts between rich and poor remained painfully marked, and unemployment was high, so high in some places that almost a quarter of those employable could find no work. The cost of poor relief rose to about £1 million a year, and in one county at least, Devon-shire, as many as one person in five had no other means of subsistence.[5] Those in work continued to receive low wages, not more than about 10d a day for agricultural labourers, 4d or so a day for women, and 1s or so for skilled craftsmen such as masons and carpenters, although some earned more, as much as 2s a day or even £1 a week, and some highly skilled craftsmen were paid as much as professional men. In the 1660s a silversmith received 3s for engraving a tankard, a music teacher £1 a month for giving lessons to two girls on the harpsichord, a barber 6d for a haircut and 1s for bleeding, a country artist £5 for painting a portrait.[6] For such people these incomes were quite satisfactory enough when meat was about 3d a pound, bacon 4d, good cheese 2d, draught ale 2d a flagon and bottled ale 6d a dozen.[7] Men like Samuel Pepys who, as a Principal Officer of the Navy, had £350 a year, could live very comfortably. And Pepys, himself, although often worried about money, certainly contrived to do so.

At one of his dinner parties in 1663 Pepys and his guests sat down to 'a great' dinner 'most neatly dressed by [his] own only mayde'. 'We had a Fricasse of rabbets and chicken,' he recorded proudly, 'a leg of mutton boiled – three carps in a dish – a great dish of a side of lamb – a dish roasted pigeons – a dish of four lobsters – three tarts – a Lampry pie, a most rare pie – a dish of anchoves – good wine of several sorts; and all things mighty noble and to my great content.' Some months later he had Lord Montagu's two daughters and niece to dinner: 'and very merry we were with our pasty, very well baked – and a good dish of roasted chickens – pease – lobsters – strawberries'.[8]

Dinner was still usually eaten in the middle of the day between about twelve and half past one, and supper, a much lighter meal, in the evenings. Some people had a snack and a drink when they got up, but breakfasts, which had been enjoyed in several households in the past, were not generally taken again until the eighteenth century. At about eleven o'clock, however, it was customary to have a 'morning draught' of ale or wine, both drinks being warmed in the winter months, the ale also being flavoured with wormwood and, later, strengthened with gin and known as purl. The draught might be accompanied by anchovies, radishes, pickled oysters or a slice of pie. Some people preferred a cup of whey, a favourite drink of lawyers on their way into Westminster Hall.[9]

In grand houses a meal might consist of three or more courses in the French manner with a final course of sweetmeats, tarts, pies and fruit; but the middle classes generally contented themselves with two courses, most if not all the dishes in each course being placed on the table at once, and sweet dishes and puddings sometimes being served with the first course as well as with the second. Forks were coming into use as well as silver *monteighs* of waters with notched brims from which wine glasses were suspended to cool. But Pepys, who had a set of forks himself, often noted their absence at other tables, even at a lord mayor's banquet. Napkins and ewers were still used instead, though the lord mayor did not even provide these which Pepys thought 'very strange'. 'It was very unpleasing that we had no napkins nor change of trenchers,' he added, 'and drunk out of earthen pitchers and wooden dishes.'[10]

Meat remained the staple diet of all those who could afford it, joints being generally preferred to minced meat, offal and made dishes. The meat most commonly served was beef, mutton or pork, much of London's supplies being bought either at the Shambles in St Nicholas Street, or at Smithfield – originally Smoothfield, a 'grassy space just outside the City walls' where Bartholomew Fair was held – or at one of those markets where all manner of other foodstuffs could be bought, such as Cheapside, a bustling market since the Middle Ages. The meat was not of high quality since it was not until the eighteenth century that improved strains of beef-cattle and sheep were developed; and, since they had no means of refrigeration, butchers could not allow their carcasses to hang long enough to make them tender.[11] Also, for much of the year fresh meat was difficult to obtain, as cattle were slaughtered in the autumn, there being no means of feeding them during the winter months. So meat still had to be preserved in brine or powdered with salt; and huge amounts of salted beef were eaten. The daily allowance for common seamen was two pounds.[12] It was a diet that, with few or no fresh vegetables, often lead to skin diseases. Housewives were instructed in cookery books how to get rid of the salty flavour of meat, but many relished the taste, as they did of other strongly preserved foods. Neat's tongue in vinegar was a popular dish. Strong Stilton cheese was served with a spoon for scooping up the maggots.[13]

Those who could get it through friends in the country served venison at parties. Pepys frequently mentions it and, while very fond of venison pasty, sometimes complained of being offered too much of it: 'We had at dinner a couple of venison pasties, of which I ate but little, being almost cloyed, having been at five pasties in three days.'[14] Pepys also enjoyed turkeys, which were driven into London in huge numbers from East Anglia, as well as pigeon and the occasional partridge, pheasant, goose and duck.

London's biggest poultry markets were the Stocks Market – which was founded on the site of the present Mansion House in the thirteenth century and took its name from what was then the only fixed pair of stocks in the City – and Leadenhall which had been established at least as early as the fourteenth century and which was named after a nearby mansion with a lead roof. Leadenhall Market had been rebuilt after the Great Fire around three large courtyards in which the stalls of butchers, fishmongers, cheesemongers and dealers in leather, wool and raw hides could also be found. There were fish markets in New Fish Street and Billingsgate where all manner of fish could be bought: in his diary Pepys mentions anchovies, carp, cod, crab, crayfish, eels, herrings, lampreys, prawns, salmon, scallops, sturgeon, teal, tench, trout and, of course, lobsters and oysters. Shellfish were cheap and plentiful, a good fat lobster costing no more than 5d or 6d in London – 8d when in short supply – and even less along the Devonshire coast and other places where they were landed in large quantities. Fish was also hawked about the town by street vendors, so was poultry and so, indeed, was almost everything else that a housewife might want.

Vegetables are not so often mentioned by Pepys in whose day Covent Garden market was no more than a few sheds grouped under the trees at the south side of a fashionable square. Yet Pepys does make passing references to cabbage, peas, asparagus, onions and cucumber, and to salads in which, though he does not say so, flowers and herbs were tossed with the lettuce, radish and cucumber, though not tomatoes which Pepys never mentions: they had originated in South America, and had probably been introduced to Europe from Mexico, but, since they were considered chill to the stomach, and a possible cause of gout and cancer, they were not to become popular in England until the beginning of the twentieth century.[15] Many vegetables were improved strains introduced from Holland, but the poor had little opportunity of eating these, confining themselves largely to the cheaper root vegetables which did not then include Virginian potatoes. Potatoes, in fact, were not often seen until the nineteenth century, despite the commendations of such advocates as Adam Smith who, as Fernand Braudel has noted, deplored the English disdain of a crop which had apparently proved its value as a food in Ireland. Usually grown for export, if grown at all, potatoes were widely suspected to be a cause of flatulence and even leprosy.[16]

Most fruits were also too expensive for the poor, the growing season being short and several varieties, apricots, melons and peaches, for example, being very limited in supply since they were grown under glass or in the sheltered gardens of the well-to-do. Oranges were imported in large quantities and the smell of orange peel was as reminiscent of the theatre as that of grease-paint. At a performance of *Henry V* in 1667, 'it was observable how a gentleman of good habit, sitting before us eating of some fruit, in the midst of the play did drop down as dead, being choked; but without much ado, Orange Mall did thrust her finger down his throat and brought him to life again'.[17] Nearly every theatre had its Orange Mall. Nell Gwyn, Charles II's delightful mistress who had been brought up in a brothel, had once been an orange-girl at the Theatre Royal.

Like many of his contemporaries, Pepys distrusted fresh fruit, believing it to be bad for the stomach, and he usually ate it cooked. He was, however, persuaded one day in 1669 to drink some fresh orange juice at the house of his cousin, Thomas Strudwick, a confectioner and provision merchant. 'Here,' he recorded, 'which I never did before, I drank a glass, of a pint I believe, at one draught, of the juice of Oranges of whose peel they make comfits; and here they drink the juice as wine, with sugar, and it is very fine drink; but it being new, I was doubtful whether it might not do me hurt.'[18] Apprehensive though he was, Pepys did occasionally eat fruit 'off the tree' and in his diary mentions apricots and peaches, cherries, figs, grapes, melons, mulberries, pears, apples, strawberries, prunes and figs, as well as a barrel of lemons which he received as a present.

Pepys, in common also with most men of his time, distrusted water as a drink, believing that, even if fresh, it was bad for the health. In many towns it was, in fact, far from fresh, being carried up from the river in leather bags strapped to the backs of horses and sold in the streets. Pepys drank wine and beer, sometimes mixed together. He frequently drank too much, complained of a hangover, was advised to drink less for the sake of his health and his memory, gave it up and found himself much better, spending less money and losing 'less time in idle company'. But then he started drinking again. As he grew older, however, he succeeded in drinking less deeply and almost only at meal times. Most of his contemporaries also drank liberally for most of their lives, considering it bad manners to sip a host's wine rather than to drink it down, and responding to frequent toasts. According to the evidence provided by the excise revenue from sales of ale and beer, English people as a whole began to drink more heavily than ever in the 1680s. The revenue from such sales dropped in the 1690s, but this was probably because by then many were drinking cheap gin instead.[19]

Beer was generally brewed in the home, but there were growing numbers of public brewers who, by 1688, were selling as many as twelve million barrels a year, that was to say an average of more than two barrels, each containing thirty-six gallons, to every man, woman and child in the country.[20] It was quite usual for a reasonably well paid working man to drink twelve pints a day. The official allowance of beer for an ordinary seaman was eight pints a day. Beer was still cheap, no more than 1d or 1½d a pint or about 6s a barrel. Ale was still cheaper; and small beer, a light brew given to children or drunk copiously in summer, was cheaper even than that.

Several kinds of ale were supplied by breweries in London, but it was said that the best, and certainly the strongest, ales came from Kent and from the north where, in certain taverns, food was provided free to those who paid for ale. As an alternative to ordinary ale some drank mum – a heavy ale, originally brewed in Brunswick, in which wheat was used instead of hops – or buttered ale which was warmed and not only flavoured with butter but also with sugar and cinnamon, or lamb's wool which was ale mixed with the pulp of roasted apples. In the West Country cider remained the favourite drink of ordinary people; and in London, cider from Devon was mixed with turnips and sold by innkeepers as a kind of claret.[21]

A true claret, Haut Brion, was the only château-bottled wine with which most gentlemen were familiar. It was imported by the London restaurateurs, the Pontaques or Pontacks whose eating-house in Abchurch Lane was as celebrated in the 1690s for its meals which cost 'one or two guineas a head', as for its proprietor, son of the President of Bordeaux, who spoke several languages, was well read in philosophy, and, as an 'eternal babbler', was described by Swift as one whose learning had driven him mad. Nearly all red wines, whether château-bottled or not, were imported from France. White wines more often came from Spain, the Canaries and Germany. There were several taverns in London that specialized in German wines, the Rhenish Wine House in Cannon Row, Westminster, being one of the best known. Some white wine was also imported from Hungary, and dessert wines from Italy, Greece and the Levant. Stored in casks, they were served at table in squat, upright bottles, the cylindrical bottle being very rarely seen until the late eighteenth century; and, until the cork stopper came into use towards the end of the century, they were invariably drunk when they were young.[22]

Wine, however, was not for the poor who, drinking great quantities of ale and beer, occupied the simplest cottages, possessed little furniture other than oak tables, benches, stools, chests and beds, and had few clothes. A man might well do with two shirts, two pairs of shoes, four pairs of breeches, two of leather and two of wool, a doublet, hat and jerkin. A woman, whose inventory survives, left five skirts, three gowns, an apron, a cloak, two hats, three waistcoats, and 'wearing linen and other necessities'.[23]

At the upper end of the social scale the days were passed, the money enjoyed, the food eaten and the clothes worn as though by inhabitants of a different world. The families of the nobility lived on incomes of up to £40,000 a year. Gregory King estimated that the average noble family had an income over fifty times greater than that of an army officer, and a hundred and fifty times greater than that of an ordinary seaman. In King's day a fair proportion of the 160 noble families were those of peers of recent creation, almost a hundred of them having been ennobled since the reign of Elizabeth; and many of these were among the richest, though fortunes could disappear as quickly as they came. Sir Lionel Cranfield, who had been apprenticed as a boy to a merchant adventurer, was created Earl of Middlesex for his services to the Crown in 1622 and died worth some £100,000. Yet the third Earl's heir died penniless. The first Duke of Chandos made so much money from his appointment as Paymaster General to the Duke of Marlborough that he was enabled to build one of the most splendid country houses in England, Canons Park. Such men as these thought nothing of spending as much on clothes as one of their servants might earn in a lifetime. The Earl of Bedford paid as much for the clothes that he and his attendants wore at the Coronation of Charles II as would have fed and clothed a farm-worker's family for ten years.[24]

Rich men strove to 'imitate women in their apparel', Anthony Wood contended in 1663, 'viz. long periwigs, patches in their faces, painting, short wide breeches like petticoats, muffs, and their clothes highly scented, bedecked with ribbons of all colours'.[25] Evelyn saw a man walking through Westminster Hall with 'as much Ribbon about him as would have plundered six shops and set up twenty Country Pedlars: All his Body was dres't like a Maypole or a Tom-a-Bedlam Cap'.[26] Even Samuel Pepys, whose income was relatively modest, did not stint himself in finery, having his cuffs edged with silver lace and his cloaks lined with plush. His shoes were made to measure and from 1661 he wore a sword, as was 'the manner now among gentlemen', sometimes also carrying a varnished walking-staff in gloved hand or a silver-headed Japan cane.[27]

The household papers of the fifth Earl of Bedford show how much a rich man was prepared to spend upon his appearance and accoutrements, upon 'rich broad gold silver wire purl lace' at £3 13s a yard and periwigs at £20 each, upon silver buckled belts, fine Holland socks, muslin cravats, gloves scented with jasmine or frangipane, silk dressing-gowns, and, in 1687, soon after their introduction from the East, umbrellas. The Earl also spent huge sums upon the maintenance of Woburn Abbey and upon Bedford House in the Strand where the profits from the family estates were stored in a chest from which sums were taken when needed for the payment of salaries, wages, tradesmen's bills and personal expenditure. In 1662 the household staff at Woburn included a receiver-general who was paid £50 a year; his assistant who had £30 a year; a lawyer who had a retaining fee of £20 a year and received additional fees for each item of business he conducted and, therefore, died a rich man; a gentleman of the chamber and a gentleman of the horse; a chaplain; a steward; a clerk of the kitchen; a cook; a house bailiff; twelve footmen; sundry porters, watchmen, pages, scullions and turnspits; a gentlewoman and her assistant; a housekeeper; and several maids, including Betty Buskin, Lydia Long, the laundrymaid, and one known simply as 'Alice-about-the-house'. The pages were clothed and fed but received no wages and had to be content with the hope of promotion and the occasional tip. The watchmen had about £1 a week and received additional payments for such regular or irregular jobs as seeing 'all candles put out every night' or 'killing rats and mice, etc.' In 1664 the total of salaries and wages for all outdoor and indoor servants came to £600.

Much more than this was spent upon food and drink and fuel. Purchases of coal appear frequently in the accounts, both of sea coal from Newcastle which was bought at St Neots and of coal from the Scottish mines which, at a cost of £1 13s a ton in 1685, was carted to Woburn usually in the earl's own wagons from the Thames-side premises of a merchant in Durham Yard. In 1654 a dozen pigeons cost 5s 6d, butter was 6d a pound, beef 1s 8d a stone, and cream 3d a pint. Prices rose thereafter: by 1663 white plums were 1s a dozen, peaches 2s a dozen and apricots 2s a pound. Oysters were 1s 6d a quart. But the rise in prices made no difference to the amount of food bought. Huge numbers of oysters were eaten, being brought up by the barrel load in a carrier's cart or special wagon from Bedford House whence they had arrived from Colchester.

Wine, bought from a wine merchant, a merchant adventurer or an impoverished gentleman who received a commission for choosing and importing a few puncheons from France, was another expensive item in the Woburn Abbey accounts. Chablis, Bordeaux, Burgundy, and Rhenish wine, Greek, Navarre and Canary wine, port wine, sherry, brandy and champagne were all carried down by bottle and cask into the cellar, the champagne, sometimes by the hogshead, sometimes by the bottle, at a price in 1676 of four dozen bottles for £6.

Coffee was also quite an expensive item, rising from 3s 6d a pound in 1689, to 4s in 1690 and 6s in 1692. Indeed, it was not until 1637, at Balliol College, Oxford, that John Evelyn first came across a man drinking coffee. This was 'one Nathaniel Conopios out of Greece who returning many years after, was made . . . Bishop of Smyrna'. The custom for coffee drinking, Evelyn added, 'came not into England til 40 years after'. In fact, the first coffee-house was established in Oxford in 1649 by a Jew who moved to London two years later and opened a similar place in Holborn; and by 1663, though coffee was suspected of being an anti-aphrodisiac and was condemned as a 'eunuch's drink', there were over eighty coffee-house owners in London, paying 1s each for their licences, charging 1d a dish for their coffee and offering also tea – which had come to England via Holland from China in about 1658 – and chocolate, which was first brought to England in 1652 and sometimes drunk enriched with eggs, sack and spices. Tea was much more expensive than coffee, although some blends cost a good deal less than others. At Woburn as much as three guineas a pound was being paid for one blend of tea in 1687 when the cheapest blend bought was 25s a pound.[28]

Tobacco was another expensive luxury, the fifth Earl of Bedford being a particularly heavy smoker of both Virginian tobacco at 2s 6d a pound and of Spanish at up to 9s a pound. A huge number of pipes were also purchased, but these were cheap, twelve gross costing no more than £1 4s in 1695.[29]

The trade in Virginian tobacco was protected by the government which prohibited the cultivation of tobacco at home. Proclamations against the growth of the plant in England were issued regularly, and without much effect, from 1619. The use of troops to destroy crops, particularly at Winchcombe, Gloucestershire, the most important centre, had begun during the Interregnum. On 19 September 1667 Pepys recorded in his diary,

She [my wife] tells me how the Lifeguard, which we thought a little while since was sent down into the country about some insurrection, was sent to Winchcombe to spoil the Tobacco there, which it seems the people there do plant contrary to law and have always done, and still been under force and danger of having it spoiled; as it hath been oftentimes, and yet they will continue to plant it.

They began to desist, however, towards the end of the century when large-scale cultivation in England came to a close.[30]

The most extravagant of the Earl of Bedford's indulgences were the regular visits he liked to make to Trinity College, Cambridge, where he had spent three years before embarking on the Grand Tour. On these visits he travelled in state, accompanied by trumpeters, harpists and bell-ringers. The accounts for one of the jaunts in 1689 have been preserved and include a list of payments which indicate how varied and how costly were both the pleasures and the obligations of a rich nobleman at that time:

|  | £ | s | d |
|---|---|---|---|
| To bill at Royston for meat and drink | 1 | 5 | 0 |
| And to the servants of the house and poor |  | 3 | 6 |
| To the ringers |  | 10 | 0 |
| To harper |  | 5 | 0 |
| Music morning and dinner | 1 | 0 | 0 |
| Crier, bellman, beadle, housekeeper | 1 | 0 | 0 |
| And to the poor's box and the prisoners' box | 2 | 3 | 0 |
| The ostler's bill | 3 | 3 | 10 |
| The bill for wine and glasses broke | 4 | 17 | 9 |
| To the poor at inn when your lordship took coach |  | 7 | 6 |
| To porters that fetched the wine |  | 2 | 0 |
| For oil of bitter almonds |  |  | 6 |
| To the servants at my lady Alington's [the Earl's daughter's house where he stopped on the way] | 14 | 2 | 6 |
| Coachman and the groom's charge all night | 1 | 11 | 4 |
| Shoeing a horse by the way |  | 1 | 0 |
| Given to a mad woman at Royston |  |  | 6 |

### Bill at the Red Lion, Cambridge

| | | | |
|---|---|---|---|
| For a large pike with all sorts of fish about it | 2 | 18 | 6 |
| For a surloin of beef | | 13 | 0 |
| For making a pasty | | 12 | 0 |
| For a shoulder, neck and a breast of mutton | | 7 | 0 |
| For a couple of geese | | 8 | 0 |
| For a dish of capons and sausages | | 9 | 6 |
| For a ham and eight chickens and cauliflowers | 1 | 10 | 0 |
| For a dish of collared pig | | 11 | 0 |
| For a 'frigize' of rabbits and chickens | | 5 | 0 |
| For salading | | 1 | 6 |
| For a dish of mince pies | | 8 | 6 |

### Second course

| | | | |
|---|---|---|---|
| For 2 dishes of all sorts of wild fowl | 1 | 15 | 6 |
| For a brace of pheasants | | 7 | 6 |
| For a brace of curlews and partridge | | 5 | 0 |
| For a dish of fat chickens and pigeons | | 8 | 6 |
| For a stand of all sorts of pickle and collared eels | | 17 | 0 |
| For a large jowl of sturgeon with a rand about it | 1 | 15 | 0 |
| For a dish of all sorts of tarts with ladies tarts about them | | 11 | 6 |
| For a dish of fruit | | 3 | 6 |
| For lemons and double re-fined sugar | | 3 | 6 |
| For oil and vinegar | | 2 | 6 |

### Supper

| | | | |
|---|---|---|---|
| For a shoulder of mutton | | 3 | 6 |
| For gherkins and capers | | | 6 |
| For a dish of wild fowl | | 6 | 0 |

The total cost of this day's meals at the Red Lion was £15 3s 6d. The following day's meals, to the cost of which was added that of cheese, bread and beer for the servants (£6 19s 8d) and of 'firing' and 'porterage', came to £18 11s. The short excursion cost over twelve times as much as the annual wages of his most highly paid footman.

Visits to Tunbridge Wells and Bath where the earl drank the waters for the alleviation of his rheumatism and gout were equally expensive. Of the two resorts the countess preferred Bath, but the earl favoured Tunbridge Wells where he would rent a house for the duration of his stay: on one occasion he took a house 'at Southborough, near Tunbridge, at £41 os od the week'.[31]

In earlier generations the rich had usually gone to the Continent for the cure of their various ailments, in particular favouring Spa in Belgium. But the discomforts and tiresome duration of foreign travel had led to the increasing popularity of English watering places, although none of them had yet attained those fashionable heights they were to reach in the next century.

Bath, indeed, before the advent of that most fastidious master of cere-monies, Richard Nash – in whose time the city was to be rebuilt in the Palladian style by the two John Woods – had rather a raffish reputation. It was a tawdry place where gentlemen came to dance in top boots, wore swords habitually and smoked in the presence of ladies. Lodgings were both dirty and expensive; sedan chairmen were rude and quarrelsome; there were no respectable assembly rooms, no recognized conventions as to dress and no methods of introduction. Duels were as common as drunkenness.

Not long after the fifth Earl of Bedford had taken his last cure, another visitor wrote:

It has been observed before, that in former times this was a resort hither for cripples; and we see the crutches hang up at the several baths, as the thank-offerings of those who have come hither lame, and gone away cured. But now we may say it is the resort of the sound, rather than the sick; the bathing is made more a sport and diversion, than a physical prescription for health; and the town is taken up in raffling, gaming, visiting, and in a word, all sorts of gallantry and levity.

The whole time indeed is a round of the utmost diversion. In the morning you (supposing you to be a young lady) are fetched in a close chair, dressed in your bathing clothes, that is, stripped to the smock, to the Cross-Bath. There the music plays you into the bath, and the women that tend you, present you with a little floating wooden dish, like a basin; in which the lady puts a handkerchief, and a nosegay, of late the snuff-box is added, and some patches; though the bath occasioning a little perspira-tion, the patches do not stick so kindly as they should.

Here the ladies and gentlemen pretend to keep some distance, and each to their proper side, but frequently mingle . . . and the place being but narrow, they converse freely, and talk, rally, make vows, and sometimes love; and having thus amused themselves an hour or two, they call their chairs and return to their lodgings.[32]

Tunbridge Wells was then more fashionable than Bath. Its waters had been publicized by Lord North who had taken a cure there in 1606 and it had subsequently been patronized by the queens of both Charles I and Charles II, though when Henrietta Maria visited the place in 1630 there was so little accommodation that she and her suite had to stay in tents on the banks of the spring.[33]

In the reign of Queen Anne – who compared the place favourably with 'Epsome, Hampstead and such like places' – a visitor wrote:

> Those people who have nothing to do anywhere else, seem to be the only people who have anything to do at Tunbridge. After the appearance is over at the Wells (where the ladies are all undressed) . . . you are surprised to see the walks covered with ladies completely dressed and gay to profusion; where rich clothes, jewels, and beauty not to be set out by (but infinitely above) ornament, dazzles the eyes from one end of the range to the other.
>
> As for gaming, sharping, intriguing; as also fops, fools, beaux, and the like, Tunbridge is as full of these, as can be desired, and it takes off much of the diversion of those persons of honour and virtue, who go there to be innocently recreated. However a man of character, and good behaviour cannot be there any time, but he may single out such company as may be suitable to him, and with whom he may be as merry as heart can wish. In a word, Tunbridge wants nothing that can add to the felicities of life, or that can make a man or woman completely happy, always provided they have money; for without money a man is no-body at Tunbridge.[34]

# PART THREE

## From Defoe to Cobbett

# 27 · 'A Tour thro' the Whole Island'

Soon after the appearance of *Robinson Crusoe* and *Moll Flanders*, Daniel Defoe published the first part of his *Tour thro' the Whole Island of Great Britain*, the best authority for early eighteenth-century England that we have. Defoe travelled through East Anglia and in the south-eastern counties from London to Land's End, in the West Country and Wales, in the Midland counties then up to Yorkshire and throughout the north-east and the north-west. And everywhere he went he saw the countryside and towns through which he passed with the observant eye of a highly skilful journalist.

Bury St Edmunds was 'the town of all this part of England, in proportion to its bigness, most thronged with gentry, people of the best fashion, and the most polite conversation. The beauty and healthiness of its situation was no doubt the occasion which drew the clergy to settle here, for they always choose the best places in the country to build in, either for richness of soil, or for health and pleasure in the situation of their religious houses.' There was also a high proportion of gentry living in Ipswich and here 'the company you meet with are generally persons well informed of the world and who have something very solid and entertaining in their society. This may happen, perhaps, by their frequent conversing with those who have been abroad.' At Yarmouth, Defoe was told that the merchants there 'cured, that is to say hanged and dried in the smoke, 40,000 barrels of merchantable red herrings in one season . . . But this is only one branch of the great trade carried on in this town. Another part of this commerce is in the exporting these herrings after they are cured; and for this their merchants have a great trade to Genoa, Leghorn, Naples, Messina and Venice as also to Spain and Portugal also exporting with their herrings very great quantities of worsted stuffe and stuffe made of silk . . . the manufactures of the neighbouring city of Norwich.' Silk was also made at Canterbury 'but the great wealth and increase of [this] city is from the surprising increase of the hopgrounds all round the place. It is within the memory of many of the inhabitants now living, and that none of the oldest neither, that there was not an acre of ground planted with hops in the whole neighbourhood, or so few as not to be worth naming, whereas I was assured that there are at this time near six thousand acres of ground so planted within a very few miles of the city.'

To the north of Canterbury, at Chatham, the chief arsenal of the Royal Navy, the buildings were 'like the ships themselves, surprisingly large, and in their several kinds beautiful. The ware-houses, or rather streets of ware-houses, and store-houses for laying up the naval treasure, are the largest in dimension, and the most in number, that are anywhere to be seen in the world.' At Reading, too, there were large storehouses and much shipping to be seen: 'The town lies on the river Kennet but so near the Thames, that the largest barges which they use may come up to the town bridge, and there they have wharfes to load and unload them. Their chief trade is by this water-navigation to and from London. They send from hence to London by these barges very great quantities of malt and meal . . . a thousand or twelve hundred quarters of malt at a time.' Even so, Reading could not, of course, be compared with Bristol, 'the greatest, the richest and the best port of trade in Great Britain, London only excepted'.

Of other towns in the west, Salisbury was remarkable not only for its cathedral but also for the variety of its clothing manufactures which employed 'the poor of great part of the county around', in marked contrast to Winchester, 'a city without trade' but of 'abundance of gentry'. Yet Defoe did not think Salisbury 'the pleasanter for that which they boast so much of: namely the water running through the middle of every street. It adds [nothing] to the beauty of the place, but just the contrary; it keeps the streets always dirty, full of wet and filth and weeds even in the middle of Summer.' Taunton was also a busy manufacturing town, not one of the looms there being idle and 'not a child in the town, or in the villages round it, of above five years old, but could (if necessary) earn its own bread'. Shrewsbury, too, was a town 'full of trade, for here too is a great manufacture as well of flannel as also of white broad-cloth which enriches all the country round it'. Chester was equally prosperous, for this was the centre for Cheshire cheese which, made also in Shropshire, Staffordshire and Lancashire, was shipped by river all over the country in enormous quantities, 14,000 tons a year going to London alone. At Chester, Defoe was much impressed by the water supply. Until recently water had been 'carried from the River Dee upon horses, in great leather vessels, like a pair of bakers' paniers, just the very same for shape and use as they have to this day in the streets of Constantinople and at Belgrade in Hungary to carry about the streets to sell for the people to drink. But now it is supplied by pipes to the city plentifully as London is from the Thames, even though some parts of Chester stand very high from the river.'

Defoe did not, however, care for the celebrated rows which served to make the city 'look both old and ugly': 'These Rows are certain long galleries, up one pair of stairs, which run along the side of the streets, before all the houses, though joined to them, and as is pretended, they are to keep the people dry in walking along. This they do indeed effectually, but then they take away all the view of the houses from the street. Nor can a stranger, that was to ride through Chester, see any shops in the city; besides, they make the shops themselves dark, and the way in them is dark, dirty, and uneven.'

Nor was Defoe much attracted by the other cathedral towns of the west. Hereford he did not consider worth describing. Worcester was 'a large, populous, old though not a very well built city . . . the houses standing too thick. The cathedral is a decayed building . . . very mean in its aspect.' Gloucester was 'an ancient middling city, tolerably built but not fine . . . The large stone bridge over the Severn . . . and the cathedral is all I see worth recording of this place.' The large towns of the Midlands, however, were another matter. Northampton was 'the handsomest and best built town in all this part of England', Warwick 'a really fine town, pleasantly situated on the bank of the Avon . . . It was ever esteemed a handsome, well-built town . . . but the face of it is now quite altered, for having been almost wholly reduced to a heap of rubbish by a terrible fire [in 1694] it is now rebuilt in so noble and so beautiful a manner that few towns in England make so fine an appearance.' Nottingham – described by Celia Fiennes as the 'neatest' place she ever saw – was 'one of the most pleasant and beautiful towns in England'; Derby 'a fine, beautiful and pleasant town' with 'more families of gentlemen in it than is usual in towns so remote'; Leicester an 'ancient, large and populous town' with a thriving trade in 'the weaving of stockings by frames'. 'One would scarcely think it possible that so small an article of trade could employ such multitudes of people as it does; for the whole county seems to be employed in it.'

The chief manufacture carried on at Nottingham was also 'framework knitting for stockings . . . and as they brew a very good liquor here, so they make the best malt and the most of it of any town in this part of England'. In the countryside around, as in Leicestershire, there were as fine cattle and sheep to be seen as anywhere in the country. In Leicestershire, indeed, 'most of the gentlemen are graziers, and in some places the graziers are so rich that they grow gentlemen; 'tis not an uncommon thing for graziers here to rent farms from 500l to two thousand pounds a year rent. The sheep bred in this county and Lincolnshire, which joins to it, are, without comparison, the largest and bear not only the greatest weight of flesh on their bones but also the greatest fleeces of wool on their backs of any sheep of England . . . The horses produced here, or rather fed here, are [also] the largest in England, being generally the great black coach horses and dray horses of which so great a number are continually brought up to London.'

Travelling north, Defoe found some of the towns gloomy and forbidding, the streets of Sheffield, for instance, being narrow and the houses 'dark and black, occasioned by the continued smoke of the forges which are always at work', Barnsley appearing as grimy and smoky 'as if they were all smiths that lived in it'. Yet most places were pleasant enough. Doncaster was 'noble, large and spacious'; Wakefield 'a large, handsome, rich clothing town full of people and full of trade'; Huddersfield 'in full enjoyment of the wealth' which the 'vast clothing trade' had bestowed upon this part of the country. York was a 'pleasant and beautiful city and better furnished than any other with provisions of every kind . . . The river being so navigable, and so near the sea, the merchants here trade directly to what part of the world they will, for ships of any burthen come up within thirty mile of the city, and small craft from sixty to eighty ton and under come up to the very city.' Leeds was 'large, wealthy and populous' and, with the exception of that at Halifax, had the greatest market for cloth in the north:

> At seven a clock in the morning, the clothiers being supposed to be all come by that time, even in the winter, the market bell rings; it would surprise a stranger to see in how few minutes, without hurry or noise, and not the least disorder, the whole market is filled; all the boards upon the trestles are covered with cloth, and behind every piece of cloth, the clothier standing to sell it . . .
>
> As soon as the bell has done ringing, the merchants and factors, and buyers of all sorts, come down, and coming along the spaces between the rows of boards, they walk up the rows, and down as their occasions direct. Some of them have their foreign letters of orders, with patterns sealed on them, in rows, in their hands; and with those they match colours, holding them to the cloths as they think they agree to; when they see any cloths to their colours, or that suit their occasions, they reach over to the clothier and whisper, and in the fewest words imaginable the price is stated; one asks, the other bids; and 'tis agree, or not agree, in a moment.
>
> The merchants and buyers generally walk down and up twice on each side of the rows, and in little more than an hour all the business is done; in less than half an hour you will perceive the cloths begin to move off, the clothier taking it up upon his shoulder to carry it to the merchant's house; and by half an hour after eight o'clock the market bell rings again; immediately the buyers disappear, the cloth is all sold, or if here and there a piece happens not to be bought, 'tis carried back into the inn, and, in a quarter of an hour, there is not a piece of cloth to be seen in the market. Thus, you see, ten or twenty thousand pounds value in cloth, and

sometimes much more, bought and sold in little more than an hour, and the laws of the market the most strictly observed as ever I saw done in any market in England.

By nine o'clock the boards are taken down, the trestles are removed, and the streets cleared, so that you see no market or goods any more than if there had been nothing to do; and this is done twice a week. By this quick return the clothiers are constantly supplied with money, their workmen are duly paid, and a prodigious sum circulates through the county every week.

Large sums of money also passed hands at Halifax where it was quite ordinary for a clothier with a large family to come to town on a market day 'and buy two or three large bullocks from eight to ten pounds a piece' and to cart them home to kill for his store. Defoe was fascinated by Halifax and the surrounding villages in which the houses of the clothiers, each standing in an acre or so of land, spread across the sides of the steep hills.

These hills were 'infinitely full of people, the people all full of business. Not a beggar, not an idle person is to be seen, except here and there an alms-house where people ancient, decrepit and past labour might perhaps be found, for it is observable that the people here, however laborious, generally live to a great age, a certain testimony to the goodness and wholesomeness of the country which is without doubt as healthy as any part of England. Nor is the health of the people lessened but helped and established by their being constantly employed and . . . working hard.'

Every clothier kept at least one horse to fetch home wool and provisions from the market, to carry yarn to the spinners, and his manufactures to the fulling-mill and, when finished, to the market to be sold. Every clothier also kept a cow or two on the enclosed land around his house; and beyond the enclosures were scattered innumerable cottages in which lived the wives and children of the workmen, all of them 'always busy, carding, spinning etc. . . . some at the dye-fat, some dressing the cloths, some in the loom, some one thing, some another, all hard at work and full employed upon the manufacture and all seeming to have sufficient business'.

Manchester, a centre of the cotton trade, 'one of the greatest, if not really the greatest mere village in England', was quite as busy and prosperous. It sent no members to Parliament, its highest magistrate was a constable, yet Defoe was not surprised to learn that it contained more than 50,000 people. In fact, its population was probably no more than 10,000, but it was certainly growing fast and the buildings of the town were obviously extending 'in a surprising manner'. There was 'an abundance not of new houses only but of new streets of houses' so that the place was almost twice as large as it had been a few years before.

Liverpool, 'one of the wonders of Britain', was growing at an equal pace. When Defoe had first visited it in 1680 it was already 'large and handsome'. On his second visit in 1700 it seemed twice as big; and on his third twice as large again. By then there was no town in England, London alone excepted, that could equal Liverpool 'for the fineness of the streets and the beauty of the buildings'. 'What it may grow to in time', he added, 'I know not.'

On the north-eastern coast, Hull was quite as prosperous as Liverpool and 'extraordinary populous, even to a fault'. Defoe believed, indeed, that more business was 'done in Hull than in any town of its bigness in Europe': 'In a word all the trade at Leeds, Wakefield and Halifax, of which I have spoken so justly and so largely, is transacted here, and the goods are shipped here by the merchants of Hull. All the lead trade of Derbyshire and Nottinghamshire, the butter of the East and North Riding, the cheese from Stafford, Warwick and Cheshire, and the corn from all the counties adjacent, are brought down and shipped here. Again, they supply all these counties in return with foreign goods of all kinds, for which they trade to all parts of the known world.' Newcastle, too, was a large and bustling port whose wide river allowed ships to sail up to the very quays. 'And whereas when we are at London and see the prodigious fleets of ships which come constantly in with coals to this increasing city,' Defoe commented, 'we are apt to wonder whence they come and that they do not bring the whole country away. So, on the contrary, when in this country we see the prodigious heaps, I might say mountains, of coals which are dug up at every pit, and how many of those pits there are, we are filled with equal wonder.'

As he rode along from town to town, Defoe noted all kinds of facts and curiosities, asked questions, recorded replies, closely observed people and customs as well as places. He wrote of the 'best and nicest oysters' that were taken at the mouth of Colchester Wharf; of the droves of geese and turkeys, some of them a thousand strong, passing down to London along the road from Ipswich, eating the stubble in the fields on the way or being carried in special carts layer upon layer, four clacking storeys in height; of 'the strange decay of the female sex . . . in the damp part' of Essex where it was frequent to meet with men that 'had five to six, to fourteen or fifteen wives, nay and some more'. He was informed that in the marshes

. . . on the other side of the river over against Candy Island, there was a farmer who was then living with the five and twentieth wife, and that his son, who was but about thirty-five years old, had already had about fourteen . . . The reason, as a merry old fellow told me, who said that he had had about a dozen and a half of wives himself, (though I found afterwards he fibbed a little) was this: That men being bred in the marshes themselves, and seasoned to the place, did pretty well with it; but that they always went up into hilly country, or to speak their own language into the uplands for a wife: that when they took the young lasses out of the wholesome and fresh air, they were healthy, fresh and clear; and well; but when they came out of their native air into the marshes among the fogs and damps, there they presently changed their complexion, got an ague or two, and seldom held it above half a year, or a year at most. And then, said he, we go to the uplands again, and fetch another; so that marrying of wives was reckoned a kind of good farm to them. It is true, the fellow told this in a kind of drollery, and mirth; but the fact, for all that, is certainly true; and that they have abundance of wives by that very means.

In the Peak District of Derbyshire, Defoe encountered a poor woman and her children living in a cave and recorded her story 'to show the discontented part of the rich world how to value their own good fortune':

Says I, good wife, where do you live. Here, sir, says she, and points to the hole in the rock. Here! says I; and do all these children live here too? Yes, sir, says she, they were all born here. Pray how long have you dwelt here then? said I. My husband was born here, said she, and his father before him. Will you give me leave, says one of our company, as curious as I was, to come in and see your house, dame? If you please, sir, says she, but 'tis not a place fit for such as you are to come into, calling him, your worship, forsooth; but that by the by. I mention it, to show that the good woman did not want manners, though she lived in a den like a wild body.

However, we alighted and went in. There was a large hollow cave, which the poor people, by two curtains hanged across, had parted into three rooms. On one side was the chimney, and the man, or perhaps his father, being miners, had found means to work a shaft or funnel through the rock to carry the smoke out at the top. The habitation was poor, 'tis true, but things within did not look so like misery as I expected. Everything was clean and neat, though mean and ordinary. There were shelves with earthen ware, and some pewter and brass. There was, which I observed in particular, a whole flitch or side of bacon hanging up in the chimney, and by it a good piece of another. There was a sow and pigs running about at the door, and a little lean cow feeding upon a green place just before the door, and a little piece of ground was growing with good barley . . .

I asked the poor woman, what trade her husband was? She said, he worked in the lead mines. I asked her, how much he could earn a day there? she said, if he had good luck he could earn about five pence a day. Then I asked, what she did; she said, when she was able to [spare time from the children] she washed the ore [and] if she worked hard she could gain three-pence a day. So that, in short, here was but eight-pence a day when they both worked hard, and that not always, and perhaps not often, and all this to maintain a man, his wife, and five small children, and yet they seemed to live very pleasantly, the children looked plump and fat, ruddy and wholesome; and the woman was tall, well shaped, clean, and (for the place) a very well looking, comely woman. Nor was there any thing that looked like the dirt and nastiness of the miserable cottages of the poor; though many of them spend more money in strong drink than this poor woman had to maintain five children with.

Having given the woman 'a little lump' of money, at the sight of which she nearly fainted before bursting into tears, Defoe went to see the lead-mine or, rather, the numerous small holes in the ground down which the miners scrambled. He was wondering at their smallness when out of one of the grooves appeared first a hand, then an arm, next a head, and finally a body, 'a most uncouth spectacle', clothed all in leather with a brimless leather hat. He carried his tools in a small basket, and endeavoured to explain their various uses, but his accent was unintelligible. He was lean as a skeleton, grey as a corpse, and panted and struggled as he pulled up about three-quarters of a hundredweight of ore which he had dragged from the vein 150 yards underground. Defoe gave him two shillings, more than he earned in four days, and he hurried off with the money to an alehouse to treat himself to a glass or two of Pale Derby. But Defoe was there before him, bought him his drink, and told him to take the shillings back to his family.

On his way to Cambridge, Defoe visited Sourbridge Fair, 'the greatest in the world', which was held in a large cornfield near Casterton where the booths were filled with the wares of goldsmiths and turners, of milliners, haber-dashers and mercers, of pewterers and drapers and clothiers, with toys and books and medicines, and with the tables, benches, jugs and cups of the keepers of taverns, brandy-shops and cooks' shops, coffee-houses and eating-rooms. Vast quantities of goods were sold and the whole countryside and all the villages and small towns around were crowded with people and even barns and stables were turned into inns.

From here Defoe went on to give an account of the races at Newmarket where he was much displeased by the drinking and the gambling, the picking of pockets, the ill manners and the prodigal insouciance with which Tregon-well Frampton, 'the cunningest jockey in England', lost 1000 guineas one day and won 2000 the next. And he was even more shocked by the infamous Horn Fair at Charlton, an annual event supposedly licensed by King John to a miller whose wife he had seduced. Here the people, many of them dressed as kings, queens and millers with horns on their heads, 'took all kinds of liberties and the women [were] especially impudent, as if it was a day that justified the giving themselves a loose to all manner of indecency and immodesty'. He thought the fair ought to be suppressed 'as a nuisance and offence to all sober people', but it was not, in fact, put down until 1872.

He described the smuggling that was carried on along the Kentish and Essex coasts where wine and brandy from France and Holland, pepper, tea, coffee, calico and tobacco were landed in such quantities that the people were 'grown monstrous rich by that wicked trade'. He complained of the difficulty of understanding the dialects of country people outside London, particularly in Somerset where they spoke in so 'boorish' a way that 'one cannot understand one half of what they say'; and of the custom, introduced, so he said, by Queen Mary, 'of furnishing houses with chinaware . . . piling [it] upon the tops of cabinets, scrutoires, and every chimneypiece, to the tops of the ceilings and even setting up shelves for [it] where they wanted such places'.

He described a mop fair, also known as a living fair, in an Oxfordshire village where men and women offered themselves for hire and indicated the kind of labour they could undertake by holding up an appropriate tool or implement, a brush, a carter's whip, a shovel, a billhook, a woolcomb. These fairs, Defoe added, were not 'so much frequented as formerly'.[1] They survived, however, until well into the nineteenth century. In *Far From the Madding Crowd*, published in 1874 and set in the 1840s, Thomas Hardy described one in Casterbridge where 'two to three hundred blithe and hearty labourers stood at one end of the street'. 'Among these, carters and waggoners were distinguished by having a piece of whip cord twisted round their hats; thatchers wore a fragment of woven straw; shepherds held their sheep-crooks in their hands; and thus the situation required was known to the hirers at a glance.'[2]

# 28 · *Countrymen, Clergymen and Farmers*

English society was divided by Defoe into seven classes: there were the great who lived 'profusely', the rich who lived 'plentifully' and the 'middle sort' who lived 'well'. Then there were those in 'the working trades' who laboured hard and felt no want, followed by country people who fared indifferently, the poor who fared hard, and, lastly, 'the miserable that really pinch and suffer want'.[1]

The landed nobility at the apex of society were as a class inordinately rich and tightly enclosed. Many of them had urban as well as country estates, the rents from both of which were increasing year by year. The Russells, earls and dukes of Bedford, who developed Covent Garden and Bloomsbury, were receiving over three times as much from their properties in London at the end of the seventeenth century as they were at the beginning. The Grosvenors, who developed parts of Mayfair and later Belgravia, were already 'infinitely rich' when Sir Thomas Grosvenor acquired the estates his wife had inherited from an old uncle; and by the 1770s, after building on the Mayfair lands had been completed, they were richer than ever. Other landowners, like Thomas Coke of Holkham, Earl of Leicester, much increased their rents by means of improved methods of farming and of estate management. They also made immense profits from the coal and timber, the slate and stone which were taken from their lands and from the industries in which they invested. And many of them increased their fortunes by accepting office at court or in the government at a time when a secretaryship of state might yield up to £9000 a year in clear profit, when a paymaster general might put away over half a million pounds during his term of office, and a sinecure could keep a man in comfort for life. By one means or another most peers contrived to make at least £5000 a year, the rough equivalent of £300,000 a year today, and some had far more than this. By 1790, so it has been calculated, 400 landowners had incomes of £10,000 a year. Several had over £20,000;

and as early as 1715 the lands of the Duke of Newcastle were bringing in
£32,000, that is to say an annual income of some £2 million in present-day
terms. By 1800 almost a quarter of England's landed wealth was owned by
peers of the realm, some twenty of whom owned more than 20,000 acres
each.[2]

They spent their money lavishly, building and improving huge houses,
laying out parks, moving villages to improve the view, buying quantities of
furniture, pictures and books, spending vast sums on gambling, clothes,
bloodstock, kennels of hounds, election expenses and troops of servants. Sir
Robert Walpole spent £1500 a year on wine at Houghton Hall and £1 a night
on candles; the Nevilles laid out £100,000 on altering Audley End; the dukes
of Devonshire maintained not only Chatsworth but also Hardwick Hall,
Bolton Abbey, Lismore Castle and Compton Place as well as Devonshire
House and Burlington House in London. In 1753 the fourth Duke additionally inherited Chiswick House, the magnificent country villa modelled
on Palladio's Villa Rotonda at Vicenza. At Canons Park, the Duke of
Chandos's house which stood in landscaped grounds of 841 acres between
Stanmore and Edgware, there were ninety-three household servants and a
private orchestra of twenty-seven musicians.[3]

Members of the nobility were anxious to preserve their caste. Some might
marry heiresses from lesser families to increase a fortune, but daughters were
expected not to marry beneath them. Indeed, those beneath were often
regarded as creatures of another species. 'It is monstrous,' the Duchess of
Buckingham complained of Methodists, 'to be told that you have a heart as
sinful as the common wretches that crawl on the earth. This is highly
offensive and insulting and at variance with high rank and good breeding.'
The Earl of Cork lamented that it was necessary at election time to open his
doors 'to every dirty fellow in the county that is worth forty shillings a year'.
'All my best floors are spoiled by the hobnails of farmers stamping about
them,' he continued. 'Every room is a pig-stye and the Chinese paper in the
drawing-room stinks so abominably of punch and tobacco that it would strike
you down to come into it.'[4]

The aristocracy managed to keep itself a small élite. It was now much rarer
than it had been in the past for a younger son to go into trade. He might
possibly accept a position with some such organization as the East India
Company or go into banking but he was more likely to enter politics, the
army or the Church. It was also 'hard to buy your way into high society', as
Dr Roy Porter has observed. 'It was easier to marry a peer than obtain a
peerage. The ascent towards the Lords was normally slow, arduous and
costly, though a few lawyers could take a faster route and become Lord
Chancellor – as did Macclesfield, Hardwicke, Camden, Thurlow and Eldon.'
National heroes like Robert Clive, a former writer in the East India Company

at Madras, and, later, Horatio Nelson, son of a Norfolk country parson, were rewarded with peerages.

But *nouveaux riches*, however *riches*, did not easily become ennobled. They could not buy a peerage – peerages were just about the one thing not for sale in Georgian England. Nor could they themselves count on marrying peers' daughters. De Quincey wrote that John Palmer [the son of a prosperous brewer] had accomplished two things very hard to do so in our little planet. He had invented mail-coaches and he had married the daughter of a Duke.[5]

Beneath the uppermost class, however, there was much more what was later to be termed social mobility. Ranks were strictly graded, each inclined to look down upon the one below, physicians regarding themselves as superior to surgeons, brewers to provision merchants, governesses to house-keepers, housekeepers to cooks, cooks to gardeners. But it was easier than it was in most other European countries to climb the slope that led from one class to the next, and numerous are the examples of those who managed to do so. The father of Henry Thrale, the brewer, had been an agricultural labourer; so had the father of the navigator, Captain Cook; Robert Dodsley, the publisher, had once been a footman; Lancelot ('Capability') Brown a kitchen-gardener; Lord Eldon was the son of a Newcastle coal factor and hence known in the royal family as 'Old Bags'; John Thomas, Bishop of Salisbury, was the son of a drayman at Nicholson's Brewery.

This, however, was highly unusual in a bishop. Nearly all Thomas's fellow-bishops were either related to noblemen or had been chaplains or tutors in noble families. Frederick Cornwallis, Archbishop of Canterbury, was a son of Lord Cornwallis; the father of Robert Hay Drummond, Archbishop of York, was the Earl of Kinnoul; H. R. Courtenay, Bishop of Exeter, was a grandson of Earl Bathhurst; the Bishop of Winchester, Brownlow North, a son of the Earl of Guilford; Thomas Thurlow, Bishop of Lincoln, brother to the Lord Chancellor. Joseph Wilcocks, Bishop of Gloucester, had been preceptor to the daughters of the Prince of Wales; and on his elevation resided 'as much as any bishop in his diocese, at least four months in the year' and kept 'a very generous and hospitable table which [made] amends for the learning he [was] deficient in'.

No longer employed as the king's civil servants, bishops had few secular duties to perform other than their attendance at the House of Lords, and so most of them were able to devote more time to their diocese than many of their predecessors had. And for this some of them at least were very highly paid, the Archbishop of Canterbury, for instance, receiving £7000 a year, the Bishop of Durham £6000. Most of the lesser clergy in their dioceses were also better paid than they had been in the past. There were still many poor clergy occupying livings worth less than £100 a year who were obliged to earn money in other ways as the poor parsons Barnabee, Adams and Trulliver all do in Henry Fielding's *Joseph Andrews* of 1742; and there were many others being paid as little as £50 a year or less to act as curates for pluralists and absentee parsons. James Marshall, who was curate of Ireby in Cumberland for over sixty years from 1777, never had more than £50 a year. To make ends meet he kept two work-horses and carted coals from Bolton collieries to Keswick, filling the carts and conducting them to market himself. The curate of a nearby parish whose stipend was no more than £28 a year eked out his living by sheep clipping. Many others taught in schools or gave private lessons.[6]

There were still many absentee parsons. About a quarter of the 10,000 parishes in England had no resident parson, and in some counties the proportion was much higher; in Devon it had reached 70 per cent by 1780. In 1808, however, a Bill required all clergymen to live in their parishes; and one man whose life was thus transformed was Sydney Smith who, though living in London, was incumbent of Foston-le-Clay, a living in the gift of the Lord Chancellor, which was in a remote part of Yorkshire, twelve miles, as Smith put it himself, from the nearest lemon. Required to reside there, he endeavoured to exchange the living for one more accessible; but as he was permitted only to exchange it for another chancery living of similar income he did not manage to do so. He moved, therefore, to Foston where there had been no resident rector for 150 years and where the parsonage house was a hovel and had to be rebuilt. He obtained permission to live temporarily nearby at Heslington which was closer to York, a city in which he discovered that, contrary to popular opinion in the south, the people had been converted to the Christian faith, wore clothes and were not addicted to cannibalism.[7]

Smith became a good and well-liked parson. He found time to entertain numerous visitors, to teach his sons until they went to their public schools, to help his wife in the education of his daughters, to write for the *Edinburgh Review*, to preach sermons, to cross swords with Methodists and devotees of Evangelical enthusiasm, to perform the duties of a magistrate, to give dinners for some of the local farmers, and to farm himself much of the extensive Foston glebe. To save time when directing activities on his farm, he stood outside his front door, shouting orders through a tremendous speaking trumpet; and, in the words of a visiting friend, 'as a proper companion' for the trumpet, he had a 'telescope slung in leather' to observe what the labourers were doing. But his farming did not prevent him from attending conscientiously to his pastoral duties, from visiting the sick and even, on the strength of his attendance at some of Christopher Pegge's lectures at Oxford, and at clinical classes at the Royal Infirmary of Edinburgh, from becoming a 'village doctor' as well as 'village comforter'. 'The poor *intirely* confided their maladies to him,' his widow wrote, 'and he had the satisfaction of being to them eminently useful. All his drugs were got from London, a record was kept of each case of sickness and of the remedies applied.' One of the rectory servants, Annie Kay, acted as his 'apothecary's boy' and made up the medicines for him in accordance to his eccentric instructions.

> There is the Gentle-jog, a pleasure to take [he explained], the Ball-dog for more serious cases; Peter's puke; Heart's delight, the comfort of all the old women in the village; Rub-a-dub, a capital embrocation. Dead-stop settles the matter at once; Up-with-it-then needs no explanation; and so on. Now, Annie Kay, give Mrs Sprat a bottle of Rub-a-dub; and to Mr Coles a dose of Dead-stop and twenty drops of laudanum.[8]

With his fellow-clergy, 'the sporting clergy of Malton', as he described them, Smith got on well enough, though many of them did not understand his jokes and others did not approve of them. In one of his sermons he asked if it were right for a 'minister of god to lead the life of a gamekeeper or a groom'. But, although he derived little pleasure from the company of his clerical neighbours, cheerfulness was always breaking in. 'I see so little of any clever men here that I have nobody to recommend,' he told Lord Brougham. 'But if you have any young horses to break I can find many clergymen who will do it for you.'

'I hear, Mr Smith', the Archbishop of York, a notable horseman himself, once said to him, 'you do not approve of much riding for the clergy.'

'Why, my Lord,' replied Smith, who often fell off his own horse, 'perhaps there is not *much objection*, provided they do not ride too well, and stick their toes out professionally.'[9]

Sydney Smith lived very well on his £400 a year exclusive of incidental emoluments and while this was much more than most country parsons received, there were now far fewer who were pitiably poor than there had been in the days of Cranmer and Laud. By the end of the eighteenth century there were only about 4000 livings worth less than £150 a year; and as methods of agriculture improved so the value of tithes and glebe farms rose.[10]

The Rev. James Woodforde – whose final diary entry typically records his dinner of roast beef despite his being so weak he could scarcely summon the strength to dress and go downstairs – lived very comfortably indeed on £400 a year at Weston Longueville, Norfolk. He was paid his tithes without too much complaint, and rewarded those who paid him with 'a frolic . . . a good dinner, surloin of beef roasted, a leg of mutton boiled and plumb puddings in plenty'. He farmed his own glebe land profitably and provided his harvest men with beef, more of his 'plumb pudding' and 'as much liquor as they would drink'. He was not over-zealous in the performance of his duties; and when he said prayers on Good Friday 1777 he was performing a duty with which he had not troubled himself before. There were many other parsons like him. 'If a rector read the service on a Sunday,' George Pryme wrote, remembering his youth in the 1780s, 'and visited the sick when sent for, it was thought quite sufficient.'[11]

Woodforde was a characteristic example of a kind of clergyman to be found in every English county. So was Samuel Johnson's old friend, the Rev. John Taylor, whose 'talk was all of bullocks'. There were others, of course, more learned, the Rev. Gilbert White, for instance, whose *Natural History and Antiquities of Selborne* has been published in numerous editions, and men like Henry Fielding's Parson Adams who was

> a perfect master of the Greek and Latin language . . . and had treasured up a fund of learning rarely to be met with in a university. He was besides a man of good sense, good parts and good nature . . . His virtue had so much endeared and well recommended him to a bishop, that at the age of fifty, he was provided with a handsome income of twenty-three pounds a year; which, however, he could not make any great figure with; because he lived in a dear country, and was a little encumbered with a wife and six children.[12]

But John Taylor, thanks to the acquisition of various appointments and preferments in addition to the valuable living of Market Bosworth in Leicestershire, was richer than many of his landowning neighbours. He was chaplain to the Duke of Devonshire, through whose influence he was appointed to a prebendal stall at Westminster which, in turn, allowed him to obtain the post of Minister of the Chapel in the Broadway, Westminster, the perpetual curacy of St Botolph Aldersgate, as well as the appointment of minister of St Margaret's. He eventually accumulated an income of some £7000 a year upon which he lived in ample comfort at his family home in Ashbourne in Derbyshire, paying infrequent visits to the parish in Leicestershire of which he was rector. Known as the King of Ashbourne, he was a justice of the peace, the owner of one of the finest breed of milch-cows in England, and a man whose habits, as Johnson was obliged to admit, were 'by no means sufficiently clerical'. He was a selfish, childless man who was always on the look out for further ecclesiastical preferments, who never voluntarily paid a debt and who left all his money to a young page, his first wife having died and his second having left him. Johnson, without finding much to talk to him about, greatly enjoyed staying with him, being driven over from Lichfield in his host's 'large, roomy post-chaise, drawn by four stout plump horses, and driven by two steady, jolly, postilions'.

Taylor's table was always laden with the best of English food, of which Johnson was frequently tempted to eat far too much – once so much, indeed, that it was feared 'he would have died of over eating, and had not a Surgeon been got to administer to him without delay a glister he must have died', a misfortune discreetly omitted from Boswell's *Life*. Taylor's house was large and comfortable, well cared for by servants, presided over by an 'upper servant, Mr Peters, a decent grave man, in purple clothes, and a large white wig, like the butler or *major domo* of a bishop'.

Such clergymen were not, of course, expected to be evangelical and were likely to be disapproved of if they were. 'We do not much like Mr Cooper's new sermons,' Jane Austen told her sister. 'They are fuller of Regeneration and Conversion than ever.'[13] Nor were parsons expected to be specially trained for their calling: a university degree was quite enough; there were no theological colleges until well into the nineteenth century. Nor did clergymen necessarily wear distinguishing clothes until, after Methodist ministers had begun to do so, the more serious clergymen in the Church of England followed suit.

Relations between Anglican clergymen and Methodists and Dissenters were usually friendly enough. Sydney Smith could not resist confiding in a humourless neighbour that he harboured one secret desire: he had always wanted 'to roast a Quaker'. Quaker babies were an impossibility, he thought. There could be no such things: they must surely all be born 'broad-brimmed and in full quake'. Yet, living in Yorkshire, where there were many members of the Society of Friends, he found it impossible not to admire them. Their behaviour during an epidemic at Thornton he considered worthy of the highest regard; and, after a visit to a prison with Elizabeth Fry, he remarked, 'She is very unpopular with the clergy. Examples of living, active virtue disturb our repose, and give birth to distressing comparisons: we long to burn her alive.' He once asked his York grocer, Joseph Rowntree, to recommend a Quaker nursemaid for the rectory at Foxton. Her faith 'would in no way be interfered with' while she was living in a clergyman's family. 'You,' he said to Rowntree, 'obtain something we do not.'[14]

Although not as broad-minded as Sydney Smith, the Church was generally inclined to be easy-going in its attitude towards Dissenters, as it was in other matters, though in some parishes, as in that of the Somerset rector, the Rev. John Skinner, rivalry was fierce. There was less tolerance of Roman Catholics. Sydney Smith felt himself to be a lonely figure when urging Catholic emancipation which was not to be granted until the Roman Catholic Relief Act of 1829. Nearly all his fellow-clergymen in Yorkshire, including his own curate, disagreed with him when he pleaded for 'no modern chains and prisons under the names of disqualifications and incapacities . . . No tyranny in belief: a free altar, an open road to heaven.'[15]

In Somerset, John Skinner had just as much trouble with the Roman Catholics in his 'detestable neighbourhood' – which was 'governed by attorneys, apothecaries and coal-heavers' – as he did with the Methodists among his parishioners. Indeed, he and one particular Roman Catholic, a farmer and 'artful fellow' from whom he drew tithes, actually came to blows after a furious quarrel in a barley field.

> He said I was a rascal [Skinner wrote in his journal]. I immediately struck him two blows in the face, one with my right hand, the other with my left. He did not return them but said, 'This is what I have been wishing for.' He then called out to the carter and said, 'He has given me a bloody nose,' and held down his head which was bleeding. I said he richly deserved what he had got, even had it been more, and added: I supposed he meant to take the law.

The man did take the law and Skinner was indicted for an assault at the Bath Assizes. He suffered it to go 'by default' and damages were assessed at £50. 'The Catholics had expected more.'[16]

Skinner found some of the Methodists in his village equally exasperating. One day he followed one Smallcombe who had taken a scythe, pickaxe and shovel from the Glebe House, 'to endeavour to ascertain whether they were his own':

> Mrs Smallcombe was in the house, and immediately began by asking what business I had on her premises. I replied I had business to visit any place in my parish; that when her husband had been so ill, and I frequently called to see and relieve him, neither she nor her husband then found fault with me for coming on the premises. She replied, if I did come then she did not send for me and never should again, neither should I ever again enter her garden. The insolence of this woman increased and her fury became so violent and her countenance so distorted she resembled one of the witches in the painting of Sir Joshua Reynolds. 'You a parson, a shepherd of the flock, to come here,' she vociferated, 'and insult a poor woman like me (because I called her 'Beldame'). You will smart for this I assure you, I assure you.' Tyler's wife, a very rank Methodist, who was in the house, then began to join in the contest and asked whether I was not ashamed of myself to call such names: that I might talk about canting Methodists, but there never was a Churchman like me in a house but the Devil was there also. I then said 'Woman, such expressions I might make you answer for in the Ecclesiastical Court, if you were not infinitely beneath my notice.'

I particularise these absurd scenes, not only because they are worth recording as curiosities but, in another point of view, they are indices of the malignity of these sectarists. I am heartily sick of the flock over which I am nominated and placed; instead of being a shepherd, as I told the methodistical beldame when she twitted me with the name, I am in fact a pig driver; I despise myself most thoroughly for suffering irritation from such vermin. Leaving these scenes of discord, I endeavoured to tranquilise my mind by visiting those more softened by sickness and sorrow.[17]

Skinner's parishioners appear to have been particularly obstreperous. But elsewhere parsons were heartily disliked as tithe-gatherers and, although nearly everyone believed in God, the churches were not as packed in the eighteenth century as popular imagination likes to suppose. 'I was at home all day,' Thomas Turner, a Sussex shopkeeper, wrote in his diary one Sunday evening, 'but not at church. O fye! No just reason for not being there.'[18] Joseph Addison considered there was less religion in England than in any neighbouring country; and Montesquieu thought that it excited nothing but laughter.[19] Lord Melbourne once said to the young Queen Victoria that his parents never went to church: 'People didn't use to go so much formerly; it wasn't the fashion.' He himself, he added, was afraid to go 'for fear of hearing something very extraordinary'; but that was in the late 1830s. A sermon certainly afforded a very suitable opportunity to settle down for such a snooze as is enjoyed by the congregation depicted in Hogarth's *The Sleeping Congregation* in which the parson preaches on the text, 'Come unto me all ye that are heavy laden and I will give thee rest', as the hour-glass – still attached to some pulpits in the late nineteenth century – marks by its dripping sand the tedious passage of time.

Most congregations, indeed, were as indifferent to their pastors' sermons as that addressed by Hogarth's short-sighted preacher. At the end of the eighteenth century only about 10 per cent of the population took Easter Communion in their parish church; and while in some areas there were churches dotted all over the landscape, in others there were far too few. In Manchester, with a population which had risen to 20,000 by 1780, there was only one parish church; and in London in 1812, though there were 186 Anglican places of worship – very few of them offering daily services – there were no less than 256 for Dissenters, even though Methodism, which had been intended by its founder, John Wesley, an Anglican clergyman, as a movement within the Church rather than a separate sect, did not yet have many committed adherents.[20] Its influence, however, was growing year by year.

Wesley, the son of a clergyman who sent him to Charterhouse and Christ Church, Oxford, was ordained in 1725 and became a Fellow of Lincoln

College, Oxford, in 1726. At Oxford he joined a group known as the Oxford Methodists, which had been formed by his brother, Charles, the evangelist, hymn writer and friend of the Rev. George Whitefield, another highly gifted preacher. It was Whitefield's example, as well as the reluctance of his fellow-clergymen to allow so uncomfortably zealous a preacher the use of their pulpits, that led to Wesley preaching in the open air, to huge crowds mainly of working-class people. By the time of his death he was said to have preached 40,000 sermons and to have travelled a quarter of a million miles; and there is scarcely a large village in England in which tradition does not point to a green, lychgate or a churchyard by which he is said to have addressed a wondering multitude.

It was not until after Wesley's death in 1791 that the final break with the Anglican Church took place and Methodism became recognized as a religious belief outside it. Throughout his lifetime there were never many who considered themselves Methodists: in 1796 there were still no more than 77,000. There were also no more than 20,000 Quakers, whereas there had been nearly 40,000 at the beginning of the century. Then there had been as many as 58,000 Baptists, 59,000 Independents and 179,000 Presbyterians. But Dissenters had been falling in number ever since, by as much perhaps as 40 per cent in the first forty years of the century.[21] And as people had turned back to Anglicanism so righteous fury with Nonconformism had abated. No longer was it likely that a High Churchman would interrupt the prayers of a congregation in a meeting house, as Justice Bradgate did at Lutterworth when he rode his horse through the door to thunder at the preacher that he lied.[22] Provided they were prepared to show an occasional conformity to the established Church, Dissenters were not even debarred from taking their seats in the House of Commons to which nearly forty were elected during the eighteenth century. Nor did practising Jews, of whom there were about 10,000, find it impossible to enter public life.

Anti-semitism in the country had certainly not abated. Faced with furious opposition, much of it from country gentlemen, the government felt obliged in 1753 to repeal an Act which had recently been passed permitting the naturalization of Jews. And there were to be no Jewish Members of Parliament until late in the nineteenth century. As late as 1889, when Lord Rothschild was appointed to succeed the Duke of Buckingham as Lord Lieutenant of Buckinghamshire, many people were deeply shocked; and the Prince of Wales, who had several close Jewish friends, felt obliged to write to Lord Carrington, a strong opponent of the appointment, in support of it. Yet ever since the Jews, expelled from the country by Edward I, had been allowed to return by Cromwell, they had been slowly gaining influence in England and had become increasingly powerful in financial circles in the City. Sampson Gideon's father, who had changed his name from the

Portuguese Abudiente on settling in England, had been admitted to the Court of the Painters' Stainers Company in 1697 and was a Freeman of the City of London. Sampson Gideon himself made an immense fortune as a financier and was the government's principal mainstay for the raising of loans during the Seven Years' War. It was considered impossible to grant him the baronetcy he desired; but this was conferred instead in 1759 upon his fifteen-year-old son then at Eton. Nathan Rothschild, who first came to England in 1797 and who founded the English branch of the great family business, was as useful to the government of his day, and had a son who was elected Member of Parliament for the City of London. By then there had been Jewish mayors of several English cities. In the 1790s Francis Place, who remembered a time when Jews were insulted in the streets, 'hooked, hunted, cuffed, pulled by the beard and spat upon', said they were now safe and believed that those 'few who would be disposed to insult them merely because they are Jews would be in danger of chastizement from the passers-by and of punishment from the police'.[23]

Despite the fury of the Gordon Riots of 1780 in London – in which papists were, in any case, only one of many targets of the rioters – Roman Catholics in the country at large were also much less abused than they had formerly been. There were, for one thing, less of them, many families having converted to Anglicanism. The 115,000 Catholics of 1720 had been reduced to less than 70,000 by 1780; and few of these were ever attacked or insulted. 'I have lived here about thirty years', the Roman Catholic Sir Henry Arundel told Lord Hardwicke, 'and thanks to the lenity of ye government, without ever having had the least molestation given me.'[24]

The life of such clergymen as John Taylor of Ashbourne was scarcely distinguishable from that of the squire he so much resembled. A portrait of the squire of Heslington was drawn by the rector, Sydney Smith:

> In a fine old house of the time of Queen Elizabeth at Heslington there resided the last of the squires, with his lady, who looked as if she had walked straight out of the Ark, or had been the wife of Enoch. He was a perfect specimen of the Trullibers of old. He smoked, hunted, drank beer at his door with his grooms and dogs, and slept over the county paper on Sundays. At first, he heard I was a Jacobin and a dangerous fellow, and turned aside as I passed: but at length, when he found the peace of the village undisturbed, harvests much as usual, Juno and Ponto uninjured, he first bowed, then called, and at least reached such a pitch of confidence that he used to bring the papers, that I might explain the difficult words to him; actually discovered that I had made a joke, laughed till I thought he

would have died of convulsions, and ended by inviting me to see his dogs.[25]

Men like this and like Fielding's Squire Western, whose custom it was every afternoon 'as soon as he was drunk, to hear his daughter play on the harpsichord', shared a common passion for hunting as well as the bottle and roast beef: Horace Walpole referred to the East Anglian variety as 'mountains of roast beef'. They spoke in the same thick dialects as their tenants whose prejudices they shared. They were patriotic and stubbornly xenophobic, particularly disliking the French. They also disliked nabobs whose fortunes inflated the cost of country life and the great lords who were intent upon buying them out. They strongly approved of the sentiments of 'Rule Britannia', Arne's setting to which was published in 1740, and of 'God save the King' which was first printed in 1744. They rejoiced in the victories of British arms which were haphazardly assembling an empire. They heartily agreed with one of their number, William Thornton of Cattel, Yorkshire, who violently opposed a proposal for a national census in the 1750s, a 'presumptuous' and 'abandoned' proposal which, if put into effect, would provide dangerous information for enemies abroad as well as enemies at home, 'placemen and tax-masters'. The proposal in short was 'totally subversive of the last remains of English liberty' in the pursuit of which William Thornton, rather than provide an account of the number and circumstances of his family, would order his servants to give any interfering official of the government 'the discipline of the horse-pond'.

Such men were eager to accept office as justices of the peace, to exercise the power that such office bestowed upon them in the granting of licences, in the maintenance of roads and bridges, workhouses and prisons, in the levying of rates and in the administration of justice, though many of them were no more qualified to do so than Henry Fielding's Mr Thrasher who 'had some few imperfections in his magisterial capacity' in that, while it might generally be held that his office required 'some knowledge of the law', had 'never read one syllable of the matter'.[26]

If once in his life [the squire] went to London on business he was noticeable in the City crowds for his horse-hair periwig, his jockey belt and his old-fashioned coat without sleeves. His library, traditionally at least, consisted of the Bible, Baker's Chronicle, *Hudibras* and Foxe's *Martyrs*, and, whether he read these works or not, his view on Puritans and Papists usually coincided with those expressed in the last two.[27]

Some squires were quite poor, struggling to survive as gentry on a few hundred pounds a year, but the increase in land values, which almost doubled between 1700 and 1790, helped most to live comfortably, particularly those whose land enabled them to make money from forestry or mining and those who invested in commerce. In 1790, so it has been calculated, beneath the 400 great landowners who had incomes of £10,000 a year and more, there were between 700 and 800 rich gentry who had up to £4000 a year, some 300 to 400 who had between £1000 and £3000, and between 10,000 and 20,000 who had between £300 and £1000.[28] Of these there were many far more industrious and astute than the Squire Westerns who slept drunkenly amidst their hounds. There were men like Mr Allworthy of Somerset who possessed, as well as one of the largest estates in the county, 'an agreeable person, a sound constitution, a solid understanding and a benevolent heart'.[29] They served conscientiously on the back-benches of the House of Commons and were respected by the yeomen who came below them in the social scale and by the tenant-farmers who rented their land.

In the late seventeenth century the yeomen, that class of countrymen between the gentlemen and the petty farmers, numbered perhaps about 120,000. Their yearly incomes were between £40 and £200 a year, their houses comfortable, of timber and plaster in some parts of the country, of brick or stone in others. They were traditionally supposed to be hardworking and prudent, and many of them were so. 'When this John and Mary were first married,' said one Devonshire yeoman of another, 'they had but little, but God did so prosper them that before she died they had 400 bullocks and great store of money and other such stuff and were as well furnished of all things in their house as any one man of their degree was in all their country.'[30]

They made or grew nearly all of their food and were generous hosts. They also had a strong sense of social responsibility, willingly acting as churchwardens and conscientiously, if less willingly, as constables, overseers of the poor or surveyors of the highways. They set great store by education and were drawn towards the teachings of the Puritans who saw hard work as an offering to God. Several leading Puritan preachers came from yeomen families.[31]

In the eighteenth century the standard of living of yeomen with small holdings began to decline. In some areas, in fact, small owner-occupiers disappeared altogether as more and more land was enclosed; and those who could not find work as agricultural labourers, or in occupations other than farming, became additional burdens on an increasing poor rate. 'I regard these small occupiers as a set of very miserable men,' wrote Arthur Young, prolific author of books on agriculture. 'They fare extremely hard, work without intermission like a horse . . . and practise every lesson of diligence and frugality without being able to soften their present lot.'[32] The Rev. John Howlett agreed with him:

The small farmer is forced to be laborious to an extreme degree; he works harder and fares harder than the common labourer; and yet with all his labour and with all his fatiguing incessant exertions, seldom can he at all improve his condition or even with any degree of regularity pay his rent and preserve his present situation. He is confined to perpetual drudgery, which is the source of profound ignorance, the parent of obstinacy and blind perseverance in old modes and old practices, however absurd and pernicious.[33]

Tenant farmers, who by the end of the century constituted three-quarters of all farmers in England, fared much better, provided their holdings were sufficiently substantial. Indeed, Arthur Young, who had himself failed dismally as a farmer of 300 acres in Essex, thought that the most successful of them made themselves ridiculous by aping the style of gentlemen, by buying pianofortes for their parlours and post-chaises for driving their wives to assembly rooms, by putting their servants into livery, sending their daughters to expensive boarding schools and their sons to university 'to be made parsons'.

There was no doubt that good money could be made from farming by those who took advantage of the new methods which were revolutionizing the science of agriculture. There were still backward areas. In the north Young thought it 'extremely melancholy' to view such tracts of land as were 'indisputably capable of yielding many beneficial crops' lying totally waste. But elsewhere, despite the hardships inflicted by enclosures, the growth of commercial farming was transforming the appearance of a countryside which Smollett described as 'smiling with cultivation'. 'I admit I was often amazed,' wrote a German visitor on a return to England at the beginning of the nineteenth century, 'to see great uncultivated areas made productive as though through magic and transformed into fine, corn-bearing fields.'[34]

'Move your eyes which side you will,' Arthur Young confirmed, 'you will behold nothing but great riches and yet greater resources.' In the county of Norfolk, half of which in the past had yielded 'nothing but sheep feed', 'those very tracts of land [were now] covered with fine barley and rye as any in the world and great quantities of wheat besides'.[35] Following the example of such agricultural innovators as 'Turnip' Townshend of Raynham, Norfolk, and the Walpoles of Houghton, Norfolk, of Thomas Coke of Holkham, of Jethro Tull, the Berkshire farmer who invented a drill for planting seeds, and of Richard Bradley, author of several books on husbandry and gardening, farmers now experimented with crop rotation and forage crops, and with new farm layouts. They made better use of the soil, improved fine English breeds, like Herefordshire cattle and Southdown sheep, as well as horses, and introduced to each other new tools and ploughs and even machinery.

Steam threshing machinery began to come into general use in several counties in the first half of the nineteenth century. By 1800 every two of the three or so million people engaged in agriculture were feeding five others, whereas they were providing food for scarcely more than three other people a century before.

Yet if farmers were generally prospering, and if tenants on such competently run estates as that of the Earl of Leicester could well afford to pay their higher rents, there were hundreds of thousands of people living in the country – where nearly 80 per cent of England's 9 million population still lived at the end of the eighteenth century – whose existence remained one of pitiable poverty.

# 29 · *Country Houses and Gardens*

Towards the end of the eighteenth century the formality and orderliness, which had been so apparent in the design and planning of country houses since the days of Inigo Jones, were beginning to be relaxed. Inigo Jones, who had designed Wilton for the Earl of Pembroke, and Roger Pratt who had built Coleshill in Berkshire for his cousin, Sir George Pratt, were both strongly influenced by Continental models; so were the architects of numerous other seventeenth-century country houses built or reconstructed all over England from Raynham Hall in Norfolk, to Ragley Hall in Warwickshire and Petworth in Sussex.

By the time Chatsworth in Derbyshire was completed in 1707 for the Duke of Devonshire, several revolutionary changes had occurred in the interiors of most large country houses. Servants no longer ate in the hall but had their own servants' hall, perhaps in the basement, the upper servants in some houses having their meals separately from the lower in the steward's parlour. The first-floor great chamber was becoming obsolete, while, on the ground floor, saloons were taking the place of parlours. Backstairs had been introduced; and dressing rooms for both husbands and wives had appeared so that, as Roger North put it, 'at rising each may retire and have [separate] accommodation complete'.[1] Indeed, in many houses, French fashion was followed, and husband and wife had separate bedrooms as well as dressing-rooms.[2]

After Vanbrugh – architect of Blenheim and Castle Howard – and the Baroque went out of fashion at the beginning of the eighteenth century, Palladianism came in.

To begin with [the historian of the country house, Mark Girouard, has written], Palladianism did not mean a change of plan in the country-house world, it only meant a change of uniform. The reign of the saloon between apartments went on – but now the ceremonial centre could be neatly expressed in terms of a temple, with a portico at one or both ends . . . The apartments could be arranged to produce houses with wings extended . . . or with . . . apartments turned back along either side of the hall and saloon to produce a compact, approximately square plan. The type with wings extended was much used for houses at the centre of great estates where show was considered essential. The results were the immensely extended façades of houses like Stowe, Wanstead or Wentworth Woodhouse. The wings-folded arrangement worked very well for houses built for people of moderate fortunes but sophisticated tastes, or for the subsidiary and more private residences of the great.[3]

Most of these houses had libraries, something which had not been common in the past when a man who owned more than 1000 books, as Lord Burghley did, was a rarity. The Countess of Shrewsbury had only six books at Hardwick and these she kept in her bedchamber. Libraries were more often to be found in country houses in the later seventeenth-century; but they were generally used for study and, like cabinets of curiosities, were not intended for communal living. In the eighteenth century, however, they became rooms of entertainment and, as well as books, often specially bound and stamped with the family crest, games and folders of prints were kept in them, sometimes also pictures, not just portraits which had filled the galleries of earlier houses but still lifes and landscapes. As they became rooms of entertainment, so they tended to grow in size; and as country gentlemen bought more pictures and sculpture, many of them acquired on the Grand Tour, so more space had to be provided for the display of these too. Architects had to bear these requirements in mind.

While libraries were becoming rooms of communal entertainment, dining-rooms were beginning to be used for no other purpose than for eating; and the large dining-table became a permanent piece of furniture in them, whereas formerly it was more general to have smaller folding tables which were carried into the room by servants who placed chairs around them as required. The food was brought to the table, course by course, by footmen who took the guests' plates to the dishes to be served. They also took their glasses to the sideboard where the butler presided over the wine.

Breakfast was served at about half past nine or ten, and usually consisted of tea or chocolate and hot buttered bread, perhaps with cheese, or toast. The German pastor, Carl Philip Moritz, was delighted by toast, an English invention. 'There is a way of roasting slices of buttered bread before the fire which is incomparable,' he wrote. 'One slice after another is taken and held to the fire with a fork till the butter soaks through the whole pile of slices. This is called *toast*.'[4] Peter Kalm, a young Swedish scientist, added that the English invented toast because their houses were so cold that to harden the bread was the only means of spreading butter.[5]

Dinner was served at about four or five and supper at ten, though by the early nineteenth century the hour of dinner had moved on to nearer seven o'clock, and luncheon was served as an additional meal in the middle of the day. After the dessert had been served at dinner the ladies retired to the drawing-room for tea or coffee, while the men remained drinking in the dining-room, sometimes for hours.[6]

In simpler homes dinner was still served in the middle of the day, although the provincial family with pretensions might sit down at two or three o'clock, like the mercer of Boswell's acquaintance who had settled in Durham and wished to impress the people there with what he supposed to be the fashionable ways of the capital. The Rector of Aston near Birmingham also had dinner at three. When Catherine Hutton went to dinner with him in 1779 the meal ended at five when the ladies went to the drawing-room for an hour, and at about six they ordered tea and asked the gentlemen to come to join them.[7]

In London this summons would probably have resulted in the gentlemen going upstairs, for town houses tended to be built to a common design, often being constructed by builders without the help of architects and with panelling and staircases following stock patterns. The kitchen was in the basement, the dining-room and parlour on the ground floor, the drawing-room on the floor above, and the bedrooms on the floor above that.

The relaxation of formality which began towards the end of the eighteenth century was commented upon by several foreign observers. 'Formality counts for nothing,' wrote the duc de La Rochefoucauld after his visit to England in 1784,

> and for the greatest part of the time one pays no attention to it. Thus, judged by French standards, the English, and especially the women, seem lacking in polite behaviour. All the young people whom I have met in society in Bury [St Edmunds] give the impression of being what we should call badly brought up: they hum under their breath, they whistle, they sit down in a large armchair and put their feet on another, they sit on any table in the room and do a thousand other things which would be ridiculous in France, but are done quite naturally in England.[8]

Two years before, Carl Moritz had commented upon the casual way in which Members of Parliament entered the Commons: 'They even come into the House in their great coats and with boots and spurs. It is not at all uncommon to see a member lying stretched out on one of the benches, while others are debating. Some crack nuts, others eat oranges. There is no end to their going in and out.'[9]

This growing informality was reflected in the abandonment of the practice of ladies and gentlemen sitting in constraining circles of chairs to talk to each other for the freedom of individual groups entertaining themselves in different ways. It was also reflected in the design of new houses. It was no longer considered essential to maintain the symmetry of a house by balancing a servants' wing with another wing on the opposite side of the main block. It was felt to be a much happier arrangement if the principal rooms of the house, not least the new breakfast-room which was also used as a morning sitting-room, could not only overlook vistas, parks and gardens but, by means of low-silled or French windows, actually open out into the garden as in the irregular houses designed by John Nash in association with Humphry Repton of which the *cottage orné* built for the Prince of Wales in Windsor Park, and later to be known as The Royal Lodge, was a charming example.[10]

The ideal garden was now considered to 'bee *irregular*' in the words of Henry Wotton, a former British ambassador in Venice, rather than formal and geometrically planned as in the Tudor fashion. The new style had been introduced slowly. In the seventeenth century the model landscape gardens had been French in style, with the axial and radial avenues, the parterres, canals and statuary, to be seen at Versailles. In the reign of William and Mary this French style had been slightly modified by Dutch influences, particularly by the more extensive use of clipped evergreens and of leaden statues. But it was not until the beginning of the eighteenth century that a strong reaction set in against French formality in landscape gardening which was now seen as a reflection of authoritarianism in politics and the arts.[11] Joseph Addison, who argued that the garden should be freed from the constraints and restrictions that the French had imposed upon it, wrote in *The Spectator* in 1712:

> I look upon the Pleasure which we take in a Garden, as one of the most innocent Delights in humane Life. A Garden was the Habitation of our first Parents before the Fall. It is naturally apt to fill the Mind with Calmness and Tranquility, and to lay all its turbulent Passions at Rest. It gives us a great Insight into the Contrivance and Wisdom of Providence, and suggests innumerable Subjects for Meditation. I cannot but think the very Complacency and Satisfaction which a Man takes in these Works of Nature, to be a laudable, if not virtuous Habit of Mind.[12]

The English garden, it was felt, should, as Alexander Pope said, 'call in the country'. It should, according to Stephen Switzer, the influential author of

*The Nobleman, Gentleman and Gardener's Recreation* (1715), allow
'Beauties of Nature' to remain 'uncorrupted by Art': 'All the adjacent
Country [should] be laid open to View, and the Eye should not be bounded
with High Walls, Woods misplac'd and several Obstructions.' It should
celebrate the rural life as Virgil and Horace had done; it should assume the
forms suggested by the 'best of landskip painters', examples of whose work
William Kent, painter and architect as well as landscape gardener, went to
Italy to collect. By making use of the ha-ha it was possible to suggest that 'the
adjacent Country was all a Garden', the garden itself comprising undulating
expanses of grass, sinuous walks and streams, classical and Gothic temples
and follies, or, where possible, genuine ruins. Calling upon such professional
architects and designers as Vanbrugh, Bridgeman, Gibbs and Kent, landowners set about remodelling their grounds; and, though the English garden
was less expensive to lay out and to maintain than the French, several of them
were ruined by their expenditure, while the results of their labours were
often derided:

> Clipt hedges, avenues, regular platforms, strait canals have been for some
> time very properly exploded [so *The World* suggested to its readers in
> 1753]. There is not a citizen who does not take more pains to torture his
> acre and half into irregularities, than he formerly would have employed to
> make it as formal as his cravat. Kent, the friend of nature, was the Calvin of
> this reformation, but like the other champion of truth, after having routed
> tinsel and trumpery, with the true zeal of a founder of a sect he pushed his
> discipline to the deformity of holiness: not content with banishing sym-
> metry and regularity, he imitated nature even in her blemishes, and
> planted dead trees and mole-hills, in opposition to parterres and
> quincunxes.[13]

Yet the extravagant and tireless gardener was not in the least deterred.
'Every Man now, be his fortune what it Will,' the publication, *Common
Sense*, declared in 1739, 'is to be *doing something* at his Place, as the
fashionable Phrase is; and you hardly meet with any Body, who, after the
first Compliments, does not inform you, that he is *in Mortar* and *moving* of
Earth; the modest terms for Building and Gardening.'[14]

Modest cost was rarely possible when executing the designs suggested by
Lancelot Brown, once kitchen-gardener at Stowe, who acquired his nick-
name, 'Capability', from his habit of observing in his amiable way when
looking over his clients' rolling acres that he saw 'great capability of improvement here'. Brown, who acquired a large fortune from his practice, endeavoured to emphasize the essential features of a site and improved them
where he could by artificial or enlarged pieces of water, carefully planted
trees, accentuated mounds and hollows in which cattle grazed, enhancing the

pleasures of the view. There were those who considered his work insipid. Among them were William Chambers who said that Brown's gardens differed 'very little from common fields, so closely is common nature copied in most of them'. Chambers himself was a devotee of orientalism which he had introduced to the royal gardens at Kew where his Chinese pagoda and other features, had, in his own opinion, transformed a 'Desart into an Eden'.[15]

Humphry Repton had a higher regard for Brown but considered that his numerous imitators, his 'illiterate followers', had betrayed his achievement. Whereas Brown had allowed the lawns to approach as close to the house as the drawing-room windows, Repton reintroduced terraces and flowerbeds, shrubberies and gravelled walks.[16] His work for an acquaintance of James Rushworth in Jane Austen's *Mansfield Park* makes Rushworth so envious that he is determined to make similar improvements to his own property:

'I wish you could see Compton,' said he, 'it is the most complete thing! I never saw a place so altered in my life. I told Smith I did not know where I was. The approach now is one of the finest things in the country; you see the house in the most surprising manner. I declare when I got back to Sotherton yesterday, it looked like a prison – quite a dismal old prison.'

'Oh, for shame!' cried Mrs. Norris. 'A prison, indeed! Sotherton Court is the noblest old place in the world.'

'It wants improvement, ma'am, beyond anything. I never saw a place that wanted so much improvement in my life; and it is so forlorn, that I do not know what can be done with it.'. . .

'Your best friend upon such an occasion,' said Miss Bertram calmly, 'would be Mr. Repton, I imagine.'

'That is what I was thinking of. As he has done so well by Smith, I think I had better have him at once. His terms are five guineas a day.'

'Well, and if they were ten,' cried Mrs. Norris, 'I am sure you need not regard it. The expense need not be any impediment. If I were you, I should not think of the expense, I would have everything done in the best style, and made as nice as possible. Such a place as Sotherton Court deserves everything that taste and money can do. You have space to work upon there, and grounds that will well reward you. For my own part, if I had anything within the fiftieth part of the size of Sotherton, I should be always planting and improving, for naturally I am excessively fond of it . . .'

After a short interruption Mr. Rushworth began again. 'Smith's place is the admiration of all the country; and it was a mere nothing before Repton took it in hand. I think I shall have Repton.'[17]

\*

William Shenstone, creator of the celebrated garden at the Leasowe's, Worcestershire, expressed in 1764 some 'Unconnected thoughts on Gardening' which found general approval:

Gardening may be divided into three species – kitchen gardening – parterre-gardening – and landskip, or picturesque gardening: which latter consists in pleasing the imagination by scenes of grandeur, beauty, or variety. Convenience merely has no share here, any farther than as it pleases the imagination . . .

A ruin may . . . afford that pleasing melancholy which proceeds from a reflexion on decayed magnificence . . . A rural scene to me is never perfect without the addition of some kind of building.

Landskip should contain variety enough to form a picture upon canvas; and this is no bad test, as I think the landskip painter is the gardener's best designer . . .

The eye should always look rather down upon water . . . Water should ever appear as an irregular shape or winding stream. Islands give beauty . . .

The side-trees in vistas should be so circumstanced as to afford a probability that they grew by nature . . .

Hedges, appearing as such, are universally bad. They discover art in nature's province. Trees in hedges partake of their artificiality. There is no more sudden, and obvious improvement, than an hedge removed, and the trees remaining; yet not in such manner as to mark out the former hedge.[18]

The garden at Grandison Hall as described by Samuel Richardson was one of which Shenstone would have largely approved and most country gentlemen in the middle of the century would have felt proud:

The park itself is remarkable for its prospects, lawns, and rich-appearing clumps of trees of large growth.

The gardens, vineyard, &c. are beautifully laid out. The orangery is flourishing; every-thing indeed is, that belongs to Sir Charles Grandison. Alcoves, little temples, seats are erected at different points of view; the orchard lawne and grass-walks, have sheep for gardeners; and the whole being bounded only by sunk fences, the eye is carried to views that have no bounds.

The orchard, which takes up near three acres of ground, is planted in a peculiar taste. A neat stone bridge in the centre of it, is thrown over the river: It is planted in a natural slope; the higher fruit-trees, as pears, in a semicircular row, first; apples at further distances next; cherries, plumbs, standard apricots, &c. all which in the season of blossoming, one row gradually lower than another, must make a charming variety of blooming sweets to the eye, from the top of the rustic villa, which commands the whole.

The outside of this orchard, next the north, is planted with three rows of trees, at proper distances from each other; one of pines; one of cedars; one of Scotch firs, in the like semicircular order; which at the same time that they afford a perpetual verdure to the eye, and shady walks in the summer, defend the orchard from the cold and blighting winds.[19]

The countryside beyond the orchard and garden was more valued than it had been in the past when 'many landowners treated their visits to their country seats like a visit to the dentist. It was something which had to be done, but the quicker it was over the better. They found the remoteness of the country acutely painful after the gay social life in London.'[20] Now, improved roads and carriages had made the countryside less remote, while farming occupied more of a gentleman's time, and country pursuits were becoming more pleasurable and, often, more exciting.

# 30 · *Interiors*

The Yorkshire home of Dr Daniel Dove, so Robert Southey related, consisted of seven rooms including the dairy and cellar:

As you entered the kitchen there was on the right one of those open chimneys which afford more comfort in a winter's evening than the finest register stove; in front of the chimney stood a wooden bee-hive chair, and on each side was a long oak seat with a back to it, the seats serving as chests in which the oaten bread was kept. They were of the darkest brown and well polished by constant use. On the back of each were the same initials as those over the door, with the date 1610. The great oak Table, and the chest in the best kitchen which held the house linen, bore the same date. The chimney was well hung with bacon, the rack which covered half the ceiling bore equal marks of plenty; mutton hams were suspended from other parts of the ceiling; and there was an odour of cheese from the adjoining dairy, which the turf fire, though perpetual as that of the Magi, or of the Vestal Virgins, did not over-power. A few pewter dishes were ranged above the trenches, opposite the door, on a conspicuous shelf. The other treasures of the family were in an open triangular cupboard, fixed in one of the corners of the best kitchen, half-way from the floor, and touching the ceiling. They consisted of a silver saucepan, a silver goblet and four apostle spoons. Here also King Charles's Golden Rules were pasted against the wall, and a large print of Daniel in the Lion's Den . . . Six black chairs were arranged against the wall, where they were seldom disturbed from their array. They had been purchased by Daniel the grandfather, upon his marriage, and were the most costly purchase that had ever been made in the family; for the goblet was a legacy.[1]

Southey was writing in the nineteenth century, but the doctor's room, like thousands of others like it, had changed little in appearance in over a hundred years. The interiors of more modish professional men and the lesser, though fashionable, gentry, however, had been transformed in the course of the eighteenth century. Their houses, preferably built on rising ground commanded a view – sites which improved methods of water supply now made more practicable – their rooms were spacious, high-ceilinged and well lit by large sash windows. Under the influence of Robert and James Adam, the Scottish architects, panelling began to disappear in the larger houses from the 1770s. But before that, as Isaac Ware wrote in his *A Complete Body of Architecture* of 1756, it was considered ideal for the reception rooms of a house. For the hall 'nothing is so well as stucco,' Ware continued, 'and for the apartment of a lady, hangings . . . this last comprehending paper, silk, tapestry and every other decoration of this kind'.[2] Silk damask was widely used as a wall covering, so, increasingly, was paper, Chinese hand-painted wallpapers being particularly popular with those who could afford them or who had generous friends serving in embassies or working as merchants in the East. Over 2 million yards of wallpaper of various kinds were sold in 1785 compared with less than 200,000 yards in 1713.[3] Prints were also pasted on walls, a form of decoration favoured by Horace Walpole and later by the Duke of Wellington. And when the Adam style came into vogue, semicircular alcoves at one end of a room and niches at intervals became common, as well as ceilings divided into compartments containing, amid festoons and scrolls, pateras and rosettes, 'cheese cakes and raspberry tarts' as they were described by one of those contemporary critics who thought the taste too showy.[4] Adam motifs could also be bought ready-made and stuck on to walls, ceilings and chimney-breasts as fancy dictated.

But these motifs, so house-owners were advised, must not distract attention from the pictures, from the works of Italian masters or those of English masters now also much admired, Hogarth and Gainsborough, Reynolds and Devis, Romney and Lawrence. In more modest households the prices demanded by such fashionable artists could not be afforded – Reynolds who regularly charged £200 for a 'whole length' was paid more than this for his Marlborough group and, so Walpole said, for his group of the Ladies Waldegrave – but there would be oil paintings by lesser-known names, a few watercolours, Cotmans perhaps, or, at least, some family portraits painted by those journeyman artists who travelled about and were prepared to capture a perfectly respectable likeness for £15 or less.

In cabinets were displays of Continental porcelain, of Chelsea, Bow and Derby, or Worcester and Spode, and of the finer pieces from Wedgwood's works which supplied pottery for all classes, 'Ornamental' and 'Useful'. On the floors were Axminster and Wilton carpets; and arranged upon them, or upon the polished floors between their edges and the skirting boards, were screens and sofas, chairs and grandfather clocks in lacquer-work cases and those pieces of furniture made to the designs recommended by Chippendale, Hepplewhite and Sheraton.

Thomas Chippendale's book of furniture designs, *The Gentleman and Cabinet Maker's Director*, first appeared in 1754. Almost every type of domestic furniture was illustrated in it, and the designs, many of them based on models in earlier English and Continental pattern books, were copied all over England as well as used for pieces made in Chippendale's own workshop in St Martin's Lane, London. George Hepplewhite's *The Cabinet Maker and Upholsterer's Guide* was published in 1788. It contained about 300 designs and was widely used as a trade catalogue by country craftsmen. Thomas Sheraton's *Cabinet-Maker and Upholsterer's Drawing Book* was issued in parts between 1711 and 1794 and was intended to bring to the notice of the trade the most up-to-date designs of the late eighteenth century.[5]

While a provincial cabinet-maker might construct an excellent mahogany or walnut table to a Chippendale or Hepplewhite design, the services of a joiner, a draper and an upholsterer had each to be called upon for the construction of a custom-made bed or comfortable chair; and the difficulties involved in getting such craftsmen to work together satisfactorily were often considerable. So were the problems encountered when building or repair work was to be done. When Henry Purefoy, the unmarried owner of an estate at Shalstone in Buckinghamshire, wanted to build a new servants' hall, he was beset with frustration. The first stone-mason he approached proved slow and forgetful, the next was scarcely an improvement. 'This is the third day you have been from my work,' Purefoy complained to him in September 1738, 'I think you are a very unworthy man to neglect it so this fine weather.' At length, after Purefoy had threatened to employ someone else, a wall high enough to take a floor was finished; but then there was trouble in getting a carpenter to come at the right time to lay it. No sooner was this work finished than there were further annoyances over fireplaces. Having decided to have one new fashionable fireplace 'in handsome red and white marble' and an existing fireplace fitted with a black marble slab, Purefoy ordered the materials from a stonecutter in London. After a delay of three months the marble arrived at Shalstone; but it was not only the wrong size but also cracked and had to have 'bits of something put into it artificially'.

Having settled the stonecutter's bill for £12 17s, Purefoy endured a further delay of two months before he could find a mason to fit the fireplace, and, when he did find one, the man fixed it so badly that fires could not be lit in it. As the room was so cold and unusable, Purefoy decided to have it painted and the floor planed, while waiting – and waiting in vain – for the mason to come back to put the fireplace in properly. This took four months, after which another mason had to be found. But by now it had been discovered that the marble slab sent from London for the other fireplace was a fake: its surface had cracked, revealing some inferior stone beneath. A replacement did not arrive from the stonecutter until a further three months had passed; and this, so friends assured Purefoy, was no better than the first one sent and would soon go the same way. Another replacement arrived. This, too, was unacceptable, being badly cracked and bound together with iron. The parlour was still unusable in June 1741 when the distressing correspondence breaks off.[6]

Although still sparsely furnished by later standards, there were far more pieces in the drawing-rooms of houses like Purefoy's than there had been at any time in previous centuries; and on winter evenings the gloom that had once shrouded the furniture was now dispelled by candles brightly burning in chandeliers and by sconces whose light was brilliantly reflected by looking-glasses in gilded frames. In cold weather, however, the house was likely to be as cold as it ever had been. In some houses braziers and portable stoves were used; and at Holkham, so Matthew Brettingham said, there was a 'Furnace beneath the Floor of the Hall, for the convenience of warming it; which it does by means of Brick Flues, that have their Funnels for the conveyance of Smoke carried up in the lateral walls'.[7] This form of central heating, though, was very unusual, and most houses had no other means of warming them than open fires, so that unless there was a fire in every fireplace some rooms were necessarily icy. When Mrs Lybbe Powys paid a visit to old Buckingham House in 1767, in 'the coldest weather possible', she was 'amazed to find so large a house so warm and attributed the phenomenon to fires being kept the whole day, even in closets'.[8]

Sanitation had also improved but little. Although not uncommon in France, bathrooms such as those described by Celia Fiennes at Chatsworth and in 1773 by Matthew Brettingham at Holkham were rarely to be found in English houses, apart from those of the richest noblemen such as the Duke of Bedford. Foreigners all agreed that English houses were clean. The Frenchman, César de Saussure, observed that not a week went by 'but well-kept houses [were] washed twice in the seven days, and that from top to bottom; and even every morning most kitchens, staircase, and entrance [were] scrubbed. All furniture, and especially all kitchen utensils [were] kept with the greatest cleanliness.'[9] Half a century later another Frenchman confirmed that in cleanliness the English seemed 'to vie with the Hollanders. The plate, hearthstones, moveables, apartments, doors, stairs, the very street doors, their locks and the large brass knockers, are every day washed, scowered or rubbed.'[10] And Peter Kalm, the Swedish scientist, discovered that English women generally had 'the character of keeping floors, steps and such things very clean'.[11]

Yet, while de Saussure believed that English men and women washed their hands, arms, faces and necks every day 'in winter as well as in summer', this was as far as most of them went and many did not trouble themselves even as much as that. Occasionally a bath might be taken in a tub of hot water; but many of the social superiors of Thomas Turner, the mid-eighteenth-century Sussex grocer, agreed with him that once a year was often enough for a bath. The smoke and soot of London made it necessary for Boswell to change his linen every day; but he would not have done so otherwise. He enjoyed living rough on his Grand Tour and in Germany exulted in not having taken his clothes off in a week. Samuel Johnson was far from alone in having 'no relish' for clean linen, while his upper-class friend, Topham Beauclerk, seemed to take a perverse pleasure in shaking the bugs out of his wig in the presence of ladies. Some of his female contemporaries were no cleaner than he was himself. When someone commented to Lady Mary Wortley Montagu on the dirtiness of her hands, she replied, 'If you call that dirty, you should see my feet!' At Chelsea, old pensioners cheerfully gambled on races between the lice extracted from beneath their coats.

In 1775 Alexander Cumming, a Scottish mathematician who had a watchmaker's business in Bond Street, took out a patent for a water-closet; and in 1778 Joseph Bramah, a cabinet-maker from Yorkshire, invented an improved model which, with various modifications, remained in use for most of the nineteenth century. But very few water-closets were yet installed and those that were, without adequate pans and traps, were unsatisfactory and smelly. Few men, perhaps, would now take Pepys's way out and relieve themselves in a fireplace, and few women were likely to be discovered, as Lady Sandwich was, 'doing something upon the pot' in a dining-room; but chamber pots were commonly placed in the drawers of sideboards so that gentlemen need not leave the table after dinner. And Hogarth thought nothing of pulling down his breeches in a churchyard and, when his friends tickled his bare bottom with a bunch of thistles, he merely went off to squat down by the church door.

Modest homes, like those of the well-to-do, were much more adequately furnished than they had been in the past, even if the most cherished pieces were oak tables, chests and settles which had been passed down in the family from generation to generation and which would long since have been thrown out of smarter houses. Many middle-class houses contained a large number of attractive ornaments, collecting being now a widespread and eclectic pursuit. Even the small houses of artisans were likely to contain several pictures and looking-glasses as well as curtains, chests of drawers, tables and beds complete with bolsters, pillows and bedspreads, sheets and blankets. The inventory of a Colchester weaver, who was taken to the workhouse in

1744, includes all these items and, in addition, numerous kitchen utensils, some of copper, candlesticks and bellows, glass dishes, pewter measures, smoothing irons, four teapots, sixteen cups and saucers, sixteen plates, two silver spoons, two chamber pots and a bird-cage.[12]

In the country it was often difficult to find a vacant cottage. In many places custom still allowed a man to build on village waste land, but he was traditionally obliged to complete the dwelling in one night; and waste lands were, in any case, being rapidly encroached upon by enclosure. Also, one of the duties upon parish constables was to ensure that no cottages were built without proper authority.[13]

There were areas, particularly in the north, where hovels still abounded; but in most villages by the end of the eighteenth century the cottages, though primitive and frequently crowded, were not as uncomfortable as neglect and poverty later made them. They certainly compared very favourably with the dreadful shacks of the peasants which Arthur Young described in his *Travels in France*. In 1788 Gilbert White maintained that in his village in Hampshire all the mud cottages had disappeared and even the poorest people now lived in brick or stone cottages which had upstairs bedrooms and glass in the windows.[14] To buy a four-bedroomed house cost no more than £150.

In London and the industrial centres, however, housing conditions were much worse. The rows of back-to-back hovels in the north and the tenement slums of London, where the occupiers of a few squalid rooms were asked to pay 2s 6d a week, and by the end of the century more than this, were already a disgrace to humanity.

# 31 · *Manners and Dress*

It was generally agreed by foreign visitors that the manners of Englishmen were slowly improving. They were still violently xenophobic, to be sure. César de Saussure said that it was 'almost dangerous for a well-dressed foreigner to walk the streets of London, for he ran a great risk of being insulted by the vulgar populace, the most cursed brood in existence. He is sure of not only being jeered at and bespattered with mud, but as likely as not dead dogs and cats will be thrown at him.'[1] The English were also inveterate swearers. Carl Moritz thought that a stranger in London might well suppose that everyone who lived there was called 'Damme', although a character in Sheridan's *The Rivals*, which was first performed in 1775, observes that the damms have had their day.[2] The people were often still cruel to animals, but perhaps not more so than in other countries; and towards the end of his life Hogarth believed that this cruelty was abating. He had produced his *Four Stages of Cruelty* 'in hopes of preventing in some degree that cruel treatment of poor animals which makes the streets of London more disagreeable to the human mind than anything whatever', and he congratulated himself that these prints, of which he was more proud than any of his other works, had helped to check the once so prevalent spirit of barbarity.[3] The English still made money out of a savage trade in slaves; but protests against the traffic were growing ever louder and it was abolished by Act of Parliament in 1807.

English people were gradually becoming politer as well as more humane. There was less spitting in the streets, less overt drunkenness and rampant whoring. There was also less eating with the fingers. And the advent of cheap cotton made clothes easier to wash and led to the far wider use of clean sheets and table napkins.[4] From about 1770, so Joseph Farington, the painter, wrote:

A change in the manners and the habits of the people of this country was beginning to take place. Public taste was improving. The coarse familiarity so common in personal intercourse was laid aside, and respectful attention and civility in address gradually gave a new and better aspect to society. The profane habit of using oaths in conversation no longer offended the ear, and bacchanalian intemperance at the dinner-table was succeeded by rational cheerfulness and sober forbearance.[5]

Vulgar words in common use at the beginning of the century were no longer heard in respectable society. The word 'respectability' itself, in the sense of 'the state, quality or condition of being respectable in point of character or social standing', first came into use in 1785. 'Prudishness' had entered the language as early as 1704, and was a word increasingly required. Codpiece Row in London was renamed Coppice Row; words like 'belly' and 'bitch' were banned from genteel tongues; popular novels were roundly condemned in such intemperate words as those used in 1793 in the *Evangelical Magazine* which castigated them as being in general 'instruments of abomination. A fond attachment to them is an irrefragable evidence of a mind contaminated, and totally unfitted for the serious pursuits of study or the delightful exercises and enjoyments of religion.'[6]

Thomas Bowdler, a physician from an ancient Shropshire family – from whose *Family Shakespeare* all words and expressions which could not 'with propriety be read aloud in a family' were deleted – was working when he died on a purified version of Gibbon's *Decline and Fall of the Roman Empire* 'with the careful omissions of all passages of an irreligious or immoral tendency'.[7]

Sensuality came to be the antonym of respectability [so Dr Porter has written]. By association, cleanliness became a cardinal virtue. For Wesley it was next to godliness, yet Hannah More rated it a higher priority, at least for the poor: 'The necessity of going to church in procession with us on the anniversary, raises an honest ambition to get something decent to wear, and the churches on Sunday are now filled with very cleanlooking women.' All in all 'Victorianism' was already casting its long shadows in the age of Victoria's grandparents. 'By the beginning of the nineteenth century,' wrote G. M. Young, 'virtue was advancing on a broad, invincible front.'[8]

This was reflected in fashions in clothes which had become far less extreme and ostentatious, and in some cases almost austere as a reflection of their wearers' approval of the styles of revolutionary France. Writing of what he called the 'era of Jacobinism' in London in 1793–4, Sir Nathaniel Wraxall observed:

It was then that pantaloons, cropped hair, and shoestrings, as well as the total abolition of buckles and ruffles, together with the disuse of hair powder, characterised the men; while the ladies having cut off those tresses which had done so much execution, exhibited heads rounded *à la victime et à la guillotine*, as if ready for the stroke of the axe.[9]

A few years earlier Carl Moritz had observed that the most usual dress in summer was 'a short waistcoat, black breeches, white silk stockings and a frock, generally of a very dark blue cloth which looks like black'. The English, he added, seemed in general to prefer dark colours.[10]

Earlier in the century young men had paraded in the most extreme Italian and French styles with glittering gold and silver buttons on their coats and diamond buckles on their shoes, with embroidered waistcoats open to reveal shirts of fine linen and the lace ends of well-ironed ties, with ruffles at the wrist, silk handkerchiefs dangling from huge pockets, gold fobs loaded with seals jingling by their stockinged legs, diamond-hilted swords swinging at the waist. They wore flamboyantly cocked hats and in cold weather often held their hands in muffs or carried canes with long tassels in their gloved hands. One such Macaroni appeared at an assembly in a coat of shot-silk, a pink satin waistcoat, breeches covered with silk net, white stockings with pink clocks, and pink satin shoes with large pearl buckles. His hair was dressed to a remarkable height and stuck full of pearl pins.[11] Samuel Johnson commented to Boswell, 'Fine clothes are good only as they supply the want of other means of securing respect.'[12] Yet even he, who was usually dressed untidily in sombre brown, astonished the audience at Drury Lane where his tragedy, *Mahomet and Irene*, was performed, by walking into one of the side boxes in a brilliant scarlet waistcoat, richly embroidered with gold lace and a gold laced hat. Later he spent no less than £30 on a new suit and Bourgeois wig to wear in Paris.

The variety of wigs that came in and went out of fashion was extraordinary. There were story wigs and bob wigs, busby wigs and scratch wigs, bag wigs, brown George wigs, riding wigs, nightcap wigs, periwigs, tie wigs, queue wigs, dark majors, grizzle majors, grizzle ties and several more. Many were extremely expensive and were in constant danger of being snatched from the head in busy streets by thieves who cut holes in the backs of hackney coaches or, disguising themselves as bakers, carried 'sharp boys' in big bread-baskets on their shoulders. They were carefully tended by peruquiers who, before powdering them, dressed them with pomatum to keep the curls in place. Their owners carried tortoise-shell wig-combs about with them in their pockets. Generously powdered, they were a minor hazard in the streets, particularly on windy days. In his poem, *Trivia*, John Gay warned his readers:

> You sometimes meet a Fop of nicest Tread
> Whose mantling Peruke veils his empty Head . . .
> Him, like the Miller, pass with Caution by
> Lest from his Shoulders Clouds of powder fly.

In the 1760s it became fashionable for gentlemen to wear their own hair, tied perhaps at the back with a ribbon as General Wolfe had done and George, Prince of Wales, was for a short time to do. But wigs were still to be seen until the 1790s; and, even after they had been generally abandoned, gentlemen continued to powder their hair. Walter Savage Landor, who entered Trinity College, Oxford, in 1793, the year of the execution of Louis XVI, was perhaps the first undergraduate to give up hair-powder. When he insisted on wearing his 'plain hair and queue tied with black ribbon', his tutor warned him: 'Take care. They will stone you for a republican.'[13] The practice of powdering hair stopped, however, soon after 1795 when Pitt imposed a heavy tax upon hair-powder. Attempts were made to find suitable alternatives: one of the Duke of Atholl's sons took out a patent for the extraction of starch from horse-chestnuts; but no satisfactory substitutes could be found and the use of hair-powder died out with the century.

Women, too, used powder and pomatum. Mary Frampton recalled dressing her sister's hair in 1780:

> At that time everybody wore powder and pomatum; a large triangular thing called a cushion to which the hair was frizzed up with three or four enormous curls on each side; the higher the pyramid of hair, gauze, feathers and other ornaments was carried the more fashionable it was thought, and such was the labour employed to rear the fabric that night caps were made in proportion to it and covered over the hair, immensely long black pins, double and single, powder and pomatum and all, ready for the next day.[14]

High headgear for women was by then, however, on the verge of going out of fashion. Earlier the hair had been piled up to a startling height.

> There is not so variable a thing in nature as a lady's headdress [Addison had written]. Within my own memory I have known it rise and fall within thirty degrees. About ten years ago it shot up to a very great height, insomuch as the female part of our species were much taller than the men. The women were of such enormous stature that we appeared as grasshoppers before them . . . I remember several ladies, who were once very near seven feet high, that at present want some inches of five.[15]

The hair was not merely piled up, it was decorated with ribbons, blossoms, fruit, ostrich feathers and even the flowers of the scarlet runner bean. In April 1777 Hannah More met some young ladies who had on their heads 'an acre and half of shrubbery, besides slopes, grass-plats, tulip beds, clumps of peonies, kitchen gardens and greenhouses'.[16] It is said that Garrick helped to abolish the fashion by appearing in the character of Sir John Bute dressed in female attire with his cap decorated with a profusion of every kind of vegetable, a huge carrot hanging below each ear.[17] Certainly, in 1786 when four ladies entered the Haymarket Theatre in extravagant head-dresses and huge nosegays on their bosoms, the entire audience ridiculed them and the play was stopped while four actresses went off to dress in similar garb and reappeared to join in the general mockery.[18]

By then tall head-dresses were an unusual sight, but the long feathers with which they were adorned remained in fashion. Queen Charlotte, whose cheeks were often brushed by them as ladies made their obeisances on being presented to her, disliked feathers intensely. 'For two or three years no one ventured to wear them at Court,' Lady Louisa Stuart said, 'except some daring spirits either too supreme in fashion to respect any other kind of pre-eminence, or else connected with the Opposition and glad to set Her Majesty at defiance.' The queen, however, had to give way eventually, and feathers were established as the orthodox head-dress at court by the end of the century.

In other respects the court lagged far behind fashion. The clothes worn there both by men and women were certainly very splendid, as they nearly always had been. The gentlemen at a birthday court, so Mrs Delany said, were arrayed in 'much finery chiefly brown with gold or silver embroidery and rich waistcoats'; and of another birthday court in 1764, Mrs Montagu wrote, 'I never saw anything equal to the Court on Wednesday. There was hardly a gentleman or gentlewoman in London who was not expiring under a load of finery. Indeed, I was one of the fools myself.' When the Duke of Bedford appeared at court in 1791 he was wearing a coat and breeches of brown striped silk, shot with green, with a white waistcoat. All these clothes 'were embroidered in silver, blue and foil and stones in wreaths of flowers for the borders and seams and the ground covered with single brilliants and silver spangles and it was estimated that it cost him £500.'[19]

Yet fine as the display was, it was not always fashionable. 'If I were to describe their clothes to you,' wrote Lady Hartford of those attending one birthday court, 'you would say you had seen them (or just such) at every birthday you can remember.' The hoop which came into fashion in about 1710 had disappeared in society by the 1780s but it was worn at court and remained a court fashion until 1820. At their coronations, both Queen Caroline in 1727 and Queen Charlotte in 1761 wore a form of dress which had already gone out of fashion by the end of the seventeenth century.[20]

Like the grotesquely tall head-dress, the hoop, the precursor of the crinoline, was much ridiculed and much attacked for its inconvenience. It was almost universally worn by fashionable ladies in the middle of the century. 'The only thing that seems general,' Mrs Pendarves told a correspondent in 1746, 'are hoops of an enormous size', although the year before the author of a pamphlet entitled 'The Enormous Abomination of the Hoop Petticoat' had condemned the style as an intolerable nuisance, maintaining that he had seen a young lady taking up the whole side of a street with her immense hooped petticoat and that another woman had walked down the aisle of a church, after receiving the sacrament, with one side of her hem brushing the pews on the right and the other side on her left.

It seemed to Oliver Goldsmith that a lady's long train was as great a nuisance and absurd an affectation as the hoop, whether held up by a page or allowed to trail on the ground, tripping up both its owner and those who trod on it.

> What chiefly distinguishes the sex at present is the train. As a lady's quality or fashion was once determined here by the circumference of her hoop, both are now measured by the length of her tail. Women of moderate fortunes are contented with tails moderately long, but ladies of true taste and distinction set no bounds to their ambition in this particular.[21]

Even after handbags had come into general use in the 1760s a lady who went out unaccompanied by a page or footman would usually carry a gold *étui* case in which had been packed small bottles of scent and aromatic vinegar and perhaps a snuff-box. She would also carry a fan.

Fans were sometimes of such large size and wielded so energetically that they were compared to windmills. The more expensive were mounted with diamonds and inlaid with jewels, and were painted with political emblems, verses from popular songs or extracts from books, pictures of fruit and flowers. Great dexterity was required for 'fluttering', and all manner of emotions could be wordlessly conveyed by the skilful manipulator, from anger and confusion to amusement and love. Addison said that it took three months' assiduous practice before the art of 'fluttering' was fully mastered.

The lady might also carry an umbrella of waxed silk or taffeta. Umbrellas had been introduced into England in the late seventeenth century. They were mentioned by Swift in 1704 and by John Gay in 1716. And in the 'Description of a City Shower' which appeared in the *Tatler* in 1710:

> The tuck'd up semstress walks with hasty strides
> While streams run down her oil'd umbrella's sides.

Umbrellas were not, however, in common use until much later and men who dared to be seen with them in public were liable to be jeered at by porters and coachmen, as were the lawyers of Lincoln's Inn who borrowed the large umbrella from Wall's coffee-house in 1714. John Macdonald, on his return to London from France in 1778, wrote that umbrellas were rarely seen

> except in noblemen and gentlemen's houses, where there was a large one hung in the hall, to hold over a lady or gentleman if it rained, between the door and the carriage. I was going to dine in Norfolk Street on Sunday. It rained. My sister had hold of my arm, and I had the umbrella over our heads. In Tavistock Street we met so many young men, calling after us, 'Frenchman, take care of your umbrella.' 'Frenchman, why do you not get a coach, Monsieur?'[22]

Jonas Hanway, the philanthropist, who is credited with having set the fashion of carrying an umbrella, had to endure the scorn of the mob for thirty years before his habit was accepted without derision. But by the time of his death in 1786 it seems from the large number of satirical prints showing people with umbrellas that they had come into common use in London.[23] Elsewhere, however, they were still an unusual sight. George Pryme, Professor of Political Economy at Cambridge, recalled that as late as 1797 there was but one umbrella in the town, this being kept in a shop in Benet Street and hired out by the hour.[24]

Ladies indicated their political inclinations by face patches as well as by the motifs on their fans, and these patches, circular or crescent-shaped pieces of black or bright red silk, velvet or paper, remained in fashion long after their political significance had been forgotten, often hiding the worst ravages of smallpox. The skin on the face was also covered with preparations as dangerous as those used in the sixteenth century. A foundation of white lead, which caused serious illnesses in the workmen who made it, was first applied; then, at least until the 1780s when the practice became less common, the cheeks were rouged, perhaps with a red leather imported from Brazil, and the colour of the lips was heightened with carmine or painted with lipsticks made from ground and coloured plaster of Paris. Eyebrows were trimmed, blackened with lead combs, or concealed behind artificial mouseskin eyebrows. False teeth and 'plumpers', small cork balls held inside the cheeks to make them appear rounder, helped their wearers to talk with a fashionable lisp. There were also false buttocks, an importation from the Continent, and pads worn over the stomach by those who wished to appear pregnant.[25]

*

Clothes were important because they indicated rank and even occupation; and it annoyed Lord Chesterfield that some young men flouted the recognized conventions.

> Most of our young fellows here display some character or other by their dress [he wrote], some affect the tremendous, and wear a great and fiercely-cocked hat, an enormous sword, a short waistcoat, and a black cravat . . . Others go in brown frocks, leather breeches, great oaken cudgels in their hands, their hats uncocked, and their hair unpowdered; and imitate grooms, stage-coachmen and country bumkins so well in their outsides, that I do not make the least doubt of their resembling them equally in their insides.[26]

Chesterfield believed that a gentleman ought to dress 'in the same manner as the people of sense and fashion of the place where he is'. If he dressed better he would show himself to be fop, if worse he would be 'unpardonably negligent'.[27] It was also generally accepted that certain professional men should be recognized by their attire. A full-bottomed wig remained the standard wear for lawyers, physicians and clergymen until the middle of the century and was still worn by some in the second half. Many physicians also carried gold-headed canes. Clergymen generally wore black or grey in town, although some habitually chose brighter colours, like the Rev. John Lind – who called upon Jeremy Bentham 'in his flowered dress of purple and gold and I know not what' – and the Rev. Charles Churchill, the poet, who shocked the Dean of Westminster by wearing leather breeches, silk stockings, a blue coat, gold-laced hat and ruffles.

While it was only the rich who could afford to follow every changing fashion, in families throughout the country magazines such as *The Fashions of London and Paris* and the coloured fashion plates in *The Lady Magazine* were eagerly awaited and studied. In the country dress was usually much simpler, of course, than it was in the town, though there were a few country gentlemen who dressed at home much as they did in London. John Howard, the future prison reformer who had a small estate in Bedfordshire, was discovered at home by Arthur Young as though he were dressed for an evening in London, wearing 'a powdered bag wig, white silk stockings, thin shoes'.[28] But Howard was an exception. Most country landowners dressed far less elegantly, and some were as negligent as Lord Effingham who, even in the House of Lords, had the appearance 'both in his person and dress of a Common Country Farmer, wearing a great coat with brass buttons, frock fashion, his hair short, strait, and to appearance uncombed, his face rough, vulgar and brown, as also his hands.'[29]

Indeed, some of the tenants on such men's estates dressed much better than they. In Oxfordshire Carl Moritz noticed in 1782 that the countrymen were dressed not in coarse frocks as they would have been in Germany, but 'with some taste, in fine good cloth'.[30] As for the women, so the author of a pamphlet declared that same year, 'they wear scarcely anything now but cotton, calicoes, muslin or silks, and think no more of woollen stuffs than we think of an old almanac'.[31] Wool, however, was still used for that ubiquitous item of country women's apparel – the red cloak, the hooded form of which was known as a riding-hood. These were still being worn at the end of the century when 'an ample crimson or scarlet cloak of finest wool, double milled and of an intense dye that threw a glimmer wherever it moved' was donned by women for church or chapel every Sunday. 'I wish you saw the number of scarlet cloaks and silk pelisses assembled in the churchyard,' wrote Sarah Hutchinson of a village in Westmorland in 1811.[32] Red cloaks were still popular in the 1820s when Mary Russell Mitford described the numbers of them in Berkshire; but by 1840, according to *The Workwoman's Guide*, they survived only in the wardrobes of elderly ladies.[33]

For countrymen a common form of working dress was a short jacket and sleeveless waistcoat in various shades of brown, breeches and buckled shoes or short boots, perhaps an apron and a black hat. In Stubbs's 'The Hay-makers' of 1782 all the men are depicted wearing wide-brimmed round black hats – as they are, too, in his 'The Reapers' of 1785 – but most of them have taken off their waistcoats and work in white, full-sleeved shirts. The working women also wear big black hats, and one of them is in a bedgown secured by an apron. Women often wore bedgowns in the fields, and sometimes discarded them and worked in their stays covered only by a short-sleeved shift and a petticoat with a handkerchief over neck and shoulders. Most countrywomen also had linen caps and nearly all had a hat made of straw or chip. These were often worn with ribbons and strings tied beneath the chin and were to be seen at every summer fair, as at Stourbridge Fair where one day the Marchioness Grey met with 'a Number of clean, tight [trim] Countrywomen and maidens tricked out with their Ribbands and straw hats to whom this is really a happy, jolly day'.[34]

By the end of the century farm labourers, carters and shepherds were all wearing smock-frocks both for work and at home and in the alehouse. They were not yet the ornamental garments they were later to become, such gathering as there was being merely to shape the garment; but those 'of a brown or light blue linen', which Marianne Thornton saw in Yorkshire in 1797, were 'extremely picturesque'. They seem to have been less favoured by the younger than the older worker for everyday wear, the young men of the village preferring to appear in more dashing clothes when they could, like the 'clodpated yeoman's son' whom a friend of George Selwyn saw at Leicester races in 1779 in a 'drab coat and red waistcoat, tight leather breeches and light grey worsted stockings, with one strap of the shoe coming out from under the buckle upon the foot; with his lank hair and silk handkerchief, new for *Reacetime*, about his neck'.[35]

# 32 · Travellers, Postmen and Innkeepers

Carl Moritz said that he would remember as long as he lived his journey from Leicester to London on his way back to Germany. The getting up alone to the top of the coach was, he thought, 'at risk of one's life'. And when he was up there, sitting at the corner of the coach next to a farmer and a blackamoor, he had nothing to hold on to but a short little handle fastened on the side. 'The moment we set off,' Moritz recalled, 'I fancied that I saw certain death awaiting me. All I could do was to take still faster hold of the handle, and to be more and more careful to preserve my balance. The machine now rolled along with prodigious rapidity over the stones through the town, and every moment we seemed to fly into the air.' As the coach began to climb a hill and consequently slowed down, Moritz thought he would be safer and more comfortable in the basket where the luggage was kept. So, despite the warnings of the black man, who said he would be shaken to death, he climbed into the basket where, when the coach began to rattle down the hill, he was so violently knocked about by the trunks and cases that he thought his last hour had come. He was unable to escape from this torture for an hour; and soon after he did get out it began to pour with rain. At Northampton he changed coaches and this time managed to obtain a seat inside. But this stage of the journey was scarcely better. It was, indeed, not so much a journey as a 'perpetual motion or removal in a close box' in which his three travelling companions were 'unfortunately all farmers who slept so soundly that even the hearty knocks of the head with which they often saluted each other did not awaken them'. After rattling and bumping through Newport Pagnell, Dunstable, St Albans and Barnet, Moritz at length arrived in London looking 'like a crazy creature'.[1]

Moritz's experiences were not in the least exceptional. There were a few travellers who agreed with César de Saussure that English roads, compared with those in other countries, were 'magnificent . . . wide, smooth and well kept'. But to most Englishmen such opinions seemed incomprehensible. 'In Summer the Roads are suffocated and smothered with Dust,' wrote Robert Phillips in 1736 in his *Dissertation Concerning the Present state of the High Roads of England, especially of those near London*,

> and towards the Winter, between wet and dry, they are deep Ruts full of water with hard dry Ridges, which make it difficult for Passengers to cross by one another without overturning. And in the Winter they are all Mud, which rises, spues and squeezes into the Ditches; so that the Ditches and Roads are full of Mud and Dirt all alike.

Such descriptions are so common that it cannot be doubted that in the first half of the eighteenth century the roads of England were deplorable. It was a well-known fact, the *Gentleman's Magazine* maintained twenty years after Phillips's *Dissertation* appeared, that a 'party of ladies and gentlemen would sooner travel [from London] to the south of France and back again than down to Falmouth'.

Coaches became stuck in the mud or overturned, their axles broke, their horses were lamed, their occupants were thrown out with the luggage into the ditch. A journey from Petworth, a distance of forty miles, undertaken by the King of Spain in 1703, took fourteen hours during which he and fellow-travellers did not once get out of the coaches, 'save only when overturned or stuck in the mud'. Six years later Ralph Thoresby, the topographer, found the roads between London and Hull atrocious, 'in some places the ice being broken by the coaches and rougher than a ploughed field, in others yet hard as iron that it battered the horses' feet'. Horace Walpole described the roads in Sussex as 'bad beyond all badness, the night dark beyond all darkness, the guide frightened beyond all frightfulness'. One Sussex lady grew so exasperated by her horses' inability to negotiate the roads which led to her parish church that she had her coach drawn there by a team of six oxen. Even the road between the court suburb of Kensington and Piccadilly was so 'infamously bad' in 1736 that Lord Hervey complained of living 'in the same solitude as if cast on a rock in the middle of the ocean'. 'All the Londoners' told him that the road between the City and Kensington was 'an impassable gulf of mud'. As late as 1763 'the roads were so bad [in Yorkshire] at particular seasons of the year that they were for want of proper forming almost impassable; and it has been known in the winter to have been eight days' journey from York to London'. In 1770 the road from Preston to Wigan in Lancashire was 'execrable'. Arthur Young knew not, 'in the whole range of language terms sufficiently expressive to describe' that 'infernal highway' in which the ruts were four feet deep in summer. 'What must it therefore be in winter?', he asked. 'The only mending it receives in places is the tumbling of some loose stones, which serve no other purpose but jolting a carriage in the most intolerable manner.' The Essex road between Billericay and Tilbury was, if possible, even worse. 'Of all the cursed roads that ever disgraced this kingdom in the very ages of barbarism' none ever equalled this, Young thought.

> It is for near twelve miles so narrow that a mouse cannot pass by any carriage . . . The ruts are an incredible depth . . . and the trees everywhere overgrow the road, so that it is totally impervious to the sun except at a few places. And to add to all the infamous circumstances which concur to plague a traveller, I must not forget the eternally meeting with chalk waggons, themselves frequently stuck fast till a collection of them are in the same situation, and twenty or thirty horses may be tacked to each to draw them out, one by one.[2]

The ordinary dangers of the road were compounded by those threatened by highwaymen. No doubt these dangers were exaggerated by contemporaries, and have subsequently been overemphasized; yet, while we may doubt that Englishmen in the 1750s really were, as Horace Walpole said they were, forced to travel even at noon as if they were going into battle, there was no doubt that highwaymen did constitute a major hazard on the road. 'I was robbed last night as I expected,' the Prime Minister, Lord North, wrote with characteristic placidity and resigned acceptance in 1774. 'Our loss was not great, but as the postilion did not stop immediately, one of the two highwaymen fired at him . . . It was at the end of Gunnersbury Lane.' The following year the Norwich coach was held up in Epping Forest; three of the seven highwaymen were shot dead before the guard was killed himself. One of the highwaymen who robbed Walpole threatened him with a pistol which exploded in his face and blackened his skin with powder and shot marks. He was left thinking that had he been sitting an inch nearer the window, the ball would have passed through his brain. In the words of one experienced traveller, highwaymen were as 'common as crows'.[3]

Foreigners, accustomed in their own countries to a strong force of *maréchaussée* to protect the roads, were astonished by this state of affairs. The number of robbers, one Swiss traveller thought, was 'amazing'. A Frenchman wrote that all the main roads within thirty or forty miles of London were '*garnis de voleurs à cheval*'. The Abbé le Blanc recorded that in the 1720s highwaymen, 'in order to maintain their rights', blatantly 'fixed up papers at the doors of the rich people about London, expressly forbidding all persons, of what condition or quality soever, to go out of town without ten guineas and a watch about them, upon pain of death'.

Sixty years later Sophie von la Roche was at a party in the country attended by several ambassadors who all came away early. 'Perhaps they needed their money for gaming,' she commented, 'and hence could not afford to give it to the highwaymen! So they decided to depart all together, as the robbers would hardly hold up four coaches at once.'

Foreign visitors could at least comfort themselves with the thought that provided they handed over their money and rings and watches quickly and without complaint – and this, they agreed, was essential – the English highwayman was unlikely to pull the trigger of the pistol he always held in his hand like a badge of office. Indeed, as the German historian Johann Wilhelm von Archenholz observed, highwaymen were 'generally very polite; they assure you they are very sorry that poverty has driven them to that shameful recourse, and end by demanding your purse in the most courteous manner'.

'I have been told,' a Frenchman confirmed, 'that some highwaymen are quite polite and generous, begging to be excused for being forced to rob, and leaving passengers the wherewithal to finish their journey.' And the Duc de Lévis agreed that '*en général, les choses se passent de part et d'autre avec beaucoup de sang-froid, et souvent même avec politesse.*'

The English newspapers of the time show that the experiences of these foreign tourists were quite common. The 'Knights of the Road', as they were flatteringly styled, were evidently much given to polite requests and gracious apologies. 'He behaved genteely,' runs a typical report, 'and by way of apology for what he did told the passengers that his distress drove him to it.'

> On Tuesday last [the *Birmingham Gazette* reported on 6 May 1751], the Shrewsbury caravan was stopped between the Four Crosses and the Welsh Harp by a single highwayman who behaved very civilly to the passengers, told them that he was a stranger in distress, and hoped that they would contribute to his assistance. On which each passenger gave him something, to the amount in the whole of about £4, with which he was mighty well satisfied, but returned some half-pence to one of them, saying he never took copper. He told them there were two other collectors on the road, but he would see them out of danger, which he accordingly did, and begged that they would not at their next inn mention the robbery nor appear against him if he should be taken up hereafter.

Since roads were still generally the responsibility of the parishes through which they passed, and since the parishes were reluctant to spend money on them for the benefit of strangers, some more reliable method of maintaining them had to be devised. Parliament was, therefore, eventually induced to pass an Act authorizing the establishment of Turnpike Trusts to erect gates and toll-bars where passengers would be required to pay a toll to pass through. At first few turnpikes were established; in remote areas there was none until after the middle of the eighteenth century. But by 1770 about 15,000 miles of roads were under trusts; and, although Lord Hervey once complained that the Turnpike Commissioners 'seldom execute what they undertake', most roads cared for by trusts were being maintained appreciably better by the end of the century than they had been at the beginning. Turnpikes, however, were bitterly resented not only because of the high tolls which the users had to pay – at the Tyburn turnpike, for example, carriages were charged 10d, horsemen 4d, and drovers 5d for twenty oxen and 2d for twenty pigs – but also because so many of those who could afford the charges were exempt. At Tyburn, mail-coaches, members of the royal family, soldiers in uniforms, parsons on parish duty, funeral processions and prison carts were all exempt; at others, Turnpike Commissioners were excused from paying the charges they had themselves imposed. And when, in 1741, extra tolls were charged on vehicles over three tons, these new rates did not apply to gentlemen's carriages, farmers' vehicles or wagons in the king's service.[4] Attacks on toll-gates were so frequent that offenders – who had at first been liable to three months' imprisonment and a whipping for a first offence and seven years' transportation for a second – were eventually liable to be hanged. This, however, did not prove a deterrent. Numerous reports of attacks on turnpike gates and toll-keepers' houses are to be read in the newspapers of the time; and the numbers of rioters were frequently large: 400 Somerset people were reported to have assaulted turnpikes in Bristol in 1749; and on another occasion it took six troops of dragoon guards to quell a body of Gloucestershire people, 'some naked with their faces blackened', who attacked a turnpike with the intention of blowing up the posts with gunpowder so that they could get their cattle to the fair without payment.

The toll-keeper's appointment was clearly not an enviable one. In danger from attack from angry people, he was also an obvious target for robbers. He was, moreover, woken up at all hours of the night. It was not surprising that toll-keepers attempted to augment their meagre pay by cheating their employers and the users of the road alike. No one respected them:

Returning by way of frolic, very late at night, on horseback, to Wimbledon from Addiscombe . . . Lord Thurlow, then Chancellor, Pitt and Dundas, found the Turnpike Gate situate between Tooting and Streatham, thrown open. Being elevated above their usual prudence, and having no Servant near them, they passed through the gate at a brisk pace, without stopping to pay the Toll; regardless of the remonstrances or threats of the Turnpike man, who, running after them, and believing them to belong to some Highwaymen, who had recently committed depredations on that road, discharged the contents of his Blunderbuss at their backs. Happily he did no injury.[5]

Turnpike trusts, which could be sold like any other business, were valuable properties: Lewis Levi, a rich stockbroker, paid £12,000 for the lease of the Tyburn turnpike trust and it proved a sound investment.[6] But turnpikes, naturally, much increased the cost of travelling. James Wood-forde paid £4 8s for his fare from Oxford to London in 1774, a distance of 100 miles; and by the end of the century he would have been charged consider-ably more. A journey from Scotland to London undertaken by stage-coach by Thomas Somerville in 1800 cost him twice as much as the £7 he had paid in 1769. Coach fares were usually about 2½d a mile in summer and 3d in winter.[7]

Yet if journeys were more expensive, they were also much quicker. In 1700 a journey from Norwich to London had taken fifty hours, by 1800 it took no more than nineteen; the ninety hours of travel between Manchester and London was reduced to thirty-three, and the 256 between Edinburgh and London to sixty. Travellers had to wait until the nineteenth century before the road improvement schemes of Thomas Telford and John McAdam were completed. But by 1800 many road surfaces were incomparably better than they had been before. The enterprising John Metcalf, though blinded by smallpox at the age of six, had built over 500 miles of good roads in Yorkshire and Lancashire when he relinquished road-making for the cotton business in 1792. Main roads were provided with milestones for the first time since the days of the Romans. After an Act of 1793 they had more signposts as well; and for the convenience of travellers there were road atlases.

The frequency and extent of services had also much improved and cross-country connections had been established. There were forty daily coaches from Birmingham, fifty-four from Manchester; the 'Exeter Flying Machine' from Bath took up passengers there from the Oxford, Newbury and Reading coaches; at Bristol it connected with the Gloucester, Worcester and Birmingham coaches, and at its destination, Exeter, with the coach going on to Plymouth. There were five daily coaches from Bath to London, the first leaving the terminal at five in the morning, the last at nine at night.

The variety of private and public transport was extraordinary. The Turnpike Act of 1803 mentioned coaches, calashes, barouches, chariots, landaus, berlins, chaises, chaises marines, cars, chairs, caravans, hearses and litters. There were also phaetons, light, open, doorless, four-wheeled car-riages with two seats which dashing young men drove at breakneck speed to the constant irritation of coachmen. For larger parties there were post-chaises which could be hired complete with postilions; for the public at large there were stage-coaches – much improved in comfort since the substitution of steel springs for leather – and mail-coaches.

These had been projected by John Palmer, a Bath theatre proprietor who on the journeys he made looking for talented actors, had observed how slow and inefficient the state post was, letters commonly taking three days to reach London from Bath. There had been no postal services at all until 1635 when the royal posts were made available to the public by the establishment of a General Post in London to carry letters out along the main post roads. Postage was charged according to the distance carried and, until the development of cross-country posts, all mail had to be sent through London. Even after cross-country posts had been established, the system was extremely slow, since letters were carried by postboys and postmen often riding very old horses.[8]

Postmen were much abused. Until the end of the century, when they were provided with red suits faced and piped with blue, they had no uniforms and were considered 'rather an inferior set of men'. There were frequent complaints of them failing to blow their horns to give notice of their coming, of them being late with their deliveries, of them delaying their journeys on the least excuse, of them staying indoors in bad weather like the postman who takes shelter from the rain in the kitchen of Framley Parsonage and accepts a bowl of tea and a slice of buttered toast, though 'the wery 'edges 'as eyes', he says, and he is reported to the postmaster in Silverbridge if he as much as stops on his rounds to pick a blackberry.[9] 'The post is grown very indolent,' runs a typical complaint in the *Verney Letters* of 1753, 'and takes it into his head not to call here unless he pleases; and on Thursday last our letters did not go. He said it was out of his way to call from Bicester to Wimslow, and he could not.'[10]

There were also frequent complaints about the expense of the post. In London, William Dockwra had set up a private penny post service towards the end of the seventeenth century. He had announced that 'Letters or Pacquets under a Pound Weight' would be conveyed 'to and from all parts within the Cities of London and Westminster, and the Out Parishes . . . for One Penny', to be paid by the sender. An extra penny was later charged for deliveries within ten miles of the General Letter Office; and this 2d rate was increased to 3d in 1711. Sending letters outside the London area was more costly still, and by the end of the century was considered by many to be prohibitive. 'Your letter is charged 8d,' a London clerk told one of his correspondents in 1717, 'but I have cheated Mr Pitt at that rate out of 3s 4d by having sent five letters by wagon.' Others asked those who were allowed to send letters free – such as officials in government service and Members of Parliament – to frank their own letters for them. A country parson wrote to Horace Walpole, Member for Lynn, in 1766 asking him to frank an enclosed letter 'by directing it . . . in his own Hand', according to the Franking Act of 1764. It was not until 1840 that a uniform penny rate covering all places in the British Isles was established in accordance with proposals outlined in Rowland Hill's *Post Office Reform*.

With his wide experience of the defects of the postal services of his day, John Palmer proposed that mail should be carried in coaches which were to have armed guards, to travel at a speed of eight or nine miles an hour, and to carry no outside passengers. The officials of the Post Office declared that Palmer's proposals were impracticable; and, when the government nevertheless decided that they should be put to the test on the London to Bristol road in August 1784, the local postmasters on the route had to be strongly warned against putting obstructions in their way. The trial runs were so promising that the Treasury suggested that the mail-coach service should be extended to Norwich, Nottingham, Liverpool and Manchester; and a year later its facilities were extended all over the country from Swansea to Birmingham, from Leeds to Dover, Exeter to Shrewsbury. By 1786 there was a regular mail-coach service between London and Edinburgh.

The four passengers inside the mail-coaches travelled in greater comfort and safety, and at far greater speed, than they did in the ordinary stage-coaches. De Quincey wrote of their marvellous velocity: 'We heard our speed, we saw it, we felt it as thrilling; and this speed was not the product of blind insensate agencies, that had no sympathy to give [like the railway trains which were to replace them] but was incarnated in the fiery eyeballs of the noblest among brutes, in his dilated nostril, spasmodic muscles, and thunder-beating hoofs.'[11]

Travelling by mail-coach, however, was not cheap: a seat on the London to Bristol run cost 28s in 1784. And the quality of the service offered in the inns *en route* was highly variable. There were some truly dreadful places. At Windsor, Carl Moritz was shown a room which 'much resembled a prison for malefactors', and upon asking for an alternative, he was advised to go on to Slough. Eventually, he found what seemed a more promising place in Windsor, but here he was also told, by a sneering chambermaid, to go elsewhere when he complained of the room he was offered. Eventually the innkeeper found him another room which he was obliged to share with a fellow-guest who proved to be drunk. 'Right under this bedroom was a tap-room,' Moritz said. 'The floor shook. Drinking songs were sung . . . I was hardly able to sleep with such a noise and bustle, and had just dozed off a little when my sleeping-partner arrived, possibly one of those from the tap-room, who knocked into my bed. With great difficulty he found [his own] and threw himself onto it just as he was – clothes, boots and all.' In the dining-room the waiter served him grumpily and afterwards demanded a tip. 'I gave him three halfpence,' Moritz recorded, 'on which he saluted me with the heartiest "God damn you, Sir!" I had ever heard. At the door stood the cross maid, who also accosted me with "Pray remember the chamber-maid!" "Yes, yes," said I, "I shall long remember your most ill-mannered behaviour,

RIGHT: Bagnigge Wells, one of the most popular of 18th-century spas, had a rather raffish reputation. Prostitutes and highwaymen were among its habitués. Its once extensive gardens are now covered by King's Cross Road.

BELOW: At the beginning of the 18th century Brighthelmstone, as Brighton was then called, was no more than a small fishing town; and it was not until Dr Richard Russell advocated its sea water as a sovereign cure for various ailments that it began to become a popular seaside spa. The Prince of Wales made it highly fashionable when he came here to live in the Marine Pavilion designed for him by Henry Holland and transformed, as depicted here, by John Nash. George Cruikshank caricatures a promenade in front of it in 1826. Various well-known Brighton visitors can be identified, including the Duke of York, standing in profile to the left and talking to the Duke of Gloucester who is flanked by the three approaching dandies; N. M. Rothschild, walking along with his fat wife to the right of the knock-kneed dandy in the foreground; Col. D'Este, acknowledging the bow of a fat parson; and Talleyrand on the extreme right.

ABOVE: Caricatures of 1814, satirizing the custom of segregating the sexes after dinner. The ladies go to the drawing-room to drink tea, the gentlemen remain in the dining-room to drink port and get drunk. Chamber-pots were commonly kept in dining-room sideboards.

BELOW: A museum of natural and artificial curiosities at 22 Piccadilly, opened in 1809 by William Bullock who had previously displayed his exhibits in Liverpool. For a time it was 'the most fashionable place of amusement in London'. Jane Austen was among the thousands of visitors.

LEFT: Thomas Rowlandson shows a coach about to leave an inn, the ostler leading up the horses, the passengers stowing their luggage inside. Rowlandson himself travelled all over England, enjoying tavern life to the full. In his day there were as many as 54 daily coaches from Manchester and from Bath five daily coaches to London alone.

BELOW: Cheapside, London, in the middle of the 18th century with Wren's steeple of St Mary-le-Bow towering above the shops. Hanging signs were as prominent in many other London streets until an Act was passed in 1762 requiring signboards to be fixed flat to the building and so make them less liable to fall off on passers-by in windy weather. Tavern keepers and certain other tradesmen, however, defied the law with impunity.

NATIONAL LOVE

LEFT: The fashions of the 1790s made breast-feeding a much more simple operation than it was later to become. The custom of employing wet-nurses had by then been abandoned by large numbers of upper-class ladies. In 1789 Lady Craven reported that 'you will find in every station of life mothers of families who would shrink with horror at the thought of putting a child from them to nurse'. And Baron von Archenholz observed at about the same time that 'even women of quality nurse their children'. The plumes which ladies of fashion then wore – as does this nursing mother – grew to such a height that the Queen complained of their inconvenience at Court.

BELOW: The pain of an amputation might be alleviated but could not be suppressed by the drugs or other means available to surgeons in the 18th century. When asked what was the most valuable invention of their time, many a Victorian unhesitatingly answered, 'anaesthetics'.

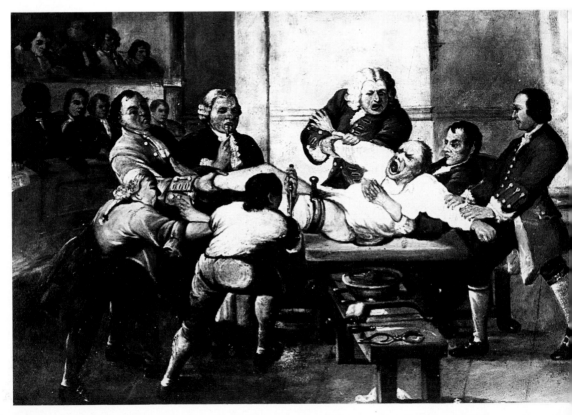

and shameful incivility"; and so I gave her nothing.'[12]

Travellers were often required to share a room, as Moritz had been, though now such inns as the one in Derbyshire – where, so Celia Fiennes said, there were four beds in a room and sometimes three people in each of them – were now rarely encountered. Nor was it likely that the traveller would come across an inn like the Rose and Crown at Nether Stowey where John Taylor, the Thames waterman turned poet, stayed in the seventeenth century and waited three hours for the boiled beef and carrots he had ordered. After this exasperating delay he was told that there was no beef: would he make do with fried eggs and parsley? Two hours later he was told that there were no eggs either. He went out to try to find some bread and butter.[13]

Yet, if inns were not so crowded or so ill-run, the service in many of them left much to be desired. A French traveller in Dover who could get no one to attend to him in the main inn in the town and so helped himself to what he could find in the kitchen was turned out of his room at three o'clock in the morning by servants who told him it was needed for someone else.[14] English travellers were likely to fare no better, being often troubled by flies and sometimes by rats as was Dr Syntax who threw his bolster and pillow and his shoes at them, but could not stop them eating his wig until an ostler came up to deal with them with two fierce cats.[15] Arthur Young classified all the inns where he had stayed during the travels which resulted in *A Tour through the Southern Counties*. Many of them were either 'bad' or 'dirty', or 'dear'. The George at Winchester was both 'dirty and dear', but that at least was also 'civil'.[16]

By the end of the century the food and accommodation at inns were both much improved, and the prices quite moderate, the more so the further the coach travelled from London.

My father [George Colman the Younger recalled] frequently observed upon the gradual lowering of charges in proportion to the distance from London: the articles enumerated in a bill for dinner, which were then cheap, not only grew cheaper as we went on, but, when we reach'd the northern counties were not enumerated at all; and, instead of swelling the account with a roast fowl, sauce for ditto, potato, melted butter for ditto, to poach'd eggs, to cheese, to toasted ditto, &c. &c., the items were all consolidated under the head of 'EATING,' against which was regularly placed the sum of One Shilling; and this for no scanty meal, but plenty of everything; fish, flesh, and fowl, and excellent of their kind.[17]

An Irish gentleman travelling in England at about the time of which Colman wrote, paid only 6d at the Lion, Liverpool, for 'a very good supper, consisting of veal cutlets, pigeons, asparagus, lamb and salad, apple-pie and tarts'.[18] At inns like this the bedrooms were also comfortable, well finished with four-poster beds, chairs, wash-stands and carpets; they had fires in the grates and warming-pans between the sheets.

Some inns were now very large establishments. The London Inn at Exeter had 'a complement of five hundred horses'; at the White Hart at Bath guests were met by liveried footmen; while at the George and Blue Boar, Holborn, the starting point for the coach to Glasgow, there were forty bedrooms, stabling for over fifty horses and seven coach-houses.[19]

When Tom Brown went to Rugby for his first term in the 1830s the journey which Thomas Hughes described and the inns at which the coach stopped were much the same as they had been thirty years before. Tom was woken up at half past two in the morning at the Peacock Inn, Islington, by the bootboy's voice: 'Now, Sir, time to get up if you please. Tally-ho coach for Leicester 'll be round in half an hour, and don't wait for nobody.' Having drunk a cup of coffee and eaten a biscuit, Tom said goodbye to his father and rushed out to climb on to the coach while the guard, having examined them by the lamps, threw a bundle of parcels into the hind boot and jumped up beside him as the coach rattled off, forty-five seconds after it had first pulled up. Tom was very cold, despite his scarf and his Petersham coat and the straw with which the guard muffled his feet and the oat sack he pulled over his knees. But

> it had its pleasures, the old dark ride . . . There was the music of the rattling harness, and the ring of the horses' feet on the hard road, and the glare of the two bright lamps through the steaming hoar-frost over the leaders' ears into the darkness; and the cheery toot of the guard's horn to warn some drowsy pikeman or the ostler at the next change.

At dawn the coach stops at a wayside inn where the coachman, guard and passengers all get down to drink a glass of purl as they stand before the fire. They are soon off again through the morning countryside, passing a market-cart or two, men in smock-frocks going to work, pipes in their mouths, a pack of hounds jogging along to a distant meet at the heel of the huntsman's hack, an early up-coach which they approach at eleven miles an hour, the coach-men gathering up their horses and passing one another with the accustomed lift of the elbow. And then, as the coachman calls out, 'Twenty minutes here gentlemen', the coach stops at another inn for breakfast.

> There is the low dark wainscoted room hung with sporting prints; the hat-stand, with a whip or two standing up in it belonging to bagmen, who are still snug in bed, by the door; the blazing fire, with the quaint old glass

over the mantelpiece, in which is stuck a large card with the list of the meets for the week of the county hounds. The table covered with the whitest of cloths and of china, and bearing a pigeon-pie, ham, round of cold boiled beef cut from a mammoth ox, and the great loaf of household bread on a wooden trencher. And here comes in the stout head waiter, puffing under a tray of hot viands; kidneys and a steak, transparent rashers and poached eggs, buttered toast and muffins, coffee and tea, all smoking hot. The table can never hold it all; the cold meats are removed to the sideboard, they were only put on for show, and to give us an appetite.[20]

# 33 · *Hunters, Poachers and Smugglers*

For many country gentlemen hunting was not so much a favourite pastime as a way of life; and so it remained for generations to come as it had been for generations past. When R. S. Surtees, the sporting novelist who came from an old Durham family, described Lord Scamperdale in *Mr Sponge's Sporting Tour* he was writing towards the middle of the nineteenth century but the character he delineated might well have stepped out of the pages of Henry Fielding and would have been as recognizable to Fielding's grandfather as to his grandson. Scamperdale was 'a coarse, broad, large-built sort of man' with clothes to correspond who, so far as he could manage it, did not spend 'a halfpenny upon anything but hunting'. He was 'stumpy and clumsy and ugly, with as little to say for himself as could well be conceived . . . a square, bull-headed looking-man, with hard, dry, round, matter-of-fact features that never looked young and yet somehow never got old'. He lived in a fine, stone Italianate house which, surrounded by a park of 800 acres, had been built at enormous cost by a forebear who had pulled down the original brick Elizabethan mansion. But, wishing to preserve the equally fine contents in good condition 'against he got married', he had the house 'put away in brown holland, the carpets rolled up, the pictures covered, the statues shrouded in muslin, the cabinets of curiosities locked, the plate secured, the china closeted'. And he lived in a small sitting-room, whose bookshelves contained, in addition to only two books, a grand quantity of old spurs, knots of whipcord, piles of halfpennies, gun charges, hunting horns and similar miscellaneous articles, mainly of a sporting character.[1]

In Scamperdale's day hunting usually meant fox-hunting. Yet, even though the enclosure of so much waste land and the destruction of so many forests had led to a severe decline in the number of herds of wild deer, stag-hunting maintained its popularity for many years after the superiority of fox-hunting had been recognized in the north and spread gradually to the south. Even after she grew too fat to ride, Queen Anne drove after the hounds in Windsor Forest which she had restocked with deer. She drove at a furious pace, 'like Jehu', Jonathan Swift told Esther Johnson, the 'Stella' of his *Journal*. She sat in a narrow, one-seated carriage with extraordinarily high wheels which carried her rattling through cornfields and across the most formidable obstacles. The taking of the quarry was celebrated by a loud blowing on a great number of horns and a knife was presented to the highest-ranking man present who cut off the animal's head. Queen Anne's young son, the Duke of Gloucester, who was to die shortly after his eleventh birthday, was given his 'baptism of blood' when he was six from hands dipped into the carcass of a deer that had been brought into the yard and killed for this specific purpose.[2]

Horses were used mercilessly. Runs of eighty miles and more were not uncommon; and at the end of one run, which lasted for six hours and in which George III took part, the stag dropped down dead before the hounds. Not twenty out of 150 horses were in at the death; several had died in the field; and tired ones were seen limping away to every village.[3]

By George III's day, however, deer were more often seen as ornamental animals in a gentleman's park than as quarry to be chased and slaughtered. Hare-hunting continued to be popular well into the nineteenth century, and there were packs of harriers in every county; yet fox-hunting was gradually gaining ground. Horses began to be bred for speed as much as for endurance; and they were also now bred for jumping, even though the more prudent riders would often dismount and lead their mounts over or around obstacles. The Belvoir, Quorn, Pytchley and Cottesmore hunts were all founded in the 1770s. Many ladies hunted as enthusiastically as men, though others only dutifully. George III's daughters went out with their father, all wearing 'blue habits faced and turned up with red, white beaver hats and black feathers'; and the Vicar of Wakefield's entire family 'on fine days rode a-hunting'.[4]

While hawking and the netting and liming of birds were all still practised, the development of the sporting gun had made shooting them more popular. The matchlock with a barrel five feet long or more had taken the place of the much shorter-barrelled flintlock; and while this was far from a reliable, not to mention far from safe, weapon – and while reloading was still a slow operation – it did make it less difficult to shoot birds on the wing. Indeed, a skilful shot like Thomas Coke of Holkham was said to have killed no less than eighty partridges with less than a hundred shots, though those less experienced, having to aim so far in front of a flying bird, were more likely to miss it than not.[5] Double-barrelled guns had been invented, but were generally considered unsatisfactory and, by some, unsportsmanlike.[6]

Fishing, like shooting, required much skill, since most rods were home-made, consisting of two or three straightened and seasoned twigs spliced together, and with lines made of horse-hair. But all the methods known to the modern angler were practised; and numerous new editions of Izaak Walton's *The Compleat Angler* had appeared since its first publication in 1653.[7]

Fish, like game, was still stolen in large quantities by poachers, despite the number of laws passed to protect the interests of the owners, particularly the great landowners. An Act of 1671 had actually restricted the right to take game, even on a man's own land, to those with estates worth more than £100 a year. And in 1723 an Act known as the Waltham Black Act introduced some fifty new capital offences, from deer stealing at night to breaking down the heads of fishponds, from cutting down trees 'planted in any avenue, or growing in any garden, orchard or plantation', to robbing 'any warren or place where conies or hares are usually kept'. This Act took its name from Waltham Chase in Hampshire where men with blackened faces had been causing violent disturbances similar to those that had occurred in the 100,000 acres of Windsor Forest. According to a proclamation issued in February that year 'great numbers of disorderly and ill-designing persons' had associated themselves under the name of Blacks and, armed and disguised, had broken into forests and parks, killed and carried off deer, rescued offenders from the constables, sent menacing letters to gentlemen demanding both venison and money, and threatened to burn down houses, farm-buildings and haystacks. They had shot at people in their homes, 'maimed their horses and cattle, broke down their gates, and cut down avenues, plantations, and heads of fish-ponds, and robbed them of the fish'.[8] The Act which these crimes provoked has been described by Sir Leon Radzinowicz as constituting 'in itself a complete and extremely severe criminal code',[9] and by E. P. Thompson as 'an astonishing example of legislative overkill', though Pat Rogers has suggested that the Blacks belonged to the 'criminal subcultures of Georgian England, that their behaviour was a real danger to peaceable men' and that the Black Act had 'a justification at this time.'[10]

Despite the severity of the Black Act, however, it seems that the Game Laws were not in general enforced very strictly until the middle of the eighteenth century. Thereafter, though, as they began to use guns, poachers were punished with far less leniency.[11] An Act of 1770 made would-be nocturnal poachers liable to six months' imprisonment; another Act of 1803 rendered them liable to hanging if they were armed and resisted arrest; and in 1816, a man, even unarmed, might be transported if caught with a net. By 1827 one seventh of all convicted criminals were poachers.[12] William Taplin, author of *Observations of the Present State of The Game in England*, said that he had never been into a farmhouse which did not contain an illegally acquired hare or a few brace of birds and that the London market was regularly supplied with hares by poachers who risked man-traps, leg-breakers and spring guns to keep in business.

Similarly, smugglers regularly supplied the market with huge quantities of lace, tobacco, wine, spirits and tea, so much tea, in fact, that dealers in it petitioned Parliament in 1736, maintaining that half the amount consumed in England had come into the country illicitly. Smuggling was carried on not only extensively but also with great skill and cunning. Lace was stuffed into geese and hams; tobacco was made into ropes, becoming scarcely distinguishable from ships' gear; brandy kegs were concealed in lobster pots and packing-cases marked 'returned Government stores'. The landsman who carried off the contraband once it had been unloaded from the ships were as expert in their way as the sailors, while the gangs who undertook to fight off coastguards were as ready to mutilate or murder an exciseman as an informer. In 1748 an informer, Daniel Chater, and an exciseman, William Galley, were murdered together:

> They began with poor Galley, cut off his nose and privities, broke every joint of him and after several hours' torture dispatched him. Chater they carried to a dry well, hung him by the middle to a cross beam in it, leaving him to perish with hunger and pain; but when they came, several days after, and heard him groan, they cut the rope, let him drop to the bottom, and threw in logs and stones to cover him. The person who gave this information, however known to the magistrates, was in disguise lest he should meet the like fate.[13]

Such atrocities caused only temporary revulsion. Smuggling was not considered a serious crime; and smugglers were regarded as romantic adventurers performing a useful service of which all sensible people availed themselves. Sir Robert Walpole, the king's principal minister, used an Admiralty barge to bring his smuggled wine up the Thames and was thought none the worse for that. Lesser men would have done the same; and, whenever they could get it, they did not hesitate to buy and drink contraband brandy, a keg of which was once left at the door of a house in the Isle of Wight where Elizabeth Sewell, the writer, once stayed with her uncle. It was a token of gratitude from the smugglers who crossed and recrossed the grounds of the house without interference.[14] A tap on a window or door late at night at the Rev. James Woodforde's parsonage in Norfolk usually heralded the arrival of the local smuggler. 'Andrews the smuggler brought me this night about 11 o'clock a bagg of Hyson Tea 6 Pd weight,' Woodforde recorded in his diary on 29 March 1777. 'He frightened us a little by whistling under the Parlour

Window just as we were going to bed. I gave him some Geneva and paid him for the tea at 10/6 per Pd . . . 3.3.0.'[15]

The traffic was far too extensive for the few customs officers and revenue cutters to control it; and such excisemen as there were were often corrupt or incompetent. The entire crew of the revenue cutter, the *Rose*, were dismissed in 1825; and at Looe a chief customs officer was convicted of collusion as both his immediate predecessors had been. Tom Paine, author of the *Rights of Man*, who had once served aboard a privateer, was dismissed from his appointment as a supernumerary officer in the excise for passing traders' returns without examining their stocks and, having been taken back into the service, was dismissed again for going off without leave. He was also suspected of having dealt in smuggled tobacco. When smuggling did begin to decline after the end of the Napoleonic Wars the reason was not so much that the preventive system had improved as that the previously high customs duties had been so much reduced that the crime was far less profitable.[16]

# 34 · *Pastimes and Pleasures*

Anxious though they were to keep their men hard at work during the time of wakes and fairs and other traditional holidays, most masters found it as difficult as Josiah Wedgwood did to prevent them wandering off to enjoy themselves whenever they could. There were few districts in England without their regular feast days or wakes, few places where a fair was not held at least once a year or where a local custom such as the bull-running at Stamford in Lincolnshire, the pancake race at Olney in Buckinghamshire, or the presentation of the Dunmow Flitch did not draw large crowds.

English people, so foreign observers thought, loved crowds and noise and bustle. They seemed to spend little time indoors, flocking together, enjoying each other's company in a rowdy, joking way. In London they walked in their hundreds in the parks and in the pleasure gardens of which there were over sixty in addition to Ranelagh and Vauxhall. A German visitor thought the medley of people in St James's Park 'astonishing', while a Frenchman described the crowds at Vauxhall as the largest he had ever seen gathered together in one place. At Vauxhall, or the New Spring Garden as it was called until 1785, admission was originally free. An entrance fee of a shilling was introduced in the 1730s, but even so 12,000 people gathered here for a rehearsal of Handel's 'Music for the Royal Fireworks' in 1749. At Ranelagh in Chelsea, where the charge for admittance was 2s 6d 'tea and coffee included' – 5s on firework nights – the grounds were equally packed. The rotunda – into which 'everybody that loves eating, drinking staring or crowding' was admitted for a shilling – was often so full that the orchestra could only just be heard above the din. At Hampstead Wells all kinds of people from fashionable ladies to Fleet Street sempstresses, from attorneys to chimney-sweeps, came to dance and to listen to the music, to promenade up and down Well Walk and to bowl and gamble on the Heath.[1]

In colder weather men pushed their way into taverns and coffee-houses.

Those who could afford the prices went to James Wyatt's Pantheon in Oxford Street, the 'winter Ranelagh', where the opening ceremony in 1772 was attended by 1500 people, and where masquerades, fêtes, *ridottos* and concerts thereafter attracted patrons in even greater numbers. Or they went to Carlisle House in Soho Square where the Viennese opera singer and courtesan Theresa Cornelys ran assembly rooms which, when Fanny Burney was taken to them in 1770, were 'so crowded' there was 'scarce room to breathe'. Or they set out for Almack's Assembly Rooms in King Street, St James's, where a voucher of admission to the weekly ball was 'the seventh heaven of the fashionable world' and where all the gentlemen had to wear knee breeches and white cravats, even the Duke of Wellington being refused admission because he was wearing trousers. And for those who could not find the money for assembly rooms there were 'cock and hen clubs', where men and women met to sing songs; 'cutter clubs' for apprentices who enjoyed themselves on the river and in riverside taverns; and political and debating clubs like that known as the House of Lords whose meetings, attended by the 'more dissolute sort of barristers, attorneys and tradesmen', were held at the Three Herrings in Bell Yard.

There were puppet shows, freak shows and waxworks, shooting galleries and football matches, brothels and chop-houses, taverns with skittle-alleys and bowling-courts, bear baitings, cockfights and prize-fights, fights between men and fights between women; and there were the marvellous continuing fairs, Bartholomew Fair at Smithfield, Mayfair which gave its name to the West End's fashionable quarter, and Southwark Fair originally lasting for three days but eventually for two weeks.[2]

Hogarth's *Southwark Fair* depicts some of the best-known performers and booth proprietors of his day, including Miller, the German Giant; Violante, the acrobat; a conjuror; a slack rope walker; a waxworks exhibitor; a troupe of players; a fortune-teller; a player of the bagpipes; a Savoyard music-grinder; a fire-eating quack; a performing dog; and James Figg, the famous pugilist, whose head was covered with black patches concealing his scars and at whose academy young gentlemen were trained to defend themselves against the attacks of footpads.[3]

At most fairs all over the country there was a ring where pugilists displayed their skills and accepted bets from amateurs who fancied their chances in battling against them. 'Anything that looks like a fight,' the Frenchman Henri Misson suggested, was 'delicious to an Englishman'. Jack Broughton who became champion of England in 1740 – and who was abandoned by his patron, the Duke of Cumberland, when he lost a fight upon which Cumberland had bet £10,000 – introduced his pupils to boxing gloves to 'secure them from the inconveniency of black eyes, broken jaws and bloody noses'. But gloves were not generally worn and fights were then crude and bloody, often

made more so by the spectators who would join in a match which was not
going the way their bets lay and jump into the ring to kick or punch one or
other of the antagonists. For this reason, towards the end of the century the
rings were raised on stages six feet or so above the ground.[4] It was on such a
stage at Stilton in Huntingdonshire that the Jewish pugilist, Daniel Mendoza,
fought 'the gentleman boxer', Richard Humphreys, in a fight which
lasted for forty minutes before Humphreys collapsed and which was continued, after his recovery, for a further ten minutes before he lost consciousness again. A subsequent fight between them, which was maintained over
seventy-two rounds, lasted for an hour and thirteen minutes.[5] Such lengthy
fights were not uncommon; nor were fights between women which were
regularly staged in London at Stoke's Amphitheatre in Islington Road.

César de Saussure gave an account of a contest between two women which
was preceded by 'a fight with wicker staves by a few rogues. They do not
spare each other, but are very skilful in giving great whacks on the head.
When blood oozes from one of the contestants a few coins are thrown to the
victor. These games pass the time till all the spectators have arrived'.

Both women [de Saussure wrote] were very scantily clothed, and wore
little bodices and very short petticoats of white linen. One of these
amazons was a stout Irishwoman, strong and lithe to look at, the other was
a small Englishwoman, full of fire and very agile. The first was decked with
blue ribbons on the head, waist, and right arm; the second wore red
ribbons. Their weapons were a sort of two-handed sword, three or three
and a half feet in length; the guard was covered, and the blade was about
three inches wide and not sharp – only about half a foot of it was, but then
that part cut like a razor. The spectators made numerous bets, and some
peers who were there some very large wagers. On either side of the two
amazons a man stood by, holding a long staff, ready to separate them
should blood flow. After a time the combat became very animated, and was
conducted with force and vigour with the broad side of the weapons. The
Irishwoman presently received a great cut across her forehead, and that
put a stop to the first part of the combat. The Englishwoman's backers
threw her shillings and half-crowns and applauded her. During this time
the wounded woman's forehead was sewn up, this being done on stage; a
plaster was applied to it, and she drank a good big glass of spirits to revive
her courage, and the fight began again, each combatant holding a dagger in
her left hand to ward off the blows. The Irishwoman was wounded a
second time, and her adversary again received coins and plaudits from her
admirers. The wound was sewn up, and for the third time the battle
recommenced . . . The poor Irishwoman was destined to be the loser, for
she received a long and deep wound all across her neck and throat. The

surgeon sewed it up, but she was too badly hurt to fight any more, and it was time, for the combatants were dripping with perspiration, and the Irishwoman also with blood. A few coins were thrown to her to console her, but the victor made a good day's work out of the combat.

Two male champions next appeared. They wore short white jackets and breeches and hose of the same colour; their heads were bare and freshly-shaven; one of them wore green ribbons, the other yellow. They were hideous to look at, their faces being all seamed and scarred. They also commenced by paying each other grotesque and amusing compliments, and then fell on each other with the same sort of weapons the women had used; but they showed more strength, vigour, and ability, if not more courage. One blow rapidly followed another; it was really surprising neither man should be killed . . . They fought five or six times running, and only stopped for the sewing up of a wound or when too exhausted to continue. After every round the victor was thrown money by his backers; but he had to exercise great skill in catching the coins, for he had a right only to those he caught in his hands; those that fell on the ground became the property of some of the numerous rascals that were standing about, who hastened to pick them up and appropriate them. The two combatants received several wounds, one of them having his ear nearly severed from his head, and a few moments later his opponent got a cut across the face, commencing at the left eye and ending on the right cheek. This last wound ended the fight and entertainment.[6]

William Hickey described a similar entertainment which he witnessed at Wetherby's, a raffish club in Drury Lane, where men and women, 'promiscuously mounted upon chairs, tables and benches', shouted encouragement at two 'she-devils engaged in a scratching and boxing match, their faces entirely covered with blood, their bosoms bare, and the clothes torn from their bodies'. In another corner of the room 'an uncommonly athletic young man' was defending himself from the assaults of three 'Amazonian tigresses' and various male members of the club who lashed out at him with their sticks. 'He, however, made a capital defence, not sparing the women a bit more than the men, but knocking each down as opportunity occurred.'[7]

The public taste for violence was also indulged by bull- and bear-baiting. The scarred and battered animals were taken around the country by their leaders and, when a sufficient crowd had gathered, they were chained to a stake and the spectators paid a shilling each to set their dogs upon them. The handlers stood by with long staves to break the fall of the dogs as the infuriated bulls tossed them high into the air. An advertisement from the *Weekly Journal* promised additional excitements:

At the Bear Garden, at Hockey-in-the-Hole, at the request of several persons of quality, on Monday, the 11th of this instant of June, is one of the largest and most mischievous bears that was ever seen in England to be baited to death, with other variety of Bull-baiting and Bear-baiting; as also a Wild Bull to be turned loose in the Same Place, with Fireworks all over him. To begin exactly at three o'clock in the afternoon, because the sport continues long.[8]

Badgers were also baited by being tied into holes in the ground by means of chains passed through their tails and then being set upon by dogs. As many as five or six dogs might be killed by a badger's strong jaws and sharp teeth before the tormented animal died itself. But none of these so-called sports was as popular as cock-fighting, the widespread practice of which is indicated by the number of words and phrases connected with it, apart from cockpit itself, which have passed into the language, including 'pit against', 'cut out for', 'scoot' and 'a clean pair of heels'.[9]

The sport appealed to all classes and was enjoyed in village churchyards, the courts of small taverns, and in specially constructed outdoor and indoor cockpits such as the New Red Lion Cockpit at Clerkenwell, the Royal Cockpit, Birdcage Walk, and the establishment, possibly at Newmarket, where the blind Lord Albemarle Bertie is seen in Hogarth's engraving gambling with his cronies on the birds he cannot see.

As soon as its sex had been determined the owner of a cock intended for fighting would cut off its comb and wattles as well as the tail as far as the rump, clip the neck feathers from head to shoulders, then trim the wings to points, and sharpen the beak. The cock's spurs would also be sharpened with a knife, though richer owners equipped their birds with steel or silver spurs. As at prize-fights enormous sums were wagered on cockfights by such patrons of the sport as the Duke of Rutland, while a poorer man might bet a pig.

The animals used are of a particular breed [wrote de Saussure]; they are large but short-legged birds, their feathers are scarce, they have no crests to speak off, and are very ugly to look at. Some of these fighting-cocks are celebrated, and have pedigrees like gentlemen of good family, some of them being worth five or six guineas . . .

The stage on which they fight is round and small. One of the cocks is released, and struts about proudly for a few seconds. He is then caught up, and his enemy appears. When the bets are made, one of the cocks is placed on either end of the stage; they immediately rush at each other and fight furiously. It is surprising to see the ardour, the strength, the courage of these little animals, for they rarely give up till one of them is dead. The noise is terrible, and it is impossible to hear yourself speak unless you shout. At Whitehall Cockpit, on the contrary, where the spectators are mostly persons of a certain rank, the noise is much less; but would you believe that at this place several hundred pounds are sometimes lost and won? Cocks will sometimes fight a whole hour before one or the other is victorious; at other times one may get killed at once. You sometimes see a cock ready to fall and apparently die, seeming to have no more strength, and suddenly it will regain all its vigour, fight with renewed courage, and kill his enemy. Sometimes a cock will be seen vanquishing his opponent, and, thinking he is dead (if cocks can think), jump on the body of the bird and crow noisily with triumph, when the fallen bird will unexpectedly revive and slay the victor. Of course, such cases are very rare, but their possibility makes the fight very exciting. Ladies never assist at these sports.[10]

Cocks were also trained to dodge the sticks that were thrown at them in the game known as cock-throwing. In this the bird was tied to a peg by a cord, and those taking part in the game paid 2d or so for three chances of hitting it with a broomstick thrown from a distance of twenty-two yards. When they succeeded in knocking the cock over, they ran towards it and if they could pick it up before it rose to its feet again they could keep it. A well-trained cock could usually avoid the stick; but there was less chance of escape for the goose in goose-riding in which the bird, with greased neck, was tied by its legs to a bough while riders took it in turns to gallop beneath, attempting to snatch off its head as they passed.

Games like this were from time to time suppressed by the local authorities but not so much because they were cruel as because they were considered a public nuisance when they took place, as they often did, in the street. In other areas the authorities felt obliged by tradition and public opinion to maintain such sports: at Beverley in Yorkshire it was still the custom – as it had been 'from time immemorial' – 'for every mayor of this town on his election, to give a bull to the populace, for the purpose of being baited, on the day of his being sworn into office'.[11]

Even racing had its cruel aspects. In one of his letters César de Saussure described the large open spaces, outlined by posts, in which the races were held, the starting and finishing pillars on which the judges sat, the jockeys' 'little shirts and tight breeches of red, blue, green or yellow cloth, and little caps of the same colour'. He wrote of the crowds of racegoers some of whom arrived in coaches, others in chaises, yet others in phaetons and many more on horseback; and of the farmers of the neighbourhood, 'all well mounted and making considerable wagers . . . their manner of talking and behaving and expressing themselves being quite peculiar to their nation . . .

their conversation artless and frank, but at the same time assured and very pleasing, if you pay no attention to the oaths they continually use'.[12]

Races were then run in a series of heats, the winner being the horse that won most heats, sometimes as many as four over a distance of four miles. Horses, bred for staying power rather than for speed, were untrained, and the jockeys more adept at jostling their rivals or even knocking them off their small saddles than in skilful riding. They whipped and kicked and attempted to unhorse each other by entwining their legs, wrote John Lawrence, the eccentric author of *A Philosophical and Practical Treatise on the Horse and on the Moral Duties of Man towards the Brute Creation*: 'I well remember a fellow . . . who was accustomed to boast of the execution he had formerly done with the but end of his whip, and the eyes and teeth he had beat out.'[13] When a jockey fell, a spectator might catch the horse and ride him past the finishing post. But winning was not always an unalloyed pleasure. The hard-drinking painter, George Morland, who kept eight horses at the White Inn, Paddington, told a friend in 1785 that, having 'commenced a new business of jockey to the races', he was angrily scolded and then whipped by 'a mob of horsemen' after losing a heat; yet, when he won at Margate, he was 'very near being killed'. 'I won the heat so completely that the other horses were half a mile behind,' he said, 'upon which near 400 sailors, smugglers, fishermen etc. set upon me with sticks, stones, waggoners' whips, fists etc. and one man took me by the thigh and pulled me off the horse.'[14]

Racing – first organized at York in 1530 – was already, however, 'the sport of kings'. The races at Newmarket had been patronized by Charles II. Queen Anne, a keen racegoer who gave plates to be run for at both Newmarket and Datchet Mead near Windsor out of secret service money, had 'appointed races to be made' at Ascot in 1711. In 1728 George II had attended the races at Newmarket 'and nothing was spared to make them successful'. George III went regularly to the races at Ascot and Egham; while his son, the future George IV, owned some of the finest horses in the country, winning no less than 185 races between 1788 and 1791, though he refused to have anything more to do with Newmarket and sold his stud after his brilliant jockey, Samuel Chiffney, had been accused there of dishonesty and questioned by the members of the Jockey Club.[15]

After the foundation of the Jockey Club in about 1750, the St Leger was established in 1776, the Oaks in 1779, the Derby in 1780; and some of the greatest jockeys in the history of the turf began to make their reputations. It was not, however, until Lord George Bentinck turned his attention to the reform of the turf in the 1830s that its principal abuses were gradually extirpated.

\*

If violence often erupted on the racecourse before Lord George Bentinck's time, so it still did during games of football, matches which were 'very inconvenient to passers-by'. A 'score of rascals' would appear in the street kicking about 'a leather ball filled with air'. 'They will break panes of glass and smash the windows of coaches,' a foreign visitor remarked, 'and almost knock you down without the slightest compunction; on the contrary, they will roar with laughter.'[16] Cricket, on the other hand, was a relatively peaceful game. 'Everyone plays it,' de Saussure said, 'the common people and also men of rank . . . They go into a large open field, and knock a ball about with a piece of wood. I will not attempt to describe this game; but it requires agility and skill.'[17]

At that time the wicket consisted of only two stumps about one foot high and perhaps two feet apart with a third stump or bail across the top. The ball was thrown along the ground as fast as possible by the bowler, and the batsman, who stood at a distance of twenty-two yards from him, attempted to hit it with a wooden bat curved like a hockey stick. In the early days of the game runs were scored by cutting notches on a stick, a method satisfactory to the innumerate player. If the batsman missed the ball, or after he had hit it and taken a run, he had to place his bat in a hole scooped out between the stumps, known as the 'popping hole', before the wicket-keeper got the ball into it first. Later, instead of getting his bat into the 'popping hole', to avoid being run out or stumped, the batsman had to place it behind a line marked about two feet from the wicket; this was, and still is, known as the popping crease.

It appears from medieval manuscript illuminations that a kind of cricket was being played in England at least as early as the thirteenth century. References to the game become more common in the sixteenth century when, for instance, one of Queen Elizabeth's coroners for Surrey deposed in court that 'when he was a scholler in the free school at Guildford, he and several of his fellowes did runne and play there at crickett and other plaies'. As the game spread across the southern counties it seems to have been frowned upon by the authorities. According to Sir William Dugdale, Oliver Cromwell, who was born in 1599, 'threw himself into a dissolute and dangerous course' and 'became famous for football, cricket, cudgelling and wrestling', acquiring the 'name of royster'. In the county of Kent, where it was played on a Sunday, the game caused particular offence. 'Maidstone was formerly a very profane town,' wrote the author of a life of Thomas Wilson who was born two years after Oliver Cromwell, 'in as much as I have seen morrice-dancing, cudgel-playing, stoolball, cricket and many other sports openly and publicly indulged in on the Lord's Day.' It was not until 1748 that it was formally decided that cricket was not an illegal game, the Court of King's Bench holding that it was 'a very manly game, not bad in itself, but

only in the ill use made of it by betting more than ten pounds on it; but that
was bad and against the law'. Soon afterwards the celebrated Hambledon
Club was formed, and the men who played in this club on Broad Ha' Penny
and Windmill Downs in Hampshire were a match for any team that could be
brought against them.[18]

By now the game was played by the well-to-do as well as by the common
people. The Gentlemen of Sevenoaks had been playing the Gentlemen of
London by the 1730s; and in the 1740s a team from Kent – captained by the
head gardener at Knole and including Lord John Sackville whose family had
lived there since the beginning of the seventeenth century – was facing an All
England team which lost by one run. In 1792, 2000 spectators watched Kent
play Hampshire. On this occasion there were evidently eleven players on
each side but in village matches there were sometimes less and often more,
sometimes as many as twenty-two.

The mixture of classes in a game which had originally been played only by
the lower was condemned in some quarters. *The British Champion* of 8
September 1743 loftily declined 'to dispute the privilege' that noblemen and
gentlemen enjoyed of making butchers, cobblers and tinkers their companions if they so wished.[19] But the appeal of the game was too wide for its
devotees to be deterred by such criticisms. It was, in any case, seen as a more
gentlemanly and sportsmanlike game than most. 'You will desire to excel all
boys at your age at cricket,' that fastidious arbiter of taste, Lord Chesterfield,
informed his son. Several distinguished habitués of the expensive and
fashionable Star and Garter tavern in Pall Mall, including the Earl of Winchilsea and Charles Lennox, later Duke of Richmond, met occasionally to
play cricket on White Conduit Fields in Islington and in 1752 they formed the
White Conduit Club. Considering it undignified to play on public land, they
arranged for Thomas Lord, their Yorkshire 'attendant', to take a lease of
private land on the site of what is now Dorset Square. The ground was
opened in 1787, the year in which some members of the White Conduit Club
formed the Marylebone Cricket Club. The two clubs were later merged, and
in 1814 the Marylebone Cricket Club moved to a new ground in St John's
Wood taken by Thomas Lord.[20]

The rules of the game had by then been much altered. A third stump had
been introduced in 1776 and the wicket had been raised to a height of
twenty-two inches. It was some time, however, before these rules were
generally observed. When Diana Sterling painted a cricket match being
played in Essex during the Regency she depicted only two stumps and a bat
far larger than the new regulations allowed. The gentlemanly players are all
in white with tall hats.[21] But, although white top hats with black bands were
preferred by more formal teams – those of the Earl of Winchilsea's being
distinguished by silver lacing – most country players wore no special clothes.

They also disdained the use of gloves and pads, and seem to have been less willing than those in London teams to welcome girls into their sides.

It was certainly not a game for delicate fingers, particularly for those who played as wicket-keepers.

> The blood of a cricketer is seldom shed from any part of the body but his fingers [wrote John Nyren, the Hambledon cricketer and author of *The Young Cricketer's Tutor*]. But the fingers of an old cricketer, so bent, so shattered, so indented, so contorted, so venerable! are enough to bring tears of envy and emulation from any eye.[22]

> We never thought of knocks [another Hambledon player told the Rev. James Pycroft]. Certainly you would see a bump heave under the stocking and even blood come through, but I never saw a man killed now you ask the question, and never saw an accident of much consequence. Fancy the old fashion before cricket shoes! I saw John Wells tear a finger nail off against his shoe buckle in picking up a ball.[23]

Gambling was carried on as eagerly at cricket matches as it was at cockfights and prize-fights and at horse races. Bookies were banned from Lord's in 1825; but huge private bets continued to change hands as they had done in the past. There was also much drinking at cricket matches, and the deeper men drank the higher they gambled.

Foreign visitors considered, in fact, that gambling was a kind of national fever. Bets were placed on everything, not only on games of chance and every sporting event and political contest but on all manner of happenings whose outcome was unknown or on anything that cropped up in conversation or led to argument. 'There is nothing, however trivial, or ridiculous which is not capable of producing a bet,' noted the *Connoisseur* magazine in 1754. Horace Walpole told the story, which thereafter became well-known, of a man who fell down in the street; immediately bets were placed as to whether he were dead or not; a sympathetic passer-by, suggesting that he should be bled, was shouted down by the gamblers as this, they protested, would affect the fairness of the betting.[24]

At White's Club, as at most similar establishments in St James's and elsewhere, a betting-book was kept in which were recorded wagers as to the duration of wars, the numbers of children various members' wives would have, whether or not Mr Cavendish would succeed in killing 'the blue bottle before he goes to bed', the ages at which people would die: 'Ld. Lincoln bets Ld. Winchilsea One Hundred Guineas that the Dutchess Dowager of Marlborough does not survive the Dutchess Dowager of Cleveland'. This was a comparatively modest wager: one wet day Lord Arlington bet £3000 upon which of two raindrops would first reach the bottom of a window-pane;

and in 1755 Sir John Bland, Member of Parliament for Ludgershall, who squandered his entire fortune playing hazard and at one stage of play found himself £32,000 down, shot himself after being ruined at the club. Suicides were not at all uncommon. In the year of Bland's death, Lord Mountford, having lost enormous sums, shot himself; and a few years later Lord Milton's eldest son did the same at the Bedford Arms in Covent Garden at the age of twenty-three. 'I tremble to think,' Lord Lyttelton wrote, 'that the rattling of a dice box at White's may one day or another (if my son should be a member of that noble academy) shake down all our fine oaks.' A typical night at White's, another member said, might involve 'dinner say at seven o'clock, play all night, one man unable to sit in his chair at three o'clock, break up at six the next morning and the winner going away drunk with a thousand guineas'.[25]

Charles James Fox, who once lost £13,000 at a single sitting to the Earl of Carlisle, was one of those who would willingly sit up all night playing cards; and once he gambled continuously for twenty-four hours, losing money at the rate of £10 a minute. His fellow-players sat intently round the table, wearing loose frieze great-coats – sometimes worn inside out to bring them luck – their laced ruffles protected by pieces of leather such as those worn by footmen when cleaning knives.

Play was carried on as assiduously and for quite as high stakes at Almack's, Brooks's Club and elsewhere as it was at White's:

> The gaming at Almack's which has taken the *pas* of White's [Walpole told Sir Horace Mann in February 1770], is worthy of the decline of our empire . . . The young men of the age lose ten, fifteen, twenty thousand pounds in an evening there. Lord Stavordale, not one and twenty, lost 11,000l. there last Tuesday, but recovered it by one great hand at hazard. He swore a great oath – 'Now if I had been playing deep I might have won millions.'[26]

Gambling was not confined either to the rich or to gentlemen. Ladies also gambled for high stakes, and several, like Lady Mornington, Lady Cassilis and Lady Archer kept gaming establishments or faro tables. Mrs Lybbe Powys described the gambling that went on at an evening party at Eastbury in 1777:

> They danced in the Saloon. No minuets that night; would have been difficult without a master of the ceremonies among so many people of rank. Two card-rooms, the drawing-room and eating-room. The latter looked so elegant lighted up; two tables at loo, one quinze, one vingt-une, many whist. At one of the former large sums pass'd. I saw one lady of quality borrow ten pieces within half an hour after she set down to vingt-une, and a

countess at loo who ow'd to every soul round the table before half the night was over. They wanted Powys and I to play at 'low loo' as they term'd it, but we rather chose to keep our features less agitated than those we saw around us.[27]

There were said to be almost as many hazard tables at Newmarket and the fashionable spas as there were in London; and it was the gambling facilities of Bath that first drew there that arbiter of taste Richard 'Beau' Nash who, as master of ceremonies, took large commissions on winnings at the gaming tables in the Assembly Rooms and was a partner in Wiltshire's as well as in other gaming-houses in the city.

Several efforts were made to suppress gambling; but they had little success, and gaming-houses continued to flourish. The *St James's Evening Post* printed a list of officials and servants that one of these establishments employed: there was a director; an 'operator' who dealt the cards at faro; two croupiers; two 'puffs' who had money given them to decoy others to play; a 'clerk' who kept an eye on the 'puffs'; a 'flasher' who went about telling the customers how often the bank had lost; a 'dunner' who saw to it that losses were promptly paid; a 'captain' who fought any gentleman who was 'peevish for losing his money'; a waiter 'to fill out wine, snuff, candles and attend in the gaming room'; an usher who showed and lit the way upstairs from the street; a porter; an 'orderly man' who walked up and down outside and gave prompt notice of the approach of constables; and a 'runner' who was employed 'to get intelligence of the justices' meetings'.[28]

Powerless to prevent gambling, the government took a profit from it by authorizing lotteries and, by an Act of 1778, compelling keepers of lottery offices to take out licences. In London these cost £50, elsewhere £10; and these high sums ensured that few licences were taken out. Whereas there were known to be as many as 400 lottery offices in London alone before 1778, no more than fifty-one offices took out licences in the whole of England as required by the Act. It was calculated that in 1796 well over 9500 men were employed in one capacity or another by licensed and unlicensed offices, both of which were frequently as crowded with poor gamblers as the fashionable gambling rooms were with the rich. An elderly tradesman told Francis Place that he had been in a lottery office one evening 'with a large number of others' when, 'all their money being gone', he 'had pulled off his waistcoat and buttoned up his coat. The other men did the same; women pulled off their petticoats and even their stockings to make a lot for the pawnbroker to raise money.'[29]

Just as men would sit up all night to gamble, so they would sit up all night to drink. Bolingbroke would go to his office in the morning straight from the dining-table with a wet napkin round his head; and, according to Gilbert Eliot, 'men of all ages [drank] abominably', Fox a 'great deal', Sheridan 'excessively', Pitt 'as much as either', and Grey 'more than any of them'. But none was a match for Dr John Campbell who – while Pitt and Sheridan were content to drink six bottles a day – was said to get through thirteen, and they were of port. Drunkenness was common in all classes: Samuel Johnson recalled that when he was young 'all the decent people in Lichfield got drunk every night, and were not the worse thought of'. In Herefordshire, so Henry Gunning wrote in his *Reminiscences*, country gentlemen regularly drank, 'in addition to their wine, a copious draught of the real *Steyre* cider, a huge tankard of which was always placed at each end of the table'. Drunkenness was not only viewed with indulgence, it was often considered an excuse for criminal behaviour.

> At a Christening at Beddington in Surrey [the *Gentlemen's Magazine* reported in 1748] the nurse was so intoxicated that after she had undressed the child, instead of laying it in the cradle she put it behind a large fire, which burnt it to death in a few minutes. She was examined before a magistrate, and said she was quite stupid and senseless, so that she took the child for a log of wood; on which she was discharged.[30]

It was quite usual to see magistrates and Members of Parliament drunk on their benches; and when the Mutiny Act was being framed it was thought advisable to include a clause providing for court martials to take place only at times of the day when its members were more likely to be sober.[31]

Both towns and villages were well supplied with alehouses and had been so for many years. In the early years of the seventeenth century one observer complained that every street in London was 'replenished' with them; and Thomas Dekker confirmed that some streets were but one 'continued alehouse'. In the county of Durham it was said that there were so many of them that it was impossible to count their numbers.[32] A government survey made in 1577 had suggested that there were then about 24,000 alehouse-keepers in England, that is to say one for every 142 inhabitants of the country.[33] There seems to have been a slight slowing down in the growth of their numbers at the beginning of the eighteenth century and a noticeable decline in proportion to the increasing population at the beginning of the nineteenth; yet, even so, in about 1700 Bristol had an alehouse for every fifty-six inhabitants, Oxford one for every sixty-two. In Kent in 1753 there was a public house for every 104 or so people, in Chester one for every ninety-two; and the numbers in other counties were comparable with these. In the 1780s John Howard, the prison reformer, wrote of 'the great and increasing number of alehouses' that he saw on his travels throughout the kingdom.

In nearly all of them great quantities of ale and small beer were consumed or were carried away in jugs, barrels and pails to be drunk at home or at work. It seems from excise records that by the late seventeenth century consumption for the whole country was as much as three quarts a week a head; and Peter Clark, who has made a detailed study of the alehouse in England, thinks that the real figure may have been nearly twice as high.[34]

Certainly, foreigners were astonished by the amount of beer that the English drank.

> Would you believe it, though water is to be had in abundance in London and of fairly good quality, absolutely none is drunk? [wrote César de Saussure]. The lower classes, even the paupers, do not know what it is to quench their thirst with water. In this country nothing but beer is drunk, and it is made in several qualities. Small beer is what everyone drinks when thirsty; it is used even in the best houses, and costs only a penny the pot. Another kind of beer is called porter, meaning carrier, because the greater quantity of this beer is consumed by the working classes. It is a thick and strong beverage, and the effect it produces, if drunk in excess, is the same as that of wine; this porter costs threepence the pot. In London there are a number of alehouses, where nothing but this sort of beer is sold. There are again other clear beers, called ale, some of these being as transparent as fine old wine, foreigners often mistaking them at first sight for the latter . . . It is said that more grain is consumed in England for making beer than for making bread.[35]

Some alehouses were, as William Vaughan said, no more than 'paltry cottages'. Others were large establishments with their own cellars and brewhouses, with rooms partitioned off into drinking cubicles, pewter tankards instead of the stone and earthenware pots still in use in the poorer places, tables and chairs as well as stools, and, perhaps, with looking-glasses, prints and maps upon the walls and several beds for the convenience of travellers. Many offered games, like ninepins and bowls, as well as drink; a few had bowling-alleys; most had benches outside the front door where customers could sit in fine weather and where the alehouse-keeper would often stand to encourage business while his children ran off to whistle at workers to remind them of the pleasures their father offered. Among these pleasures might be a pretty wife, like Mrs Walker of William Walker's alehouse which Conand Barton frequented more to see her 'than for the ale'. Or there might be a girl on the premises, a servant or a lodger perhaps, who would allow customers to take her to bed. A Worcestershire victualler arranged for one Elizabeth Hodges to entertain customers 'upon his own bed

. . . and his wife put her apron before the window to shadow them'. Barnaby Rich said that a man might have 'his pot of ale, his pipe of tobacco and his pocksy whore and all for his 3d'.[36]

By the middle of the eighteenth century the number of disreputable tippling establishments appears to have decreased. Alehouses were becoming more like taverns and were often referred to – as taverns and smaller inns were referred to – as public houses. The old ale-stakes were replaced by inn signs; food was more widely available; cakes and pies as well as bread and cheese and even roast meat were sold; tobacco and snuff were also to be had; newspapers were provided; women were more often seen as customers; and instead of being asked to share a room or a bed, travellers were more likely to be offered a choice of rooms in which they could enjoy a meal by a blazing fire. In Smollett's *The Life and Adventures of Sir Launcelot Greaves*, which was published about 1760, there is a country alehouse whose kitchen was 'paved with red bricks, remarkably clean, furnished with three or four windsor chairs, adorned with shining plates of pewter and copper sauce-pans nicely scoured, while a cheerful fire of sea-coal blazed in the chimney'.[37]

Yet while alehouses were becoming more decent and respectable, most gin-shops and brandy-shops were certainly not. These proliferated at an extraordinary rate after 1700, there being, so William Maitland estimated in 1737, no less than 8659 of them in London alone. Many of them were in cellars where the customers drank standing up or took their spirits away with them. They were generally kept, the Middlesex justices protested, not by licensed victuallers and vintners but by 'chandlers, weavers, tobacconists, shoemakers, carpenters, barbers, tailors, dyers, labourers, and others'.[38] There were less of them in the provinces, but there spirits, frequently smuggled, were sold in most alehouses.

In London spirits were sold not only in shops but 'even in the streets and highways', so a committee of justices reported in 1726, 'on bulks set up for that purpose, in wheelbarrows and privately in garrets, cellars, backrooms and other places . . . Such who sell fruit or herbs in stalls sell geneva, and many inferior tradesmen begin now to keep it in their shops for their customers, whereby it is scarce possible for soldiers, seamen, servants or others of their rank, to go anywhere, without being drawn in . . . In the hamlet of Bethnal Green above forty weavers sell it. And if we may judge what will happen in other workhouses now erecting, by what has already happened in that of St Giles in the Fields, we have reason to fear the violent fondness and desire of this liquor, which unaccountably possesses all our poor, may prevent in great measure the good effects proposed by them.'[39]

By 1743 over 8 million gallons of gin were being sold in London a year.[40] It was sold in factories, as well as workhouses, in barbers' shops, in brothels and in prisons; in the King's Bench Prison, 120 gallons of gin were sold every week 'besides other spirits in proportion'. It was sold in common lodging-houses where men and women 'often strangers to each other, lie promiscuously, the price of a double bed being no more than threepence as an encouragement to lie together. But as these places are thus adapted to whoredom, so are they no less provided for drunkenness, gin being sold in them at a penny a quartern, so that the smallest sum of money serves for intoxication.' The bodies of men, women and children could be seen lying dead drunk where they had fallen, in the middle of the day, as well as at night in many of the streets of the slum quarters of St Giles, Whetstone Park and Spitalfields. In the gin cellars rows of bodies sat on the straw, propped up against the walls until the effects of the spirit wore off and they could start drinking again.

In Hogarth's admonitory *Gin Lane*, the scene is the slum of St Giles and in the background can be seen the spire of Hawksmoor's recently finished church of St George's Bloomsbury, emphasizing by its ornate elaboration the degradation and ugliness below. The central figure is a bedraggled woman who sprawls half naked at the top of a flight of steps, staring in front of her with an expression on her drunken face of senseless and grotesque amusement as she reaches for a pinch of snuff. A baby till lately sucking at her breast falls unregarded on to the cobblestones beneath. By her scabrous legs sits a corpse-like ballad-seller leaning back exhausted against a wooden rail. 'Buy my ballads,' the poor wretch who served Hogarth as a model for this character used to croak, 'and I will give you a glass of gin for nothing.' Above him in the street are men brawling in front of a distillery, women selling their kitchenware to a pawnbroker, little charity girls sipping, a baby choking, a starving man gnawing at a dog's bone. A young woman is laid into her coffin; in a garret dangles a man who has hanged himself; a nearby house is toppling into ruins. The sordid gin cellar bears over the doorway the celebrated legend:

> Drunk for a penny
> Dead drunk for two pennies
> Clean straw for nothing.

It was scarcely an exaggerated picture: a man set to watch the door of a gin shop on Holborn Hill between the hours of seven and ten in the evening counted 1411 persons going in and out, excluding children, the children from seven to fourteen years of age as intoxicated as their parents.[41] In letters, pamphlets and sermons, in the reports of parliamentary committees and in charges to juries, the evil consequences of the excessive drinking of gin were constantly deplored.

These accursed spirituous liquors which to the shame of our Government are to be so easily had and in such quantities drunk have changed the very nature of our people [one writer protested], and they will if continued to be drunk, destroy the very race . . . There is not only no safety of living in this town [London] but scarcely any in the country now, robbery and murder have grown so frequent. Our people have become what they never were before; cruel and inhuman.[42]

There were cases enough to support his words. When in 1734 Judith Dufour, a dipsomaniac 'never in her right mind but always roving', collected her baby from a workhouse where it had been 'new clothed', she strangled it and left the naked body in a ditch. She sold the new clothes for 1s 4d and spent the money on gin. A few years later, so the *Gentleman's Magazine* reported, 'There were executed at Tyburn, July 6, Elizabeth Banks for stripping a child; Catherine Conway, for forging a seaman's ticket; and Margaret Harvey for robbing her master. They were all drunk.'

Should the drinking of this poison be continued in its present height, during the next twenty years [wrote the Bow Street magistrate, Henry Fielding], there will by that time be few of the common people left to drink it . . . Gin is the principal sustenance (if it may be so called) of more than a hundred thousand people in the metropolis . . . The intoxicating draught itself disqualifies them from any honest means to acquire it, at the same time that it removes sense of fear and shame and emboldens them to commit every wicked and desparate enterprise.[43]

In the early 1740s, when gin drinking was out of control, there were twice as many burials as baptisms in London; and 'can it be necessary to add to this shocking loss', asked Corbyn Morris, 'the sickly state of such infants as are born who with difficulty pass through the first stages of life and live very few of them to years of manhood? . . . Enquire from the several hospitals in this City, whether any increase of patients and of what sort, are daily brought under their care. They will all declare, increasing multitudes of dropsical and consumptive people arising from the effects of spirituous liquors.' Even when the worst years were over, an eighth of all deaths of adults in London were attributed by doctors to the excessive drinking of spirits.[44]

The government was slow to heed the warnings. In a Parliament largely occupied by landowners dedicated to the principles of *laissez faire* and self-aggrandisement it was difficult to pass any measures which interfered with agricultural interests; and the money derived by farmers and land-owners from the distillation of spirits from English grain was an important source of their income. Acts were passed to restrict consumption, but they had little effect, and stronger measures were firmly opposed on various grounds such as those put forward by William Pulteney who declared that they would 'produce such riots and tumults as may endanger our present establishment, or at least [could] not be quelled without spilling blood . . . and putting an end to the liberties of the people'. At length in 1751, how-ever, an Act was passed which did have good effects; and thereafter, with the duty on spirits much increased and its sale in chandlers' shops forbidden, the poor began to return to beer. 'The lower people of late years have not drank spirituous liquors so freely as they did before the good regulations and qualifications for selling them,' it was confidently asserted in 1757. 'The additional excise has raised their price, improvements in the distillery have rendered the home-made distillations as wholesome as the imported. We do not see the hundredth part of poor wretches drunk in the streets.'[45]

By 1784 the home consumption of British spirits had fallen to one million gallons a year; and an American visitor to England, while noting the enormous amount of beer and porter drunk by the common people, added that they drank 'but little ardent spirits because its excessive dearness [placed] it almost beyond their reach'.[46]

# 35 · *Marriage and Divorce*

'We saw a light in the parson's chamber,' says Captain Basil in Farquhar's *Stage Coach* of 1704, 'went up and found him smoking his pipe. He first gave us his blessing, then lent us his bed.'

Marriage in Farquhar's day, and for many years before and after it, was certainly not difficult to contract. Nor were common law marriages which were recognized by the authorities. According to ecclesiastical law, promises made verbally before witnesses, such as 'I do take thee to my wife' or 'I do take thee to my husband', constituted irrevocable commitments for life, even though weddings in church to other persons might subsequently take place. There were local variations; but it was generally agreed that a binding marriage had occurred provided that there were witnesses to the mutual undertaking, that the man kissed the woman and gave her a present – usually a gold ring or even half a gold ring – and that sexual intercourse took place.[1]

In 1604 it had been ordained that a church wedding – by then generally recognized as a prerequisite of any proper marriage, whatever the law had to say upon the matter – must take place during the morning after eight o'clock, that it must be held in the parish church of either the bride or the bridegroom, that banns must be read for three weeks running before the ceremony to allow objections to the marriage to be heard, and that no one might marry before the age of twenty-one without the permission of parents or guardians.[2] But there were many ways of evading these canons. 'Every man may privately have a wife in every corner of London,' so it was claimed in a parliamentary debate, 'or in every town he has been in, without it being possible for them to know of one another.'[3] There were, for instance, churches which claimed exemption from jurisdiction, one of them being St James's, Duke Place, where, between 1664 and 1691, about 40,000 quick marriages took place; while there was 'such a coupling at St Pancras that they stand behind one another, as 'twere in a country dance'.[4] Also, there were

numerous clergymen who were prepared to conduct a brief marriage ceremony without asking embarrassing questions, provided they were given an
appropriate fee. In London, Fleet marriages – which were not declared
illegal until after the middle of the eighteenth century – were notorious. They
were performed without licence, first in the chapel of the Fleet Prison and
then in nearby taverns and houses, several of which bore signs depicting a
male and female hand clasped together above the legend 'Marriages Performed Within'. The marriages were mostly conducted by clergymen who
were imprisoned in the Fleet for debt and were allowed the 'Liberties of the
Fleet', that is to say were permitted to move about freely within a certain area
immediately surrounding the prison. They could be seen standing beneath
the hanging signs awaiting custom, like one described as 'a squalid profligate
fellow clad in a tattered plaid night gown with a fiery face and ready to couple
you for a dram or a roll of tobacco'. The more usual fee varied between a
couple of guineas for a well-dressed couple and three shillings or so for a
couple that evidently could afford no more. If they had been brought in from
the streets the tout had his share, as did the tavern-keeper if the ceremony
took place on his premises. The couple could have an official-looking
document if this were wanted – backdated when bastard children had to be
legitimized – while all records could conveniently be lost if a secret or
bigamous marriage were required. Nor was it only in London that these
fly-by-night marriages could be contracted. In several country villages –
Fledborough in Nottinghamshire, for example – there were known to be
parsons prepared to conduct them.

After clandestine marriages were outlawed by Lord Hardwicke's Marriage
Act, which came into operation in 1754, marriages conducted in taverns or
private houses, or in places far removed from the parish where the bride or
bridegroom lived, were to be declared invalid; and enforcement of the law
was to be entrusted to secular rather than ecclesiastical courts, clergymen
who broke it being liable to fourteen years' transportation. The Act also
decreed that only the church wedding, not the verbal promise, was binding
and that all church weddings had to be entered on the parish register.

While marriages could be easily contracted before Lord Hardwicke's
Marriage Act, the formalities to be observed in a conventional marriage
among the gentry and well-to-do yeomen families were nevertheless elaborate. In Yorkshire, for example, it was customary for the prospective
bridegroom's father, or the young man himself, to write to the father of his
intended bride 'to know if he shall be welcome to the house':

> If the notion he thought well of, and embraced, then the young man goeth
> perhaps twice to see how the maid standeth affected. Then if he see that
> she be tractable, and that her inclination is toward him, then the third time

that he visiteth, he perhaps giveth her a ten-shilling piece of gold, or a ring of that price; or perhaps a twenty-shilling piece, or a ring of that price; then 10s the next time, or the next after that, a pair of gloves of 6s 8d a pair; and after that, each other time, some conceited toy or novelty of less value. They usually visit every three weeks or a month, and are usually half a year, or very near, from the first going to the conclusion.

So soon as the young folks are agreed and contracted, then the father of the maid carrieth her over to the young man's house to see how they like of all, and there doth the young man's father meet them to treat of a dower, and like-wise of a jointure or feoffment for the woman. And then do they also appoint and set down the day of the marriage, which may perhaps be about a fortnight or three weeks after, and in that time do they get made the wedding clothes, and make provision against the wedding dinner, which is usually at the maid's father's.

Then so soon as the bride is [attired] and that they are ready to go forth, the bridegroom comes, and takes her by the hand, and saith: 'Mistress, I hope you are willing', or else kisseth her before them, and then followeth her father out of the doors. Then one of the bridegroom's men ushereth the bride . . . to church.

A dinner followed the church service, but the bride and bridegroom did not immediately go away together. Instead, a month or so elapsed before the husband went to fetch his wife, accompanied by 'some of his best friends, and young men his neighbours'.[5] This period was known as the 'honeymoon', a word which did not until later come to mean the holiday which the bride and bridegroom took together, the bride usually being accompanied by a companion until the middle of the nineteenth century. Before the honeymoon holiday became an accepted practice for those who could afford it, the first night of a marriage was often attended by banter and by a ritual almost as public as that which traditionally accompanied the wedding night of an heir to the throne who would be undressed by his gentlemen, while the bride was being undressed by her ladies, then conducted to the bridal bed whose curtains were drawn back to reveal the couple together before being closed again for the night. It was customary for the bride to wear gloves; and as late as 1708 a girl who had questioned this practice in the correspondence columns of *The British Apollo* was told that since it was 'the custom and fashion to go into the bridal bed with gloves on, we think it not genteel to go to bed without'.[6]

Love was rarely a matter for consideration in most upper-class marriages; and, indeed, it was suggested that a marriage charged with excessive passion might result in the birth of unnatural children, a 'cursed progeny [of] woeful imps'.[7] 'Beg first the assistance of God', James Houblon, a rich merchant, advised his daughters when they began to 'undertake the matching' of their children, 'and see that you match them in families that fear the Lord and have gotten their Estates honestly.'[8] After the Civil War it had become so common a practice for merchants such as Houblon to arrange socially satisfactory marriages for their daughters and granddaughters that Sir William Temple condemned it as 'a public grievance'; and Sir William Morice lamented that his own daughters were 'commodities lying on [his] hands', pushed out of the marriage market by 'merchants' daughters that weigh so many thousands'.[9] While it was generally considered quite proper, however, for a gentleman's son to marry a merchant's daughter for her worldly goods, it was by no means so for the merchant's son to marry the gentleman's daughter. Lord Sandwich, for instance, was far from being alone in deciding that he would rather see his daughter 'with a pedlar's bag at her back', provided her husband was a gentleman, than have her demean herself by a marrying a mere citizen.[10]

In Sandwich's day a father's decision was usually final in such matters. In 1701 a young lady wrote to *The Athenian Oracle* – a magazine that answered questions from young ladies – to ask for advice: she had vowed to leave her parents as soon as an opportunity offered itself because they had treated her so unkindly; she now had the chance to do so: did her vow take precedence over her duty to her father. 'Your vow does not oblige you,' she was advised categorically, 'for your Body is the Goods of your Father, and you cannot lawfully dispose of your self without his knowledge and consent, so that you ought to beg God Almighty's Pardon for your Rashness.'[11]

Indeed, it long remained the custom among the gentry for the father of the intended bride to be consulted before any steps towards marriage were taken. In the 1740s one Mr Grosvenor, having lost all his money gambling, decided he would have to look for a rich wife. He was offered one by his friend Hungerford who invited him down to the country to see the property that would one day be his if he married the Hungerfords' only daughter and heir. Grosvenor accepted the offer to view the property and the girl, and asked his man of affairs, a barrister named Elers, to accompany him so that he could look through the title deeds and, if all was satisfactory, draw up the conveyances. On arrival, however, Grosvenor was disappointed in the human part of the bargain: he found Miss Hungerford, while good-natured enough, a plain, clumsy, plump, 'unfashioned girl with little knowledge of any sort and no accomplishments'. He sadly confessed to Mr Elers that he did not much fancy her, that she was 'a sad encumbrance upon the estate'. When Elers demurred, Grosvenor suggested that the lawyer should take the whole thing over himself. The father was, therefore, consulted; he agreed; the daughter then consented 'with blushes and becoming filial duty' to marry the lawyer. So the match was settled.[12]

*

In the upper and landed classes the eldest sons and heirs almost invariably married so as to produce heirs themselves. Younger sons, however, did not marry as a matter of course, about a fifth of them remaining bachelors, either by choice or, more usually, through financial necessity. In the seventeenth century upper-class daughters were also less often likely to be married than their female forebears had been a century before, since the practice of keeping estates intact for the benefit of the male heir had meant that there was less money and property available for his siblings. So, whereas only 10 per cent of daughters in landed families were still spinsters at the age of fifty in the sixteenth century, the proportion rose to 15 per cent in the early seventeenth century and to almost 25 per cent between 1675 and the end of the century. The proportion of unmarried women in the country as a whole at this time seems to have been much lower than this, perhaps no more than 9 or 10 per cent.[13]

Marriages in the early seventeenth century were not usually contracted at nearly so early an age as the plays of Shakespeare suggest. One might suppose from *Romeo and Juliet*, as Peter Laslett has indicated, that girls were commonly married when they were about fourteen, as Juliet was herself, and sometimes at twelve or thirteen, as her mother was. In fact, girls were very rarely married at fourteen, virtually never at twelve and less often in their late teens than they are now, although the age of consent was fourteen for a boy and twelve for a girl.[14] An examination of 1000 licences issued by the diocese of Canterbury in 1619–60 to people marrying for the first time, revealed that only one girl gave her age as thirteen, four as fifteen and twelve as sixteen. All the rest were seventeen or over, 85 per cent more than nineteen; the average age was about twenty-four. The bridegrooms were, in general, about three or four years older than the brides. These couples were, in fact, only slightly younger than are those who get married today when the average age for men is between twenty-eight and twenty-nine and for women twenty-five to twenty-six.[15]

In the landed classes the average age of brides was slightly younger than that of poorer girls, but not appreciably so, while bridegrooms from these classes were of much the same age as those who were artisans and who would have to wait until they had acquired the necessary means to support a wife. Similarly, the younger son of a squire might have to wait until he had established himself in a profession and, by the eighteenth century, might be in his middle thirties before he had done so.[16]

There were, of course, occasional arranged marriages in which one or both parties were very young indeed, no more than eleven or twelve. But these were exceptional cases. The age of sexual maturity in women was probably not as early then as it is now. Certainly, it has fallen in western countries within the last few generations. In mid-nineteenth-century Norway, which has the longest records known, girls began to menstruate when they were just over seventeen; but 100 years later they had begun to do so, as they had in England, at about thirteen and a half.[17]

At whatever age the partners were when they contracted it, a marriage was unlikely to be of long duration, for the poor about seventeen to nineteen years on average in the seventeenth century and twenty-two in the eighteenth, and for the children of squires about twenty-two in the earlier period and thirty in the later.[18] Life expectancy was short: three score years and ten was accepted as the span of man's life on earth, but few people lived to seventy and those who did were considered to be very old. In the seventeenth century when no more than about 5 per cent of the population was over sixty, life expectancy at birth was probably no more than twenty-two or twenty-three; and although a child who lived to adulthood had a much better chance of surviving into old age than a baby had, a bride or bridegroom probably had the prospect of no more than twenty-five or thirty years of life together as compared with the forty-five or so today[19] This relatively high mortality rate ensured that remarriage was common, particularly in the case of widowers who were better placed to find wives than widows were husbands. Indeed, about a quarter of all marriages in the seventeenth century were remarriages. At Clayworth, a deeply studied village in Nottinghamshire, there were, towards the end of the century, seventy-two husbands, twenty-one of whom had been married more than once, three of these four times and one five times. Of the seventy-two wives, nine had been married before.[20]

Contrary to popular belief families were not large, even though many women spent most of their adult lives pregnant. From the late sixteenth century until the early twentieth the average size of a household in England was less than five people. Couples had parents or parents-in-law living with them less often than they do now, partly because the parents did not live as long as their modern counterparts, and partly because housing was not only relatively easier to come by – there usually being one or two vacant dwellings in any village – but also cheaper, a simple cottage costing no more to build than the sum a labourer might expect to earn in three years. Also, married couples did not have as many babies as is commonly supposed. There were, of course, celebrated exceptions: Ann Hackett, a Kentish girl who married when she was eighteen, had given birth twenty times twenty-three years later; James Smith, the architect, had eighteen children by his first wife who died in 1699 and fourteen by his second; and it is well known that Queen Anne became pregnant nearly twenty times, though most of her babies that survived their birth died in infancy. In most families, however, the numbers of children were kept low not only by the rate of infant mortality which meant that nearly a third of all children died before they were fifteen, but also by the practice of birth control – usually, it is presumed, *coitus interruptus* – and by neglect or accident, an inexperienced mother's carelessness in the early and critical weeks, perhaps, or a smothering in a bed shared with both parents and, in many cases, with other children as well. Moreover, since she was not likely to enter into marriage before her middle twenties, and her menopause would begin when she was about forty, there were not many years in which a wife could give birth. The number of children she was likely to have was further inhibited by the contraceptive effects of breast-feeding which usually lasted for at least eighteen months, lactation generally preventing menstruation for that period in under-nourished women and for six months in those well fed. This applied less, of course, to upper-class women who generally employed wet-nurses for their babies and were, therefore, more likely to conceive sooner after the birth of a child than poorer women. Also, since the rich wife was usually younger than the poor, and since malnutrition in poor homes reduced both male sexual appetite and female fecundity, more children were born, and were likely to survive, in the homes of the well-to-do than in those of the indigent.[21]

As wife and mother, and as daughter, a woman continued to be regarded as subordinate to her husband, less among artisans, shopkeepers and labourers – where the woman was part of a working team – than among the gentry; but in all classes, to a greater or lesser extent. Lawrence Stone suggests that it is highly significant of popular attitudes towards women in the early seventeenth century that Joseph Swetman's *The Arraignment of Lewd, Idle, Froward and Unconstant Women*,

> a savage anti-feminist piece of polemic, went through no less than ten editions between its first publication in 1616 and 1634, although it also generated some fierce rebuttals . . . The theoretical and legal doctrines of the time were especially insistent upon the subordination of women to men in general, and to their husbands in particular . . . and many women accepted these ideas. Defoe's Roxana (who declared that 'the very nature of the marriage contract was . . . nothing but giving up liberty, estate, authority and everything to a man') grimly reflected that 'a wife is looked upon as but an upper servant'. The treatment of wives by their husbands naturally differed widely from individual to individual, but one gets the impression that the casual insouciance expressed in the diary of a small Lancashire gentleman, Nicholas Blundell, on 24 September 1706 was far from uncommon: 'My wife felt the pains of labour coming on her. Captain Robert Fazakerley and I went a-coursing.'[22]

It was commonly accepted that women were in general less intelligent than men and it was even supposed that the female brain was biologically different from the male. On her death the clever Duchess of Newcastle, who had borne no children, was described as an exception to the rest of 'her frail sex . . . who have Fruitful Wombs but Barren Brains'.[23] In fact, it was not that women were less intelligent but that most of them were less well educated and denied the opportunities enjoyed by men. In the spheres allotted to them, as Lady Antonia Fraser has shown in her study of women's lot in seventeenth-century England, they performed their tasks with practised skill, and were frequently honoured accordingly. In the City a foreign traveller observed that at 'all banquets and feasts', wives were 'shown the greatest honour', being placed at the upper end of the table where they were served first. The same respect was shown to them in other towns where wives often kept their husbands' apprentices under firm control. In the country, women trained servants, looked after poultry and pigs, took charge of the garden and orchard, managed the dairy, dealt with sales at market, kept farm accounts, were responsible for household management and the family medicines, cooked, made wine and cider, brewed ale, mended, made and embroidered clothes. And in times of danger they displayed as much courage and resource as their husbands and fathers. In the Civil War, both as chatelaines and as servants, they defended castles and strongholds with as much resource as their forebears had shown during the Wars of the Roses; they raised funds; they served as nurses and some fought as soldiers. At Basing House they turned lead into bullets; at Corfe Castle they bravely defended the upper ward; during the siege of Gloucester they laboured in the fortifications and earthworks with 'cheerful readiness'. 'Our maids and others,' a pamphleteer recorded of this siege, 'wrought daily without the works in little mead, in fetching in turf, in the very face of our enemy.' In London also, led by the lady mayoress with her own entrenching tool, women helped to build the fortifications; while at Bristol 200 women evidently went up to the parliamentary commander to offer to stand in the mouth of the cannon to ward off the shot. At Nantwich women saved Dorford House by putting out the 'terrible fire in the brushwood ricks'.[24]

After the Civil War it began to be recognized that women were enjoying a new-found independence, and many men, and some women, too, deplored the fact. Lord Clarendon wrote with distaste of young women conversing 'without circumspection and modesty'; and the Duchess of Newcastle complained of women 'affecting a Masculinacy' and imitating the behaviour of men: the recent fighting had led them 'to Swagger, to Swear, to Game, to Drink, to Revell, to make Factions'. They even began to preach, which made Sir Ralph Verney – who strongly deprecated the practice of women taking notes in sermons – reflect that St Paul would have 'fixed a Shame' upon them. They preached at the General Baptist Church in Bell Alley in London; they preached in their houses; they preached in Kent, in Cambridgeshire and

Wiltshire. Mary Milbrowe, a bricklayer's wife, preached from a high brick pulpit in her husband's parlour.[25]

In the next century, after political and philosophical theories had helped further to modify attitudes, women gained further measures of independence. Admittedly, it was still true in many cases, as John Shebbeare said in 1758, that in France woman was 'the companion in the hours of reason and conversation' while in England she was 'the momentary toy of passion'. And there were still those who agreed with Thomas Gisborne, whose *Enquiry into the duties of the female sex* was published in 1797, that if education induced women to ape the *salon* leaders of Paris, then women would be better left uneducated. Indeed, in Derek Jarrett's words, 'the *salons* of the French revolutionary period shocked English public opinion even more than those of the *ancien régime* had done, so that more and more women were driven back into that unwholesome world of repressed domesticity which Jane Austen was to describe with telling precision'.[26] Yet, if there were repeated demands that women should remain the 'gentle guardians of domestic happiness', there were increasing numbers of women who were becoming recognized as conversationalists more than able to hold their ground with men and as writers and scholars whose works commanded respect. Samuel Johnson expressed the belief that 'a man is in general better pleased when he has a good dinner on his table than when his wife talks Greek'. But he relished the company of intelligent women and held them in high esteem.

There was, as a whole, less agreement with Milton's view that 'woman was created for man', that he was 'for God only, she for God in him'. It was still theoretically the case, as William Blackstone, the eighteenth-century jurist, put it, that the husband and wife were one, and that the husband was that one, or, as *The Lawes Resolutions* maintained: 'that which the husband hath is his own . . . That which the wife hath is the husband's.' By law her children still belonged to their father and she had no rights over them, even were she to become a widow, unless she were specifically named as their guardian in his will. By law, also, she could still not take anything with her if she was provoked beyond endurance to leave her husband, and he could force her to go back to him. Should he then murder her he might be hanged, but if she murdered him, she was liable to the penalty of being burned alive – a woman who killed her husband was, in fact, burned at Tyburn in 1725. Yet, although a husband acquired by marriage complete control of his wife's property, she was now much more likely to have a decisive influence over its disposal, as well as a personal allowance provided for her by the marriage contract. She was also more likely to be able to arrange a separation from her husband should she wish to do so.

Separations were, however, much more easily arranged by the rich and by the poor than they were by those in between. Since the Reformation the annulment of a marriage could be obtained only if a prior contract to another person could be proved, if husband or wife bore certain family relationships to each other, if the husband had shown himself impotent over a period of three years, or if either husband or wife had left home and had not since been seen for seven years. And only in cases where a marriage had been annulled for these reasons, could either party legally remarry, adultery and cruelty notwithstanding. By the end of the seventeenth century, however, it had become possible, though extremely expensive, to obtain a divorce by private Act of Parliament. It was also possible to divorce a wife who agreed to take part in the ancient custom known as wife-sale in which she was taken to market with a halter round her neck and sold to the highest bidder, usually a purchaser who had already agreed to buy her. This was a custom which, both illegal and constantly condemned as immoral, continued until at least 1887.[27] In *The Mayor of Casterbridge*, written in the 1880s and set in the 1840s, Thomas Hardy described such a wife-sale at a fair in Weydon-Priors in Upper Wessex, basing his description on accounts of actual sales in the *Dorset County Chronicle*:

> 'Will anybody buy her?' said the man.
> 'I wish somebody would,' said she firmly. 'Her present owner is not at all to her liking.'
> 'So we are agreed about that. Gentlemen, do you hear? It's an agreement to part . . .'
> 'Now who's auctioneer?'
> 'I be,' promptly answered a short man, with a nose resembling a copper knob, a damp voice, and eyes like button-holes. 'Who'll make an offer for this lady?'
> 'Five shillings,' said someone, at which there was a laugh . . .
> 'I'll tell you what – I won't sell her for less than five guineas,' said the husband . . . 'I'll sell her for five guineas to any man that will pay me the money, and treat her well; and he shall have her for ever, and never hear aught o' me. But she shan't go for less. Now then – five guineas – and she's yours. Susan, you agree?'
> She bowed her head with absolute indifference.
> 'Five guineas,' said the auctioneer, 'or she'll be withdrawn. Do anybody give it. The last time. Yes or no?'
> 'Yes,' said a loud voice from the doorway.[28]

Wife-sales were not, however, considered a possible way out of an unendurable marriage for most people in England who, at the same time, could not afford the parliamentary route followed by the rich. The case of

Elizabeth Oxinden is characteristic of that of a wronged middle-class wife. She had been married when she was fourteen to Tom Oxinden whose family had been attracted to her by her money. But Oxinden soon fell in love with another man's wife with whom he ran away. The passion cooled; and when Mrs Oxinden next heard of her husband he had become a highwayman. He was soon apprehended and sentenced to imprisonment. Although deserted by a man now in gaol, Elizabeth Oxinden still felt bound to him; and it was not until she heard that he had died in prison that she was free to marry again.[29]

Marriages arranged without reference to the feelings of the bride and bridegroom – and with sole regard to the increase of family fortunes – were, by the beginning of the eighteenth century, becoming less and less common. In the upper classes, when large sums of money and extensive estates were involved, there were still such marriages as that contracted in the 1780s for a daughter of Lord Spencer who said, 'I had not the least guess about it till the day papa told me . . . I wish I could have known him a little better first.'[30] Also stories were still told of parents locking up and beating recalcitrant daughters, as Elizabeth Paston had beaten her stubborn child, Agnes; but such treatment was now almost universally frowned upon and, as Professor Stone has observed, it would be hard to find a more convincing demonstration of the new attitude towards parental control over marriage among provincial townspeople and country gentry than the story of a Banbury attorney named Aplin, and of his daughter who helped her father in his office. Also working in his office as an articled clerk was Richard Bignell, an enterprising young man of humble birth, who fell in love with Miss Aplin and, when he was qualified as an attorney himself, asked her father for permission to marry her. The request was rejected 'with the utmost scorn'. And when Mr Aplin discovered that his daughter had married despite his prohibition, he threw her out of his house, declaring that he wanted nothing more to do with her. Strongly disapproving of his harsh conduct, his clients one by one withdrew their business from his charge and transferred it to his pleasant and industrious former young clerk who had in the meantime set up on his own.[31]

It was by now generally agreed that before marriage was contracted, there should ideally be some mutual affection on both sides, even if only as a precaution against immediate adultery. 'The greatest pleasure I can feel is to know that you are happy,' Lord Pembroke told his son who had asked his father for an additional allowance so that he could marry a poor girl whom he loved rather than a rich one for whom he did not care. 'If you are happy, my dear George, I must be so . . . It would have been lucky for us had you found a thirty thousand pounder as agreeable to you as Elizabeth . . . [But] *n'en parlons plus.*'[32]

Also, by the eighteenth century there were far more opportunities than there had formerly been for young men and women of the wealthier classes to meet each other. They did so not only at private parties, receptions and balls, but also at fairs and race-meetings, at smart watering-places and assembly rooms, and above all, during the London season, already established by 1705 as a period during which the fashionable élite gathered together in the metropolis. 'The English have much more opportunity of getting to know each other before marriage, for young people are in society from an early age; they go with their parents everywhere,' remarked the duc de La Rochefoucauld. 'Young girls mix with the company and talk and enjoy themselves with as much freedom as if they were married.'[33]

Although it was Samuel Johnson's contention that all marriages would be better arranged by the Lord Chancellor than by the parties concerned – and although many arranged marriages certainly did turn out very well – it was generally felt by foreign observers that the opportunities offered by English society for young people to meet others of their class, and consequently to choose partners for themselves, did lead to more companionable marriages than were readily encountered on the Continent.

> Husband and wife are always together and share the same society [the duc de La Rochefoucauld continued]. It is the rarest thing to meet the one without the other. The very richest people do not keep more than four or six carriage-horses, since they pay all their visits together. It would be more ridiculous to do otherwise in England than it would to go everywhere with your wife in Paris. They always give the appearance of perfect harmony, and the wife in particular has an air of contentment which always gives me pleasure.[34]

Attitudes towards the upbringing of children were also changing. In the past parents had been advised to keep their children in deferential awe of them at all times; and, because of the high rate of infant mortality, had learned to bear the loss of their offspring, as Montaigne confessed to doing, 'not without regret, but without great sorrow'. Wealthier parents, indeed, saw little of them. As babies they were given over to the care of wet-nurses – in whose charge they were twice as likely to die as they were if fed at home – and on their return would be cared for by nursemaids and governesses until it was time for them to go to school or be placed in the charge of tutors. When away from home they were likely to receive few visits from their parents and few letters. William Blundell, a Lancashire gentleman, told his girls they must not expect to hear from their parents more than about once a year. He had not

wanted daughters, anyway. 'My wife has much disappointed my hopes in
bringing forth a daughter, which, finding herself not so welcome in this
world as a son, hath made already a discreet choice of a better,' he wrote
heartlessly after the death of his sixth female child. Having despatched two of
her surviving sisters to foreign nunneries, he replied to their complaint that
they hardly ever heard from home, 'When business requires no more, your
mother or I do commonly write to our children once (and seldom oftener) in
little less than a year. We hope they will be pleased with this.'[35]

For children living with their parents discipline was strict. Once released
from the physical restraints of their swaddling clothes – which were, until
about the middle of the eighteenth century considered essential if the child
were not to do some injury to itself or were not to suffer from some deformity
of the limbs – the girls might well, for the sake of their figure and deportment,
be forced into some such iron bodice as caused the death of Elizabeth Evelyn
at the age of two. Thereafter, both boys and girls were frequently subjected
to a regime intended to crush their natural stubbornness and wilful independence. If schoolmasters were liable to wield their birches with frequent
intemperance, so were parents, even if mothers and fathers were not, as John
Aubrey claimed they were in the days of his youth, given to beating their
children as severely as masters of the House of Correction whipped their
charges. Certainly Lady Abergavenny whipped her daughter so savagely for
so long that her husband was drawn into the room of punishment by the
child's shrieks, whereupon the mother threw the girl to the ground with such
force that she broke her skull and killed her.[36]

Whether or not taught to be subservient by physical intimidation, the
seventeenth-century child was expected to show respect to parents by
kneeling in their presence to seek their blessing every morning. In many
families the sons, even when grown up, would not presume to keep their hats
on or even to sit down uninvited in their parents' presence, while daughters
would remain kneeling until bade to stand up. 'Gentlemen of thirty and forty
years old,' wrote John Aubrey, 'were to stand like mutes and fools
bareheaded before their parents; and the daughters (grown women) were to
stand at the cupboard-side during the whole time of their proud mother's
visit, unless (as the fashion was) leave was desired, forsooth, that a cushion
should be given to them to kneel upon . . . after they had done sufficient
penance in standing.'[37]

By the end of the century, however, it was noticed that children were being
treated by their parents in a much more kindly way. It was still believed, as
John Locke taught in his *Some Thoughts Upon Education*, that the small
child should be ruled by 'fear and awe'; and there were still those who agreed
with Hannah More that it was 'a fundamental error to consider children as
innocent beings, whose little weaknesses may perhaps want some correction,

rather than as beings who bring into the world a corrupt nature and evil dispositions'. But it was now more generally held that the power that parents exercised by right over their offspring should be maintained by 'love and friendship'. 'He that would have his son have a respect for him and his orders,' Locke insisted, 'must himself have a great reverence for his son.' The elaborate politeness of demeanour in a parent's presence was no longer required; and children were beginning to be recognized not as miniature adults in constant need of correction but as immature beings whose feelings should be understood and whose concerns and interests catered for. Children's books, written to entertain rather than educate or elevate, were now produced in large quantities; board games which were both instructive and amusing began to appear; so did geographical jigsaw puzzles, while dolls' houses and dolls with changeable clothing began to be mass-produced. Children playing with hoops and hobby horses were introduced regularly into family portraits.

In many conservative homes children were still soundly whipped. One of the sisters of the Prince of Wales, who was born in 1762, recalled how she had seen both him and his brother, Prince Frederick, 'held by their tutors to be flogged like dogs with a long whip'.[38] And the children of Mrs Thrale, the eldest of whom was born in the same year as the Prince of Wales, had to grow accustomed to being beaten by their mother and knocked about by her fists when they misbehaved or failed to learn their lessons properly. But such treatment was now the exception rather than the common rule. Most parents were not only prepared to give more time to their children but also to heed the advice of James Nelson, author of the influential *Essay on the Government of Children* of 1756, who condemned 'severe and frequent whipping' as very bad practice: 'It inflames the skin, it puts the blood in a ferment; and there is besides a degree of ignominy attending it, which makes it very unbecoming.' Yet even so, Nelson believed that in his day less harm was being done to children by harsh punishment than by extreme permissiveness; and undoubtedly there were houses in which the antics of uncontrolled children profoundly shocked their parents' guests. One such child was the adopted son of the eccentric Princess Caroline, William Austin, who was dangled over the dining-room table to snatch his favourite sweetmeats from the dishes, knocking over the guests' wine glasses in the process.

> Once he cried for a spider on the ceiling [Lady Hester Stanhope recalled], and, though they gave him all sorts of playthings to divert his attention, he would have nothing but the spider. Then there was such a calling of footmen, and long sticks, and such a to-do . . . The P[rince]ss used to say to Mr Pitt, 'Don't you think he is a nice boy?' To which Pitt would reply, 'I don't understand anything about children.'[39]

While 'Willikin' was allowed to play on the dining-table, another notoriously indulged child, the son of Henry Fox, first Lord Holland, was permitted to enjoy himself under it; and on one occasion at Holland House, when the children entered the dining-room towards the end of the meal at a grand dinner party, he expressed an urgent desire to climb into the cream bowl. At his father's request it was placed on the carpet so that he could paddle about it in his petticoats to his heart's content. At a subsequent dinner party at Holland House a pig roasted at the kitchen fire was served with the traditional apple in its mouth and a note in verse from the chef: 'While at the fire I foam'd and hiss'd, A fox's cub upon me piss'd.' The guests greeted this intelligence with applause.[40] Such extravagant indulgence towards a child did not always cause as much harm as James Nelson predicted. Lord Holland's son grew up to be that most delightful statesman, Charles James Fox. William Austin, however, died in a Chelsea lunatic asylum.

In many of the wretched overcrowded homes of the poor the arrival of yet another baby was a disaster. Elder brothers and sisters might be put out as servants or to some other kind of child labour from the age of seven or even six, but even so it often proved beyond the means or the wit of parents to feed a further child. Unwanted babies were left out in the streets to die or were strangled and thrown on to dung heaps or into open drains. Those that survived were an irksome charge upon the parish and were put out to parish nurses, notorious as gin drinkers, who were known to maim or disfigure them so that when they were old enough to go out begging they might by exciting pity be the more successful. These nurses made further profit out of their charges by hiring them out to beggars at four pence a day; but if a baby appeared too sickly to survive and thus fail to become an ultimate source of profit to the nurse it was soon despatched by 'the infernal monster' who would 'throw a spoonful of gin down the child's throat which instantly strangles the babe. When the searchers come to inspect the body and enquire what distemper caused death, it is answered "convulsions".' The Sessions Papers of the period are full of terrible stories of wanton cruelty to children, of children being starved by drunken parents or parish nurses, being forced to become prostitutes at the age of eleven or twelve when they were already 'half eaten up with the foul distemper' of venereal disease, being ferociously beaten as apprentices in workshops.

It was the sight of babies exposed in the streets, abandoned by their parents and left to die on dunghills that persuaded Captain Thomas Coram, a shipwright and master mariner, to devote the rest of his life to the welfare of poor children. With the assistance of various rich patrons he took over some houses in Hatton Garden in 1741, and then arranged for the building of a foundling hospital in Lamb's Conduit Fields. Originally intended for limited numbers of children, the hospital was misguidedly opened to children all over the country in 1756. Word of this new, unique hospital soon spread fast and children appeared in such immense numbers, being dumped on the doorsteps in baskets brought from as far away as Yorkshire, often dying and sometimes dead, that it proved impossible to cope with them. In the first four years of its being opened as a hospital for the whole country, about 10,000 children died in it. Rules of admission had, therefore, to be made: only the first children of unmarried mothers were to be admitted; the babies had to be less than a year old; the fathers must have deserted both mother and child; and the mothers must have been of good repute before their 'fall'. Babies accepted were sent out to foster-parents in the country until they were four or five years old and were then brought back to the hospital to be educated. The governors arranged indentures for the boys when they reached the age of fourteen and thereafter supervised their apprenticeship.

Coram died in 1751, his private finances having fallen into such sad disarray that he was obliged to depend upon an annuity of £161 paid for by his friends. The foundation of his hospital had, however, proved the urgent need for such an institution, and by prompting numerous other philanthropic endeavours, was a turning point in the social history of the eighteenth century.[41]

# 36 · Sex

I was really unhappy for want of women [James Boswell wrote in his journal a few days after his arrival in London in 1762]. I thought it hard to be in such a place without them. I picked up a girl in the Strand; went into a court with intention to enjoy her in armour. But she had none. I toyed with her. She wondered at my size, and said if I ever took a girl's maidenhead, I would make her squeak. I gave her a shilling, and had command enough of myself to go without touching her. I afterwards trembled at the danger I had escaped. I resolved to wait cheerfully till I got some safe girl or was liked by some woman of fashion.[1]

For a time Boswell did wait, but when he thought he had found a 'safe girl' in a handsome actress from Covent Garden Theatre, he contracted gonorrhoea from her, the third time he had suffered from this complaint, the two previous infections taking ten weeks and four months respectively to cure. When he was cured of this infection he picked up a whore in St James's Park and, on this occasion, he did 'engage in armour' but he found that a sheath, which he had never worn before, dulled his satisfaction, though the girl who submitted to his 'lusty embraces' was 'a young Shropshire girl, only seventeen, very well looked'. The next week, however, he wore a sheath again when he strolled into the Park and took the first whore he met, an ugly, thin girl whose breath smelled of spirits. He 'never asked her name'. Thereafter he regularly 'performed concubinage in armorial guise' with a variety of whores, with 'a strong, plump, good-humoured girl called Nanny Baker', with 'a jolly young damsel' whom he picked up at the bottom of the Haymarket and engaged upon Westminster Bridge, with a 'low, abandoned, perjured, pilfering creature' who picked his pocket in Privy Garden, with several streetwalkers who patrolled the courts in the Temple, and with a 'fine fresh lass', an officer's daughter, born in Gibraltar. There were also two pretty girls who asked him to take them with him to a tavern – where in a private room he bought them wine, fondled them and then took them 'one after the other, according to their seniority' – and a monstrous big whore whom he had 'a great curiosity to lubricate as the saying is' after he met her in the Strand. But after she had displayed 'all the parts of her enormous carcase' to him in a tavern, she asked so much that he declined and walked off 'with the gravity of a Barcelonian bishop'. 'I had an opportunity tonight,' Boswell added, 'of observing the rascality of the waiters in these taverns. They connive with the whores, and do what they can to fleece the gentlemen. I was on my guard, and got off pretty well. I was so much in the lewd humour that I felt myself restless and took a little girl into a court; but wanted vigour. So I went home, resolved against low street debauchery.'

On one occasion he was persuaded not to use a sheath by a girl who said 'the sport was much pleasanter without it'; and the next day he much regretted the lapse, though he suffered no serious ill effects. A few years later, however, having been persuaded by General Clark that medicinal oil was as effective a protection as a condom, he contracted gonorrhea again after making love to two girls at the same time. This was his ninth infection, but it was not his last. In 1769, during a visit to a Dublin brothel, he caught the disease again, and had to go to London for another tedious and painful cure which included the application of a camphor liniment and mercury plaster to his genitals, daily doses of a pint of Kennedy's Lisbon Diet Drink which cost half a guinea each, and minor surgery.[2]

The condoms – Casanova called them 'English overcoats' – which might have saved Boswell from several of his infections had not been in use in England for long, though they were widely used in France where Mme de Sévigné commended them in 1671. They had not been available to Samuel Pepys and were little used at all until the eighteenth century when advertisements urged 'gentlemen of intrigue' to buy 'those bladder policies or implements of safety, which infallibly secure the health of customers'. Made of sheep gut or fish skin, they were secured in place by a red ribbon tied around the scrotum, and were sold at first at a shop in St Martin's Lane, then at others in Half Moon Street and Orange Court, Leicester Fields, where they were advertised as being supplied to 'apothercaries, chymists, druggists etc . . . ambassadors, foreigners, gentlemen and captains of ships etc going abroad'.

They seem rarely to have been used in Boswell's day as contraceptives. By far the most common form of birth control remained *coitus interruptus*; and, although not a reliable method, it was much more efficacious than most other measures employed. Quacks offered powders which if taken with warm ale prevented conception. Folklore advocated various spices, the juice of the herb savin, commonly known as Cover Shame, as well as marjoram, rue, parsley, thyme, bracken and lavender, either taken singly or in specified proportions. Honeysuckle was recommended in both Nicholas Culpeper's edition of the *College of Physicians' Directory* and in the almanacs of John Swan who advised his readers that its juice, drunk continuously for thirty-seven days, would render a man sterile for ever. Rue was said to make him impotent. A man's sexual desires could also be dampened by castor oil, lettuce, and a mixture of radish root and agaric, boiled in barley water and drunk when cool.[3]

Women were told they might inhibit conception by using uterine douches composed of castor oil, camphor and rue, or pessaries of ground bitter almonds. These would kill the seed which it was supposed was secreted by the ovaries – the counterpart of a man's testicles – the existence of the female 'egg' then being unknown.[4] Men were counselled to bathe their penises in vinegar or henbane juice, or even to be cupped to reduce the heat of the blood and, therefore, the generative power of their semen. Both men and women were told that conception was less likely if intercourse were performed with much violent activity. When conception occurred an abortion might be induced by the means whereby Lady Alderley brought about hers: 'a hot bath, a tremendous walk, and a great dose'.[5]

All these methods were condemned out of hand by those who took the biblical story of Onan as proof of God's disapproval of wasting seed. For them sexual intercourse, even in marriage, was to be practised only with a view to conception. As for masturbation, this was not only sinful but – with girls as well as boys – led to lassitude, indigestion, disorder of the lungs and the nervous system, boils, convulsions, epilepsy, and even death. The evils of the practice were luridly set out in *Onania or the Heinous Sin of Self-pollution, and all its frightful Consequences in Both Sexes Considered*, a pamphlet by an anonymous clergyman which was published in 1710 and which, fifty years later, had sold 38,000 copies in nineteen editions.[6]

While masturbation could not very well be made a crime, many other sexual activities were, though not incest which did not become a secular offence until the twentieth century. In the late sixteenth century and until about 1660 constables were authorized to enter houses where they supposed fornication or adultery was taking place. They would arrest the offenders, have them put in prison or taken before a justice of the peace who might order them to be whipped or to stand penitentially in white sheets not only in church but also in the market-place. It has been calculated that between 1558 and 1603 in the county of Essex – whose population of adults was about 40,000 – as many as 15,000 people were summoned to court for sex offences, that is to say about 330 persons a year or one per cent of the adult population. In their adult lives, in fact, a quarter of all men and women in Essex were likely to be accused of some sexual offence.[7]

Punishments varied in severity. Giving birth to a bastard child, which might become a burden on the parish, was often treated harshly, the father being served with a maintenance order, and, until the beginning of the eighteenth century, both he and the mother were liable to be stripped to the waist and whipped through the streets. Adultery was made a capital crime by an Act of 1650, though the man might escape execution by pleading that he did not know the woman was married, and the woman by proving that her husband had left her more than three years before. Juries were, however, disinclined to return verdicts which might result in the death of the accused; and apparently only one woman was sentenced before the Act was repealed.[8] The public was less sympathetic in cases of bestiality and buggery. Bestiality had become a capital offence in 1534, and, with a brief interval, remained so until 1861.[9] And for most of this period it was widely believed that such sexual union could result in the birth of monsters 'partly having the members of the body according to the man, and partly according to the beast'. The dead body of a monster believed to have been begotten by a young man on a sheep was once nailed up as a gruesome warning in the porch of a Sussex church. Women, it was believed, could give birth to monsters, too. Anthony Wood once went to see the deformed child of an Irishwoman which was 'originally begot by a man, but a mastiff dog or monkey gave the [man's] semen some sprinkling'.[10]

Buggery was still a capital offence and men found guilty of this crime were liable to be pilloried as well as hanged. In the sixteenth and seventeenth centuries, it seems, homosexual practices were quite rare and were regarded tolerantly. It was not until the end of the seventeenth century that a Puritan crusade led to raids on homosexual brothels, and later, in 1727, under pressure from the Societies for the Reformation of Manners, to arrests, prosecutions and executions.[11] In 1772 Captain Robert James was executed for sodomy; and in the 1780s one of two homosexuals pilloried in London was furiously attacked by the mob, even though the constriction of the pillory itself had led to his going black in the face and blood issuing from his nostrils, eyes and ears. When the pillory was opened he 'fell down dead upon the stand of the instrument. The other man was likewise so maimed and hurt by what was thrown at him that he lay there without hope of recovery.'[12]

While supporting severe punishments for sexual offences, seventeenth-century theologians emphasized the importance of restraint in lawful marriage. Carnal desires were not to be over-indulged; excessive passion in marriage was evil; there was to be no intercourse in Lent or on Sundays during the hours of divine service; supposedly unnatural positions in which, for instance, the wife's body was on top of the husband's or in which the woman was entered from behind were forbidden, as, of course, were anal and oral sex. For reasons of health, also, copulation must not take place too frequently, since the expenditure of semen weakened a man's resistance to disease and contributed to impotence in old age. Furthermore, women, being innately lascivious, should not have their sexuality aroused too often.

John Evelyn advised his son against 'intemperance' which would not only lead to 'unfortunate expectations' in his bride, but would also 'dull the sight, decay the memory and shorten life'. It was most unwise to make love on a full stomach, in the hours of daylight, or when it was either very cold or very hot.[13]

Yet for all the legal prohibitions, the writings and preaching of theologians, and the warnings of medical men, Englishmen and Englishwomen in the seventeenth and eighteenth centuries seem to have been by no means inhibited sexually. The lower middle classes were undoubtedly prudish; but the views of the upper classes were reflected in the pronouncement of Mrs Manley who described sexual pleasure as an inestimable delight, 'the greatest that human nature is capable of enjoying'. Erasmus Darwin considered it the 'chef d' oevre, the masterpiece of nature'.

> Now that you know what's what, and the best and worst that man can do unto you, you will give me leave to wish you joy [Lord Monmouth wrote to his niece shortly after her wedding, adding, for the benefit of her unmarried sister who was ill], you may tell her that such an ingredient as you have had of late would do her more good than any physick she can take. But she is too good and too handsome to lack it long if she have a mind to it . . . But you will be better to preach this doctrine to her now that you have tried it yourself.[14]

It was generally agreed that the illnesses which afflicted unmarried girls were dispelled by copulation, and that the female orgasm was an aid to conception; while for men sexual activity was often deemed essential to health and the retention of semen deleterious. 'I was afraid I was going to have an attack of gout the other day,' Lord Carlisle once said. 'I believe I live too chaste. It is not a common fault with me.'[15] All but the severest Puritans believed that provided it was performed at appropriate times and without immoderate lust, there was nothing sinful about marital sex, 'whatever hypocrites', in Milton's words, 'austerely talk'.[16] The medieval phrasing of the marriage service – 'with my body I thee worship' – was adopted in the Protestant Prayer Book of 1548, and, while attempts were made to alter it at the Savoy Conference between Anglicans and Presbyterians in 1661, it has continued into our own day.[17]

The open freedom with which Englishwomen greeted visitors with kisses had long delighted foreigners. 'Wherever you come you are received with a kiss by all,' Erasmus had written in 1499. 'When you take your leave, you are dismissed with kisses; you return, kisses are repeated. They come to visit you, kisses again; they leave you, you kiss them all round. Should they meet you anywhere, kisses in abundance; in fine, wherever you move, there is nothing but kisses.' It was a habit that persisted. In 1620 it was said that saluting strangers with a kiss was considered immodest in a foreigner, but merely civil in England, and at the end of the eighteenth century it was still considered 'the form of salutation peculiar to our nation'.[18]

As Samuel Pepys's diaries strongly indicate, women in the late seventeenth century rarely raised a strong objection to more intimate contact than kissing. Pepys was fascinated by the prostitutes that he saw at their doors in Fleet Alley, Long Acre, Drury Lane and in Moorfields, but tempted though he was to enter their houses, he resisted the impulse; and when he did once go into one, the 'jade', thinking, so he supposed, that he would not give her enough money, 'would not offer to invite to do anything' and he was glad 'to escape without any inconvenience'. Numerous other women, however, he kissed and fondled and stroked, and if he was not always permitted to do everything that he wanted to do, he was never, it seems, very firmly rebuffed except on Sunday 18 August 1667 when he went to St Dunstan-in-the-West to hear a sermon by the vicar and stood by 'a pretty, modest maid whom [he] did labour to take by the hand and the body'.

> But she would not [he recorded]; but got further and further from me, and at last I could perceive her to take pins out of her pocket to prick me if I should touch her again, which seeing, I did forbear, and was glad I did espy her design. And then I fell to gaze upon another pretty maid in a pew close to me, and she on me; and I did go about to take her by the hand, which she suffered a little.[19]

Pepys was then thirty-five years old and had been married twelve years, and for most of that time he had found other women as irresistible as they were accommodating, and quite prepared to take advantage of his desire for them to ask for posts or promotion for their husbands. He pursued Mrs Bagwell, the wife of a ship's carpenter, with whom he went to dinner at Deptford, and after dinner he 'found occasion of sending [her husband] abroad': 'And then alone,' he continued in the mixture of foreign languages and code he employed to describe such adventures, *'elle je tentoy à faire ce que je voudrais, et contre sa force je le faisoy, bien que pas à mon content-ment.* By and by, he coming back, I took leave and walked home.'

Pepys also made advances to Mrs Daniel, wife of a naval officer, who wanted 'to help her husband to the command of a little new pleasure-boat building': 'And here I had opportunity *para besar elle and tocar sus mamelles, so as to make mi mismo espender* with great pleasure.' He seduced Betty Martin, a linen draper in Westminster Hall whose husband, a would-be purser, was 'a sorry little fellow'. With her on first acquaintance he was 'exceeding free in dallying, and she not unfree to take it'. He afterwards took her to a Rhenish wine house where he bought her a lobster:

> And I do so towse her and feel her all over, making her believe how fair and good a skin she has; and indeed, she hath a very white thigh and leg but monstrous fat. When weary, I did give over, and somebody having seen some of our dalliance, called aloud in the street, 'Sir, why do you kiss the gentlewoman so?' and flung a stone at the window – which vexed me – but I believe they could not see me towsing her; and so we broke up and went out the back way, without being observed I think; and so she towards [Westminster Hall] and I to White-hall, where taking water, I go to the Temple.

Later he made love to her at 'the cabaret at the Cloche in the street du roy' – where 'after some caresses, *je l'ay foutée sous de la chaise deux times*' – at 'the old house at Lambeth-marsh', where he ate and drank and had 'pleasure of her twice', and at the Trumpet Tavern, King Street, Westminster, where he had pleasure of her again: 'And she, like an impudent jade, depends upon my kindness to her husband; but I will have no more to do with her, let her brew as she hath baked.'

There was also Mrs Burrows, widow of a naval officer, 'a mighty pretty woman and very modest', who came to him 'to get her ticket paid for her husband's service' and who was persuaded to go out with him into 'the fields of Uxbridge way: I had her lips as much as I would'. And one Sunday in 1666 when he met her at Betty Martin's house, despite her modest demeanour, she allowed him to tumble her and another of his friends, Doll Powell, 'all afternoon as [he] pleased'. There was also Diana Crisp, the daughter of a woman with whom he once lodged; and Betty Mitchell, wife of the keeper of a strong-water house, who did 'hazer whatever I did'. And there was the actress, Mrs Knepp, with whose breasts he played both in a coach and when she was in bed; and then, having the opportunity to be bold, put his hand 'abaxo de her coats and tocar su thighs and venter – and a little of the other thing . . . and tocar her corps all over'. And there were the two sisters, Frances and Sarah Udall, serving maids at the Swan, New Palace Yard; and Jane Welsh, 'a very pretty innocent girl', maidservant to his barber, Richard Jervas, who vexed him much by supplying him with a periwig infected with nits; and there was his wife's maid and companion, Deb Willet, of whom he had 'a great mind for to have the maidenhead'. She was combing his hair one night, 'which occasioned the greatest sorrow to [him] that he ever knew: For my wife, coming up suddenly, did find me imbracing the girl con my hand sub su coats; and endeed, I was with my main in her cunny'.

A dreadful row followed upon this discovery, and Deb was dismissed. Pepys, however, tracked her down at her new employer's:

And there she came into the coach to me . . . and at last yo did make her tener mi cosa in her mano, while my mano was sobra her pectus, and so did hazer with grand delight. I did nevertheless give her the best counsel I could, to have a care of her honour and to fear God and suffer no man para haver to do con her – as yo have done – which she promised. Yo did give her 20s. and directions para laisser sealed in paper at any time the name of the place of her being, at Herringman's my bookseller in the Change – by which I might go para her.

The next day Pepys recorded the sequel in his diary:

Up, and at the office all the morning, with my heart full of joy to think in what a safe condition all my matters now stand between my wife and Deb and me; and at noon, running upstairs to see the upholsterers, who are at work upon hanging my best room and setting up my new bed, I find my wife sitting sad in the dining-room; while inquiring into the reason of, she begun to call me all the false, rotten-hearted rogues in the world, letting me understand I was with Deb yesterday; which, thinking impossible for her even to understand, I did a while deny; but at last did, for the ease of my mind and hers, and for ever to discharge my heart of this wicked business, I did confess all; and above-stairs in our bed-chamber there, I did endure the sorrow of her threats and rows and curses all the afternoon. And which was worse, she swore by all that was good that she would slit the nose of this girl, and be gone herself this very night from me . . . So, with most perfect confusion of face and heart, and sorrow and shame, in the greatest agony in the world I did pass the afternoon . . . But at last I did call for W. Hewers [his clerk in the Navy Office] and . . . he obtained what I could not, that she would be pacified upon condition that I would give it under my hand never to speak with Deb while I live . . . So before it was late, there was, beyond my hopes as well as desert, a tolerable peace; and so to supper, and pretty kind words, and to bed, and there yo did hazer con ella to her content.[20]

A hundred years later Boswell found maidservants as compliant as Pepys found the girls at the Swan, New Palace Yard. On his way from Edinburgh to meet Samuel Johnson at Ashbourne in 1777, he took pleasure in fondling the maids, 'licentiously loving wenches', at every inn where he stopped. At

Liverpool he played with the chambermaid both in the evening and when she was taking the sheets off the bed the next morning, though she would not allow him to enter her fully. At Leek he was allowed to fondle the chambermaid as well as the serving-maid who brought him his tea. There is no reason to suppose that the women he and Pepys encountered were peculiarly accommodating; nor apparently were those enjoyed by William Hickey who attributed his abiding 'attachment to women of loose and abandoned principles' to his childhood experiences with his nurse, 'a wanton little baggage', who took him into her bed every night until dismissed from the household, having already been dismissed from that of the Duchess of Manchester for having seduced her thirteen-year-old son.[21] Indeed, it seems, that most women in their day took pleasure in sex and were, like men, unselfconsciously intrigued by all its manifestations and quite ready to regard with indulgence the results of its illicit practice. Illegitimate children were accepted quite casually both in the upper and in the professional classes. Lady Oxford had so many children by different husbands that they were known as the Harleian Miscellany, while the two bastards of Erasmus Darwin, the physician and grandfather of the naturalist, were treated just as they would have been had he been married to their mother. 'I often dined with him,' wrote Horace Walpole of Lancelot Blackburne, Archbishop of York. 'His mistress, Mrs Cruwys, sat at the head of the table, and Hayter, his natural son by another woman, and very much like him, at the bottom, as chaplain.'

Homosexuality was generally still more severely frowned upon than it had been in the sixteenth and seventeenth centuries and still savagely punished on occasions, much to the satisfaction of the mob. Yet it seems, among the upper classes at least, there was a growing tendency to regard homosexuality as no more than an unfortunate predilection which appears to have been more openly admitted by the time William Beckford was despatched on the Grand Tour in 1777 after his emotional entanglement with a young boy. Certainly, despite the activities of the Societies for the Reformation of Manners, there remained several homosexual clubs and brothels, or 'molly houses', in London and they seem to have been quite as well patronized as the more conventional brothels of Covent Garden. One of them had been frequented in the earlier years of the century by the corrupt, homosexual City Marshal, Charles Hitchen, who took his young assistant there one night, telling him that 'he would introduce him to a company of He-Whores'.

The man, not rightly comprehending his meaning, asked him if they were hermaphrodites. 'No, ye fool you. They are sodomites such as deal with their own sex, instead of females.' . . . No sooner [had they entered] but the Marshal was complimented by the company with the title of Madam and Ladyship . . . a familiar language peculiar to the house. The man was not long there before he was more surprised than at first. The men calling one another 'my dear', and hugging, kissing, and tickling each other, as if they were a mixture of wanton males and females, some telling others they ought to be whipped for not coming to school more frequently. The Marshal was very merry in this assembly and dallied with the young sparks with a great deal of pleasure.[22]

Dildoes were used by upper class women in the eighteenth century, and could be bought at a shop in St James's Street by whose proprietor they were imported from Italy; and most courtesans had birches as part of their equipment, as does the prostitute in one of the plates of Hogarth's *A Harlot's Progress*.

'Where are the instruments of pleasure?' asks the man of his mistress in Thomas Shadwell's *The Virtuoso*. 'I was so used to it at Westminster School I could never leave it off since . . . Do not spare thy pains. I love castigation mightily.'[23] There was a celebrated flagellants' brothel in Charlotte Street, another one in Tavistock Court, and flagellants' clubs in Jermyn Street.

Pornography was extremely popular. In Pepys's day most pornographic books were imported from France which continued to supply them until the middle of the eighteenth century. Pepys himself came across one, *L'Escholler de Filles*, in the shop of John Martin, a bookseller at Temple Bar, and finding it 'the most bawdy, lewd book' he ever saw, was 'ashamed of reading in it'. However, he soon afterwards bought a copy in plain binding from a bookseller in the Strand and the following night read it in his chamber, persuading himself that it would do him 'no wrong to read for information sake'. But 'it did hazer my prick para stand all the while', he recorded, 'and una vez to decharger'.[24]

After Pepys's death pornographic books in English became available in large quantities. So did pornographic prints and sex manuals like Aristotle's *Masterpiece*; while models of female reproductive organs could be examined in waxwork shows. John Cleland, a former pupil at Westminster School who had left employment in the East India Company after a quarrel with members of the Council at Bombay, produced *Fanny Hill, or the Memoirs of a Woman of Pleasure* in 1750. This was so successful that the bookseller, who bought the manuscript from him for twenty guineas, was said to have made the enormous sum of £10,000 out of it. Cleland followed *Fanny Hill* with *Memoirs of a Coxcomb* but, after being summoned before the Privy Council, he was offered a pension of £100 provided he made 'a worthier use of his talents', and no more pornography from his pen appeared. There were numerous other writers to supply the demand, however; and several pornographic magazines were published, including *The Covent Garden Magazine, or Amorous Repository* and *The Ranger's Magazine, or the Man of Fashion's*

*Companion*. There were also directories such as Jack Harris's *The Whore-monger's Guide to London* and his *List of Covent Garden Ladies*, the 1786 edition of which described, in a list of over a hundred tempting prostitutes, one of seven years' experience whose 'coral-tipped clitoris still forms the powerful erection'.[25]

There were immense numbers of prostitutes available. Von Archenholz estimated that there were at least 50,000. Some were extremely smart, elegant and as rich as Kitty Fisher who was said to have once shown her indifference to money and scorn of the men who paid her by eating a thousand-pound note in a sandwich. A few courtesans married their lovers, like the Gunning sisters who married respectively the Earl of Coventry and the Duke of Hamilton. Many were as fresh-faced and young as the 'so called light girls, all with fine blooming figures, well dressed and true to their name' whom Sophie von la Roche saw in a box at Sadler's Wells. 'Not one of them looked older than twenty, and every one so made that the best father or husband would be proud of having a virtuous daughter or wife with such stature and good features.'[26] Many more were as unappetising as the twelve who were produced for Casanova's inspection at the Star tavern and dismis-sed, one after the other, with a shilling.[27] Some were grasping and ill-natured; others as generous as the 'very pretty little girl' who accosted the young William Hickey 'under the Piazza of Covent Garden', conducted him to her 'dirty, miserable bed' in a 'very indifferent-looking apartment up three pairs of stairs in a dark, narrow court out of Drury Lane' and then refused the half guinea he offered her, insisting on going out for change, and then declining to accept more than five shillings, though Hickey subsequently discovered that 'she had not at that time a single sixpence in her possession'.[28]

# 37 · *Theatres and Shows*

One of King Charles II's first public acts after his Restoration to the throne had been to issue a royal warrant granting two of his friends, Sir William D'Avenant, the poet and playwright, and Thomas Killigrew, an indifferent dramatist who was groom of his bedchamber, the exclusive right to revive the theatre in London by forming two separate companies of players. Killigrew's was to be known as the King's Company, and D'Avenant's as the Duke's, since it was under the patronage of the king's brother, the Duke of York. As the only licensed theatrical entrepreneurs in London, D'Avenant and Killigrew were free to present 'tragedies, comedies, plays, operas, music scenes and all other entertainments of the stage whatsoever'. They could charge whatever they deemed 'reasonable'; they could build theatres wherever they chose; and they were permitted to employ actresses in their respective companies. Despite their monopoly patents, however, the king's two favoured friends found it difficult to enforce their rights. Other companies declined to walk quietly off their stages. Indeed, the king himself attended a performance given by the Red Bull company under the management of Michael Mohun; and Pepys's first visit to a theatre after the Restoration was to John Rhodes's company which, with Thomas Betterton in the cast, gave performances at the Cockpit Theatre in Drury Lane. Pepys also attended a performance at the Salisbury Court Theatre by a company of players under the direction of George Jolly who had been acting on the Continent during the Interregnum.[1] The two principal companies soon established their pre-eminence, however, the King's at the Vere Street Theatre, then at the Theatre Royal in Bridge Street and finally at the Theatre Royal, Drury Lane; the Duke's at the Lincoln's Inn Fields Theatre, then at the Dorset Garden Theatre and ultimately at Covent Garden.

At first the plays performed were usually new renderings of old plays, versions of Shakespeare and Jonson and of Beaumont and Fletcher; but then came those comedies of manners, like Congreve's *Love for Love*, the heroic plays of Dryden and such tragedies as Otway's *Venice Preserv'd*. In comedy parts, while gestures and movements were performed in a traditionally stylized manner, the words were delivered with far more naturalness than was expected of the tragedian, who accompanied his extravagant gestures with a reverberating intonation that echoed round the galleries. Actors were renowned for their performances in particular kinds of role; and audiences did not take kindly to their being cast in parts outside their usual type. Samuel Sandford, for example, who had joined D'Avenant's company at Lincoln's Inn Fields Theatre soon after its formation, and who was celebrated as a stage villain, was once cast as an honest statesman. The audience, so Colley Cibber recalled in his autobiography, sat impatiently through four acts waiting for the true and evil nature of the man to be revealed; and when, at last, finding that 'Sandford was really an honest man to the end of the play, they fairly damned it, as if the author had imposed upon them the most incredible absurdity'.[2] Audiences were never slow to demonstrate their displeasure, either at the poor quality of an unacceptable or boring piece, which they would hiss and boo off the stage, or at the inability of actors to remember their lines, a not uncommon failing when a play's run was rarely more than two or three days and so many new parts had to be learned.

A large proportion of the members of any audience came to see each other rather than the play. The Restoration theatre, indeed, has been described as 'the toy of the upper classes',[3] and its audiences as mainly composed of 'courtiers and their satellites . . . noblemen in the pit and boxes, the fops and beaux and wits or would-be wits who hung on to their society, the women of the court . . . the courtesans with whom these women of quality moved and conversed on equal terms'.[4] 'Women of doubtful character, "Vizard Masks", as they were euphemistically styled, flocked the side-boxes, in the pit, and in the upper gallery . . . So numerous did they become that in 1688 John Crowne, the dramatist, could declare that they made up "half the pit and all the galleries".'[5]

Certainly there were many courtesans in most audiences, as well as aristocratic fops who paid an additional charge to visit the actresses behind the scenes; certainly, too, actresses did not enjoy a high reputation for purity; nor, for that matter, did actors. The delightful Nell Gwyn, a star of the Theatre Royal, seems to have had numerous lovers before she became the king's mistress; while Mrs Pepys had good cause to be jealous of Elizabeth Knepp. On 24 January 1669 Pepys recorded in his diary, 'I to talk to Tom Killigrew, who told me and others, talking about the play-houses, that he is fain to keep a woman on purpose, at 20s a week, to satisfy eight or ten of the young men of his House [the Theatre Royal, Drury Lane], whom till he did so he could never keep to their business, and now he doth.'[6]

Yet perfectly respectable women went to the theatre regularly; and sometimes, like Mrs Pepys, they went without their husbands. The middle gallery usually contained a number of 'citizens' wives and daughters', according to the author of *The Country Gentleman's Vade Mecum* of 1699, as well as of 'serving-men, journey-men, and apprentices'. Above them, the upper gallery was full of servants; below them, in the pit, were squires and the richer citizens and their wives, as well as 'beaus, bullies and whores . . . wits and censurers'. In the boxes sat 'persons of quality', who had paid 4s each for the seats, four times as much as the price of admission to the upper gallery.[7]

The first performances of new plays were generally most exciting events.

We sat at the office all morning, [runs a characteristic entry in Pepys's diary], and at noon home to dinner; and my wife being gone before, I go to the Duke of York's playhouse, where a new play of Etheriges called *She would if she could*. And though I was there by 2 a-clock, there was 1000 people put back that could not have room in the pit; and I at last, because my wife was there, made shift to get into the 18d box [the middle gallery] – and there saw; but Lord, how full was the house.[8]

On a later occasion, when Thomas Shadwell's comedy, *The Sullen Lovers, or the Impertinents*, was being first performed, Pepys arrived three and a half hours before the play began 'to get a good place' in the pit, paid a poor man to keep his seat for him, and returned after spending an hour at his bookseller's to find the theatre 'quite full'.[9]

The performances generally started at half past three throughout the reign of Charles II, though by 1695 four o'clock seems to have been a more usual time; by 1703 five or half-past five; in 1706, and for many years afterwards, six o'clock. But it was never possible to reserve a seat, even a seat in a box, though a whole box could be taken in advance. Doors always opened long before the performance, and there was usually a wild scramble to secure a good place. There were vociferous protests when the Drury Lane management proposed to open their doors earlier than usual because this was felt unfair to those who could not leave their work in time to get a seat.

Even when the house was full, people would push and squeeze their way on to the benches; and on one occasion, so Frederick Reynolds, the dramatist, related, a place was obtained at Drury Lane by a cunning late-comer:

The riot and struggle for places can scarcely be imagined . . . Though a side box close to where we sat, was completely filled, we beheld the door burst open, and an Irish gentleman attempt to make entry, *vi et armis* –

'Shut the door, box-keeper!' loudly cried some of the party – 'There's room by the pow'rs!' cried the Irishman, and persisted in advancing. On this, a gentleman in the second row, rose, and exclaimed, 'Turn out that black-guard!' 'Oh, and is that your mode, honey?' coolly retorted the Irishman. 'Come, come out, my dear, and give me satisfaction, or I'll pull your nose, faith, you coward, and *shillaly* you through the lobby!'

This public insult left the tenant in possession no alternative; so he rushed out to accept the challenge; when, to the pit's general amusement, the Irishman jumped into his place, and having deliberately seated and adjusted himself, he turned round, and cried, 'I'll talk to you after the play is over.'[10]

The seats in the pit, which cost 2s 6d until almost the end of the eighteenth century (prices being doubled for first performances) were the most popular with regular playgoers and critics. But if the pit, as Dryden confirmed, was the best place from which to see and hear a play, it could also be the noisiest when young men came 'drunk and screaming' into it, like the youths described in Shadwell's *The Virtuoso* who rush raging in to 'stand upon the Benches, and toss their full Periwigs and Empty Heads, and with their shrill unbroken Pipes, cry, "Dam-me, this is a Damn'd Play. Prithee, let's to a whore, Jack!"'.[11] Drunk and rowdy men were certainly often to be seen at the theatre. Sir Charles Sedley, Sir Thomas Ogle and Lord Buckhurst once all got drunk at the Cock Tavern in Bow Street, exhibited themselves in obscene postures on the balcony of Covent Garden and 'gave great offence to passengers by very unmannerly discharges upon them'. Sedley after being fined for his conduct commented that he thought he must be the first man that 'had ever paid for easing himself *a posteriori*'.[12] On such occasions brawls frequently erupted, as they did in August 1675, when Sir Thomas Armstrong stabbed one Mr Scrorp to death during a performance of *Macbeth*, and in February 1679 at the Duke's Theatre after a gentleman made an insulting reference to the king's mistress, the Duchess of Portsmouth.

After the accession of William and Mary, there was a strong reaction against the stage and attempts were made to prevent the young from attending playhouses or, at least, to make the places more respectable. In 1696 the Lord Chamberlain ordered that no plays should be performed without licence; and, in 1697, that all scurrilous sentiments and expressions of profanity be deleted from them. In 1700 the Grand Jury of the City of London proposed 'to the court at the old Baily, that for any person to goe to play houses was a public nuisance; and that the putting up bills in and about this Citty for playes was an encouragement to vice and prophanesse; and prayed that none be suffered for the future'. The request was granted and playhouse bills were forbidden. But the prohibition was evidently ignored since, soon afterwards, the Grand Jury of Middlesex made further complaints about bills being posted and in 1703 complained:

We the Grand Jury of the county of Middlesex do present, that the Plays which are frequently acted in the playhouses in Drury-Lane and Lincoln's-Inn-Fields in this County are full of prophane, irreverent, lewd, indecent, and immoral expressions, and tend to the great displeasure of Almighty God and to the corruption of the auditory, both in their principles and their practices. We also present, that the common acting of plays in the said play-houses very much tend to the debauching and ruining the youth resorting thereto, and to the breach of the peace, and are the occasions of many riots, routs and disorderly assemblies, whereby many murders and other misdemeanors have been frequently done, and particularly the barbarous murder of Sir Andrew Slanning, which was very lately committed as he came out of one of the said playhouses; further that the common acting of plays at the said play-houses is a public nuisance.[13]

In 1704 fresh efforts were made to 'reform all indecencies and abuses of the stage which have occasioned great disorders'. It was, therefore, commanded by royal decree that 'no person of what quality soever' should presume to go 'behind the scenes or come upon the stage, either before or during the acting of any play, that no woman be allowed or presume to wear a vizard mask', and that no persons should come into a theatre 'without paying the price established for their respective places'.[14]

There were still only two patent theatres, Drury Lane and Covent Garden, but both were large. In the early 1740s, so it has been calculated, nearly 8500 people were attending them each week, and by the late 1750s almost 12,000. In 1780 Drury Lane had seating for about 2000 and after 1794, when the theatre was rebuilt, 3611. Covent Garden held some 2100 people in 1782, and after it had been altered in 1792, just over 3000.[15] (The seating capacity today is 2141.) The monopoly of the two theatres was reinforced by the Theatres Act of 1737 which was passed by the government to restrain the activities of Henry Fielding whose ballad-opera, *The Welsh Opera, or, the Grey Mare the Better Horse*, had been performed at the unlicensed Haymarket Theatre six years before. Opposition to this piece, which attacked both political parties and satirized the royal family, was strong enough to induce Fielding to offer his next, less contentious plays to Drury Lane. In 1734 his *Don Quixote in England* was produced at the Haymarket and this and subsequent plays which audaciously and outspokenly satirized Sir Robert Walpole's administration induced the government to bring in the Act which confirmed Drury Lane and Covent Garden as the only two legitimate theatres, established a strict censorship and brought about the closure of the unlicensed theatres.

Ways of evading the Act were found, however. The Haymarket reopened and was taken over in 1747 by Samuel Foote, a brilliant mimic who some years later, after losing a leg in a cruel practical joke in which the Duke of York was involved, managed to obtain a patent from the king for the summer months. So the 'Little Theatre in the Hay', as it had been known, became the Theatre Royal. At the same time, other theatres, charging about 6d a seat, sprang up all over London to cater for the larger, less discriminating, increasingly middle-class audiences which were being found for the new sentimental comedies, the ballad-operas which became so popular after the success of John Gay's *The Beggar's Opera*, the pantomimes, the burlettas and those other entertainments of an age of which it was complained that nothing would go down 'but Ballad-Operas and Mr Lun's Buffoonery'.[16]

Lun was the stage-name of John Rich, the theatrical manager whose appearances as Harlequin were largely responsible for the enormous success of eighteenth-century pantomimes: his own ran for the then astonishing number of forty or even fifty consecutive performances. These pantomimes were a remarkable mixture of comic dumb show, opera, mythological masque and such mechanical spectacles as presented themselves to the audience when the curtain rose upon one of Rich's productions, *A Dramatick Entertainment, call'd Harlequin a Sorcerer*: 'dark rocky caverns, by the side of a Wood, illumin'd by the Moon; Birds of Omen promiscuously flying, Flashes of Lightning faintly striking'.[17]

In the 1770s spoken dialogue was introduced into pantomimes. But, despite the success of Colman's *The Genius of Nonsense*, this was not generally considered an improvement; and after 1786 the pantomime reverted to its earlier type, in which the noise of the audience fully compensated for the silenced voices on the stage.[18] The comments in the stage directions of *The British Stage; or, The Exploits of Harlequin: A Farce* give a good idea of the part the spectators were expected to play in one of Rich's shows:

Enter the Dragon, spitting Fire . . . (The whole Audience hollow with Applause, and shake the very Theatre). [An ass] endeavours to mount the Dragon, falls down, the Dragon is drawn up in the Air by Wires.

(The Audience ring with Applause).

Enter Windmill.

Harl [equin]. Advance, Mr Windmill, and give some Entertainment to this great Assembly.

(The Audience hollow and huzza, and are ready to break down the House with Applause).

They dance with the Ghosts, Devils, and Harlequin.

(The Audience clap prodigiously).[19]

In these audiences pickpockets abounded, and prostitutes were numerous, though these generally kept to their own special parts of the house. Drunkenness and fighting were still quite common; duels took place in the aisles and on the stairs and, on one occasion at least, upon the stage when other accommodation was deemed too restricting. A drunken earl once staggered across the stage during a performance of *Macbeth*, struck one of the actors who politely remonstrated with him, and, when a second blow was returned, drew his sword and, with several companions, did such damage to the theatre that it had to be closed for two days.[20] 'This night,' Richard Cross wrote in his diary on 26 December 1757, 'by the Crowd upon the upper Gallery Stairs two Women and a Man were killed.'[21] And J. P. Malcolm recorded, 'We witness constant disputes often terminating in blows, and observe heated bodies stripped of the outward garments, furious faces, with others grinning horribly.'[22]

Sometimes the disturbances turned into riots. There were riots in 1737 when a French company was granted a licence to perform at the Little Theatre, Haymarket; there were riots when prices were raised at Drury Lane; and there were riots when managements attempted to end the custom of allowing people into the theatres at half price after the end of the third act of the main item on the programme. Seats were torn up, curtains pulled down, sconces and mirrors smashed, box partitions splintered.

In 1755, when war with France threatened, there were further riots when a show, *The Chinese Festival*, directed by a supposed Frenchman (actually Swiss) and with a few French actors in the cast, was put on at Drury Lane:

The inhabitants of the boxes, from the beginning of the dispute, were inclined to favour the exhibition of the Festival, and very warmly espoused the cause of the managers against the plebeian part of the audience, whom they affected to look down upon with contempt. The pit and galleries became more incensed by this opposition of the people of fashion, and entered into a strong alliance to stand by each other, and to annoy the common enemy. Several gentlemen of rank being determined to conquer the obstinacy of the rioters, they jumped from the boxes into the pit with a view to seize the ringleaders of the fray. The ladies at first were so far from being frightened at this resolution of the gentlemen, that they pointed out the obnoxious persons with great calmness. Swords were mutually drawn, and blood shed . . . The contest between the boxes and the other parts of the house was attended with real distress to the managers, for they knew not which party they could oblige with safety. One would not give way to the other, and they seemed to be pretty equally balanced: at last, after much mutual abuse, loud altercation, and many violent blows and scuffles, the combatants fell upon that which could make no resistance, the materials before them. They demolished the scenes, tore up the benches, broke the lustres and girandoles, and did in a short time so much mischief to the inside of the theatre, that it could scarce be repaired in several days.[23]

There was evidently an ever-present need for the rows of sharp spikes which can be seen in Hogarth's *The Laughing Audience* separating the men in the pit from the sedate musicians in the orchestra.

Even when there was no violence, the uproar in the theatre was sometimes deafening, particularly when the first work of a dramatist, who had previously given offence to some part of the audience, was performed. The opening performance of Miller's *Hospital for Fools* in 1739, for instance, was shouted down because his earlier *Coffee-House* was taken to have cast aspersions upon a favourite meeting-place of some young lawyers of the Temple. This was at a

time when it was the Fashion to condemn them all, right or wrong, without being heard; and when Parties were made to go to new Plays to make Uproars, which they called by the odious name of *The Funn of the first Night*. And on the very Night I am speaking of . . . not one single Word was heard that the Actors spoke, the noise of These First-Night Gentlemen was so great. However the Actors went thro' it and the Spectators might see their Mouths wag, and that was all.

Similarly, West's *Hecuba* was 'not heard' when it was presented at Drury Lane, because 'a rout of Vandals in the Galleries intimidated the young Actresses, disturbed the Audience, and prevented all Attention'. The second performance of *Three Hours after Marriage* was 'acted like a ship tost in a tempest', while Colley Cibber's *The Refusal,* though it had nothing to do with politics, was loudly hissed as soon as the first words of the prologue were spoken, since his previous play *The Non-Juror* had given offence to the Jacobites. And Hugh Kelly's *A Word to the Wise* was treated in the same way because the author had changed his political opinions and become a supporter of the government. 'The people refused to give his play a hearing and easily overcame the small group who insisted on it being presented.'[24]

'I will wager you five hundred pounds,' says a character in Boaden's *The Modish Couple* – proposing a bet that would certainly not have been accepted at the time –

that half a Score of us shall quite demolish the best Piece that can come on any Stage . . . We strike up such a Chorus of *Cat-calls*, *Whistles*, *Hisses*, *Hoops and Horse-laughs* that not one of the Audience can hear a Syllable, and therefore conclude it to be very sad stuff – The Epilogue's spoke, the Curtain falls, and so the poor Rascal is sent to the Devil.[25]

At the first performance of *The Rivals* an apple was thrown at the Irish actor taking the part of Sir Lucius O'Trigger. 'He stepped forward, and with a genuine rich brogue, angrily cried out, "By the pow'rs, is it personal? Is it me or the matter?" '[26] And in 1762 'there was a great riot at Covent Garden playhouse without the least plea or pretence whatever', according to a newspaper report:

[This was] occasioned by the gentry in the upper gallery calling for a hornpipe, though nothing of the sort was expressed in the bills. They went so far as to throw a quart bottle and two pint bottles upon the stage, which happily did no mischief, but might have been productive of a great deal.[27]

Nor was it only such demands and antagonism to the author or leading members of the cast that led to uproar.

At night I went to Covent Garden and saw *Love in a Village* by Isaac Bickerstaffe, a new comic opera [Boswell recorded in his journal on 8 December 1762] . . . I saw it from the gallery but I was first in the pit. Just before the overture began to be played, two Highland officers came in. The mob in the upper gallery roared out, 'No Scots! No Scots! Out with them!', hissed and pelted them with apples. My heart warmed to my countrymen, my Scotch blood boiled with indignation. I jumped up on the benches, roared out, 'Damn you, you rascals!,' hissed and was in the greatest rage. I am very sure at that time I should have been the most distinguished of heroes. I hated the English.[28]

Another night, at Drury Lane, 'in a wild freak of youthful extravagance', Boswell 'entertained the audience prodigiously', so he flattered himself, 'by imitating the lowing of a cow'. 'I was so successful in this boyish frolic that the universal cry of the galleries was, "*Encore* the cow! *Encore* the cow!". In the pride of my heart I attempted imitations of some other animals, but with very inferior effect. My reverend friend [his companion, Dr Hugh Blair], anxious for my *fame*, with the air of utmost gravity and earnestness addressed me thus: "My dear sir, I would confine myself to the cow." '[29]

The uproar before the play begins is indescribable [wrote a German visitor, Friedrich von Schütz] . . . Not only orange-peels but sometimes even glasses of water or other liquids are thrown from the gallery into pit and boxes, so that frequently spectators are wounded and their clothing is soiled. In short, such outrages are committed in the name of freedom that one forgets one is in a playhouse which claims in its avertisements the title of Royal Theatre. In Germany such disorder would never be tolerated even at a marionette theatre in a village inn. At Drury Lane I wished to look around at the gallery in order to examine its structure, but a heap of orange-peels, striking me with considerable force in the face, robbed me of all curiosity. The best plan is to keep your face turned towards the stage and thus quietly submit to the hail of oranges on your back. On one occasion my hat was so saturated (I really do not know with what watery ingredients) that I was compelled to have it cleaned next day at the hatter's.

His neighbour's hats fared no better; nor did that of a nearby lady who, nevertheless, assured him that 'the audience had been on its best behaviour today'.[30]

Another German, Johann Wilhelm von Archenholz, confirmed that the 'uproar of the common people in the theatre before the curtain rises [was] simply frightful':

A foreigner, unfamiliar with such outbursts, imagines he is facing a field of battle on which the combatants are ready to break one another's necks . . . Before going to the theatre, one fills one's pockets with oranges, which serve the double purpose of refreshment and entertainment . . . But the peels are often hurled by the occupants of the gallery into the pit, or they land there if they miss the proscenium, at which they are usually aimed . . . They are so heaped up by the time for the curtain to rise that a servant must enter with a broom.[31]

In theatres outside London the noise was quite deafening. At the theatre in Richmond in 1777, Johann Georg Busch was startled by a number of voices crying out, 'Throw her down! Throw her down!' He thought the words must apply to an actress who was giving a 'very mediocre performance'. 'The actors paused, and I was prepared for the worst,' Busch wrote. 'Then something really was thrown down from the gallery, I know not what . . . Similar disturbances occurred in those quarters several more times, and each time the actors, being quite accustomed to such interruptions, very calmly paused.'[32]

Towards the end of the century there seems to have been a marked improvement in the behaviour of theatre audiences. Foreigners praised the way in which the spectators refrained from applause and laughter 'until the end of the speech or song, disturbing neither the listener in his attention nor the actor in the performance of his role'. 'This unbearable jubilation and shouting of the French over every little trifle' was never heard in England, except when an irrepressible youth raised his voice. English audiences became absorbed in the play, unlike audiences in Italy where it was 'customary to play cards in the loges' and where it was 'in poor taste for ladies to pay attention to what takes place on the stage'. When Mrs Bellamy played in *Oedipus* in London she was so overcome by the tragedy of her role that she had to be carried off the stage unconscious. Most members of the audience, overcome themselves, quietly left the theatre.

There was also now widespread acclaim for the thoroughness with which English actors memorized their parts, unlike those in other countries where the prompter came to the aid of the performers 'whenever they showed the slightest uncertainty'.[33]

Much of the credit for the improvements noticed in the English theatre was due to David Garrick, who, in the words of Edmund Burke, 'raised the character of his profession to the rank of a liberal art'. Garrick had arrived in London from Lichfield with Samuel Johnson who said that when he entered the city his friend had no more than three halfpence in his pocket. Soon tiring of the wine merchant's business which he managed to establish with an elder brother, Garrick set his heart upon becoming an actor but, after some experience in the provinces, he was rejected by both Drury Lane and Covent Garden and had to make his formal debut in 1741 as Richard III at a theatre in Goodman's Fields, Whitechapel, which was soon afterwards closed through the influence of the patent theatres. Garrick's success was not immediate. His 'easy and familiar yet forcible style in speaking and acting', as his first biographer called it, came as a surprise to audiences accustomed to the measured declamations and stiff mannerisms of James Quin who remarked after seeing his young rival: 'If the young fellow is right, I and the rest of the players have been all wrong.' Soon, it was generally agreed that they *had* been wrong; and Garrick, acknowledged as the greatest actor of his time, took over the management of Drury Lane where most of the best actresses of the day appeared with him, among them Peg Woffington (for several years his mistress), Kitty Clive, Mrs Cibber, Mrs Bellamy and Mrs Abington. During the thirty-odd years he spent at Drury Lane many reforms in the theatre were instituted: the audience was finally driven from the stage; concealed stage-lighting was introduced as well as cut-out scenery designed for him by the Alsatian painter, de Loutherbourg. Performers still appeared in haphazardly anachronistic costume, often grabbing for themselves the most splendid garments from the stock wardrobe so that a maid might well be seen far more sumptuously dressed than her mistress. While characters like Falstaff and Richard III traditionally wore costumes suitable to their periods, other members of the cast were clothed in eighteenth-century dress. When Garrick himself played King Lear he wore a white wig, silk hose, lace ruffles, high-heeled shoes with diamond buckles, and no beard; as Macbeth he came on stage – as Spranger Barry also did – in the uniform of an officer in the Seven Years' War; and, when he defied convention by appearing in *Othello* in Moorish robes instead of a military uniform, the audience ridiculed such eccentricity. But, however strangely inappropiate their attire, the performers in Garrick's companies were not permitted the extravagant gestures, the slow delivery and tiresome pauses of the past. Even the great Kitty Clive – whose custom it had been occasionally to let 'her eyes wander from the stage into the boxes' in search of her friends and acquaintances and would give them 'a comedy nod or curtsy' – was rebuked by Garrick and told always to keep her eyes on her fellow-performers as the convincing production of the play demanded.[34]

Garrick, who knew from his own experience in Ipswich how valuable was the training to be gained in the provinces, advised the young people who came to him in the hopes of going on the stage to serve their apprenticeship with Griffith's company in Norwich.[35] There were several other provincial companies to which he might have sent them; and the numbers of provincial theatres were growing all the time as inn yards and town halls were being replaced as playhouses by specially built theatres which, in several cases, were granted royal patents, those in Bath and Norwich in 1768, in York and Hull in 1769, in Liverpool in 1771, and in Chester in 1777.[36]

The life of an actor in the provinces continued, however, to be hard. Actors who went on tour from the London theatres during the summer vacation often had an enjoyable time; so did those who were based in the county towns and travelled with companies on regular country circuits; but there were hundreds of small troupes who travelled long distances and worked long hours for a very meagre living. Many of them were recruited by country managers in one of those taverns around Covent Garden where unemployed and would-be actors and comedians congregated. They were asked what parts they had played and how many lines they could master overnight; and then, if chosen, they were sent off to join the company with barely enough money for the journey, sometimes no more than half a guinea per hundred miles which they might be asked to repay out of their share of the profits of the company. The profits were shared out in equal parts, the manager taking five shares to compensate him for his expenses in running the company. Shares were rarely large, and most strolling actors could not have survived without such extra payments as were made for delivering handbills at a shilling a day in the town and two shillings a day in the country, and their benefit performances from which they received all the profits, less expenses. Gradually salaries began to take the place of the sharing system; but there were conservative managers who clung to the old ways, like the one encountered by Sylvester Daggerwood who would have nothing to do with any 'paltry salary scheme'. There were managers, too, who dressed in fine clothes and silver-laced hats while their players were in rags, who left their companies in the lurch when offered a London engagement, who never announced a final night and crept out of town before the bills were paid, who failed to find money for wagons and left their actors and their actresses to carry their scenery and wardrobes to the next town on their shoulders.[37]

There was rarely very much to carry. One strolling actress, Mrs Charke, described a property box in her company as containing a few scabbardless, rusty swords and one or two superannuated mopsticks 'transmigrated into Tragedy Truncheons'. The company described in Breval's *The Strollers* could boast of a second-hand dragon; but this unfortunately had lost a wing and two claws in an over-boisterous opera.[38]

Shabby as they were, sometimes even 'in a deplorable pickle, ragged and emaciated', the players contrived to make a good show when they entered a town, waving handbills in the air to the sound of drum beats, dressed in bright if tawdry clothes, cocked hats, ruffles, embroidered waistcoats and flounced skirts, all liberally supplied with spangles and feathers. They lodged in inns or the houses of tradesmen, and used barns to store their properties in and to put on their costumes, as the actresses do in Hogarth's lively picture. If no theatre or town hall was available, they would sometimes stage their plays in a barn, a 'horrid wreck of a barn', perhaps, such as that described in George Parker's memoirs, 'with a few bits of candle stuck in clay to light the dismal hole'.[39] Or they would take a room in an inn which they would do their best to transform into an inviting theatre. John Bernard remembered how the manager of his company took a large room in an inn and from its ceiling suspended a 'collection of green tatters' for a curtain – whatever the material, the colour of the curtains had always traditionally to be green. The manager then

> Erected a pair of paper screens right-hand and left for wings; arranged four candles in front of said wings to divide the stage from the orchestra (the fiddlers' chairs being legitimate division of the orchestra from the pit), and with all spare benches of the inn to form boxes, and a hoop suspended from the ceiling (perforated with a dozen nails, to receive as many tallow candles) to suggest the idea of a chandelier, he had constructed and embellished what he denominated a Theatre.[40]

Hard as was their life, most strolling players would have had no other. They complained of grasping managers; but there were others who were trusted and even loved, who would willingly turn their hands to any task from painting scenery to printing handbills, who, like the one described by S. W. Ryley in the *Itinerant* (1808), 'if he had money which was rarely the case, he laughed and lent it; if he had none he laughed and did without'. 'We players are a set of merry, undone dogs,' one of them is quoted by Ryley as having remarked contentedly, 'and though we often want the means of life, we are seldom without the means of mirth.'[41]

The booths of strolling players were often to be seen at fairs alongside those of acrobats and freaks, foreign musicians and singers, rope-dancers and posture-dancers, fortune-tellers and keepers of strange animals such as bears that 'daunce like any ladies while "tat, tat, tat, tat," says the little penny Trumpet'. A late seventeenth-century ballad lists some of the fair's attractions:

> Here are the rarities of the whole fair!
> Piper-le-Pim, and the wise Dancing Mare;
> Here's valiant St George and the Dragon,
> a farce,
> A girl of fifteen with strange moles on
> her arse,
> Here is Vienna Besieged, a rare thing,
> And here Punchinello, shown thrice to
> the King.[42]

The plays were generally far from sophisticated, consisting for the most part of crude farces and drolls, of spectacles representing recent events and occasional political squibs, though these were not so popular in the eighteenth century as they had been earlier.[43] 'Everything was done to such a Perfection of Uncoothness,' wrote Ned Ward of one 'dwarf comedy, Sir-named a Droll entitled, "The Devil of a Wife"'. It was 'the strangest Hodg-Podg that ever was Jumbled together'. Yet he had to admit that it was 'an excellent Farce to please an Audience of such Fools'.[44] Later commentators, while admitting the crudity of the shows, were equally entertained.

By the middle of the century at Bartholomew Fair and elsewhere the players' booths had become much more elaborate and comfortable. Pantomimes and ballad-operas were presented as well as such farces as 'The Whore of Babylon, the Devil and the Pope'. Actors, giving as many as nine performances a day, could earn five or six guineas a week, far more than the 25s a week which was as much as they could expect to earn even in the best provincial companies. The booths, constructed of stout wooden boards, were described as being 'of extraordinary Largeness'. Some had two galleries, in addition to the pit and boxes, and a balcony on which the players marched about in costume and attracted audiences by the blare of trumpets. In the early years of the century prices were not much cheaper than those demanded at ordinary permanent theatres, 2s 6d for boxes, 1s 6 for the pit, 1s for the first gallery and 6d for the upper gallery. But towards the end of the century they became cheaper: at St Bartholomew's Fair in 1784 a seat in an upper gallery could be had for 3d.[45]

Repeated attempts were made by the authorities to close or restrict fairs and to shut down the players' booths which were condemned as the corrupters of morals of servants and children, gathering places of 'Loose, Idle, Disorderly People, who were taught there to mock their betters', and – at Bartholomew Fair at any rate – to ridicule 'the Grandeur of the City', even to laugh at a 'Lord-Mayor (as in the Renown'd Play of Whittington)' and to find amusement in the sight of a drunken porter representing 'an alderman in a Scarlet Gown'. The collapse of a booth in August 1749, and the consequent death of two spectators, furnished an excuse for the prohibition of show booths the following year; but they soon appeared again, and further decrees against them had to be issued. When the authorities tried to enforce these decrees there was usually a riot. In 1743 the Borough authorities ordered the bellman to cry around the fairground at Southwark that all performers offering plays would be taken up as vagrants and punished and that the fair should be limited to three days. This so incensed the debtors in the nearby Marshalsea Prison – who had been accustomed to receiving by way of charity a share of the money collected by the booth-keepers – that they began to hurl stones over the wall at the crowd, killing a child and injuring several other people. Some years later a similar announcement at Bartholomew Fair resulted in the enraged populace breaking the windows 'of almost every inhabitant of Smithfield'.[46]

One of the most popular of all entertainments at fairs were the puppet shows which by the 1760s had become the main attraction at Bartholomew Fair where, in 1790, eight of the thirteen entertainments offered were being given by puppeteers. Shows with glove puppets had been known in England since the fourteenth century; but by the eighteenth the gloves had become marionettes, two or even three feet tall, expertly manipulated by wires. Puppet plays had been allowed to continue after the theatres had been closed in 1642; and after the Restoration they had become extremely popular. Pepys records having seen 'an Italian puppet play', the best he 'ever saw, and great resort of gallants', 'within the rayles' in Covent Garden in May 1662.[47] And between then and 1668 he mentions as many as six different puppeteers in his diary, the best of them being Signor Bologna, also known as Policinello or Punchinello, after the chief character in his performances, the hook-nosed, hump-backed character whose name was eventually shortened to Punch. Bologna was given a gold chain and medal by Charles II for a much admired performance at Whitehall where the stage for his marionettes measured twenty feet by eighteen.[48]

Puppet shows were given in booths at fairs, in hired rooms in inns, and at street corners. Like plays in the theatre, they were announced by pictorial handbills, by drums, flags and banners. Admittance was a penny or two-pence, and the show lasted for about half an hour. Some puppeteers were quite incompetent. Ned Ward complained of 'a senseless dialogue between Punchenello and the Devil' which was conveyed 'to the ears of the listening rabble through a tin squeaker'; while Joseph Strutt remembered in his youth having seen wretched displays of

> wooden figures, barbarously formed and decorated, without the least degree of taste or propriety. The wires that communicated the motion to them appeared at the tops of their heads, and the manner in which they were made to move evinced the ignorance and inattention of the managers; the dialogues were mere jumbles of absurdity and nonsense, intermixed with low moral discourses passing between Punch and the fiddler, for the orchestra rarely admitted of more than one minstrel; and these flashes of merriment were made offensive to decency by the actions of the puppets.[49]

Yet the more expert manipulators of marionettes had many admirers until the end of the eighteenth century when suddenly their popularity declined and their place was once more taken by the glove puppeteer who travelled about the streets and in the country with his theatre on his back, giving performances in the open air, or in an empty stable by the light of a few flaming candles stuck in a hoop – as Codlin and Harris do in *The Old Curiosity Shop* – his wife or an assistant collecting what they could from those who stopped to watch them, thankful to get three shillings for a performance, but giving ten performances or more on a summer's day, passing the secrets of his craft on to his son so that it remained among a very few families.[50]

One of the puppeteers, a man named Piccini who was born in 1745, was described by another old showman:

> Everyone in London knowed him, Lords, dukes, princes, squires and vagabonds, all used to stop to laugh at his performances, and a funny old fellow he was. He always carried a rum bottle in his pocket, and drunked out of this unbeknown behind the baize afore he went into the frame, so that it should lay in his power to give the audience a most excellent perform-

ance . . . He was past performing when I bought my show off him, and
werry poor . . . He had spent all he had got in drink and in treating friends
. . . At last he reduced himself to want, and died in the workhouse.[51]

It was an end to which many circus performers also came.

The circus originated with those acrobats, rope-dancers and trainers of
animals who had been encountered at fairs for generation after generation.
These were brought together in the 1760s by equestrian performers who
rented fields in which to exhibit their feats, and offered the public both trick
horse-riding and the familiar diversions of the fair. The most celebrated,
though not the first, equestrian acrobat to have done so was Philip Astley
who, with his wife, performed a comic act of atrocious horsemanship called
'The Taylor riding to Brentford' and who in 1773 added to his equestrian
turns, the antics of 'the Sagacious Dog', the acrobatics of a Veronese family
who built themselves into a pyramid, Polish and Spanish gymnasts, Madame
Paliasette and her family on the tight-rope, and Madame Margeretta who
stood on one leg on a slack wire while balancing thirteen full glasses on a
tobacco pipe.[52] In 1779 Astley, a large, boorish former cavalryman with a
stentorian voice who prided himself on knowing 'what would catch John
Bull', opened a canvas-covered ring near Westminster Bridge, naming it the
Royal Grove, and, after a fire, rebuilding it as the famous Astley's
Amphitheatre. Here he presented dancing horses and fox hunts, fireworks
and waterworks, ventriloquists and conjurors, sword fights and melodramas,
and Joseph Grimaldi, the great clown, who had first appeared at Drury Lane
at the age of two in 1781.

> Dear, dear, what a place it looked, that Astleys! [wrote Charles Dickens
> who went there often when he was a young man and the performances were
> just as they had been fifty years before]. With all the paint, gilding and
> looking-glass, the vague smell of horses suggestive of coming wonders, the
> clean white sawdust down in the circus, the company coming in and taking
> their places, the fiddlers looking carelessly up at them while they tuned
> their instruments, as if they didn't want the play to begin, and knew it all
> beforehand! What a glow was that which burst upon them all, when that
> long, clear, brilliant row of lights came slowly up; and what the feverish
> excitement when the little bell rang and the music began in full earnest . . .
> Then the play itself! The horses, the firing . . . the forlorn lady . . . the
> tyrant . . . the man who sang the song with the lady's maid and danced
> the chorus . . . the pony who reared up on his hind legs when he saw
> the murderer . . . the clown who ventured on such familiarities with the
> military man in boots . . . the lady who jumped over the nine and twenty

ribbons and came down safe upon the horse's back – everything was delightful, splendid and surprising.[53]

Modelled on places like Astley's – and on the Royal Circus and Equestrian Philharmonic Academy, which Charles Dibdin, a former composer at Covent Garden, and the horse showman, Charles Hughes, opened in Blackfriars Road in 1782 – circuses were soon being built all over the country, several of them of imposing size: Ryan's Amphitheatre in Birmingham held 2000 people, the Amphitheatre in Leeds 3000. Most of them were built of wood and were none too secure. The gallery of the circus at Bristol collapsed in 1799, resulting in many casualties; and a circus at Norwich was later blown down in a gale. But although tents were used at Liverpool in 1788, there is no further record of these until the 1840s when the example of a circus owner, who had seen circus tents in America, was widely copied. By the end of the nineteenth century tents were being made large enough to accommodate 7000 people.

# 38 · *Quacks, Diseases and Cures*

The mountebank who stands upon the stage in laced hat and embroidered coat in Hogarth's *Southwark Fair* is representative of a type of quack encountered everywhere in eighteenth-century England. Assisted by their Merry-Andrews who eagerly endorsed their claims, such charlatans made handsome profits by dispensing to a gullible public a variety of highly coloured pills and medicines whose curative properties were said to be infallible. Travelling through Moorfields in June 1781 Samuel Curwen came across a 'stage doctor on an elevated scaffold covered with a ragged blanket, discoursing to the more dirty-faced ragged mob; demonstrating to their satisfaction no doubt, the superior excellence of his nostrums to those of the dispensary, and the more safe and secure state of patients under his management than hospitals and common receptacles of sick and wounded poor'.[1]

Most of these mountebanks claimed to be able to cure all kinds of diseases and complaints from syphilis to corns and toothache. A handbill distributed in London in the middle of the eighteenth century advertised the expertise of one Dr Cerf, 'lately arrived from France':

> Well-known for curing all kinds of disorders, both internal and external; likewise the SECRET DISEASE, let it be ever so inveterate, without any hindrance of business and in as short a time as the case will admit of. Trusses to be disposed of for all kinds of ruptures.
>
> Any person that cannot attend personally, by sending their morning urine, may be faithfully informed of their complaint, and receive such medicines as are proper for their disorder, on the most reasonable terms. Advice given by a physician every afternoon, from four till six o'clock; and to the poor (gratis) from seven till eight in the morning.
>
> The doctor may be spoke with in all languages; and letters (post paid) will be immediately attended to.

Likewise speedily cures all sorts of corns, without the least pain, so that the patient may walk or jump about again in a few minutes. Chilblains ever so bad cured in a short time. Also cures the most violent tooth-ach in an instant. Draws teeth, preserves those that are decaying, and puts in artificial ones in the most perfect manner.

N.B. A back door with a latch, by which persons may let themselves into the surgery.

Patients may be accommodated with lodgings at the doctor's house.[2]

The nostrums prescribed, not only by unqualified practitioners, were quite as bizarre as those recommended in the Middle Ages. Snails mashed with bay salt and mallows were advanced as cures for ague; Venetian soap as well as 'your own Youren when warm' and woodlice ground up with sugar and nutmeg were recommended for cancer; the juice of wild cucumber for dropsy; fishes' eyes for toothache; dung tea, stewed owls and crushed worms for a variety of other complaints. Joanna Stevens, who refused to reveal the secrets of a universal cure until an Act of Parliament was passed providing her with £5000, issued on receipt of this amount from the Treasury various recipes requiring the admixture of powdered snails and Alicante soap, calcined eggshells, wild carrot seeds, hips and haws burned to blackness and stirred up in further amounts of soap and honey.

Advertisements for pills, powders and tinctures filled column after column in the newspapers. At 'Mr Dunstan's toy shop at the Rose and Crown, under St Dunstan's Church, Fleet Street', so readers of the *Spectator* were informed, a cure for stuttering which had 'stupendous effects' could be purchased for 2s 6d per pot, 'with directions'. And at 'Mr Payne's, at the Angel and Crown in St Paul's Churchyard' sufferers from 'Loss of Memory or Forgetfulness' could buy for the same price a pot of 'a grateful electuary' which would enable them to 'remember the minutest circumstances of their affairs etc. to a wonder'.

Not all these improbable remedies were ineffective. Having been told that a stye might be cured by rubbing it with the tail of a black cat, James Woodforde determined to 'make a trial of it' and soon afterwards felt his 'eyelid much abated by the swelling'. An acquaintance of Thomas Gray recovered from dropsy after prescribing himself 'a boiled chicken entire and five quarts of small beer'; while Horace Walpole was a firm believer in Dr James's Antimonial Fever Powders which he swore he would take if his house caught fire and which, he was firmly convinced, would have saved the life of Oliver Goldsmith who had asked to be given a dose on his deathbed.

These powders, a combination of oxide of antimony and phosphate of lead, were the invention of Dr Robert James who had been at school with Samuel Johnson. He was said to have been drunk every day for twenty years and was damned by Johnson as a rascal after having apologized for taking a whore about with him in a coach by explaining that 'he always took a swelling in his stones' if he abstained for too long from sexual intercourse. Yet although undoubtedly a 'very lewd fellow both *verbo* and *facto*', James was the author of a medical dictionary in three stout volumes and his powders were so highly regarded that they were prescribed for George III. They were but one of numerous supposed sovereign remedies which were swallowed or applied by all kinds of patients, hypochondriacs and valetudinarians. There were Dr Belloste's pills for rheumatism at a guinea the box, Parke's pills for the stone at 2s 6d per pill, Velno's vegetable syrup for venereal disease, Daffy's Elixir, Godfrey's Cordial, Scots pills and Indian root. There was, pre-eminently, tar-water whose virtues were extravagantly broadcast by the philosopher and prelate Dr George Berkeley, for several years Bishop of Cloyne. 'It is impossible to write a letter now without tincturing the ink with tar-water,' the Archbishop of York was assured in 1744. 'This is the common topic of discourse both among the rich and poor, high and low, and the Bishop of Cloyne has made it as fashionable as going to Vauxhall or Ranelagh.'[3]

Some of these cures were harmless and perhaps even, on occasions, efficacious; but others were certainly not: the practice of quietening children with such drugs as Godfrey's Cordial – which was commonly given to children at the Foundling Hospital – and with other proprietary concoctions consisting largely of laudanum and spirits, resulted in innumerable fatalities. William Buchan maintained in his *Domestic Medicine* (1769) that as many as half infant mortalities in London were due to the administering of dangerous soporifics.[4] Even those doctors who sensibly emphasized the importance of diet in the maintenance of good health often had strange ideas as to what constituted a proper diet. Derek Jarrett cites George Cheyne, author of *The Natural Method of Cureing the Diseases of the Body* (1742), as an advocate of the consumption of meat in the winter, of fruit and vegetables in the summer, or milk and turnips all the year round for chronic distempers and, for acute distempers, 'teas made of saponaceous or aromatic seeds'.[5]

Most quacks, like most doctors, had their favourite cure. Dr John Hancock, chaplain to the Duke of Bedford, advocated cold water and stewed prunes, while Dr John Moore, of Abchurch Lane, warmly recommended his own worm powders, which earned him an apostrophe from Alexander Pope:

> O learned friend of Abchurch Lane,
> Who sett'st our entrails free,
> Vain is thy art, thy powder vain,
> Since worms shall eat e'en thee.

Profiting by their patients' anxiety to believe such claims as that advanced by Dr Benjamin Thornhill – who advertised in the *Evening Post* his 'infallible cure for the gout' and 'never-failing remedy for the colic' – many medical practitioners made large fortunes. Thornhill himself, according to Steele, 'died worth five hundred pounds per annum, though he was not born to a half penny'. William Read, who was knighted as a mark of royal favour, had once been an illiterate tailor and in one of his advertisements asserted that for twenty-five years he had been 'in the practice of couching cataracts, taking off all sorts of wens, curing wry necks, and hair-lips without blemish though never so deformed'. He gave grand parties at which Swift, once a guest, much admired the punch served 'in golden vessells'. His contemporary, the self-styled occulist, Roger Grant, was also probably illiterate; he had been a cobbler and a Baptist Preacher and afterwards, 'putting out eyes with great success', acquired wealth comparable to Read's. Joshua Ward, who was once perhaps a footman, having invented the famous 'drop and pill' – with which he claimed to be able to cure every human malady – treated Lord Chesterfield, Gibbon and Henry Fielding among many other noble and famous patients. And, although his pill, which contained a large proportion of antimony, was said to have killed as many as it cured, and although, in addition, it was established in a court action that, apart from a nodding acquaintance with pharmacy, Ward was quite destitute of medical knowledge, he was especially exempted by name when in 1748 an Apothecaries Act was introduced into Parliament to restrain unlicensed persons from compounding medicines. After treating the king for a sprained thumb, Ward was accorded the best thanks of the House of Commons and allowed the privilege of driving his carriage through St James's Park. He died, a very rich man, in 1761.

As invalids of all classes flocked to him, so too they did to Sarah Mapp, the daughter of a bone-setter and a bone-setter herself, who practised her art in London at the Grecian Coffee House in Devereux Court and at Epsom where, according to the *London Magazine*, ' 'tis reckoned she gets near 20 guineas a day, she executing what she does in a quick manner'. Certainly she attracted so many people to the town that she was offered a hundred guineas by the local authorities to remain there a year. Equally successful in his way was Dr de Mainauduc, a *soi-disant* pupil of Mesmer, whose hypnotized patients included 'one duke, one duchess, one marchioness, two countesses, one earl, one baron, three baronesses, one bishop, five right honourable gentlemen and ladies, two baronets, seven Members of Parliament, one clergyman, two physicians, seven surgeons, besides ninety-two ladies and gentlemen of respectability'. But of all quacks none was more celebrated than James Graham to whose lavishly furnished Temple of Health crowds of people in search of 'the whole art of enjoying health and vigour of body and mind' were drawn by handbills delivered from door to door by immensely tall servants in splendid liveries and gold-laced cocked hats. At the Temple of Health, which moved to Schomberg House, Pall Mall, from Adelphi Terrace in 1779, the walls were hung with 'walking sticks, ear trumpets, visual glasses, crutches etc left as most honourable trophies by deaf, weak, paralytic and emaciated persons, cripples etc who being cured had no longer need of such assistance'. There was also a 'celestial bed' for conceiving perfect children 'as even the barren must do when so powerfully agitated in the delights of love'. This bed, which was hired out at £100 per night, was said by its owner to have cost £60,000, had a dome lined with mirrors, coloured sheets and mattresses 'filled with strongest, most springy hair, produced at vast expense from the tails of English stallions'. It also played music and, in 1781, was attended, so it was claimed, by Emma Lyon, later Lady Hamilton, posing as the Goddess of Health. Graham died in a lunatic asylum.[6]

The treatment of the mentally disturbed in private mad-houses and public lunatic asylums was often appallingly cruel and intended to be so for the benefit of the patients. As a seventeenth-century physician observed, 'Maniacs often recover much sooner if they are treated with torture and treatment in hovels instead of with medicaments.'[7] It continued to be generally held in the eighteenth century that madmen were best controlled by beating and other methods of coercion, by being flung into baths of cold water and frequently bled and purged. At Manchester Royal Lunatic Asylum, which was opened in 1766, the treatment, so one of its doctors wrote, consisted in repeated bathing, constant dosing with opium and other drugs, 'blood-letting . . . vomiting . . . purgatives . . . and calomel given until the patient's mouth was sore'.[8] Even the Rev. Francis Willis, an elderly clergyman with an Oxford medical degree who was called in to help look after George III when the king's mind was affected by porphyria, was a strong believer in the strictest discipline. Considered by some, so Lord Sheffield said, 'not much better than a mountebank, and not far different from some of those' that were confined in his mad-house in Lincolnshire, Willis tied his royal patient to his bed, enclosed him in a straitjacket, stuffed handkerchiefs in his mouth to keep him quiet when he was being reprimanded, blistered him when it was considered necessary 'to divert the morbid humours' from his head, and doctored him with a formidable variety of medicines. He was given calomel and camphor, digitalis, quinine, and, as an emetic, tartarized antimony which made him so sick that he knelt on his chair fervently praying that he might either be restored to his senses or allowed to die.[9]

Public sympathy for the king helped to improve the lot of patients at the Bethlehem Royal Hospital in London, more generally known as Bedlam, where, until 1770, visitors were admitted to look at the patients many of whom were chained to cells in galleries like caged animals in a menagerie. 'You can get a sight of these poor creatures, little windows being let into the doors,' a visitor wrote after a visit in 1725. 'On holidays numerous persons of both sexes, but belonging generally to the lower classes, visit this hospital, and amuse themselves watching these unfortunate wretches, who often give them cause for laughter. On leaving this melancholy abode, you are expected by the porter to give him a penny.'[10]

This hospital existed at the beginning of the fourteenth century as an annexe to the Priory of St Mary Bethlehem, but it probably then cared for patients suffering from general complaints, and it was not until 1377 that 'distracted' patients were looked after, that is to say were kept chained to the wall by leg or ankle and when violent ducked in water. In 1547, when the priory was dissolved, the mayor and corporation bought the site from the king and re-established the hospital as a lunatic asylum. Not until the Bethel Hospital at Norwich was opened at the beginning of the eighteenth century was a new hospital built in England intended solely for the insane.[11] And although others soon followed thereafter – Sophie von la Roche was told that there were 300 lunatic asylums in London alone – many insane people were kept locked up at home, like the first Mrs Rochester at Thornfield Hall in *Jane Eyre* and the 'madwoman of Cwmgwanon' who, so the Rev. Francis Kilvert was told, 'they keep locked up in a bedroom alone, for she will come down amongst them stark naked. She had broken the windows and all the crockery . . . threatens to wring her daughter-in-law's neck . . . Then she will set to and roar till they can hear her down the dingle . . . nearly half a mile [away].'[12] The nurses employed to look after such people were frequently no more tender than Betsy Prig who, so Mrs Gamp tells us in *Martin Chuzzlewit*, 'has nussed a many lunacies and well she knows their ways, which putting em right close afore the fire, when fractious, is the certainest and most compoging'.[13]

By Betsy Prig's day, however, the treatment of the insane in asylums had become more humane; and it was generally accepted that the mentally deranged were not incurable lunatics possessed by devils but people who were ill, who could be treated and might be cured. There were far more institutions like the Retreat which Louis Simond had visited at York. This was 'admirably managed, and almost entirely by *reason* and kindness: it was instituted by Quakers. Most of the patients move about at liberty, without noise and disorder.'[14] Commissioners in Lunacy were established as a permanent body in 1828 and were required to visit hospitals and submit reports.[15]

Much mental illness, so it was supposed, was caused by masturbation which was also held to be a common prelude to self-destruction, so prevalent an occurrence that it was sometimes known as the 'English disease'. The light-hearted referred to suicide as a joke: in 1755 an advertisement in the *Gentleman's Magazine* drew its readers' attention to a preparation called 'Stygian Spirit' which enabled gentlemen who found life intolerable to commit suicide even while in company without upsetting their companions. And some years later the Earl of Pembroke told a friend about a Frenchman who, having spent a long time in Salisbury, contracted the 'English disease' and hanged himself *'à l'anglaise'*.[16] In his *De l'Esprit des Lois* (1748) Montesquieu devoted a whole chapter to the English habit of suicide, in which he mentioned the right which English people sometimes exercised of driving a stake through the heart of a suicide unless he could be shown to be insane at the time of his criminal act. The corpse of a London bookseller who killed his child and then shot himself in 1755 was carried off by his friends and buried secretly when a note was found placing the blame upon his creditors rather than upon his own disturbed state of mind. The Lord Mayor ordered that the body should be dug up and reburied at Moorfields crossroads with the customary stake through the heart.[17]

Despite the claims of doctors and quacks, no effective cure could be found for smallpox which, after the disappearance of plague, became the most feared of all diseases, particularly for children and in industrial towns.[18] In one town alone 589 children died between 1769 and 1774; and in London there were 3500 deaths from smallpox in 1796.[19] In earlier centuries the victims of the disease had been quite likely to recover, even though they were often scarred for life, many as badly as Mrs Seward whose disfigurement, Pepys thought 'would make a man weep to see'. In the sixteenth century the young Richard Allington had sadly observed on his death-bed: 'Maisters, I must needes die, which I assure you I never thought wolde cum to pass by this disease, consyderinge that it is but the small pocke.'[20] But since then the severity of the disease and the likelihood of it proving fatal had much increased; and in the eighteenth century the fatality rate rose to one death in every six or seven attacks.[21]

In certain cases it was shown that the disease might be prevented in children and adults by placing them in contact with a person suffering from it, much in the same way that attempts were made to prevent hydrophobia by plucking a hair from a rabid dog and placing it upon the wound or getting the patient to swallow it. John Evelyn, two of whose own daughters died of smallpox, described such a case in the household of Mrs James Graham of Bagshot:

> Her eldest son, was now sick there of the small pox, but in a likely way of recovery; & other of her Children ran about, & among the infected, which she said she let them do on purpose that they might whilst young, passe

that fatal dissease, which she fancied they were to undergo one time or other, & that this would be the best: The severity of this cruel dissease so lately in my poore family confirming much of what she affirm'd.[22]

Experiments with transplanting matter from a mildly affected patient to one in need of protection were first made in Italy and in Constantinople. And in 1721, during a smallpox epidemic in London, Lady Mary Wortley Montagu, whose husband was British ambassador in Constantinople, had her little daughter inoculated in the presence of various physicians. Her son had already been inoculated in Constantinople and had suffered few ill effects. The girl, too, recovered quickly; and the doctors, impressed by the mildness of her attack and by the reports from Constantinople which had been publicized in London by Dr John Woodward, repeated the experiment with almost equal success, first upon some Newgate prisoners, who were promised reprieves for submitting to it, and then upon charity schoolchildren. There were, however, dangers in this form of inoculation with smallpox. Not only did the induced disease occasionally take a severe course, two or three deaths occurring with every hundred inoculations, but unless the person inoculated was kept isolated the disease was likely to spread. This method of prevention was therefore rarely practised after 1728.[23] A subsequent and supposedly improved method, which substituted shallow for deep insertions and usually produced a local rather than a general infection, proved to be scarcely more effective.[24] Yet many felt the dangers of inoculation were less to be feared than a severe attack of smallpox, and in certain areas the method continued to be widely practised.

> This morning [Parson Woodforde wrote in his journal on 3 November 1776] Dr Thorne of Mattishall came to my House and inoculated my two servants, Ben Legate and little Jack Warton. Pray God my people and all others in the Small Pox may do well. Several Houses have got the Small Pox at present in Weston . . . Nov. 4: My inoculating folks took their salts very well this morning and drank very well of Water Gruel . . . The inoculated people had for supper Rice Milk, and I am afraid Molly put some eggs in the same . . . I am astonished at her. Nov. 8: I paid the Dr. for inoculating our people 10s 6d. I gave him also towards inoculating a poor family: 10s 6d. Ben's arms look much inflamed . . . much forwarder than the boy's . . . Nov. 12: Dr Thorne told Ben that he might now live as he used to do before Inoculation; [but] that Jack should live low as yet.

These inoculations were successful enough; but in other places they were carried out in a most hurried and haphazard way. A Bath surgeon of long experience wrote:

When the inoculating rage once takes place whole parishes are doomed, without the least attention to age, sex or temperament . . . with no previous preparation, no after treatment or concern. Are not scores and hundreds seized upon at once, for the incisions, scratchings, puncturings and threadings? . . . And whether they may or may not receive the infection is just as little known or cared about.[25]

Yet, despite the dangers, inoculation – or variolation as it is better described – continued to be practised until the end of the eighteenth century when a far more satisfactory method of protection was devised.[26]

It had long been known that cowherds and milkmaids were for the most part immune from smallpox, but it was generally supposed that contact with the cows protected them rather than the disease of the cows known as cowpox which the animals passed to the persons who milked them through a scratch or lesion on the hands. It was, however, observed that farmworkers who had contracted cowpox did not thereafter suffer from smallpox when that disease visited their villages; and in 1774, during an epidemic of smallpox that swept across Dorset, a farmer near Yeovil allowed two of his men, who had both had cowpox, to nurse the smallpox sufferers. They did so with no ill effects; and, reassured by this, the farmer took some matter from one of his diseased cows and rubbed it into scratches which he made with a darning needle on the arms of his wife and two sons. The farmer was condemned for his inhumanity; but this experiment also was a success. None of his family contracted smallpox; and a local doctor who was told the story sought and received permission to inoculate the two sons with cowpox. No reaction followed; but the doctor does not appear to have tried the experiment on other patients.[27]

At this time a former pupil of the celebrated surgeon John Hunter was in practice at Berkeley in Gloucestershire. This was Edward Jenner who had been studying the relationship between smallpox and cowpox since a milkmaid had said to him: 'I cannot take smallpox for I have had cowpox.' In 1778 Jenner was consulted by a Berkeley woman who, as one who had had cowpox, wanted to know whether she ought to be inoculated against smallpox which had at that time claimed many victims in the district. Jenner inoculated her from a smallpox pustule and observed that there were only the slightest after-effects. He subsequently inoculated several other people who had had cowpox; and they, too, escaped the more serious disease. Finally in 1796, during an outbreak of cowpox on two dairy farms near Berkeley, Jenner was ready to make the vital test.

The more accurately to observe the progress of the infection [he wrote] I selected a healthy boy about eight years old for the purpose of inoculation

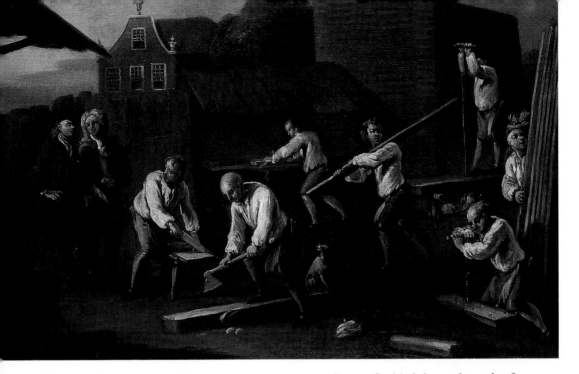

ABOVE: Joiners and carvers at work in a carpenter's yard as portrayed by Hogarth. Gentlemen's houses were in Hogarth's day (1697–1764) generally built under the direction of architects. But frequently houses were based on designs in pattern books.

BELOW: George Stubbs's haymakers of 1785. Women, seen here working industriously with long-handled rakes, often wore bedgowns in the fields, and sometimes worked in their stays covered only by a short-sleeved shift and a petticoat with a handkerchief over neck and shoulders.

FAR LEFT: St James's Fair, Bristol: detail from an early 19th-century evocation by Samuel Colman. As well as being popular entertainments, fairs still supplied the wants, in the way of clothes, provisions and household goods, of hundreds of thousands of country people.

LEFT: The cobbled streets of 18th-century Bristol were worn smooth by the constant passage of the horse-drawn sledges seen on the right. In the 17th century Bristol had begun to grow into the largest city in England after London, with a flourishing trade in tobacco, sugar, cotton, manufactured goods and slaves. Defoe described it as 'the greatest, the richest and the best port of trade in Great Britain, London only excepted'. In the early 18th century as many as 30,000 slaves left Bristol every year. Later this trade was centred upon Liverpool where the painter, Fuseli, said he could 'smell everywhere the blood of slaves'.

BELOW: Between the Cotswold hills and the Vale of Evesham: Dixton Manor House, Gloucestershire, a characteristic West Country landscape in the 18th century.

ABOVE: Old Somerset House by Canaletto, who spent most of the years 1746–56 in England and who painted this view of the house when it was occupied by foreign ambassadors. The original Renaissance palace was built in 1547–50 by Lord Protector Somerset; it later became a royal palace and, having been much altered and enlarged, was replaced by the building designed by William Chambers, Robert Smirke and James Pennethorne.

RIGHT: Covent Garden, London's best-known fruit and vegetable market, started in 1656 as a few temporary stalls erected in the garden of Bedford House, home of the Earl, later Duke, of Bedford. The surrounding area had been developed by the fourth Earl who called in Inigo Jones as architect. Jones built three sides of a square of tall terraced houses looking inwards onto a large open courtyard. In his instructions to his architect, the Earl said that the development would require a church but, being a low churchman, he did not want it to be 'much better than a barn'. 'Well, then,' replied Jones, 'you shall have the handsomest barn in England.' The church, dedicated to St Paul, was consecrated in 1638. A hundred years later the market was flourishing.

LEFT: *The Charitable Lady* by William Redmore Bigg. The lady, accompanied by her children and attended by her black servant, is wearing clothes fashionable in the late 1780s.

BELOW: *Mr Howard Offering Relief to Prisoners* by Francis Wheatley. John Howard, a Bedfordshire landowner, made a series of tours throughout the country, investigating the conditions of prisons and prisoners. By his efforts, and the revelations incorporated in his book, *The State of Prisons in England and Wales* (1777), some reforms of their appalling administration were effected.

A detail from *The Iron Forge*, painted by Joseph Wright of Derby in
1772, one of numerous pictures which he exhibited between 1765
and 1773 and in which he experimented in the portrayal of figures
illuminated by candlelight or fire. Wright, the son of a Derby
attorney, has been described as 'the first professional painter to
express the spirit of the Industrial Revolution'.

with the cowpox. The matter was taken from a suppurated sore on the hand of a dairy Maid who was infected by her master's Cows, and it was inserted on the 14th May 1796 into the arms of the Boy, by means of two superficial incisions, each about three quarters of an inch long . . . During the whole of [the ninth day after this] he was perceptibly indisposed, and had rather a restless night; but, on the following day, he was perfectly well . . . On the 1st of July following this Boy was inoculated with Matter immediately taken from a smallpox Pustule. Several punctures and slight incisions were made in both his arms, and the matter was well rubb'd into them, but no disease followed.[28]

Jenner, however, was a cautious man; and it was not until after he had conducted several more successful experiments that, in 1798, he published his influential *Enquiry into the Causes and Effects of the . . . Disease . . . Known by the name of Cow Pox*. This pamphlet was severely criticized by medical men, attacked by clergymen and journalists and ridiculed by satirists: James Gillray in his *The Cow-Pock – or the Wonderful Effects of the New Inoculation* portrayed a scene in the Smallpox and Inoculation Hospital at St Pancras where Jenner is seen gashing the arm of a young woman with a knife while a boy holds up a bucket labelled 'Vaccine Pock hot from ye Cow'. From other patients, cows' horns and heads sprout grotesquely from noses, ears, foreheads, breeches and petticoats.[29]

Gradually, however, as several distinguished doctors lent their support to vaccination, the prejudice against it was overcome; and those who objected to being injected with matter from sick animals were comforted to know that the operation was equally successful if the matter came from human beings. In 1808 Isaac Cruikshank produced a caricature in strong contrast to Gillray's. In it Jenner is seen about to be crowned by a cherub with a laurel wreath; he is holding a vaccination knife, whose blade is inscribed 'Milk of human Kindness', while three old-fashioned doctors, practicers of inoculation, run off with much larger and blood-soaked knives, crying: 'Curse on these Vaccinators we shall all be starved.' The ground around them is strewn with children dead or dying of smallpox.[30]

By then, in fact, outbreaks of the disease, thanks to vaccination, were already becoming increasingly less severe. About half the children born in British towns were vaccinated between 1800 and 1870; and in 1853 vaccination of infants within four months of their birth was made compulsory. There was a serious epidemic of smallpox in 1870–72 in which over 40,000 people died, nearly 10,000 of them in London. But in those years the efficacy of vaccination was conclusively shown: in the worst year, 1871, 821,856 children were born in England and Wales; of these nearly 80,000 died before they could be vaccinated, but of the rest almost 94 per cent were successfully treated. After the epidemic was over the number of deaths from the disease rapidly declined.[31]

The problems of disease in eighteenth-century England were greatly exacerbated by the dreadful housing conditions in which most people lived, by primitive systems of drainage and by inadequate or contaminated water supply. In towns houses were built as quickly as possible, and families flocked into them, often crowding into a single room and having to share what water could be obtained from the communal taps with several other families. They also had to share an outside privy, usually a filthy, overflowing earth closet, with all the inhabitants of a court or row. Those few houses which had water-closets made conditions worse rather than better; for these early water-closets discharged their effluent into brick sewers where in dry weather it remained to stagnate and in wet was carried along with the drain water from the streets to be discharged into a canal or the river from which the water supply of the town was drawn. Nor were the cottages in which many farmworkers lived any better than those of factory hands. Nor were the houses of the rich much healthier than those of the poor; they were more spacious and less overcrowded to be sure, but their sanitary defects were quite as obnoxious. Even at Windsor Castle, as late as 1861, 'nothing had been done to improve the drains in connection with the various water closets, sinks, etc.', so the Lord Chamberlain reported. 'The noxious effluvia which escapes from the old drains and the numerous cesspools still remaining, is frequently so exceedingly offensive as to render many parts of the castle almost uninhabitable.' The queen herself had contracted typhoid fever several years before; the Prince Consort is believed to have died of it, though he may also have been suffering from cancer; and their eldest son, the Prince of Wales, became dangerously infected with the disease during a visit to Lord Londesborough's country house near Scarborough whose noisome drains resulted in the death of his fellow-guest, the Earl of Chesterfield.

While houses remained so unwholesome it could not be a matter of surprise that typhoid and other mysterious fevers, 'those strange and fatal feavers' as Samuel Pepys had called them, raged from time to time all over the country. 'The fever,' wrote Mrs Gaskell in *Mary Barton* in 1848 – and she could well have been writing of her great-grandmother's day – 'was of a low, putrid typhoid kind; brought on by miserable living, filthy neighbourhood and great depression of mind and body. It is virulent, malignant and highly infectious. But the poor are fatalists with regard to infection, and well for them it is so, for in their crowded dwellings no invalid can be isolated.' This was in Manchester. In London 'fever' featured in the Bills of Mortality as a steady item year after year, seldom falling below 1000 deaths and in 1741, during a general epidemic of typhus, rising to 7500.[32] In the countryside 'fever' was also a constant menace. 'Mr du Quesne's man, Robert, a very old servant, very ill in the Fever that prevails so much in Norfolk now,' wrote Parson Woodforde in his journal on 28 June 1781. 'Very bad at Norwich. Fifty three were buried last week there.' On 1 July he added, 'Poor Robert England, Mr du Quesne's old servant died this afternoon in the Fever that rages much.'

When deaths from 'fever' began to decline other epidemic diseases carried off men, women and children by the thousand, the Bills of Mortality recording whooping cough, measles, scarlatina, infantile diarrhoea and, later, cholera, among the principal causes of death.[33] Even when death did not result and was not expected, illness was often a prolonged trial: wounds were quickly infected and suppurated for days on end; gastric upsets from eating bad food were common; decayed teeth produced permanent septic foci; alcohol and laudanum might relieve pain but surgical operations without anaesthetics were as much to be dreaded as they had ever been; and death was a constant spectre.

'Bring me the candle, Brown,' said Keats to his friend when he first realized he was dying of consumption. 'Let me see the blood . . . It is arterial blood I cannot be deceived . . . That drop of blood is my death warrant. I must die.'[34]

Tuberculosis, both glandular and pulmonary, was a common complaint; and, in the seventeenth century at least, scrofula – a state of constitutional weakness characterized mainly by defective nutrition of the tissues which renders them a ready prey to tuberculosis – seems to have been particularly virulent. It was also known as the King's Evil since it had been believed from the time of Edward the Confessor that it could be cured by a touch from the sovereign's hands. Edward III had given public displays of his ability to cure sufferers from the disease; Henry VII had the 'Ceremonies for the Healing' inserted in the Service Book; Elizabeth I laid her long white fingers on the afflicted flesh of thousands of her subjects; and James I, although he clearly found the process distasteful, did the same. Charles II is said to have touched nearly 100,000 scrofulous people, over 6000 of them in the year of his Restoration. William III continued the ceremony grudgingly, repeating, 'God grant you better health and more sense' after each laying on of his hand and eventually abandoned the practice altogether. It was revived by Queen Anne who insisted on having persons suffering from the disease brought into her presence even when she herself was dying. Samuel Johnson, whose operation for scrofula on the glands of his neck and a later attack of smallpox left him scarred for life, was one of those whom she touched. This was in March 1712 when he was not yet three years old, but he claimed to have a 'confused but somehow a sort of solemn recollection of a lady in diamonds, and a long black hood', and he greatly prized the golden touchpiece she gave him, a thin medallion on a white ribbon, which he wore round his neck till he died. Two years after this, when George I came to the throne, the ceremony was abandoned, not to be revived. Belief in the healing power of the monarch survived, however, well into the twentieth century. Before the Second World War afflicted people in Norfolk pressed round George VI in the hope of curing themselves by touching him.

Pulmonary tuberculosis, called by John Bunyan, 'The Captain of the Men of Death', also appears to have been widespread in the seventeenth century. Indeed, according to John Locke, writing in 1685, as many as a fifth of all deaths in London were caused by this disease. One seventeenth-century victim was Pepys's brother, of whom the diarist wrote, 'About eight o'clock my brother began to fetch his spittle with more pain and to speak as much but not so distinctly; till at last the phlegm getting the mastery of him and he beginning as we thought to rattle, I had no mind to see him die . . . and so withdrew . . . Before I came back he was dead.'[35]

It was a disease usually associated with towns, but country people were not immune, though the distance between villages did inhibit the spread of the disease.[36] In the Middle Ages and the England of the Tudors it may have been, as is sometimes suggested, a disease to which the upper classes were more prone than the lower: Henry VII and his son, Prince Arthur, both probably died of it, as did King Henry's grandson, Edward VI, whose complaint was, no doubt, aggravated by hereditary syphilis. But during the eighteenth century the disease was far more common among the poor than the rich, miners, brassworkers, stonecutters and pregnant women working in industry being particularly susceptible.[37] There were, however, numerous victims in comfortable homes such as that of Parson Woodforde where his maid, Molly, died in 1785 'in the last stage of a consumption . . . very sensible of her approaching end and happily resigned to it'.

In London the increase in the death rate from pulmonary tuberculosis appears to have culminated in about 1800 and thereafter to have fallen slowly. In industrial towns the death rate probably remained high slightly longer.[38] Yet, during the first five years after the introduction of death registration in 1838 about 60,000 people were listed as having died from the disease; and in the early 1850s there were still over 50,000. Consumption, in fact, killed more people in nineteenth-century Britain than smallpox, typhus fever, scarlet fever, measles and whooping cough put together.[39] There was no recognized cure, and many patients considered it useless to consult a doctor. One of these was Emily Brontë whose sister, Charlotte, wrote:

I told you Emily was ill in my last letter . . . A more hollow, wasted, pallid aspect I have not beheld. The deep, tight cough continues; the breathing after the least exertion is a rapid pant; and these symptoms are accompanied by pains in the chest and side . . . In this state she resolutely refuses to see a doctor. She will give no explanation of her feelings; she will scarcely allow her feelings to be alluded to.[40]

A few years before Emily Brontë's death, a Warwickshire doctor, George Boddington, had published his *Treatment and Care of Pulmonary Consumption*; and in 1843 he had established a small hospital for consumptives at Sutton Coldfield. But while it was generally agreed that the balanced diet and rest he advocated for his patients might do them good, his insistence that they should also be allowed into the fresh air as often as possible was ridiculed, and he felt obliged to give up his project. Other sanatoria were soon afterwards opened, however, and fresh air, good food and rest became the recognized treatment. Although there were never enough beds for all sufferers from the disease, the incidence of tuberculosis began to fall at the end of the century; but, even so, it was not until the advent of pasteurization, tuberculin testing, mass radiography, modern anti-tuberculous drugs and Bacille Calmette-Guerin vaccinations, that the disease was finally brought under control.

Cholera was conquered more quickly. Endemic in India, it did not reach Britain until October 1831 when cases of a 'new disease' were reported from houses on the quay in Sunderland. The disease spread rapidly. Twenty-two thousand people died before the beginning of June 1832 and by the end of that year cholera had visited most parts of England. In Staffordshire nearly 700 people died within two months at Bilston, and at Tipton in a family of fourteen only two survived. The most frightening aspect of the disease was the suddenness with which its victims perished. An attack of violent diarrhoea and vomiting was followed by agonizing cramps in the limbs and abdomen, thirst and fever. After three to twelve hours, the symptoms advanced with rapidity, the skin became dry and a dusky blue or purple in colour, the eyes sank in their sockets, the features were pinched, the pulse at the wrist imperceptible, the voice reduced to a hoarse whisper. Death often took place within a day, sometimes within a few hours.

There was another outbreak in 1848–9 in which there were at least 50,000 deaths in England and Wales and probably as many as 70,000, about 14,000 of them in London, 180 of these in an orphanage in Tooting. Other crowded cities, mainly the poorer quarters of them, also suffered severely, notably Liverpool and Wolverhampton. There were a further 10,675 deaths in London in 1854 and in 1866 more than 5000 people died within three weeks.[41]

Some medical authorities held that the disease was caused by aerial poison produced by the putrefaction of corpses or rotting vegetables. In 1849, however, a pamphlet was published with the title *On the Mode of Communication of Cholera*. This suggested that the infection from the sick could be transmitted to food and that it might also be carried by water. Its author was John Snow.

The son of a Yorkshire farmer, Snow was better known as an anaesthetist than as an expert on cholera. His attention had been drawn to the properties of ether which had been recently introduced in America as an anaesthetizing agent. Having made improvements in the methods of its administration, Snow had demonstrated its use in the dental out-patient room at St George's Hospital, and in 1853 had administered chloroform to Queen Victoria during the birth of Prince Leopold. But he had also been interested in the problem of cholera ever since he had served as an unqualified assistant during the epidemic of 1831–2; and in the epidemic of 1854 he was able to confirm his belief that cholera is a water-borne disease. In the outbreak of that year over 600 deaths occurred in the Broad Street area of London, the inhabitants of only twelve of the forty-nine houses in Broad Street itself escaping death. Snow traced the source of the infection to a pump which provided water for the area, and after he had persuaded the Vestry of St Pancras to remove the handle from the pump, the incidence of cholera in the district fell sharply. Even so, it was some time before Snow's contentions were generally accepted; but in the 1866 epidemic, which occurred when London's main drainage system was almost complete, three quarters of the deaths were in the East End, many of them in those areas from Aldgate to Bow as yet unconnected to the system. These districts were supplied by the East London Company from Old Ford Reservoir whose waters, grossly polluted, were supplied without filtration. 'The area of intense cholera was almost exactly the area of this particular water supply,' declared the medical officer for health, 'nearly if not absolutely filling it and scarcely, if at all, reaching beyond it.' These outbreaks of cholera and the work of John Snow and of William Budd, a Bristol doctor who had simultaneously come to conclusions similar to Snow's, emphasized the urgent need for a pure water supply and for further sanitary reform.[42]

# 39 · *Operators and Tooth-drawers*

Few complaints were more common or more troublesome than toothache; and in the eighteenth century the methods of treating, extracting and replacing bad teeth had improved very little since the Middle Ages when tooth-drawers, wearing necklaces of teeth round their necks and sewed into their belts, would declaim their skill at fairs, promising painless extractions and giving rise to the adage, 'to lie like a tooth-drawer'. John Gay described the most commonly resorted to of dentists, the barber, whose sign and inscription, 'Shaving, bleeding and teeth drawn at a touch', can be seen hanging next door to the Rummer Tavern in Hogarth's *Night*:

> His pole with pewter basons hung
> Black rotten teeth in order strung,
> Rang'd cups, that in the window stood,
> Lin'd with red rags to look like blood,
> Did well his threefold trade explain,
> Who shav'd, drew teeth and breath'd a vein.[1]

But teeth were treated and pulled out not only by barbers but also by blacksmiths, hairdressers, apothecaries, farriers and even by cobblers, watchmakers, jewellers and wood-turners.

Several of those in dental practice were women. In the middle of the eighteenth century among those practising in London were a Mrs Silvie of Porter's Street, Newport Market; Hannah Crippen who continued 'her late husband's business as Dentist and Phlebotomist' in Baldwin's Gardens; Mme Rauxcourt who had acquired her knowledge from 'the most famous Monsier Caperon of Paris, dentist to the King of France'; Signora Foggioni who could cure toothache by placing a finger on the affected tooth, and, to prove that there was no trickery involved, washed her hands in full view of the patient; and Catherine Madden of West Smithfield whose cures were so efficacious that she guaranteed 'no recurrence of the trouble'. Mrs Lewis of Bath attended ladies in their own homes; and Mrs de St Raymond of York was not only a 'Dentist and Operator' on teeth and gums, but also filled hollow teeth, made loose ones firm, straightened children's irregular teeth, supplied efficacious dentifrice at 2s 6d the box, and bored holes in ladies' ears for rings.[2] It was a doctor who extracted several teeth from the Rev. Francis Kilvert's acquaintance, William Hulbert, but he was no gentler nor more expert than the ordinary itinerant tooth-drawer:

> And whilst the doctor was pulling out the [seven] teeth, [so Kilvert said] he felt three tumours (he called them 'knubs') in Hulbert's head. These he insisted on cutting out on the spot, and Hulbert brought the whole lot, 'snags' [stumps] and 'knubs' home in his pocket. 'It made I sweat,' he said. 'It was all over in ten minutes, but the place was like a butcher's shop and once I should have liked to knock the doctor through the door.'[3]

Instruments used were pliers which might prove effective with a loose tooth; keys with claws that engaged over the crown and were rapidly twisted in the mouth to dislocate the tooth from its socket; pelicans which had claws resembling the bird's beak and dragged more recalcitrant teeth out sideways; and tools which, by twisting the teeth round sharply, dragged out the roots. A skilful practitioner might perform these operations without too much agony to the patient but a clumsy, heavy-handed one might – as Ambrose Paré, the expert surgeon to the French court, had warned – dislocate the jaw or even bring part of it away. Certainly, rough use of the pelican could result in good teeth being pulled out with the decayed: Paré recorded the case of a poor countryman who had three sound teeth removed by a tooth-drawer's bungling apprentice and was warned by the youth that if he complained his master would charge him for taking out three teeth instead of one; so the man hurried off with his drawn teeth in his pocket and his painful one still in his mouth.[4]

All kinds of powders and tinctures were used to preserve teeth and thus avoid the pain of losing them, and all sorts of preparations were recommended to prevent the bad breath resulting from decay. 'To take away the stinking of the mouth,' one early seventeenth-century authority proposed, 'wash mouthe with water and vinegar and chew masticke then washe mouth with the decoction of Annis seeds, mints and cloves sodden in wine.'[5] It was recommended that the teeth should be picked clean after meals, not with the point of a knife but with a wooden stick, that they should be rubbed with a cloth or sponge – brushes were rarely used until the middle of the nineteenth century – and that the mouth should be rinsed out with some such home-made preparation as a mixture of honey, myrrh, juniper root and rock alum. Roasted turnip parings were also said to be efficacious when placed behind the ear. Ladies with bad teeth or bad breath found fans extremely useful in disguising the one and discreetly wafting away the fumes of the other.

Numerous patent powders and tinctures were advertised in the newspapers. In December 1717 the *Daily Courant* advertised a tincture which 'infallibly fastened loose teeth to admiration and caused the flesh to grow up to the teeth again when almost quite eaten away'. The same issue of this paper carried an advertisement for a powder which made the teeth as white as ivory, 'tho' never so black or yellow':

> It effectually preserves them from rotting or decaying, continuing them sound to exceeding old age. It wonderfully cures the scurvy in the gums, prevents rheum or defluxions, kills worms at the roots of the teeth, and thereby hinders the tooth-ach. It admirably fastens loose teeth.[6]

As late as 1821 readers of *The Times* were assured that

> A Discovery has lately been introduced which bids fair to supersede the necessity of a dentist. Hudson's Botanic Tooth Powder is a certain remedy and preventative for all disorders of the Mouth. It not only cleans and beautifies the Teeth, but preserves them from decay to the latest period of life. It makes them white, fastens such as are loose, prevents those decayed from growing worse, removes the tartar, and cures the scurvy in the gums, leaving them firm and of a healthy redness. It is an antidote for gum-boils, swelled face, and that excruciating pain called tooth-ache; and so certain and undeviating in its effects, that there never was an instance of any person who used it ever having the tooth-ache or tooth decay; and though so efficacious an antiseptic, it is so innocent that the contents of a box may be swallowed by an infant without any danger.[7]

Another advertiser recommended a cure for toothache guaranteed to banish the pain for at least fifteen years, to keep teeth firm in their sockets and to prevent decay. This was a cure, 'effected in three seconds', 'by fumigation or steam from foreign herbs which destroys the nerve without causing any pain to the patient'.

When such prophylactics proved ineffective a visit to the tooth operator could no longer be delayed; and perhaps, if the painful tooth was not too far gone, it might be saved by cutting out the decay and filling the cavity. Gold leaf had been occasionally used as a filling material since the fifteenth century; but in the eighteenth molten lead or gutta percha were more usual materials, and in the early nineteenth a dangerous amalgam of mercury and silver scrapings. But filling was rarely practised. A bad tooth was generally pulled out, the patient sitting or lying on the floor, before chairs came into common use, with his head held between the operator's knees and his limbs perhaps bound with leather straps to limit the inconvenience of struggling. Good teeth were cleaned with metal scrapers and sticks dipped in *aqua fortis* which, while undoubtedly making them white, eventually destroyed them.

When a tooth was extracted it was often replaced with another healthy one taken from another person's jaw, a method recommended by John Hunter who published his *Natural History of the Human Teeth* in 1771 and who advocated as a cure for toothache burning the ear lobe with a hot iron.[8] Rowlandson's *Transplanting of Teeth* (1787) shows a fashionable dentist performing this operation. He is Bartholomew Ruspini, self-styled 'Operator for the Teeth, Gums etc.', who arrived in England in 1759, established himself at first in Bath and ultimately in St Alban's Street, not far from the Prince of Wales's mansion, Carlton House. Having become rich through his practice, and through his patent dentifrice which preserved the teeth and rendered them 'perfectly white', he married into one of the oldest families in Northumberland.[9] Ruspini is shown extracting a tooth from a chimney-sweep which he is about to place in the mouth of a lady who has had one of her own bad teeth pulled out for the purpose. A ragged boy and a girl, crying with pain, leave the room, holding their cheeks in their hands. A placard on the door reads, 'Money given for live teeth'.[10]

Some poor people sold all their teeth for the benefit of the rich in need of a sound set; and a dentist would pull them out one after the other, trying each one for size in the holes in his patient's gums. Some dentists, following the lead of Charles Allen, author of the first book in English which dealt exclusively with dentistry, *The Operator for the Teeth* (1685), disapproved of the transplantation of human teeth, which was likely to transmit disease, particularly syphilis. But Allen considered it 'very profitable and advantageous' to transplant the teeth of sheep and dogs, goats and baboons into human jaws.[11] Animal teeth were rarely used, however, and as the demand for human teeth from the living out-stripped supply, recourse was had to grave-robbers – who knew that, even when a corpse was decomposed, its teeth were saleable at up to £30 a set – and to dealers in teeth taken from the bodies of dead soldiers on battlefields. So-called 'Waterloo teeth' were shipped over in thousands from the Continent after the end of the Napoleonic Wars; and in the 1860s, so the *Pall Mall Gazette* reported, certain dentists no longer troubled to make artificial teeth, relying instead on the teeth sent across the Atlantic in barrels by tooth-drawers from the battlefields of the American Civil War.[12]

For those who could not bear the thought of any form of transplant and eventually became toothless there were masticators, which resembled nutcrackers and crushed hard food into an easily managed pulp. There were also sets of false teeth. These had been known for centuries, even in the ancient world: dentures of the bridge-work type have been found in Etruscan tombs of 700 B.C. But until recent years they were neither comfortable nor sightly, and often had to be removed for eating. Robert Herrick described a set which looked exactly as though they had been made from a bone handle:

> Glasco had none, but now some teeth has
> > got;
> Which though they furre, will neither
> > ake, or rot.
> Six teeth he has, whereof twice two are
> > known
> Made of a Haft, that was a mutton-bone.
> Which not for use, but merely for the
> > sight,
> He wears all day, and draws those teeth
> > at night.

Eighteenth-century advertisements promised false teeth that appeared to be natural. John Watts, an 'Operator' who applied 'himself wholly to the said business' in Racquet Court, Fleet Street, offered in 1711, 'Artificial teeth set in so well as to eat with them, and not to be distinguish'd from natural, not to be taken out at night, as is by some falsely suggested, but may be worn years together. They are an ornament to the mouth and greatly help the speech.'[13]

Most sets, in fact, impaired rather than improved the speech; and 150 years later they did not fit much better than they had in the days of Queen Anne. 'That it is a much easier task to make artificial teeth ornamental than useful,' a textbook on dentistry affirmed in 1846, 'may be inferred from the fact that in by far the greatest number of cases, they are much too insecure in the mouth to admit of any attempt at complete mastication of the food without displacement.'[14]

Lord Palmerston's dentures were so loose, indeed, according to Disraeli, that they would 'fall out of his mouth when speaking, if he did not hesitate and halt so in his talk'.

Until the 1790s false teeth were generally made of bone, of hippopotamus or walrus ivory, or, in the most expensive sets, of silver, mother of pearl or enamelled copper attached to an ivory base. In 1753 Lord Hervey, hitherto toothless, though not yet forty, appeared before the Duchess of Portland with the 'finest set of Egyptian pebble teeth you ever saw'. In 1792 dentures began to be made of porcelain paste supplied by the Wedgwood pottery company; and by 1804 the manufacturer claimed that 12,000 of his porcelain dentures were in use. Even these, however, were not very convincing, the teeth not being separated from each other, merely shaded; while the gold coil springs which were used to hold them in were not at all easy to manage. Later false teeth were made of vulcanite and celluloid which, being inflammable, was liable to cause such accidents as that which overtook Sydney Dark, editor of the *Church Times*, one day in the Savile Club.

> He had dozed off in one of the armchairs with a lighted cigarette [Sir Compton Mackenzie recalled]. Suddenly he leapt up with fumes coming from his mouth; that lighted cigarette had set fire to his false teeth. This is not just one more Savile story; I saw those fumes with my own eyes and I heard Sydney Dark's shout of dismay as he leapt up and hauled the denture out of his mouth.[15]

Dentures sometimes rotted in the mouth, as did those of a lady who had had a set wired to her remaining sound teeth. 'Having been called in to examine the mouth of a lady of quality who felt herself gradually declining in a slow fever,' wrote the medical man whom she consulted, 'I found that the artificial teeth of animal substance which she had were become black and exhaled a fetid and insupportable smell. I did not hesitate to declare that the fever was occasioned and continued by the absorption of the infected matter which came off the infected teeth.'[16]

Throughout the eighteenth and for much of the nineteenth century dentists remained a rather despised group on the fringes of the medical profession. Some earned large sums of money. The Prince Regent's dentist, Charles Dumergue, was paid a regular fee of 100 guineas a year by that one royal patient alone;[17] and by 1859, so an American dentist calculated on a visit to England, certain practitioners were earning £25,000 a year.[18] Yet in 1817 a dentist was defined as 'an artisan who confines himself to the extraction of teeth and to several operations required by their defects, redundancies, accidents or disorders . . . The head surgeons of London deem this branch of their art beneath notice and generally decline interfering in it.' In 1838 it was complained that: 'dentistry, as we find it called, is growing into a profession which numbers nearly as many members as surgery. Great rogues many of them are.' And as late as 1849 a dentist was described simply and dismissively as one 'who cleans and extracts teeth'.[19]

Soon afterwards, however, the reputation of dentists began to improve. In 1856 both the College of Dentists of England and the Odontological Society of London were founded; and in 1860, after an amending clause had been added to the Medical Act of 1858, the first examinations were held to determine the fitness of male candidates to practise dental surgery: women were not eligible for diplomas in England until 1912. In 1878 a rather inadequate Dentists Act was passed establishing a register of persons entitled to practise dentistry under the control of the General Medical Council and providing for improved dental education. And at last in 1921, since previous Acts had not prevented unqualified people from continuing to set up 'dental surgeries' and 'dental consulting rooms', a new Dentists Act was passed which, while allowing those already practising to continue doing so, made dental practice a profession which was in future open only to those who had passed the requisite examinations.

# 40 · 'Youth are Expeditiously Instructed'

She was very fond of me, and I was always good with her, though perhaps naughty enough at home [wrote William Hore, recalling the dame school to which he was sent in the 1780s]. She lived in one room, a large underground kitchen; we went down a flight of steps to it. Her bed was always neatly turned down in one corner. There was a large kitchen grate and in cold weather there was always a good fire in it, by which she sat in a carved wooden armchair with a small round table before her on which lay a large Bible, open, on one side, and on the other a birch rod. Of the Bible she made great use, of the rod very little, but with fear we always looked upon it. There, on low benches, books in hand, sat her little scholars.[1]

This pleasant scene is offset by others less attractive. According to Thomas Holcroft, the novelist, who was the son of a shoemaker, children were sent to dame schools 'rather to keep them out of the way than to learn anything'.[2] And many children did not learn anything, even how to read: in the parish of Islington between 1767 and 1814 about 75 per cent of poor boys and 76 per cent of poor girls were illiterate.[3] The Rev. George Crabbe, the Suffolk poet, describes two infants' schools which were perhaps more representative than the one attended by William Hore:

> Yet one there is, that small regard to Rule
> Or Study pays, and still is deem'd a school;
> That, where a deaf, poor patient widow sits,
> And awes some thirty Infants as she knits;
> Infants of humble, busy wives, who pay
> Some trifling price for Freedom through the day . . .
> Poor Reuben Dixon has the noisiest school
> Of ragged lads, who ever bow'd to Rule;

Low is his Price – the Men who heave our Coals
And clean our Causeways, send him Boys in Shoals.

These schools were certainly cheap. Few charged more than 3d a week per child and some no more than 1½d. Even so, many parents could not afford them. James Lackington, born in Somerset in 1746, wrote, 'As I was the eldest and my father for the first few years a careful hardworking man, I fared something better than my brothers and sisters. I was put for two or three years to a day school kept by an old woman . . . But my career of learning was soon at an end, as my Mother became so poor that she could not afford the mighty sum of twopence per week for my schooling.'[4] The standard of teaching was generally commensurate with these low prices, and was usually undertaken by untrained women.

It is commonly thought so tiresome an undertaking to teach children to Spell and Read English, that a peevish School-master is not judged to have Patience enough to do it [one commentator observed in 1710]. And therefore they are sent to a Mistress, supposing she may be more fit to deal with them in their tender Years; where partly thro' the Ignorance of many such Teachers, and partly Neglect, the Children often spend whole Years to little Advantage.[5]

One of those who could testify to these wasted years was William Lovett, who was born in 1800 and later became a Chartist: he was sent 'to all the dame schools of the town' before he could master the alphabet, and at one of them spent much of the time incarcerated in the coal cellar for misbehaviour.[6]

Some male teachers were very young, others cruel. John Collier, better known as Tim Bobbin, the dialect poet and caricaturist, became an itinerant schoolmaster at the age of fourteen. And at one of the schools Francis Place attended, he was taught by boys little older than himself. His first school, to which he was sent at the age of seven in 1778, was 'kept by a tall stout well-looking man named Jones, proverbially "savage Jones". This name he got . . . in consequence of the frequent punishments he inflicted on the boys and the delight he seemed to take in punishing them. There were about 120 boys in this school.' They sat at desks in two large schoolrooms under the eyes of the master and the usher who were so placed that they could see all the pupils who were called up to be tested in groups of six. 'If any one failed he was obliged to go out and stand at a short distance from the master holding out first one hand and then the other to receive on each a stroke with a stout cane, the strokes were from two to twelve, in extreme cases fourteen.' Place confessed that he learned very little.

The whole concept of even attempting to teach the poor was often called into question. Hannah More, writing in 1795, considered that 'to teach good principles to the lower classes is the most likely way to save the country. Now in order to do this we must teach them to read.'[7] But other, more insistent voices, were raised against this proposition. 'Does it necessarily follow that the lower classes will become more industrious, more virtuous, more happy, by learning how to read?' asked one opponent of education for the poor. 'Certainly not . . . What ploughman who could read the renowned history of Tom Hickethrift, Jack the Giant-Killer, or the Seven Wise Men, would be content to whistle up one furrow and down another from dawn in the morning to the setting of the sun?' A Member of Parliament, Davies Giddy, agreed with him: 'Giving education to the labouring classes of the poor . . . would be prejudicial to their morals and happiness; it would teach them to despise their lot in life, instead of making them good servants in agriculture and other laborious employments. Instead of teaching them subordination, it would render them fractious and refractory.' 'It is safest for both the Government and religion of the country,' the Bishop of London concurred in 1803, 'to let the lower classes remain in that state of ignorance in which nature has originally placed them.'[8]

Nevertheless, the work of the charity schools continued and expanded, it being generally held that 'Children are made tractable and submissive by being early accustomed to Awe and Punishment and Dutiful Subjection. From such timely Discipline the Publick may expect Honest and Industrious Servants.' As Eliza Cook put it in her 'Song for the Ragged Schools',

> Better build schoolrooms for 'the boy'
> Than cells and gibbets for 'the man'.[9]

By 1787, so it was estimated, there were about 250,000 children at charity schools in the country, most of them the deserving children of soldiers, sailors, petty tradesmen, servants and mechanics rather than those of the very poor. Their education was largely paid for by private subscribers, most of them middle-class people living in the area where the school was established. At a charity school in the parish of St Margaret's, Westminster, the six initial subscribers were, typically, a cheesemonger, a draper, a bookseller and three general dealers.[10]

In these schools great emphasis was laid upon religion and moral teaching. Girls at Sheffield in 1789 were taught to pray: 'Make me dutiful and obedient to my benefactors and charitable to my enemies. Make me temperate and chaste, meek and patient, true in all my dealings and content and industrious in my station.' And they were instructed:

Do no wrong.
It is a sin to steal a pin.
Swear not at all, nor make a Bawl.
Use no bad words.
Live in peace with all as much as you can.[11]

There was much reading of the Bible and the Book of Common Prayer and, as in the industrial schools which became favoured foundations at the beginning of the nineteenth century, there were also long hours of vocational training and the teaching of craft skills. Industrial charity schools were usually established in areas where there was little employment for children, as, for instance, at Lewisham, Epping, Kendal, St Albans, Bristol and Norwich. Pupils were taught to spin wool and flax, to put heads on pins and given training in domestic service. They earned from 1s to 2s 6d. a week.[12] Vocational training at ordinary charity schools included such specialized crafts as shoemaking which was taught at the Blue Cap School at Nantwich, Cheshire.[13] Arithmetic was usually taught only to those who could read and write, and, as in the seventeenth century, rarely at all to girls, who were put to needlework, spinning and knitting instead. Singing was discouraged as unsuitable from the 1820s onwards; while the reading of popular ballads and chapbooks was frequently forbidden. At the Wesleyan charity school at Leytonstone, where the day began at four o'clock in the morning for the children who had to light the fires, and at five o'clock for the rest, there were no toys and no times set aside for play.[14]

The teachers, whose social status was low, had often drifted into the profession from other employment in which they had failed or been dismissed, or had perhaps, like Parson Woodforde's relative, taken it up when invalided out of the army. They were in general as ill paid as they had ever been. Some were paid for each child they taught, others a low salary. In the 1730s John Collier earned £10 a year, an income he supplemented in the evening by teaching adults and taking on work as a 'hedge-lawyer', writing wills and indentures and giving legal advice. In 1744 Silas Todd, who had been appointed to his post by John Wesley, was paid 10s a week for a nine-hour day; he was assisted by an usher and four monitors but had no holidays. At a charity school in Soho the masters did slightly better with a minimum of £30 a year, rising to £36 in 1790, though female teachers earned no more than £26.[15]

The food supplied to their pupils was generally unpalatable and sometimes inadequate. Even at Christ's Hospital – which in the 1780s had about 700 pupils of whom nearly a third, so Coleridge thought, were the sons of clergymen – the diet was 'very scanty'.

Every morning a bit of dry bread and some small beer [so Coleridge recalled]. Every evening a larger piece of bread and cheese or butter . . . For dinner – on Sunday boiled beef and broth; Monday, bread and butter and milk and water; on Tuesday, roast mutton; Wednesday, bread and butter, and rice milk; Thursday, boiled beef and broth; Saturday, bread and butter and pease-porritch. Our food was portioned and excepting on Wednesdays I never had a belly full. Our appetite was *damped*; never satisfied and we had no vegetables.[16]

For some poor children the only education to be had was at Sunday Schools. These had been founded by Robert Raikes, a businessman and journalist from Gloucester, who had been concerned by the numbers of ragamuffin children employed in the pin-making trade who ran wild on Sundays, 'cursing and swearing in a manner so horrid as to convey to any serious mind an idea of hell'. He paid a Mrs King 1s 6d a day to teach the catechism and reading in her house. At first it was stipulated that the children, who were to be between six and fourteen years old, should be clean; but when his school was firmly established it was found that many of the children who came were too destitute for proper cleanliness; and so, he said, 'I now reject none on that footing. All that I require are clean hands, clean face and their hair combed. If you have no clean shirt come in what you have on.'[17]

A pupil named Bourne who was at the school in about 1800 was questioned about it in his old age. He replied:

No writing was taught in the school in my time. We used to learn 'Reading-made-easy' Book, the Collects, Bible and Testament. That is those who could read . . . Mr Raikes used always to come to school on Sundays and inquire what the children had learnt and whether they had been 'good boys'. If there had been extra bad boys then he would punish them himself . . . An old chair was laid on its two front legs, downwards so, and then the young 'un was put on so, kicking and swearing all the time . . . Then Mr Raikes would cane him. I knew a boy he could never draw a tear from – we used to say he couldn't feel . . . Mr Raikes could do nothing with him and one day he caught him by the hand and pressed the tips of his fingers on the bars of the stove or fireplace.
Q: Was he burnt?
Bourne: Blistered a bit . . . What I think hurt [Mr Raikes] most was to hear boys cursing and swearing at each other in church. We were at church one morning and a boy named Philpotts (we called him Mugs) stuck a big shawlpin into a boy who was nodding. He jumped up into the air with pain and yelled and swore and flew at 'Mugs'. The beadles came and turned them out. I saw Mr Raikes's face and I have never forgotten his look.[18]

After the establishment of the first Sunday School, others rapidly followed. In 1784 there were 1800 pupils at the Manchester interdenominational schools alone. By 1800 about 200,000 children were attending Sunday Schools; and by the 1820s nearly every working-class child had attended Sunday School at some time or another.[19]

While the numbers and influences of Sunday Schools were growing, grammar schools were generally in decline. 'Whoever will examine the state of the grammar schools in different parts of this Kingdom will see to what a lamentable condition most of them are reduced,' Lord Chief Justice Kenyon declared in 1795. 'Empty walls without scholars and everything neglected but the receipt of the salaries and emoluments.'[20] A few grammar schools continued to thrive. Between 1740 and 1765 there were nearly 200 boarders at Manchester Grammar School – almost half of whom went on to university after a classical education there – and almost 500 day boys, mostly the sons of local tradesmen, who were given a good grounding in mathematics and science.[21] Few grammar schools were in as parlous a condition as that at Shaftesbury, which was closed in 1780 for lack of pupils, or the one at Monk's Kirby, Warwickshire, where the master claimed that he had 'nothing to do'.[22] Yet many found it difficult to attract pupils, particularly those that had had to increase their fees because inflation had so drastically reduced the value of their endowments. At Bath Grammar School in 1820, boarders were being charged as much as fifty-five guineas a year.[23]

There were no local children at this school; and at others, too, local tradesmen were actively discouraged from taking up free places, for which the original statutes provided. Fee-paying boarders, taken in their place, allowed these schools to become indistinguishable from public schools.[24]

Many parents were deterred from sending their sons to grammar schools by the continuing emphasis on the classics which in many schools were taught, in accordance with their statutes, to the exclusion of nearly all other subjects. A few grammar schools succeeded in changing their statutes by Act of Parliament, as did the school at Macclesfield which was consequently permitted to offer lessons 'not only in grammar and classical learning, but also in writing, arithmetic, navigation, mathematics and the modern languages'. Others, while providing 'a liberal education in Latin and Greek', offered additional lessons for a fee. At Burnsall Grammar School, Wharfedale, for example, Latin was taught without charge, but 8d a week was required for lessons in writing and 1s for those in arithmetic. But there remained many schools that continued to offer nothing but the classics, and some were defiantly proud to do so. In the early nineteenth century the prospectus of St Paul's School carried this warning: 'At St Paul's we teach nothing but Latin and Greek. If you want your son to learn anything else you must have him taught at home, and for this purpose we give him three half holidays a week.'[25]

For a more general education parents turned to those private schools which offered suitable instruction for boys destined for the universities, the army or the navy, or for careers in business and the professions. The prospectus of the Islington Academy resembled many another:

> Youths are generally boarded, tenderly treated and expeditiously in-structed in the languages, writing, arithmetic, merchants' accounts and mathematics, with dancing, drawing, music, fencing and every other accomplishment required to form gentleman, scholar and the man of business upon reasonable terms.[26]

> All proper regard will be paid to the morals and Behaviour of the Pupils [promised the proprietors of Mr Pulman's Academy at Leeds]. Such as are modest and diffident, will be treated with Tenderness . . . Those who, by an honest ambition, strive to excel will be regarded with peculiar Marks of Favour and Esteem; and such as are rebellious, obstinate or incorrigible, must be removed from the Academy.[27]

At their academy for girls 'over against the vicarage in Leeds', Jane Stock and her daughter taught 'all sorts of Needlework, and Patterns drawn on Cloth or Canvas after the newest Fashion, likewise Paistry, Huswifry, Pickling and Sweet meats'.[28]

Most of these private academies were not expensive, but the advertise-ments for some hint at horrors later to be witnessed at such Yorkshire schools as Dotheboys Hall. For an inclusive fee of £12 a year for boys under fourteen, £14 for those already fourteen, £14 14s for fifteen-year-olds and £5 15s plus a 10s 6d entrance fee for boys of sixteen and over, Ephraim Sanderson's school at Aberford, 'a very healthful Situation on the Great North Road betwixt Ferrybridge and Wetherby' undertook in 1788 to look after the board, washing and tuition of any boy 'all year round, without holidays if necessary'.[29]

If most private academies were careful to stress the tender treatment their charges might expect, no such promises were made by the public schools. The reputation of some public schools had, indeed, fallen so low by the late eighteenth century that many parents, who could well have afforded to do so, refused to send their children to them. In 1779 Oundle had only five pupils, Rugby in 1798 'scarcely a single boy'.[30]

In his poem, *Tirocinium,* Cowper wrote:

> Would you your son should be a sot or dunce,
> Lascivious, headstrong, or all these at once;
> That, in good time, the stripling's finish'd taste
> For loose expense and fashionable waste,
> Should prove your ruin, and his own at last
> Train him in public with a mob of boys.

In nearly every public school bullying and savage corporal punishment were rife. 'Many a white and tender hand, which the fond mother had passionately kissed a thousand times, have I seen whipped until it was covered with blood,' an Old Etonian recalled of the early eighteenth century; 'perhaps for smiling, or for going a yard and a half out of the gate, or for writing an O for an A, or an A for an O.'[31] In the 1790s parents of boys at Oundle wrote to complain of masters giving boys 'violent Blows on the Loins with the fist doubled up' and hitting them on the head, occasioning lumps 'as large as a Walnutt'.

> My eldest son had cause to complain . . . severely of his master beating him and the rest of the children unmercifully and setting them unreasonable tasks [one letter of complaint runs], for which he desired that I would not insist upon his going there any more as he declared to me he would rather go to Dung Cart or hard work than go to Mr Evanson's School [Oundle]. He likewise declared that his master did beat William Kettle in such manner that the child when he was called up by him wou'd fall a crying, that his master wou'd knock him down with his fist . . . I saw his back very green eight days after his Ill treatment.[32]
>
> My dear Mother [a boy at Westminster School wrote home in the early nineteenth century], if you don't let me come home, I die – I am all over ink and my fine clothes have been Spoilt. I have been tost in a blanket, and seen a ghost.
> I remain, my dear, dear mother,
> Your dutiful and most unhappy son,
> Freddy.[33]

Another Westminster boy recalled, 'I have been woken many times by the hot points of cigars burning holes in my face.'[34]

There were frequent revolts against such treatment. In 1793 at Winchester there was a 'Great Rebellion' in which boys fired pistols and threw stones from the tower; in 1797 at Rugby pupils blew up the headmaster's door and had to be read the Riot Act; in 1818 there was another riot at Winchester, this time so serious that it had to be quelled by soldiers with bayonets. There were also disturbances at Harrow in 1808 when senior boys paraded about with banners declaring 'Liberty and Rebellion', but on this occasion the protest was not against the brutality of masters but against the curtailment of the elder boys' rights to flog the juniors.[35]

The public schoolboy's curriculum was dominated by the classics to an even greater extent that that of the grammar schoolboy. 'His sole and exclusive occupation is learning Latin and Greek,' wrote Sydney Smith in the *Edinburgh Review* in 1810. 'He has scarcely a notion that there is any other kind of excellence; and the great system of facts with which he is most perfectly acquainted are the intrigues of the heathen gods: with whom Pan slept – with whom Jupiter – whom Apollo ravished.'[36]

The 1798 timetable of the sixth form at Rugby shows how emphatic this domination was. The Iliad, Virgil, Tully, 'Latin Authors' 'Greek Poetry', Latin verses, Greek grammar, Homer, Juvenal, Horace, Ovid, these are the subjects that regularly appear, week in, week out.[37]

Yet, despite the violence and the narrowness of the studies – and despite the temporary decline of some of the notoriously ill run – most upper-class children in the eighteenth century were sent to a public school. Two-thirds of the sons of peers attended one or other of nine famous schools, Eton, Harrow, Westminster, Winchester, Shrewsbury, Rugby, Charterhouse, Merchant Taylors' or St Paul's. Half of these attended Eton or Westminster, and 72 per cent of ministers of state had attended either one or the other.[38]

Not all boys at Eton, of whom there were 380 in 1788, were unhappy there. Humphrey Senhouse, who came from a Cumbrian family engaged in trade with the West Indies, wrote home letters of the utmost contentment:

> Notwithstanding the School Exercises of which there are a good many, I find time to go to the playing fields and get my shins broke at football which I think excellent sport, for we have the best balls and the best ground for playing I ever saw . . . I like my new room exceedingly [he continued when in his second year] and think I should prefer it to any room in the House for it is both a very pretty clean and warm room and has so fine a prospect out of the window . . . I have a full view of the River Thames and can see barges going up and down the river . . . I am at present very happy at Eton for as I know all the customs of the school now I am not at a loss about doing anything as I was at first.[39]

Yet these sentiments were not so common or so sincere, perhaps, as those expressed by a contemporary of Senhouse who wrote from Eton in 1791, 'My Dame is as Damned a fool as ever; the Bitches (for I can't with propriety call them Maids) as impertinent as ever and your humble servant as disatisfied as ever with this cursed place.'[40]

In 1837, taking note of the gambling, cockfighting and drinking in the town that went on at Eton – and echoing the belief of Henry Fielding, himself an Old Etonian, that public schools were 'the nurseries of all vice and immorality' – the *Quarterly Journal of Education* declared, 'Before an Eton Boy is ready for University he may have acquired a confirmed taste for gluttony and drunkenness, an appetite for brutal sports and a passion for female society of the most degrading kind.'[41]

# 41 · *Universities, Academies and the Grand Tour*

It was widely agreed in the second half of the eighteenth century that the universities, like grammar schools, had fallen into discredit. They had also become much more expensive, the fees rising far faster than the cost of living. In 1720 it had cost about £50 a year to maintain a commoner; thirty years later £90 would barely cover his expenses, and this figure was to rise to between £200 and £250 in the middle of the nineteenth century.[1] In writing from Oxford to his father for more money in 1727, William Pitt, after listing the prices he had had to pay for various items, added, 'I have too much reason to fear you may think some of these articles too extravagant, as they really are, but all I have to say for it is humbly to beg you would not attribute it to my extravagance but to ye custom of this place, where we pay for most things at too high rate.'[2]

The heavy cost of the universities, combined with the decline in their reputation, led to a gradual decrease in the numbers of undergraduates. There were 460 freshmen a year in the 1660s but less than 250 a year by 1800.[3] The decrease was particularly noticeable among the poorer undergraduates, since inflation had much reduced the value of the endowments available to them, while the decline of the grammar schools had made a satisfactory preliminary education more difficult to obtain. Whereas in 1711, 27 per cent of Oxford freshmen were of plebeian origin, the proportion fell to 17 per cent in 1760 and to a mere one per cent in 1810.[4]

The curriculum was still, of course, predominantly classical, so that Mr Farish of Magdalene College, Cambridge, who in 1794 gave lectures in the botanical gardens on such subjects as smelting and dyeing, bridge construction and the making of gunpowder, was a Fellow worthy of special remark.[5] Benjamin Marshall, an Oxford undergraduate of the early eighteenth century, gave his former headmaster at St Paul's an account in Latin of his day which, while apparently more conscientiously spent than were most days by his contemporaries, gives a fair indication of the kind of studies which one of the rare strict tutors might have expected of them:

|            | Rise before dawn. |
|------------|-------------------|
| 6 a.m.     | Public Latin prayers. |
|            | Breakfast |
|            | A walk with my friends, half an hour. |
|            | Study of the Minor Prophets. |
|            | Study of the poem of Tograeus. |
| 9 a.m.     | Study of Philosophy. |
| 10 a.m.    | To my Tutor, Mr Pelling, who expounds some portion of Philosophy to me and my friends. |
| 11 a.m.    | Luncheon. |
|            | With my friends to coffee-house, where we discuss public affairs. |
| 1 p.m.     | Study of the Koran. |
| 4 p.m.     | Study of Aristotle's Rhetoric. |
| 6 p.m.     | Dinner. |
|            | Read Horace's Odes or Martial's epigrams, or mix with my friends in a sociable way. |
| 9 p.m.     | Public Latin prayers. In the morning we pray for success upon our doings, and in the evening we return thanks for such success as has been secured.[6] |

Most undergraduates seem to have spent their days far less industriously. Edward Gibbon, who entered Magdalen College, Oxford, shortly before his fifteenth birthday, was flattered to receive a velvet cap and silk gown which distinguished a gentleman commoner from a plebeian student and which enabled him to 'command, among the tradesmen of Oxford, an indefinite and dangerous credit'. He was given a key to the 'numerous and learned library' and was shown into 'three elegant and well furnished rooms in the new building'. But the next fourteen months – until he professed himself a Roman Catholic and had to leave the college – were 'the most idle and unprofitable' of his whole life. The Fellows were 'decent, easy men who supinely enjoyed the gifts of the founder; their days were filled by a series of uniform employments; the chapel and the hall, the coffee-house and the common room, till they retired, weary and well satisfied, to a long slumber'. Gibbon's tutor virtually ignored him, never summoning him to attend 'even the ceremony of a lecture', and receiving him but once in his rooms. 'The tutor and pupil lived in the same college as strangers to each other.'[7]

Evidently Gibbon's idleness was far from exceptional. 'They are perfectly their own masters,' commented the *Gentleman's Magazine* on rich undergraduates in 1798, 'and they take the lead in every disgraceful frolic of juvenile debauchery. They are curiously tricked out in cloth of gold, of silver and of purple, and feast most sumptuously throughout the year.'[8]

Looking back on his undergraduate days at Oxford in 1763–5, the Earl of Malmesbury considered that the two years he was up at Merton were 'the most unprofitably spent of his life. The discipline of the University happened at this particular moment to be so lax that a Gentleman Commoner was under no restraint and never called upon to attend either lectures, or chapel or hall.'[9]

The one rule which appears to have been strictly enforced was that against mixing with ordinary townspeople; and an undergraduate friend of Parson Woodforde was actually sent down for 'carousing with some low-life People', whereas a clergyman who complained of being attacked by a mob of drunken undergraduates shouting Jacobite slogans and other 'Treasonable and Seditious Expressions', was complacently informed by the Vice-Chancellor that 'nothing could prevent young fellows getting in liquor'.[10]

The rules of Merton College in 1747 enjoined tutors to ensure that 'no pupil . . . do contract any Intimacies with Tradesmen or their Families; nor accept of invitations to their Houses, nor introduce them to Entertainments at his chamber'.[11]

Otherwise, life was most comfortable and little regulated. At Hertford College, Oxford, in 1747 each undergraduate had three rooms and two servants; and at Christ's College, Cambridge, in 1748 Humphrey Senhouse was 'very well pleas'd with [his] situation in every particular'. Senhouse's meals were 'very good and always well done'. Those of the Fellows were even better.[12] Dining with the Warden of New College in 1774, James Woodforde had 'a most elegant dinner indeed':

> The first Course was Cod & Oysters, Ham, Fowls, boiled Beef, Rabbits smothered with Onions, Harroco of Mutton, Pork Griskins, Veal Collops, Puddings, Mince Pies, Roots etc – The Second Course was a very fine rost Turkey, Haunch of Venison, a brace of Woodcocks, some Snipes, Veal Olive, Trifle, Jelly, Blomonge, Stewed Pippins, Quinces preserved etc . . . Madeira, Old Hocke and Port wines to drink etc. A desert of Fruit after Dinner – we stayed till near 8.

Among the undergraduates there was much drinking of tea, and more of ale and claret, port and arrack-punch. Extracts from the accounts of Humphrey Senhouse indicate how enjoyable a time most undergraduates had. Among items commonly listed appear port, sherry, claret, horse-hire to Newmarket, 'two barrels of oysters', china teapots, cream jugs, decanters, goblets, pipes and tobacco.[13]

Examinations were oral and were considered by critics no more than a formality. They were even said to be conducted during drinking bouts or on horseback. John Scott, later Lord Chancellor Eldon, maintained that his examination in Hebrew and History for his Bachelor's degree in 1770 consisted of just two questions:

EXAMINER: What is the Hebrew for the place of a Skull?
SCOTT: Golgotha.
EXAMINER: Who founded University College?
SCOTT: King Alfred.
EXAMINER: Very well, sir, you are competent for your degree.[14]

At Cambridge, however, examinations seem to have been rather more conscientiously conducted. 'We got into the theatre at eight in the morning,' wrote a candidate for the bachelor's degree in 1753, 'all that day, all the next and the forenoon of the next we sit to be examined by the officers of the University, and by the Masters of Arts . . . On the Friday morning we are severally invested with the Cap of the degree by the Vice Chancellor.'[15]

Certainly the examinations undergone by aspiring Fellows of Trinity College, Cambridge, seem to have been severe enough. Richard Cumberland gave an account of his examination by the Master in 1752:

[He was sitting] in a chamber up stairs, encompassed with large folding screens, and over a great fire, though the weather was uncommonly warm: he began by requiring of me an account of the whole course and progress of my studies in the several branches of philosophy . . . When he had held me a considerable time under this examination, I expected he would have dismissed me, but on the contrary he then proceeded . . . to demand of me an account of what I had been reading before I had applied myself to academical studies . . . He bade me give him a survey account of the several great empires of the ancient world, the periods when they flourished, their extent when at the summit of their power, the causes of their declension and dates of their extinction . . . He gave me a sheet of paper written through in Greek with his own hand, which he ordered me to turn either into Latin or English, and I was shewn into a room containing nothing but a table furnished with materials for writing, and one chair. I was required to use dispatch . . . When I had given in my translation in Latin I was remanded to the empty chamber with a subject for Latin prose and another for Latin verse.[16]

Since the universities were renowned for idleness and debauchery, many parents chose to send their sons to Dissenting Academies instead. 'The education of my children in a right way is what I have much at heart and I

forsee many dangers in sending them to the university,' wrote Lord Kilker-
ran in 1743. 'I have been of the opinion that the better way is to send them to
an academy under virtuous people.'[17] At Charles Morton's Academy,
Newington Green, there were 'not a few knights' and baronets' sons and one
Lord's son who were sent hither to avoid the debaucheries of the University',
wrote Samuel Wesley, their fellow-student, 'though some of em made
themselves sufficiently remarkable while they were with us.'[18]

These Dissenting Academies were cheap as well as respectable. At Jen-
ning's Academy in 1720, £8 10s sufficed for half a year's board and tuition,
and an additional 10s 5d was charged for books. It could not very well have
charged more, since the majority of students came from modest homes.
Samuel Mercer, the son of a Lancashire cheese factor, was at Northampton
Academy in 1750 studying to be a Nonconformist minister like many other
students at such places:

> My gown is so far gone that it will scarce last me till a few weeks longer [he
> told his father]. I have bought a new wig which I stood in great need of. I
> wore my old one till it was not worth a penny . . . And I have bespoke a
> new pair of boots which I cannot possibly do without (as you would agree)
> if you knew what I undergo by going into the country towns to repeat
> sermons . . .
>
> Dear Father – I should esteem it not only a great favour, but as a great
> honour paid to me if you would be so good as . . . to make a present to the
> doctor of a couple of cheshire cheeses, and likewise to send my Dame for
> she is a widow and behaves very well to me. I hope, father you will not
> forget.[19]

At the Northampton Academy, as at other similar establishments, the
students were far more closely supervised than they were at the universities.
They had to get up at six o'clock for roll-call, prayers and private reading.
There were more prayers before breakfast, lectures between ten o'clock and
two when there was a short break for dinner. After dinner there were tutorials
and further lectures before supper at nine. The gate was locked at ten, and
the students were expected to retire to their rooms at half past.[20]

There were fines for breaking the rules, 1d being demanded for missing
the early-morning roll-call, 2d for being late for a lecture or absent from
prayers, 1s for being out after the locking of the gate. No students were 'to go
into a Publick House to drink there on penalty of a public censure for the first
time and a forfeiture of a shilling the second'. They were, however, allowed
to have tea with their tutor in his parlour, provided they took their own tea
and sugar with them. But only the most privileged students were allowed to
make toasted cheese in their rooms, which was considered a most extravagant

habit. There were two weeks' holiday at Christmas and six at Whitsun.[21]

At many academies the dominant subjects were theology and ethics, Bible Study, the classics and history, mostly English, ecclesiastical and Jewish history. But at Kibworth Academy in Leicestershire the syllabus also included astronomy, mechanics, hydrostatics, geometry, algebra and French, though this was studied 'without regard to pronunciation', with which the proprietor, John Jennings, honestly admitted 'he was not acquainted'.[22]

At Warrington Academy the emphasis was placed upon subjects likely to be useful for those going into trade, upon book-keeping, drawing and designing, shorthand, mathematics, French (with stress here upon correct pronunciation), geography and upon the commercial details, such as the coinage, of the countries studied.[23] At Newington Green Academy students had the benefit not only of 'a fine garden, bowling green and fish pond' but also of 'a laboratory and some not inconsiderable rarities with air pump, thermometer and all sorts of mathematical instruments'.[24]

Many of the subjects offered at these Dissenting Academies were also available, at a price, in courses of public lectures. A course of lectures in mathematics was offered at Manchester in 1719 and a series in chemistry in Scarborough in 1733. And Richard Kay, the son of a Lancashire physician, attended lectures in Manchester between 1741 and 1743 on geography, anatomy, trigonometry and general science.[25]

Courses of lessons in French were widely popular and advertisements similar to the following in a 1751 edition of the *Cheshire Courant* could be read in numerous papers all over the country:

> Monsieur Reillie lately from Paris begs leave to inform the public that he intends to teach the French tongue, in a method the most concise and intelligent that has hitherto been practised, with due accent as spoke by the nobility in Paris and Blois. Attendance will be given at the Widow Shereman's, staymaker, in Bridge Street, Chester from nine to eleven in the forenoon and from two to four in the after; the other hours he reserves for the use of such gentlemen and ladies as choose to be taught in their own houses.[26]

Many young gentlemen had already learned French on the Grand Tour, an aristocratic institution which had long been accepted as an important, if not an essential part of upper-class education and which, so Adam Smith declared in 1776, had been brought into repute by 'the discredit into which the universities [were] allowing themselves to fall'.[27]

Although it was not until the eighteenth century that it assumed its peculiar significance, the Grand Tour was not a new institution. In Eliza-

bethan England – a century before Richard Lassels in his *Voyage of Italy* of
1670 first used the phrase in a printed work – the Grand Tour had been
recognized as a means of gathering information which could be turned to the
nation's advantage, and of training young gentlemen in the arts of diplomacy.
Sir Philip Sidney, for example, later to be appointed English amabassador to
the Emperor, Rudolf II, had been trained for this important post by a long
tour of Europe. Following a preliminary education at Shrewsbury and Christ
Church, Oxford, and a few months spent at Queen Elizabeth's court, Sidney
had left England in 1572 for Paris. Accompanied by a half-Italian tutor, three
servants and four horses, he had travelled through France, Germany, the
Low Countries and Italy, learning the languages and the ways of foreign
courts. Thereafter, despite the dangers and discomforts which attended a
European tour, the number of Englishmen who travelled abroad as part of
their education and training increased year by year. They were expected to
spend their time while abroad gaining knowledge rather than enjoying
themselves in idleness. They must make an effort not only to perfect their
mastery of foreign languages but also to learn all they could about the history,
geography, trade, climate, crops, minerals, food, clothes, customs, fauna,
flora, politics, laws, art and military fortifications of the district. On entering
a strange town the tourist should at once ascend the highest steeple to gain a
good view of it and pick out the buildings worthy of further inspection.

Having inspected these buildings he must make drawings of them, take the
necessary measurements, endeavour to learn how any curious details were
executed, list their valuable contents and striking furnishings, constantly
bearing in mind his future as inheritor and patron. 'Take particular note of
the French way of furnishing rooms,' Lord Annandale advised his nephew
who was making the Grand Tour in 1725 and who, some time after his
return, could expect to become the owner of a fine country house, 'especially
with double doors and windows and door curtains and finishing them with
looking-glass, marble, painting, and gilded stucco.'

The tourist was advised in one of those numerous books written for his
guidance never to travel by night and never to travel alone; to avoid the
company of young women in the interests of virtue and of old women because
they always want the best seats; if travelling by sea, to keep clear of the sailors
who are sure to be covered with vermin and to remove his spurs, otherwise
they would be stolen while he was being sick; always to carry something to eat
on a journey both as a means of assuaging hunger and of keeping off starving
dogs; on reaching his inn at night to look behind all the big pictures or
looking-glasses in the room to make sure they do not hide secret doors.[28]

He was expected to return from his travels with a broadened mind as well
as a good command of foreign languages, a new self-reliance and self-
possession as well as a highly developed taste and grace of manner. Some did

do so, but many did not. France and Italy were full of young Englishmen such as the one Dr John Moore came across in Rome who, having ordered a post-chaise and four horses to come to his lodgings, drove through 'churches, palaces, villas and ruins with all possible expedition' to get all his sightseeing done in the shortest possible time so that he could settle down to enjoy himself, perhaps in the manner of James Boswell who 'sallied forth of an evening like an imperious lion', having resolved to have a different girl every day. Many such young men returned from their Grand Tour with scant command of French or Italian and little improvement in their store of general knowledge. Samuel Johnson, who considered that the Grand Tour was generally undertaken at far too early an age, complained of one particular young lord whom he had only once heard speak of what he had seen and then it was merely to tell a tiresome story of 'a large serpent in one of the pyramids of Egypt'.

> A young man who goes abroad at seventeen or eighteen and returns home at one-and-twenty [Adam Smith concluded] . . . commonly returns more conceited, more unprincipled, more dissipated and more incapable of any serious application either to study or to business, than he could well have become in so short a time had he stayed at home.[29]

The influence of the Grand Tour on English taste was, nevertheless, profound, and the experiences of the discerning tourist eventually brought about a lasting transformation of English art and manners. The third Earl of Burlington, champion of the Italian architects, Palladio and Scamozzi, was only one of numerous rich Englishmen who upon their return built houses in the classical Italian style, decorated them under the influence of Continental models and surrounded them with gardens in the romantic manner of Nicolas Poussin and other landscape artists whose work they had admired abroad. At the same time the treasures which found their way into England, either as purchases made on the Grand Tour or in consequence of tastes formed on Continental travels, were of an extraordinary range.

# 42 · *Masters and Workers*

Foreign visitors to England in the middle of the eighteenth century repeatedly stressed the comfortable circumstances in which most people seemed to be placed, the complacent contentment with which they regarded their country and their own lot, the satisfaction which the middle classes took in making money and all but the very poor took in spending it. It was a view of a country widely shared by its own inhabitants. 'You would not know your country again,' Horace Walpole told Sir Horace Mann who had left it to become assistant to the British Envoy in Florence in 1737 some fifty years before. 'You left it as a private island living upon its means. You will find it the capital of the world.' And Tobias Smollett, who was so cantankerous and captious in France and Italy, had words of high praise for England which was 'smiling with cultivation: the grounds exhibiting all the perfection of agriculture, parcelled out into beautiful enclosures, corn fields, lay pasture, woodland and commons'.

Industrial output was soaring, and by 1790 the value of exports was almost twice as high as it had been eight years before and by the end of the century totalled 22 million pounds. The merchant marine had increased from 3300 vessels in 1702 to 9400 in 1776. Trade with the colonies had created the largest free trade area in the world, while demand for goods at home was increasing fast with the growth of population, there being nearly 9 million people in England and Wales when the first official census was taken in 1801, 3 million more than there had been in 1760. Over two-thirds of the people still lived in the country, and agriculture was still the largest occupation, but towns were growing fast. Liverpool, where Fuseli, the painter, thought that he could 'everywhere smell the blood of slaves' – in 1771, 107 slave ships sailed from Liverpool – was now one of the largest towns in the kingdom with 78,000 inhabitants in 1801, more than any other provincial city, except Manchester which with Salford had 84,000.

The mill towns of Lancashire were larger than all but two or three towns had been anywhere in England at the beginning of the century. Wigan had a population of nearly 11,000, Blackburn and Preston of almost 12,000, Bolton of more than 12,000 and Stockport of nearly 15,000.[1]

Between 1770 and 1830 the national income doubled. By 1797 there were 290 banks in the country; by 1821 there were 370, all issuing their own notes.[2] Vastly increasing amounts were being expended on insurance and advertising. It has been estimated that whereas the average family was buying £10 worth of British-made goods a year in 1688, £25 worth was purchased in 1750 and £40 worth by 1811.[3]

More canals were being dug, more navigable rivers extended, more mines opened up, more factories built. A small factory could be started for £2000 or even less: Abraham Walker established his iron foundry in Sheffield for no more than £600 in 1741, and by 1801 the business was worth £235,000. Most entrepreneurs were self-made men, the sons of yeomen or tradesmen, and many were Dissenters, a high proportion of them Quakers like Abraham Darby, the iron-smelter. Many of these men were hard taskmasters; most laid down strict rules for their men's conduct: Abraham Crowley, the iron-master, built houses for his workers but he required them to be at home in them by nine o'clock at night, and, while he paid poor relief, those in receipt of it had to wear a badge labelled, 'Crowley's Poor'. All were ambitious. 'I shall ASTONISH THE WORLD ALL AT ONCE,' Josiah Wedgwood told his partner, 'for I hate piddling you know.' His was no piddling enterprise. Yet large as his Etruria works were, there were numerous other factories all over the country which could be compared with it. Robert Peel, of Haworth, Peel and Yates, calico printers, was proud to be the employer of 'some fifteen thousand persons'.[4]

Like all his fellow-manufacturers, Peel introduced machinery whenever it was profitable to do so; and it was probably through fear that the introduction of new machinery would provoke the jealousy of his handloom workers that he moved a branch of his business to Tamworth in Staffordshire from Blackburn. Handloom weavers did, indeed, burn down a factory in Manchester after the introduction there of a new power loom; but such attacks were, as yet, quite rare, and most workers were prepared to tolerate the innovations so long as the opportunities of employment kept pace with the rapid increase in population. They took pride in producing articles of fine workmanship.

> With regard to the neatness and solidity of work of all kinds they succeed better in the least towns of England, than in the most considerable cities of France [wrote the Abbé le Blanc] . . . The English artisan has the quality, extremely commendable, and peculiar to him, which is, never to swerve

from the degree of perfection in his trade which he is master of: whatever he undertakes he always does as well as he can. The French workman is far from deserving this commendation.[5]

The range of inventions with which workers had to grow accustomed was extraordinary. Nearly 1000 new patents were taken out between 1760 and 1789. The flying shuttle, invented by John Kay, a clockmaker, doubled the output of weavers; James Hargreaves's spinning jenny had a similar effect on the work of spinners; Henry Cort, a naval supplier, devised a new process of converting pig-iron into wrought iron, Abraham Darby one of smelting cast-iron in furnaces with coke; Thomas Newcomen, a Devonshire ironmonger, invented an improved machine for pumping water out of flooded mines. In 1775 came James Watt's steam engine, and Crompton's 'mule'; in 1776 the first iron bridge spanning a river was completed; in 1789 a new power loom was invented by Edmund Cartwright, a clergyman; and in 1815 Sir Humphry Davy perfected his safety lamp. By 1800 the output of coal had risen to nearly 14 million tons a year, compared with less than 5 million tons in 1750.[6]

The later years of that period, however, had witnessed growing discontent. Coalminers were relatively well paid; but in some areas they had to deliver the coal as well as mine it, while in many they were expected to spend at least part of their wages in shops owned by the mine-owners, and occasionally they received all their wages in goods rather than in money.

Working conditions in the mines were appalling, as they were in many factories where women and children laboured alongside men, thousands of them in the cotton industry. Women and children also worked in coalmines and in lead, tin and copper districts, breaking, sorting and washing ore and pulling and pushing wagons. They also worked in lime-kilns and Peter Kalm was distressed to see women carrying as many as three immense baskets of chalk on their heads at a time, smashing up the chalk, labouring – 'mostly like slaves' – for 8d a day.[7] Indeed, there were few industries for which women and children were considered unsuitable, just as there were few families which could survive without the wages, considerably less than those of men, which they took home. William Hutton, the son of a wool-comber, recalled that when he was a child 'consultations were held about fixing [him] in some employment for the benefit of the family'. 'Winding quills for a weaver was mentioned, but died away,' he wrote in his memoirs, 'stripping tobacco for the grocer, in which I was to earn fourpence a week', was mentioned next. Eventually, when he was seven years old, he was sent to work in a silk factory in Derby.[8]

Other children began their working life when they were five. They were taken over by mill-owners who lodged them in crowded sheds near the factory gates and kept them at work for as long as they could stay awake. It was not until 1819 that it was made illegal to employ children under nine in cotton-mills and to keep older children at work for more than twelve hours a day. And even then, since there were no factory inspectors, the law was easily and frequently evaded.

Children were employed in the field to grub up weeds, pick fruit, scare crows, cart away stones; and in the cities many found employment as crossing-sweepers or chimney-sweeps' climbing-boys. Most of these climbing-boys were poor children supplied by the parish authorities, as few parents prepared to consign their children to such hard and dangerous work could afford to pay the fees due on apprenticeship. In 1767 and 1778 laws were passed, largely through the efforts of Jonas Hanway, which required that the premiums due should be paid in two instalments. This at least ensured that the sweep had an interest in keeping the boy alive until the second instalment was paid.[9] Many did not survive, however, since not only was cancer of the scrotum an occupational disease but fatal accidents were common. Boys were burned and suffocated; and, although they were half-starved to keep them thin enough to climb up narrow chimneys, they often got stuck in them.

Towards the end of the century women were less often seen working hard with men in the fields. It was not only that agricultural tools had become heavier, but also that unemployment among male labourers was rising. Farmers were laying men off and choosing, when there was work to be done, to employ paupers whom the overseers of the poor offered to them at cheap rates.

In the view of most well-to-do observers, poverty was a necessary if regrettable state; and poor labouring people, while essential to the economy of the country, were not necessarily honourable. Their work was for the benefit of society, but would not be performed unless poverty drove them to it. The world could not subsist without poverty, in the opinion of Soame Jenyns, the well-born Member of Parliament for Cambridgeshire and prolific author of *A Free Enquiry into the Origin and Nature of Evil*, 'for had all been rich, none could have submitted to the demands of another, or the drudgeries of life'. Henry Fielding agreed with him. So did George Hickes, the Bishop of Thetford, who in a sermon declared that the poor were

necessary for the establishment of Superiority, where there must be Members of Dishonour, as well as Honour, and some to serve and obey, as well as others to command. The poor are the Hands and Feet of the Body

Politick . . . who hew the Wood, and draw the Water of the Rich. They Plow our Lands, and dig our Quarries, and cleanse our Streets.[10]

It was 'GOD's own appointment', another clergyman observed, 'that some should be Rich and some Poor, some High and some Low'.[11] It was Samuel Johnson's opinion that mankind were 'happier in a state of inequality and insubordination'. And Johnson's friend Hannah More, whose poetry he praised with such flattering extravagance, observed: 'Scarcity has been permitted by an all WISE and gracious Providence . . . to show the poor how immediately dependent they are upon the rich.'

Arthur Young concluded that 'everyone but an idiot' knew that 'the lower classes must be kept poor' or they would 'never be industrious'. When food prices rose this was not a reason for higher wages but for stricter economy on the part of those who were required to pay the prices demanded.[12]

Indeed, by the end of the century it was commonly agreed that the problems of the poor were caused not so much by poverty itself as by vice, by drunkenness, gambling and excessive sexual indulgence. In 1797 Frederick Morton Eden argued persuasively against this theory in his *The State of the Poor* which demonstrated how hard life was for the indigent even when their lives were models of sobriety and prudence. But no easy solutions to the problem were offered. Nor were they by Thomas Malthus, whose *Essay on Population* of 1798 foresaw a world whose population increased faster than the means of subsistence.[13]

It was only right and proper, customary morality argued, that for the sake of the well-being of society and of stable government, the poor should be provided with adequate subsistence to fulfil their duties. But they should expect no more than this, and should be thankful that they received no more; for men and women who worked hard kept their bodies exercised and healthy and their minds free from the mental problems that perplexed the minds of the rich. Modest wages also prevented them from drinking too much. When workmen earned large sums, said George Fordyce, the Scottish physician who helped to found the Society for the Improvement of Medical and Chirurgical Knowledge in 1793, they merely spent it 'in drinking'. They were always idle when they had 'any money left so that their life [was] spent between labour . . . and perfect idleness and drunkenness'. The women of the overpaid also passed 'very disorderly lives'.[14]

This was a view almost universally shared. Francis Place, a champion of radicalism and the right of combination, wrote at the beginning of the nineteenth century that 'until lately, all the amusements of the working people of the metropolis were immediately concerned with drinking – choir clubs, chanting clubs, lottery clubs, and every variety of club, intended for amusement, were always held at public houses'. It was also commonly agreed that even if they were not spent on drink, excessive wages would be wasted on some other form of luxury or debauchery.

There was no such agreement, however, upon what constituted an excessive wage. In the country – though there were still large numbers of self-employed men such as thatchers and tinkers – most workers were now wage-earners, as, indeed, they were in the towns. And in the early years of the century, when labour was in relatively short supply, employers were able to keep wages down. They varied from district to district and season to season, and were sometimes implemented by allowances of beer or cider or food, and, for young men who did not live in their own cottages, of accommodation also. But, except at harvest time, men were unlikely to earn more than 10d to 1s 3d a day – haymakers in Islington were earning 1s 4d a day in 1775 – and women, employed at less strenuous tasks such as weeding, earned only about half as much as men. When travelling in England in 1748 Peter Kalm discovered that one farmer he came across in Hertfordshire paid no more than 8d to 10d a day for which he required twelve hours' work. The farmer gave the men beer but no food. In Essex, Kalm, found rates a little more generous at 9s a week for hired labourers, but again no food was provided, only beer.

Nor were most men able to remain in employment for the full 300 or so working days a year. They were more likely to be taken on as hired labourers for less than 250 days, either for general labour or for specific tasks such as spreading manure, digging turnips, threshing, hedging or building fences; and in winter they were hard pressed to survive. Those who could do so obtained other work in rural industries, as assistants to tailors or shoemakers, or relied upon the wages their women and children could earn, as spinners in East Anglia at 4d a day perhaps, as glove-makers in Oxfordshire and Dorset, lace-makers in Buckinghamshire, or straw-plaiters in Bedfordshire.[15] In some villages, indeed, these rural industries rivalled agriculture as the principal occupation of the poor. Professor W. G. Hoskins has shown that in one such village, Wigston Magna in Leicestershire, where framework knitting was already widespread at the beginning of the century, a third of the inhabitants were engaged in manufacturing by the 1760s.[16] In other households in Wigston Magna tailors and shoemakers combined their trades with the cultivation of land.[17] Elsewhere, men moved from one occupation to another as demands for their labour required. In Dorset, for example, farmworkers turned their hands to rope-making, tanning and quarrying stone; in Banbury, Oxfordshire, they turned to weaving; in Cornwall tin-miners worked in the pilchard fishery when they needed the extra money the busy autumn season offered; while in Selborne in Hampshire, as Gilbert White said, 'beside the employment in husbandry the men work in hop gardens, of which we have many; and fell and bark timber. In the spring and summer the women weed the corn; and enjoy a second harvest in September by hop-picking.'[18]

Low as wages were, they were not excessively so for those who could by one means or another find regular work, for prices were also low and remained so until the 1760s. Both the political economists, Adam Smith and Malthus, agreed that wages kept apace of prices in these years;[19] and Dr R. W. Malcolmson has suggested that 'the real wages of the labouring people were probably slightly higher around 1760 than they had been at the beginning of the century'.

However, from the 1760s provisions ceased to be cheap. Average annual grain prices rose significantly from the mid 1760s, reaching unprecedented heights during the last decade of the century. Wheat, for instance, which cost 34s a quarter in 1780, cost 58s by 1790 and was as much as 128s by 1800 . . . It also seems . . . that wage rates on the whole, though they increased almost everywhere, tended to lag behind prices, or at best just kept up with inflation (and even this was not common in the 1790s). The only districts that unquestionably experienced a general increase in real wages during the last third of the century were those with rapidly expanding industrial economies, notably the West Riding of Yorkshire, south Lancashire and the Birmingham region. Real wages in most country districts during these decades were undoubtedly eroded, and in London they were probably in decline by the 1790s if not before. As the nineteenth century opened the real wages of most labouring people in most parts of England were probably lower – sometimes just slightly, sometimes quite strikingly – than they had been in the 1760s.[20]

This decline in wages was accompanied not only by a growing disinclination on the part of employers to allow their workers such traditional perquisites as dockers' 'sweepings' and miners' free coal but also by hardship occasioned by the continuing enclosure of common lands which, so it was complained, utterly ruined families who for centuries had enjoyed the rights of pasturage, of feeding pigs, of collecting fuel, nuts and berries and of materials for thatching. 'An amazing number of people,' wrote the rector of Cookham, Berkshire, 'have been reduced from a comfortable state of partial independence to the precarious condition of mere hirelings, who when out of work immediately come on the parish.'[21] Arthur Young, who recognized the benefits to commercial farming of enclosure, had to admit that it caused widespread hardship: 'By nineteen out of twenty Enclosure Bills the poor are injured and most grossly . . . The poor in the parishes may say with truth,

Parliament may be tender of property. All I know is, I had a cow; and an Act of Parliament has taken it from me.'

The diet of the poor consequently became more meagre and for the first time the bread which formed so large a part of it was as likely to be bought in a shop as baked at home. Even so, while one family in five was in receipt of poor relief, the worker who received regular wages ate quite well, and at least some of those who had to look to the parish for financial help contrived to buy butter and lard to spread on their bread, and bacon to eat with it. One Oxfordshire labourer, who had three children and earned no more than 9s a week, spent £2 10s a year on tea and sugar which was only 10s a year less than he spent on rent.[22]

Although better wages could generally be earned in the town or in collieries than on the land, the movement from the countryside into the industrial centres was at first quite slow: by 1800 about two-thirds of the country's population were still living in the country. Yet, the industrial towns which Defoe had described would scarcely have been recognized by him sixty or seventy years later when the population of Birmingham, that 'largest mere village in England', had risen from about 12,000 to 45,000 and that of Liverpool from some 6000 to nearly 40,000; nor would the work-places which they contained, the mills and factories of Manchester and Leeds, the potteries of north Staffordshire, the foundries of Sheffield, the mines around Newcastle and Durham, the glassworks and distilleries of Bristol, the shoe workshops of Northampton, the hosiery works in Leicester and Nottingham, the ship-repair yards of Hull, the naval dockyards at Chatham, the harbours of Folkestone, Whitby, Lowestoft and of several other thriving seaports. London, the city of Defoe's birth whose population had risen from about 575,000 in 1700 to nearly 700,000 in 1800, was not only by far the largest city in England but also by now the largest in Europe. It had few big industries of national importance, other than shipbuilding and, in Spitalfields, silk-weaving; but it found employment for innumerable skilled and unskilled men in the building trade, for tens of thousands of domestic servants and shop assistants, and for all manner of craftsmen and their apprentices. So, to a far lesser extent, did the provincial, market and cathedral towns of England where small businesses attended to the needs of local communities, where the staffs of numerous inns looked after wayfarers and the houses of gentlemen were tended by innumerable servants.

Foreign and native visitors were alike much struck by the attractiveness of these small provincial towns. But they were often either distressed or overwhelmed by the industrial towns of the Midlands and North, and by the condition of those who were obliged to work in them. They were ready to admit that there was compensation for the vigorous workmen in full employment who might earn as much as £3 a week, the amount which some maidservants were paid in a year. On an income like this a man could afford to eat meat fairly regularly, to have white rather than brown rye or barley bread on their tables, to drink tea – which was much stronger than it was in poor households where the same leaves were used time after time – and to indulge a growing taste for sugar, 5 million pounds of which were consumed in 1760. Yet in most large towns there were streets in which the poverty was appalling. 'I found some in their cells, others in their garrets, half starved with cold and hunger, added to weakness and pain,' John Wesley wrote in 1753. 'But I found not one of them unemployed who was able to crawl about the room. So wickedly, so devilishly false is that common objection, "They are poor because they are idle".'[23]

Working long hours, commonly from dawn to dusk six days a week, workers suffered from a variety of industrial diseases for which there was no cure nor even treatment. 'The collier, the clothier, the painter, the gilder, the miner, the makers of glass, the workers in iron, tin, lead, copper, while they minister to our necessities or please our tastes and fancies,' the *Gentleman's Magazine* conceded in 1782, 'are impairing their health, and shortening their days.' Lead-miners contracted plumbism, butchers anthrax; coalminers – who spent more time underground as pits grew deeper and some of whom slept as well as worked underground – ran the risk not only of contracting silicosis but also of being killed when a pit prop – or a pillar of coal used as a prop – collapsed or when there was an explosion caused by fire-damp, as there was at Chester-le-Street in 1708 when a hundred miners were killed and at Bensham in 1710 when eighty more lost their lives.[24] And everywhere tired workers were being mutilated by primitive unguarded machinery.

In Birmingham, so Robert Southey said, every man stank of train oil and emery and had a complexion 'composed of oil and dust smoke-dried'. 'Some I have seen with red eyes and green hair; the eyes affected by the fires to which they are exposed, and the hair turned green by the brass works.'[25] Of Manchester, Edmund Burke, comparing British workers to slaves in other countries, wrote, 'I suppose there are in Great Britain upwards of a hundred thousand people employed in lead, tin, iron, copper and coal mines . . . An hundred thousand more at least are tortured without remission by the suffocating smoke, intense fires and constant drudgery necessary in refining and managing the production of those mines.'[26]

There were factory-owners who prided themselves upon the conditions in which their workforce spent their long days of up to thirteen hours. Among these were men like Richard Arkwright, a former barber's apprentice who invented a carding machine and spinning frame and built the first factory to contain water-driven machinery in 1777; Josiah Wedgwood, the potter, whose workmen lived under his firm paternalistic care in a village near

Burslem which he had constructed for them near his mansion, Etruria Hall; and Robert Owen, the son of a saddler and ironmonger, the conduct of whose 1300 workers at New Lanark Mills was marked by 'silent monitors', labels of different colours indicating the various grades of good and bad behaviour.

Visitors to factories such as these were impressed by the numbers of men employed, and by the regimented manner in which they performed their work. Louis Simond described a visit in 1810 to a manufactory in Birmingham in which 'no mark of ill-humour' was discernible. 'These people [who were earning between sixteen and sixty shillings a week], are well broken to taxation,' he wrote. 'They complain indeed, but it is just as they complain of their climate, from habit, or as we see children continue crying, long after they have forgotten the cause of their tears.'

The manufactories are mostly of hardware and glass, and are less unhealthy, although more dirty, than those of Manchester and Glasgow, which require heat and confined air, and clog the lungs with floating particles of cotton. By means of late improvements, the smoke of innumerable coal fires is consumed, and the atmosphere much clearer than formerly.

In one place, 500 persons were employed in making plated ware of all sorts, toys and trinkets. We saw there patent carriage steps, flying down and folding up of themselves, as the door opens or shuts; chairs in walking-sticks, pocket-umbrellas, extraordinary cheese-toasters, and a multitude of other wonderful inventions. In another place, 300 men produce 10,000 gun barrels in a month. We saw a part of the process – enormous hammers, wielded by a steam-engine, of the power of 120 horses, crushing in an instant red hot iron bars.[27]

In nearly all factories discipline was harsh. In many the men were expected to work in silence except perhaps when required to sing a song in praise of the virtues of their employer. While bonuses were occasionally awarded, punishments were imposed for insubordination. At Wedgwood's works – where the master admitted he would have thrashed his men 'right heartily' if he could for presuming to take their traditional time off to go to Burslem Wakes – a worker who answered an overseer back was immediately dismissed, and one who 'conveyed ales or liquor into the manufactory' was fined 2s. At Marshal's flax-spinning mill at Leeds all employees from managers and overseers to oilers, spreaders, spinners and reelers had their precise duties allocated to them and if they were found 'a yard out of their ground' or in transgression of any rule, they were 'instantly turned off as unfit for their situation'. Monitors ensured that men did not arrive late for work or leave early, that was to say, in Ambrose Crowley's iron foundry, after five o'clock in the morning or before eight o'clock at night.

J. L. and Barbara Hammond cited the fines imposed upon spinners in one Manchester workshop where the temperature rose to 84 degrees Fahrenheit:

|  | s. | d. |
|---|---|---|
| Any spinner found with his window open | 1. | 0 |
| Any spinner found dirty at his work | 1. | 0 |
| Any spinner found washing himself | 1. | 0 |
| Any spinner leaving his oil can out of its place | 1. | 0 |
| Any spinner putting his gas out too soon | 1. | 0 |
| Any spinner spinning with gaslight too long in the morning | 2. | 0 |
| Any spinner heard whistling | 1. | 0 |
| Any spinner being five minutes after last bell rings | 1. | 0 |
| Any spinner being sick and cannot find another must pay for steam per day | 6. | 0 |
| Any spinner found in another's wheel-gate | 1. | 0 |
| Any spinner neglecting to send his sweepings three mornings in the week | 1. | 0 |
| Any spinner having waste on his spindles | 1. | 0[28] |

# 43 · Clothworkers and Machine-breakers

Although Louis Simond thought the workers in the manufactory he visited in Birmingham were content enough, there was, in fact, widespread and growing discontent both in town and country. In the first year of the century it was remarked that the common people were 'very rough and savage in their Dispositions, being of levelling Principles, and refractory to Government, insolent, and tumultuous'. They were consumed with envy, another observer contested, railing at their betters, 'misconstruing their most commendable Actions' and loudly complaining that the 'good Things of the World are chiefly enjoy'd by those who do not deserve them'.[1] These were to remain familiar complaints for many years during which outbreaks of violent disorder were constantly expected by those who had most to lose and whose fears were exacerbated by the threats they received. One characteristic threat was addressed in 1762 to a Lancashire justice of the peace who was held to be one of those responsible for the high price of bread:

> This his to asquaint you that We poor of Rosendale Rochdale Oldham Saddleworth Ashton have all mutaly and firmly agreed by Word and Covinent and Oath to Fight and Stand by Each Other as long as Life doth last for We may as well be all hanged as starved to Death and to see ower Children weep for Bread and none to give Them nor no liklyness of ever mending . . . If You dont amaidatley put a Stopp and let hus feel it the next Saturday We will murder You all that We have down in Ower List and Wee will all bring a Faggot and burn down Your Houses and make Your Wifes Widdows and Your Children Fatherless. Take care.[2]

Other similar letters were addressed to employers and to landlords. One such was received in 1787 by the clothiers of Newbury who were told:

You Gentlemen are Agreed to Beat down the Price of the Weavers. Work is already so Low They Cannot get A livelywood like Almost any Other Trade . . . Youre Lives As Well as Our are Not Insured One Moment . . . Prepare your selves for A Good Bonfire at Both Ends At Each Your Dwellings . . . I May as well Dey with a Houlter As Be Starved to Death . . .[3]

A landlord intent upon closing a common in 1799 was warned that should he commit that 'bloudy act' it would not be in his power to say he was safe from the hands of his enemies. 'For Whe like birds of pray will prively Lye in wait and spil the bloud of the aforesaid Charicters whose names and plaices of abode are as putrified sores in our nostrils.'[4]

The objectives of all these protesters were strictly limited, and those who wished to turn such violent upheavals as the Jacobite rebellions into national revolutions were disappointed. The disturbances, nevertheless, were frequent and serious enough. There were riots over enclosures and over the price and unfair distribution of corn, over enclosures and turnpike tolls, new machinery and taxes, over the activities of recruiting officers and press gangs and excise officials and gamekeepers. There were riots during heated labour disputes, hotly contested elections and balloting for the newly organized militia which was likely to bear more heavily upon the poor than upon the rich.

The London mob was particularly unruly; and in 1780 during the Gordon Riots – named after Lord George Gordon, leader of the Protestant Association – an estimated 850 people lost their lives and the damage to property was incalculable. The trouble started with a march by some 50,000 people to demonstrate their opposition to the repeal of anti-Roman Catholic legislation. But the organizers soon lost control of the crowd. Some demonstrators broke away to plunder and burn Roman Catholic chapels; and by the evening of 5 June the mob, no longer confining attacks to Catholics, had begun a campaign of general destruction, directed particularly against Irish property and Irishmen who were condemned as wage-cutting blacklegs. Prisons were destroyed, distilleries pillaged, the houses of magistrates and lawyers attacked. Assaults were made on Downing Street and on the Bank of England which was defended by militiamen and by clerks who melted down inkwells for bullets. After four days of tumult troops at length restored order. Gordon was acquitted of high treason, but twenty-one ringleaders were hanged. 'Such a time of terror,' Samuel Johnson told Mrs Thrale, 'you have been fortunate in not seeing.'[5]

Outside London the forest regions of the country were considered to be exceptionally dangerous and turbulent. Quarrels between landlords, as well as royal officials, and local people, who were being deprived of their traditional common rights and the resources of the forest, often erupted into violence. Cannock Chase in Staffordshire, Cranborne Chase in Dorset, the Forest of Dean in Gloucestershire, Kingswood Forest near Bristol, the Forest of Selwood in Somerset and the forests of the south-east were all said to be filled with poachers and malcontents, coiners, deer-stealers, fugitive criminals, highwaymen, rough country folk and pests of society abandoned to idleness, vice and profligacy. The vicinity of Wychwood Forest in Oxfordshire, according to Arthur Young, was 'filled with poachers, deer-stealers, thieves and pilferers of every kind: offences of almost every description abound so much that the offenders are a terror to all quiet and well-disposed persons; and Oxford gaol would be uninhabited, were it not for this fertile source of crimes'.[6]

In nearly all areas food riots were common. In the years 1756–7 alone there were over 100 disturbances in thirty different counties. One market day in May 1757 in Taunton angry housewives forced the farmers to bring down the price of wheat from 8s 6d to 6s 6d a bushel; and there were similar incidents at Yeovil and Salisbury, in Staffordshire and at Bewdley in Worcestershire where the market was put 'in a great Confusion by the Assembling of a Number of Women who cut open some Bags of Wheat' and insisted on their being sold at the price they had fetched in Kidderminster a few days before. At Exeter in April 1757, when the townsmen heard that the farmers had agreed to hold out for 15s a bushel for wheat, they 'sent their Wives in great numbers to Market, resolving to give no more than 6s per Bushel, and, if they would not sell it at that Price, to take it by Force'.

> And such Wives, as did not stand by this Agreement, were to be well flogg'd by their Comrades. Having thus determined, they marched to the Corn-Market, and harangued the Farmers in such a Manner, that they lowered their Price to 8s 6d. The Bakers came; and would have carried all off at that Price, but the Amazonians swore, that they would carry the first man who attempted it before the Mayor; upon which the Farmers swore they would bring no more to Market; and the sanguine Females threatened the Farmers, that, if they did not, they would come and take it by Force out of their Ricks. The Farmers submitted.[7]

The rioters were rarely intent upon theft and as a general rule conscientiously ensured that the farmers were paid what was considered a fair price.

> The Price of Wheat was raised so high in the Market at Barnstable [so *Jackson's Oxford Journal* reported in July 1766], that the Poor, who are in great Distress, joined in a Body, and compelled the Farmers to sell it at

Five Shillings per Bushel. Some of the Farmers refusing to take the Money, the Poor were honest enough to tie it up carefully for them in their Sacks. And as soon as they had taken it at a low Price sufficient to supply their Necessities, they dispersed, leaving the Farmers to make what Price they could of other People.[8]

There were frequent riots, too, during industrial disputes when employers tried to reduce wages or increase work, or when a worker agreed to accept a lower rate than his fellows. There were riots, for instance, at Frome in Somerset in 1726 when weavers were threatened with a reduction in wages and an increase in work. Large numbers of them, styling themselves regulators, broke into the houses of their masters, 'and where their Demands were complied with, and smooth Words given, they did no harm, but where there was any hesitation, or what they call uncivil Treatment, the Windows paid for it'. A few years later other weavers near Bristol attacked 'one of their Fraternity for working under Price', ducked him in the river and beat him so severely that he lost an eye.[9]

Such incidents were common. So were attempts by workers to combine together to frustrate what they took to be the unfair designs of their masters and the selfish behaviour of their fellows. Framework knitters in Nottinghamshire, journeymen tailors in Norwich, button-makers in Cheshire, miners in Durham, building workers in Manchester, needle-makers and nailers in the west Midlands and Birmingham and shipwrights as well as stay-makers in London were among the numerous workers who at one time or another in the century acted collectively in industrial disputes. The government reacted sharply to restrict these labour combinations and to make combination itself illegal. A whole series of Acts were passed against them: by 1799 there were nearly fifty. And then there came the Combination Acts of 1799 and 1800 which made illegal the association of two or more people for the purpose of obtaining wage increases or improving working conditions. Offenders against the Acts would be sentenced to three months' imprisonment by a single magistrate.[10]

Although the first was intended to prevent combinations of masters as well as workers, these Acts marked a further stage in the increasingly hostile relationship between employers and workers. Soon after the middle of the century, the economist, the Rev. Josiah Tucker, the son of a farmer, complained that in the woollen districts of the Cotswolds, Wiltshire and Somerset – as indeed elsewhere – those who worked for a master clothier, who might employ 1000 people, looked upon him not only as their paymaster but also 'sometimes as their Tyrant'.

Besides, as the Master is placed so high above the Condition of the Journeyman [Tucker continued], both their Conditions approach much nearer to that of a Planter and Slave in our American colonies, than might be expected in such a Country as England. The Master, for Example, however well-disposed in himself, is naturally tempted by his Situation to be proud and over-bearing, to consider his People as the Scum of the Earth, whom he has a Right to squeeze whenever he can; because they ought to be kept low, and not to rise up in Competition with their Superiors. The Journeymen on the contrary, are equally tempted by their Situation, to envy the high Station, and superior Fortunes of their Masters, and to envy them the more, in Proportion as they find themselves deprived of the Hopes of advancing themselves to the same Degree by any Stretch of Industry, or superior Skill. Hence their Self-Love takes a wrong Turn, destructive to themselves, and others. They think it no Crime to get as much Wages, and to do as little for it as they possibly can, to lie and cheat, and do any other bad Thing; provided it is only against their Master, whom they look upon as their common Enemy, with whom no Faith is to be kept.[11]

Towards the end of the century such attitudes became more and more common, the prejudices against increasingly successful associations of workers and trade clubs more pronounced, and class distinctions more divisive. When the nineteenth century began, inflation and the economic consequences of the war with revolutionary France were exacerbating the general discontent and providing opportunities for the ideas of the radicals and Tom Paine to gain ground. Despite temporary setbacks the economy was expanding fast, yet most poor people were receiving little benefit from this expansion. 'In visiting the labouring families of my parish,' wrote the Rev. David Davies, the rector of Barkham, Berkshire, in 1795, 'I could not but observe with concern their mean and distressed condition . . . Yet I could not impute the wretchedness I saw either to sloth or wastefulness.' Five years later nearly 30 per cent of the population was being paid poor relief. And by 1812 the annual expenditure on poor rates had grown from about 2 million pounds in 1780 to 8 million.[12]

By then the relationship between employers and employed in many industries had been worsened by the introduction of new machinery. There had been several isolated attacks upon machinery before the Combination Acts were passed: in Lancashire in the 1750s spinners attacked the jennies invented by James Hargreaves; in the 1770s in Nottinghamshire hosiers smashed scores of Arkwright's stocking-frames; and at Birkacre in 1776 'a most riotous and outrageous mob . . . armed in warlike manner . . . destroyed most of the machinery [of a carding factory] and afterwards set fire to and consumed the whole Buildings, and Every Thing therein contained'.[13] After the passing of the Combination Acts such attacks upon machinery, and the destruction of tools and workshops, became more frequent and more destructive. The workers from three trades in particular felt vulnerable to the introduction of modern machinery, and it was among them that the violence to be known as Luddism erupted in its terrifying fury.

Clothworkers from the West Riding, cotton-weavers from south Lancashire, and framework knitters from the midland counties of Nottinghamshire, Leicestershire and Derbyshire were all skilled tradesmen who took pride in their work and jealously guarded the traditional privileges to which their expertise entitled them. This was especially true of the Yorkshire clothworkers who considered themselves superior to other workers in the district. They earned as much as thirty shillings a week – almost three times the average wage in the Yorkshire clothing trade. Now, however, their pride was being undermined by the growing interest in two cloth-dressing machines: the gig-mill, used to raise the nap on woollens, and the shearing frame, a new invention that trimmed away the superfluous nap. The gig-mill was not a modern invention. It had been known for centuries, but in Yorkshire – with the exception of a few villages outside the main centres of trade – the clothworkers had so far successfully resisted its introduction; in Leeds not a single employer had dared set one up in his factory.

Not all the clothworkers were blindly prejudiced against gig-mills and shearing frames. Indeed, most of them were prepared to come to terms with machinery provided it did not throw them out of work without compensation. Practical suggestions were made for a tax on machine-worked cloth, the proceeds to be paid to unemployed croppers until new work was found for them. Many small employers were willing to negotiate on these terms and, in the meantime, contributed generously to the 'sick clubs' and 'institutions' which their workers founded as an alternative to the trade unions which the law denied them.

The richer and more powerful employers were decidedly less sympathetic, however. So, too, were the authorities in London where Parliament, perturbed by the growing unrest in the country, removed by a series of enactments all the protection and privileges that the clothworker had previously enjoyed. He now could do nothing but face the gig-mill and the shearing frame with implacable enmity. When various Yorkshire employers took advantage of their workers' weakened position to install the machinery, violence could no longer be averted.

In the Midlands, meanwhile, the framework knitters (or stockingers, as they were also called) were edging toward violence in much the same way. Their main grievance was not so much machinery as their employers' attempts to save money by cutting down on labour and the quality of goods.

Framework knitters had never been well paid, but they took pride in their traditions and skill. They made gloves and shirts, cravats and pantaloons, as well as stockings, and they were deeply offended by the shoddy articles, disreputable to their trade, that now resulted from slapdash techniques and the use of unskilled labour.

They had other grievances as well. Most of them still worked at home, paying rent to the master hosiers not only for their cottages but also for their looms; and their rents were being constantly and arbitrarily increased. Moreover, specialists were now often paid at rates appropriate to unskilled men.

Following the example of the Yorkshire clothworkers, the framework knitters at first tried to protect their interests by constitutional means, but when these attempts failed the stockingers also felt forced to resort to violence.[14]

By the end of 1811 it was clear that the consequent outbreaks of violence were carefully planned and deliberate; they were no longer the work of shouting mobs urged on by rabble-rousers but of disciplined gangs led by masked men whose orders were implicitly obeyed. 'The rioters appear suddenly in armed parties, under regular commanders,' a provincial news-paper reported. 'The chief commander, be he whomsoever he may, is styled *General Ludd*.'

The name was soon familiar throughout the country. It appeared as a signature at the bottom of inflammatory handbills and at the end of dire warnings to employers whose machinery had been marked for destruction. It appeared in ballads and in broad-sheets. While nurses of middle-class children frightened their charges with it, conjuring up visions of a terrifying ogre, the children of the poor were taught to venerate it and to remember it in their prayers. 'The dread name Ludd' was invoked at night in taverns and alehouses; it was mentioned with fear and apprehension at the dinner tables of the rich. Men said that to disobey an order given on its authority was to risk immediate death.

Those who knew the real Ned Ludd could only be astonished by his sudden rise to fame, for he was a simpleton living in an obscure village in Leicestershire, where he was the natural butt of heartless children. One day, provoked beyond endurance by his tormentors, he chased one of the children into a nearby cottage. He lost track of the child there, but he did find two knitting frames and vented his anger on them instead. Thereafter in that district poor Ned Ludd was automatically blamed whenever frames were smashed. Within ten years the convenient scapegoat had become a legend, and straw effigies of 'the renowned General Ludd' were carried in procession through the northern and midland villages, accompanied by the standard-bearers waving red flags. Under the name of Luddites, the machine-breakers became members of an underground revolutionary movement with a definite, if unsystematic, programme of action.

They were certainly not indiscriminate in their destruction. The workshops and knitting frames of good and honest employers were left untouched. 'In one house last night,' runs a typical newspaper report about the marauders, 'they broke four frames out of six; the other two, which belonged to masters who had not lowered their wages, they did not meddle with.' It soon became common for hosiers to protect their machinery by posting notices that read: 'This frame is making full-fashioned work at the full price.' But no frame was completely safe until the Luddites had given it their sanction.

Calling themselves 'inspectors from the committee', groups of Luddites would visit a village and summon the workers to the local inn. After collecting money for men already thrown out of work because their frames had been broken, the 'inspectors' designated the frames to be destroyed in the future. These orders were invariably obeyed, for the Luddites were known to be as merciless as they were just. Anyone breaking their rules was sure to be severely punished, even hanged.

By the beginning of February 1812, the Luddites' campaign in the Midlands was gradually coming to a halt. They had achieved a considerable measure of success: most employers had been forced to increase their men's wages, dismiss unapprenticed boys and women, and improve the quality of goods. But the attacks also ceased because great numbers of troops had moved into the area, and the government had introduced a Bill that would make frame-breaking a capital offence.

No sooner had the authorities appeared to have gained control over the situation in the Midlands, however, than Luddism broke out with even greater virulence in Yorkshire and Lancashire. Workers there were urged in the name of 'General Ludd, Commander of the Army of Redressers', to 'follow the noble example of the brave citizens of Paris who in sight of 30,000 tyrant redcoats brought a tyrant to the ground'. Employers received letters threatening murder unless their 'detestable' shearing machines were pulled down.

Many employees did pull down their machines, and the shops of those who declined to do so were attacked at night by gangs of workers with blackened faces. Men wielding huge iron hammers known as 'Enochs' – after the firm of blacksmiths who made them – smashed doors, shattered shearing frames, and demolished gig-mills. As in Nottinghamshire, the Luddites operated with military discipline, marching towards their objective in silent ranks, ten abreast. And 'as soon as the work of destruction was completed', the *Leeds Mercury* informed its readers, 'the Leader drew up his men, called over the roll, each man answering to a particular number instead of his name; they then fired off their pistols, . . . gave a shout, and marched off in regular military order.'

On one attack on the premises of a Stockport manufacturer who had installed a steam loom, the demonstrators were led by two men dressed as women and calling themselves General Ludd's wives; in another subsequent attack on a mill at Middleton they armed themselves with muskets and carried out a military assault in which several of them were killed and many wounded.

By the spring of 1812, scarcely any smaller manufacturers in Yorkshire were still using machinery, and the Luddites felt that the time had come to march against the big mills whose owners had hired guards. There were two mills in particular that the Luddites were determined to destroy, William Horsfall's mill near Huddersfield and William Cartwright's at Rawfolds in Liversedge. They decided to attack Cartwright's mill first.

With the help of troops, Cartwright, who never left his mill, barricaded it against attack and placed a vat of concentrated sulphuric acid at the top of the stairs to tip on the heads of any Luddites who might succeed in breaking down the door. He successfully drove off the attack, wounding several of the armed workers, two of them mortally. One of these two was John Booth, nineteen years old, a harness-maker's apprentice and the son of a former cropper who was a clergyman in the neighbourhood. As he lay dying amidst the fumes of the aqua fortis that had been applied to the stump of his amputated leg, a pugnacious High Tory parson hovered over him in the hope that he might confess the names of his accomplices. He refused to speak, however, until he knew he was dying, and then he motioned to Robertson to come closer. 'Can you keep a secret?' he whispered. With eager expectation Robertson replied that he could. 'So can I,' gasped Booth, closed his eyes, and died.[15]

Cartwright's successful defence of his mill marked a turning point in the history of Yorkshire Luddism. Thereafter, no other mill was assaulted in force; and Cartwright himself became a hero to the authorities, to army officers, Tory squires, magistrates and parsons alike. The clothworkers, of course, detested him more than ever. He received some grudging approval when a soldier who had refused to fire on the Luddites, and who was sentenced to receive 300 lashes outside his mill, was unbound after twenty-five at Cartwright's request. But this leniency scarcely softened the hatred he aroused during his subsequent relentless pursuit of those Luddites who had survived the attack on his mill.

Despite the thoroughness of this pursuit, however, not a single man was arrested. Thousands of troops patrolled the West Riding; scores of spies were employed; whole villages of working people, who must have known at least some of the men involved, were rigorously questioned. But there was a conspiracy of total silence. As two London magistrates who had been sent north reported to the Home Office: 'Almost every creature of the lower order, both in town and country, are on the Luddites' side.'

Thus supported and protected, the Luddites now decided to take action against the other big mill-owner whom they had marked down for punishment, William Horsfall, a man who was hated even more than Cartwright and who had been heard to proclaim his ardent desire to 'ride up to his saddle girths' in Luddite blood. But Horsfall's mill was so well protected by soldiers and by cannon mounted on the roof, that its owner was attacked instead. He was mortally wounded by a fusillade of musket balls as he rode home from Huddersfield one morning in 1812.

Soon afterwards those responsible for the murder were apprehended and taken to York gaol, together with numerous other suspected Luddites and their supporters. Among these were hatters and shoemakers as well as clothworkers, cardmakers and coalminers, tailors, butchers, watermen, carpet weavers and apprentices. The youngest was a boy of fifteen, the oldest nearly seventy. Many were illiterate; a few had criminal records; the greater number were honest men who had never been in trouble before. As the *Leeds Mercury* reported of those accused of the worst crimes, 'they were young men on whose countenances nature had not imprinted the features of assassins'.

Several of them were sentenced to imprisonment in a penal colony, seventeen to be hanged, including five men of good character who, on the flimsiest evidence, were convicted of having taken part in the assault on Cartwright's mill. On being asked if he thought that so many men should be hanged on one beam, the judge is said to have pondered the question at some length before delivering the whimsical reply, 'Why, no, Sir, I consider they would hang more comfortably on two.'

For a time it had seemed that the Luddites might provoke a national revolution. Horsfall's murder had been preceded by a powerful Luddite assault at Westhoughton, where a steam-powered mill had been invaded and its power looms demolished; it had been followed a fortnight later by the murder of the prime minister, Spencer Perceval, by John Bellingham, a mentally deranged commercial agent ruined by the war, who was acclaimed by the Luddites as a hero. In Lancashire people openly expressed their joy at his deed; in London, huge crowds applauded him; in Nottingham, mobs paraded through the town 'with drums beating and flags flying in triumph'; in Yorkshire, notices offering rewards for the Prince Regent's head, now that the prime minister had been disposed of, were posted on the walls.

The vice-lieutenant of Yorkshire declared his belief that England was taking the 'direct road to an open insurrection'. Had there been some national leadership or even national policy with which the Luddites could have identified themselves, this open insurrection, which the government constantly dreaded, might well have broken out. But what little reliable evidence exists suggests that Luddism was essentially a spontaneous movement: its local leaders had little connection with one another and no settled policies of long-term reform. In the districts where they operated, the Luddites retained their hold on the working communities long after the days of machine-breaking were over, but by the summer of 1812 the crisis of Luddism was past. There were isolated instances of machine-smashing and rioting well on into the autumn, and as late as 1817 a large factory at Loughborough in Leicestershire was attacked by masked men armed with blunderbusses, their leaders shouting, 'Ludds, do your duty well!' This was the final demonstration of the Luddites' declining power, and afterwards James Towle, the last of the Luddite heroes, was executed.[16]

Yet for years the spirit of the Luddites lingered on. Those who survived the gallows or escaped transportation handed down Luddite legends, sang Luddite songs, and carefully preserved Luddite secrets. They were proud of their part in an underground movement that was considered to be an important stage in the development of the working class, far more significant than the outbursts of violence that gave Luddism its subsequent notoriety. Machinery was, after all, only part of a general factory system the Luddites had vainly strived to destroy. As E. P. Thompson has pointed out, Luddism erupted at a time when the old paternalist legislation that had to some extent protected the worker from the unscrupulous manufacturer and unjust employer was being swept away; when the 'shadowy image of a benevolent corporate state' – in which artisans occupied a lowly but nevertheless respected position in society – was being rapidly dispersed. Artisans and journeymen felt themselves 'thrust beyond the pale of the constitution' and robbed of those few rights they had previously enjoyed.[17]

'As a body of ingenious artisans employed on materials of great value,' the experienced silk-workers of Derby protested to the master hosiers, 'we conceive ourselves entitled to a higher station in society.' Instead of that, they – and tens of thousands of skilled workers in other trades – were to be given over to what they considered little better than slavery in vast, depressing factories where their identities would be lost, where they and their children would be exploited and oppressed, confined for all their working lives in demeaning and incessant labour.[18]

# 44 · *Rick-burners, Paupers and Chartists*

A century after Daniel Defoe published his *Tour thro' the Whole Island of Great Britain*, William Cobbett, the essayist who had recently started a seed-farm at Kensington, embarked upon a journey through the southern counties similar to the one that Defoe had undertaken. Much of what he saw distressed and angered him. On 11 October 1822 he arrived at Weyhill on the day of the sheep fair which he had first attended forty-six years before. In those days the sheep sellers carried home about £300,000; now they were lucky to make £70,000. 'The countenance of the farmers were descriptive of their ruinous state,' Cobbett wrote. 'I never in all my life, beheld a more mournful scene. There is a horse-fair upon another part of the Down; and there I saw horses keeping pace in depression with the sheep . . . Met with a farmer who said he must be ruined, unless another "good war" should come! This is no uncommon notion. They saw high prices with war, and they thought that the War [the war against Napoleon's France] was the cause.'

On the last day of that month Cobbett rode through Windsor Forest, 'that is to say upon as bleak, as barren, and as villainous a heath as ever man set his eyes on'. 'Here are new enclosures without end,' he continued. 'And there are new houses too, here and there, over the whole of this execrable tract of country . . . But farm-houses have been growing fewer and fewer; and it is manifest to every man who has eyes to see with, that the villages are regularly wasting away . . . In all the really agricultural villages and parts of the kingdom, there is a shocking decay, a great dilapidation and constant falling down of houses . . . The labourers' houses disappear also.'

'The villages are all in a state of decay,' he wrote when further south in Hampshire. 'The farm-buildings dropping down, bit by bit . . . If this infernal system could go on for forty years longer, it would make all the labourers as much slaves as the negroes are.' Their wages, in these years of agrarian depression between the days of subsistence farming under the traditional open-field system and the prosperous times yet to come, were pitiably low. In Wiltshire, Cobbett came upon thirty or more men digging a field of about twelve acres. They were being paid 9d a day which was 'as cheap as ploughing'. 'But if married, how are their miserable families to live on 4s 6d a week?' Cobbett asked. 'And if single they must and will have more by poaching, or by taking without leave.'

Charity was no solution, Cobbett insisted. One Sunday a little girl of whom he asked the way was wearing a camlet gown, white apron and plaid cloak and was carrying a book in her hand. She told him that Lady Baring of Grange Park had given her the clothes and had taught her to read and to sing hymns and spiritual songs. Later that morning he saw 'not less than a dozen girls clad in the same way'. 'It is impossible not to believe that this is done with a good motive,' he commented. 'But it is possible not to believe that it is productive of good. It must create hypocrites, and hypocrisy is the great sin of the age.'

In the valley of the Avon, Cobbett was shocked by the impoverishment of the countryside: 'It is manifest that the population of the valley was, at one time, many times what it is now; for, in the first place, what were the twenty-nine churches built for? The population of the twenty-nine parishes is now but little more than half of that of the single parish of Kensington; and there are several of the churches bigger than the church of Kensington . . . These twenty-nine churches would now not only hold all the inhabitants, men, women and children, but all the household goods, and tools, and implements of the whole of them, farmers and all . . . The villages down this Valley of Avon, and, indeed, it was the same in every part of this county, used to have great employment for the women and children in the carding and spinning of wool for the making of broad-cloth. This was a very general employment for the women and girls; but it is now wholly gone.'

In Somerset he found that the 'poor creatures of Frome' had had to pawn all their things, 'all their best clothes, their blankets and sheets; their looms; any little piece of furniture they had'. And yet here were 'new houses in abundance, half finished; new gingerbread "places of worship", as they are called; great swaggering inns; parcels of swaggering fellows going about, with vulgarity imprinted upon their countenances, but with good clothes upon their backs'. 'Of all the mean, all the cowardly, reptiles that ever crawled on the face of the earth,' Cobbett wrote in another bitterly indignant passage after riding into Worcestershire, 'the English landowners are the most mean and the most cowardly; for, while they support the churches in their several parishes, while they see their own parsons pocket the tithes and the glebe-rents, while they see the population drawn away from their parishes to the WENS [the towns], they suffer themselves and their neighbours to be taxed, to build new churches for the monopolizers and tax-eaters in those WENS! Never was there in this world a set of reptiles so base as this. Stupid as many of them are, they must clearly see the flagrant injustice of making depopulated parishes pay for the aggrandizement of those who have caused the depopulation.'[1]

The resentment among labouring country people which Cobbett had witnessed and shared had already erupted in disturbances in various parts of the country. In Northamptonshire in 1799, for example, troops of yeomanry escorting wagons loaded with fencing had been stopped by a crowd of some 300 people who had lit a bonfire in the road. The Riot Act had been read and several arrests made before the wagons passed. On the whole, as John Clarke has said, the enclosure commissioners carried out their tasks with commendable impartiality.[2] But the combination of manorial and tithe rights inevitably led to the share of the village land owned by the lord of the manor – and sometimes by the rector – being increased; while those who had made part of their living by exercising their rights to common land – and those who had made use of it without legal right – were deprived of their independence, and not always compensated by the opportunity of work on the large farms which enclosure created.

In 1830 there were serious riots all over England in protest against enclosures, low wages, the employment of 'strangers', and the farm machines, mainly threshing machines, which were held to be keeping men out of work. From Wiltshire to Sussex and as far north as Carlisle, gangs of men, sometimes with blackened faces and reported to be in women's clothes, often carrying flags and blowing horns, cut down fences, destroyed machinery and burnt down ricks and barns. Most of the attacks were preceded by threatening letters, many signed by 'Captain Swing'. One characteristic letter ran, 'This is to inform you what you have to undergo gentelmen if providing you Dont pull down your messhenes and rise the poor men's wages the married men give tow and six pence a day the singel tow shillings or we will burn down your barns and you in them this is the last notis.'[3]

On occasions when the rioters clashed with yeomanry blood was shed and lives were lost. This happened near Salisbury on 25 December when the owner of the Pyt House estate, roused by his steward early in the morning, rode out to find 400 labourers armed with bludgeons and crowbars with which they had smashed three threshing machines in local farms. They told him they wanted 2s a day in wages, otherwise they would smash his machines too. Neither appeals nor threats deterred them; and his barns were broken into and his machines destroyed before a troop of yeomanry arrived from Hindon. The labourers fought with their bludgeons and bars, hatchets, pick-axes and hammers; the yeomanry with muskets; one labourer was killed, several others were wounded, and twenty-five arrested.

More commonly, however, the destruction and arson were carried on without bloodshed. Special constables were sometimes beaten up, men who would not join in the rioting were thrown into the village pond, and ferocious threats were frequently uttered. 'Blast my eyes,' a man was heard to shout in a Wallingford public house, 'I will smash the bloody buggers' heads, six at a time!' 'Be damned,' another man called out, 'if we do not beat the bloody place down!' But although 'violent language was often heard and formidable weapons carried round,' so the Attorney General reported, 'there has been such an absence of cruelty as to create general surprise.'[4]

The property of landowners and parsons was mostly at risk; ordinary farmers, particularly small farmers, often sympathized with the labourers who were prepared to accept that their employers would pay higher wages if they did not have to pay such high rents. At Horsham, Sussex, indeed – so the county's High Sheriff maintained – the farmers 'were known secretly, to be promoting the assembling of the people'. Certainly, both farmers and labourers assembled in the church where, so a local lady said, they occupied

> every tenable place within the walls, and by their shouts and threatening language [showed] their total disregard for the sanctity of the place. I am ashamed to say the farmers encouraged the labouring classes who required to be paid 2s 6d a day, while the farmers called for a reduction of their rents & the tithes by one half. Mr Simpson [the parson] in a very proper manner gave an account of the revenues of his living, and after shewing that he did not clear more than £400 per annum, promised to meet the gentlemen & farmers & to make such a reduction as they could reasonably expect. Mr. Hurst held out so long that it was feared blood would be shed. The doors were shut till the demands were granted; no lights were allowed; the iron railing that surrounds the monument was torn up, and the sacred boundary between the chancel & alter overleaped before he would yield; at last the three points were gained & happily without any personal injury. The Church is much disfigured. Money was afterwards demanded at different houses for refreshment &, if not obtained with ease, the windows were broken. Today the Mob is gone to Shipley and Rusper.[5]

By the time the risings were brought under control there were nearly 2000 rioters held in prison awaiting trial. Suspecting that local magistrates might be too lenient upon them, the Government ordered special commissions to conduct trials in those counties where the disturbances had been most alarming. Of the prisoners tried 800 were acquitted or bound over; 644 were sent to prison; 505 were sentenced to transportation, and of these 481 sailed for the Australian colonies. Seven prisoners were fined, one was whipped and nineteen were hanged, most of them for arson. As E. J. Hobsbawm and George Rudé have observed, in terms of death sentences and executions, the punishments followed the pattern of the times. 'Yet in terms of men transported, they were quite remarkably severe . . . In the south of England, there were whole communities that, for a generation, were stricken by the blow. From no other protest movement of the kind – from neither Luddites nor Chartists, nor trade unionists – was such a bitter price exacted.'[6]

Several attempts to form trade unions had been made after the repeal of the ineffective Combination Acts in 1824 and the subsequent passing of the Reform Act of 1832 which, while welcomed by the middle classes, was a profound disappointment to radicals and the militant working class. One national union, the National Association for the Protection of Labour, which was believed to have recruited 100,000 members, disintegrated soon after its foundation, following a succession of quarrels between its leaders. Two years later the Grand National Consolidated Trades Union was established; but, although this at one time claimed to have half a million members, it, too, was rent by internal disagreements. And when, in 1834, in the Dorset village of Tolpuddle, six trade unionists – the members of whose combination had had their wages reduced from 9s to 6s – administered oaths to their fellow-workers, they were arraigned under the Mutiny Act of 1749 and sentenced to seven years' transportation.

In that same year the grievances of the poor were much exacerbated by the Poor Law Amendment Act which sought to remedy the evils of a system whereby a labourer's wages were fixed immutably at a figure that took no account of the cost of living, being supplemented, in cases of severe necessity, by a pitifully meagre dole from the parish. The so-called Speenhamland system, which had spread from Berkshire to other places, originated with a decision by local magistrates in 1795 to provide outdoor relief – on a scale based on the price of bread and the size of the family concerned – both to those who were unemployed and to those whose earnings fell below the settled scale, thus in effect subsidizing the wages of the lowest paid. Since the amount of the dole depended upon the number of mouths a labourer had to feed, families had tended to grow larger, young men and women had come to town in search of work, and industrial workers had become almost as ill paid as those who worked on the land. Furthermore, the supplementation of inadequate wages out of the poor-rate killed any incentive there might otherwise have been to hard work and destroyed the workers' self-respect. Under the new Poor Law there were to be no supplementary allowances; there were to be no inducements for men to live as idle paupers; those without the means of livelihood were to be consigned to workhouses where rules were to be imposed with such strictness, and food was to be distributed with such economical care, that no one would enter them while hard work was an alternative.

Workhouses already had a bad name. By 1776 there were nearly 2000 of them, many of them built under a general Workhouse Act of the 1720s. They were often farmed out to contractors who made what profit they could out of them; and the death rate in them was appallingly high. Jonas Hanway, who believed that babies up to three years old consigned to workhouses in London were not likely to live for much more than a month, went so far as to say that 'parish officers never intend that parish infants should live'. Parson Wood-forde, after visiting a workhouse in Norfolk in 1781, had observed, 'About 380 Poor in it now, but they don't look either healthy or cheerful, a great Number die there, 27 have died since Christmas last.'

The condition of workhouses had not since improved. With barns, ricks and threshing machines, they had been one of the principal targets of the rioters of 1830 who took care not to harm the inmates. At Headley in Hampshire, the master testified, they left the sick ward untouched; but, having removed the infants, put them in beds in the yard, covered them over and 'kept them from harm all the time', they pulled the rest of the building down 'until not a room was left entire'.

It was generally accepted by the middle classes that the new law of 1834 was, as Dr Arnold of Rugby called it, 'a measure in itself wise and just'. 'But standing alone and unaccompanied by others of a milder and more positively improving tendency', it wore, Arnold added, 'an air of harshness' which would 'embitter the feelings of the poorer classes still more'.[7] And embitter them it did. It was intended that distinctions should be made between those who could not work and those who chose not to do so; but these distinctions were rarely made, and in many workhouses the respectable poor and such foundlings as Oliver Twist were incarcerated with men and women who might well have been in prison. Dickens's description of the workhouse diet as constituting 'three meals of thin gruel a day, with an onion twice a week, and half a roll on Sundays' was not, of course, meant to be taken as exact; yet the officially approved allowances were not very much more generous, while children under nine years of age were to be dieted 'at discretion'. The bowl of gruel and small piece of bread, which Oliver and his companions eat hungrily in the bare stone hall of the workhouse, cannot have been too uncommon a meal; nor was the beadle, Mr Bumble, choleric and fat, as proud of his oratorical powers as of his own importance, exceptional in being an incompetent official which the new system of poor relief inherited from the old.

The New Poor Law revived the unrest of 1830. When a proposal was made to alter the workhouse at Wroughton in Wiltshire the parishioners demonstrated their disapproval of the measure by walking out of the church *en masse* and smoking their pipes in the graveyard. At Christian Melford there were riots against the rules that separated men from their wives in the workhouses. There were subsequent riots in Sussex and in other counties, too.

The injustices of the Poor Law and the failure of attempts to develop trade unionism were among the complaints voiced by that movement for political reform known as Chartism. The movement took its name from The People's Charter of 1838 which was largely drafted by William Lovett, son of a Cornish master mariner, and his radical friends in the London Working Men's Association. This Charter made six demands of the government. It required annual parliaments, universal male suffrage and vote by secret ballot, equal electoral districts, an end to property qualifications for Members of Parliament and the introduction of salaries for them. These demands were taken up by other Working Men's Associations throughout the country, all determined, in the words of Benjamin Wilson, the Halifax Chartist and Methodist, to obtain 'a voice in making the laws they were called upon to obey'.

Chartism attracted mass support and aroused the deepest fears. Its leaders declared that they would have the Charter 'peaceably' if they could, but 'forcibly' if they must. At immense meetings of supporters, hatred of the governing classes was loudly voiced and the class solidarity of the workers passionately acclaimed. There were rallies in the open on public holidays – one at Halifax on Whit Monday 1839 was said to have attracted a crowd of 200,000 – and there were meetings at night.

> Working people met in their thousands and tens of thousands to swear devotion to the common cause [wrote a Chartist of demonstrations in the factory districts of Lancashire]. It is almost impossible to imagine the excitement caused by these manifestations. The people met at a starting point, from whence, at a given time, they issued in huge numbers, formed into procession, traversing the principal streets, making the heavens echo with the thunder of their cheers on recognizing the idols of their worship in the men who were to address them, and sending forth volleys of the most hideous groans on passing the office of some hostile newspaper, or the house of some obnoxious magistrate or employer. The banners containing the most formidable devices, viewed by the red light of the glaring torches, presented a scene of awful grandeur . . .
>
> The uncouth appearance of thousands of artisans who had not time from leaving the factory to go home and attend to the ordinary duties of cleanliness, and whose faces were therefore begrimed with sweat and dirt, added to the strange aspect of the scene. The processions were frequently of immense length, sometimes containing as many as fifty thousand people; and along the whole line there blazed a stream of light, illuminating the lofty sky, like the reflection from a large city in a general conflagration. The meetings themselves were of a still more terrific character. The very appearance of such a vast number of blazing torches

only seemed more effectually to inflame the minds alike of speakers and hearers.[8]

It seemed on occasions that the demands of the Chartists could not be resisted. In August 1839 a general strike was attempted; and later that year an insurrection broke out in Newport, Monmouthshire, which was suppressed with greater loss of life to the civilian population than any other outbreak of the nineteenth, or, for that matter, of the eighteenth century, greater even than the so-called Peterloo Massacre of 1819 in which fifteen people were killed when a crowd of 60,000 people, gathered near the centre of Manchester to hear the great orator Henry Hunt speak on the urgent need for parliamentary reform, were charged by mounted troops. The immediate objective of the demonstrators in 1839 was the release of Henry Vincent, the Chartist orator, from Newport gaol. About 7000 armed men, mostly miners and iron-workers, marched through the streets of the town and were suddenly fired upon by soldiers when they reached the Westgate Hotel in its centre. At least twenty-two of them were killed.[9]

Chartism itself survived. In 1842 a petition presented to Parliament contained 3 million signatures; and in 1848, the year of revolutions on the Continent, when a massive demonstration was planned in London, it was feared, or hoped, that revolution was about to break out in England too. But the government was resolute. Huge numbers of police were brought into London; 150,000 special constables were enrolled; yeomanry regiments were called up. One Chartist leader declared that the government had proved itself too strong for the workers. Another, the Irish orator, Fergus O'Connor, already suffering from the disease which was to kill him, urged the crowds to depart.[10] Thereafter Chartism, which had consistently failed to build an efficient national organization, gradually declined and eventually disintegrated. The reforms its leaders sought were slow to come.

# 45 · *Below Stairs*

'Does your father keep a coach?' a clergyman's daughter was asked soon after arriving for her first term at a smart boarding school in the late eighteenth century.

'No.'

'How many servants have you?'

'Four.'

'Dear! Only think, Miss's papa does not keep a coach, and they have only four servants.'[1]

Four was certainly considered a modest number of servants for a gentleman to employ at that time. The Rev. John Trusler, author of a book of advice on such matters, recommended that a country squire even of modest means could not manage with less than five. Parson Woodforde, with his quite modest income of about £300 a year, employed a staff of this number, a farming-man who sometimes helped in the house, a footman, a yard-boy and two maids. Woodforde's two clergyman friends, du Quesne and Jeanes, also had five servants. Clergymen and squires of ampler incomes usually had more. The Rev. George Betts, Francis Sitwell, Henry Purefoy and Sanderson Miller all had seven; and John Custance, a Norfolk landowner, ten. Even ten was considered parsimonious by Giles Jacob, author of *The Country Gentleman's Vademecum*, who proposed that the average, fairly large country family should have twenty servants. Many did have as many, and several had more. Mrs Philip Lybbe Powys described an establishment of 1786 which was 'so numerous' she thought it 'uncomfortable – house-steward, man-cook, two gentlemen out of livery, under-butler, Mrs Pratt's two footmen, Mr Pratt's two, upper and under coachmen, two grooms, helpers, etc., etc. These are menservants; female ones, I dare say, in proportion.'[2] There were households enough with over forty servants.

The sixth Duke of Somerset employed twenty-six menservants alone in the 1720s; and at his London house the Duke of Bedford had forty-two male and female servants in 1771. Thomas Coke had about sixty in 1820; and Joseph Farington calculated in 1816 that at Wentworth Woodhouse, which was 'princely in all respects', seventy servants sat down to dinner every day in the servants' hall and a further thirty upper servants in the housekeeper's room.[3] Even Horace Walpole's friend, Mary Berry, considered that it was impossible to live without 'pinching economy and pitiful savings' with fewer than three menservants and four women. Walpole himself at Strawberry Hill had a staff of about ten.[4]

The wealthy middle classes had almost as many servants as the upper: Henry Thrale, the brewer, kept about twenty servants at Streatham; while in the 1770s, John Baker, a lawyer, employed a valet, a coachman, a postilion, a gardener, a boy, a housekeeper, a housemaid, a laundry-maid, a dairymaid and a general maid. By then ordinary tradesmen were taking pride in the number of servants they employed. 'About five and twenty years ago,' remarks the father of Smollett's Humphry Clinker, whose *Expedition* was published in 1771, 'very few even of the most opulent citizens of London kept any equipage, or even any servants in livery . . . At present, every trader in any degree of credit, every broker and attorney, maintains a couple of footmen, a coachman and a postillion.'

In the eighteenth century there were more people working as domestic servants than were employed in any other occupation, except agriculture. In 1851 this still held true; and there were by then almost a million of them, as compared with about 700,000 twenty years before.[5] This represented 13 per cent of the working population. By 1891 the proportion had risen to a peak of nearly 16 per cent, as compared with a far smaller proportion, and a total of no more than 103,000 resident domestic servants, mostly women, in 1961.[6] Commenting on the figures in the census of 1881, the Registrar-General wrote:

Of females above five years of age, one in nine was a domestic servant . . . and of girls between fifteen and twenty years of age no less than one in three was a domestic servant. Such, at least, was the case according to the returns; but . . . there is reason to believe that a considerable number of servant girls who are not yet fifteen years old represent themselves as having reached that age, so as to be more readily taken into service.[7]

As the total number of servants rose in the late nineteenth century, so did the households of the larger country houses: the Duke of Westminster had a staff of over 300 at Eaton Hall.[8] And between the loftiest of the upper servants and the humblest of the lower there were as many grades and ranks as there were in the hierarchy of aristocracy itself. At the annual mop fairs in the country the various grades of lower servants could still be seen advertising themselves by distinctive utensils – cooks with basting ladles, housemaids with brooms or mops, milkmaids with pails – while in the registry offices in towns upper servants provided particulars of their rank and past experience. At the London Society for the Encouragement of Faithful Servants an applicant's name was never placed on the books unless evidence of two years' service in one place could be produced.[9]

Among the upper servants were included the house steward and his female counterpart, the housekeeper. The house steward was usually a most impressive figure quite capable of keeping a large staff in order as well as looking after the household accounts and ordering the supplies. Lord Ernest Hamilton always remembered the steward at his family home, Chesterfield House, Mayfair, a stately figure in a short frock-coat and with a pointed grey beard. 'Good morning, Burgh,' Lord Ernest would say when he met this imposing servant in the passage or on the stairs; and the steward would flatten himself against the wall and reply: 'Your most obedient, my lord.'[10]

Housekeepers, who presided over the store-room, kept the housekeeping accounts, made the drawing-room tea, and wore no uniform, were usually quite as imposing. Basing the character upon recollections of his own grandmother, who had been appointed housekeeper at Crewe Hall, Cheshire, in 1785 at a salary of eight guineas a year, Dickens described Mrs Rouncewell, housekeeper at Chesney Wold:

> Mrs Rouncewell is rather deaf, which nothing will induce her to believe. She is a fine old lady, handsome, stately, wonderfully neat, and has such a back, and such a stomacher, that if her stays should turn out when she dies to have been a broad old-fashioned family fire-grate, nobody who knows her would have cause to be surprised.[11]

Next in rank below the house steward in the male hierarchy was the groom of the chambers whose many duties at Burley, country house of the Earl of Nottingham, were listed as follows:

> You must be careful of the furniture, brushing and cleaning every morning that which is in constant use, and the rest also once in the week or oftener if need be.
>
> You must make fires in the hall, parlour, etc., where required, keeping clean the hearths and often coming in to repair them, and at night to snuff ye candles.

You are to attend in the Hall when there is Company, and also at other times, but in this last you shall be relieved by ye footmen in turns.

You must take care of all keys in your custody, not to break them, but especially yt they be not lost.

You must bar all the windows, *lock all the outward doors every night when the family is in bed, and rise so early as to open them in time for such as have occasion to come into the house*, and to take care to put out all fires and candles at night.

When any strangers lodge here you must diligently attend ym. taking care that there be fires, candles, etc., in good order, and that nothing be wanting.

You are to ring the bell for prayers and lay the cushens and take them away when done, and to keep them and all the furniture of the chappell (when ready) clean.[12]

After the groom of the chambers came the butler who looked after the wine, presided over the dining-room and made regular rounds of the reception rooms, ensuring that all was in order, the blinds drawn if necessary, the fires burning satisfactorily and the newspapers well aired, neatly cut and folded, and, in some houses, ironed.[13] The butler's day was long; but not as long as the valet's who had to wake his master in the morning with his shaving water and to wait up until he saw fit to go to bed, helping him undress and taking clothes and shoes away for washing, brushing and polishing. The valet's counterpart was the lady's-maid who had not only to look after her mistress's clothes but also brush her hair, tie it in curling papers at night, and apply lotions and ointments to her skin.

Last of the upper servants were the cooks and chef, well-rewarded specialists, the most talented of whom were the envy of all their masters' friends and neighbours. In the eighteenth and early nineteenth centuries the richer households had confectioners and bakers as well as male roasting cooks, female assistant cooks, kitchen maids and kitchen boys. Some had French chefs as well. Antonin Carême was for a time employed at Carlton House by the Prince Regent who offered him the enormous salary of £500 a year and a pension of £250 a year to persuade him to return to London after he had left to enter the service of Baron Rothschild. Alexis Soyer was chef to the Duke of Sutherland and the Marquess of Waterford before his appointment to the Reform Club. The extravagant Duke of Buckingham also had a French chef as well as an English roasting cook and an Italian confectioner, and, when advised to get rid of the confectioner on the grounds of economy, was said to have plaintively remonstrated: 'Good God! Mayn't a man have a biscuit with his glass of sherry?'

Leading the ranks of the under servants were the footmen. It was their duty to take coals into the reception rooms, clean the boots and plate, trim lamps, lay the breakfast and, in livery of knee breeches, silk stockings and powdered hair, to wait at table; and, in the afternoons, to answer the front door; or, if on carriage duty, to attend their masters or mistresses, standing on the platform at the back of the coach, ready to jump down to lower folding steps as soon as the horses were brought to a halt by the coachman. When their employers went out walking, the footmen would follow them at a respectful distance, hurrying ahead to knock on a door when a call was to be made. In the days of sedan chairs they walked in front of the chairmen, clearing a path. On Sundays they walked behind their mistresses to church carrying the prayer books.

In his journal, William Tayler, footman to the widow of a rich East India Company merchant who had become Member of Parliament for Queensborough, gave an account of a Sunday in his 'very buisy' life in the 1830s:

> I got up at half past seven, cleaned the clothes and knives [and] lamps, got the parlour breakfast, lit my pantry fire, cleared breakfast and washed it away, dressed myself, went to church, came back, got parlour lunch, had my own dinner, sit by the fire and red the Penny Magazine and opnd the door when any visitors came. At 4 o'clock had my tea, took the lamps and candles up into the drawing room, shut the shutters, took glass, knives, plate and settera into the dining room, layed the cloth for dinner, took the dinner up at six o'clock, waited at dinner, brought the things down again at seven, washed them up, brought down the desert, got ready the tea, took it up at eight o'clock, brought it down at half past, washed up, had my supper at nine, took down the lamps and candles at half past ten and went to bed at eleven.[14]

Usually on Sundays, Tayler went to see his wife and children; and this was the only day in the week on which he did see them. There were three maidservants in the house but he was the sole footman, and he consequently had to perform many duties which in other households would have been done by the second or third footman or by the under-butler. As well as footmen and under-butlers, larger households would also employ watchmen and grooms, postilions, lamp-men and candle-men, odd-men, and steward's-room-men, pages and ushers of the hall, office clerks and plate burnishers, hall-boys, servant's-hall-boys, boot-boys, messenger-boys and, of course, gardeners and garden-boys. Some households could still boast of musicians, chaplains, librarians and tutors, others of birdkeepers and apiarists; one even had an old man living in a hermitage instead of the stuffed hermits to be seen peering lugubriously out of grottoes elsewhere.[15] At Chatsworth, and at Belvoir, there was a resident upholsterer; at Longleat there was a chimney-sweep as well as a courier who made all arrangements for the family's journeys; at Belvoir there was a watchman who went about the terraces and battlements and along the paths, and if a guest woke in the night in the castle he 'would hear a padded foot on the gravel outside and a voice, not loud enough to waken but strong enough to reassure, saying "Past twelve o'clock. All's well."'

In her memoirs Lady Diana Cooper, third daughter of the eighth Duke of Rutland, remembered how at Belvoir in the 1890s 'the gong rang for dressing-time, getting louder and louder, as it approached down the unending passage':

The gong man was an old retainer, one of those numberless ranks of domestic servants which have completely disappeared and today seem fabulous. He was admittedly very old. He wore a white beard to his waist. Three times a day he rang the gong – for luncheon, for dressing-time, for dinner. He would walk down the interminable passages, his livery hanging a little loosely on his bent old bones, clutching his gong with one hand and with the other feebly brandishing the padded-knobbed stick with which he struck it. Every corridor had to be warned and the towers too, so I suppose he banged on and off for ten minutes, thrice daily.

Then there were the lamp-and-candle men, at least three of them, for there was no other form of lighting. Gas was despised, I forget why – vulgar I think. They polished and scraped the wax off the candelabra, cut wicks, poured paraffin oil and unblackened glass chimneys all day long. After dark they were busy turning wicks up and down, snuffing candles, and de-waxing extinguishers. It was not a department we liked much to visit. It smelt disgusting and the lamp-men were too busy. But the upholsterer's room was a great treat. He was exactly like a Hans Andersen tailor. Crosslegged he sat in a tremendous confusion of curtains and covers, fringes, buttons, rags and carpets, bolsters, scraps (that could be begged off him), huge curved needles like scimitars, bodkins, hunks of beeswax to strengthen thread, and hundreds of flags. The flags on the tower-top, I suppose, got punished by the winds and were constantly in need of repair. I never saw him actually at work on anything else. There were slim flags for wind, little ones for rain, huge ones for sunshine, hunting flags, and many others.

The water-men are difficult to believe in today. They seemed to me to belong to another clay. They were the biggest people I had ever seen, much bigger than any of the men of the family, who were remarkable for their height. They had stubbly beards and a general Bill Sikes appearance. They wore brown clothes, no collars and thick green baize aprons from chin to knee. On their shoulders they carried a wooden yoke from which hung two gigantic cans of water. They moved on a perpetual round. Above the ground floor there was not a drop of hot water and not one bath, so their job was to keep all jugs, cans and kettles full in the bedrooms, and morning or evening to bring the hot water for the hip-baths. We were always a little frightened of the water-men. They seemed of another element and never spoke but one word, 'Water-man,' to account for themselves.[16]

At Belvoir, in addition to these innumerable menservants, there was 'a regiment of maids' under the control of Lena, the head housemaid, and Mrs Smith, the housekeeper, 'sparkling with jet arabesques'. There were also, as there were in all other large country houses, ladies'-maids and house-maids, still-room maids and scullery-maids, kitchen-maids, laundry-maids and dairymaids. At Holkham in 1851 there were, as well as a housekeeper, a female cook and a female baker, five housemaids, three nursery-maids, three kitchen-maids, four laundry-maids, two charwomen, a lady's-maid, a dairy-maid, a nurse and a governess.

The domestic offices in which the maids and menservants performed their various duties were as numerous as their own ranks. There were housemaids' pantries on the upper floors, butlers' pantries and sculleries below; there were linen-rooms and knife-rooms and lamp-rooms, leather-rooms and boot-rooms, gun-rooms and brushing-rooms, wash-houses and mangling-rooms, ironing-rooms, folding-rooms and airing-rooms. And in many of these rooms lists of strict rules were displayed instructing servants in the correct methods to be employed in carrying out their duties, and warning them against the improper use of materials and of such tools as knife-cleaning machines. At Longleat in the 1830s there was a list of materials which included over 600 towels, all of them marked and each designated for a particular use; there were also nearly as many cloths – special china cloths and dusters for the housemaids, glass cloths for the butler, pocket cloths for the footmen, rubbers for the kitchen-maids, lamp cloths for the porter, horn cloths for the servants'-hall-boy.[17] The dustpans were all numbered: each housemaid had her own and had to learn how to hold it, together with a candle, in one hand so that she could use the brush with the other. She also had to learn how to polish the metal fittings on furniture with fine sand, how to polish paintwork with cream dressing, how to sweep carpets with damp tea leaves, how to take off old polish with vinegar and put on new with beeswax and turpentine; how to wash high ceilings with soda and water while standing on the top of step-ladders; how to dust down brocaded walls and rub them over with tissue paper and then with silk dusters; how to unstring and scrub Venetian blinds; how to take up carpets; how to whiten corridors with pipe-clay and spread French chalk on a floor before a ball; how to make a bed and black a bedroom grate with a mixture of ivory black, treacle, oil, small beer and sulphuric acid. She also had to remember at what time the sunlight came into various rooms so that the blinds could be drawn to protect the furniture. And she was very poorly paid.

The wages of domestic servants had never been high. In the eighteenth century they varied widely from place to place and much depended upon a servant's experience and upon the perquisites which might be expected. The rates recommended in books such as John Mordaunt's *Complete Steward* of 1761 and advertisements in newspapers both indicate that wages in themselves were rarely an inducement to those seeking work in domestic service. Mordaunt's list of recommended wages gives £4 a year for an under-housemaid, £5 for a head housemaid, £5 for an under-footman, £7 for a head footman, and only £3 for a postilion. In 1740 a footman was engaged for no more than £2 15s a year by a gentleman in Sussex; while in 1770 a Lancashire baronet was able to employ a cook for as little as £5 a year. Some advertisements offered higher rates: one, for a footman-gardener in 1762, gave notice that the would-be employer was willing to pay between £10 and £12 a year; another, for a porter in 1792, offered up to £16.[18] Wages certainly improved as the century progressed. James Woodforde was paying his footman £3 a year in 1766; but in the 1780s he felt obliged to increase this to five guineas and by 1787 he was paying £8.[19] In the nineteenth century wages continued to rise, but they did so very slowly and women's much more slowly than men's. In the course of the 1850s and 1860s housemaids' wages went up from about £11 to £14 a year; and cooks' from about £11 to £17. Yet there were still some poor maids-of-all-work who were paid no more than 2s a week, though skilled and pretty lady's-maids could earn more than cooks, and the wages of nursemaids increased to about £17 a year.[20] At Holkham in 1865 a young lady's-maid was getting £18 a year, the scullery-maids £12 a year, the cook £50, the coachmen £40 each, the valet £60, the gardener £90, the German governess £80 and the French governess £105 (which was £5 more than the Rev. Alex Napier, Lord Leicester's librarian). By 1894 the valets' wages had gone up to £70 a year; the kitchen-maids were being paid between £16 and £24; and the housemaids between £12 and £22.[21]

In the eighteenth century servants had generally been compensated for low wages by ample food, by the provision of clothes and by various other allowances. Those who did not want beer were often supplied with beer money; and when the family was away they were given extra board money to cater for themselves. In large eighteenth-century houses, according to the duc de La Rochefoucauld, there was 'a supply of cold meat, tea and punch' on the servants' tables 'from morning to night'.[22] Another observer considered that 'servants in great families wantonly' ate five times as much meat as nature really required. Jonas Hanway said that in some houses the domestic staff had meat three times a day; and certainly at Canons, the Duke of Chandos's servants had one and a half pounds of beef every Tuesday, Thursday and Sunday, the same amounts of mutton on Monday and Friday and of pork on Wednesday and Saturday. They also had 'pastries, jellies and tarts' and fruit 'in the greatest profusion'.[23]

In most eighteenth-century houses, however, there seems to have been a marked difference between the food eaten by the lower servants in the servants' hall and that enjoyed by the upper servants in the steward's or housekeeper's room, the 'Pug's Parlour' as it came to be known, a 'pug' being an upper servant in a large establishment. The food at the steward's table at the Duke of Kingston's house, Thoresby Hall, would not, so it was said, have disgraced 'a gentleman of ten thousand a year'; but that in the servants' hall was far less appetising; and, according to Nancy Woodforde, a butler and housekeeper were quite capable of entertaining 'so much company that the other servants were kept short of everything that they ought to have'.[24]

Hungry servants in large houses, however, seem to have been rare; and in the later nineteenth century unknown. At Longleat in the 1890s luncheon was announced by a handbell rung in the servants' hall where the lower servants took their places standing at the table until the upper servants, led by the housekeeper and butler, arrived from the steward's room. The butler then indicated that they might all sit down, whereupon, after grace had been said, the meat course was served. After this the upper servants left the servants' hall to have the rest of the meal in the privileged quiet of the steward's room. At Welbeck the two classes of servants did not mix except on Twelfth Night when a splendid ball was given for all the servants, tenants and their families as well as the local tradesmen. On this occasion they were attended to by fifty hired waiters, while an orchestra from London played in the huge underground ballroom. On other days the upper servants ate in the steward's room where their meals, served on fine china and accompanied by wine, were of the highest quality. They had clean napkins every day, and their own silver napkin rings. At supper the men wore smoking jackets and the women dress blouses.[25] Toasts were regularly drunk to the duke and duchess and their family.

> The food was of the best and no stint [recalled an upper servant in the household of a Scottish baronet], wine and whiskey were provided in the steward's room – beer and ale for the servants in the hall. The health of Sir H– and my Lady were drunk every night, in both rooms, the butler proposing it in the steward's room and the under butler in the servants' hall. A rap on the table, then in a reverential tone came the toast – 'Sir H– and my Lady.'

'With all my heart,' was the response.

The second toast given in old families is the 'Young Family', but as there was no young family's health to propose, it was substituted by another, 'Our noble selves.' It was the custom to fill a half-pint horn and drain it off for each toast. The ale was strong . . . and two horns were as much as could be taken in safety, which put some of the drinkers in a merry mood for the rest of the evening.[26]

Servants in smaller households also usually ate well. Mrs Prinsep's footman described dinners of roast beef and vegetables, dumplings and damson pie, and 'very good table ale' of which 'everyone could have as much as they liked'. But maids who were the only servants of poorer familes often did go hungry like Elsie, the maid-of-all-work, in Arnold Bennett's *Riceyman Steps*, who for days on end does not eat 'enough to satisfy a cat'; and one night, in the grip of a tyrannical appetite, she is discovered by her mistress in the light of a candle 'not merely eating bacon but eating raw bacon'.[27]

Lilian Westhall, maid-of-all-work to a dentist and his wife in Chiswick would have sympathized with Elsie. Up at six in the morning, she worked a seventeen-hour day for 5s a week, making sure that the whole house was spotless for her mistress who 'explained she was very particular':

The meals I remember well. For breakfast I had bread and dripping. There were often mice dirts on the dripping to be scraped off first. Dinner was herring, every day; tea was bread and marge. I didn't have a bath during the month I was there, I wasn't given the opportunity; no time to comb my hair properly.

My room was in the attic. There was a little iron bed in the corner, a wooden chair and a washstand. It was a cold, bare, utterly cheerless room. At night I used to climb the dark stairs to the gloomy top of the house, go over to my bed, put the candle on the chair, fall on my knees, say my prayers, and crawl into bed too tired to wash.[28]

Maidservants in houses like this were usually relegated to the attics, although in terrace houses in London and other towns they often slept in the basement like the succession of maids employed at between £8 and £12 a year by Thomas and Jane Carlyle at 5 Great Cheyne Row, Chelsea. There were two dark kitchens in the basement of the eight-roomed house; one at the back, which was used as a washhouse, the other at the front, where the cooking was done on an antiquated range. In the back kitchen – a cheerless, stone-paved room where Thomas Carlyle emptied buckets of cold water over himself as he stood in a tin bath – the maid kept her clothes. And in the front kitchen, when her hard day's work was done at last, she lay down to sleep, but not until the master had finished his pipe, which he liked to smoke by the dying embers of the fire, sitting up late, while beyond the door in the cold back kitchen the maid waited anxiously for the sounds that heralded his departure upstairs to bed. She then could go to her own – which was infested with bugs – after a supper of cold porridge.

Yet if the maidservants disliked working for a temperamental mistress and a selfish master who, according to his wife, 'considered it a sin against the Holy Ghost to set a chair or a plate two inches off the spot they have been used to stand on', the Carlyles were equally dissatisfied with their maidservants, thirty-four of them in thirty-two years. There was Jane, a clumsy, dreamy creature, who poured water over her mistress's foot instead of into the coffee-pot and who became so absorbed in reading her book that she forgot to light the fire. There was a 'mutinous Irish savage' with 'a face like a Polar Bear', and a primitive Scottish girl, who loved answering the door but failed to announce the boisterous actress, Fanny Kemble, being 'entirely in a non-plus whether she had let in a leddy or a gentleman', and who had a tiresome 'follower' in the shape of a soldier, by whom she seems to have become pregnant. There was Helen, who was dirty and drank and whom her mistress discovered one day 'lying on the floor, dead-drunk, spread out . . . with a chair upset beside her, and in the midst of a perfect chaos of dirty dishes and fragments of broken crockery'. After her came 'The Beauty' who spent her time looking through keyholes and reading Mrs Carlyle's letters and who left complaining that she could not live in a house that was 'such a muddle'; an 'old halfdead' woman with a 'shocking bad temper'; and 'a little girl . . . who could not cook a morsel of food or make a bed, or do any civilised thing'.[29]

In households larger and more generous than the Carlyles', servants enjoyed various allowances and perquisites, other than food and beer money, which made their low wages acceptable. Many could look forward to cast-off clothing. The Duke of Kingston's valet regularly received 'his wardrobe before Easter Newmarket meeting and the Saturday before October meeting'.[30] Other servants were given old clothes when their conduct was deemed satisfactory. New liveries were not, however, necessarily the property of the servant who wore them. James Woodforde told a newly employed footman in 1785 to remember that his livery and greatcoat were not given to him but only to be worn while employed in his master's service;[31] and at Hatfield, towards the end of the nineteenth century, liveries which had been used for a year belonged to the servants who had worn them; those worn for less than a year were Lord Salisbury's property and had to be given back to him 'on leaving service'.[32]

Occasionally servants were driven to complain of the threadbare clothes which were provided for them. 'I humbly beg your ladyship will be pleased to consider my clothing,' Lady Strafford's gamekeeper felt obliged to write to her, 'for with walking about the park and woods I am got as ragged as a sheep; its upwards of two years since I had any and my lord was pleased to be so good as tell me I should have a frock every year and a plush coat every two years, and a laced hat as other noblemen's keepers had.'[33] Most employers however, were anxious to ensure that their servants' appearance did their masters credit. Indeed, rich employers vied with each other to provide their servants with liveries that were not merely impressive but startling in their richness. Jonas Hanway declared that in the past it had been 'a rare thing to see any gold or silver lace on the clothes of a domestic servant in livery'; yet now footmen appeared 'in rich vestments, besilvered and begilded like the servants of sovereign princes'.[34] Ten years later Lord Derby's coachmen were described, 'with their red feathers and flame coloured silk stockings', as looking 'like so many figurantes taken from behind the scenes of the Opera House'.[35] Even maidservants, so Carl Moritz said, were turned out in a way that reflected the greatest credit upon the households from which they came:

> The appearance of the female domestics will, perhaps, astonish a foreign visitor more than anything in London. They are in general handsome and well-clothed. They are usually clad in gowns well adjusted to their shapes, and hats adorned with ribbands. There are some who even wear silk and sattin.[36]

Such items of clothing as shirts and neckwear and, usually, shoes had to be provided by the servants themselves; and it was often difficult for a man applying for a new appointment to judge how to dress when presenting himself for interview. John Macdonald, who had twenty-eight different masters in thirty-nine years of service, once appeared for an interview in 'a gold laced vest and other things in form', only to be informed that he was considered unsuitable for the post since he 'looked more like a gentleman than a servant'. Determined not to repeat his mistake, he presented himself for his next appointment in the plainest clothes and was again rejected, his prospective employer's footman explaining, 'I am sorry I did not tell you to dress yourself finer, for Sir Francis is very nice.'[37]

For Macdonald one of the great pleasures of being a footman was the opportunity it gave him of walking about 'in good clothes with rich vests', in wearing the 'genteelest' livery, 'richly trimmed with silver'. Another pleasure was that of travelling. With one of his several masters, the Earl of Galloway's brother, Macdonald went all over the country from hunt to hunt, 'to Oxfordshire, to Blenheim, to Lord Foley's, to Lord Thanet's, Stow-in-the-Wold, Cheltenham in Gloucestershire, Hampshire and Bedfordshire'.[38] Indeed, many men entered domestic service largely because of the opportunities it offered for wearing fine clothes, for travel, for sexual adventures and for social advancement. It was very rarely, of course, that a footman could rise so far as to marry his employer, like Lady Henrietta Wentworth's footman; and it was almost as rarely that a female servant married her master like Samuel Richardson's Pamela and the cook of Boswell's attorney acquaintance who was taken as his wife 'because she dressed a lovely bit of collop'. But servants did expect to take on some of the social standing of their masters and mistresses; and were very happy to be known by their names. It might be considered demeaning for a footman to lose his own name and be referred to as John or Robert or by whatever name footmen were known in a particular household to save the family the trouble of remembering what their real names were; yet there was always the chance that they would one day be promoted to the post of butler and then be known by their proper surname and be addressed by other servants as 'Mister'; just as one day a maid might become a housekeeper and be known as 'Mrs' whether she were married or not. And in the meantime it was quite pleasurable, when their employers were on visits to other houses, to be addressed by noble titles. The Earl of Leicester's granddaughter was once amused to hear one manservant call out to another, 'I say, Stanhope, did you clean Rosebery's boots?'[39]

Association with the great was supposed to confer a kind of gentility upon those who worked for them; and the more distinguished the master or mistress the more respect his footmen or maids felt was their due. A lady's-maid, in referring to a grocer in a copy of the *Carlton House Magazine*, is made to remark, 'Such low people are beneath our attention, though some have the *frontery* to put themselves upon a footing with a nobleman's attendant.'

> We sometimes condescend indeed to talk with them in familiar terms, as if they were our equals [she continues], and this has encouraged them to be arrogant. That enormous mass of a woman, our butcher's wife in St James's Market, accosts me with as much freedom and as little *embarrassment* as if she had belonged to a family of rank as well as myself. But I always discountenance such people and convince them that I know how to support the *spear* of life to which my stars have elevated me.[40]

Servants as socially pretentious as this abounded. The Rev. William Jones, writing at the beginning of the nineteenth century, described a 'great mushroom man' named Rogers who had begun his career in Lord Monson's stables. Jones could scarcely credit the man's humble beginnings, for he had risen to be steward and in the discharge of his duties and the collection of the estate rents, he assumed an air of such consequence it seemed 'that he supposed the house and land to be his own'.[41]

This man's rise through the hierarchy of domestic service – or the move from service in a lesser to a greater house – was what many servants set their hearts upon; and it was an ambition often realized. Messenger-boys became footmen, footmen rose to be butlers, butlers were appointed stewards. William Lanceley, who began his working life as hall-boy to the local squire, rose to be steward to the Duke of Connaught.[42] Nancy Bare, who was taken from a Hampshire poorhouse to work as a weeder in the gardens of a local family, later became a kitchen-maid. She performed her duties so well that after she had been 'carefully instructed in all branches of education', she was taken on as a lady's-maid.[43]

Also, a career in domestic service frequently led to more profitable careers in other fields. Many domestics became innkeepers: John Macdonald saved enough to open a hotel. Others became landladies of lodging-houses; coachmen and grooms set up as dealers in saddlery; footmen became grocers, like the royal footman, William Fortnum, who opened a shop quite close to the site of the present store that still bears his name. The Duke of Chandos's valet, having saved money and 'gained information' at Canons, became a surgeon.

These were the fortunate ones. So were the servants in such families as that of William Hogarth, a strict but kindly master and 'a punctual paymaster', who painted them all looking remarkably contented, and that of the Yorkes of Erddig in North Wales where their portraits were also painted and where their masters wrote verses about them.

The low wages of servants were also frequently offset by various traditional perquisites such as candle-ends and empty bottles, the dripping, bones and cinders sold by cooks, by the old carriage wheels sold by coachmen, by commissions and presents from shopkeepers, and, perhaps, by legacies and gifts.

No perquisites had been more widely resented by those from whom they were exacted than the tips known as vails. The diaries of foreign visitors to England in the eighteenth century are full of complaints about the importunities of servants who expected or demanded vails, who lined up in rows when a guest departed from a house to receive the gratuity appropriate to their calling. In some houses, so Jonas Hanway said, the servants actually adopted a fixed scale of rates for all the various services provided for guests.[44] 'If a Duke gives me a Dinner four Times a Week,' Baron de Pollnitz complained, 'his Footmen would pocket as much of my Money as would serve my Expenses at the Tavern for a Week.'[45] Johann von Archenholz agreed that it was cheaper to pay for a meal in a tavern than accept an invitation from a man of quality. And César de Saussure recorded:

If you wish to pay your respects to a nobleman and to visit him, you must give his porter money from time to time, else his master will never be at home for you. If you take a meal with a person of rank, you must give every one of the five or six footmen a coin when leaving. They will be ranged in file in the hall, and the least you can give them is one shilling each, and should you fail to do this, you will be treated insolently the next time. My Lord Southwell stopped me one day in the park, and reproached me most amicably with my having let some time pass before going to his house to take soup with him. 'In truth, my lord,' I answered, 'I am not rich enough to take soup with you often.' His lordship understood my meaning and smiled. This is an abuse that noblemen and gentlemen have vainly endeavoured to abolish.[46]

Englishmen knew only too well that the guest who declined to pay vails was more than likely to regret it. He was 'a marked man'. If he asked for beer, he would be given a piece of bread; if he asked for wine, he would receive, after a long delay, 'a mixture of the whole sideboard in a greasy glass'. Nobody would notice his empty plate; and he would be served 'fish sauce with his mutton and pickles with his apple pye'.[47]

The custom had become so widespread that the amount a servant might expect to receive in vails was set out in advertisements, and was an important factor in the computation of wages. In an issue of the *Daily Advertiser* in 1765 the unusually high remuneration of £17 a year was offered to a footman, but then came the explanation: 'the vails are small.' The same newspaper contained an advertisement for a footman's place at only £8 a year; but in this case the value of the vails was said to double the figure.

Efforts by employers to stamp out the practice of giving vails met with furious objection from servants, although in some households the master's command that no vails should be accepted was quickly obeyed. One of William Hogarth's sitters, a Mr Cole, offered a small tip to a servant who opened the door for him on his departure: 'But the man very quickly refused it, telling me it would be as much as the loss of his place if his master knew it. This was so uncommon, and so liberal in a man of Mr *Hogarth's* profession at that time of day, that it struck me, as nothing of the sort had happened to me before.'[48] In Scotland the movement to abolish the custom gained ground rapidly after 1760 when a gallery full of riotous servants in Edinburgh attempted to prevent the performance of Townley's *High Life Below Stairs* which presented members of their calling in a particularly unfavourable light. But in England employers who forbade their servants to accept vails often lost them to others who allowed them to do so; and in 1761, so the *London Chronicle* reported, an admiral's valet, denied his customary gratuities, cut to pieces the hat of one of his master's guests and made plans to sprinkle the clothes of others with aqua fortis. Sir Francis Dashwood, a leading opponent of vails-giving, was told in a threatening letter that he would 'sartenly lose his life if he persisted in denying tips to Sarvants that has but nine Pounds tha cannot ceepe a Wife and Female'.[49]

In 1764 there were 'great riots at Ranelagh among those *beings*, the footmen', according to the Earl of Malmesbury's mother; 'and there was fighting with drawn swords, for some hours.' Riots broke out again two days later with increased violence. But already the custom of vails collecting had been abandoned in many houses; and by 1771 it was said not to be suffered 'in any genteel familes'. In 1778 Lord Hutchinson found that it was 'laid down almost everywhere'; and ten years later, although one or two large households still maintained the practice – and continued to do so well into the nineteenth century – it had elsewhere quite died out, an example, so Hannah More declared, of what could be done by the example of 'the Great'.[50]

Hannah More, however, still had occasion to complain of another imposition, the practice whereby guests were expected to place money for playing-cards beneath candlesticks for the butler or the groom of the chamber. Her contemporaries also complained of the impositions levied both by porters who required tips to open gates or doors – and who were always ready to inform the close-fisted that their masters were not at home – and by housekeepers, butlers and others who charged such large fees for showing people round their master's houses that Dr John Shebbeare said as much money was laid out upon visiting houses as was spent on building them. Agreeing with Shebbeare, Horace Walpole once protested that he would have to marry his housekeeper at Strawberry Hill if only to recoup the fortune the house had cost him.

Country houses were customarily opened to any respectable visitors who called and asked permission to enter. When Elizabeth Bennet visits Pemberley in Jane Austen's *Pride and Prejudice*, she is immediately admitted to the hall on applying to see the place; the housekeeper comes to take her round and, after being shown 'all of the house that was open to general inspection', she takes leave of the housekeeper, 'a respectable-looking, elderly woman', and is consigned to the gardener at the hall door.[51] Similarly, on his tour of England in 1810–11, Louis Simond, the indefatigable American sightseer, found no difficulty in gaining admittance to the country houses he passed on his travels. At Hatfield 'there was some doubt whether' he should be allowed in 'as the Duke of Clarence was expected on a visit, the Marquess of Salisbury being already come to receive his noble visitor, and the whole house in the full tide of preparation. But the servants, good souls [were] very unwilling to disappoint strangers and [he] saw all.'[52]

Elsewhere Simond found the servants only too willing to admit him because of the fees and tips they were anxious to exact. 'The domestics of these noble houses,' he commented, 'are generally as obsequious as innkeepers, and for the same motives.' At Chatsworth he was soon surrounded by 'porters, footmen and gardeners'; and at Blenheim, so he recorded,

> We were first conducted to a small house on the left, containing a humble appendage to the glory of the Marlboroughs, viz. a cabinet or gallery of old china; and were made to undergo the sight of a whole series of dishes and teapots, mostly very coarse, rude, and ugly. The guardian of these treasures is, very properly, a female. Whether she perceived our unworthiness, I do not know, but there seemed to be a sort of tacit agreement between us to dispatch the business as quickly as possible. Having paid our fees, we drove on . . . [and were soon] overtaken by a gardener, who came after us au grand galop, mounted on an ass, to direct our admiration to particular spots (all tame enough), and get his 2s 6d. On the limits of his jurisdiction, the park, he delivered us over to another cicerone, an old servant who descanted on the architecture. He committed us to the charge of another domestic, our fifth guide (a great division of labour), who opened to us a small theatre, used formerly by the family and their friends. A sixth man took us round the pleasure-grounds.
>
> The seventh guide was a coxcomb of an upper servant, who hurried us through the house. The fees of all our different guides amounted to nineteen shillings. The annual income of the Duke of Marlborough is estimated at L. 70,000. There are eighty house-servants; one hundred out of doors, of whom thirty are for the pleasure-grounds.[53]

In some houses, for example at Canons, it was understood that the fees would be handed over to the owner for the maintenance of the fabric and the defraying of household expenses; but in most the servants pocketed the money themselves and thus added considerable amounts to their income. In her will the old housekeeper at Warwick Castle left the younger members of the family, to whom she was devoted, no less than £20,000 which she was said to have collected over many years from visitors to their home.[54]

Although savings on the scale of the Warwick Castle housekeeper were highly exceptional if not unique, many upper servants were able to save part of their earnings. Lower servants, however, were hard put to it to do so; and 'we must remember', as the *Edinburgh Review* advised its readers in 1862, 'that the [class of domestic servants as a whole] does not consist of butlers at £50 a year or lady's-maids with about the same pay in money or gifts':

We must include a million and more of general servants, housemaids, middle-class cooks and nurserymaids, whose wages lie between £18 and £8 a year . . . Of the 400,000 maids-of-all-work few have more than £10 a year and many have no more than £8. It is absurd to talk of their laying by money . . . How much can the housemaid lay by of her £10, £12 or £15 a year, or the middle-class cook out of her £12, £15 or £18? Some persons who lecture them on improvidence assume that out of £15 they might lay by £10, and so on; but any sensible housewife will say at once that this is absurd. The plainest and most economical style of dress, respectable enough for a middle-class kitchen, cannot, we are assured, be provided for less than £6 in the country and £7 in town. Then, is the maidservant never to do a kind thing to her own family or anybody else – never to pay postage – never to buy a book or anything that is not wearable? . . .

'The number of old servants who are paupers in workhouses is immense . . .' we learn from Prince Albert's address to the Servants' Provident Society on 16 May 1849. How can the position of the domestic servant ever be elevated if the career ends in the workhouse? . . .[55]

In the years immediately following the appearance of this article, the wages of servants did improve slightly as alternative work in factories and shops, particularly for women, became more plentiful. In the first (1861) edition of Mrs Beeton's *Book of Household Management* wages of £7 10s to £11 (with tea, sugar and beer) were recommended for general servants, £12 to £26 for cooks and £25 for valets. In the 1888 edition these figures were increased to as much as £16 for general servants, to a minimum of £16 for cooks and of £35 for valets. At the same time the total number of domestic servants in England and Wales was growing year by year as increasing numbers of middle-class families felt able to afford them. It was estimated in the 1850s that a man with £500 a year ought to be able to afford three servants, and that one with £1000 should be able to employ six. At that time there were some 850,000 men and women employed in domestic service in England and Wales, about 575,000 of them female general servants. By 1871 the total number had increased to over 1,300,000, and general maidservants to over 780,000. The numbers continued to increase between 1871 and 1911 but by then the growth was slower than that of the population as a whole, while the proportion of young girls entering domestic service was falling sharply.[56]

For those who remained in service as general maidservants life continued to be hard. They still commonly worked far longer hours than women in factories, and when the factories were silent they had to work on. They were still kept in uniform, in black dresses in the afternoons with white aprons and caps; they were still often required to share a room or even a bed with another maid if there was a second servant in the household; they were still provided with books of prayers which instructed them to seek divine help in bearing rebukes with patience and in preserving them from idleness and 'wasting the time which is another's'; and they still slept beneath framed biblical texts bearing some such injunction as that from Ephesians: 'Servants be obedient to them that are your masters according to the flesh, with fear and trembling, in singleness of your heart.'[57]

# 46 · Shops and Shopping

Walking down 'lively' Oxford Street in 1786, Sophie von la Roche was deeply impressed by the splendid shops on either side, their façades brightly lit by oil lamps, their doors open until ten o'clock at night. She passed a watch-maker's, then a shop selling fans and silk, then one for china and glass. She thought the spirit booths were 'particularly tempting', with their crystal flasks of every shape and form, each one with a light behind 'which makes all the different coloured spirits sparkle'. Just as alluring were the confectioners and fruiterers, 'where, behind the handsome glass windows, pyramids of pineapples, figs, grapes, oranges and all manner of fruits' were on show. Most of all she admired a stall with Argand lamps 'situated in a corner house and forming a really dazzling spectacle. Every variety of lamp, crystal, lacquer and metal ones, silver and brass in every possible shade'. Even the butchers' shops struck her as being 'deliciously clean'. There was 'no blood anywhere, no dirt: the shop walls and doors were all spruce, balance and weights brightly polished'.[1]

Behind the great glass windows of London's shops, Sophie von la Roche wrote in another enthusiastic passage, 'absolutely everything one can think of is neatly, attractively displayed, in such abundance of choice as to make one greedy':

> Now large slipper and shoe-shops for anything from adults down to dolls, can be seen; now fashion-articles or silver or brass shops, boots, guns, glasses, the confectioner's goodies, the pewterer's wares, fans, etc. . . . There is a cunning devise for showing women's materials. They hang down in folds behind the fine, high windows so that the effect of this or that material, as it would be in a woman's dress, can be studied.[2]

Had she turned down Charles Street from Oxford Street and gone through Soho Square into Greek Street, Sophie von la Roche would have come to the magnificent showrooms of Josiah Wedgwood who had moved here from Great Newport Street in 1774. In these rooms Wedgwood's wares were displayed in cabinets along the walls and on large tables, laid out as though a dinner party were about to be given. Salesmen discreetly moved about between the columns that rose from the polished floor to the plastered ceiling; and on stands against the walls sets of vases were arranged in patterns which every few days were 'so alter'd, revers'd and transform'd as to render the whole a new scene'. It was Wedgwood's declared aim 'to amuse and divert, please, astonish, nay, even to ravish the Ladies'.[3]

In their attempts to attract customers shopkeepers in the West End were replacing small panes of bottle-glass with larger plate-glass windows, through which their goods could more clearly be seen, encroaching upon pavements with bow-windows, painting and gilding their fronts and fitting up the insides of their shops with 'fine shelves, shutters, boxes, glass doors, sashes and the like'. Yet even in London such smart and well-lit shops were still rare, and in provincial cities almost unknown. The size of a shop window rarely permitted an inviting display of goods. A single straw hat, a phial of cordial or a pair of boots unsually indicated what kind of merchandise was to be found within.

Most shopkeepers still lived above or behind their shops which were dark and poky; many sold their goods through open windows, as their predecessors had done for centuries past; some had no more than a shed leaning against the wall of a house and serving both as shop and home for the poor tradesman.

There had been a time in the recent past when the shopping streets had been bedecked with painted signboards and models which advertised a shop's existence and, since houses were not yet numbered, helped customers and porters to find them. The first tradesmen's signs, introduced by the Romans, had been bas-reliefs in stone. These had given way to emblems, usually of wood, painted or carved and fixed above the door; and these, in turn, to those heavy, creaking boards which, seeming to vie with each other for attention, were so striking a feature of the streets of large cities. They hung out at right angles to the street on heavy wrought-iron brackets, and grew bigger and bigger in size until they almost completely blocked off sun and air from some narrow streets and were a hazard in all. They frequently fell down 'to the great danger and injury of the inhabitants'; and occasionally brought with them the whole front of the building to which they were attached. One that tumbled into Bird Lane in London, with a roar of collapsing bricks and masonry, killed four people who happened unluckily to be passing beneath it.

The earliest signs and models were quite simple and were intended to indicate the trade of the shopkeeper whose premises they advertised – three hats or a beaver for a hatter, three golden balls for a goldsmith, walnuts for cabinet-makers, mulberries for silk merchants, leopards for skinners, civet cats for perfumers, Adam and Eve for fruiterers, a dog and a bear for an inn where animal baiting was offered as supplementary entertainment. But the presence of a particular shop beneath its distinctive sign was never to be guaranteed. Premises were sold or re-let, new owners or tenants came in, yet the signs stayed where they were. Addison claimed he had seen the sign of a goat outside a perfumer's, a king's head above a sword cutler's, a boot above a cook-shop and a cobbler living under a roasted pig. Many signboards were extremely complicated, for when a tradesman bought an existing business he often incorporated the sign of that business, whose customers he hoped to retain, with his own. Also, when apprentices set up their own businesses they frequently used their former masters' devices and combined them with others of their own invention. Moreover, since certain streets were known for the particular trades practised there, it became essential to make variations in the signs and symbols used by the individual tradesmen. Shared premises, too, led to further variations and to the necessity of the pairing of devices when one sign had to serve for two tradesmen occupied in quite different trades. This explains some of the more incongruously paired tradesmen's signboards such as the Bull and Bedpost, the Three Nuns and Hare, the Whale and Gate and the Goat and Compasses (sometimes supposed to be a corruption of God Encompasseth Us).

Despite their inconvenience and the dangers they posed for the public, it was not until 1762 that an Act was passed forbidding hanging signboards in the City of London and Westminster. From that year signs had to be fixed flat to the wall of the building, an order that heralded the advent of the modern shop-front fascia. Tavern-keepers, however, seem to have defied the law with impunity; and so did certain other tradesmen. But by 1800 signboards had almost completely given way to shop fascias, often with gilded and carved lettering. By then, too, numbering of shops and houses had been introduced: an act of 1765 had required the Court of Common Council to affix name tablets to the corners of each street, square and lane; three years later only twelve streets had been so named, but by 1770 only a quarter of London's streets did not have name plates and in the rest both numbers and trade signs were displayed.[4]

The number of shops in London, and in the country as a whole, was extraordinary. In his *History and Survey of London*, William Maitland suggested that in 1732 almost a quarter of all houses in the capital were either shops or taverns selling food or drink, and this estimate did not take into account all the shops of other kinds. Some of these establishments would scarcely have been recognized as shops, since no taxes or rates were levied upon those who sold goods from their houses; and there were many who took advantage of this to become occasional tradesmen, dealing in any merchandise they were able to make or buy. Yet the proportion of full-time shopkeepers to the population of the capital as a whole was certainly very high, and remained so as long as it was customary for provincial shopkeepers to come to London shops for their supplies.[5] By 1800 there were over 150 shops in Oxford Street alone.[6]

England was, indeed, as Adam Smith observed before Napoleon, 'a nation of shopkeepers'. And most of these shopkeepers dealt in as wide a variety of foods and household goods as Thomas Turner, the mid-eighteenth-century Sussex village shopkeeper who was a grocer as well as a draper, a hatter and haberdasher as well as an undertaker, who sold drugs as well as ironmongery, gloves as well as stationery, and who also dealt in hops and wheat.

Shops such as Turner's were, and for many years remained, an essential part of working-class life. Their owners were prepared to sell their stock in the smallest quantities, supplying essential items on credit and sometimes making handsome profits from the interest that accrued.[7] The poor were well advised to keep on good terms with them, for shopping could be a tricky business, involving haggling over the price and possible disagreements about the coins or paper money offered. Counterfeit money abounded. So did silver coins which constant use had worn thin or clipping had damaged; and a shopkeeper offered a handful of these was likely to put them on the scales and, if they failed the test, to ask the customer for more to make up the weight. Bank notes were less troublesome; but every year one or other of the private banks that issued them went bankrupt, while the notes of even the most prosperous banks were accepted only locally. As for counterfeit money, Defoe said that 'if you went but to buy a pair of gloves or stockings or any trifle at a shop, you went with bad money in one hand and good money in the other, proffering first the bad coins to get them off if possible, and then the good if the other was rejected'.[8]

Bargaining over prices gradually died out as fixed-price sales became more general. It seems that the first shop to have adopted the new practice was Flint and Palmer's on London Bridge which opened its doors at eight o'clock one morning in the middle of the century to reveal all the variety of goods they sold with price tags.

Not much time was allowed for bargaining, a price being fixed for everything and, compared with other houses, cheap [wrote Robert Owen, the social reformer who worked there as a boy]. If any demur was made or much hesitation, the article asked for was withdrawn, and as the shop was generally full from morning till late in the evening, another customer was attended to.[9]

The firm's customers were at first astonished by this new practice but when it became evident that Mr Palmer was fair and consistent in his prices, it became so popular that the shop was crowded until eleven o'clock at night and other shops began to follow suit. One of them was that of James Lackington, whose bookshop, 'The Temple of the Muses' in Finsbury Square, was one of the sights of London. On the top of the building was a dome with a high pole from which flew a flag when Mr Lackington was in residence. In the middle of the shop was a huge circular counter around which, it was said, a coach and six could be driven, so large were the premises. A wide staircase led to the 'lounging-rooms' and the first of a series of galleries with bookshelves. The books got shabbier and cheaper as the customers ascended, the 'neat' copies being in the lower galleries, the 'damaged' in the upper.

In the seventeenth century books were offered for sale unbound, the loose sheets lying on shelves and tables, and the title pages hanging on posts outside, so that the purchaser could choose the style and colour of the binding, having his entire library, if he wished, bound in green and gold-blocked calf. If he was not sure that he wanted to commit himself to buying a particular book by asking the bookseller to bind it for him, he could read the loose sheets in the shop, sitting at one of the reading desks in the window, or he could take them home and read them there before making up his mind. Towards the end of the eighteenth century, however, books were sold ready bound and in 1780 James Lackington decided to mark 'plainly in every book, facing the title, the lowest price' that he would take for it, making no exception, 'not even to nobility'. He also resolved to 'give no person whatever any credit'.

> I was determined to make this resolution from various motives [he wrote in his memoirs]. I had observed that when credit was given, most bills were not paid within six months, some not within a twelve-month and some not within two years . . . When I communicated my ideas on this subject to some of my acquaintances I was much laughed at and ridiculed. It was thought I might as well attempt to re-build the Tower of Babel as to establish a large business without giving credit.[10]

Soon afterwards, however, cash sales at fixed prices were so common in all shops that an assistant who had become a highly skilled and fluent haggler or 'chafferer' in the markets of the East End of London found his talents wasted in a draper's shop in the City.[11] 'The method of business of having only one price was just then coming into fashion,' one such assistant explained, referring to the early years of the nineteenth century, 'and all the best houses had adopted it, many of them preferring to let customers go away unserved rather than break through the rule.'[12] By the 1850s bargaining was virtually unknown in this kind of shop: a visiting Frenchman observed that if an attempt was made to negotiate a price lower than that asked, the shop assistant 'thinks at first that you have misunderstood him but when he understands what you are driving at, he stiffens visibly like a man of honour to whom one has made a shady proposal'.[13] Even so, it was still considered rather vulgar in many of the better shops to put price labels on goods for sale; and this did not become a general practice until the advent of the department store on the lines of the Bayswater emporium of William Whiteley who had so many different items for sale in the 1870s that he styled himself 'The Universal Provider', offering to supply 'anything from a pin to an elephant at short notice'.[14]

The assistants at Whiteley's, many of whom lived on the premises, worked from seven o'clock in the morning until eleven at night. And at all times they were expected to keep a sharp eye open for shoplifters, for whom nineteenth-century dresses might well have been designed: one shoplifter at Whiteley's was caught hiding under her clothes forty-two silk handkerchiefs, two pairs of gloves, several lengths of ribbon and over twenty-four yards of velvet.[15]

Robert Owen remembered how at Flint and Palmer's he and his companions sometimes did not finish their work of tidying the unsold goods on the counters and rolling up the lengths of material until two o'clock in the morning, and then they had scarcely enough energy left to pull themselves up the banisters to the attic where they slept for five hours until their daily round began again.[16] Owen, who had had previous experience in a draper's shop in Northamptonshire, was paid £25 a year, but others of his fellow shop assistants received much less than that. And in some establishments the staff did not even have beds to go to, being provided instead with hammocks which were slung over the counters when the last customers had departed or on truckle beds which were pushed out of sight when it was time to open the shutters for business again.

Working conditions for shop assistants did not much improve during the nineteenth century. In the north they were now more likely to live at home, and to work for rather shorter hours than they had been in the past. But in the south hours remained long, shops frequently not closing until ten o'clock at night on weekdays and midnight on Saturdays. In 1883 a working day of seventeen hours was still quite common. It remained so for adults well into the next century, though by then the Shop Hours Act of 1886 had prevented shopkeepers from keeping assistants under eighteen at work for more than seventy-four hours a week.[17]

In most shops, assistants – nearly all male until the end of the century – were still required to live in; and in many of the higher class houses the juniors had to work for two or three years, being provided with no more than their board and lodging while they were learning the trade.

When Owen left London for Manchester in the 1780s, various streets in the capital had already become fashionable shopping centres. Among them was Bond Street where shop-gazing was as popular then as it is now, and where many of the shopkeepers let off their upper rooms as lodgings to well-to-do bachelors. But it was not until the beginning of the nineteenth century that a street was designed purely as a shopping street; one of the earliest of these was Woburn Walk in Bloomsbury which was designed as a shopping centre by Thomas Cubitt in 1822. There were by then, however, several shopping arcades, the earliest of which, Royal Opera Arcade, was built by John Nash and G. S. Repton at the back of the Haymarket Opera House in 1816–18. This was soon followed by Burlington Arcade, Piccadilly, which was designed in 1819 by Samuel Ware for Lord George Cavendish of Burlington House with the original intention of preventing passers-by throwing oyster-shells and other rubbish into his garden. It soon became a highly fashionable shopping centre, the rooms above the small, smart shops being rented by prostitutes for the entertainment of their richer customers.

The shops of the West End seemed a world apart from the dingy chandlers' shops to the east. Here not only candles and links were sold but all manner of goods from soap and sand to coal and cats' meat. Market women came for breakfast, maidservants for packets of sand; many were treated to a dram of gin to warm them or induce them to return; farthings were not despised as payment and when credit was denied, a shift, apron or cap was left until the money due was paid.[18] This kind of shop lasted well into the nineteenth century.

> Then comes a shop where they sell cats' meat, coal, cow-heels, wood and tripe [wrote Francis Place of one establishment in Lock's Fields in about 1830]. And ever and anon a load of coals comes in and black clouds of dust arise as they are emptied into the shop, settling on the cow-heels and the tripe, and the pillars of pudding. Yet these they eat all up, and as one of them once remarked, 'the dust does instead of pepper.'[19]

Many of these shops were in cellars which also served as premises for cobblers, for scrap-metal merchants, for the owners of 'green shops' that sold roots and firewood, and as milk cellars where women, who had collected milk from nearby farms, left it to stand so that they could skim off the cream before watering the rest and carrying it away on their rounds. Some cellars served as cowsheds; and as late as the 1880s, before 'railway milk' drove them out of business, there were still about 700 licensed cow-houses in London. But whether from a London cow-house or a farm in the suburbs the milk was often in a disgusting state by the time it reached the customer.

> The produce of faded cabbage leaves and sour draff, it was [in the jaundiced opinion of the testy Tobias Smollett] lowered with hot water, frothed with bruised snails, carried through the streets in open pails, exposed to the foul rinsings discharged from doors and windows, spittle, snot and tobacco quids from foot-passengers, overflowings from mud-carts, spatterings from coach wheels, dirt and trash chucked into it by roguish boys for the joke's sake, the spewings of infants who have slabbered in the tin measure which is thrown back in that condition among the milk for the benefit of the next customer; and, finally, the vermin that drops from the rags of the nasty drab that vends this precious mixture, under the respectable title of milk-maid.[20]

Dealers in old clothes also traded from cellars, seldom coming forth in the world, as Dickens observed, 'except in the dusk and coolness of the evening' when they could be seen sitting in chairs, smoking their pipes and watching their children play in the gutter. 'Their countenances bear a thoughtful and dirty cast, certain indications of their love of traffic; and their habitations are distinguished by that disregard of outward appearance, and neglect of personal comfort, so common among people who are constantly immersed in profound speculation, and deeply engaged in sedentary pursuits.'[21]

Although Dickens supposed in the 1830s that Monmouth Street, one of London's second-hand clothes markets, would continue to be as it had been for a century, the burial place of fashions until there were no more fashions to bury, by the 1860s it had become an old boot and shoe market where most of the cobbling was done with brown paper and blacking. Houndsditch, however, remained an old clothes market throughout the nineteenth century and visitors to it were advised 'to leave their watches and valuables at home and not to take offence at a little "Bishopsgate banter"'.

While old clothes shops tended to congregate in particular areas, rag and bottle shops could be found everywhere. In these far more was offered for sale and far more was bought by their owners than the rags and bottles from which they got their name. One offered the highest prices for 'wax and sperm pieces, old copper, brass, pewter etc., lead, iron, zinc, steel, etc., old horse hair mattresses, waste paper, old books, all kinds of coloured rags, bones, phials, broken flint glass, wearing apparel, furniture and timber'. The description of Mr Krook's shop in *Bleak House* could have been applied to dozens of others:

In one part of the window was a picture of a red paper mill, at which a cart was unloading a quantity of sacks of old rags. In another, was the inscription, BONES BOUGHT. In another, KITCHEN-STUFF BOUGHT. In another, OLD IRON BOUGHT. In another, WASTE PAPER BOUGHT. In another, LADIES' AND GENTLEMEN'S WARDROBES BOUGHT. Everything seemed to be bought, and nothing to be sold there. In all parts of the window, were quantities of dirty bottles: blacking bottles, medicine bottles, ginger-beer and soda-water bottles, pickle bottles, wine bottles, ink bottles. There was a little tottering bench of shabby old volumes, outside the door, labelled 'Law Books, all at 9d.'[22]

Unsavoury as he made Krook's shop appear, Dickens spared his readers a description of the sickening stench that emanated in such places from the rags and 'kitchen stuff' and from sacks full of bones that were scattered about the floor. Their owners, however, seemed quite unconscious of the foulness of the atmosphere in which they lived. One of them, 'in speaking of the many deaths among his family, could not conjecture to what cause it could be owing'.[23]

As well as rag and bottle shops there were cookshops in the poorer quarters of all large towns. In the seventeenth century cookshops had been frequented by men of Pepys's class. They had generally been cheaper than taverns which charged prices comparable with those of the King's Head, Charing Cross – where a meal at the host's table cost 2s 6d and one at the second table 1s – and they were much cheaper than Chatelin's, the French eating-house in Covent Garden, where dinner might cost as much as 6s 8d. Pepys himself often had a meal in a cookshop, sometimes took its dishes home or hired the cook for a party.[24] But a century later cookshops were the common resort of the poor.

Boswell once saw Samuel Johnson in Clifton's eating-house in Butcher Row and was 'surprised to perceive him' in such a place, since the mode of dining, or rather being fed, at [these] houses in London, is well known to be particularly unsocial as there is no ordinary, or united company, but each person has his own mess, and is under no obligation to hold any intercourse with any one'. Taverns were consequently much more to Johnson's taste. He sometimes ate at home, but as he informed Mr and Mrs Thrale, 'a general anarchy' prevailed in his kitchen, and the roasting there was 'not magnificent', for they had no jack.

'No jack! Why how do they manage without?'

'Small joints, I believe, they manage with a string, and larger are done at the tavern. I have some thoughts (with a profound gravity) of buying a jack, because I think a jack is some credit to a house.'

'Well, but you'll have a spit, too?'

'Why, sir, no. That would be superflous, for we shall never use it; and if a jack is seen a spit will be presumed.'

When he did dine at home, as he usually did on a Sunday, Johnson therefore preferred to rely upon food provided by the cookshop rather than his own kitchen. 'I generally have a meat pye on Sunday,' he told Boswell. 'It is baked at a public oven, which is very properly allowed, because one man can attend it; and thus the advantage is obtained of not keeping servants from church to dress dinners.' In fact when Boswell dined with Johnson one Sunday, expecting 'some strange, uncouth ill-drest dish', he had not only meat pie but 'a very good soup, a boiled leg of lamb and spinach and a rice pudding'.

In 1773, though, there were few cookshops which a man with Johnson's well-developed taste for good food would have cared to patronize. They catered for people who could afford to spend a few pennies only and who were prepared to eat what was offered them in sheets of old paper either at the counter or in the streets outside. Nevertheless, for hungry young men prepared to spend as much as 7d there were cookshops that did provide at least a satisfying if not an elegant meal, such as the one enjoyed by Defoe's two thieves in Rosemary Lane where they had 'three pennyworth of boiled beef, two pennyworth of pudding, a penry brick as they called it or loaf, and a whole pint of strong beer [with] a mess of beef broth into the bargain'.[25]

# 47 · *Pedlars and Markets*

Those disinclined to go to a cookshop had their wants supplied by the street traders who hawked all kinds of food about from morning till night. Throughout the eighteenth and nineteenth centuries the streets of London and other large cities were the regular market-place of itinerant vendors as they had been for centuries past. Merchandise of almost every description was carried and 'cried' along lanes, down alleys and into courts, so that the din of the vendors' voices, competing for attention and custom, was an integral part of town life and often astonished country visitors. All kinds of food were offered: 'Buy my fat chickens!'; 'Buy my flounders!'; 'Twelve pence a peck, oysters!'; 'Sixpence a pound fair cherries!'; 'Crab! Crab! Any Crab!'; 'Hot baked wardens!'; Lemons and Oranges, fresh and fair!'

Many of the cries were chanted in a loud, repetitive sing-song with the emphasis on the appropriate word: 'Buy my ropes of hard *onions*!'; 'Delicate *cucumbers*!'; 'Buy a dish of great *eels*!' Vendors kept strictly to the wares in which they specialized, wet, dry or shellfish, poultry, game or cheeses, vegetables, fruit or flowers. There were sellers of pea soup and pickled whelks, of sheep's trotters and baked potatoes, of ham sandwiches and ginger beer, of curds and whey and rice, of pastry, gingerbread and watercress, of muffins, boiled puddings and spiced wine. And along with the vendors of food came the hawkers of cigars and walking-sticks, spectacles and dolls, cutlery, goldfish, dogs and shells, whips and crackers, ballad sheets and shirt buttons, wash leathers and rat poison, all crying their wares, singing their songs, making their progress known by trumpet calls like the newspaper men, or ringing bells as the muffin men did, or rattling pots and coins on their trays. Then came the men offering services or trying to tempt domestic servants to let them have, in exchange for a knicknack, a rabbit skin which they could dispose of to a felt-hat maker or the remains of a joint of meat which they could take to a cookshop: 'Any kitchen stuff have you maids?';

'Maids, any cunny skins?'; 'Old chairs to mend!'; 'Knives or scissors to grind!'; 'Sweep! Chimney sweep!'; 'Wood to cleave!'; 'Brass pots to mend!'; 'Corns to pick!'; 'Dust O! Dust O! Dust O! Dust oy-eh!'

The dustmen went by in their hooded caps with leather flaps hanging down behind their necks, leading a horse and box-cart, stopping outside the houses where there was ash and rubbish to collect, filling their buckets from the dustbins, emptying their loads into the carts, then trundling them away to the dustyard where men, women and children would be hard at work on the mountainous heaps of rubbish, the women in black bonnets, their dirty cotton dresses tucked up behind them, banging their iron sieves against their leather aprons, separating the 'brieze' from the 'soil' – the 'brieze' or coarse, cindery dust being despatched to the brickfields, the finer 'soil' being sold as manure. Broken bricks, old books, kettles, rags, bones and oyster-shells all found their appropriate market.

The numbers of men, women and children who made their living in the streets of the country's cities were immense. Henry Mayhew, the first volumes of whose masterly social survey, *London Labour and the London Poor*, were published in 1851, estimated that in London alone the number of costermongers – 'that is to say those street sellers attending the London "green" and "fish" markets' – appeared to be 'from the best data at [his] command, now 30,000 men, women and children'.

> The costermongering class extends itself yearly [Mayhew continued]; and it is computed that for the last five years it has increased considerably faster than the general metropolitan population. This increase is derived from all the children of costermongers following the father's trade, but chiefly from working men, such as the servants of greengrocers or of innkeepers, when out of employ, 'taking a coster's barrow' for a livelihood; and the same being done by mechanics and labourers out of work. At the time of the famine in Ireland, it is calculated, that the number of Irish obtaining a living in the London streets must have been at least doubled.[1]

Costermongers – who got their name from 'costard', a large, ribbed apple – were a rough, quarrelsome, mostly illiterate set of men much given to fighting, drinking and gambling, to tattooing their arms and throwing bricks at policemen. Anxious to keep the secrets of their trade from the police and potential rivals they spoke to each other in an esoteric language, incomprehensible to the uninitiated, which involved the use of an extensive cryptic vocabulary and an ability to pronounce words backwards. 'I tumble to your Barrikin' meant 'I understand you'; 'cool the esclop', 'look at the police'; 'flatch kanurd', half drunk; and 'a top of reeb', a pot of beer. Few costermongers troubled to marry the women they lived with; most – although not above cheating their customers – were honest among themselves and kind to their donkeys and children, though 'perhaps in a rough way'; hardly any had been inside a church or could read or write. Mayhew reported the conversation he had with one of them, almost verbatim, omitting oaths and slang:

Well, times is bad, Sir . . . When I served the Prince of Naples not far from here (I presume he alluded to the Prince of Capua) I did better . . . He was a good customer, and was very fond of peaches. I used to sell them to him, at 12s the plasket when they was new. The plasket held a dozen, and cost me 6s at Covent-garden – more sometimes; but I didn't charge him more when they did. He was the Prince o' Naples, was my customer; but I don't know what he was like, for I never saw him. I've heard that he was the brother of the King of Naples. I can't say where Naples is, but if you ask at Euston-square, they'll tell you the fare there and the time to go it in. Why don't you ask at the square? I never heard of the Pope being a neighbour of the King of Naples. Do you mean living next door to him? But I don't know nothing of the King of Naples, only the prince. I don't know what the Pope is. Is he any trade? It's nothing to me, when he's no customer of mine. I have nothing to say about nobody that ain't no customers. My crabs is caught in the sea, in course. I gets them at Billingsgate. I never saw the sea, but it's salt-water, I know. I can't say whereabouts it lays. I believe it's in the hands of the Billingsgate salesmen. I've worked the streets and the courts at all times. I've worked them by moonlight, . . . I can't say how far the moon's off us. It's nothing to me, but I've seen it a good bit higher than St Paul's. I don't know nothing about the sun. Why do you ask? It must be nearer than the moon for it's warmer, – and if they're both fire, that shows it. It's like the taproom grate and that bit of a gas-light; to compare the two is. What was St Paul's that the moon was above? A church, sir; so I've heard. I never was in a church. O, yes, I've heard of God; he made heaven and earth; I never heard of his making the sea; that's another thing, and you can best learn about that at Billingsgate.[2]

'No, I never heard about this here creation you speaks about,' another costermonger said to Mayhew.

In coorse God Almighty made the world, and the poor bricklayers' labourers built the houses afterwards – that's *my* opinion; but I can't say, for I've never been in no schools and knows nothing about it. I have heered a little about our Saviour. They seem to say he was a goodish kind of man; but if he says as how a cove's to forgive a feller as hits you, I should say he know'd nothing about it. In coorse the gals lads goes and lives with thinks our walloping 'em wery cruel, but we don't. Why don't we? Why, because we don't . . . On a Sunday I goes out selling. As for going to church, why, I can't afford it – besides, to tell the truth, I don't like it well enough. Plays, too, ain't in my line much. I'd sooner go to a dance – it's more livelier . . . The songs are out and out, and makes our gals laugh. The smuttier the better, I thinks. Bless you, the gals like it as much as we do . . . When I was fourteen I took up with a gal . . . I used to walk out of a night with her and give her half-pints of beer at the publics. She were about thirteen, and used to dress werry nice.

Costermongers' children were very rarely sent even to Ragged Schools and were put to work at an early age, usually before they were seven; and when the boys were about fourteen they started in business on their own and with a woman of their own, settling the arrangement by giving the girl a silk handkerchief which was usually taken back after a time, either as a gambling pledge or as a scarf for themselves. Costermongers were renowned for 'dressing flash', as they called it, and were inordinately proud of their silk neckerchieves and, indeed, of all their clothes. Most wore a kind of uniform of long cord waistcoats with huge and numerous pockets and shining brass or mother-of-pearl buttons, seamed trousers fitting tightly at the knee and billowing out over highly polished boots, and a worsted skull-cap or a cloth cap pulled very much down on one side of a head covered with ringlets at the front and with long hair, 'Newgate-Knocker style', hanging down over the ears. The general costume of the women was a black straw bonnet with a few ribbons or flowers, a printed cotton gown with a silk handkerchief tucked into the neck, and petticoats worn short, 'ending at the ankles just high enough to show the whole of the much admired boots'.

> The life of the coster-girls is as severe as that of the boys [Mayhew thought]. Between four and five in the morning they have to leave home for the markets, and sell in the streets until about nine. Those that have more kindly parents, return then to breakfast, but many are obliged to earn the morning's meal for themselves. After breakfast, they generally remain in the streets until about ten o'clock at night; many having nothing during all that time but one meal of bread and butter and coffee, to enable them to support the fatigue of walking from street to street with a heavy basket on their heads.[3]

Yet once they had 'learnt the markets' – and such tricks of the trade as boiling oranges to make them swell – and were able to fend for themselves, costermongers lived quite comfortably. Taking the more prosperous with the less successful, the English with the Irish and the men with the women, Mayhew estimated that 10s a week was, perhaps, 'a fair average of the

earnings of the entire body the year through'; but some made well over £1 10s
a week. They could afford to frequent 'two-penny hops' and those rowdy and
bawdy temporary theatres known as penny gaffs; and they could spend a
good deal on drink and food as well as upon clothes. They always managed to
have what they called a 'relish' for breakfast and tea, 'a couple of herrings, a
bit of bacon, or what not'; and while waiting for a market would often spend a
shilling on the cakes, crisp butter biscuits and 'three cornered puffs sold by
the Jews'. 'The owners toss for them, and so enable the young coster to
indulge his two favourite passions at the same time – his love of pastry and his
love of gambling.' For dinner on weekdays they commonly had saveloys or
meat pies with a pint of beer or a glass of neat gin, and on Sundays a shoulder
of mutton with plenty of potatoes or a dish of kidney puddings, hot eels,
pickled whelks and oysters.

There were thousands of street sellers, though, who could never afford
such fare, men who, having failed in other occupations, had come to the trade
late in life and never learned to bargain successfully at the markets. 'They're
inferior salesmen, too,' one of their more enterprising and experienced
competitors said of them. 'And if they have fish left that won't keep, it's a
dead loss to them', for

they aren't up to the trick of selling it cheap at a distance where the coster
ain't known; or of quitting it to another, for candle-light sale. Some of
these poor fellows lose every penny. They're mostly middle-aged when
they begin costering. They'll generally commence with oranges or herrings. We pity them. We say, 'Poor fellows! they'll find it out by-and-by.'
It's awful to see some poor women, too, trying to pick up a living in the
streets by selling nuts or oranges. It's awful to see them, for they can't set
about it right; besides that, there's too many before they start. They don't
find a living, it's only another way of starving.[4]

Mayhew's volumes contain numerous examples of the pitiable plight to
which the poorest and least successful street sellers were reduced. One young
orphaned flower-girl of fifteen told him how she contrived to make a home for
her younger brother and sister with the 6d a day she earned from selling
primroses, carnations and violets in the streets. She paid 2s a week for a bed
in a dark, bare, dank room in Drury Lane which was rented by an Irishman
and his wife whose own bed was separated from hers by an old curtain. She
shared the bed with her brother, aged thirteen, and her sister, eleven; and
she was proud that she 'could get them a bit of bread and had never troubled
the parish'. The two girls went out on their rounds every morning, wearing
torn, dark print frocks and broken black chip bonnets. The elder sister had a
pair of worn-out shoes, the younger went barefoot. 'We live on bread and

tea,' the elder said, 'and sometimes a fresh herring of a night. Sometimes we don't eat a bit all day when we're out; sometimes we take a bit of bread with us . . . My sister can't eat taturs; they sicken her . . . We never pawned anything; we have nothing they would take in at the pawnshop.'

A younger girl, aged eight, described an even more pitiable life. She was one of those who could be seen every morning at the cress market, haggling with the saleswomen over the price, shivering in their thin dresses as they washed the leaves at the pump, their fingers aching with cold. She had been 'very near a twelve month on the streets,' she said, her 'long rusty hair standing out in all directions', shuffling her feet 'for fear that the large carpet slippers that served her for shoes would slip off':

I go about the streets with water-creases, crying, 'Four bunches a penny, water-creases!! . . . My mother learned me to needle-work and to knit when I was about five. I used to go to school, too; but I wasn't there long. I've forgot all about it now, it's such a time ago. The master whacked me . . . He hit me three times, ever so hard, across the face with his cane. The creases is so bad now that I haven't been out with 'em for three days. They're so cold, people won't buy 'em; for when I goes up to them, they say, 'They'll freeze our bellies.' Besides, in the market, they won't sell a ha'penny handful now – they're ris to a penny and tuppence. I used to go down to market along with another girl, as must be about fourteen, 'cos she does her back hair up. When we've bought a lot, we sits down on a door-step, and ties up the bunches. We never goes home to breakfast till we've sold out; but, if it's very late, then I buys a penn'orth of pudden, which is very nice with gravy . . . We children never play down there [in the market] 'cos we're thinking of our living. No; people never pities me in the street – excepting one gentleman, and he says, says he, 'What do you do out so soon in the morning?' but he gave me nothink – he only walked away.

It's very cold before winter comes on reg'lar – specially getting up of a morning. I gets up in the dark by the light of the lamp in the court . . .

I always give mother my money, she's so very good to me. She don't often beat me. She's very poor, and goes out cleaning rooms sometimes, now she don't work at the fur. I ain't got no father, he's a father-in-law. No; mother ain't married again – he's a father-in-law. He grinds scissors, and he's very good to me. No; I don't mean by that that he says kind things to me, for he never hardly speaks. When I gets home, I puts the room to rights: mother don't make me do it, I does it myself. I cleans the chairs, though there's only two to clean. I takes a tub and scrubbing-brush and flannel, and scrubs the floor – that's what I do.

I don't have no dinner. Mother gives me two slices of bread-and-butter and a cup of tea for breakfast, and then I go to till tea, and has the same. We has meat of a Sunday, and, of course, I should like to have it every day. Mother has just the same to eat as we has, but she takes more tea – three cups, sometimes. No; I never had no sweet-stuff; I never buy none – I don't like it. Sometimes we has a game of 'honeypots' with the girls in the court, but not often. I knows a good many games, but I don't play at 'em, 'cos going out with creases tire me. On a Friday night, too, I goes to a Jew's house till eleven o'clock on a Saturday night. All I has to do is to snuff the candles and poke the fire. You see they keep their Sabbath then, and they won't touch anything; so they gives me my wittals and 1½d, and I does it for 'em.

I am a capital hand at bargaining. They can't take me in . . . I know the quantities very well. When I've bought 3d of creases, I ties 'em up into as many little bundles as I can. They must look biggish, or the people won't buy them, some puffs them out as much as they'll go . . . I'm past eight, I am. I can't read or write but I know how many pennies goes to a shilling, and two ha'pence goes to a penny, and four fardens goes to a penny. I knows, too, how many fardens goes to tuppence – eight. That's as much as I wants to know for the markets.[5]

This little girl rarely earned more than 3d or 4d a day, but other street sellers, like the more successful costermongers, made enough to live quite comfortably. One, a tin-ware seller, had begun his working life as a pantry-boy. After some time he resolved to join the army but on the day of his enlistment into the 60th Rifles he had broken his leg and been permanently crippled. He had then found employment in a dust-yard at 10s a week, and had subsequently lived a vagrant life, sleeping in the arches of the Adelphi and eating the rotten oranges and other rubbish in the market at Covent Garden. He had contracted cholera and been admitted to a workhouse. On his discharge had had gone to work in a coal-shed for 10s a week, but was soon dismissed. He then 'began to think seriously of some way of living'. He borrowed enough to buy 200 oranges and with the profits from their sale set himself up as a sugar boiler. From sugar boiling he turned to selling rings at a penny each, then, having bought a bundle of old umbrellas and taken the trouble to study the way they were made, he began in business as an umbrella repairer and salesman. For three years he prospered well enough; then decided he could do better as a mender and maker of saucepans and pots. 'And I succeeded so well,' he said, 'that I abandoned the rainy-day system, and commenced manufacturing articles in tin-ware, such as [I now] sell in the streets, namely funnels, nutmeg graters, penny mugs, extinguishers, slicers, save-alls . . . and thanks to the Lord I am better off than ever I expected to be.'[6]

\*

Covent Garden Market, where this man went for scraps of food, had for long been London's biggest and busiest fruit and vegetable market. Established in 1656 as a few temporary stalls erected in the garden of Bedford House, it had become a thrice-weekly market by the end of the seventeenth century. It was not, however, until the closure of the other fruit and vegetable markets in London that it assumed its unrivalled pre-eminence. The Stocks Market, founded in the thirteenth century on the site of the present Mansion House and rebuilt after the Great Fire, had been closed in 1737; its successor, the Fleet Market, was cleared for the construction of Farringdon Street in 1826–30; and thereafter Covent Garden became so crowded that several large new buildings had to be constructed. From six in the morning it was packed with carts, vans, donkeys and barrows; with porters making their way through the crowds, their teeth clenched as they carried columns of heavy hampers on their heads; with apple women sitting on porters' knots and smoking pipes; with small flower-girls running past with bundles of violets; with costers in corduroy suits, greengrocers in blue aprons and countrymen in smocks and tattered straw hats. The flagstones were covered with walnut husks, grape skins and bits of white paper from crates of lemons, and they were stained green with squashed cabbage leaves. The air was filled with the smell of bruised or squashed fruit, of oranges, onions and bitter herbs. Charles Dickens, like Tom Pinch in *Martin Chuzzlewit*, enjoyed many a pleasant stroll in Covent Garden, 'snuffing up the perfume of the fruits and flowers', lingering at the doors of the herbalists, 'gratefully inhaling scent as of veal-stuffing yet uncooked, dreamily mixed up with capsicums, brown paper and seeds', 'catching glimpses down side avenues of rows and rows of old women, seated on inverted baskets shelling peas'.[7]

Although 'all was bustle and confusion' at Covent Garden, there was no shouting as in other markets, rather a low murmuring hum, as of the sea at a distance. The row at Billingsgate, however, was deafening. Here, amid piles of smelly brown baskets, shining wet fish on slabs, herring scales, huge black oyster bags and fishmongers' carts, salesmen and hucksters tried to shout each other down as they stood in their white aprons on top of their tables and competed for their customers' attention, crying, 'Ye-oo! Ye-o-o! Turbot! Turbot! All alive turbot! . . . Oy! Oy! Oy! Now's your time! Fine grizzling sprats! All large and small . . . Hullo! Hullo! Hullo! Here! Fine cock crabs! All alive O! O! O! . . . Here! Here! Here you are, governor, had-had-had-haddick! All fresh and good! . . . Now or never, now or never, five brill and one turbot – have that lot for a pound!' Inured to the din, foul-mouthed women with cods' tails dangling from their aprons elbowed their way through the crowds; and porters pushed behind them in their bobbing hats which were so called after the shilling charge their wearers made for their services and which were said to have been modelled on the leather helmets worn by Henry V's bowmen at Agincourt. Sailors wandered about in striped guernseys and red worsted caps; and the customers themselves walked from table to table, asking, 'What's the price, master?', picking up a sole to smell it, knocking a crawling lobster back into its heap, peering into herring barrels and sackfuls of whelks, turning over smelts on their marble slabs.

Billingsgate had been a market for well over eight centuries. Smithfield, the meat market, was almost as old; and since at least the twelfth century had been a market for cattle and horses, pigs and sheep as well. Despite the constant complaints of the inconvenience of unruly and stampeding cattle being driven through the streets of the City, of beasts – tormented by drunken herdsmen – taking refuge in houses, and of 'bulls in china shops', the sale of live cattle continued at Smithfield until 1855 when it was transferred to the Metropolitan Cattle Market in Islington. Before that Smithfield was a shambles as well as a market. Blood flowed through the streets and entrails were dumped in the drainage channels. The scene was described by Dickens:

It was market-morning. The ground was covered, nearly ankle-deep, with filth and mire; a thick steam, perpetually rising from the reeking bodies of the cattle, and mingling with the fog, which seemed to rest upon the chimney-tops, hung heavily above. All the pens in the centre of the large area, and as many temporary pens as could be crowded into the vacant space, were filled with sheep; tied up to posts by the gutter side were long lines of beasts and oxen, three or four deep. Countrymen, butchers, drovers, hawkers, boys, thieves, idlers, and vagabonds of every low grade, were mingled together in a mass; the whistling of drovers, the barking of dogs, the bellowing and plunging of oxen, the bleating of sheep, the grunting and squeaking of pigs, the cries of hawkers, the shouts, oaths, and quarrelling on all sides, the ringing of bells and roar of voices, that issued from every public-house; the crowding, pushing, driving, beating, whooping, and yelling; the hideous and discordant din that resounded from every corner of the market; and the unwashed, unshaven, squalid, and dirty figures constantly running to and fro, and bursting in and out of the throng; rendered it a stunning and bewildering scene which quite confounded the senses.[8]

Apart from Covent Garden, Billingsgate and Smithfield there were other specialist markets all over London. There was the watercress market in Farringdon Street, a sad place where, long before daylight the buyers gathered beneath the gas-lamps over the iron gates, dressed in every kind of rags, some with their baskets over their heads, like hoods, some with shallows fastened to their backs with straps, others with rusty tea trays.

Just as the clocks are striking five, a stout saleswoman enters the gates, and instantly a country-looking fellow, in a waggoner's cap and smock-frock, arranges the baskets he has brought up to London. The other ladies are soon at their posts, well wrapped up in warm cloaks, over their thick shawls, and sit with their hands under their aprons. The customers come in by twos and threes, and walk about, looking at the cresses, and listening to the prices asked. Every hamper is surrounded by a black crowd, bending over till their heads nearly meet, foreheads and cheeks lighted up by the candle in the centre. The saleswomen's voices are heard above the noise of the mob, sharply answering all objections that may be made to the quality of their goods. 'They're rather spotty, mum,' says an Irishman, as he examines one of the leaves. 'No more spots than a new-born babe, Dennis,' answers the lady tartly, and then turns to a new comer . . .

As the morning twilight came on, the paved court was crowded with purchasers . . . and the gas-man came round with his ladder to turn out the lamps. Then every one was pushing about; the children crying, as their naked feet were trodden upon, and the women hurrying off, with their baskets or shawls filled with cresses, and the bunch of rushes in their hands . . .

As it grew late, and the crowd had thinned; none but the very poorest of the cress-sellers were left. Many of these had come without money, others had their halfpence tied up carefully in their shawl-ends, as though they dreaded the loss. A sickly-looking boy, of about five, whose head just reached above the hampers, now crept forward, treading with his blue naked feet over the cold stones as a cat does over wet ground. At his elbows and knees his skin showed in gashes through the rents in his clothes, and he looked so frozen, that the buxom saleswoman called to him . . . He went up to her, and, as he stood shivering on one foot, said, 'Give us a few old cresses, Jinney,' and in a few minutes was running off with a green bundle under his arm.[9]

East of Farringdon Street Market, beyond St Paul's Cathedral, was Houndsditch where oranges, lemons and nuts were sold by Jews and where, when the market was closed, a few sickly hens could be seen wandering about, turning over the heaps of dry leaves that the oranges had been packed in. Here the walls of the houses, blackened with soot and apparently in the last stages of dilapidation, concealed rooms elegantly furnished by their Jewish owners with Spanish mahogany, Morocco leather, Turkey carpets, ormolu chandeliers and gilt-framed looking-glasses.

As well as from less prosperous Jews in Monmouth Street, second-hand clothes could be bought at numerous markets from Saffron Hill to Shoreditch, in Petticoat Lane and Rosemary Lane, where all kinds of other articles were also offered for sale. Food markets, most of which stayed open till late at night, were even more common. Displayed by the light of oil- or grease-lamps or candles stuck inside turnips or sieves were russet apples and Yarmouth bloaters on toasting forks; gingerbread and lemonade and baked potatoes; onions, grapes, pies and muffins; whelks and mackerel (six for a shilling), live soles and mussels (a penny a quart); and any amount of turnips: 'Here's your turnips, ho! ho! hi! What do you think of these then? A penny a bunch! Hurrah for free trade!' And, competing for attention with the vendors of food, were men and women and children selling bootlaces and crockery, tea trays, and combs, pens, cough drops and corn plasters.

In all large towns in the provinces there were similar markets, though in smaller places the stall-holders were likely to be not middlemen and hawkers but the men and women who had themselves grown or made what they had to sell. There was never a shortage of customers. Over half the shops in England today are food shops, but in Victorian times most people bought their food in markets; and in many towns the municipal authorities provided large, well-lit buildings in which markets could be held. Liverpool's authorities were one of the first to do so: in their city a covered market hall, gas-lit and with a supply of fresh water, was in use by the early 1820s.[10] When the Jubilee Market at Covent Garden was completed in 1904 there were few large towns in England that did not have a covered market such as that still in use at Oxford.

Outside the towns, fairs, markets and pedlars still supplied the wants of hundreds of thousands of country people. A small village might have a cobbler, a baker, perhaps a butcher and a grocer who kept a few items of drapery. Small towns had their shoemakers' shops, their butchers and bakers, their grocers and drapers. Most of them had coal and timber merchants, corn-chandlers and tailors. Aldeburgh in Suffolk, for example, which had a population of 1300 in the 1830s had, in addition to eight inns, six shoemakers, four drapers who also stocked groceries, two haberdashers, three bakers, two chemists, four tailors, three milliners, five blacksmiths, a saddler, a coachmaker, a hairdresser, and a carrier who transported goods two days a week to and from Ipswich. There were, however, no fishmongers, no greengrocers and no butchers, the provisions which these resident tradesmen would have supplied being available in the markets which were held every Wednesday and Saturday. There were also local fairs in March and May.[11] And it was upon such fairs and markets that country people relied for all that their local shops could not supply.

To them the cottager of the 1880s still went for his 'store pig', the shepherd for his bells, and the agricultural labourer for his linen gaberdine – the good old garment of his Saxon forefathers – and for his leather gaiters. 'At country fairs everything sells,' wrote a travelling salesman who took his goods from one fair to the next, 'bridles, saddles, whips, guns, padlocks, saws, etc., etc., all goods of amounts varying from a shilling to three pounds and upwards.'[12]

This man, a cheapjack, travelled all over the country with his horse and cart and at least £100 of stock, standing on the tailboard of his cart when he arrived at his destination, offering his goods with a beguiling stream of comic patter to attract a crowd around him. 'I used to go out with a lot of goods on the Wednesday to Romford Market,' he recalled, 'on Thursday to Bishop Stortford, Friday to Chelmsford, Saturday to Colchester, Monday to Hadleigh, Wednesday to Bury St Edmunds, Thursday to Diss, and on the Saturday to Norwich . . . that is on the market days as they fall to each of the above places . . . The best fairs are those held in the autumn, as Peterboro, Cantbury, Maidstone, Maldon, Colchester, etc.'[13]

The recollections of another cheapjack reveal the hazards of the trade. He had begun his working life in Kent at the age of five or six when he was sent out with a roll of matches and strict instructions not to come home without the money received from their sale. Thrashed by a drunken father when he did not sell them all, he ran away one morning soon after his eighth birthday with nine-pennyworth of matches, determined never to return. He made his way to Deptford, staying in lodging-houses on the way, paying twopence for the share of a third, fourth, fifth or even sixth part of a bed, and each day saving a penny from his profits to buy brimstone to make more matches, begging the wood from carpenters. From selling matches he progressed to selling song sheets in public houses, and was taught to read the words on them by a kindly old soldier; then he turned to selling tapes and thread, then to rabbit and hare skins. When he was twelve he went to Norwich and began to sell phosphorus boxes – 'a piece of phosphorus was stuck in a tin tube, the match was dipped into the phosphorus, and it would ignite by friction' – but a constable, 'considering they were dreadful affairs, and calculated to encourage and assist thieves and burglars', took him to the private house of a magistrate who, 'equally horrified', sent him to prison for a month. Upon his release he was given a shilling with which he purchased some songs; and he travelled to Yarmouth to sell them to sailors. After a few weeks he had made 12s with which he purchased 'some hardware at the swag-shop and commenced hawking'. He did well, made £5, 'bought a neat box and started to sell a little Birmingham jewellery'. 'I was now respectably dressed,' he said, 'was getting a living, and had entirely left off stopping at common lodging-houses. But I confined my visits to small villages – I was afraid of the law; and as I was pursuing my calling near Wakefield, a constable inquired for my hawker's licence. I had none.' He was sent to prison again and lost his box of goods; but when he came out he went to Leeds and, at a fair there, met a cheapjack who offered him regular employment as his assistant and a steady wage besides all he 'could get above a certain price placed upon each of the goods'. After fifteen months he had saved £25. He bought a hawker's licence, started up on his own; and when he told his story in the late 1840s had a good stock of goods worth at least £50. He was married and had a family. He travelled only in the summer; his wife stayed at home looking after their little swag-shop which always turned in 'at least the family expenses'.[14]

Pedlars had to pay £4 for their licences, but this was considered far from excessive by shopkeepers who regarded cheapjacks as a serious threat to their own trade, and had long thought them so. 'There is not any commodity to be named that can be in any way ported but that the Pedlar doth carry it about all the country to sell,' an aggrieved pamphleteer had written in 1684. 'People (after a while) will have little or no occasion to come to the Cities or Market Townes for anything.' Fifty years later another writer complained, 'The Shopkeeper has the Milk where the Pedlar has the Cream; the Shopkeeper has the Gleanings where the Pedlar has the Harvest.'[15] Pedlars were accused of carrying stolen and smuggled goods, of cheating their customers, of damaging the trade not only of country town shopkeepers but of London merchants, too, since retailers in the provinces no longer found it necessary to come to the capital for their stock now that they could buy all they wanted from the caravans of travelling salesmen whose heavily laden packhorses tramped through the roads of every county.

Pedlars did have their champions, though. When the government decided to bring in a Shops Tax and, as compensation to the shopkeepers, to make all peddling illegal, there was an outcry from the manufacturers of linen, wool and cotton goods who protested that they would be driven out of business were it not for travelling salesmen and the so-called Scotch Drapers who called from house to house in the industrial districts of the north, selling 'hosiery, drapery and other necessary articles' on credit in the manner of tallymen, collecting weekly sums and offering new goods when the score was settled. Manufacturers contended that in the mill villages of the West Riding alone, Scotch Drapers were owed some £40,000 by 'labouring mechanics' and 'manufacturers'. It was also maintained that hawkers and pedlars had 'contributed greatly to the Extension of many of the Manufacturers of both England and Scotland by introducing them into Parts of the Country where they could not otherwise have been Sold'.

Many great and important Advantages are derived from the said useful and industrious Class of Tradesmen [one petition from Cumberland emphasized], the Quantity of goods bought and disposed of by them being considerably more extensive than has been generally conceived, and the Mode of Sale which is wholly confined to small Villages and Places remote from general Markets tends very greatly to diffuse the Manufacturers of the Kingdom in general and is a source of great convenience to those Inhabitants who live at a Distance from the principal Towns, great Quantities of goods of almost every Description being vended in detail, which the remote Inhabitants could not find Leisure to seek; and when Necessity might compel him to go from Home, the Expence of his Journey would frequently be as great as the Object of his Purchase.[16]

The protests were heeded: the pedlars were spared; and while their numbers declined in the nineteenth century as more shops were opened in country places, they survived – and many prospered – throughout and beyond the Victorian age.

# PART FOUR

## From the Victorians to Modern Times

It has long been supposed that the English nobility had survived so successfully because it was much more open to the middle classes than the French
and thus had not aroused that violent antipathy which the *tiers état* had felt
for the *noblesse*. But a recent study of estates in three representative
counties, Northamptonshire, Hertfordshire and Northumberland, has indicated that this supposition may be wrong, that, unlike the landed upper
classes in other countries, those in England were careful to keep their large
estates in manageable holdings within their families, to improve and enlarge
them by money acquired from rich brides, and to ensure by legal instruments
that they remained within the family, secure from the effects of partible
inheritance, unwelcome outsiders being kept at arm's length. In the three
counties mentioned no more than 137 'men of business' bought a country seat
between the Dissolution of the Monasteries and 1880.[1]

The riches of the most wealthy of English landed families were prodigious.
Disraeli assured Queen Victoria that the Duke of Bedford, the 'wealthiest of
all her subjects', had an income absolutely exceeding £300,000 a year, a sum
which might perhaps be compared with about £20 million today, or, at a time
when the pound was worth $4.86, an equivalent of almost 90 million dollars a
year. Later on in the century, the Duke of Westminster was enjoying an
annual income of £250,000 from his London properties alone, the Duke of
Buccleuch's estate brought him £217,000 a year, the Duke of Devonshire's
£181,000, the Duke of Northumberland's £176,000, the Marquess of Bute's
£150,000. The Duke of Marlborough, who lived in the grandest style at
Blenheim Palace, was relatively poor with a mere £37,000 a year (about £2.25
million in present-day terms) from an estate of less than 25,000 acres, a very
small estate compared with that of the Duke of Buccleuch who had 460,000
acres or the Duke of Sutherland who owned 1,358,000, an area larger than

the counties of Bedfordshire, Berkshire and Buckinghamshire put together. In all there were forty-four great landowners who had over 100,000 acres each and many more whose income – derived from stocks and shares, royalties from minerals or docks, from rich wives, as well as from land – exceeded £100,000 when income tax was 2d in the pound.

Most of them lived in a style of appropriate grandeur. The Duke of Rutland's guests at Belvoir were awoken in the morning by a military band; at Inveraray Castle, the Duke of Argyll's were given strident notice that it was time to change for dinner by his grace's personal bagpipers; at Petworth, Lord Egremont stabled 300 horses; at Eaton Hall, Cheshire, where guests were entertained 'on a truly royal scale', they could look out upon grounds tended by forty gardeners.

At Blenheim Palace, guests of the Duke of Marlborough sat down to dinners of alarming richness. First two soups, one hot and one cold were served simultaneously; then two kinds of fish, again one hot and one cold. After the fish came an entrée, then a meat dish, followed by a sorbet. This was followed by game – grouse or partridge, pheasant, duck, woodcock or snipe. In the summer, when there was no game, there were quails from Egypt, fattened in Europe, and ortolans from France 'which cost a fortune'. 'An elaborate sweet followed, succeeded by a hot savoury with which was drunk the port so comforting to English palates,' the ninth duke's American wife recalled. 'The dinner ended with a succulent array of peaches, plums, apricots, nectarines, raspberries, pears, and grapes, all grouped in generous pyramids among the flowers that adorned the table.'[2]

The duke, a fastidious, sarcastic and autocratic man, considered an hour quite long enough for the consumption of this huge meal; and after that time had elapsed his duchess, having 'collected eyes', would dutifully rise to her feet to lead the ladies to the long library where an organist would be playing Bach or Wagner or a Viennese orchestra would strike up a waltz.

In some houses the meals served were even more elaborate than the dinners at Blenheim. Poached turbot and salmon mayonnaise would follow the hot and cold, clear and thick soups; two subsequent dishes – turkey and roast mutton, perhaps – would be accompanied by several entrées, such as cutlets, *vol-au-vent*, fillets of leveret or sautéd fillets of fowl. These would be succeeded by two roasts; and, as well as sorbet and game, there would be numerous *entremets* – lobster salad, maraschino jelly, truffles with champagne. Those with delicate appetites would merely pick at a selection of these dishes; but others might help themselves to all. The Prince of Wales was a celebrated, though not apparently uniquely exceptional, trencherman whose great appetite was not in the least affected by the huge cigars and the Egyptian cigarettes he smoked in such quantities. After drinking a glass of milk in bed, he would fortify himself for a morning's shooting with platefuls of bacon and eggs, haddock and chicken, toast and butter, the kind of breakfast, in fact, served at Trollope's Plumstead Episcopi where the household sat down to 'dry toast and buttered toast, muffins and crumpets; hot bread and cold bread, home-made bread, baker's bread, wheaten and oaten bread . . . eggs in napkins and crispy bits of bacon under silver covers . . . and little fishes . . . and devilled kidneys frizzling on a hot-water dish'. Soon after breakfast an hour or two in the fresh air would sharpen the prince's appetite for hot turtle soup. Yet this would in no way impair his appetite for luncheon at half past two, just as a hearty luncheon would not prevent his appearing in the hall at Sandringham where, as his band played appropriate tunes, he would help himself to poached eggs, *petits fours*, preserved ginger, rolls, scones, hot cakes, cold cakes, sweet cakes and that particular species of Scotch shortcake of which he was especially fond.

The dinner which followed at half past eight consisted usually of at least twelve courses; and it was not unknown for him to take a liberal sample of every one. He had as evident a relish for rich as for simple food, and would tuck into Scotch broth, Irish stew and plum pudding with as much zest as into caviare, plovers' eggs and ortolans. He was once noticed to frown upon a bowl of boiled ham and beans, but this, he hastened to explain, was not because he despised such fare but 'because it should have been bacon'. He would enjoy several dozen oysters in a matter of minutes, setting the fashion for swallowing them between mouthfuls of bread and butter; and then would go on to more solid fare, to sole poached in Chablis and garnished with oysters and prawns, or to chicken and turkey in aspic, quails and pigeon pie, grouse and partridge; and the thicker the dressing, the richer the stuffing, the creamier the sauce, the more deeply did he seem to enjoy each mouthful. No dish was too rich for him. He liked his pheasant stuffed with truffles and smothered in oleaginous sauce; he delighted in quails packed with *foie gras* and served with oysters, truffles, mushrooms, prawns, tomatoes and cro-quettes. He never grew tired of boned snipe, filled with forcemeat as well as *foie gras* and covered with truffles and Madeira sauce. And, after eating all this food for dinner, he would advise his guests to have a good supper before going to bed, strongly recommending grilled oysters which were his own favourite refreshment at that time of night. On his bedside table was placed a cold chicken in case he became hungry during the night.[3]

His passion for food was shared by many if not most contemporaries of his class. At Marienbad a photograph was taken of him in earnest conversation with the Prime Minister, Sir Henry Campbell-Bannerman. So serious did both men appear, the one striking his palm with a clenched fist in emphasis of some point to which the other was listening with close attention, that when the picture appeared in an illustrated paper it was captioned: 'Is it peace or war?' When shown the paper by his private secretary, Sir Henry asked if he would like to know what actually was being discussed. It transpired that the question under such intense examination was whether halibut was better baked or boiled.[4]

Splendid as the food was in the grand houses at which the prince was so demanding, though appreciative, a guest, it rarely arrived on the table hot; for the dining-room was often separated from the kitchen by long, draughty corridors down which servants endlessly tramped with trays and trolleys. The dining-room at Blenheim Palace was a good 300 yards from the kitchen, and in some houses the two rooms were separated by distances even greater than that. At one of these, the food was so cold that, when the champagne was served, the Earl of Beaconsfield was heard to exclaim sardonically: 'Thank God for something warm at last.'[5]

The method of serving dinner varied from house to house. The old-fashioned preferred to retain the eighteenth-century practice of having several dishes on the table at once, the gentlemen helping themselves when the covers had been removed, offering to help their neighbours, and sending a servant to fetch anything they could not reach. In other houses service was *à la russe*, each course being served separately and handed round by servants in white gloves who either offered the dishes first to the ladies and then to the gentlemen or went straight round the table from one guest to the next.

The Duchess of Marlborough grew to 'dread and hate' the dinners at Blenheim, not only those dinners eaten alone with her husband – who sulkily pushed his plate away from him, backed his chair from the table and, crossing one leg over the other, endlessly twisted the ring on his little finger – but also those formal dinners which entailed a great deal of preliminary worry as, indeed, did the whole arrangement of a weekend house party. She resented the 'amount of trouble' these regular visits of twenty-five or thirty weekend guests always gave her. For, so she recalled,

> my round of the thirty guest-rooms, accompanied by the housekeeper, was apt to reveal some overlooked contingency too late to be repaired; a talk with the chef more often disclosed an underling's minor delinquency; orders to the butler invariably revealed a spiteful desire to undermine the chef – a desire that, if realised, I knew would jeopardise the culinary success of my party. Menus had to be approved and rooms allotted to the various guests. I had, moreover, spent hours placing my guests for the three ceremonial meals they would partake with us, for the rules of precedence were then strictly adhered to, not only in seating arrangements but also for the procession in to dinner. Since it was then considered ill-bred not to answer all letters oneself, I had no secretary. There was therefore a considerable amount of purely mechanical work to be done – dealing with correspondence, answering invitations, writing the dinner

cards and other instructions which appear necessary to ensure the smooth progression of social amenities – which took up a great deal of my time . . . The seating arrangements caused endless trouble but were greatly facilitated when I discovered a Table of Precedence and against the name of every peer the number of his rank. I was glad to know my own number, for, after waiting at the door of the dining-room for older women to pass through, I one day received a furious push from an irate Marchioness who loudly claimed that it was just as vulgar to hang back as to leave before one's turn.[6]

The duchess rarely enjoyed these weekends even when there were no unpleasantnesses with either guests or servants. She received her guests in the Italian garden where tea-tables had been laid, and after tea they would amble through the pleasure grounds until it was time to change for dinner. The duchess then showed the guests to their bedrooms, and 'shuddered' at the sight of washstands with pitchers and basins prominently displayed against a background of magnificent tapestries depicting the battles of the Great Duke, and of round bathtubs surrounded by hot and cold water jugs, soap and sponge bowls, towels and mats, all strangely incongruous beneath heroic forms of dying horses and dead soldiers.[7]

The guests were often as reluctant to go to these weekends as the duchess was to receive them. One of them, Arthur Balfour, described a big weekend party given for the Prince and Princess of Wales:

There is a big party here . . . To begin with (as our Toast lists have it) 'the Prince of Wales and the rest of the Royal family –' or if not quite that, at least a quorum, namely himself, his wife, two daughters and a son-in-law. There are two sets of George Curzons, the Londonderrys, Grenfells, Gosfords, H. Chaplin, etc., etc. We came down by special train – rather cross most of us – were received with illuminations, guards of honour, cheering and other follies, went through agonies about our luggage, but finally settled down placidly enough.

Today the men shot and the women dawdled. As I detest both occupations equally I stayed in my room till one o'clock and then went exploring joining everybody at luncheon. Then, [there was the] inevitable photograph . . . and here I am writing to you.[8]

To the Duchess of Marlborough, Sundays seemed particularly tedious, 'interminably long for a hostess who had no games wherewith to entertain her guests. Golf and tennis had not yet become the vogue', and would not, in any case, have been played on a Sunday. The guests trooped off to church at Woodstock for Matins and then to the palace chapel for Evensong. In between these two services 'promenades were the fashionable pastime, and the number of *tête-à-tête* walks she could crowd into an afternoon became the criterion of a woman's social success'. The duchess had known 'some unattractive women, who, unfortunately for their peace of mind, were as vain as they were self-conscious', and preferred to spend the afternoon in their rooms pleading a headache than to acknowledge that they had not been invited to go for a walk.[9]

At country houses less respectable than Blenheim Palace, however, house-parties could be highly pleasurable. Lady Brooke, later Countess of Warwick, for instance, spent an immense amount of money on hers and took pains to ensure that all her guests enjoyed themselves to the full. One of her parties lasted a week, the guests being transported by a special train which ran from London and back every day, and actors being engaged to play the parts of chessmen in the gardens, arrayed in fantastic costumes.

According to Elinor Glyn, who lived nearby at Durrington House and often attended her neighbour's house-parties at Easton Lodge, those with a taste for sexual intrigue and illicit liaisons found their hostess an ever-willing and resourceful collaborator, always careful to warn her guests that the stable yard bell rang at six o'clock in the morning, thus providing them with a reliable alarm in case they had to return to a previously unoccupied bed.

> In the staircase hall [Mrs Glyn wrote], there was a tray, on which stood beautifully cleaned silver candlesticks . . . one of which you carried up to your room, even if you did not need it at all. It might be that in lighting it up for you, your admirer might whisper a suggestion of a rendezvous for the morning; if not, probably on your breakfast tray you would find a note from him, given by his valet to your maid, suggesting where and when you might chance to meet him for a walk . . . Supposing you had settled to meet the person who was amusing you in the saloon, say, at eleven, you went there casually at the agreed time, dressed to go out, and found your cavalier awaiting you. Sometimes Lady Brooke would be there too, but she always sensed whether this was an arranged meeting or an accidental one. If it was intended, she would say graciously that Stone Hall, her little Elizabethan pleasure house in the park, was a nice walk before lunch, and thus make it easy to start. Should some strangers who did not know the ropes happen to be there, too, and show signs of accompanying you on the walk, she would immediately engage them in conversation until you had got safely away.[10]

Once the intending lovers had come to an understanding, it would usually be agreed that something would be left outside the lady's bedroom door to signify that she was alone and that the coast was clear; but a pile of sandwiches on a plate, formerly a favourite sign, had fallen into disfavour since the greedy German diplomat, Baron von Eckardstein, seeing some in a corridor at Chatsworth, had picked them up and eaten them all on the way to his room, much to the consternation of the countess who had placed them there.

Baron von Eckardstein had been asked to Chatsworth to meet Joseph Chamberlain to discuss Anglo-German relations; and house-parties often did serve as an excuse and as a meeting place for informal conferences of this kind. But most were organized purely for pleasure; and, in the opinion of the Hon. Sir Harold Nicolson, writing of those given in Edwardian times – which differed little from those given half a century earlier – they were 'the most agreeable form of social intercourse that the world has ever known'.

Awakened by their valets with brass cans of hot water for shaving and with trays of tea, toast and biscuits, the gentlemen would arrive in the dining-room at about half past nine. 'The smell of last night's port had given place to the smell of this morning's spirit of wine. Rows of little spirit lamps warmed rows of large silver dishes.' As well as hot food, there would be cold hams and tongues, galantine, pheasant and ptarmigan laid out on a separate table; on a third there would be porridge; on a fourth jugs of lemonade and water; on a fifth coffee and Indian and China tea, the China indicated by yellow ribbons, the Indian by red. At the centre table,

> bright with Malmaisons and toast racks, no newspapers were, at this stage, allowed . . . A pleasant sense of confederacy and sin hung above the smell of the spirit lamps. For had they not all been brought up to attend family prayers? And had they not all eluded that obligation? It was true of course that the host and hostess had at nine proceeded to the family chapel and heard the butler reading a short collect for the day. But the guests had for their part evaded these Victorian obligations. The corporate evasion gave to the proceedings an atmosphere of dash. There was no insincerity in the bright gaiety with which they greeted each other, with which they discussed how he or she had slept. 'A little kedgeree, Lady Maude?' 'Oh, thank you, Mr Stapleton.' Evidently it was all going well.

After breakfast they would go to church, after luncheon for a drive in a large motor-car, after tea they would play bridge, after dinner they would return to the bridge tables, and after a supper of devilled chicken they would go to bed. In the morning their valets would pack their fruit salts and their shooting-sticks, and they would be driven to the railway station to go back to London. 'Their carriages would meet them, horses champing bits at the arrival platform.' In the train they would have picked up the *Morning Post* and read with satisfaction a list of their own names as members of the house-party. 'They returned to Curzon Street feeling very pleased indeed. And next Saturday it would all begin again.'[11]

# 49 · *Dressing, Smoking and Social Rank*

For ladies, one of the principal preoccupations of the house-party was the problem of clothes and the need to keep changing them. Breakfast in the dining-room demanded an elegant costume of velvet or silk, or perhaps, a riding habit; before luncheon these clothes were discarded for tweeds, suitable wear for joining the guns and watching a drive or two; at tea-time tweeds gave way to an elaborate tea-gown; and then it was time to change for dinner when the maids brought out satins or brocades which were worn with a great display of jewels. 'All these changes necessitated tremendous outlay, since one was not supposed to wear the same gown twice.'[1]

Putting on these costumes was a lengthy business, for the flimsy, figure-revealing, often transparent, frocks of the Regency had long since given way to dresses of an increasingly cumbersome, figure-concealing fussiness. In the 1830s a footman in the employment of a rich widow confided to his diary how deeply the immodest clothes of his mistress's young guests shocked his sense of propriety:

> It's quite disgusting to a modist eye to see the way the young ladies dress to attract the notice of the gentlemen. They are nearly naked to the waist, only just a little bit of dress hanging on the shoulder, the breasts are quite exposed except a little bit comeing up to hide the nipples. Plenty of false haire and teeth and paint. If a person wish to see the ways of the world, they must be a gentleman's servant then they mite see it to perfection.[2]

This footman died in 1892 and by then he would have had no cause for such complaint. The high-waisted and straight-hanging style of the early years of the nineteenth century had first given way to the much more elaborate style of the 1830s with the waists lowered and the skirts belled, then to the fashions of the 1840s with skirts, supported by masses of petticoats bunched at the waist which made the crinoline 'a physical and mechanical necessity'. The crinoline had been in full swing in the 1850s and remained in fashion, disliked though it was, until the late 1860s. But this, in turn, had given place to the flounces, polonaises and bustles of the 1870s, and, eventually, a more manageable style developed with the greater freedom and activity of late Victorian life.[3] Leg-of-mutton sleeves, however, outlasted the century as did those long, trailing skirts which had to be held up before their wearers could move about in them. So also did corsets which even young girls wore to compress their waists as near as possible to the required eighteen inches and which were frequently responsible for fainting fits and occasionally for permanent ill-health.

Some advanced women took to the bloomer – a short skirt with loose trousers gathered round the ankles – a form of dress recommended by the advocate of women's rights, Amelia Jenks Bloomer; but most ladies considered this sort of apparel quite shockingly *outré*, though the bloomer both concealed and impeded female legs rather than revealed their charms. Knickers began to be worn in 1890, though in a very apologetic kind of way at first being long and wide and frilled at the edges so that if they were seen at all, they would look like the petticoats they were intended to replace. At the end of the century the customers of Harrods, the fashionable department store, were not being offered underclothes much more liberating than these. The store's 1895 catalogue offered unappetising longcloth knickers with trimmed edgings and longcloth drawers at 1s 6d the pair, cambric combinations with 'trimmed Torchon Lace Insertion' at 3s 11½d, and nainsook camisoles at 1s 11½d.[4] At this time a separate blouse might have been worn by a lady playing tennis, but even for this activity she still wore a long though not a trailing skirt, and she normally kept her corset on as well, even on the hottest summer days.

False hair and hair dyes were still employed in the 1880s but a painted face was rarely seen except on the stage or in those establishments in the Haymarket from whose very doors the eyes of respectable ladies were averted. Sarah Bernhardt appeared in polite society with white powder on her face and black lines around her eyelids to emphasize her eyes. But actresses were allowed a certain licence which would never have been extended to ladies; and it was another actress, Ellen Terry, who noted how 'astonishing' it seemed when Bernhardt, while talking to Henry Irving, 'took some red stuff out of her bag and rubbed it on her lips'.[5]

If a lady wanted to use cosmetics, she had to do so with such discretion that the effects appeared to be only the slightest improvement upon nature. Lip-salves containing a hint of carmine might perhaps be used by those with the excuse of a chapped skin; and rich and daring ladies might secretly visit such establishments as Madame Rachel's in New Bond Street where 'Chinese

Leaves for the Cheek and Lips', 'Circassian Beauty Wash', 'Favourite of the Harem's Pearl White', 'Magnetic Rock Dew Water of the Sahara', 'Venus's Toilet' and similar preparations were offered for sale at prices commensurate with the magical ingredients that they were alleged to contain. Madame Rachel's 'Royal Arabian Toilet of Beauty', a course of baths, ranged in price from 100 to 1000 guineas. Most ladies, however, apprehensive of being detected in some unseemly artifice, had to be content with soap and water, sponge and brush, to bring the contrast of colour to a pale face.

Towards the end of the century, while obvious lip colouring was still unusual, rouged cheeks were more often seen in upper-class society, so were kohl-shadowed eyes, eyelashes painted with mascara and thickened with coconut oil, and lightly coloured, highly polished finger-nails. In Oscar Wilde's *A Woman of No Importance* of 1894 a character comments that there are now only two kinds of women in society, 'the plain and the coloured'; and two years later Max Beerbohm lamented:

> It is useless to protest. Artifice must queen it once more in town . . . For behold! The Victorian era comes to an end and the day of sancta simplicitas is quite ended. The old signs are here and portents to warn the seer of life that we are ripe for a new epoch of artifice. Are not men rattling the dice-box and ladies dipping their fingers in the rouge-pot?[6]

The clothes of a late-Victorian gentleman were scarcely more suited to his various occupations than were those of his wife and daughters until the less formal wear required for playing games had their effect upon the dress worn at other times. In the 1830s black was the established colour for business and professional wear, though for sport and upon social occasions of all kinds other colours were acceptable from brown and grey to green and blue. Even for evening dress black did not become universal until late Victorian times. Breeches were being discarded for trousers in the 1830s except by elderly gentlemen of conservative tastes. The trousers had flaps buttoned across the waist, were usually worn very tight and were often extremely colourful: Brougham's were of tartan, Macaulay's of nankeen, Disraeli's of green velvet. Coats for wearing outdoors had full skirts for riding and were closely buttoned; those worn indoors had lapels rolled well back to reveal an expanse of linen, neck-cloth, glittering jewels and brightly embroidered waistcoats.[7] David Copperfield wears a gold watch and chain, a ring upon his little finger, a long-tailed coat, straw-coloured kid gloves, shoes too small for him, and a great deal of pomade on his hair. It sometimes takes him two hours to dress, and in his buttonhole he sports a flower, a 'pink camellia japonica, price half a crown'. His tastes are those of his creator who loved to parade the streets in 'crimson velvet waistcoats, multi-coloured neck-ties with two breast pins joined by a little gold chain, and yellow kid gloves'. At a banquet given in honour of the actor William Charles Macready, in 1851, Dickens appeared 'in a blue dress coat faced with silk and aflame with gorgeous brass bottons, a [waistcoat] of black satin, with a white satin collar, and a wonderfully embroidered shirt'.[8] Later on in the century such dandified clothes were considered insufferably vulgar; and the well-dressed gentleman in town wore a frock coat with a black waistcoat, a tall black top-hat, a silk cravat, and wide tubular trousers which touched the ground at the heel of the boot and rose over the instep in front. In the country, less formal though not too brightly coloured attire was now considered acceptable. What were to become known as sports coats and business suits were often seen in fashionable country houses in the late 1860s, when a gentleman could also walk the streets without fear of ridicule in the headgear recently put on sale by the London hatter, John Bowler, or in summer in a round, flat straw hat with a silk ribbon, known as a boater. Many gentlemen, however, still wore black frock coats in the country: if Millais's portrait is to be believed, John Ruskin wore his when climbing mountains; and Lord Salisbury certainly went so far as to don his for shooting rabbits. As late as the 1890s the Prince of Wales could be seen riding down Rotten Row in a long coat and silk hat.

The prince, of course, was an expert on all matters sartorial and was a supremely important influence in the development of male fashion. 'My dear fellow,' he once said ('more in sorrow than in anger') to a groom-in-waiting who was to accompany him to a wedding, 'where is your white waistcoat? Is it possible you are thinking of going to a *wedding* in a black waistcoat?' And to a secretary who had thought it odd to present himself 'in a sort of Stock Exchange' attire for a visit to a picture gallery and had thought it prudent to question the instructions, the prince replied: 'I thought everyone must know that a short jacket is always worn with a silk hat at a private view in the morning.' He himself was infallible. He even knew what the answer was when the Russian ambassador asked him if it would be proper for him to attend race-meetings while in mourning: 'To Newmarket, yes, because it means a bowler hat, but not to the Derby because of the top hat.'[9]

Although generally conservative, even reactionary in some respects, trying to prevent the demise of the frock coat, reviving the fashion of wearing knee-breeches with evening dress, and deriding those who wore Panama hats, the prince originated some new fashions and made others respectable. His adoption of a short, dark blue jacket with silk facings, worn with a black bow tie and black trousers while on a voyage to India, led to the general acceptance of the dinner jacket; his fondness for the loose, waist-banded Norfolk jacket made this type of coat popular all over England; while photographs of him wearing a felt hat with a rakishly curved brim brought back from Homburg, or a green, plumed Tyrolean hat from Marienbad, led to hundreds of thousands of similar hats being sold at home. He found it more comfortable – then decided it looked elegant – to leave the bottom button of his waistcoat undone, and soon no gentleman ever did that button up.

The prince also did much to make smoking more acceptable. His mother disliked the habit intensely. She had once been seen puffing on a cigarette at a summer picnic to keep the midges away, but her aversion to smoking indoors was so extreme that when two of her younger sons entered her room suddenly one day to offer their condolences upon some disaster, they thought it as well to apologize profusely for having dared to appear before her in their smoking jackets. Even Prince Albert had not presumed to smoke in her presence; and at Osborne House, the mansion that Thomas Cubitt, with his royal master at his elbow, designed for the royal family on the Isle of Wight, a special smoking-room was built, the only room with a lonely A above the door instead of an A intertwined with a V. The queen could always detect the smell of tobacco on documents which were sent up to her; and her Assistant Private Secretary, Frederick Ponsonby, once received a sharp injunction not to smoke while decoding telegrams which made the smell of their official box 'most obnoxious'. He and his colleagues took to carrying peppermints in their pockets in case a summons to the queen came at a moment when their breath was sure to offend her.[10]

> Smoking at Windsor [Ponsonby wrote in his memoirs] necessitated a very long walk for the guests, as the billiard room, which was the only room in which smoking was allowed, was a long way off. In conceding the billiard-room to smokers the Queen thought she was really doing all that was necessary. If any gentleman wished to indulge in the disgusting habit of smoking he should go away as far as possible.

When her third daughter, Princess Helena, married Prince Christian of Schleswig-Holstein, Queen Victoria heard to her horror that he smoked.

> It was not so bad as if he drank, but still it was a distinct blemish on his otherwise impeccable character. The Queen, however, decided to be broad-minded and actually to give him a room where he could indulge in this habit. A small room was found near the servants' quarters which could only be reached by crossing the open kitchen courtyard, and in this bare room was placed a wooden chair and table. She looked upon this room as a sort of opium-den. Later when Prince Henry of Battenberg married Princess Beatrice he induced the Queen to alter this barbarous smoking-room, and although she insisted on its being more or less in the servants'

quarters, it could be reached without going out of doors, and it was suitably furnished with armchairs, sofas, and writing-tables.[11]

The queen's dislike of smoking was widely shared. Lord Melbourne always made 'a great row about it' and, if he smelled tobacco, 'swore perhaps for half an hour'. The Duke of Wellington required his guests to smoke in the servants' hall; Sir John Boileau never repeated an invitation to a guest who had been caught smoking; and George Murray, Bishop of Rochester, confessed that he would have refused a candidate for ordination if it came to light that he had been smoking in his bedroom when staying in the Bishop's Palace.[12]

After the smoking-room was installed at Osborne in 1845, however, most country houses were provided with rooms where the host and his male guests could smoke and tell stories free from the constraints imposed by the company of ladies, most securely so at Bryanston which was built by Norman Shaw for Lord Portman in 1890 and in which there was a completely masculine wing of billiard-room, smoking-room, sitting-room, lavatories and bachelor bedrooms.[13] Smoking-rooms were not innovations. There were, for example, such rooms at Canons in 1727 and at Kedleston in 1767; but towards the end of the eighteenth century smoking had gone out of fashion among the upper classes. Heavy smokers, like the fifth Earl of Bedford, and those who chewed tobacco while talking, as the Duke of Albemarle had done, became virtually unknown in England, though pipes were smoked and cigars handed freely around in the courts of Germany, as young men on the Grand Tour had often noticed. The German Prince Pückler-Muskaü, who arrived in England on a tour in 1826 and next year attended a dinner given in honour of the king's brother, the Duke of Sussex, was surprised to notice that cigars were offered to him and to the other gentlemen after the ladies had left. It was the first time he had seen this done in England.[14] But then the Duke of Sussex had been at Göttingen university and had spent much of his time abroad; and it was known that he had acquired a taste for tobacco in Germany. It was not for another generation that cigar-smoking in England became general.

By then billiard-rooms as well as smoking-rooms had become integral parts of most gentlemen's country houses, and guests who did not appear in them for a convivial smoke or game after the ladies had retired were liable to be dragged out of bed to conform to a recognized social convention. There were still, however, houses which were not provided with smoking-rooms. One such was Cragside, Northumberland, built by Norman Shaw for Lord Armstrong, the inventor, scientist and armaments manufacturer in the 1870s; and it was 'curious to see', so *The Onlooker* observed in 1901, 'a row of Japanese or other foreign naval officers, in charge of some war vessel building at the famous Elswick works [apart from Krupps, the biggest armament factory in the world] sitting on the low wall outside the front door, puffing away for all they were worth'.[15]

Smoking-rooms and billiard-rooms were far from being the only new requirements of most owners and builders of country houses. The ninth Duke of Marlborough was exceptional in his reluctance to install new bathrooms and lavatories. In his day nearly all large country houses were well supplied with water-closets and, if bathrooms were not so common, there was usually running water on every floor. Some had had showers, baths and water-closets for many years. By 1813 the Earl of Moira had installed at least six water-closets at Donington Park in Leicestershire; and both he and the countess had their own bathroom, his leading off his study and powdering-room, hers off her dressing-room. By the 1840s the Duke of Buckingham had at least nine water-closets at Stowe, four bathrooms and a shower-bath.[16]

At the same time candles were being replaced by oil. Belvoir Castle was already mostly lit by oil in the 1830s, as many as 600 gallons being used in the sixteen or seventeen weeks of 'the season of his Grace's residence'.[17] Gas was also coming into favour; but this was very expensive and, although in use at the Marine Pavilion, Brighton, before the Prince Regent succeeded to the throne as George IV in 1820, it was generally considered too hot and too smelly for domestic use. At Brighton guests were constantly complaining of the excessive heat of the rooms.[18] But by the end of the century gaslight had become almost universal; and in some houses, had already been replaced by electricity. Cragside was the first private house in England to be properly fitted with electric light, Swan lamps being installed throughout the house by the end of 1880.[19] Electricity was introduced into Hatfield soon afterwards; and twenty years later several other houses were also lit by electricity and many more had central heating.

While the interiors of country houses were being altered to make them more comfortable and convenient, the outsides of many were also being transformed. Classical, eighteenth-century façades were being swallowed up by the Gothic and neo-Elizabethan exteriors such as those which enveloped the earlier Shadwell Park in Norfolk and the Earl of Carnarvon's house at Highclere. The Gothic and Elizabethan styles were also usually preferred for new houses rather than the Italianate. Prince Albert chose the Italianate for Osborne; but far more representative was Eaton Hall as rebuilt by Alfred Waterhouse for the Duke of Westminster in the 1870s at a cost of about £600,000. Gothic houses such as this eschewed the porticoes, the sham fortifications and those machicolations which Wyatville had incorporated into the fabric at Windsor Castle and which, hitherto unknown there, were, it was to be hoped, no longer of practical use. But late Victorian domestic

architecture, while generally rejecting the impression of a fortress, did often
contrive to hint at a kind of comfortable, Anglican monasticism. Architects
and their clients had a strong taste for stained glass and tracery, for chapels
and for such inscriptions carved over lintels as, 'Except the Lord buildeth the
house they labour in vain that build it.' At Eaton Hall, where bells played
'Home Sweet Home' when the Duke returned from London, a tall tower and
a chapel contrived to dominate the rest of the building.

While some of the most imposing of Victorian country houses were built or
reconstructed by aristocratic families, Burges's Cardiff Castle by Lord Bute,
for example, and the neo-Georgian Bryanston by Lord Portman, there were
others which were built for men or the sons of men who had made fortunes in
banking, in industry, from newspapers or shipping. Lord Wolverton's house
at Iwerne Minster was built with the profits of railways; Arthur Wilson's
Tranby Croft with those of ships. A cotton tycoon built Orchardleigh House
in Somerset, a wool millionaire Milner Field in Yorkshire; the printer and
principal proprietor of *The Times* spent some £120,000 reconstructing Bear
Wood in Berkshire. These new owners, joining in the field sports of the older
families, sending their sons to expensive schools, obeying the rules of
upper-class society, were eventually accepted by the ancient aristocracy,
without being welcomed into it. Yet, while they were eager to share in the
enjoyment of prestige and influence, they were not at all anxious to usurp it.
Nor had the middle classes, who had no pretension to landed estates, any
desire to see the eclipse of nobility. 'It is not our aim to overthrow the
aristocracy', an industrialist told Hippolyte Taine in the 1860s.

> We are ready to leave the government and high offices in their hands. For
> we believe . . . that the conduct of national business calls for special men,
> born and bred to the work for generations, who enjoy an independent and
> commanding position. Besides, their titles and pedigree give them a
> quality of dash and style . . . But [there must] be no mediocrities and no
> nepotism. Let them govern, but let them be fit to govern.[20]

The Victorian aristocracy certainly adapted itself skilfully to the changing
conditions of the time. The lessons of the European revolutions of 1848 had
not been lost upon it; nor had the aspirations of the Chartists. The arrogance,
frivolity and selfish extravagance which had characterized so many noblemen
during the regency and reign of George IV were discarded for different,
more responsible and worthy attributes. It was a revealing sign of the times
that Lord Hatherton contended that in 1810 only two gentlemen in Staffordshire had family prayers and that by 1850 only two did not.

There were still eccentric and profusely wasteful aristocrats such as the
fifth Duke of Portland who had an underground tunnel a mile and half long

built between Welbeck Abbey and the nearby town of Worksop so that his curtained carriage could be driven to the railway station, lifted on to the train and transported to London without his being seen. When he arrived in London, this duke – who was known to have any maid who encountered him in the corridors at Welbeck dismissed on the spot – was driven to his town house where huge ground-glass and cast-iron screens, 200 feet long and eighty feet high, ensured that he was protected from his neighbours' prying eyes.[21] There were still also such flamboyant figures as the Earl of Cardigan, leader of the most famous cavalry charge in history, seducer of women and savage snob, whose career showed that while most noble families contrived to conceal their black sheep and to hide their skeletons in cupboards, there remained aristocrats not merely irresponsible and immoral but brazenly so. Yet far more characteristic of his time was the first Duke of Westminster, once Liberal Member of Parliament for Chester, subsequently supporter of Gladstone in the Lords, philanthropist, Christian, Lord-Lieutenant, honorary colonel of yeomanry, model landlord, promoter of education, sportsman, art collector, race-horse breeder, good and faithful husband – though his first wife was often unfaithful to him – and kind father of fifteen children.[22]

'Before the example of a court, virtuous, humane and beneficient, the attitude of the British upper classes has undergone a noble change,' wrote the Rev. Charles Kingsley in 1862. 'There is no aristocracy in the world, and there never has been, as far as I know, which has so honourably repented . . . which has so cheerfully asked what its duty was, that it might do it . . . The whole creed of our young gentlemen is becoming more liberal, their demeanour more courteous, their language more temperate.'[23] Even the radical politician, Richard Cobden, was obliged to conclude at the same time that in his experience the upper classes had 'never stood so high in relative social and political rank'. Certainly they contrived with marked success to hold on to their positions of power. In the 1865 House of Commons over three-quarters of the members were connected with the peerage by marriage, descent or interest. And those of the upper class who were not politicians, and were not occupied exclusively with the management of their estates, were likely to be at least active in local government and recognized by their acknowledged inferiors as being worthy both of responsibility and respect.

# 50 · *Workers on the Land*

'When I was ten I left school to work on a farm for £3 a year and my keep,' recalled Tom Mullins, an old farmer who had started his working life in the early 1870s at the age of seven as a 'half-timer' at a rope-works in Leek, Staffordshire, where he had earned 1s 6d a week by turning the handle of a machine. On the farm he helped to drive the horses, and 'when there were two [he] had to walk between them while leading and often got trodden on'.

> We often had difficulty in getting our horses and wagons across flooded streams. Often my clothes were quite wet when I took them off at night and still wet when I put them on again next morning . . . I was always hungry at that place, but after a year I moved to a bigger farm where the living was better . . . On Sundays I walked ten miles home to have dinner with my parents, and then walked ten miles back to start milking . . . I then went to work on a farm belonging to Michael Bass. He was an easy man to talk to and you did not realize he was titled. I often went to his house for the hot soup, meat and dripping which were distributed free to the poor of the parish . . . One of my jobs was to take letters to the post-box, and this I did not like doing for the lane ran alongside a dark wood where rough men wandered about. When I was ten I milked and tended seven cows single-handed.

Mullins left Bass's farm to work on a milk-round in Leek, then found employment at a farm near Manchester where the family lived 'like pigs' and expected him to exist on bread and dripping. So he left there after a week, and returned to Staffordshire where he worked as a carter on a seventy-five-acre farm. There was little machinery in Staffordshire in those days, he said, and, indeed, steam-ploughs and steam-driven threshing machines were still far from common in several other counties as well. Mullins's master would not have even a horse in the field, insisting that hard manual work was best and requiring his men to cut corn with a short 'badging' hook and hay with a scythe. Little artificial manure was used. Cows' urine was poured into tanks, carted out to the fields in barrels and spread with a long-handled ladle; night-soil was bought from contractors who collected it in the towns; and women earned 18d a day by following the horses grazing in the pastures and breaking up the dung with long forks. Mullins himself was earning £16 a year and his keep by the time he was seventeen, 'the highest wage a man could get'. Yet while wages were low, people managed to live on them and even save a bit, since, as he said, money went so much further then than now. 'Bread was 3d the quarten loaf, milk 3d a quart, tobacco 3d an ounce (what a cry went up when it was raised to 3½d), while beer was 2d a pint.' The year's work ended at Michaelmas 'when all farm workers took a week's holiday, and then went to the Hiring Fair, about October, 10th . . . other holidays were May Day and Well-dressing.'[1]

In 1902 when, after more than thirty years of hard work, Mullins had saved enough to rent his own farm, the number of people working on the land had fallen to 712,000, only 12,000 of them women, whereas in 1851 there had been 1,343,000, about 143,000 of them women, apart from 364,000 indoor farm servants of both sexes.[2]

Many women farm labourers worked in gangs by which was meant, in the words of an official report, 'a number of persons, men, women, girls, lads and boys, employed by and under the control of one person who lets them out to different farmers in turn for certain kinds of work'.[3] Following a series of inquiries inspired by Lord Shaftesbury in the 1860s these gangs were eventually brought under control by the Gangs Act of 1868; but before that the workers employed in them, up to about thirty in each gang, worked in conditions which horrified the commissioners appointed to investigate them. Working hours were long, rates of pay low: children received no more than 4d a day, women 8d, the same amount paid to the few men, mostly disabled by illness or infirmity, who could get no other work. The gangmaster, acting as foreman, paid wages even lower than these if he could, pocketing all the profits he could make after having agreed with the farmer the price to be paid for the hoeing, weeding, stone-picking or other work that the gang were set to do.

Since gangs were usually employed on large farms in thinly populated areas, the workers often had to walk long distances from the villages and were often 'placed in situations where they [could] procure no shelter from rain or inclement weather' and were consequently subject to 'intermittent fever, rheumatism, scarlet fever, pleurisy . . . consumption' and maladies occasioned by their eating their midday meal while sitting on the damp ground.

As well as an unhealthy life, it was, as the commissioners declared, an extremely immoral one. No attention was paid by the gangmaster to the habits or character of the women he employed; and if they were not immodest when they entered his employment they soon became so. Decent people were shocked when a gang of women and boys walked past their houses, shouting obscenities at each other, engaged in 'loud and coarse conversation, with great thick boots, and buskins on their legs', the petticoats of the women tucked up between their bare legs as they wore them in the fields.

A Lincolnshire doctor, who had been in practice in Spalding for twenty-five years, told the commissioners that he was convinced that the gang system was the 'cause of much immorality'. Many girls as young as thirteen or fourteen had been brought into the infirmary pregnant; and he had himself witnessed 'gross indecencies between boys and girls of fourteen to sixteen years of age'. 'The evil in the system,' he considered, 'is the mixture of the sexes under no control. The gangers pay these children once a week at some beer house, and it is no uncommon thing for the children to be kept waiting at the place till eleven or twelve o'clock at night.'[4]

Gangmasters themselves often exercised a kind of droit du seigneur over their employees. In a case heard at Downham Market in 1866, a gangmaster was accused of assaulting a girl aged thirteen who deposed that he threw her to the ground and pulled up her clothes. 'It was in the sight of the gang,' she added. 'We were sitting down to our dinners . . . The other boys and girls in the gang were around me. I called out. The others laughed. He said, "Open your legs more" . . . He was lying on me flat. I could not get up . . . He had a stick . . . He has threatened to flog us if we told any tales.'[5]

Referring to this case, a Member of Parliament observed that there would be far more 'if children dared to speak'. Certainly it was generally assumed that young women in agricultural gangs were easy prey for such insatiable fornicators as the author of *My Secret Life*.

'You can always have a field girl,' this man was advised in his youth by his cousin, a wealthy farmer's son. 'Nobody cares. I have had a dozen or two.' He himself seized upon one of about fifteen who, however, resisted him. He overpowered her, violated her, then offered her money to stem her tears, clinking the gold sovereigns in his hand. 'What a temptation they must have been,' he thought, 'to a girl who earned ninepence a day and was often without work at all.' At this moment the farm foreman appeared. The girl, hesitating, pouting, wriggling her shoulders, was persuaded to take a sovereign but said she would tell her sister what had happened. 'None o' that, gal,' the gangmaster warned her, 'an' I hears more on that, you won't work here any more, nor anywhere else in this parish. I knows the whole lot on you. I knows who got yer sister's belly up . . . and I knows summut about you, too. Now take care, gal . . . Say you nought. That be my advice.' The girl, muttering, went her way.[6]

In the earlier years of the century the wages not only of workers in gangs but in the farming industry generally were almost uniformly low, lower in the south and west of the country than in the north and falling in some areas to as little as 6s a week, rising to about 11s or 12s a week in 1832. Thereafter they had risen gradually but erratically, losing ground in such wet years of disastrous harvests as 1879 and varying much from one part of the country to another. By the end of the century ordinary farm labourers in counties where agriculture was the main if not the only means of livelihood were receiving about 15s a week; those in counties where other industries forced up farm wages got about £1. Men with experience as cowmen or shepherds could earn rather more, but a good deal less than they might have been paid in a town. There were, however, certain allowances which could make life more agreeable, milk and potatoes, perhaps, beer or cider, fuel and a cottage.[7] On certain estates, like those of the Prince of Wales or the Duke of Bedford, the cottage might be quite comfortable; but for the most part labourers' cottages, until at least the 1870s, were leaky, draughty, ancient, overcrowded dwellings, little better than the hovels of the Middle Ages: in 1873 it was estimated that 'one third of the agricultural houses of Great Britain required to be rebuilt'.[8] In the Midlands and Lancashire they were generally of brick, in the Cotswolds and much of Yorkshire of stone, elsewhere of timber, wattle and daub, in Scotland commonly and Ireland nearly always of turf.

In the Oxfordshire village in which Flora Thompson spent her childhood and to which she gave the name Lark Rise, 'a few of the houses had thatched roofs, whitewashed outer walls and diamond-paned windows, but the majority were just stone or brick boxes with blue-slated roofs. The older houses were relics of pre-enclosure days and were still occupied by descendants of the original squatters, themselves at that time elderly people.' Apart from one old couple who owned a donkey and cart which they hired out by the day to neighbours, a retired farm bailiff who was said to have 'well feathered his own nest' during his years of employment, an old man who owned and worked upon an acre of land, a stone-mason who walked three miles to work in the nearest town every day, and the local innkeeper, all the other men in the village were employed as agricultural labourers.

Some of the cottages had two bedrooms, others only one, in which case it had to be divided by a screen or curtain to accommodate both parents and children.

Often the big boys of a family slept downstairs, or were sent to sleep in the second bedroom of an elderly couple whose own children were out in the world. Except at holiday times, there were no big girls to provide for, as they were all out in service. Still it was often a tight fit, for children swarmed, eight, ten or even more in some families, and although they were seldom all at home together, the eldest often being married before the youngest was born, beds and shakedowns were often so closely packed that the inmates had to climb over one bed to get into another . . . When the wind cut across the flat land to the east, or came roaring down from the north, doors and windows had to be closed, but then, as the hamlet people said, they got more than enough fresh air through the keyhole.

In nearly all the cottages there was but one room downstairs, and many of these were poor and bare, with only a table and a few chairs and stools for furniture and a superannuated potato-sack thrown down by way of hearthrug. Other rooms were bright and cosy, with dressers of crockery, cushioned chairs, pictures on the walls, and brightly coloured hand-made rag rugs on the floor. In these there would be pots of geraniums, fuchsias, and old-fashioned, sweet-smelling musk on the window-sills. In the older cottages there were grandfathers' clocks, gate-legged tables, and rows of pewter, relics of a time when life was easier for country folk.

The interiors varied, according to the number of mouths to be fed and the thrift and skill of the housewife, or the lack of those qualities; but the income in all was precisely the same, for ten shillings a week was the standard wage of the farm labourer at that time in that district.[9]

Poor and cramped as many of the cottages in Lark Rise were, however, some of those that the Rev. Francis Kilvert entered in the 1870s as curate at Clyro near Hay-on-Wye were much poorer still. In one the bedroom was a 'dark hovel hole almost underground'. Here an old man of eighty-two lay dying next to 'a fair haired little girl of 4 years old'. In another the bedroom was 'a low and crazy loft in the roof' which was so dark that it was impossible to discern the features of the occupants. 'A small and filthy child knelt or crouched in the ashes of the hearth before a black grate and cold cinders. No one else was in the house and the rain splashed in the court and on the roof and the wind whistled through the tiles. Almost all the glass was smashed out of the bedroom or rather bed loft window, and there was only a dirty cloth hanging before the ruin of the window to keep the wind away.'[10]

The size of the farms upon which the occupants of such places worked varied widely from district to district. Yeomen farming their own (usually quite modest) acreages were now a dying breed. Most farmers rented their land from the gentry and either hired labour by the year if the size of their farm warranted it or worked the land themselves with the help of their families if it did not. Large farms were tending to grow larger and small farms fewer. In the Cotswolds and East Anglia, for example, there were several large farmers who had held the same land for generations and were, in the words of W. Johnston, writing in 1850, permitted to 'mix with the landowners in their field sports'. This association was, however, 'upon a footing of understood inferiority, and the association exists only out of doors, or in the public room of an inn after a cattle-show or an election. The difference in manners of the two classes does not admit of anything like social and family intercourse'.[11] The gulf between the large farmer and the smallholder was almost equally wide, the latter being 'scarcely above the labourers in education or in general manner of life'.[12]

In Yorkshire there were both large farms of over 1000 acres in extent and smallholdings of less than twenty. The large farms commonly employed several men and women who were provided with board and lodging – often in primitive buildings presided over by elderly female caretakers and cooks – as well as with wages which were rarely paid more than three times in the year. They were engaged on an annual basis at the Martinmas hirings and usually moved on to a new farm when their year's employment was over.[13] The tenants of some of the smallholdings in the West Riding continued to eke out their meagre living with industrial labour as their forebears had done in the eighteenth century.

They have looms in their houses [wrote James Caird, the agriculturist, in 1851], and unite the business of weavers and farmers. When trade is good the farm is neglected; when trade is dull the weaver becomes a more attentive farmer. His holding is generally under twenty acres, and his chief stock consists of dairy cows, with a horse to convey his manufactured goods and his milk to market. The union of trades has been long in existence in this part of the country, but it seldom leads to much success on the part of the weaver-farmer himself, and the land he occupies is believed to be the worst managed in the district.[14]

Men like these and the agricultural labourer, the ignorant, 'tall, long, smock-frocked, straw-hatted, ankle-booted fellow' of William Howitt's description, lived hard lives which few looked back upon with contentment and satisfaction.

Admittedly, some farm labourers remembered being happy and well fed with 'any amount of bread and bacon, and plenty of home-brewed beer, and, in the winter, a sure, drowsy place by the kitchen fire'. Most, however, recalled less happy times, rising at dawn to work until sunset for their paltry wages, eating bread and potatoes with an occasional piece of bacon and an apple dumpling, often going to bed hungry. One, no doubt characteristic, family in Yorkshire, had bread and treacle for breakfast, and sometimes a little tea made from used leaves collected from a local inn; for dinner there was broth obtained from a nearby farm three days a week, potatoes and possibly dumplings; supper was like breakfast with the occasional addition of an apple pie. It was estimated that by now about 2 million people in Britain lived largely on potatoes. In Ireland 4 million – nearly half the total population in 1841 – did so; and when the Irish crop failed hardship and famine were inevitable. In successive years after 1845 the Irish crop was blighted and hundreds of thousands of people died either by starvation or of the fevers that attended malnutrition. Many more, perhaps a million, emigrated within the six years before 1851, most of them to America, but many to England where they not only poured into the industrial towns – between a third and a fifth of Manchester's and Liverpool's labouring populations were composed of Irish immigrants[15] – but also into the countryside, swelling the number of casual agricultural labourers and adding to the problems of farming communities.

During the 1870s conditions began gradually to improve in most areas as Joseph Arch's agricultural trade union became effective. But towards the end of that decade a general depression in agriculture affected the livelihoods of workers in most parts of the country. A generation or so before, a foreign observer had expressed the opinion that 'English agriculture taken as a whole [was] at this day the first in the world'.[16] But in 1877 its prosperity was beset by widespread outbreaks of rinderpest. An exceptionally wet summer in 1878 was followed in 1879 by the worst and wettest that most farmers could remember and this time it was accompanied by an outbreak of liver-rot in sheep. That year was 'a disastrous one for agriculture', one farmer recorded in his diary, having 'had a very bad yield of corn & sheep rotten & doing very bad'.[17] Four years later there was a violent epidemic of foot-and-mouth disease.

During these years the growth of railways in the United States, the rapid spread of farm machinery there and the increasing cheapness of ocean-going steamer transport combined to make it possible for American farmers to export great quantities of prairie-wheat. The price of English wheat consequently plummeted and soon almost half the country's grain, nearly all of which had previously been supplied at home, was coming from abroad. In the wake of the wheat came imports of frozen meat, of live cattle, and of a cheap substitute for butter. Farm wages fell sharply once more; many farmers went bankrupt; whole tracts of land were abandoned to birds of prey; almost 100,000 labourers left the land to find work in the towns; and over a million people emigrated. Yet by the end of the century, after a series of more productive and healthier seasons, it was generally agreed that life for poor country people was less harsh than it had been. There was more variety in their diet; wages, so one of them said, seemed to 'go a bit further'; women and children were far less often to be seen working singly or in gangs in the fields. Already by 1881 there were only 68,000 boys under fifteen working on the land as compared with 106,000 thirty years before and no more than 40,000 women as compared with 144,000 in 1851.[18] In all there were still over a million people occupied in agriculture but this was by now only 12 per cent of the total population whereas the 1,388,000 so employed in 1851 had represented a proportion of over 20 per cent.[19]

While the lot of the agricultural labourer was less unenviable than it had been in the earlier years of the century, his way of life continued to be an impoverished one; and so it remained throughout the Edwardian era. In about 1906 the average weekly earnings of a farmworker had risen no higher than 17s 6d, well below the figure of 21s 8d which Seebohm Rowntree considered the minimum sum a man living in York would require to support a wife and three children with the basic necessities of life.[20] Some farm-workers earned considerably less than this. One, a labourer with a wife and five children living in the Wiltshire village of Corsley in 1906, had no more than 15s a week. The rent of his cottage was 1s 6d a week, and other regular outgoings included 2s 5d a month to a Friendly Society and 5s a year for an allotment. One typical week in January he and his wife spent 13s 4¾d and with this sum were able to purchase three pounds of sugar (5½d), half a pound of tea (8d), one and a half pounds of butter, (1s 6d), two ounces of tobacco (6d), half a pound of lard (2½d), quarter of a pound of suet (2d), half a pound of currants (1½d), one pint of beer (2d), one pound of soap (3d) and a pair of stockings (6½d). Other purchases were small quantities of bacon (1s 4d), oranges (2d), Quaker oats (5½d), cheese (9d), baking powder (1d), papers (2d), coal (1s 2½d), milk (6½d), oil (2½d) and bread (3s). When clothes had to be bought or the parents were ill, the amount spent on food had to be severely reduced. It was estimated that a third of all the families living in the village were existing below what had come to be known as the poverty line.[21]

There were certain compensations. Various Allotment Acts, for instance, had enabled many labourers, like this man in Corsley, to provide their families with fresh vegetables, though farmers did not like their men having these plots of land which, so they felt, took up too much of their time and energy, and the men themselves often enough found them scarcely worth the trouble of maintaining, because of the depredations of the protected game of the landlord. Also, membership of a pig club gave labourers the opportunity of acquiring a little extra meat without undue expense, while membership of a union, such as the Eastern Counties Agricultural Labourers' and Small-holders' Union, formed in 1906, might bring occasional benefits through united action against avaricious employers.[22] At the same time, the govern-ment endeavoured to help small farmers by a Smallholdings Act of 1907 which eventually led to the establishment of about 14,000 new holdings, extending over 200,000 acres, before the outbreak of the First World War. Yet, while the number of smallholdings was increasing and the dairy industry was growing – with a twofold increase in the area of permanent grassland between 1870 and 1914 – arable farming was sharply declining, the corn area of the country being diminished by 30 per cent in the fifty or so years before 1914. By 1909 the number of agricultural workers in the country had fallen to 750,000, and many villages, so C. F. G. Masterman wrote that year, were now becoming bereft of craftsmen practising such traditional skills as those of smiths and wheelwrights and were largely occupied by the old and by children. In the remoter villages changes were less pronounced; but in these places the inhabitants were inward-looking and inbred communities, some of which had no more than three or four surnames in the entire parish.[23]

Despite the decline in agriculture – which was by now contributing little more than 6 per cent to the national product – there were still many farmers who were evidently very comfortably off. They did not presume to interfere too much in the running of local affairs or to have political views at variance with their landlords', generally preferring to grumble about the weather or low prices rather than the iniquities of Lord John Russell or Mr Gladstone. Gabriel Oak in Thomas Hardy's *Far From the Madding Crowd*, which was first published in 1874, is typical of his kind. A deliberate, slow, steady man, large in frame and modest by nature, he had formerly been a shepherd. 'By sustained efforts of industry and chronic good spirits', he had been enabled to lease a farm. When he smiled

> the corners of his mouth spread till they were within an unimportant distance of his ears, his eyes were reduced to chinks, and diverging wrinkles appeared round them, extending upon his countenance like the rays in a rudimentary sketch of the rising sun . . . He wore a low-crowned felt hat, spread out at the base by tight jamming upon the head for security in high winds, and a coat like Dr Johnson's; his lower extremities being encased in ordinary leather leggings and large boots.
>
> Mr Oak carried about him, by way of watch, what may be called a small silver clock; in other words, it was a watch as to shape and intention, and a small clock as to size. This instrument being several years older than Oak's grandfather, had the peculiarity of going either too fast or not at all. The smaller of its hands, too, occasionally slipped round on the pivot, and thus, though the minutes were told with precision, nobody could be quite certain of the hour they belonged to. The stopping peculiarity of his watch Oak remedied by thumps and shakes, and he escaped any evil consequences from the other two defects by constant comparison with and

observations of the sun and stars, and by pressing his face close to the glass of his neighbours' windows, till he could discern the hour marked by the green-faced time-keepers within . . . On Sundays he was hampered by his best clothes and umbrella . . . He went to church but yawned privately by the time the congregation reached the Nicene creed, and thought of what there would be for dinner when he meant to be listening to the sermon.[24]

Gabriel Oak had no social pretensions, but there were naturally some farmers who behaved in the way that Arthur Young had condemned a century earlier, who bought expensive furniture, put their servants into livery and sent their children to smart schools. But all these things, Young objected, 'imply a departure from that line which separates these different orders of being [gentlemen and farmers]. Let these things, and all the folly, foppery, expense, and anxiety, that belong to them, remain among gentlemen; a wise farmer will not envy them.'[25]

Some farmers, nevertheless, did continue to envy them. Richard Jefferies, the naturalist, himself a Wiltshire farmer's son, described in a book published in 1880 how a farmer's daughter who had been to an expensive boarding-school reacted to the prospect of marriage on returning home to her country town after her last term.

A banker's clerk at least – nothing could be thought of under a clerk in the local banks; of course, his salary was not high, but then his 'position'. The retail grocers and bakers and such people were quite beneath one's notice – low, common persons. The 'professional' tradesmen (whatever that may be) were decidedly better, and could be tolerated. The solicitors, bank managers, one or two brewers (wholesale – nothing retail), large corn factors or coal merchants, who kept a carriage of some kind – these formed the select society next under . . . the clergy and gentry.[26]

# 51 · *Towns, Factories and Public Health*

Every year, even before the depression of British farming in the 1870s, tens of thousands of men, women and children left the country for the towns which by 1851, for the first time, contained more people than the country and, by 1881, over twice as many. Most found it difficult to settle in places the sheer size of which was intimidating. The population of Greater London, which had been scarcely more than a million in 1801, had risen to well over 2 million by 1841, was over 3 million in 1861, and increased to almost 4 million in 1871, to 4,713,441 in 1881 and to 5,571,968 in 1891. It was still the largest city in the western world. Whereas no other in England had had more than 100,000 inhabitants at the beginning of the nineteenth century, when the 1851 census was taken there were nine. The population of Leeds had risen to 172,000, that of Birmingham to 233,000, Manchester's to 303,000. Four years later, when the population of Britain as a whole stood at just over 23 million (compared with 56 million in European Russia, 37.5 million in France, 34 million in Austria and 32 million in the United States) Manchester's and Birmingham's population, as well as Liverpool's, had increased to nearly half a million, and there were over twenty other towns with more than 100,000 inhabitants each, most of them industrial towns, the growth of such places as Exeter and Norwich being far more modest.

The smoky, foreboding aspect of these industrial towns was made familiar to Dickens's middle-class readers, many of whom had never seen them, by his description of Coketown in *Hard Times* which he wrote after going to Preston in Lancashire, where the workers had been on strike for almost six months. He had gone there to see for himself how the poor passed their lives in such a place – such a depressing, 'nasty' place, as he discovered it to be.

It was a town of red brick, or of brick that would have been red if the smoke and ashes had allowed it; but as matters stood it was a town of unnatural red and black like the painted face of a savage. It was a town of machinery and tall chimneys, out of which interminable serpents of smoke trailed themselves for ever and ever, and never got uncoiled. It had a black canal in it, and a river that ran purple with ill-smelling dye, and vast piles of building full of windows where there was a rattling and a trembling all day long, and where the piston of the steam-engine worked monotonously up and down like the head of an elephant in a state of melancholy madness. It contained several large streets all very like one another, and many small streets still more like one another, inhabited by people equally like one another, who all went in and out at the same hours, with the same sound upon the same pavements, to do the same work, and to whom every day was the same as yesterday and tomorrow, and every year the counterpart of the last and the next.[1]

Towns like this, usually covered in soot and dust and overcast by smoke, could but add to the unhappiness of those newly arrived from the country. 'I drew near the town and the tall chimneys of the factories became visible through the dense clouds of smoke,' recalled a former factory worker of his first sight of Leeds, whose population had risen to 207,000 in 1861 when it was the sixth largest town in the country. It exhibited

the many marks by which a manufacturing town may always be known, viz. the wretched, stunted, decrepit and frequently mutilated appearance of the broken down labourers, who are generally to be seen in the dirty, disagreeable streets; the swarms of meanly-clad women and children, and the dingy, smoky, wretched looking dwellings of the poor.[2]

For the sake of cheapness, thousands of cottages were still built back-to-back, with privies in front and open ashpits in the streets, with a cellar for coal and food, and with one small room, as a Unitarian missionary wrote, 'to do all the cooking, washing and the necessary work of a family in, and another of the same size for all to sleep in'. Even worse than these were those dwellings around dark, airless, noisome courts – whose occupants were obliged to share a privy and a tap – and those dark cellars in which, so one authority estimated, as many as 50,000 workers spent their nights in Manchester and almost as many in Leeds. Friedrich Engels, the German-born author of *The Condition of the Working Class in England*, who for twenty years from 1849 worked in a Manchester textile firm founded by his father, described the state of the poorer quarters of these northern towns. He wrote of the water from polluted rivers flooding into the cellars; of the vain attempts of their inhabitants to repair the rutted, broken streets outside with shovelfuls of ashes; the holes filled with refuse and excrement; the cottages 'cramped almost to suffocation with human beings both day and night'; the slums of Huddersfield; the lodging houses of Manchester, 'hot-beds of unnatural vice'; the engorgement of the sewers and the consequently high rate of mortality in Leeds; the death rate of the poor in Liverpool where, according to an official report, the average age at death of the 'gentry and professional persons' was thirty-five, of 'tradesmen and their families' twenty-two, and of 'labourers, mechanics and servants' fifteen; and the 'little pitch-black stinking river' that flowed through Bradford.

> The interior of Bradford is as dirty and uncomfortable as Leeds [Engels wrote]. Heaps of dirt and refuse disfigure the lanes, alleys and courts. The houses are dilapidated and dirty and are not fit for human habitation . . . The workers' houses at the bottom of the valley are packed between high factory buildings and are among the worst-built and filthiest in the whole city. Such conditions are to be found in the other towns of the West Riding . . . such as Barnsley and Halifax.[3]

London was as bad as anywhere and in some districts worse. Hippolyte Taine, whose *Notes sur Angleterre* was published in 1871, described 'one of the poor neighbourhoods' down by the river where 'low houses, poor streets of brick under red-tiled roofs cross each other in every direction'.

> It is in these localities [he wrote], that families have been discovered with no other bed than a heap of soot; they had slept there during several months . . . One observes the narrow lodgings, sometimes the single room, wherein they are all huddled in the foul air. The houses are most frequently one storied – low, narrow – a den in which to sleep and lie. What a place of residence in winter, when, during the weeks of continuous rain and fog, the windows are shut![4]

Soon after Taine wrote these words, Charles Booth, the rich co-founder of the Booth Steamship Company, came to London from Liverpool and for seventeen years immersed himself in the detailed study of poverty which was to result in the many-volumed *Life and Labour of the People in London*. Having closely examined the ways of life of some 90,000 people in various parishes in East London and Hackney, he divided them into eight classes. At the lowest level were some 11,000 'occasional labourers, loafers and semi-criminals' whose food was of the 'coarsest description' and whose only luxury was drink; their life was the 'life of savages, with vicissitudes of extreme hardship and occasional distress'. Slightly above them Booth placed 100,000 of those whom he described as 'very poor', living on the casual earnings of two or three days' work a week. Then came 75,000 people with intermittent earnings, such as dockers, coal-heavers and waterside porters, who were in and out of work according to the season or the amount of work available for them; these were also deemed 'poor'. So were the next class of people, 129,000 of them, who were in receipt of 'small regular earnings'. Then came the largest group of 377,000 people who had 'regular standard earnings' of from 22s to 30s a week; after them Booth listed 121,000 of the best paid of the artisans; and after them the smaller numbers of the lower middle class and the upper middle class. Almost half of all these people were 'poor' by the criteria Booth devised to define the term; and over 30 per cent of the population of London as a whole lived on the verges of his poverty line or below it.

Booth estimated that a man categorized as 'very poor' and with a wife and three children to look after would spend on average about 15s a week and this would absorb the whole of his income. About 9s would be spent on food, about 5s 9d on rent, heating and lighting, and the remaining few pence on clothes and whatever other necessaries it might prove essential to provide. Artisans with 'regular standard earnings' could afford to spend over twice as much. Booth provided the example of a casual dock labourer of thirty-eight, Michael H. who was 'in poor health fresh from the infirmary':

His wife of forty-three is consumptive. A son of eighteen who earns 8s regular wages as a car man's boy, and two girls of eight and six, complete the family. Their house has four rooms but they let two. Father and son dine from home; the son takes 2d a day for this. The neighbouring clergy send soup two or three times a week, and practically no meat is bought. Beyond the dinners out, and the soup at home, the food consists principally of bread, margarine, tea, and sugar. No rice is used nor any oatmeal; there is no sign of any but the most primitive cookery, but there is every sign of unshrinking economy; there are no superfluities, and the prices are the lowest possible – 3½d per quarten for bread, 6d per lb for so-called butter, 1s 4d for tea, and 1d for sugar. The accommodation costs about 17s a month. On firing, etc., the H——s spent 10s 4d in the five weeks – as much as, and more than, many with double the means; but warmth may make up for lack of food, and invalids depend on it for their lives. Allowing as well as I can for the meals out, and the charitable soup, I make the meals provided by Mrs H—— for her family to cost 1d per meal per person (counting the two little girls as one person). A penny a meal is very little, but expended chiefly in cheap bread, cheap butter, cheap tea, and cheap sugar.[5]

Other families which Booth offered as examples included those of Mr R., a blind man with a weekly pension of 5s 6d; Thomas B., a wharf labourer; and a widow with two grown-up children. Mr R. had a wife, who earned a little money in the season, picking fruit and hops, and three grown-up daughters, the eldest, 'a rough girl who ruined her health at the lead works', being an occasional sack-maker and bottle-washer. The other two daughters worked in a seed factory and gave their mother between 11s and 13s a week between them. The total housekeeping money of this family was 17s 6d a week; and they lived, 'to the greatest possible extent, from hand to mouth', buying almost everything on credit from one shop and every week putting in and taking out of pawn the same set of garments for which the broker charged 4d. The two working girls spent 2d a day on their dinners at work; the meals they had at home costing 3d a head for dinner on Sundays and 1½d for other meals. Tea formed a large part of their purchases at the corner shop to which they resorted as often as a middle-class housewife would go to her canister, making as many as three trips a day and buying 'pinches' at ¾d each.

The widow managed rather better than the Rs. She herself earned 7s a week; her daughter, aged twenty-three, received up to 15s in a good week as an envelope-folder; while her twenty-one-year-old son, who had no regular work, contrived to bring home 5s or so. Their living, with the cost of meals working out at 1¾d each, was very bare, their only luxury an occasional bottle of ginger-beer.

The dock labourer earned 21s a week, his wife a little extra, sometimes 3s 6d, by needlework; and although he had five children under ten at home and a girl out at service who still received both money and clothes from her parents, he was able to live quite comfortably, thanks to 'steadiness on his part and good management on the part of the wife'. He had all his meals at home with the family for whom, in an average week, he was able to supply eight pounds of meat at 5d a pound, five pounds of fish at 3d, thirty pounds of potatoes, thirty-four pounds of bread, three pounds of flour, one and a quarter pounds of butter and seven pounds of sugar.

Booth went on to describe in detail the appearance and inhabitants of various London streets. One of these, Shelton Street, St Giles, may be taken as characteristic:

Shelton Street was just wide enough for a vehicle to pass either way, with room between curb-stone and houses for one foot-passenger to walk; but vehicles would pass seldom, and foot-passengers would prefer the roadway to the risk of tearing their clothes against projecting nails. The houses, about forty in number, contained cellars, parlours, and first, second and third floors, mostly two rooms on a floor, and few of the 200 families who lived here occupied more than one room – which in rare instances would be curtained off. If there was no curtain, anyone lying on the bed would perhaps be covered up and hidden, head and all, when a visitor was admitted, or perhaps no shyness would be felt. Drunkenness and dirt and bad language prevailed, and violence was common, reaching at times even to murder. Fifteen rooms out of twenty were filthy to the last degree, and the furniture in none of these would be worth twenty shillings, in some cases not five shillings. Not a room would be free from vermin, and in many life at night was unbearable. Several occupants have said that in hot weather they don't go to bed, but sit in their clothes in the least infested part of the room. What good is it, they said, to go to bed when you can't get a wink of sleep for bugs and fleas? The passage from the street to the back door would be scarcely ever swept, to say nothing of being scrubbed. Most of the doors stood open all night as well as all day, and the passage and stairs gave shelter to many who were altogether homeless. The little yard at the back was only sufficient for dustbin and closet and water-tap, serving for six or seven families. The water would be drawn from cisterns which were receptacles for refuse, and perhaps occasionally a dead cat. The houses looked ready to fall, many of them being out of the perpendicular. Gambling was the amusement of the street. Sentries would be posted, and if the police made a rush the offenders would slip into the open houses and hide until danger was past. Sunday afternoon and evening was the hey-day time for this street. Every doorstep would be crowded by those who sat or stood with pipe and jug of beer, while lads lounged about, and the gutters would find amusement for not a few children with bare feet, their faces and hands be-smeared while the mud oozed through between their toes.

Among the inhabitants of Shelton Street were Mr Mulvaney who collected the rents from other occupiers; a widow with three children who made a 'fair living as a costermonger, very clean, careful, and kindly disposed'; a rough Covent Garden porter who spent most of what he earned on drink before he came home, then swore and knocked his wife about; a woman of French origin who claimed to be an officer's widow and got her living by begging and picking up odds and ends in the street; Mrs Shane, an Irishwoman, seller of water-cresses, 'rather tidier than some, though given to drink at times'; a family of Irish costermongers who would only open their door wide enough 'to afford a glimpse of wall covered with pictures and shut it again'; a woman whose husband had emigrated to America and whose children were locked up in her room while she went out into the streets selling oranges; an alcoholic, paralysed by drink, whose family were 'filthy and lived like pigs – both sights and smells were sickening'; Mrs Varney, a respectable woman who obtained a living by selling fowls; a prostitute who lived with her mother, 'a notorious drunkard'; a murderer who asserted that he 'did not believe in anything but beer'; a charwoman, 'clean and steady,' with a husband crippled by rheumatism and worn out with pain; another market porter who 'drank the largest part of his earnings, came rolling and roaring upstairs into his room' and lived 'like a demon' with a wife who also spent most of what she could lay her hands on in the public house; a very pious Roman Catholic woman whose two daughters worked in the City; a scavenger employed by the Board of Works, 'a martyr to asthma', whose room was 'most offensive and swarming with vermin'; 'a very decent man who had formerly been a pugilist, a hard hitter and hard drinker, as his battered face testified, now an abstainer and very respectable'; a mysterious young woman 'of quiet manners and doubtful character'; a shiftless, though sober, furniture repairer whose mother was a nurse; Mrs Berry, 'a widow, paralysed so as to be almost speechless, who pushed a barrow and sold mussels in the street'; Mrs O'Brien who 'sold lights in the streets, exciting pity with her suffering children' while her husband was in hospital; a drunken and violent chimney-sweep who lived with a woman whom, occasionally assisted by his sons and by another woman, he abused and insulted and slowly battered to death; a polite young man who made toys in the form of wooden mice; a music-hall bouncer; a vendor of shellfish; Mr Warner, a cobbler who bought old shoes, patched them up with paper, paste and polish and disposed of them in Dudley Street where they sold for 1s a pair 'warranted' and fell apart on the first wet day; and Mr and Mrs Park who had five children.

> This man, now about forty-eight years old, had served in India as a soldier, and was discharged in ill-health suffering from pains in the head and loss of memory due to fracture of the skull and sunstroke . . . He does house painting when he can get it, which is rare. The mother works hard for her children and attends . . . every mission-hall. This brings her soup three or four times a week and sometimes a loaf of bread . . . At Christmas she may contrive to get two or three Christmas dinners from different places. The room here was full of rubbish – all in it would not fetch 10s; the dirty walls covered with little pictures never taken down. Vermin abounded and the stench was awful. These people have had seven children but about eight years ago two of them, aged nine and eleven, going to school in the morning, have never been heard of since.[6]

For those who had no rooms of their own there were numerous lodging-houses, and 'lower still in reputation, "furnished houses", and houses where stairways and corners are occupied nightly by those without any other shelter'. The registered lodging-houses were reasonably well run and orderly. They had common kitchens with open fires on the ground floor and dormitories above. The quarters for single women were large rooms packed so close with broken-down truckle beds that there was only just enough room to walk between them; married couples, or those who claimed to be such, were assigned to rooms boxed off by wooden partitions. The many un-licensed lodging-houses, however, were like 'visions of hell' in which every conceivable crime had been committed and in which prostitutes, many of them children, abounded. Tens of thousands slept in such places down by the docks, around Drury Lane, St Giles's, Ratcliffe Highway and Whitechapel. The charge was generally no more than 2d a night for a bundle of rags on a bunk and the use of the fire in the kitchen by which would be crowded a ragged assortment of labourers, pickpockets, Billingsgate porters, beggars and sailors, vagrants and drunkards, and men fallen from better positions, 'usually through drink, clerks in holy orders, educated men, school teachers, merchants, reduced to the lowest condition'. Wearing a weird array of clothes, shiny with age and grease – some barefooted, others in boots with the toes cut off so that they could get their feet into them – they sat at tables round the walls, drying the ends of cigars they had picked up in the streets, or crowded round the fire toasting herrings or bits of meat stolen from a butcher's stall. For a penny reduction in the fee it was possible to sleep on the floor of the kitchen and many did so, women as well as men, girls and boys, most of them having taken the precaution of getting drunk if they could afford it for there was no sleep otherwise to be had.

Booth described two such places in Parker Street. One, which accommo-dated fifty to sixty men, was entered 'down some steps from a back yard into a rough kind of cavern, and then through a door into the kitchen which was more like a dungeon than anything else'. In the other, also underground, about seventy women squatted round the coke fire. Their hair was matted, their faces and hands filthy, their ragged clothing 'stiff with accumulations of beer and dirt, their underclothing, if they have any at all, swarming with vermin. Many of them are often drunk . . . Bad as this house is here described, it was worse in the days of Mrs Collins, a gigantic woman profusely bedecked with rings, who grew enormously fat and died weighing nearly thirty stone. She made her living by combining the role of lodging-house keeper with that of procuress.'[7]

Even among the very poor there were, of course, innumerable families who contrived to live in decency if not in comfort; and many of those with regular earnings lived in contentment in two or three rooms in Battersea or Clapham with clean coverings on the floors, curtains at the unbroken windows, picture postcards on the walls, Staffordshire figures, a few other ornaments, as well as a tin tray and a looking-glass on the shelf above the fireplace, a cloth on the table and sheets on the bed. Indeed, several contemporary observers, critical as they were of the unpleasant conditions in which they had to work, conceded that the homes of artisans were sometimes quite pleasant. A writer in *The Cornhill Magazine* in 1862 found that in 'nearly all the cottages' in one mining village, 'and especially those tenanted by respectable families' the furniture was 'of a superior order':

> The bedstead is pretty sure to be a mahogany four-poster, with imposing pillars, clean white furniture, and a quilted coverlet. It is placed in the best room as an ornamental piece of furniture, and beside it will frequently stand a mahogany chest of drawers, well polished, and filled with linen and clothes. An old-fashioned eight-day clock, in a good case, usually flanks the four-poster. In the best ordered pit dwellings I have often seen also good chairs, china, bright brass candlesticks, and chimney ornaments; every one of these items being kept scrupulously clean, for cleanliness is the pride of the pitman's wife. Herself probably the daughter of a pitman, she cherishes all the old associations of a similar home, and what constituted her mother's pride stimulates hers: things must indeed be in a bad state when the four-poster, the eight-day clock, the little ornaments of the chimney-piece, and the chest of drawers are poor or neglected.[8]

The houses of the more respectable factory workers of Lancashire were also quite comfortable. A writer in the *Fortnightly Review* compared their dwellings very favourably with those of operatives in London who were obliged to inhabit 'a portion of a tenement, often in the attic' where 'privacy is unknown':

> The dwellings of the [better-off Lancashire] operatives are mostly long rows of two-storied buildings, with a couple of rooms on each floor, the rental of which varies according to size and situation, from 2s 6d to 4s 6d a week, the landlord generally paying the rates. The furniture of the living room may consist of a dresser, an eight-day clock, kitchen sofa, and a couple of rocking-chairs on either side of the fire-place. The walls are usually adorned with two or three framed engravings or coloured lithographs. The better-paid workmen improve upon this a little. Their front apartment on the ground-floor is dubbed a parlour, and its furniture includes a small book-case if the man be studious, or if, as is not infrequent, he has a taste for music, a piano.[9]

Nor were the conditions in which all operatives had to work as unpleasant as some of the more partisan writers would have liked their readers to suppose. Fry's chocolate and cocoa works at Bristol, for example, was described in a government report of 1866 as so well run that it was 'a pleasure to visit the place'. There was a schoolroom and a chapel into which every morning at a quarter to nine, after work had been going on for some time, the employees proceeded looking 'bright and fresh', the men and boys in canvas jackets, the girls in neat aprons. They sat down in 'an orderly way' 'the little girls in front, then the elder and women, then the boys and, at the back, the men, each taking down the Bibles from the shelves as they entered'.[10]

The firm of Thomas Adams and Company, lace warehousemen of Nottingham, was another example of one that paid close attention to the welfare of its employees. The building was light and airy, and a large room was set aside as a canteen where hot meals were provided for all who did not go home for dinner. As well as a chapel and a schoolroom equipped with books and maps, there were washrooms, a savings bank, a book club and a sick club which secured medical attention for those who fell ill while in the firm's employ. Similar favourable reports were given of a match factory in London, 'a very nicely conducted place', according to a report of 1863; there was 'nothing unpleasant or objectionable here'.[11]

Such reports were offset, however, by the great number of condemnations of dark, ill-ventilated, rowdy and wretched factories from whose grim discipline many workers recoiled in horror. Among these were handloom weavers, obsolescent artisans of whom there were still 800,000 in the 1840s, more than in any other single occupational group, except that of farm labourers. Whole families of handloom weavers earned no more than 8s a week between them; yet, even so, framework knitters commonly had less, for though they might earn 10s a week, they had as much as a third of this deducted for candles, needles and the rents of the frames they used in their own cottages or in the small workshops of a master stockinger.[12]

Although so ill-rewarded for their labour that many of them had to exist on a diet composed largely of porridge and potatoes, these outworkers clung tenaciously to their occupation since the alternative was constant hunger or the loss of independence. The outworker could at least work at his own speed and in his own way, and have a drink when he wanted one, free from the strict regime and monotony of the factory.

There were, it had to be admitted, certain advantages in working in places such as that huge mill built on the banks of the Aire by the Bradford manufacturer, Sir Titus Salt. For close to his mill, Sir Titus, the son of a cloth merchant turned farmer, provided over 800 good, small houses for his men and their families as well as a school, a chapel, a park, an infirmary, baths and a dining-hall. But, in return for these benefits, all employees at Saltaire had to submit themselves to a firm discipline: they were not allowed to touch any alcohol, even beer; and notices to this effect were displayed about the works. The men employed by William Fairbarn, owner of a Lancashire engineering works, were also well provided for; but they, too, were forbidden to drink alcohol, were instantly dismissed if they did so, and were sternly admonished if they appeared ill-dressed in the streets on a Sunday.

The unvarying dreariness of life in most mid-nineteenth-century factories was described by William Dodd in his *Factory System Illustrated*. He cited the example of a pathetic 'specimen of a great proportion of the factory girls in Manchester'. Every morning she hurried from her room, having been woken by the watchman's tap on the bedroom window, her meagre breakfast tied up in a handkerchief.

> The bell rings as she leaves the threshold of her home. Five minutes more and she is in the factory . . . The clock strikes half past five; the engine starts and her day's work commences. At half past seven the engine slacks its pace for a short time till the hands have cleaned the machinery and swallowed a little food. It then goes on again, and sometimes at full speed till twelve o'clock when it stops for dinner.[13]

Before she went home for dinner this girl had to clean the machine which sometimes took her so long she had no time for food. Once the machines started again they continued clanking and whirring until seven o'clock at night. 'She then comes home, and throws herself into a chair exhausted. This is repeated six days in the week (save that on Saturdays she may get back a little earlier, say an hour or two) . . . She looks very pale and delicate and has every appearance of an approaching decline.'

Factory girls like this were paid between 5s and 10s a week, their younger sisters and brothers from 2s 6d to 5s. Mill workers got 12s to 24s a week depending upon the degree of skill and experience required in their particular job. Men of exceptional skill could command as much as 30s. These highly practised engineers and craftsmen considered themselves, and were considered to be, a cut above the ordinary labouring class, artisans almost on a par with stone-masons, carpenters, compositors, shoemakers and tailors, the best paid of whom might have as much as £2 a week to spend. These were the men who belonged to trade unions from which they were anxious to ensure that common, unskilled labourers continued to be excluded. They were as far above the common labourer as the clerks of the city, though more poorly paid, were above them in the subtly graduated social scale. In Bradford, as Professor Harrison has noted, 'the skilled woolcombers did not drink in the same pubs with more lowly members of the textile fraternity'.[14]

In Bradford, as in many another large industrial town, towering above the poor houses of the people were public edifices of increasing size, impressiveness and dignity. More building was carried out in England in the nineteenth century, in fact, than in all the centuries that preceded it. Town hall and law

LEFT: A lady's maid dressing her mistress in a crinoline. The crinoline had been in full swing in the 1850s and remained in fashion, disliked though it was, until the 1860s. After the demise of the crinoline, bustles came into fashion again.

BELOW: The kitchen at Keele Hall, Staffordshire, at the turn of the century. From left to right are the culinary maid, the third chef, the second chef and the head chef, the butcher, the fishmonger, the head gardener, the first English cook and the second English cook. These were only a few of the entire domestic staff. The Duke of Westminster had a staff of over 300 at Eaton Hall, the Duke of Westminster's income exceeding £250,000 a year from his London properties alone, that is to say about £15 million a year in present-day terms. But a man with a relatively modest income of £1,000 a year, so it was estimated in the 1850s, should have been able to employ at least six servants. There were 1,300,000 men and women employed in domestic service in 1871.

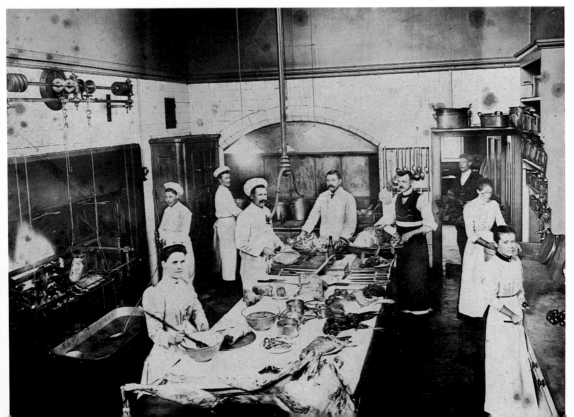

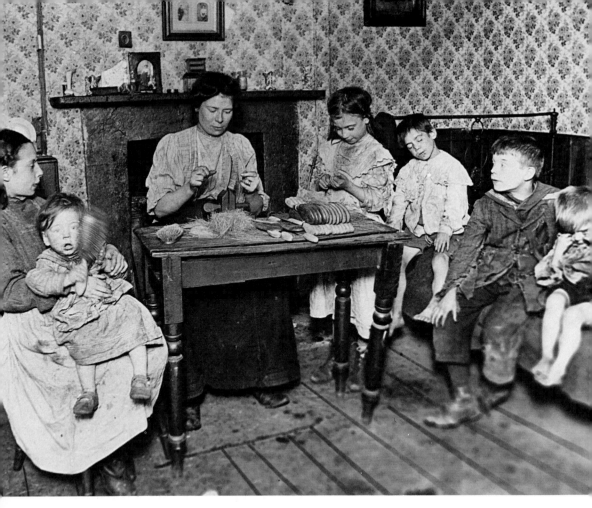

ABOVE: Making brushes in Bethnal Green in the late 19th century. Such work was paid for by the piece, so the children were put to work as soon as they were old enough. There were reports of families working continuously for 18 hours at a stretch and even longer.

LEFT: Hungry children waving meal tickets outside the Edinburgh Castle Mission. Appalled by the living conditions of poor children in London, Dr Barnardo, who had come to study at the London Hospital in 1866, started a Ragged School in Stepney. His first home for destitute boys was at Stepney Causeway. A number of 'Dr Barnardo's Homes' such as this one soon followed it.

LEFT: A family in the hop fields in 1880. For many poor families a week or so working as a hop-picker in Kent was the only holiday they had. George Orwell, who went hop-picking in the 1930s, wrote: 'My hands cut to bits, I felt a wreck at the end of it. It was humiliating to see that most of the people there looked on it as a holiday . . . In fact it is because hopping is regarded as a holiday that the pickers will take such starvation wages.'

BELOW: Whitby market, Yorkshire, in 1884. In large towns the stall-holders were likely to be middlemen and hawkers but in smaller places they were men and women who had themselves grown or made what they had to sell. From the early Middle Ages Whitby market had been celebrated for the quality of its fish.

TOP LEFT: A so-called 'bus conductorette' in 1917, taking her advertisement-covered bus to Upper Street, Islington. As men left for the Front in the First World War, there was far more work for women to do and opportunities to demonstrate that they could do it well. The number of bus conductresses rose from a few hundred in 1914 to 2,500 in 1918. In the transport industry as a whole the numbers of women employed increased from 18,000 in 1914 to 117,000 in 1918. Many of the recruits were former domestic servants.

CENTRE LEFT: A Bank Holiday picnic at Easter, 1923. The Bank Holiday Act passed in 1871 had added extra holidays on Boxing Day, Easter Monday, Whit Monday and the first Monday in August to the national holidays of Sundays, Good Friday and Christmas Day. When this photograph was taken an Austin Seven motor car cost about £120. There were 132,000 cars on the road by 1914, two million by 1939.

BELOW: The Grand Hotel and South Sands at Scarborough in about 1900. Seaside resorts had begun to replace inland spas as fashionable holiday retreats in the 18th century. Earlier versions of the bathing-machines shown here had been in use in Scarborough since 1735.

courts, hospitals and schools, museums and galleries, government offices and warehouses, university colleges and libraries, clubs, hotels and theatres, large blocks of healthy if intimidating model dwellings for artisans, all appeared in a variety of styles from Greek to Byzantine, from Gothic to Elizabethan. There were prisons designed to look like medieval castles, railway stations like Renaissance French *châteaux*, banks like Roman temples.

The size and style of public buildings were frequently influenced by considerations neither practical nor aesthetic. When George Gilbert Scott entered the competition organized in 1856 for new government offices in Whitehall, all his Gothic designs were at first accepted. But Whig advocates of the classical style – warmly supported by Lord Palmerston and angrily attacked by their political opponents in both Houses of Parliament – condemned the Gothic taste as too much associated with conservatism and with the High Church movement; and so orders were given for an Italian design to be submitted instead.

Rivalries of a different kind led to the building of a town hall at Leeds at far greater expense than had originally been proposed. For, when the mayor of Bradford announced that his city's recently constructed St George's Hall was 'the best known specimen' of such a building in all England, eleven feet wider than Birmingham town hall, even loftier than Exeter Hall in London and capable of containing concert audiences of over 3000 people, the merchants of Leeds were much irritated by the claims. They commissioned a young Yorkshire architect, Cuthbert Brodrick, to build a fine town hall of which they could be just as proud. When the queen came to Leeds for the official opening in 1858, Brodrick's massive classical structure was certainly an impressive sight, longer than London's Guildhall, higher than Birmingham's town hall, wider than Westminster Hall. That it was larger than Bradford's St George's Hall went without saying. So imposing was it, in fact, that, as Asa Briggs has noted, it provided inspiration for at least three other town halls, that of nearby Morley (usually profoundly suspicious of Leeds), Portsmouth and Bolton.[15] By the end of the century there was scarcely a town in the country that did not possess an imposing town hall, a monument to civic pride only occasionally overshadowed by the knowledge that in almost every city, out of sight of the hall's proud towers and serried windows, were – as it was said of Birmingham in 1875 – other quarters in which little else was to be seen but 'bowing roofs, tottering chimneys, tumbledown and often disused shopping, heaps of bricks, broken windows and coarse, rough pavements, damp and sloppy'.[16] In these areas the ill-health of the people was a cause of deep concern.

*

In 1842 the *Report of an Enquiry into the Sanitary Conditions of the Labouring Population of Great Britain* was issued by the Poor Law Commission. It was based largely on the findings of the Secretary of the Commission, Edwin Chadwick, an industrious, opinionated and domineering man who had been trained as a barrister and had been an intimate friend of Jeremy Bentham. The report was a horrifying indictment and was to have far-reaching effects. For years the conditions which it revealed had been unknown or ignored; and attempts to deal with the problems of sanitary reform and public health had been half-hearted and sporadic. Threats of dangerous outbreaks of disease had occasionally prompted the government into action: fear of yellow fever being introduced into the country from abroad in the early nineteenth century had led to the establishment of a Board of Health; but this had been dissolved when the fever did not arrive. Later, following a serious outbreak of cholera on the Continent, another Central Board of Health was established, but this too was disbanded when the danger was past. And it was not until the painstaking inquiries of Chadwick and his colleagues were made known that the Public Health Act of 1848 established a General Board of Health which was more than a temporary expedient. Thereafter Medical Officers of Health were appointed; and serious attempts began to be made to deal with polluted water supply, grossly inadequate sewage disposal and the other evils which encouraged and spread disease and death.

> The prisons [Chadwick had written] were formerly distinguished for their filth and bad ventilation; but the descriptions given by Howard of the worst prisons visited in England (which he states were the worst he had seen in Europe) were exceeded in every Wynd in Edinburgh and Glasgow inspected by Dr Arnott and myself. More filth, worse physical suffering and moral disorder than Howard describes are to be found amongst the cellar populations of the working people of Liverpool, Manchester or Leeds and in large portions of the metropolis.[17]

The mortality rate among people forced to live in such places could readily be appreciated by studying the figures for life expectancy. These were closely related to class: in eight districts which Chadwick examined, life expectancy among the upper classes was forty-three years, among tradesmen thirty, and for labourers only twenty-two.[18] And it was erroneous to suppose, Chadwick insisted, that 'greater sickness and mortality' could be ascribed to children employed in factories than among those

> who remain in such homes as these towns afford to the labouring classes. However defective the ventilation of many of the factories may yet be, they

are all of them drier and more equally warm than the residences of the parents . . . It is an appalling fact that, of all who are born of the labouring classes in Manchester, more than 57% die before they attain five years of age; that is before they can be engaged in factory labour, or in any other labour whatsoever.[19]

Even in a country town such as Windsor which, 'from the contiguity of the [castle], the wealth of the inhabitants and the situation', might have been expected to be superior to other towns, sanitary conditions were quite as bad as anywhere else and health as much endangered. 'From the gas-works at the end of George Street a double line of open, deep, black and stagnant ditches extends to Clewer-lane. From these ditches an intolerable stench is perpetually rising, and produces fever of a severe character.'[20]

The 1848 Public Health Act which followed upon this report was limited in scope and effectiveness. It granted local authorities permission to set up Local Boards of Health rather than obliged them to do so, while the General Board of Health, which it established and which was reconstructed in 1856, lasted only until 1858. And by then Chadwick whose autocratic manner had offended medical men and local authorities alike, had been dismissed, much to the pleasure both of *The Times* which preferred to take its 'chance of cholera and the rest than to be bullied into health' and of those who agreed with the *laissez-faire* opinions of a writer in *The Economist* who averred: 'Suffering and evil are nature's admonitions; they cannot be got rid of; and the impatient attempts of benevolence to banish them from the world by legislation, before benevolence has learnt their object and their end, have always been more productive of evil than good.'[21]

Yet the Public Health Act did mark 'the first clear acceptance by the state of responsibility for the health of the people'; while the General Board of Health, in the words of John Simon – who became the first medical officer of the Privy Council after the board's demise – awoke in the whole country 'a conscience against filth'.[22]

Simon, who remained medical officer until 1876, was a man whose character was in striking contrast to Chadwick's. Diplomatic, patient, persuasive, he was to a considerable extent responsible for a whole series of enactments which helped to transform the nation's health, among them the Sanitary Act of 1866, the Factory Act of 1867, the Artizans' and Labourers' Dwellings Act of 1868, the Vaccination Act of 1871 and the Public Health Act of 1872 which divided the country, apart from London, into districts each responsible for appointing a Sanitary Inspector as well as a Medical Officer of Health and for supervising the administration of the sanitary laws. Finally in 1875 came the 'Great Public Health Act' which provided a complete statement of the powers and duties of local sanitary authorities and covered all manner of subjects from the prevention of epidemics to the foundation of infirmaries, from offensive trades to adulterated foods, from housing and the purchase of land for public amenities to the cleaning of streets and the inspection of markets and slaughterhouses.[23]

Between the passing of this Act and 1900 the mean annual death rate fell from over twenty-three to well under nineteen per thousand of the population for men, and from over twenty to less than seventeen for women.[24]

# 52 · *Mines, Brickfields and Sweat-shops*

In March 1862 the readers of *The Cornhill Magazine* were offered an account of 'Life and Labour in the Coal-fields'. The writer described his being lowered in an iron cage to the dark passages leading to the coalfaces, their roofs supported by pillars of coal which were themselves to be knocked down when the mine was exhausted. Along these passages boys dragged or pushed laden baskets to the crane which hauled them up to be carried away by the pit ponies; and beyond the boys, struggling with their loads, could be seen the 'real getters of the coal, the so-called hewers':

> Their work is the most peculiar we have witnessed. In a small, corner-like recess, full of floating coal-dust, foul and noisome with bad air and miscellaneous refuse and garbage, glimmer three or four candles, stuck in clay or there may be only a couple of Davy lamps. Close and deliberate scrutiny will discover one hewer nearly naked, lying upon his back, elevating his short sharp pickaxe a little above his nose, and picking into the coal-seam with might and main; another is squatting down and using his pick like a common labourer; a third is cutting a small channel in the seam, and preparing to drive in wedges. By one or other kind of application the coal is broken down, but if too hardly embedded, gunpowder is employed, and the mineral blasted; the dull, muffled, roof-shaking boom that follows each blast startling the ear . . . At the busiest hours of the day here are in all some four hundred living human beings in the different parts of the vast mine [but] there is only one time in the twenty-four hours when we can see all these people together and that is the hour of loosening or stopping work. At that hour let us take our stand at the bottom of the shaft.
>   The long-wished-for minute arrives, and is signalled, not by clock or bell, but by one long, shrill, resonant cry, coming from the top of the shaft and the banksman's lips. 'Loose; l-o-o-s-e; l-o-o-s-e-' is the one word thrice

repeated, but drawled and drawn out into vocal lengths of some seconds' duration. The cry is taken up by men below, and rings from mouth to mouth and gallery to gallery, until the remotest corners of the pit are echoing with the welcome sound. Down fall picks from the hands of hewers, and implements of all kinds are left by human beings of all ages. Every five or ten minutes shows us gang after gang winding their dim and perilous way to the base of the shaft; to that little circle of light which, like a fairy ring, lies brightly upon the black coal floor. On it stands the empty cage; into that get the men and boys as they arrive, and up they go, black and weary.[1]

Writing some years earlier, before the passing of the Hours of Labour in Factories Act of 1844 and its subsequent amendments, another observer, Friedrich Engels, described the utter exhaustion of the miners, particularly the children, as they wandered home from the pit. Basing his accounts on official reports as well as upon his own observations, Engels described the long and toilsome days of the miners who worked for twelve or more hours at a stretch, frequently undertaking double shifts so that they spent twenty-six hours without coming to the surface, having no set times for meals but eating when they could. Their children – mostly over eight, though some were no more than four – were employed underground, as children had been for generations, in opening and shutting ventilation doors as well as in carting lumps of coal in heavy, wheel-less baskets and tubs.

The tubs have to be hauled over the bumpy ground of the underground passages, often through wet clay or even water [Engels wrote]. Sometimes they have to be hauled up steep inclines and are brought through passages which are so narrow that the workers have to crawl on their hands and knees . . . All the children and young people employed in hauling coal and ironstone complain of being very tired. Not even in a factory where the most intensive methods of securing output are employed do we find the worker driven to the same limits of physical endurance as they are in the mines. Every page [of the official reports] gives chapter and verse for this assertion. It is a very common occurrence for children to come home from the mine so exhausted that they throw themselves on to the stone floor in front of the fire. They cannot keep awake even to eat a morsel of food. Their parents have to wash them and put them to bed while they are still asleep. Sometimes the children actually fall asleep on their way home and are eventually discovered by their parents late at night. The women and older girls are also habitually exhausted owing to the brutal way in which they are overworked. The most obvious consequence of their unnatural physical exertions is that all the strength in their bodies is concentrated into muscular development.[2]

Some parts of their bodies were overdeveloped by the strain of their exertions, while others were 'crippled owing to lack of nourishment'. Nearly all miners were physically stunted, 'except those in Warwickshire and Leicestershire [who worked] under particularly favourable conditions'; and most were bandy-legged or knock-kneed or had some spinal or other deformity. Among both boys and girls puberty was delayed, sometimes until the eighteenth year. J. C. Symons encountered one boy of nineteen who, except for his teeth, had the physique of a boy aged between eleven and twelve. The crippling of women was particularly noticeable, and many women were forced to undergo exceptionally painful and sometimes fatal confinements due to distortion of the pelvis. Diseases of the lungs and heart, internal pains, indigestion and the distressing complaint known as 'black spittle' were all widespread; and life expectancy was very low.

Coalminers in all districts, *without exception* become prematurely aged and unfit for work after they are forty years old [Engels continued, basing his comments on the *First Report* (1842) of the Children's Employment Commission]. It is generally agreed that a miner is practically an old man [at that age]. That is true of the coalhewers. The loaders, who lift heavy lumps of coal into the tubs, become old when they are 28 or so, so that there is a saying in the coal districts: Loaders are old men before they are young ones. It is very rare indeed to come across a miner who is 60 years of age. Even in South Staffordshire, where the coal mines are relatively healthy, comparatively few miners reach the age of 51.[3]

At the beginning of the 1840s there were 118,000 coalminers in Britain, 2350 of them women. The men earned between 15s and 25s a week, the women a good deal less. As the Shaftesbury Commission discovered in 1842 'a girl of twenty [would] work for 2s a day or less, while a man of that age would want 3s 6d'.

The men work in a state of perfect nakedness [the commission reported], and are in this state assisted in their labours by females of all ages, from girls of six years old to women of twenty-one, these females being themselves quite naked down to the waist . . . 'One of the most disgusting sights I have ever seen,' says the Sub-Commissioner, 'was that of young females, dressed like boys in trousers, crawling on all fours, with belts round their waists and chains passing between their legs . . . In one pit, the chain, passing high up between the legs of two of these girls, had worn large holes in their trousers; and any sight more disgustingly indecent or revolting can scarcely be imagined – no brothel can beat it. On descending Messrs. Hopwood's pit at Barnsley, I found assembled round the fire, boys and girls . . . stark naked down to the waist, their hair bound up with a tight cap, and trousers supported by their hips. Their sex was recognisable only by their breasts, and some little difficulty occasionally arose in pointing out to me which were girls and which were boys, and which caused a good deal of laughing and joking . . . In [other] pits the system is even more indecent; for . . . at least three-fourths of the men for whom the girls 'hurry' work stark naked, or with a flannel waistcoat only. [A miner was quoted as saying], 'I have worked a great deal where girls were employed in pits. I have had children by them myself, and have frequently had connexion with them in the pits. I am sure that this is the case especially in pits about Lancashire.' 'I am certain the girls are worse than the men in point of morals [another miner said] and use far more indecent language . . . I have known myself of a case where a married man and a girl who hurried for him had sexual intercourse often in the bank where he worked.' 'I have worked in a pit since I was six years old [reported one Betty Wardle]. I have had four children, two of them were born while I worked in the pits. I worked in the pits whilst I was in the family way. I had a child born in the pits, and I brought it up in the pit shaft in my skirt.'

A female miner, Betty Harris, aged thirty-seven, described her work in the mines:

I have a belt round my waist, and a chain passing between my legs, and I go on my hands and feet. The road is very steep, and we have to hold by a rope, and, when there is no rope, by anything we can catch hold of. There are six women and six girls and boys in the pit I work in: it is very hard work for a woman. The pit is very wet where I work, and the water comes over our clog-tops always, and I have seen it up to my thighs; it rains in at the roof terribly; my clothes are wet through almost all day long . . . My cousin looks after my children in the daytime. I am very tired when I get home at night; I fall asleep sometimes before I get washed. I am not so strong as I was, and cannot stand my work as well as I used to. I have drawn till I have had the skin off me; the belt and chain is worse when we are in the family way. My feller has beaten me many a time for not being ready. I were not used to it at first, and he had little patience: I have known many a man beat his drawer.

Seventy years later there was still very little mechanization in the mines, and a day's work remained very hard. One Welsh miner, who started working underground at Mountain Ash, Glamorgan, on his fourteenth birthday in 1915, told George Ewart Evans:

> I was fourteen in the morning and I went to work that night . . . Well, the men – they told me, 'You put that coal into that tub by there; and after you've done, you have a little spell till I'm ready for you again.'
>
> That was my first night underground; and when I came home in the morning, I was very tired. Every penny counted in those days. I was having twelve shillings a week. That was my wages: six days a week, Monday to Saturday . . .
>
> I was frightened, I'll say that, first of all when I went into the face because seeing everything in front of you in darkness and only this little oil-lamp I had going in, and naturally it was a bit frightening. I had a little box of food, a tommy-box it was called, and a little tin jack of water. That was the standard equipment for a collier at that time, with the Davy lamp. No electrical lamps, no cap-lamp.
>
> At that time it was done with no machinery. The mandril, the shovel and the curling-box – these were your tools. I was working in a seam that was roughly two feet six inches high. Your mate would send you to the top end of where you were working; you'd have to drag this curling-box of coal down; and take the curling-box of muck back up to keep filling in behind you. The coal went into the tub or dram; and the rubbish into the place to pack behind you for safety – to help keep the roof up.[4]

Men, women and children in the chain- and nail-making trades were required to work quite as hard as miners, in conditions almost as bad and for less money. The men earned at most 5s a hundredweight and they were able to produce no more than three hundredweight a week, while the women often earned less than 5s a week. 'We do not live very well,' one of them admitted. 'Our most living is bacon.' Another, a girl of fifteen, 'stated that she did not get enough to eat, even of bread and potatoes'. A doctor confirmed that the workers were nearly always hungry.

One of the worst abuses was the masters' habit of forcing the workers either to accept part of their wages in food or to buy their food and other necessities at shops owned by them or by their relations or friends, where prices were inflated. 'They tell their men, or at least it is understood, "If you do not buy my groceries, we will not buy your nails."'

This elaboration of the truck or tommy system, which the navvies also found so irksome, was common in many other industries and was widely resented, as Benjamin Disraeli, who had studied the official reports, well knew. In his novel *Sybil*, published in 1845, he records a conversation between a group of black-faced miners in the Rising Sun who complain bitterly of the butties, or middlemen who contract to supply a certain amount of coal for an agreed sum and who pay the wages of the colliers under contract to them in goods.

'The question is,' said Nixon, looking round with a magisterial air, 'what *is* wages? I say 'tayn't sugar, 'tayn't tea, 'tayn't bacon. I don't think 'tis candles; but of this I be sure, 'tayn't waistcoats . . . Comrades you know what has happened; you know as how Juggins applied for his balance after his tommy-book was paid up, and that incarnate nigger Diggs [a butty and owner of a tommy shop] has made him take two waistcoats. Now the question arises, what is a collier to do with waistcoats? Pawn 'em I s'pose to Diggs' son-in-law, next door to his father's shop, and sell the tickets for sixpence . . . The fact is we are tommied to death . . .'

'And I have been obliged to pay the doctor for my poor wife in tommy,' said another. ' "Doctor," I said, says I, "I blush to do it, but all I have got is tommy, and what shall it be, bacon or cheese?" "Cheese at tenpence a pound," says he, "which I buy for my servants at sixpence! Never mind," says he, for he is a thorough Christian, "I'll take the tommy as I find it." ' . . .

'Juggins has got his rent to pay, and is afeard of the bums,' said Nixon; 'and he has got two waistcoats!'

'Besides,' said another, 'Diggs' tommy is only open once a-week, and if you're not there in time, you go over for another seven days. And it's such a distance, and he keeps a body there such a time; it's always a day's work for my poor woman; she can't do nothing after it, what with the waiting, and the standing, and the cussing of Master Joseph Diggs; for he do swear at the women.'

'This Diggs seems to be an oppressor of the people,' said a voice from a distant corner of the room.

Master Nixon looked around, smoked, puffed, and then said, 'I should think he wor; as bloody-a-hearted butty as ever jingled.'

'But what business has a butty to keep a shop?' inquired the stranger. 'The law touches him.'

'I should like to know who would touch the law,' said Nixon; 'not I for one. Them tommy-shops is very delicate things; they won't stand no handling, I can tell you that.'

'But he cannot force you to take goods,' said the stranger; 'he must pay you in current coin of the realm, if you demand it.'

'They only pay us once in five weeks,' said a collier; 'and how is a man to live meanwhile?'

'Ay, ay,' said another collier; 'ask for the young Queen's picture, and you would soon have to put your shirt on, and go up the shaft.'

'It's them long reckonings that force us to the tommy-shops,' said another collier; 'and if a butty turns you away because you won't take no tommy, you're a marked man in every field about.'[5]

The factory inspectors had an impossible task in endeavouring to ensure that the provisions of the Factory Acts were observed, since the employers paid runners to warn of their approach and made it clear that workers who complained of their treatment might well find themselves out of work. Extracts from the Acts were to be found pinned on the workshop wall at the time of the inspectors' visits, only to be stowed back in a drawer as soon as they had gone. 'It is quite a common thing,' said a minister from Dudley, a centre of the chain-making industry, 'for these people to work even thirteen or fourteen hours a day . . . In fact, you may go through the district when it is pitch dark, and there are no lamps in some parts, you will hear these little forges going and people working in them, and you wonder when they are going to stop.'

A nailer's usual day is from 5 or 6 a.m. till 9 or 10 p.m. [recorded one worker in the industry from Halesowen near Birmingham]. That is many hours to be stiving up in a hot shop, but some work till 11 or 12 or later if the master wants the work quickly . . . Some children begin at eight years old . . . I should not like my boy now 5, to begin before 8, and he shan't if I can help it, but if I am anyways obligated he must. He is but a little mossel, and if I were to get that little creature to work I should have to get a scaffold for him to stand on, to reach, and with that it would be like murder-work, as you may say.[6]

Children did, however, work in nailers' workshops before they were eight, as they – and women of all ages – did in the brickfields where the conditions of labour were as degrading as they were in the mines and in agricultural labour gangs.

I consider that in brickyards [a factory inspector reported in 1865] that the degradation of the female character is most complete . . . I have seen females of all ages, nineteen or twenty together (some of them mothers of families), undistinguishable from men, excepting by the occasional peeping out of an earring, sparsely clad, up to the bare knees in clay splashes, and evidently without a vestige of womanly delicacy, thus employed, until it makes one feel for the honour of a country that there should be such a condition of human labour existing in it.

I questioned one such group in a brickyard in South Staffordshire as to how many of them could read, and found that only one out of twenty was so qualified . . . Lest my evidence should seem partial, or as seen only through the medium of inspectorship, permit a master brick-maker to give his own version of the story.

'I am a brick and tile manufacturer and sanitary pipe maker, in the neighbourhood of Tipton, midway from Birmingham and Wolverhampton. I employ about fifty work-people, about half of whom are women and children. A flippancy and familiarity of manners with boys and men grows daily in the young girls. Then, the want of respect and delicacy towards females exhibits itself in every act, word, and look; for the lads are so precocious and the girls so coarse in their language and they sing unblushingly before all, whilst at work, the lewdest and most disgusting songs.

'The overtime work is still more objectionable, because boys and girls, men and women, are not then so much under the watchful eye of the master, nor looked upon by the eye of day.

'All these things, the immorality, levity and coarse pleasures, awful oaths, lewd gestures, and conduct of the adults and youths, exercise a terrible influence for evil on the young children.

'It is quite common for girls employed in brickyards to have illegitimate children. Of the thousands whom I have met with I should say that one in every four, who had arrived at the age of twenty, had an illegitimate child.'[7]

'They become rough and foul-mouthed,' another observer reported of the women workers of the brickfields of Staffordshire. 'Clad in a few dirty rags, their bare legs exposed far above the knees, their hair and faces covered with mud, they learn to treat with contempt all feelings of modesty and decency. During the dinner hour they may be seen lying about the yards asleep, or watching the boys bathing in some adjoining canal.'[8]

Dickens, who knew only too well what the brickmakers' communities were like, described one near Chesney Wold which was visited by the self-righteous philanthropist Mrs Pardiggle. He has Esther Summerson describe the scene:

The brickmaker's house was one of a cluster of wretched hovels in a brickfield, with pigsties close to the broken windows, and miserable little gardens before the doors, growing nothing but stagnant pools. Here and there, an old tub was put to catch the droppings of rain-water from a roof, or they were banked up with mud into a little pond like a large dirt-pie. At the doors and windows, some men and women lounged or prowled about . . .

Mrs Pardiggle, leading the way with a great show of moral determination, and talking with much volubility about the untidy habits of the people, conducted us into a cottage at the farthest corner, the ground-floor room of which we nearly filled. Besides ourselves, there were in this damp offensive room – a woman with a black eye, nursing a poor little gasping baby by the fire; a man, all stained with clay and mud, and looking very dissipated, lying at full length on the ground, smoking a pipe; a powerful young man, fastening a collar on a dog; and a bold girl, doing some kind of washing in very dirty water. They all looked up at us as we came in, and the woman seemed to turn her face towards the fire, as if to hide her bruised eye; nobody gave us any welcome . . . 'I want an end to these liberties took with my place,' (growled the man upon the floor). 'You haven't no occasion to be up to it. I'll save you the trouble. Is my daughter a washin? Yes, she is a washin. Look at the water. Smell it! That's wot we drinks. How do you like it, and what do you think of gin, instead! An't my place dirty? Yes, it is dirty – it's nat'rally dirty, and it's nat'rally onwholesome; and we've had five dirty and onwholesome children, as is all dead infants, and so much the better for them, and for us besides. Have I read the little book wot you left? No, I an't read the little book wot you left. There an't nobody here as knows how to read it . . . How have I been conducting of myself? Why, I've been drunk for three days; and I'd a been drunk four, if I'd a had the money. Don't I never mean for to go to church? No, I don't never mean for to go to church . . . And how did my wife get her black eye? Why, I giv' it her; and if she says I didn't, she's a Lie.'[9]

Dreadful as workers' conditions were in mines and brickfields, however, it was generally agreed by contemporary observers that those who worked in sweat-shops had to endure lives even more pitiable. As late as 1890 a Parliamentary committee, appointed to report on the sweating system, heard of

a double room, perhaps nine by fifteen feet, in which a man, his wife and six children slept and in which same room ten men were usually employed, so that at night eighteen persons would be in this one room . . . with . . . three or four gas jets flaring, a coke fire burning in the wretched fireplace, sinks untrapped, closets without water and altogether the sanitary condition abominable. [In another tailoring workshop] the water closet is in the shop itself, the females sit within three feet of it . . . There is great want of decency, and it is easy to imagine what follows on such contamination . . . There is a sky-light which, when broken, exposes the workers to the rain. On complaints being made the sweater says, 'If you can't work go home.' . . . In nine cases out of ten the windows are broken and filled up with canvas; ventilation is impossible and light insufficient . . . There is to be found all the trade refuse in the room.

One witness who appeared before the committee said: 'You can tell when work is being done on the Sabbath by the blinds being drawn.' Another confessed: 'I am almost ashamed to say what my food is . . . I might get meat once in six months.'

Most workers in tailoring sweat-shops were paid by the piece. A woman might get 7½d for a coat and by working fifteen hours she could make four coats in the day, earning 2s 6d. But out of this she had to pay 3d for getting the button-holes worked, and 4d for trimmings. Men were paid slightly more than women, but rarely received more than 15s a week, when they were paid at all. For wages were as uncertain as work was irregular. Sometimes, one workman said, 'we have nothing to do for weeks and weeks'. Then there would be a rush of work and he would be constantly employed from six o'clock in the morning until midnight. Other witnesses worked for twenty-two hours at a stretch; one had worked for forty.

In almost every occupation workers lived in fear of losing their jobs and, since there were more people looking for work than vacancies to fill, they clung to employment so anxiously that their masters were able to make demands upon them which today would seem utterly intolerable. Men, unskilled as well as skilled, were often required to pay hiring charges for the tools they had to use or to provide their own. Men working in ironworks even had part of their pay stopped for 'clay to repair the furnaces'; and, as Professor Best has noted, the clerical staff at a Burnley mill in 1852 were recommended to bring their own coal to work to fuel the office stove during cold weather. The management did, however, provide 'brushes, brooms, scrubbers and soap' so that the clerks could clean their offices 'forty minutes before prayers'.

Complaint was likely to lead to dismissal, and dismissal to reliance upon the inadequate and humiliating outdoor relief provided by the Poor Law.

We read of dock labourers fighting to get to the front of the crowd outside the dock gates, of skilled workmen, clerks and shop-assistants dyeing their hair black so as to look younger and brisker than they actually felt. After sixty, wrote the coolest statistician of the period, 'a man becomes unfit for hard work, and if he loses his old master, cannot find a new one. In some trades, a man is disabled at fifty-five or fifty. A coal backer is considered past work at forty.'[10]

It is usually reckoned that the strongest man cannot last more than twenty years at the business [Henry Mayhew confirmed]. Many of the heartiest of [coalbackers] are knocked up through the bursting of blood-vessels and other casualties, and even the strongest cannot continue at the labour three days together. After the second day's work, they are obliged to hire some unemployed mate to do the work for them.

The coalbackers are generally at work at five o'clock in the morning, winter and summer. In the winter time, they have to work by the light of large fires in hanging caldrons, which they call bells.

Many of the backers are paid at the public-house; the wharfinger gives them a note to receive their daily earnings of the publican, who has the money from the merchant. Often the backers are kept waiting an hour at the public-house for their money, and they have credit through the day for any drink they may choose to call for. While waiting, they mostly have two or three pots of beer before they are paid; and the drinking once commenced, many of them return home drunk, with only half their earnings in their pockets. There is scarcely a man among the whole class of backers, but heartily wishes the system of payment at the public-house may be entirely abolished. The coalbackers are mostly an intemperate class of men. This arises from the extreme labour and the over-exertion of the men, the violent perspiration and the intense thirst produced thereby. Immediately a pause occurs in their work, they fly to the public-house for beer. One coalbacker made a regular habit of drinking sixteen half-pints of beer, with a pennyworth of gin in each, before breakfast every morning.[11]

Yet almost any kind of work was preferable to the kind of life to which a man might be reduced had he to depend upon a local authority for his livelihood. At Andover in 1847 paupers were put to bone-crushing: they were so ill fed that they fought each other for the putrid gristle from the horses' bones.[12]

# 53 · 'No One Knows the Cruelty'

After 1842 women and children under ten years of age were by law excluded from underground mining. Yet for many years thereafter both were still to be found working underground, just as they were still to be seen working in other places equally unpleasant. The Children's Employment Commission discovered innumerable examples of children working full-time in industry at four or five years old in the 1860s; and, when they worked at home, they were put to their tasks as soon as they could be taught to use their fingers and for as long as they could be kept awake.

The commissioners reported cases of small boys and girls working for as little as 1s 6d a week in the pottery factories of Staffordshire, and working extremely hard, in fearfully hot temperatures and in 'the poisoned atmosphere of the dipping house'. They were required to 'come in before the men in the morning to light the fires in the stoves and to stay after the men have done work to sweep out the shops'. The commissioners also found little children working in match factories where the smell was 'quite suffocating and one would think unendurable for any length of time'.

A wretched place, the entrance to which is through a perfectly dark room [reported a witness of one typical match factory]. Outside at the back the arrangements are even worse. There is a water-butt with a little tub of sickly green water in it. Here, I was told, the children wash. Beyond this is the yard . . . a few feet wide, filled in the middle with a stagnant gutter . . . Here the children eat their meals . . . At the end of this yard, with an open cesspool in front of it, is a single privy, common to all and in a very bad state.

There were children, too, in boot factories, where they had to sit so close together at work that they 'not frequently' struck each other in the face or eye with their needles: 'many have lost an eye in this way'. Children were also employed in milliners' factories like the one in Manchester in which they were kept at work, so an inspector of factories reported, for 'unreasonably long hours', in rooms heated by steam 'almost to suffocating point and so impregnated with gas that most of the young creatures complain almost continually of sore throats, loathing of the stomach, dizziness or vertigo and headaches'. Many other children worked in steel- and ironworks such as John Brown and Company's in Sheffield where upwards of 6000 persons were employed, many of them 'exposed to considerable heat and to the dangers from flying flakes of masses of red hot metal'. Yet others ground cast metal, 'the unhealthiest kind of grinding known', work which – without a fan – 'almost certainly doomed them to much suffering and early death, probably at latest by the age of 30, perhaps much earlier'. That climbing boys still suffered as horribly as they had in the eighteenth century was made all too clear by the evidence the commission collected from master sweeps. One from Manchester deposed:

In learning a child, you can't be soft with him, you must use violence. I shudder now when I think of it. I myself have gone to bed with my knee and elbow scraped and raw, and the inside of my thighs all scarified. We slept five or six boys in a kind of cellar with the soot bags over us, sticking in the wounds sometimes. That and some straw were all our bedclothes . . . Dozens die of consumption . . . They are filthy in their habits. Lads often wear one shirt right on till it is done with. I have been for fifteen months without being washed except by the rain. Why I have been almost walking away with vermin.

The usual age at which boys begin now is from six upwards [another sweep reported]. I began myself at a little over five. They are generally the children of the poorest and worst-behaved parents who want to get rid of them and make a little bit of money by it as well. It is as bad as the Negro slavery, only it is not so known . . . The use of boys for climbing seems to harden the women more than the men. Only lately [1863] a woman who had put her child to a sweep followed me and threatened to pull my hair for speaking against having climbing boys . . . I had myself formerly boys as young as 5½ years, but I did not like them. They were too weak. I was afraid they might go off . . . They go off just as quietly as you might fall asleep in the chair, by the fire there . . . I have known eight or nine sweeps lose their lives by the sooty cancer. The [private] parts which it seizes are entirely eaten off. There is no cure for it once it has begun.

At one time the number of climbing boys was brought very low [according to the vivid account of George Ruff, master-sweep of Nottingham]. But lately they have been very much increased . . . The law against climbing boys is a dead letter here. At first a paid agent was employed by some ladies and gentlemen in the town to watch the sweeps, but he was given up . . . The use of boys is much encouraged by the fact that many householders will have their chimneys swept by boys instead of by machinery . . . I have been sent away even from magistrates' houses, and by some cases even by ladies who have professed to pity the boys, for refusing to use them . . .

No one knows the cruelty which they undergo in learning. The flesh must be hardened. This is done by rubbing it, chiefly on the elbows and knees with the strongest brine, as that got from a pork-shop, close by a hot fire. You must stand over them with a cane, or coax them by a promise of a halfpenny, etc. if they will stand a few more rubs.

At first they will come back from their work with their arms and knees streaming with blood, and the knees looking as if the caps had been pulled off. Then they must be rubbed with brine again, and perhaps go off at once to another chimney. In some boys I have found that the skin does not harden for years.

The best age for teaching boys is about six. That is thought a nice trainable age. But I have known two at least of my neighbours' children begin at the age of five. I once saw a child only 4½ years in the market-place in his sooty clothes and with his scraper in his hand . . .

Nottingham is famous for climbing boys. This is on account of the chimneys being so narrow. A Nottingham boy is or was worth more to sell.

A boy of about 7 or 8 was stolen from me once. As he was in the street a man seized him in his arms, carried him off to a lodging-house, and stupefied him with drugged tea. After the tea the child fell into deep sleep and lost all his appetite. An inspector and I traced him to Hull. The boy was so glad to find that 'master' had come. The man had said that if they had got him to France, they should have had £10 for him.

Formerly the sweeps, as they said themselves, had three washes a year, viz. at Whitsuntide, Goose Fair [October], and Christmas. But now they are quite different. This is owing a great deal I think to a rule which we brought about of taking no orders after twelve midday, and washing then. The object of this was to let boys go to school in the afternoon.

At first most did, but they do not now. A lady complained to me because she could not get her chimney done, and said, 'A chimney sweep, indeed, wanting education! what next?'

The day's work here generally begins at about 4 or 4½ a.m., and lasts for 12 hours, including going round for orders. A man and boy together will earn in a fair full day 6s, but perhaps one day they may sweep 20 chimneys, another half-a-dozen.

The younger boys are more valuable, as they can go up any chimney.

When they get too big to climb, which in town chimneys is about 15, or 16, in the large country chimneys a few years older, they are unfitted for other employments.[1]

There were few occupations in which children, and their parents, did not incur some kind of danger to limb or health. Most dippers in the Potteries sooner or later suffered from painter's colic or paralysis and many were crippled at an early age; workers in match factories contracted diseases of the lungs or lost their jaws, some as early as eleven or twelve years old; turners in the ribbon trade in Coventry 'suffered in the brain and spinal cord, and some have died of it'. Newspapers were full of reports of accidents in factories, many of them fatal. In a matter of a few summer weeks of one year the *Manchester Guardian*, in addition to various other serious injuries, recorded several deaths in Lancashire factories; one boy died 'from lockjaw after his hand had been crushed by the wheels of a machine'; three days later another 'youth died of dreadful injuries after being caught in a machine'; soon afterwards an 'Oldham girl died after being swung round fifty times in machinery belting, every bone in her body being broken'; three days after this 'in Manchester a girl fell into a blower [a machine used in preparing raw cotton] and died as a result of serious injuries'.[2]

As for deformities and diseases caused by excessive labour in factories, a Leeds surgeon testified to the Factories Enquiry Commission that among hundreds of working children he had examined, distortions of the spine, knock knees, fallen arches, varicose veins, leg ulcers and chronic dyspepsia were all common.

Innumerable cases of scrofula, affections of the lungs, mesenteric diseases have also occurred [he said]. Asthmatic cases, and other affections of the lungs, particularly of those who are employed in the dusty parts of the mill, not infrequently occurr . . . The nervous energy of the body I consider to be weakened by the very long hours and a foundation laid for many diseases . . . The general appearance of the children in Leeds immediately struck me as much more pallid, the firmness of the fibre much inferior . . . and [their size] more diminutive . . . than the children of the adjacent country.[3]

It would be natural to draw the conclusion that these poor children, like their parents, must of necessity be 'badly nourished' and 'badly clothed', Friedrich Engels wrote.

And there is ample evidence to bear this out. The vast majority of the workers are clad in rags. The material from which the workers' clothes are made is by no means ideal for its purpose. Linen and wool have practically disappeared from the wardrobes of both men and women, and have been replaced by cotton . . . Even if the workers' clothes are in good condition they are unsuitable for the climate . . . The heavy cotton, though thicker, stiffer and heavier than woollen cloth . . . of which gentlemen's suits are made . . . does not keep out the cold and wet to anything like the same extent as woollens . . . The growing habit of going about barefoot in England has been introduced by Irish immigrants [there were so many of these that by 1871 there were no less than 567,000 Irish-born people living in England and Wales, almost 200,000 of them in Lancashire]. In all factory towns we can now see, particularly women and children, going about barefooted and this custom is gradually being adopted by the poorer class of English.[4]

From the inadequate clothes of the poor in the industrial towns of the north, Engels turned his attention to their food and found that equally unsatisfactory:

The workers only get what is not good enough for the well-to-do. The very best food is to be had in all the big towns of England, but it is expensive, and the worker, who has only got a few coppers to spend, cannot afford it. The English worker is not paid until Saturday evening. In some factories wages are paid on Fridays, but this desirable reform is far from general. Most workers can only get to market on Saturdays at four, five or even seven o'clock in the evening, and by that time the best food has been purchased in the morning by the middle classes. When the market opens, there is an ample supply of good food, but by the time the worker arrives the best has gone. But even if it were still there, he probably could not afford to buy it. The potatoes purchased by the workers are generally bad, the vegetables shrivelled, the cheese stale and of poor quality, the bacon rancid. The meat is lean, old, tough and partially tainted. It is the produce either of animals which have died a natural death or of sick animals which have been slaughtered. Food is generally sold by petty hawkers who buy up bad food and are able to sell it cheaply because of its poor quality . . .
    Both producers and shopkeepers adulterate all foodstuffs in a disgraceful manner, with a scandalous regard for health.[5]

Engels's strictures may have been partisan but they were not unduly exaggerated. The *Liverpool Mercury* provided numerous examples of the ways in which butter was adulterated, sugar mixed with pounded rice, cocoa with fine brown earth, tea leaves with 'sloe leaves and other abominations', pepper with dust, flour with chalk. Shopkeepers and tradesmen were regularly prosecuted – in 1844 eleven butchers were punished for selling tainted meat – yet 'the impudent and dangerous practices continued'.

'Is it your opinion that adulteration is very prevalent?' an expert witness, a doctor, was asked by a Parliamentary committee in the 1850s.

'I find adulteration to be very prevalent [he replied]. It may be stated generally that it prevails in nearly all articles which it will pay to adulterate . . . The adulterations practised are very numerous . . . Bread is adulterated with mashed potatoes, alum and sometimes with sulphate of copper . . . coffee with roasted wheat . . . saw dust, mangel-wurzel and a substance resembling acorns . . . flour with alum . . . milk with water and annatto [a cheap fruit juice] . . . tea with . . . sycamore and horse chestnut leaves . . . vinegar with sulphuric acid . . .Most of those articles are not simply adulterations of an innocuous character, but they are many of them injurious to health, and some of them even poisonous. I think there can be no question but that is the case.'[6]

Towards the end of the century, however, adulteration of food seems to have presented less of a problem, and the diet of most working people began to improve. Certainly there were improvements in factory conditions, and in the lot of women and children as the Factory Acts were extended and more and more trades were brought under government control. After 1868 it was illegal to employ children under eight in agricultural gangs; after 1870 it was required that all children under ten should go to school; in 1874 it became illegal to employ children younger than that full-time. By the time the 1881 census was taken there were appreciably less children in regular work than there had been twenty years earlier.

At the same time working hours were growing shorter. Operatives in the textile industries had, after a long struggle, been granted a sixty-hour week in 1850; and in 1874 this had been lowered to fifty-six and a half hours' work, ten hours from Mondays to Fridays and six and a half hours on Saturdays. These shortened hours of labour, as well as Saturday half holidays, were thereafter gradually extended to other industries also. By the Bank Holiday Acts of the 1870s further holidays were given for most though by no means all workers on Boxing Day, Easter Monday, Whit Monday and the first Monday in August.

Work also began to be less dangerous. In the 1870s 1000 miners were still being killed every year in underground disasters, and many more were being injured; almost as many railway workers were losing life or limb: no less than 767 were killed in 1875 and nearly 3000 injured. Before the campaign of Samuel Plimsoll, brewery manager turned coal merchant, resulted in the implementation of the Merchant Shipping Acts, countless numbers of sailors lost their lives at sea through the overloading of vessels. But by the time the century came to an end, government intervention, a more enlightened approach to their workforces on the part of masters and managers, and improved safety measures had combined to ensure that the horrifying figures of earlier years had been greatly reduced.

# 54 · *Middle Classes and Class Distinctions*

Writing in 1887, the year of the queen's jubilee, the novelist and historian of London, Sir Walter Besant, whose life almost exactly spanned the Victorian age, suggested that in any useful study of the times in which he was living 'the great middle class', which was 'supposed to possess all the virtues [and] to be the backbone, stay and prop of the country', ought to have a chapter to itself.

Besant himself had been born in 1836 in a middle-class home in Portsmouth, the fifth of the ten children of a moderately prosperous merchant and, looking back to the days of his youth, he described how different the middle class was then from what it had since become.

> In the first place [he wrote], it was far more a class apart. In no sense did it belong to society. Men in professions of any kind (except in the Army and Navy) could only belong to society by right of birth and family connections; men in trade – bankers were still accounted tradesmen – could not possibly belong to society. That is to say, if they went to live in the country they were not called upon by the county families, and in town they were not admitted by the men into their clubs, or by ladies into their houses . . . The middle class knew its own place, respected itself, made its own society for itself, and cheerfully accorded to rank the deference due.

Since then, however, the life of the middle classes had undergone great changes as their numbers had swelled and their influence had increased. Their already well-developed consciousness of their own importance had deepened. More critical than they had been in the past of certain aspects of aristocratic life, they were also more concerned with the plight of the poor and of the importance of their own values of sobriety, thrift, hard work, piety and respectability as examples of ideal behaviour for the guidance of the lower orders. Above all they were respectable. A French schoolmaster, Paul

Blouet, recorded that while staying with an English family, one of the sons offered to accompany him on a Sunday morning walk. As they were leaving the house Blouet picked up his walking stick. 'Take an umbrella,' the young man advised him. 'It looks more respectable.'[1]

There were divergences of opinion as to what exactly was respectable and what was not: in some families drinking in moderation and going to dances and the theatre were considered perfectly acceptable activities, in others 'fast'. There were, nevertheless, certain conventions which were universally recognized: wild and drunken behaviour was certainly not respectable, nor were godlessness or overt promiscuity, nor an ill-ordered home life, unconventional manners, self-indulgence or flamboyant clothes and personal adornments.[2] In her remarkable novel *The Young Visiters*, the alarmingly observant Daisy Ashford shows how, even at the early age of nine, a Victorian girl understood the importance of clothes in the appurtenances of a gentleman. Her hero, Mr Salteena, 'an elderly man of 42' who is upon his own admission 'not quite a gentleman but you would hardly notice it', is even sent a top-hat when he is invited to stay with one Bernard Clark, a friend 'inclined to be rich'. It is a most splendid top-hat, 'very uncommon', Mr Salteena is assured, 'of a lovly rich tone rarther like grapes with a ribbon round compleat'. Mr Salteena's own clothes – his 'white alpacka coat to keep off the dust and flies', his compleat evening suit (which he wears for dinner at Clark's 'sumpshuous' house, Rickare Hall, because he believes it 'the correct idear'), not to mention the 'ruby studs he had got in a sale' – are quite put in the shade by it. At the Crystal Palace, where it is hoped Mr Salteena may grow more gentlemanly and seemly by mixing with the earls and dukes who have 'privite compartments' there, his clothes are examined with distaste by the Groom of the Chambers, Edward Procurio. This very superior servant, who smiles upon Mr Salteena 'in a very mysterious and superier way' when he carries in his early-morning beverage, continues to smile to himself as he pulls up the blinds:

> Oh thank you cried Mr Salteena feeling very towzld compared to this grand fellow. Then to his great surprise Procurio began to open the wardrobe and look at Mr Salteena's suits making italian exclamations under his breath. Mr Salteena dared not say a word so he swollowed his tea and eat a Marie biscuit hastily. Presently Procurio advanced to his bed with a bright blue serge suit. Will you wear this to-day sir he asked quietly.

The Earl of Clincham, under whose tutelage Mr Salteena is placed at Crystal Palace, is advised by Bernard Clark that his pupil 'is not quite the right side of the blanket as they say, in fact he is the son of a first rate butcher but his mother was a decent family called Hyssops of the Glen so you see he is not so bad and is desireus of being the correct article'. Lord Clincham does his best with his rather mere material, supervises his instruction (for a suitable fee) in such matters as 'proper Grammer, clothes and etiquett to menials', and arranges an introduction both to various members of the Aristokracy and to the Prince of Wales who wears a lovely ermine cloak and a small but costly crown as he laps up strawbery ice-cream and complains that all he wants is peace and quiet and a little fun. 'Who did you say you were?' he asks Mr Salteena in a puzzled tone.

Lord Hyssops responded our hero growing purple at the lie.

Well you are not a bit like the Lord Hyssops I know replied the Prince could you explain matters.

Mr Salteena gazed helplessly at the earl who had grown very pale and seemed lost for the moment. However he quickly recovered.

He is quite alright really Prince he said. His mother was called Miss Hyssops of the Glen.

Indeed said his royal Highness that sounds correct but who was your father eh.

Then Mr Salteena thourght he would not tell a lie so in trembly tones he muttered, My poor father was but a butcher your Highness a very honest one I may add and passing rich he was called Domonic Salteena and my name is Alfred Salteena.

The Prince stroked his yellow beard and rarther admired Mr Salteena for his truthful utterance – Oh I see he said well why did you palm off on my menials as Lord Hyssops eh.

Mr Salteena wiped his swetting brow but the earl came to the rescue nobly. My fault entirely Prince he chimed in, as I was bringing him to this very supearier levie I thought it would be better to say he was of noble birth have I offended your Royal dignity.

Not much said the prince it was a laudible notion.

The concern for social standing which pervades the whole of Daisy Ashford's book – and which was one that she must have heard endlessly discussed by the grown-ups in her family – was an almost universal pre-occupation in middle-class society. Trollope, well aware of this, elaborates the problems presented to Miss Thorne of Ullathorne when making her arrangements for her *fête champêtre*. She had arranged for the quality to have a breakfast and the non-quality to have a dinner, and two marquees had been erected for these two banquets, that for the quality on the garden side of a deep ha-ha and that for the non-quality on its paddock side. But

No one who has not had a hand in the preparation of such an affair can understand the manifold difficulties which Miss Thorne encountered in her project.

In the first place there was a dreadful line to be drawn. Who were to dispose themselves within the ha-ha, and who without? To this the unthinking will give an off-hand answer, Oh, the bishop and such like within the ha-ha; and Farmer Greenacre and such like without. True, my unthinking friend; but who shall define these such-likes? It is in such definitions that the whole difficulty of society consists. To seat the bishop on an arm chair on the lawn and place Farmer Greenacre at the end of a long table in the paddock is easy enough; but where will you put Mrs. Lookaloft, whose husband, though a tenant on the estate, hunts in a red coat, whose daughters go to a fashionable seminary in Barchester, who calls her farm house Rosebank, and who has a pianoforte in her drawing-room? The Misses Lookaloft, as they call themselves, won't sit contented among the bumpkins. And yet Mrs. Lookaloft is no fit companion and never has been the associate of the Thornes and the Grantlys. And if Mrs. Lookaloft be admitted within the sanctum of fashionable life, if she be allowed with her three daughters to leap the ha-ha, why not the wives and daughters of other families also? Mrs. Greenacre is at present well contented with the paddock, but she might cease to be so if she saw Mrs. Lookaloft on the lawn.

As it happens the Lookalofts do manage to gain admittance to the quality precinct, much to the consternation of the footman.

But he had not the courage to tell a stout lady with a low dress, short sleeves, and satin at eight shillings a yard, that she had come to the wrong tent; he had not dared to hint to young ladies with white dancing shoes and long gloves, that there was a place ready for them in the paddock. And thus Mrs. Lookaloft carried her point, broke through the guards, and made her way into the citadel. That she would have to pass an uncomfortable time there, she had surmised before. But nothing now could rob her of the power of boasting that she had consorted on the lawn with the squire and Miss Thorne, with a countess, a bishop, and the county grandees, while Mrs. Greenacre and such like were walking about with the ploughboys in the park. It was a great point gained by Mrs. Lookaloft, and it might be fairly expected that from this time forward the tradesmen of Barchester would, with undoubting pens, address her husband as T. Lookaloft, Esquire.[3]

Such snobberies extended throughout society. Paul Blouet discovered that English boys began 'swaggering about their social position' as soon as they left the nursery; and he recorded how amusing it was to follow a group of public schoolboys on their way home. The sons of professional men pointed out other boys and commented, 'Sons of merchants, don't you know!' But 'these are not without their revenge, as they look at a group close by, "Sons of clerks, you know!" But you should see the contemptuous glances of the latter as they pass the sons of shopkeepers, "Tradespeople's sons, I believe!"'[4]

To be considered middle class a certain minimum income was required, a certain style of family life and a certain form of employment, preferably professional. In the eighteenth century there were only three professions – apart from those of the army and navy – the law, the church and medicine. These were still regarded as superior to all others, but some additional occupations were now beginning to rank with them in social acceptability. Among these occupations were those of architects, surveyors and engineers; actuaries, senior civil servants and accountants; writers and artists (provided they were respectable); schoolmasters (if they taught in good schools); and, though in a rather lower class, Nonconformist ministers, dentists and veterinary surgeons. There were recognized classes, too, in the superior professions. There was a world of difference between a fashionable London doctor and a medical practitioner in the service of a Poor Law Union, just as there was still a social gap, though increasingly less marked, between a physician and a surgeon. Although not likely to be treated with the hauteur of Lady Carlisle – who, considering it beneath her dignity even to address her physician directly, instructed her maid to 'inform the doctor that he may bleed the Countess of Carlisle' – the family physician with an ordinary general practice would not normally expect to be acknowledged as an equal by the squire and would not presume to consider his daughter a suitable match for the squire's son. Nor would he be asked to stay to dinner as would the well-to-do London doctor whose advice was sought in most cases of grave illness in families who could afford his fees. The social standing of general practitioners rose, however, with the passing of the Medical Act of 1858 which, among other reforms in the profession, required doctors to pass examinations before practising; and thereafter doctors from good families such as Trollope's Thomas Thorne, who marries the heiress, Miss Dunstable, became far less of a rarity; while it was also less rare for the children of a physician to rise in the world as do those of Dr Roberts, the physician from Exeter, a man 'of no private means but enjoying a lucrative practice', whose son goes to Harrow with the rich Lord Lufton and whose daughter marries him.

If the medical profession was a hierarchy within the larger hierarchy of Victorian society, so was the legal profession. The president of the Law

Society and the rich lawyers of his acquaintance with their grand and spacious offices in Chancery Lane and Lincoln's Inn Fields – and their membership of the Conservative Club (founded in 1840) or the Junior Carlton (1864), the New University Club (1864), the Devonshire Club (1875), the National Liberal Club (1882), or one of those numerous other clubs established for the growing numbers of the prosperous middle class – were very different people from the solicitors whom Dickens had known when himself a clerk with Messrs Ellis and Blackmore. These professional men in the lower social reaches of their profession, who appear in one Dickens novel after another, occupy offices as dingy and unsavoury as those of Mr Vholes whose 'chambers are on so small a scale that one clerk can open the door without getting off his stool while the other who elbows him at the same desk has equal facilities for poking the fire. A smell as of unwholesome sheep, blending with the smell of must and dust, is referable to the nightly (and often daily) consumption of mutton fat in candles, and to the fretting of parchment forms and skins in greasy drawers.'[5]

The clerks who worked in such places – and who, together with the growing army of clerks in other offices, large and small, constituted so large a proportion of the lower middle class – were themselves, as Dickens said, divided into several grades:

> There is the salaried clerk who devotes the major part of his thirty-shillings a week to his personal pleasure and adornment, repairs half-price to the Adelphi at least three times a week, dissipates majestically at the cider cellar afterwards, and is a dirty caricature of the fashion which expired six months ago. There is the middle-aged copying clerk, with a large family, who is always shabby, and often drunk. And there are the office lads in their first surtouts [overcoats], who feel a befitting contempt for boys at day-schools, club as they go home at night, for saveloys and porter, and think there's nothing like 'life'.[6]

> There is also the articled clerk who 'has paid a premium and is an attorney in perspective, who runs a tailor's bill, receives invitations to parties, knows a family in Gower Street and another in Tavistock Square, goes out of town every vacation to see his father . . . and who is, in short, the very aristocrat of clerks'. Yet when he has completed his apprenticeship and becomes an attorney, he is not likely to find himself as socially acceptable as he would have done had he become a barrister, or for that matter an army officer or a clergyman. When her cousin announced her intention of marrying an attorney, Lady Amelia de Courcy advised her strongly against it. A clergyman would have been a far better proposition since 'clergymen – particularly

the rectors and vicars of country parishes – do become privileged above other professional men'.[7]

The sporting parson, however, was becoming a figure of the past. There were still several clergymen who were also landowners and even a few, like Thomas Sweet-Escott, a Somerset rector, who passed on to their ordained sons both their manor houses and their livings. Yet most Victorian clergymen were much more likely to resemble the Rev. Patrick Brontë than the Rev. Laurence Sterne; and Victorian hostesses were most unlikely to entertain in their dining-room such a sporting parson as the one who passed Squire Osbaldeston a note under the table to the effect that their hostess was his mistress and gave him 'some extremely odd evidence to that effect'. There remained, however, an unbridgeable social gap between most Anglican clergymen and all but a few of their parishioners. In Lark Rise

> the Rector visited each cottage in turn, working his way conscientiously round the hamlet from door to door . . . When he tapped . . . at a cottage door there would come a sound of scuffling within, as unseemly objects were hustled out of sight, for the whisper would have gone round that he had been seen getting over the stile and his knock would have been recognized. The women received him with respectful tolerance. A chair was dusted with an apron and the doing of housework or cooking was suspended while his hostess, seated uncomfortably on the edge of one of her own chairs, waited for him to open the conversation. When the weather had been discussed, the health of the inmates and absent children inquired about, and the progress of the pig and the prospect of the allotment crops, there came an awkward pause, during which both racked their brains to find something to talk about. There was nothing. The Rector never mentioned religion. That was looked upon in the parish as one of his chief virtues, but it limited the possible topics of conversation. Apart from his autocratic ideas, he was a kindly man, and he had come to pay a friendly call, hoping, no doubt, to get to know and to understand his parishioners better. But the gulf between them was too wide; neither he nor his hostess could bridge it. The kindly enquiries made and answered, they had nothing more to say to each other, and, after much 'ah-ing' and 'er-ing', he would rise from his seat, and be shown out with alacrity.[8]

As in the case of lawyers and medical men, there was a wide disparity both between the incomes of clergymen and between their relative social standing. Bishops almost invariably came from old families. In 1868, when A. C. Tait, a member of a family that had owned large estates in Scotland, was appointed Archbishop of Canterbury, the Archbishop of York was closely related to the

Earl of Marchmont. And in this same year, to take a representative selection, the Bishop of Bath and Wells was Lord Auckland; the Bishop of Norwich was a son of the Earl of Chichester; the Bishop of Winchester was the old Etonian younger brother of a former Archbishop of Canterbury; the Bishop of Lichfield's father was first cousin of his namesake, the eighteenth-century wit and man of fashion, George Augustus Selwyn; the Bishop of Oxford was a son of the philanthropist William Wilberforce, who came from an ancient Yorkshire family; and the Bishop of Durham was the son of a baronet. In the diocese of the Bishop of Barchester there are several clergymen as well born as these. Theophilus Grantly, the rich Archdeacon, has a daughter who marries the heir of the Marquess of Hartletop; the sister of the Rector of Framlingham marries a nobleman whose income is between £15,000 and £20,000 a year. There are others who, though poor, are recognized as gentlemen, as the Rev. Josiah Crawley, Vicar of Hogglestock, is; while there are some, like the bishop's dreadful chaplain, the Rev. Obadiah Slope, who are expressly stated to be not. When Dr Stanhope, who spends much of his time in Italy, meets Slope for the first time he is amazed, for, 'in spite of his long absence, he knew an English gentleman when he saw one'. And when Mr Crawley expresses to the archdeacon his regrets that he cannot provide a dowry for his daughter, who is to marry the archdeacon's son, the archdeacon replies, 'My dear Crawley, I have enough for both', and he interrupts the vicar's protests that he wished they stood 'on more equal grounds' by rising from his chair and declaring, 'We stand on the perfect level on which such men can meet each other. We are both gentlemen.'[9]

There were numerous examples of such wide differences in fortune between fellow-clergymen in every diocese. There were several extremely profitable bishoprics, like that of Durham which was worth – as was the archbishopric of Canterbury – £19,000 a year; and there were more than 100 benefices in the Church of England worth over £2000 a year. There were a good many more as valuable as the living of Framley which brings to the incumbent an income of £900 upon which he can employ a footman, a groom, a cook and a gardener as well as maidservants to help his wife run the parsonage.[10] But most Anglican clergymen, not so well connected, had less than £400 a year and a few had no more than £50.

The incomes of the poorest curates still compared most unfavourably, in fact, with men of similar education in other professions. In 1850 one authority wrote that 'young people of good position' could get married 'comfortably on £500 a year and expectations';[11] and in 1857, when *Barchester Towers* was published, Mrs Eleanor Bold was considered to be excessively well provided for with £1200 a year. Mrs Beeton considered that an income of as little as £150 a year justified the employment of a maid of all work; that a man earning £500 a year could afford a cook, one with £750 a bootboy as well as a cook and a housemaid, and one with £1000 a year a manservant, two housemaids and a cook. But an income of much less than £150, on which so many clergy were expected to survive, was too little for the support of a gentlemanly life.

Many office clerks, the most numerous class of salaried men, had no more than £150 and some less. Apprentice clerks employed on leaving school might get as little as £20 a year, and junior clerks with such institutions as banks and insurance companies could not expect more than about £80. Indeed, the reports of a Lancashire statistician suggest that even these figures might be high: he reckoned that the average salary of clerks in the Manchester area did not exceed £60 and that of responsible cashiers was only £100.[12] Anthony Trollope's income when he started work as a clerk in the General Post Office in 1834 was £90 a year, and after seven years it had risen no higher than £140.[13] In the 1870s one firm of solicitors reported that twenty-one of its clerks were earning less than £100 a year, twenty-five had less than £200, six less than £300 and only two over £300. The Mersey Docks and Labour Board in Liverpool, with a staff of about 300 clerks, employed ninety-six of them at under £100 a year, ninety-five at under £200, and only twenty-three at £200 to £500. Clerks in the Civil Service were slightly better paid. Junior clerks had about £125 to £300 a year; assistant clerks £300 to £600; senior clerks up to £900; while chief clerks started at about £1000.[14]

Most clerks, in fact, earned little more than skilled artisans. In the professions, however, rewards could be much higher. This was admittedly not true of the army; but then there were few officers who had no more than their pay to live on, and none at all in the smartest and most expensive regiments in which commissions changed hands for large sums. The *Army List* published an official list of 'Prices of Commissions'. That for July 1854 gives the following figures for the various ranks from cornet and ensign to lieutenant-colonel:

*Foot Guards*

| | |
|---|---|
| Lieutenant-colonel | £9000 |
| Major | £8300 |
| Captain | £4800 |
| Lieutenant | £2050 |
| Ensign | £1200 |

*Life Guards*

| | |
|---|---|
| Lieutenant-colonel | £7250 |
| Major | £5350 |
| Captain | £3500 |
| Lieutenant | £1785 |
| Cornet | £1260 |

### Dragoons

| | |
|---|---|
| Lieutenant-colonel | £6175 |
| Major | £4575 |
| Captain | £3225 |
| Lieutenant | £1190 |
| Cornet | £840 |

### Regiments of the Line

| | |
|---|---|
| Lieutenant-colonel | £4500 |
| Major | £3200 |
| Captain | £1800 |
| Lieutenant | £700 |
| Ensign | £450 |

These sums, large as they were, were frequently exceeded. The Earl of Lucan, for example, paid £25,000 for the command of the 17th Lancers. And it was not uncommon for poorer officers, talented though they might be, to remain throughout their careers blocked on the path to promotion by lack of money. It was not until the country had been shocked by the course of the Franco-Prussian War of 1870–71 that the Secretary of State for War, Edward Cardwell, was able, among other reforms, to abolish the purchase of commissions.

In professions other than the army rewards could be high. The headmaster of a good public school could command a salary of at least £1000; so could, it was estimated in 1851, 'a physician who is becoming popular' and, according to a writer in the *Contemporary Review*, 'a young married lawyer'. A promising barrister could earn £5000 a year; while celebrated lawyers in the 1880s were receiving over £15,000 a year, and doctors of the standing of Sir William Jenner earned almost as much. Jenner himself left £375,000.

In the earlier years of the century, so *A New System of Practical Domestic Economy* advised, a man with £5000 a year could not only maintain an establishment of thirteen male and nine female servants, but also ten horses, a coach, a curricle, a tilbury and a gig. And, so the same authority maintained, a man with £1000 a year could afford, in addition to his footman and three female servants, a coachman, two horses and a four-wheeled carriage.[15]

The carriage was all important. It should preferably be a four-wheeled carriage such as a barouche, but the possession of a light two-wheeled, one-horse carriage, a gig or a curricle, might entitle a family to be known as 'carriage people' and to be respected by shopkeepers as representing part of that valued custom known as 'the carriage trade'. An income of at least £600 a year was required to maintain an equipage of the most modest kind; a four-wheeled carriage complete with two horses, coachman, stabling and coach-house indicated an income considerably larger than that. In all there were, in 1856, slightly more than 200,000 people with their own private carriages.[16] One of them was Charles Dickens who could not disguise his pride when his success enabled him first to acquire a 'small chaise with a smaller pair of ponies' and then a 'more suitable equipage' cared for by a groom.

As he prospered, Dickens not only bought more expensive carriages, he also bought larger and more imposing houses, moving from Doughty Street to Devonshire Terrace, Regent's Park, a large house of ' "undeniable" situation and excessive splendour', which he took for £160 a year, paying £800 for the remaining twelve years of the lease; then moving to an even larger and grander house in Tavistock Square, for which he paid £1450 for a forty-five year lease; and, in 1856, buying a country house, Gad's Hill Place in Kent, for £1700.[17]

For 'carriage people' a commodious house was, of course, as necessary as the equipage itself. In the country house of, say, a moderately prosperous solicitor in the middle of the century, as well as bedrooms and dressing-rooms for the family and guests, there would be servants' rooms and nurseries approached by a back staircase. The domestic offices would be separated from the reception rooms by a swing door covered in red or green baize. As in the larger houses of the conservative upper classes, bathrooms were still rare; so were pipes for gas and hot water. 'There was no bathroom at Down,' wrote Charles Darwin's granddaughter of his house in Kent, 'nor any hot water except in the kitchen, but there were plenty of housemaids to run about with big brown-painted bath-cans.'[18] When Dr Proudie becomes Bishop of Barchester his wife finds that the house in the close to which she is to move has 'no gas; none whatever, but in the kitchen and passages [and] there is no hot water laid on anywhere above the ground floor. Surely there should be means of getting hot water in the bedrooms without having it brought in jugs from the kitchen.' She soon has gas installed; but many middle-class houses remained without it for many years yet.

Oil lamps and candles were used for lighting [recalled a vicar's daughter of her life in Hertfordshire in the 1850s and early 1860s]. There were no bathrooms then, and all hot water and cold water had to be carried from the kitchen and scullery. But we all had baths each day in spite of that . . . Our drawing-room was papered with a buff and gilt Fleur-de-Lys pat-terned paper. There were bookshelves and pier glasses and woolwork ottomans and an upright grand piano with faded red silk fluted across the front and a very fine harp . . . The carpet was red with a buff pattern and my mother had a davenport [a small writing-table] sacred to her own use. In the best bedrooms there were four-post beds with damask curtains, though brass beds were by then becoming fashionable . . . After the nurse left, our household consisted of a cook, house-parlour-maid and a girl. The wages were £18, £16 and £6. A widow who lived in a cottage nearby came in to bake and to help when required. She always wore her bonnet and clattered about the kitchen and scullery in pattens. The family then were my father and mother and myself and two brothers who came on visits, as did, later, grandchildren. Our income then I think, was about £800 a year. We kept an open carriage called a Stanhope . . . a groom, one horse and a groom-gardener who also pumped and looked after the fowls and pigs . . . There was a park-like field, a small flower garden and excellent kitchen garden and stables.[19]

In towns the well-to-do middle class generally lived in detached villas well away from the commercial centre. The larger villas had extensive gardens surrounded by walls and, often, a lodge with a gatekeeper to keep unwanted callers, beggars and pedlars at bay. In London, and in such towns as Cheltenham, Bath, Brighton, Leamington, and Bristol, terrace houses were still considered fashionable; but, except in Scotland, flats were not so. It was not until later in the century that mansion flats became acceptable to the prosperous middle class. The blocks around Ashley Place, Westminster, were built in the 1850s but it was not before the 1870s and 1880s that a growing demand for large flats led to such developments as Norman Shaw's Albert Hall Mansions of 1879.[20]

As more and more prosperous middle-class people moved into flats, so, too, did the rather less well-to-do move into semi-detached houses, the first of which had been built at St John's Wood where, as early as 1796, a firm of auctioneers had recommended the laying-out of a grand circus ringed with pairs of semi-detached houses. The circus did not materialize but the pairs of houses did, spreading along the banks of the canal, up Wellington Road towards Hampstead and Finchley, and inaugurating a form of domestic architecture which was soon afterwards to be seen in every town in England.[21] At the same time row upon row of small terrace houses, many with bow windows in the front rooms, stained glass over the front doors and small brick-walled gardens at the front and back, were being built for the respectable lower middle classes who lived behind their heavy curtains in domestic seclusion if not always in that domestic harmony of Charles Kingsley's ideal.

Charles Pooter, a clerk in a mercantile office in the City, lives in a house much like this, No. 12 Brickfield Terrace, Holloway, known as 'The Laurels'. This has a porticoed front door, a stuccoed balustrade protecting the house from the street, heavy facings surrounding the windows, and an out-of-scale parapet projecting several feet above the level of the flat roof, which gives the front façade a false impression of height. Lace curtains, and a half-closed blind in the sitting-room, conceal the occupants from view; the back of Mrs Pooter's dressing-table looking-glass is all that can be seen in her bedroom window. In addition to the basement there are six rooms in the house in one of which sleeps a maid. As in most other lower-middle-class houses of this time – the late 1880s and early 1890s – the lighting is by gas and a geyser noisily supplies hot water in a small bathroom.

On his return from the City by omnibus, Mr Pooter enjoys a meat-tea, reads the newspaper or *Exchange and Mart*, listens to his wife playing the cottage piano (bought on the three years' system), or does a few odd jobs about the house. 'There is always something to be done: a tin-tack here, a venetian blind to put straight, a fan to nail up or part of a carpet to nail down', all of which he can do, he assures us, with his pipe in his mouth. Occasionally his friend Cummings (a keen tricyclist and regular reader of *Bicycle News*), comes in for a game of dominoes or bezique, a glass or two of whiskey (price 36s for a dozen bottles) or a smoke in the breakfast parlour. Sometimes Mrs Cummings and other friends call and then Mrs Cummings sings a song or two, or they play consequences or more noisy games like 'Monkeys and Cutlets' or listen to Mr Fosselton of the local amateur dramatic society, the Holloway Comedians, doing his priceless imitation of Henry Irving. On Sundays Mr and Mrs Pooter always go to church, often twice; and Mr Pooter takes it as 'a great compliment' when the curate asks him to take round the plate. He also thinks it a great impertinence when the grocer's boy has the cheek to bring his basket to the front door.[22]

Both Mr Pooter and his wife are sticklers for propriety as were nearly all members of their class for whom books of etiquette and guides to deportment – together with manuals of domestic economy and publications such as *Party Giving on Every Scale* and *Dont: Mistakes and Improprieties more or less prevalent in Conduct and Speech* – were published in ever-growing numbers and were so widely read that many of them became best-sellers in numerous editions.

One of these manuals advised its female readers that

Soup should be eaten with a table spoon, and not with a dessert. Fish should be eaten with a silver fish-knife and fork. All made dishes, such as rissoles, patties, etc., should be eaten with a fork only. In eating asparagus a knife and fork should be used. Salad should be eaten with a knife and fork. Jellies, blancmanges, iced puddings, etc., should be eaten with a fork . . . When eating cheese, small morsels of cheese should be placed with a knife on small morsels of bread, and the two conveyed to the mouth with the thumb and finger, the piece of bread being the morsel to hold as the cheese should not be taken up in the fingers, and should not be eaten off the point of the knife. As a matter of course, young ladies do not eat cheese at dinner parties.[23]

Every activity of a lady's day was covered by these manuals. She was instructed how to behave in any circumstance in which she might find herself, and told what clothes to wear and how to wear them. Virtuous women had a 'repugnance to excessive luxury' in underclothing; they never wore 'too much lace embroidery or ribbons and bows'; to wear a garter below the knee was 'against all rules of taste'; night chemises must have long sleeves and reach down to the feet. If face powder were worn it must be applied so modestly that its effects could be mistaken for those of a slight natural bloom. When asked to dance, according to *Society Small Talk* (1879), a lady did not reply, 'I shall be happy', a phrase that had quite 'disappeared in Company'. Less eager responses, after a glance at the dance card, were more lady-like. Recommended replies were, 'I will give you a dance if you will come for it a little later. I am engaged for the next three', or 'I am afraid I have not one to spare except number fourteen, a quadrille.'

Control over the countenance was an essential part of good manners, readers of *The Habits of Good Society* were informed. On gracefully entering a drawing-room – not rushing in 'head-foremost' – a lady should look for her hostess, a smile upon her face, granting 'an elegant bend to common acquaintance', then accepting the hand extended to her with 'cordial press-ure' rather than shaking it. 'Let her sink gently into a chair . . . Her feet should scarcely be shown and not crossed.'

It was also essential to master the rules governing the presentation of visiting cards:

A lady's card is larger than a gentleman's. The former may be glazed, the latter not . . . A young lady does not require a separate card so long as she is living with her mother . . . Cards should be delivered in person, and not sent by post. A lady should desire her manservant to inquire if the mistress of the house at which she is calling is 'at home.' If 'not at home,' she should hand him three cards: one of her own and two of her husband's . . . If the answer is in the affirmative, she should, after making the call, leave two of her husband's cards on the hall-table, and neither put them in the card-basket nor offer them to her hostess, all of which would be very incorrect. When the mistress of the house has a grown-up daughter or daughters, the lady leaving cards should turn down one corner of her

visiting card – the right-hand corner generally – to include the daughter
. . . in the call.[24]

Books of etiquette were addressed to men as well as to women:

Don't tuck your napkin under your chin or spread it upon your breast [one
of these authorities advised]. Don't eat from the end of your spoon, but
from the side. Don't gurgle, or draw in your breath, or make other noises
when eating soup . . . Don't bite your bread. Break it off [but not] into
your soup . . . Don't expectorate on the sidewalk . . . Don't use slang.
There is some slang that, according to Thackeray is gentlemanly slang,
and other slang that is vulgar. If one does not know the difference, let them
avoid slang altogether . . . Don't use profane language . . . Don't use
meaningless exclamations . . . Don't call your servants girls . . . Don't
conduct correspondence on postal-cards . . . Don't sit cross-legged. Pretty
nearly everybody of the male sex does – but nevertheless, don't . . . Don't,
however brief your call, wear overcoat or overshoes into the drawing-
room. If you are making a short call, carry your hat and cane in your hand,
but never an umbrella . . . Don't attempt to shake hands with everybody
present. If host or hostess offers a hand, take it; a bow is sufficient for the
rest. Don't in any case, offer to shake hands with a lady. The initiative
must always come from her. By the same principle don't offer your hand to
a person older than yourself, or to any one whose rank may be supposed to
be higher than your own, until he has extended his.

When meeting a female acquaintance in the street a man must wait until he
received a bow. 'You then lift your hat quite off your head [though] you have
no need, as they do in France, to show the world the inside thereof, so you
immediately replace it. In making this salute you bend the body slightly. If,
as should rarely occur, you happen to be smoking, you take your cigar from
your mouth with the other hand.'

In addition to these books on etiquette there were also numerous works on
domestic economy. Kitchiner's *Cook's Oracle* and *Housekeeper's Oracle*,
published in the 1820s were still referred to, as were Hayward's *Art of Dining*,
Carême's *Maître d Hotel Français*, Soyer's *The Modern Housewife* and the
works of Louis Eustache Ude. Margaret Dodd's *Cookery Book* of 1830 was
followed by Eliza Acton's *Modern Cookery in All its Branches*; Mrs Rundell's
*New System of Domestic Cookery, Formed upon Principles of Economy and
Adapted to the Use of Private Families; Domestic Duties, or Instructions to
Young Married Ladies on the Management of Their Households*; and, in
1861, the first one-volume edition of the celebrated *Household Management*

by Mrs Beeton, a publisher's wife who died before she was thirty, having given birth to her fourth son.

Mrs Beeton and Alexis Soyer both offered suggestions for quite simple meals as well as for dinner parties. Here, for example, are Mrs Beeton's recommendations for a week's 'plain family dinners' for a comfortably off middle-class household:

SUNDAY

Clear Gravy Soup. Roast Haunch of Mutton. Sea Kale. Potatoes. Rhubarb Tart. Custard in Glasses.

MONDAY

Crimped Skate and Caper Sauce. Boiled Knuckle of Veal and Rice. Cold Mutton. Stewed Rhubarb and Baked Custard Pudding.

TUESDAY

Vegetable Soup. Toad in the Hole, made from the remains of cold mutton. Stewed Rhubarb and Baked Plum Pudding.

WEDNESDAY

Fried Soles. Dutch Sauce. Boiled Beef, carrots, suet dumplings. Lemon Pudding.

THURSDAY

Pea Soup made from liquor that beef was boiled in. Cold Beef. Mashed Potatoes. Mutton Cutlets and Tomato Sauce. Macaroni.

FRIDAY

Bubble and Squeak, made with remains of cold beef. Roast Shoulder of Veal, stuffed, and spinach and potatoes. Boiled Batter Pudding and Sweet Sauce.

SATURDAY

Stewed Veal and Vegetables, made from remains of the shoulder. Broiled rumpsteaks and oyster sauce. Yeast Dumplings.

When guests were to be entertained and impressed, less simple fare was naturally recommended, although Mrs Beeton did not favour the extravagance of eighteenth-century menus. One of her recommendations for a dinner party for twelve people begins with soup *à la Reine* and Julienne soup, followed by turbot with lobster sauce and slices of salmon *à la Genevese*. As entrées she suggests croquettes of leveret, fricandeau of veal, and *vol au vent* with stewed mushrooms. Then come guinea fowls and forequarter of lamb; and – after charlotte *à la Parisienne*, orange jelly, meringues, ratafia ice pudding and lobster salad with sea kale – dessert and ices.

Dinner parties and the proper seating of guests were almost as important in middle-class as in upper-class society.

The regular round of formal dinner parties was very important in Cambridge [wrote the daughter of a professor]. In one house the parties were generally of twelve or fourteen people, and everybody of dinner-party status was invited strictly in turn. The guests were seated according to the Protocol, the Heads of Houses ranking by the dates of the foundation of their colleges, except that the Vice-Chancellor would come first of all. After the Masters came the Regius Professors in the order of their subjects. Divinity first; and then the other Professors according to the dates of the foundations of their chairs, and so on down all the steps of the hierarchy. It was better not to invite too many important people at the same time, or the complications became insoluble to hosts of only ordinary culture. How could they tell if Hebrew or Greek took precedence, of two professorships founded in the same year? And some of the grandees were very touchy about their rights, and their wives were even more easily offended.[25]

In most middle-class households about a third of their total income was spent upon food;[26] and much attention was paid to the furnishing of dining-rooms, as has evidently been the case with the Veneerings' in which 'a great looking glass above the sideboard reflects the table and the company and the flowers and the candles and the champagne chalice'.[27] Certainly Archdeacon Grantly has strong views on the importance of dining-room tables. He considers a dining-room measuring only sixteen feet by fifteen far too cramped; and when Mr Arabin suggests a round table he is horrified: round tables are the most abominable pieces of furniture ever invented. A dining-room table should be a goodly board which can be extended almost indefinitely to accommodate the requisite number of guests. It should also be almost black with perpetual polishing and shine like a looking-glass. He connects round tables with oak, and the unseemly new fashion of spreading a cloth on the table with Dissenters and calico-printers who know no better.[28]

When *Barchester Towers* was published in 1857 the elegant comfort of early Victorian rooms had given way to the fussiness and elaborate ornamentation which had become so popular and spread so fast after the Great Exhibition of 1851 had opened its doors upon an awesome display of voluptuously ornate and ingenious objects and upon interiors overwhelming in their richness. 'Wherever you can rest there decorate,' was the advice of John Ruskin, the champion of the Gothic revival whose influence on the decorative arts was decisive; and, in eager obedience to this doctrine, the

Victorians rejected the restraint and simplicity in interior decoration that their grandparents had so much admired. Bareness was looked upon with profound disapproval; rooms were crowded with a jumble of exotically decorated furniture, ornaments, pictures, looking-glasses, screens, and bric-à-brac of every kind. Dining-room tables, frequently required to accommodate twenty-four guests, were covered with epergnes and cruets, salvers and urns, candlesticks, silver breadbaskets, bon-bon dishes and wine coolers. Plain, rose-coloured silk-lined walls were overlaid with flocked and patterned papers. Back-to-back settees stood upon the thick pile of Brussels carpets. Porcelain figures, papier-mâché boxes and cut-glass bowls were set above white marble fireplaces beside French clocks, candelabra and gilt-framed chimney glasses. On console tables stood models of Swiss chalets brought back from Lausanne and on grand pianos Benares trays, presents from sons and nephews in the Poona Horse. The embroidered handles of bell pulls hung down beside huge landscapes and seascapes, prints, silhouettes and oleographs, sepia photographs of dead relatives, and reproductions of the pictures of Sir Edwin Landseer, Frith, Mulready and Lord Leighton. Spring-upholstered chairs and sofas banished earlier, less plushy seats to the attic or the saleroom. Towards the end of the century, under the influence of the prophet of craftsmanship, William Morris, the more sophisticated Victorians sent their now unfashionable 'Exhibition art' to the saleroom also. Morris – whose designs for wallpaper, fabrics, carpets and furniture began a new chapter in the history of interior decoration – urged people to have nothing in their houses except those objects that they knew to be useful or believed to be beautiful; and gradually they began to take heed of his advice. For more than a generation, though, the English, as Ralph Waldo Emerson said, were gripped by a passion to 'deck and improve' their homes with expensive furniture, pictures, ponderous mirrors, table lamps and padded chairs.[29]

One of the most ubiquitous pieces of middle-class Victorian furniture was the davenport, a small writing-table the prototype of which had been made for Captain Davenport by the firm of Gillow in the eighteenth century. Numerous variations on the basic form were produced; and every morning in thousands of homes all over England women could be seen sitting down at their davenports occupied in one of a weekday morning's principal activities, in writing notes and letters, answering and issuing invitations, checking household accounts.

After the middle of the century most women used steel pens made in Birmingham with bone, cedar or ebonized handles, quill pens being favoured only by the old-fashioned – the penknives, which had formerly been essential for trimming and sharpening the quills, now usually being used for other purposes. Fountain pens came into general use in the late 1880s; and by

1895 Harrods store was offering several different types from 2s 6d to half a guinea, the Lacon fountain pen, the 'only one with a Transparent Barrel which enables the writer to see at a glance when the ink requires to be replenished', costing 7s 9d. Ink had formerly been made at home from powdered galls mixed with camphor; but in 1832 Dr Henry Stephens, who had been supplying his friends with an excellent mixture, decided to manufacture it commercially. Soon after bottled ink had appeared in the shops, machine-made blotting paper was also available. This had been manufactured since 1859 by the nephew of John Slade, originator of 'Slade's Original Hand-Made Blotting', who had recognized the possibilities in a batch of faulty writing paper which had soaked up the ink applied to it. Fine sand was, however, still used to dry ink occasionally, as it had been for centuries; and pounce was, indeed, still in use for drying ink on hand-written documents in solicitors' offices in the 1920s.

Before the machine-made envelopes manufactured by Messrs de la Rue and Hill became popular in about 1850, letters were generally sealed by a wafer. Rowland Hill mentioned 'the little paper bags called envelopes' in 1839; and Mulready designed an envelope which was put on the market when adhesive stamps were introduced with the Penny Postage in 1840. But these early envelopes proved to be largely unsaleable and great numbers of them had to be destroyed.[30] Soon afterwards, however, they were available in all shapes, colours and sizes – from Dark Silurian Double Thick and unglazed Turkay Mill to Azure-laid Papyrus Antiqua – and, like mourning writing paper, with five different sizes of black borders, Italian, narrow, middle, broad and extra broad.[31]

After luncheon, her letters all written, the lady of the house would go out to pay calls, leave cards or merely to take 'carriage exercise'. She would return, perhaps, for afternoon tea; and in the evenings after dinner settle down to her needlework or woolwork while her husband read aloud or her daughters played the piano. Some might copy music or sketch, or model fruit in wax or press flowers into albums or make pictures with shells or look at photographs through stereoscopes or play a game of cribbage or halma. And, in the more religious houses, there would be family prayers in the evening as well as in the morning, the servants coming into the room to kneel down in front of chairs facing the wall on one side, the members of the family on the other, the master of the household, also on his knees, reading from a prayer book at a table in the middle.

On Sundays servants and family prayed together in church where they were similarly divided.

> The servants wore bonnets on Sundays and went to church and sat in their own pews [an old Edwardian lady wrote, recalling her childhood in the

1850s]. There were boxed-in pews in those days where the quality sat in state and the poor people waited in church until the gentlefolk had made their way out. The men and women of the lesser orders were separated, the men sitting on one side, the women on the other . . . Before oil lamps were used there were tall iron candlesticks fastened to the end of each pew.[32]

# 55 · *Leisure Hours*

Describing the life he had known in Manchester in the 1860s, Thomas Wright, alias 'the journeyman engineer', recalled most vividly the excited anticipation with which people waited on Saturdays for the ringing of the one o'clock bell that signalled the end of the week's work. They relished being able to stroll home unhurriedly to their dinner and, after dinner, having the time to smoke their pipes 'still in a leisurely and contemplative manner unknown to them at other times'. Then they would go down to the public baths, taking their clean clothes with them to put on when they had washed, and bringing away their working clothes with them. After that, attired in cord or moleskin trousers, black coats and waistcoats, caps 'of somewhat sporting character' and mufflers 'more or less gaudy', they would go out shopping with their wives, or stroll round the town, looking in the shop windows, 'particularly of newsagents where illustrated papers and period-icals are displayed', or they might go booming about the town with a factory band, parade up and down a suburban field in the uniform of the local volunteer corps, go to the greyhound races or, perhaps, go out pigeon-flying.

> Pigeon-flying was a weekly sport, especially among the tattooed men in the poorer quarters of the parish [wrote Richard Church of his childhood in Battersea], costers with flat black caps and hoarse voices, chokers instead of collars and ties, and boots of a ginger-yellow. These men, scrubbed and shaved, red-faced and 'blue-lipped', would rattle off on their carts behind ponies and donkeys . . . anxiously guarding long wicker baskets out of which floated the soft sub-chorus of pigeon voices, and the fidget of crowded feathers.[1]

Families with young children might go to public parks. Following com-plaints that it was 'scarcely in the power of the factory workmen to taste the breath of nature or to look upon its verdure', three parks had been opened in 1847 in Manchester, the first town to have such open spaces after Birkenhead.[2] Three years later a park was opened in Bradford; soon afterwards there was one in Bolton; and by the end of the century there was scarcely a town in England which had not provided one. Most towns also by then had museums and public libraries, either run by the local authorities or by private institutions, Manchester being the first large town to take advantage of the Free Libraries Act of 1850 which enabled up to a halfpenny rate to be spent on library services provided two-thirds of the ratepayers approved of the levy.

As well as museums and public libraries there were concert halls and mechanics' institutes, literary and philosophical societies, lecture rooms and art galleries. Outings were organized by Sunday Schools, trade unions, friendly societies, and Nonconformist chapels; readings and talks with lantern slides were provided by missionary societies and mutual improvement groups; concerts were given by choral societies and amateur orchestras. There were, indeed, opportunities enough for those who wanted to improve their minds, to widen the range of their interests or to pursue an artistic or cultural inclination, to do so. And there were, as it was frequently regretted, ample opportunities for the pursuit of more raffish and self-indulgent pleasures. The author of *Liverpool Life: Its Pleasures, Practices and Pastimes*, which was published in 1856, found that a man wandering about the city on a Saturday night could certainly have met with a perfectly respectable gathering of artisans and middle-class families enjoying a show combining wholesome comedy with sentimental songs and monologues. But he would also have come across numerous low dance-halls and smoky taverns, places where prostitutes and 'dollymops' paraded up and down among the customers; concert rooms where vulgar songs were sung and more or less naked girls adopted *poses plastiques*; fairgrounds like the one on the corner of Lime Street and Roe Street where a 'medical galvanist' gave an obscene demonstration of the effects of laughing gas and where the targets in the shooting gallery included the Duke of Wellington, Napoleon III, Prince Albert and the Queen.[3] The Saturday night wanderer would also have passed countless taverns and gin palaces where drinking continued for most of the night.

The number of such places in the country as a whole was enormous, particularly in poorer quarters of large towns where there were even more than the national average in 1861 of one for every 186 people in England and Wales. The amount of alcohol consumed in these places was astonishing. In 1875, 'the most bibulous year on record', the consumption stood at 1.3 gallons of spirits and 34.4 gallons of beer per head of the population.[4] Never again were the English to drink so much. Even of wine, of which well over half a gallon was drunk per head in the early 1870s, the consumption was higher than it was to be until after the Second World War. Public drunkenness was common, particularly on such occasions as Derby Day, at other race meetings, and at such prize-fights as that celebrated contest in a Hampshire field in 1860 when thousands of spectators came by train to see Tom Sayers, the small and doughty English champion, knocked down repeatedly by the huge American John C. Heenan in a drawn fight of thirty-seven rounds that lasted over two hours. There was also much drunkenness after football matches.

Until the introduction of the Saturday half holiday in the middle of the century, football had almost been forgotten as a popular working-class game and – although condemned by most boards of governors and headmasters as a vulgar activity fit only, in the words of Samuel Butler, Headmaster of Shrewsbury School, for 'butchers' boys and farm labourers' – it had been taken over and kept alive by the public schools. Under a variety of different rules, or, more often, loosely observed customs, it had been played at Charterhouse and Westminster, at Harrow and Eton, at Winchester, Shrewsbury and Rugby; and at most of these schools it was a rough and tumble game in which handling of the ball and a good deal of violent tackling and hacking were allowed. All schools, however, except Rugby, insisted that when caught the ball had to be dropped and kicked with the feet, the Rugby players alone being permitted to hold on to the ball and run with it. At the universities attempts were made from time to time to agree upon some commonly accepted set of rules by which players might be bound; but it was not until the Football Association was founded in 1863 that such regulations were drawn up, and even then not all teams chose to accept them. Blackheath School, for example, insisted upon retaining the old indulgences which had permitted the kicking of shins and the handling of the ball – as in the version of the game played at Rugby – and from their method of playing football, or soccer as it was colloquially known from 1891, the game of Rugby football developed.

Attempts were made by well-meaning gentlemen players from the public schools and universities to introduce the game under Football Association rules to the working classes in industrial areas. But these attempts met at first with little success; and when in 1871 the Old Harrovian Secretary of the Football Association established a competition for a challenge cup open to all the fifty clubs by then affiliated to the Association, only fifteen accepted, nearly all of them clubs formed by public school old boys' societies. One or other of these clubs won the cup for the first eleven years of the competition until, in 1883, the Old Etonians were beaten by Blackburn Olympics, a team largely composed of iron foundry and cotton workers, who took the cup north to the strains of brass bands and the cheers of supporters described as 'a northern horde' distinguished by their 'uncouth garb' and 'strong oaths'.[5]

By then a large number of other working-class clubs had been formed, many of them founded by church or chapel congregations. Among them were Aston Villa, Birmingham City, Bolton Wanderers, Everton, Liverpool and Wolverhampton Wanderers. Others were founded by schools, among them Queen's Park Rangers (Droop Street School) and Leicester City (Wyggeston School); by cricket teams, as in the case of Derby County, Preston North End, Sheffield Wednesday and Sheffield United; or by factories and industrial firms, like Manchester United (which was formed by workers employed by the Lancashire and Yorkshire Railway Company), West Ham United (founded by men from the Thames Iron Works) and Crewe Alexander (established by railwaymen whose meetings were held at the Alexander Hotel).[6]

Most of the successful teams came from the north. Between 1883 and 1915 the Football Association Cup was won only once, in 1901, by a southern team, Tottenham Hotspur; and the wide and growing popularity of the game in the northern and Midland counties led to charges being made for tickets of admission to football grounds, then to the introduction of professional players, the best of whom, however, received no more than the wages of a skilled artisan. By 1910 there were 6000 professional footballers in the country, and ever increasing numbers of football supporters. The cup final, which had been watched by no more than 17,000 in 1888, attracted a crowd of 120,000 in 1913. After the outbreak of war the next year the number of matches played that autumn and winter rapidly declined, as clubs called upon players and spectators alike to join up. By the end of 1914 some 500,000 men, about half the total number of volunteers, had enlisted through the agency of football clubs. But professional football had by then become, as it was to be again when the war was over, the principal entertainment of a large majority of the working class.

At the same time cricket, which appealed to a far wider social range, was becoming a nationally popular game as county sides developed, as the All-England and United All-England elevens toured the country, as such players as W. G. Grace – the large, bearded doctor who played for Gloucester County – became household names, and as the first visit by an Australian team in 1878 inaugurated a rivalry which was to be pursued in the continuing struggle for the Ashes, the remains of a bail burned by Australian supporters mourning their eleven's defeat by the Marylebone Cricket Club in 1883.

As cricket and soccer matches drew ever larger crowds, new games were invented and old ones modernized. Rugby football, governed since 1871 by the Rugby Union, an organization that banned professionalism within its member clubs, developed into a game which was almost as popular with the middle classes as association football was with the workers; and in South

Wales, Lancashire and on the Scottish border, where it was played professionally, rugger – like soccer, a slang word that came from the universities – attracted large crowds of working-class supporters. Tennis, an adaptation of the medieval game, was patented in 1874 under the name of 'Sphairistike' by an army officer whose original rules were altered three years later by the Wimbledon All England Croquet and Lawn Tennis Club. Golf, which had been played in Scotland for centuries and since 1608 at Blackheath, where it had been introduced by James I's Scottish courtiers, was also growing in popularity, the Royal North Devon Club having been founded in 1864 at Westward Ho and the Royal Liverpool Club at Hoylake in 1869, the year in which polo was introduced from India. Women as well as men played golf and in 1885 were considered to do so expertly enough to be admitted to the full courses from the shorter ones to which they had previously been relegated. They also, of course, played croquet, a game which had come over from France by way of Ireland and whose white hoops and coloured post could be seen on the lawn behind nearly every middle-class house.

Inside those houses in the evenings, since inactivity was considered reprehensible, not to say immoral, all the members of the family occupied themselves in playing games or reading or in some other educational or artistic pursuit. Some would draw or paint, while others did fancy-work, rolled paper-work or embroidery; they made models in wax or pictures with shells; pressed flowers in books; painted trays; decorated bellpulls; pasted postcards and pictures from magazines onto screens; sewed dresses from the cut-out paper patterns in the *Englishwoman's Domestic Magazine*. There were kaleidoscopes to play with, and stereoscopes, and zoetropes which, when quickly revolved, made pictures of animals run and jump. There were magic lanterns and folios of prints, watercolours and photographs to look at. There were jigsaws and all kinds of games to play, card games and board games, paper and pencil games, whist and loo, piquet and Pope Joan, halma, solitaire and corinthian. Above all there was patience, and there was music.

In the houses of the richer families, professional musicians were employed to perform before the guests; but in less privileged households the entertainment had to be provided by the members of the family and their guests themselves. No self-respecting middle-class home was without a piano; few daughters were not taught to play, though far from all played tunefully; and most fathers liked to sing. The result seems often to have been the kind of party that the wife of the Rev. Archer Clive, Rector of Solihull, regretted having given one Sunday evening in 1846:

> It was not a success. There was too much bad music tonight. A little is all very well, but tonight it was the staple. The wretched Iringhams and

Edwards brought their young children, to do them good as they said, not thinking of the harm to us. The Crowthers played something wrong all through the first bar, and then got up a horrid glee for two pianoforte players, one harp and four voices, which was truly dreadful for discord. I sang as badly as usual. And Archer . . . set off on the wrong note and kept steadily wrong all the way.[7]

While young children were not often taken to musical parties, adults joined in children's games with unremitting zest. They played blindman's buff, hide-and-seek, hunt the thimble, come-and-sit-ye-down-by-me-love, charades, twirl the teacher, musical chairs, postman's knock, shadow buff, my lady's toilet and an extraordinary variety of other games whose rules – such as they were – have long since been forgotten. And when the company collapsed exhausted, there was sure to be some member of the party who could keep them entertained with a conjuring trick or a comic song or by making a tortoise from muscat raisins and their stalks, by carving a pig out of an apple, or constructing a set of vampire's fangs from an orange peel.

The excitement engendered at these evening parties frequently came close to hysteria, particularly at Christmas, when the party season was at its height. 'Such dinings, such dancings, such conjurings, such blind-man's buffings, such kissings-out of old years and kissings-in of new years!' wrote Dickens of one happy Christmas when his children were young. He had taken them to a party given by his friend, the actor William Charles Macready, and had performed a country dance with Mrs Macready; displayed his remarkable skill as a conjuror, producing a plum pudding from an empty saucepan and heating it up over a fire in Clarkson Stanfield's top hat ('without damaging the lining'), changing a box of bran into a live guinea-pig. After supper the guests had all got 'madder than ever' with the 'pulling of crackers, the drinking of champagne and the making of speeches'. Then the dancing started and Dickens's friend, John Forster, had seized Jane Carlyle round the waist and whirled her into the thick of it. 'Oh, for the love of heaven let me go!' she cried out. 'You are going to dash my brains out against the folding doors!' 'Your brains!' he had answered. 'Who cares about their brains here? *Let them go!*'

At Dickens's own house on Christmas Day, as in thousands of others, the family sat round the big mahogany table in the dining-room, surrounded by the holly and ivy which covered the walls and dangled from the gas brackets; and when the flaming pudding came in they would greet it by clapping, and Dickens would give his traditional toast, 'Here's to us all! God bless us!' The toast would be repeated on New Year's Eve as the church bells pealed; then one of his daughters would play the piano, and there would be dancing, and the master would lead off with the cook, jigging about and clapping his hands

ABOVE: A brickfield in Lancashire.
Conditions in brickfields in the 19th
century were acknowledged to be as bad
as they were in the mines and the worst
factories. Dickens's description of the
brickmaker's house in *Bleak House* was
taken from life. It was 'one of a
cluster of wretched hovels in a
brickfield, with pigsties close to the
broken windows, and miserable little
gardens before the doors, growing
nothing but stagnant pools.'

RIGHT: *Fête in Petworth Park* (1835,
detail) by William Frederick
Witherington. The west front of
Petworth had been built in the 1680s for
the sixth Duke of Somerset either by a
Frenchman or by an English architect
strongly influenced by French ideas.
The third Earl of Egremont was a most
indulgent landowner, allowing the
villagers to play bowls and cricket on his
lawns whenever they liked and to
scribble on his walls and even the glass
of his windows.

ABOVE: In this painting by James Hayllar which was exhibited at the
Royal Academy in 1889, a little girl takes one of her father's tenant
families around the picture gallery at the hall. The smocks the tenant
and the older man are wearing were formerly used purely as
protective clothing, but were now worn, often elaborately
ornamented, as an everyday garment and even on Sundays.

RIGHT: The hall and staircase of a country house in 1882, in a
painting by Jonathan Pratt. In obedience to the advice of John
Ruskin, the later Victorians rejected the restraint and simplicity so
much admired by their forebears and crowded their rooms with a
jumble of furniture, pictures, looking-glasses, screens, busts,
carpets, rugs, bric-à-brac of every kind, and with what Sir Osbert
Lancaster called 'an extraordinary love of plant life which manifested
itself in every interior', aspidistras, palms, rubber-plants and ferns.

Frith's *Ramsgate Sands*, painted in 1854, depicts the variety of
enjoyments which a seaside holiday afforded – paddling and digging
in the sand, performances by trained mice, Nigger Minstrels, Punch
and Judy men, performing rabbits, whelks and jellied eels and
ginger beer. While children play their fathers read newspapers or
look out to sea through telescopes; their mothers, in straw bonnets
and crinolines, work at their embroidery or read books. Queen
Victoria bought the painting for Buckingham Palace.

ABOVE: Frith's *Many Happy Returns of the Day*. A celebration of middle-class family life. The children's high chairs were known as Astley-Cooper chairs. Designed by Sir Astley Paston Cooper, the orthopaedic surgeon, for the purpose of training children to sit upright, they were brought into the dining-room when children were permitted to join the grown-ups for a meal or for children's parties such as this.

LEFT: In this detail from his *Game of Draughts*, Thomas Faed portrays a game in a family far less comfortably provided for than that shown in Frith's *Many Happy Returns of the Day*. Many of the poorest families, however, had boxes of simple and often home-made games, as Henry Mayhew discovered when questioning children in the streets in the 1850s.

LEFT: A detail from *Beach Scene* by Ernest Proctor. The larger holiday resorts grew rapidly in the 1920s and 1930s. Blackpool, for example, had a resident population of over 100,000 in 1931 and seven million visitors a year. Yet in smaller, less frequented seaside places there were scarcely more working-class holiday-makers to be seen than there had been in Cornwall in the 1890s.

BELOW: Helen McKie's impression of Waterloo Station one afternoon in the Second World War evokes the hurry, excitement and anxiety of those days. Among the land girls, the marching soldiers and women of the Auxiliary Territorial Service, the sailors and Wrens, the paratroopers and highlanders, the military policemen and RAF officers, the Free French officer, the American and Indian soldiers and the Chelsea Pensioner there is scarcely a civilian to be seen.

to make everyone join in, doing lively, encouraging pirouettes behind those who were slow to do so.[8]

Nearly everyone looked forward to the Christmas festivities then, to the parties and the presents under the Christmas tree; the kissing under the mistletoe, the visit of Father Christmas; the carolers with their lanterns singing in the snow; the walk to church where, for once in the year, grown-ups pretended not to notice if the girls whispered or the boys let spiders loose across the hymnbooks in the family pew; the drives to dances in the pony-cart with straw and hot bricks piled on the floor to keep the feet warm, and hot baked potatoes held in muffs; the evenings by the fire reading books and newspapers and magazines.

The number of these published was enormous, as were the circulation figures of the more widely-read periodicals, such as *The Cornhill Magazine*, *Fraser's Magazine*, *Punch* and Dickens's *Household Words*. *The Illustrated London News*, which was founded in 1842, was soon selling 60,000 copies an issue. Sales reached 130,000 in 1851 after the paper had published drawings of Joseph Paxton's designs for the Crystal Palace. The next year, after a special issue had been devoted to the Duke of Wellington's funeral, sales rose to 150,000; and in 1855, partly due to the reproduction of Roger Fenton's photographs of the Crimean War and the abolition of the newspaper tax, they rose to 200,000 copies a week. By 1863 well over 300,000 copies were being sold.[9] *All the Year Round*, a magazine established in 1859 in which *A Tale of Two Cities* was serialized, also sold 300,000 copies a week.[10]

The circulation of newspapers was not so high as that of these popular magazines – even after 1855 when the 'newspaper Tax', which had once been as high as 4d, was abolished – but there were far more newspapers published than there are today. In 1861, when its price was 3d, the circulation of *The Times* was rather more than 60,000. At that time *The Times* had no rival: the *Daily News* had no more than 6000, the *Morning Post* a mere 4500. But soon the circulation of the *Daily News*, which sold for a penny, overtook that of *The Times*; and so did that of the *Daily Telegraph*, while racy Sunday papers such as *Lloyd's* and *Reynold's* sold far more copies than any of them. Weekly newspapers sold in even greater numbers. Well over 2.2 million copies of these were sold in London; and in the provinces there were few large towns without a weekly as well as a daily paper. Some towns had several: there were no less than seven in Cheltenham; Newcastle-on-Tyne had five as well as five dailies. There were over 100 papers serving the London suburbs.[11]

The demand for religious and educational literature was almost insatiable. Religious tracts, books of sermons and religious family papers like the *Christian World*, *Leisure Hour* and *Christian Herald*, were all published in huge numbers. In 1864 the total circulation of monthly periodicals of a religious nature published in London was almost 2 million; and the number of religious books published each year was equally impressive. According to the *Publisher's Circular* of 1870, new books on religious matters far outstripped publications on any other subject. 'Juvenile works and tales' came a poor second, and these included many more books of a religious nature. Books of sermons sold particularly well and many a clergyman made far more out of publishing them than he received as his stipend.

Yet at the same time there was an equally voracious demand for books of entertainment, from romantic novels and melodramatic tales of crime to the works of Trollope, Dickens, Thackeray and George Eliot. Widely read, these authors were well rewarded. Anthony Trollope was paid £3000 by the proprietors of *The Cornhill Magazine* for *The Small House at Allington* in 1864; Thackeray was given £6000 for *The Virginians*; in 1869 Dickens received £7500 against the profits of the first 25,000 copies of *The Mystery of Edwin Drood*; and George Eliot was offered £10,000 for *Romola* in 1862. Scores of thousands of people subscribed to Charles Edward Mudie's 'Select Circulating Library' which stocked 2000 copies of George Eliot's *The Mill on the Floss* and well over 3000 copies of her *Silas Marner*.[12]

On most afternoons in the middle of the century an immense and rowdy crowd of Londoners, porters, dockers, costermongers, pale-faced dustmen, black-faced sweeps, their wives and girlfriends, could be seen in Waterloo Road, jostling and shouting at each other around the doors of the Royal Victoria Theatre. As soon as the money-taker had taken up his post the customary wild rush for the staircase began, men jabbing and pushing at the backs in front of them, girls – several of them with babies in their arms – shrieking and clutching their bonnets. Having parted with their threepences (three-halfpence for infants) they tumbled into the gallery which held two thousand people and sat packed close together on the benches, young boys at the back drawing their knees to their chins and rolling over the massed heads below to force a place for themselves near the front. Beneath the sputtering gas jets the men took off their coats, revealing cross braces over white shirts or, here and there, an expanse of bare shoulder through a ragged vest, while the women removed their bonnets and hung them along the iron railings – or on the spiked partition boards that separated the gallery from the rest of the vast theatre – where they served as targets for the customary bits of orange peel and nutshell. The noise was so deafening that when the orchestra began playing it was impossible to hear a note of music, the puffed out cheeks of the trumpeters and the flailing drumsticks being the only indication that the overture had begun. Sooner or later a fight was sure to begin, and then everyone stood up whistling and shouting until the commotion suddenly stopped as the curtain rose to shouts of 'Silence!' 'Order!' 'Ord-a-a-a-r!'[13]

As at numerous other similar theatres in London and the provinces, melodramas were followed by farces and burlesques; and in the intervals between the pieces, while sellers of ham sandwiches, pigs' feet and porter hawked their wares, there were dances and comic songs, Highland flings and reels, recitations, ballads, monologues, clowns, acrobats and posture artists. Indeed, the entertainment offered by such theatres had changed little in a hundred years. The number and variety of theatres, however, had greatly increased to cater for the hundreds of thousands of working men and women both in London and the provinces who, though earning less than £2 a week, would spend every other evening watching some performance or another.

There were immense theatres like Astley's, rebuilt in 1862, and smaller theatres where highly coloured versions of Shakespeare and plays about ancient Rome alternated with ballets, pantomimes and cabarets. There were respectable provincial theatres which featured programmes of 'vocal enter-tainments' and 'repertoires of old and new pieces' followed by performances featuring 'infant geniuses' or 'Ethiopian marionettes'. There were also decidedly disreputable places of entertainment such as Sadler's Wells, described by Dickens as 'a bear garden, resounding with foul language, oaths, cat-calls, shrieks, yells, blasphemy, obscenity'; and there were 'penny gaffs', those upper floors of shops where disreputable entertainers took part in obscene dances or sang coarse songs and where 'the most immoral acts' were represented by performers, 'rude pictures' of whom in their 'most humorous' attitudes were displayed outside beneath coloured lamps. And there were numerous private theatres where stage-struck amateurs paid fees to play the parts, most of these amateurs, so Dickens said, being 'dirty boys, low copying-clerks in attorneys' offices, capacious headed youths from City counting-houses, Jews whose business, as lenders of fancy dress [was] a sure passport to the amateur stage, shopboys who now and then [mistook] their master's money for their own, and a choice miscellany of idle vagabonds. The lady performers [paid] nothing for their characters, and, it is needless to add, [were] usually selected from one class of society.'[14]

There were song and supper rooms of which Evans Late Joys in King Street, Covent Garden, haunt of wealthy Bohemians, was one of the best known; and there were tavern concert rooms that developed into the music-halls of which the Canterbury in Westminster Bridge Road was one of the earliest. This was opened in 1852 by Charles Morton, the 'Father of the Halls', who built and managed numerous similar places over a period of more than fifty years, including the Tivoli, the Palace, the Alhambra and the Empire. J. E. Ritchie, author of *The Night Side of London*, described a visit to the Canterbury in the 1850s:

A well-lighted entrance attached to a public-house indicates that we have reached our destination. We proceed up a few stairs, along a passage lined with handsome engravings, to a bar. We pay 6d if we take a seat in the body of the hall, and 9d if we ascend into the gallery.

We make our way leisurely along the floor of the hall, which is well lighted, and capable of holding 1500 people. A balcony extends round the room in the form of a horse-shoe.

At the opposite end to that at which we enter is the platform, on which are placed a grand piano and a harmonium on which the performers play in the intervals when the previous singers have left the stage.

The chairman sits just beneath them. It is dull work for him, but there he must sit drinking and smoking cigars from seven to twelve o'clock.

The room is crowded, and almost every gentleman has a pipe or cigar in his mouth. Evidently the majority present are respectable mechanics or small tradesmen, with their wives and daughters and sweethearts. Now and then you see a few fast clerks and warehousemen. Everyone is smoking, and everyone has a glass before him; but the class that come here are economical, and chiefly confine themselves to pipes and porter.[15]

Most of Morton's other music-halls were as respectable as the Canterbury; but there were music-halls far less so. In these the customers came to eat and drink, to talk to the barmaids or to pick up one of the prostitutes who strolled in the promenades, rather than to watch the performances. But after the authorities had required that liquor should be served in bars outside the auditorium rather than within it, and after the tables and chairs of the earlier halls had been replaced by rows of fixed seats, music-halls became increasingly reputable and grew fast in size and numbers. By 1868 there were twenty-eight music-halls in London and 300 in the rest of the country. There were ten in Sheffield, nine in Birmingham and eight in both Manchester and Leeds.[16] In the 1880s more and even larger halls were built and the older ones reconstructed and enlarged. The Tivoli Music Hall in the Strand, which was erected at a cost of £300,000, not only had a restaurant adjoining the enormous auditorium but private dining-rooms as well. The subsequent variety houses, like Edward Moss's London Hippodrome opened in 1900, and the Coliseum in St Martin's Lane, designed in 1904 for Oswald Stoll, were equally impressive. So were the theatres which Moss and Stoll and their rivals built in the provinces.[17]

While music-halls and variety houses grew ever more large and sumptuous, the prices of seats did not greatly increase. At the Canterbury in the early days, the cheaper tickets cost 6d; in the 1860s at the South London Palace of Varieties in Lambeth, which could accommodate audiences of up to 4000, gallery seats were 3d, balcony and stalls 1s; and at the Oxford Music

Hall, Tottenham Road, the price of a ticket for a good seat plus a five-course meal was 2s 6d. A generation later music-hall seats cost little more. The rewards of the performers, on the other hand, increased rapidly, though the pay of the best had never been low: Morton's singers at the Canterbury got as much as £20 a week.[18] Blondin, the tightrope performer, and the Channel swimmer, Captain Webb, who both appeared at the Alhambra, received up to £100 a performance in the 1880s; Dan Leno, the comedian, who was earning £5 a week in his early career at the Foresters', Whitechapel, could command £100 a week at Drury Lane in performances in pantomimes, shows in which the most popular stars, like Vesta Tilley, could regularly earn £350 a week and some as much as £500. Famous actors, who could be induced to appear in playlets or excerpts at variety houses, received even more: Herbert Tree was once paid £750 a week at the Palace and Sarah Bernhardt £1000 at the Coliseum.[19]

While music-halls and variety houses prospered, theatres which presented less popular productions began to attract a new kind of audience. For this the queen was to some extent responsible. At the beginning of her reign, when wishing to provide a dramatic entertainment for her guests, she had summoned various performers to Windsor. But since then she had attended the Prince of Wales's Theatre for a performance of *The Corsican Brothers*, a romantic drama adapted from the French by Dion Boucicault; and this visit to a public theatre, which provoked a good deal of criticism at the time, led to many families, who would not have dreamed of entering such places a generation earlier, becoming regular theatregoers. They now found that they could with perfect propriety go to the Prince of Wales's whose fortunes were made by Tom Robertson, an accomplished dramatist and stage-manager who insisted, as Garrick had done, that actors perform their parts in a natural way, without that declamatory, histrionic method of speaking which had been adopted in most theatres since the time of Sarah Siddons and which Charles Mathews and his wife, Madame Vestris, had vainly endeavoured to supersede at the Olympic and the Criterion. They could also go with propriety to the Haymarket to which the actor-manager, Squire Bancroft, and his wife, Marie Wilton, moved in 1879; to the Court Theatre which was co-managed by John Hare before he moved to the St James's and in which tea and coffee were served in the interval instead of spirits; to the Criterion where Charles Wyndham became manager in 1876; to the Lyceum where Ellen Terry acted with Henry Irving, whose performances determinedly rejected any compromise with the more restrained style of acting upon which Tom Robertson insisted; and to the Savoy where the operas by Gilbert and Sullivan had restored the reputation of the musical stage.

By the end of the century, indeed, the theatre became fashionable rather than raffish. The curtain rose later and the audience arrived in the smart evening clothes they had worn at dinner or were to wear at an after-theatre supper party. The orchestra stalls, a seat in which cost 10s 6d at the Prince of Wales's, gradually absorbed the pit; while the tiers of public boxes above the pit gave way to dress and upper circles, private boxes, and, almost out of sight, the gallery. The discontinuation of half-price seats after the start of the performance reduced the length of the programme; while the extension of the practice of booking seats not only gradually eliminated the unseemly scramble for places but also encouraged longer runs.[20]

The provincial theatre was also transformed. Whereas in the past a famous London actor or actress would go on tour with a few associates and perform with local companies, now complete productions came from London by rail and staged their shows in theatres of ever-increasing splendour. The Grand Theatre and Opera House at Leeds, for example, was equipped with scene shops, rehearsal rooms, paint shop and pottery, a gas-making plant, a concert hall and 'grand saloon' as well as a large stage and an auditorium to accommodate 3200 people, 2600 of them seated, and 600 standing.[21]

While these large theatres continued to prosper into the twentieth century, so did the smaller more recent provincial repertory theatres. The Gaiety repertory theatre in Manchester which opened in 1907 was followed two years later by a similar theatre in Liverpool and by another in Birmingham in 1913.[22] By the 1920s Oxford and Bristol also had repertory theatres; and the number of amateur dramatic societies was growing so fast all over the country that in 1939 it was estimated that there were as many as 10,000.[23]

# 56 · *The Flesh and the Spirit*

'Sexual indulgence before the age of twenty-five,' a widely-read medical textbook of the 1830s advised, 'not only retards the development of the genital organs, but of the whole body, impairs the strength, injures the constitution and shortens life.' By the end of the century the admonitory tone of such works as this had changed very little. Dr William Acton – an authority on diseases of the urinary and generative organs and author of a book on the subject which remained in print long after his death in 1875 – was of the confirmed opinion that 'much of the languor of mind, confusion of ideas, and inability to control the thoughts of which married men complain' arose from sexual excess. It was essential that these sensual feelings should be 'sobered down'. Fortunately for husbands, their wives were 'not very much troubled with sexual feelings of any kind'.

> What men are habitually, women are only exceptionally [Acton wrote]. It is too true, I admit, as the divorce courts show, that there are some few women who have sexual desires so strong that they surpass those of men . . . I admit, of course, the existence of sexual desires terminating even in nymphomania, a form of insanity which those accustomed to visit lunatic asylums must be fully conversant with; but, with these sad exceptions, there can be no doubt that sexual feeling in the female is in the majority of cases in abeyance . . . The best mothers, wives and managers of households know little or nothing of sexual indulgence. Love of home, children, and domestic duties, are the only passions they feel . . . A modest woman seldom desires any sexual gratification for herself. She submits to her husband, but only to please him; and, but for the desire of maternity, would far rather be relieved from his attentions.[1]

To seek relief in masturbation, that 'most vicious' form of incontinence, was not only a danger to health but might even result in death. Masturbation could, and often did, lead to consumption, curvature of the spine and insanity. Those who practised it could be recognized by their stunted frames, their underdeveloped muscles, sunken eyes, pasty complexions, acne, damp hands and skin. Parents should closely 'watch their children' for the tell-tale signs, and supervise a regimen of sponge-baths, showers and 'gymnastic exercises regularly employed and carried to an extent just short of fatigue'.

Acton was also, with far more justification, considered to be an expert on prostitution which, like most of his contemporaries, he considered to be inevitable and of which he assumed many if not most of his male, middle-class readers would have had personal experience before marriage. The numbers of prostitutes in the country was known to be immense, though estimates as to their numbers varied widely. W. T. Stead, who exposed in the *Pall Mall Gazette* the scandalous trade in the bodies of young children, calculated that in 1885 there were as many as 60,000 in London alone. Other, no doubt exaggerated, estimates put the figure as high as 80,000. Whatever their number, it was generally agreed that there were far more in the middle years of the century than there were in the later, most noticeably in the streets off the Haymarket and the Strand which, so one observer of low life commented, was 'a favourite place for doxies to go to relieve their bladders'.

> The police took no notice of such trifles, provided it was not done in the great thoroughfare [he continued], (although I have seen at night women do it openly in the gutters of the Strand). In particular streets I have seen them pissing almost in rows; yet they mostly went in twos and threes . . . one usually standing up (to provide a screen) . . . Indeed the pissing in all the bye-streets of the Strand was continuous, for although the population of London was only half of what it is now, the number of gay ladies seemed double.[2]

They were to be found in brothels and in dancing-rooms, in pleasure gardens and in the streets. They could be met through the offices of procuresses, in 'introducing houses' patronized by the 'many wealthy, indolent, sensual men of London' who, in Acton's words, 'obtained for their money a superior class of prostitute . . . presented to them as maid, wife or widow'. They could be visited in numerous 'accommodation houses', rooms above coffee-houses, taverns and shops which could be rented for an hour or so 'for the most part openly, or when not exactly so, on exhibition of a slight apology for travelling baggage . . . Their tariffs are various, and the accommodation afforded ranges between luxury and the squalor of those ambiguous dens, half brothel and half lodging-house, whose inhabitants pay their twopence nightly.' The more expensive rooms cost about 5s in the 1850s, but by the 1870s the cost had risen to 10s or more in the West End. For this, as one habitué of such places testified, a customer could expect 'red curtains, looking-glasses, wax lights, clean linen, a huge chair, a large bed, and a cheval glass, large enough for the biggest couple to be reflected in'.[3]

The anonymous author of the eleven volumes of sexual memoirs entitled *My Secret Life*, which has been described by Steven Marcus as 'the most important document of its kind about Victorian England', estimated the income of one of the most fashionable courtesans of his acquaintance as being up to £70 a week on which she kept 'several servants and a brougham'. He himself, however, though rich enough, declined to pay her prices, believing that there was 'wonderfully little difference between the woman you have for five shillings and the one you pay five pounds, excepting in the silk, linen and manners'. In his youth in the 1840s and 1850s

> a sovereign would get any woman and ten shillings as nice a one as you needed. Two good furnished rooms near the Clubs could be had by women for from fifteen to twenty shillings per week, a handsome silk dress for five or ten pounds, and other things in proportion. So cunt was a more reasonable article than it is now [about 1880], and I got quite nice girls at from five to ten shillings a poke, and had several in their own rooms, but sometimes half a crown extra for a room elsewhere. [One of them] was young, handsome, well made, and in the Haymarket would now get anything from one to five pounds; yet I had her several times for three or four shillings a time.

Most prostitutes were young, many of them being driven to the life they led, so Acton said, by 'cruel biting poverty' and a large proportion of them returning 'sooner or later to a more or less regular course of life'. Thousands were under thirteen which was, until 1885, when it was raised to sixteen, the age of consent. Some were under ten. The author of *My Secret Life*, who confessed to having paid £200 for a little virgin when he was inexperienced in such matters, once violated a ten-year-old girl, reflecting afterwards that he might 'as well have the broaching of a little cunt, and pay for it, as let a coster lad have it for nothing'. After all, as the little orphan girl's 'aunt' told him, 'she had taken charge of her and prevented her going to the workhouse. She was in difficulties, she must live, the child would be sure to have it done to her some day. Why not make a little money by her? Someone else would if she did not. So spoke the fat, middle-aged woman.'

Such girls were easily supplied and fulfilled a constant and eager demand, so a former brothel-keeper told Stead:

A keeper who knows his business has his eyes open in all directions. His stock of girls is constantly getting used up, and needs replenishing, and he has to be on the alert for lively 'marks' to keep up the reputation of his house.

The getting of fresh girls . . . is easy enough. I have gone and courted girls in the country under all kinds of disguises, occasionally assuming the dress of a parson . . . and got them in my power to please a good customer . . . I bring her up, take her here and there giving her plenty to eat and drink, especially drink . . . I contrive it so that she loses her last train . . . I offer her nice lodgings for the night . . . My client gets his maid . . .

Another very simple mode of supplying maids is breeding them. Many women who are on the streets have female children. They are worth keeping . . . I know a couple of very fine little girls now who will be sold before long. They are bred and trained for the life. They must take the first step sometime, and it is bad business not to make as much out of that as possible. Drunken parents often sell their children to brothel-keepers. In the East End you can always pick up as many fresh girls as you want.

Young children could also be acquired from women who masqueraded as foster-parents or baby-farmers but who were, in fact, professional infanticides or dealers in children. One of them, who advertised her adoption agency in the newspapers, charged £5 for her services which included 'everything'. When she was arrested several children, dying of starvation, were found in her house as well as numerous pawn tickets for their clothing. She was hanged in 1870; but other similar agencies continued in business and child abuse remained a horrifying problem, despite the efforts of the National Society for the Prevention of Cruelty to Children which was founded in 1889.[4]

It was always easy to find young girls who, while indignantly denying that they were 'gay', were prepared to act as prostitutes occasionally.

'How long have you been gay?' [one of these girls, dressed like the child of 'a decent mechanic', was asked by a man who had picked her up in the Strand one day and taken her to a bawdy house].

'I ain't gay,' said she, astonished.

'Yes you are.'

'No I ain't.'

'You let men fuck you, don't you?'

'Yes, but I ain't gay.'

'What do you call gay?'

'Why the gals who come out regular of a night, dressed up, and gets their living by it.'

'Don't you?'

'No, Mother keeps me.'

'What is your father?'

'Got none. He's dead three months back. Mother works and keeps us. She's a charwoman, and goes out on odd jobs.'

'Don't you work?'

'Not now,' said she in a confused way. 'Mother does not want me to. I take care of the others.'

'What others?'

'The young ones . . . But what do you ask me all this for?'

'Only for amusement. Then you are in mourning for your father?'

'Yes, it's shabby ain't it? I wish I could have nice clothes. I've got nice boots, ain't they?' – cocking up one leg – 'a lady gived 'em me when father died. They are my best.'

'Are you often in the Strand?'

'I do if mother's out for the day.'

'Does she know you are out?'

'Bless you, no. She'd beat me if she knew. When she be out I locks them up and takes the key and then I goes back to them . . .'

'They may set fire to themselves.'

'There ain't no fire.'

'What do you do with yourself all day?'

'I washes them. I give them food if we've got any, then washes myself. Then I looks out the winder.'

'Wash yourself?'

'Yes, I washes from head to foot, allus.'

'Have you a tub?'

'No, we've only got a pail and a bowl, but I'm beautiful clean . . . I buy things to eat (she went on in answer to a question as to how she spent the money men paid her). I can't eat what mother gives us. She'd give us more, but she can't. So I buy foods, and gives the others what mother gives me . . . If mother's there I eat some. Sometimes we have only gruel and salt . . .'

'What do you like?'

'Pies and sausage rolls,' says the girl, smacking her lips and laughing. 'Oh, my eye, ain't they prime – oh!'

'That's what you went gay for?'

'I'm not gay.'

'Well what you let men fuck you for?'

'Yes.'

'Sausage rolls?'

'Yes. Meat pies and pastry, too.'[5]

This girl seemed happy enough; and so did many other so-called 'dolly-mops' and prostitutes interviewed by Henry Mayhew and his colleagues. 'I am not tired of what I am doing,' one of them, the twenty-three-year-old daughter of a tradesman from Yarmouth, said. 'I rather like it. I have all I want . . . What do you think will become of me? What an absurd question! I could marry to-morrow if I liked.'[6]

How did I come to take this sort of life [another girl said breezily]. Well, I'll tell yer . . . It's easy to tell. I was a servant gal away down in Birmingham. I was tired of workin' and slavin' to make a livin', and gettin' a bad one at that! What o' five pun' a year and yer grub, I'd sooner starve I would! After a bit I went to Coventry, cut Brummagem, as we calls it in those parts, and took up with the soldiers as was quartered there. I soon got tired of them. Soldiers is good – soldiers is – to walk with and that, but they don't pay; cos why, they ain't got no money. So I says I'll go to London and I did. I soon found my level there . . . One week with another I makes nearer on four pounds nor three – sometimes five. I 'ave done eight and ten . . . And now I think I'll be off. Good night to yer.[7]

There were, however, many girls whose misery was pitiable. One of them, a good-looking girl of sixteen whose hands were swollen with cold, told her pathetic story. She had been a maidservant in the house of a tradesman whose wife beat her cruelly 'with sticks as well as with her hands'. She ran away and took shelter in a lodging-house where she stayed for about three months, living on the three shillings she had saved and the money she was given when she pawned her best clothes. When all her money was gone she became the mistress of a fifteen-year-old pickpocket. She herself at that time was twelve. One day her young lover was arrested and sent to prison; and she was sorry because he had been kind to her, although she was 'made ill through him'. She broke some windows in St Paul's Churchyard so that she could get into prison and be cured of her disease. She was 'scolded very much in the Compter on account of the state [she] was in, being so young'. When she was released she was given 2s 6d; but this did not last long, and she was 'forced to go into the streets for a living'.

I continued walking the streets for three years [she went on] sometimes making a good deal of money, sometimes none, feasting one day and starving the next . . . I was never happy all the time, but I could get no character and could not get out of the life. I lodged all this time at a lodging house in Kent Street. They were all thieves and bad girls . . . The beds were horrid filthy and full of vermin. There was very wicked carryings-on. We lay packed on a full night, a dozen boys and girls squeezed into one bed

. . . I can't go into all the particulars, but whatever could take place between boys and girls did take place . . . I am sorry to say I took part in these bad ways myself . . . Some boys and girls slept without any clothes and would dance about the room that way . . . Wicked as I was, I felt ashamed . . .

At three years' end I stole a piece of beef from a butcher. I did it to get into prison. I was sick of the life I was leading, and didn't know how to get out of it . . . When I got out I threatened to break windows again. I did that to get into prison again . . . and thought I would stick to prison rather than go back to such a life. I got six months for threatening. When I got out I broke a lamp next morning for the same purpose and had a fortnight. That was the last time I was in prison. I have since been leading the same life as I told you of and lodging at the same houses, and seeing the same goings on. I hate such a life now more than ever. I am willing to do any work that I can in washing and cleaning . . .[8]

When this sad report appeared in the *Morning Chronicle* public interest in prostitution, the 'social evil' – and concern about the spread of venereal disease – were becoming more intense year by year and reached their height in the 1860s when discussion raged as to the merits and iniquities of the Contagious Diseases Acts. The first of these acts was passed in 1864 ostensibly to deal with the problems presented by the incidence of venereal disease in the army which was so high that Florence Nightingale could maintain that 'fully one half of all sickness' in soldiers serving at home was 'owing to the disease of vice'. She herself suggested that if soldiers – only a very few of whom were allowed by army regulations to get married – had better living conditions and recreational activities, they would be less inclined to consort with prostitutes. But others maintained that, since prostitution was inevitable, it would be sensible to regulate it in the manner of certain countries on the Continent. The periodical inspection of men in the army had been abolished in 1859, partly out of a wish to increase their self-esteem; but there was no reason, so those in favour of regulation argued, why the women whom they slept with should not be required to undergo inspection. After all, in eleven garrison towns, so it was estimated by the Inspector-General of Hospitals, there were well over 7000 prostitutes, nearly 1000 of whom were believed to be diseased.

The Contagious Diseases Acts, which were passed with scant opposition, enabled the authorities to require women found soliciting to be examined in a certified hospital, and, if found to be diseased, to be detained so that a cure could be effected. The Acts were at first limited to certain garrison and dockyard towns; but when it was proposed that they should apply to the whole country, and that prostitutes should be licensed and regulated everywhere, there was widespread protest both from those who condemned the policy as unwarranted state intervention and from 'moralists, feminists, individualists, and opponents of medical pretension and military arrogance'.[9]

Prominent among these campaigners were H. J. Wilson, the Sheffield radical; James Stansfeld, the friend of Mazzini and Liberal cabinet minister who gave up a promising career to devote his energies to the cause; and Josephine Butler, a kinswoman of Earl Grey and wife of the Principal of Liverpool College, an impassioned, eloquent if sometimes almost hysterical reformer, who heatedly drew attention to the double standards of sexual morality which, by enforcing the examination of women but not of men, presumed that it was the female, not the male, who was responsible for spreading the disease. After years of campaigning the Acts were repealed in 1886. It had been accepted by then that, although they had brought about some improvement, they had not been nearly as effective as their supporters maintained. Certainly, cases of venereal disease in the army went on diminishing after the repeal of the Acts, continuing a trend that had begun before they were passed.

While prostitution undoubtedly remained widespread throughout the Victorian period; while seduction of maidservants by the sons or masters of the house was still common enough, often expected, and sometimes encouraged by the maids themselves; while, so Acton maintained, large numbers of men made a 'sport and habit' of debauching any pretty working-class girl whom they fancied, most middle-class Victorians were genuinely shocked by sexual promiscuity. They were sincerely convinced that a better, more fulfilled and enjoyable life could be lived in the care and comfort of a family and in the earnest pursuit of wealth and of a respected place in society, than in the manifestly transient and probably deleterious pleasures of sex. And in this belief they were strengthened by a religious faith which was of profound significance to them.

Its precepts permeated their nurseries. At their public schools they were told, as Dr Arnold's pupils were told at Rugby, that 'religious and moral principles' were above all required of them: these principles were even more important than 'gentlemanly conduct' which was itself to be more highly regarded than intellectual ability. In their adult lives they were conscious always that the probity of their conduct was God's concern: straight dealing would be rewarded, dishonesty punished in an after-life. There were still, of course, men like Lord Melbourne who had assured the young queen in 'his amusing way' that religion must never be allowed to 'interfere with private life'. But men such as these were now in the minority. For most religion was a dominant force in their lives. Children in the schoolroom, Members of

Parliament in the chamber, clerks in the counting-house, all began their days with communal prayers, just as servants and family joined in prayer when the day's work was done.

Differences of belief were wide and methods of worship various. One March Sunday in 1851, when a census was taken of people attending places of worship in England and Wales, numerous denominations had to be taken into account from Anglicans high and low, to Roman Catholics (their numbers vastly swollen by Irish immigration) and to Nonconformists of all kinds, from Unitarians (about 37,000) to Mormons (some 18,000). In all, well over 7 million out of a total population of 18 million attended some place of worship, a proportion ten times as great as it was to be a hundred years later. Even so, contemporaries were shocked by the large numbers of those who stayed away, predominantly working-class people living in large towns many of whom were inclined to believe that the Church of England was for the middle classes, as did Joseph Arch, founder of the National Agricultural Labourers' Union and a Primitive Methodist preacher.

> I never took Communion in the parish church in my life [Arch wrote]. When I was seven years old I saw something which prevented me once for all . . . First, up walked the squire to the communion rails; the farmers went up next; then up went the tradesmen, the shopkeepers, the wheel-wright, and the blacksmith; and then, the very last of all, went the poor agricultural labourers in their smock frocks. They walked up by themselves; nobody else knelt with them; it was as if they were unclean . . . I said to myself, 'If that's what goes on – never for me.'[10]

Many working people felt like Arch and thought that, if they were to go to a Christian service at all, one held in a Nonconformist chapel was likely to be more in their line, though there were acknowledged social divisions in dissenting congregations also: Unitarians and Quakers, for example, were regarded as being superior to Primitive Methodists, and Congregationalists to Baptists.

In Yorkshire on that Sunday in 1851 of the 983,000 or so people who went to a place of worship, 600,000 went to a Dissenters' chapel or meeting-house, 431,000 of them to a Methodist chapel. In London, as Charles Booth discovered, there was little regular church attendance among the poor. One foggy Sunday morning – a 'proper day for churchgoing', he supposed – he looked in at the King's Cross Mission to the Masses on his way to Charlotte Street. 'In the body of the church there were only a few people scattered about,' he noticed. 'The masses certainly do not come in the morning nor, I found later, do any very large numbers come in the evening.'[11]

For the middle classes, though, church attendance was almost *de rigueur*, if not always either profitable or pleasurable. 'My back still aches in memory of those long services,' a writer recalled of his middle-class childhood in the 1870s. 'Nothing was spared us – the whole of the "Dearly Beloved", never an omission of the Litany, always the full ante-Communion service, involving a sermon of unbelievable length.'

Sermons usually were long. Those of the Rev. C. H. Spurgeon, the Calvinistic preacher for whom the Metropolitan Tabernacle was built, were measured in hours rather than minutes. Yet he was so spell-binding an orator that all 6000 seats in the Tabernacle were often filled half an hour before he began to speak and the 'aisles were solid blocks and many stood throughout the service, wedged in and prevented from escaping by the crowd outside who . . . stood in throngs as far as the sound could reach'.[12]

After going to church most middle-class people stayed at home. And for those who had no homes to go to, Sundays could be days of unutterable gloom as Arthur Clennam discovers when he returns from Marseilles:

It was a Sunday evening in London, gloomy, close and stale. Maddening church bells of all degrees of dissonance, sharp and flat, cracked and clear, fast and slow, made the brick and mortar echoes hideous. Melancholy streets in a penitential garb of soot, steeped the souls of the people who were condemned to look at them out of windows, in dire despondency. In every thoroughfare, up almost every alley, and down almost every turning, some doleful bell was throbbing, jerking, tolling, as if the Plague were in the city and the deadcarts were going round. Everything was bolted and barred that could by possibility furnish relief to an overworked people. No pictures, no unfamiliar animals, no rare plants or flowers, no natural or artificial wonders of the ancient world – all taboo with that enlightened strictness, that the ugly South sea gods in the British Museum might have supposed themselves at home again. Nothing to see but streets, streets, streets. Nothing to breathe but streets, streets, streets. Nothing to change the brooding mind, or raise it up.[13]

Provincial towns were just as gloomy on Sundays as London, if not more so; and the active members of such societies as those founded for Promoting the External Observance of the Lord's Day and for the Suppression of Public Lewdness were determined to keep them so. When bands were given permission to play in the new public parks in Manchester and Salford in 1856, 'the opposition on the part of the Sabbatarian public was so strongly expressed that the experiment was soon abandoned'. The Sabbatarians were not, however, always successful in their claims. Theatres and pleasure gardens were closed on Sundays, but not all taverns or shops. Sunday postal services were reduced in 1850, but were not altogether abandoned. Despite vociferous objections Sunday trains and omnibuses still ran. The Queen herself came down from Scotland to Euston on a Sunday, though, having broken her journey at Crewe, she got up very early so as to arrive in London before morning service and not cause undue offence to the Sabbatarians whose prejudices she thought 'overdone'. 'You know I am not at all an admirer or approver of our very dull Sundays,' she told her daughter, the Princess Royal, 'for I think the absence of innocent amusement for the poor people, a misfortune and an encouragement of vice.'[14]

There were households, like the Ruskins', in which Sundays were observed so strictly that the pictures were turned to the wall and only cold meals were served so that the servants had time to worship and study, as the members of the family did themselves; but there were many others as respectable in which the adults read novels or even a Sunday newspaper – though preferably not the scandalous stories in *Reynold's Weekly News* – while the children were allowed to play quiet games and to look at their magazines, the *Monthly Packet* perhaps or *Little Folks*.

# 57 · *Passengers and Drivers*

'Them Confugion steamers,' cries Mrs Gamp, the gin-loving old midwife in *Martin Chuzzlewit*, shaking her umbrella at the Antwerp packet to emphasize her detestation of those 'hammering and roaring, and hissing and lamp-iling . . . sputtering noisy monsters' of steam engines. 'Them Confugion steamers,' she goes on, 'has done more to throw us out of our reg'lar work, and bring events on at times when nobody counted on 'em (especially them screeching railroad ones), than all the other frights that ever was took.'[1]

Such frights had never disturbed Samuel Pickwick's countryside through which stage-coaches rattled along from inn to inn as they had for centuries. To be sure, there had then been a few local railways; but they had mostly been on the coalfields and even there steam had not yet altogether displaced horse power. But that early nineteenth-century landscape was now being transformed, and conservative Englishmen were aghast at the change. As early as 1838 the Duke of Wellington, who could never reconcile himself to 'these accursed railways', was complaining that they had 'totally destroyed our convenient communications' and 'even deranged' the post. Ten years later he was still expressing his decided opinion that

> People never acted so foolishly as we did in allowing of the Destruction of our excellent and commodious [post roads] in order to expend Millions Sterling on the Rail Roads! It appears to me to be the Vulgarest, most indelicate, most inconvenient, most injurious to Health of any mode of conveyance that I have seen in any part of the World! Mobs of well dressed Ladies and Gentlemen are collected at every Station, to examine and pry into every Carriage and the actions of every Traveller. If an unfortunate Traveller wishes to quit His Carriage, he is followed by one of these well dressed Mobs as a Hunted animal is by Hounds, till he is forced again in His Carriage![2]

Despite such protests railways continued to proliferate, and there were those, unlike the Duke, who welcomed them. Watching a train on the Rugby line, Thomas Arnold said: 'I rejoice to see it, and think that feudality is gone for ever.'[3] The extensive building which had been encouraged by the success of the Liverpool and Manchester line soon gathered momentum. By 1840 Southampton was a terminus; in 1841 the Great Western line reached Bristol. By 1848 about 5000 miles of track had been laid; the line to Dover had been completed; and the London and North-Eastern Counties Company's line ran to Ipswich, Colchester, Cambridge and Norwich.[4] By 1852 all the main railway lines of England had either been finished or authorized. Hereford, Yeovil and Weymouth were exceptional in having no railway station; and in these places the need was soon supplied.[5] By 1875 nearly 500 million passengers were being transported by rail each year and the whole tenor of English life, as well as the appearance of the countryside, had been altered for ever. 'It was only yesterday,' exclaims one of Thackeray's characters, 'but what a gulf between now and then. *Then* was the old world. Stage-coaches, more or less swift riding horses, packhorses, highwaymen . . . But your railroad starts a new era . . . We who lived before railways and survive out of the ancient world, are like Father Noah and his family out of the Ark.'[6]

Embankments and cuttings, bridges, viaducts and tunnels took the lines across and under the landscape in every direction, while signal boxes, plate-layers' huts, coal yards, water-towers and Gothic railway stations, with diapered brickwork and fretted barge-boards, sprang up as though overnight.

Armies of men who had originally worked on canals and were hence known as navigators – or, more commonly, navvies – had marched across the country with picks and shovels, wheelbarrows and lanterns on their backs to undertake the formidable task of construction. They were a rough, tough set of men, wearing a kind of uniform of corduroy trousers, stout boots, jackets and brightly coloured scarves, and dressing as flamboyantly as costermongers when off duty. They were proud of their strength but, according to one of their number, 'wonderfully tender-hearted, too. A navvy will cry the easiest thing as is. If you'd only talk a little good to him you can make a navvy burst out crying like a child in a few minutes, if you'd only take him the right way.'[7] In the mid-1840s they numbered about 200,000, many of them agricultural labourers attracted to the hard work by the relatively high wages paid. Pickmen and shovellers were paid between 22s 6d and 24s a week in 1846, skilled men, such as bricklayers and masons, 33s. The labourers, working in gangs and often in rows under a foreman, were expected to shovel about twenty tons of earth and rock a day. The work was dangerous as well as hard. In wet weather the men often slipped as they were pushing their wheelbarrows up the steep planks from the bottom of cuttings; in all weathers there was danger from blasting and from collapsing tunnels. The Woodhead tunnel, built between 1839 and 1845 between Sheffield and Manchester, cost the lives of thirty-two men; a further 140 were seriously injured; and there were 400 other accidents.[8] Compensation was rarely received from the railway companies or the contractors; the most that could usually be expected was some small contribution from a sick club.[9]

Few navvies, however, had families to worry about. They were followed about by young women who were their concubines and by older women who did their cooking; they slept in wood or even mud huts in shanty towns, as many as thirty in a room in the larger huts, one above the other in tiers of bunks, much to the disgust of the outsider. 'In these huts they lived . . . in a state of utter barbarism,' wrote John Francis in 1851, 'with man, woman and child mixing in promiscuous guilt, with no possible separation of the sexes . . . Dissoluteness of morals prevailed. There were many women, but few wives. Loathsome forms of disease were universal. Work often went on without intermission on Sundays as well as on other days.'[10]

Navvies remained together in their gangs, moving from one completed line to the next, going wherever the contractors sent them. Their intake of liquor – ten pints of strong ale a day was usual – was matched by the quantities of food they ate. This was mostly bread and meat and was consumed at the rate of two pounds of each a day.[11] In order to check their drunkenness, the contractors paid them as infrequently as they could, advancing credit against purchases to be made at the 'tommy' shop, the employers' store, where prices were generally far higher than they were in the nearest village. Yet they often contrived to get drunk, and then fights would break out, and these would sometimes develop into riots involving the local people who grew to dread the establishment of a rowdy navvy camp in their neighbourhood.[12]

While the navvies sweated and drank, and the railway mania continued unabated, fortunes were made and lost. George Stephenson, builder of the famous *Rocket* and of the Liverpool and Manchester Railway, was born the son of a poor colliery fireman and died, rich and respected, at a large country house in Derbyshire. Stephenson's protégé, Thomas Brassey, contractor for the Great Northern Railway among others, died worth many million pounds. George Hudson, a Yorkshire farmer's son, the ebullient, broad-spoken 'Railway King', became a millionaire, Lord Mayor of York, a Member of Parliament, and the owner of a huge house in London which is now occupied by the French Embassy. When he went abroad in 1849 he left investors in companies he had promoted with losses totalling £80 million. Yet after Hudson's disgrace railway lines spread across the country as fast as ever, while those who expressed their strong disapproval of them gradually fell into silence. Landowners took a kinder view of the new means of transport when it was seen how much money could be made out of it and how, thanks to the muscles of the navvies, the tracks could be kept out of sight of drawing-room windows by cuttings and tunnels. Almost everyone who could afford to do so invested in railway shares; and railway bills and the relative merits of narrow and broad gauges became the subject of heated debate at dinner parties. According to Thackeray the mania spread to the servants' hall: Lady Clavering's butler is well on the way to making his fortune while his mistress struggles to comprehend stock-exchange terminology.[13]

While the countryside was being transformed by the building of the railways, so were the towns, particularly London. The earlier termini, in London as elsewhere, were on the outskirts of cities; but after the building of Euston and Paddington stations in the 1830s, it was evident that more central stations would be acceptable; and these were soon provided. With the exception of St Paul's, now Blackfriars, which was built in 1886, and Marylebone, completed in 1889, all London's main railway termini were built in less than forty years between 1836 and 1874. And as railway companies scrambled to buy land, as bridges and viaducts were built, as cuttings and tunnels were dug, as locomotive sheds, repair shops, platforms, ticket offices and refreshment rooms were constructed, as marshalling yards, shunting areas and interminable rows of coal bunkers were laid out, houses were demolished wholesale and residential areas completely changed their character. Twenty thousand people were obliged to abandon their homes by the building of the London and Birmingham Railway, most of them, unwilling or unable to move far away, crowding into already overpopulated areas nearby, pouring in their hundreds into houses abandoned by the middle-classes who took advantage of the railway to move even further out from London's centre. The railway companies had a legal responsibility for the people whose homes they destroyed; but it was not always observed, and the new houses which were provided were frequently offered to tenants at rents they could not afford. Nine hundred houses were demolished by the North London Railway Company for the laying of two miles of track; and it was found beyond the company's means to rehouse their occupants adequately. In all, between 1853 and 1883, 56,000 people were displaced by railway lines in London.

Charles Dickens, who had himself witnessed the disruptive effect of railway building in the inner suburbs, described in *Dombey and Son* how it utterly changed the neighbourhood of Camden Town:

Houses were knocked down, streets broken through and stopped; deep pits and trenches dug in the ground; enormous heaps of earth and clay thrown up; buildings undermined and shaken, propped by great beams. Here, a chaos of carts, overthrown and jumbled together, lay topsy-turvy at the bottom of a steep unnatural hill; there, confused treasures of iron soaked and rusted in something that had accidently become a pond. Everywhere were bridges that led nowhere . . . and piles of scaffolding and wildernesses of brick.[14]

As it was with Camden Town, so it was with the area around York Road which, after the London and South Western Railway's construction of Waterloo Station, finally degenerated from the pleasant, residential area it had been in the earlier decades of the century to mid-Victorian London's most squalid and notorious red-light district.

Yet, as Dickens recognized, the railways brought benefits to the people as well as distress. They promoted the growth of new towns and virtually created others such as Crewe. They led to the decline of some small ports, but brought prosperity to others, Cardiff, Fleetwood, Barry and Southampton among them.[15] They made possible the building and expansion of suburbs, like King's Norton and Northfield outside Birmingham, in which men could live and travel every day to work. Samuel Smiles wrote in 1879 of the number of new small towns of from 10,000 to 20,000 inhabitants which had sprung up around London in the past twenty years. Guildford and Dorking were now within reach of the city; and while Clapham and Bayswater, yesterday's suburbs, had become 'as it were parts of the great metropolis', Brighton and Hastings were 'but the marine suburbs of London'. The rail journey from Watford, Barnet and Reigate was now quicker than the drive in horse-drawn vehicles from places much closer to Lombard Street and the Bank. There were 300 stations 'in actual use' within five miles of Charing Cross.[16]

Railways also made it possible for fresh food and milk to pass quickly from town to country; they carried 'inland coal' to householders everywhere, transporting 2.5 million tons of it from the north Midlands fields alone by 1865;[17] and they widened the horizons of people who were enabled to travel beyond the confines of the enclosed communities from which they had rarely been able to escape before, who gradually discarded their suspicions of the outside world and learned both that their fellow-countrymen were much like themselves, sharing the same concerns, and that many of them lived in conditions of shocking squalor. Thus it is on the railway journey to Leamington that Mr Dombey first realizes the extent of the industrial horrors that he and men like him have allowed to remain undisturbed for so long, although it never occurs to him to reflect that 'the monster who has brought him there has let the light of day on these things, not made or caused them':

> Everything around is blackened. There are dark pools of water, muddy lanes, and miserable habitations far below. There are jagged walls and falling houses close at hand, and through the battered roofs and broken windows, wretched rooms are seen, where want and fever hide themselves in many wretched shapes, while smoke and crowded gables, and distorted chimneys and deformity of brick and mortar penning up deformity of mind and body, choke the murky distance.

In this passage Dickens also conveys the novel excitement of railway travel:

> Through the hollow, on the height, by the heath, by the orchard, by the park, by the garden, over the canal, across the river, where the sheep are feeding, where the mill is going, where the barge is floating, where the dead are lying, where the factory is smoking . . . away, with a shriek and a roar and a rattle, and no trace to leave behind but dust and vapour . . . Louder and louder yet, it shrieks and cries as it comes tearing on.[18]

Indeed, at first the prospect of being driven along an iron track at great speed was too much for many would-be travellers to contemplate. When it was learned that the carriages on the Woolwich to London line would travel at eighteen miles an hour a writer in the *Quarterly Review* protested, 'We should as soon expect the people of Woolwich to be fired off upon one of Congreve's ricochet rockets as trust themselves to the mercy of such a rate.' In those days thirty miles an hour was still considered a very fast speed; and one traveller on the Manchester to Liverpool line in 1835 was 'completely horrified' by the train's speed. As he told his sister:

> At six o'clock we were all on our way to the much talked of railhead. On reaching this office, as soon as you have paid your fare, you are commanded to walk upstairs to the coach rooms . . .
> Reaching the top, there you behold a range of coaches of large dimension fastened close to each other. Some are closed like our Leeds coach, and others are open on the sides – in order to have a view of the country, as I thought, and of their manner of proceeding. We all took our place in an open one . . . Before starting I took a survey of all around, first placing my little ones safe. The steam carriage which propels each train is something like a distilling wagon and have each a name of no inviting character, for instance, Fury, Victory, Rapid, Vulcan, Tiger and so on.

A few minutes after we started, not very fast at first, but, in less than five minutes, off we went like a shot from a gun. No sooner did we come to a field than it was a mile behind us, but this was nothing in comparison with meeting a long train of carriages from Liverpool. I was never so frightened in my life than at this moment; I shrank back completely horrified in my seat; I do not think the train was more than 2 seconds in passing, yet it was as long as Holywell Hill. We were then going at a full 34 miles an hour, consequently they passed us at double that time.

It is impossible to form any idea of the rapidity of moving. Several other trains passed us, but as I was aware of their approach they no longer alarmed me as at first. The first 17 miles we went in 32 minutes. I am much disappointed in the view of the country, the railway being cut through so many hills you have frequently for miles only clay mounds on each side of you – consequently no splendid prospect can attract your attention. Even when the railway is on a bridge or at an elevation above the usual track of land, you are not charmed by that diversity of prospect which is to be met with in ordinary stage coach travelling. That has a decided superiority over this new work of man . . . Previous to entering Liverpool, you go through a dark, black, ugly, vile abominable tunnel 300 yards long, which has all the horrors of banishment from life – such a hole as I never wish to go through again.[19]

Many of the smaller lines did not presume to the velocity of the Manchester to Liverpool. The Eastern Counties line was one of them. So notoriously slow was it, indeed, that a robust youth of sixteen, discovered to be travelling at half price, pleaded that he had been under twelve when the 'train started'.[20] But by 1842 when Queen Victoria arrived at Paddington Station from Slough, after her first experience of railway travel, the seventeen-mile journey had taken just twenty-three minutes, at an average of forty-four miles an hour. Prince Albert thought this rather dangerous. 'Not so fast next time, Mr Conductor, if you please,' he is often said to have requested. Six years later, however, the *Great Britain* steam engine was roaring into London, carrying its carriages along at more than a mile a minute. Many passengers still found such speeds alarming. A German travelling in England in the 1840s found 'riding in an open and shaking carriage so elevated' most startling. It was 'really frightening' to be 'dragged along backwards by the snorting engine with such rapidity, under thundering bridges, over lofty viaducts, and through long dark tunnels filled with smoke and steam!' By and by, however, he became accustomed even to this.[21] Most passengers, in fact, did soon grow accustomed to the hurtling speeds, though still astonished by them. 'So rapid are the communications,' wrote Dr Dionysius Lardner in 1850, 'that it is frequently announced that this professor or artist will, on

Monday evening, deliver a lecture or entertainment in Liverpool, on Tuesday in Manchester, on Wednesday in Preston, on Thursday in Halifax and so forth.'[22]

While speeds improved, the safety of the passengers did not. There were fifteen times as many fatal accidents in England as there were in Germany, many of them the fault of the passengers themselves who were constantly attempting to board moving trains, jumping off to pick up their hats, sitting on the tops of the carriages and falling over the sides of the open, seatless trucks which were the only form of accommodation at first provided for third-class travellers. In the railway companies' reports there are frequent references to these accidents: 'Injured, jumped out after his hat'; 'fell off, riding on the side of a wagon'; 'skull broken, riding on the top of a carriage, came into collision with a bridge'; 'fell out of a third-class carriage while pushing and jostling'; 'guard's head struck against a bridge, attempting to remove a passenger who had improperly seated himself outside'. Of the serious accidents reported to the Board of Trade one year, twenty-two happened to persons who had 'jumped off when the carriages were going at speed, generally after their hats, and five persons were run over when lying either drunk or asleep upon the line'.[23]

Uncomfortable as their accommodation was, passengers were at first charged at the rate of 1½d a mile.[24] This rate was reduced in 1844 to 1d a mile for third-class passengers who were, by order of Parliament, provided with at least one train a day on every line. Still cheaper fares were introduced in the 1860s; and in the early 1870s the Midland Railway set the example of providing third-class carriages on every train.[25]

The Railway Act of 1844, as well as introducing the so-called daily 'Parliamentary trains' for third-class passengers, also required that they must have protected seating accommodation; and in 1870 their carriages were made a good deal less uncomfortable. They were still badly lit, though; and even in the second-class carriages passengers had to take candles with them if they wanted to read at night. Candles could be bought, together with books, newspapers and magazines, from W. H. Smith & Son who opened their first bookstall at Euston Station in 1848 and who subsequently opened 200 more bookstalls on the Great Western and London and North Western Railways. On occasions brimstone matches served the purpose of candles as Francis Kilvert discovered one day in May 1870 when travelling to the Bath Flower Show:

Found the first train going down was an Excursion train and took a ticket for it. The carriage was nearly full. In the Box tunnel as there was no lamp, the people began to strike foul brimstone matches and hand them to each other all down the carriage. All the time we were in the tunnel these lighted matches were travelling from hand to hand in the darkness. Each match lasted the length of the carriage and the red ember was thrown out of the opposite window, by which time another lighted match was seen travelling down the carriage. The carriage was chock full of brimstone fumes, the windows both nearly shut, and by the time we got out of the tunnel I was almost suffocated. Then a gentleman tore a lady's pocket handkerchief in two, seized one fragment, blew his nose with it, and put the rag in his pocket. She then seized his hat from his head, while another lady said that the dogs of Wootton Bassett were much more sociable than the people.[26]

Those embarking on long journeys had to take food as well as matches with them, since until 1882 there were no restaurant cars, except for first-class passengers travelling short distances. Even then, as there were no corridors, passengers intending to eat in the restaurant car had to get out when the train stopped at a station and walk along the platform. Corridor coaches were, however, being built by the early 1890s; and sleeping-carriages, introduced on the North Eastern line soon afterwards for first-class passengers only, were also becoming general. There were no lavatories, though, except on the royal train where they were provided for Queen Victoria whose ladies, not permitted to use them, had to get out when the train stopped at secluded places on its way to Scotland.[27]

While passengers were being transported around the country in ever faster and more comfortable trains, journeys in cities were becoming easier too, if not always quicker or safer: an illustration in an 1864 issue of *The Illustrated London News* depicts a traffic jam on the corner of Brick Street and Park Lane in London in which nervous or angry pedestrians, coachmen, drovers and passengers are embroiled in a jumble of barking dogs, sheep and long-horned cattle. The horses of a carriage and pair have come face to face with a costermonger's donkey cart, while a hansom cab, whose top-hatted occupant is arguing with its driver, attempts unsuccessfully to overtake a crowded omnibus on its way to Paddington.

The omnibus had first appeared in London prints towards the end of the eighteenth century, though the name did not come into general use until 1829 when a 'new vehicle, called the omnibus, commenced running this morning [4 July] from Paddington to the City'. The name had originated in France where at the shop of a M. Omnès in Nantes, the terminus of a service of large-capacity passenger vehicles, a slogan was displayed advertising the service with a pun on the shopkeeper's name – *Omnes Omnibus* ('All for Everyone'). George Shillibeer, a former midshipman who had set up a small business in Paris after having trained as a coach-builder in Long Acre, was responsible for introducing the 'new carriages on the Parisian mode' to

England. His first two carriages ran from the Yorkshire Stingo at Paddington to the Bank, the fare being 1s, later increased to 1s 6d for inside passengers, 1s remaining the price for those on top. Each omnibus, which had windows at the sides and back, was drawn by three bays, harnessed abreast, and carried up to twenty passengers. Soon Shillibeer had increased the number of his omnibuses to twelve, running in various parts of London; but, having relinquished his business in the centre of London to start a new service of omnibuses to Greenwich and Woolwich, he was ruined by the opening of the Greenwich Railway; and his enterprise was developed by others, notably the London General Omnibus Company. This was formed in 1856 and thereafter omnibuses, or buses as they were colloquially known – De Tivoli's Patent Buses which ran between Paddington and the Bank being particularly comfortable models – became one of the principal means of passenger transport not only in London but in all the larger towns of England. Horse-drawn omnibuses did not finally disappear until the First World War; but by then motor buses were in general use, the first licence having been issued for these in 1897. And by 1913 there were 3000 motor omnibuses on the London streets. It was not until 1925, however, that the tops of some buses were enclosed and the 'outside' passengers, still known as such, were sheltered from the rain.[28]

The first conductors, some of whom were said to be the sons of army officers, were celebrated for their courtesy and efficiency. But by the 1850s they were better known for their dishonesty, their cockiness and for their determination to crowd as many passengers into the bus as possible. Attempts were made to check their honesty by employing women to get on to the omnibus, to count the number of fares – differentiating between 'insides' and 'outs' and short and long journeys – and then to fill in a form for the proprietor at the terminus. But the conductors, or 'cads' as they were commonly known, soon learned to recognize the spy whose returns could, in any case, never be reliable.

Drivers suspected of dishonesty were immediately dismissed, and many were discharged without good reason. Being an omnibus conductor was not an enviable occupation as one of them pointed out:

The worst part of my business is its uncertainty. I may be discharged any day, and not know for what. I never get to a public place, whether it's chapel or a playhouse, unless, indeed, I get a holiday, and that is once in two years. I've asked for a day's holiday and been refused. I'm quite ignorant of what's passing in the world, my time's so taken up. We only know what's going on from hearing people talk in the 'bus. I never care to read the paper now, though I used to like it. If I have two minutes to spare,

I'd rather take a nap than anything else. We know no more politics than the back-woodsmen of America, because we haven't time to care about it. I've fallen asleep on my step as the bus was going on, and almost fallen off. I have often to put up with insolence from vulgar fellows, who think it fun to chaff a cad, as they call it. There's no help for it. Our masters won't listen to complaints: if we are not satisfied we can go. It takes every farthing of our wages to live well enough, and keep a wife and family.[29]

Even so, most passengers seem to have regarded omnibus conductors less as men deserving pity than as impertinent upstarts to be prodded with umbrellas, to be distrusted whenever answering questions as to the destination of their vehicles, and in constant need of correction for their cheeky manners. In 1842 the stipendiary magistrate at Marlborough Street Police Court was moved to observe 'in very indignant tones' that it was necessary to protect the public 'and females in particular' against 'the ruffianly conduct of omnibus conductors'.[30] Charles Dickens, who compared the pleasurable variety of an omnibus journey with the tedium of one by coach, wrote of one conductor who had taken

more old ladies and gentlemen to Paddington who wanted to go to the Bank, and more old ladies and gentlemen to the Bank who wanted to go to Paddington, than any six men on the road; and, however much malevolent spirits may pretend to doubt the accuracy of the statement, they well know it to be an established fact that he has forcibly conveyed a variety of ancient persons of either sex to both places, who had not the slightest or most distant intention of going anywhere at all.[31]

The great boast of another conductor of Dickens's highly coloured but apparently not entirely misleading description was that he could 'chuck an old gen'l'm'n into the buss, shut him in, and rattle off, afore he knows where it's a-going to' – a feat which he frequently performed. 'We are not aware that it has ever been precisely ascertained how many passengers our omnibus will contain,' Dickens added. 'The impression on the cad's mind evidently is, that it is amply sufficient for the accommodation of any number of persons that can be enticed into it.'

'Any room?' cries a very hot pedestrian.
'Plenty o' room, sir,' replies the conductor, gradually opening the door, and not disclosing the real state of the case until the wretched man is on the steps.
'Where?' inquires the entrapped individual with an attempt to back out again.

'Either side, sir,' rejoins the cad, shoving him in and slamming the door. 'All right, Bill.'[32]

Bill, the driver, would no doubt have been as likely to complain of his long hours as most conductors were. One driver, a former builder, told Henry Mayhew:

It's a hard work is mine; for I never have any rest but a few minutes, except every other Sunday, and then only two hours . . . If I was to ask leave to go to church, I know what the answer would be – 'You can go to church as often as you like, and we can get a man who doesn't want to go there' . . . If I'm blocked [in a traffic jam] I must make up for the block by galloping; but if I'm seen to gallop and anybody tells our people, I'm called over the coals . . . It's not easy to drive a bus; but I can drive and must drive to an inch; yes, sir, to half an inch.[33]

Omnibus drivers were considered to be for the most part a sober and respectable class of men. This was not the case, however, with cabmen and the drivers of hackney coaches. These usually came to the occupation from a variety of other employments. Some had been costermongers or green-grocers, others grooms or footmen, barmen, innkeepers, shop assistants, pawnbrokers or saddlers; several had criminal records; one, in the 1860s, was said to be a baronet. Mayhew was informed 'on excellent authority' that a tenth, 'or to speak beyond the possibility of cavil, a twelfth of the whole number', either lived with women of the town or were supported 'on the wages of the women's prostitution'. Certainly they knew where all the brothels were; and one cabman remembered how he used to drive Lord Barrymore 'in his rounds of the brothels'. 'His Lordship used always to take his own wine with him'; and, after waiting up until daylight, the cabdriver took him, 'girls and all – fine dressed-up madams – to Billingsgate, and there left them to breakfast at some queer place or to slang with the fish-wives'.[34]

In the 1860s there were about 4600 cabdrivers in London in all. Of these about 2000 were their own masters and were much more respectable than the employed 'loose fellows' who had drifted into the life, believing it to be 'both idle and exciting'. Their reputation for heavy drinking led to the building, at the expense of various philanthropists, of London's cabmen's shelters where they could provide themselves with a cheap meal and a hot non-alcoholic drink. There were at one time over sixty of these shelters, a few of which still remain.

The drivers' vehicles were mostly *cabriolets*, a French importation, like the omnibus. By the middle of the nineteenth century, cabs had almost entirely replaced the hackney coaches which had plied for hire in the London streets since the early seventeenth century and of which there were over 1000 by the early nineteenth. The *cabriolet*, which had arrived in 1823, was drawn by a single horse and carried two passengers under a hood, the driver being seated outside the hood on the offside of the vehicle. In 1834 Joseph Aloysius Hansom, a joiner's son who became an architect, introduced his 'Patent Safety Cab', a vehicle whose abnormally large wheels and body near the ground reduced the risk of accidents. In the developed hansom cab the driver was seated on top of the vehicle; and in later versions he was mounted behind the cab with his reins going over the roof in which there was a window through which he could communicate with his passengers. In 1865 the hansom cab was joined by the growler, a four-wheeled cab drawn by a single horse with space for a third passenger beside the driver; and men who had taken to summoning cabs by blasts on the silver whistle that hung from their watch-chains now signalled their requirements by a single blast for a hansom and a double blast for a growler.[35] By 1904 there were 7499 hansom cabs in London and 3905 growlers. There were also by then several mechanically driven cabs. These, powered by electric batteries and weighing two tons – far heavier than the hansom's eight hundredweight – were introduced in 1897 but they had a short life, being extinct before 1901. In 1904 they were replaced by petrol-engined motor cabs of which there were 8397 at the outbreak of the First World War. The taximeter, which gave the taxicab its present name, was in general use from 1907.[36]

Both hansoms and growlers survived into the days of the motor cab. Indeed, as late as 1927 there were still twelve hansoms in London and 100 growlers; and there was still one horse-drawn cab operating in 1947. The horse-drawn tramcar was also seen for several years after the motor omnibus had been introduced in 1897. Tramcars, with wheels running in metal tracks, had first appeared in London in 1861 when an American entrepreneur, George Francis Train, who had introduced them the year before in Birkenhead, received permission to lay tracks along Victoria Street from Westminster Abbey to Pimlico. The trams ran every five minutes, carrying forty-eight passengers, half of them outside. But as the lines stood fourteen inches above the road surface, they were strongly objected to by the owners and drivers of other vehicles and were removed before the year was over. Despite Train's failure, three other tramways were authorized for the outskirts of London in 1869; and these lines eventually expanded into a large network covering most of London apart from its central area. The tramcars, which had a vertical iron ladder at each end, changed little after the brief appearance of steam trams and compressed air trams and the invention of electric traction, though most were then roofed over. Powered either by overhead lines or by live rails set in conduits between the tracks, these electric tramcars, the first of which were operated at Northfleet in Kent in 1889, were a popular means of transport until briefly superseded by the trolley-bus or 'trackless tram'.

Trams have been called the 'gondolas of the people',[37] a description that echoes Disraeli's celebration of the hansom cab as the 'Gondola of London'; and before the end of the nineteenth century they were to be seen in large towns all over the country, from Plymouth to Leeds – where the first electric tram was seen at Roundhay as early as 1891 – much reducing the time it took people to travel to work and enabling them to get to football grounds and shops and their children to get to school. After the Tramways Act of 1870 had allowed local authorities to buy private tramways by compulsory purchase after twenty-one years of operation, sixty-one local authorities took advantage of this legislation, though there were still eighty-nine undertakings managed by private enterprise.[38]

When electric trams first appeared in London the congestion in the streets had been slightly alleviated by the building of the underground. Proposals for this revolutionary scheme were put forward by Charles Pearson, the enterprising surveyor to the City of London, to a Royal Commission which had been appointed in 1845 to consider the problems of traffic which were threatening to become insuperable. The streets in the centre of the city were daily choked not only by tens of thousands of pedestrians, by 20,000 equestrians, by herds of innumerable animals bumping into each other on their way to market, by omnibuses, hansoms and growlers, but also by thousands of other carriages, vans and carts, gigs, tilburies, phaetons, landaus, broughams, dogcarts and donkey-carts.

Pearson, therefore, proposed that, since there was no longer room for people to move about comfortably at street level, they should be transported beneath it. Objections to such a quixotic idea were immediate and numerous: the houses above the lines would collapse into the tunnels; digging holes in the ground for such a purpose must surely be contrary to the laws of God; the Duke of Wellington warned that one day a French army would suddenly arrive in London by train without anyone even knowing that it had landed on the English shore.

Pearson persisted, however, and, having persuaded several rich men that underground railways would not only ease traffic congestion and enable working people to live in healthier districts outside central London but that they would also be highly profitable, his scheme was eventually accepted. But it was not until May 1862 that the first section of the Metropolitan Line was opened for an inaugural journey upon which W. E. Gladstone, at that time Chancellor of the Exchequer, seated in top-hat and morning coat beside his wife, was one of the passengers. The next year the line was opened to the public and on its first day it carried 30,000 passengers in open trucks behind a

steam engine from Paddington to Farringdon Street in the City. So successful was the line, in fact, that by the end of 1864 no fewer than 259 projects for
underground railways in and around London had been presented.

At first the lines were dug by what was known as the 'cut and cover'
method, that was to say by following the lines of existing roads to avoid
paying for property, digging a deep trench, supporting the earth at the sides
with brick walls, laying the tracks, roofing over them, then restoring the road
surface. The District and Circle lines were both built by this method. Later
tunnels were built with the help of cast-iron circular shields, originally
patented by Marc Brunel. These were used in the construction of the City
and South London railway (later part of the Northern Line), the world's first
electric tube railway which was opened in 1890 from Stockwell to King
William Street. It was a deep tube, with platforms forty feet below ground
from which passengers were taken back to the surface by hydraulic lifts. The
apprehension which such a mode of transport initially aroused was soon
overcome by its speed and comfort, and by the cheapness of its 2d flat rate
fare. In its first two weeks this electric railway carried 165,000 passengers,
and its success led to a wave of other railway promotions until there were over
100 miles of underground lines in the London area.[39]

While thousands of people were going to work by underground railways in
late Victorian London, thousands, too, all over the country, were going by
bicycle. Compared with other means of cheap transport the bicycle had come
late upon the scene. In 1839 a Scottish blacksmith named Macmillan had
invented a primitive kind of bicycle driven by cranks rather than pedals; but,
little better than a hobbyhorse, it had never become popular, and it was not
until the 1860s – when two Frenchmen, Pierre and Ernest Michaux, built a
more sophisticated machine which became known as a *vélocipède* – that a
bicycle became accepted as a feasible means of transport. The Coventry
Sewing Machine Company made 400 of the Michaux bicycles for export to
France, but the outbreak of the Franco-Prussian War obliged the company to
sell them in England where, it was soon found, a keen market for bicycles
existed and where, up till then, most machines were clumsy contraptions like
the one Tom Mullins bought for 2s 6d which 'had a wooden frame and
handlebars, but no chains or pedals, you simply pushed it along with your
feet'. Other machines were made by village blacksmiths and, while fast
enough going downhill, were so heavy that they demanded a great deal of
energy when the road took an upward turn.

In 1870 James Stanley, a young foreman at the Coventry company, built
the first 'penny farthing', a high bicycle with a front wheel much larger than
the rear; but this was also difficult to ride and it was not until the low-framed
Rover 'safety bicycle' with wheels of equal size was introduced in 1880,

followed in 1888 by the invention of a pneumatic tyre by a Belfast veterinary surgeon, John Boyd Dunlop, and by the improvement of the free wheel in the early 1890s, that bicycling became a pleasure. It was eagerly adopted by all classes, particularly by the lower middle classes, and by women who found it both a healthy exercise and a liberating experience which they could share on equal terms with men.

> There are bicycling clubs in every part of England [wrote T. H. S. Escott in 1897]. A favourite rendezvous in the neighbourhood of London is Bushey Park, and there, when the weather is fine, as many as a thousand bicyclists congregate. During the summer, too, in the heart of the city, when the business traffic of the day is done and the streets are clear, an active scene may often be witnessed by gas-light. Under the shadow of the Bank and the Exchange, the asphalt thoroughfare is covered with a host of bicycle riders, performing a series of intricate evolutions on their iron steeds.[40]

All over the country bicycles were now to be seen. In Cambridge the daughter of the Plumian Professor of Astronomy was 'just about at the right age to enjoy it' when the 'bicycling craze came in'. 'At first even "safety bicycles" were too dangerous and improper for ladies to ride,' she recalled. 'They had to have tricycles. My mother had (I believe) the first female tricycle in Cambridge; and I had a little one, and we used to go out for family rides, all together.' Her father led the way on his bicycle; her brother stood miserably on the bar behind their mother, 'holding on for all he was worth'. Before the advent of the pneumatic tyre she found it hard to keep up with the others, 'pounding away on hard tyres, a glorious but not a pleasurable pastime'. 'Then one day at lunch,' she continued, 'my father said he had just seen a new kind of tyre, filled with air, and he thought it might be a success. And soon after that everyone had bicycles . . . and [they] became the smart thing in society . . . We were then permitted to wear baggy knickerbockers, horridly improper, but rather grand . . . I only once saw a woman (not, of course, a *lady*) in real bloomers.'[41]

The small motor-car was also soon to be recognized as a pleasurable and cheap form of private transport, cheaper at least than a private carriage. Before the death of Queen Victoria there were numerous small cars on the roads. They were quite reliable – in the words of a correspondent whose letter was published in *The Autocar* in 1901 – and were capable of reaching respectable speeds 'with very few involuntary stops'.[42] The Queen herself had an Electric Victoria whose driver sat on a platform above the rear wheels looking over the heads of the two passengers. It cost £570, could cover up to forty miles on one charge, and was driven at a speed of about twelve miles an hour. This was quite fast enough for the Queen; and would have been illegal before the repeal in 1896 of a law which prohibited vehicles being driven on public roads at more than four miles an hour and which required them to be preceded by a man carrying a red flag. To celebrate the repeal of this law, and the raising of the speed limit to twelve miles an hour, a group of motorists burned their red flags and drove off to Brighton in what was to be the first of a series of regular events, later to be known as Veteran Car Runs, in which motor cars made between 1895 and 1905 are driven from Hyde Park Corner to Madeira Drive, Brighton.

Although considered quite fast enough by most pedestrians, a speed of twelve miles an hour – raised in 1903 to twenty miles an hour on roads deemed suitable – was thought not nearly fast enough by most motorists, many of whom regularly exceeded it. Among these was Edward VII who in 1898, while Prince of Wales and staying at Highcliffe Castle in Hampshire, had been driven at forty miles an hour in a Daimler by a fellow-guest. When he had his own cars, among them a sixty-five-horse-power Mercedes, the King liked to be driven much faster than that. Unaffected by the traffic laws of his realm, he often congratulated himself upon having raced along the Brighton road in 1906 at sixty miles an hour. Other motorists had to grow accustomed to being overtaken by a large car, without number plates but with the Royal Arms on the door panels, in which a bearded figure sat on the blue Morocco back seat, smoking a large cigar, as he urged his chauffeur on with impatient gestures and gruff commands to ever greater speeds.[43]

The King's luxurious cars were, of course, extremely expensive both to buy and to run; and most people still considered, as *The Illustrated London News* put it in 1905, that the motor-omnibus, which had 'come to stay, had the same attraction for the masses as the motor car had 'for the classes'.[44] But small cars were available for well under £200 and these could be run for about 4d a mile. The Vanguard, a cheap, economical car introduced in 1908, was designed especially for doctors.

By 1910 over 100,000 cars had been registered as compared with 23,000 in 1903 when registration became compulsory; and by 1914 the number had risen to 132,000. Most of these were either imported or were assembled in England for Henry Ford's company in Detroit; but by the time war broke out William Morris's factory in Oxford was producing his bull-nosed Morris-Oxfords which did up to fifty miles on a gallon of petrol, could travel at fifty miles an hour, and cost £165. The increasing cheapness of private transport was beginning to bring about a transformation in English society as momentous as that brought about earlier in the century by the coming of the railways.

# 58 · Law and Order

When Mr and Mrs Manning were hanged on the roof of Horsemonger Lane gaol in 1849, Charles Dickens was 'astounded and appalled by the wickedness' of the spectacle. 'You have no idea what the hanging of the Mannings really was,' he told a friend. 'The conduct of the people was so indescribably frightful that I felt for some time afterwards almost as if I were living in a city of devils.'[1] As late as 1864, at the execution of Franz Müller for the murder of a bank clerk in a railway carriage, *The Times* reported that 'robbery and violence, loud laughing, oaths, fighting, obscene conduct and still more filthy language reigned round the gallows far and near'. The spectators comprised the most 'incorrigible dregs' of London – 'sharpers, thieves, gamblers, betting men, the outsiders of the boxing ring . . . the rakings of cheap singing halls and billiard rooms'.[2]

For centuries such scenes had been common at public executions, yet it was not until 1868 that a private Member's Bill – introduced by J. T. Hibbert and providing for the future carrying-out of executions within prison walls – was accepted by the government; and it was to be a further century before sentence to death by hanging was abandoned.

It had long been held that capital punishment was an essential deterrent not only for murder but for crimes against property too. In the early years of the nineteenth century Lord Ellenborough, the Lord Chief Justice, had strenuously opposed a suggestion that shoplifters found guilty of stealing less than 10s should not be hanged. He was convinced, he said, 'with the rest of the judges, that public expediency [required] there should be no remission of the terror denounced against this description of offenders. Such will be the consequences of the repeal of this statute that I am certain depredations to an unlimited extent would immediately be committed.'[3]

It was a familiar argument. It had been advanced against Sir Samuel Romilly who had urged his fellow-Members to remember that 'cruel punishments have an inevitable tendency to produce cruelty in the people' and who had committed suicide in a sudden access of despair after the failure of yet another of his Bills attempting to reduce the number of capital offences. And it had been advanced against Sir Thomas Fowell Buxton who had declared in a parliamentary debate: 'We rest our hopes on the hangman; and in this vain and deceitful confidence in the ultimate punishment of crime, forget the very first of our duties – its prevention.'

In Fowell Buxton's day an extraordinary number of crimes were punishable by death. According to his own estimate, there were as many as 223 of them, four made capital in the reign of the Plantagenets, twenty-six in the reign of the Tudors, thirty-six in the time of the Stuarts and no less than 156 since.[4] Apart from such crimes as treason, murder, piracy, arson, stealing, rape, sodomy and various breaches of the game laws, which had been capital offences for many years, it was an offence punishable by death to send a letter demanding money signed with a fictitious name, to impersonate a Chelsea Pensioner, to make a false entry in the books of the Bank of England, to strike a Privy Councillor, to damage Westminster Bridge, to refuse to remain in quarantine, and to commit many other crimes, more or less reprehensible, some of which had not even been crimes, let alone capital ones, before.[5]

Admittedly the numbers of malefactors hanged were not so high as they had been in previous centuries; but executions were still common enough. A witness giving evidence to a parliamentary committee said that he had twice seen forty men hanged in a single day; and out of every twenty criminals hanged, so it was estimated, eighteen were less than twenty-one years old. Many were under fifteen. In 1801 a boy aged thirteen was hanged for breaking into a house and stealing a spoon; two sisters aged eight and eleven were hanged at Lynn in 1808; as late as 1831 a boy of nine was hanged at Chelmsford for setting fire to a house; and two years later another boy of nine was sentenced to death for pushing a stick through a cracked shop window and taking two pennyworth of printer's colour.[6] Yet there were those who argued that the failure of executions to reduce the rate of crime was due to hanging being *Not Punishment Enough*. This was the title of a pamphlet whose author recommended breaking on the wheel, hanging alive in chains and whipping to death as punishments more likely to serve the purposes of deterrence. Others advocated castration and branding.

The arguments of the reformers, however, gradually began to gain ground. It could not, after all, be denied that the so-called 'Bloody Code' was not only bloody but that it did not work, that while men were being publicly hanged for robbery, burglary and housebreaking, these crimes had been increasing for many years, were still increasing and continued to increase.

In 1819 the House of Commons carried a motion for the appointment of a Committee of Inquiry into the Criminal Laws; and although the practical achievements which followed the committee's Report were negligible, the long debates served to keep the reform of the criminal law in the public mind and to prepare the way for the work which Robert Peel began soon after his appointment to the Home Secretaryship in 1821. By a series of Acts passed between 1823 and 1827 Peel abolished capital punishment for several offences and made it possible for courts to abstain from pronouncing the death sentence for all convicted persons except murderers. He also abolished Benefit of Clergy and reduced over 300 confused statutes into four intelligible Acts. Gibbeting was abolished in 1834, the pillory in 1837. In 1831 out of 1601 persons sentenced to death, only fifty-two were executed, and three years later the City of London was obliged to dismiss one of its two salaried executioners as there was so little work for him to do.[7]

Peel realized, as few other reformers had done, that reform of the criminal law was dependent upon police reform and it was towards the reorganization of the police that he cautiously but surely moved. He had to contend with deeply ingrained prejudices. For generations Englishmen had preferred to rely upon the severity of the criminal law, and the offer of rewards to those who brought criminals to justice, rather than upon a professional police. The very word police – a French word not used in official English until 1714 – was, in its modern sense, unknown. The idea of policemen paid by the government might be all very well for Frenchmen, it was widely held, but such a concept would never do for the freedom-loving island race of Englishmen. Besides, so it was also argued, the cost of a professional police force would be prohibitive. The loss of hundreds and thousands of pounds worth of goods and money stolen each year was more acceptable than the supposedly exorbitant cost of paying enough men to prevent it.

So the enforcement of law and the maintenance of order were left in the hands of voluntary associations or armed civilians; trained bands of respectable citizens like John Gilpin; military guards; watchmen and constables, often decrepit and sometimes corrupt; thief-takers who were paid for the convictions they were able to contrive; and magistrates and their staffs, very few of whom were as competent as those at Bow Street in the days of Sir Thomas de Veil, Henry Fielding, his blind half-brother Sir John, and of the parish constables who were trained there, the prototypes of the celebrated Bow Street Runners. The more successful Sir John Fielding's men and his horse and foot patrols had become, however, the less the government had been prepared to support him. As soon as crime seemed less prevalent, his allowances had been reduced; and after his death the reputation of the Bow Street Runners began to decline.[8]

Occasionally a series of crimes or outbreaks of violence prompted calls for a more efficient system of law enforcement. The Gordon Riots in London had made people aware of the problems presented by a large and unruly underworld, growing year by year and scarcely submerged beneath the level of respectable life; but calls for a professional police, based on the better aspects of the French police, went unheeded. And when in 1811 there were several horrifying murders in Ratcliffe Highway, and the incompetence of justices and parish constables was once more revealed, the *Morning Post* expressed a common sentiment when it declared that 'either respectable householders must determine to be their own guardians, or we must have a regularly enlisted armed police under the orders of proper officers'. Yet the panic engendered by the murders soon relapsed into complacency. 'They have an admirable police at Paris,' wrote John William Ward, 'but they pay for it dear enough. I had rather half a dozen people's throats be cut in Ratcliffe Highway every three or four years than be subject to domiciliary visits, spies and all the rest of Fouché's contrivances.'[9]

There had been a similar reaction in 1820 after a battalion of the 3rd Foot Guards mutinied during a riot. 'In my opinion,' the Duke of Wellington told the Earl of Liverpool, the Prime Minister, 'the government ought, without the loss of a moment's time to adopt measures to form either a police [force] in London or a military corps, which should be of a different description from the regular military force, or both.'[10]

Yet it was not until 1829, seven years after Lord Liverpool had appointed him Home Secretary, that Peel's Metropolitan Police Act at last became law. This Act provided for a new force of paid constables commanded by two Justices, later called Commissioners, who were given offices in Whitehall Place, the back of which opened on to a courtyard known as Scotland Yard. When the two Commissioners – a barrister and an army officer – moved to these offices a new era in the history of police had begun.

Less than three months after its establishment, Wellington wrote to Peel to congratulate him upon 'the entire success of the London police'. Almost the whole of the metropolis had been divided into police divisions, sections and beats; and constables armed with short wooden batons and wearing top hats and blue tail coats, with the number and letter of their division on their collars, had appeared in the streets. The force had certainly been organized with remarkable speed, but it aroused widespread resentment among the public at large and there was much dissatisfaction among the constables themselves. They were very poorly paid and the commissioners' difficulties in finding suitable men were reflected in the number of dismissals – nearly 5000 – between 1830 and 1838. In these years there were also more than 6000 resignations, most of them being 'not altogether voluntary'.[11] Superintendents received £200 a year, inspectors £100, sergeants 22s 6d a week and constables (after 2s had been deducted for their uniforms) 19s a week. Their pay remained low throughout the century in the early years of which they supplemented it by asking householders on their beats for a Christmas box.[12]

The dislike and distrust of the police extended to almost all classes of people until 1833 when about 500 constables were called out to control a political demonstration in Cold Bath Fields. The mob threw stones at them and three of them were stabbed and one killed. At the subsequent inquest on the dead constable, a prejudiced jury – against all the evidence – brought in a verdict of 'justifiable homicide', while the government attempted to shuffle responsibility on to the Commissioners. Even the most extreme radicals who had been in the crowd acknowledged that both the jury's verdict and the government's behaviour were grossly unfair, and a reaction in favour of the police set in. Former critics of the system found good things to say of the force; parishes outside the Metropolitan district asked to be taken into it; and soon provincial towns were asking for police officers trained in London to come to their help.

For in the provinces, where the old parochial system still prevailed, crime was rising fast as criminals, driven out of London by the new force, began to operate there. The proportion of known bad characters to the general population had risen, so it was calculated in 1837, to one in forty-five in Liverpool, to one in thirty-one in Bristol and as high as one in twenty-seven in Newcastle-on-Tyne.[13] Two years later an Act was passed permitting counties to raise and equip paid police forces. Essex was the first county to take advantage of this Act and the results were so immediately favourable that the adjoining counties of Suffolk, Hertfordshire and Cambridgeshire were encouraged to follow Essex's example. Other counties, some of them in the face of strong opposition, did the same. By May 1853, however, there were still twenty-two counties completely without a professional police force, and in these counties those who had been robbed were liable to be presented with a bill similar to that presented to a poor man in Wiltshire whose boots were stolen by a thief. He chased the man and, having caught him, handed him over to a constable who eventually presented him with an account for a sum far in excess of the value of his boots:

|  | £ | s | d |
|---|---|---|---|
| To apprehending prisoner |  | 2 | 6 |
| To maintaining prisoner |  |  |  |
| (2 days) |  | 3 | 0 |
| To guard watching (one night) |  | 2 | 6 |
| Conveyance of prisoner at 9d |  |  |  |
| a mile and allowance to |  |  |  |
| constable at 8d a mile | 2 | 15 | 5 |

| | | |
|---|---|---|
| 3 days' loss of time | 15 | 0 |
| Hire of conveyance, coach and other fares | 1 1 | 2 |
| | 4 19 | 7[14] |

The man to whom this bill was presented might have been considered lucky to find a constable willing to help him at all, for many could not. One constable, in a far from exceptional instance, apologized for not being able to come out to quell a riot but he 'sent his staff by bearer'.[15] Men understandably felt that they must continue to protect their houses from burglars with spring guns and man-traps – although these had been declared illegal in 1827 – and in Cambridgeshire they chased thieves with bloodhounds.[16] This unsatisfactory state of affairs was brought to an end at last in 1856 when a Police Act made it obligatory for all counties to raise and maintain a professional constabulary.

The prisons to which sentenced malefactors were committed were still under local control. A hundred years before about half of them were privately owned and conditions in them had been appalling. As John Howard, author of *The State of Prisons in England and Wales*, had discovered, they were generally so disgusting that more people died in them of that 'putrid, contagious and very pestilential' disease known as gaol fever than were executed. Prisoners were starved and beaten, chained to stone floors and forced to pay for 'easement of irons' by gaolers who made large sums by selling gin to those who could afford it. The overcrowding in prisons had been alleviated by the transportation of criminals at first to America and then to Australia and – when these convenient dumping grounds for the unwanted had to be abandoned – by the incarceration of men in the now idle convict ships. But, if less crowded, prisons were no less unpleasant; and two Inspectors of Prisons appointed in 1835 found that in many conditions had scarcely improved in 100 years. In Newgate, for example – although, thanks to the unremitting efforts of Elizabeth Fry, 'more system and a greater semblance of decorum was maintained' in the female side – the main part of the prison was a disgrace to humanity. Men convicted of homosexual offences were shut up in the same wards as young boys awaiting trial and slept on the same rope mats with them; minor offenders were put with hardened criminals awaiting transportation; lunatics with those who were pretending to be mad. The ward which a newcomer entered was settled by prisoners, known as wardsmen, to whom the governor assigned this duty and to whom bribes were openly paid. Most of the prisoners were in rags; food was served out by the wardsmen who made as much money out of this duty as they could.

The days were passed in idleness, debauchery, riotous quarreling, immoral conversation, gambling, instruction in all nefarious processes, lively discourse upon past criminal exploits, elaborate discussion of others to be perpetrated after release. No provision whatever was made for the employment of prisoners. Drink, in more or less unlimited quantities, was still to be had . . . Women saw men if they merely pretended to be wives . . . Perhaps the worst feature of the visiting system was the permission accorded to male prisoners to have access to the female side.[17]

Newgate, which covered a site upon which a prison had stood since the twelfth century, had been rebuilt in 1780–83 after its destruction in the Gordon Riots. Since then other modern prisons had appeared in London. In 1821 Millbank Penitentiary had been completed on lines suggested by Jeremy Bentham's *The Panopticon or Inspection House*. In the shape of a six-pointed star, it was a gloomy place on marshy ground by the banks of the river where the Tate Gallery now stands. It sprawled over seven acres, and one warder after several years of service still had to mark the walls with chalk so that he did not lose his way in the three miles of labyrinthine passages and winding staircases. Prisoners were confined to separate cells, where they made shoes and stitched mailbags, and were forbidden to communicate with each other during the first half of their sentences. Both the locality and the diet were extremely unhealthy and in 1822–3 epidemics of scurvy and cholera swept through the prison, killing thirty inmates. The male survivors were removed to hulks while the building was being fumigated, the women being pardoned, as this was felt to be the only way of restoring their health.

By the time Millbank was reopened, plans for a number of other prisons had been approved. In 1842 a large new penitentiary was completed at Pentonville and by 1848 no less than fifty-four other prisons had been built on the same plan, having rows of single cells arranged in tiers and in separate blocks radiating from a central hub like the spokes of a wheel. Apart from Wormwood Scrubs, which was built in 1874, and Dartmoor, begun in 1806 for French prisoners of war but made into a convict prison in 1850, nearly all the large English prisons were built in the 1840s and 1850s, many of them like Reading prison, which was considered 'the finest building in Berkshire after Windsor Castle', combining 'with the castellated, a collegiate appearance'. Holloway, finished in 1852, was also described as a 'noble building of the castellated Gothic style'.[18]

Pentonville, a characteristic example, had 520 small cells, thirteen feet by seven, with little windows on their outside walls and doors opening on to the narrow landings in the galleries. They were 'admirably ventilated', a visitor wrote, and had 'even the luxuries of a water-closet', though water-closets were later replaced by the communal, evil-smelling 'recesses' because they were constantly getting blocked and their pipes were used as a means of communication. The occupants of the cells, in obedience to a system of prison discipline developed in America, were forbidden to talk to each other and when permitted to take exercise tramped along in silent rows, wearing masks of brown cloth over their faces. In chapel, which they had to attend every day, they sat in little cubicles, their heads visible to the warder on duty but hidden from each other. Men caught trying to talk to their neighbours were confined in refractory cells completely dark for as long as three weeks on end. Mental disturbances were common. An official report admitted that 'for every sixty thousand persons confined in Pentonville there were 220 cases of insanity, 210 cases of delusions, and forty suicides'.[19]

Breakfast consisted of ten ounces of bread and three-quarters of a pint of cocoa; dinner was half a pint of soup (or four ounces of meat), five ounces of bread and one pound of potatoes, supper a pint of gruel and five ounces of bread. Work lasted from six o'clock in the morning until seven o'clock at night.

In other prisons, since the provision of useful work was often considered either impossible or undesirable, the inmates were kept occupied in such pointless tasks as picking old rope to pieces long after the use of iron in the building of ships had made oakum almost unsaleable. The treadwheel and the crank were also advocated not only as punishments but also as means of occupation which would not threaten the livelihood of honest men and which were purposeless, therefore degrading, and exhausting, therefore deterrent. The treadwheel, a big iron frame of steps around a revolving cylinder, could be fitted to a mill or used for pumping water; and the crank, a wheel like the paddle wheel of a steamer fitted into a box of gravel which the prisoner had to turn by means of a handle, could also be used for productive purposes. But it was rarely that either was. Prisoners, male and female, trudging up the steps in their separate compartments on the wheel might work as they did at Cold Bath Fields Prison for six hours a day and achieve nothing but the climbing of 8640 feet.

In some prisons the inmates were not only obliged to lead lives of unutterable dreariness but were also subjected to cruel tyranny. A Royal Commission appointed to inquire into allegations of cruelty in prisons in 1854 found that prisoners in Birmingham prison, including boys, were savagely and continually whipped, and a straitjacket, 'an engine of positive torture', was frequently employed. At Leicester prison, no convict was allowed a meal on weekdays until he had completed his required number of revolutions on a special type of crank which made the labour of turning it one of agonizing difficulty. One man, the commission understood, had had only nine of the prison's inadequate meals in three weeks of working days.[20]

The revelations of such cruelties led to demands that prisons should be brought under national control. They were so by a Prison Act of 1877; but this Act endorsed the silent system, approved 'hard bodily labour' by crank, treadmill, shot-drill and capstan, and authorized the use of chains and irons, confinement in refractory cells on bread and water, and flogging. Indeed, conditions in some prisons remained almost as bad after the passing of the Act as they had been at the beginning of the century.

At Chatham, according to another Royal Commission which made its report in 1879,

> Prisoners severely mutilated themselves and threw themselves beneath the wheels of the railway wagons in the dock basins in their efforts to escape from the fearful place. If they did not die they were flogged. 'There was no reason,' the Governor said, 'why they should not be flogged, because they had only mutilated an arm or a leg.'

Because they were so badly fed, the convicts at Chatham were driven to eating live worms and frogs and rubbish and at Portland, Dartmoor and other prisons they melted candles in their gruel to make it more satisfying.[21]

Concern was expressed about 'the moral condition' in which men left such prisons as these and about 'the serious number of recommittals'. There was, in fact, 'ample cause for a searching enquiry into the main features of prison life'. A Departmental Committee of Inquiry into Prisons was consequently set up under the chairmanship of Herbert Gladstone; and in 1898 a new Act was passed incorporating most of the committee's recommendations, including the limitation of corporal punishment and the introduction of remission of sentences conditional upon good behaviour. Yet the difficulties of translating legislation into practice remained; and visitors to prisons were still deeply shocked by the conditions which they found. A visitor to Dartmoor in 1906 wrote:

> As I walked along the endless landings and corridors in the great cellular blocks I saw something of the 1,500 men who were then immured in Dartmoor. Their drab uniforms were plastered with broad arrows, their heads were closely shaven . . . Not even a safety razor was allowed, so that in addition to the stubble on their heads, their faces were covered with a sort of dirty moss, representing the growth of hair that a pair of clippers could not remove . . . As they saw us coming each man turned to the nearest wall and put his face closely against it, remaining in this servile position until we had passed him. This was a strictly ordered procedure, to avoid assault or familiarity, the two great offences in prison conduct.[22]

The Gladstone Committee had warned of the effect on a man's subsequent behaviour of confinement in cells but the effect of contamination in a prison like this might be equally disastrous. 'The average man was inextricably dragged down by the conduct and example of the men around him, whose company he could not escape. Within a year, he was almost unrecognizable in speech and habit and point of view.'[23]

At least something was being done for young offenders, although the early Reformatory Schools Acts insisted on initial periods of imprisonment, and regulations about how the reformatories should be run were rare, while punishments in them were often extremely harsh. The Rev. Sydney Turner, in charge of the Redhill Reformatory, for example, advocated severely punishing boys by isolating them for a few days in unheated cells on a diet of bread and water and by whipping them 'with as much solemnity and form as possible'.[24] But after the return of Evelyn Ruggles-Brise, chairman of the Prison Commissioners, from America where he had studied the growing system of state reformatories, a building in the village of Borstal in Kent was taken over as an institution where boys, who might otherwise be sent to prison, could be trained 'mentally, morally and physically' by an experienced staff. Within four years the experiment seemed so promising that the prison commissioners asked the Home Secretary for legislation to establish the Borstal system as an official one, and to permit the courts to sentence boys and girls between sixteen and twenty-one to reformatories for up to three years. The request was granted by the Prevention of Crimes Act of 1908; and with the help and encouragement of Sir Alexander Paterson, the most understanding and far-sighted of the prison commissioners, the Borstal system grew and prospered. In 1930 a Borstal without walls or wire was opened near Nottingham; and four years later the first 'open prison' in England was started near Wakefield. At last, after so many years, steps were being taken to prevent crime by the reformation and rehabilitation of the criminal rather than by his degradation and humiliating punishments. The problems of contamination, however, remained. 'I learnt more about thieving from the chaps there than anywhere else,' one former Borstal boy told a magistrate;[25] and another complained that he was bullied by the other boys: 'there was a lot of sexual stuff went on in that place . . . If you refused you got beaten up.'[26]

Hard as Sir Alexander Paterson tried to turn Borstals into real reformatories and prisons into more than squalid places of confinement, the fundamental problems remained unsolved at his death and have not been solved today.

So long as the country had no professional police force, soldiers and militiamen were liable to be called to the scenes of disturbances and to arrest troublemakers. Their policing duties had not endeared them to the public and they had generally been regarded as oppressors rather than protectors. 'Military service does not bring distinction in England as it does in many parts of Europe,' it was observed in the time of the Duke of Wellington, 'and, as the profession of arms is not held here in the first estimation, the better class of peasantry do not leave the plough or the shuttle for the sword. Consequently the recruits of infantry regiments are . . . often drawn from the refuse of manufacturing towns, for instance from destitute workmen who enroll themselves in the army through necessity.'[27] William Cobbett, who enlisted in the West Norfolk Regiment in 1785 and was rapidly promoted to sergeant-major, while complaining of the impossibility of living on the miserable pay, spoke warmly of soldiers, their fundamental decency and lack of hypocrisy. But few of his contemporaries shared his opinions. General Wolfe had described his men as 'dirty, drunken, insolent rascals . . . terrible dogs to look at'. 'I knew their discipline to be bad and their valour precarious,' he had added. 'No nation ever paid so many bad soldiers at so high a rate.' Wellington, whose contempt was mixed with admiration, later described his soldiers as scum who enlisted only for drink.

In the Middle Ages men had been pressed into service whether they were willing to take arms or not. Some of the more adventurous eagerly accepted the pay which was appreciably more than they could have expected for hired labour in their villages. But, although they were rarely kept on active service for more than three months at a stretch, most peasants were reluctant to accept the summons of the King's Commissioners of Array even when pay was offered in advance. Desertions were common. Of 16,000 men ordered to be at Carlisle in June 1300, only 3000 were still under the king's command in August. Some had died; others had served their allotted time; but most had crept home.[28] As the fourteenth century progressed, and the wars of Edward III demanded more and more recruits, enrolment became an ever-present danger, and the categories of those liable for muster were widened on occasions to include all able-bodied men between sixteen and sixty.

Since then increasing reliance had been placed upon voluntary service; and, as the rewards of a soldier's life were so meagre and conditions often intolerable, few except vagrants and vagabonds were persuaded to enlist. There was a time after the Civil War when the New Model Army had imposed the strictest discipline upon its troops, when soldiers, if not popular, were generally respected. But the moral fervour associated with the New Model Army had soon evaporated, and soldiers, billeted in private houses where they were frequently drunk and violent, became more disliked than ever. After the Restoration, despite the strong prejudice against it, a standing army was achieved and by the Militia Act of 1661 the management of national defence was placed in the hands of the king. But recruits remained of a very low standard. As Defoe observed, 'the poor starve, thieve or turn to soldier'; and when insufficient numbers joined through necessity, the ranks were made up with imprisoned debtors, drafted into the service and with unemployed or 'notoriously idle' men sent to the colours by magistrates with statutory powers of enlistment. In the American War crisis of 1779 orders were issued to press all London's rogues and vagabonds into the army.[29] Samuel Johnson considered that felons and life guardsmen were equally undesirable in respectable society.

Since the billeting of troops in private houses had been declared illegal in the reign of William III, however, the public at large had had less cause for complaint about the behaviour of troops; and as more barracks were built, and rooms in taverns and inns were less often commandeered, soldiers and civilians tended to regard each other with less resentment. Indeed, for a time during the Napoleonic wars soldiers were accorded the wary respect that had formerly been reserved for sailors. Even so, the conditions in which most of them were required to live when stationed at home were often deplorable. Married men – limited to six in a company – were allocated a corner of the barrack room where blankets or screens of canvas were hung up between the beds. For almost 100 years since the end of the seventeenth century pay had been fixed at 2s 6d a day for cavalry troopers, 1s 6d for dragoons and 8d for private soldiers in the infantry. Out of this the men had to feed themselves, and, in the case of mounted troops, their horses. Moreover, various deductions were exacted from time to time, one shilling in the pound for Chelsea Hospital, for example, payments for medicines and subscriptions to regimental auditors for purposes not always well defined. Pay had been increased in 1797 so that all troops thereafter were entitled to at least a shilling a day; there were also enlistment bounties of four or five guineas and a bread allowance of 1½d a day. But the bounties were soon spent, and for most soldiers their pay proved quite inadequate. Furthermore, uniforms were extremely uncomfortable and tight-fitting, while the powdered and clubbed pigtails, which were officially abolished in 1804 but which did not finally disappear until 1814, not only caused discomfort but endless trouble. Flogging was a constant threat. In 1809 Cobbett was sentenced to two years' imprisonment for taking up in his *Political Register* the case of a soldier who had received 500 lashes for alleged mutiny; and such punishments were far from uncommon. Sentences of 2000 lashes were not unknown. In 1836 the Articles of War limited a sentence by a general court martial to 200 lashes and a sentence by a regimental court martial to 100. But the maximum number of lashes were frequently imposed, and the whole regiment was paraded to watch them being applied. In the 1860s a young officer described a flogging witnessed by 600 troops at Aldershot. Many of them were young soldiers and over 100 fainted. Officers, too, fell out and 'tried to recover their composure while sitting on the shafts of empty carts'.[30]

There was still an unbridgeable gulf between officers and their men. Reforms carried out by the Duke of York as Commander-in-Chief had improved the quality of officers. A Royal Military College had been established, and, while infantry and cavalry officers continued to purchase their commissions – until the reforms carried out by Edward Cardwell, Secretary for War between 1868 and 1874 – artillery and engineer officers were not required to buy rank or promotion, though promotion did for them, as often as not, depend upon seniority rather than merit. Yet after the Crimean War, in which the failings of the army had been painfully revealed, the chasm between officers and men remained as wide as ever, the officers being almost exclusively upper class or upper middle class from the older public schools or such more recent schools as Wellington – which, founded in 1856, supplied more cadets to the Royal Military College at Sandhurst than any other – the other ranks still being recruited from the lowest ranks of society and from the half starved poor in the towns and villages of Ireland: in 1878, 39,121, soldiers out of 178,064 in the army were Irish. A sergeant in the 13th Regiment calculated that out of every 120 recruits, eighty were 'labourers and mechanics out of employment' who turned to the army for support, sixteen were idle men who thought that a soldier's life might prove an easy one, nine were either criminals or bad characters falling back on the army as a last resort, and eight were discontented and restless men in search of a more varied existence. Only two out of every 120, in this sergeant's opinion, were respectable men who had joined the army because misfortune had driven them to it, and only one was motivated by ambition.[31] A generation later, towards the end of the century, this was still largely true. In a study of late Victorian poverty it was estimated that 90 per cent of all recruits were working class, 7 per cent former shop assistants or clerks and only one per cent from the 'servant-keeping class'.[32] It was now accepted that Tommy Atkins was quite likely to be a decent enough fellow at heart, as he often appeared in the poems and stories of Rudyard Kipling, but he was still more likely to be regarded as a creature to be pitied rather than admired and, as Kipling himself admitted, 'single men in barracks don't grow into plaster saints'. Notices could still be seen in the windows of public houses warning: 'Men in uniform not admitted.'[33]

Reforms in the army were, however, slowly being made, though pensions remained low and pay meagre. Medical services, for instance, were gradually improving to deal with soldiers whose health was far poorer than that of the civilian population and whose rate of death from tuberculosis alone was five times that of the people as a whole. In 1859 flogging was restricted to a limited number of offenders; nine years later it was decreed that it could be inflicted only on active service; and the last flogging took place in 1881. Education in the army also improved; by 1871 school attendance had been made compulsory for recruits and every major garrison had a library and several had writing- and reading-rooms. Between 1858 and 1899 the literacy rate among recruits rose rapidly; while the number of officers attending the Staff College, established in 1858, also increased. Drunkenness was less widespread, while regimental temperance societies and the Army Temperance Association became more influential. And sports which were shared by all ranks, as were amateur theatricals, helped to bridge the divide that separated officers from men.

At the same time the barrier between the army and the nation as a whole was becoming less marked, particularly so after the Anglo-Boer War of 1899–1902 in which almost half the combatants on the British side, apart from colonial troops, were volunteers (later territorials), yeomanry and militia.[34] During the First World War the barrier almost disappeared altogether, since most soldiers were by then in any case either volunteers or conscripted from civilian life. There were also by then many more officers who had risen from the ranks. In his day the career of William Robertson – who had enlisted as a lancer in 1877, was promoted troop sergeant-major in 1885, commissioned in 1888 and died a field-marshal – was highly unusual; but by 1918 there were numerous officers of field rank who had joined the army as privates.

After the First World War, however, the army was again dissociated from the nation at large. For most officers their careers once more became of less interest than their sporting and social pleasures, while for other ranks a soldier's life was usually seen, as it had been in the past, as an escape from poverty and unemployment. There was to be another war before attitudes changed yet again.

# 59 · *Homes and Holidays*

In 1925, in the publication *Metro-Land*, a Middlesex builder advertised for sale 'Semi-Detached Brick Built Villas within 3 minutes of North Harrow, 5 minutes West Harrow Stations. Train journey about 16 minutes to Baker Street or Marylebone'. The three-bedroomed houses with bow windows to ground and upper floors, electric light, 'large gardens' and 'facilities for garage' were offered for £750 leasehold, and £920 freehold. Four-bedroomed houses were also advertised from £950 to £1450. Rates were 8s in the pound, and advances were granted on the properties by the Middlesex County Council under the Housing Acts 1890–1924. 'Hundreds,' the advertisement claimed, 'have been satisfied.'[1]

The Housing Act of 1924 was the most recent of several Acts which had encouraged house building by granting subsidies. An earlier Act of 1922 had subsidized building by private firms; and the 1924 Act had subsidized houses built by local authorities. By the late 1930s well over 300,000 houses were being built every year; and when war was declared in 1939 more than 4 million houses had been built since 1918, about half of them for sale, most of the rest for rent by local councils. By 1940 the total amount outstanding on mortgages was nearly £700 million; and there were 1.5 million borrowers in the country, one in eight of all families, many of whom had been required to put down no more than £25 as a deposit. The houses they occupied in the sprawling suburbs that encircled the large towns were neat and comfortable. The specifications for a typical semi-detached house erected in North Ilford in 1934 and costing £745 had three bedrooms, all with electric fires; a bathroom with 'white glazed tiles to dado height', 'porcelain enamelled bath with marbled panels', 'lavatory basin bracketed out from wall; heated linen cupboard; heated chromium towel rail. Separate W.C.' On the ground floor the drawing-room (16ft 3in. by 11ft 9in.) had a fireplace with tiled surround and mahogany mantel, and 'a five-light, semi-circular bay window'; the dining-room had casement doors to the garden; both floor and walls of the kitchen were tiled. There was a gas cooker in the kitchen and electric power points in most rooms.[2]

While such houses were being built all over the country, efforts were being made to control their environment. At the beginning of the First World War the Town Planning Institute had demanded 'the emancipation of all communities from the beast of ugliness';[3] and by the end of the 1930s, various approved urban and rural schemes had been brought into operation under the Town and Country Planning Act of 1932. Garden cities had been created on the lines of Welwyn Garden City, which had been founded in 1920, and Wythenshawe near Manchester where 7000 houses had been built before 1939. On the outskirts of London, garden suburbs had appeared, among them Hampstead Garden Suburb laid out by Raymond Unwin and Barry Parker – designers of Letchworth Garden City – on some 250 acres between Golders Green and East Finchley. And the Green Belt Act of 1938 created around London a broad band of mostly farmland, parkland and recreation ground in which building development was to be carefully controlled, the pleasures of the countryside were to be provided within easy reach of the city-dweller, and the unrestricted growth of the tentacles of the metropolis were to be prevented from spreading into the so far undeveloped landscape.

For the poor, however, housing conditions were often still pitiably inadequate; and despite the large number of new council houses, two-thirds of all householders continued to pay rent to private landlords, a large proportion of them having to part with as much as a third of their incomes for inadequate accommodation, in many cases without a piped water supply. Overcrowding remained a major problem in many large cities, particularly in the north. Nearly 50,000 people were severely overcrowded in Manchester, almost 40,000 in Leeds and 68,000 in Birmingham; while in County Durham 20 per cent of the population were overcrowded, and the proportion was even higher in parts of London. The 1931 census revealed that as many as 35 per cent of the population in England and Wales as a whole were living more than two to a room, and 15 per cent more than three to a room. Nearly half the families in Islington, Finsbury and Shoreditch were sharing their houses, with two or even three families to a house; and in Stepney over 50,000 people were living two or more to a room.[4]

Towards the end of the 1930s, however, conditions did begin slowly to improve in most places. In York, for example, most slums had been demolished and replaced; overcrowding had been reduced to 2 per cent of the population; and a piped water supply and satisfactory drainage were almost universal. Here and elsewhere there would have been further improvements had it not been for the outbreak of war. During the war the house completion rate dropped from 330,000 a year to about 5000 in 1944–5; and, while numerous houses due for demolition had to be left standing, over 450,000 other houses were destroyed in air raids or rendered uninhabitable. When the war ended the housing shortage was one of the most urgent problems that the new government had to face.

Parked outside increasing numbers of suburban houses in the 1930s there was a small motor-car. The figure of 132,000 cars in 1914 had increased to about 2 million by 1939; while interest in cars – fostered by the Motor Show, first held at Earl's Court in 1937 – had spread and deepened all over the country. As well as becoming more numerous, cars were also becoming cheaper. In 1932 an Austin Seven could be bought for less than £120, not much more than half its price ten years before; and it could be driven at far higher speeds than were permitted before the speed limit was raised from twenty-two miles an hour in 1930. Accidents were, however, common. There were over 7000 road deaths in 1934 – the year before driving tests were introduced – scarcely less than the 7779 deaths in 1972, though there were by then eight times as many vehicles on the roads.[5]

In the evenings many of the family cars of the 1930s could be seen parked outside cinemas. It had already been estimated in 1917, when there were well over 3000 cinemas in the country, that about half the population went to the cinema once a week. The number of cinemas rose to nearly 5000 in 1939 and many of these could accommodate over 4000 people, the cheapest seats costing no more than sixpence. By then some 20 million tickets were being sold every week. Every large town had several cinemas. In York there were ten in 1939 and half the population went to one or other of them once a week.[6] Returning to Bolton in the 1980s, Leslie Halliwell, the historian of the cinema, discovered that only one cinema survived; in his youth there had been twenty-eight.[7]

The influence of the cinema was pervasive. According to the *New Survey of London Life and Labour*, it could be traced not only 'in the clothes and appearance of the women' but also 'in the furnishings of their houses':

> Girls copy the fashion of their favourite film star . . . In all classes of society they wear 'Garbo' coats and wave their hair *à la* Norma Shearer or Lilian Harvey. It is impossible to measure the effect the films must have on the outlook and habits of the people . . . Certainly today the cinema is *par excellence* the people's amusement.[8]

Although it did not rival the cinema as a mass entertainment, broadcasting was also becoming popular. Five years after the British Broadcasting Company's daily programmes started from Savoy Hill in 1922, well over 2.25

million licences had been issued at 10s each; and by the late 1930s there were over 8 million. Wireless sets could be purchased for £1 and, while John Reith, the first Director-General of the BBC, maintained that to have exploited 'so great an invention for the pursuit and purpose of entertainment alone would have been a prostitution of its powers', popular entertainment was offered, dance music as well as classical music. Indeed, in the 1930s such dance bands as those of Jack Payne and Henry Hall could be heard every night, and more people listened to them than went to dance-halls, popular as these were, particularly the larger and celebrated places like the Palais de Danse in Hammersmith, the first to enable those who came alone to hire partners.

While middle-class people tended to go out more often in the evenings than their parents and grandparents had done, the hours spent in reading at home seem to have increased rather than diminished. Certainly far more books, newspapers and magazines were published per capita than ever before. Nearly 15,000 books were published in 1939 compared with just over 8,500 in 1914; and almost 27 million books were sold in 1939, over three times as many as had been sold ten years before. In the same period borrowings from public libraries increased at an even greater rate, from about 85 million in 1924 to more than 247 million in 1939.[9]

As well as public libraries there were mobile libraries and commercial libraries varying in size from the small stock held by village shopkeepers to the large stores available at branches of Boot's chemist shops. Book clubs prospered, and in 1935 Allen Lane published the first Penguins, sixpenny paperbacks.

Magazines proliferated, children's magazines like the *Boy's Own Paper*, *Rainbow*, *Dandy*, *Beano* and *Film Fun*; women's magazines such as *Woman's Journal*, *Woman and Home*, *The Lady*, *Woman's Own* and, most widely read of all, *Woman* launched in 1937 and costing 2d; political and literary weeklies, including the *Spectator*, a survivor from 1828, and the *New Statesman*, founded in 1913; magazines which came to be known as glossies, among them *Harper's Bazaar* and *Vogue*; magazines for country people like *Field* and *Country Life*; magazines containing pictures of smart parties such as those in the *Tatler*; news magazines of which *Picture Post*, with a circulation of more than 2 million in 1939, was by far the most successful; and a bewildering variety of specialist magazines catering for bird fanciers, model-makers, stamp collectors, cyclists, cinemagoers, gardeners, golfers, publicans and sinners.

Sales of newspapers also increased dramatically, notably those of the popular national newspapers. The *Daily Express* was selling nearly 2.5 million copies a day in 1939; the *Daily Herald* about 2 million; and the

*Daily Mail* (established by Lord Northcliffe in 1896 and selling initially at
½d) and *Daily Mirror* about 1.5 million each. Circulation of the so-called
'quality' papers was also growing rapidly: *The Times*, which had sold less
than 50,000 copies a day before the First World War, was now selling
213,000, the *Daily Telegraph* 640,000 compared with 230,000. The two
Sunday newspapers, the *News of the World* and *The People*, sold more than
7 million copies between them. In 1939 it was estimated that, in all, nearly
70 per cent of the population over sixteen years old read a national newspaper and over 80 per cent a Sunday paper.[10]

While more money than ever before was spent on reading, so it also was
on holidays.

Sea-water, so an eighteenth-century Brighton doctor, Richard Russell, had
advised, was a sovereign remedy for all kinds of complaints from tumours
and abscesses to tuberculosis and gonorrhoea. It was beneficial both to
bathe in it and to drink it, either on its own, a pint or so before breakfast, or
in conjunction with concoctions of crabs' eyes, vipers' flesh, burned
sponge, cuttlefish bones, snails and woodlice.[11] After 1850 very few people
were to be found who continued to advocate sea-water as a medicine, but
sea bathing was becoming increasingly popular. Indeed, bathing had been
recommended as a cure long before Dr Russell's day and at least as early as
1735 bathing-machines – small sheds on wheels in which the occupants
were dragged by horses into the water – were in use on the beach at
Scarborough and were soon afterwards to be seen at Brighton and other
seaside resorts.[12]

These resorts were gradually replacing the inland spas as fashionable
holiday retreats. King George III had favoured Weymouth where no
sooner had 'he popped his royal head under water than a band of music,
concealed in a neighbouring machine, struck up "God save great George
our King"'.[13] His son, the Prince of Wales, preferred Brighton; his daughter-in-law, Princess Caroline, went to Worthing; his granddaughter,
Princess Charlotte, was taken to Southend and Bognor; and his great-
granddaughter, Princess Victoria, later spent childhood holidays at Ramsgate and Broadstairs.

It was not until the coming of cheap public transport, however, that
these places were frequented by the common people. Before that the poor
had been obliged to spend their holidays at home, and while most of them
enjoyed a number of days off work, either on permitted holidays or on such
stolen breaks as 'St Monday' or even 'St Tuesday', the week-long holiday
was very rare. But first cheap steamboats taking passengers to Gravesend
and Southend, Margate and Ramsgate and, from Liverpool, to the Wirral
and Rhyl, and then the railways enabled wage-earners to go to the seaside

for prices they could afford. In the days of the stage-coach it cost about 21s to travel inside from London to Brighton, whereas by 1844 the third-class railway fare was only 4s 2d and in the second half of that year some 360,000 passengers made the journey. In 1859, 73,000 people went to Brighton in one week alone.[14]

Seaside resorts grew rapidly in consequence. The population of Brighton rose from less than 66,000 in 1841 to over 123,000 in 1901; that of Blackpool more than tripled in fourteen years from 1857 and increased from 8000 in 1871 to 47,000 in 1907. Welsh seaside villages grew rapidly into towns, as did the fishing villages of the Isle of Wight.

There was a world of difference socially between these various resorts. In the north Scarborough was described as 'a fashionable watering-place' in the 1840s, and Blackpool at that time was also frequented by the gentry and wealthy merchants of Lancashire. Lytham and St Annes-on-Sea were both developed as residential resorts for the prosperous, while Fleetwood was more favoured by workers in the Lancashire cotton towns. In Wales, the seaside resorts being further away from the large towns, the visitors were more genteel; so were they for the most part in the west of England, except at Weston-super-Mare where day-trippers came from Bristol at 1s a head return: Torquay was considered so far from London that in the 1860s to say that you were going there 'was to create a feeling of envy and astonishment amongst your friends and acquaintances'.[15] There was no branch-line to Lyme Regis, which had been Jane Austen's favourite seaside place, until 1903. And in the 1890s, when Leslie Stephen took his family to Cornwall – his daughter Virginia Woolf ever afterwards considered that to catch a mackerel in a Cornish bay 'was the greatest excitement under the moon' – there was scarcely a working-class holiday-maker ever to be seen along the entire coast.[16]

In the south, so Professor Perkin has observed, resorts within easy reach of London were 'subtly graduated in the social hierarchy of middle-class values':

[Margate was] merely for tradespeople, [its neighbour, Ramsgate, for] the somewhat higher class depicted in broad cloth and silk in W. P. Frith's painting of *Ramsgate Sands*, Dickens's Broadstairs in between, the first self-described 'select' resort for a still superior class, while Gravesend and Southend were 'low', a target for day-tripping clerks, shop assistants and artisans. Eastbourne and St Leonards, on the other hand, were for the social élite and were developed respectively by the Duke of Devonshire and Sir James Burton, the architect, on spacious lines for a superior clientele, for whom even Brighton was too noisy and vulgar.[17]

Bournemouth also prided itself on being highly select. In 1861 its population was no more than 1750. Donkeys were banned on the beach and day excursionists were not encouraged. On Sundays sea bathing was forbidden until 1914; the cafés were closed; the bands did not play and the trams did not run. The Winter Gardens were not opened until 1877; and R. L. Stevenson, who lived here between 1884 and 1887, pronounced that the daily round was as monotonous as a weevil's in a biscuit.[18]

By then in most other seaside resorts, however, great efforts had been made and much money expended on attracting as many visitors as could be accommodated. Piers had been built; zoological gardens laid out; shooting-galleries and waxwork shows created. There were regular performances in music-halls, Punch and Judy shows on the beach; bands played in the pleasure gardens, Nigger Minstrels strummed their banjos on the promenade; and the sellers of ginger beer, whelks and jellied eels set up their stalls.

Frith's *Ramsgate Sands*, which was painted in 1854 and bought by Queen Victoria for Buckingham Palace, depicts the variety of entertainments to be found on the beach. Children are shown paddling and digging in the sand with wooden spades; men read newspapers or peer out to sea through telescopes; the women, in their straw bonnets and crinolines, shaded by their parasols from the harmless rays of the pale sun, work at their embroidery, look at books, pretend not to look at exhibitors of trained mice, and carefully ignore the men selling whelks and ships in bottles. Behind them Nigger Minstrels dance and sing; a Punch and Judy man beats his drum to attract children to the next drama of Jack Ketch the hangman, the Blind Man and Toby the dog; and little girls stand on tiptoe to watch the antics of a performing rabbit.

Bathing was considered more of a health-giving duty than a pleasure. Up till the 1870s it was usual for men to bathe naked, as women, too, had done in the eighteenth century. In 1872 Francis Kilvert found 'a delicious feeling of freedom in stripping in the open air [on the sands at Weston-super-Mare] and running down naked to the sea, where the waves were curling white with foam and the red morning sunshine glowing upon the naked . . . bathers'. But two years later, at Shanklin on the Isle of Wight, Kilvert found that it was no longer considered proper to go into the sea unclothed: men were now expected to adopt what he called the detestable custom of wearing drawers; and by the 1870s even drawers were considered immodest and had been replaced by bathing costumes with three-quarter-length sleeves and legs reaching to the knees.

Ladies dressed themselves in heavy serge with elbow-length sleeves and baggy bloomers concealed by thick, full skirts. In these they stepped from their bathing-machines and, usually concealed from the beach by a hood, they were helped down into the water by male or female dippers, the women – usually fat and frequently drunk – being clothed in waterproof wrappings and a large bonnet.

> A little table on which lay a great book stood within a railing enclosing all the bathing-machines [a Scottish lady recalled of holidays at Ramsgate].
> Each party, on entering the gate of this enclosure, set their names down in the book, and in their turn were conducted to a bathing-machine, roomy boxes upon wheels, shaded at one end by a large canvas hood that reached the water when the horse at the other end had proceeded with it to a sufficient depth; the driver then turned his carriage round with the hood to the sea, and, unhinging his traces, went in search of another fare, leaving the bathers to the care of a woman in a blue flannel jacket and petticoat and a straw bonnet, who soon waded into view from another machine, and lifting up the canvas shade stood ready to assist in the fearful plunge. The shock of a dip was always agony.[19]

Ladies' bathing places were set widely apart from the men's; and at Southport, where they were separated by at least 100 yards, pleasure boats were prohibited on pain of a fine of 5s from approaching within thirty yards of the female area. The beaches, however, were lined with voyeurs with telescopes and opera glasses and 'no more sense of decency than so many South Sea islanders'. At Brighton, before the advent of male bathing costumes, ladies were said to behave with an 'almost heathen indecency', sitting on their camp stools and watching the men emerge from the sea to climb naked up the steps of the machines.[20] Dr A. B. Granville, author of *The Spas of England and Principal Sea-Bathing Places*, considered it a stain upon the gentility of Brighton that men should be permitted thus to expose themselves.

Others considered it far more disgraceful that the accommodation and food provided at seaside resorts was so execrable. Most people stayed in furnished apartments rather than hotels or boarding-houses, but they all seemed to have been almost equally uncomfortable. Jane Carlyle, staying at a hotel in Ryde reputed to be the most expensive in Europe, found that 'the cream was blue milk, the butter tasted of straw and the "cold fowl" was a lukewarm one and was as tough as leather'. She moved out into lodgings only to be plagued by bugs. Nathaniel Hawthorne also found that because a hotel was expensive it was not necessarily good. He was asked to pay like a nabob but was served with 'joints, joints, joints, sometimes perhaps a meat pie which weights upon your conscience, with the idea that you have eaten the scraps of other people's dinners'. 'The dinner was very bad,' wrote a guest at a hotel in Brighton; 'a

sprawling bit of bacon upon a bed of greens; two gigantic antediluvian fowls
. . . a brace of soles that perished from original inability to flounder into the
Ark, and the fossil remains of a dead sirloin of beef.'[21]

At Blackpool it was the usual practice for visitors to rent anything from a
whole house to a single bedroom from a landlady who undertook to cook the
food which the visitors themselves brought in. Overcrowding was commonplace, and three or four people were often crammed into a single bed. 'They
used to be content so long as they were at Blackpool,' said one old resident, 'if
they were crammed a dozen in a bed, but now they grumble if there's only
five.' Another resident, a landlady perhaps letting her imagination run away
with her, observed in 1898, 'They will not be packed together as they used to
be in Blackpool, from eleven to nineteen in a bedroom.'[22]

Hundreds of thousands of visitors avoided this discomfort by coming
down just for the day. Cheap day-tickets had been offered on the Liverpool
and Manchester line as early as 1830; in 1840 the Sunday Schools of
Manchester organized an excursion for 40,000 children on the Leeds and
Manchester Railway; and in 1841 Thomas Cook, a young wood-turner and
Secretary of the South Midland Temperance Association, organized an
excursion from Leicester to a temperance demonstration at Loughborough.
The fare was 1s return and the ticket included tea, ham sandwiches, dancing,
cricket and other games.

> On the day appointed [Thomas Cook recalled] about five hundred passen-
> gers filled some twenty or twenty-five open carriages – they were called
> 'tubs' in those days – and the party rode the enormous distance of eleven
> miles . . . We carried music, and music met us at the Loughborough
> station. The people crowded the streets, filled windows, covered the
> housetops and cheered all along the line . . . All went off in the best style
> and in perfect safety we returned to Leicester; and thus was struck the
> keynote of my excursions.[23]

Soon afterwards outings for workers began to be organized by employers,
some of whom – in nearly all cases those employing clerks and shop assistants
– also started the practice of granting holidays with pay. For all workers there
were more official holidays after the Bank Holiday Act of 1871 which added
to the existing national holidays at Christmas, Good Fridays and Sundays,
extra holidays on Boxing Day, Easter Monday, Whit Monday and the first
Monday in August. At first the observance of these new holidays was far from
general; but within a year the August Bank Holiday, according to *The Times*,
had already acquired 'at least as decisive a popular acceptance as the old
traditional Holydays. Last year . . . people scarcely realized their opportun-

ity. But yesterday [the August Bank Holiday of 1872] was all but universally observed.'[24]

A decade or so later the practice of granting paid holidays began to spread to firms employing manual workers. 'A great proportion' of employees on the London and North Western Railway, for example, received a week's holiday with pay in 1890. But this, it was emphasized, was not a right but a reward for good conduct. And it was not until the next century that holidays with pay became more general. Even so, only 1.5 million workers were enjoying holidays with pay in 1925 when a Bill for compulsory annual paid holidays was introduced into Parliament without success; and in 1938, when the Holidays with Pay Act was passed, less than half the national workforce earning £250 a year or less was receiving the benefits the Act proposed. Yet the total number of families going away on holiday had risen dramatically. In the 1880s, when the average annual earnings of adult male manual workers had been about £60 a year, there had been little to spare in most families for holidays. But since then wages had risen and prices had fallen, so that by 1902 Charles Booth could write that going on holiday was 'one of the most remarkable changes in habits in the last ten years'.[25] In 1934, according to *The New Survey of London Life and Labour*, about half the work people in the capital were taking holidays away from home; and in 1937 the total number of holiday-makers away from home for a week or more was estimated to be 15 million.[26]

The holiday resorts grew rapidly to cope with the vastly increased summer trade. Blackpool, which was said to be able to accommodate half a million people in a single night and had 7 million visitors a year, had a resident population of over 100,000 in 1931. Brighton's population had risen to 147,000, Southend's to 120,000, Bournemouth's to 116,000, Southport's to 78,000, Hastings's to 65,000 and Eastbourne's to 57,000. The amenities provided by most resorts had much improved and, in many, large sums had been spent in providing swimming pools, carparks, bowling greens, dance-halls, tennis courts and such buildings as Hastings's White Rock Pavilion which was opened in 1927 at a cost of £100,000.[27]

The accommodation available at the seaside was also much more comfortable, and, except in the large hotels, not expensive. At Eastbourne board residence ranged from £2 10s to three guineas a week (£2 a week in the winter);[28] and at Blackpool, where most landladies now provided food themselves, the difference between the minimum rates for apartments and full board was usually a modest 3s 6d. Some landladies, however, clung to the old method. One of these was Mrs Cavanagh whose boarding house in Vance Road in the 1930s was fondly remembered by one of her regular guests:

We used to do our own buying in when we got there and we had a shelf in a cupboard . . . and each day we would go and buy our own meat or fish for the day and Mrs Cavanagh did all the cooking and everything was lovely. Mr Cavanagh was in the background doing all the washing up etc. We went each year and she had something altered in the house each time. We still went after we were married and it cost us 28s per week for a double bed and all the cooking . . . We went thirteen years running three times a year, it was like home from home. I remember one very wet day and Mrs Cavanagh said you all have no need to go out at all. After dinner was cleared she brought out the cards, and we were all having such a good time when who should come in but the landlady, a white bucket filled with ice cream and wafers to go with it, she had been to Pablo's round the corner and had it filled. She was a grand person and there was always tears as we had to leave. My husband was the only chap she would give a pint pot of tea to, all the others had to have cups.[29]

Even in the more select resorts the social atmosphere was now much more relaxed, with bands playing on Sundays, motor omnibuses running and holiday-makers swimming. Mixed bathing was now universally permitted – it had been allowed at Bexhill as early as 1902 – and tents or cabins on the beach had replaced bathing-machines; in most places it was customary for bathers to change in their rooms and then 'cover up' for the walk to the beach – 'mackintosh bathing', it was called.

We used to book up for a week in Southend at a bed and breakfast [one old person recalled of holidays in the 1930s]. You'd have your breakfast and then go out all day. We'd have cockles and mussels with salt and vinegar for tuppence a plate. There'd be stalls all along the road where you could get a basin of eels, winkles or shrimps. The Italians used to make their own 'Hokey-Pokey' [ice-cream]. You'd take a cup to their stall and they'd ask you what flavour you wanted. You'd say 'Top her up, Jack' if they stopped too soon. They would keep it cool in a can surrounded by ice . . . For us Londoners, Southend was the place. If you were a bit richer it was Margate and Ramsgate. If you were very rich you could go to Bournemouth. We never thought of going to places like Spain or Portugal. The only time we heard about such places was when a war was on.[30]

Some richer families went on holidays, parents and children together. Esther Stokes, a girl from an upper-middle-class Roman Catholic family, went every year with her mother and father to Cornwall. They travelled by train from Paddington in a coach which they had to themselves. 'All the family used to be in the front part of this coach and the maids used to be in the back,' she recalled. 'We were very excited about the journey for two reasons, one was that we always had tongue sandwiches . . . and the other was it was the only time we saw the maids without caps . . . All the maids went with us and the caretakers would move into the London house.'[31]

In other families the parents stayed in a hotel with the older children while the younger ones stayed in a boarding-house with their nanny. But in some, like that of Joan Poynder, the daughter of a baronet, 'parents didn't have holidays in that sort of way. They went on shooting parties or stayed with friends or something.'[32]

Many families less well off stayed in holiday camps. One of the earliest of these was Cunningham's Young Men's Holiday Camp which had been established towards the end of the nineteenth century and attracted about 50,000 visitors a year to its site at Douglas on the Isle of Man. Here the campers, all of them men, had to sign a pledge not to drink alcohol during their holiday, nor to use improper language. They slept in candle-lit tents and were expected to join in team-games and communal sing-songs. The camp remained in business, still teetotal and still banning women, until its sale in 1945.[33]

This was not the kind of holiday camp that William Butlin, a travelling showman born in South Africa, envisaged when on holiday in Wales in the early 1920s. He was 'astounded at the way the guests were treated' in the small boarding-house at Barry where he was staying. They were required to leave after breakfast and were 'not made welcome again until dinner in the evening'. 'Watching these unhappy holiday makers [he] thought, "What they need is a place where there are things to do when it rains".'[34]

Some years later Butlin bought a sugar-beet field for £300 three miles from Skegness where the first Butlin's Holiday Camp opened in 1936, the guests paying 35s to £3 a day, according to the time of the season, for accommodation, three meals a day and free entertainment. The next year a second Butlin's camp was built at Clacton, and 'Butlin Special' trains were run to take campers there. Soon there were further Butlin's camps at Filey and Pwllheli; and by 1939 there were as many as 200 holiday camps in all in the country with rooms for 30,000 people a week. The Butlin camps alone had 100,000 guests that year.

J. A. R. Pimlott, author of *The Englishman's Holiday*, described a holiday at the Clacton holiday camp where a camp commandant was assisted by house captains and ' "Red coats", so called from their blazers, whose main job is to organize the entertainments'. In addition to these supervisors there were two orchestras

and other full-time entertainers including the Frogmen (under-water swimmers), a theatre organist, 'Uncle Mac' (entertaining the 'Kiddies'), and a camp cartoonist. The chief radio announcer and his assistants are responsible for Radio Butlin which has an important role in the whole organization. There are a number of other entertainers, apart from visiting artists, and a whole host of employees are engaged upon catering, cleaning, maintenance and administration . . . Discipline does not present a serious problem. On the whole the campers are well contented, but at the least sign of rowdiness or other misconduct a firm hand is applied, and where necessary the camper's money is returned and he is told to leave.

There were games and coach trips, swimming and dancing competitions and 'organized ambles', campers' concerts, 'grand carnivals' with decorated motor-cars and bicycles, 'Kiddies' Fun', parades of 'Holiday Lovelies', fancy-dress galas and 'Toddlers' Tea Times'. There were billiard rooms, shops, tennis courts, bowling greens, a gymnasium, a Palm Court tea-lounge, a Jolly Roger bar, a Smugglers' Cave Bar and a sick bay. On Sundays divine service was held in the ballroom. The campers slept in chalets. The bathrooms and lavatories were labelled 'Lads' and 'Lassies'. Meals were eaten in two dining-halls accommodating over 600 people at a time at two sittings.[35]

Since nearly all the entertainments were free, campers would not spend much more than £5 or £6 each on a week's stay (children up to ten years old were half price). Yet there were scores of thousands of families for whom such prices were far beyond their means; and many of them went hop-picking in Kent where the conditions in which they lived were often appalling but not much worse than they were used to at home. 'It wasn't a bad life,' wrote George Orwell who went hop-picking himself in the early 1930s. 'But what with standing all day, sleeping rough and getting my hands cut to bits, I felt a wreck at the end of it. It was humiliating to see that most of the people there looked on it as a holiday . . . In fact it is because hopping is regarded as a holiday that the pickers will take such starvation wages.'[36]

Yet there were those who regarded hop-picking not just as a holiday but as a most enjoyable one. 'It was a marvellous holiday,' one old former hop-picker recalled. 'And you were always pleased because you were getting paid for it at the same time.'

A hop-picking holiday gave you health [was another verdict]. The fumes from the hops did you a lot of good. That's why a lot of people went. I'd take the children with me, cooking implements and the necessary food. Parents hid their children under the train seats to avoid paying for them. It wasn't a genteel holiday . . . You'd get up at about six in the morning and see people frying egg and bacon on the embers. We'd pick hops from seven in the morning until six in the evening.[37]

Most children did not much enjoy themselves, though:

I went to the hop-fields once, because the family always went, but it was terrible really. We had to sit or lie of a night-time in a big barn. One night they started saying there was earwigs around. I stayed awake all night. If I'd had cotton wool I'd have put it in my ears, but I hadn't, so I sat up all night with my hands over my ears.[38]

# 60 · Wars and Aftermaths

A few days after war was declared in August 1914 the first recruiting appeal appeared:

YOUR KING AND COUNTRY NEED YOU
A CALL TO ARMS

An addition of 10,000 men to his Majesty's Regular Army is immediately necessary in the present grave National Emergency. Lord Kitchener [the Secretary for War] is confident that this appeal will be at once responded to by all who have the safety of our Empire at heart.[1]

The response was overwhelming. Recruiting offices were at once crowded with volunteers. By the end of the next month 750,000 men had joined up; by the end of the year over a million. In January 1918 the British Army numbered 4.4 million men; and although conscription had been introduced in 1916, the proportion of conscripted soldiers was only about a third of the total mobilized.[2] Workers were as eager to join as young men from the universities and public schools; and, while at first one or two voices were raised in protest, these were soon drowned by the general enthusiasm. 'When one sees young men idling in the lanes on Sunday,' Arnold Bennett, once a pacifist, recorded in his journal, 'one thinks: "Why are they not at war?" All one's pacific ideas have been rudely disturbed. One is becoming militarist.' There were, indeed, very few people in the country who did not wholeheartedly support the war which was, in H. G. Wells's phrase, 'The War that Will End War'.[3]

Propaganda reflected and intensified the public mood. Stories emanating from the government's War Propaganda Bureau – or invented by the proprietors or editors of newspapers whose headlines grew ever larger and blacker – spread hatred of the enemy while glorifying the British cause.

Newspaper stories of German atrocities in Belgium were followed by rumours that soldiers of the 'alien enemy' had cut off the breasts of nurses, that the corpses of slain English soldiers were being rendered down in the Kaiser's laboratories for fat and tallow. Posters depicted a little girl asking her father, 'Daddy, what did you do in the War?' White feathers were handed out by women to young men in civilian clothes. A boxed announcement in the *Daily Mail* advised its readers to 'refuse to be served by an Austrian or German waiter. If your waiter says he is Swiss, ask to see his passport.' Stones were thrown at German dogs. And, when reports that the Kaiser had described the British Expeditionary Force as 'contemptible' were followed in May 1915 by the sinking of the *Lusitania* and the consequent drowning of 2000 passengers, then by the first Zeppelin raids, and, in October, by the execution of the English nurse Edith Cavell, attacks on shops and other property owned by foreigners increased in numbers and intensity. Directed not only against people of German descent, or with German-sounding names, but also against Russians and Jews, Swiss and even Chinese, the riots spread from Manchester to Leeds, from Liverpool to London. Pork butchers' shops were smashed and looted; factories employing foreign labour were besieged; and in London foreign restaurants and the premises of hairdressers came under attack.[4]

The 3000 cinemas in the country, supplied with material by the Cinema Division of the Department of Information, provided a steady flow of propaganda which, while applauding the heroism of the British soldiers and deploring the perfidy of the Germans, glossed over the horrors of the fighting in which they were both engaged and the appalling loss of life. By the end of November 1914 the British had already suffered almost 90,000 casualties; six months later the number had risen to nearly 400,000. When the war was over it was estimated that 850,000 men had been killed; and of the 8 million men who had been mobilized, 2 million had been wounded. In 1922 almost a million war pensions were being paid.

A high proportion of the killed and wounded were officers, many of whom had received their commissions on the strength of certificates granted by the Officer Training Corps of the public schools and universities, and many more of whom had gone straight from school to France as second lieutenants before even reaching that not very high standard of efficiency that the granting of a certificate demanded. About one in five of officers from public schools were killed, the exact numbers for Eton being 1157 fatal casualties out of 4852 Old Etonians who served overseas. About one in five of the undergraduates from Oxford and Cambridge who served in the army were also killed; so were one in five of the peerage. By the end of 1914 six peers, ninety-five sons of peers, sixteen baronets, eighty-two sons of baronets, six knights and eighty-four knights' sons had already been killed.[5] The losses among the working classes were proportionately not so severe, partly because many of their occupations excused them from conscription and partly because so large a number of men from poor families failed to pass the standards set by the National Service Medical Boards: in a few industrial areas almost three-quarters of those examined were deemed unfit for overseas duty.

In order to reinforce units depleted by heavy casualties, the government felt obliged to reduce the standards originally set. At first recruits had to be five feet eight inches tall, but this requirement was soon amended to five feet five and then to five feet three. As losses mounted, and since conscription brought in fewer men than had been expected, the ranks of the army were filled with soldiers who in earlier times would have been discharged, or rejected out of hand. Before the war was over even those who had lost a hand or a foot were kept on to perform what duties they could still undertake, while about half the infantry soldiers in France were not yet nineteen years old.

For those who stayed at home there was more than enough work, and wages were considerably higher than they had been before the war. Munitions factories were producing immense quantities of tanks and guns, aeroplanes, rifles and shells not only for Britain's army but also for the armies of its allies, including that of America whose entry into the war was crucial to victory. In these and other factories and workshops the rate of increase in wages for both skilled and unskilled workers was almost unprecedented, since the demands of trade unions were felt to be virtually irresistible when labour was in such short supply. A shipyard riveter, for example, whose wages were 37s 9d a week before the war began, was earning 74s 9d when it was over; while the wages of a bricklayer's labourer rose from 29s 1d to 65s 2d.[6] At the same time prices rose sharply: by June 1915 the cost of food was very nearly a third higher than it had been a year before; and by September 1916 it had risen in large towns by 68 per cent and in villages by 62 per cent. The increase in the cost of some foods was far higher even than this. The price of eggs had almost doubled; and sugar was over one and a half times as expensive as it had been in 1914. There were demonstrations against these increases in different parts of the country; one, organized by the National Union of Railwaymen, took place in Hyde Park in August 1916. But, for most workers, wages rose higher than prices; meals in factory canteens remained reasonable – 'Sausage and Mash, 2½d, Mince and Mash, 2d, Patties 1d, Beans, 1d, Stewed Fruit, 1d, Milk Pudding 1d' – and, despite the high cost of sugar, people were eating more sweets and chocolates than ever.

'There are now no poor in Newcastle-upon-Tyne,' the *Daily Mail* reported; and in the West End of London a shop manager said that his new clientele – 'rather different than before the war . . . hardly so discriminating'

– were 'certainly more free with money': 'Many of our regular West End clients are economizing, but evidently there is a new and prosperous section of the community taking their places. This new section is so well off that no article is approved unless it is costly.'[7]

Similar reports came from shops in much poorer quarters. A man whose mother kept a corner shop in a slummy part of Salford said that 'some of the poorest in the land started to prosper as never before':

> In spite of the war, slum grocers managed to get hold of different and better varieties of foodstuffs of a kind sold before only in middle-class shops and the once deprived began to savour strange delights . . . One of our customers, wife of a former foundry labourer, both making big money now on munitions, airily inquired one Christmas time as to when we were going to stock 'summat worth chewin'. 'Such as what?' asked my father, sour-faced. 'Tins o' lobster,' she suggested, 'or them big jars o' pickled gherkins!'
>
> Furious, the old man damned her from the shop. 'Before the war,' he fumed, 'that one was grateful for a bit o' bread and scrape!'[8]

There could be no doubt, in fact, that many working-class women and children were being better fed than they had been before the war. It was reported in 1918 that School Medical Officers in London had found that the percentage of children 'in a poorly nourished condition' was less than half the percentage in 1913.

The improved lot of women was particularly noticeable. As men left for the front there was far more work for women to do and opportunities to demonstrate that they could do it well. They worked for as much as £2 a week in munitions factories: almost a million of them were doing so by the end of the war, compared with just over 200,000 at the beginning; they worked in the auxiliary branches of the armed services; they worked on the land; they worked as nurses – there were 45,000 nurses in 1917 – they were employed in clerical work and as bus conductresses. The numbers of conductresses rose from a few hundred in 1914 to 2500 in 1918, those of female clerks and typists from 33,000 to 102,000. 'No woman worker is in greater demand than the shorthand typist,' the *Daily Mail* reported as early as September 1915. Her wages had risen from £1 to 35s a week and she could be seen 'dining out alone or with a friend in the moderate-priced restaurants in London' and 'smoking the customary cigarette'. The growing independence and self-confidence of women was noted in other ways. 'They appear more alert, more critical of the conditions under which they work, more ready to make a stand against injustice than their pre-war selves,' the *New Statesman* commented. 'They have a keener appetite for experience and pleasure and a tendency . . . to protest against wrongs even before they become "intolerable".'[9] They took to wearing shorter skirts – 'extraordinarily short' in many cases, one newspaper noted disapprovingly – revealing not only feet and ankles but 'even more of the stockings'. Some went so far as to emulate the girls who worked on the land and who wore trousers after they had finished work as well as in the fields and cow-sheds. Many others abandoned the old-fashioned camisole for the brassière, an item but recently admitted to the catalogue of fashionable shops. Most spent a good deal more on make-up than they would have dreamed of doing before the war.

The contribution which women made to the war effort was recognized by political concessions. Before the outbreak of war the women's movement had not progressed far since the publication in 1792 of Mary Wollstonecraft's feminist manifesto, *A Vindication of the Rights of Women*. Admittedly, the social position of women had constantly been questioned; and in 1882 the Married Women's Property Act had enabled women to own their own property. But men still controlled women's work and education and continued to deny them the right to vote. A number of Bills intended to extend the franchise to women failed to win sufficient support, and were, indeed, condemned by many women themselves. Queen Victoria's disapproving views on the subject of women's rights were widely shared by her sex. The frustrations which these failures aroused led to the emergence of a militant feminist movement and to the foundation of the Women's Social and Political Union. The demonstrations of the suffragettes, their attacks on property, the death of Emily Wilding Davison after running onto the course at Epsom during the Derby, brought widespread attention to their movement but aroused as much indignation as sympathy. And it was not until the war, when the Women's Social and Political Union threw its influence behind the struggle for victory, and when the essential contribution of women, other than as mothers and housekeepers, to the success of the nation was recognized at last, that the battle for the vote was won. In 1918, the prejudice of some influential anti-feminists being at last overcome, the vote was granted to women aged thirty and over, subject to some educational and property qualifications, by the Fourth Reform Act. This was followed by the Sex Disqualification (Removal) Act of 1919, which ensured that no one should be disqualified from exercising any public office or appointment by sex, and then, in 1928, by an act granting women full voting equality with men.

The war had also forced the country to realize that, just as more should be done by the State for women, so should more attention be paid to the needs of children, the number of whom aged fourteen and under in work had increased by four times during the war. In 1918 the first important Education Act for fifteen years raised the school-leaving age to fourteen, and the Minister of Education, H. A. L. Fisher, insisted that a child's education should continue after this age and that parents should not be required to pay fees in state elementary schools.

In the years following the war, however, many of Fisher's hopes remained unrealized. Almost three-quarters of children between the ages of eleven and fourteen in elementary schools were receiving no advanced instruction, merely a repetition of lessons they had already been taught. Only just over 5 per cent were being given advanced instruction and only one in 200 was at a junior technical school. Almost a quarter contrived to leave school before they were fourteen. As few as 7 per cent managed to reach the grant-aided secondary schools. Six per cent attended private schools, including the public schools.

The number of young people who went on to university was extremely small, less than eight students for every 10,000 people in the country in 1926 and of these only just over a quarter were girls. Most of them came from a very small selection of schools even after the founding of new university colleges such as those at Exeter and Southampton, Nottingham and Leicester. Less than five in 1000 children from state elementary schools reached university at all.

The school-leaving age was due to be increased to fifteen on 3 September 1939 but it was on that day that war broke out again. The measure had to be postponed as a fifth of the country's schools were destroyed in air raids; and it was not until the Education Act of 1944 that secondary education for all children became a reality.

As well as accelerating the women's movement towards equality with men and prompting advances in education, the war at once strengthened the trade-union movement and stimulated demands for social reform. 'For the first time in the history of this country since the Black Death,' the prime minister was told in 1915, 'the supply of labour has not been equal to the demand.' It was a situation of which the trade unions were quick to take advantage. There were times when the unions – several of whose leaders became associated with, or even members of, the government – seemed close to losing touch with their members; and on Clydeside and elsewhere unofficial strikes were repeatedly called by shop stewards in defiance of union executives. Yet by the end of the war the number of those belonging to trade unions had risen from just over 4 million to well over 6.5 million; and in 1920 stood at 8.3 million; while the percentage of women who were members of unions rose from only 8 per cent to over 20 per cent, an increase largely due to the flight of women from occupations which were not organized, such as domestic service.[10] Thereafter governments were increasingly obliged to pay careful notice to the demands of organized labour as well to the people's demands for social reform. A Ministry of Reconstruction was established in order to investigate such matters as housing which had been a principal cause of much social unrest during the war; Ministries of Pensions and Health were also created; and after Lloyd George won a general election, in which the issues of public welfare played a crucial part, a serious attempt was made to reduce the still immense gap between the rich and the poor by increases in death duties and in taxes upon high incomes. Income tax which had stood at 1s 2d in the pound in 1913–14 had risen to 6s by 1918–19; and, whereas a man with an earned income of £10,000 a year had paid only just over 8 per cent of it in tax before the war, he was obliged to part with more than 40 per cent by the time the war was over. A man with an unearned income of £10,000 had been able to keep about £8000 in 1913, but by 1919 he was left with less than £5000 after tax had been paid.[11]

In the months immediately following the war there was widespread unrest in the country. Militant members of trade unions threatened and organized strikes. There were race riots in several seaports; violent disturbances at army camps over the slow rate of demobilization; and clashes between the police and crowds of young people. The town hall was burned down at Luton; shops in Liverpool, where the police went on strike, were smashed and looted; troops and tanks were sent into the streets of Clydeside. In February 1919 the miners, railwaymen and the transport workers joined forces in the so-called 'Triple Alliance' which had been making plans for a general strike in the autumn of 1914 and which now renewed the call for unified action. The miners were prepared for a fight to the finish; but on Friday 5 April 1921, 'Black Friday' as it came to be known, the transport and railway unions, under more conciliatory leadership, called off their strike; and the miners, left on their own, were defeated. Thereafter wages fell in other industries, too, on some occasions after an unsuccessful strike, on others after ineffectual threats of strike action.

The post-war boom was over. *The Economist* declared that 1921 was 'one of the worst years of depression since the industrial revolution'; and by June that year the numbers of unemployed passed 2 million.[12] Yet, as Asa Briggs has observed, there was 'little pressure inside England for revolutionary change'. The Labour Government which came to power in 1924 did nothing to suggest that it wished to carry through a radical programme.

Nor did a second minority Labour government in office from 1929 to 1931 . . . Indeed, faced with economic crisis, Labour's prime minister, Ramsay MacDonald, who had been a pacifist during the War, chose (without a general election) to head a 'national' government consisting predominantly of Conservatives. Clearly the social framework of the country, by then tested by severe economic depression, had not changed as much as many of the commentors of 1919 and 1920 had suggested. Nor should the General Strike called on 3 May 1926 in support of the miners, a unique event in English history, be considered evidence to the contrary.[13]

The call to strike was at first completely successful. Scarcely a single trade-union member disobeyed it. But the Conservative Government, which had been returned to power in 1924 under Stanley Baldwin, was able to call upon thousands of volunteers to drive buses and trains, unload ships and to act as special constables. The official *British Gazette* attained a circulation of 2 million, while other newspapers – which might have advanced opinions in support of the strikers – remained unpublished. The British Broadcasting Corporation supported the view that the strike was unconstitutional, allowing the prime minister to broadcast but not the eloquent A. J. Cook, General Secretary of the Miners' Federation, or other strikers' leaders. On 12 May the strike was called off unconditionally, to the 'intense relief' of the people everywhere, in the words of the editor of the Labour newspaper, the *Daily Herald*. By the end of the year the miners had been forced to accept lower earnings and an eight-hour day.[14]

From now until the Second World War mass unemployment was a constant shadow over English life, there being never fewer than a million people out of work and, in 1922–3, nearly 3 million, a quarter of the insured working population as compared with 3,177,200 in April 1985 representing just over 11 per cent of the workforce. Moreover, as John Stevenson has observed, since official statistics excluded large groups of workers – among them farmworkers, the self-employed and married women – the total numbers were almost certainly higher than the government's figures revealed.[15] To obtain unemployment benefit under the National Insurance Scheme, which had been introduced in 1911, it was necessary to attend a labour exchange every day. A man with a wife and three children might then receive 23s a week, about a third of the average wage earned by those in work. But many workers, agricultural labourers among them, were not covered by National Insurance and these, when they lost their jobs, had to turn to the Poor Law or to private charity. Meagre as they already were, unemployment benefits were reduced after the financial crises of 1931, and to obtain any 'dole' at all after six months – during which he had to prove he was genuinely seeking work even in those areas where no work was available – a man was obliged to undergo a means test carried out by an official of the Public Assistance Committee who was authorized to enter his house to establish that he was not living in undue comfort, to inquire into the amount of his savings and of any wages or pensions received by other members of his family. The most he could receive, having passed the means test, was 15s 3d a week; and many thousands of unemployed were considered ineligible even for this. After months of unemployment, usually depressed and bored and often ill-fed, men tended to fall into apathy; and those who witnessed the 'hunger marches' were struck as much by the looks of despair in the eyes of the men who tramped down from the north and from Wales through the Home Counties to London as by their thin, white faces and the poor clothes hanging from their bony shoulders.

The Communist-backed National Unemployed Workers Movement, which organized most of the marches, had as many as 100,000 members at one time; yet this was but a very small proportion of the total of unemployed, and its leaders blamed the apathy of those who did not join it as much as they blamed the Labour Party for its lack of wider support. Drawn neither to the extreme Left nor to the extreme Right of the British Union of Fascists, which, founded by Sir Oswald Mosley in 1932, had less than 50,000 members, most of the unemployed waited in silent resignation for better days to come.

Deeply sunk in poverty though so many of them were, the unemployed were, however, not alone in their plight. In some industries in the 1920s and 1930s wages were so low that a man might even be better off on 'the dole' than in work. Agricultural labourers who were earning about £48 a year on average in 1906, were getting no more than £82 in 1924 and £89 in 1935, despite the rise in the cost of living; and over a quarter of the entire employed population in 1938 were earning less than £2 10s a week. Domestic servants frequently had no more then £1, some had no more than 5s; shop assistants commonly had to make do with 10s a week. Surveys carried out between 1924 and 1937 in various towns on Merseyside, in London, Bristol and York suggested that an unacceptably high proportion of the population was living in circumstances ranging from 'primary poverty' to 'utter destitution'. Seebohm Rowntree estimated that in 1935–6 almost 20 per cent of the people of York could be described as poor. Herbert Tout came to similar conclusions after a study of conditions in Bristol in 1937.

Survival for the poor was both a struggle and a challenge; and experience and ingenuity were often needed. After his bankruptcy Helen Forrester's father was driven to discover how essential it was to know the ropes of poverty in Liverpool:

> There were agencies in the town, he was told, which would provide the odd pair of shoes or an old blanket for a child. There were regimental funds willing to provide a little help to old soldiers. He gathered other scraps of

information, which were revelations to a man who had never had to think twice about the basic necessities of life. An open fire, he was assured, could be kept going almost all day from the refuse of the streets, old shoes, scraps of paper, twigs, wooden boxes, potato peelings; if one was very ill or had a broken bone, the outpatients departments of most of the local hospitals would give some medical care. Pawnbrokers would take almost anything saleable, and one could buy second-hand clothing from them. Junk yards would sometimes yield a much needed pram wheel or a piece for an old bike.[16]

Middle-class people from homes like that of this man's childhood were as unaware of conditions in the poorest homes of large towns as Dickens's 'amazing Alderman' was unaware of the real existence of the slum known as Jacob's Island which was described in *Oliver Twist*. And when the Second World War led to the arrival in country districts of families evacuated from city slums, the owners of houses who were asked to take them in were appalled by their dirty, inadequate clothes, their skin diseases and head-lice, their extraordinary tastes in food, their incomprehensible accents and their 'insanitary habits', such as defecating on newspapers which were then wrapped up and thrown on the fire, a practice which, so it was believed, resulted from a reluctance in their own families to use a communal outdoor lavatory. In all about 1.5 million of those who were eligible under the official evacuation scheme chose to take advantage of it – another 2 million made private arrangements – but most of them liked the country no better than many of their hosts liked them. And by the end of 1939 almost a million of them, encouraged by the evident reluctance or inability of the Germans to carry out the air raids that had been predicted, were thankful to go home.

While poverty remained an intractable problem in Britain between the wars, the majority of the people lived in relative comfort, real wages for those in reasonably well paid regular employment in the 1920s having gone up 20 per cent since the war and the average working week having been reduced from fifty-five to forty-eight hours. Several major industries were in decline, but other, newer ones were growing fast. The output of coal fell sharply in the late 1920s and early 1930s; so did its export, particularly to France, formerly one of the industry's best customers, which was now receiving coal from Germany by way of reparations. Seams had been exhausted by the immense demand of the war years; and oil was becoming recognized as an alternative fuel. Although 40 per cent of Britain's merchant fleet had been lost in the war, shipbuilding, after the needs of peace-time trade had been met, came to a complete halt. Cotton exports slumped dramatically; so did those of iron and steel; manufacturing production generally continued to fall while that of

America, which had risen by over 20 per cent in the war, and that of Japan, which had gone up by over three-quarters, continued to increase rapidly. There was some recovery of earlier losses by 1935; but by 1937 Britain's share of world trade, which had been a third in 1870 and a seventh in 1914, had fallen still further to a tenth. And, after the collapse of the New York Stock Exchange in 1929, the total value of British exports fell from £729.3 million in that year to £390.6 million in 1931, and unemployment rose to new heights. Yet the motor vehicle, chemical, construction, textile, printing, consumer and electricity supply industries were all expanding fast and providing work for large numbers of well-paid men and women. The electricity industry alone was employing over 350,000 people by 1939 when two-thirds of the houses in the country were lit by electric light; even more workers, about 400,000, were employed in making the more than half million motor vehicles produced that year. Large and prosperous industrial combines such as Imperial Chemical Industries and Unilever employed tens of thousands more. So did the new chain stores such as Woolworths, which had opened the company's first English shop in Liverpool in 1909, and Marks and Spencer, which owed their origins to a stall in Leeds market set up by a Polish immigrant in 1884 and which was to have over 250 stores in the country by 1939 when its turnover was ten times as great as it had been a decade earlier. The number employed in the distributive trades generally rose from 1,773,000 in 1920 to 2,039,000 in 1929 and continued to rise thereafter.

As families became smaller in size and as earnings grew, those in regular employment found that their standard of living continued to improve. Workers at Ford's factory at Dagenham could earn £4 or £5 a week in 1935; and, while workers in potteries had less than £4 a week and miners rather less than £3, prices were low enough for most working-class families in receipt of regular wages to live without hardship, spending far more on fresh food – almost twice as much on fresh fruit, vegetables, meat, butter and eggs – than they had done in the past, but also filling their shopping baskets with tinned soups and cornflakes, cocoa and granulated coffee, custard powders and all manner of sweets and chocolates, yet still finding enough money left over to buy clothes, to smoke and to drink, and to pay a far higher proportion of their income on insurance, medical care, trade union subscriptions, and pleasure.

Far more was spent on tobacco than had been before the war. Expenditure rose from about £40 million in 1914 to £204 million in 1939 and £564 million by 1945. By 1948, 80 per cent of men and over 40 per cent of women bought cigarettes, smoking on average about twelve or thirteen a day. The consumption of beer, on the contrary, declined from some 34 million barrels a year in 1910–13 to only about half that amount in the 1930s. The consumption of spirits, which were far more highly taxed than they had been in the past, also fell sharply. And, whereas before the war public houses remained open throughout most of the day – in London from five o'clock in the morning until half an hour after midnight, elsewhere from six in the morning until ten or eleven at night – after the passing of the Intoxicating Liquor (Temporary Restriction) Act in August 1914 licensing authorities were encouraged to impose more limited opening hours. In London 'a transformation of the night scenes' became immediately apparent.

> Great traffic centres, like the Elephant and Castle, at which immense crowds usually lounge about until 1 o'clock, have suddenly become peaceful and respectable [the *Brewers' Gazette* reported]. The police, instead of having to 'move on' numbers of people who have been dislodged from the bars at 12.30 at night, found very little intoxication to deal with.[17]

Other observers, however, were not so impressed by the efficacy of the Act, Lloyd George among them. 'We are fighting Germany, Austria and Drink,' he declared in a speech in March 1915, 'and, as far as I can see, the greatest of these deadly foes is Drink.' In an effort to defeat that particular foe, he prompted the king to give up alcohol for the duration of the war as an example to the people. His Majesty promptly concurred, having his cellars locked and his dinner guests handed a list of soft drinks including ginger ale which Lord Rosebery reluctantly chose as the nearest thing to alcohol he was likely to get and suffered from a fearful attack of hiccups in consequence. Queen Mary's jug of fruit cup was, however, liberally if discreetly spiced with champagne, and the king, himself, when the meal was over, so his eldest son said, retired to his study 'to attend to a small matter of business. The matter in question was tacitly assumed to be a small glass of port.'[18]

Despite the king's well-publicized example, reports of excessive drinking throughout the country continued to disturb the government, and further measures to curb it were deemed necessary. In June 1915, under the comprehensive and widely resented Defence of the Realm Act known as *Dora*, a Central Control Board was established to impose further restrictions upon the sale and consumption of liquor; and soon afterwards, in areas where heavy drinking was thought to be hindering the war effort, the sale of alcohol was forbidden before noon and throughout the afternoon after half past two. The traditional practice of buying drinks for other customers in public houses was also forbidden.

> Yes, no treating [recalled a worker in the East Anglian hay trade]. You couldn't go into a public house, two on you and say, 'Give us two pints o' beer and I'll pay for them.' That was against the law. The pubs got restricted, and it got so they didn't have the beer. Sometimes they weren't

open above two days a week because they never had the beer. It was more or less rationed to them . . . Some of them boys came home here [to Bungay] on leave and would go into a pub. There was a notice up: *Regular Customers Only*, and only one pint! Yes, there were terrible rows down there. Chaps smashed the windows because the landlord wouldn't serve them . . . Before the war some of the pubs would be open all night nearly. Open again at six in the morning. I've been down there [at The Crown in Carlton] at 6.30 in the morning and seven or eight of 'em have been drunk as lords. There was more beer spilled on the floor then than is drunk now.[19]

By limiting the sale of beer, decreasing gravity – though the price increased from 3d a pint to as much as 10d – restricting the sale of spirits, and controlling opening hours, the government did eventually manage to reduce the incidence of drunkenness throughout the country. In 1914 average weekly convictions for drunkenness had been 3388 in England and Wales; by the end of 1918 they had dropped to 449; and after the war they remained far lower than they had been before it. It was still possible in some districts to find public houses open all day long and far into the night, but after the Licensing Act of 1921 this was no longer the case. By then drunkenness, previously 'half admired as a sign of virility', was regarded 'as, on the whole, rather squalid and ridiculous'.[20]

Just as the First World War had a profound effect upon people's drinking habits, so it changed certain attitudes towards sexual morality. One of the most popular songs of the war years was 'There's a Girl for Every Soldier'; and in most towns soldiers on leave found this to be only too satisfactorily true, although many of those who had gone so far as to marry in haste lived to regret their imprudence. There were almost three times as many divorces in 1920 as there had been in the years immediately before the war.

There were also far more men and women who had had some kind of sexual experience before marriage. One survey suggested that, while less than 20 per cent of married women born before 1904 had had such experience before their marriages, 36 per cent of those born between 1904 and 1914 and almost 40 per cent of those born between 1914 and 1924 had been sexually intimate either with their future husbands or with other men. There was at the same time an increased awareness and tolerance of contraception. Whereas in mid-Victorian times, so it has been estimated, only about a fifth of women practised contraception, well over three-quarters of those who married between 1918 and 1939 did so. And, while in 1900 a quarter of all married women had a baby every year, in 1930 this was true of only one in eight. Apart from total abstention or abstention except at those times when conception was least likely, *coitus interruptus* remained the most common method of birth control; but other methods were becoming more widely known. For the poor there were home-made pessaries manufactured from lard and flour, cocoa-butter and quinine; there were sponges and douches. For those who could afford them there were vaginal syringes; there were diaphragms and by the early 1930s these had been made more reliable by the introduction of improved contraceptive jellies. There were also rubber condoms, so much more effective than the 'armour' with which Boswell had had to make do. By the 1930s 2 million rubber sheaths were being produced by the largest manufacturer in the country and large numbers were also being imported.[21] 'When I left England in 1911,' wrote Sir Robert Bruce Lockhart, 'contraceptives were hard to buy outside London or other large cities. By 1913 every village chemist was selling them.'[22]

When the Second World War broke out, birth control had become respectable. The Roman Catholic Church maintained its opposition to all forms of contraception other than what had become known as the use of the 'safe period'; but the Anglican Church had long since abandoned the teaching that sexual intercourse was permissible only when the procreation of children was intended. The Ministry of Health had authorized advice on contraception being given in Maternity Welfare Centres; and the Family Planning Association ran numerous birth-control clinics all over the country. For the change in the climate of opinion much credit was due to Dr Marie Stopes, a palaeobotanist by profession, who had been the first woman to join the science faculty at Manchester University. Her first marriage had been annulled on her suit of non-consummation; and it was after her second marriage to a man also interested in birth control that her own passionate devotion to the problem and to sex education in general was intensified. Her first book *Married Love* was published in 1918 and caused a sensation; almost half a million copies were sold within five years. Her next book, *Wise Parenthood*, was even more successful and widely influential.

While contraception became more widespread, abortions were still common, particularly among the poorer classes. Before 1938 it was illegal in England for a doctor to end the pregnancy of a woman unless her life was in danger. In that year, after a gynaecological surgeon, Aleck Bourne, operated on a girl of fourteen (who had been raped and made pregnant by some guardsmen) and then reported his operation to the police, it was established that therapeutic abortion could be justified if there were reasonable grounds for supposing that a continued pregnancy would permanently impair the mother's mental or physical health. But it was not until after the Second World War that the law governing abortion became more relaxed; and in the meantime criminal and back-street abortions were of daily occurrence: as late as the 1960s it was estimated that 300 were performed every day in England.[23] Those carried out at home were induced by the usual methods of drinking gin, lying in hot baths, jumping off tables, falling downstairs and ingesting a variety of real or supposed abortifacients, including soap, gunpowder, pennyroyal, aloes, vinegar, quinine, slippery elm, expectorants, tobacco and a potion made by boiling together water, olive oil and lead oxide.

Smaller families led to an improvement in living standards not only for the poor who had fewer children to feed and clothe but also for the middle classes who had less to pay in school bills and in wages for increasingly expensive nursemaids, governesses or for the few day nurseries which then existed. They also made it easier for women to go out to work. Over 6 million women had jobs outside the house in 1931, an appreciable increase on those who went out to work before the war; and, although most of these were unmarried women, the proportion of married working women was increasing all the time: by 1951, while less than a quarter of married women went out to work, this was twice as many as had done so a generation earlier and a far higher proportion than in nearly all other countries in Europe.

For middle-class women the number of occupations available was growing – if growing slowly – all the time. The struggle to enter the professions had admittedly been a hard one. Elizabeth Garrett Anderson and Sophia Louisa Jex-Blake, two leading pioneers of medical education for women, had both experienced great difficulty in qualifying, since no medical school in England would accept them as pupils nor any examining body as candidates. Elizabeth Garrett Anderson eventually took the examinations of the Society of Apothecaries, having been advised that the Society's charter made refusal impossible; but no sooner had the Apothecaries reluctantly granted her the necessary licence in 1865, than they changed their constitution. She was consequently for many years the only female member of the British Medical Association. Miss Jex-Blake, sister of the headmaster of Rugby, after studying medicine in Edinburgh, was thwarted in her attempt to sit for examination by the College of Surgeons by the prompt resignation of the entire body of examiners. It was not until 1877, three years after she had founded the London School of Medicine for Women, that clinical experience was at last made available for women by the London (afterwards the Royal) Free Hospital. It was not until 1919 that restrictions upon women entering the professions, including law as well as medicine, were removed by the Sex Disqualification (Removal) Act; not until 1922 that a woman was called to the English Bar; and not until 1929, ten years after Lady Astor had become the first woman to take her seat in the House of Commons as Conservative Member for the Sutton division of Plymouth – formerly represented by her husband – that a woman became a Privy Councillor and Cabinet Minister when Margaret Bondfield was appointed Minister of

Labour. She held office for only two years, however; and it was many years before another woman held a Cabinet appointment.

In the 1920s and 1930s there were women mayors and magistrates to be found in every county; but their numbers were very small. Twenty-four women were elected to Parliament in 1945; but this was still only a very small fraction of the number of men. Indeed, women were still generally far from sharing equal rights with men. A series of enactments had certainly removed the more obtrusive of women's legal disabilities. They no longer had to prove grounds other than adultery for obtaining a divorce; and they could possess and sell property on the same terms as men. Their clothes also suggested a new freedom. Skirts became much shorter; waistlines, liberated from constriction, gradually disappeared altogether; silk stockings became commonplace, underclothes far lighter and more alluring, sports clothes more practical, swimming costumes more revealing, hairstyles much simpler. Before the First World War the suffragettes had been urging women to discard the long tresses and elaborate coiffures which were symbols of female bondage; and during the war long hair came close to being considered unpatriotic, since women in the services and nurses were not permitted it and women working with machinery would have found it dangerous. After the war short hair became fashionable: shingling, the fringe and the boyish style known as the Eton crop were all the rage. Lips were more vividly painted, for a time in the artificial shape of the cupid's bow; nails were coloured, lacquered and varnished; eyebrows were plucked and replaced by pencilled lines. By the early 1930s about £500,000 a year was being spent on promoting beauty preparations in the rapidly expanding advertising business which, by the time the Second World War broke out, was spending in all nearly £10 million a month.[24]

Yet, while many of the aims of the early feminists had been achieved by 1939, and while the war brought about further improvement in their lot, in 1945 women still laboured under numerous disadvantages. In many occupations, including the Civil Service, they received less than men for the same work; they were expected to abandon their appointments when they married; and, even when they were permitted to stay on, they were most unlikely to find their posts held for them if they left them to give birth.

Their children were, at least, far more likely to survive infancy than the children of their great-grandparents had been; and they themselves were far less likely to die from puerperal fever or from any other of the dangers attending childbirth in the past. The treatment of sickness generally had dramatically improved since Florence Nightingale had observed in 1863 that 'the very first requirement in a hospital is that it should do the sick no harm'.[25] At that time few hospitals had met that requirement; and it was often as difficult to get into those that did as to survive treatment in those that did not. In 1859 the rules of Salop Infirmary had provided

> That no woman big with child, no child under seven years of age (except in extraordinary cases, such as fractures, stone, or where couching, trepanning or amputation is necessary), no persons disordered in their senses, suspected to have smallpox or other infectious distemper, having habitual ulcers, cancers not admitting to operation, epileptic or convulsive fits, consumptions, or dropsied in their last stage, in a dying condition, or judged incurable, be admitted as inpatients, or inadvertently admitted, be suffered to continue.[26]

Patients at other hospitals were liable to be denied food or to be discharged for breaking such rules as those established by the governor of Guy's Hospital who ran it 'despotically' for half a century and provided by Rule V that 'if any patient curse or swear or use any prophane or lewd talking, and it was proved on them by two witnesses, such patient shall, for the first offence, lose their next day's diet, for the second offence lose two days' diet, and the third be discharged'.[27] The loss of diet, however, was considered no great punishment. In most large London hospitals the food provided consisted of a pint of water gruel or porridge for breakfast, eight ounces of meat or six ounces of cheese for dinner, and broth for supper. Patients might also receive up to a pound of bread a day and two to three pints of beer, but no vegetables or fruit.[28]

Those who were denied admission to hospital could frequently regard themselves as fortunate. Even in the 1890s there were numerous institutions like the workhouse in which the editor of the *British Medical Journal* found the sick 'lying on plank beds with chaff mattresses about three inches thick between their weary bodies and the hard uneven planks . . . Some idiots and imbeciles share the wards with these patients. The infants occupy a dark, stone-paved room, bare of furniture, with no rug for the babies to crawl or lie upon and no responsible persons to see to their feeding and cleanliness.'

Most hospitals, in fact, were extremely bleak and insanitary institutions where the standard of nursing was abysmal, where drunkenness and sexual escapades were common, and where the risk of cross-infection was acute. Standards of nursing gradually improved after reforms initiated by the Anglican Nursing Sisterhoods – in particular by Sister Mary Jones, whose nurses were responsible for tending the patients of King's College Hospital – and by Florence Nightingale whose work in the Crimean War had brought her fame, influence and a decisive say in the disposal of large sums of money. The Nightingale School of Nursing was opened in 1860 at St Thomas's Hospital which was rebuilt on a new site a few years later to designs approved by Miss Nightingale. The building cost £330,000 and provided beds for nearly 600 patients in seven detached blocks.

> Every ward on each floor has two hydraulic lifts: one small lift for food or medicines, one larger one for taking up patients or nurses [*The Illustrated London News* reported]. Every ward has its own bathrooms, lavatories and closets detached from others and its separate shoots for sending down dust and ashes . . . dressings and other things. Natural ventilation is as much as possible depended on . . . All the building is fireproof . . . The walls of each ward are coated with Parian cement which, while not as cold, is almost as hard and non-absorbent, and quite as smooth, as marble.

When the new St Thomas's Hospital was opened by Queen Victoria in 1871 there were far too few hospitals in the country to provide for the needs of the sick, even though the State's responsibility for providing hospitals for the poor had been recognized by the Metropolitan Poor Act of 1867. Ten years before the opening of St Thomas's, when the population of England and Wales was rather more than 20 million, there were less than 12,000 beds in 117 hospitals, compared with 250,000 beds in some 3000 hospitals in 1939; and as late as 1896 a census of the sick poor revealed that of 58,550 cases only just over 22,000 were in general infirmaries, the rest being looked after in workhouses.[29]

Most people, therefore, even when seriously ill, had to be looked after at home, as they had been at the beginning of the century when there were only about 3000 patients in hospitals in the entire country.[30]

The first district nurse did not appear until 1857; and, a generation later, the only doctors available to the destitute were the 'parish doctors', practitioners of scant competence employed, usually part-time, by the local Boards of Guardians. 'The great majority of wage-earners, however,' as F. F. Cartwright has written, 'depended upon the sixpenny doctor, often an able but over-worked general practitioner who received patients in his surgery, gave them a cursory examination, and invariably supplied a bottle of more or less harmless medicine, bright colour and pungent flavour being the most desirable qualities.'[31] He also provided his patient with a certificate enabling him to draw sick pay from any benefit society or club of which he happened to be a member.

Towards the end of the nineteenth century death and sickness rates, particularly death rates of children and of adult deaths from tuberculosis, began to fall. At the same time surgical operations became less painful and less perilous. Chloroform had been first administered as an anaesthetic in 1847 by Sir James Simpson who had already used ether to relieve the pains of childbirth; and after 1884, when it was discovered that cocaine produced insensitivity to pain if applied to the eye, local anaesthesia was quickly developed. Antiseptic surgery with a carbolic spray was introduced by Joseph Lister in 1865, and was soon followed by the sterilization of surgical instruments.

A fearful epidemic of influenza in 1918–20 was responsible for over 150,000 deaths, the highest in proportion to population since the cholera outbreak of 1849.[32] And this upset the encouraging trend of health statistics for a time. But thereafter more nourishing diets and improvements in housing, sanitation, hygiene and water supply encouraged the rising standards of health and an increase in the average height and weight of children. So did improvements in medical skills and treatment. Insulin proved effective in the treatment of diabetes, salvarsan in that of syphilis, sulphonamides in cases of pneumonia. After the 1930s diphtheria was brought under control by immunization; and experiences gained by doctors in World War II led to advances in both cosmetic surgery and blood transfusions.

Hospital treatment, however, often proved extremely expensive. Free only for the very poor, it had to be paid for by most patients; and even those whose contributions to National Insurance were regularly maintained were not covered for certain specialist services including dentistry and ophthalmic treatment: tooth decay was consequently widespread and spectacles were on sale in large stores where customers tried on one pair after another until they found the one that suited them best. Harrods and the more expensive shops sent out sets of trial lenses 'for the convenience of country customers'.

The National Insurance Act, applying to some 13 million workers with wages of less than £160 a year, had come into force in 1913. But it was not until 1919 that a general health scheme began to be established by the creation of a Ministry of Health by Lloyd George's Coalition Government, and not until the 1920s that a drastic reform of the Poor Law, under which the treatment of the sick had previously been administered, was undertaken by a Conservative Minister of Health, Neville Chamberlain. By 1938, although the National Insurance Act had been extended to cover nearly 20 million people, there were many, including the dependents of the insured, the self-employed and most of the middle classes, who were still not covered by its provisions.

The government's reaction to the outbreak of war in 1914 had been slow. The Defence of the Realm Act had given it extensive powers; but it was not until the end of 1916 that the Ministries of Labour, Shipping and Food were established; not until 1917 that the railways and mines came under government control; and not until February 1918 that rationing was introduced. The reaction to the threat of the Second World War was far quicker: two Emergency Powers Acts were introduced within months; new Ministries were quickly established; petrol rationing was imposed; men up to the age of forty-one were made liable to conscription; a fair distribution of clothes and certain foods was ensured by a system of rationing by 'points'; rent controls were extended to nearly all unfurnished houses; food subsidies were introduced in December 1939; not long afterwards cheap 'utility clothing' appeared in the shops; air-raid shelters were made, and gas-masks distributed.

A quite new and horrible type of warfare was expected, and immense numbers of civilian casualties were forecast. In the First World War there had been occasions when the fighting at the front seemed far removed from the relative comforts of Blighty, when the soldiers were wholly out of sympathy with the denizens of Civvy Street. Siegfried Sassoon, a brave young officer in the Royal Welch Fusiliers who, after being wounded, came on convalescent leave to London, wrote of his desire to see the jolly complacency of a theatre audience violently disrupted:

> I'd like to see a tank come down the stalls
> Lurching to rag-time tunes of Home Sweet Home
> And there'd be no more jokes in music-halls
> To mock the riddled corpses of Bapaume

There was no such widespread feeling in the Second World War during which 264,000 fighting men were killed, less than a third of the 908,000 who died in 1914–18. Nothing much happened on the home front at first and, when the raids did begin, casualties were not on the terrible scale that had been predicted. Yet by the beginning of January 1941 over 13,000 civilians had been killed in London and nearly 18,000 badly injured. And on the night of 10–11 May that year there were over 3000 casualties, 1436 of them fatal. In all 60,000 civilians were killed in the war and 35,000 merchant seamen.

As in the First World War, women played a vital role in victory. Conscription of women was introduced – as it had not been in the earlier war – at first for those between twenty and thirty years of age, then, after 1943, for those from eighteen and a half to fifty. But in practice only women between the ages of nineteen and twenty-four were called up, and these could choose between serving in the various auxiliary services – in which they would not be called upon to use a gun or other weapon unless they agreed to do so in writing – joining the Civil Defence or taking up some kind of specified civilian employment. Married women living with their husbands were exempt, so were the mothers of children under fourteen whether married or not. In 1944 there were almost half a million women in the Women's Royal Navy Service, the Auxiliary Territorial Service and the Women's Auxiliary Air Force, mostly volunteers. There were only 1072 female conscientious objectors compared with 60,000 men.

A further 200,000 women served in the Woman's Land Army, while 260,000 worked in government ordnance factories and very nearly half the posts in the Civil Service were held by women.

It had been expected [so Arthur Marwick has written], that where women were substituted for men it would require three women to do the work of two men, but in fact a one to one substitution proved perfectly possible; this was partly because modern technology had rendered sheer strength less essential to industrial work. In a previous generation the symbol of female rights which had been gained at the end of a previous war was the vote; now, though there had been no organized movement comparable with that of the suffragists and suffragettes, the symbol was equal pay.[33]

A Royal Commission on Equal Pay was accordingly appointed in the last year of the war. The members of this commission suggested that 'conventions and prejudices' had been 'crumbling fairly fast in recent years' and that the record of what women had been able to achieve in war had exerted and [would] continue to exert a lasting influence in breaking down whatever elements of the old-fashioned or irrational remains in the public's estimation of the capabilities of women'.[34]

Despite these remarks the commission, with three of its women members dissenting, did not wholeheartedly recommend equal pay on the grounds that it would not be in the interests of women for them to receive it, since it would have adverse effects on the expansion of women's employment. Nevertheless the movement for equal pay 'had received an enormous accession of strength from the war experience'.[35]

The war, by submitting men and women, rich and poor to many of the same dangers and deprivations, had also helped to forge a national unity which had seemed unattainable in 1926. 'Hitler,' the London correspondent of the *New York Herald* reported, 'is doing what centuries of English history have not accomplished – he is breaking down the class structure of England.' At the same time the government's measures to keep down the cost of living by food subsidies, rent controls and other means proved successful. Between the outbreak of war and 1945 – a period of full employment – wages increased by more than half, but the cost of living during that time rose only by 30 per cent. Most foods, except bread and potatoes, remained rationed, yet vegetables, grown everywhere, including Hyde Park and Windsor Castle, were usually in ready supply. The Ministry of Food, under the direction of Lord Woolton, a former chairman of Lewis's, the department store, was highly effective; the meals supplied in schools, works canteens and the so-called

British Restaurants were high in nutritional value. Babies were provided with concentrated orange juice.

Although the prime minister himself was principally concerned with winning the war, others were already planning the better society which it was hoped would be created when the fighting was over. Already in 1942 Sir William Beveridge, Director of the London School of Economics, had issued a Report on Social Security in which was proposed not only a social insurance scheme, national health service and child allowances, but also measures to ensure full employment and widespread reforms in housing and education. In 1945 a Labour government under Clement Attlee was returned with a large majority to carry out a programme of limited nationalization.

'No such opportunity has ever been given to any nation before – not even by the French Revolution,' Lloyd George had declared towards the end of the First World War. 'The nation is now in molten state . . . We cannot return to the old days, the old abuses, the old stupidities.' Such sentiments were now repeated. The hopes expressed have yet to be realized.

# References

For full bibliographical details see Sources (pp. 738–53).

PART ONE

1 *Castles, Lords and Chatelaines*

1 Platt (*Medieval England*), 2–16,
   83–9, 176–7; Mitchell and Leys (*A
   History of the English People*),
   203–7; Oman, (*Castles*) *passim*;
   Braun, *passim*.
2 *Ibid.*; W. H. St John Hope,
   *Windsor Castle* (1913), vol. 1,
   15–84.
3 Cook, 2–14; Girouard (*Life in the
   English Country House*), 30–9; M.
   Wood, 35–65.
4 Kenneth Hare (*Sir Gawain and
   the Green Knight: A Fourteenth-
   Century Poem Done into Modern
   English* (2nd ed., 1948), 18.
5 Rickert, 87.
6 Furnivall *Booke of Courtesy*,
   291.
7 Platt, op. cit., 185.
8 *Northumberland Household Book*,
   quot. Coulton (*Social Life*), 383.
9 *Ibid.*
10 Girouard, op. cit., 49–50.
11 Labarge (*A Baronial Household*),
   82.
12 *Fifteenth Century Schoolbook*, para.

31, quot. Labarge, op. cit., 81.
13 Labarge, op. cit., 86–101.
14 T. Wright, 348–57.
15 W. E. Mead, *The English
   Mediaeval Feast* (1931), 102–3.
16 Mitchell and Leys, op. cit., 250–57;
   Girouard, op. cit., 25–6; Labarge,
   op. cit., 102–110.
17 Peter of Blois, *Epistolae*, quot.
   E. B. Morgan, 77.
18 *Monumenta Germaniae Scriptores*,
   XXXII, 219, quot. Coulton, op.
   cit., 30.
19 Quot. Girouard, op. cit., 30.
20 *Ibid.*, 47–50.
21 A. Hammond, *The Book of
   Chessmen* (1950), *passim*.
22 N. Davis, vol. 1, 72, 124.
23 U. T. Holmes, *Daily Living in the
   Twelfth Century, based on the
   Observations of Alexander
   Neckham* (1952), 273–4.
24 Girouard, op. cit., 54–8; M. Wood,
   367–88.

2 *Cottagers and Peasants*

1 Hilton (*The English Peasantry*), 49.
2 *Walter of Henley's Husbandry*, 201.
3 Hilton, op. cit., 42.

4 Chaucer, *The Canterbury Tales*, trans. Nevill Coghill.
5 Bennett (*Life on the English Manor*), 80–81.
6 *Ibid.*
7 F. W. Maitland (ed.), *The Court Baron*, iv, 53.
8 I. Gollancz, *The Parlement of the Three Ages* (1915), quot. Bennett, op. cit., 270.
9 Coghill, see note 4.
10 Bennett, op. cit., 147.
11 *The Ledger Book of Vale Royal Abbey*, quot. Bennett, op. cit., 146.
12 *Pierce the Ploughman's Crede*, ed. W. W. Skeat.
13 Hilton, op. cit., 102–3.
14 *Ibid.*, 99.
15 Bennett, op. cit., 244–5.
16 Hilton, op. cit., 58.
17 Ashley (*The People of England*), 39–40, 42–3.
18 Bennett, op. cit., 283.
19 *Ibid.*, 300.
20 Rothwell (ed.), *English Historical Documents, 1189–1327* (1955).

### 3 Plague and Revolt

1 Deaux, 118.
2 *Ibid.*
3 Creighton, vol. 1, 121.
4 Twigg, *passim*.
5 Shrewsbury, 27; Cartwright, 62.
6 Deaux, 128.
7 Shrewsbury, 147; Trevelyan, 8.
8 Ziegler, *passim*.
9 Quot. A. Briggs (*A Social History*), 88.
10 Statutes of the Realm, ii, 2, quot. Trevelyan, 12.
11 McKisack, 405–23; Hilton (*Bond Men Made Free*), *passim*.

### 4 Churches, Monks and Friars

1 *The Knight of La Tour-Landry*, 41–2; Owst (*Preaching in Medieval England*), 161; Coulton (*Medieval Panorama*), 182–4.
2 *Northumberland Household Book*, 323.
3 Moorman, 89.
4 Bennett (*Life on the English Manor*), 325; Coulton, op. cit., 157–76.
5 Coulton, op. cit., 172–5, 178; Coulton (*Social Life*), 260–61.
6 *Ibid.*, 178; Bennett (*The Pastons*), 224–5.
7 Coulton (*Medieval Panorama*), 194.
8 Bennett (*The Pastons*), 195.
9 *Ibid.*, 197–8.
10 *Stonor Letters and Papers*, ed. C. L. Kingsford, 291.
11 Bennett (*The Pastons*), 202; Capes; Stephens, *passim*.
12 Capes, 267.
13 *Oxford Dictionary of the Christian Church*, 558.
14 Knowles (*Monastic Order and Religious Orders*); Mitchell and Leys (*A History of the English People*), 85–91; Coulton, op. cit., 269–71.
15 *The Autobiography of Giraldus Cambrensis*, trans. H. Butler (1937); Coulton (*Social Life*), 116–17.
16 Coulton (*Medieval Panorama*), 274–5.
17 *Ibid.*, 168–75, 266–70; Knowles (*The Monastic Order*), 107–10.
18 Chaucer, *The Canterbury Tales*, trans. Nevill Coghill.
19 Mitchell and Leys, op. cit., 96–7; Power (*Medieval English Nunneries*), 200–47.
20 Coulton, op. cit., 276.
21 Mitchell and Leys, op. cit., 95.
22 Platt (*Medieval England*), 70–73; Brooke (*The Coming of the Friars*), *passim*.

### 5 Drinking and Playing

1 P. Clark, 8.
2 *Ibid.*, 11.
3 *Ibid.*, 24.
4 *Ibid.*, 30.
5 *Ibid.*, 30.
6 *Piers Plowman* modernized by H. W. Wells, 1935.
7 Wilkins, *Concilia Magnae Britanniae et Hiberniae*, 1937, quot. Bennett (*The Pastons*), 265; *The Lives of the Berkeleys*, ed. J. Maclean (1883–5), vol. 1, 378.
8 Bennett, op. cit., 271.
9 Quot. Hone, 551.
10 Strutt (*Manners, Customs*), vol. 2, 331–9.
11 Oman (*The Art of War*, revised and ed. John H. Beeler, 1953); Roger Ascham, *Toxophilus, the Schole of Shooting* (1545).
12 John Stow, *Survey of London*, ed. C. L. Kingsford (1908).
13 *Ibid.*
14 Alexander Neckham, *De Naturis Rerum*, trans. Thomas Wright (1863); Platt (*Medieval England*), 190–91.
15 H. Y. Thompson, *A Lecture on Some English Illuminated MSS* (1902), quot. Mitchell and Leys (*A History of the English People*), 211, 213.
16 *Joys and Frivolities of Courtiers*, quot. Hassall, 183.
17 *The Master of Game by Edward, second Duke of York; the Oldest English Book of Hunting*, ed. W. A. and F. Baillie-Grohman (1909), quot. Hassall, 182.
18 J. Armitage Robinson, *The Abbot's House at Westminster* (1911), quot. Coulton (*Social Life*), 396.
19 Quot. Coulton, op. cit., 395–6.
20 Quot. Bennett (*Life on the English Manor*), 278.

### 6 Wayfarers and Pilgrims

1 F. M. Stenton, 3; Labarge (*A Baronial Household*), 153–4.
2 Anderson, 64.
3 Hey, 65; Anderson, 68.
4 Quot. Bennett (*The Pastons*), 133.
5 Jackman, 14.
6 Pratt, 29.
7 Quot. Bennett, op. cit., 132.
8 Anderson, 134.
9 *Ibid.*, 133.
10 *Ibid.*, 63.
11 Jusserand, 61.
12 *Ibid.*, 106.
13 Anderson, 133.
14 Pratt, 13.
15 Jackman, 29.
16 *Ibid.*, 63.
17 *Ibid.*, 66.
18 John Stow, *Annales* (1601), 201.
19 Jackman, 42.
20 Hey, 77.
21 Anderson, 70–71; Pratt, 12.
22 Labarge, op. cit., 158–9; J. F. Willard ('Inland Transport'), 361.
23 Bennett, op. cit., 155; Labarge, op. cit., 157.
24 Jackman, 232.
25 Jusserand, 54, 98–9; Anderson, 134.
26 Willard, op. cit., 247, 366–7; Hey, 119, 91–2, 122; Jackman, 27.
27 F. M. Stenton, 17; Labarge, op. cit., 161; Jusserand, 73.
28 Pratt, 18; Willard, op. cit., 364.
29 Anderson, 68; Labarge, op. cit., 162–3; Bennett, op. cit. 160–62.
30 F. M. Stenton, 20.
31 Willard, op. cit., 371; Hey, 119.
32 *Ibid.*, 371.
33 *Ibid.*, 362.
34 *Ibid.*, 373; Jackman, 25.
35 Hey, 175.
36 Jackman, 27; Guilford, 44.
37 Quot. Jackman, 34.
38 Guilford, 61.
39 Bennett, op. cit., 131.

40 *Ibid.*, 139.
41 Jusserand, 77.
42 *Ibid.*, 150–52.
43 Bennett, op. cit. 141.
44 *Ibid.*
45 *Ibid.*, 140–41.
46 Pratt, 28.
47 Bennett, op. cit., 163; Pratt, 22; Jusserand, 87.
48 Guilford, 53.
49 *Ibid.*, 54.
50 Jusserand, 41.
51 R. W. Eyton, *Court, Household and Itinerary of Henry II* (1878); A. R. Myers, *The Household of Edward IV* (1959); Hubert Hall, *Court Life Under the Plantagenets* (1890), 242–9; William Thoms, *The Book of the Court* (1838), 213–44.
52 *King Edward II's Household and Wardrobe Ordinances*, ed. Furnivall (1876); Jusserand, 104–7.
53 Jusserand, 105.
54 Labarge (*Medieval Travellers*); Jusserand, 125–6.
55 Jusserand, 126–9.
56 *Ibid.*, 129.
57 Anderson, 86–7.
58 P. Clark, 29; Jusserand, 64.
59 Jusserand, 206.
60 Anderson, 80.
61 Tighe and Davis, *Annals of Windsor* (1858), 232.
62 Jusserand, 343–4.

## 7 *Tournaments, Pageants and Miracles*

1 Maurice Keen, *Chivalry* (1984).
2 Froissart, *Chronicles*, trans. Lord Berners.
3 Malory, *Le Morte d'Arthur* (preface by Prof. John Rhys, Everyman's Library; 1906); E. K. Chambers, *Arthur of Britain* (new ed. 1966).
4 Quot. Coulton (*Medieval Panorama*), 240.
5 Quot. Thoms, 222.
6 Quot. Coulton, op. cit., 243.
7 *Ibid.*, 243–4.
8 Wickham, vol. 1, 15, 22; Poole, vol. 2, 622–3; Strutt (*Manners, Customs . . .*), 129–43; *Lamdsdowne Collection*, quot. T. E. Harwood, *Windsor Old and New* (1929), 161.
9 Wickham, vol. 1, 22.
10 Coulton, op. cit., 142.
11 W. H. St John Hope, *Windsor Castle* (1913), vol. 1, 111–12.
12 Denholm Young, 'The Tournament in the 13th Century', *Essays Presented to F. M. Powicke*, 254; Wickham, vol. 1, 17–18, 54; Stow, vol. 1, 95; Chambers (*The Mediaeval Stage*), vol. 2, 167.
13 Walsingham's *Historia Anglicana*, ed. H. T. Riley (1863), vol. 1, 331.
14 Wickham, vol. 1, 51–109.
15 Stow, vol. 1, 220–31; James Hamilton Wylie, *The Reign of Henry V* (1929), vol. 2, 209–27.
16 Chambers, op. cit., vol. 2, 6, 174–5; Coulton, op. cit., 687; 'Liturgical Drama', *Oxford Companion to the Theatre* (3rd ed.), 581.
17 Chambers, op. cit., vol. 1, 90–92, vol. 2, 118, 138, 139, 243–4; Wickham, vol. 1, 173; Hartnoll, 43; Tydeman, 209; Nicoll (*The Development of the Theatre*), 64; Hartnoll, 45.
18 Coulton, op. cit., 688.
19 Quot. Tydeman, 203.
20 *Ibid.*, 205–6.
21 *Ibid.*, 206; Chambers, op. cit., vol. 2, 140.
22 Nicoll, op. cit., 60.
23 Hartnoll, 46.
24 Tydeman, 226.
25 *Ibid.*
26 *Ibid.*, 228–32.
27 Chambers, op. cit., vol. 2, 116.
28 *Oxford Companion to the Theatre* (3rd ed.), 601; Chambers, op. cit., vol. 1, 207.

29 Wickham, vol. 1, 202–3.
30 Chambers, op. cit., vol. 1, 195–7.
31 Nicoll, op. cit., 152; Chambers, op. cit., vol. 2, 262–3.
32 Chambers, op. cit., vol. 1, 47.
33 *Ibid.*, 46, 49–50.
34 Holt, 112, 137.
35 Chambers, op. cit., vol. 1, 50, 56.
36 *Ibid.*, 55.
37 *Ibid.*, 45.

## 8 *Town Life*

1 Hilton (*The English Peasantry*), 77.
2 Platt (*The English Medieval Town*), 15.
3 Hilton, op. cit., 85.
4 *Ibid.*, 78–81.
5 Platt, op. cit., 15.
6 A. S. Green, vol. 1, 14–15.
7 *Ibid.*, vol. 1, 12, 18–19, vol. 2, 32–3.
8 Platt, op. cit., 23.
9 *Ibid.*, 105, 107–9.
10 A. S. Green, vol. 1, 127–45.
11 *Ibid.*, vol. 2, 298–9.
12 *Ibid.*, 251.
13 *Ibid.*, 170–256.
14 Platt (*Medieval Southampton*), 94.
15 A. S. Green, vol. 2, 29–31.
16 *Ibid.*
17 Platt (*The English Medieval Town*), 69–70.
18 *Ibid.*, 49–50.
19 *Ibid.*, 25.
20 Mitchell and Leys (*A History of the English People*), 176.

## 9 *Daughters and Wives*

1 Pollock and Maitland, *History of English Law*, vol. 1, 482; Mitchell and Leys (*A History of the English People*), 64.
2 Bennett (*The Pastons*), 81.
3 *Paston Letters, passim*; Bennett, op. cit., 43–6.
4 *Ibid.*; Bennett, op. cit., 52–4; Barber, 65.

## 10 *Pupils and Masters*

1 *Italian Relations of England*, Camden Society, 1847, 24.
2 Ascham, *The Scholemaster*, ed. E. Arber (1870), 47.
3 Orme (*English Schools*), 123, 128–9.
4 Sylvester, 17–18.
5 Sir Thomas Elyot, *The Boke Called the Governour*, 1541.
6 F. J. Furnivall (*The Babees Book*), 403–4.
7 Sylvester, 21–3.
8 Orme, op. cit., 170, 190.
9 *Ibid.*, 61–9.
10 Sylvester, 28.
11 Orme, op. cit., 69.
12 *Ibid.*, 101.
13 *Ibid.*
14 Sylvester, 29–30.
15 Leach, 280–81.
16 Orme, op. cit., 124.
17 Rashdall, 673.
18 Orme, op. cit., 130.
19 *Ibid.*, 122–5.
20 Sylvester, 21–3, 25; Orme, op. cit., 96; Cobban, 149.
21 Orme, op. cit., 244.
22 *Ibid.*, 179–80.
23 *Ibid.*, 217, 118; Sylvester, 26–7.
24 Orme, op. cit., 118–19; Sylvester, 17; Clanchy, 194.
25 Orme, op. cit., 119.
26 *Ibid.*, 161–2.
27 *Ibid.*, 152.
28 *Ibid.*, 159.
29 *Ibid.*, 78.
30 Sylvester, 25.
31 Orme, op. cit., 160.
32 Sylvester 20–21.
33 Orme, op. cit., 117, 133; Sylvester, 22, 23; Clanchy, 173.
34 Orme, op. cit., 34.
35 *Ibid.*, 51.
36 *Ibid.*, 25–6.
37 *Stonor Letters and Papers*, ed.

C. L. Kingsford, xlvi; Bennett (*The Pastons*), 114.
38 Bennett, op. cit. 116–17; Clanchy, 189–91.
39 Orme, op. cit., 31, 36.

## 11 *Scholars and Students*

1 V. H. H. Green, 19; Cobban, 97–102; Rashdall, vol. 2, 105.
2 *Ibid.*
3 Quot. Sylvester, 59–60.
4 Rashdall, vol. 2, 396; John Ayliffe, *The Antient and Present State of the University of Oxford* (1714), quot. Morris, 16.
5 Cobban, 105.
6 Quot. Morris, 16–17.
7 Anthony Wood, *History and Antiquities of the University of Oxford* (1674), quot. Morris, 17–20; Rashdall, vol. 2, 403–6.
8 Rashdall, vol. 2, 411–12.
9 V. H. H. Green, 20, 31; Rashdall, vol. 2, 393, 614.
10 G. H. Cooper, *Annals of Cambridge*, vol. 1, 160.
11 Anstey (ed), *Munimenta Academica*, vol. 1, 304–5, quot. Sylvester, 74.
12 Cobban, 107; Rashdall, vol. 2, 415; Sylvester, 62.
13 Rashdall, vol. 2, 389.
14 Quot. Sylvester, 61.
15 *Ibid.*, 64.
16 Chaucer, *The Canterbury Tales*, trans. Nevill Coghill.
17 *Victoria County History of Oxfordshire*, vol. 3, *passim*.
18 Sylvester, 66–7; Morris, 20–21.
19 Rashdall, vol. 2, 671–2; V. H. H. Green, 23; Morris, 39.
20 V. H. H. Green, 6, 23; Rashdall, vol. 2, 413–15, 625–6, 672.
21 Rashdall, vol. 2, 165–7; V. H. H. Green, 21.
22 Rashdall, vol. 2, 165–7; V. H. H. Green, 21.

23 Sylvester, 71; V. H. H. Green, 20.
24 Quot. V. H. H. Green, 27.
25 Guilford, 274.
26 V. H. H. Green, 26.
27 Sylvester, 60.
28 Rashdall, vol. 2, 351, 658; Morris, 10; Coulton (*Social Life*), 61.
29 Cobban, 142, 204–5, 215; Sylvester, 73; V. H. H. Green, 13.
30 Cobban, 18, 208, 226–9.
31 Sylvester, 76.

## 12 *Crime and Punishment*

1 L. O. Pike, vol. 1, 243–50; Jeudwine, 151.
2 Quot. Bennett (*The Pastons*), 182–3.
3 *Ibid.*, 187.
4 Barber, 35–6.
5 L. O. Pike, vol. 1, 204, 226, 243–4; Stephen, vol. 1, 17–27.
6 Coulton (*Medieval Panorama*), 379.
7 L. O. Pike, vol. 1, 195–6.
8 *Ibid.*, 226.
9 Bennett, op. cit., 178.
10 *Ibid.*, 176.
11 L. O. Pike, vol. 1, 229–30.
12 *Ibid.*, 240.
13 Stone, 'Literacy and Education in England', 43.
14 Quot. Jusserand, 165–6.
15 L. O. Pike, vol. 1, 199.
16 Bennett, op. cit., 174.
17 Mitchell and Leys (*A History of the English People*), 152–3.
18 L. O. Pike, vol. 1, 220; Jeudwine, 188.
19 Coulton (*Social Life*), 178.
20 Pike, vol. 1, 414.

## 13 *Doctors and Patients*

1 Coulton (*Social Life*), 452–3.
2 Horton-Smith, *Johannes de Mirfield of St Bartholomew's*, 79–80.
3 Coulton, op. cit., 507.
4 Quot. Jusserand, 186–7.

5 Quot. Coulton, op. cit., 502.
6 *Ibid.*, 506.
7 John Aderne, E.E.T.S. (1910), 103, quot. Coulton, op. cit.
8 Thomas (*Religion and the Decline of Magic*), 51, 56.
9 Horton-Smith, op. cit., note 2, 192.
10 *Ibid.*, 81–5.
11 Andrew Boorde, *Dyetary of Health*, ed. F. J. Furnivall (1870).
12 Cartwright, 44.
13 *Ibid.*, 23–5.
14 *Ibid.*, 22–3.
15 Coulton, op. cit., 445–6; Cartwright, 26–9.
16 Coulton, op. cit., 449.
17 Cartwright, 27.
18 *Ibid.*, 28.
19 Coulton, op. cit., 456.
20 Cartwright, 29.
21 R. M. Clay, *The Mediaeval Hospitals of England* (1909), 42.
22 Quot. Cartwright, 33.
23 Clay, op. cit., note 21, 49.
24 *Ibid.*, 78.
25 *Ibid.*, 82.
26 *Ibid.*, 94.
27 Creighton, vol. 1, 241.
28 *Ibid.*, 200.
29 *Ibid.*, 202.
30 Stow, 142.
31 Creighton, vol. 1, 267, 314–16.
32 *Ibid.*, 314.
33 Stow, 149.
34 Braudel (*The Structures of Everyday Life*), 88.
35 Creighton, vol. 1, 419.
36 *Ibid.*, 421.
37 *Ibid.*, 426.
38 *Ibid.*, 423–5.

PART TWO

14 *Villagers, Vagrants and Vagabonds*

1 Toulmin Smith (ed.), *The Itinerary of John Leland*; Rowse (*The England of Elizabeth*), 33.
2 William Camden, *Britannia* (1586); Rowse, op. cit., 71.
3 Rowse, op. cit., 71; Trevelyan, 149–55.
4 John Norden, *Speculum Britanniae* (1625).
5 Tusser, 135.
6 Rowse, op. cit., 74.
7 Burton (*The Early Tudors*), 136.
8 Emmison, 56.
9 Rowse, op. cit., 69.
10 A. Briggs (*A Social History*), 126.
11 Trevelyan, 137.
12 W. G. Collingwood, *Elizabethan Keswick*; Rowse, 127.
13 A. Briggs op. cit., 126.
14 Trevelyan, 189.
15 Dodd, 135; Trevelyan, 190–91.
16 Dickens; Scarisbrick, *passim*.
17 H. S. Darby, *Hugh Latimer* (1953).
18 Harrison, vol. 2, 87.
19 Hall, *Society in the Elizabethan Age*, quot. Byrne (*Elizabethan Life*), 115.
20 Byrne, op. cit., 116.
21 Dodd, 137.
22 W. K. Jordan, *Philanthropy in England, 1480–1660* (1959); Dodd, 127, 138.
23 Aydelotte, 15.
24 Harrison, vol. 1, 59.
25 *King Lear*, Act 2, sc. iii.
26 Aydelotte, 26.
27 *Ibid.*
28 Thomas Dekker, *Lanthorne and Candle-light*, quot. Aydelotte, 39.
29 Mitchell and Leys (*A History of the English People*), 475.
30 Quot. Byrne, op. cit., 152.
31 Quot. Aydelotte, 29–30.
32 Aydelotte, 68–9.
33 Lansdowne MSS., quot. Aydelotte, 168.
34 Quot. Aydelotte, 81.
35 Thomas Wright, *Elizabeth and her Times* (1838), vol. 2, 251.

36 Aydelotte, 83–4.
37 *Ibid.*, 104.

## 15 *Priests, Parishioners and Recusants*

1 Simon Fish, *The Supplication of the Beggars*, quot. Trevelyan, 102.
2 Scarisbrick, 1.
3 Trevelyan, 102.
4 Mackie, 370–401.
5 Mathew, 107.
6 *Ibid.*, 112.
7 Trevelyan, 180.
8 Rowse (*The England of Elizabeth*), 370.
9 J. E. Neale, 220.
10 Dodd, 76.
11 A. T. Hart, (*Man in the Pulpit*), 84.
12 Caraman (*The Other Face*), 172.
13 *The State Civil and Ecclesiastical of the County of Lancaster*, quot. Caraman, op. cit., 174.
14 *The Life and Death of Edward Jennings*, quot. Caraman, op. cit., 108.
15 Mathew, 47.
16 John Mush, *The Life of Margaret Clitherow*, ed. William Nicholson (1849), 222.
17 Mathew, 46; Mackie, 552; Caraman, op. cit., 189.
18 Trevelyan, 178–81.
19 Rowse, op. cit., 423.
20 Dodd, 79.
21 W. Harrison, vol. 1, 227.

## 16 *Country Houses and Country People*

1 Cook, 40, 67; Rowse (*The England of Elizabeth*), 3–5; W. Harrison, vol. 2, 229–34.
2 Cook, 40; Platt (*The English Medieval Town*), 42.
3 Cook, 43.
4 *Ibid.*, 43.
5 Girouard (*Robert Smythson*), passim.
6 Girouard (*Life in the English Country House*), 87–104.
7 Emmison, 25.
8 Buxton, 66.
9 G. S. Thomson, 280.
10 Buxton; Rowse, op. cit.; Cook; Girouard, op. cit.
11 Burton (*The Early Tudors*), 261–2.
12 *Ibid.*, 227.
13 Hentzner, 147.
14 Burton, op. cit., 256.
15 Hentzner, 153.
16 Quot. Cook, 80.
17 *Ibid.*, 104.
18 Tusser, 187–8.
19 Burton (*The Elizabethans*), 26.
20 *Ibid.*, 109.
21 Braudel (*The Structures of Everyday Life*), 205–6.
22 Levine Lemnie, *The Touchstone of Complexions*.
23 Braudel, op. cit., 167–72.
24 Fynes Moryson, *Itinerary* (1907), 223–4.
25 Byrne (*Elizabethan Life*), 33–4.
26 Emmison, 36, 61–2, 69.
27 Dodd, 71; Byrne, op. cit., 130.
28 Emmison, 47–54.
29 Burton (*The Early Tudors*), 150–51.
30 Emmison, 56–8.
31 *Ibid.*, 38–9, 44–5, 46, 64–9.

## 17 *Animals and Sportsmen*

1 Emmison, 62, 96–7; Dodd, 13; Girouard (*Life in the English Country House*), 110; Burton (*The Elizabethans*), 44.
2 Burton, op. cit., 42.
3 Girouard, op. cit., 112.
4 Byrne (*Lisle Letters*), 150.
5 Thomas (*Man and the Natural World*), 105.
6 Burton, op. cit., 153.
7 Thomas, op. cit., 106.
8 *Ibid.*, 107.
9 *Ibid.*, 109.
10 *Ibid.*

11 *Ibid.*
12 *Ibid.*
13 *Ibid.*, 29.
14 D. Harris Willson, *King James VI and I* (1956), 180–2.
15 Elizabeth Jenkins, *Elizabeth the Great* (1958), 199.
16 Neale, 220.
17 Mitchell and Leys (*A History of the English People*), 209.
18 Walvin, 7, 9, 12–15.
19 Dodd, 114; Mitchell and Leys, op. cit., 403.
20 Byrne (*Elizabethan Life*), 210–11.
21 Walvin, 5.
22 Burton (*The Early Tudors*), 205.

18 *Readers and Music Makers*

1 Coulton (*Social Life*), 232; Trevelyan, 79.
2 Orme (*English Schools*), 24–5, 83–5; Bennett (*The Pastons*), 84; E. Gordon Duff, *English Fifteenth Century Books* (1918); N. F. Blake, *Caxton and His World* (1969).
3 Rowse (*The Elizabethan Renaissance: The Cultural Achievement*); Buxton; Duff, see note 2.
4 'Bible (English Versions)', *Oxford Dictionary of the Christian Church*.
5 Dodd, 83, 86.
6 Byrne (*Elizabethan Life*), 257.
7 Burton (*The Elizabethans*), 203.
8 Rowse, op. cit., 101–2, 104–6, 116–19.
9 Buxton, 173.
10 Burton, op. cit. 198.
11 Byrne, op. cit., 223.
12 Emmison, 70–71, 74–5.
13 Dodd, 116.
14 Burton, op. cit., 197; Byrne, op. cit., 222.
15 Dodd, 116.
16 Wickham, vol. 1, 218–19.
17 Chambers (*The Elizabethan Stage*), vol. 1, 202–3.

18 John Summerson, *Inigo Jones* (1966), 21–3; Carola Oman, *Henrietta Maria* (1936).

19 *Clothes and Class*

1 Doreen Yarwood, *English Costume* (1953); C. W. Cunnington, *Handbook of English Costume in the 16th Century* (1962); Lester and Kerr, *Historic Costume* (1967); Burton (*The Elizabethans*), 37–9; Rowse (*The Elizabethan Renaissance*), 189–90.
2 Gunn, 72.
3 *Ibid.*, 76–7; William Vaughn, *Naturall and Artificial Directions for Health* (1600).
4 Sir Hugh Platt, *Delightes for Ladies* (1602), 27.
5 W. Harrison, vol. 2, 47; A. Briggs (*A Social History*), 113; Buxton, 24; Sir Thomas Smith, *De Republica Anglorum*, quot. Rowse (*The England of Elizabeth*), 244.
6 W. Harrison, vol. 2, 48.
7 William Lambarde, *Perambulation of Kent* (1596), 14.
8 Hoskins, quot. Rowse, op. cit., 226.
9 Briggs, op. cit., 113.
10 *Ibid.*, 118.
11 Byrne (*Elizabethan Life*), 120–1; Briggs, op. cit., 116.
12 Rowse, op. cit., 225.
13 *Ibid.*, 23.

20 *Citizens, Masters and Journeymen*

1 *The London Encyclopaedia*, 'Population'.
2 Stow, 296.
3 Philippa Glanville, *London in Maps* (1972).
4 Quot. Byrne (*Elizabethan Life*), 70.
5 Breton, *A Flourish upon Fancy*, quot. Byrne, op. cit., 72.
6 Dekker, *The Seven Deadly Sinnes of London* (1606).

7 Rowse (*The England of Elizabeth*), 158–9.

8 Byrne, op. cit., 148–9; Harbage, 56.

9 Thomas Dekker, *Shoemaker's Holiday, or the Gentle Craft* (1600).

## 21 *Women and Children*

1 Tusser, 153–60.

2 *Ibid.*, 168–74.

3 Anthony Fitzherbert, *Book of Husbandry* (1523), quot. Byrne (*Elizabethan Life*), 133–4.

4 D. M. Meads (ed.), *The Diary of Lady Margaret Hoby, 1559–1605* (1930).

5 Byrne, op. cit., 177.

6 Dodd, 69.

7 Watson, 13, 53.

8 R. O'Day, 89.

9 Byrne, op. cit., 186.

## 22 *Actors and Playgoers*

1 Thomas Dekker, *The Seven Deadly Sinnes of London*, 1606.

2 Harbage, 57.

3 *Ibid.*, 84; Chambers (*The Elizabethan Stage*), vol. 2, 532, 548.

4 Harbage, 61.

5 Brown, 51.

6 Gurr, 7.

7 Harbage, 41.

8 Quot. Bentley, vol. 6, 209–10.

9 Bradbrook, 97; Brown, 55; Chambers, op. cit., vol. 2, 552.

10 Harbage, 95, 111.

11 Bradbrook, 107.

12 J. P. Collier, *The History of English Dramatic Poetry*, vol. 1, 452–3; Bentley, vol. 1, 25.

13 Quot. Harbage, 97.

14 *Ibid.*

15 Bradbrook, 98; Wickham, vol. 2, 67–8; Ordish, 94–5; Roose-Evans, 20–21.

16 Hartnoll, 74–5.

17 Quot. Roose-Evans, 17.

18 *Hamlet*, Act 2, sc. ii.

19 Gurr, 85; Chambers, op. cit., vol. 2, 556.

20 Quot. Chambers, op. cit., vol. 2, 532.

21 Gurr, 39; Bentley, vol. 6, 36, 65; Brown, 12; Harbage, 61.

22 Byrne (*Elizabethan Life*), 230–33; Bentley, vol. 1, 136; Hartnoll, 81; Chambers, op. cit., vol. 2, 143, 177; Bradbrook, 63.

23 Chambers, op. cit., vol. 4, 323.

24 Quot. Bentley, vol. 6, 54.

25 Harbage, 16–17; Chambers, op. cit., vol. 1, 287–93, 313; Brown, 42.

26 Wickham, vol. 2, 116.

27 Quot. Bradbrook, 69–70.

28 Chambers, op. cit., vol. 4, 198–9.

29 *Ibid.*, 321.

30 *Ibid.*, 322.

31 Wickham, vol. 2, 9, 18; Chambers, op. cit., vol. 1, 202, 281; Gurr, 28; Bentley, vol. 2, 690.

32 Bentley, vol. 6, 113.

33 *Ibid.*

34 Bentley, vol. 6, 114; W. C. Hazlitt, *English Drama and Stage* (1869), 67–9.

## 23 *'Whole Counties Became Desperate'*

1 Ivan Roots, *The Great Rebellion* (1966); C. V. Wedgwood, *The Great Rebellion: The King's War, 1641–1647* (1958); Austin Woolrych, *Battles of the English Civil War* (1961); Samuel Rawson Gardiner, *History of the Great Civil War* (1893).

2 Ashley (*The People of England*), 94, 96–7; A. Briggs (*A Social History*), 134.

3 Briggs, op. cit., 134.

4 Wallace Notestein, *English Folk*, quot. Trevelyan, 239.

5 Quot. Briggs, op. cit., 142.

6 Ashley, op. cit., 99.

7 Briggs, op. cit., 149.
8 Gregory King, *Natural and Political Observations and Conclusions upon the State and Condition of England, 1696* (1801).
9 Quot. Hart (*The Man in the Pew*), 107–8.
10 *Ibid.*, 108.
11 Quot. Trevelyan, 278.
12 Ashley, op. cit., 102–3; Trevelyan, 224–6; G. S. Thomson, 191.
13 King, see note 8, quot. Trevelyan, 277.
14 Briggs, op. cit., 154.
15 Quot. Trevelyan, 254.
16 Notestein, 186.
17 Hart, op. cit., 246.
18 L. O. Pike, vol. 2, 186, 188–9.
19 *Ibid.*, 180–81.
20 Thomas (*Religion and the Decline of Magic*), 540, 210, 253, 278–9.
21 *Ibid.*, 547.
22 *Ibid.*, 546.
23 Lewinsohn, 128–35; L. O. Pike, vol. 2, 236–7; *The Discovery of Witches . . . by Matthew Hopkins, Witchfinder* (1647).
24 John Gaule, *Select Cases of Conscience Touching Witches and Witchcraft* (1646).
25 L. O. Pike, vol. 2, 236–7.
26 Sydney, vol. 1, 281; L. O. Pike, vol. 2, 289–90.
27 Radzinowicz, vol. 1, 217–18; Horn (*The Rural World*), 161.

24 *Schoolboys and Schoolgirls*

1 R. O'Day, 7.
2 B. Simon, 21.
3 Cressy, 33–4.
4 *Ibid.*, 2.
5 R. O'Day, 41; Stone ('The Educational Revolution in England'), 44.
6 B. Simon, 373; Cressy, 50, 104.
7 Raistrick, 11.
8 Adamson, 206.
9 Sylvester, 175.

10 *Ibid.*, 171.
11 *Ibid.*, 196.
12 *Ibid.*, 171.
13 Cressy, 68.
14 R. O'Day, 168.
15 Quot. Byrne (*Elizabethan Life*), 195.
16 Cressy, 66.
17 *Ibid.*, 65.
18 *Ibid.*, 38.
19 Gathorne-Hardy (*The Public School*), 38.
20 Cressy, 92.
21 R. O'Day, 174.
22 B. Simon, 20.
23 R. O'Day, 17–19, 24.
24 *Ibid.*, 9–20.
25 Stone ('Literacy and Education in England'), 99.
26 Cressy, 27.
27 Sylvester, 191.
28 R. O'Day, 32; Gathorne-Hardy, op. cit., 44.
29 R. O'Day, 32.
30 Byrne, op. cit., 181.
31 Adamson, 23–4; Buxton, 192; Byrne, op. cit., 191.
32 Cressy, 82.
33 *Ibid.*, 88.
34 Kamm, 76.
35 Fraser, 120.
36 Cressy, 107.
37 R. O'Day, 186.
38 Quot. Kamm, 38.
39 *Ibid.*, 60.
40 Fraser, 121–2.
41 J. H. Jesse, *Continuation of Memoirs of the Court of England* (1901), vol. 1, 196.
42 *An Account of the Conduct of the Duchess of Marlborough* (1742), 172.
43 Fraser, 122.
44 *Ibid.*, 129; Cressy, 178.
45 Fraser, 138.
46 *Ibid.*, 322; Kamm, 59.
47 Fraser, 320.
48 Cressy, 113; Fraser, 324.

49 Fraser, 327.
50 Cressy, 114.
51 Adamson, 210; Kamm, 65.
52 Adamson, 206–7.
53 R. O'Day, 187; Kamm, 59, 69, 76.
54 Frances Parthenope Verney,
   *Memoirs of the Verney Family
   During the Civil War* (1892).

### 25 *Undergraduates and Tutors*

1 R. O'Day, 90.
2 *Ibid.*, 90–91.
3 Kearney, 23.
4 W. Harrison, vol. 2, 202.
5 Stone ('The Educational Revolution
   in England'), 45.
6 Stone, op. cit., 56; R. O'Day, 104.
7 R. O'Day, 107–8.
8 Rowse (*The England of Elizabeth*),
   515–16.
9 Quot. Byrne (*Elizabethan Life*),
   203; Sylvester, 150.
10 J. Simon, 18.
11 Stone, op. cit., 71.
12 Quot. Morris, 69–70.
13 Cressy, 116, 128.
14 R. O'Day, 94.
15 V. H. H. Green, 80.
16 *Ibid.*, 75–7.
17 Anthony Wood, *History and
   Antiquities of the University of
   Oxford* (1674), quot. Morris, 58.
18 Morris, 78–80.
19 John Aubrey, *Brief Lives*, ed.
   Richard Barber (1975), 187.
20 Quot. Morris, 96.
21 Cressy, 119.

### 26 *'Roasted Chickens – Pease –
   Lobsters – Strawberries'*

1 G. C. Moore-Smith (ed.), *The
   Letters of Dorothy Osborne* (1928),
   89.
2 Ashley (*Life in Stuart England*),
   107.
3 *Ibid.*, 109.
4 *Ibid.*, 14.
5 *Ibid.*, 21.

6 Bryant (*The England of Charles II*),
   163.
7 *Ibid.*, 205.
8 Pepys, vol. 4, 95.
9 Bryant, op. cit., 104.
10 Pepys, vol. 4, 354; vol. 10, 144.
11 Pepys, vol. 10, 145.
12 Bryant, op. cit., 105.
13 *Ibid.*, 105; Pepys, vol. 10, 145.
14 Pepys, vol. 3, 190.
15 Jane Grigson, *The Vegetable Book*
   (1978), 505.
16 Braudel (*The Structures of
   Everyday Life*), 170.
17 Pepys, vol. 8, 516–17.
18 *Ibid.*, vol. 9, 477.
19 *Ibid.*, vol. 10, 104.
20 Bryant, op. cit., 100.
21 *Ibid.*, 101.
22 Pepys, vol. 10, 106.
23 Ashley, op. cit., 32.
24 G. S. Thomson, 108–10.
25 A. Wood, 172.
26 Quot. Bryant, op. cit., 152.
27 Pepys, vol. 10, 99.
28 G. S. Thomson, *passim*.
29 *Ibid.*, 182.
30 Pepys, vol. 8, 442.
31 G. S. Thomson, 216–20, 222.
32 Defoe, 360.
33 Godfrey (*Social Life under the
   Stuarts*), 100.
34 Defoe, 142.

### PART THREE

### 27 *'A Tour thro' the Whole Island'*

1 Defoe, *passim*.
2 Thomas Hardy, *Far From the
   Madding Crowd* (1874), ch. 6.

### 28 *Countrymen, Clergymen and
   Farmers*

1 Earle, 129.
2 Ashley (*The People of England*),
   118; Porter, 69, 81; A. Briggs
   (*A Social History*), 170.

3 Porter, 75.
4 *London Encyclopaedia*, 818.
5 Porter, 60, 64, 80.
6 Horn (*The Rural World*), 149.
7 A. Bell, 85.
8 *Ibid.*, 105–6.
9 *Ibid.*, 118.
10 Trevelyan, 359.
11 Woodforde (*Diary*), *passim*; Porter, 189.
12 Henry Fielding, *Joseph Andrews* (1742).
13 R. W. Chapman (ed.), *Jane Austen's Letters* (1932), 467.
14 A. Bell, 105.
15 *Ibid.*, 124.
16 Skinner, 274, 283.
17 *Ibid.*, 191–2.
18 Turner, 182.
19 Porter, 185.
20 *Ibid.*, 191.
21 *Ibid.*, 195.
22 Trevelyan, 295.
23 Quot. Porter, 287.
24 *Ibid.*, 187.
25 A. Bell, 85.
26 Henry Fielding, *Amelia* (1751), Book 1, ch. 2.
27 Trevelyan, 206.
28 Mingay (*English Landed Society*), 54.
29 Henry Fielding, *Tom Jones* (1749).
30 Ashley (*Life in Stuart England*), 42.
31 *Ibid.*, 44.
32 Quot. Porter, 84.
33 *Ibid.*
34 Quot. A. Briggs, op. cit., 172.
35 *Ibid.*

29 *Country Houses and Gardens*
1 Quot. Girouard (*Life in the English Country House*), 150.
2 *Ibid.*
3 *Ibid.*, 160.
4 Moritz, 35.
5 Kalm, 13.
6 Girouard, op. cit., 203–4, 208, 272.
7 Jarrett, 165.

8 Rochefoucauld, 219.
9 Moritz, 127.
10 Girouard, op. cit., 214–20; John Summerson, *The Life and Work of John Nash* (1980), 94–5.
11 Hunt and Willis, 7–8.
12 Joseph Addison, *The Spectator* No. 477, 6 September 1712, quot. Hunt and Willis, 145–7.
13 Quot. Hunt and Willis, 274.
14 *Ibid.*, 19.
15 John Harris, *Sir William Chambers* (1970), 32–9.
16 Hunt and Willis, 31.
17 Jane Austen, *Mansfield Park* (1814), ch. 6.
18 William Shenstone, 'Unconnected Thoughts on Gardening' (1764), quot. Hunt and Willis, 289–97.
19 Samuel Richardson, *The History of Sir Charles Grandison* (1753–4).
20 Girouard, op. cit. 218.

30 *Interiors*
1 Robert Southey, *The Doctor* (1834–7).
2 Isaac Ware, *A Complete Body of Architecture* (1756), 469–70.
3 Porter, 240.
4 Oliver Brackett, 'The Interior of the House', in Turberville (*Johnson's England*), vol. 2, 148.
5 J. Fleming and H. Honour, *The Penguin Dictionary of Decorative Arts* (1977), 184, 374–5, 931; John Gloag, *A Short Dictionary of Furniture* (1969), 229, 389, 606.
6 Eland, vol. 1, 53–60; Jarrett, 158.
7 Matthew Brettingham, *The Plans, Elevations, and Sections of Holkham in Norfolk*, vol. 1, quot. Brackett, 139.
8 *Passages from the Diary of Mrs Lybbe Powys, 1756–1808*, 116.
9 Saussure, 157.
10 Quot. Brackett, op. cit., 134.
11 Kalm, 12–13.
12 Porter, 237.

13 Jarrett, 152.
14 Marshall (*English People*), 8; Jarrett, 153.

31 *Manners and Dress*

1 Saussure, 111.
2 Moritz, 59.
3 P. Quennell, 208.
4 Porter, 321, 323, 325.
5 Farington, vol. 2, 24.
6 Quot. Porter, 326.
7 Thomas Bowdler (ed.), *Gibbon's History of the Decline and Fall of the Roman Empire, for the Use of Families and Young Persons*, 6 vols (1826).
8 Quot. Porter, 326.
9 Wraxall, vol. 1, 99.
10 Moritz, 88.
11 Talbot Hughes, 'Costume' in Turberville (*Johnson's England*), vol. 1, 394.
12 James Boswell, *Life of Johnson*, 2 vols (1791), 29 March 1776.
13 Forster (*Life of Landor*), quot. Sydney, vol. 1, 110–11.
14 Quot. Buck, 169.
15 Sydney, vol. 1, 90.
16 *Ibid.*, 92.
17 *Ibid.*
18 Roche, 5.
19 Buck, 21.
20 *Ibid.*, 11–13.
21 Sydney, vol. 1, 95.
22 John Macdonald (*Life and Travels*), 382–3.
23 Talbot Hughes, op. cit., note 11, 393.
24 Sydney, vol. 1, 115.
25 Gunn, 114–15.
26 Chesterfield, vol. 1, 249–50.
27 *Ibid.*
28 Buck, 92.
29 Quot. Porter, 277.
30 Moritz, 92.
31 Quot. Trevelyan, 389.
32 Buck, 130.
33 *Ibid.*, 131.
34 *Ibid.*, 125–6.
35 J. H. Jesse, *George Selwyn and his Contemporaries* (1843), quot. Buck, 138.

32 *Travellers, Postmen and Innkeepers*

1 Moritz, 128–30.
2 Sydney, vol. 2, 6, 7, 10, 24; A. Young (*A Tour through the North of England*), 430–1.
3 Patrick Pringle, *Stand and Deliver: The Story of the Highwaymen* (1951); Charles Harper, *Half-Hours with the Highwaymen*, 2 vols (1908).
4 H. L. Beales, 'Travel and Communications' in Turberville (*Johnson's England*), vol. 1, 131; 'Turnpikes', *London Encyclopaedia*, 895.
5 Wraxall, vol. 2, 473.
6 Mark Searle, *Turnpikes and Toll-Bars*, 2 vols (n.d.); 'Turnpikes', *London Encyclopaedia*, 895.
7 Beales, op. cit., note 4, 141.
8 *Ibid.*, 140–41; Mitchell and Leys (*A History of the English People*), 506; Joyce, *History of the Post Office* (1893).
9 Anthony Trollope, *Framley Parsonage* (1861), ch. 9.
10 Quot. Mitchell and Leys, 530.
11 Quot. Beales, op. cit., note 4, 140.
12 Moritz, 124.
13 John Taylor, *Wanderings in the West* (1870), 16–17.
14 Mitchell and Leys, 520.
15 *Ibid.*, 522.
16 A. Young (*A Tour through the Southern Counties*), 197.
17 George Coleman, *Random Recollections* (1795), vol. 1, 215.
18 An Irish Gentleman, *Journey through England* (1752), 12; quot. Beales, op. cit., note 4, 148.
19 Richardson and Eberlein, 22.

20 Thomas Hughes, *Tom Brown's Schooldays* (1857), ch. 4.

### 33 *Hunters, Poachers and Smugglers*

1 Robert Surtees, *Mr Sponge's Sporting Tour* (1853), ch. 24.
2 G. M. Hughes, *A History of Windsor Forest* (1890), 73.
3 Ingram Cobbin, *Georgiana* (1820), 25.
4 E. D. Cuming, 'Sports and Games' in Turberville (*Johnson's England*), vol. 1, 366–7; G. M. Hughes, op. cit., 70.
5 Trevelyan, 407.
6 Cuming, op. cit., note 4, 369.
7 *Ibid.*, 371.
8 E. P. Thompson (*Whigs and Hunters*), 27.
9 Radzinowicz, vol. 1, 77.
10 E. P. Thompson, op. cit., 195.
11 Peter B. Munsche, *Gentlemen and Poachers: The English Game Laws, 1671–1831* (1981), quot. Malcolmson, 148.
12 Porter, 153.
13 *Gentleman's Magazine* (1748), quot. Jarrett, 54.
14 *The Autobiography of Elizabeth M. Sewell* (1907), quot. Mitchell and Leys (*A History of the English People*), 719.
15 Woodforde (29 March 1787).
16 H. N. Shore, *Smuggling Days and Smuggling Ways* (1929); Mitchell and Leys, op. cit., 715.

### 34 *Pastimes and Pleasures*

1 Jacob Larwood, *The Story of the London Parks* (n.d.); E. Beresford Chancellor, *The Pleasure Haunts of London* (1925); *London Encyclopaedia*; Hole (*A Dictionary*).
2 Altick (*The Shows of London*); *London Encyclopaedia*, 805–6.
3 Ireland and Nichols, vol. 1, 161–84.

4 E. D. Cuming, 'Sports and Games' in Turberville (*Johnson's England*), vol. 1, 378.
5 *Memoirs of the Life of Daniel Mendoza*, ed. Paul Magriel (1951), 65–6.
6 Saussure, 277–80.
7 *Memoirs of William Hickey*, ed. P. Quennell, 48–9.
8 Sydney, vol. 1, 177.
9 Cuming, op. cit., note 4, 372.
10 Saussure, 281–2.
11 Malcolmson, 102.
12 Saussure, 291.
13 John Lawrence, *History and Delineation of the Horse* (1809), quot. Cuming, op. cit., 364.
14 Gilbey and Cuming, *George Morland: His Life and Works* (1907), 46–7.
15 Christopher Hibbert, *George IV* (1972), vol. 1, 109–10; Roger Mortimer, *Jockey Club*, 44–6.
16 Saussure, 294–5.
17 *Ibid.*, 295–6.
18 Altham and Swanton, 70.
19 Cuming, op. cit., note 4, 378–9.
20 Trevelyan, 408; *London Encyclopaedia*, 484, 500–1, 953; John Arlott (ed.), *From Hambledon to Lords* (1948); Altham and Swanton.
21 *Mrs Hurst Dancing*, ed. G. E. Mingay (1981), 32.
22 E. V. Lucas (ed.), *The Hambledon Men: Being a new edition of John Nyren's Young Cricketer's Tutor and The Cricketers of my Time* (1954), 121.
23 *Ibid.*, 136.
24 Walpole, vol. 7, 334.
25 Percy Colson, *White's, 1693–1950* (1951).
26 Walpole, vol. 14, 292.
27 *Passages from the Diary of Mrs Lybbe Powys, 1756–1808*, 186.
28 Sydney, vol. 1, 229.
29 *Ibid.*, 228.

30 Quot. Porter, 35.
31 Trevelyan, 315.
32 P. Clark, 39.
33 *Ibid.*, 43.
34 *Ibid.*, 39, 59, 109, 158.
35 Saussure, 158.
36 P. Clark, 66–9, 83, 149.
37 *Ibid.*, 187–95, 199.
38 *Ibid.*, 239.
39 George (*London Life*), 32.
40 *Ibid.*, 35.
41 Cadogan, 25.
42 *Ibid.*, 20.
43 Henry Fielding, *An Enquiry into the Causes of the Late Increase of Robbers* (1751).
44 George, op. cit., 28.
45 *Ibid.*, 38.
46 *Ibid.*, 39.

### 35 *Marriage and Divorce*

1 Laslett (*The World We Have Lost*), 152.
2 Stone (*The Family, Sex and Marriage*), 30–31.
3 *Ibid.*, 33.
4 *Ibid.*, 32.
5 Quot. Laslett, op. cit., 101.
6 Stone, op. cit., 223.
7 Fraser, 26.
8 *Ibid.*
9 *Ibid.*, 269.
10 *Ibid.*
11 *Ibid.*, 275.
12 Stone, op. cit., 195.
13 *Ibid.*, 39–40.
14 Fraser, 12; Laslett, op. cit. 84.
15 Laslett, op. cit., 85.
16 Stone, op. cit., 44; Laslett, op. cit., 86.
17 Laslett, op. cit., 87.
18 Stone, op. cit., 46.
19 Laslett, op. cit., 105.
20 *Ibid.*, 104; Stone, op. cit., 46.
21 Stone, op. cit., 52, 54; Laslett, op. cit., 107.
22 Quot. Stone, op. cit., 136–8.
23 Fraser, 4.

24 *Ibid.*, 43, 44–8, 181–2, 185, 201.
25 *Ibid.*, 244–5.
26 Jarrett, 118, 128.
27 Stone, op. cit., 35.
28 Thomas Hardy, *The Mayor of Casterbridge* (1886), ch. 1.
29 Fraser, 291–2.
30 Stone, op. cit., 212.
31 *Ibid.*, 193.
32 *Ibid.*, 203.
33 Rochefoucauld, 217.
34 *Ibid.*, 219.
35 Stone, op. cit., 87.
36 *Ibid.*, 122.
37 Quot. Stone, op. cit., 122.
38 *Recollections of the Early Years of the Present Century by the Hon. Amelia Murray* (1868).
39 *Stanhope Memoirs: Memoirs of the Lady Hester Stanhope as related by herself in conversation with her physician*, vol. 2, 234.
40 Loren Reid, *Charles James Fox* (1969), 10.
41 George (*London Life*), 42–9; *London Encyclopaedia*, 291–2.

### 36 *Sex*

1 Boswell (*London Journal*), 7t
2 Boswell, 250–358; Frederick A. Pottle, *James Boswell: The Earlier Years, 1740–1769* (1966), 96–120.
3 Stone (*The Family, Sex and Marriage*), 226, 341; Reay Tannahill, *Sex in History* (1980), 336; Fraser, 66–7.
4 Fraser, 67.
5 *Ibid.*, 66.
6 Stone, op. cit., 320.
7 *Ibid.*, 324.
8 *Ibid.*, 325; Fraser, 233.
9 Thomas (*Man and the Natural World*), 39.
10 *Ibid.*, 135.
11 Bray, *passim*.
12 James Prior, *Life of Burke* (1826), quot. Sydney, vol. 2, 304.
13 Fraser, 52.

14 *Ibid.*, 51.
15 Porter, 278.
16 Fraser, 51.
17 Stone, op. cit., 325–6.
18 *Ibid.*, 325.
19 Pepys, vol. 8, 389–90.
20 *Ibid.*, vol. 5, 351; vol. 4, 417; vol. 1, 220; vol. 4, 203, 317; vol. 5, 17, 219, 242; vol. 9, 337, 366–7, 367–8.
21 *Memoirs of William Hickey*, ed, P. Quennell, 8.
22 *An Answer to a . . . libel, entitled a Discovery of the Conduct of receivers and thieftakers . . . written by C——s H——n wherein is prov'd . . . who is originally the Grand Thieftaker*, etc. (1718).
23 Stone, op. cit., 279.
24 Pepys, vol. 9, 21–2, 58–9.
25 Stone, op. cit., 336.
26 *Sophie in London 1786*, 133.
27 Casanova, *Memoirs*, vol. 2, 163–4; Jarrett, 137.
28 Hickey, op. cit., note 21, 23.

### 37 *Theatres and Shows*

1 Pepys, vol. 10, 431–3.
2 Colley Cibber, *Apology*, ed. R. W. Lowe (1889), vol. 1, 132–3.
3 Nicoll (*Restoration Drama*), 12.
4 Pepys, vol. 10, 443.
5 Nicoll, op. cit., 14.
6 Pepys, vol. 9, 425.
7 *Ibid.*, vol. 10, 444.
8 *Ibid.*, vol. 9, 54.
9 *Ibid.*, 183.
10 *Life and Times of Frederick Reynolds*, vol. 1, 90–91.
11 Quot. Summers, 37.
12 Dobbs, 34.
13 Quot. Pedicord, 41–2.
14 Summers, 90–91.
15 Pedicord, 2.
16 Nicoll (*A History of English Drama*), vol. 2, 10–11.
17 *Ibid.*, 254.
18 W. J. Lawrence, 'The Drama and the Theatre' in Turberville (*Johnson's England*), 175.
19 Nicoll, op. cit., vol. 2, 257.
20 Pedicord, 48–9, 52; *Daily Courant*, 14 December 1702.
21 Quot. Pedicord, 48.
22 Malcolm, vol. 2, 408–9.
23 Lawrence, op. cit., note 18, vol. 2, 187.
24 Kelly, 55.
25 Nicoll, op. cit., vol. 2, 14.
26 *Ibid.*, vol. 3, 6.
27 Quot. Alwin Thaler, *Shakespeare to Sheridan* (1922), 145.
28 Boswell (*London Journal*), 98.
29 Boswell, *Journal of a Tour to the Hebrides*, ed. Frederick A. Pottle and Charles Bennett (1963), 119.
30 Kelly, 150–51.
31 *Ibid.*, 55.
32 *Ibid.*, 72.
33 *Ibid.*, 54, 55, 66.
34 Hartnoll, 122; W. J. Lawrence, op. cit., note 18, 186–7; Carola Oman, *David Garrick* (1958).
35 George Parker, *A View of Society and Manners*, vol. 1, 189.
36 Rosenfeld (*Strolling Players*), 2.
37 *Ibid.*, 5, 28, 112.
38 *Ibid.*, 23.
39 Parker, op. cit., 222.
40 John Bernard, *Retrospections of the Stage* (1830), quot. Rosenfeld, op. cit., 22.
41 Quot. Rosenfeld, op. cit., 16.
42 Speaight (*Punch and Judy*), 42.
43 Rosenfeld (*The Theatres of the London Fairs*), 7, 144.
44 Ward, 10.
45 Rosenfeld, op. cit., 2, 60, 40, 150, 158.
46 *Ibid.*, 63, 74.
47 Pepys, vol. 3, 80.
48 Speaight, op. cit. 39.
49 *Ibid.*, 62.
50 *Ibid.*, 113.
51 P. Quennell (*Mayhew's London*), 432.

52 Speaight (*A History of the Circus*), 24–8.
53 Charles Dickens, *The Old Curiosity Shop* (1841), ch. 39.

### 38 *Quacks, Diseases and Cures*

1 Samuel Curwen, *Journal*, 317.
2 Quot. Menzies Campbell, 190.
3 Sydney, vol. 1, 312.
4 Jarrett, 69.
5 *Ibid.*, 221.
6 Brian Fothergill, *Sir William Hamilton* (1969), 198; James Graham, *A Sketch . . . of Dr Graham's Medical Apparatus* (1780); Sydney, vol. 1, 317–23.
7 Dainton, 141.
8 *Ibid.*, 152.
9 Ida MacAlpine and Richard Hunter, *George III and the Mad Business* (1970), 54, 78, 79.
10 Saussure, 93.
11 Dainton, 145.
12 Kilvert, 4 July 1871.
13 Charles Dickens, *Martin Chuzzlewit* (1844), vol. 2, ch. 21.
14 Simond, 109.
15 Dainton, 163–5.
16 Quot. Jarrett, 210.
17 *Ibid.*, 220.
18 Cartwright, 75; J. D. Rolleston, 25.
19 Cartwright, 78–9.
20 Rolleston, 15.
21 Creighton, vol. 2, 544.
22 Evelyn, vol. 4, 468.
23 Cartwright, 81.
24 *Ibid.*, 82.
25 Creighton, vol. 2, 512.
26 Cartwright, 83.
27 *Ibid.*, 84.
28 *Ibid.*, 85; Dorothy Fisk, *Dr Jenner of Berkeley* (1959).
29 *Catalogue of Personal and Political Satires*, British Museum 9924, 12 June 1802.
30 *Ibid.*, BM 11093, 20 June 1808.
31 Rolleston, 18; Cartwright, 90; Gale, 139.
32 Creighton, vol. 2, 13.
33 Gale, 131–6.
34 Walter Jackson Bate, *John Keats* (1967), 559.
35 Pepys, vol. 5, 76.
36 Creighton, vol. 2, 122; Gale, 124.
37 Creighton, vol. 2, 122–4.
38 Gale, 124.
39 Cartwright, 123.
40 Winifred Gérin, *Emily Brontë* (1971).
41 Creighton, vol. 2, 793, 841; Cartwright, 105–6.
42 John Snow, *On Cholera* (new ed., 1965).

### 39 *Operators and Tooth-drawers*

1 Quot. Menzies Campbell, 237.
2 *Ibid.*, 260–61.
3 Kilvert, 37–9.
4 *Ibid.*, 148–9.
5 Thomas Vicary, *The English Man's Trasure* (1613), quot. Laver, (*Taste and Fashion from the French Revolution to the Present Day*), 20.
6 Menzies Campbell, 191.
7 Laver, op. cit., 42–3.
8 Bremner, 396.
9 Menzies Campbell, 53–6.
10 M. D. George, *Catalogue of Personal and Political Satires*, vi, 745, BM 7766.
11 Bremner, 395.
12 Menzies Campbell, 238.
13 *Ibid.*, 189.
14 Horatio Pass, *Artificial Teeth and Palates* (1840), quot. Laver, op. cit., 4.
15 Compton Mackenzie, *Octave Six*, 179.
16 Laver, op. cit., 56.
17 Christopher Hibbert, *George IV* (1972), vol. 1, 174.
18 Menzies Campbell, 252.
19 *Ibid.*, 237–8.

### 40 'Youth are Expeditiously Instructed'

1 Quot. Neuburg, 48.
2 *Ibid.*, 40.
3 *Ibid.*
4 *Ibid.*, 42.
5 *Ibid.*, 17–18.
6 *Ibid.*, 54.
7 Martin, 7.
8 Neuburg, 417.
9 M. G. Jones, 73.
10 *Ibid.*, 22, 44.
11 *Ibid.*, 75, 78.
12 *Ibid.*, 156.
13 R. O'Day, 254.
14 Neuburg, 36–7.
15 *Ibid.*, 18, 23, 24, 30–31.
16 Quot. Sylvester, 207–9.
17 Martin, 9; Sylvester, 256.
18 Sylvester, 259–60.
19 R. O'Day, 256–8.
20 Martin, 40.
21 R. O'Day, 201.
22 Martin, 33.
23 R. O'Day, 200.
24 *Ibid.*, 201.
25 Martin, 33; R. O'Day, 203; Raistrick, 15, 28.
26 R. O'Day, 208.
27 Sylvester, 250–51.
28 *Ibid.*, 253.
29 *Ibid.*, 252–3.
30 *Ibid.*, 204.
31 R. O'Day, 201.
32 Sylvester, 198–9.
33 Martin, 40.
34 *Ibid.*, 28.
35 *Ibid.*, 29.
36 *Ibid.*, 40.
37 Sylvester, 204–6.
38 R. O'Day, 204.
39 Sylvester, 259–60.
40 E. Hughes, 319–31.
41 Martin, 29–30.

### 41 Universities, Academies and the Grand Tour

1 R. O'Day, 198.
2 I. Parker, 83.
3 R. O'Day, 196–7.
4 *Ibid.*, 147.
5 Sylvester, 217.
6 Quot. Morris, 156–7.
7 Edward Gibbon, *Memoirs* (1792), quot. Morris, 152–3.
8 Quot. Morris, 165.
9 *Ibid.*
10 *Ibid.*, 145–6, 160.
11 Sylvester, 219.
12 *Ibid.*, 216; E. Hughes, 301.
13 E. Hughes, 315.
14 Quot. Morris, 151.
15. E. Hughes, 307.
16 Sylvester, 219–20.
17 I. Parker, 89.
18 *Ibid.*, 59.
19 Sylvester, 245–6.
20 I. Parker, 86.
21 Sylvester, 237, 240–43.
22 *Ibid.*, 233–7.
23 *Ibid.*, 246–7.
24 R. O'Day, 213.
25 *Ibid.*, 210.
26 *Ibid.*
27 Sylvester, 231–2.
28 John Moore, *A View of Society and Manners in Italy* (1792); Sir Thomas Nugent, *The Grand Tour*, 4 vols (1749); James Howell, *Instructions for Forreine Travel* (1642).
29 Quot. Sylvester, 231–2.

### 42 Masters and Workers

1 Porter, 152, 205, 224, 330, 336; A. Briggs (*A Social History*), 170; Ashley (*The People of England*), 116; Trevelyan, 388–9.
2 Ashley, op. cit., 123–4.
3 Porter, 336.
4 *Ibid.*, 346.
5 Quot. Porter, 334.

6 Ashley, op. cit., 120–3; Porter, 212, 329.
7 Kalm, 179.
8 Quot. Malcolmson, 57–8.
9 Jarrett, 64, 84.
10 Quot. Malcolmson, 13.
11 *Ibid.*, 14.
12 Jarrett, 89.
13 *Ibid.*, 110.
14 Quot. Porter, 106.
15 Quot. Malcolmson, 37, 43.
16 Hoskins (*The Midland Peasant*), 228.
17 *Ibid.*, 204.
18 Malcolmson, 45.
19 Ashley, op. cit., 117.
20 Malcolmson, 145–6.
21 *Ibid.*, 56.
22 Porter, 108.
23 *Ibid.*, 102.
24 Trevelyan, 285, 321.
25 Robert Southey, *Letters from England*, vol. 1, 36.
26 Quot. A. Briggs, op. cit., 177.
27 Simond, 118.
28 Hammonds (*The Town Labourer*), 19–20.

### 43 *Clothworkers and Machine-breakers*

1 Quot. Malcolmson, 109.
2 Quot. Porter, 118.
3 Malcolmson, 120–21.
4 *Ibid.*, 128.
5 J. Paul de Castro, *The Gordon Riots* (1926); Christopher Hibbert, *King Mob: Lord George Gordon and the Riots of 1780* (1958).
6 Arthur Young, *General View of the Agriculture of Oxfordshire* (1813); Malcolmson, 112.
7 Malcolmson, 118.
8 *Ibid.*, 119.
9 *Ibid.*, 125.
10 Hammonds (*The Town Labourer*), 127–9.
11 Quot. Malcolmson, 150–51.

12 Porter, 110; Ashley (*People of England*), 133.
13 Quot. Porter, 354.
14 E. P. Thompson (*Making of the English Working Class*), 529–89
15 *Ibid.*, 614.
16 *Ibid.*, 656–7.
17 *Ibid.*
18 *Ibid.*; Hammonds (*The Skilled Labourer*), *passim*.

### 44 *Rick-burners, Paupers and Chartists*

1 Cobbett, *passim*.
2 Clarke, 33.
3 Hobsbawm and Rudé, 182.
4 *Ibid.*, 212.
5 *Ibid.*, 112–13.
6 *Ibid.*, 263.
7 Humphry House, *The Dickens World* (2nd ed., 1942), 93.
8 R. G. Gammage, *The History of the Chartist Movement* (1894), quot. Best, 187–8.
9 D. J. V. Jones, *passim*.
10 A. R. Schoyen, *The Chartist Challenge* (1958); Donald Read and Eric Glasgow, *Feargus O'Connor: Irishman and Chartist* (1961); Mark Hovel, *The Chartist Movement* (1925); Hammonds (*The Age of the Chartists*).

### 45 *Below Stairs*

1 Hecht, 3.
2 Powys, 222–3.
3 Hartcup, 17.
4 Hecht, 6.
5 Porter, 100; Ashley (*People of England*), 136; Burnett (*Useful Toil*), 138.
6 Best, 121.
7 *Ibid.*, 124.
8 *Ibid.*, 122.
9 Young, vol. 2, 144.
10 Hartcup, 41.
11 Charles Dickens, *Bleak House* (1853), ch. 7.
12 Hecht, 51.

13 Hartcup, 47.
14 Quot. Burnett, op. cit., 176.
15 Hole (*English Home-Life*), 96.
16 Diana Cooper, *The Rainbow Comes and Goes* (1958), 34–6.
17 Hartcup, 67.
18 Hecht, 150–51.
19 *Ibid.*, 153.
20 Best, 124.
21 Hartcup, 91–3.
22 Hecht, 114.
23 *Ibid.*, 7, 14, 112.
24 *Ibid.*, 111.
25 Hartcup, 26.
26 Burnett, op. cit., 190.
27 Arnold Bennett, *Riceyman Steps* (1923), part 4, ch. 7.
28 Burnett, op. cit., 216.
29 Thea Holme, *The Carlyles at Home* (1965), *passim.*
30 Hecht, 115.
31 Woodforde, vol. 2, 212.
32 Girouard (*Life in the English Country House*), endpapers.
33 Quot. Hecht, 117.
34 *Ibid.*, 121.
35 *Ibid.*, 126.
36 Moritz, 159.
37 Macdonald, 179–80.
38 *Ibid.*, 95, 236.
39 Hartcup, 28.
40 Quot. Hecht, 180.
41 *Ibid.*, 185.
42 William Lanceley, *From Hall-Boy to House-Steward* (1925).
43 Hecht, 183–4.
44 *Ibid.*, 159.
45 *Ibid.*, 161.
46 Saussure, 194.
47 Hecht, 162.
48 P. Quennell (*Hogarth's Progress*), 186.
49 Hecht, 167.
50 *Ibid.*, 168.
51 Jane Austen, *Pride and Prejudice* (1813), ch. 43.
52 Simond, 145.
53 *Ibid.*, 122–3.

54 Hecht, 171; Hartcup, 24.
55 Quot. Burnett, op. cit., 160–61.
56 Burnett, op. cit., 139.
57 *Ibid.*, 174.

## 46 *Shops and Shopping*

1 Roche, 25, 141.
2 *Ibid.*, 87.
3 Quot. D. Davis, 201.
4 Bryant Lillywhite, *London Signs* (1972); *London Encyclopaedia*, 841–2.
5 D. Davis, 189.
6 A. Briggs (*A Social History*), 178.
7 J. F. C. Harrison (*The Early Victorians*), 93–4.
8 D. Davis, 184.
9 *The Life of Robert Owen by Himself*, ed. M. Beer (1920), 25–7.
10 Quot. D. Davis, 187.
11 *Ibid.*, 293.
12 *Ibid.*, 291.
13 *Ibid.*
14 *London Encyclopaedia*, 960.
15 Mitchell and Leys (*A History of the English People*), 560.
16 *The Life of Robert Owen*, see note 9, 19.
17 D. Davis, 260–61.
18 *Ibid.*, 216.
19 *Ibid.*, 223.
20 *Ibid.*, 206.
21 Charles Dickens, *Sketches by 'Boz'* (1836), ch. 6.
22 Charles Dickens, *Bleak House* (1853), ch. 5.
23 P. Quennell (*Mayhew's London*), 268.
24 Pepys, vol. 10, 417–18.
25 Daniel Defoe, *Colonel Jack* (1722), quot. D. Davis, 218.

## 47 *Pedlars and Markets*

1 P. Quennell (*Mayhew's London*), 28.
2 *Ibid.*, 56–7.
3 *Ibid.*, 86.
4 *Ibid.*, 31.

5  P. Quennell (*Mayhew's Characters*), 89–92.
6  *Ibid.*, 96–9.
7  Charles Dickens, *Martin Chuzzlewit* (1844), ch. 40.
8  Charles Dickens, *Oliver Twist* (1838), ch. 21.
9  P. Quennell (*Mayhew's London*), 110–11.
10  D. Davis, 253.
11  *Ibid.*, 265–6.
12  *Ibid.*, 263–4.
13  Charles Hindley, *The Life and Adventures of a Cheap Jack* (1876), quot. D. Davis, 264.
14  P. Quennell (*Mayhew's Characters*), 73–6.
15  D. Davis, 240.
16  Quot. D. Davis, 246.

PART FOUR

48  *Owners of the Land*

1  Stone (*An Open Elite?*), *passim*.
2  Balsan, 84.
3  Philip Magnus, *King Edward VII* (1964); Christopher Hibbert, *Edward VII: A Portrait* (1976); *King Edward VII: Biographical and Personal Sketches and Anecdotes* (1910); Sir Sidney Lee, *King Edward VII*, 2 vols (1925–7).
4  John Wilson, *C.B.: A Life of Sir Henry Campbell-Bannerman* (1973), 145.
5  Robert Blake, *Disraeli* (1969), 681.
6  Balsan, 81–3.
7  *Ibid.*, 82.
8  E. C. Dugdale, *A. J. Balfour* (1936), 179.
9  Balsan, 84.
10  Quot. Anthony Glyn, *Elinor Glyn: A Biography* (1955), 186–7.
11  Nicolson, 85–7.

49  *Dressing, Smoking and Social Rank*

1  Balsan, 93.
2  Quot. Burnett (*Useful Toil*), 182.
3  Young, vol. 1, xiv.
4  *Victorian Shopping*, 807–19.
5  Gunn, 139.
6  Max Beerbohm, *In Defence of Cosmetics* (1896), quot. Gunn, 140.
7  Young, op. cit., xix.
8  J. P. Collier, *An Old Man's Diary* (1872); John Coleman, *Fifty Years of An Actor's Life* (1904), vol. 2, 23–4; Edgar Johnson, *Charles Dickens* (1953), vol. 1, 410, 497; Christopher Hibbert, *The Making of Charles Dickens* (1967), 112–13.
9  Ponsonby, 150, 202–3, 213, 221, 224.
10  Viscount Mersey, *A Picture of Life, 1872–1940* (1941), 359; Ponsonby, 16; Elizabeth Longford, *Victoria R.I.* (1964), 417.
11  Ponsonby, 17.
12  Girouard (*Life in the English Country House*), 295.
13  Girouard (*The Victorian Country House*), 26.
14  Pückler-Muskaü, vol. 1, 44.
15  Girouard, op. cit., 146.
16  Girouard (*Life in the English Country House*), 265, 276.
17  *Ibid.*, 265.
18  Christopher Hibbert, *George IV* (1973), vol. 2, 126–7.
19  Girouard (*The Victorian Country House*), 142.
20  Taine, 155.
21  Hermione Hobhouse, *Lost London* (1971), 49.
22  Gervase Huxley, *Victorian Duke* (1967).
23  Charles Kingsley, *Alton Locke* (1862), quot. Girouard, op. cit., 3.

50  *Workers on the Land*

1  Burnett (*Useful Toil*), 64–7.

2 Reader, 72; Best, 60.
3 E. R. Pike (*Documents of the Victorian Golden Age*), 216.
4 Children's Employment Commission, 6th report, quot. Pike, op. cit.
5 *Ibid*.
6 Quot. Marcus, 137–8.
7 Reader, 62–3.
8 Best, 86.
9 Flora Thompson, *Lark Rise* (1939), ch. 1.
10 Kilvert, 2 July, 20 October 1870.
11 W. Johnston, *England As It Is*, quot. Reader, 54.
12 Reader, 55.
13 J. F. C. Harrison (*The Early Victorians*), 61–2.
14 Quot. Harrison, op. cit., 60–61.
15 *Ibid*., 70.
16 Léonce de Lavergne, *The Rural Economy of England* (1855), quot. Young, 5.
17 Quot. Reader, 60.
18 Best, 128.
19 *Ibid*., 127.
20 Rowntree, 8.
21 Davies, quot. Bishop, 64.
22 Bishop, 64.
23 Reader, 67; Bishop, 62; Masterman (*The Condition of England*), 172.
24 Thomas Hardy, *Far From the Madding Crowd* (1874), Ch. 1.
25 A. Young (*A Tour through the Southern Counties*), 124.
26 Quot. Best, 273.

51 *Towns and Factories*

1 Charles Dickens, *Hard Times* (1854), ch. 5.
2 William Dodd, *The Factory System Illustrated* (1842), quot. J. F. C. Harrison (*The Early Victorians*), 40.
3 Engels, 78–80.
4 Taine, 134.
5 Booth (*Life and Labour*), 98.
6 *Ibid*., 108–24.

7 *Ibid*., 127.
8 J. R. Leifchild, 'Life and Labour in the Coal-fields', *The Cornhill Magazine* (1862), quot. E. R. Pike (*Documents of the Victorian Golden Age*), 68.
9 W. A. Abram, 'Social Condition and Political Prospects of the Lancashire Workman', *Fortnightly Review* (October 1868), quot. E. R. Pike, op. cit.
10 Childrens' Employment Commission, 5th Report (1866), quot. E. R. Pike, op. cit., 188.
11 Quot. E. R. Pike, op. cit., 117, 189.
12 J. F. C. Harrison, op. cit., 52–7.
13 Quot. Best, 50–51.
14 J. F. C. Harrison, op. cit. 48.
15 A. Briggs (*Victorian Cities*), 182.
16 *Ibid*., 229–30.
17 Lewis, 219.
18 Cartwright, 103.
19 Watkin, 39–40.
20 *Ibid*., 38.
21 Trevelyan, 530.
22 Watkin, 48; Lloyd, 252.
23 Cartwright, 112.
24 Watkin, 49.

52 *Mines, Brickfields and Sweat-shops*

1 J. R. Leifchild, 'Life and Labour in the Coal-fields', *The Cornhill Magazine*, quot. E. R. Pike (*Documents of the Victorian Golden Age*), 68–9.
2 Engels, 279.
3 *Ibid*., 281.
4 G. E. Evans (*The Days that We Have Seen*), 124–5.
5 Benjamin Disraeli, *Sybil* (1845), Book III, ch. 1.
6 Children's Employment Commission, 3rd Report, 1864.
7 Reports of Inspectors of Factories, 1864 (Robert Baker's Reports), quot. E. R. Pike, op. cit., 212.
8 F. D. Longe's Report on the

Brickfields of Staffordshire
(Children's Employment
Commission, 5th Report, 1866),
quot. E. R. Pike, op. cit., 214.
9 Charles Dickens, *Bleak House*
(1853), ch. 8.
10 Quot. Best, 96.
11 P. Quennell (*Mayhew's London*),
541.
12 Cole and Postgate, 315.

53 *'No One Knows the Cruelty'*
1 Children's Employment
Commission Reports, quot. E. R.
Pike (*Documents of the Victorian
Golden Age*), 113–45.
2 Quot. Engels, 186.
3 *Ibid.*, 175–7.
4 *Ibid.*, 78–80.
5 *Ibid.*, 80, 82.
6 Report of the Select Committee
appointed to inquire into the
Adulterations of Food, Drinks and
Drugs, 1st Report (1854–5), quot.
E. R. Pike, op. cit., 295–6.

54 *Middle Classes and Class
Distinctions*
1 Quot. Best, 284.
2 J. F. C. Harrison (*The Early
Victorians*), 131, 143; Best, 283–4;
Read, 24.
3 Anthony Trollope, *Barchester
Towers* (1857), ch. 39.
4 Quot. Best, 272.
5 Charles Dickens, *Bleak House*
(1853), ch. 39.
6 Charles Dickens, *Pickwick Papers*
(1837), ch. 30.
7 Anthony Trollope, *Doctor Thorne*
(1858), quot. Best, 270.
8 Flora Thompson, *Lark Rise* (1939),
ch. 14.
9 Anthony Trollope, *The Last
Chronicle of Barset* (1867), ch. 83.
10 Anthony Trollope, *Framley
Parsonage* (1861), Chs 1 and 9.
11 Young, vol. 1, 107.

12 Best, 110.
13 Anthony Trollope, *Autobiography*
(1883).
14 Best, 107–9.
15 Young, vol. 1, 104–5.
16 J. F. C. Harrison, op. cit., 135.
17 Edgar Johnson, *Charles Dickens*, 2
vols (1953).
18 Raverat, 126.
19 Young, vol. 1, 90.
20 *London Encyclopaedia*, 11; Best,
34.
21 *London Encyclopaedia*, 726.
22 George Weedon Grossmith, *Diary
of a Nobody* (1892).
23 *Manners and Rules of Good Society*
(1888), 111.
24 *Ibid.*, 20; E. R. Pike (*Documents of
the Age of the Forsytes*), 35–47.
25 Raverat, 33.
26 J. F. C. Harrison, op. cit., 133.
27 Charles Dickens, *Our Mutual
Friend* (1865), ch. 2.
28 Trollope, op. cit., note 3, ch. 19.
29 Burton (*The Early Victorians*), 91.
30 Young, vol. 1, 93–4.
31 *Victorian Shopping*, 1220–21.
32 Young, vol. 1, 101.

55 *Leisure Hours*
1 Richard Church, *Over the Bridge*
(1955), 52.
2 A. Briggs (*Victorian Cities*), 132.
3 Hugh Shimmin, *Liverpool Life*
(1856), quot. Best, 238.
4 Altick (*Victorian People*), 185.
5 Walvin (*The People's Game*), 74.
6 *Ibid.*, 58.
7 A. Clive, quot. Christopher
Hibbert, *Daily Life in Victorian
England* (1975), 34.
8 Edgar Johnson, *Charles Dickens*, 2
vols (1953); Christopher Hibbert,
*The Making of Charles Dickens*
(1967); John Forster, *The Life of
Charles Dickens*, 3 vols (1871–4).
9 Christopher Hibbert, *The
Illustrated London News Social*

*History of Victorian Britain* (1976), 13.

10 Johnson, op. cit., vol. 2, 947.
11 Best, 249.
12 Altick, op. cit., 196.
13 P. Quennell (*Mayhew's London*). London.
14 Charles Dickens, *Sketches by 'Boz'*, 'Private Theatres' (1836).
15 Quot. Haddon, 28.
16 Delgado, 53.
17 Victor Glasstone, *Victorian and Edwardian Theatres* (1975); *London Encyclopaedia*, 188, 474.
18 Howard, 226; Haddon, 22.
19 Haddon, 72–95, 153.
20 Rowell, 103.
21 Glasstone, 62–4.
22 Rowell, 138.
23 L. Hudson, 209.

### 56 The Flesh and the Spirit

1 William Acton, *Prostitution* (1870), quot. Marcus, 31.
2 *My Secret Life*, quot. Marcus, 98.
3 *Ibid.*, 99.
4 Behlmer, *passim*.
5 *My Secret Life*, quot. Marcus, 106–7.
6 P. Quennell (*Mayhew's London*), 37.
7 *Ibid.*, 54.
8 Quot. *Westminster Review*, vol. 53 (1850), 496–7, quot. E. R. Pike (*Documents of the Victorian Golden Age*), 353–5.
9 McHugh, 16.
10 Quot. Horn (*The Rural World*), 160.
11 *Charles Booth's London*, 327.
12 *London Encyclopaedia*, 513.
13 Charles Dickens, *Little Dorrit* (1857), ch. 3.
14 Elizabeth Longford, *Victoria R.I.* (1964), 214; Christopher Hibbert, *Queen Victoria in her Letters and Journals* (1984).

### 57 Passengers and Drivers

1 Charles Dickens, *Martin Chuzzlewit* (1844), ch. 40.
2 *Wellington and His Friends, Letters of the First Duke*, ed. 7th Duke (1965), 266–7.
3 Quot. Young, vol. 2, 291.
4 Reader, 17; Young, vol. 2, 206.
5 Best, 89.
6 A. Briggs (*Victorian Cities*), 14.
7 Quot. Burnett (*Useful Toil*), 60.
8 J. F. C. Harrison (*The Early Victorians*), 64.
9 *Ibid.*
10 Quot. Christopher Hibbert, *Daily Life in Victorian England* (1975), 83.
11 J. F. C. Harrison, op. cit., 65.
12 Terry Coleman, *The Railway Navvies* (1965).
13 William Makepeace Thackeray, *The History of Pendennis* (1848–50).
14 Charles Dickens, *Dombey and Son* (1848), ch. 6.
15 Best, 89.
16 Reader, 87.
17 Young, vol. 1, 26.
18 Dickens, op. cit., note 14, ch. 20.
19 Charles Young, 6 August 1835, quot. Kennedy, 7–8.
20 Young, vol. 2, 295.
21 Quot. Mitchell and Leys (*A History of the English People*), 162.
22 Young, vol. 1, 20.
23 S. Legg (ed.), *The Railway Book*, quot. Kennedy, 9–10.
24 Young, vol. 2, 293.
25 Best, 91.
26 Kilvert, 18 May 1870.
27 Mitchell and Leys, op. cit., 570.
28 *London Encyclopaedia*, 884–5.
29 P. Quennell (*Mayhew's London*), 567–8.
30 *The Illustrated London News*, vol. 1, 46, quot. Mitchell and Leys, op. cit., 568.

31 Charles Dickens, *Sketches by 'Boz'* (1836), ch. 17.
32 *Ibid.*, ch. 16.
33 P. Quennell, op. cit., 566–7.
34 *Ibid.*, 570.
35 Mitchell and Leys, op. cit., 568.
36 *London Encyclopaedia*, 889.
37 Hoggart, 120.
38 A. Briggs, op. cit., 15.
39 *London Encyclopaedia*, 899–900.
40 Quot. Reader, 199.
41 Raverat, 247.
42 Quot. Reader, 200.
43 C. W. Stamper, *What I Knew . . . Reminiscences of Edward VII* (1913).
44 Reader, 199.

#### 58 *Law and Order*

1 Collins, 240.
2 Cadogan, 246.
3 *Parliamentary Debates* (1811), XIX, quot. Charles Reith, *A New Study of Police History* (1956).
4 *Parliamentary Debates* (1819), XXXIX.
5 Radzinowicz, vol. 1, 611–59.
6 Koestler and Rolph, *Hanged by the Neck* (1961), 32.
7 Gerald Gardiner, *Capital Punishment as a Deterrent* (1956), 28, 69.
8 Pringle (*Hue and Cry*), 240–49; Reith, op. cit., note 3; W. L. Melville Lee, *A History of Police in England* (1901), *passim*.
9 J. W. Ward, *Letters to Ivy* (1905), quot. Radzinowicz, vol. 3, 347.
10 Charles Reith, *The Police Idea* (1938), 215.
11 Lee, op. cit., note 8, 240.
12 Radzinowicz, vol. 2, 256.
13 *First Report of the Constabulary Commissioners*, 13, quot. Lee, op. cit., note 8, 272.
14 Lee, op. cit., note 8, 286–7.
15 *Ibid.*, 290.
16 *Ibid.*, 283.

17 Arthur Griffiths, *The Chronicles of Newgate* (1884), 407–11.
18 Collins, 7; *London Encyclopaedia*, 388.
19 Albert Crew, *London Prisons* (1933), 88.
20 *Report of Royal Commission* (1854), quot. George Ives, *A History of Penal Methods* (1914), 193.
21 *Report of the Royal Commission* (1879), 355, 627, 680; Collins, 21.
22 Quot. S. K. Ruck, *Paterson on Prisons* (1951).
23 *Ibid.*
24 Quot. Melville Hinde, *The British Penal System, 1773–1950* (1951), 108.
25 Sir Leo Page, *The Young Lag* (1950), 260.
26 *Ibid.*
27 Quot. Laffin, 105.
28 J. E. Morris, *The Welsh Wars of Edward III*, 301.
29 H. C. B. Rogers, 61.
30 Farwell, 97.
31 Quot. Laffin, 128.
32 Farwell, 84–5.
33 *Ibid.*, 94.
34 Johnston, 42.

#### 59 *Homes and Holidays*

1 Jackson, 256.
2 *Ibid.*
3 A. Briggs (*A Social History*), 288.
4 Marwick (*Britain in the Century of Total War*), 177.
5 Stevenson (*British Society*), 390–1.
6 *Ibid.*, 396.
7 Leslie Halliwell, *Seats in all Parts* (1985).
8 Quot. Marwick, op. cit., 185.
9 Stevenson, op. cit., 398.
10 James Curran and Jean Seaton, *Power with Responsibility: The Press and Broadcasting in Britain* (1981); Stevenson, op. cit., 402.
11 Musgrave, 48–52.
12 *Ibid.*, 48–52.

13 D'Arblay, vol. 5, 36.
14 Perkin (*The Age of the Railway*), 213.
15 Clunn, 273.
16 Nigel Nicolson (ed.), *Virginia Woolf's Letters*, vol. 3, 517.
17 Perkin, op. cit., 214.
18 Manning-Saunders, 701.
19 Grant, 106.
20 Pimlott, 130.
21 *Ibid.*, 126–7.
22 Walton (*The Blackpool Landlady*), 125.
23 S. Legg (ed.), *The Railway Book*, quot. Kennedy, 27–8.
24 Pimlott, 148.
25 Quot. Perkin, op. cit., 230.
26 Pimlott, 240.
27 *Ibid.*, 245.
28 Hern, 133.
29 Walton, op. cit., 180.
30 *Fifty Years Ago*, 43.
31 T. Thompson, 137.
32 *Ibid.*, 158, 219.
33 Jill Drower, *Good Clean Fun* (1982).
34 Butlin,
35 Pimlott, 276–9.
36 George Orwell, *Collected Works* (1970), vol. 1, 9.
37 *Fifty Years Ago*, 45.
38 *Ibid.*, 46.

### 60 *Wars and Aftermaths*

1 Marwick (*The Deluge*), 35.
2 Stevenson (*British Society*), 47.
3 Arnold Bennett, *Journal, 1896–1932*, 98; Marwick, op. cit., 48.
4 Stevenson, op. cit., 56.
5 *Ibid.*, 53.
6 *Ibid.*, 79.
7 C. S. Peel, *How We Lived Then*, 68, quot. Marwick, op. cit., 125.
8 Robert Roberts, quot. Stevenson, op. cit., 82.
9 *New Statesman*, 23 June 1917, quot. Marwick, op. cit., 94.

10 Stevenson, op. cit., 88.
11 *Ibid.*, 92.
12 A. J. P. Taylor, 140–46.
13 A. Briggs (*A Social History*), 266.
14 G. A. Phillips, *The General Strike: The Politics of Industrial Conflict* (1976); M. Morris, *The General Strike* (1976); P. Renshaw, *The General Strike* (1975).
15 Stevenson, op. cit., 266.
16 Quot. Stevenson, op. cit., 139.
17 *Brewers' Gazette*, 26 September 1914, quot. Marwick, op. cit., 64.
18 Duke of Windsor, *Family Album* (1960), 54.
19 G. E. Evans (*The Days That We Have Seen*), 140–41.
20 *New Survey of London Life and Labour*, ix (1935), 245.
21 Stevenson, op. cit., 153.
22 Lockhart, 79.
23 John Hewetson, 'Birth Control, Sexual Morality and Abortion', *Twentieth Century*, Winter 1962–3.
24 Gunn, 154; Stevenson, op. cit., 113.
25 Abel-Smith, 1.
26 *Ibid.*, 37.
27 *London Encyclopaedia*, 349.
28 Abel-Smith, 10.
29 Cartwright, 158–9.
30 Abel-Smith, 1.
31 Cartwright, 161.
32 Marwick, op. cit., 257.
33 Marwick (*Britain in the Century of Total War*), 293.
34 *Report of Royal Commission on Equal Pay*, 1944–6, quot. Marwick, op. cit., 293.
35 Marwick, op. cit. 294.

# Sources

Abel-Smith, Brian, *The Hospitals,
1800–1948: A Study in Social
Administration in England and
Wales* (1964)

Abrams, Mark, *The Condition of the
British People, 1911–1945* (1946)

Adamson, J. W., *Pioneers of Modern
Education 1600–1700* (1905)

Aldburgham, Alison, *Shops and
Shopping 1800–1914* (1981)
*Silver Fork Society 1814–1840*
(1983)

Aldcroft, Derek, and Michael Freeman
(eds), *Transport in the Industrial
Revolution* (1983)

Allen, M. E. A., *Plants that Changed
Our Gardens* (1974)

Altham, H. S., and Swanton, E. W.,
*A History of Cricket* (1948)

Altick, Richard D., *The Shows of
London* (1978)
*Victorian People and Ideas* (1973)

Altschul, Michael, *A Baronial Family
in Medieval England: The Clares,
1217–1314* (1965)

*Albion's Fatal Tree: Crime and Society
in Eighteenth Century England*
(Studies by Douglas Hay, Peter
Linebaugh, John S. Rule, E. P.
Thompson and Cal Winslow,
1975)

Anderson, R. M. C., *The Roads of
England* (1932)

Archenholz, J. von, *A Picture of
England* (1791)

Armitage, W. H. G., *Four Hundred
Years of English Education* (1970)

Ashley, Maurice, *Life in Stuart
England* (1964)
*The People of England: A Short
Social and Economic History*
(1982)

Ashton, T. S., *Studies in the Industrial
Revolution* (1960)

Ausubel, Herman, *In Hard Times:
Reformers under the Late
Victorians* (1960)

Aydelotte, Frank, *Elizabethan Rogues
and Vagabonds* (1913)


Bagley, J. J., *Life in Mediaeval
England* (1960)

Balsan, Consuelo Vanderbilt, *The
Glitter and the Gold* (1958)

Barber, Richard, *The Pastons* (1981)

Barley, M. W., *The English Farmhouse
and Cottage* (1961)

Barnes, D. G., *History of the English
Corn Laws* (1930)

Barnett, Corelli, *Britain and Her Army*
(1970)

Barraclough, Geoffrey (ed.), *Social Life in Early England* (1960)

Barrow, W. S., *Feudal Britain* (1956)

Bédarida, François, *A Social History of England, 1851–1975* (trans., A. S. Forster, 1979)

Behlmer, George K., *Child Abuse and Moral Reform in England, 1870–1908* (1984)

Bell, Alan, *Sydney Smith* (1980)

Bell, Florence, Lady, *At the Works* (1907)

Beloff, Max, *Public Order and Popular Disturbances 1660–1714* (1938)

Benjamin, Bernard, *Health and Vital Statistics* (1968)

Bennett, H. S., *Life on the English Manor: A Study of Peasant Conditions, 1150–1400* (1937)
*The Pastons and their England: Studies in an Age of Transition* (1922)

Bentley, G. E., *The Jacobean and Caroline Stage* (7 vols, 1941–68)

Best, Geoffrey, *Mid-Victorian Britain 1851–75* (1971)

Bishop, James, *The Illustrated London News Social History of Edwardian Britain* (1977)

Black, Eugene C. (ed.), *Victorian Culture and Society* (1973)

Blake, Robert (ed.), *The English World: History, Character and People* (1982)

Blythe, Ronald, *The Age of Illusion: England in the Twenties and Thirties* (1963)

Booth, Charles, *The Aged Poor in England and Wales* (new ed., 1984)
*Life and Labour of the People of London*, 17 vols (1889–1903)

Boswell, James, *Boswell's London Journal, 1762–1763* (ed. Frederick A. Pottle, 1950)
*Life of Johnson* (ed. R. W. Chapman, new ed. G. D. Fleeman, 1970)

Boucé, Paul-Gabriel (ed.), *Sexuality in 18th-Century Britain* (1982)

Boulton, William B., *Amusements of Old London* (1901)

Bovill, E. W., *The England of Nimrod and Surtees* (1959)
*English Country Life, 1760–1830* (1962)

Bradbrook, M. C., *The Rise of the Common Player: A Study of Actor and Society in Shakespeare's England* (1962)

Brailsford, Dennis, *Sport and Society: Elizabeth to Anne* (1969)

Brander, Michael, *The Victorian Gentleman* (1975)

Branson, Noreen, *Britain in the Nineteen Twenties* (1978)
and Heinemann, M., *Britain in the Nineteen Thirties* (1971)

Braudel, Fernand, *Civilization and Capitalism, 15th–18th Century* (3 vols, *The Perspective of the World*; *The Structures of Everyday Life*; *The Wheels of Commerce* trans. Siân Reynolds, 1981–4)

Braun, Hugh, *The English Castle* (1936)

Bray, Alan, *Homosexuality in Renaissance England* (1983)

Bremner, M. D. K., *The Story of Dentistry* (1954)

Briggs, Asa, *A Social History of England* (1983)
*The Age of Improvement* (1959)
(ed.), *How They Lived, 1700–1815* (1969)
(ed.), *The Nineteenth Century* (1985)
(ed.), *They Saw It Happen, 1897–1940* (1960)
*Victorian Cities* (1963)

Briggs, Susan, *Keep Smiling Through* (1975)

Brooke, Iris, *History of English Costume* (1972)

Brown, Ivor, *Shakespeare and the Actors* (1970)

Browning, Andrew, (ed.), *English · Historical Documents 1660–1740* (1953)

Bryant, Arthur, *The Age of Elegance 1812–1822* (1950)
*The England of Charles II* (1934)
*English Saga 1840–1940* (1940)
*The Years of Endurance* (1942)
*The Years of Victory* (1944)

Buck, Anne, *Dress in Eighteenth-Century England* (1979)

Burke, Thomas, *English Night-Life* (1941)

Burnett, John, *A History of the Cost of Living* (1969)
*Destiny Obscure: Autobiographies of Childhood, Education and Family from the 1820s to the 1920s* (1982)
*Housing: A Social History, 1815–1970* (1978)
*Plenty and Want: A Social History of Diet in England from 1815 to the Present Day* (1966)
(ed.), *Useful Toil: Autobiographies of Working People from the 1820s to the 1920s* (1974)

Burton, Elizabeth, *The Early Tudors at Home, 1485–1558* (1976)
*The Early Victorians at Home, 1837–1861* (1972)
*The Elizabethans at Home* (1958)
*The Georgians at Home, 1714–1830* (1967)
*The Jacobeans at Home* (1962)

Buxton, John, *Elizabethan Taste* (1963)

Byrne, Muriel St Clare, *Elizabethan Life in Town and Country* (1954)
(ed.), *The Lisle Letters* (selected and arranged by Bridget Boland, 1983)

Bythell, Duncan, *The Sweated Trades: Outwork in 19th-Century Britain* (1978)

Cadogan, Edward, *The Roots of Evil* (1937)

Calder, Angus, *The People's War: Britain 1939–1945* (1971)
and Dorothy Sheridan, *Speak for Yourself: A Mass-Observation Anthology, 1937–1949* (1984)

Calder, Jenni, *The Victorian Home* (1977)

Campbell, J. Menzies, *Dentistry Then and Now* (1981)

Campbell, Mildred, *The English Yeoman under Elizabeth and the Early Stuarts* (1960)

Camplin, Jamie, *The Rise of the Plutocrats: Wealth and Power in Edwardian England* (1978)

Cannadine, David, *Lords and Landlords: The Aristocracy of the Towns, 1774–1967* (1980) (ed.), *Patricians, Power and Politics in Nineteenth-Century Towns* (1982)

Cape, W. W., *The English Church in the Fourteenth and Fifteenth Centuries* (1900)

Caraman, Philip (ed.), *The Other Face* (1960)
*The Years of Siege: Catholic Life from James I to Cromwell* (1966)

Cartwright, F. F., *A Social History of Medicine* (1977)

Cecil, Robert, *Life in Edwardian England* (1969)

Chadwick, D., *Social Life in the Days of Piers Plowman* (1922)

Chalmers, Patrick, *Racing England* (1939)

Chambers, E. K., *The Elizabethan Stage* (4 vols, new ed., 1951)
*The Mediaeval Stage* (2 vols, 1903)

Chandos, John, *Boys Together: English Public Schools, 1800–1864* (1984)

*Charles Booth's London* (ed. Albert Fried and Richard Elman, 1969)

Chaucer, Geoffrey, *The Canterbury Tales* (trans. into modern English by Nevill Coghill, 1951)

Chesney, Kellow, *The Victorian Underworld* (1970)

Chesterfield, Lord, *The Letters of the*

*Earl of Chesterfield to his Son*
(2 vols, ed. C Strachey, 1932)

Cholmondeley, R. H., *The Heber
Letters, 1783–1832* (1950)

Clanchy, M. T., *From Memory to
Written Record* (1979)

Clapham, J. H., *An Economic History
of Modern Britain* (3 vols,
1926–38)

*The Railway Age, 1820–1850* (1926)

Clark, Alice, *Working Life of Women in
the 17th-Century* (1919)

Clark, G. Kitson, *An Expanding
Society: Britain, 1830–1900*
(1967)

*The Making of Victorian England*
(1962)

Clark, J. C. D., *English Society
1688–1832: Ideology, Social
Structure, and Political Practice
during the Ancien Régime* (1985)

Clark, Peter, *The English Alehouse: A
Social History 1200–1830* (1983)

Clark, Peter, and Slack, Paul, *Crisis
and Order in English Towns,
1500–1700* (1972)

*English Towns in Transition,
1500–1700* (1976)

Clarke, John, *The Price of Progress:
Cobbett's England, 1780–1835*
(1977)

Clunn, Harold, *Famous South Coast
Pleasure Resorts* (1929)

Cobban, A. B., *The Mediaeval
Universities: Their Development
and Organisation* (1975)

Cobbett, William, *Rural Rides* (ed. and
with an introduction by George
Woodcock, 1967)

Cole, G. D. H., and Filson, A. W.,
*British Working-Class Movements:
Select Documents, 1789–1875*
(1951)

Cole, G. D. H., and Postgate,
Raymond, *The Common People,
1746–1946* (1956)

Collins, Philip, *Dickens and Crime*
(1962)

Cook, Olive, *The English Country
House* (1974)

Corfield, P. J., *The Impact of English
Towns* (1982)

Coulton, G. G., *Medieval Panorama:
The English Scene from Conquest
to Reformation* (1947)

*The Mediaeval Village* (1925)

*Social Life in Britain from the
Conquest to the Reformation* (1919)

Creighton, Charles, *A History of
Epidemics in Britain* (2 vols, 1891)

Cressy, David, *Education in Tudor and
Stuart England* (1975)

Critchley, T. A., *A History of Police in
England and Wales, 900–1966*
(1967)

Croker, John Wilson, *The
Correspondence and Diaries of the
Late John Wilson Croker* (3 vols,
ed. Louis J. Jennings, 1885)

Cruikshank, R. J., *Charles Dickens and
Early Victorian England* (1949)

Cuddon, J. A., *Dictionary of Sports
and Games* (1979)

Dainton, Courtney, *England's
Hospitals* (1961)

D'Arblay, Mme, *Diary and Letters* (ed.
C. F. Barrett, 1842)

Daunton, M. J., *House and Home in
the Victorian City: Working-Class
Housing, 1850–1914* (1983)

Davidson, Caroline, *A Woman's Work
is Never Done: A History of
Housework in the British Isles,
1650–1950* (1982)

Davies, Maud F., *Life in an English
Village* (1909)

Davis, Dorothy, *A History of Shopping*
(1966)

Davis, Norman, *Paston Papers and
Letters of the Fifteenth Century*
(2 vols, 1971, 1976)

Deaux, George, *The Black Death 1347*
(1969)

Defoe, Daniel, *A Tour Through the
Whole Island of Great Britain* (ed.

with an introduction and notes by
Pat Rogers, 1971.)

Delgado, Alan, *The Annual Outing and Other Excursions* (1977)
*Victorian Entertainment* (1971)

Dickens, A. G., *The English Reformation* (1964)

Dobbs, Brian, *Drury Lane* (1972)

Dobson, C. R., *Masters and Journeymen* (1980)

Dodd, A. H., *Life in Elizabethan England* (1967)

Dodds, J. W., *The Age of Paradox* (1953)

Driver, Christopher, *The British at Table 1940–1980* (1983)

Du Boulay, F. R. H., *An Age of Ambition: English Society in the Late Middle Ages* (1970)

Dyos, H. J., and Wolff, Michael (eds), *The Victorian City: Images and Realities* (1973)

Earle, Peter, *The World of Defoe* (1976)

Eland, G. (ed.), *Purefoy Letters, 1735–53* (2 vols, 1931)

Ellacott, S. E., *A History of Everyday Things in England, 1914–1968* (1968)

Elton, G. R., *England under the Tudors* (2nd ed., 1974)

Emmison, F. G., *Tudor Food and Pastimes* (1964)

Engels, Friedrich, *The Condition of the Working Class in England* (trans. and ed. W. O. Henderson and W. H. Chaloner, 1958)

Englander, David, *Landlord and Tenant in Urban Britain, 1838–1918* (1983)

Evans, George Ewart, *From Mouths of Men* (1976)
*The Days that We Have Seen* (1975)

Evans, Joan (ed.), *The Flowering of the Middle Ages* (1985)

Evans, Joan, *The Victorians* (1966)

Evelyn, John, *The Diary of John Evelyn* (6 vols, ed. E. S. de Beer, 1955)

Ewing, Elizabeth, *Dress and Undress: A History of Women's Underwear* (1978)

Farington, Joseph, *The Farington Diary* (ed. J. Grieg, 1922–28)

Farwell, Byron, *For Queen and Country: A Social History of the Victorian and Edwardian Army* (1981)

Fiennes, Celia, *The Illustrated Journeys of Celia Fiennes 1685c–1712* (ed. Christopher Morris, 1984)

*Fifty Years Ago: Memories of the 1930s* (ed. Age Exchange Theatre Company, 1983)

Fisher, F. J. (ed.), *Essays in the Economic and Social History of Tudor and Stuart England* (1960)

Fitzgerald, Percy, *A New History of the English Stage* (1882)

Fitzherbert, John, *The Boke of Husbandrie* (1523)

Flinn, M. W., and Smouth, T. C., *Essays in Social History* (1974)

Fox, Barclay, *Barclay Fox's Journal* (ed. R. L. Brett, 1979)

Fraser, Antonia, *The Weaker Vessel: Woman's Lot in Seventeenth-Century England* (1984)

Furnivall, F. J. (ed.), *The Booke of Courtesy* (1868)
*The Booke of Nurture* (1868)
*Manners and Meals in Olden Time* (1868)

Gale, A. H., *Epidemic Diseases* (1959)

Gathorne-Hardy, Jonathan, *The Public School Phenomenon* (1977)
*The Rise and Fall of the British Nanny* (1972)

Gay, John, *Trivia, or The Art of Walking the Streets of London* (1716)

George, M. Dorothy, *British Museum Catalogue of Political and Personal Satires, Vols 6–11* (1938–54)
*England in Johnson's Day* (1928)
*English Political Caricature, 1793–1832* (2 vols, 1959)
*London Life in the XVIIIth Century* (1925)
Girouard, Mark, *Life in the English Country House* (1978)
*Robert Smythson and the Elizabethan Country House* (1983)
*The Victorian Country House* (1971)
Godfrey, Elizabeth, *Home Life Under the Stuarts 1603–1649* (1903)
*Social Life under the Stuarts* (1904)
Goodenough, Simon, *The Country Parson* (1983)
Goodwin, A. (ed), *The European Nobility in the Eighteenth Century* (2nd ed., 1967)
*The Friends of Liberty* (1979)
Gough, Richard, *History of Myddle* (ed. D. Hey, 1981)
Grant, Elizabeth, *Memoirs of a Highland Lady, 1797–1827. The Autobiography of Elizabeth Grant of Rothiemurchus* (revised and ed. Angus Davidson, 1950)
Graves, Robert, and Hodge, Alan, *The Long Week-End: A Social History of Great Britain 1918–1939* (1940)
Greaves, Richard L., *Society and Religion in Elizabethan England* (1981)
Green, A. S., *Town Life in the Fifteenth Century* (2 vols, 1894)
Green, V. H. H., *A History of Oxford University* (1974)
Gregg, Pauline, *A Social and Economic History of England* (1975)
*A Social and Economic History, 1760–1980* (1983)
Greville, Charles, *The Greville Memoirs, 1814–1860* (8 vols, ed. Lytton Strachey and Roger Fulford, 1938)

Grimaldi, Joseph, *Memoirs of Joseph Grimaldi* (ed. Richard Findlater, 1968)
Guilford, E. L., *Travellers and Travelling in the Middle Ages* (1924)
Gunn, Fenja, *The Artificial Face: A History of Cosmetics* (1973)
Gurr, Andrew, *The Shakespearean Stage, 1574–1642* (2nd ed., 1980)

Haddon, Archibald, *The Story of the Music Hall* (1935)
Hammond, J. L. and Barbara, *The Age of the Chartists* (1930)
*The Skilled Labourer* (1919)
*The Town Labourer* (1917)
*The Village Labourer* (1920)
Harbage, Alfred, *Shakespeare's Audience* (1941)
Harris, Mary Dormer, *Life in an Old English Town* (1898)
Harrison, Brian, *Drink and the Victorians* (1971)
Harrison, J. F. C. *Learning and Living* (1961)
*The Early Victorians, 1832–51* (1971)
Harrison, William, *Description of England* (1577, 3 vols, 1887)
Hart, A. Tindal, *The Country Clergy in Elizabethan and Stuart Times* (1958)
*The Eighteenth-Century Country Parson* (1955)
and Carpenter, Edward, *The Nineteenth Century Country Parson* (1954)
*The Man in the Pew, 1538–1660* (1966)
Hartcup, Adeline, *Below Stairs in the Great Country Houses* (1980)
Hartley, Dorothy, *Food in England* (1955)
*The Land of England* (1979)
*Water in England* (1964)
Hartnoll, Phyllis, *A Concise History of the Theatre* (1968)

Hassall, W. O. (ed.), *How They Lived: An Anthology of Original Accounts Written Before 1485* (1962)

Haswell, Jock, *The British Army* (1975)

Havins, Peter J. Neville, *The Spas of England* (1976)

Hearnshaw, F. J. C. (ed.), *Edwardian England* (1933)

Hecht, J. Jean, *The Domestic Servant Class in Eighteenth-Century England* (1956)

Hentzner, Paul, *A Journey into England in the Year 1598* (1759)

Hern, Anthony, *The Seaside Holiday* (1967)

Hey, David, *Packmen, Carriers and Packhorse Roads* (1980)

Hill, Bridget, *Eighteenth-Century Women: An Anthology* (1984)

Hill, Christopher, *Change and Continuity in 17th Century England* (1975)
*The World Turned Upside Down* (1972)

Hilton, Rodney, *Bond Men Made Free: Mediaeval Peasant Movements and the English Rising of 1381* (1973)
*A Medieval Society: The West Midlands at the End of the Thirteenth Century* (1966)
*The English Peasantry in the Late Middle Ages*: The Ford Lectures for 1973 and Related Studies (1965)
and Fagan, H., *The English Rising of 1381* (1950)

Himmelfarb, Gertrude, *The Idea of Poverty: England in the Early Industrial Age* (1984)

Hinde, Thomas, *A Field Guide to the English Country Parson* (1983)

Hindley, Geoffrey, *England in the Age of Caxton* (1979)

Hobsbawm, E. J., *Industry and Empire: An Economic History of Britain since 1750* (1968)

and Ranger, Terence, *The Invention of Tradition* (1983)
and Rudé, George, *Captain Swing* (1969)
*Labouring Men: Studies in the History of Labour* (new ed., 1985)

Hodges, Cyril, *The Globe Restored* (1953)

Hoggart, Richard, *The Uses of Literacy* (1958)

Hole, Christina, *A Dictionary of British Folk Customs* (1978)
*English Home-Life, 1500–1800* (1947)

Holme, Thea, *The Carlyles at Home* (1965)

Holmes, G. A., *The Estates of the Higher Nobility in the Later Middle Ages* (1957)

Holmes, Geoffrey, *Augustan England: Professions, State and Society, 1680–1730* (1983)

Holt, J. C., *Robin Hood* (1982)

Hone, William, *Every Day Book* (1840)

Hopkins, Donald R., *Princes and Peasants: Smallpox in History* (1983)

Horn, Pamela, *Labouring Life in the Victorian Countryside* (1976)
*The Rural World, 1750–1850: Social Change in the English Countryside* (1980)

Hoskins, W. G., *The Midland Peasant: The Economic and Social History of a Leicestershire Village* (1957)
*Provincial England* (1963)

Hotson, Leslie, *The Commonwealth and Restoration Stage* (1928)

Howard, Diana, *London Theatres and Music Halls* (1970)

Hudson, Derek, *Munby: Man of Two Worlds* (1972)

Hudson, Lynton, *The English Stage, 1850–1950* (1951)

Huggett, Frank E., *A Day in The Life of a Victorian Farmworker* (1972)

Hughes, Edward, *North Country Life in the Eighteenth Century* (1965)

Hughes, M. V., *A London Family*

*1870–1900* (new ed., 1981)

Hughes, Philip, *The Reformation in England* (1963)

Hunt, John Dixon, and Willis, Peter, *The Genius of the Place: The English Landscape Garden 1620–1820* (1979)

Hunter, Donald, *Health in Industry* (1959)

Huxley, Anthony, *An Illustrated History of Gardening* (1979)

Ireland, John, and Nichols, John, *Hogarth's Works: With Life and Anecdotal Descriptions of His Pictures* (3 vols, 1883)

Jackman, W. T., *The Development of Transport in Modern England* (1962)

Jackson, A. A., *Semi-Detached London: Suburban Development, Life and Transport, 1900–1939* (1973)

Jacques, David, *Georgian Gardens: The Reign of Nature* (1983)

Jarrett, Derek, *England in the Age of Hogarth* (1974)

Jennings, Humphrey, *Pandaemonium* (1985)

Jennings, Louis J. (ed.), *The Croker Papers* (3 vols, 1885)

Jeudwine, J. W., *Tort, Crime and Police in Medieval Britain* (1917)

Jones, David J. V., *The Last Rising: The Newport Insurrection of 1839* (1985)

Jones, E. L., and Mingay, G. E. (eds), *Land, Labour and Population in the Industrial Revolution* (1967)

Jones, M. G., *The Charity School Movement* (new ed., 1964)

Johnson, Wendell Stacy, *Living in Sin: The Victorian Sexual Revolution* (1979)

Johnston, S. H. F., *British Soldiers* (1977)

Judges, A. V. (ed.), *The Elizabethan Underworld* (1930)

Jusserand, J. J., *English Wayfaring Life in the Middle Ages (XIVth Century)* (trans. Lucy Toulmin Smith, 2nd ed., 1920)

Kalm, Pehr (Peter), *Account of a Visit to England* (trans. J. Lucas, 1892)

Kamm, Josephine, *Hope Deferred: Girls' Education in English History* (1965)

Kearney, H. F., *Scholars and Gentlemen: Universities and Societies in Pre-Industrial Britain* (1970)

Kee, Robert, *The World We Left Behind: A Chronicle of the Year 1939* (1984)

Keen, Maurice, *Chivalry* (1984)
*The Outlaws of Medieval England* (1963)

Kelly, J. A., *German Visitors to English Theaters in the 18th Century* (1936)

Kendall, Paul Murray, *The Yorkist Age: Daily Life during the Wars of the Roses* (1962)

Kennedy, Ludovic (ed.), *A Book of Railway Journeys* (1980)

Kenyon, J. P., *Stuart England* (1978)

Kilvert, Francis, *Journal of a Country Curate: Selections from the Diary of Francis Kilvert 1870–79* (1977)

Knowles, David, *The Monastic Order in England* (1940)
*The Religious Orders in England* (1948)

Labarge, Margaret Wade, *A Baronial Household of the Thirteenth Century* (1965)
*Medieval Travellers: The Rich and Restless* (1982)

Laffin, John, *Tommy Atkins: Story of the English Soldier* (1966)

Langland, William, *The Vision of William Concerning Piers the*

Langland, William – *cont.*
  *Plowman* (ed. W. W. Skeat, 1886)
Lasdun, Susan, *Victorians at Home*
  (1981)
Laslett, Peter, *Family Life and Illicit
  Love in Earlier Generations* (1977)
  *The World We Have Lost* (3rd ed.,
  1983)
Laver, James, *The Age of Illusion*
  (1972)
  *Taste and Fashion From the French
  Revolution to The Present Day*
  (1937)
  *Victorian Vista* (1954)
Lawson, J., and Silver, H., *A Social
  History of Education in England*
  (1973)
Leach, A. F., *Schools of Mediaeval
  England* (1915)
Lee, A. J., *The Origins of the Popular
  Press in England, 1855–1914*
  (1976)
Lennard, Reginald (ed.), *Englishmen
  at Rest and Play, 1558–1714*
  (1931)
Lewinsohn, Richard, *A History of
  Sexual Customs* (trans. Alexander
  Mayce, 1958)
Lewis, R. A., *Edwin Chadwick and the
  Public Health Movement,
  1832–1854* (1952)
*Lisle Letters*, see Byrne
Lloyd, Wyndham E. H., *One Hundred
  Years of Medicine* (1968)
Lockhart, Robert Bruce, *Your England*
  (1955)
Lockhead, Marion, *The Victorian
  Household* (1964)
*London Encyclopaedia* (ed. Ben
  Weinreb and Christopher Hibbert,
  new ed., 1985)
Longmate, Norman, *The
  Breadstealers: The Fight Against
  the Corn Laws, 1838–1846* (1984)
Low, Donald A., *That Sunny Dome: A
  Portrait of Regency Britain*
  (1977)
Lowerson, John, and Myerscough,

  John, *Time to Spare in Victorian
  England* (1977)
Lucy, Mary Elizabeth, *Mistress of
  Charlecote: The Memoirs of Mary
  Elizabeth Lucy* (introduced by
  Alice, Lady Fairfax-Lucy (1983)
Lufkin, Arthur, *A History of Dentistry*
  (1983)

Macdonald, John, *Memoirs of an
  Eighteenth-Century Footman* (ed.
  John Beresford, 1927)
  *Travels in Various Parts* (1790)
MacFarlane, Alan, *Marriage and Love
  in England, 1300–1840* (1986)
  *The Origins of English Individualism*
  (1978)
McFarlane, K. B., *England in the
  Fifteenth Century: Collected
  Essays* (1983)
  *The Nobility of Later Mediaeval
  England* (1973)
McHugh, Paul, *Prostitution and
  Victorian Social Reform* (1980)
MacKerness, E. D., *A Social History of
  English Music* (1964)
Mackie, J. D., *The Earlier Tudors* (1952)
McKisack, Mary, *The Fourteenth
  Century* (1962)
Maitland, F. W., *Township and
  Borough* (1898)
Malcolm, James Peller, *Anecdotes of the
  Manners and Customs of London
  in the Eighteenth Century* (2 vols,
  1808)
Malcolmson, R. W., *Life and Labour in
  England, 1700–1780* (1981)
Manning-Saunders, Ruth, *Seaside
  England* (1951)
Marcus, Steven, *The Other Victorians*
  (1966)
Marshall, Dorothy, *Eighteenth-Century
  England* (1962)
  *The English Domestic Servant in
  History* (1969)
  *English People in the 18th Century* (1956)
  *The English Poor in the Eighteenth
  Century* (1926)

*Industrial England, 1776–1851* (1973)

Martin, Christopher, *A Short History of English Schools 1750–1965* (1979)

Marwick, Arthur, *Britain in the Century of Total War* (1968)
*The Deluge: British Society and the First World War* (1965)
*Women at War, 1914–1918* (1977)

Mason, Tony, *Association Football and English Society, 1863–1915* (1982)

Masterman, C. F. G., *The Condition of England* (1910)
*England after the War* (1923)
*From the Abyss* (1902)

Mathew, David, *Catholicism in England* (1938)

Maxwell, Sir Herbert (ed.), *The Creevy Papers* (1903)

Mayhew, Henry, *London Labour and the London Poor* (3 vols, ed. Peter Quennell, 1950–51)
*The Unknown Mayhew: Selections from the* Morning Chronicle *1849–1850* (ed. E. P. Thompson and Eileen Yeo, 1971)

Meacham, Standish, *A Life Apart: The English Working Class 1890–1914* (1977)

Middlemas, Keith, *The Pursuit of Pleasure: High Society in the 1900s* (1977)

Midmer, Roy, *English Mediaeval Monasteries, 1066–1540* (1979)

Mingay, G. E., *English Landed Society in the 18th Century* (1963)
*The Gentry* (1976)
(ed.), *Mrs Hurst Dancing; and Other Scenes from Regency Life, 1812–1823* (1981)
*Rural Life in Victorian England* (1977)
(ed.), *The Victorian Countryside* (1981)

Mitchell, R. J., and Leys, M. D. R. *A History of the English People* (1950)
*A History of London Life* (1958)

Moorman, J. R., *Church Life in England in the Thirteenth Century* (1945)

Morgan, E. B. (ed.), *Readings in English Social History* (1923)

Morgan, Kenneth O. (ed.), *The Oxford Illustrated History of Britain* (1984)

Moritz, C. P., *Travels in England in 1782* (trans. P. E. Matheson, 1924)

Morpurgo, J. P. (ed.), *Life Under the Stuarts* (1950)

Morris, Jan, *The Oxford Book of Oxford* (1978)

Morsley, Clifford, *News from the English Countryside, 1750–1850* (1979)
*News from the English Countryside, 1851–1950* (1983)

Moryson, Fynes, *An Itinerary containing his ten years Travels* (1617)

Mount, Ferdinand, *The Subversive Family* (1982)

Muggeridge, Malcolm, *The Thirties* (1940)

Musgrave, Clifford, *Life in Brighton* (1970)

Neale, J. E., *Queen Elizabeth I* (1934)

Neale, R. S., *Class in English History, 1680–1850* (1981)

Neuburg, Victor, *Popular Education in 18th Century Britain* (1971)

Nicoll, Allardyce, *The Development of the Theatre* (new ed., 1966)
*The Garrick Stage: Theatres and Audiences in the Eighteenth Century* (1980)
*A History of English Drama 1660–1900* (1952–59)
*A History of Restoration Drama 1660–1700* (1940)
*Masks, Mimes and Miracles: Studies in the Popular Theatre* (new ed., 1963)

Nicolson, Harold, *Small Talk* (1937)

Notestein, Wallace, *English Folk: A Book of Characters* (1938)

Nowell-Smith, Simon (ed.), *Edwardian England* (1964)

O'Day, Alan, *The Edwardian Age: Conflict and Stability, 1900–1914* (1979)

O'Day, Rosemary, *Education and Society 1500–1800* (1982)

Oman, C. W. C., *The Art of War in the Middle Ages* (new ed., 1953)
*Castles* (1926)

Ordish, T. F., *Early London Theatres* (1950)

Orme, Nicholas, *English Schools in the Middle Ages* (1973)
*From Childhood to Chivalry: The Education of the English Kings and Aristocracy, 1066–1530* (1984)

Orwell, George, *The Road to Wigan Pier* (1937)

Owst, G. R., *Literature and Pulpit in Mediaeval England* (1933)
*Preaching in Medieval England* (1926)

Padfield, Peter, *Rule Britannia: The Victorian and Edwardian Navy* (1981)

Pagnamenta, Peter, and Overy, Richard, *All Our Working Lives* (1984)

Palliser, David, *The Age of Elizabeth* (1983)

Parker, Irene, *Dissenting Academies in England* (new ed., 1969)

Parker, J. H., *Domestic Architecture of the Middle Ages* (1852–9)

Parry, A. W., *Education in England in the Middle Ages* (1920)

*Paston Letters, see* Davis, N.; and Barber

Patten, John, *English Towns, 1500–1700* (1978)

Paulson, R., *Hogarth: His Life, Art and Times* (2 vols, 1971)

Pearson, Geoffrey, *Hooligan: A History of Respectable Fears* (1983)

Pedicord, E. W., *The Theatrical Public in the Time of Garrick* (1954)

Pepys, Samuel, *The Diary of Samuel Pepys* (11 vols; a new and complete transcription ed. Robert Latham and William Matthews, 1970–83)

Perkin, Harold, *The Age of the Railway* (1970)
*The Origins of Modern English Society, 1780–1880* (1969)

Petrie, Sir Charles, *Scenes of Edwardian Life* (1965)

Phythian-Adams, Charles, *Continuity, Fields and Fission* (1978)

Pike, E. Royston, *Human Documents of the Age of the Forsytes* (1969)
*Human Documents of the Industrial Revolution in Britain* (1976)
*Human Documents of the Victorian Golden Age* (1967)

Pike, Luke Owen, *A History of Crime in England* (1873–6)

Pimlott, J. A. R., *The Englishman's Holiday* (1947)

Place, Francis, *The Autobiography of Francis Place* (ed. M. Thale, 1972)

Platt, Colin, *The Castle in Medieval England and Wales* (1982)
*The English Medieval Town* (1976)
*Medieval England: A Social History and Archaeology from the Conquest to A.D. 1600* (1978)
*Medieval Southampton: The Port and Trading Community, A.D. 1000–1600* (1973)

Plumb, J. H., *The Commercialisation of Leisure in Eighteenth-Century England* (1973)
*England in the Eighteenth Century* (1950)
*Georgian Delights* (1980)
*Studies in Social History* (1955)

Ponsonby, Frederick, *Recollections of Three Reigns* (1951)

Poole, Austin Lane, *Medieval England* (1958)

Porter, Roy, *English Society in the Eighteenth Century* (1982)

Postan, M. M., *The Medieval Economy and Society* (1972)

Power, Eileen, *Mediaeval English Nunneries* (1922)
*Some Mediaeval People* (1924)
*The Wool Trade in English Mediaeval History* (1941)

Powys, Lybbe, *Passages from the Diary of Mrs Philip Lybbe Powys, 1756–1808* (ed. Emily J. Climenson, 1899)

Pratt, E. A., *A History of Inland Transport and Communication* (new ed.; 1970)

Pringle, Patrick, *Hue and Cry* (1955)
*The Thief Takers* (1958)

Prior, Mary (ed.), *Women in English Society 1500–1800* (1985)

Pückler-Muskaü, Prince, *Tour in England, Ireland and France 1826–8* (2 vols, 1832)

Quennell, Marjorie, and C. H. B., *A History of Everyday Things in England* (4 vols, 1918–1934; new eds, revised Peter Quennell, 1958–61)

Quennell, Peter, *Hogarth's Progress* (1955)
(ed.) *London's Underworld* (1950)
*Mayhew's Characters* (1971)
*Mayhew's London* (1950)

Radzinowicz, Leon, *A History of English Criminal Law* (1948–56)

Raistrick, E., *Village Schools: An Upper Wharfedale History* (1971)

Rashdall, H., *Universities of Europe in the Middle Ages, Vol. 2* (1895)

Raverat, Gwen, *Period Piece: A Cambridge Childhood* (1954)

Raymond, John (ed.), *The Baldwin Age* (1960)

Read, Donald, *Edwardian England* (1972)

Reader, W. J., *Victorian England* (new ed., 1974)

Reed, Michael, *The Georgian Triumph, 1700–1830* (1983)

Reynolds, Susan, *An Introduction to the History of Mediaeval Towns* (1977)

Richardson, A. E., and Eberlein, H. D., *The English Inn, Past and Present* (1925)

Rickert, Edith (ed.), *The Babees Book: Medieval Manners for the Young* (1908)

Robins, Keith, *The Eclipse of a Great Power: Modern Britain, 1870–1975* (1983)

Roche, Sophie von la, *Sophie in London* (ed. Clare Williams, 1933)

Rochefoucauld, duc de La, *A Frenchman in England, 1784* (trans. S. C. Roberts, 1933)

Rogers, H. C. B., *The British Army of the Eighteenth Century* (1977)

Rogers, J. E. Thorold, *The History of Agriculture and Prices* (1882)

Rogers, Pat, *Grub Street* (1972)

Rolleston, J. D., *The History of the Acute Exanthemata* (1937)

Roose-Evans, James, *London Theatre from the Globe to the National* (1977)

Rosenfeld, Sybil, *Strolling Players and Drama in the Provinces, 1660–1765* (1939)
*The Theatres of the London Fairs in the 18th Century* (1960)

Rowell, George, *The Victorian Theatre* (1978)

Rowley, Trevor, *The Norman Heritage 1066–1200* (1983)

Rowntree, B. Seebohm, *Poverty: A Study of Town Life* (new ed., 1984)

Rowse, A. L., *The Elizabethan Renaissance: The Cultural Achievement* (1972)
*The Elizabethan Renaissance: The Life of the Society* (1971)
*The England of Elizabeth: The Structure of Society* (1950)

Rudé, George, *The Crowd in History* (1964)
*Hanoverian London* (1971)

Sala, George Augustus, *Twice Round the Clock, or the Hours of the Day and Night in London* (1858)
Salter, Emma Gurney, *Tudor England Through Venetian Eyes* (1930)
Salusbury, G. T., *Street Life in Medieval England* (1948)
Salzman, L. F., *English Life in the Middle Ages* (1926)
Samuel, Raphael (ed.), *Village Life and Labour* (1975)
Saussure, César de, *A Foreign View of England in the Reigns of George I and George II* (trans. Madame van Muyden, 1902)
Scarisbrick, J. J., *The Reformation and the English People* (1983)
Scott, A. F., *Everyone a Witness: The Norman Age* (1976)
*The Georgian Age* (1970)
Scott, W. S., *The Georgian Theatre* (1946)
Seaman, L. C. B., *Life in Britain Between the Wars* (1970)
Seebohm, F., *English Village Community* (1883)
*Shakespeare's England* (1926)
Sharpe, J. A., *Crime in Seventeenth-Century England: A County Study* (1983)
Shelton, Arthur J., *English Hunger and Industrial Disorders* (1973)
Sheppard, E. W., *A Short History of the British Army to 1914* (1926)
Sheppard, Francis, *London 1808–1870: The Infernal Wen* (1971)
Shrewsbury, J. F. D., *A History of Bubonic Plague in the British Isles* (1970)
Simon, Brian (ed.), *Education in Leicestershire 1540–1940* (1968)
Simon, Joan, *Education and Society in Tudor England* (1966)
Simond, Louis, *An American in*

*Regency England* (ed. Christopher Hibbert, 1968)
Skelley, Alan Ramsay, *The Victorian Army at Home* (1977)
Skinner, John, *Journal of a Somerset Rector, 1803–1834*, ed. Howard and Peter Coombs (new ed., 1984)
Slack, Paul, *The Impact of Plague in Tudor and Stuart England* (1985)
Smith, Maurice, *A Short History of Dentistry* (1958)
Smith, Robert A., *Late Georgian and Regency Britain* (1984)
Smyth, John, *Lives of the Berkeleys* (ed. Sir J. Maclean, 1883)
Southern, Richard, *The Staging of Plays before Shakespeare* (1973)
Speaight, George, *A History of the Circus* (1980)
*Punch and Judy: A History* (1970)
Springall, L. Marion, *Labouring Life in Norfolk Villages, 1834–1914* (1936)
Stenton, D. M., *The English Woman in History* (1957)
Stenton, F. M., 'The Road System of Mediaeval England', *Economic History Review*, vol. VII (1936)
Stephen, Sir James Fitzjames, *A History of the Criminal Law of England* (1883)
Stevenson, John, *British Society 1914–15* (1984)
*Popular Disturbances in England, 1700–1870* (1979)
and Cook, Chris, *The Slump: Society and Politics During the Depression* (1977)
Stone, Lawrence, *The Crisis of the Aristocracy, 1558–1641* (1965)
'The Educational Revolution in England', *Past and Present* (1964)
*The Family, Sex and Marriage in England, 1500–1800* (1977)
'Literacy and Education in England', *Past and Present* (1969)
and Stone, Jeanne C. Fawtier, *An Open Elite? England 1540–1880* (1984)

*Stonor Letters and Papers* (ed. C. L. Kingsford, 1924)

Stow, John, *A Survey of London, 1598* (ed. C. L. Kingsford, 1908)

Strutt, Joseph, *Manners, Customs . . . of the People of England* (3 vols, 1774–6)
*Sports and Pastimes of the People of England* (1801)

Summers, Montague, *The Restoration Theatre* (1934)

Sydney, William Connor, *England and the English in the Eighteenth Century* (2 vols, 1892)

Sylvester, D. W., *Educational Documents 800–1816* (1970)

Symonds, John Addington, *The Memoirs of John Addington Symonds* (ed. Phyllis Grosskurth, 1984)


Taine, Hippolyte, *Notes on England* (trans. Edward Hyams, 1957)

Taylor, A. J. P., *English History, 1914–45* (1965)

Taylor, Christopher, *Village and Farmstead: A History of Rural Settlement in England* (1983)

Thomas, Keith, *Man and the Natural World: Changing Attitudes in England, 1500–1800* (1983)
*Religion and the Decline of Magic: Studies in Popular Beliefs in Sixteenth and Seventeenth-Century England* (1971)

Thompson, Denys (ed.), *Change and Tradition in Rural England* (1980)

Thompson, E. P., *The Making of the English Working Class* (1983)
*Whigs and Hunters: The Origin of the Black Act* (1975)

Thompson, Flora, *Lark Rise to Candleford* (1945)

Thompson, F. M. L., *English Landed Society in the 19th Century* (1963)

Thompson, Thea, *Edwardian Childhoods* (1981)

Thoms, William J., *The Book of the Court* (1838)

Thomson, Gladys Scott, *Life in a Noble Household, 1641–1700* (1936)

Thomson, John A. F., *The Transformation of Mediaeval England 1700–1830* (1983)

Titow, J. Z., *English Rural Society, 1200–1350* (1969)

Tomkeieff, O. G., *Life in Norman England* (1966)

Traill, H. D., and Mann, J. S., *Social England: A Record of the Progress of the People* (new ed., 1902–4)

Trevelyan, G. M., *English Social History: A Survey of Six Centuries, Chaucer to Queen Victoria* (3rd ed., 1946)

Trevor-Roper, Hugh, *The Gentry, 1540–1640* (1953)
*Religion, the Reformation and Social Change* (1967)

Trewin, J. C., *The Edwardian Theatre* (1976)

Trotter, Eleanor, *Seventeenth-Century Life in a Country Parish* (1919)

Trustram, Myna, *Women of the Regiment: Marriage and the Victorian Army* (1984)

Turberville, A. S. (ed.), *English Men and Manners in the Eighteenth Century* (1920)
*Johnson's England: An Account of the Life and Manners of His Age* (2 vols, 1933)

Turner, Thomas, *The Diary of Thomas Turner, 1754–1765* (ed. David Vaisey, 1984)

Tusser, Thomas, *Five Hundred Points of Good Husbandry* (1573, new ed., 1984)

Twigg, Graham, *The Black Death: A Biological Reappraisal* (1984)

Tydeman, William, *The Theatre in the Middle Ages 800–1576* (1978)

Urquhart, Judy, *Animals on the Farm: Their History from the Earliest Times to the Present Day* (1983)

Verney, Margaret M., *Memoirs of the Verney Family* (1899)
*Victorian Shopping: Harrods 1895 Catalogue* (introduction by Alison Aldburgham, 1972)
Vinogradoff, Paul, *The Growth of the Manor* (1905)
  *English Society in the Eleventh Century* (1908)
  (ed.), *Oxford Studies in Social and Legal History* (9 vols, 1912–27)
Vives, J. L. de, *Tudor Schoolboy Life* (trans. Foster Watson, 1908)

Waller, P. J., *Town, City and Nation: England 1850–1914* (1983)
Walpole, Horace, *Letters* (ed. W. S. Lewis, 39 vols, 1937–79)
*Walter of Henley's Husbandry, together with an anonymous Husbandry, Seneschaucie etc.* (ed. E. Lamond, 1890)
Walton, John K., *The Blackpool Landlady* (1978)
  *The English Seaside Resort: A Social History, 1750–1914* (1983)
Walvin, James, *Beside the Seaside: A Social History* (1978)
  *The People's Game: A Social History of British Football* (1975)
  *The Black Presence* (1971)
Ward, Edward, *London Spy* (1703)
Watkin, Brian, *Documents on Health and Social Services* (1945)
Webb, R. K., *The British Working-Class Reader, 1790–1848* (1955)
Wedgwood, C. V., *The Common Man in the Civil War* (1957)
White, R. J., *The Age of George III* (1968)
  *Life in Regency England* (1963)
  *Waterloo to Peterloo* (1957)

Whiteley, William T., *Artists and their Friends in England, 1700–1799* (1928)
Wickham, Glynne, *Early English Stages, 1300–1600* (3 vols, 1959–1972)
Willard, J. F., 'Inland Transport in England during the Fourteenth Century', *Speculum*, vol. 1 (1926)
  'The Use of Carts in the Fourteenth Century', *History*, Vol. XVII (1932–3)
Williams, Alfred, *Life in a Railway Factory* (1915)
Williams, E. N., *Life in Georgian England* (1962)
Williams, Percy, *Life in Tudor England* (1964)
Williams, Raymond, *Culture and Society, 1780–1950* (1958)
  *The Long Revolution* (1961)
Wilson, Charles, *England's Apprenticeship, 1603–1763* (1965)
Wilson, C. Anne, *Food and Drink in Britain* (1973)
Wilson, Derek, *England in the Age of Thomas More* (1978)
Wilson, F. M., *Strange Island: Britain through Foreign Eyes* (1955)
Wilson, John Dover (ed.), *Life in Shakespeare's England* (1949)
Wingfield-Stratton, Esmé, *The Squire and his Relations* (1956)
Wohl, Anthony S., *Endangered Lives: Public Health in Victorian Britain* (1984)
  (ed.), *The Victorian Family* (1978)
Wood, Anthony, *History and Antiquities of the University of Oxford* (1674)
Wood, Margaret, *The English Mediaeval House* (1965)
Woodforde, James, *The Diary of a Country Parson, 1758–1802* (5 vols, ed. John Beresford, 1924–31)

Woods, Robert, and Woodward, John,
  *Urban Disease and Mortality in
  19th-Century England* (1984)
Woods, William, *England in the Age of
  Chaucer* (1976)
Woodward, Marcus, *The Countryman's
  Jewel: Days in the Life of a
  Sixteenth-Century Squire* (1934)
Wraxall, Sir Nathaniel, *Historical
  Memoirs of My Own Time* (1815)
Wright, Lawrence, *Clean and Decent*
  (1960)
Wright, Thomas, *The Homes of Other
  Days: A History of Domestic
  Manners and Sentiments in
  England* (1871)

Wrightson, Keith, *English Society,
  1580–1680* (1982)

Youings, Joyce, *Sixteenth-Century
  England* (1984)
Young, G. M., *Early Victorian
  England, 1830–1865* (2 vols, 1932)
Young, Arthur, *The Farmer's Tour
  through the East of England
  1770–1* (1771)
  *Six Months' Tour Through the North
  of England* (1771)
  *A Six Weeks' Tour Through the
  Southern Counties* (1768)

Ziegler, Philip, *The Black Death* (1969)

# Illustration Credits

BLACK AND WHITE

Cooks and scullions in the kitchen. Bodleian
MS. 264 f.170
Servants preparing and serving a meal, from
the Luttrell Psalter. Fotomas Index
Administering medicine. Mansell Collection
Ladies travelling in a coach. British Library
MS. Add 42130 f.181ᵛ
The Pilgrim. British Library MS. Cotton
Avii f.93ʳ
Monk and woman in stocks. British Library
MS. Roy 10E iv f.187ʳ
Chess game. British Library MS. Add
12228 f.236
Bear-baiting. British Library MS. Add
42130 f.161
Farming pursuits, from the Luttrell Psalter.
Mansell Collection
Craftsmen constructing a wall, from the
Life of St Alban. Trinity College,
Dublin/Visual Arts Library

Sir Thomas More and his family, c. 1527 by
Holbein. Private Collection/Granada
Publishing Archive
The burning of Anne Askew and others at
Smithfield, from Acts and Monuments by
John Foxe (martyrologist), 1576. British
Library/Granada Publishing Archive
Visscher's map of London, Pl. II, c. 1616.
Mansell Collection
The Great Plague in 1665. Mansell
Collection
Matthew Hopkins, 'Witchfinder General',
from 'Black Cats and Broomsticks'; Haggs
Castle Museum, Glasgow/Visual Arts
Library

'The Humours of Bagnigge Wells', printed
for Carington Bowles. The Museum of
London/Visual Arts Library
'Beauties of Brighton', 1826, by George
Cruikshank. E. T. Archive
'L'Après-Dînée des Anglais', showing the
segregation of the sexes. British Museum
ref: M. D. George 12350 & 12351
Bullock's Museum. Reproduced by courtesy
of the Guildhall Library, London
Coaching scene by Thomas Rowlandson.
E. T. Archive
The Church of St Mary-le-Bow in
Cheapside, London, c. 1750. Reproduced
by courtesy of the Museum of London
'The Elegant Mother', c. 1796, by James
Gillray. Mansell Collection
The Amputation. E. T. Archive

'The Troubles of the Crinoline', c. 1860.
London Stereoscopic Society Photo. BBC
Hulton Picture Library
The kitchen at Keele Hall, Staffordshire.
From the Sneyd Papers, University of
Keele Library
Making brushes. Salvation Army/Visual
Arts Library
Children outside a Dr Barnardo home. Dr
Barnardo Photo/Visual Arts Library
Whitby market, Yorkshire, 1884.
Photograph by Frank Meadow Sutcliffe,
courtesy of the Sutcliffe Gallery, Whitby
Family in the hopfields, c. 1880, by William
Henry Boyer. Visual Arts Library
The Grand Hotel, Scarborough, by G. W.
Wilson. Courtesy of Aberdeen University
Library

Bank Holiday picnic, Easter 1923. BBC Hulton Picture Library

Bus conductorette, *c.* 1917. BBC Hulton Picture Library

### COLOUR

15th-century farmyard. MS. 311 Virgil. Reproduced by courtesy of the Earl of Leicester, Holkham Hall © Coke Estates Ltd

Walled herb garden. British Library MS. Add 19720 f.165

Childbirth scene. British Library MS. Harl 2278 f.13ᵛ

The marriage of John of Portugal to Philippa of Lancaster. British Library MS. Roy 14 EIV f.284

15th-century tournament. Reproduced by courtesy of His Grace the Archbishop of Canterbury and the Trustees of Lambeth Palace Library

Sir Geoffrey Luttrell with his wife and daughter. British Library MS. Add 42130 f.202ᵛ

The Peasants' Revolt. British Library MS. Roy 18 EI f.175

Winchester College with warden, fellows and scholars. The Chaundler Manuscript, New College MS. 228, reproduced by courtesy of the Warden and scholars of New College, Oxford

Lord Cobham and family, *c.* 1567, by Hans Eworth. Reproduced by courtesy of the Marquess of Bath, Longleat House, Wiltshire

Elizabeth Vernon, Countess of Southampton, *c.* 1600. Anon. Reproduced by courtesy of the Duke of Buccleuch and Queensberry, KT, Boughton House, Kettering

A view of Longleat, by Jan Siberechts (1627–1700). Reproduced by courtesy of the Marquess of Bath, Longleat House, Wiltshire. Photograph Bridgeman Art Library

Queen Elizabeth I dancing with Robert Dudley, Earl of Leicester. By permission of Viscount de l'Isle, VC, KG from his collection at Penshurst Place, Kent

The Thames at Richmond, Flemish School. Reproduced by courtesy of the Fitzwilliam Museum, Cambridge

King Charles I dining in public, by Gerrit Houckgeest (1600–61). Reproduced by gracious permission of HM the Queen

William, 2nd Earl of Salisbury, *c.* 1626, by George Geldorp. Reproduced by courtesy of the Marquess of Salisbury/Hatfield House

The Carpenter's Yard, by William Hogarth (1697–1764). Reproduced by courtesy of Sydney Sabin

Haycarting, by George Stubbs (1724–1806). Reproduced by courtesy of the Walker Art Gallery, Liverpool

Dixton Manor House, Glos. Anon. British School, 18th century. Courtesy of Cheltenham Art Gallery and Museums/ Bridgeman Art Library

St James's Fair, Bristol, by Samuel Coleman. Reproduced courtesy of the City of Bristol Museum and Art Gallery/ Bridgeman Art Library

Broad Quay, Bristol. British School, *c.* 1735. Reproduced by courtesy of the City of Bristol Museum and Art Gallery

Covent Garden Market and Piazza, *c.* 1750, by Samuel Scott. Reproduced by courtesy of the Museum of London

Old Somerset House from the Thames, by Canaletto (1697–1768). Reproduced by courtesy of Mr and Mrs Harry A. Brooks. Photograph from the Metropolitan Museum, NY

The Charitable Lady, *c.* 1781, by William Redmore Bigg (1755–1828). Reproduced by courtesy of the Philadelphia Museum of Art: given by Mr and Mrs Harald Paumgarten

Mr Howard offering Relief to Prisoners, by Francis Wheatley (1747–1801). Private Collection

The Iron Forge, 1772, by Joseph Wright of Derby. Reproduced from the Broadlands Collection by permission of Lord Romsey

Brickfields, Liverpool. British School, 19th Century. Reproduced by courtesy of the Walker Art Gallery, Liverpool

Fête in Petworth Park, Sussex, 1835, by W. F. Witherington (1785–1865). Reproduced by courtesy of the National Trust

The Picture Gallery at the Hall, Southport, by James Hayllar (1829–1920). Fine Art Photographic Library

The Hall and Staircase of a Country House, 1882, by Jonathan Pratt (1835–1911). Bridgeman Art Library

Ramsgate Sands, 1854, by W. P. Frith (1819–1909). Reproduced by gracious permission of HM the Queen

Many Happy Returns of the Day, 1853, by W. P. Frith. Reproduced by courtesy of Harrogate Art Gallery

A Game of Draughts, by Thomas Faed (1826–1900). Reproduced by courtesy of the Graves Art Gallery, Sheffield

Beach Scene, by Ernest Proctor (1886–1935). Courtesy of Whitford & Hughes, London/Bridgeman Art Library

Waterloo, 1939–45, by Helen McKie. National Railway Museum, York/Bridgeman Art Library

# Index of Names

# Index of Subjects

abbeys, 80–81, 104, 156
Abingdon, 105
abortion, 399, 702–3
actors, *see* theatre
Acts of Parliament, Act of Uniformity, 258;
Apothecaries', 429; Bank Holiday, 599;
Combination, 480, 482, 492; Contagious
Diseases, 639–40; Defence of the Realm, 700,
707; Education (1918 *and* 1944), 694;
Emergency Powers, 707; Fourth Reform, 693;
Free Libraries 622; Gangs, 559; Green Belt,
676; Holidays with Pay, 684; Hours of Labour
in Factories, 582; Housing, 675; Intoxicating
Liquor (Temporary Restriction), 700;
Licensing, 701; Married Women's Property,
693; Metropolitan Police, 664; Metropolitan
Poor, 706; Militia, 671; National Insurance,
707; Police, 666; Poor Law Amendment, 492;
Prevention of Crimes, 670; Prison, 669; Public
Health (1848), 580, 581; Public Health (1872),
581; Public Health (1875), 581–2; Railway,
651; Reform, 492; Riot, 455, 490; Sex
Disqualification (Removal), 693, 703; Shop
Hours, 520–21; Smallholdings, 565–6; Town
and Country Planning, 676; Tramways, 657;
Waltham Black, 360; Workhouse, 493
advertising, 467; handbills, 430; mountebanks,
426–7, 429; rapidly expanding business, 704;
for servants, 503; tooth powders and tinctures,
443
agriculture (*see also* animal husbandry *and*
enclosure of land), children employed, 469,
558; crops, 173; decline in, 566; decline in corn
growing, 34; depression, 488–9, 564; farm
boy's work, 558–9; farm labourers' wear, 345,
535; farmers with social pretensions, 567; glebe
farming, 311, 312; improved methods, 256–7;
labouring gangs, 559–61; largest occupation,
284, 466, 497; mediaeval, 21–2; mop fairs,
307; percentage of labourers in population,

565; revolution, 321–2; riots, 254, 479–80,
490–91; size of farms, 562–3; smallholdings,
20, 565–6; unemployment, 469; wages, 471,
558, 559, 561; weaver-farmers, 563; Women's
Land Army, 709
Aldeburgh, 535
alehouses, 52, 53, 79, 375–7
allotments, 565
animal husbandry, disease, 178, 564; horse
rearing, 301–2; improved breeds of cattle and
sheep, 321; mediaeval peasants', 20; sheep
farming, 34, 173, 177, 301, 488
animals (*see also* horses *and* sports),
bloodhounds, 666; cruelty to, 337, 368, 369;
deer, 358, 359; donkeys, 681; draught animals,
173; London traffic congestion, 657;
slaughtered during plague, 163, 164;
Smithfield Market, 533; in Tudor times,
208–10
apprentices, chimney sweeps, 469; clothes, 234;
craftsmen, 105; from Foundling Hospital, 396;
holiday, 247; tradesmen's signs and emblems,
517
archery, 57–8, 185, 212
architecture, Baroque, 323; Chester rows, 301;
continental influence, 323; crenellation, 4;
Gothic railway stations, 645; late Victorian
domestic, 555–6; nineteenth century public
buildings, 579; Norman halls, 4; Palladian,
294, 323–4; Reading Gaol, 667; sixteenth
century evolution, 194
aristocracy, country houses, 555–6; Dissolution,
177; First World War casualties, 690; incomes
in seventeenth century, 289; landed nobility,
208–9; peerages conferred, 209–10; permitted
to read Bible, 217; responsibility and duty,
556, 557; Roman Catholics, 188; weakening
authority, 99
army (*see also* World War, First *and* Second),
Auxiliary Territorial Service, 708; barracks,

'cross-biting', 185; dance halls and taverns, 622; directories of, 407; earnings, 240; in eighteenth-century, 407; expelled from Oxford, 125, 132; gin and, 378; mid nineteenth-century, 634–5; music-halls, 630; Pepys and, 402; public concern over, 639; theatre, 409, 414; vagabonds, 180
public health, *see* disease
public houses, 377, 593, 700–701
public schools (*see also individual schools*), 454–7; First World War casualties, 690; football, 623; headmaster's salary, 610; Officers' Training Corps, 690; religious and moral principles, 640; tenets taught, 640
punishment and penalties, 142–8 *passim*; capital, 379, 389, 661–3; gibbeting, 663; manor courts, 139; pillory, 663; transportation, 491, 492, 666; under Puritans, 260–61; Waltham Black Act, 360
*for*: breaches of guild rules, 99; breaking curfew, 74; breaking sanctuary, 145; consorting with gipsies, 180; ejecting ballast, 71; hawk theft, 61; murder, 389; road obstruction, 63–4; sabbath breaking, 43; serving meat in Lent, 175–6; sexual offences, 28, 399, 400; vagrancy, 182, 183
*of*: actors, 246, 251, 260; agricultural rioters, 491–2; apprentices, 234; army personnel, 672, 673–4; Bethlehem Hospital patients, 160; burgesses of Oxford, 134; children, 112–15, 267, 393, 394; Eton boys, 269; factory workers, 475; Gordon Rioters, 478; Guy's Hospital patients, 705; Luddites, 486; members of Inns of Court, 137; miracle players, 92; Norman minstrel, 94; Oxford University students, 128–9, 130, 132; pirates, 231; Prince of Wales, 394; prisoners, 666, 668, 669; recusants, 191; reformatory inmates, 670; schoolboys, 239, 269, 449, 455; schoolmasters, 269; suicides, 432; traitors, 231; whores and hangers-on, 76; witches, 262–4; wives, 107
Puritans, 258; Civil War, 253; 'Dissenting Academies', 272; homosexuality, 400; law under, 260; marital sex, 401; theatre, 247; yeomen, 320

quack doctors, *see* disease *and* medicine

Ragley Hall, 323
railways, accidents, 651; amenities, 652; avoidance of fares, 687; benefits brought by, 648; cheap day-tickets, 683; demolition of housing, 647; description of 1835 journey, 649–50; fares, 651; fortunes made in, 646; government control of, 707; investment in, 647; lighting, 651–2; navvies, 645–6; speed, 649, 650; strike, 695; transport of goods, 648; transport holidaymakers, 679–80; travellers, 648–9; underground, 657–8

Raynham Hall, 323
Reading, 51, 266, 300, 667
Reformation, 186
relics, holy, 80
religion, Bible reading and religious controversy, 217; books and periodicals, 625–6; denominations in mid nineteenth-century, 641; import in Victorian life, 640–41
rents, Cambridge, 129; controlled, 708, 709; farm labourer's cottage, 565; inflation after Dissolution, 177; private landlords, 676; railways and London rents, 647; slums, 336; wages and, 491
Repton School, 266
rewards, factory workers' bonuses, 475
Riot Act, 455, 490
riots, against draining fens, 254; agricultural, 490–91; attacks on turnpikes, 351; Chartist, 494–5; Cold Bath Fields, 665; Evil May Day, 176; following First World War, 695; footmen at Ranelagh, 511; Gordon Riots, 318, 478, 664, 667; in late eighteenth-century, 478–80; Luddism, 482–7; Northamptonshire, 490; at Oxford, 124–8; Peasants' Revolt, 36–8, 146; price inflation, 691; at public schools, 455–6; rioters pull down workhouse, 493; suppression of fairs, 422; theatre audiences, 414–15; in Tudor times, 176–7; xenophobic, 176
rivers, extension of navigable rivers, 467; hazards of travel by, 71; Humber crossing, 77; pirates, 71; river transport, 70–71, 86, 304; Severn traffic, 284; silting-up, 233; Thames traffic, 300, 361
road accidents, 677
roads, eighteenth-century, 347–9, 352; floods, 73; mediaeval, 63–4; repair and maintenance, 65–6; sixteenth-century, 64–5; Turnpike Trusts, 350–51
Roman Catholicism, 187–92; attendance at university, 279; contraception, 702; emancipation, 314; exclusion from public office, 258; Gordon Riots, 318, 478; Irish immigration and, 641; James II, 258; Skinner and, 315; Sydney Smith's attitude to, 314; toleration of, 318
Rotherham School, 115, 120, 268
royal households, 75–6
Royal Lodge, The, 326
Royal Military College, Sandhurst, 673, 674
Royal Navy, 283, 300; Women's Royal Naval Service, 708
Royal Society, 256–7
Rugby School, 454, 455, 456, 623, 640

Sabbatarians, 642, 643
St Albans, 118, 451
St James's Palace, 158, 195, 211
St Paul's Cathedral, 87
St Paul's School, 116, 117, 271, 453–4, 456

364–6; cock-fighting, 367; cock-throwing, 368; cricket, 211–12, 370–72; croquet, 625; fencing, 197; fishing, 359–60; football, 212–13, 370, 623–5; golf, 625; hare-coursing, 211; hawking, 61, 211, 359; hunting, 60–61, 208, 210, 358–9; Laudian Code, 281; mediaeval, 58; Newmarket races, 306; pigeon-flying, 621; prize-fights, 623; proscribed at Universities, 279; racing, 368–9; shooting, 359; tennis, 211, 625; tilting, 59, 231; under Puritans, 260; wrestling, 58
staircases, 323, 325
Stanton Harcourt, 5
Stokesay Castle, 4
Stourbridge Fair, 105, 306, 345
Stowe, 324, 327, 555
Strawberry Hill, 497, 511
street vendors, 525–6, 529–31
strikes, 495, 568, 694, 696
suffrage, 494, 693
suicide, 373, 431–2, 662, 668
Sunday Schools, 452, 622, 683
Sundays, at Blenheim, 545; Bournemouth, 681; navvies work on, 646; seaside, 685; Victorian 642–3
sweat-shops, 591–2

taverns, 523, 622
taxes, death duties, 695; hair powder, 340; income, 695; newspaper, 627; poll, 36, 38; rates, 675; spirits, 380; tolls charged 'by cartload', 69; turnpikes, 350–51
teeth, decay widespread, 707; dental profession, 446–7; false, 343, 427, 445–6; hygiene, 442–3; masticators, 444–5; sale of, 444; tooth-drawers, 441; treatment, 442, 443–4
theatre (*see also* cinema), actors, 245–7, 260, 419–20, 421, 550; amateur theatricals, 674; behaviour of audiences, 411, 414–18; Boswell at, 416; censorship, 411, 413; circus, 424–5; costume, 419; Covent Garden, 408, 411, 416, 418; eighteenth-century, 412–14; first London theatres, 243–4; Garrick's influence on, 418–19; managers, 420, 421; miracle plays, 90–93; mumming plays, 93; music halls, 629–31, 681; nativity plays, 89–90; orange-girls, 287; pantomime, 413; penny gaffs, 529; prices, 410, 411; private theatres, 244–5; provincial, 419–20, 632; puppet shows, 422–3; reform, 411–12; Restoration, 408–10; royal patents, 408, 412, 419; shut by plague, 246, 247; sixteenth-century, 240–49; strolling players, 180, 419–22 *passim*; suppressed, 249–51; Theatre Royal, Drury Lane, 408–10 *passim*, 412, 416–18 *passim*, 424
Theobalds, 199, 207–8
thief-takers, 663
thieves, *see* criminals
Thoresby Hall, 504

tips, vails, 509–11, 512
tobacco, alehouses, 377; cigar-smoking, 554; cost, 291; expenditure on, 699; price, 559; Prince of Wales, 542, 553; Queen Victoria dislikes, 553–4; smoking rooms, 553–5; smuggling, 361, 362; trade, 291–2; women smokers, 692, 699
Tolpuddle Martyrs, 492
tommy shops, 487, 646
tools (*see also* utensils), brewing, 53; coalmining, 585; dental instruments, 442; farming, 173, 559; hiring charges, 592; mop fairs, 307, 498; navvies, 645
tournaments, 84–6
Tower of London, 36, 37
towns, industrial, 473–4, 568–70; mediaeval 97–104; nineteenth-century migration to, 568; small provincial, 473; Sundays in provincial, 642–3
toys, 394
trade, cloth, 302–3; cotton, 303; distributive trades' employees, 699; fourteenth-century, 98; guilds, 99; prosperity, 467; slave, 284, 466; slump, 698–9; tobacco, 291–2; wool, 31, 34, 98, 173, 254
trade unions, agricultural, 564, 565; Chartism and, 494; Combination Acts, 480, 482; early, 492; First World War, 691, 694; membership, 694; militancy, 695; outings organized, 622; Tolpuddle Martyrs, 492
Tranby Croft, 556
transport (*see also* railways *and* travel), bicycles, 658–9; cabmen, 655; *cabriolets*, 655–6; carriages, 68–9; carting, 290; carts, 69–70, 74, 231; coaches, 347, 348, 352; eighteenth-century, 352; fares, 352; General Strike, 696; growlers, 656; hackney coaches, 655; hansom cabs, 656; holidays and cheap public transport, 679; horse, 67–8, 69, 303; litters, 68; mail-coaches, 352–3, 354; motor-cars, 659–60, 677; omnibuses, 643, 652–5 *passim*, 660, 692; post-chaise, 314, 352; Queen Anne's hunting carriage, 359; river, 70–71, 86, 304; sedan chairs, 294, 500; in sixteenth-century London, 231–2; stage-coaches, 680; steamboats, 679; Sunday, 643; taxicabs, 656; traffic jam, 652; tramcars, 656–7; transport workers strike, 695; trolley-buses, 657
travel, alehouses, 79; dangers of, 72–4; eighteenth-century, 347, 352; inns, 77–8; in large parties, 74; mail-coach, 354; pilgrims, 79–80; railway opens opportunity for, 648; rich households, 76–7; royal household, 75–6; servants and masters, 507; by train, 649–50
trees, 198, 254, 329–30
truck system, 587, 646
Tunbridge Wells, 294, 295
turnpikes, 350–52

umbrellas, 342–3
unemployment, agriculture, 469, 490, 564;
  between First and Second World Wars, 695,
  696–7, 699; early nineteenth-century, 489; fear
  of, 592; seventeenth-century, 284; sheep
  farming, 173; in Tudor times, 176, 177, 178;
  unemployment benefit, 696–7
universities (*see also* education, Cambridge *and*
  Oxford), 458–61; age of students on entry,
  135; begging scholars, 183; curriculum in
  eighteenth century, 458; duration of courses,
  134–5; expense, 133–4; football, 623;
  medicine, 155, 157; Officer Training Corps,
  690; poor scholars, 134, 135, 277–8; theology,
  136
utensils (*see also* tools), drinking, 11, 376;
  kitchen, 336; mediaeval cottagers' domestic,
  19; mediaeval dining, 5, 6, 13, 133; roasting
  jack, 523–4; table silver, 202, 285; washing,
  132

vagabonds, criminals, 179–80, 184–5;
  Dissolution of Monasteries, 179; enlistment in
  army, 671, 672; legislation, 182–3, 185;
  number in seventeenth-century, 255;
  punishment, 182, 183; roaming, 179–80; skills
  and tricks, 181; Statute of Liveries responsible
  for, 178; at theatre, 240, 242
vermin, 335, 355, 403, 573, 595
vineyards, 11, 200
visiting cards, 614–15
Vyne, the, 197

Wadley, 201
wages and salaries, between First and Second
  World Wars, 694, 697, 698; Chartists'
  demands, 494; Combination Acts, 480; fee for
  inoculation, 433; fixed rates, 176; increase
  during First World War, 691; inequality
  between men's and women's, 704; inflation
  after Black Death, 34; Luddism and, 484; paid
  in food and drink, 53; perquisites supplement,
  468, 472; Poor Law Amendment Act, 492;
  prices and, 254; riots over, 490–91; Royal
  Commission on Equal Pay, 709; seventeenth-
  century, 255, 257–8, 284–5; Tolpuddle
  Martyrs, 492
*in various trades and professions*: actors, 91,
  246, 420, 421, 631; agriculture, 177–8, 471,
  558, 559, 562, 563, 564, 565, 697; army, 672;
  chain- and nail-making, 587; children at
  industrial charity schools, 451; children in
  pottery factories, 594; chimney sweeps, 596;
  clergy, 192–3, 310–11, 312, 608; clerks, 609;
  clothworkers, 482; coalminers, 468, 585, 587;
  costermongers' earnings, 528–9; domestic
  servants, 503, 505, 512, 513, 612; dentists,
  446; eighteenth century labourers, 472; factory
  workers, 699; footballers, 624; framework

knitters, 483; hired labourers, 177–8;
  household staff at Woburn, 290; lead miners,
  305; male manual workers, 684; mediaeval
  doctors, 150; mediaeval peasants, 27, 28, 31;
  messengers, 68; Metropolitan Police, 664–5;
  miners, 699; minstrels, 95; navvies, 645;
  nineteenth century London labouring classes,
  571–2; paviour, 103; Pepys, 285; porters, 70;
  pottery workers, 699; Prince Regent's chef,
  499; prostitutes, 409, 638; Sarah Mapp, 429;
  schoolmasters and tutors, 119–20, 268, 451;
  shop assistants, 520; sixteenth-century
  workers, 234; Sydney Smith, 312; tailoring
  sweat-shop workers, 592; water-cress seller,
  530; weavers and knitters, 577; whipping boy,
  113; women labourers, 468
Wakefield, 91, 302, 304, 670
Walsingham, 80, 110, 111
Wanstead, 324
Wardour Old Castle, 195
Warwick Castle, 512
watch and ward, 100, 101
water supply, Chester, 300; disease, 436, 440;
  drinking, 288; and health standards, 707;
  house sites, 332; Ingatestone, 205; London
  slums, 573; mediaeval, 103; north London,
  231; piped, 676; pollution, 165
weapons, cannon, 486; highwaymen's, 350; for
  killing birds, 211; long-bow, 58; of Luddites,
  485, 487; Margaret Paston asks for, 140; of
  mediaeval brigands, 139; mediaeval musters-at-
  arms, 100; proscribed under Laudian Code,
  280; sporting guns, 359; swords, 339; trials by
  combat, 141–2; used in 1830 riots, 490
Wedgwood pottery, 445
Welbeck Abbey, 504, 557
Wellington College, 673
Welwyn Garden City, 676
Wentworth Woodhouse, 324, 497
Westminster Abbey, *prologue*
Westminster School, 239, 455, 456, 623
Weymouth, 465, 679
Whitby, 473
Whitehall Palace, 211, 220, 230
wigs, Beauclerk, 335; cost of periwigs, 290;
  Elizabeth I, 224; Gay on, 340; John Taylor's
  servant, 314; nit-infested, 403; professional
  men, 344; Samuel Mercer buys, 462; variety,
  339; wig-snatchers, 339
Wilton House, 323
Winchester, 80, 103, 300, 355
Winchester College, age of pupils, 120;
  classroom, 117; curriculum, 116; football, 623;
  riots, 455; sons of peers, 456; warden's salary,
  119; William of Wykeham, 115
windows, cottage, 336; fourteenth-century, 12;
  French, 326; Hardwick Hall, 194; King's
  College, Cambridge, 132; long gallery, 197;
  plate-glass, 516; sash, 332; shop, 516